INTERNATIONAL BUSINESS
A MANAGERIAL PERSPECTIVE

INTERNATIONAL BUSINESS
A MANAGERIAL PERSPECTIVE

RICKY W. GRIFFIN
Texas A&M University

MICHAEL W. PUSTAY
Texas A&M University

Addison-Wesley Publishing Company

Reading, Massachusetts • Menlo Park, California • New York • Don Mills, Ontario • Wokingham, England

Amsterdam • Bonn • Sydney • Singapore • Tokyo • Madrid • San Juan • Milan • Paris

Executive Editor:	Michael Payne
Senior Sponsoring Editor:	Beth Toland
Associate Editor:	Janice Jutras
Editorial Assistant:	Erin J. Murray
Executive Editor, Development:	Mary Clare McEwing
Senior Development Editor:	Sue Gleason
Managing Editor:	Kazia Navas
Senior Production Supervisor:	Loren Hilgenhurst Stevens
Senior Production Coordinator:	Beth F. Houston
Production Services:	Jane Hoover, Lifland et al., Bookmakers
Production Technology Manager:	Laurie Petrycki
Electronic Production Administrator:	Sally Simpson
Technical Art Specialist:	Robert Chamberlain
Electronic Production Specialist:	Tricia Deforge
Copy Editor:	Laura Michaels, Mountainview Publications
Art and Design Director:	Karen Meyer Rappaport
Art Development Editor:	Meredith Nightingale
Prepress Buying Manager:	Sarah McCracken
Art Buyer:	Joseph Vetere
Illustrator:	Maryland CartoGraphics, Inc.
Photo Researcher:	Susan Van Etten
Permissions Editor:	Mary Dyer
Text Design:	Karen Gourley-Lehman
Cover Design:	Karen Meyer Rappaport
Marketing Manager:	Craig Bleyer
Marketing Coordinator:	Theresa D. Riley
Senior Manufacturing Manager:	Roy Logan
Manufacturing Supervisor:	Hugh Crawford
Film Output Source:	Pre-Press Co., Inc.
Printer:	R. R. Donnelley & Sons Company

Reprinted with corrections September, 1996.

Photo credits appear on page xxxi, which constitutes a continuation of the copyright page.

Library of Congress Cataloging-in-Publication Data

Griffin, Ricky W.
    International business : a managerial perspective / by Ricky W.
Griffin, Michael W. Pustay. — 1st ed.
        p.   cm.
    ISBN 0-201-58653-3
    1. International business enterprises—Management.   I. Pustay,
Michael W.   II. Title.
HD62.4.G74   1995
658'.049—dc20   95-9000
                                                                    CIP

3 4 5 6 7 8 9 10-DOW-9897

Ricky W. Griffin is the Lawrence E. Fouraker Professor of Business Administration and professor of management at Texas A&M University. He is also director of the Center for Human Resource Management at Texas A&M. After receiving his Ph.D. from the University of Houston in 1978, he joined the faculty at the University of Missouri–Columbia before moving to Texas A&M University in 1981.

Professor Griffin teaches international management, organizational behavior, human resource management, and general management. He has taught both undergraduate and graduate students, participated in numerous executive training programs, and taught in Europe. A member of the Academy of Management, he has served as division chair of that group's Organizational Behavior division. He also is a member of the Southern Management Association and the board of directors of the Southern Management Association.

Professor Griffin has written several successful textbooks, including *Management, Organizational Behavior* (with Greg Moorhead), and *Business* (with Ron Ebert). He is currently conducting research on workplace violence in Canada and job design differences and similarities among firms in Japan, Europe, and the United States.

Michael W. Pustay is professor of management at Texas A&M University. He currently serves as associate director of the Center for International Business Studies and as associate director of the Center for International Business Education and Research at Texas A&M. He is the North American editor of the British journal *Transport Reviews.* Professor Pustay received his B.A. in economics *summa cum laude* from Washington and Lee University in 1969 and his Ph.D. in economics from Yale University in 1973. He taught at Purdue University and Bowling Green State University prior to joining Texas A&M's business school faculty.

Professor Pustay, who has taught international business for 10 years, focuses his teaching and research efforts on international business and business-government relations. His work has appeared in such professional journals as the *Journal of Management, Southern Economic Journal, Land Economics,* and *Transportation Journal.* He is currently researching the role of regional trading blocs on the world economy and the impact of domestic economic policies on international competition.

Professor Pustay is a member of numerous professional organizations, including the Academy of International Business, the American Economic Association, the Association for Canadian Studies in the United States, and the Transportation Research Forum. He has served as a consultant for a variety of public and private organizations, including the U.S. Department of Transportation, the Small Business Administration, the Civil Aeronautics Board, and Houston Power & Light.

To my parents—Ione Dyer and James Griffin.
R.W.G.

To my parents—Catherine and Walter Pustay.
M.W.P.

Contents

PART 1

INTRODUCTION TO INTERNATIONAL BUSINESS   2

CHAPTER 1

An Overview of International Business   4

Case: The Business of the Olympics   5

What Is International Business?   8

Why Study International Business?   9

    Going Global: A Rose by Any Other Name . . .   10

International Business Activities   10

The Extent of Internationalization   13

The Evolution of International Business   16
    The Early Era of International Business   16
    Going Global: Trying to Blend In   17
    International Business Growth since World War II   19

Reasons for International Business Growth   27

An Overview of the Contents of This Book   29

Chapter Review   31
Building Global Skills   32
Closing Case: The Rise and Fall of the British Sportscar   33
Chapter Notes   34

CHAPTER 2

Global Marketplaces and Business Centers   36

Case: The First Rule: Know the Territory   37

The Structure of the World Economy   40

The Marketplaces of North America   **41**
   The United States   **41**

   Going Global: Classifying Countries by
      Income Level   **42**

   Canada   **43**
   Mexico   **46**
   Central America and the Caribbean   **47**

The Marketplaces of Western Europe   **48**

**The Marketplaces of Eastern and
Central Europe**   **50**
   The Former Soviet Union   **50**
   Central Europe   **54**

The Marketplaces of Asia   **56**
   Japan   **56**
   Australia and New Zealand   **58**
   The Four Tigers   **59**
   India   **62**
   China   **62**
   Southeast Asian Countries   **64**

The Marketplaces of Africa   **64**

The Marketplaces of South America   **66**

Chapter Review   **68**
Building Global Skills   **70**
Closing Case: The Chinese Treasure Chest   **71**
Chapter Notes   **73**

POINT/COUNTERPOINT: Helping Developing
   Nations: Aid or Trade?   **74**

PART 2

THE INTERNATIONAL ENVIRONMENT   **76**

CHAPTER 3

International Trade and Investment Theory   **78**

Case: Caterpillar: Making Money by
   Moving Mountains   **79**

**International Trade and the World
Economy**   **81**

**Classical Country-Based Trade
Theories**   **82**
   Mercantilism   **82**
   Absolute Advantage   **83**
   Comparative Advantage   **85**
   Comparative Advantage with
      Money   **86**
   Relative Factor Endowments   **87**

Modern Firm-Based Trade Theories   **90**
   Country Similarity Theory   **90**

   Going Global: Extending the Product
      Life Cycle   **91**

   Product Life Cycle Theory   **91**
   Global Strategic Rivalry Theories   **94**
   Porter's National Competitive
      Advantage   **96**

Overview of International Investment   **99**
   Types of International Investments   **99**
   Foreign Direct Investment and the
      United States   **100**

International Investment Theories   **101**
   Ownership Advantages   **102**
   Internalization Theory   **102**
   Eclectic Theory   **103**

**Factors Influencing Foreign Direct
Investment**   **103**
   Supply Factors   **103**
   Demand Factors   **106**
   Political Factors   **108**

Chapter Review   **109**
Building Global Skills   **110**
Closing Case: Komatsu's Challenge   **111**
Chapter Notes   **112**

POINT/COUNTERPOINT: Should Nations Encourage
   Foreign Direct Investment?   **114**

CHAPTER 4

The International Monetary System and the Balance of Payments   116

Case: The Plunging Dollar in the News   117

History of the International Monetary System   119
The Gold Standard   119
The Collapse of the Gold Standard   120
The Bretton Woods Era   122
The End of the Bretton Woods System   128
Performance of the International Monetary System since 1971   129
Going Global: Buying Bad Debts for Good Causes   137

The Balance of Payments Accounting System   137
The Major Components of the BOP Accounting System   138
The U.S. Balance of Payments in 1993   144
Defining Balance of Payments Surpluses and Deficits   146

Chapter Review   148
Building Global Skills   150
Closing Case: Recent U.S. BOP Performance: Is the Sky Falling or Not?   151
Chapter Notes   153

CHAPTER 5

Foreign Exchange and International Financial Markets   154

Case: Exchange-Rate Chaos   155

The Economics of Foreign Exchange   157
The Demand for Foreign Exchange   157
The Supply of Foreign Exchange   158
Determination of the Equilibrium Price   158
Going Global: A Brief Hint   159

Balance of Payments Equilibrium   160
Fixed Exchange-Rate System   161
Flexible Exchange-Rate System   163
Pros and Cons of the Two Types of Exchange-Rate Systems   165

The Structure of the Foreign-Exchange Market   166
The Role of Banks   166
Spot and Forward Markets   169
Arbitrage and the Currency Market   173
Going Global: Big Mac Currencies   176

The International Capital Market   180
Major International Banks   180
The Eurocurrency Market   183
The International Bond Market   184
Global Equity Markets   185
Offshore Financial Centers   186

Chapter Review   186
Building Global Skills   188
Closing Case: Can Nomura Remain Number One?   188
Chapter Notes   191

PART 3

THE NATIONAL ENVIRONMENT   192

CHAPTER 6

Formulation of National Trade Policies   194

Case: Desmarais Is Tired of Being Dumped On   195

Rationales for Trade Intervention   196
Industry-Level Trade Theories   197
National Trade Policies   201

Barriers to International Trade 205
  Tariffs **205**
  Nontariff Barriers **209**
  Going Global: An Unlevel Playing Field **213**

Promotion of International Trade 217
  Subsidies **217**
  Foreign Trade Zones **218**
  Export Financing Programs **220**

Controlling Unfair Trade Practices 221
  Countervailing Duties **221**
  Antidumping Regulations **222**
  Super 301 **223**

Chapter Review 224
Building Global Skills 225
Closing Case: Harley-Davidson: Back in
  Hog Heaven **226**
Chapter Notes 228

POINT/COUNTERPOINT: Should Unfair Trade Laws
  Be Enforced? **230**

CHAPTER 7

**International Cooperation among
Nations 232**

Case: On the Road to the New EC **233**

**The General Agreement on Tariffs and
Trade 234**
  How the GATT Works **235**
  The Uruguay Round **237**
  The Future of the World Trade
    Organization **240**

Regional Economic Integration 242
  Forms of Economic Integration **242**
  The Impact of Economic Integration on
    Firms **244**

The European Union 246
  Completing the Common Market—
    EC '92 **247**

The Creation of the European Union 251
  Governing the European Union **253**
  Going Global: Lobbying the European
    Union **256**

Other Regional Trading Blocs 257
  The North American Free Trade
    Agreement **257**
  Other Free Trade Agreements **260**

International Commodity Arrangements 264
  Organization of Petroleum Exporting
    Countries **264**
  The Multifibre Arrangement **265**

Chapter Review 265
Building Global Skills 267
Closing Case: Will Whirlpool Clean Up
  in Europe? **267**
Chapter Notes 270

CHAPTER 8

Legal and Political Forces 272

Case: Toys 'R' Us Takes on the World **273**

Differences in Legal Systems 275
  Common Law **276**
  Civil Law **276**
  Religious Law **277**
  Bureaucratic Law **277**

Home Country Laws 278
  Going Global: The Law Is the Law **279**
  Restrictions on Trading with Unfriendly
    Countries **279**
  Indirect Effects on International
    Competitiveness **281**
  Extraterritoriality **281**
  Going Global: The Ethics of
    Bribery **283**

The Impacts of MNCs on Host Countries 284
  Economic and Political Impacts **284**
  Cultural Impacts **285**

Host Country Laws   285
   Ownership Issues   **286**
   Intellectual Property Rights   **287**
   Other Host Country Controls   **289**

**Dispute Resolution in International
Business   291**

The Political Environment   293
   Political Risk   **293**
   Doing Business in Centrally Planned
     Economies   **296**
   Doing Business in Formerly Centrally Planned
     Economies   **297**

Chapter Review   301
Building Global Skills   303
Closing Case: The Best Little Creamery
   in Texas   **304**
Chapter Notes   305

CHAPTER 9
The Role of Culture   308

Case: Finding a Cross-Cultural Tour Guide   **309**

Characteristics of Culture   311

Elements of Culture   312
   Social Structure   **313**
   Going Global: The Impact of Japanese Culture
     on Business   **314**
   Language   **315**
   Going Global: International Communication:
     A Primer   **322**
   Communication   **323**
   Religion   **326**
   Values and Attitudes   **330**

Cultural Differences and Ethics   334

Cultural Clusters   334

A Final Word   337

Chapter Review   337
Building Global Skills   338
Closing Case: Hollywood Abroad   **339**
Chapter Notes   340

PART 4

MANAGING IN THE INTERNATIONAL
ENVIRONMENT   **342**

CHAPTER 10
International Strategic Management   344

Case: Global Mickey   **345**

**What Is International Strategic
Management?   348**

**Components of an International
Strategy   349**
   Scope of Operations   **350**
   Resource Deployment   **350**
   Distinctive Competence   **351**
   Synergy   **352**

**Developing International
Strategies   352**
   Going Global: Disney Is
     Synergy   **353**
   Mission Statement   **353**
   Environmental Scanning and the
     SWOT Analysis   **355**
   Strategic Goals   **357**
   Tactics   **357**
   Control Framework   **358**

Levels of International Strategy   358
   Corporate Strategy   **358**
   Business Strategy   **362**
   Functional Strategies   **364**

Foreign Market Analysis 364
 Assessing Alternative Foreign Markets 365
 Evaluating Costs, Benefits, and Risks 370

Chapter Review 371
Building Global Skills 372
Closing Case: Motorola 373
Chapter Notes 374

CHAPTER 11

Modes of Entry into International Business 376

Case: Heineken Brews Up a Global Strategy 377

Choosing a Mode of Entry 378

Exporting to Foreign Markets 382
 Forms of Exporting 384
 Additional Considerations 386
 Export Intermediaries 389

International Licensing 393
 Basic Issues in International Licensing 393
 Going Global: "Easier Done Than Said" 394
 Advantages and Disadvantages of International Licensing 397

International Franchising 398
 Basic Issues in International Franchising 398
 Advantages and Disadvantages of International Franchising 399

Specialized Entry Modes for International Business 400
 Management Contract 400
 Turnkey Project 400

Foreign Direct Investment 401
 The Greenfield Strategy 402
 The Acquisition Strategy 403
 Joint Ventures 404

Chapter Review 404
Building Global Skills 406
Closing Case: Blockbuster Fast-Forwards Overseas 406
Chapter Notes 407

CHAPTER 12

International Strategic Alliances 410

Case: The European Cereal Wars 411

International Corporate Cooperation 413
 Comparison of Joint Ventures and Other Types of Strategic Alliances 413
 Growth in Strategic Alliances 415

Benefits of Strategic Alliances 415
 Ease of Market Entry 415
 Shared Risk 417
 Shared Knowledge and Expertise 418
 Synergy and Competitive Advantage 418

Scope of Strategic Alliances 420
 Comprehensive Alliances 420
 Going Global: Small Alliances Can Be Profitable 421
 Functional Alliances 422

Management of Strategic Alliances 425
 Selection of Partners 425
 Form of Ownership 427
 Joint Management Considerations 430

Pitfalls of Strategic Alliances 432
 Incompatibility of Partners 432
 Access to Information 432
 Distribution of Earnings 433
 Potential Loss of Autonomy 434
 Changing Circumstances 434

Chapter Review 435
Building Global Skills 436
Closing Case: Ford and Mazda Share the Driver's Seat 437

Chapter Notes **438**

POINT/COUNTERPOINT: What Role Should Foreign
MNCs Play in South Africa? **440**

CHAPTER 13

Organization Design for International Business **442**

Case: Ford's New Global Design **443**

The Nature of International Organization Design 444

Initial Impacts of International Activity on Organization Design 446
  The Corollary Approach **446**
  The Export Department **447**
  The International Division **447**

Global Organization Designs 448
  Global Product Design **449**

  Going Global: Daimler-Benz Is More Than
    Mercedes **451**

  Global Area Design **452**
  Global Functional Design **454**
  Global Customer Design **456**
  Global Matrix Design **457**
  Hybrid Global Designs **458**

Related Issues in Global Organization Design 459
  Centralization versus Decentralization **459**
  Role of Subsidiary Boards of Directors **461**
  Coordination in the Global Organization **462**

Corporate Culture in International Business 464
  Creating the Corporate Culture in
    International Business **464**
  Managing the Corporate Culture in
    International Business **465**

Managing Change in International Business 466
  Reasons for Change in International
    Business **466**

Types of Change in International
    Business **467**

Chapter Review 468
Building Global Skills 470
Closing Case: Unilever's Unique Design **470**
Chapter Notes 471

CHAPTER 14

Managing Behavior and Interpersonal Relations **474**

Case: The Sony Way **475**

Basic Perspectives on Individual Differences 478
  Social Orientation **478**
  Power Orientation **480**
  Uncertainty Orientation **482**
  Goal Orientation **485**
  Time Orientation **486**

Motivation in International Business 486
  Need-Based Models across Cultures **487**
  Process-Based Models across Cultures **489**
  The Reinforcement Model across
    Cultures **490**

Leadership in International Business 490

Decision Making in International Business 492
  Models of Decision Making **492**
  The Normative Model across Cultures **494**
  The Descriptive Model across Cultures **496**

Groups and Teams in International Business 497
  The Nature of Group Dynamics **497**
  Managing Cross-Cultural Teams **497**

  Going Global: The Best and the
    Brightest **498**

Chapter Review 499
Building Global Skills 500

Closing Case: People Propel Rank Xerox **501**

Chapter Notes **502**

CHAPTER 15

Controlling the International Business **504**

Case: Remaking Siemens **505**

Levels of Control in International Business **507**
    Strategic Control **507**
    Going Global: The Importance of Control **510**
    Organizational Control **511**
    Operations Control **514**

Managing the Control Function in International Business **515**
    Establishing International Control Systems **515**
    Essential Control Techniques **520**
    Behavioral Aspects of International Control **522**

Controlling Productivity in International Business **524**
    Productivity around the World **525**
    Managing Productivity **525**

Controlling Quality in International Business **527**
    Quality around the World **528**
    Total Quality Management **530**

Controlling Information in International Business **533**
    The Role of Information **533**
    Managing Information **534**

Chapter Review **535**
Building Global Skills **536**

Closing Case: A New Face for Laura Ashley **537**

Chapter Notes **539**

PART 5

MANAGING INTERNATIONAL BUSINESS OPERATIONS **542**

CHAPTER 16

International Marketing **544**

Case: Nestlé: The Swiss Giant **545**

International Marketing Management **547**
    International Marketing and Business Strategies **547**
    The Marketing Mix **549**
    Standardization versus Customization **550**

Product Policy **553**
    Standardized Products or Customized Products? **553**
    Legal Forces **554**
    Cultural Influences **555**
    Going Global: International Marketing Ethics **556**
    Economic Factors **556**
    Brand Names **557**

Pricing Issues and Decisions **557**
    Pricing Policies **558**
    Market Pricing **559**

Promotion Issues and Decisions **561**
    Advertising **562**
    Personal Selling **566**
    Sales Promotion **567**
    Public Relations **567**
    Going Global: Sales Promotions Can Be Too Successful **568**

Distribution Issues and Decisions **569**
    International Distribution **569**
    Channels of Distribution **570**

Chapter Review **574**
Building Global Skills **576**
Closing Case: Levi Strauss: Clothing
    the World **576**
Chapter Notes **577**

CHAPTER 17

**International Operations
Management** **580**

Case: Coloring the World **581**

**The Nature of International Operations
Management** **583**
    The Strategic Context of International
        Operations Management **584**
    Complexities of International Operations
        Management **585**

Production Management **585**
    Sourcing and Vertical Integration **586**
    Location Decisions **592**
    International Logistics and Materials
        Management **596**
    Going Global: Just-in-Time Inventory
        Management **597**

International Service Operations **598**
    Characteristics of International
        Services **599**
    The Role of Government in International
        Services Trade **600**
    Managing Service Operations **601**

Chapter Review **602**
Building Global Skills **603**
Closing Case: Principles to Fasten
    Onto **606**
Chapter Notes **607**

POINT/COUNTERPOINT: Should International
    Businesses Promote Human and Worker
    Rights? 610

CHAPTER 18

International Financial Management **612**

Case: KLM's Worldwide Financial
    Management **613**

Financial Issues in International Trade **614**
    Choice of Currency **615**
    Credit Checking **615**
    Method of Payment **616**
    Financing Trade **624**

Managing Foreign-Exchange Risk **626**
    Transaction Exposure **626**
    Translation Exposure **629**
    Going Global: Financial Derivatives: Blessing
        or Curse? **630**
    Economic Exposure **631**

Management of Working Capital **634**
    Minimizing Working Capital
        Balances **634**
    Going Global: Colfax and Fowler's Cash Flow
        Solution **635**
    Minimizing Currency Conversion
        Costs **635**
    Minimizing Foreign-Exchange Risk **637**

International Capital Budgeting **638**
    Net Present Value **638**
    Internal Rate of Return **640**
    Payback Period **640**

**Sources of International Investment
Capital** **641**
    Internal Sources of Investment Capital **641**
    External Sources of Investment
        Capital **642**

Chapter Review **644**
Building Global Skills **645**

Closing Case: Janssen Pharmaceutica Cures Its
Currency Ills **646**

Chapter Notes **648**

Closing Case: Globalization of Accounting
Services **679**

Chapter Notes **681**

CHAPTER 19

International Accounting and Taxation **650**

Case: There's No Comparison **651**

National Differences in Accounting **652**
The Roots of Differences **652**
Differences in Accounting Practices **655**
Impact on Capital Markets **657**
Impact on Corporate Financial
Controls **660**
Accounting in Centrally Planned
Economies **660**

Efforts at Harmonization **661**

**Accounting for International Business
Activities** **662**
Accounting for Transactions in Foreign
Currencies **663**
Foreign-Currency Translation **664**

International Taxation Issues **669**
Transfer Pricing **670**
Tax Havens **673**

Going Global: The Ethics of Tax Havens and
Transfer Pricing **674**

**Taxation of Foreign Income by the
United States** **674**
Taxation of Exports **674**
Taxation of Foreign Branch Income **675**
Taxation of Foreign Subsidiary
Income **675**

Resolving International Tax Conflicts **676**
Tax Credits **676**
Tax Treaties **676**
"Bashing" of Foreign Firms **677**

Chapter Review **677**
Building Global Skills **679**

CHAPTER 20

International Human Resource Management and Labor Relations **684**

Case: Training for the World **685**

**The Nature of Human Resource
Management** **686**
Strategic Significance of HRM **688**

International Managerial Staffing Needs **689**
Scope of Internationalization **689**
Centralization versus Decentralization
of Control **691**
Staffing Philosophy **691**

Recruitment and Selection **693**
Recruitment of Managers **694**
Selection of Managers **696**
Expatriation and Repatriation Issues **698**

Training and Development **700**
Assessing Training Needs **700**
Basic Training Methods and
Procedures **701**
Developing Younger International
Managers **702**

Performance Appraisal and Compensation **703**
Assessing Performance in International
Business **703**
Determining Compensation in International
Business **704**

Going Global: The American
Advantage **706**

Retention and Turnover **708**

**Human Resource Issues for
Nonmanagerial Employees** **709**
Recruitment and Selection **709**
Training and Development **710**

Compensation and Performance
　Appraisal　**711**

Labor Relations　712
　Comparative Labor Relations　**712**
　Collective Bargaining　**712**
　Union Influence and Codetermination　**713**

Chapter Review　714
Building Global Skills　715

Closing Case: "You Americans Work Too Hard"　**716**
Chapter Notes　717

Comprehensive Cases　721
Glossary　732
Company Index　745
Brand Name Index　751
Subject Index　753

O PRODUCE STUDENTS WHO WILL BE COMFORTABLE AND EFFECTIVE IN A WORLDWIDE MARKETPLACE—this is our vision in writing this book. When we began planning this book several years ago, we and members of Addison-Wesley's editorial and production staff held numerous meetings with faculty to discuss the needs of students taking their first course in international business. We were immediately struck by the fact that interest in international business has never been higher. Students are well aware of the importance of international business and its impact on their careers and everyday lives. Yet they often feel overwhelmed by the amount of new knowledge they must assimilate in order to master the subject. Further, many of the existing textbooks are written in needlessly technical terms and seem to be concerned only with students who are specializing in international business. However, *all* students—even those who will never have an overseas assignment—need to be knowledgeable about the global economy.

Preface

This is why we feel so strongly about our vision for this book. We want students to attain "cultural literacy" in international business. That is, we want them, for example, to be able to talk knowledgeably with a visiting executive from a French multinational corporation or to understand and analyze the impact on themselves and their firms of trade negotiations with Japan, devaluation of the Mexican peso, economic growth in China or Brazil, or the collapse of a British bank. To accomplish this task, we present in the text a comprehensive discussion and analysis of international business and the environment in which international businesses compete. We describe the global economy, the forces that have created this economy, and the businesses—both large and small—that compete in it.

Distinctive Coverage

We approach the study of international business from the standpoint of *managers* who must function in a global competitive environment. Our presentation of international accounting in Chapter 19 is a good example of how we do this. Some books attempt to make students into international accountants; we leave that task to specialized accounting courses. Our coverage, in line with our vision, provides students with information about those aspects of international accounting that are necessary for them to function effectively as managers. Our goal is to equip students with the knowledge, tools, and insights necessary to succeed in a business environment that is becoming increasingly and inevitably global.

Chapter by Chapter. We have organized our coverage of international business to progress from the broad, general context of international business to the more specific managerial and operational elements of managing in an international business environment. We begin in Part 1 by devoting two chapters to introducing students to the contemporary international business world. Chapter 1 provides a broad overview of international business—what it is, how it has evolved, the reasons for its growth, and its importance to students. Chapter 2—

a unique chapter among international business textbooks—equips students with a basic foundation in economic geography. In addition to detailed maps of the world's major marketplaces, we provide students with relevant historical, political, and economic information about these marketplaces so that they can better understand and appreciate the impacts of these factors on opportunities available to contemporary businesses.

Part 2 describes the international environment of business—the institutional framework that shapes the opportunities available to firms. Our discussion of international trade and investment theories, the international monetary system, the balance of payments, the foreign exchange market, and the global capital market gives students the information they need to succeed in the global marketplace.

Part 3 shifts from the international environment to the domestic environment. This part explores how domestic politics, laws, and culture affect international business activities. It also examines the formulation of national trade policies and cooperative agreements among countries to promote their mutual prosperity.

Part 4 describes the overall set of issues and challenges associated with managing international businesses. The major topics discussed are international strategic management, modes of entry into international markets (with special emphasis on strategic alliances), international forms of organization design, behavioral processes in different cultures, and issues associated with international control. Several elements of Part 4 are unique. This is the only book in the market, for example, to devote full chapters to coverage of strategic alliances, organization design, behavioral processes, and control in international business. Such coverage is clearly warranted because these are all fundamental business functions.

Part 5 focuses on how international businesses manage specific business operations. Separate chapters explore marketing, operations management, finance, accounting, and human resource management—all from an international business perspective.

Currency. Throughout the book, we have made every effort to be as current and up to date as possible in the presentation of theories, concepts, and examples. This book was electronically produced at the publisher's home office, so we had the luxury of being able to update it up to the last minute. Here are some examples of current issues we cover:

▶ The financial disaster at Baring Bank (Ch. 15)

▶ Intellectual property and U.S.-China trade conflicts (Ch. 8)

▶ Depreciation of the Mexican peso (Ch. 2)

▶ The impact of the Uruguay Round on international business (Ch. 7)

▶ The Clinton administration's attempts to control transfer prices used by multinational corporations (Ch. 19)

▶ Uses and abuses of financial derivatives (Ch. 18)

▶ Ethical obligations to honor human and workers' rights in developing countries (Ch. 16)

Historical Perspective. While we do not wish to overwhelm students with history, we have tried to provide relevant historical and political background information to allow them to better understand the environment in which international businesses compete. For example, Chapter 4 examines the political forces that induced the World Bank to create its various subsidiaries. Chapters 2 and 7 discuss the political infighting among members of the European Union and how businesses can exploit these differences to achieve their goals. As future managers, students need to be aware of how these political and historical issues affect the world today.

Examples. International business is one of the liveliest subjects taken by business majors, yet many existing textbooks manage to make it dry and lifeless. We think good examples are critical to students' mastery of the material, so we include more than 1000 company examples to illustrate the theory and practice of international business. We have worked hard to find a variety of relevant and memorable ones. For example, Chapter 6 discusses the complexity of classifying imported goods for tariff and quota purposes. To address this issue, we discuss the importation of Star Trek dolls into the European Union. Students learn that the question of whether Mr. Spock is human or nonhuman is of interest to customs officials and international businesspersons as well as to Trekkies.

Furthermore, many international business textbooks focus on large firms and almost exclusively on Japanese, German, British, and U.S. examples. The authors of these books also fail to realize the types of businesses in which nonindustrialized, less developed countries are involved. This limiting of exposure to a handful of manufacturing firms and a select group of countries means that students miss the opportunity to learn about the truly *global* aspects of international business. While our book presents a balanced coverage of material taken from the major industrial powers, it also covers events in less visible countries; for example, Belgium, Canada, Kenya, Mexico, Namibia, the Philippines—even the Spratly Islands. Maps, photographs, cases, boxes, and our unique Building Global Skills exercises supplement and expand the book's coverage of these wide-ranging examples.

Ethics. No international business textbook would be complete without a detailed presentation of ethics. In this book, we integrate throughout the text the ways in which ethical issues affect international business. Ethical insights are also found in many of the Going Global boxes and Point/Counterpoints, as well as in selected Building Global Skills exercises and Closing Cases (see Learning Features below for a description of these features).

Our book looks at three levels of ethical behavior: individual, organizational, and governmental. For example, as future managers, students must consider whether bribery is ever appropriate, whether they should obey foreign laws they believe are unjust, and whether they should comply with local customs and cultures they find inappropriate or abhorrent. They must also confront ethical issues at an organizational level: for example, does a firm have a moral responsibility to monitor the human and workers' rights policies of its foreign subcontractors and should a firm take into account the impact of its investment policies on local entrepreneurs? Finally, students must grapple with the ethical issues facing countries: for example, whether a government's sole responsibility is to its citizens, regardless of the impact its actions have on the world economy and whether developed countries have obligations to promote the economic prosperity of poorer countries.

Learning Features

In addition to providing thorough and comprehensive coverage of international business, we include a complete, integrated learning system designed to help students master the book's material. Each chapter opens with an outline and a series of learning objectives and closes with a summary, review questions, and discussion questions. The book offers numerous learning features designed to enhance the students' understanding, several of which are unique to this book.

Point/Counterpoint. All too often, students are exposed only to a single point of view in international business textbooks. They don't understand the ways in which two countries or firms can perceive the same situation in different ways. Our Point/Counterpoint feature addresses this teaching and learning challenge by taking important but controversial issues relevant to international business today and providing a discussion—in almost a debate format—of opposite points of view. We include one of these features in each of the book's five parts:

► Trade versus aid: What is the best means of stimulating the economies of developing countries? (Part 1, Ch. 2)

► Should countries encourage or discourage foreign direct investment? (Part 2, Ch. 3)

► Should countries enforce antidumping regulations? (Part 3, Ch. 6)

► What responsibilities do foreign multinational corporations wanting to enter the South African market have to that market's emerging nonwhite business community? (Part 4, Ch. 12)

► Should international businesses promote human and worker rights in developing countries? (Part 5, Ch. 17)

For each of these, the book does not supply a *right* answer. Instead, the basic pros and cons of each side are highlighted and discussed. Accompanying questions are designed to stimulate classroom discussion and provide food for thought for students. Where appropriate, we have highlighted ethical implications of these debates.

Cases. Cases are also an important learning feature. Each chapter's opening case is designed to introduce the student to a particular international business or situation that is relevant to the chapter. This case then serves to motivate the material that opens the chapter and is referenced throughout the chapter as a running example. For example, the opening case of Chapter 10, the strategic management chapter, discusses EuroDisney. Disney's strategy formulation and implementation processes are then used as a running example throughout the chapter.

The chapters' closing cases provide a different perspective on the material covered in the chapter and include several questions that help students analyze the case itself in light of the chapter content. Some cases enable students to delve more deeply into important issues. For example, Chapter 3's opening case involves Caterpillar, and its closing case involves Komatsu, Caterpillar's chief rival. This combination allows the student to discover how changes in the external environment affect competition within an industry. Similarly, Chapter 12's closing case involves the Ford-Mazda strategic alliance, while Chapter 13's opening case examines Ford's 1994 organizational restructuring. This arrangement allows for a natural transition between discussions of strategic goals and structural issues.

Finally, at the end of the book, we include four additional cases for analysis. These cases are longer than the chapter cases and relate to various international business topics and issues that span the contents of several chapters. Thus they serve an integrative function as well as allow instructors and students to examine issues more deeply. For example, "The Ethics of Global Tobacco Marketing" draws on material found in Chapter 3 (international trade), Chapter 6 (national trade policies), Chapter 8 (domestic laws and politics), Chapter 9 (culture), and Chapter 16 (marketing), as well as the discussion of ethics found throughout the text.

Maps. Too few U.S. students today can identify the countries of Western Europe, let alone those that comprise the Four Tigers. Our book includes almost forty maps, including nine in Chapter 2 alone, to help students better visualize where various countries and firms are located and how international business transactions occur. The maps also help students better understand political boundaries and national geography, for example:

▶ Chapter 2 presents a topographic map of South America to demonstrate the physical barriers to trade among South American countries.

▶ Chapter 3 uses a map to demonstrate the economic interdependence of Indonesia, Malaysia, and the Philippines.

▶ Chapter 18 includes a map that helps students visualize a complex, multi-country countertrade deal.

The maps also contain "talk boxes" to highlight aspects important to international businesses. For example, in Chapter 2, the map of the former Soviet Union highlights ethnic differences among the new countries that resulted from the breakup of that empire, and the map of Asia focuses on the wide differences in incomes among countries located on the largest continent.

Photographs. Photographs are integrated throughout the chapters and serve to reinforce and/or expand the material covered. Each has a content-driven caption that explains its importance and relevance to the text. For example, one in Chapter 9 illustrates the cultural adaptation of Barbie dolls that are manufactured in Indonesia and destined for the Asian market. Others, in Chapter 16, depict differences in advertising messages in rich and poor countries.

Going Global Boxes. All chapters contain one or more boxed features called "Going Global." Each feature highlights an especially interesting and important concept, topic, or example that justifies extra attention. Many also address ethical issues, for example:

▶ The ethics of bribery

▶ The linking of trade with human rights

▶ The uses and abuses of financial derivatives

▶ The ethics of transfer pricing

Building Global Skills. Most international business textbooks present theory and concepts but do not provide students with the opportunity to use these in practice. If students are to truly understand international business and master the theories presented, they must take an active role in the learning process. The Building Global Skills exercises found at the end of each chapter require students, alone or in groups, to solve problems, find information in the library, analyze, and critique. Some examples of these exercises are as follows:

▶ Chapter 2 asks students to obtain basic information about the Belgian economy, which requires them to learn about sources of international business data. They will use such knowledge throughout the rest of the course.

▶ Chapter 12 invites students to evaluate potential joint venture partners, requiring them to apply the concepts introduced in the chapter.

▶ Chapter 18 asks students to develop a currency netting operation so that they can experience first-hand the complexities of dealing with numerous currencies and also learn implications of transfer pricing in a more vivid way than they would by simply reading about them.

Ancillaries

Many busy instructors find themselves teaching several different classes and/or teaching classes with large enrollments. To encourage more effective instruction and to help instructors use their time more efficiently, we have developed a high-quality set of ancillary materials for instructors.

Instructor's Resource Manual. The Instructor's Resource Manual, prepared by Veronica Horton of Middle Tennessee State University, contains many valuable materials for all faculty, especially those new to teaching international business. Suggested course outlines will assist instructors in preparing both lectures and class discussions. Detailed chapter outlines, lecture support, and discussions of introductory and end-of-chapter cases are prepared for each chapter. Study questions complement the multiple-choice questions in the Test Bank (see the next item) and may be copied and distributed for students to help them focus on key elements for each chapter.

Test Bank. The Test Bank, prepared by Sesan Kim Sokoya of Middle Tennessee State University, includes the correct answer for each question and the text page on which the answer is found. Discussion questions that may be used either in essay exams or in class discussion are included in the Instructor's Resource Manual. Each chapter includes 45–60 questions, all of which have been reviewed and edited from a student's perspective. Misleading words and phrases, "all of the above" and "none of the above" answers, and trivia-type questions have been eliminated.

Test Generator. The electronic Test Generator for IBM computers allows faculty to personalize exams and easily add, edit, or delete questions from the Test Bank. The order of questions may be scrambled and multiple versions of a test may be prepared. Answer sheets are generated for each test designed.

Videos. A video collection is available from the publisher to adopters free of charge, in addition to a video guide which provides detailed summaries of each tape.

Transparencies. Approximately 110 color acetates and transparency masters which contain a selection of figures, tables, and charts drawn from the text are available.

Acknowledgments

The cover of this book identifies two authors by name. In reality, *International Business: A Managerial Perspective* represents a true team effort involving literally dozens of skilled professionals. While any and all errors of fact, omission, and emphasis are solely our responsibility, we would be remiss if we did not acknowledge those who helped us create this book.

First of all, a dedicated team of publishing experts from Addison-Wesley played an integral part in shaping this book into its final form. Our acquisitions editor, Beth Toland, and our developmental editor, Sue Gleason, were especially important to our work. Barbara Rifkind, Chip Price, Michael Payne, Meredith Nightingale, Loren Hilgenhurst Stevens, Beth Houston, Erin Murray, and Janice Jutras were all major players at one stage or another as we moved from blank sheets of paper to bound book. Jane Hoover of Lifland et al., Bookmakers also played a major role in producing the book.

Next, we must humbly acknowledge the contributions of our colleagues at other universities. Veronica Horton and Sesan Kim Sokoya of Middle Tennessee State University have produced an outstanding instructor's manual and test bank to supplement the main text. A large team of reviewers and focus group participants also contributed mightily to our work. The reviewers, for example, pored over the manuscript through each draft, providing suggestions and noting weaknesses, all with the same goal: to produce a new generation of international business textbook for today's students. These reviewers continuously displayed conscientious and expert oversight to the development of the manuscript, and we tip our hats to each and every one of them:

Dara Khambata
American University

Philip Van Auken
Baylor University

David Oh
California State University
Los Angeles

Jean Boddewyn
CUNY Bernard Baruch College

Robert Kemp
Drake University

Jeffrey Rosensweig
Emory University

Charles Newman
Florida Atlantic University

Robert Vichas
Florida Atlantic University

Bill Renforth
Florida International University

Bill Anthony
Florida State University

Bruce Johnson
Gustavus Adolphus College

Jeffrey Krug
Indiana University

John Stanbury
Indiana University–Kokomo

Gary Hannen
Mankato State University

Basil Janavaras
Mankato State University

Cathy Rich-Duval
Merrimack College

Sesan Kim Sokoya
Middle Tennessee State
University

Susan Douglas
New York University

John Scheidhut
North Dakota State University

Heidi Vernon-Wortzel
Northeastern University

Sharon Browning
Northwestern Missouri State University

Nader Shoostari
Radford University

Tom Bates
San Francisco State University

Thomas Jones
Southern Oregon College

Johnny Duisend
Stetson University

Arieh Ullmann
SUNY–Binghamton

George Westacott
SUNY–Binghamton

Donald Howard
University of Akron

Larry Barton
University of Nevada–Las Vegas

Rose Knotts
University of North Texas

Gary Dicer
University of Tennessee

Michael Song
University of Tennessee

Esra Gencturk
University of Texas–Austin

Jerry Ralston
University of Washington

Scott Kramer
University of Wisconsin

Robert Aubey
University of Wisconsin–Madison

Dharma deSilva
Wichita State University

At Texas A&M University, we have had the good fortune to work with one of the finest groups of professional colleagues anyone could imagine. We gratefully acknowledge the assistance of A. Benton Cocanougher, dean of the College of Business Administration and Graduate School of Business and Dick Woodman, head of the department of management, for fostering an environment that promotes and rewards diverse creative and intellectual work. We also appreciate the support of other colleagues whose expertise and insights have been incorporated into this manuscript. These include Benito Flores, Julian Gaspar, Rafael Gely, Bob Hoskisson, Arvind Mahajan, Ramona Paetzold, Glenn Rowe, Steve Salter, and Asghar Zardkoohi.

Our secretary, Phyllis Washburn, also played an integral part in the development and preparation of this book. Her professionalism and skill were key ingredients in our ability to write it. Thank you, Phyl, for all that you do.

Finally, we would also like to acknowledge the contributions made by our families—Glenda, Dustin, and Ashley Griffin and Zandy, Scott, and Katie Pustay. They didn't write a single word of the book or draw any of the maps or artwork, but their imprint can be found on everything we do. They support us, encourage us, and inspire us. They give our work—and our lives—meaning. It is with all our love and affection that we thank them.

Photo Credits

About the Authors

Page v (top and bottom): Mike Pustay.

Part 1

Page 2: Reuters/Bettmann. Page 3: Lincoln Potter/Liaison International.

Chapter 1

Page 13: Courtesy, Boeing Aircraft Group. Page 14: Courtesy, ABB Archive.

Chapter 2

Page 53: Guis/Figaro Magazine/Liaison International. Page 60 (left): Jasmin/ Liaison International. Page 60 (right): Steve Proehl/The Image Bank.

Point/Counterpoint

Page 74: Reuters/Bettmann. Page 75: Lincoln/Potter/Liaison International. Text sources: "Food Crisis for 34m Africans," *Financial Times,* August 5, 1994, p. 3; "World Bank Attacked for Backing Nyerere," *Financial Times,* July 27, 1994, p. 12; "World Bank Laments Its Tanzania Role," *Financial Times,* July 27, 1994, p. 3; "Empty Promises," *The Economist,* May 7, 1994, pp. 11–12; "The Kindness of Strangers," *The Economist,* May 7, 1994, pp. 19–22; "Developed Nations Want Poor Countries to Succeed on Trade, But Not Too Much," *Wall Street Journal,* September 20, 1993, p. A10.

Part 2

Page 76: © Susan Van Etten. Page 77: Courtesy, The Seattle Mariners.

Chapter 3

Page 83: The Granger Collection. Page 88: James Pozarik/Liaison International.

Point/Counterpoint

Page 114: Courtesy, The Seattle Mariners. Page 115: © Susan Van Etten. Text sources: "Cause for Concern Behind the South Pacific Smiles," *Financial Times,* August 8, 1994, p. 3; Sun Bae Kim, "Foreign Direct Investment: Gift Horse or Trojan Horse," *Weekly Letter* (Federal Reserve Bank of San Francisco), March 20, 1992.

Chapter 4

Page 122: UPI/Bettmann. Page 129: Copyright © 1971 by The New York Times Company. Reprinted by permission. Photo by Susan Van Etten. Page 137: © Susan Van Etten.

Chapter 5

Page 166: Hashimoto/Sygma. Page 170: © Larry Lefkowitz/Tech Photo Inc.

Part 3

Page 192: © Susan Van Etten. Page 193: © Susan Van Etten.

Chapter 6

Page 207: All STAR TREK® elements © 1995 by Paramount Pictures. All rights reserved. Photo by Susan Van Etten. Page 211: Courtesy, Collin Street Bakery.

Point/Counterpoint

Page 230: © Susan Van Etten. Page 231: © Susan Van Etten. Text sources: Lisa Zagaroli, "U.S. Rules Japan Not Dumping Minivans," *Boston Globe,* June 25, 1992, p. 33; "ITC, in Big Blow to U.S. Laptop Makers, Tacks Steep Duties on Japanese Screens," *Wall Street Journal,* August 16, 1991, p. B3; "Laptops: U.S. Pulls Plug on a Domestic Industry," *Wall Street Journal,* August 12, 1992, p. A10; Hiroshi Matsumoto, "Legal Harassment of Foreign Firms: The Case of the U.S. Steel Industry," *Pacific Basin Quarterly,* No. 20 (Fall 1993), p. 31; Tracy Murray, "The Administration of the Antidumping Duty Law by the Department of Commerce," in Richard Boltuck and Robert E. Litan, eds., *Down in the Dumps* (Washington, D.C.: Brookings Institution, 1991), pp. 23–63.

Chapter 7

Page 239: David Hasselhoff/Sygma. Page 250: Deville-Photo News/Liaison International.

Chapter 8

Page 278: © Terry O'Neil. Page 299: B. Swersey/Liaison International.

Chapter 9

Page 325: Sally Weiner Grotta/The Stock Market. Page 329: © Robin Moyer/Time Magazine.

Part 4

Page 342: © Susan Van Etten. Page 343: Werner Frankenfeld/Liaison International.

Chapter 10

Page 346: UPI/Bettmann. Page 369: © 1992 Malcolm Linton/Black Star.

Chapter 11

Page 386: Mike Mazzaschi/Stock Boston. Page 399: Peter Menzel/Stock Boston.

Chapter 12

Page 413: Bachmann/Stock Boston. Page 423: Museum of Modern Art.

Point/Counterpoint

Page 440: Werner Frankenfeld/Liaison

International. Page 441: © Susan Van Etten. Text sources: Alan Chi, Alta Campbell, and Patrick J. Spain (eds.), *Hoover's Handbook of World Business 1993* (Austin, Tex.: Reference Press, 1993), pp. 616–617; "The Color of Money Is Starting to Change," *Business Week,* March 14, 1994, p. 42; "Doing the Right Thing in South Africa?" *Business Week,* April 27, 1992, pp. 50–64; "All Roads Lead Out of South Africa," *Business Week,* November 3, 1986, pp. 24–25; "Soweto Gets Huge New Mall—But Not Everyone Happy" and "We're Still Treated Like Slaves," *Houston Chronicle,* October 30, 1994, p. 26A.

Chapter 13
Page 463: © Hashimoto/Sygma. Page 465: Peter Turner/Black Star.

Chapter 14
Page 482 (left and right): Mike Pustay. Page 496: Richard Wood/The Picture Cube.

Chapter 15
Page 519: © Wendy Stone/Liaison International. Page 522: Eric Vandeville/Liaison International.

Part 5
Page 542: Pablo Fridman/Liaison International. Page 543: John Chiasson/Liaison International.

Chapter 16
Page 562 (left): Nicholas DeVore/Tony Stone Worldwide. Page 562 (right): Mike Yamashita/Woodfin Camp & Associates. Page 563: Courtesy Ford Motor Company. Photo by Susan Van Etten.

Chapter 17
Page 587: © Susan Van Etten. Page 598: © Susan Van Etten.

Point/Counterpoint
Page 610: Pablo Fridman/Liaison International. Page 611: John Chiasson/Liaison International. Text sources: "Levi Tries to Make Sure Contract Plants in Asia Treat Workers Well," *Wall Street Journal,* July 28, 1994, pp. A1, A6; "Levi's Law," *Far Eastern Economic Review,* April 14, 1994, p. 60; Tim Smith, "The Power of Business for Human Rights," *Business & Society Review* (Winter 1994), pp. 36–38.

Chapter 18
Page 623: Chip Hires/Liaison International. Page 640: Courtesy, Placer Dome Inc.

Chapter 19
Page 659: Porter Gifford/Liaison International. Page 678: Liaison International.

Chapter 20
Page 692: Courtesy Author Andersen & Co. Page 701: Jean-Lou Bersuder/Sipa Press.

INTERNATIONAL BUSINESS
A MANAGERIAL PERSPECTIVE

INTRODUCTION TO INTERNATIONAL BUSINESS

I

Promoting Global Prosperity

All countries have not shared equally in the postwar growth of the world's economy. An important issue facing the global community is how to stimulate economic growth in the world's poorest countries. Are less developed countries best helped by trade or by aid? (See "Point/Counterpoint" on pages 74–75.)

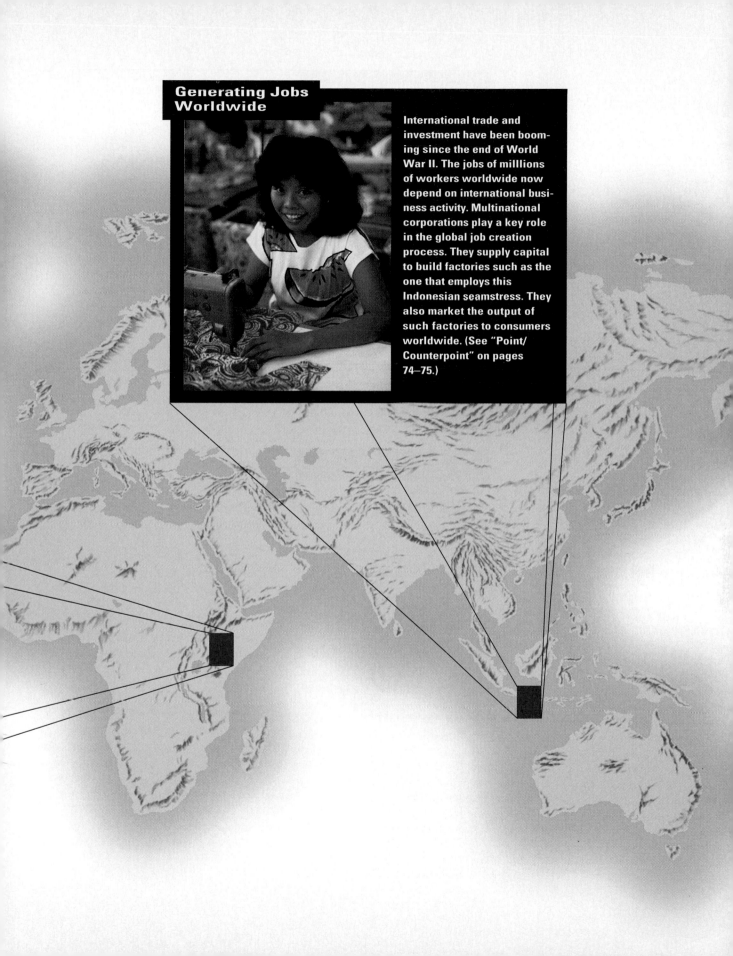

Generating Jobs Worldwide

International trade and investment have been booming since the end of World War II. The jobs of milllions of workers worldwide now depend on international business activity. Multinational corporations play a key role in the global job creation process. They supply capital to build factories such as the one that employs this Indonesian seamstress. They also market the output of such factories to consumers worldwide. (See "Point/Counterpoint" on pages 74–75.)

An Overview of International Business

Chapter Outline

What is international business?

Why study international business?

International business activities

The extent of internationalization

The evolution of international business

The early era of international business
International business growth since World
War II

Reasons for international business growth

An overview of the contents of this book

After studying this chapter you should be able to:

Discuss the meaning of international business.

Explain the importance of understanding international business.

Identify and describe the basic forms of international business.

Discuss the evolution of international business.

Describe international business during the 1950s, the 1960s, and the 1970s.

Characterize the global environment from the 1980s forward, focusing on global competitiveness and the emerging global marketplace.

Describe the growth of international business over the last half-century.

T HE MODERN OLYMPIC GAMES HAVE OFTEN REFLECTED THE prevailing world order. (The first modern summer games were held in 1896; the winter games were added in 1920.) Adolf Hitler sought to use the 1936 games in Berlin to showcase the superiority of the Nazi political system. Arab terrorists used the 1972 games in Munich as a platform for a highly publicized attack against Israeli athletes, killing 16 people. The United States led a boycott of the 1980 games in Moscow to protest the Soviet invasion of Afghanistan. And the Soviet Union reciprocated during the 1984 games in Los Angeles with a boycott of its own. ▌▌ Given that international business and the global economy play such a dominant role in the world today, it should come as no surprise that the Olympic games have also come to reflect international business at its most intense. The games are governed by the

The Business of the Olympics[1]

International Olympic Committee (IOC), which is based in Switzerland. The IOC decides where the games will be held and which sports will be represented and oversees the selection of judges and referees. Each country wanting to send athletes to compete in the games establishes a national committee to organize its Olympic effort. These committees are supervised by and report to the IOC. The IOC has an annual budget of hundreds of millions of dollars, yet the cost of running the games far exceeds this budget. Thus the IOC relies heavily on the host cities to help cover much of the cost. And each national committee is responsible for raising the funds to sponsor its own teams. ▌▌ Potential host cities must prepare elaborate presentations for the IOC and make substantial commitments in terms of facilities, a volunteer workforce, and related organizational support. For example, as part of its winning bid to host the 1998 Winter Olympics, Japan promised to build a new high-speed rail line between Tokyo and Nagano, the proposed site of the games. Further, the infighting to be selected is vicious. For example, China threatened a trade war with the United States after the U.S. Senate passed a resolution that hurt Beijing's chances to host the Summer Olympics in 2000, a prize eventually seized by Sydney, Australia. ▌▌ Why would a city want to host the Olympic games? Most compete for the privilege because the games would thrust them into the international spotlight and because tourism associated with the games would boost their economies. For example, when Atlanta was awarded the 1996 Summer Olympics, that city's officials estimated that over 150,000 people per day would visit the city during the 17-day event. And the tourism benefits are long-lived; for example, skiers, skaters, and snowboarders continue to enjoy the facilities at previous Olympic sites such as Lillehammer, Calgary, Albertville, and Lake Placid, pouring money into the local economies long after the Olympic torch has been extinguished. The games also are frequently a catalyst for improvements in a city's infrastructure. For example, the high-speed rail line between Tokyo and Nagano will halve the travel time between the two cities—a benefit that will continue for local residents and future visitors. ■■ Because of the high cost of running the Olympics— the 1996 Summer Olympics in Atlanta will cost in the neighborhood of $1.6 billion—both the IOC and national Olympic committees are always on the alert for ways to generate revenue. Television coverage provides one significant source of revenue for both the IOC and national committees. For example, the European Broadcasting Union, a consortium of 17 state-owned broadcasters, paid $90 million for the European rights to televise the 1992 games and $240 million for the 1996 games. NBC paid $401 million for the more valuable U.S. broadcast rights for the 1992 games and $456 million for the 1996 games. The EBU and NBC, in turn, will sell advertising time to companies eager to market their goods to Olympic fans throughout Europe and the United States. ■■ Another important source of revenue for the IOC and each national committee is corporate sponsors. Many firms have come to believe that being associated with the games confers a high degree of prestige and status. They can participate in Olympic sponsorship in various ways. The highest-profile—and most expensive—level is that of worldwide sponsor. Firms that market their products to consumers throughout the world, such as Coca-Cola, Eastman Kodak, and Visa, pay millions of dollars to be official Olympic sponsors. The primary benefit of sponsorship is that sponsors get priority advertising space during Olympic broadcasts, if they choose to buy it. For example, Coca-Cola will pay $60 million above and beyond its sponsorship fee for television advertising during the 1996 games. Not only will this provide valuable advertising exposure for the firm, but it also keeps rival PepsiCo from buying any advertising time during Olympic broadcasts. ■■ Firms also pay for licenses to market their products or services in conjunction with the Olympics. For example, during the 1992 games, Evian was the games' official water, Ray Ban the official sunglasses, Bell the official bicycle helmets, and Reebok provided the suits some athletes wore during medal ceremonies. ■■ Sponsorship is even more complex at the level of national teams. National teams typically maintain ongoing and costly training programs and facilities for which there is usually little publicity. Thus opportunities to raise money from the public are limited. Teams consequently depend heavily on corporate sponsorships to cover their costs. But because of the international character of both the games and the businesses, unusual partnerships of teams and firms often are created. For example, Subaru, a Japanese firm, is an official sponsor of the U.S. ski team. Seiko, another Japanese firm, also supports U.S. Olympic teams. Eastman Kodak supports 24 national Olympic teams, and Coca-Cola supports 82 as part of its efforts to maintain a domestic image within each of those individual countries. ■ ■ ■ ■ ■

The Olympic games are supposed to be about sportsmanship and the joys of athletic competition. But in a world of rapidly expanding international markets, they also have come to be about money and international economic competition. Cities on six continents vie to host the games, television and radio networks bid for the rights to broadcast them, and manufacturers of everything from athletic shoes to sunglasses compete for the opportunity to have world-famous athletes showcase their products on the international stage. Millions of dollars hinge on the success of each city, network, and manufacturer in its efforts to become affiliated with the games. Very clearly, then, the Olympics are international business in every sense of the word.

Moreover, the forces that have made the Olympics a growing international business are the same as those that affect firms worldwide as they compete in domestic and foreign markets. Changes in communications, transportation, and information technology not only ease domestic firms' foreign expansion but also aid foreign firms in their invasion of the domestic market. Those millions of dollars spent on the Olympics by television networks and corporate advertisers are symptomatic of the internationalization of business—the result of the desire of firms such as Coca-Cola, Sony Corporation, and Daimler-Benz to market their products to consumers worldwide.

The global economy profoundly affects your daily life—from the products you buy to the prices you pay to the interest you are charged to the job you hold. By writing this book, we hope to help you become more comfortable and effective in this burgeoning international business environment. To operate comfortably in this environment, you need to learn the basic ideas and concepts—the common body of knowledge—of international business. Further, you must understand how these ideas and concepts affect managers as they make decisions, develop strategies, and direct the efforts of others. You also need to be conversant with the fundamental mechanics and ingredients of the global economy and how they affect people, businesses, and industries. You need to understand the evolution of this economy and the complex commercial and political relationships among Asia, Europe, North America, and the rest of the world.

To help ensure your future effectiveness in the international business world, we plan to equip you along the way with the knowledge, insights, and skills that are critical to your functioning in a global economy. To that end, we have included hundreds of examples to help demonstrate how international businesses succeed—and how sometimes they fail. You also will read boxed tips and examples about global companies ("Going Global"), and you will have the chance to practice your growing skills in end-of-chapter "Building Global Skills" exercises and cases.

What Is International Business?

Any business transaction between parties from more than one country is part of international business. Examples of such transactions include buying raw materials or inputs in one country and shipping them to another for processing or assembly, shipping finished products from one country to another for retail sale, building a plant in a foreign country to capitalize on lower labor costs there, or borrowing money from a bank in one country to finance operations in another. The parties involved in such transactions may include private individuals, individual companies, groups of companies, and/or governmental agencies.[2]

How does international business differ from domestic business? Simply put, domestic business involves transactions occurring within the boundaries of a single country, while international business transactions cross national boundaries. More substantively, international business can differ from domestic business for a number of reasons, including the following:

▶ The countries involved may use different currencies, forcing at least one party to convert its currency into another.

▶ The legal systems of the countries may differ, forcing one or more parties to adjust their behavior to comply with local law. Occasionally, the mandates of the legal systems may be incompatible, creating major headaches for international managers. For example, U.S. law promotes equal employment opportunities for women, while Saudi Arabian law discourages the employment of women when they will have to interact with adult males to whom they are not related.

▶ The cultures of the countries may differ, forcing each party to adjust its behavior to meet the expectations of the other. For example, U.S. businesspeople prefer to start meetings on time and to get down to specifics quickly, whereas Latin American businesspeople are less concerned about promptness and more concerned with learning more about the people with whom they are doing business.

▶ The availability of resources differs by country. One country may be rich in natural resources but poor in skilled labor, while another may enjoy a productive, well-trained workforce but lack natural resources. Thus the way products are produced and the types of products that are produced vary among countries.

In most cases the basic skills and knowledge needed to be successful are conceptually similar whether one is doing business domestically or internationally. For example, the need for marketing managers to analyze the wants and desires of target audiences is the same regardless of whether the managers are engaged in international business or purely domestic business. But although international and domestic business are conceptually similar, there is little doubt that the complexity of skills and knowledge needed for success is far greater for international business. International businesspeople must be knowledgeable about cultural, legal, political, and social differences among countries. They must choose the countries in which to sell their goods and from which to buy inputs. International businesses also must coordinate the activities of their foreign subsidiaries, while dealing with the taxing and regulatory authorities of both their home countries and all the countries in which they do business.

Why Study International Business?

There are many different reasons why students today need to learn more about international business. First, almost any large organization you work for will have international operations or be affected by the global economy. You need to understand this increasingly important area in order to better assess career opportunities and to interact effectively with other managers. For example, as part of your first job assignment, you could be part of a project team that includes members from Mexico, Uruguay, Peru, and the United States. A basic grasp of international business would help you to understand more fully why this team was formed, what the company expects it to accomplish, and how you might most effectively interact with your colleagues.

Small businesses also are becoming more involved in international business. If after graduation you plan to start your own business, you may find yourself using foreign-made materials or equipment, competing with foreign firms, and perhaps even selling in foreign markets. For example, a small U.S. firm may buy raw materials from BASF AG (German), communications equipment from Northern Telecom (Canadian), office equipment from Canon (Japanese), business forms from Moore Corporation (Canadian), and manufacturing equipment and machines from the Daewoo Group (Korean).

You also need to study international business because you may eventually work for a firm that is owned by a corporation headquartered in another country. British Petroleum PLC, Siemens AG, and Toyota, for example, employ thousands of U.S. citizens. Overall, more than 2 million U.S. citizens work in foreign-owned manufacturing operations.[3] And this figure doesn't include those employed by foreign-owned service operations or those working outside the United States.

Still another reason for you to study international business is to keep pace with your future competitors. Business students in Europe have traditionally learned multiple languages, traveled widely, and had job experiences in different countries. And more European universities are launching business programs, many of which require students to spend one or more semesters in different countries. Japanese students, too, are actively working to learn more about foreign markets and cultures, especially those of the United States and European countries. These students, training to become managers, will soon be in direct competition with you, either in jobs with competing companies or in positions within your own company. You need to ensure that your global skills and knowledge will aid your career, rather than allowing their absence to hinder it.[4]

You also need to study international business in order to stay abreast of the latest business techniques and tools, many of which are developed outside the United States. For example, Japanese firms have pioneered inventory management techniques such as **just-in-time (JIT) systems**. Under JIT, suppliers are expected to deliver necessary inputs just as they are needed. Similarly, European firms such as Volvo and Japanese firms such as Honda were among the first to experiment with such labor practices as empowerment, quality circles, autonomous work groups, and cross-functional teams to raise the productivity and satisfaction of their workforces. Managers who remain ignorant of the innovations of their international competitors are doomed to fail in the global marketplace.

GOING GLOBAL

A Rose by Any Other Name ...

Most people in the United States are familiar with the abbreviation **Inc.** and are accustomed to seeing business names such as Burlington Northern, Inc. and Lands' End, Inc. The term, of course, stands for *incorporated* and means that the liability of the company's owners is limited to the extent of their investments if the company fails or encounters financial or legal difficulties. But other countries have different terminology when dealing with this concept of *limited liability.*

For example, Germany uses three different terms to reflect different forms of limited liability. **Aktiengesellschaft (AG)** is used for a large, publicly held firm that must have a management board and a board of directors. Examples include Deutsche Bank AG and Volkswagen AG. **Kommanditgesellschaft auf Aktien (KGaA)** is used for a firm that is owned by limited partners but has at least one shareholder with unlimited liability. Henkel KGaA, a German chemicals manufacturer, is an example. Finally, **Gesellschaft mit beschränkter Haftung (GmbH)** applies to smaller, privately held companies.

In Japan, **kabuskiki kaisha (KK)** is used for all limited-liability companies. In the Netherlands **BV (besloten vennootschap)** refers to a privately held, limited-liability firm and **NV (naamloze vennootschap)** to a publicly held, limited-liability firm, such as Philips Electronics NV. The United Kingdom also distinguishes between privately held and publicly held limited-liability companies, using **Ltd.** for the former and **PLC** for the latter. Examples are Swire Pacific Ltd. and Glaxo Holdings PLC. Italy uses **Spa (la società per azioni)** to denote a limited-liability firm, for example, Benetton Group Spa and Fiat Spa. France uses **SA (société anonyme)** for the same purpose, as in Carrefour SA and Hachette SA.

Finally, you need to study international business to obtain cultural literacy. As global cultures and political systems become even more intertwined, understanding and appreciating the similarities and differences of the world's peoples will become increasingly important. You will more often encounter colleagues, customers, suppliers, and competitors from different countries and cultural backgrounds. Knowing something about how and where their countries and companies fit into the global economy—or at least knowing where to go to find that information—can help you earn their respect and confidence as well as give you a competitive edge in dealing with them (see "Going Global"). Conversely, if you know little or nothing about the rest of the world, you may very well come off as being provincial, arrogant, or simply inept. And this holds true regardless of whether you are a manager, a consumer, or just an observer of world events.

International Business Activities

Historically, international business activity first took the form of exporting and importing. **Exporting** is the selling of products made in one's own country for use or resale in other countries. **Importing** is the buying of products made in other countries for use or resale in one's own country. Today many firms' first ventures into the international marketplace begin with exporting or importing. In this way they often can limit their investments to little more than the value of what is being traded, thereby controlling their direct financial risk in their initial international endeavors.

Exporting and importing activities often are subdivided into two groups:

1 Trade in goods, that is, tangible products such as clothing, computers, and raw materials. Official U.S. government publications call this type of trade **merchandise exports and imports**. The British call it *visible trade*.

2 Trade in services, that is, intangible products such as banking, travel, and accounting activities. In the United States this type of trade is called **service exports and imports**. The British call it *invisible trade*.

Figure 1.1 shows the volume of merchandise trade among the Americas, Europe, and Asia.

Exports are often critical to a firm's financial health. Over 58 percent of the sales of one of the largest U.S. exporters, Boeing Aircraft Company, are to foreign customers. Approximately 70,000 jobs in the Seattle area are directly attributable to Boeing's exports. But international sales often are equally important to smaller firms, particularly those that serve niche markets. For example, Lixi is a medical technology firm based in Downer's Grove, Illinois. In a typical year 55 percent of its sales come from abroad.[5] And trade is important to countries as well, as Fig. 1.2 shows.

Exporting also is important in an economy's service sector. Today services generate over 60 percent of the gross domestic products (GDPs) of the world's industrialized countries and account for an increasing proportion of global imports and exports.[6] Consulting, communications, transportation, tourism, and information services, for example, are all becoming more important in international trade, partly because they help facilitate other forms of international business.[7] For example, in 1983 U.S. service exports equaled $64 billion, or 24 percent of total U.S. exports of goods and services. By 1993 that figure had reached $185 billion, or 29 percent of total exports of goods and services.

The second major form of international business activity is **international investments**—capital supplied by residents of one country to residents of another. Traditionally, such investments are divided into two categories:

FIGURE 1.1

Merchandise Trade among Asia, Europe, and the Americas, 1992

Source: GATT, *International Trade Statistics*, 1993, p. 8.

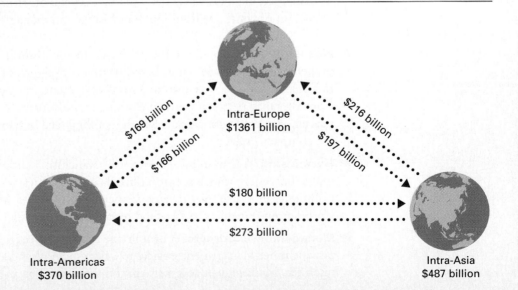

Intra-Europe $1361 billion

$169 billion

$166 billion

$216 billion

$197 billion

$180 billion

$273 billion

Intra-Americas $370 billion

Intra-Asia $487 billion

FIGURE 1.2

**Merchandise
Exports as a
Percentage of GDP
for Some Key
Countries**

Source: World Bank, *World
Development Report*, 1994,
pp. 166–167, 186–187.

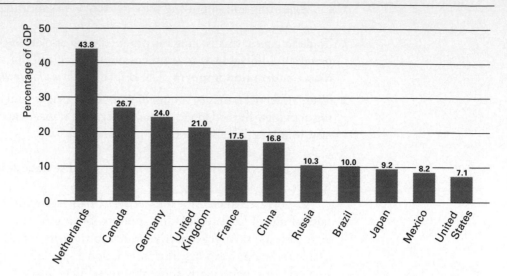

1. **Foreign direct investments (FDI)** are investments made for the purpose of actively controlling property, assets, or companies located in host countries. (The country in which the parent company's headquarters is located is called the **home country**; any other country in which it operates is known as a **host country**.) An example of FDI is the 1990 purchase of all the common stock of Jaguar Motor Company (U.K.) by Ford Motor Company. After the purchase, Ford installed its own executives to oversee Jaguar's operations and integrate them into Ford's European procurement and marketing programs.

2. **Portfolio investments** are purchases of foreign financial assets (stocks, bonds, and certificates of deposit) for a purpose other than control. An example of a portfolio investment is the purchase of 1000 shares of Sony's common stock by a Dutch pension fund. With this investment, the pension fund was trying to raise the attractiveness of its asset portfolio rather than to control Sony's decision making. For the same reason many investors in recent years have bought shares of mutual funds that specialize in foreign stocks and bonds.

International business activity can take several other forms, among the most important of which are licensing, franchising, and management contracts:

▶ **Licensing.** A firm in one country licenses the use of some or all of its intellectual property (patents, trademarks, brand names, copyrights, or trade secrets) to a firm in a second country in return for a royalty payment. For example, the Walt Disney Company may permit a German clothing manufacturer to market children's pajamas embroidered with Mickey Mouse's smiling face in return for a percentage of the company's sales.

▶ **Franchising.** A firm in one country (the franchisor) authorizes a firm in a second country (the franchisee) to utilize its brand names, logos, and operating techniques in return for a royalty payment. For example, McDonald's Corporation franchises its fast-food restaurants worldwide.

▶ **Management contracts.** A firm in one country agrees to operate facilities or provide other management services to a firm in another country for an agreed-upon fee. Management contracts are common, for example, in the upper end of

International business is extremely important to Boeing. In 1993, for example, the firm's exports exceeded $14 billion. Boeing sells aircraft to virtually every major airline in the world. Its biggest competitors are McDonnell Douglas, a U.S.-based firm, and Airbus Industrie, a European consortium of aerospace firms.

the international hotel industry. Hoteliers such as Marriott and Hilton often do not own the expensive hotels outside the United States that bear their brand names but rather operate them under management contracts.

The Extent of Internationalization

To aid in understanding international business activity, experts have categorized firms according to the extent of their international activities. The broadest category is **international business**, an organization that engages in cross-border commercial transactions with individuals, private firms, and/or public-sector organizations. But note that we have also used the term *international business* to mean cross-border commercial transactions. Whenever you see this term, you need to determine from the context in which it is being used whether it is referring to a general process involving transactions across borders or a single organization engaging in specific transactions across borders.

The term **multinational corporation (MNC)** is used to identify firms that have extensive involvement in international business. A more precise definition of a multinational corporation is a firm "that engages in foreign direct investment and owns or controls value-adding activities in more than one country."[8] In addition to owning and controlling foreign assets, MNCs typically buy resources in a variety of countries, create goods and/or services in a variety of countries, and then sell those goods and services in a variety of countries. They generally coordinate their activities from a central headquarters, but also allow their affiliates or subsidiaries in foreign markets considerable latitude in adjusting their operations to local circumstances.

IBM is a good example of an MNC. This computer firm imports electronic components to the United States from over 50 foreign countries, exports its computers to over 130 foreign countries, and has direct investments in 45 countries. While many people think of IBM as a U.S. firm, it earns more than half its sales and profits abroad. Other well-known MNCs include Daimler-Benz, Nestlé, Toyota, and Unilever. Table 1.1 lists the world's largest industrial MNCs.

Multidomestic corporations tailor their operations to the various national markets in which they compete. Asea Brown Boveri, Ltd. (ABB), an electrical engineering firm that is legally Swedish but headquartered in Switzerland is one such company. As shown here, the firm employs a workforce that reflects considerable diversity.

Because some large MNCs—such as accounting partnerships and Lloyd's of London—are not true corporations, some writers distinguish between multinational corporations and *multinational enterprises (MNEs)*. Further, not-for-profit organizations—such as the IOC and the International Red Cross—are not true enterprises, so the term *multinational organization (MNO)* can be used when one wants to refer to both not-for-profit and profit-seeking organizations. Because of the common use of *multinational corporation* in the business press, however, we use it in this book, even though technically its use should be restricted to businesses that are legal corporations.

The term *multinational corporation* generally can be applied to most of the world's larger, well-known businesses. At times, however, this terminology is too broad, and more precise terms are needed to further categorize MNCs. International business experts often find it useful to refer to three different types of MNCs:

1 A **multidomestic corporation** views itself as a collection of relatively independent operating subsidiaries, each of which is focused on a specific domestic market and is free to customize its products, marketing campaigns, and production techniques to best serve the needs of its local customers. The multidomestic approach is particularly useful when distinct differences exist among national markets; economies of scale in production, distribution, and marketing are low; and coordination costs between the parent corporation and its foreign subsidiaries are high. Because each subsidiary needs to be responsive to the local market, the parent typically delegates much power and authority to managers of its subsidiaries in host countries.

2 A **global corporation** views the world as a single marketplace and strives to create standardized goods and services that will meet the needs of customers worldwide. The underlying philosophies of a multidomestic corporation and a global corporation are antithetical. The former believes consumers in each country are basically different; the latter believes consumers are basically similar regardless of their nationalities. A global corporation thus views the world market as a single entity as it develops, produces, and sells products. It seeks to capture economies of

TABLE 1.1

The World's Largest Industrial Corporations, 1993

RANK	CORPORATION	SALES $ MILLIONS	PROFITS $ MILLIONS	PROFITS RANK	ASSETS $ MILLIONS	ASSETS RANK	EMPLOYEES NUMBER	EMPLOYEES RANK
1	General Motors (U.S.)	133,621.9	2,465.8	7	188,200.9	3	710,800	1
2	Ford Motor (U.S.)	108,521.0	2,529.0	6	198,938.0	2	322,200	7
3	Exxon (U.S.)	97,825.0	5,280.0	1	84,145.0	7	91,000	66
4	Royal Dutch/Shell Group (U.K./Neth.)	95,134.4	4,505.2	2	99,664.6	4	117,000	43
5	Toyota Motor (Japan)	85,283.2	1,473.9	21	88,150.0	5	109,279	51
6	Hitachi (Japan)	68,581.8	605.0	69	87,217.7	6	330,637	6
7	International Business Machines (U.S.)	62,716.0	(8,101.0)	494	81,113.0	8	267,196	9
8	Matsushita Electric Industrial (Japan)	61,384.5	227.0	164	80,006.2	9	254,059	11
9	General Electric (U.S.)	60,823.0	4,315.0	3	251,506.0	1	222,000	14
10	Daimler-Benz (Germany)	59,102.0	364.0	119	52,271.3	11	366,736	4
11	Mobil (U.S.)	56,576.0	2,084.0	11	40,585.0	27	61,900	102
12	Nissan Motor (Japan)	53,759.8	(805.5)	481	71,564.0	10	143,310	30
13	British Petroleum (U.K.)	52,485.4	923.6	41	45,828.9	19	72,600	86
14	Samsung (South Korea)	51,345.2	519.7	82	50,492.4	15	191,303	18
15	Philip Morris (U.S.)	50,621.0	3,091.0	5	51,205.0	14	173,000	21
16	IRI (Italy)	50,488.1	NA		NA		366,471	5
17	Siemens (Germany)	50,381.3	1,112.6	35	46,194.6	18	391,000	3
18	Volkswagen (Germany)	46,311.9	(1,232.4)	489	45,586.7	20	251,643	12
19	Chrysler (U.S.)	43,600.0	(2,551.0)	493	43,830.0	24	128,000	38
20	Toshiba (Japan)	42,917.2	112.5	255	52,252.8	12	175,000	20

scale in production and marketing by concentrating production in a handful of highly productive factories and creating global advertising and marketing campaigns. Because of the global corporation's need to coordinate its worldwide production and marketing strategies, it often concentrates power and responsibility at the parent's headquarters.[9]

3 A **transnational corporation** seeks to combine the benefits of global-scale efficiencies (the hallmark of a global corporation) with the benefits of local responsiveness (the advantage of the multidomestic approach). In transnational corporations,

> key activities and resources are neither centralized in the parent company, nor decentralized so that each subsidiary can carry out its own tasks on a local ... basis. Instead, the resources and activities are dispersed but specialized, so as to achieve efficiency and flexibility at the same time. Further, these dispersed resources are integrated into an interdependent network of worldwide operations.[10]

A high degree of interdependence among operating units is required in order for the transnational corporation to combine global efficiencies with local responsiveness;

thus these firms often require complex organizational structures and two-way coordination mechanisms between the parent and its subsidiaries. In practice, they tend to centralize decision making at the parent's headquarters for some functions (such as production and research and development, which require uniform standards and benefit from economies of scale) and decentralize it at the local level for others (such as marketing and human resource management, which may need to be attuned to local cultural differences).

Yet another category of international business exists, although presently only hypothetically. There is no generally accepted term for these organizations, so we will refer to them as world companies. A **world company** is a firm that transcends national boundaries and in so doing loses its national identity. Presently the term represents a theoretical level of internationalization that may or may not ever be achieved in reality. No company has actually reached this level, although some are moving toward it.[11] One firm that is approaching this hypothetical level is Nestlé. While legally a Swiss company, Nestlé has 95 percent of its assets and earns 98 percent of its revenues outside Switzerland. Fewer than 10 percent of Nestlé's employees are Swiss. Moreover, its CEO is German and only five of its top ten executives are Swiss. Another example is Asea Brown Boveri, Ltd. (ABB), an electrical engineering firm that is legally Swedish but is headquartered in Switzerland. About half of ABB's stock is owned by investors outside these two countries. Its top managers are Swiss, Swedish, and German, but its official language, which is used for intracorporate communications and meetings, is English.[12] Service firms such as Reuters (a news agency), Bertelsmann (a publishing company), and Citicorp (a banking corporation) also are moving toward such a worldwide perspective. The "Going Global" feature summarizes how some firms are becoming increasingly involved in charitable giving in different countries as a way of better blending into the cultures of those countries.

The Evolution of International Business

Although the volume of international business has exploded in recent years, its origins developed thousands of years ago. Indeed, many events of the past have played a major role in defining contemporary markets, trade patterns, and financial centers. Moreover, history has played a major role in shaping the faces of many of today's dominant international businesses.[13]

The Early Era of International Business

International business originally consisted of international trade. Trade between nations can be traced back as far as 2000 B.C., when tribes in Northern Africa took dates and clothing to Babylonia and Assyria in the Middle East and traded them for spices and olive oil. This trade continued to expand over the years, encompassing more regions and a growing list of resources and products. Even the Olympic games have their roots in this early era, with the first being held in Greece in 776 B.C. By 500 B.C. Chinese merchants were actively exporting silk and jade to India and Europe, and common trade routes were being established.

GOING GLOBAL

Trying to Blend In

MNCs often find it useful to blend into the local scene. A manager at Rank Xerox, for example, once remarked that his firm tries to look "as European as possible." He argued that this made European customers more likely to see the firm as a local enterprise rather than as a monolithic multinational based in some far-off setting.

In an effort to blend in better, many MNCs are becoming increasingly involved in charitable giving in the countries in which they do business. For example, DuPont recently gave 1.4 million water-jug filters to eight African countries to help local citizens remove debilitating parasites from drinking water. Alcoa teamed up with local authorities in southern Brazil to help build a sewage treatment plant to serve 15,000 rural residents. Heinz has funded infant nutrition studies in China and Thailand to help local officials better understand their citizens' dietary needs. And IBM donated computer equipment and loaned programmers to Costa Rica's National Parks Foundation to help that country develop strategies for preserving its rain forests.

U.S. MNCs are not alone in these efforts. For example, Toyota has made donations to the Boston Pops Orchestra. Mitsui and Company contributes over $500,000 annually to educational and other nonprofit groups in the United States. Honda has become a significant contributor to the United Negro College Fund. And foreign-owned firms throughout the United States have increased their commitment to and involvement in such programs as the United Way and local charitable groups.

Sources: "Charity Doesn't Begin at Home Anymore," *Business Week*, February 25, 1991, p. 91; "Japanese Firms Embark on a Program of Lavish Giving to American Charities," *Wall Street Journal*, May 23, 1991, pp. B1, B5.

Success in international trade often led to political and military power. First Greece and then the Roman Empire prospered in part because of exploitation of international trade. Ancient wars were fought to maintain trade dominance. For example, the Northern African city of Carthage became an international business center that rivaled Rome in the third century B.C., as merchants from Europe brought precious metals and glass to trade for the grains, ivory, and textiles offered by African merchants. Over a period of 100 years, Rome fought three bloody wars with Carthage to maintain its trade supremacy, finally beating the Carthaginians in 146 B.C. The victorious Romans burned the city and plowed salt into the soil (so that crops could not grow) to ensure that Carthage would never again rise as a rival.

During the Middle Ages, Italy became a focal point for international business because of its central location in what was then the world market. The political and military strength of Venice, Genoa, and Florence reflected their roles as major centers of international commerce and banking that linked trade routes between Europe and China.[14] Indeed, some of today's most significant trading relationships were established during this period. Some of the more important international trade routes of the era are illustrated in Map 1.1.

In 1453 these trade routes were severed when the Turks conquered Constantinople (now Istanbul) and gained control of the Middle East. Europe's trade with China had been particularly profitable, so European governments became interested in finding new ocean routes to the Far East. Backed by the Spanish government, Christopher Columbus sailed west from Europe looking for such routes. His landing in the Caribbean islands instead served to identify an important new source of

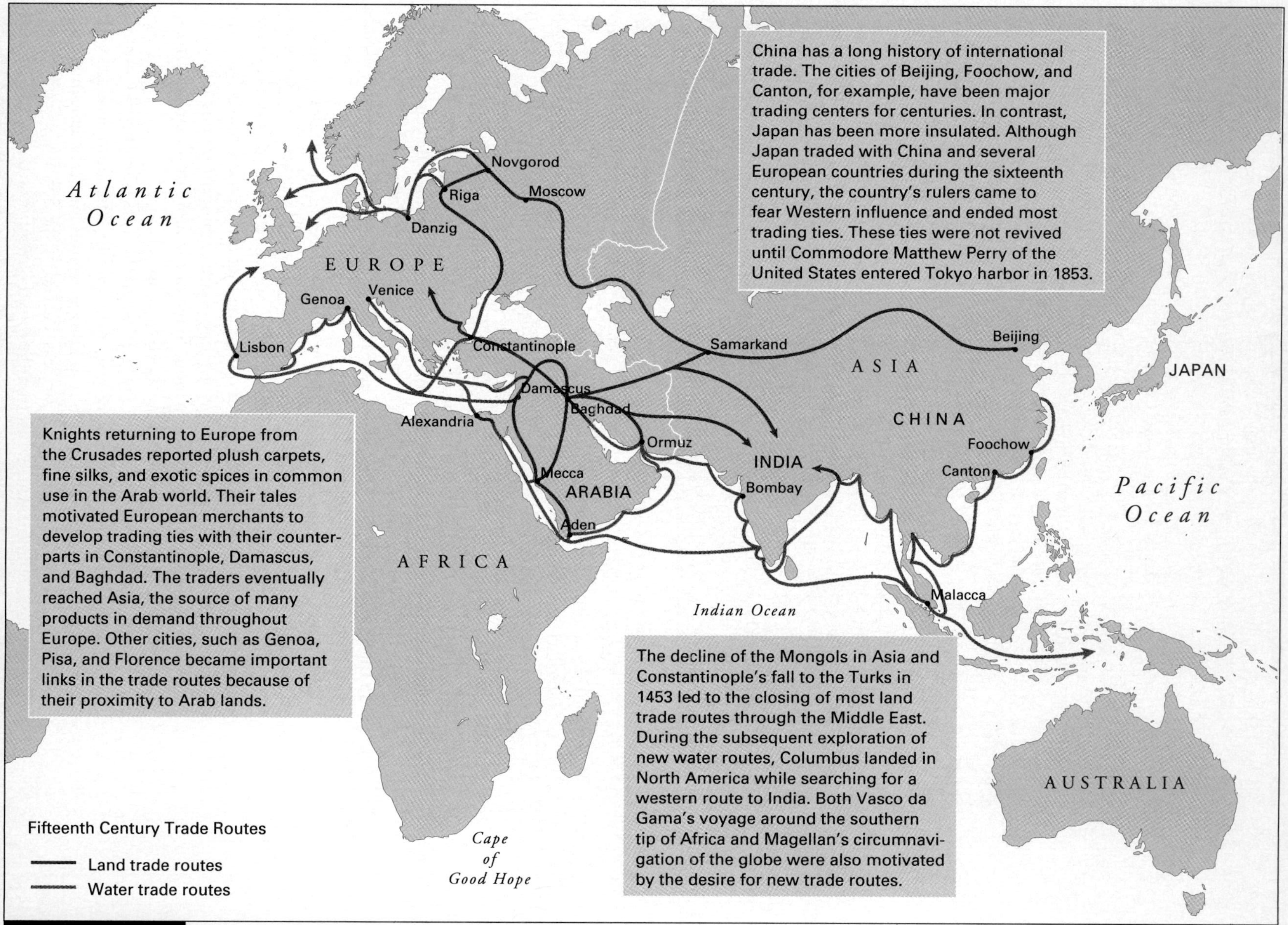
China has a long history of international trade. The cities of Beijing, Foochow, and Canton, for example, have been major trading centers for centuries. In contrast, Japan has been more insulated. Although Japan traded with China and several European countries during the sixteenth century, the country's rulers came to fear Western influence and ended most trading ties. These ties were not revived until Commodore Matthew Perry of the United States entered Tokyo harbor in 1853.
Knights returning to Europe from the Crusades reported plush carpets, fine silks, and exotic spices in common use in the Arab world. Their tales motivated European merchants to develop trading ties with their counterparts in Constantinople, Damascus, and Baghdad. The traders eventually reached Asia, the source of many products in demand throughout Europe. Other cities, such as Genoa, Pisa, and Florence became important links in the trade routes because of their proximity to Arab lands.
The decline of the Mongols in Asia and Constantinople's fall to the Turks in 1453 led to the closing of most land trade routes through the Middle East. During the subsequent exploration of new water routes, Columbus landed in North America while searching for a western route to India. Both Vasco da Gama's voyage around the southern tip of Africa and Magellan's circumnavigation of the globe were also motivated by the desire for new trade routes.
Atlantic Ocean
Novgorod
Moscow
Riga
Danzig
EUROPE
Genoa
Venice
Lisbon
Constantinople
Samarkand
Beijing
ASIA
JAPAN
CHINA
Damascus
Baghdad
Alexandria
Ormuz
INDIA
Foochow
Canton
Mecca
ARABIA
Bombay
Pacific Ocean
Aden
AFRICA
Malacca
Indian Ocean
AUSTRALIA
Cape of Good Hope
Fifteenth Century Trade Routes
Land trade routes
Water trade routes

MAP 1.1 **Ancient Trade Routes**

resources and, eventually, led to the colonization of the Americas by European countries. At the same time, new trade routes to India and China were opened by Vasco da Gama's voyage around the Cape of Good Hope to India in 1498 and Ferdinand Magellan's voyage around the world from 1519 to 1522.

As European countries colonized the Americas, new avenues of trade opened. Settlers throughout the Americas sold raw materials, precious metals, and grains to Europe in exchange for tea, manufactured goods, and other commodities. Most of the American territories eventually became independent countries and important contributors to the world economy.

Another phenomenon of great importance to international business developed during the colonial period and the subsequent Age of Imperialism: the growth of FDI and MNCs, both of which involve foreigners supplying and controlling investments in a host country. European capitalists from such imperialist powers as Great Britain, France, the Netherlands, Spain, Belgium, and Portugal, nurtured new businesses in their colonial empires in the Americas, Asia, and Africa, establishing networks of banking, transportation, and trade that persist to this day. The earliest of these firms founded during this period include the Dutch East India Company (established 1600), the British East India Company (1602), and the Hudson's Bay Company (1670). These and latter-day trading companies such as Jardine Matheson Holdings, Ltd., owned copper mines, tea and coffee estates, jute and cotton mills, rubber plantations, and the like as part of their global trading empires.[15]

In the nineteenth century the invention and perfection of the steam engine, coupled with the spread of railroads, dramatically lowered the cost of transporting goods over land and thereby made larger factories more economical. This development in turn broadened the extent of FDI. The forerunners of such large contemporary multinational corporations as Unilever, Ericsson, and Royal Dutch Shell took their first steps on the path to becoming international giants by investing in facilities throughout Asia, Europe, and the Americas during this period. New inventions promoting technological change further stimulated FDI. For example, in 1852 Samuel Colt built a factory in Great Britain to produce his famous firearms, and later in the century Dunlop built factories in Belgium, France, and Japan to exploit its tire-making expertise.[16]

International Business Growth since World War II

Although international trade has been common for five millennia and international investment for five centuries, these two forms of international business activity have enjoyed unprecedented growth in the past five decades. Figure 1.3 illustrates growth trends in world merchandise exports for each ten-year period since 1950. The trend is both obvious and dramatic—world exports have increased steadily at a significant pace. In 1950 they were around $53 billion.[17] In 1992 they were estimated to be slightly over $3.6 trillion, accounting for 15.5 percent of the world's $23 trillion economy. Most economists expect this trend to continue for the rest of this century and well into the next.

The statistics for FDI tell much the same story. As Table 1.2(a) indicates, in 1967 the total stock (or cumulative value) of FDI received by countries worldwide was slightly over $105 billion, but this figure doubled by 1973 and doubled again

FIGURE 1.3

**The Growth
of World
Merchandise
Exports since 1950**

Source: *International
Monetary Fund Supplement
on Trade Statistics*
(International Monetary
Fund, Washington, D.C.:
1990).

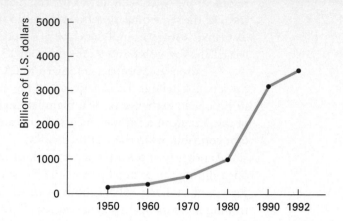

by 1980. Current worldwide FDI is over $1.2 trillion. As you might expect, the
source of most FDI is developed market economies, which have consistently
accounted for about 97 percent of all direct investments in foreign countries, as
the first highlighted line in Table 1.2(b) indicates. Now let's look more closely at
some significant shifts in the stock of FDI over the past 20 years:

1 As shown in the second highlighted line in Table 1.2(b), the United States is becoming a less important source of FDI. FDI by U.S. firms has continued to increase in
absolute terms but has shrunk in relative terms. The United States accounted for
over half of the stock of FDI in 1967 but only 30.5 percent in 1988.

2 Japan's and Germany's importance as sources of FDI has increased dramatically
over the same period, as shown by the third and fourth highlighted lines in
Table 1.2(b).

3 Note from the first two highlighted lines in Table 1.2(a) that the share of FDI
received by the developed countries has increased over the past 20 years, as has
that of the United States. This trend reflects a shift toward FDI motivated by
penetration of large consumer markets and away from FDI designed to exploit
natural resources.[18]

4 Finally, although FDI by Japan has increased [see Table 1.2(b)], Japan's role as a
destination country has remained about the same [Table 1.2(a)].

The growth of international trade and investment reflects the economic,
political, and technological forces that are leading to the globalization of industries and the marketplace. Let's briefly review the evolution of international business over the past half-century to see how these forces have interacted to create
today's economic and political climate.

The Golden Era of U.S. Business: 1945–1960. Consider the situation at
the end of World War II in 1945: air, ground, and sea battles had devastated
much of Europe; most Japanese business centers had been bombarded into rubble;
and of the major industrial powers, only the United States had an infrastructure
and industrial base that was unscathed. As a result, U.S. businesses faced relatively
little foreign competition at home and also enjoyed considerable success abroad.

TABLE 1.2

Destination and Source of FDI, 1967–1988 (billions of U.S. dollars)

a. Destination of FDI by major host countries and regions

COUNTRIES/REGIONS	1967 Value	1967 Percent of total	1973 Value	1973 Percent of total	1980 Value	1980 Percent of total	1988 Value	1988 Percent of total
Developed market economies	73.2	69.4	153.7	73.9	403.4	78.5	959.5	78.7
Western Europe	31.4	29.8	73.8	35.5	186.9	36.4	444.5	36.5
UK	7.9	7.5	24.1	11.6	63.0	12.3	119.6	9.8
Germany	3.6	3.4	13.1	6.3	47.9	9.3	83.5	6.8
Switzerland	2.1	2.0	4.3	2.1	14.3	2.8	23.2	1.9
United States	9.9	9.4	20.6	9.9	83.0	16.2	328.9	27.0
Other*	31.9	30.2	59.3	28.5	133.5	26.0	175.7	14.4
Japan	0.6	0.6	1.6	0.8	3.3	0.6	10.4	0.9
Developing countries	32.3	30.6	54.7	26.3	110.3	21.5	259.8	21.3
Africa	5.6	5.3	10.2	4.9	13.1	2.6	30.9	2.5
Asia	8.3	7.9	15.3	7.4	34.9	6.8	114.0	9.3
Latin America and the Caribbean	18.5	17.5	28.9	13.9	62.3	12.1	114.9	9.4
Other†	NA	NA	0.3	0.1	NA	NA	NA	NA
Total	105.5	100.0	208.1	100.0	513.7	NA	1219.3	NA

* Other developed economies: Australia, Canada, Japan, New Zealand, South Africa.
† Other developing countries: Fiji, Papua New Guinea, Saudi Arabia, Turkey, Yugoslavia, Kuwait, UAE.
NA = not available

b. Source of FDI by major home countries and regions

COUNTRIES/REGIONS	1967 Value	1967 Percent of total	1973 Value	1973 Percent of total	1980 Value	1980 Percent of total	1988 Value	1988 Percent of total
Developed market economies	109.3	97.3	205.0	97.1	535.7	97.2	1108.8	97.2
United States	56.6	50.4	101.3	48.0	220.3	40.0	345.4	30.5
United Kingdom	15.8	14.1	15.8	7.5	81.4	14.8	183.6	16.2
Japan	1.5	1.3	10.3	4.9	36.5	6.6	110.8	9.8
Germany	3.0	2.7	11.9	5.6	43.1	7.8	103.4	9.1
Switzerland	2.5	2.2	7.1	3.4	38.5	7.0	44.1	3.9
Netherlands	11.0	9.8	15.8	7.5	41.9	7.6	77.5	6.8
Canada	3.7	3.3	7.8	3.7	21.6	3.9	50.7	4.4
France	6.0	5.3	8.8	4.2	3.8	3.8	56.2	5.0
Italy	2.1	1.9	3.2	1.5	7.0	1.3	39.9	3.5
Sweden	1.7	1.5	3.0	1.4	7.2	1.3	26.2	2.3
Other**	5.4	4.8	20.0	9.5	17.4	3.2	64.0	5.6
Developing countries	3.0	2.7	6.1	2.9	15.3	2.8	31.7	2.8
Total††	112.3	100.0	211.1	100.0	551.0	100.0	1140.5	100.0

** Australia, Austria, Belgium, Denmark, Finland, Greece, Ireland, New Zealand, Norway, Portugal, South Africa and Spain.
†† Including a small amount of outward FDI by centrally planned economies, especially in 1980 and 1988.

Source: From John H. Dunning, *Multinational Enterprises and the Global Economy*. Wokingham, England: Addison-Wesley Publishers Ltd., 1993. Reprinted with permission.

During the 1950s American Motors (now a part of Chrysler), Chrysler, Ford and General Motors sold all the automobiles they could produce. General Electric and RCA were leading electronics suppliers in most world markets. U.S. Steel and Bethlehem Steel faced virtually no foreign competition. Boeing, McDonnell Douglas, and Lockheed dominated the commercial aircraft market internationally. There were, of course, non-U.S. firms that were successful during this era. But giant U.S. corporations were the primary global suppliers for most industries. Indeed, by the decade's end, 70 of the world's 100 largest businesses were based in the United States.

Quite understandably, the energies of the other major combatants were focused on rebuilding their own economies and infrastructures. Japan, Germany, the Soviet Union, and France had to reconstruct or repair their highways, railroads, and communications systems. A fair amount of this reconstruction in Western Europe was financed with direct or indirect aid from the United States through the Marshall Plan. The **Marshall Plan**, named for U.S. Secretary of State George C. Marshall, was a massive aid program to help European countries work together to rebuild themselves. Some of the work was performed by U.S. firms, thus generating profits for the firms and jobs for U.S. workers. But much of the work in each country was done by local businesses. Thus the reconstruction process revitalized both the infrastructures and the economies of those countries.

The U.S. military also directly affected many foreign economies in the 1950s. For example, during the Korean conflict the United States based many of its supply operations in Japan, resulting in a tremendous infusion of capital, jobs, and technology to that country. Massive postwar U.S. troop deployments throughout Europe also created a similar benefit for European countries. Partly because of U.S. support, many industrialized countries, such as France, Italy, and Japan, achieved annual GNP growth rates of 10 percent or more throughout the 1950s. Thus, while U.S. firms were reaping benefits from their work in reconstructing other countries, they and the U.S. government were nevertheless helping to resurrect the economies of other countries that eventually would become their major competitors. By the end of the 1950s, the process of rebuilding the infrastructures of Europe and Japan was essentially completed.

The Resurgence of Europe and Japan: 1960–1980. As the 1960s began, European and Japanese firms were well prepared to reclaim their traditional shares of the international marketplace.[19] The stage was set for foreign companies to aggressively seek new market opportunities and to expand their operations abroad. For example, Nissan Motor Company started shipping cars to the United States in 1958 under the Datsun name. It established the Nissan Motor Corporation in Los Angeles in 1960 and built its first factory abroad, in Mexico, in 1961. That same year, Alcan Aluminum (Canadian) opened its first foreign plant, in the United States. In 1962 Fuji initiated a joint venture with Xerox to build copiers. In 1967 Mazda introduced its rotary engine in Japan, and the Daewoo Group was created in Korea. And Toyota shipped its first Corona to the United States in 1965, followed by its first Corolla in 1968.[20] The initiatives undertaken by European and Asian firms during this period created the underpinnings of the complex global competitive environment in which firms operate today.

Nor was global expansion limited to industrial firms. For example, in 1961 Japan Air Lines launched the first nonstop flights between Japan and Europe. Deutsche

Bank AG expanded from 345 branches in 1957 to 1100 by 1970, many of them in other European countries and in the Far East, Middle East, and North Africa. Other countries' banks and service firms also were expanding rapidly into foreign markets.

Of course, U.S. firms were expanding their global operations as well. For example, in the 1960s Ford built manufacturing facilities in England and Germany. In 1960 Polaroid was selling film in 10 countries; by 1969 it was selling film in 62. Borden, too, expanded aggressively into foreign markets in the 1960s, as did Merck, IBM, Caterpillar, and Goodyear. By 1970, 64 of the world's 100 largest firms were U.S.-based.

In the 1970s, however, several events weakened the position of the United States in the world economy.[21] Some were a backlash from a decade of heated competition. Others resulted from unpredictable turns in the world economy. During the 1950s and the 1960s demand for products and services had been so great that U.S. businesses did not have to be overly concerned with costs, efficiency, or quality. At the same time, however, many companies in other countries had been waging fiercely competitive domestic battles and had grown quite proficient at using cost and quality for gaining competitive advantage. The Japanese in particular had long been dedicated to maximizing product quality and were among the first to realize that efforts to increase quality actually lowered, rather than increased, costs. Thus, during the 1970s Japanese firms were perhaps better prepared for global competition than were most U.S. ones.[22]

Another significant but unforeseen event of the 1970s was the change in world oil prices and supplies. At that time the Middle Eastern countries took center stage in the global economy (see Map 1.2). The key oil-exporting countries in the region (Libya, Iran, Saudi Arabia, Kuwait, and others) forged a strong cartel, the Organization of Petroleum Exporting Countries (OPEC), which limited production of crude oil and simultaneously raised prices. OPEC's actions affected countries and companies around the world and triggered a massive wealth redistribution from oil-consuming to oil-producing countries. OPEC's policies had a particularly heavy impact on the United States because much of the competitive strength of the U.S. economy was based on the country's cheap energy policies. U.S. consumers and businesses faced the difficult task of adjusting their behavior and purchasing decisions in light of higher energy prices. For example, petrochemical companies such as DuPont, Monsanto, and Dow Chemical had prospered in international markets by converting low-priced petroleum into petrochemicals, plastics, and synthetic fibers. They had to rethink their operating practices and even their corporate missions in light of dramatically higher input costs. The adjustment problem was worsened by the U.S. government's inconsistent and constantly changing energy policies, which alternately created shortages and surpluses in critical markets for electricity, gasoline, and natural gas. Airlines and industrial consumers dependent on reasonably priced energy from reliable sources were particularly victimized by these shifting governmental policies. Further, the U.S. automobile industry suffered major losses in market share because its products were much less fuel-efficient than those of its Japanese competitors.

These forces enabled firms from Europe, Japan, and elsewhere to significantly increase their shares of the U.S. and world markets. With the enhanced profits generated by the increased demand for their products, these firms were able to expand their manufacturing capacities and increase their research and development

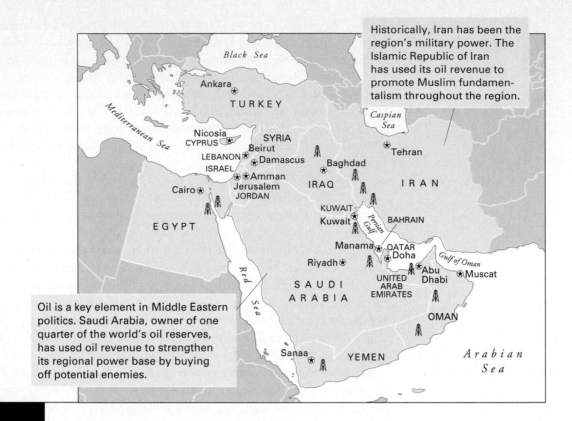

Historically, Iran has been the region's military power. The Islamic Republic of Iran has used its oil revenue to promote Muslim fundamentalism throughout the region.

Oil is a key element in Middle Eastern politics. Saudi Arabia, owner of one quarter of the world's oil reserves, has used oil revenue to strengthen its regional power base by buying off potential enemies.

MAP 1.2

The Middle East

expenditures. During the 1970s entire industry structures shifted.[23] For example, the Japanese came to dominate the steel and electronics industries. European automakers ruled the high end of the market, while Japanese automakers displaced General Motors, Ford, and Chrysler as leaders in the market's middle and low end. Japanese banks, fueled by the success of Japan's manufacturing sector, came to reign over the world financial system. By the end of the 1970s, the number of U.S. firms among the world's 100 largest had dropped to 49.

The New Global Marketplace: 1980 to the Present. By the end of the 1970s managers at many U.S. firms had begun to realize their companies could no longer remain complacent and still expect continued growth and prosperity, let alone world leadership. Many managers also realized that the emerging global marketplace not only posed monumental threats but also offered enormous opportunities. They began paying more attention to what their competitors from abroad were doing and emulating those competitive practices that were most effective, while improving on those that were less so.

One manifestation of this new interest was several best-selling books such as William Ouchi's *Theory Z* (1981), that focused on how Japanese organizations differed from their U.S. counterparts. Ouchi noted that Japanese organizations were highly participative and every worker contributed to making the highest-quality products possible. In contrast, many U.S. firms were highly centralized and workers were given little input into how the organizations were run. As these differences became clear, many U.S. firms began copying the competitive management tactics of Japanese firms. For example, they adopted such techniques as quality circles, autonomous work groups, JIT systems, and statistical quality control procedures because they believed those techniques contributed to Japanese success.[24]

However, U.S. firms discovered that simply imitating Japanese practices did not always work in the highly individualistic U.S. culture. This discovery reinforced the importance of carefully assessing the extent to which specific practices are transferable across cultures. Thus U.S. firms, by emulating their foreign competitors in some areas and using new ideas and strengths developed from their own experiences in others, became better able to compete. For example, Ford and Chrysler, following the lead of Honda and Toyota, began emphasizing product quality, and subsequently each was able to regain lost market share and profitability. Companies in the electronics industry, such as Texas Instruments and Motorola, were reminded of the importance of research and development and cost control by Japanese competitors such as Hitachi and Toshiba. And Eastman Kodak redoubled its product development and marketing efforts after closely studying Fuji. In virtually every international market the increasingly intense competition meant that firms that relied on the old way of doing things fell by the wayside— pushed aside by innovative, quality-conscious competitors better able to satisfy the needs of customers worldwide.[25]

As MNCs in Europe and Japan grew in size and wealth, they also began to escalate their direct investment in the United States. This strategy became popular for several reasons. Some firms wished to quickly establish a major presence in the U.S. market. Canada's Campeau Corporation achieved this goal by buying several prominent U.S. retailers, including Allied Stores (owners of Jordan Marsh and Stern's, among others) and Federated Department Stores (whose key properties included Bloomingdale's and Lazarus). Other MNCs acquired U.S. firms for their unique assets; for example, music libraries and copyrights motivated Bertelsmann AG's purchase of RCA Records and Sony's purchase of CBS Records. Some MNCs acquired U.S. assets as part of their globalization strategies; an example is KLM's investment in Northwest Airlines or Hoechst AG's acquisition of Celanese. Other FDI has been motivated by political and/or marketing factors. Mazda, Nissan, and Toyota have built auto assembly plants in the United States to defuse political criticisms and to counteract "Made in America" advertising campaigns by GM, Ford, and Chrysler.

By the dawn of the 1990s, a competitive global economy was beginning to take shape.[26] There was no single moment in time that marked the beginning of the global era. But today managers in every international business know that the rules of the game have changed dramatically. The old rules, already made brittle by the changes wrought during the 1960s and 1970s, were shattered during the highly competitive 1980s. And the new rules are still being written as the 1990s close out this century.[27]

As Fig. 1.4 shows, three geographic marketplaces now dominate the world economy:

1 United States and Canada

2 The European Union (EU)

3 Japan

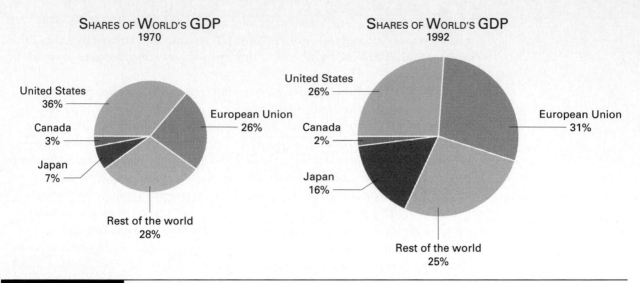

FIGURE 1.4

The World Economy:
1970 and 1992
Source: World Bank, *World Development Report*, 1994.

While other marketplaces are important, and promise to become even more so in the years ahead, these three regions produce and consume the majority of the world's output of goods and services. Chapter 2 discusses each of these major marketplaces, as well as developing marketplaces, in more detail.

The structures of many industries are changing in response to the globalization of the world economy.[28] While some industries remain essentially domestic in nature (such as commercial printing, residential construction, health services, and regional transportation), an increasing number are truly global in nature (including automobiles, consumer electronics, chemicals, and aviation). In these global industries individual firms find that, to compete effectively, they must serve all the world's major markets. For some industries, these global pressures result from economies of scale in production, marketing, or research and development (R&D). For example, aircraft manufacturers such as Boeing, McDonnell Douglas, and Airbus Industrie must sell their products to customers worldwide in order to amortize their multibillion-dollar R&D costs. Matsushita Electric Industrial Co., the Japanese giant whose brand names include JVC, Panasonic, and Quasar, has successfully sought market leadership not only in Japan but also in Europe and the United States in order to maximize the value of those brand names. Similarly, airlines such as Delta, American, and United have recognized that their carefully constructed hub-and-spoke systems designed to corral domestic passengers can also capture international ones. Other industries, such as accounting, advertising, banking, express parcel delivery, legal services, and telecommunications are globalizing because their customers are globalizing. For example, no fewer than three international telecommunications consortia were launched in the early 1990s with the explicit strategy of meeting the communications needs of the world's 100 largest companies. Of course, in between these extremes are other industries that have a clear international dimension but still have many firms with limited international operations. These industries include furniture, mining, publishing, and retailing.[29]

Reasons for International Business Growth

Our brief history of international business provides clear and dramatic documentation of the rate of international business growth in recent years. But why has this growth occurred? And why is international business activity likely to continue to escalate during the next several years? Several factors have contributed to this growth: market expansion, resource acquisition, competitive forces, technological changes, social changes, and changes in government trade and investment policies.

Market expansion is perhaps the most significant catalyst for international business growth.[30] As the productive capacities of firms' factories outgrow the size of their home markets, firms often internationalize their operations to seek new marketing opportunities. In many smaller economies, such as those of Singapore, Switzerland, and the Netherlands, firms quickly recognized that they had to look beyond national boundaries if they were to continue to grow. For example, one of the first international businesses was Nestlé. Because its home country, Switzerland, is so small, Nestlé was shipping milk to 16 different countries as early as 1875. In contrast, the large size of the U.S. market has resulted in many U.S. firms remaining content to sell only within that market. This attitude is disappearing as more U.S. companies recognize the rich commercial opportunities available outside the United States.

International business activity also is growing as firms seek to facilitate *resource acquisition.* These resources may be materials, labor, capital, or technology. In some cases, organizations must go to foreign sources because certain products or services are either scarce or unavailable locally. For example, U.S. grocery wholesalers buy coffee and bananas from South America, Japanese firms buy forest products from Canada, and firms worldwide buy oil from the Middle East. In other cases, firms simply find it easier and/or more economical to buy from other countries. For example, firms in many countries buy their communications equipment from Northern Telecom because they can obtain a complete system relatively inexpensively, which is easier than buying from multiple vendors and then assembling the components. Some firms move their manufacturing facilities abroad because of cheaper labor; for example, Sony and Matsushita Electric have stereo assembly plants in Malaysia. And as world financial systems open up, many firms are seeking capital from foreign investors and lenders. For example, Disney used European investors for over half of the financing for its European theme park outside Paris.

Competitive forces also spur growth in international business activity. Because of economies of scale and the financial strength that comes with larger organizational size, smaller firms often have difficulty competing with larger ones. Thus, when a firm's competitors begin to grow by expanding into new foreign markets, that firm may have little choice but to follow suit. For example, Mazda struggled for years because it lacked the resources of its larger domestic competitors—Toyota and Nissan. It entered the U.S. market in order to keep pace with these Japanese rivals. In the early 1990s, Mazda aggressively introduced several new models that exploit market niches (such as the Miata convertible) and increased its worldwide automobile production. It adopted these tactics to increase its market share, sales, and profits, with the eventual goal of putting it on an equal footing with its major competitors. Similarly, the H.J. Heinz Company, a U.S. food processing firm, recently decided to increase its international presence largely because it felt the need to keep pace with its primary competitors—Nestlé, Kellogg, and Philip Morris—each of which has operations in several foreign markets. A vivid demonstration of this need to keep up with one's competitors can be seen in Central and Eastern Europe, especially Russia. As these formerly inaccessible markets open, literally hundreds of businesses have raced to capture new customers. Each one realizes that if it falls behind its competitors, it may have a difficult time ever catching up.

Technological changes—particularly in communications, transportation, and information processing—are another important cause of the growth in international business activity. Think about the difficulties of conducting business internationally when the primary form of transportation was the sailing ship, the primary form of data processing was pencil and paper, and the primary form of communication was the letter delivered by a postman on horseback. Transportation improvements in the past 150 years—from sailing ship to steamship to seaplane to modern jet airliners—mean that a manager in London no longer needs to spend weeks traveling in order to confer with colleagues in Bombay, Toronto, or New York. The increasing ability of computers to rapidly handle and process vast quantities of information allows firms to manage offices and factories located in every corner of the globe. Exxon, for example, relies on its computers to adjust continuously the output of its refineries and the sailings of its tanker fleet in order to meet changes in worldwide demand for its products. Changes in communications technology, such as the advent of facsimile transmission and electronic mail, enable a manager in Tokyo to receive reports from colleagues in Amsterdam, Abidjan, and Auckland in minutes rather than days. These technological advances make managing a business far easier today than executives would have dreamed possible just a few decades ago and so have facilitated expansion into international markets.

Social changes also have served to increase international business activity. Products and services too strongly identified with a particular culture were once shunned in certain societies. During the 1950s, for example, U.S. consumers avoided Japanese products, partly because they perceived those products to be of poor quality and partly because of lingering resentment from World War II. Similarly, Kellogg struggled in its attempts to open markets in Europe and Pacific Asia partly because many people in those regions traditionally did not eat processed cereals for breakfast: Europeans ate bread and natural grains, and fish was the choice in much of Asia. But because of long and intensive advertising campaigns, Kellogg is now finding its products becoming more accepted abroad. Today, as consumers worldwide tune into MTV and CNN, they are more likely than in the past to seek out foreign-made products. This global awareness boosts sales of such products as exotic bottled waters from France, television sets from Japan, and expensive cars from Germany.

Finally, changes in *government trade and investment policies* have expanded growth opportunities for international businesses. In the past 40 years, countries have negotiated reductions in import tariffs (taxes placed on imported goods) and eliminated barriers to FDI within their borders. Many of the reductions were negotiated through the General Agreement on Tariffs and Trade (GATT), a Geneva-based organization to which most of the world's major trading countries belong. Regional accords, such as the EU and the North American Free Trade Agreement (NAFTA), also have resulted in relaxed trade and investment barriers among their members. Consequently, international business has become more important to the world's economy.

An Overview of the Contents of This Book

As we noted earlier, our mission with this book is to help you become comfortable and effective in the competitive global economy. We use the fundamental perspective of a manager or employee who is or will be competing in the international arena and focus on identifying the major similarities and differences in doing business in domestic versus international settings. That is, we start with the assumption that most users of this book will eventually work for or own a business that is affected by international business activity.

To provide you with the common body of international business knowledge and skills to use in international business, we have structured the contents to move from relatively macro, or general, issues to increasingly micro, or specific, issues that managers deal with regularly. Our rationale is that managers must fully understand the context of international business in order to work effectively within that context. This broad, general context provides the backdrop within which all international business occurs. At each increasingly specific level within that context, the international manager is faced with more specific and operational issues, problems, challenges, and opportunities.

Part I comprises Chapters 1 and 2. Chapter 1 has supplied some background definitions and a history of how the contemporary global business environment evolved to its present form. Chapter 2 provides a wealth of economic and geographical information about the world's major marketplaces and business centers. Together Chapters 1 and 2 lay a foundation of the common body of international business knowledge that provides a useful context for the later chapters. Chapter 2 is especially important because of its coverage of international economics and geography.

Parts II through V follow a logical progression of topics, moving from the broad, general issues confronting international business to increasingly more specific, focused issues that managers face daily (see Fig. 1.5). Part II discusses in more detail the *international* environment itself, addressing the overall context of international business and introducing many of the global forces and conditions that affect organizations and managers. Part III describes the *national* environment of international business—the more specific country-level environmental context of today's organizations.

Part IV adopts the perspective of a specific organization, focusing on general management issues such as international strategies, modes of entry into foreign markets, joint ventures and strategic alliances, organization design, individual behavior, and control in international business. Part V covers the management of specific international business functions: marketing, operations, finance, accounting, and human resource management.

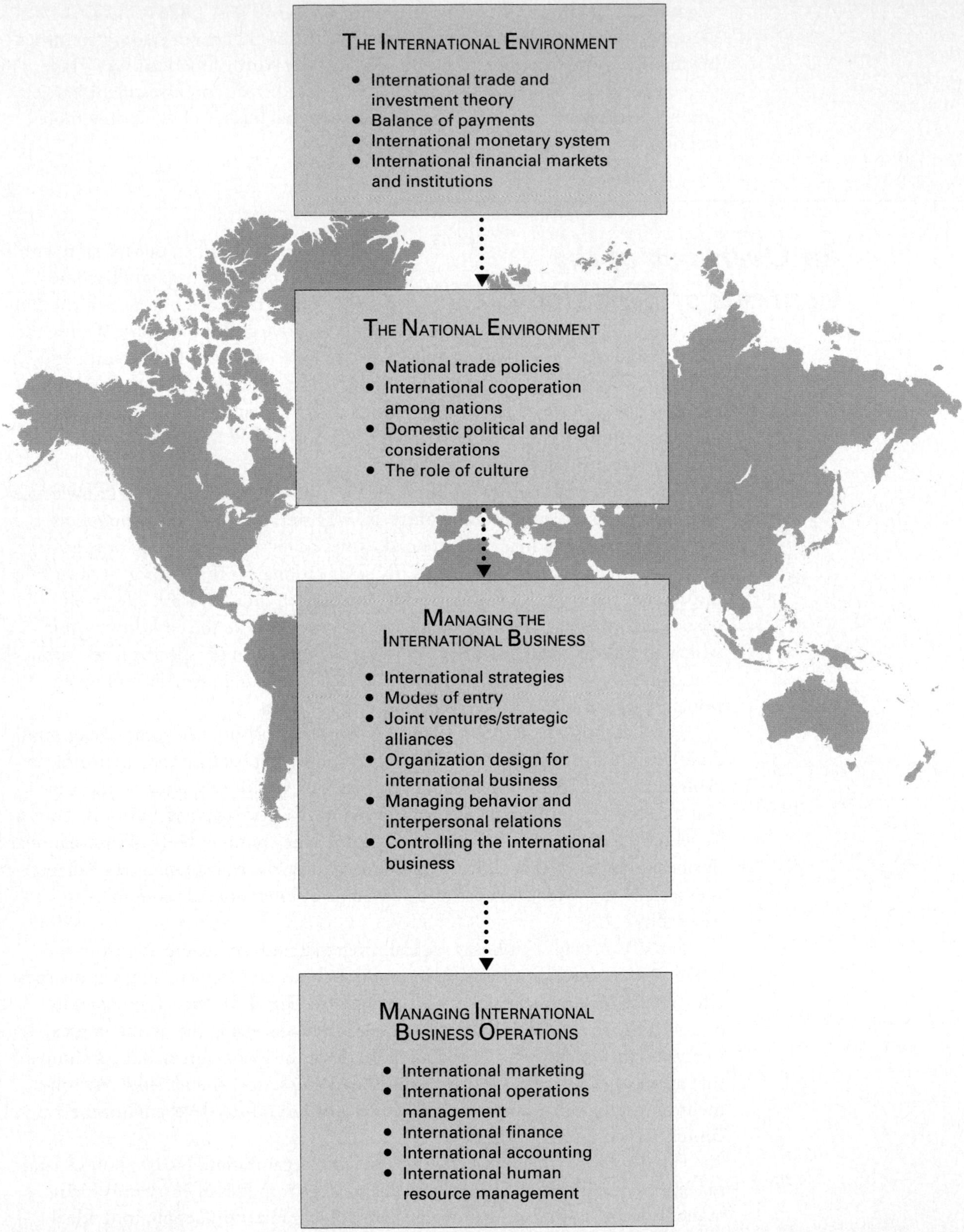

THE INTERNATIONAL ENVIRONMENT

- International trade and investment theory
- Balance of payments
- International monetary system
- International financial markets and institutions

THE NATIONAL ENVIRONMENT

- National trade policies
- International cooperation among nations
- Domestic political and legal considerations
- The role of culture

MANAGING THE INTERNATIONAL BUSINESS

- International strategies
- Modes of entry
- Joint ventures/strategic alliances
- Organization design for international business
- Managing behavior and interpersonal relations
- Controlling the international business

MANAGING INTERNATIONAL BUSINESS OPERATIONS

- International marketing
- International operations management
- International finance
- International accounting
- International human resource management

FIGURE 1.5 Framework for This Book

CHAPTER REVIEW

Summary

International business encompasses any business transaction that involves parties from more than one country. These transactions can take various forms and can involve individual companies, groups of companies, and/or government agencies.

International business can differ from domestic business because of differences in currency, legal systems, cultures, and resource availability.

Studying international business is important for several reasons:

▶ Any organization you work for, even if small, is likely to be affected by the global economy.

▶ You some day may work for a foreign-owned firm.

▶ You need to keep pace with other managers who are learning to function in international settings.

▶ You need to be culturally literate in today's world.

International business activity can take various forms. Exporting involves selling products made in one's own country for use or resale in another country. Importing involves buying products made in other countries for use or resale in one's own country. Foreign direct investment is investment made for the purpose of controlling property, assets, or companies located in foreign countries. Other common forms of international business activity include licensing, franchising, and management contracts.

An international business is one that engages in commercial transactions with individuals, private firms, and/or public-sector organizations that cross national boundaries. Firms with extensive international involvement are called multinational corporations, or MNCs. Special forms of multinational corporations include multidomestic corporations, global corporations, and transnational corporations.

Evidence of international business activity can be traced back thousands of years; many of today's major international trading patterns have evolved over several centuries. During the 1950s the United States dominated the global economy because many other industrialized countries were rebuilding after World War II. But international competition began to increase during the 1960s and eventually led to the end of U.S. dominance in the 1970s. In the 1980s many U.S. firms gradually began to regain their competitiveness. As the 1990s dawned, global marketplaces and global industries were becoming fairly well-defined.

International business has grown dramatically in recent years because of market expansion, resource acquisition, competitive forces, technological changes, social changes, and changes in government trade and investment policies.

Review Questions

1. What is international business? How does it differ from domestic business?

2. Why is it important for you to study international business?

3. What are the basic forms of international business activity?

4. How do merchandise exports and imports and service exports and imports differ?

5. What is portfolio investment?

6. Identify and describe the various kinds of international businesses that exist today.

7. Briefly summarize the evolution of international business.

8. How did World War II shape international business? How might business have shaped the war?

9. Trace the U.S. role in international business through the 1950s, 1960s, and 1970s.

10. What are the basic reasons for the recent growth of international business activity?

Questions for Discussion

1. Do you think true world companies will ever really exist? Why or why not?

2. If the trade routes through the Middle East had not been closed in 1453, how might the history of international business have been different?

3. What types of firms were likely to prosper during World War II? What types were more likely to have suffered during the war?

4. Why do some industries become global while others remain local or regional?

5. Under what circumstances might a firm want to decrease its level of international activity?

6. Does your college or university have any international programs? Does this make the institution an international business? Why or why not?

7. What are some of the skill differences that may exist between managers in a domestic firm and those in an international firm?

8. Would you want to work in a foreign-owned firm? Why or why not?

9. Are the Olympics and business too intertwined? What are the pros and cons of the increased commercialization of the Olympics?

10. How is managing the IOC similar to and different from managing a business?

 **BUILDING GLOBAL SKILLS**

List ten different products you use on a regular basis, such as your alarm clock, camera, car, coffee maker, computer, razor, sneakers, telephone, television, or VCR—perhaps even your favorite movie, shirt, fruit juice, or type of recording tape.

After you have developed your list, go to the library and research the following for each item:

1. What firm made the item?

2. In which country is that firm based?

3. What percentage of the firm's annual sales comes from the United States? What percentage comes from other countries?

4. Where was the item most likely manufactured?

5. Why do you think it was manufactured there?

Follow up by meeting with a small group of your classmates and completing these activities:

1. Discuss the relative impact of international business on your daily lives.

2. Compile a combined list of the ten most common products the average college student might use.

3. Try to identify the brands of each product that are made by U.S. firms.

4. Try to identify the brands of each product that are made by non-U.S. firms.

5. Does either of your lists of ten products include items that have components that are both U.S.-made and non–U.S.-made?

CLOSING CASE

The Rise and Fall of the British Sportscar [31]

Imagine being the world's largest exporter of a product and controlling the lion's share of the world's biggest market for that product. Now imagine first losing the export title and then being forced to drop completely out of the business—all in relatively few years. Could such a debacle occur? Yes—and it involved the British firms that first created, then dominated, and eventually dropped out of the market for low- to- mid-priced sportscars.

During the first six decades of this century, the MG Car Company became a major player in the British auto industry. Mirroring the strategy used by Alfred Sloan, president of GM from 1923 to 1937, MG developed and sold a variety of cars in every price range. This allowed the firm to sell entry-level cars to young families and later to get them to "trade up" to more expensive models. One part of the MG product line was an inexpensive, two-seat sportscar called—simply enough—the MG; the Morris and the Riley were two of the firm's most successful family cars.

At the conclusion of World War II, two things happened to create a golden opportunity for MG. First, the British government, in dire need of hard currency, pressured domestic automobile manufacturers to export 70 percent of their output to the United States, where hard currency was readily available. To reinforce this pressure, the British government restricted domestic sales of automobiles. Thus MG, along with other British automakers, began shipping large quantities of cars to the U.S. market.

The second factor underlying MG's golden opportunity was unexpected demand in the United States. While most British models were undistinguishable from their U.S. counterparts, the MG sportscar was unique—it essentially had no competitors. Moreover, since many U.S. soldiers had already seen and admired the MG during the war, they eagerly snapped up every unit the firm could ship to dealers in the United States. Thus, the MG emerged as one of the hottest exports from Britain after the war. Indeed, that country was the world's largest exporter of automobiles from 1947 until the early 1960s, fueled in part by the extraordinary success of the MG.

Of course, the MG was not the only sportscar made in Britain, and its success was quickly noticed. Triumph Motor Company made some modifications to its own sportscar line and, in 1950, began shipping units to the United States. And Jaguar, which had been selling its cars in the United States for decades, increased its sales and marketing efforts dramatically. Throughout the 1950s and into the 1960s, MG controlled the low-priced segment of the U.S. sportscar market, Triumph controlled the mid-priced segment, and Jaguar controlled the higher-priced niche.

Blinded by a decade of success, however, the British firms made a classic error of many highly successful businesses—they grew complacent. Each firm saw its position in both the world and the U.S. market as totally secure, refusing to acknowledge that it faced potential competitive threats. For example, the British firms did not continue to invest in new technology, and, as a result, their production methods became relatively inefficient as other automakers built new, more modern plants. Similarly, with demand for their products so strong, the British firms saw little reason to improve the quality and reliability of those products. And when change was necessary, they tended to approach it superficially. For example, when the U.S. government mandated that all cars sold within the United States had to have stronger bumpers, MG simply added larger, bulkier bumpers to its sportscars without altering their design in any other way.

Because the British firms enjoyed what was essentially a monopoly in the U.S. sportscar market, these weaknesses were hidden from managers. In the 1960s, however, two events occurred that led to the eventual downfall of British sportscar makers. The first event took place in 1964, when Ford unveiled the Mustang. Its jaunty styling, low price, and "muscle car" image made it a big success and soon a formidable competitor for the MG and the Triumph. This weakened MG and the other British firms and, more significantly, revealed their vulnerabilities to all their competitors. Unfortunately for Ford, however, its managers also failed to fully understand the sportscar market. They soon began to add features and gimmicks to the Mustang while also increasing its size and price, overlooking the fact that simplicity, small size, and low price were three determinants of the car's appeal. Thus Ford began to lose momentum and the British companies breathed a brief—and unjustified—sigh of relief.

Waiting in the wings were the Japanese, led by Nissan (which used the name "Datsun" in the United States during this era). The Datsun 240-Z, introduced in the United States in 1969, was in its own way a bigger success than the Mustang. Nissan avoided Ford's mistake of forgetting its target market. The 240-Z had numerous innovative mechanical and design features, was more reliable than other sportscars, and sold for about the same price as the Triumph. Soon the Datsun 240-Z ruled the highways and crippled its British competitors. Two years after the car was introduced it was the best-selling sportscar in the United States, and a year later it was outselling the MG and the Triumph combined in that market.

As a result of financial difficulties caused by loss of market share, MG merged with Triumph to create what was known as British Leyland Motor Corporation. Managers hoped that this combination would have the size and clout to regain the top market position and to compete more effectively with both U.S. and Japanese firms. The new firm quickly tried to develop new products, but these were poorly designed and underengineered, having numerous flaws and weaknesses when they hit the market. Among the more spectacular failures for British Leyland was the Triumph TR7, a wedge-shaped car designed to compete with the Datsun 240-Z. The TR7 sold a respectable 32,743 cars in the United States in 1975 (its first full year of production), but sales dropped to only 22,939 the next year and continued to plum-

met until the model was eventually discontinued in 1981. The TR7 took with it British Leyland's entire sportscar line; the firm announced it was abandoning the sportscar market altogether. Today, the only British-made sportscar sold in the United States is the Jaguar, now produced by a division of Ford.

The British sportscars did leave an interesting legacy, however. One of the most successful sportscars introduced in recent years is the Mazda Miata. The Miata was intentionally designed and marketed to evoke memories of the 1950s in general and the MG in particular. The Miata is small, with only two seats, has a spartan but functional interior and a jaunty overall look, and carries a modest price tag. Its tremendous success serves to remind the automobile world of a bygone era and to help managers remember the importance of keeping focused on their markets and in tune with their customers.

Case Questions

1. What are the basic lessons international managers can learn from the experiences of the British sportscar manufacturers?

2. Can you identify any firms today that have the same market position as that occupied by the British automobile manufacturers during the 1950s?

3. If you were a British auto executive today, would you consider reentering the sportscar market? Why or why not?

4. Ford recently introduced a new model of the Mustang designed to take the car back to its roots. Comment on the success of this effort.

CHAPTER NOTES

1. "Catalonia Basks in the Olympic Light," *World Press Review*, January 1992, pp. 17–18; "NBC's Olympic Gamble," *Newsweek*, January 13, 1992, p. 44; "The Olympics: Brought to You By ...," *USA Today*, July 21, 1992, pp. 1B, 2B; "Let the Bidding Begin for the TV Rights to '96 Olympics, and Watch It Heat Up," *Wall Street Journal*, August 7, 1992, p. B1; "Going for the Gold, Merchandisers and Retailers Promote the Olympics Two Years in Advance," *Wall Street Journal*, December 7, 1993, pp. B1, B16; "Japan's Nagano, Site of 1998 Games, Faces

Problems of Olympic Proportions," *Wall Street Journal,* March 15, 1994, p. A14; "Olympics Strategy Has Its Rewards," *USA Today,* February 21, 1994, pp. 1B, 2B.

2. See Mira Wilkins, "The Conceptual Domain of International Business" (paper presented at a conference entitled "Perspectives on International Business: Theory, Research, and Institutional Arrangements," University of South Carolina, May 21–23, 1992).

3. *Survey of Current Business* (Washington, D.C.: U.S. Department of Commerce), January 1994, p. 37.

4. Jeremy Main, "B-Schools Get a Global Vision," *Fortune,* July 17, 1989, pp. 78–86.

5. "The Little Guys Are Making It Big Overseas," *Business Week,* February 27, 1989, pp. 94–96.

6. "The *Fortune* Global Service 500," *Fortune,* August 22, 1994, pp. 180–208.

7. Hermann Simon, "Lessons from Germany's Midsize Giants," *Harvard Business Review,* March–April 1992, pp. 115–125.

8. John H. Dunning, *Multinational Enterprises and the Global Economy* (Wokingham, England: Addison-Wesley Publishing Company, 1993), p. 3.

9. See Erdener Kaynak (ed.), *The Global Business* (New York: International Business Press, 1993) for a discussion of global corporations.

10. Christopher Bartlett and Sumantra Ghoshal, *Transnational Management* (Homewood, Ill.: Irwin, 1992), p. 14.

11. Larry Hirschhorn and Thomas Gilmore, "The New Boundaries of the "Boundaryless" Company," *Harvard Business Review,* May–June 1992, pp. 104–115.

12. "The Stateless Corporation," *Business Week,* May 14, 1990, pp. 98–104.

13. Richard Thurnwald, *Economics in Primitive Communities* (London: Oxford University Press, 1932).

14. Simcha Ronen, *Comparative and Multinational Management* (New York: John Wiley & Sons, 1986).

15. S. D. Chapman, "British-based Investment Groups before 1914," *Economic History Review,* Vol. 38 (1985), pp. 230–235.

16. John H. Dunning, op. cit., pp. 106ff.

17. *International Monetary Fund Supplement on Trade Statistics* (Washington, D.C.: International Monetary Fund, 1990).

18. John H. Dunning, op. cit., p. 21.

19. Richard J. Barnett and Ronald E. Muller, *Global Reach— The Power of the Multinational Corporations* (New York: Simon and Schuster, 1974).

20. Alan Chai, Alta Campbell, and Patrick J. Spain, *Hoover's Handbook of World Business 1993* (Austin, Tex.: The Reference Press, 1992).

21. Michael E. Porter, "The Competitive Advantage of Nations," *Harvard Business Review,* March–April 1990, pp. 73–93.

22. Lloyd Dobyns and Clare Crawford-Mason, *Quality or Else* (Boston: Houghton Mifflin, 1991).

23. Michael Prowse, "Is America in Decline?" *Harvard Business Review,* July–August, pp. 34–45.

24. David A. Ricks, Brian Toyne, and Zaida Martinez, "Recent Developments in International Management Research," *Journal of Management,* June 1990, pp. 219–245.

25. Sylvia Nasar, "America's Competitive Revival," *Fortune,* January 4, 1988, pp. 44–52.

26. Michael E. Porter, *The Competitive Advantage of Nations* (New York: Free Press, 1990).

27. Rosabeth Moss Kanter, "Transcending Business Boundaries: 12,000 World Managers View Change," *Harvard Business Review,* May–June 1991, pp. 151–164.

28. Michael A. Hitt, Robert E. Hoskisson, and Jeffrey S. Harrison, "Strategic Competitiveness in the 1990s: Challenges and Opportunities for U.S. Executives," *The Academy of Management Executive,* May 1991, pp. 7–22.

29. Richard I. Kirkland, Jr., "Entering a New Age of Boundless Competition," *Fortune,* March 14, 1988, pp. 40–48.

30. Raj Aggarwal, "The Strategic Challenge of the Evolving Global Economy," *Business Horizons,* July–August 1987, pp. 38–44.

31. Timothy R. Whisler, "Defeating the Triumph," *Audacity,* Fall 1993, pp. 17–25; "Triumph Takes a Holiday," *Automobile Quarterly,* Fall 1993, pp. 23–35; "Triumph Before Tragedy: The Odyssey of the TR Sports Car," *Automobile Quarterly,* Summer 1990, pp. 10–29.

CHAPTER

2

Global
Marketplaces
and
Business
Centers

Chapter Outline

The structure of the world economy

The marketplaces of North America   The United States
                                              Canada
                                              Mexico
                                              Central America and the Caribbean

The marketplaces of Western Europe

The marketplaces of Eastern and   The former Soviet Union
Central Europe   Central Europe

The marketplaces of Asia   Japan
                                              Australia and New Zealand
                                              The Four Tigers
                                              India
                                              China
                                              Southeast Asian countries

The marketplaces of Africa

The marketplaces of South America

After studying this chapter you should be able to:

Describe the value of economic geography to international businesspeople.

Evaluate the impact on business of the political and economic characteristics of the various world marketplaces.

Appreciate the uses of national income data in making business decisions.

Discuss North America as a major marketplace and business center in the world economy.

Describe Western Europe as a major marketplace and business center in the world economy.

Discuss the problems facing the economies of the former communist countries of Eastern and Central Europe.

Discuss Asia as a major marketplace and business center in the world economy.

Assess the development challenges facing African and South American countries.

A FTER THE IRON CURTAIN BEGAN TO RISE IN 1989, WESTERN FIRMS and their advertising agencies eagerly moved into Central European markets where consumers were hungry for high-quality consumer goods. However, they unexpectedly ran up against government regulators unsympathetic to the hyperbole and exaggerations of most advertising, and they also faced political controversies they were unprepared for. ▌▌ For example, when Unilever introduced its OMO detergent to the Hungarian market with claims that the detergent's stain-removing power was greater than that of "ordinary detergent," government regulators fined the company $25,000. They judged the ad unfair because Hungarian shoppers would presume that "ordinary detergent" referred to the unbeloved locally produced product. When IBM advertised its entrance into the Czechoslovakian market in 1991 it was sensitive to the ethnic and political infighting between Czechs and Slovaks. Its billboards used the politically correct name "Czecho-Slovakia" to appease Slovak nationalists. Of course, in so doing, it upset Czech nationalists. Or consider Procter & Gamble's (P&G) decision to introduce its Wash & Go shampoo to Polish consumers by mailing product samples to their homes—the first time this common U.S. marketing approach was used in Poland. Because the samples were so valuable in consumer goods–starved Poland, many mailboxes were broken into and the shampoo samples stolen. To reduce the ill will it created, P&G offered to repair the damaged mailboxes.[1] ▌▌ Cargill, a large Minneapolis grain company, finally received permission in 1993 to build a $30 million soybean processing plant to serve the booming South Korean soybean market. However, it had to wait for over four and a half years for official Korean governmental permission to proceed. One reason for the delay was that the daughter of the head of Dongbang Corp., an important South Korean food processor that would be hurt by the new Cargill plant, is married to the son of South Korea's president. In a country in which close family ties exist among the political, military, and business leadership, Cargill perhaps would have been wise to adopt a less direct approach to entering the market or at least to spend additional time laying the political groundwork for its entry application.[2] ▌▌ In August 1992 DHL International sought to trumpet the speediness of its courier services in the fast-growing Asian market by placing a seemingly amusing ad in the *Asian Wall Street Journal* and the *International Herald Tribune*. The ad pictured a DHL courier and five Asian heads of state along with text that questioned, "Who keeps the world's fastest moving economies moving faster?" However, Indonesian President Suharto, one of the five heads of state depicted in the ad and Indonesia's ruler since

The First Rule: Know the Territory

he seized power in 1968, was not amused at being compared to a mere courier. That country's Information Minister, denouncing the ads as unethical and contrary to the "moral values of Indonesian culture," promptly canceled circulation of both newspapers in the country. While both newspapers and DHL quickly printed apologies for the misunderstanding, none are likely to be invited to the presidential palace any time soon.[3] ∎∎∎∎∎

Businesses trying to internationalize their operations often blunder because they fail to obtain vital information. Ignorance of basic geography, market characteristics, and politics may lead to lost profits or, in the extreme, may doom a venture to failure. Linguistic and cultural ties, past political associations, and military alliances play significant roles in the world pattern of trade and investment and in shaping the opportunities available for businesses today. For example, London's contemporary importance as a world financial center arises from the political and military power of the British Empire in the nineteenth century. Tiny Hong Kong thrives as a conduit for international trade and investment for China because of geographical proximity and because they share a common culture and language.[4] Similarly, Austria serves as a bridge between Western and Eastern Europe because of transportation, educational, and cultural linkages that remain from the 600-year reign of the Hapsburg dynasty over the Austro-Hungarian empire.

Take a moment now to assess your own understanding of today's important global marketplaces and business centers by answering the following questions:

1 How far apart geographically are Tokyo and Singapore?
2 What is Ukraine's capital?
3 What is Brazil's official language?
4 What countries border France?
5 Which is farther south: Miami, Florida, or Monterrey, Mexico?

It is perhaps surprising that many people cannot answer these questions. People often think, for example, that Tokyo and Singapore are close neighbors. In fact, they are over 3300 miles apart, about the same distance that separates New York from London and Montreal from Paris. People also may not know that Kiev is Ukraine's capital (many pick St. Petersburg), that Portuguese is Brazil's official language (many pick Spanish, the dominant language throughout the rest of South America); that France's neighbors are Andorra, Belgium, Luxembourg, Monaco, Germany, Switzerland, Italy, and Spain (many people can name some, but few can name all); and that Miami is farther south than Monterrey (people "know" Mexico is south of the United States). Anyone involved in international business needs to know the basic structure of the world economy and where on a globe or map to find the major countries and cities that are home to the world's major marketplaces and business centers. (See Map 2.1.) This chapter provides a basic understanding of the geographical, economic, and political foundations of the world economy.

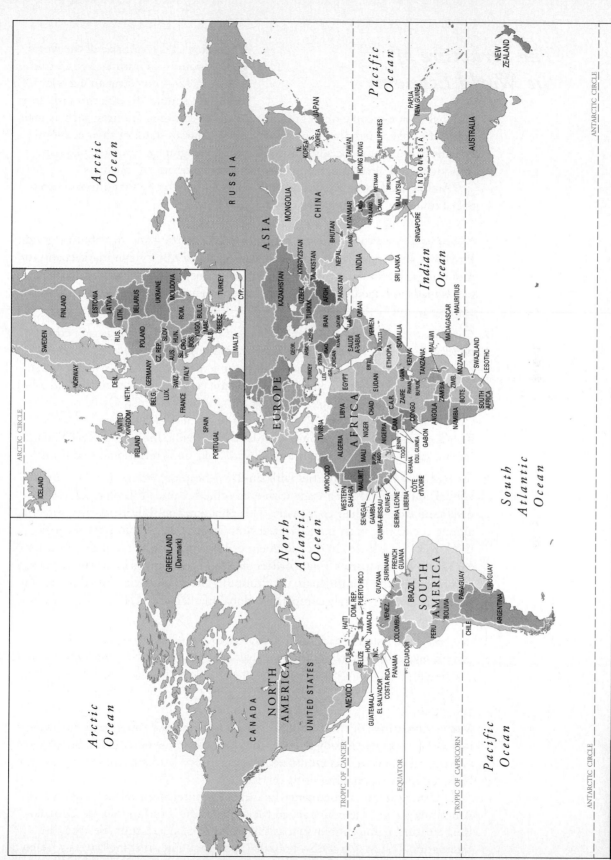

MAP 2.1   **World Map**

The Structure of the World Economy

Because of the vast size of the world economy—an estimated $23 trillion in 1992—providing an overview of it is not simple. To ease this task, international businesspeople often group countries by common features, such as their political systems (democracy, monarchy, or totalitarian state) or their economic systems (communist, socialist, or free market). Geography, however, plays an important, and often underappreciated, role in international business.

Among the factors of cultural and economic geography that affect international trade and investment flows are

1 *Shared borders*. Proximity lowers the costs of transporting and distributing goods. Proximity also makes it easier for firms to stay abreast of foreign markets and to monitor the performance of their foreign investments and operations. For example, Canada and the United States are major trading and investment partners, as are France and Germany.

2 *Common heritage*. Countries that have a common heritage arising from ethnic or political bonds often have strong international business relations. For example, much of China's initial trade and investment activity with the Western democracies was funneled through Hong Kong because geographical proximity and ethnic and family ties between capitalist Hong Kong and communist China overcame Cold War hostilities. Similarly, trade and investment ties between the United Kingdom and its former colonies of Australia, Canada, India, and New Zealand remain strong because of common political, legal, and educational traditions.

3 *Similar income levels*. Countries with similar per capita incomes (see "Going Global" on page 42) often trade with each other because of similarities in the needs and wants of their consumers. This phenomenon is particularly noticeable among the world's most industrialized countries and often colors the strategic thinking of large firms. In the judgment of Kenichi Ohmae, managing director of McKinsey & Company's Tokyo office, the world economy is increasingly being dominated by the **Triad:** Japan, the European Union, and the United States. To survive in the increasingly competitive global market any MNC must, according to Ohmae,

> become an insider in each of the Triad regions. Failure in any one would be like losing one leg of a tripod, with a consequent loss of stability. Transforming branches of the enterprise into insiders at overseas locations through one's own effort, or indirectly through effective tie-ups with local firms, is now a matter of corporate life or death.[5]

Many MNCs have operationalized Ohmae's warning and recognized the importance of competing globally in order to expand their customer bases. Such global strategic thinking typifies industries such as airlines, banking, securities, automobiles, computers, and accounting services.

Other experts, recognizing the increasing integration of the large North American market, have broadened the scope of the Triad to include Canada, thus creating a grouping known as the **Quad**. The Quad countries provide international businesses with a pool of 776 million high-income buyers with common needs and account for 75 percent of the world's GDP.

4 *Ownership of natural resources.* Countries with many natural resources sell them to those with fewer. For example, Saudi Arabia, with abundant oil reserves, sells crude oil to the rest of the world. Canada, with its extensive forests, is the world's largest exporter of forest products.

Because most students using this book have already taken college courses in economics and political science, we concentrate here on providing an overview of the *economic geography* of the world marketplace. We examine the major centers of international business and analyze existing patterns of trade among them. Factors that we will discuss within this geographical framework include population, income, trading and investment patterns, and the public infrastructure (transportation facilities, communications networks, and utilities). We will also explore an individual country's history to the extent that it illuminates that country's contemporary character. We hope you will consider this chapter as an economic travel guide for the international businessperson.

The Marketplaces of North America

North America includes the United States, Canada, Mexico, Greenland, and the countries of Central America and the Caribbean.

The United States

The United States has only the world's third-largest population and fourth-largest land mass, yet it possesses the largest economy. With a 1993 gross domestic product (GDP) of $6.4 trillion, it accounts for approximately 26 percent of the world's GDP. As Map 2.2 shows, the United States enjoys the highest per capita income of the North American countries.

The United States occupies a unique position in the world economy because of its size and political stability. It accounts for about one seventh of world trade in goods and services. It is the prime market for lower-income countries trying to raise their standards of living through export-oriented economic development strategies and for firms from higher-income countries trying to attract business from the country's large, well-educated middle class. The U.S. dollar serves as the **invoicing currency**, that is, the currency in which the sale of goods and services is denominated, for about half of all international transactions and is an important component of foreign-currency reserves worldwide.[6] Because of its political stability and military strength, the United States also attracts **flight capital**, that is, money sent out of a politically or economically unstable country to one perceived as a safe haven. Citizens unsure of the value of their home country's currency often choose to keep their wealth in dollars. An estimated 75 percent of the 1.2 billion U.S. $100 bills in circulation are held outside the United States.[7] The United States also is an important recipient of long-term foreign investment. Foreigners have invested an estimated $445 billion in U.S. factories, equipment, and property.

Although international trade has become increasingly more important in the past decade, it is a relatively small component of the U.S. economy. U.S. exports

GOING GLOBAL

Classifying Countries by Income Levels

Often the single most important piece of information needed by international businesspeople about a country is its income level. Income levels provide clues about the purchasing power of residents, the technological sophistication of local production processes, and the status of the public infrastructure. Such information is useful to international businesses that are contemplating exporting to a new market or investing in a local economy. For example, higher-income countries often offer prime markets for expensive consumer goods, such as luxury automobiles, advanced consumer electronic goods loaded with the latest features, and expensive status goods like Scotch whiskeys and French perfumes. Lower-income countries offer a better market for lower-priced staple goods. Such economies also may interest firms seeking access to large pools of low-wage workers. On the other hand, in these countries electricity distribution often is unreliable and roads often are in disrepair, so a firm needing a reliable public infrastructure might want to look elsewhere.

A country's income is normally measured as the total market value of its output of goods and services produced during some time period, such as a year. Until the 1990s most governmental statisticians calculated the **gross national product (GNP)**, a measure of the market value of goods and services produced by property and labor owned by the country's residents. In the 1990s most governmental accounting systems focus on the **gross domestic product (GDP)**, a measure of the market value of all goods and services produced in the country. The difference between GNP and GDP is subtle: GNP focuses on ownership of production, whereas GDP concentrates on the location of production. For example, the dividends returned to Japan by Nissan's U.K. subsidiary, which assembles automobiles in Sunderland, England, would be included in Japan's GNP, but not in its GDP. In most cases, international businesspeople can ignore this difference and use whichever measure is more easily obtainable, for the relative difference between a country's GNP and GDP is usually small. For example, in 1993 the U.S. GNP was $6378.1 billion, and the U.S. GDP was $6377.9 billion—a difference of only 0.003 percent. So an international market researcher who has GDP information about one country and GNP information about a second can compare the two without worrying that the results will be terribly distorted.

In assessing a foreign country as a potential market, international marketers often ignore total GNP or total GDP and instead look at **per capita income**—the average income per person in a country. Per capita GDP is calculated by dividing the country's total GDP by its population. Which income concept to use—total GDP or per capita GDP—depends on the problem facing the business. Total GDP indicates the economy's overall size, which may be important in a market assessment for durable equipment or bulk goods such as grain, steel, or cement. Per capita income indicates the average income of consumers, which may be important when marketing upscale personal care products or consumer durables.

of goods and services in 1993 totaled $641.7 billion, but were only 10.1 percent of U.S. GDP. However, this figure is somewhat misleading. Because of the country's large size and large internal market, trade that might be counted as international in smaller countries is considered domestic in the United States. For example, the money spent for a hotel room in neighboring Belgium by a Dutch motorist trapped in a thunderstorm 50 miles from home late at night is counted in the international trade statistics of both Belgium and the Netherlands. A similar expenditure by a Connecticut motorist stuck in New Jersey after watching a football game at the Meadowlands is a purely domestic transaction.

As discussed throughout this book, MNCs heavily influence international trade and investment. In 1993, the world's 500 largest industrial corporations had total sales of $5.4 trillion. Given the importance of the United States in the world economy, it should come as no surprise that 159 of these corporations, or about

For example, China has a large GDP—$506 billion—but a very low per capita income —$470. In contrast, Switzerland has a much smaller population and correspondingly smaller GDP—$241 billion—yet Swiss residents enjoy a per capita income of $36,080. Thus China may represent a better market for agricultural products than for 31-inch color TVs.

International marketers also are concerned about a country's **income distribution**—the relative numbers of its rich, middle-class, and poor. This information is not evident from GNP or GDP alone. Manufacturers of expensive prestige items such as Rolls-Royces are interested in the number of millionaires in the country, while producers of consumer durables such as refrigerators and automobiles may want to know the size of the country's middle class.

One important source of these income statistics is the World Bank, an agency of the United Nations. The World Bank divides the world's countries into high-income, middle-income, and low-income categories. High-income countries are defined as those that enjoy annual per capita incomes of at least $8356. The high-income group comprises three clusters of countries. One is the **Organization for Economic Cooperation and Development (OECD)**. The OECD includes 25 market-oriented democracies—19 Western European countries, 3 Pacific Rim countries (Japan, Australia, and New Zealand), Canada, and the United States (Mexico joined the OECD in 1994 but is classified as middle-income). The second cluster comprises oil-rich Kuwait, Saudia Arabia, and the United Arab Emirates. The third cluster consists of smaller industrialized countries—Hong Kong, Israel, and Singapore.

Middle-income countries have per capita incomes of more than $675 but less than $8356. This category includes the former communist countries of Central and Eastern Europe, which generally enjoyed high levels of development in the 1930s but stagnated economically since World War II. Other countries in this category, such as Taiwan, Brazil, Mexico, and South Korea, have been undergoing successful industrialization and economic growth and may be elevated to the high-income category by the end of this decade.

Lower-income countries, often called *developing countries,* have per capita incomes of $675 or less. This category includes some countries, such as Indonesia, whose economies are growing substantially because of external aid, sound domestic economic policies, FDI, and/or exploitation of valuable natural resources. Officially labeled "underdeveloped" by the United Nations General Assembly in 1971, these countries have the potential for above-average economic growth. Other countries, designated "undeveloped" and "least developed" by the United Nations, have low literacy rates, per capita incomes, and economic growth. They are less attractive to international businesses because they offer less consumer demand and lack the public infrastructure necessary for reliable production and distribution of goods and services. A prime example of this latter category is Somalia, an East African country wracked by drought, civil war, and starvation.

Sources: *Survey of Current Business,* vol. 73, no. 9 (September 1993), p. 9; Central Intelligence Agency, *The World Factbook 1991* (Washington, D.C.: U.S. Government Printing Office, 1991), p. 376; World Bank, *World Development Report 1994* (Washington, D.C.: World Bank, 1994).

32 percent, are headquartered in the United States, including 32 of the largest 100 (see Fig. 2.1). GM is currently the world's largest industrial company, with 1993 sales of $133.6 billion.[8]

Canada

Canada has the world's second-largest land mass, although its population is only 27.4 million. Eighty percent of the population is concentrated within a 100-mile band along the country's southern border with the United States. Much of Canada's political and economic history reflects its close geographical and economic ties to the United States as well as its attempts to maintain a cultural identity separate from its more populous southern neighbor. The Liberal Party, under the leadership of Prime Minister Pierre Trudeau (1968–1979, 1980–1984), adopted nationalistic and protectionist policies designed to minimize U.S. influence on the Canadian

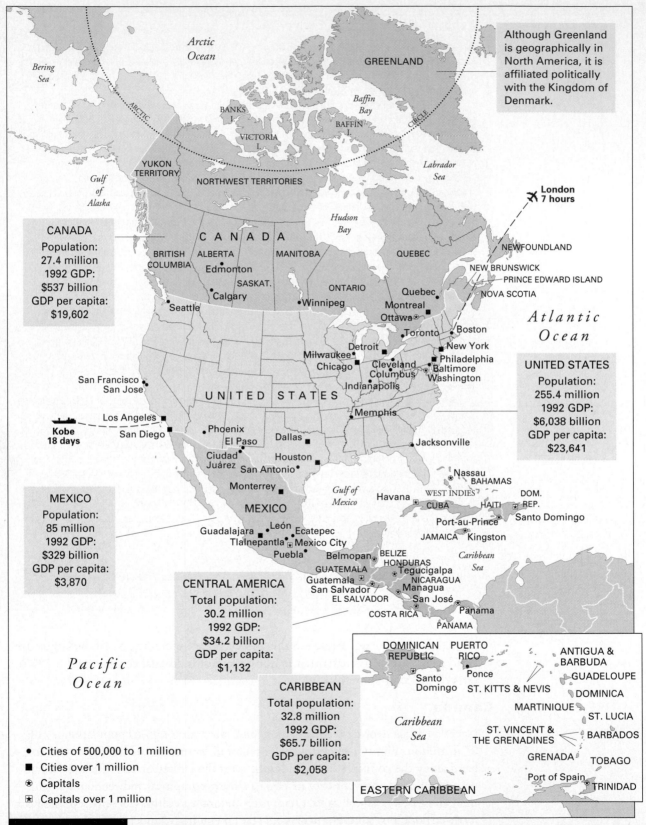

Although Greenland is geographically in North America, it is affiliated politically with the Kingdom of Denmark.

CANADA
Population:
27.4 million
1992 GDP:
$537 billion
GDP per capita:
$19,602

✈ London
7 hours

UNITED STATES
Population:
255.4 million
1992 GDP:
$6,038 billion
GDP per capita:
$23,641

Kobe
18 days

MEXICO
Population:
85 million
1992 GDP:
$329 billion
GDP per capita:
$3,870

CENTRAL AMERICA
Total population:
30.2 million
1992 GDP:
$34.2 billion
GDP per capita:
$1,132

CARIBBEAN
Total population:
32.8 million
1992 GDP:
$65.7 billion
GDP per capita:
$2,058

Pacific Ocean

Arctic Ocean

Bering Sea

Gulf of Alaska

GREENLAND

BANKS I.

VICTORIA I.

Baffin Bay

BAFFIN I.

ARCTIC CIRCLE

YUKON TERRITORY

NORTHWEST TERRITORIES

Labrador Sea

C A N A D A

BRITISH COLUMBIA

ALBERTA

SASKAT.

MANITOBA

Hudson Bay

QUEBEC

NEWFOUNDLAND

NEW BRUNSWICK

PRINCE EDWARD ISLAND

NOVA SCOTIA

Edmonton

Calgary

Winnipeg

Quebec

Montreal

Ottawa

Toronto

Boston

New York

Philadelphia

Baltimore

Washington

Atlantic Ocean

Seattle

ONTARIO

San Francisco

San Jose

Detroit

Milwaukee

Chicago

Cleveland

Columbus

Indianapolis

U N I T E D   S T A T E S

Memphis

Los Angeles

San Diego

Phoenix

El Paso

Dallas

Ciudad Juárez

San Antonio

Houston

Jacksonville

Monterrey

M E X I C O

Gulf of Mexico

Havana

Nassau

BAHAMAS

WEST INDIES

CUBA

HAITI

DOM. REP.

Santo Domingo

Port-au-Prince

JAMAICA

Kingston

Caribbean Sea

Guadalajara

León

Ecatepec

Tlalnepantla

Mexico City

Puebla

Belmopan

BELIZE

HONDURAS

GUATEMALA

Tegucigalpa

Guatemala

NICARAGUA

San Salvador

Managua

EL SALVADOR

San José

COSTA RICA

Panama

PANAMA

DOMINICAN REPUBLIC

PUERTO RICO

ANTIGUA & BARBUDA

Santo Domingo

Ponce

GUADELOUPE

ST. KITTS & NEVIS

DOMINICA

MARTINIQUE

ST. LUCIA

Caribbean Sea

ST. VINCENT & THE GRENADINES

BARBADOS

GRENADA

TOBAGO

Port of Spain

TRINIDAD

EASTERN CARIBBEAN

- Cities of 500,000 to 1 million
- Cities over 1 million
- ✹ Capitals
- ⊕ Capitals over 1 million

MAP 2.2 **North America**

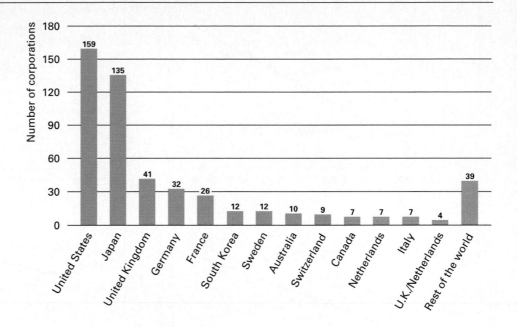

FIGURE 2.1

Headquarters of the World's Largest Industrial Corporations in 1993 by Country
Source: *Fortune,*
July 25, 1994.

economy. These policies were later reversed by Progressive Conservative Brian Mulroney, elected Prime Minister in 1984. Mulroney opened the Canadian economy, reduced state influence on business by deregulating important industries and selling state-owned enterprises (for example, Air Canada) to the private sector, and forged closer economic ties with the United States. Then, in October 1993, Mulroney's party was voted out of office, and Liberal Jean Chretien was elected Prime Minister. So far, Chretien's government has maintained Canada's economic openness. For example, shortly after taking office, Chretien agreed to endorse ratification of the North American Free Trade Agreement (NAFTA), which promises to increase trade among Canada, Mexico, and the United States and to maintain Canada's access to the U.S. market (see Chapter 7 for more discussion of NAFTA).

The importance to the Canadian economy of access to the U.S. market cannot be underestimated. Exports are vital to the economy, accounting for 27 percent of its 1992 GDP. Canada's most important exports reflect its rich natural resources: forest products, petroleum, minerals, and grain. The United States is the dominant market for Canadian goods, receiving 76 percent of Canada's $131.7 billion in exports in 1992. Two-way trade between the U.S. and Canada forms the single largest bilateral trading relationship in the world.

International investors have long been attracted to Canada because of its proximity to the huge U.S. market and the stability of its political and legal systems. Canada's excellent infrastructure also contributes to the performance of its economy. The importance of this factor is reflected in Fig. 2.2, which indicates the close linkage between infrastructure and income level. Lack of infrastructure is often an impediment to a country's economic development, for low-wage countries are not necessarily low-cost ones: "If power is expensive and intermittent, ... if transport is problematic and ... cumbersome, then the fact that [workers] make a few cents less a day is not going to make much of a difference to an investor."[9] Recognizing that its telecommunications, transportation, and utilities

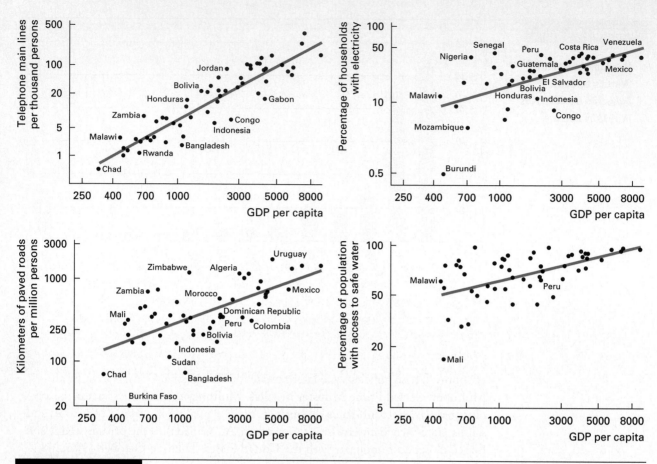

FIGURE 2.2

Per Capita Availability of Major Infrastructure

Source: World Bank, *World Development Report 1994*, p. 16.

networks, which rank among the world's best, lower costs of doing business and raise its appeal as a market and production site for international businesses, Canada has paid close attention to maintaining the quality of its infrastructure.

However, a major threat to Canada's political stability—and to its ability to attract foreign investment—is the longstanding conflict between French-speaking Canadians (most of whom live in the province of Quebec) and English-speaking Canadians. A strong separatist movement has existed in Quebec since the 1960s, and English-speaking Canada has been pressured to adopt policies to diffuse separatism. This conflict has affected domestic and international businesses in many ways. For example, firms exporting products to Canada must be aware of the country's bilingual labeling laws. Also, the riskiness of loans to Quebec firms would increase substantially, at least in the short run, if the province were to become a separate nation.

Mexico

The third major economic power in North America is Mexico. Mexico's political history, like Canada's, is tied to its geography. Now the world's largest Spanish-speaking nation, Mexico declared its independence from its Spanish conquerors in 1810. Its modern boundaries were not established, however, until after its unsuccessful wars with Texan rebels (1836) and the United States (1846–1848). In the 1850s the Mexican economy was wracked by a civil war, which led to a period of political instability until General Porfirio Diaz seized control of the government in

1876. Diaz's 35-year reign encouraged foreign investment in key sectors of the economy, including oil, mining, and railroads. However, his policies became increasingly unpopular as Mexican patriots claimed that the country's resources were being used to benefit foreigners (in other words, U.S. citizens), rather than Mexicans. A peasants' revolt led by Francisco Madero, Venustiano Carranza, Emiliano Zapata, and Pancho Villa ended Diaz's rule in 1911.[10]

Modern Mexican political history begins with the adoption of the 1917 Mexican Constitution, which embodies the nationalistic spirit of the peasants' revolt. Like the United States, Mexico is a federal system whose head of government, a president, is elected by popular vote every six years. Mexican politics have been dominated by the Institutional Revolutionary Party (PRI), which has won every presidential election since its founding in 1929. Historically, the PRI promoted a program of economic nationalism under which Mexico discouraged foreign investment and erected high tariff walls to protect its domestic industries.

President Miguel de la Madrid began to abandon these policies in 1982 after the country's inflation rose as high as 132 percent annually, its trade balance fell into deficit, and it was unable to service its massive external debts. President Carlos Salinas de Gortari, after his election in 1988, completed the reversal of the PRI's traditional economic policies. He reduced the government's role in the economy by selling many publicly owned firms, such as Aeromexico and Telefonos de Mexico. Salinas also opened more sectors of the economy to foreign investors and lobbied vigorously for the passage of NAFTA.

As a result of NAFTA and Salinas's economic reforms, Mexico attracted much attention from international businesses seeking new markets, sources of inputs, and production facilities. For example, after NAFTA's passage retail chains like J.C. Penney, Dillards, and Wal-Mart expanded rapidly to serve the shopping needs of Mexico's growing middle class.[11] Unfortunately, in 1994 foreign investors' confidence in the Mexican economy was shaken by the country's growing political instability and its expanding deficit. Newly elected President Ernesto Zedillo was forced to allow the peso to devalue in December 1994; within six weeks, the peso's value had fallen 45 percent. The arrest of former president Salinas's brother in March 1995 on grounds that he masterminded a political assassination raised new doubts about the country's future. To restore Mexico's economic health, Zedillo faces the difficult challenge of simultaneously reducing the trade deficit, rebuilding political stability, and bolstering the confidence of foreign investors.

Central America and the Caribbean

The North American continent is also occupied by 20 other countries that are divided geographically into two groups: Central America and the island states of the Caribbean. Collectively their populations equal 63 million—over double Canada's. However, their total GDP of $100 billion is far less than Canada's $537 billion. With a few exceptions (notably Costa Rica), the economic development of these countries has suffered from:

▶ Political instability

▶ Chronic U.S. military intervention

▶ Inferior educational systems

▶ A weak middle class

▶ Economic policies that have created large pockets of poverty

▶ Import limitations by the United States and other developed countries on Central American and Caribbean goods, such as sugar and clothing

The Marketplaces of Western Europe

Western European countries are among the world's most prosperous and compose the second component of Kenichi Ohmae's Triad. They can be divided into two groups: (1) members of the European Union (EU), and (2) other countries in the region (see Map 2.3).

The EU, which we discuss in greater detail in Chapter 7, comprises 15 countries that are seeking to promote European prosperity by reducing mutual barriers to trade and investment. In the past decade, the EU has made tremendous strides in achieving this objective. With a GDP of $7.2 trillion and a population of 369 million, it is the world's richest market. EU members can be subdivided into three groups:

1 The rich, populous, and politically powerful: Germany, France, the United Kingdom, and Italy

2 The rich, less populous, and less politically powerful: Denmark and the Benelux countries (Belgium, the Netherlands, and Luxembourg), as well as Austria, Finland, and Sweden, which joined the EU in 1995.

3 The relatively poor: Greece, Ireland, Portugal, and Spain

The World Bank classifies the countries in the first two groups, as well as Spain and Ireland, as high income and the remaining members of the third group as middle income. The EU members are free-market–oriented, parliamentary democracies. However, government intervention and ownership generally play a more important role in these countries' economies than in that of the United States.

From an economic perspective, Germany is the EU's most important member. With a 1992 GDP of $1.8 trillion, it possesses the world's third-largest economy, after those of Japan and the United States. It is a major player in international business; in recent years the title of world's largest exporter has bounced back and forth between Germany and the United States. Whether Germany is the leader or the runner-up in any given year depends on the value of its currency, the deutsche mark, relative to the dollar in that year. Because of the strength of the German economy and the government's strict anti-inflation policies, the mark has become the dominant currency in Europe. Thus, in practice the Bundesbank, the German central bank, controls the monetary policy of the EU.

Politically, France exerts strong leadership within the EU. The French government has been a leading proponent of increased political, economic, and military union within Europe and of strengthening the powers of the EU's government. France also has advocated restricting free trade in commodities important to its economy, such as agricultural goods, automobiles, fish, and semiconductor chips.

France's positions have not gone unchallenged, however. The United Kingdom in particular has steadfastly resisted French initiatives to expand governmental

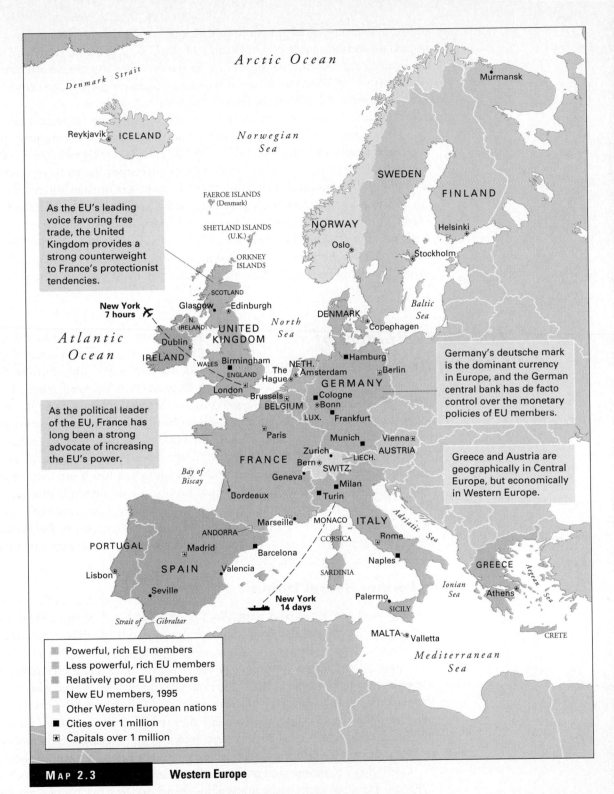

As the EU's leading voice favoring free trade, the United Kingdom provides a strong counterweight to France's protectionist tendencies.

As the political leader of the EU, France has long been a strong advocate of increasing the EU's power.

Germany's deutsche mark is the dominant currency in Europe, and the German central bank has de facto control over the monetary policies of EU members.

Greece and Austria are geographically in Central Europe, but economically in Western Europe.

Powerful, rich EU members
Less powerful, rich EU members
Relatively poor EU members
New EU members, 1995
Other Western European nations
Cities over 1 million
Capitals over 1 million

MAP 2.3   **Western Europe**

intervention in the EU market. The United Kingdom's Conservative government has been trying to increase the role of free-market forces within the British economy. It believes that transferring political power from the national governments of EU members to the EU's supranational government will lead to increased governmental control of the European economy. Also, as a traditionally strong supporter of free trade, the United Kingdom provides an important counterweight to French protectionist tendencies. Because of the U.K.'s free-trade policies, London has been a center of international business activity since the nineteenth century. Along with New York and Tokyo, it is a major international finance center, employing over 300,000 in the financial services sector alone.

The U.K. is a major exporter and importer of goods, an important destination for and source of foreign investment, and the home to the headquarters or regional divisions of numerous MNCs. In 1992, U.K. firms generated $190 billion in merchandise exports, approximately 21 percent of the country's GDP, with the bulk of these goods destined for other EU members or the United States.

Western European countries that are not EU members include Iceland, Malta, Norway, and Switzerland, plus several "postage stamp" countries such as Andorra, Monaco, and Liechtenstein. Classified as high income by the World Bank, collectively these countries account for 1 percent of the world's GDP. Like their EU neighbors, they are free-market–oriented, parliamentary democracies.

The Marketplaces of Eastern and Central Europe

No region of the world is undergoing as much economic change as is Eastern and Central Europe. Soviet leader Mikhail Gorbachev's 1986 reform initiatives of *glasnost* (openness) and *perestroika* (economic restructuring) triggered a political, economic, and social revolution. Eastern Europe now comprises the 15 separate countries that resulted from the disintegration of the Soviet Union in 1991 (see Map 2.4). (Geographically, several of these countries are in Asia, but since they share economic problems with their European counterparts, they are discussed in this section.) Central Europe is composed of Albania, Austria, and the former Soviet satellite states of Bulgaria, Czechoslovakia (now the Czech Republic and Slovakia), Hungary, Poland, and Romania. It also includes Bosnia-Herzegovina, Croatia, Macedonia, and Slovenia, which were carved out of Yugoslavia (see Map 2.5 on page 54).

The Former Soviet Union

The Union of Soviet Socialist Republics (Soviet Union or USSR) emerged from the wreckage of the Russian empire, which was caused by its defeat in World War I. In the chaos that followed the March 1917 abdication of Czar Nicholas II, the Communist Party seized control of the Russian government and established the Soviet Union in the name of the workers and peasants. The communists outlawed the market system, abolished private property, and collectivized the country's vast rich farmlands. By so doing, they succeeded in reducing the enormous income inequalities that had existed under czarist rule. Despite this success the population's standard of living increasingly fell behind that of the Western democracies.

Gorbachev's economic and political reforms led to the Soviet Union's collapse in 1991 and the subsequent declarations of independence by the 15 Soviet republics. In 1992, 11 of the newly independent countries (all but Estonia, Georgia, Latvia, and Lithuania) agreed to form the Commonwealth of Independent States (CIS). The exact powers and the future of the CIS are uncertain. The most important of these new countries is the Russian Federation (Russia), which was the dominant

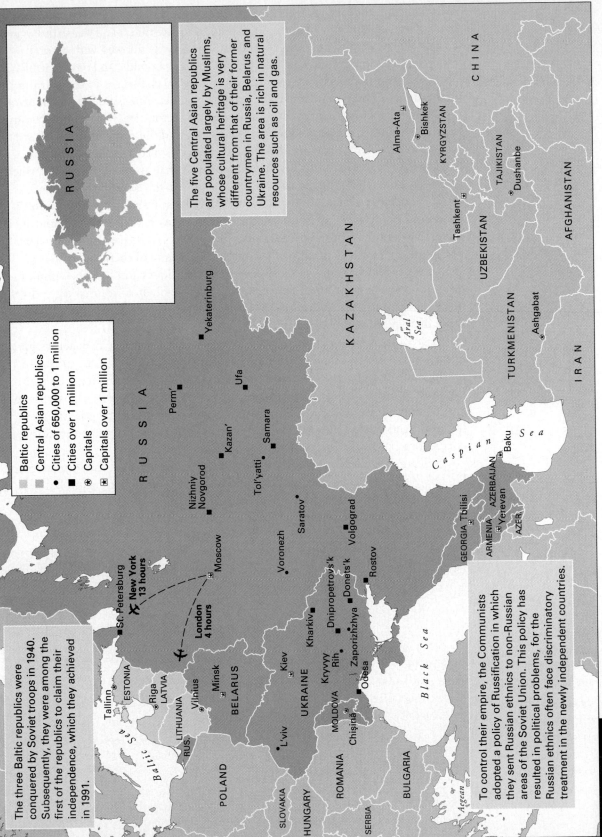

The three Baltic republics were conquered by Soviet troops in 1940. Subsequently, they were among the first of the republics to claim their independence, which they achieved in 1991.

The five Central Asian republics are populated largely by Muslims, whose cultural heritage is very different from that of their former countrymen in Russia, Belarus, and Ukraine. The area is rich in natural resources such as oil and gas.

To control their empire, the Communists adopted a policy of Russification in which they sent Russian ethnics to non-Russian areas of the Soviet Union. This policy has resulted in political problems, for the Russian ethnics often face discriminatory treatment in the newly independent countries.

Baltic republics
Central Asian republics
• Cities of 650,000 to 1 million
■ Cities over 1 million
✳ Capitals
⊞ Capitals over 1 million

MAP 2.4   **Eastern Europe**

republic within the former Soviet Union. As an independent state, Russia is the world's largest country in land mass (6.5 million square miles) and the sixth-largest in population (149 million people). The country is well endowed with natural resources, including gold, oil, natural gas, minerals, diamonds, and fertile farmland.

Russia and the other former republics face many challenges in transforming their economies from communist to capitalist systems. One issue is **privatization**, the selling of state-owned property to the private sector. For 75 years, the communist leadership had denounced private ownership and the profit concept; thus privatization represents a major philosophical change as well as an economic one. Russia is further along in the privatization process than most of the other former republics. Since the initiation of President Boris Yeltsin's economic reforms in 1992, 70 percent of state-owned industries have been transferred into private hands and over two thirds of the country's workforce of 75 million is employed in the private sector.[12] But in 80 percent of the newly privatized firms, managers and employees own 51 percent of the shares. Too many of these enterprises are run by management teams that use Soviet-era techniques and lack the vision, the desire, and the basic business skills to operate profitably in a free market.[13] In the other new countries privatization has been slowed by political infighting and resistance of Soviet-installed managers to change.

A second challenge is controlling inflation. Rather than close factory gates and lay off workers, many of the new governments have sought to subsidize inefficient, obsolete state-owned factories that are not yet privatized by printing more money. The ensuing inflation is eroding faith in the new governments and destroying the value of their citizens' savings. Faith in the governments has also been eroded by their inability to curb organized crime and widespread corruption.

Still another challenge is determining who is responsible for the former Soviet Union's international obligations. Negotiations among the former republics over ownership of Soviet assets (such as government-owned gold, naval vessels, and the nuclear arsenal) and responsibility for Soviet debts will take some time to complete.

Moscow street vendors, such as these young entrepreneurs selling *matrushka* (nesting dolls) and Communist Party banners, have mushroomed as a result of the privatization of the Russian economy. But the economic transformation has not been easy on average Russians, many of whom have suffered from rising inflation and unemployment.

But the major challenge facing Russia and the other former republics is overcoming the lack of political consensus. For example, half of the members of the current Russian parliament (elected in 1993) have little sympathy for Yeltsin's market-oriented reforms. Some of these dissidents want to strengthen state control over the economy; others want to reassert Russian military authority over the other new countries in the region—which Russians refer to as "the near abroad." The political instability of the area makes conducting international business there highly risky. Armed insurrections have arisen within Russia as ethnic groups, as in Chechnya, for example, have struggled to free themselves from Moscow's rule. Pro-Russia and anti-Russia factions are struggling for control of Belarus and Ukraine. Armenia and Azerbaijan have fought over treatment of their respective ethnic minorities. Moreover, Western firms are often caught up in bureaucratic squabbling over which government agency has the authority to make decisions. Occasionally, a Western firm will strike an agreement with one state agency, only to have a second issue a deal-threatening edict. For example, White Nights, a joint venture of Anglo-Suisse (a Houston-based oil services firm), Philbro (a subsidiary of Salomon Inc.), and a Russian state-owned enterprise called Varyeganneftegas, was established in 1991 to incorporate secondary production methods in the Siberian oil fields. The joint venture almost disintegrated when in January 1992, after the agreement was signed and operations had commenced, the Russian Ministry of Finance imposed a $5 export tax on each barrel of oil and later a 23 percent excise tax on production. The project was made unprofitable by this unexpected tax load. Only after two years of negotiations did the Russians promise to reduce the tax burden on the company.[14]

Nonetheless, Russia and the other Eastern European countries present international businesses with rich opportunities. Although they can sell their commodities (gold, oil, and natural gas) on the world market, they have found very little demand there for the shoddy, ill-designed, and often obsolete consumer goods produced by Soviet industries. Thus these countries need help. In order to manufacture and market all types of high-quality goods, private and state enterprises are eagerly seeking Western capital and technology by forming joint ventures with Western firms. Virtually every large MNC and thousands of small businesses are flocking to these new nations to access the potentially lucrative market of 290 million that opened with the collapse of the Soviet Union. For example, sensing rich opportunities due to poor existing communications infrastructure, Hughes Network Systems, a unit of GM, teamed up with San Francisco-Moscow Teleport, Inc. to construct the world's first broad-based wireless telephone system for the 3.6 million residents of Tatarstan (an ethnic republic within Russia).[15] Because of the political importance of these 15 new countries, the Western nations have facilitated such private initiatives by providing grants and development assistance to strengthen the economies.

Central Europe

Central European countries that were aligned with the former Soviet Union also face serious challenges. Poland, Hungary, Slovakia, Bulgaria, Romania, and the Czech Republic have different abilities to respond to the disintegration of the Soviet bloc. However, they share some common problems. (Because East Germany has been reintegrated into the Federal Republic of Germany, it faces its challenges as part of the much stronger German economy.)

Communist support of heavy industry and indifference to pollution contributed to environmental havoc throughout much of Central Europe. One particularly devastated region is the industrial triangle between Dresden, Katowice, and Mlada Boleslav.

Following the revolutions of the 1980s, four of Yugoslavia's six republics broke away to become independent nations. The status of the two remaining republics, Serbia and Montenegro, remains uncertain. While some blood was shed when Macedonia, Slovenia, and Croatia separated from Yugoslavia, several hundred thousand lives have been lost in Bosnia-Herzegovina's quest for independence. At issue is the extent of Serbia's control over the Balkan peninsula.

Albania is Europe's poorest country, the result of its Stalinist-style economy which eliminated the private sector. Albania split from the Soviet bloc in 1961, believing the bloc's policies were insufficiently Marxist. Because of its isolation, Albania has received little aid or FDI from North America or Western Europe.

London 3 hours

New York 15½ days

Former Yugoslavia
- Cities of 350,000 to 1 million
- ⊛ Capitals
- ⊠ Capitals over 1 million

MAP 2.5   **Central Europe**

The first common problem is the loss of export markets within the Soviet bloc. The former Soviet Union and its satellite states developed a regional trading bloc called the Council for Mutual Economic Assistance (COMECON) to integrate their economies tightly. The former Soviet Union benefited from COMECON by dictating the goods and services each satellite country should specialize in. The satellites benefited by having guaranteed markets within COMECON for their exports and by receiving subsidized goods from the Soviet Union in order to maintain their political fealty. Of particular value was the crude oil they received at prices well below world market prices.

With the 1989 collapse of Central European communism COMECON broke down and was finally abandoned in 1991. The former satellite states had to adjust to the loss of guaranteed export markets. For example, many COMECON armaments factories were located in the Slovakian portion of Czechoslovakia. After COMECON disintegrated, Slovakian military goods lost their natural market and unemployment rates in that region skyrocketed. These economic pressures contributed to the 1993 split of Czechoslovakia into two countries (Slovakia and the Czech Republic).

A second common problem is the restructuring of the various Central European economies from centrally organized communist systems to decentralized market systems. The Czech Republic is further along in this process than are the other former Soviet satellites. Prime Minister Vaclav Klaus has enjoyed strong support for his efforts to build a society based on democracy and a free market. Klaus's privatization program utilized vouchers, which were sold to Czech citizens for a nominal 1000 Czech crowns (about $34) and gave them the right to purchase shares in state-owned industries. By the summer of 1994 these vouchers were worth between 20,000 and 30,000 crowns; not only did the average Czech benefit financially from the program but 80 percent of the Czech economy was privatized. More importantly, the Czech economy has been booming. Foreign direct investment, particularly from Germany, has flowed into the country to take advantage of highly skilled but inexpensive (by German standards) Czech labor. In 1994 the Czech Republic's unemployment rate was 3.5 percent, the lowest in Europe. The country's average income approximates that of Portugal, classifying it as middle income by the World Bank's definition.[16]

The economic restructuring of Hungary and Poland has also advanced significantly, although it is not as far along as that of the Czech Republic. In 1990 Poland's first post-communist government adopted a policy of "shock therapy" to reform the economy. State employees, farmers, and welfare recipients were hurt by the rapid transformation to a free-market economy and reductions in state subsidies. Yet buying patterns suggest that overall citizens are benefiting from Poland's economic policies (see Table 2.1). Hungary, which in 1968 instituted market-oriented reforms within the context of communism, known as **market socialism**, or, more colorfully, "goulash communism," has also benefited from FDI from Europe and the United States—about $4.5 billion in 1991 and 1992 alone. As a result of these earlier reforms, the small business sector of Hungary's economy is particularly strong, accounting for 40 percent of the country's GDP. Hungary's primary problem is controlling its government deficits, which amounted to 7 percent of GDP in 1992.[17]

Economic reforms are less advanced in Albania, Bulgaria, and Romania, because these countries have not developed a political consensus as to the direction

TABLE 2.1

Ownership of Consumer Durables in Poland (per 100 households)

	1985	1990	1992
Cars	27.2	33.2	41.4
Color televisions	23.1	67.1	91.4
VCRs	N/A	20.1	53.4
Washing machines	38.7	63.5	69.7

Source: *The Economist*, April 16, 1994.

they want their economies to take. The situation is far worse in the former Yugoslavia. Conflict among Croats, Bosnian Muslims, and Serbs has devastated the economies of the region and discouraged many MNCs from investing there until peace is achieved.

The Marketplaces of Asia

Asia is home to over half the world's population, yet it produces only 25 percent of the world's GDP. As shown in Map 2.6, the continent contains some of the world's fastest-growing market-oriented economies, including Japan, Hong Kong, and South Korea, as well as the world's largest communist economy, China. Asia's importance to international business cannot be minimized. The region is a source of both high-quality and low-quality products and of both skilled and unskilled labor. It is both a major destination for foreign investments by MNCs and a major supplier of capital to non-Asian countries. More importantly, its aggressive, efficient entrepreneurs have increasingly put competitive pressure on European and North American firms to improve the productivity and quality of their operations.

Japan

Japan, an island country of 125 million people, rose from the ashes of World War II to become the world's second-largest economy (with a GDP of $3.7 trillion in 1992) and an important member of the Triad. Between 1980 and 1992, the Japanese economy grew at an average annual rate of 3.6 percent—double the growth rate of the U.S. economy. Japan's per capita GDP in 1992 was $29,360.

Japan's rapid growth in the past 50 years is due in part to the partnership between its Ministry of International Trade and Investment (MITI) and its industrial sector. MITI has used its formal and informal powers to guide the production and investment strategies of the country's corporate elite. Immediately after World War II, MITI encouraged Japanese firms to concentrate their efforts on such basic industries as steel and shipbuilding. As other countries entered these industries, MITI and Japan's MNCs shifted their focus to producing automobiles, consumer electronics, and machinery.

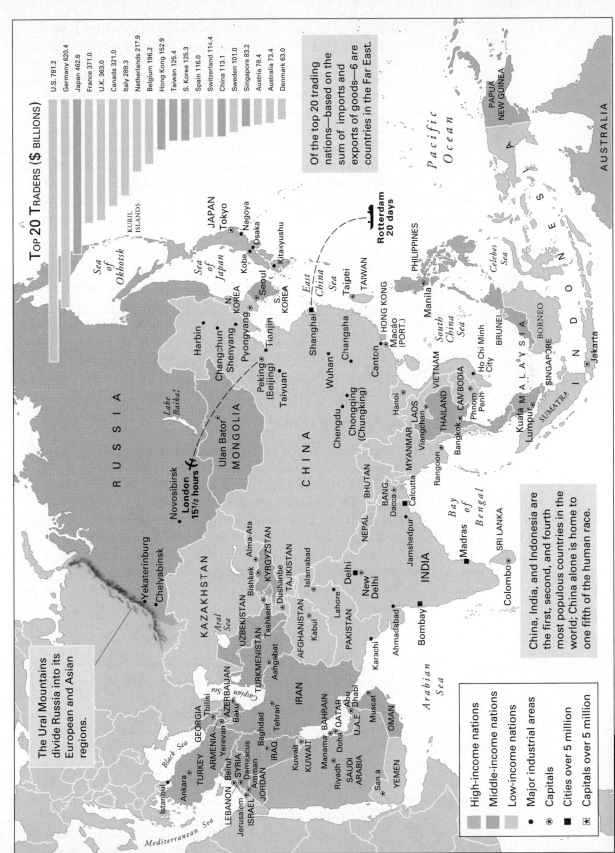

TOP 20 TRADERS ($ BILLIONS)

U.S. 781.2
Germany 620.4
Japan 462.6
France 371.0
U.K. 363.0
Canada 321.0
Italy 289.3
Netherlands 217.9
Belgium 196.2
Hong Kong 152.9
Taiwan 125.4
S. Korea 125.3
Spain 116.0
Switzerland 114.4
China 113.1
Sweden 101.0
Singapore 83.2
Austria 78.4
Australia 73.4
Denmark 63.0

Of the top 20 trading nations—based on the sum of imports and exports of goods—6 are countries in the Far East.

The Ural Mountains divide Russia into its European and Asian regions.

China, India, and Indonesia are the first, second, and fourth most populous countries in the world; China alone is home to one fifth of the human race.

Rotterdam 20 days

London 15½ hours

High-income nations
Middle-income nations
Low-income nations
• Major industrial areas
⊛ Capitals
■ Cities over 5 million
✶ Capitals over 5 million

Asia

MAP 2.6

MITI has been aided by Japan's concentrated industrial structure. Japanese industry is controlled by large families of interrelated companies, called *keiretsu*, that are typically centered around a major Japanese bank. The bank takes primary responsibility for meeting the keiretsu's financing needs. The members often act as suppliers to each other, thus making it more difficult for outsiders to penetrate Japanese markets. Members are also protected from hostile takeovers by an elaborate system of cross-ownership of shares by which members of a keiretsu own shares in one another. Toyota Motors, for example, owns 19 percent of the common stock of Koito Manufacturing, and other members of Toyota's keiretsu own 40 percent of Koito's stock. Koito in turn is the primary supplier for Toyota's automotive lighting needs. Keiretsu members often rely on a *sogo sosha*, an export trading company, to market their exports worldwide. Typically the sogo sosha is also a keiretsu member.

Although most political commentators note that exports have spurred Japan's postwar growth, exports are a smaller portion of Japan's GDP—only 9.2 percent—than is the case for many countries, such as Germany (24.0 percent) and France (17.5 percent). Yet Japanese exports have become a lightning rod for international criticism because of the perception that Japan employs unfair trading practices to market its exports while using numerous nontariff barriers to restrict imports from its domestic market (we'll discuss this further in Chapter 6). The large balance of trade Japan has enjoyed in the past decade has enabled it to expand its purchases of overseas assets. It is now the world's largest creditor country.

Australia and New Zealand

Australia and New Zealand are the other traditional economic powers in Pacific Asia. Although they share a common cultural heritage, significant differences exist between the two countries, which are separated by 1200 miles of ocean (see Map 2.7). Australia's 17.5 million people live in an area of 2.97 million square miles. Because of the aridity of much of the continent, most of the population is concentrated in the coastal regions, with approximately 40 percent living in either Sydney or Melbourne. With a 1992 GDP of $295 billion, Australia is the world's fifteenth-largest economy. It is rich in natural resources but suffers from a relatively small workforce. As a result, its exports, which account for 12.9 percent of GDP, are concentrated in natural resource industries (such as aluminum, zinc, and coal) and in land-intensive agricultural goods (such as wool, beef, and wheat).

New Zealand's 3.4 million people live on two main islands—the more populous North Island and the more scenic but less temperate South Island. With a GDP of $42 billion and a per capita GDP of only $12,300 in 1992, New Zealand has been the slowest-growing of the OECD countries in the post–World War II period. Much of the blame for this was placed on overregulation of the country's business sector. As a result, beginning in 1984, the Labor Party began systematically deregulating and privatizing the economy, including such key industries as telecommunications, transportation, and financial services. Trade is extremely important to the country; 1992 exports of $9.3 billion constituted 22.6 percent of its GDP. Over half of New Zealand's exports are attributable to its extensive pasture lands—these exports include dairy products, meat, and wool. Australia, Japan, and the United States account for approximately half of New Zealand's exports and imports.

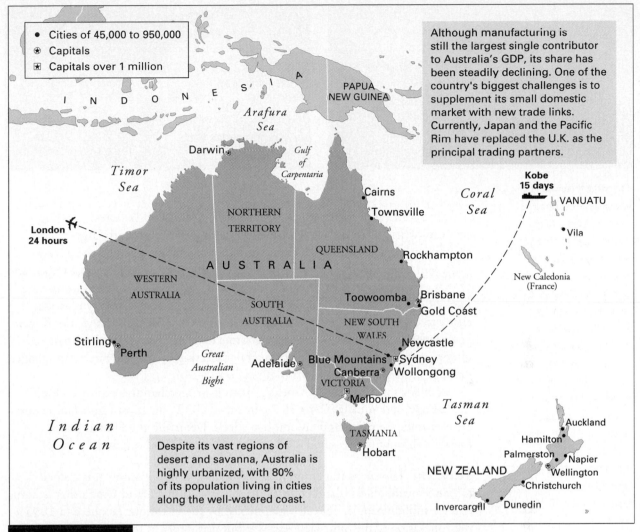

- Cities of 45,000 to 950,000
- ⊛ Capitals
- ⊞ Capitals over 1 million

Although manufacturing is still the largest single contributor to Australia's GDP, its share has been steadily declining. One of the country's biggest challenges is to supplement its small domestic market with new trade links. Currently, Japan and the Pacific Rim have replaced the U.K. as the principal trading partners.

INDONESIA

Arafura Sea

Darwin

Gulf of Carpentaria

Timor Sea

Kobe 15 days

Coral Sea

VANUATU

Vila

London 24 hours

NORTHERN TERRITORY

Cairns
Townsville

New Caledonia (France)

QUEENSLAND

Rockhampton

AUSTRALIA

WESTERN AUSTRALIA

SOUTH AUSTRALIA

Toowoomba   Brisbane
Gold Coast

NEW SOUTH WALES

Newcastle

Stirling
Perth

Great Australian Bight

Adelaide   Blue Mountains   Sydney
Canberra   Wollongong

VICTORIA

Melbourne

Tasman Sea

Auckland

Hamilton

Palmerston   Napier

Wellington

Indian Ocean

TASMANIA
Hobart

NEW ZEALAND

Despite its vast regions of desert and savanna, Australia is highly urbanized, with 80% of its population living in cities along the well-watered coast.

Christchurch

Invercargill   Dunedin

MAP 2.7

Australia and New Zealand

The Four Tigers

Pacific Asia is one of the world's most rapidly industrializing regions. South Korea, Taiwan, Singapore, and Hong Kong in particular have made such rapid strides since 1945 that they are collectively known as the "Four Tigers," a reference to the Chinese heritage that three of the four share. You may also see the four referred to as the newly industrialized countries (NICs) or the newly industrialized economies (NIEs), because Hong Kong is not legally a country and whether Taiwan is an independent country is a sensitive diplomatic issue.

South Korea. The Republic of Korea, more commonly known as South Korea, was born of the Cold War. After the Soviets declared war on Japan in August 1945, the Korean peninsula north of the 38th parallel was occupied by Soviet troops, and the area south of the 38th parallel fell under U.S. influence. North Korean troops invaded South Korea in 1950, triggering the Korean War. Three years of bloody conflict ensued. Peace talks at Panmunjom left the peninsula divided into communist North Korea and capitalist South Korea approximately along the prewar boundaries.

The contrast between the economic performance of communist North Korea (left) and that of capitalist South Korea (right) has been dramatic. After the Korean War ended in 1953, both countries ranked among the world's poorest. Housing, food, and other consumer goods are still scarce in North Korea, and its per capita income is only $1,000. The export-oriented economic policies of South Korea have generated an economic boom. The country's per capita income is $6,790, and it is a major force in the world economy.

Since the 1960s South Korea has been one of the world's fastest-growing economies: its 1992 GDP of $296 billion made it the fourteenth largest. This growth has been accomplished through tight cooperation between the government and a handful of large, privately owned conglomerates. The most important of these conglomerates, or *chaebol*, are Samsung, Hyundai, Daewoo Group, and Lucky-Goldstar. Leaders of the chaebols are in many cases related by marriage either to one another or to top government officials.[18] In many ways, the Korean government has tried to follow the economic path established by the Japanese: discouragement of imports, governmental leadership of the economy, and reliance on large economic combines for industrialization.

A major source of South Korea's growth is its merchandise exports, which totaled $76 billion in 1992, or 25.7 percent of GDP. The most important exports are electronics, textiles, and automotive goods. Japan and the United States together account for over half of the country's exports and imports.

Taiwan. Taiwan, as the Republic of China is commonly known, is a small (13,885 square miles) island country off the coast of mainland China that is home to 21.1 million people. Taiwan was annexed by the victorious Japanese in 1895 at the conclusion of the Sino-Japanese War but was returned to Chinese control at the end of World War II. In the civil war that followed, the Chinese communists under Mao Tse Tung defeated Chiang Kai-Shek's armies. Chiang's troops and government fled to Taiwan in 1949.

Declaring the island "the Republic of China" and himself the rightful governor of the mainland, Chiang undertook to develop the Taiwanese economy to support a promised invasion of the mainland. Redistribution of land from large estate holders to peasants increased agricultural productivity. Reliance on family-owned private businesses[19] and export-oriented trade policies has made Taiwan one of the world's fastest-growing economies over the past three decades, with a real growth rate averaging over 9 percent annually. Exports were $82.4 billion in 1992, or 39.4 percent of the country's GDP of $209 billion. The United States is the destination of 29 percent of Taiwan's exports, followed by Hong Kong (19 percent) and the EU (17 percent).

Taiwan's economic development has been so fast-paced that it can no longer compete as a low-wage manufacturing center. Consequently Taiwanese businesses more recently have focused on high-value-added industries such as electronics and automotive products. However, they still need low-wage workers. Despite the lack of diplomatic relations between Taiwan and China, these businesses increasingly are investing in factories and assembly plants in China in order to access the low-wage workers they need. Private estimates of total Taiwanese investment in the mainland range as high as $10 billion.[20]

Singapore. The Republic of Singapore is a former British colony and a small island country (only 239 square miles) off the southern tip of the Malay peninsula. Since becoming independent in 1965, the country has been governed by a parliamentary democracy. To remedy chronic unemployment Lee Kuan Yew, the country's first Prime Minister, who served from independence until 1991, emphasized development of labor-intensive industries such as textile production. This economic policy proved so successful that Singapore shifted to higher-value-added activities such as oil refining and chemical processing in the late 1960s and high-tech industries such as computers and biotechnology in the late 1970s. Today Singapore has a population of 2.8 million and an unemployment rate of only 2.7 percent. In fact, it suffers from a labor shortage and can no longer compete with such countries as Honduras and Indonesia in the production of price-sensitive, labor-intensive manufactured goods.

In 1992 Singapore's per capita income was $15,730 and its exports totaled $63.4 billion, or *138 percent* of its GDP of $46 billion. That figure is not a misprint. Singapore thrives on **re-exporting**. Singapore's firms take advantage of the country's excellent port facilities to import foreign goods and then re-export them to another country (particularly neighboring Malaysia). Besides being an important port and center for oil refining, Singapore provides sophisticated communications and financial services for firms in Pacific Asia.

Hong Kong. Of the Four Tigers, the one whose future is the most uncertain is Hong Kong. Currently a British Crown Colony, this island group is scheduled to be ceded back to China in 1997. China has promised to designate Hong Kong a Special Administrative Region and honor its British-based laws and political rights. However, because of the slaughter of pro-democracy demonstrators at Tiananmen Square in 1989, many Hong Kong residents fear the Beijing government will not respect its treaty obligations once the British leave.

Over 5.6 million people are packed into Hong Kong's small (411 square miles) land mass, an island of capitalism surrounded by the world's largest communist country. Hong Kong offers highly educated, highly productive labor for industries such as textiles and electronics and provides banking and financial services for much of East Asia. Hong Kong also has thrived as an entrepôt for China, receiving goods from it and preparing them for shipment to the rest of the world, and vice versa. Moreover, as a result of common culture and geography, Hong Kong entrepreneurs often act as intermediaries for companies around the world that want to conduct business with China. For example, the Hong Kong subsidiary of the Quanta Group built the new McDonald's restaurant in Xiamen, a mainland Chinese city that lies opposite Taiwan.[21]

Export statistics for Hong Kong reflect its trade services to China. Hong Kong exported $119.5 billion of goods in 1992, or 139 percent of its $86 billion GDP. Half of its exports are bound for China or the United States. Of Hong Kong's $82.4 billion in imports, China supplied 37 percent, followed by Japan (16 percent), Taiwan (9 percent), and the United States (8 percent). Hidden in Hong Kong's trade statistics is its role as a bridge between Taiwan and its political enemy, China. Because Taiwanese goods are somewhat politically tainted in China, and vice versa, Hong Kong provides the valuable service of converting goods produced by one political enemy into Hong Kong goods so that they can be exported to the other political enemy.[22]

India

India is the world's second most populous country, with approximately 884 million people in 1992. It also is one of the poorest countries, with a per capita GDP of only $310. Agriculture accounts for over 70 percent of employment, but only 35 percent of GDP. Although India's economy has expanded substantially since 1945, continued population growth of almost 2 percent a year has slowed per capita income growth.

India was part of the British empire until 1947, when British rule ended. The Indian subcontinent subsequently was partitioned along religious lines into India, where Hindus were predominant, and Pakistan, where Muslims were dominant. The eastern part of Pakistan became the independent nation of Bangladesh in 1971. The new country of India adopted many of the formalities of the British governmental system, including the parliamentary system, a strong independent judiciary, and a professional bureaucracy. For most of its postwar history, the country has relied on state ownership of key industries, including power, transportation, and heavy industry, as a critical element of its economic development efforts.

India's bureaucracy can be cumbersome and slow to provide documents necessary to conduct business within the country. Until 1991 India discouraged foreign investment, limiting foreign owners to minority positions in Indian enterprises and imposing other onerous requirements. For example, as a condition for remaining in the country, India in the 1970s retroactively required the Coca-Cola Company to divulge its secret soft-drink formula. Coca-Cola refused and chose to leave the market. Coca-Cola subsequently reentered the market as a result of Prime Minister Rao's 1991 market-opening reforms.

During the Cold War, India was loosely aligned with the Soviet bloc. The Indian economy was hurt by the former Soviet Union's collapse and the subsequent loss of markets for its goods. For example, Russia normally accounted for 60 percent of India's tea exports. Russia's cash shortages caused it to cancel tea orders, resulting in the threat of bankruptcy for numerous small tea plantations in eastern India.[23]

Because of India's large domestic market and the importance of heavily subsidized and globally uncompetitive firms in its economy, international trade has not been as important to it as it is to other countries. In 1992, India exported $19.8 billion, only 9.2 percent of its GDP of $215 billion. Recognizing that India's international uncompetitiveness was harming the country's economic growth, in 1991 the Indian government launched a series of economic reforms, which included lessening restrictions on FDI. These reforms have attracted foreign companies, such as Colgate Palmolive and ABB, to expand their presence in the Indian market.

China

With over 1.1 billion people, China is the world's most populous country. It also is one of the world's oldest, ruled by a series of emperors from 2000 B.C. until the early 1900s, when a republic was founded. A chaotic civil war facilitated a Japanese invasion in 1931. After expulsion of the Japanese at the end of World War II, the civil war renewed. Finally, in 1949 the communist forces of Mao Tse-Tung defeated the nationalist army led by General Chiang Kai-Shek.

Communism in China under Mao Tse-Tung went through several stages. The "Great Leap Forward" was a program undertaken from 1958 to 1960 to force industrialization through the growth of small labor-intensive factories. The program's failure led eventually to the "Cultural Revolution" in 1966, during which youthful communist cadres indiscriminately purged any Communist Party member suspected of deviating from Mao's doctrines. Neighbor turned against neighbor. Family members turned on each other. Professors' books were destroyed, and farmers were brought in from the countryside to teach in the universities or to practice medicine. The political chaos that followed set back the country's economic progress, as many of its most productive and educated members were exiled to the countryside to repent their ideological sins.

After Mao's death in 1976, the government adopted limited free-market policies that called for returning agriculture to the private sector and allowing entrepreneurs to start small businesses such as restaurants and light manufacturing. Foreign companies were permitted to establish joint ventures with Chinese firms. As a result, FDI in China and economic growth soared, as did hopes for increased political freedom. However, Communist Party leaders were unwilling to relinquish their powers. The conflict that resulted led to the massacre of pro-democracy demonstrators in Beijing's Tiananmen Square in June 1989. Western countries quickly demonstrated their objections to the massacre by cutting off aid and investment capital to China.

Nonetheless, China is following a unique path. It continues to adopt market-oriented economic policies under the Communist Party's watchful eye. In the 1980s it established numerous special enterprise zones to attract foreign capital. It also has invested in many Hong Kong companies to better learn the ways of capitalism. In July 1992 the Chinese government granted all enterprises increased independence from the state's central planners, including the right to engage in international trade, the ability to negotiate with foreigners, and the freedom to adjust production, merge, or go bankrupt without permission from governmental planners. As a result, China's economy is becoming increasingly schizophrenic. Half of the country's output is produced by state enterprises noted for their low productivity and shoddy products; the remainder is produced by private firms. For example, in the Wenzhou region, which is home to 6.5 million people, private entrepreneurs have responded to economic liberalization by creating 153,000 small businesses and 42 private banks. Over 88 percent of Wenzhou's output is produced by the private sector. Typical of these firms is the Zhejiang Spark Industrial Automatic Meter Industrial Development Group. A machinist employed by the state-owned meter factory who hadn't been paid for a year started the firm with borrowed money. The privately owned Zhejiang factory now annually sells $2 million in meters and gauges to petroleum and chemical refineries.[24]

Private-sector development has attracted the attention of firms worldwide. FDI sextupled from $4 billion in 1991 to $25 billion in 1993.[25] Of particular note are the increased investments in China by Chinese investors living in Taiwan, Hong Kong, and Singapore, who see the country as a source of hard-working, low-cost labor, an increasingly scarce commodity in their own communities.

China's exports totaled $85 billion in 1990, or 16.8 percent of its GDP of $506 billion. Hong Kong and Macau (a small Portuguese colony near Hong Kong) accounted for 43 percent of China's exports and 22 percent of its imports. Most of Hong Kong and Macau's trade with China represents re-exports to or from some third country.

Southeast Asian Countries

Asia is home to numerous other countries at various stages of economic development. Of particular note are Thailand, Malaysia, and Indonesia, countries with low labor costs that have been recipients of significant FDI in the 1980s and 1990s. As labor costs have risen in their homeland, many Japanese MNCs have sprinkled these three countries with satellite plants designed to supply low-cost parts to parent factories in Japan.

Another potentially important economy in this region is Vietnam. At the end of the Vietnam War, the U.S. government imposed a trade embargo on this country; most industrialized countries followed suit. Over the last several years, however, most of those countries have dropped their embargoes and businesses from them have been setting up shop in Vietnam. Many experts believe that Vietnam is poised for a major economic surge similar to that of the Four Tigers.[26] Pressure from major U.S. MNCs that saw how aggressively their foreign competitors were moving into Vietnam resulted in President Clinton's dropping the U.S. trade embargo in early 1994. Consequently, experts believe the Vietnamese economy will increase in importance throughout the 1990s.

The Marketplaces of Africa

The African continent, shown in Map 2.8, is home to 663 million people and 55 countries. Most of Africa was colonized in the late nineteenth century by the major European powers (France, Spain, Belgium, Germany, Italy, Portugal, and Great Britain) for strategic military purposes or to meet domestic political demands. The tide of colonialism reversed beginning in the mid-1950s, as one by one these countries surrendered power over their African colonies. Vestiges of colonialism remain in today's Africa, affecting opportunities available to international businesses. For example, Chad, Niger, and the Côte d'Ivoire (Ivory Coast) retain close economic and cultural ties to France. They link their currencies to the French franc and follow French legal, educational, and governmental procedures. Because of these ties, French manufacturers, financial institutions, and service-sector firms often dominate international commerce with these countries. Similarly, the public institutions of Kenya, Zimbabwe, and the Republic of South Africa are modeled along British lines, giving British firms a competitive advantage in these countries.

The history of the newly independent African countries since 1960 has not always been happy. After obtaining their independence, many of these countries attempted to expand their economies along socialist principles. But developmental efforts were hindered by political unrest and civil war, which often occurred along tribal lines, as authoritarian, one-party governments were installed throughout the continent. In the past decade, however, Africa appears to be shifting away from

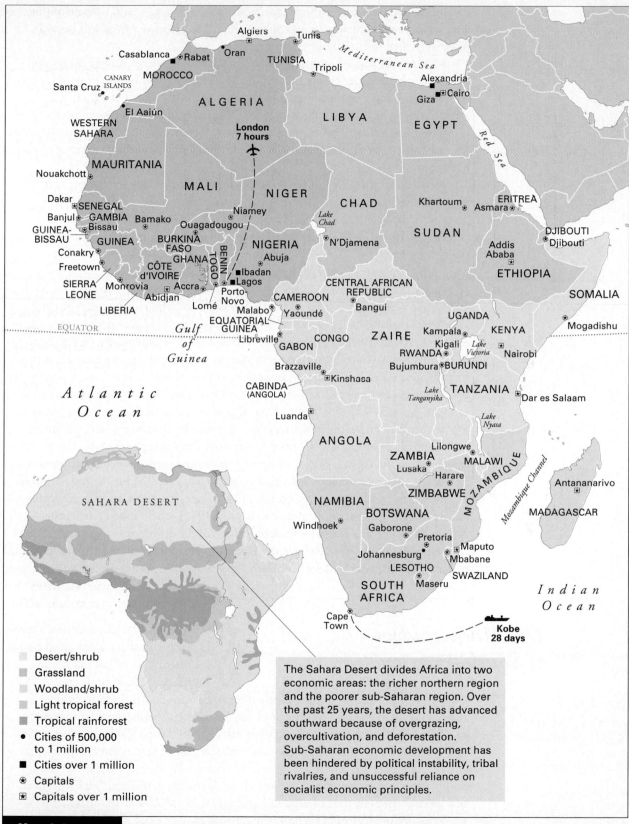

London
7 hours

Kobe
28 days

Desert/shrub
Grassland
Woodland/shrub
Light tropical forest
Tropical rainforest
• Cities of 500,000
   to 1 million
■ Cities over 1 million
⊛ Capitals
⊠ Capitals over 1 million

The Sahara Desert divides Africa into two
economic areas: the richer northern region
and the poorer sub-Saharan region. Over
the past 25 years, the desert has advanced
southward because of overgrazing,
overcultivation, and deforestation.
Sub-Saharan economic development has
been hindered by political instability, tribal
rivalries, and unsuccessful reliance on
socialist economic principles.

MAP 2.8   **Africa**

socialist economics and authoritarian politics and toward market-oriented policies and multi-party democracies. As political stability returns, Africa will become more attractive to international businesses.

Much of Africa's economy is tied to its natural resources. Libya enjoys the continent's highest per capita income—$5800 in 1992—because of its substantial oil reserves. However, the support of terrorist organizations by Libya's Revolutionary Leader Muammar Qadhafi has prompted Western countries to ostracize Libya and cut off economic aid to it. Crude oil production also accounts for one half of the GDPs of Angola, Gabon, and Nigeria and one quarter of that of Algeria.

Agriculture also is important to many African countries. For some, agricultural products are their major exports. For example, coffee, cocoa, and palm oil account for 80 percent of Côte d'Ivoire's exports, and coffee and tea comprise 80 percent of Rwanda's. Unfortunately, the population in many African countries is largely employed in subsistence farming. These countries include Gambia, Mozambique, Sierra Leone, Tanzania, Zaire, and Zambia.

As its economies grow, Africa will become a more attractive market for MNCs and a source of low-cost labor. The African island of Mauritius, which lies 900 kilometers east of Madagascar in the Indian Ocean, provides a model of successful economic development for African countries. Formerly dependent on sugar cane, Mauritius has become an important center for textile and apparel manufacturing by providing a tax-free zone for goods destined for export. Mauritius's economy has been growing at a real rate of 6.1 percent annually, and its unemployment rate is only 2.4 percent. Another likely center of growth is South Africa, which possesses fertile farmland and rich deposits of gold, diamonds, chromium, and platinum. Until the 1970s, many MNCs used South Africa as the base for their African operations. Then the United Nations imposed trade sanctions against the country because of the government's apartheid policies (which called for the separation of blacks, whites, and Asians). As a result of these external pressures, the government extended voting rights to all of its citizens in 1994. Nobel Peace Prize winner Nelson Mandela was elected president in May 1994 in the country's first multiracial elections. When the new government completes its social reforms and political stability returns, South Africa will likely attract significant foreign investment.

The Marketplaces of South America

South America's 13 countries, shown in Map 2.9, share a common political history as well as many economic and social problems. A 1494 papal decree divided colonization privileges regarding the continent between Portugal (Brazil) and Spain (the rest of the continent). Spanish and Portuguese explorers subjugated the native populations, exploited their gold and silver mines, and converted their fields to sugar cane, tobacco, and cacao plantations. By the end of the eighteenth century, the hold of the two European empires on their South American colonies had weakened. Led by such patriots as Simon Bolivar, one colony after another won its independence. By 1825 the Spanish flag remained flying over only Cuba and Puerto Rico.

The independent South American countries have not enjoyed a happy economic history. Descendants of the European colonialists have dominated their

During the late 1980s, many South American governments stimulated economic growth by adopting policies promoting free trade and private enterprise, thereby increasing the continent's appeal to U.S., European, and Asian MNCs. Chile now has one of the most free-market economies in the world.

International business in South America is affected by its physical geography. The Andes Mountains make it difficult to transport goods between Pacific Coast countries and their inland neighbors. Other mountain ranges, as well as the dense forests of the Amazon River Basin, similarly limit transport of goods.

- Cities of 350,000 to 1 million
- ■ Cities over 1 million
- ⊛ Capitals
- ⊠ Capitals over 1 million

MAP 2.9   **South America**

economies, resulting in huge income disparities. Often these nations have been characterized by political instability, frequent changes in governments (often headed by military dictators), and inward-looking economic policies that have generated inflation, inefficient production, and widespread poverty.

For much of the post–World War II period most South American countries followed what international economists call **import substitution policies** as a means of promoting economic development. With this approach, a country attempts to stimulate the development of local industry by discouraging imports via high tariffs and nontariff barriers. (The opposite of import substitution is **export promotion**, whereby a country pursues economic growth by expanding its exports. This is the developmental approach successfully adopted by Taiwan, Hong Kong, and Singapore, as discussed earlier in this chapter.) For most South American industries, however, the domestic market is too small to enable domestic producers to gain economies of scale through mass production techniques or to permit much competition among local producers. Thus prices of domestically produced goods tend to rise above prices in other markets. These policies benefit domestic firms that face import competition. But they cripple the ability of a country's exporters to compete in world markets because the companies must pay higher prices for domestically produced inputs than do their foreign competitors. Inevitably, the government must subsidize these firms and often nationalize them in order to preserve urban jobs. The high costs of doing this are passed on to taxpayers and to consumers through higher prices, but over time, the government runs a budget deficit. The result is inflation and destruction of middle-class savings.

Many major South American countries—including Argentina, Brazil, Chile, and Venezuela—adopted these well-intentioned but ultimately destructive import substitution policies. In the late 1980s, however, they began to reverse their policies. They lowered tariff barriers, sought free-trade agreements with their neighbors, privatized their industries, and positioned their economies to compete internationally. Chile, for example, now has one of the strongest free-market orientations in the world. These policy shifts are expanding South America's role in world trade, attracting foreign capital to the continent, and increasing productivity and per capita incomes.

CHAPTER REVIEW

Summary

Geography plays an important role in international business. International trade and investment flows are often affected by cultural and economic geography—factors such as shared borders, similar income levels, ownership of natural resources, and common ethnic and political heritages. International businesspeople who understand geographic principles can better select new markets and new countries in which to invest.

A key indicator of a country's desirability to international businesses is its per capita income, which provides information about its consumers and its value as a production site. The World Bank has developed a commonly used scheme for classifying income levels; it divides the world's countries into high-income, middle-income, and low-income categories based on per capita income.

The Quad countries—Japan, members of the EU, the United States, and Canada—are of particular importance to MNCs. Some experts believe that firms cannot succeed in the global economy unless they have a significant presence throughout these areas.

The North American market—Canada, Mexico, the United States, Central America, and the island countries of the Caribbean—is one of the world's largest and richest. The United States and Canada have the largest bilateral trading relationship in the world. Mexico's economic reforms, initiated in 1982, have made it a more important force in the world economy.

Another large, rich market for international businesses is Western Europe, particularly the 15-member EU. The EU members are free-market–oriented, parlimentary democracies.

With the 1989 collapse of European communism, Eastern and Central European countries are undergoing a transition from communism to capitalism. Most have adopted market-oriented policies in order to stimulate economic growth. Their growth prospects and unmet consumer demand are attractive to many North American and European MNCs.

Asia is home to several of the fastest-growing economies of the postwar period. Japan and the Four Tigers—South Korea, Hong Kong, Singapore, and Taiwan—have grown dramatically because of economic policies that focus on export promotion. Because of the economic successes of Japan and the Four Tigers, other countries such as India and China have begun to reverse their inward-looking economic policies. Australia and New Zealand are also important economies in this region.

The African countries are among the world's poorest. Their economies primarily rely on natural resources and agriculture. After declaring independence from their European colonizers in the 1950s and 1960s, most of these nations adopted socialist economic principles and subsequently suffered substantial political unrest. In the 1980s, however, several African countries became more market-oriented and politically stable, thus raising their attractiveness to international businesses.

The South American countries have been independent since the early nineteenth century. While many are rich in natural resources and farmlands, the continent's economic development since World War II has been hindered by chronic political unrest and import-substitution policies. In the 1980s, however, key South American nations—including Argentina, Brazil, and Chile—shifted toward more market-oriented, export-promotion growth strategies. Privatization and reduced governmental regulation have prompted renewed interest from international businesses in the continent.

Review Questions

1. Discuss the cultural and economic geographical factors that affect international trade and investment activity.

2. What is the Triad? What is the Quad? Why are they important to international businesses?

3. How do differences in income levels and income distribution among countries affect international businesses?

4. Describe the U.S. role in the world economy.

5. How did COMECON's breakup affect its members?

6. What is a sogo sosha?

7. Who are the Four Tigers? Why are they important to international businesses?

8. What is a chaebol?

9. What special problem do investors in Hong Kong face?

10. Discuss the reasons for Africa's slow economic development in the past three decades.

11. How did import-substitution policies affect the economies of Brazil and Argentina?

Questions for Discussion

1. Regional trading blocs, such as the EU and NAFTA, are growing in importance. What are the implications of these trading blocs for international businesses? Are they helpful or harmful? How may they affect a firm's investment decisions?

2. Discuss the problems facing Central and Eastern European countries in the 1990s. What opportunities are available to international businesses in these countries?

3. Many American and European businesspeople argue that the keiretsus system in Japan acts as a barrier to foreign companies' entering the Japanese market. Why do you think they believe this?

4. Ethnic ties, old colonial alliances, and shared languages appear to affect international trade.

Why might this be so? If true, how does this affect international businesses' strategies regarding which markets to enter?

5. What can African countries do to encourage more foreign investment in their economies?

 **BUILDING GLOBAL SKILLS**

Success in international business often depends on a firm's obtaining information it needs about foreign countries and markets so that it can make exporting, importing, and investment decisions. Fortunately, many published sources of information are available to help firms do this. Among the most useful are the following.

Survey of Current Business The U.S. Department of Commerce publishes the *Survey of Current Business* monthly. The survey is a basic source of statistical data on the U.S. economy. It provides detailed, accurate, and up-to-date analyses of international trade and investment activities affecting the United States.

The World Factbook The U.S. Central Intelligence Agency publishes *The World Factbook* annually. This document provides basic geographic, ethnic, religious, political, and economic information on all countries. It is particularly useful because it compiles data about small, obscure, and politically controversial areas. For example, the Falkland Islands, the object of a short war in 1982 between the United Kingdom and Argentina, both of which claim ownership of the islands, has its own entry, as does the Iraq–Saudia Arabia Neutral Zone. Or, if you were an executive for Crestone Energy Corporation, which was hired by China's government in 1992 to hunt for oil and gas around the Spratly Islands, *The World Factbook* is one of the few sources available in which you could learn that the islands, many of which are under water at high tide, have no permanent population yet are claimed and garrisoned by five different countries— China, Malaysia, the Philippines, Taiwan, and

Vietnam. Armed with this information, you would realize that Crestone's explorations would be extremely sensitive and possibly the target of political conflict.[27]

Background Notes The U.S. State Department periodically publishes short (10–14 pages) profiles of individual countries called *Background Notes*. Each is intended to provide government employees with a quick overview of a country's geography, culture, living conditions, political orientation, economic policies, and trading patterns. *Background Notes* are particularly useful for briefing employees who are given temporary assignments in a foreign country.

World Development Report Published annually by the staff of the World Bank, the *World Development Report* presents numerous tables detailing information about World Bank members, including population, income and income distribution, infrastructure, government expenditures, trade, production, living standards, health, education, and urbanization.

International Trade Statistics Published annually by the General Agreement on Tariffs and Trade (GATT), *International Trade Statistics* summarizes trade flows among regions of the world. It also provides export and import data by country and by product group (such as agriculture, mining, or manufacturing).

Commodity Trade Statistics Published by the United Nations, *Commodity Trade Statistics* provides detailed data, compiled annually, on each country's exports and imports, which are classified by commodity and by country of destination or origin. It is an excellent source of minutia, for example, the value of pork exports from Denmark to Portugal in 1994.

However, it is rather clumsy to use when time-series information is required, for example, Denmark's total exports from 1983 to 1994.

Balance of Payments Statistics, International Financial Statistics, and Direction of Trade Statistics These reports are published by the International Monetary Fund (IMF). *Balance of Payments Statistics,* issued annually, contains data about balance of payments performances of IMF members. The monthly *International Financial Statistics* offers international and domestic financial data on members' domestic interest rates, money and banking indicators, prices, and exchange rates. *Direction of Trade Statistics* details the exports and imports of each IMF member on a quarterly basis.

World Economic Outlook The IMF publishes *World Economic Outlook* annually. The publication provides detailed analyses of the past year's performance of the world economy, as well as analyses for regions and individual countries. It also includes an assessment of the future prospects for each economy.

National Trade Data Bank (NTDB) One of the newest data sources, the NTDB is distributed monthly by the U.S. Department of Commerce. It is packed with information assembled from other data sources, including some of those listed here. NTDB differs from the others in its format: it is distributed on a CD-ROM disk. An annual subscription costs $360. (It is also available on the Internet for free.) Many university libraries and all federal depository libraries receive the NTDB. Because an enormous amount of data can be crammed on a CD-ROM disk, the NTDB contains databases not readily available elsewhere. Suppose, for example, that your company produces mountain

bikes and is looking for a German distributor. The NTDB provides information on whether any existing German sporting equipment distributor is interested in distributing foreign-made mountain bikes. The NTDB also contains *A Basic Guide to Exporting,* a step-by-step guidebook developed by the U.S. Department of Commerce to assist first-time exporters. This guide contains an extensive list of other standard sources of information often used by international businesses.

Assignment

Go to your library and examine each of these standard references. (If your library subscribes to the NTDB, make an appointment with a reference librarian to play with it so that you can appreciate its capabilities.) Then answer the following questions:

1. What was the total value of U.S. imports from Belgium last year? Of U.S. exports to Belgium?

2. What is the total level of U.S. investments in Belgium? Of Belgian investments in the United States?

3. Profile the economy of Belgium: What is its GDP? What is its per capita income? How fast is its economy growing? What are its major exports and imports? Who are its major trading partners?

4. Profile the people of Belgium: What languages do they speak? What is their average educational level? What is their life expectancy? How fast is the population growing?

CLOSING CASE

The Chinese Treasure Chest[28]

China's vast population and untapped business potential make it one of the world's largest potential commercial treasure chests. Businesses that are able to enter and function effectively in the Chinese market face an enviable future. But those that attempt to

exploit the Chinese market without fully understanding its complexities are certain to fail.

It is easy to understand the allure of China for international businesses. The country offers over 1.1 billion consumers whose per capita income is rising rapidly. Already over 60 million Chinese residents have annual incomes of $1000 or more, the level at which experts believe consumerism begins to emerge. These consumers, in turn, will want to buy everything from McDonald's hamburgers to fashion apparel to color televisions. However, because the Chinese economy for so long has been controlled and limited by its political leaders, there is a shortage of suppliers to meet this rising consumer demand.

China is sending clear signals that it wants to move toward an open-market economy. Even though its political system is communistic, it is seeking foreign investors and new suppliers to fuel its economic growth. For example, the country is investing heavily in improving its infrastructure in order to make itself more attractive to foreign firms. New national expressways, rail lines, and duty-free trade zones are springing up all over, and new dams are being planned and built to generate energy needed for future growth.

Firms that risk entering the Chinese market are finding one surprise after another—some good, some not so good. For example, in 1992 Motorola, the U.S. electronics giant, built a small, makeshift factory in the northern Chinese port city of Tianjin to manufacture electronic paging devices. The firm expected demand for the pagers to be minimal in China and thus planned to ship most of them to other Asian markets. To Motorola's surprise, the factory's entire weekly output of 10,000 pagers is being sold exclusively in China. But Motorola has had to invest more heavily than expected in training local employees to work in a market-oriented business and to emphasize quality in manufacturing. Still, the company is so enamored of the Chinese market that it is building two new plants in Tianjin, representing a total investment of $400 million, to produce everything from cellular telephones to advanced microprocessors. Other U.S. firms are following suit; for example, Eastman Kodak and Heinz also have announced plans to build plants in Tianjin.

But China's international business appeal is not restricted to U.S. firms. Siemens and Philips are among the European firms moving aggressively into China. And Asian firms are doing the same. Even Taiwanese firms see the potential in China. For example, a few years ago, Taiwan's Chung Shing Textile Company opened a plant in Shanghai to make underwear for shipment to Western markets. But local demand has been so great that the plant's total output of Three Guns underwear has been snapped up by buyers for local Chinese department stores.

Meanwhile local Chinese firms are trying to keep a piece of the action for themselves. Local firms producing everything from furniture to processed food are desperately trying to remain competitive. A few Chinese businesses, such as Brilliance China Automotive Holdings and Shanghai Petrochemical, are even listed on the New York Stock Exchange. Unfortunately, many lack modern production equipment, and their managers do not fully understand the nature of free-market competition.

Not everyone agrees that doing business successfully in China is a sure thing. The country has had an historical problem with rampant inflation. To counter this, the Chinese government has routinely resorted to devaluing the country's currency, a step that simultaneously devalues all foreign investments. Political instability also is a major concern of international businesses. China's leadership continues to promote free-market business practices even as it attempts to maintain its tight control over all other aspects of the country. The risk is that as Chinese consumers grow more accustomed to free-market practices, they will begin to demand more freedom in other areas of their lives. Thus the potential for civil unrest will likely remain a fact of life for some time.

Case Questions

1. Assess the potential advantages and disadvantages of the Chinese market for international businesses.

2. What advice would you give a firm that is considering entry into the Chinese market?

3. What kinds of products are most likely to succeed in China in the short run? Which may need more time to be accepted?

CHAPTER NOTES

1. "Eastern Europe Poses Obstacles for Ads," *Wall Street Journal,* July 30, 1992, p. B6.

2. "South Korea Contract Award Spotlights Marriage of the Nation's Political and Business Families," *Wall Street Journal,* August 21, 1992, p. A6.

3. "Two Papers Are Halted in Indonesia Due to Ad," *Wall Street Journal,* August 10, 1992, p. B8.

4. British dominion over Hong Kong will end in 1997, when political control of the Crown Colony is to be returned to China.

5. Kenichi Ohmae, "The Triad World View," *Journal of Business Strategy,* Vol. 7, No. 4 (Spring 1987), p. 18.

6. Morris Goldstein et al., "Policy Issues in the Evolving International Monetary System," Occasional Paper #96, International Monetary Fund, Washington, D.C. (June 1992), p. 8. According to Goldstein, the U.S. dollar was used as the invoicing currency for 46 percent of exports from the six largest economies (the United States, Japan, Germany, France, Italy, and the United Kingdom) in 1987; for 53 percent of Eurocurrency deposits in 1990; for 67 percent of all external bank loans from 1985 to 90; and for 46 percent of external bond issues from 1985 to 90.

7. "Counterfeit Bills Confound Detectors at the Fed, Sleuths at the Secret Service," *Wall Street Journal,* July 3, 1992, p. A8.

8. *Fortune,* April 18, 1994, p. 220.

9. "Sinecures vs. Sewing Machines," *Wall Street Journal,* August 7, 1992, p. A12.

10. T. R. Fehrenbach, *Fire and Blood* (New York: Bonanza Books, 1985), pp. 440–497.

11. Jim Carlton, "Mexico Offers Promise for Idled Developers," *Wall Street Journal,* August 21, 1992, p. B1; "Penney Pushes Abroad in Unusually Big Way as It Pursues Growth," *Wall Street Journal,* February 1, 1994, p. A1.

12. "Russian Private Sector Dominant," *Wall Street Journal,* August 10, 1994, p. A4.

13. "Aux armes capitalists," *Financial Times,* June 30, 1994, p. 17.

14. "Russia Is Expected to Ease Taxes on Oil and Foreign Investors, U.S. Aide Says," *Wall Street Journal,* May 8, 1994, p. A8; "Russia Gives Oil Venture a Tax Break," *Houston Chronicle,* July 23, 1992, p. 2B.

15. "In Quest for Billions, GM's Hughes To Bring Phones to Tatarstan," *Wall Street Journal,* August 21, 1992, p. A1.

16. "Czech Republic Makes a Smooth Transition to Ways of the West," *Wall Street Journal,* July 6, 1994, p. A1; "Czechs opt for early payout on state shares," *Financial Times,* January 24, 1994, p. 12.

17. "Rejoined: A Survey of Eastern Europe," *The Economist,* March 13, 1993, p. 15.

18. "South Korea Contract Award Spotlights Marriage of the Nation's Political and Business Families," *Wall Street Journal,* August 21, 1992, p. A6.

19. Family-owned businesses tend to be small by world standards. Only one Taiwanese company is a member of *Fortune's* Global 500: state-owned Chinese Petroleum, which had annual sales of $8.2 billion in 1993 and is the world's 186th-largest company.

20. "Taiwan Struggles with 'Mainland Fever'," *Wall Street Journal,* August 21, 1992, p. A7.

21. Ibid.

22. "Taiwan Trade Surplus, at Odds with Policy, Increased 6.4% in 1991," *Wall Street Journal,* January 7, 1992, p. A14.

23. "India's Tea Industry Faces Crisis," *Wall Street Journal,* August 21, 1992, p. A6.

24. "Free Enterprise Comes Naturally to Residents of Wenzhou, China," *Wall Street Journal,* August 13, 1992, p. A1.

25. John J. Curran, "China's Investment Boom," *Fortune,* March 7, 1994, pp. 116ff.

26. Colin Leinster, "Vietnam—Business Rushes To Get In," *Fortune,* April 5, 1993, pp. 98–104.

27. "Spratly Islands Dispute in Southeast Asia Spotlights U.S. Role in Regional Security," *Wall Street Journal,* July 27, 1992, p. A6; Central Intelligence Agency, *The World Factbook 1991* (Washington, D.C.: U.S. Government Printing Office, 1991), p. 291.

28. John J. Curran, "China's Investment Boom," *Fortune,* March 7, 1994, pp. 116–124; "China—The Emerging Economic Powerhouse of the 21st Century," *Business Week,* May 17, 1993, pp. 54–68; "Taiwanese Firms Are Returning to China with Aim of Investing for Long Term," *Asian Wall Street Journal Weekly,* December 12–13, 1993, pp. 2, 4.

in the world. It is an importer, purchasing parts from Asian, European, and North American suppliers. Cat is an international investor, owning and operating factories in 12 countries. It also is an international borrower, seeking short-term and long-term capital from investors and banks throughout the world. The company is involved in the international licensing of technology, both in purchasing the right to use innovative technology developed by foreign firms and in selling the use of its own technologies to other foreign firms. It also franchises the rights to sell its equipment to 65 U.S. dealers and 118 foreign dealers. ■ ■ Of course, given the fierceness of international competition, Caterpillar's future is no more assured than that of any other global enterprise. Its arch-rival, Komatsu Ltd., enjoyed lower labor costs in the 1980s and a reputation for producing innovative, high-quality products. In the early 1980s, Komatsu undercut Cat's prices to U.S. customers by as much as 40 percent, causing an 11 percent erosion in Cat's domestic market share. Slashing its own prices, Cat stopped the market-share losses, although its profitability suffered. Since 1987, Cat has invested $2.1 billion in plant modernization to improve manufacturing quality and flexibility and has developed new inventory control systems to cut inventory costs. The increasing value of the yen since 1985 has helped these efforts by eroding Komatsu's cost advantage. Cat also is working with its 4000 suppliers to improve the quality of parts and supplies. ■ ■ Further, to maintain its worldwide dominance, Cat reined in its labor costs. In 1992 it fought a bitter five-month strike by the United Auto Workers in order to slow down wage increases, relax productivity-robbing work rules, and shrink its labor force. But workers remain unhappy with the company. Since the strike, the company has suffered through 11 more union walkouts and 95 unfair labor practice complaints issued by the National Labor Relations Board. Caterpillar faces the challenge of improving its labor relations because it must rely on these same workers to improve productivity and the quality of its output in the face of Komatsu's competition.[2] ■ ■ ■ ■ ■

Caterpillar is a microcosm of the complex business relationships that bind firms and countries in the contemporary global marketplace. In this chapter we analyze the underlying economic forces that shape and structure the international business transactions conducted by Caterpillar and thousands of other firms. We discuss the major theories that explain and predict international trade and investment activity. These theories introduce you to the economic environment in which firms compete. They also help firms sharpen their global business strategies, identify promising export and investment opportunities, and react to threats posed by foreign competitors. These theories also can help you understand why a firm like Caterpillar can be simultaneously an exporter, importer, international investor, international borrower, franchiser, and licensor and licensee of technology.

International Trade and the World Economy

T**rade** is the voluntary exchange of goods, services, assets, or money between one person or organization and another. Because it is voluntary, both parties to the transaction must believe they will gain from the exchange, or else they would not complete it. **International trade** is trade between residents of two countries. The residents may be individuals, firms, nonprofit organizations, or other forms of associations. Why does international trade occur? The answer follows directly from our definition of trade: both parties to the transaction, who happen to reside in two different countries, believe they benefit from the voluntary exchange. Behind this simple truth lies much economic theory, business practice, government policy, and international conflict—topics we cover in this and the next four chapters.

Total international merchandise trade in 1992 was $3.6 trillion, or approximately 16 percent of the world's $23.0 trillion GDP; trade in services in that year amounted to $1 trillion.[3] The Quad countries accounted for more than two thirds of the world's merchandise exports (see Fig. 3.1). Such international trade has important direct and indirect effects on national economies. On the one hand, exports spark additional economic activity in the domestic economy. Caterpillar's $3.6 billion in exports generate orders for its U.S. suppliers, wages for its U.S. workers, and dividend payments for its U.S. shareholders, all of which in turn create income for local automobile dealers, grocery stores, and others that then add to their own payrolls. On the other hand, imports can pressure domestic suppliers to cut their prices and improve their competitiveness. Failure to respond to foreign competition may lead to shut-down factories and unemployed workers. Because of international trade's obvious significance to businesses, consumers, and workers, scholars have attempted to develop theories to explain and predict the forces that motivate such trade. Governments use these theories when they design policies they hope will benefit their countries' industries and citizens. Businesses use them to identify promising markets and profitable internationalization strategies.

FIGURE 3.1

Sources of the World's Merchandise Exports, 1992

Source: World Bank, *World Development Report 1994,* pp. 186–187.

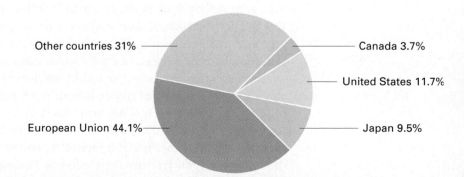

Other countries 31%

Canada 3.7%

United States 11.7%

Japan 9.5%

European Union 44.1%

Classical Country-Based Trade Theories

The first theories of international trade developed with the rise of the great European nation-states in the sixteenth century. Not surprisingly, these early theories focused on the country in examining patterns of exports and imports. As we discuss in more detail later in this chapter, these country-based theories are particularly useful for describing trade in commodities—standardized, undifferentiated goods such as oil, sugar, or lumber that are typically bought on the basis of price rather than brand name. However, as MNCs rose to power in the middle of this century, scholars shifted their attention to the firm's role in promoting international trade. The firm-based theories developed after World War II are useful in describing patterns of trade in differentiated goods—those such as automobiles, consumer electronics, and personal care products, for which brand name is an important component of the customer's purchase decision. In this section we examine the classical, country-based theories of international trade; in the next section we explore the more modern, firm-based theories.

Mercantilism

Mercantilism is a sixteenth-century economic philosophy that maintains that a country's wealth is measured by its holdings of gold and silver. According to mercantilists, a country's goal should be to enlarge those holdings. To do this it should strive to maximize the difference between its exports and its imports by promoting exports and discouraging imports. The logic was transparent to sixteenth-century policymakers: if foreigners buy more goods from you than you buy from them, then the foreigners have to pay you the difference in gold and silver, enabling you to amass more treasure. Mercantilist terminology is still used today, for example, when television commentators and newspaper headlines report that a country suffered an "unfavorable" balance of trade—that is, its exports were less than its imports.

At the time mercantilism seemed to be sound economic policy—at least to the local king. Large gold and silver holdings meant he could afford to hire armies to fight other countries and thereby possibly expand his kingdom. Politically, mercantilism was popular with many manufacturers and their workers. Export-oriented manufacturers favored mercantilist trade policies, such as those establishing subsidies or tax rebates, that stimulated their sales to foreigners. Domestic manufacturers threatened by foreign imports endorsed mercantilist trade policies, such as those imposing tariffs or quotas, that protected them from foreign competition. These businesses, their workers, their suppliers, and the local politicians representing the communities in which the manufacturers had production facilities all praised the wisdom of the king's mercantilist policies.

However, most members of society are hurt by such policies. Governmental subsidies of the exports of certain industries are paid by taxpayers in the form of higher taxes. Governmental import restrictions are paid for by consumers in the form of higher prices because domestic firms face less competition from foreign producers. During the Age of Imperialism, governments often shifted the burden of mercantilist policies onto their colonies. For example, under the Navigation Act of 1660 all European goods imported by the American colonies had to be shipped from Great Britain. The British prohibited colonial firms from exporting

Great Britain's mercantilist policy was a major contributor to the political unrest in its American colonies. Colonial merchants and manufacturers resented British taxes and regulations that hindered the growth of American firms and protected British industries. The Boston Tea Party and similar incidents led to armed conflict and ultimately to independence for the 13 colonies.

Americans throwing the Cargoes of the Tea Ships into the River at Boston

certain goods that might compete with those from British factories, such as hats, finished iron goods, and woolens. To ensure adequate supplies of low-cost inputs for British merchants, the British required some colonial industries to sell their output only to British firms. This output included rice, tobacco, and naval stores (forest products used in shipbuilding).[4] This particular mercantilist strategy ultimately backfired—it contributed to the grievances that led to the overthrow of the British Crown in the American colonies.

Because mercantilism does benefit certain members of society, mercantilist policies are still politically attractive to some firms and their workers. Modern supporters of such policies, called **neo-mercantilists**, or **protectionists**, include such diverse U.S. groups as the American Federation of Labor-Congress of Industrial Organizations, textile manufacturers, steel companies, sugar growers, and peanut farmers.

Such protectionist attitudes are not limited to the United States. North Americans and Europeans have long complained that Japan limits the access of foreign goods to its market. For example, it took 40 years of negotiations before Japan grudgingly agreed in 1993 to allow the importation of foreign rice, and even then it limited rice imports to less than 10 percent of its market. And Asian and North American firms criticize the Europeans for imposing barriers against imported goods such as beef, automobiles, and video cassette recorders. Such finger-pointing is amply justified: nearly every country has adopted some neo-mercantilist policies in order to protect key industries in its economy.

Absolute Advantage

Neo-mercantilism has superficial appeal, particularly to patriots who want to strengthen their country's economy. Why shouldn't a country try to maximize its holdings of gold and silver? According to Adam Smith, the Scottish economist who is viewed as the father of free-market economics, mercantilism's basic problem is that it confuses the acquisition of treasure with the acquisition of wealth. In *An Inquiry into the Nature and Causes of the Wealth of Nations* (1776), Smith attacked the intellectual basis of mercantilism and demonstrated that mercantilism actually *weakens* a country. He maintained that a country's true wealth is measured by the wealth of all its citizens, not just that of its king; thus a country's goal should be to maximize its citizens' wealth. In so doing the country will also become wealthy and strong, offering the king a larger base on which to levy taxes.

In Smith's view, mercantilism robs individuals of the ability to trade freely and to benefit from voluntary exchanges. Moreover, in the process of avoiding imports at all costs, a country must squander its resources producing goods it is not suited to produce. The inefficiencies caused by mercantilism reduce the wealth of the country as a whole, even though certain special-interest groups may benefit.

Smith advocated free trade among countries as a means of enlarging a country's wealth. As we explain later in this chapter, free trade enables a country to expand the amount of goods and services available to it by specializing in the production of some goods and services and trading for others. But which goods and services should a country export and which should it import? In answer to this question, Smith developed the **theory of absolute advantage**, which suggests that a country should export those goods and services for which it is more productive than other countries are and import those goods and services for which other countries are more productive than it is.

Absolute advantage can be demonstrated through a numerical example. Assume, for the sake of simplicity, that there are only two countries in the world, France and Japan; only two goods, wine and clock radios; and only one factor of production, labor. Table 3.1 shows the output of the two goods per hour of labor for the two countries. In France 1 hour of labor can produce either 2 bottles of wine or 3 clock radios. In Japan, 1 hour of labor can produce either 1 bottle of wine or 5 clock radios. France has an absolute advantage in the production of wine: 1 hour of labor produces 2 bottles in France but only 1 in Japan. Japan has an absolute advantage in the production of clock radios: 1 hour of labor produces 5 clock radios in Japan but only 3 in France.

If France and Japan are able to trade with one another, both will be better off. Suppose France agrees to exchange 2 bottles of wine for 4 clock radios. Only 1 hour of French labor is needed to produce the 2 bottles of wine bound for Japan. In return, France will get 4 clock radios from Japan. These 4 clock radios would have required 1.33 hours of French labor had France produced them itself rather than buying them from the Japanese. By trading with Japan rather than producing the clock radios itself, France saves 0.33 hour of labor. It can use this freed-up labor to produce more wine, which in turn can be consumed by French citizens or traded to Japan for more clock radios. By allocating its scarce labor to produce goods for which it is more productive than Japan and then trading them to Japan, France can consume more goods than it could have done in the absence of trade.

TABLE 3.1

The Theory of Absolute Advantage: An Example

| | OUTPUT PER HOUR OF LABOR | |
	France	Japan
Wine	2	1
Clock radios	3	5

Japan is similarly better off. Japan uses 0.8 hour of labor to produce the 4 clock radios to exchange for the 2 bottles of French wine. Producing the 2 bottles of wine itself would have required 2 hours of labor. By producing clock radios and then trading them to France, Japan saves 1.2 hours of labor, which can be used to produce more clock radios that the Japanese can consume themselves or trade to France for more wine.

Comparative Advantage

The theory of absolute advantage makes intuitive sense. Unfortunately, it is flawed. What happens to trade if one country has an absolute advantage in both products? The theory of absolute advantage incorrectly suggests that no trade would occur. David Ricardo, an early nineteenth-century British economist, solved this problem by developing the **theory of comparative advantage**, which states that a country should produce and export those goods and services for which it is *relatively* more productive than are other countries and import those goods and services for which other countries are *relatively* more productive than it is.[5]

The difference between the two theories is subtle: absolute advantage looks at *absolute* productivity differences; comparative advantage looks at *relative* productivity differences. The distinction occurs because comparative advantage incorporates the concept of opportunity cost in determining which good a country should produce. The **opportunity cost** of a good is the value of what is given up in order to get the good. Most of us apply the principles of comparative advantage and opportunity cost without realizing it. For example, a brain surgeon may be better at both brain surgery and lawn mowing than her neighbor's teenaged son is. However, if the surgeon is comparatively better at surgery than at lawn mowing, she will spend most of her time at the operating table and pay the teenager to mow her lawn. The brain surgeon behaves this way because the opportunity cost of mowing the lawn is too high: time spent mowing is time unavailable for surgery.

Let's return to the example in Table 3.1 to contrast absolute and comparative advantage. Recall that France has an absolute advantage in wine and Japan has an absolute advantage in clock radios. The theory of absolute advantage says that France should export wine to Japan and Japan should export clock radios to France. As Table 3.1 shows, France also has a comparative advantage in wine: with 1 hour of labor it produces 2 times as much wine as does Japan, but only 0.6 times as many clock radios. Thus France is *relatively* more productive in wine. Japan has a comparative advantage in clock radios. With 1 hour of labor it produces 1.67 times as many clock radios as France does, but only 0.5 times as much wine. So Japan is *relatively* more productive in clock radios. The theory of comparative advantage says that France should export wine to Japan and Japan should export clock radios to France. For the example in Table 3.1, the theory of absolute advantage and the theory of comparative advantage both yield the same outcome.

Now let's change the facts some. Suppose productivity stays the same in Japan but doubles in France as the result of new job training programs. Table 3.2 shows this new situation. France now can produce 4 bottles of wine or 6 clock radios per hour of labor. France now has an absolute advantage in *both* wine and clock radios: for each hour of labor France can produce 3 more bottles of wine (4 minus 1) or 1 more clock radio (6 minus 5) than Japan can. According to the theory of absolute advantage, no trade should occur because France is more productive than Japan in producing both goods.

TABLE 3.2

The Theory of Comparative Advantage: An Example

	OUTPUT PER HOUR OF LABOR	
	France	**Japan**
Wine	4	1
Clock radios	6	5

The theory of comparative advantage, on the other hand, indicates that trade should still occur. France is 4 times better than Japan is in wine production but only 1.2 times better in clock radio production. (Alternatively, Japan is only 0.25 as good as France in wine production but 0.83 as good in clock radio production.) France is comparatively better than Japan in wine production, while Japan is comparatively better than France in clock radio production.

By the theory of comparative advantage, France should export wine to Japan and Japan should export clock radios to France. If they do so, both will be better off. In the absence of trade, 1 bottle of wine will sell for 1.5 clock radios in France and for 5 clock radios in Japan. If Japan offers to trade 2 clock radios for 1 bottle of wine, France will be better off—*even though France has an absolute advantage in clock radio production.* Without trade, sacrificing 1 bottle of wine domestically would yield France only 1.5 clock radios in increased production. With trade, France could get 2 clock radios by giving up 1 bottle of wine to Japan. France gets more clock radios per bottle of wine given up by trading with Japan than by producing the clock radios domestically.

Japan also gains. Without trade, Japan has to give up 5 clock radios to get 1 more bottle of wine. With trade, Japan has to give up only 2 clock radios to obtain 1 more bottle. Japan gets more wine per clock radio given up by trading with France than by producing the wine domestically. Even though France has an absolute advantage in both wine and clock radio production, both countries gain from this trade. It is comparative advantage that motivates trade, not absolute advantage.

Comparative Advantage with Money

The lesson of the theory of comparative advantage is simple but powerful: *You're better off specializing in what you do relatively best. Produce (and export) those goods and services you are relatively best able to produce, and buy other goods and services from people who are relatively better at producing them than you are.*

Of course, Tables 3.1 and 3.2 are both simplistic and artificial. The world economy produces more than two goods and services and is made up of more than two countries. Barriers to trade may exist, someone must pay to transport goods between markets, and inputs other than labor are necessary to produce goods. Even more important, the world economy uses money as a medium of exchange. Table 3.3 introduces money into our discussion of trade and incorporates these assumptions:

1 The output per hour of labor in France and Japan for clock radios and wine is as shown in Table 3.2.

> ### TABLE 3.3
>
> ## The Theory of Comparative Advantage with Money: An Example
>
> | | COST OF GOODS IN FRANCE | | COST OF GOODS IN JAPAN | |
> | --- | --- | --- | --- | --- |
> | | **French-Made** | **Japanese-Made** | **French-Made** | **Japanese-Made** |
> | Wine | Fr18 | Fr40 | ¥450 | ¥1000 |
> | Clock radios | Fr12 | Fr8 | ¥300 | ¥200 |
>
> Note: For example, 1 hour's worth of French labor can produce 4 bottles of wine at a total cost of Fr72, or an average cost of Fr18 per bottle. At an exchange rate of 25 yen per franc, a bottle of French-made wine will cost ¥450 (450 = 18 × 25).

2 The hourly wage rate in France is 72 francs (Fr).

3 The hourly wage rate in Japan is 1000 yen (¥).

4 One French franc is worth 25 yen.

In the absence of trade, a bottle of wine in France costs Fr18, the equivalent of ¥450, and clock radios cost Fr12, the equivalent of ¥300. In Japan a bottle of wine costs ¥1000 (Fr40), and clock radios cost ¥200 (Fr8).

In this case trade will occur because of the self-interest of individual entrepreneurs (or the opportunity to make a profit) in France and Japan. For example, buyers for Galeries Lafayette, a major Paris department store, observe that clock radios cost Fr12 in France and the equivalent of only Fr8 in Japan. To keep their cost of goods low, these buyers will order clock radios in Japan, where they are cheap, and sell them in France, where they are expensive. Accordingly, clock radios will be exported by Japan and imported by France, just as the law of comparative advantage predicts. Similarly, wine distributors in Japan observe that a bottle of wine costs ¥1000 in Japan but the equivalent of only ¥450 in France. To keep their cost of goods as low as possible, buyers for Japanese wine distributors will buy wine in France, where it is cheap, and sell it in Japan, where it is expensive. Wine will be exported by France and imported by Japan, as predicted by the law of comparative advantage.

Note that none of these businesspeople needed to know anything about the theory of comparative advantage. They merely looked at the price differences in the two markets and made their business decisions based on the desire to obtain supplies at the lowest possible cost. Yet they benefit from comparative advantage because prices set in a free market reflect a country's comparative advantage.

Relative Factor Endowments

The theory of comparative advantage begs a broader question: What determines the products for which a country will have a comparative advantage? To answer this question, two Swedish economists, Eli Heckscher[6] and Bertil Ohlin,[7] developed the **theory of relative factor endowments,** now often referred to as the **Heckscher-Ohlin theory.** These economists made two basic observations:

I *Factor endowments (or types of resources) vary among countries.* For example, Argentina has much land, Saudi Arabia has large crude oil reserves, and China has a large pool of unskilled labor.

2 *Goods differ according to the types of factors that are used to produce them.* For example, wheat requires land, oil production requires crude oil reserves, clothing requires unskilled labor.

From these observations Heckscher and Ohlin developed their theory: *a country will have a comparative advantage in producing products that intensively use resources (factors of production) it has in abundance.* Thus Argentina has a comparative advantage in wheat growing because of its abundance of land; Saudi Arabia has a comparative advantage in oil production because of its abundance of crude oil reserves; and China has a comparative advantage in clothing manufacture because of its abundance of unskilled labor.

The Heckscher-Ohlin theory suggests a country should export those goods that use intensively those factors of production that are relatively abundant in the country. The theory was tested empirically after World War II by economist Wassily Leontief using input-output analysis, a mathematical technique for measuring the interrelationships among the sectors of an economy. Leontief believed the United States was a capital-abundant and labor-scarce economy. Therefore, according to the Heckscher-Ohlin theory, he reasoned that the United States should export capital-intensive goods, such as bulk chemicals and steel, and import labor-intensive goods, such as clothing and footware.

Leontief used his input-output model of the U.S. economy to estimate the quantities of labor and capital needed to produce "bundles" of U.S. exports and imports worth $1 million in 1947 (see Fig. 3.2).[8] (Each bundle was a weighted average of all U.S. exports or imports in 1947.) He determined that in 1947 U.S. factories utilized $2.551 million of capital and 182.3 person-years of labor, or $13,993 of capital per person-year of labor, to produce a bundle of exports worth $1 million. He also calculated that $3.093 million of capital and 170.0 person-years of labor, or $18,194 of capital per person-year of labor, were used to produce a bundle of U.S. imports worth $1 million in that year. Thus U.S.

The Heckscher-Ohlin theory predicts that a country will have a comparative advantage producing goods that intensively use resources the country has in abundance. For example, Australia's abundance of land has given it a comparative advantage in the production of wool and mutton.

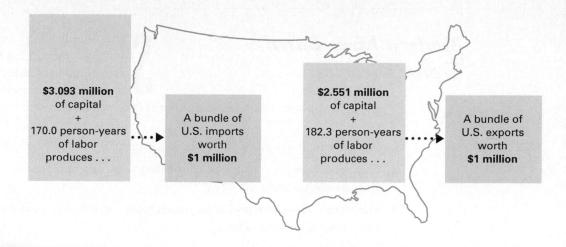

FIGURE 3.2

U.S. Imports and Exports, 1947: The Leontief Paradox

imports were more capital-intensive than U.S. exports. Imports required $4201 ($18,194 – $13,993) more in capital per person-year of labor to produce than exports did.

These results were not consistent with the predictions of the Heckscher-Ohlin theory: U.S. imports were nearly 30 percent more capital-intensive than were U.S. exports. The economics profession was distraught. The Heckscher-Ohlin theory made such intuitive sense, and yet Leontief's findings were the reverse of what was expected. Thus was born the **Leontief paradox**.

In the past 40 years numerous economists have repeated Leontief's initial study in an attempt to resolve the paradox. The first such study was performed by Leontief himself. He thought trade flows may have been distorted in 1947 because much of the world economy was still reeling from World War II. Using 1951 data he found that U.S. imports were 6 percent more capital-intensive than U.S. exports were. Although this figure was less than that in his original study, it still disagreed with the predictions of the Heckscher-Ohlin theory.[9]

Some scholars argue that measurement problems flaw Leontief's work. Leontief assumed there are two homogeneous factors of production: labor and capital. Yet other factors of production exist, most notably land, human capital, and technology—none of which were included in Leontief's analysis. Failure to include these other factors may have caused him to mismeasure the labor intensity of U.S. exports and imports. Many U.S. exports are intensive in either land (such as agricultural goods) or human knowledge (such as computers, aircraft, and services).[10] Consider the products sold by one of the leading U.S. exporters, Boeing Aircraft Company. Leontief's approach measures the physical capital—the plants, property, and equipment—and the physical labor used to construct Boeing aircraft but fails to gauge adequately the role of human capital and technology in the firm's operations. Yet human capital—the well-educated engineers who design the aircraft and highly-skilled machinists who assemble it—and technology—the sophisticated management techniques that control the world's largest assembly lines—are more important to Boeing's success than mere physical capital and physical labor. Leontief's failure to measure the role that these other factors of production play in determining international trade patterns may account for his paradoxical results.

Modern Firm-Based Trade Theories

Since World War II, international business research has focused on the role of the firm rather than the country in promoting international trade. Firm-based theories have developed for several reasons:

1 The growing importance of MNCs in the postwar international economy

2 The inability of the country-based theories to explain and predict certain aspects of international trade

3 The failure of Leontief and other researchers to empirically validate the country-based Heckscher-Ohlin theory

Unlike country-based theories, firm-based theories incorporate factors such as quality, technology, brand names, and customer loyalty into explanations of trade flows. Because firms, not countries, are the agents for international trade, the newer theories explore the firm's role in promoting exports and imports.

Country Similarity Theory

Country-based theories, such as the theory of comparative advantage, do a good job of explaining interindustry trade among countries. **Interindustry trade** is the exchange of goods produced by one industry in country A for goods produced by a different industry in country B, such as the exchange of French wines for Japanese clock radios. Yet much international trade consists of **intraindustry trade**, that is, trade between two countries of goods produced by the same industry. For example, Kodak sells film made in U.S. factories to Japan, and Fuji sells film made in Japanese factories to the United States. Japan exports Toyotas to Germany, while Germany exports BMWs to Japan. Intraindustry trade accounts for approximately 40 percent of world trade,[11] and it is not predicted by country-based theories.

In 1961 Swedish economist Steffan Linder sought to explain the phenomenon of intraindustry trade.[12] Linder hypothesized that international trade in manufactured goods results from similarities of preferences among consumers in countries that are at the same stage of economic development. In his view, firms initially manufacture goods in order to serve their domestic market. As they explore exporting opportunities, they discover that the most promising foreign markets are in countries in which consumers' preferences resemble those of their own domestic market. For example, Sony first sold its Walkman radio domestically. Observing the product's success in Japan, the firm quickly expanded its distribution to Canada, Europe, and the United States because their consumers' incomes and preferences resemble Japan's. Linder's **country similarity theory** suggests that most trade in manufactured goods should be between countries with similar per capita incomes and that intraindustry trade in manufactured goods should be common. This theory is particularly useful in explaining trade in differentiated goods such as automobiles, expensive electronics equipment, and personal care products, for which brand names and product reputations play an important role in consumer decision making.

GOING GLOBAL

Extending the Product Life Cycle

Many organizations have found that if they can extend the life cycles of their products they can prolong earnings streams and generate additional profits. One MNC successfully doing this is Boeing, the world's largest commercial aircraft maker and one of the largest exporters in the United States. Its key products include the 737, the 747, the 757, and the new 767.

Boeing delivered its first 737 in 1967. The plane, which was especially well-suited for mid-range domestic routes, sold well for several years; many carriers initially bought 20 or 30 at a time. But in the mid-1970s it began to lose ground. One of its most formidable competitors was the McDonnell Douglas DC-9, which had about the same passenger capacity but was faster and somewhat more fuel-efficient.

Boeing officials decided the 737's life cycle was ending and were preparing to cease its production. At the last minute, however, they tried one last measure to extend the plane's life cycle. The firm began marketing the plane to fledgling airlines in developing countries. Instead of trying to sell 20 planes at a time to KLM or United, they intended to sell one or two at a time to small airlines in countries in Africa, South America, and other developing regions.

After surveying that market, Boeing realized that it first had to make a few modifications in the basic 737 aircraft so that it would better fit local conditions. For example, pilots in those developing regions were not as skilled as their U.S. or European counterparts and tended to "bounce" more during landing. So Boeing engineers redesigned the 737's landing system to be better able to handle extreme landing conditions.

Boeing's plan was a big success. The firm sold enough 737s, albeit in small quantities, to justify keeping the plane in production. And as those small airlines began to grow, they continued to buy 737s, as well as occasionally upgrading to newer and larger Boeing aircraft. Surprisingly, domestic orders also continued to come in on a regular basis. As a result the firm continues to make the 737 today. The plane recently became the largest-selling commercial aircraft in aviation history.

Sources: "How Boeing Does It," *Business Week*, July 9, 1990, pp. 46–50; Andrew Kupfer, "How To Be a Global Manager," *Fortune*, March 14, 1988, pp. 52–58; Shawn Tully, "Can Boeing Reinvent Itself?" *Fortune*, March 8, 1993, pp. 66–73.

Product Life Cycle Theory

Product life cycle theory, which originated in the marketing field to describe the evolution of marketing strategies as a product matures, is a second firm-based theory of international trade (and, as we will see, of international investment). As developed in the 1960s by Raymond Vernon of the Harvard Business School, international product life cycle theory traces the roles of innovation, market expansion, comparative advantage, and strategic responses of global rivals in international production, trade, and investment decisions.[13] (See "Going Global.")

According to Vernon's theory the international product life cycle consists of three stages (see Fig. 3.3):

1 New product

2 Maturing product

3 Standardized product

In Stage 1, the *new product stage,* a firm develops and introduces an innovative product, such as a photocopier or a personal computer, in response to a perceived

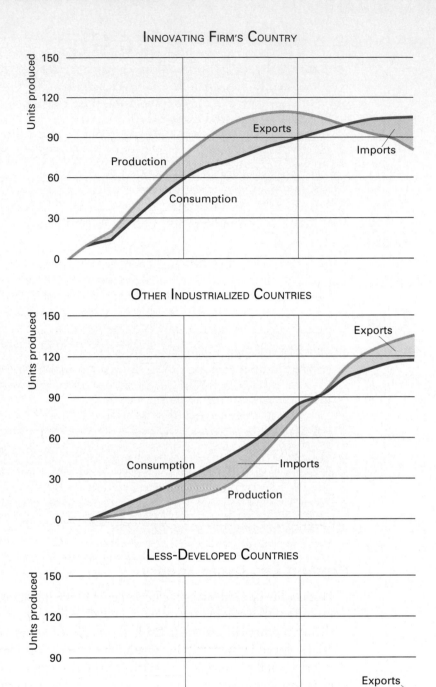

need in the domestic market. Because the product is new, this innovating firm is uncertain whether a profitable market for it exists. The firm's marketing executives must closely monitor customer reactions to ensure the new product satisfies consumer needs. Quick market feedback is important, so the product is likely to be initially produced in the country in which its research and development occurred, typically a developed country like Japan, Germany, or the United States. Further, because the market size also is uncertain, the firm usually will minimize its investment in manufacturing capacity for the product. Most output initially is sold in the domestic market and export sales are limited.

For example, in the early days of the personal computer industry the small producers that populated the industry had their hands full trying to meet the burgeoning demand for their product. Apple Computer typified this problem. Founded on April Fool's Day in 1976, its initial assembly plant was located in cofounder Steve Jobs's garage. The first large order for its homemade computers—50 units from a local computer hobbyist store that summer—almost bankrupted the firm because it lacked the financing to buy the necessary parts.[14] But Apple survived because of the nurturing environment in which it was born, California's Silicon Valley. Home to major electronics firms such as Hewlett-Packard, Intel, and National Semiconductor, the Valley was full of electrical engineers who could design and build Apple's products and venture capitalists who were seeking the "next Xerox." It was the perfect locale for Apple's sales to grow from zero in 1976 to $7.8 million in 1978 and $8.0 billion in 1993.

In Stage 2, the *maturing product stage*, demand for the product expands dramatically as consumers recognize its value. The innovating firm builds new factories to expand its capacity and satisfy domestic and foreign demand for the product. Domestic and foreign competitors begin to emerge, lured by the prospect of lucrative earnings. In the case of Apple, the firm introduced a hand-assembled version of its second model, the Apple II, at a San Francisco computer fair in spring 1977. Within three years Apple had sold 130,000 units and expanded its production facilities beyond Jobs's garage. To serve domestic and foreign customers, Apple IIs were manufactured in California and Texas and distributed from warehouses in the United States and the Netherlands.

In Stage 3, the *standardized product stage*, the market for the product stabilizes. The product becomes more of a commodity, and firms are pressured to lower their manufacturing costs as much as possible by shifting production to facilities in countries with low labor costs. As a result, the product begins to be imported into the innovating firm's home market (by either the firm or its competitors). In some cases imports may result in the complete elimination of domestic production.

The personal computer industry is in the early phase of the standardized product stage. In the U.S. market low-priced brand-name imports from new producers such as South Korea's Hyundai and Samsung have threatened the more established U.S. manufacturers. Taiwanese manufacturers such as Tatung, Mitac International, First International, and TECO Information Systems—none of them household names in the United States—annually export to the United States over 3 million personal computers, many of which are produced under contract for foreign distributors. To meet the challenge of these new competitors Apple shifted some of its production to plants in Ireland and Singapore to take advantage of lower-priced labor. Apple also decided to squeeze more value out of its well-known brand name by broadening its product line, invading high-growth niches in the microcomputer market, expanding its distribution network, and slashing its overhead expenses in order to price its products more competitively.[15]

According to the international product life cycle theory, domestic production begins in Stage 1, peaks in Stage 2, and slumps in Stage 3. Exports by the innovating firm's country also begin in Stage 1 and peak in Stage 2. By Stage 3, however, the innovating firm's country becomes a net importer of the product. Foreign competition begins to emerge toward the end of Stage 1, as firms in other industrialized countries recognize the product's market potential. In Stage 2 foreign competitors expand their productive capacity, thus servicing an increasing portion of their home markets and perhaps becoming net exporters. But as competition intensifies in Stage 2, the innovating firm and its domestic and foreign rivals seek to lower their production costs by shifting production to low-cost sites in less developed countries. Eventually, in Stage 3, the less developed countries may become net exporters of the product.

Global Strategic Rivalry Theory

More recent explanations of the pattern of international trade, developed in the 1980s by such economists as Paul Krugman[16] and Kelvin Lancaster,[17] examine the impact on trade flows of global strategic rivalry between MNCs. According to this view, firms struggle to develop some sustainable competitive advantage, which they can then exploit to dominate the global marketplace. Like Linder's approach, global strategic rivalry theory predicts that intraindustry trade will be commonplace. However, it focuses on strategic decisions firms adopt as they compete internationally. These decisions affect both international trade and international investment.

For example, after deregulation in 1978 U.S. airlines created hub-oriented route systems and frequent flier programs to lure passengers to their domestic and international flights. As a result, over the past decade European airlines have been losing market share in the transatlantic market to U.S. carriers. To reverse this decline, KLM purchased an interest in Northwest Airlines, so that KLM could funnel traffic from Northwest's domestic flights onto its transatlantic flights, effectively turning Northwest's hubs and frequent flier program from a competitive disadvantage into an advantage. To keep up with KLM, major European rivals British Airways and SAS purchased substantial interests in USAir and Continental.[18] Other firms are playing similar games in their own industries as they attempt to leverage their own strengths and neutralize those of their rivals.

Firms competing in the global marketplace have numerous ways of obtaining a sustainable competitive advantage. The more popular ones are

▶ Owning intellectual property rights

▶ Investing in research and development

▶ Achieving economies of scale or scope

▶ Exploiting the experience curve

Owning Intellectual Property Rights. A firm that owns an intellectual property right—a trademark, brand name, patent, or copyright—often gains advantages over its competitors. For example, copyright laws require foreign film distributors and movie theaters that want to show *The Lion King* to buy the right to do so from the Walt Disney Company, the maker of the movie and holder of its copyright. Owning prestigious brand names enables Ireland's Waterford Wedgewood Company, France's Louis Vuitton, and Canada's Seagram Company (Chivas Regal) to charge premium prices for their upscale products. And Coca-Cola and PepsiCo compete for customers worldwide on the basis of their trademarks and brand names.

Investing in Research and Development. Research and development (R&D) is a major component of the total costs of high-technology products. For example, Boeing spent $2 billion dollars developing the 747 jet and $4.5 billion designing its new 777 aircraft.[19] Firms in the computer, pharmaceutical, and semiconductor industries also spend large amounts on R&D to maintain their competitiveness. Because of such large "entry" costs, other firms often hesitate to compete against these established firms. Thus the firm that acts first often gains a **first-mover advantage**.

However, knowledge does not have a nationality. Firms that invest up front and secure the first-mover advantage have the opportunity to dominate the world market for goods that are intensive in R&D. According to the global strategic rivalry theory, trade flows may be determined by which firms make the necessary R&D expenditures. Why is the United States a large exporter of commercial aircraft? Because Boeing is one of the few firms willing to spend the large sums of money required to develop new aircraft and because Boeing just happens to be headquartered in the United States.

Firms with large domestic markets may have an advantage over their foreign rivals in high-technology markets because they often are able to obtain quicker and richer feedback from customers. With this feedback they can fine tune their R&D efforts, thus enabling them to better meet the needs of their domestic customers. This knowledge can then be utilized to serve foreign customers. For example, U.S. agricultural chemical producers such as Monsanto and Eli Lilley have an advantage over Japanese rivals in developing soybean pesticides because the U.S. market for such pesticides is large while the Japanese market is small. Knowledge gained in the U.S. pesticide market can be readily transferred to meet the needs of Japanese farmers. Often firms will locate their R&D and marketing facilities near important customers. For example, DuPont wanted to be closer to French farmers, who constitute Europe's largest market for pesticides and herbicides, so it moved the European headquarters of its agricultural chemicals division from Geneva to Paris.[20]

Achieving Economies of Scale or Scope. Economies of scale or scope offer firms another opportunity to obtain a sustainable competitive advantage in international markets. **Economies of scale** occur when a product's average costs decrease as the number of units produced increases. **Economies of scope** occur when a firm's average costs decrease as the number of different products it sells increases. Firms that are able to achieve economies of scale or scope enjoy low average costs, which give them a competitive advantage over their global rivals. For example, France's Michelin Company, the world's largest tire producer, has aggressively expanded its capacity in order to capture economies of scale in production, distribution, and marketing. Sony has sought economies of scope by broadening its consumer electronics product line. It uses its reputation as an innovative, high-quality producer of such goods as televisions to help sell camcorders, VCRs, and CD players.

Exploiting the Experience Curve. Another source of firm-specific advantages in international trade is exploitation of the experience curve. For certain types of products, production costs decline as the firm gains more experience in manufacturing the product. For example, the cost of constructing Liberty Ships in World War II declined as employees gained more experience in fabricating the ships. Boeing, with its vast experience in coordinating the manufacture of complex, sophisticated aircraft, benefits similarly from this phenomenon.

The presence of an experience curve may in fact govern global competition within an industry. For example, a strong experience curve exists in semiconductor chip production. Unit cost reductions of 25–30 percent with each doubling of a firm's cumulative chip production are not uncommon.[21] Any firm attempting to be a low-cost producer of so-called commodity chips—such as 256K and 1MB memory chips—can achieve that goal only if it moves further along the experience curve than its rivals do. Both U.S. and Asian chip manufacturers have often priced their new products below current production costs in order to capture the sales necessary to generate the production experience that will in turn enable them to lower future production costs. Because of their technological leadership in manufacturing and their aggressive, price-cutting pricing strategies, Asian semiconductor manufacturers such as NEC and Samsung have begun to dominate the production of low-cost, standardized semiconductor chips.[22] On the other hand, innovative U.S. semiconductor firms such as Intel and Motorola utilize the experience curve to maintain leadership in the production of higher-priced, proprietary chips, such as the 486 and Pentium chips that form the brains of newer microcomputers.

Porter's National Competitive Advantage

The most recent contribution to international trade theory comes from Harvard Business School professor Michael Porter. In *The Competitive Advantage of Nations,* an influential book published in 1990, Porter develops the **theory of national competitive advantage**, which states that success in international trade comes from the interaction of four country- and firm-specific elements:

▶ Factor conditions
▶ Demand conditions
▶ Related and supporting industries
▶ Firm strategy, structure, and rivalry

Porter represents these four elements as the four corners of a diamond (see Fig. 3.4).

Factor Conditions. A country's endowment of factors of production affects its ability to compete internationally. While the importance of factor endowments was the centerpiece of the Hecksher-Ohlin theory, Porter goes beyond the basic factors considered by the classical trade theorists—land, labor, capital—to include more advanced factors such as the educational level of the workforce and

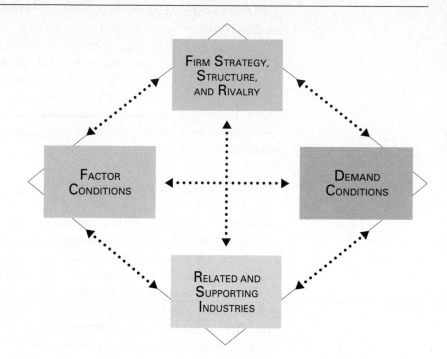

the quality of the country's infrastructure. His work stresses the role of factor creation through training, research, and innovation.

Demand Conditions. The existence of a large, sophisticated domestic consumer base often stimulates the development and distribution of innovative products, as firms struggle for dominance in their domestic market. But in meeting their domestic customers' needs firms continually develop and fine tune products that also can be marketed internationally. Thus pioneering firms can stay ahead of their international competitors as well. For example, Japanese consumer electronics producers maintain a competitive edge internationally because of the willingness of Japan's large, well-off middle class to buy the latest electronic creations of Sony, Toshiba, and Matsushita. After being fine-tuned in the domestic market, new models of Japanese camcorders, big screen TVs, and VCRs are sold to eager European and North American consumers.

Related and Supporting Industries. The emergence of an industry often stimulates the development of local suppliers eager to meet that industry's production, marketing, and distribution needs. An industry located close to its suppliers will enjoy better communication and the exchange of cost-saving ideas and inventions with those suppliers. Competition among these input suppliers leads to lower prices, higher-quality products, and technological innovations in the input market, in turn reinforcing the industry's competitive advantage in world markets. For example, as we noted earlier, Apple's path-breaking personal computer was first made in Steve Jobs's California garage in the mid-1970s. As demand for personal computers exploded, supplier firms located in the Silicon Valley in order to be closer to Apple and other personal computer manufacturers. The local availability of sophisticated software, disk drive, and computer chip suppliers strengthened the competitive advantage of California personal computer manufacturers in world markets.

Ironically, the suppliers may outlive the original industry. For example, Houston, Texas, became the center of the oil industry after the discovery of oil at Spindletop in 1901. While Texas is no longer the leading oil producer, the technologies developed during boom times by Houston oilfield services firms in such diverse areas as seismological exploration, maritime drilling, and oilfield firefighting have enabled those firms to remain international leaders in these markets.

Firm Strategy, Structure, and Rivalry. The domestic environment in which firms compete shapes their ability to compete in international markets. To survive, firms facing vigorous competition domestically must continuously strive to reduce costs, boost product quality, raise productivity, and develop innovative products. Firms that have been tested in this way often develop the skills needed to succeed internationally. Further, many of the investments they made in order to succeed in the domestic market (for example, in R&D, quality control, brand image, and employee training) are transferable to international markets at low cost. Such firms have an edge as they expand abroad. Thus, according to Porter's theory, the international success of Japanese automakers and consumer electronics goods manufacturers and of U.S. personal computer manufacturers is due to intense domestic competition in these firms' home countries.

Porter holds that national policies may also affect firms' international strategies and opportunities in more subtle ways. Consider the German automobile market. German labor costs are very high, so German automakers find it difficult to compete internationally on the basis of price. But, as most auto enthusiasts know, no speed limits exist on Germany's famed *autobahns*. So German automakers such as Daimler-Benz, Porsche, and BMW have chosen to compete on the basis of quality and high performance by engineering chassis, engines, brakes, and suspensions that can withstand the stresses of high-speed driving. Consequently these firms dominate the world market for high-performance automobiles.

Porter's theory is a hybrid: It blends the traditional country-based theories that emphasize factor endowments with the firm-based theories that focus on the actions of individual firms. Countries (or their governments) play a critical role in creating an environment that can aid or harm firms' ability to compete internationally, but firms are the actors that actually participate in international trade. Some firms succeed internationally; others don't. Porsche, Daimler-Benz, and BMW successfully grasped the opportunity presented by Germany's decision to allow unlimited speeds on its highways and captured the high-performance niche of the worldwide automobile industry. But Volkswagen and Opel chose to focus on the broader middle segment of the German automobile market, ultimately limiting their international success.

In summary, no single theory of international trade explains all trade flows among countries. The classical, country-based theories are useful in explaining interindustry trade of homogeneous, undifferentiated products such as agricultural goods, raw materials, and processed goods like steel and aluminum. The firm-based theories are more helpful in understanding intraindustry trade of heterogeneous, differentiated goods, such as Sony televisions and Caterpillar bulldozers, many of which are sold on the basis of their brand names and reputations. And, in many ways, Porter's theory synthesizes the features of the existing country-based and firm-based theories.

Overview of International Investment

As we have discussed, international business takes many forms, trade being the most obvious. The second major form of international business activity is international investment, whereby residents of one country supply capital to a second country. For many MNCs international trade and international investment are alternative mechanisms for exploiting the sustainable competitive advantages discussed earlier in the chapter.

Sometimes trade and investment are *substitutes* for each other. For example, Honda was the first Japanese automaker to construct a major assembly plant in the United States. Built in 1982 in Marysville, Ohio, the plant was a substitute for international trade because it prompted Honda to export fewer cars from its Japanese plants to the United States, thereby reducing international trade.

At other times, international trade and investment may be *complementary.* For example, in order to reduce production costs, Compaq Computer, headquartered in Houston, Texas, employs 1100 workers at two factories in Scotland's "Silicon Glen"—the region between Glasgow and Edinburgh where 10 percent of the world's personal computers are produced.[23] U.S.-bound exports from Compaq's Scottish factories illustrate the complementary relationship between international trade and investment.

Types of International Investments

International investment, as discussed in Chapter 1, is divided into two categories: portfolio investment and foreign direct investment (FDI). The distinction between the two rests on the question of control: does the investor seek an active management role in the firm or merely a return from a passive investment?

Portfolio investments represent passive holdings of securities such as foreign stocks, bonds, or other financial assets, none of which entail active management or control of the securities' issuer by the investor. Modern finance theory suggests that foreign portfolio investments will be motivated by attempts to seek an attractive rate of return as well as the reduction of risk that can come from geographically diversifying one's investment portfolio. Sophisticated money managers in New York, London, Frankfurt, Tokyo, and other financial centers are well aware of the advantages of international diversification. In 1993 U.S. citizens purchased $120.0 billion of foreign securities, bringing their total holdings of such securities to $518.5 billion. Foreigners purchased $80.0 billion of U.S. corporate, state, and local securities, raising their total holdings of such securities to $733.2 billion.[24]

Foreign direct investment (FDI) is acquisition of foreign assets for the purpose of controlling them. U.S. government statisticians define FDI as "ownership or control of 10 percent or more of an enterprise's voting securities...or the equivalent interest in an unincorporated U.S. business."[25] Perhaps the most historically significant FDI in the United States was the $24 Dutch explorer Peter Minuet paid local Native Americans for Manhattan Island.[26] The result: New York City, one of the world's leading financial and commercial centers.

FDI may take many forms, including:

▶ Purchase of existing assets in a foreign country

▶ New investment in property, plant, and equipment

▶ Participation in a joint venture with a local partner

An example of the first form is Ford's 1990 purchase of Jaguar Motor Company for $2.5 billion, after a takeover battle in which Ford fought for management and control of Jaguar's prestigious line of fine automobiles. The second form is illustrated by Toyota's $800 million investment in new property, plant, and equipment for its Georgetown, Kentucky, automobile assembly facility. The third form is demonstrated by Caterpillar's joint venture with Mitsubishi Heavy Industries to produce and sell earth-moving equipment in Japan.

Perhaps surprisingly, FDI can be politically controversial, even in developed countries such as the United States. The "Point/Counterpoint" following this chapter discusses this issue.

Foreign Direct Investment and the United States

Like international trade, FDI mostly occurs among the developed countries (refer back to Table 1.2). The stock of FDI in the United States at the end of 1993 totaled $445.3 billion, an increase of $19.6 billion over 1992 (see Table 3.4a). Japan was the most important source of this FDI, accounting for $96.2 billion, or 21.6 percent of the total. The countries listed by name in Table 3.4a account for 88 percent of total FDI in the United States.[27]

The stock of FDI by U.S. residents in foreign countries totaled $548.6 billion at the end of 1993, up by $49.6 billion over 1992 (see Table 3.4b). Most of this FDI was in other developed countries, particularly the United Kingdom ($96.4 billion) and Canada ($70.4 billion). The countries listed by name in Table 3.4b account for 62 percent of total FDI from the United States.[28]

Looking at Table 3.4, you may wonder why the small island chains of Bermuda and the Netherlands Antilles are so important. They serve as offshore financial centers, which we'll discuss in Chapter 5. Many U.S. companies set up finance subsidiaries in such centers to take advantage of low taxes and business-friendly regulations. Similarly, many financial services companies from other countries establish such subsidiaries as the legal owners of their U.S. operations.

Over the past decade outward FDI has remained larger than inward FDI for the United States (see Fig. 3.5), but both categories have more than doubled. While inward and outward flows of FDI are not perfectly matched, the pattern is clear: Most FDI is made by and destined for the most prosperous countries. In the next section we discuss how this pattern suggests the crucial role MNCs play in FDI.

TABLE 3.4

Patterns of FDI for the United States, end of 1993 (billions of dollars)

a. Sources of FDI in the United States

Japan	$ 96.2
United Kingdom	95.4
Netherlands	68.5
Canada	39.4
Germany	34.7
France	28.5
Switzerland	21.4
Bermuda and the Netherlands Antilles	8.5
Other European countries	22.3
All other countries	30.4
Total	$ 445.3

b. Destinations of FDI from the United States

United Kingdom	$ 96.4
Canada	70.4
Germany	37.5
Switzerland	32.9
Japan	31.4
Bermuda and the Netherlands Antilles	28.2
France	23.6
Netherlands	19.9
Other European countries	58.9
All other countries	149.4
Total	$ 548.6

Source: *Survey of Current Business*, June 1994, p. 72.

International Investment Theories

Why does FDI occur? A sophomore taking his or her first finance course might answer with the obvious: average rates of return are higher in foreign markets. Yet given the pattern of FDI between countries that we just discussed, this answer is not satisfactory. Canada and the United Kingdom are both major sources of FDI *in* the United States and important destinations for FDI *from* the United States. Average rates of return in Canada and the United Kingdom cannot be simultaneously below that of the United States (which would justify inward U.S. FDI) and above that of the United States (which would justify outward U.S. FDI). The same pattern of two-way investment occurs on an industry basis. In 1992, for example, U.S. firms invested $250 million in the chemical industry in Belgium, while Belgian firms invested $168 million in the U.S. chemical industry. This pattern cannot be explained by national differences in rates of return. We must search for another explanation for FDI.

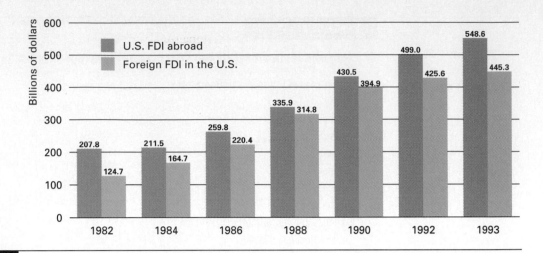

FIGURE 3.5

**Outward and
Inward U.S. FDI,
1982–1993**

Source: Data from "Direct
Investment Positions on a
Historical-Cost Basis, 1993:
Country and Industry Detail" by
Sylvia E. Bargas and Jeffrey H.
Lowe, *Survey of Current
Business*, June 1994, p. 72.

Ownership Advantages

More powerful explanations for FDI focus on the role of the firm. Initially researchers explored how firm-specific ownership (or monopolistic) advantages affected FDI. The **ownership advantage theory** suggests that a firm owning a valuable asset that creates a monopolistic advantage domestically can use that advantage to penetrate foreign markets through FDI. The asset could be, for example, a superior technology, a well-known brand name, or economies of scale.[29] This theory is consistent with the observed patterns of international and intraindustry FDI discussed earlier in this chapter. Caterpillar, for example, built factories in Asia, Europe, Australia, South America, and North America in order to exploit proprietary technologies and its brand name. Its chief rival, Komatsu, has constructed plants in Asia, Europe, and the United States for the same reason.

Internalization Theory

The ownership advantage theory only partly explains why FDI occurs. It does not explain why a firm would choose to enter a foreign market via FDI rather than exploit its ownership advantages internationally through other means, such as exporting its products, franchising a brand name, or licensing technology to foreign firms. For example, McDonald's has successfully internationalized by franchising its fast-food operations outside the United States, while Boeing has relied on exporting in order to serve its foreign customers.

Internalization theory addresses this question. In doing so it relies heavily on the concept of transaction costs. **Transaction costs** are the costs of entering into a transaction, that is, those connected to negotiating, monitoring, and enforcing a contract. A firm must decide whether it is better to own and operate its own factory overseas or to contract with a foreign firm to do this through a franchise, licensing, or supply agreement. **Internalization theory** suggests that FDI is more likely to occur—that is, international production will be *internalized* within the firm—when the costs of negotiating, monitoring, and enforcing a contract with a second firm are high. For example, Toyota's primary competitive advantages are its reputation for high quality and its sophisticated manufacturing techniques—neither of which are easily conveyed by contract. So Toyota has chosen to maintain ownership of its overseas automobile assembly plants. Conversely, the internalization theory holds, when transaction costs are low, firms are more likely to contract with outsiders and internationalize by licensing their brand names or franchising their business operations. For example, McDonald's is the premier expert in the United States in devising easily enforceable franchising agreements. Because McDonald's is so successful in reducing transaction costs between itself and its franchisees, it has continued to rely on franchising for its international operations.

Eclectic Theory

Although internalization theory addresses why firms choose FDI as the mode for entering international markets, it ignores the question of why production, either by the company or a contractor, should be located abroad. That is, is there a location advantage to producing abroad? This issue was incorporated by John Dunning in his **eclectic theory**, which combines location advantage, ownership advantage, and internalization advantage to form a unified theory of FDI. This theory recognizes that FDI reflects both *international* business activity and business activity *internal* to the firm.[30] According to Dunning, FDI will occur when three conditions are satisfied:[31]

1 *Location advantage.* Undertaking the business activity must be more profitable in a foreign location than undertaking it in a domestic location. For example, Caterpillar produces bulldozers in Brazil to enjoy lower labor costs and avoid high tariff walls on goods exported from its U.S. factories.

2 *Ownership advantage.* The firm must own some unique competitive advantage that overcomes the disadvantages of competing with foreign firms on their home turfs. This advantage may be a brand name, ownership of proprietary technology, the benefits of economies of scale, and so on. Caterpillar enjoys all three of these advantages over its Brazilian competitors.

3 *Internalization advantage.* The firm must benefit more from controlling the foreign business activity than from hiring an independent local company to provide the service. Control is advantageous, for example, when it is expensive to monitor and enforce the contractual performance of the local company,[32] when the local company may misappropriate proprietary technology, or when the firm's reputation and brand name could be jeopardized by poor behavior by the local company. All these factors are important to Caterpillar.

Factors Influencing Foreign Direct Investment

Given the complexity of the global economy and the diversity of opportunities firms face in different countries, it is not surprising that numerous factors may influence a firm's decision to undertake FDI. These can be classified as supply factors, demand factors, and political factors (see Table 3.5).

Supply Factors

FDI may be motivated by a firm's efforts to control its own costs. Some of the most important supply factors that may influence a firm's decision to undertake FDI are

► Production costs
► Logistics
► Availability of natural resources
► Access to key technology

Production Costs. Firms often make FDI in new plant, property, and equipment in order to lower production costs. Foreign locations may be more attractive than domestic sites because of lower land prices, tax rates, or commercial real estate rents or because of better availability and lower cost of skilled or unskilled labor. For example, Concord Camera, a small producer of inexpensive cameras, shifted its production from northern New Jersey to Baoan, China. By doing so it lowered its wage rates from $8 per hour to $8 per week.[33] Similarly personal computer production initially was centered in California's Silicon Valley, where most of the research and development that created personal computers was conducted. But as the industry boomed, labor costs and land values there soared. Many microcomputer manufacturers have subsequently shifted some of their production to locations such as Scotland, Singapore, and Taiwan where labor and land costs are lower.

As communities grow (or shrink), their attractiveness or unattractiveness as potential production sites changes. For example, South Korea was once a production center for low-priced sneakers sold by the millions by discounters such as Kmart and Wal-Mart. But the rising prosperity and wages of South Koreans eliminated the country's ability to compete at the low end of the market. South Korea's sneaker industry has contracted and now concentrates on producing more expensive, fashion-oriented sneakers under license from Nike, Reebok, and other major companies. China now dominates the low end of the sneaker market.

Technological change also affects production costs and the attractiveness of FDI. McGraw-Hill moved the maintainance of the circulation files of its 16 magazines from the New York City area to Loughrea, Ireland, to take advantage of Ireland's low labor costs, English-speaking population, generous tax abatements, and sophisticated fiber-optic telephone network. Technology has permitted this back-office operation to be physically housed in Ireland but directly linked to McGraw-Hill's mainframe computers at its Hightstown, New Jersey, corporate headquarters. As an added benefit the Irish facility can utilize the corporate mainframe computers during off-peak times, since Ireland is five time zones ahead of New Jersey.[34]

TABLE 3.5

Factors Affecting the FDI Decision

SUPPLY FACTORS	DEMAND FACTORS	POLITICAL FACTORS
Production costs	Customer access	Avoidance of trade barriers
Logistics	Marketing advantages	Economic development incentives
Resource availability	Exploitation of competitive advantages	
Access to technology	Preservation of brand names and trademarks	
	Customer mobility	

MAP 3.1

The Tuna Industry in Indonesia and the Philippines

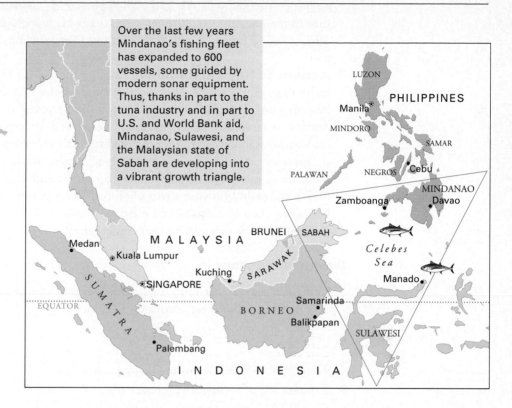

Over the last few years Mindanao's fishing fleet has expanded to 600 vessels, some guided by modern sonar equipment. Thus, thanks in part to the tuna industry and in part to U.S. and World Bank aid, Mindanao, Sulawesi, and the Malaysian state of Sabah are developing into a vibrant growth triangle.

Logistics. If transportation costs are significant, a firm may choose to produce in the foreign market rather than export from domestic factories. For example, Heineken has utilized FDI extensively as part of its internationalization strategy because its products are primarily water. It finds it cheaper to brew its beverages close to where its foreign consumers live than to transport them long distances from its Dutch breweries. International businesses also often make host-country investments in order to reduce distribution costs. For example, Citrovita, a Brazilian producer of orange-juice concentrate, operates a storage and distribution terminal at the Port of Antwerp rather than ship to European grocery chains directly from Brazil. It can take advantage of low ocean shipping rates to transport its goods in bulk from Brazil to the Belgian port. It then uses the Antwerp facility to repackage and distribute concentrate to its customers in France, Germany, and the Benelux countries.

Availability of Natural Resources. Firms may make FDI to access natural resources that are critical to their operations. For example, an integrated international oil company explores, produces, refines, and markets petroleum-based products. Because of the decrease in oil production in the United States, U.S.-based international oil companies have been forced to make significant investments worldwide in order to obtain new oil reserves. Often international businesses negotiate with host governments to obtain access to raw materials in return for FDI. For example, Manila's Ayala Corporation built tuna canneries on the northern Indonesian island of Sulawesi as part of a deal with the Indonesian government to allow Philippine tuna boats based in the southern Philippine island of Mindanao to fish its territorial waters (see Map 3.1). This deal in turn has benefited both countries: over 8000 people in the Philippines and Indonesia are now employed in nine canneries and on 600 fishing vessels, part of an operation that annually exports $34 million of tuna to North American and European consumers.[35]

Access to Key Technology. Another motive for FDI is to gain access to technology. Firms may find it more advantageous to acquire ownership interests in an existing firm than to assemble an in-house group of research scientists to develop or reproduce an emerging technology. For example, many Japanese pharmaceutical manufacturers have invested in small U.S. biogenetics companies as an inexpensive means of obtaining cutting-edge biotechnology. Similarly, Taiwan's Acer Inc., a manufacturer of personal computers and workstations, paid $100 million in the early 1990s for a pair of Silicon Valley computer companies in hopes of leveraging their technology and existing distribution networks to boost Acer's share of the U.S. personal computer market.[36]

Demand Factors

Firms also may engage in FDI in order to expand the market for their products. The demand factors that encourage FDI include

► Customer access

► Marketing advantages

► Exploitation of competitive advantages

► Preservation of brand names and trademarks

► Customer mobility

Customer Access. Many types of international business require firms to have a physical presence in the market. For example, fast-food restaurants and retailers must provide convenient access to their outlets for competitive reasons. KFC can't provide its freshly prepared fried chicken to Japanese customers from its restaurants in the United States; it must locate outlets in Japan to do so. And Benetton's success in broadening its customer base is due to its opening of a large number of new stores worldwide.

Marketing Advantages. FDI may generate several types of marketing advantages. The physical presence of a factory may enhance the visibility of a foreign firm's products in the host market. If production costs are lower in the host market, the firm may be able to reduce the price of its products to host-country consumers, thereby expanding its sales. The foreign firm also gains from "buy local" attitudes of host-country consumers. For example, through ads in such magazines as *Time* and *Sports Illustrated*, Toyota has publicized the beneficial impact of its Georgetown, Kentucky, assembly plant on the U.S. economy (see Fig. 3.6). The Kentucky plant also insulates Toyota from problems caused by the yen's increasing value, which is eroding the profitability of its exports to the United States.

Exploitation of Competitive Advantages. FDI may be a firm's best means to exploit a competitive advantage that it already enjoys. An owner of a valuable trademark or brand name may chose to operate in foreign countries

FIGURE 3.6

Toyota Ad on the Economic Benefits of the Firm's FDI in the United States.

Source: Toyota Motor Corporate Services of North America, Inc. Reprinted with permission.

Think OF IT AS economic FUEL injection.

AT TOYOTA, we're committed to building in America. In fact, almost half the Toyota passenger vehicles sold in America are built in our Kentucky and California plants. And over the last three years, we've doubled our

U.S. made parts purchasing to over $4.4 billion per year. From our manufacturing facilities to our U.S. research and design centers, our operations here provide more than 16,000 direct jobs and give an economic boost to communities right across America.

Toyota's Camry manufacturing plant, Georgetown, Kentucky.

INVESTING IN THE THINGS WE ALL CARE ABOUT. **TOYOTA**

For more information about Toyota in America write Toyota Motor Corporate Services, 9 West 57th Street, Suite 4900-BB, New York, NY 10019.

rather than export to them. Often this decision depends on the product's nature. For example, Coca-Cola and PepsiCo could not successfully penetrate foreign markets by exporting their products from the United States because of the high cost of transporting bottled soft drinks long distances. So they have internationalized their operations by establishing bottling facilities worldwide.

Firms also may make FDI in order to exploit technologically based or experientially based advantages. For example, Pari Mutuel Urbain (PMU) operates 7000 off-track betting facilities in Europe. It developed an ingenious network of computers, on-site terminals, and satellite communications to make it France's seventh-largest service company with annual revenues of $6 billion. PMU's success in harnessing modern communications technology to meet the needs of horse-racing fans has boosted its French business by 25 percent and enabled it to expand its off-track betting operations into Switzerland and Monaco.[37]

Preservation of Brand Names and Trademarks. An important consideration in a firm's internationalization strategy is the need to preserve the reputation and integrity of not only the firm but also its brand names and trademarks.

For example, Levi Strauss Company possesses a highly visible, internationally known brand name. Its worldwide reputation for producing high-quality products could be threatened if it licensed the use of its brand name internationally to independent foreign firms and those firms then used inferior raw materials or adopted inappropriate quality-control measures. To ensure uniformly high-quality production and distribution of its clothing in all its markets, Levi Strauss manufactures approximately half of its clothing in its own domestic and overseas factories and closely monitors the production of its carefully selected independent contractors.[38]

Customer Mobility. A firm's FDI also may be motivated by FDI of its customers or clients. If one of a firm's existing customers builds a foreign factory, the firm may decide to locate a new facility of its own nearby, thereby enabling it to continue to supply its customer promptly and attentively. Equally as important, it reduces the possibility that some competitor in the host country will step in and steal the customer. For example, Japanese parts suppliers to the major Japanese automakers have responded to the construction of Japanese-owned automobile assembly plants in the United States by building their own factories, warehouses, and research facilities there. Their need to locate facilities in the United States is magnified by the automakers' use of JIT inventory management techniques, which minimize the amount of parts inventory held at an assembly plant, thus severely disadvantaging a parts-supply facility located in Japan.

Similar problems confront firms in the service sector. As manufacturing firms internationalize, service providers need to expand their horizons to meet their customers' needs. For example, accounting giants Peat Marwick Mitchell and KMG merged in 1987. The merger produced KPMG, the world's largest accounting firm, with 6100 partners and annual revenues of $6.0 billion. KPMG operates 820 offices in 125 countries, so as its clients internationalize, it is ready to meet their local accounting requirements, no matter how far-flung their global operations.[39]

Political Factors

Political factors may also enter into a firm's decision to make FDI. Firms may invest in a foreign country in order to avoid host-country trade barriers or to take advantage of host-government economic development incentives.

Avoidance of Trade Barriers. Firms often build foreign facilities in order to avoid trade barriers. In the late 1970s and early 1980s, for example, U.S. automakers lobbied Congress to limit Japanese automobile imports. Before Congress could act, the Japanese government announced in 1981 that it would impose a voluntary export restraint (VER) on the Japanese automakers, thereby limiting the number of Japanese autos imported into the United States. To get around the VER, the Japanese auto companies built assembly plants in the United States. This move also fractured the political coalition in the United States that was developing against them. U.S. workers employed in the Japanese-owned assembly plants now provide new political support in the United States for their employers.

Economic Development Incentives. Most democratically elected governments—local, state, and national—are vitally concerned with promoting the economic welfare of their citizens, many of whom are, of course, voters. Many governments offer incentives to firms to induce them to locate new facilities in the governments' jurisdictions. Governmental incentives that can be an important catalyst for FDI include reduced utility rates, employee training programs, infrastructure additions (such as new roads and railroad spurs), and tax reductions or tax holidays. Often MNCs benefit from bidding wars among communities eager to attract them and the jobs they bring. For example, Kentucky's state government put together a $125 million incentive package that won the state Toyota's first wholly-owned U.S. automobile assembly plant. And Alabama provided Daimler-Benz with $300 million in incentives in order to capture that firm's new plant.

CHAPTER REVIEW

Summary

International trade is an important form of international business—over $4.6 trillion of goods and services were traded between residents of different countries in 1992. Most of this trade involved the wealthy Quad countries. International trade affects domestic economies both directly and indirectly. Exports stimulate additional demand for products, thus generating income and employment gains. Imports lower consumer prices and pressure domestic firms to become more efficient and productive.

Because of trade's importance to businesses and governments worldwide, scholars have offered numerous explanations for its existence. The earliest theories, such as absolute advantage, comparative advantage, and relative factor endowments, relied on characteristics of countries to explain patterns of exports and imports. These country-based theories help explain trade in undifferentiated goods such as wheat, sugar, and steel.

Coincident with the rise of the MNC, postwar research focused on firm-based explanations for international trade. Country similarity, product life cycle, and global strategic rivalry theories focus on the firm as the agent for generating trade and investment decisions. These firm-based theories help explain intraindustry trade and trade in differentiated goods such as automobiles, personal care products, and consumer electronics goods.

International investment is the second major way in which firms participate in international business. International investments fall into two categories: portfolio investments and FDI. FDI has risen in importance as MNCs have increased in size and number.

Dunning's eclectic theory suggests that FDI will occur when three conditions are met: (1) A foreign location is superior to a domestic location, (2) the firm enjoys a competitive advantage that can be utilized to generate monopolistic profits in foreign markets, and (3) the firm finds it cheaper (because of transaction costs) to produce the product itself rather than hire a foreign firm to do so.

Numerous factors can influence a firm's decision to undertake FDI. Some FDI may be undertaken to reduce the firm's costs. Such supply factors include production costs, logistics, availability of natural resources, and access to key technology. The decision to engage in FDI may be affected by such demand factors as developing access to new customers, obtaining marketing advantages through local production, exploiting competitive advantages, preserving the reputations of brand names and trademarks, and maintaining nearness to customers as they internationalize their operations. Political considerations may also play a role in FDI. Often firms use FDI to avoid host-country trade barriers or to capture economic development incentives offered by governments.

Review Questions

1. What is international trade? Why does it occur?

2. How do the theories of absolute advantage and comparative advantage differ?

3. Why are Leontief's findings called a paradox?

4. How useful are country-based theories in explaining international trade?

5. How do interindustry and intraindustry trade differ?

6. Explain the impact of the product life cycle on international trade and international investment.

7. What are the primary sources of the competitive advantages firms use to compete in international markets?

8. What are the four elements of Porter's diamond of national competitive advantage?

9. How do portfolio investments and FDI differ?

10. What are the three parts of Dunning's eclectic theory?

11. How do political factors influence international trade and investment?

Questions for Discussion

1. In our example of France's trading wine to Japan for clock radios, we arbitrarily assumed the countries would trade at a price ratio of 1 bottle of wine for 2 clock radios. Over what range of prices can trade occur between the two countries? (*Hint*: In the absence of trade what is the price of clock radios in terms of wine in France? In Japan?) Does your answer differ if you use Table 3.2 instead of Table 3.1?

2. In the public debate over NAFTA's ratification Ross Perot said he heard a "giant sucking sound" of U.S. jobs headed south because of low wage rates in Mexico. Using the theory of comparative advantage, discuss whether Perot's fears are valid.

3. Why is intraindustry trade not predicted by country-based theories of trade?

4. **a.** What factors did Daimler-Benz consider in deciding to build a new automobile assembly plant in the United States? In Alabama? Rank these factors in order of importance.

   b. Who benefits and who loses from the new plant in Alabama?

   c. Is the firm's decision to build the new plant consistent with Dunning's eclectic theory?

BUILDING GLOBAL SKILLS

The U.S. market for computers is almost completely dominated by U.S. firms such as IBM, Apple, Compaq, Dell, and Hewlett-Packard. The U.S. market for consumer electronics is dominated by Japanese firms and brands such as Sony, JVC, Panasonic, Mitsubishi, and Toshiba. However, the U.S. automobile market includes both strong domestic firms such as Ford and Chrysler and formidable Japanese competitors such as Toyota and Honda.

Your instructor will divide the class into groups of four or five and assign each group one of the three industries noted above. To begin, discuss within your group your individual views as to why the specific state of affairs described above exists.

Next analyze the industry assigned to your group from the standpoint of each country-based and firm-based theory of international trade discussed in this chapter. Try to agree on which theory is the best predictor and which is the worst predictor of reality for your specific industry.

Next reconvene as a class. Each group should select a spokesperson. Each spokesperson should indicate the industry that the person's group discussed and identify the best and worst theories selected. Note the points on which the groups who analyzed the same industries agree.

Finally, separate again into your small groups and discuss the areas of common disagreements. Also discuss the following questions:

1. Do some theories work better than others for different industries? Why?

2. What other industries can you think of that fit one of the three patterns noted in the opening paragraph?

3. Do the same theories work as well in making predictions for those industries?

4. Based on what you know about the Japanese market, decide whether the same pattern of competitiveness that exists in the United States for the computer, consumer electronics, and automobile industries also holds true for that market. Why or why not?

CLOSING CASE

Komatsu's Challenge[41]

This chapter opened with a discussion of the international business activities of Caterpillar, Inc. But Cat's success has not gone unchallenged. For the past two decades its preeminence has been imperiled by low-priced, high-quality goods produced by Komatsu Ltd., a relative newcomer to the industry. Komatsu had virtually no presence in the key U.S. market in 1970. Within 15 years it had captured almost 20 percent of Cat's home turf.

Komatsu is the parent corporation of a group of 62 affiliated companies that produce construction equipment and industrial machinery. Founded in 1921, it has focused on manufacturing high-quality products and offering strong product support. Until Komatsu decided to attack the construction equipment market dominated by Caterpillar, its main strength lay in the production of forklifts and other materials-handling equipment, for which Komatsu is generally recognized as the world leader.

Like many Japanese companies, Komatsu traditionally relied on exports rather than FDI to serve its foreign customers. During its initial assault on the U.S. market in the 1970s, it enjoyed lower wage rates than Caterpillar did. However, during the 1980s its labor-cost advantage began to shrink as wages rose in Japan. It anticipated cost escalation as a result of the yen's rising value, which reduced the profitability of export sales from its Japanese factories, and shifted some of its production to overseas plants via FDI. Komatsu built overseas plants in Indonesia (in 1982), Mexico, the United Kingdom,

and Brazil and in 1985 completed its first U.S. facility. The foreign plants aided communication with local customers, reduced delivery times, and improved delivery of parts to Komatsu's dealers. In a recent report to its shareholders Komatsu said the goal of its globalization strategies is "full localization" in its key markets of Asia, Europe, and North America.

Komatsu adopted several strategies as it grew from a specialist in forklift trucks to a broad-based producer of construction equipment. It systematically expanded its product line to help its dealers better compete against Caterpillar's well-established distributors. New products included innovations such as underground construction equipment and underwater robots. It also teamed up with foreign producers. For example, to penetrate the closed Indian market Komatsu established a long-term production arrangement with Bharat Earth Movers, Ltd., an Indian government-owned firm, to produce bulldozers, graders, and excavators. And it entered the Korean market by licensing Dong-A Motor Co. to produce Komatsu-designed dump trucks.

Komatsu is well positioned to exploit the large Japanese construction market. It recognized the growing shortage of skilled workers and so allocated R&D resources to develop labor-saving robots for use at construction sites and increased its production of prefabricated building materials. Komatsu has enjoyed steady growth in sales to the Japanese market. With annual domestic sales of $5.0 billion, it holds a comfortable lead over its chief domestic rival, the partnership between Cat and Mitsubishi Heavy

Industries, which sold $2.8 billion of construction equipment in Japan in 1993.

Komatsu is having more problems in the North American market. Like most Japanese manufacturers, its initial postwar successes in North America were attributable to its skilled but low-paid workforce that produced quality products at prices that undercut those of U.S. firms. However, Japanese economic growth created labor shortages that in turn forced domestic wages higher. Komatsu enjoyed booming sales in the U.S. market in the early 1980s because of the dollar's high value against the yen. But by the decade's end this exchange-rate advantage had disappeared, and increases in the yen's value relative to the dollar's eroded Komatsu's labor-cost advantage. (By 1992 Komatsu's labor costs were estimated to be only 6–25 percent below Caterpillar's labor costs of $32 per hour. Subsequent increases in the yen's value have probably eliminated this gap.) To increase its competitiveness in the U.S. market Komatsu formed a joint venture in 1988 with Dresser Industries. Dresser contributed its existing plants, while Komatsu offered its more advanced machinery and sophisticated manufacturing technology.

So far Komatsu Dresser has not been successful, and its profits have proven disappointing. Its share of the U.S. market has fallen from 20 percent to 18 percent since its founding, while Caterpillar's has risen from 34.5 percent to 36.4 percent during the same period. Both Komatsu Dresser and Cat were struck by the UAW in late 1991. Hoping to restore peaceful labor relations and output levels, Komatsu Dresser quickly yielded to the union's demands, while Cat's bitter five-month strike gained that firm more flexible work rules that promise improved productivity. In addition, Komatsu Dresser's $200 million program to modernize its factories is dwarfed by Cat's $2.1 billion investment in revitalizing its plants. Further Komatsu Dresser's dealership network is weaker than Cat's. The net worth of Cat's 65 U.S. dealers is over $1.9 billion; that of Komatsu Dresser's 60 dealers is only $300 million. Consolidating Komatsu's dealers with Dresser's distributors also has been costly, as former Komatsu and former Dresser dealers with overlapping territories have battled with each other rather than focusing on the threat from Caterpillar. And U.S.-born managers of Komatsu Dresser are resentful of being excluded from informal Friday evening management gatherings—conducted in Japanese—where key operating decisions often are made.

Case Questions

1. How does Komatsu gain from manufacturing abroad rather than exporting from its Japanese plants?

2. How does the yen's increased value against the dollar affect Komatsu's ability to export?

3. How can Komatsu improve Komatsu Dresser's profitability?

CHAPTER NOTES

1. Caterpillar Inc. *1990 Annual Report,* p. 15.

2. Ronald Henkoff, "This Cat Is Acting like a Tiger," *Fortune,* December 19, 1988, pp. 69ff; "Cat vs. Labor: Hardhats, Anyone?" *Business Week,* August 26, 1991, p. 48; Caterpillar Inc. *1993 Annual Report;* "Union and company waging 'holy war,'" *Bryan–College Station Eagle,* August 7, 1994, p. C1.

3. General Agreement on Tariffs and Trade, *International Trade Statistics,* 1993, p. 1.

4. Arthur M. Schlesinger, *The Colonial Merchants and the American Revolution 1763–1776* (New York: Facsimile Library, 1939), pp. 16–20.

5. David Ricardo, *The Principles of Political Economy and Taxation* (Homewood: Irwin, 1963). (Ricardo's book was first published in 1817.)

6. Eli Heckscher, "The Effect of Foreign Trade on the Distribution of Income," reprinted in *Readings in the Theory of International Trade,* eds. H. S. Ellis and L. A. Metzler (Homewood: Irwin, 1949). (Translated into English from the original 1919 Swedish article.)

7. Bertil Ohlin, *Interregional and International Trade* (Cambridge, Mass.: Harvard University Press, 1933).

8. Wassily Leontief, "Domestic Production and Foreign Trade; the American Capital Position Re-examined," reprinted in *Readings in International Economics,* eds. R. Caves and H. Johnson (Homewood: Irwin, 1968).

9. Wassily Leontief, "Factor Proportions and the Structure of American Trade: Further Theoretical and Empirical Analysis," *Review of Economics and Statistics,* Vol. 38 (Nov. 1956), pp. 386–407.

10. Donald B. Keesing, "Labor Skills and Comparative Advantage," *American Economic Review,* Vol. 56 (May 1986), pp. 249–258.

11. F. Clairmonte and J. Cauvanagh, "TNCs: The Ever Grasping Drive," *Development Forum,* 1985.

12. S. B. Linder, *An Essay on Trade and Transformation* (New York: Wiley, 1961).

13. R. Vernon, "International Investment and International Trade in the Product Cycle," *Quarterly Journal of Economics,* Vol. 80 (May 1966), pp. 190–207.

14. Michael Moritz, *The Little Kingdom: The Private Story of Apple Computer* (New York: William Morrow, 1984).

15. Apple Computer, Inc., *1991 Annual Report,* p. 5.

16. P. Krugman, "Intraindustry Specialization and the Gains from Trade," *Journal of Political Economy,* Vol. 89 (October 1981), pp. 959–973.

17. K. Lancaster, "Intra-industry Trade under Perfect Monopolistic Competition," *Journal of International Economics,* Vol. 10 (May 1980), pp. 151–175.

18. Michael W. Pustay, "Toward a Global Airline Industry: Prospects and Impediments," *Logistics and Transportation Review,* Vol. 28, No. 1 (March 1992), pp. 103–128.

19. Laurence S. Kuter, *The Great Gamble: the Boeing 747* (University, Ala.: The University of Alabama Press, 1973), p. vii.

20. Michael E. Porter, "New Global Strategies for Competitive Advantage," *Planning Review,* May/June 1990, p. 14.

21. Andrew R. Dick, "Learning by Doing and Dumping in the Semiconductor Industry," *Journal of Law and Economics,* Vol. 34, No. 1 (April 1991), p. 134.

22. Fred Warshofsky, *The Chip War* (New York: Scribner's, 1989), pp. 131–132.

23. "Scotland becomes high-tech giant," *Houston Chronicle,* May 11, 1992, p. 4B.

24. *Survey of Current Business,* June 1994, p. 69.

25. A. Quijana, "A Guide to BEA Statistics on Foreign Direct Investment in the United States," *Survey of Current Business,* February 1990, pp. 29–37.

26. Grant T. Hammond, *Countertrade, Offsets and Barter in International Political Economy* (St. Martin's Press: New York, 1990), p. 3.

27. *Survey of Current Business,* June 1994, p. 77.

28. Ibid., p. 74.

29. The initial argument was presented in Stephen Hymer's 1960 doctoral dissertation. The full argument is presented in Hymer's *The International Operations of National Firms* (Cambridge, Mass.: M.I.T. Press, 1976).

30. P. Krugman and M. Obstfeld, *International Economics* (Glenview, Ill.: Scott, Foresman, 1988), p. 159.

31. J. Dunning, "Explaining Changing Patterns of International Production: In Defence of the Eclectic Theory," *Oxford Bulletin of Economics and Statistics,* Vol. 41 (November 1979).

32. O. Williamson, *Markets and Hierarchies* (New York: Free Press, 1983).

33. "Small Firms Face Big Headaches in Far-Flung Ventures," *Wall Street Journal,* July 1, 1991, p. B2.

34. "American Firms Send Office Work Abroad to Use Cheaper Labor," *Wall Street Journal,* August 14, 1991, p. A1.

35. Rigoberto Tiglao, "Growth Zones," *Far Eastern Economic Review,* February 10, 1994, pp. 40ff.

36. "Acer Is Still Searching for the Password to the U.S.," *Business Week,* May 18, 1992, p. 129.

37. Peter Mikelbank, "I've Got the Cheval Right Here," *Sports Illustrated,* November 11, 1991, pp. 9–10.

38. Levi Strauss, Form 10-K for the Fiscal Year Ended November 25, 1990, p. 9.

39. Hoover et al. (eds.), *Hoover's Handbook of World Business 1992* (Austin, Tex.: Reference Press, 1992), p. 225.

40. James R. Thompson, "The Toyota Decision," *Economic Development Review,* Fall 1989, p. 21; "States' Bidding War over Mercedes Plant Made for Costly Chase," *Wall Street Journal,* November 24, 1993, p. A1.

41. "Going for the Lion's Share," *Business Week,* July 18, 1988, p. 71; Komatsu Ltd. *Annual Report 1991,* p. 2; "Maybe Caterpillar Can Pick Up Where It Left Off," *Business Week,* April 27, 1992, p. 35; "Komatsu Throttles Back on Construction Equipment," *Wall Street Journal,* May 13, 1992, p. B4; Larry Green, "Confidence in Tomorrow," *Equipment Management,* April 1990, pp. 30–36; "A Dream Marriage Turns Nightmarish," *Business Week,* April 29, 1991, pp. 94–95.

Dollar Falls to New Low Against Yen; Fears Over Japanese Politics Are Cited—
The dollar fell to a record low against the yen yesterday on fears that the latest
political convulsions in Japan have left U.S. efforts to conclude a trade agreement
with that nation in disarray....[4] ▌▌ *West Europe's Export-Driven Recovery Could
Be Derailed by Dollar's Weakness*—The driving force behind Europe's nascent
economic recovery has been export orders from the world's faster-growing
regions: the United States, Latin America, and Southeast Asia, which widely use
the dollar as a trading currency. West European economies do two thirds of their
trading among themselves. But with domestic demand still weak, the more
European countries prosper by selling overseas, the more business confidence
grows and inventories are restocked, often with orders to each other. That add-on
effect could accelerate consumer and business spending, broadening growth and
providing jobs for West Europe's nearly 20 million unemployed. But traumatized
currency markets could spoil the party if a weakening dollar continues to make
U.S. exports cheaper abroad and squeezes European exporters out of key
markets.[5] ▌▌▌▌

Stories like these appear in the world's financial press daily. They are avidly read
by managers, for they deal with topics vital to international businesspeople. What
is the value of the dollar today? What will its value be next month? Will foreign
governments stimulate their economies, thereby increasing export opportunities
next year? Will imports be a greater challenge in the future? Will trade wars break
out, thereby damaging access to foreign markets?

Underlying these headlines are the operations of the international monetary
system. An international monetary system arises because most countries have
their own currencies. A means of exchanging these currencies is needed if business
is to be conducted across national boundaries. The **international monetary
system** establishes the rules by which countries value and exchange their currencies. It also provides a mechanism for correcting imbalances between a country's
international payments and its receipts. Further, the cost of converting foreign
money into a firm's home currency—a variable critical to the profitability of
international operations—depends on the smooth functioning of the international monetary system.

International businesspeople also monitor the international monetary system's
accounting system, the balance of payments. The **balance of payments (BOP)
accounting system** records international transactions and supplies vital information about the health of a national economy and likely changes in its fiscal and
monetary policies. BOP statistics can be used to detect signs of trouble that could
eventually lead to governmental trade restrictions, higher interest rates, accelerated inflation, reduced aggregate demand, or general changes in the cost of doing
business in any given country.

History of the International Monetary System

Today's international monetary system can trace its roots to the ancient allure of gold and silver, both of which served as media of exchange in early trade between tribes and in later trade between city-states. Silver, for example, was used in trade among India, Babylon, and Phoenicia as early as the seventh century B.C.[6] As the modern nation states of Europe took form in the sixteenth and seventeenth centuries, their coins were traded on the basis of their relative gold and silver content.

The Gold Standard

Ancient reliance on gold coins as an international medium of exchange led to the adoption of an international monetary system known as the gold standard. Under the **gold standard**, countries agree to buy or sell their paper currencies in exchange for gold on the request of any individual or firm and—in contrast to mercantilism's hoarding of gold—to allow the free export of gold bullion and coins.[7] In 1821 the United Kingdom became the first country to adopt the gold standard. During the nineteenth century, most other important trading countries—including Russia, Austria-Hungary, France, Germany, and the United States—did the same.

The gold standard effectively created a fixed exchange-rate system. An **exchange rate** is the price of one currency in terms of a second currency. Under a **fixed exchange-rate system**, the price of a given currency does not change relative to each other currency. The gold standard created a fixed exchange-rate system because each country tied, or **pegged**, the value of its currency to gold. The United Kingdom, for example, pledged to buy or sell an ounce of gold for 4.247 pounds sterling, thereby establishing the pound's **par value**, or official price in terms of gold. The United States agreed to buy or sell an ounce of gold for a par value of $20.67. The two currencies could be freely exchanged for the stated amount of gold, making £4.247 = 1 ounce of gold = $20.67. This implied a fixed exchange rate between the pound and the dollar of £1 = $4.867, or $20.67/£4.247.

As long as firms had faith in a country's pledge to exchange its currency for gold at the promised rate when requested to do so, many actually preferred to be paid in currency. Transacting in gold was expensive. Suppose Jardine Matheson, a Hong Kong trading company, sold £100,000 worth of tea to Twining & Company, a London distributor of fine teas. If it wanted to be paid in gold by Twining & Company upon delivery of the tea, Jardine Matheson had to bear the costs of loading the gold into the cargo hold of a ship, guarding it against theft, transporting it, and insuring it against possible disasters. Moreover, because of the slowness of sailing ships, Jardine Matheson would be unable to earn interest on the £100,000 payment while the gold was in transit from London to Hong Kong. On the other hand, if Jardine Matheson was willing to be paid in British pounds, Twining could draft a check to Jardine Matheson and give it to the firm's London agent. The London agent could then either immediately deposit the check in Jardine Matheson's interest-bearing London bank account or transfer the funds via telegraph to the firm's account at its Hong Kong bank.

From 1821 until the end of World War I in 1918, the most important currency in international commerce was the British pound sterling, a reflection of the United Kingdom's emergence from the Napoleonic Wars as Europe's dominant economic and military power. Most firms worldwide were willing to accept either gold or British pounds in settlement of transactions. As a result, the international monetary system during this period is often called a **sterling-based gold standard**.[8] The pound's role in world commerce was reinforced by the expansion of the British Empire. The Union Jack flew over so many lands (see Map 4.1)—for example, present-day Canada, Australia, New Zealand, Hong Kong, Singapore, India, Pakistan, Bangladesh, Kenya, Zimbabwe, South Africa, Gibraltar, Bermuda, and Belize—that the claim was made that "the sun never set on the British Empire." In each British colony, British banks established branches and used the pound sterling to settle international transactions among themselves. Because of the international trust in British currency, London became a dominant international financial center in the nineteenth century, a position it still holds.[9] The international reputations and competitive strengths of such British firms as Barclays Bank, Thomas Cook, and Lloyd's of London stem from the role of the pound sterling in the nineteenth-century gold standard.

The Collapse of the Gold Standard

During World War I, the sterling-based gold standard unraveled. With the outbreak of war, normal commercial transactions between the Allies (France, Russia, and the United Kingdom) and the Central Powers (Austria-Hungary, Germany, and the Ottoman Empire) ceased. The economic pressures of war caused country after country to suspend their pledges to buy or sell gold at their currencies' par values. After the war, conferences at Brussels (1920) and Genoa (1922) yielded general agreements among the major economic powers to return to the prewar gold standard. Most countries, including the United States, the United Kingdom, and France, readopted the gold standard in the 1920s despite the high levels of inflation, unemployment, and political instability that were wracking Europe.[10]

The resuscitation of the gold standard proved to be short-lived, however. The standard was doomed by economic stresses triggered by the worldwide Great Depression. The Bank of England, the United Kingdom's central bank, was unable to maintain its new pledges under the gold standard. On September 21, 1931, it allowed the pound to **float**, meaning that the pound's value would be determined by the forces of supply and demand and the Bank of England would no longer guarantee to redeem British paper currency for gold at par value.[11]

After the United Kingdom abandoned the gold standard, a "sterling area" emerged as some countries, primarily members of the British Commonwealth, pegged their currencies to the pound and relied on sterling balances held in London as their international reserves.[12] Other countries tied the value of their currencies to the U.S. dollar or the French franc. The harmony of the international monetary system degenerated further as some countries—including the United States, France, the United Kingdom, Belgium, Latvia, the Netherlands, Switzerland, and Italy—engaged in a series of competitive devaluations of their currencies. By deliberately and artificially lowering (devaluing) the official value of its currency, each nation hoped to make its own goods cheaper in world markets, thereby stimulating its exports and reducing its imports. Any such gains were

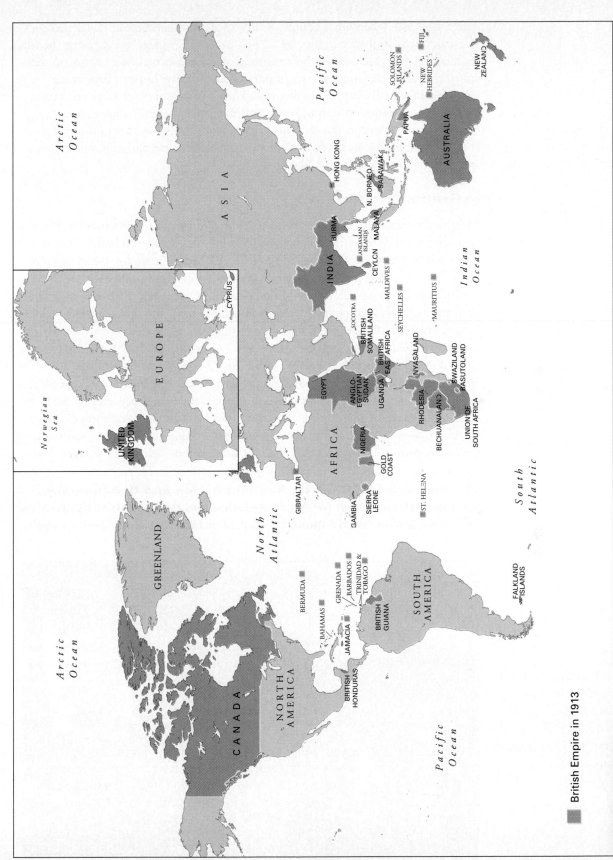

The British Empire in 1913

■ British Empire in 1913

MAP 4.1

offset, however, when other countries also devalued their currencies. (If two countries each devalue their currency by 20 percent, neither gains an advantage because each currency's value relative to the other remains the same.) Most countries also raised the tariffs they imposed on imported goods in the hope of protecting domestic jobs in import-competing industries. Yet as more and more countries adopted these **beggar-thy-neighbor policies**, international trade contracted, hurting employment in each country's export industries. More ominously, this international economic conflict was soon replaced by international military conflict—the outbreak of World War II in 1939.

The Bretton Woods Era

Many politicians and historians believe the breakdown of the international monetary system and international trade after World War I created economic conditions that helped bring about World War II. Inflation, unemployment, and the costs of rebuilding war-torn economies created political instability that enabled fascist and communist dictators (Hitler, Mussolini, and Stalin) to seize control of their respective governments. Determined not to repeat the mistakes that had caused World War II, Western diplomats struggled to create an economic environment that would promote worldwide peace and prosperity. In 1944 representatives of 44 countries met at a resort in Bretton Woods, New Hampshire, to construct the postwar international monetary system. The Bretton Woods conferees agreed to renew the gold standard on a modified basis. They also agreed to the creation of two new international organizations to assist the rebuilding of the world economy and the international monetary system: the International Bank for Reconstruction and Development and the International Monetary Fund.

The International Bank for Reconstruction and Development.
The **International Bank for Reconstruction and Development (IBRD)** is the official name of the **World Bank**. Established in 1945, the World Bank's initial

By creating the World Bank and the International Monetary Fund, the delegates to the 1944 Bretton Woods conference sought to promote world peace and prosperity.

goal was to help finance reconstruction of the war-torn European economies. With the assistance of the Marshall Plan, the World Bank accomplished this task by the mid-1950s. The Bank then adopted a new mission—to build the economies of the world's developing countries.

As its mission has expanded over time, the World Bank created three affiliated organizations:

1 The International Development Association
2 The International Finance Corporation
3 The Multilateral Investment Guarantee Agency

Together with the World Bank, these constitute the **World Bank Group** (see Fig. 4.1). The World Bank is currently owned by the 176 member countries that have contributed to its capital stock, which totaled $166 billion in 1993. In reaching its decisions, the World Bank uses a weighted voting system that reflects the economic power and contributions of its members. The United States currently controls the largest bloc of votes (17 percent), followed by Japan (7 percent), Germany (5 percent), the United Kingdom (5 percent), France (5 percent), and Canada (3 percent). From time to time, the voting weights are reassessed as economic power shifts or as new members, such as Russia, Slovenia, and Ukraine, join the World Bank. To finance its lending operations, the World Bank borrows money in its own name from international capital markets. Interest earned on existing loans provides it with additional lending power. New lending by the World Bank has averaged $17 billion per year in the 1990s.[13]

According to its charter, the World Bank may lend only for "productive purposes" that will stimulate economic growth within the recipient country. An example of such a loan is the $120 million provided to Romania in 1993 to rehabilitate and modernize its national highways. The World Bank cannot finance a trade deficit, but it can finance an infrastructure project, such as a new railroad or harbor

---

Organization of the World Bank Group

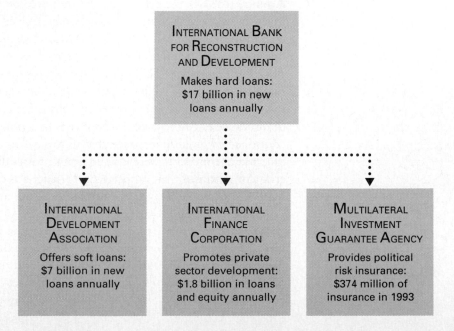

facility, that will bolster a country's economy. It may lend only to national governments or for projects that are guaranteed by a national government, and its loans may not be tied to the purchase of goods or services from any country. Most important, the World Bank must follow a **hard loan policy**; that is, it may make a loan only if there is a reasonable expectation that the loan will be repaid. This policy means that most loans go to countries that are well along the path of economic development because they are most likely to repay their loans.[14]

The hard loan policy was severely criticized in the 1950s by poorer countries, who complained it hindered their ability to obtain World Bank loans. In response, the World Bank established the **International Development Association (IDA)** in 1960. The IDA offers **soft loans**, loans that bear some significant risk of not being repaid. Its lending efforts focus on the least-developed countries. A typical loan is the $92 million provided in 1993 to improve rural water supplies to 1200 villages (total population, 4.8 million) in the mountainous southern Indian state of Karnataka. The IDA obtains resources from the initial subscriptions its members make when joining it, from transferred World Bank profits, and from periodic replenishments contributed by richer countries. In the 1990s IDA disbursements have averaged $7 billion per year—about 40 percent of the World Bank's loan volume.[15]

The two other affiliates of the World Bank Group have narrower missions. The **International Finance Corporation (IFC)**, created in 1956, is charged with promoting the development of the private sector in developing countries. Acting like an investment banker, the IFC, in collaboration with private investors, provides debt and equity capital for promising commercial activities. For example, in 1992 the IFC lent Uganda's Clovergem Fish and Food Ltd. $900,000 to build a processing plant so that the firm could export fish to Europe. The IFC also invested $17.8 million in the newly privatized Cementarny a Vapenky Mokra, the Czech Republic's largest cement manufacturer. In 1993 the IFC provided $1.8 billion of financing to supplement $15.2 billion of capital raised from other sources for private-sector projects.

The other World Bank affiliate, the **Multilateral Investment Guarantee Agency (MIGA)**, was set up in 1988 to overcome private-sector reluctance to invest in developing countries because of perceived political riskiness—a topic covered more thoroughly in Chapter 8. MIGA encourages direct investment in developing countries by offering private investors insurance against noncommercial risks. For example, MIGA insured two Japanese investors in a fertilizer plant in Bangladesh for $9.9 million in 1991 to protect them against government seizure of the plant and against war or other civil disturbances. It also provided $9.4 million of insurance to two separate investors (an American firm and a Luxembourg firm controlled by Swedish interests) that were developing cellular telephone networks in Chile; the investors were insured against losses due to war, civil disturbance, government seizure of their property, and restrictions on currency transfer.[16] In 1993 MIGA underwrote $374 million of political risk insurance.

The World Bank Group is often embroiled in international political controversy. For example, as part of its drive to promote private enterprise in developing countries, the U.S. government under President Bush lobbied the World Bank to make more direct loans to the private sector and to coordinate its lending policies more closely with the IFC. The U.S. position has been resisted by the World Bank's staff, as well as by the governments of European and developing countries, which fear that increased loans to the private sector may jeopardize the AAA credit rating of the World Bank's bonds.[17] Because the World Bank is a major source of capital to developing countries, such debates are of great interest to international businesses. World Bank loans fund major construction projects throughout less-developed economies, thereby providing business opportunities for international construction companies, steel manufacturers, cement makers, and others. Further, these loans generate economic activity in the recipient countries, thus boosting the market for foreign and domestically produced consumer goods and services.

Paralleling the efforts of the World Bank are the **regional development banks**, such as the African Development Bank, the Asian Development Bank, and the Inter-American Development Bank. These organizations promote the economic development of the poorer countries in their respective regions. The most recently created regional development bank is the European Bank for Reconstruction and Development. It was established by the Western countries to assist in the reconstruction of Central and Eastern Europe after the collapse of the region's communist regimes. The regional development banks and the World Bank often work together on development projects. In 1990, for example, the Asian Development Bank and the World Bank jointly financed the construction of a water treatment and distribution system in Manila to reduce the need for poor Filipino families to carry water from public taps to their homes.[18]

The International Monetary Fund. The Bretton Woods attendees believed that the deterioration of international trade in the years after World War I was attributable in part to the competitive exchange-rate devaluations that plagued international commerce. To ensure that the post–World War II monetary system would promote international commerce, the Bretton Woods Agreement called for the creation of the **International Monetary Fund (IMF)** to oversee the functioning of the international monetary system. Article I of the IMF's Articles of Agreement lays out the organization's objectives:

1 To promote international monetary cooperation

2 To facilitate the expansion and balanced growth of international trade

3 To promote exchange stability, to maintain orderly exchange arrangements among members, and to avoid competitive exchange depreciation

4 To assist in the establishment of a multilateral system of payments

5 To give confidence to members by making the general resources of the Fund temporarily available to them and to correct maladjustments in their balances of payments

6 To shorten the duration and lessen the degree of disequilibrium in the international balances of payments of members

Membership in the IMF is available to any country willing to agree to its rules and regulations. As of February 1995, 179 countries were members. To join, a country must pay a deposit, called a **quota**, partly in gold and partly in the country's own currency. The quota's size primarily reflects the global importance of the country's economy, although political considerations may also have some effect. The size of a quota is important for several reasons.

1 A country's quota determines its voting power within the IMF. From time to time, quotas have been adjusted, which has led to much political bickering among members. For example, the quotas assigned to Russia and other former republics of the Soviet Union when they joined the IMF in 1992 totaled about 5 percent of the IMF's total quota. This reduced the voting strengths of the United States, the United Kingdom, Canada, Australia, and many others. Currently the United States controls 19.1 percent of the votes in the IMF. The United Kingdom commands the next-largest block (6.6 percent), followed by Germany (5.8 percent), France (4.8 percent), Japan (4.5 percent), and Saudi Arabia (3.4 percent).

2 A country's quota serves as part of its official reserves (we discuss official reserves later in the chapter).

3 The quota determines the country's borrowing power from the IMF. Each IMF member has an unconditional right to borrow up to 25 percent of its quota from the IMF. IMF policy allows additional borrowings contingent on the member country's agreeing to IMF-imposed restrictions—called **IMF conditionality**—on its economic policies; such restrictions might include the elimination of export subsidies or a reduction in the domestic money supply. Local politicians and interest groups often bitterly protest the IMF's conditionality requirements. For example, in the negotiations leading to Russia's joining the IMF (and its immediate borrowing of $1 billion from it), Russian politicians balked at the IMF's condition that price controls on domestic energy prices be eliminated. Similarly, Poland's parliament grudgingly cut the country's 1992 budget after the IMF suspended credit to it because of its deficit spending.[19]

A Dollar-Based Gold Standard. The IMF and the World Bank provided the institutional framework for the postwar international monetary system. The Bretton Woods participants also addressed the problem of how the system would function in practice. All countries agreed to peg the value of their currencies to gold. For example, the par value of the U.S. dollar was established at $35 per ounce of gold. However, only the United States pledged to redeem its currency for gold at the request of a foreign central bank. Thus the U.S. dollar became the keystone of the Bretton Woods system (see Fig. 4.2). Why this central role for the U.S. dollar? In the early postwar years, only the U.S. and Canadian dollars were convertible currencies, that is, ones that could be freely exchanged for other currencies without legal restrictions. Countries had faith in the U.S. economy and so were willing to accept U.S. dollars to settle their transactions. As the British pound sterling had been in the nineteenth century, the U.S. dollar became the preferred vehicle for settling most international transactions. The effect of the Bretton Woods conference was thus to establish a U.S. dollar-based gold standard.

Because each country established a par value for its currency, the Bretton Woods Agreement resulted in a fixed exchange-rate system. (Figure 4.2 shows the structure of exchange rates at the end of the Bretton Woods era.) Under the Agreement, each country pledged to maintain the value of its currency within ±1 percent of its par value. If the market value of its currency fell outside that range, a country was obligated to intervene in the foreign-exchange market to bring the value back within ±1 percent of par value. This stability in exchange rates benefited international businesses, since the Bretton Woods system *generally* provided an assurance that the value of each currency would remain stable.

Note the use of the qualifier *generally*. Under extraordinary circumstances, the Bretton Woods Agreement allowed a country to adjust its currency's par value.

FIGURE 4.2

Role of the U.S. Dollar in the Bretton Woods System

Note: Par values as of December 31, 1970.

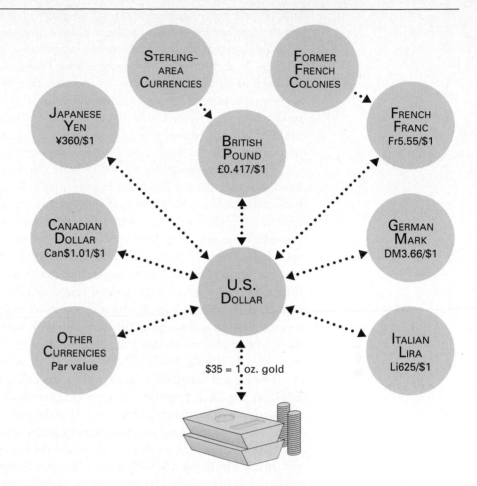

Accordingly, the Bretton Woods system is often described as using an **adjustable peg** because currencies were pegged to gold but the pegs themselves could be altered under certain conditions. For example, under the system the British pound's par value was first set at $2.80. (Technically, the par value was pegged to an ounce of gold, which then could be translated into dollars at a rate of $35.00 per ounce. Most businesspeople ignored this technicality and focused on the implicit par value of a currency in terms of the U.S. dollar.) Thus the Bank of England was obligated to keep the pound's value between $2.772 and $2.828 (±1 percent of $2.80). Suppose pessimism about the British economy caused the pound's market price to fall to $2.76. The Bank of England would be required to defend the value of the pound by selling some of its gold or U.S. dollar holdings to buy pounds. This move would increase the demand for pounds, and the market price would return to within the legal range—from $2.772 to $2.828.

This arrangement worked well as long as pessimism about a country's economy was temporary. But if a country suffered from structural macroeconomic problems, major difficulties could arise. For example, in the late 1960s, Labour governments striving for social justice dominated British politics, and British unions secured higher wages, better working conditions, and protective work rules. At the same time, however, British productivity decreased relative to that of its major international competitors. As a result, the United Kingdom suffered large, continuous BOP deficits. The Bank of England had to intervene continually in the foreign-currency market, selling gold and foreign currencies to support the pound. But in so doing, the Bank's holdings of official reserves, which were needed to back up the country's Bretton Woods pledge, began to dwindle. International currency traders began to fear the Bank would run out of reserves. As that fear mounted, international banks, currency traders, and other market participants became unwilling to hold British pounds in their inventory of foreign currencies. They began dumping pounds on the market as soon as they received them. A vicious cycle developed: as the Bank of England continued to drain its official reserves to support the pound, the fears of the currency-market participants that the Bank would run out of reserves were worsened.

The situation resembles a run on a bank. Banks never have enough cash on hand to honor all their liabilities. However, as long as everyone trusts that their bank will give them their money if they need it, no one worries. If people lose that trust and withdraw more of their money than the bank has on hand, the bank could be in trouble. The Bretton Woods system was particularly susceptible to speculative "runs on the bank," for there was little risk in betting against a currency in times of doubt. For example, speculators distrustful of the Bank of England's ability to honor the United Kingdom's Bretton Woods pledge could convert their pounds into dollars. If they guessed right and the pound were devalued, they could make a quick financial killing. If they guessed wrong and the Bank of England maintained the pound's par value, the speculators could always reconvert their dollar holdings back into pounds at no penalty.

The United Kingdom faced a "run on the bank" of this type in November 1967. The Bank of England could not counter the flood of pounds dumped on the market by speculators and was forced to devalue the pound by 14.3 percent (from $2.80 to $2.40 per pound). France faced a similar run in 1969 and had to devalue the franc. These devaluations tested the international business community's faith in the Bretton Woods system. But the system faced its true Waterloo when the dollar came under attack in the early 1970s.

The End of the Bretton Woods System

These runs on the British and French central banks were a precursor to a run on the most important bank in the Bretton Woods system—the U.S. Federal Reserve Bank. Ironically, the reliance of the Bretton Woods system on the dollar ultimately led to the system's undoing. Because the supply of gold did not expand in the short run, the only source of the liquidity needed to expand international trade was the U.S. dollar. Under the Bretton Woods system, the expansion of international liquidity depended on foreigners' willingness to continually increase their holdings of dollars. Foreigners were perfectly happy to hold dollars as long as they trusted the integrity of the U.S. currency, and during the 1950s and 1960s the number of dollars held by foreigners rose steadily.

As foreign dollar holdings increased, however, people began to question the ability of the United States to live up to its Bretton Woods obligation. This led to the **Triffin paradox**, named after the Belgian-born Yale University economist Robert Triffin, who first identified the problem. The paradox arose because foreigners needed to increase their holdings of dollars to finance expansion of international trade. But the more dollars they owned, the less faith they had in the ability of the United States to redeem those dollars for gold. The less faith foreigners had in the United States, the more they wanted to rid themselves of dollars and get gold in return. But if they did this, international trade and the international monetary system might collapse because the United States didn't have enough gold to redeem all the dollars held by foreigners.

As a means of injecting more liquidity into the international monetary system while reducing the demands placed on the dollar as a reserve currency, IMF members agreed in 1967 to create **special drawing rights (SDRs)**. IMF members can use SDRs to settle official transactions at the IMF. Thus SDRs are sometimes called "paper gold." As of 1993, approximately 21.4 billion SDRs, representing about 2 percent of the world's total reserves, had been distributed to IMF members in proportion to their IMF quotas. An SDR's value is currently calculated daily as a weighted average of the market value of five major currencies—the U.S. dollar, German mark, French franc, Japanese yen, and pound sterling—with the weights revised every five years.[20] As of May 1995, the SDR was worth $1.54 in U.S. dollars.

While SDRs did provide new liquidity for the international monetary system, they did not reduce the fundamental problem of the glut of dollars held by foreigners. By mid-1971, the Bretton Woods system was tottering, the victim of fears about the dollar's instability. In the first seven months of 1971, the United States sold one third of its gold reserves.[21] It became clear to the marketplace that the United States did not have sufficient gold on hand to meet the demands of those who still wanted to exchange their dollars for gold. In a dramatic address on August 15, 1971, President Richard M. Nixon announced that the United States would no longer redeem gold at $35 per ounce. The Bretton Woods system was ended.

President Nixon's decision to end the U.S. dollar's central role in the Bretton Woods system was front-page news around the world.

In effect, the bank was closing its doors. After Nixon's speech, most foreign currencies began to float, their values being determined by supply and demand in the foreign-exchange market. The value of the U.S. dollar fell relative to most of the world's major currencies.

But the nations of the world were not yet ready to abandon the fixed exchange-rate system. At the **Smithsonian Conference**, held in Washington, D.C. in December 1971, central bank representatives from the Group of Ten (see Table 4.1) agreed to restore the fixed exchange-rate system but with restructured rates of exchange between the major trading currencies. The U.S. dollar was devalued to $38 per ounce but remained inconvertible into gold, and the par values of strong currencies such as the yen were revalued upward. Currencies were allowed to fluctuate around their new par values by ±2.25 percent, which replaced the narrower ±1.00 percent range authorized by the Bretton Woods Agreement.

Performance of the International Monetary System since 1971

Free-market forces disputed the new set of par values established by the Smithsonian conferees. Speculators, believing the dollar and the pound were overvalued, sold both and hoarded currencies they believed were undervalued, such as the Swiss franc and the

TABLE 4.1

The Groups of Five, Seven, and Ten

	GROUP OF FIVE	GROUP OF SEVEN	GROUP OF TEN	PERCENTAGE OF WORLD GDP
	United States	United States	United States	25.7
	Japan	Japan	Japan	15.9
	Germany	Germany	Germany	7.8
	France	France	France	5.7
		Italy	Italy	5.3
	United Kingdom	United Kingdom	United Kingdom	3.9
		Canada	Canada	2.1
			Netherlands	1.4
			Belgium	1.0
			Sweden	1.0
Cumulative Percentage of World GDP	59.0	66.4	69.8	

German mark. The Bank of England was unable to maintain the pound's value within the ±2.25 percent band and in June 1972 had to allow the pound to float downward. Switzerland let the Swiss franc float upward in early 1973. The United States devalued the dollar by 10 percent in February 1973. By March 1973, the central banks (see Table 4.2 for a list of the most important of the central banks) conceded they could not successfully resist free-market forces and so established a flexible exchange-rate system. Under a **flexible (or floating) exchange-rate system**, supply and demand for a currency determine its price in the world market. Since 1973, exchange rates among many currencies have been established *primarily* by the interaction of supply and demand. We use the qualifier *primarily* because central banks sometimes try to affect exchange rates by buying or selling currencies on the foreign-exchange market. Thus the current arrangements are often called a **managed float** (or, more poetically, a **dirty float**), because exchange rates are not determined purely by private-sector market forces.

The new flexible exchange-rate system was legitimized by an international conference held in Jamaica in January 1976. According to the resulting **Jamaica Agreement**, each country was free to adopt whatever exchange-rate system best met its own requirements. The United States adopted a floating exchange rate. Other countries adopted a fixed exchange-rate by pegging their currencies to the dollar, the French franc, or some other currency.

The European Monetary System. Of particular note is the strategy adopted by EU members in the belief that flexible exchange rates would hinder their ability to create an integrated European economy. Dissatisfied with the outcome of the Smithsonian Agreement and freed by the Jamaica Agreement to do what they wanted, the EU members in 1979 created the **European Monetary System (EMS)** to manage currency relationships among themselves. Most EMS members chose to participate in the EU's **exchange-rate mechanism (ERM)**. ERM participants pledged to maintain fixed exchange rates among their currencies within a narrow range of ±2.25 percent and a floating rate against the U.S. dollar and other currencies. Italy, however, was at first allowed a wider ±6 percent range. The United

TABLE 4.2

Key Central Banks

COUNTRY	BANK
Canada	Bank of Canada
France	Bank of France
Germany	Bundesbank*
Italy	Bank of Italy
Japan	Bank of Japan
United States	Federal Reserve Bank
United Kingdom	Bank of England

*Although we have provided the English translation for most of these banks, by convention English-language news media use the term *Bundesbank* for the German central bank, rather than its English translation, "Federal Bank."

Kingdom initially chose not to join the ERM (it joined in 1990). The EMS members also created a new index currency, the European Currency Unit. The **European Currency Unit (ECU)** is a weighted "basket" of the currencies of the EU members that is used for accounting purposes within the EU (see Fig. 4.3). The ECU is now well established in international financial markets and is often used as the denomination for bonds, traveler's checks, and bank deposits and loans. For example, ECU-denominated bank loans and deposits are estimated to total 80 billion ECU, or approximately $100 billion.

The EMS has helped EU members fight inflation and promote intra-EU investment, in part because the zealous anti-inflation philosophy of the Bundesbank (Germany's central bank) has dominated EU monetary policy. However, the EMS is not flawless. During its first ten years, the fixed exchange rates established by the ERM had to be adjusted 39 times because of differences in the monetary policies of EU members.[22] The ERM suffered several near fatal blows in September 1992: turmoil in the currency market forced the United Kingdom and Italy to abandon the ERM "temporarily," compelled Spain and Portugal to devalue their currencies drastically, and caused the remaining EMS members to broaden the currency fluctuation range from the original ±2.25 percent to ±15 percent. (See the opening case of Chapter 5 for insights into these events.) Subsequently, the EMS members have focused on rebuilding the credibility of the ERM.

Table 4.3 (on pages 134–135) shows the current status of the world's exchange-rate arrangements. The current international monetary system is based on flexible exchange rates, although some countries have chosen to maintain fixed rates. For example, as just discussed, ERM members have constructed a fixed exchange-rate system among themselves, while some other countries have voluntarily adopted a fixed exchange rate against the U.S. dollar, the French franc, or some other currency. Under the current international monetary system, currencies of one country grouping float against the currencies of other country groupings. For example, the U.S. dollar group floats against the yen, the deutsche mark, the Canadian dollar, the Australian dollar, and the French franc currency group.

FIGURE 4.3

Composition of the ECU in 1993

Note: The currencies grouped as "Other currencies" here are the Danish krone, the Irish punt, the Portuguese escudo, the Greek drachma, and the Luxembourg franc. The currencies of Austria, Finland, and Sweden are not included here because they did not join the EU until 1995.

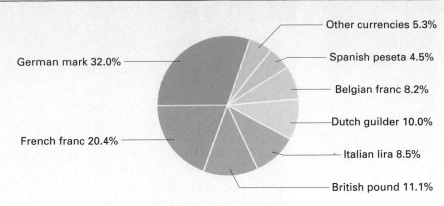

- German mark 32.0%
- Other currencies 5.3%
- Spanish peseta 4.5%
- Belgian franc 8.2%
- Dutch guilder 10.0%
- Italian lira 8.5%
- British pound 11.1%
- French franc 20.4%

PERCENTAGE SHARE OF EACH CURRENCY IN THE ECU

Other Postwar Conferences. The international monetary system that has grown out of the Jamaica Agreement has not pleased all the world's central banks all the time. Since 1976, they have met numerous times to iron out policy conflicts among themselves. For example, U.S. complaints that an overvalued dollar was hurting the competitiveness of U.S. exports and allowing cheap imports to damage U.S. industries prompted finance ministers of the Group of Five (see Table 4.1) to meet in September 1985 at the Plaza Hotel in New York City. The meeting led to the **Plaza Accord**, whereby the central banks agreed to let the dollar's value fall on currency markets. And fall it did. From its peak in February 1985, it plummeted almost 46 percent against the deutsche mark and 41 percent against the yen by the beginning of 1987. Fearing that continued devaluation of the dollar would disrupt world trade, finance ministers from the Group of Five met again, this time at the Louvre in Paris in February 1987. The **Louvre Accord** signaled the commitment of these five countries to stabilizing the dollar's value. However, the foreign-exchange market was once again thrown into turmoil in 1990, in this case by the onset of the Persian Gulf hostilities. The values of key currencies have continued to fluctuate in the 1990s. Figure 4.4 shows changes in the dollar's value against the yen and the mark since the collapse of the Bretton Woods system.

These fluctuations in currency values are of great importance to international businesses. Depreciation in the value of a firm's home currency makes it easier for the firm to export and helps a domestic firm defend itself from the threat of imports. Appreciation has the opposite effect. Recall from the discussion of the Caterpillar-Komatsu rivalry in Chapter 3 that the strong dollar caused Caterpillar problems in the early 1980s and the weak dollar (and strong yen) caused Komatsu problems in the late 1980s. Currency fluctuations also affect international investment opportunities. For example, the appreciation of the mark against the dollar since 1985 has made it more difficult for Bayerische Motoren Werke to sustain its sales of BMWs in the United States. The company's solution was to build an automobile assembly plant near Spartanburg, South Carolina, a move designed to lower the company's production costs and raise its visibility in the North American market.

The International Debt Crisis. The flexible exchange-rate system instituted in 1973 was immediately put to a severe test. In response to the Israeli victory in the Arab-Israeli War of 1973, Arab nations imposed an embargo on oil shipments

FIGURE 4.4

Exchange Rates of the Dollar versus the Yen and the Deutsche Mark, 1960–1994

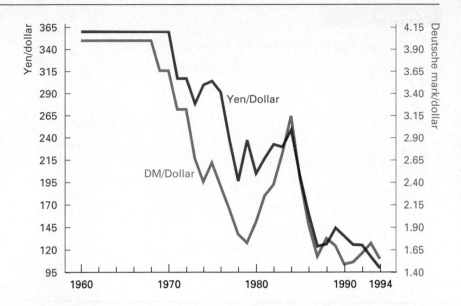

to countries such as the United States and the Netherlands, which had supported the Israeli cause. As a result, the Organization of Petroleum Exporting Countries (OPEC) succeeded in quadrupling world oil prices from $3 a barrel in October 1973 to $12 a barrel by March 1974. This rapid increase in oil prices caused inflationary pressures in oil-importing countries. For example, in the United States inflation rose from 6.1 percent in 1973 to 11.1 percent in 1974. In 1974 alone, $60 billion in wealth was transferred from oil-importing countries to oil-exporting countries. The new international monetary arrangements absorbed some of the shock caused by this upheaval in the oil market, as exchange rates adjusted to account for changes in the value of each country's oil exports or imports. The currencies of the oil exporters strengthened, while those of the oil importers weakened.

This enormous transfer of wealth raised certain economic concerns. The higher oil prices acted as a tax on the economies of the oil-importing countries. Some economists feared that worldwide depression would develop as consumer demand fell in the richer countries. Other economists worried that because trade in oil was denominated in dollars, international liquidity would dry up as dollars piled up in Arab bank accounts. Neither of these fears was realized. Many of the oil-exporting countries went on spending sprees, using their new wealth to improve their infrastructures or to invest in new facilities (particularly petroleum refineries) to produce wealth for future generations. The unspent petrodollars were deposited in banks in international money centers such as London and New York City. The international banking community then recycled these petrodollars through its international lending activities to help revive the economies damaged by rising oil prices.

Unfortunately, the international banks were too aggressive in recycling these dollars. Many countries borrowed more than they could repay. Mexico, for example, borrowed $90 billion, while Brazil took on $67 billion in new loans. The financial positions of these borrowers became precarious after the oil shock of 1978–1979, which was triggered by the toppling from power of the Shah of Iran. The price of oil skyrocketed from $13 a barrel in 1978 to over $30 a barrel in 1980, triggering another round of worldwide inflation. Interest rates on these loans rose, as most carried a

TABLE 4.3

Exchange-Rate Arrangements (as of September 30, 1993)*

| | | | CURRENCY PEGGED TO | | |
U.S. Dollar	French Franc	Russian Ruble	Other Currency	SDR	Other Composite†
Angola	Benin	Armenia	Bhutan	Libya	Algeria
Antigua & Barbuda	Burkina Faso	Azerbaijan	(Indian	Myanmar	Austria
Argentina	Cameroon	Belarus	rupee)	Rwanda	Bangladesh
Bahamas, The	Central African Republic	Kazakhstan	Estonia	Seychelles	Botswana
Barbados	Chad	Turkmenistan	(deutsche		Burundi
Belize	Comoros		mark)		Cape Verde
Djibouti	Congo		Kiribati		Cyprus
Dominica	Côte d'Ivoire		(Australian		Fiji
Grenada	Equatorial Guinea		dollar)		Hungary
Iraq	Gabon		Lesotho		Iceland
Liberia	Mali		(South		Jordan
Marshall Islands	Niger		African		Kenya
Oman	Senegal		rand)		Kuwait
Panama	Togo		Namibia		Malawi
St. Kitts & Nevis			(South		Malta
St. Lucia			African		Mauritania
St. Vincent and			rand)		Mauritius
the Grenadines			San Marino		Morocco
Suriname			(Italian lira)		Nepal
Syrian Arab Republic			Swaziland		Papua New
Yemen, Republic of			(South		Guinea
			African		Solomon Islands
			rand)		Thailand
					Tonga
					Vanuatu
					Western Samoa
					Zimbabwe

* For members with dual or multiple exchange markets, the arrangement shown is that in the major market.
† Comprises currencies which are pegged to various "baskets" of currencies of the members' own choice, as distinct from the SDR basket.
‡ Exchange rates of all currencies have shown limited flexibility in terms of the U.S. dollar.
** Refers to the cooperative arrangement maintained under the European Monetary System.
†† Includes exchange arrangements under which the exchange rate is adjusted at relatively frequent intervals, on the basis of indicators determined by the respective member countries.

Source: IMF, *International Financial Statistics*, March 1994, p. 8. Reprinted with permission.

floating interest rate, further burdening the heavily indebted nations. The international debt crisis formally began when Mexico declared in August 1982 that it could not service its external debts. Mexico requested a rescheduling of its debts, a moratorium on repayment of principal, and a loan from the IMF to help it through its debt

continued

FLEXIBILITY LIMITED IN TERMS OF A SINGLE CURRENCY OR GROUP OF CURRENCIES		MORE FLEXIBLE		
Single Currency‡	Cooperative Arrangements**	Adjusted According to a Set of Indicators††	Other Managed Floating	Independently Floating
Bahrain	Belgium	Chile	Cambodia	Afghanistan, Islamic State of	Latvia
Qatar	Denmark	Colombia	China, Puerto Rico	Albania	Lebanon
Saudi Arabia	France	Madagascar	Croatia	Australia	Lithuania
United Arab Emirates	Germany	Nicaragua	Ecuador	Bolivia	Moldova
	Ireland		Egypt	Brazil	Mongolia
	Luxembourg		Greece	Bulgaria	Mozambique
	Netherlands		Guinea	Canada	New Zealand
	Portugal		Guinea-Bissau	Costa Rica	Nigeria
	Spain		Indonesia	Dominican Republic	Norway
			Israel	El Salvador	Paraguay
			Korea	Ethiopia	Peru
			Lao P.D. Rep	Finland	Philippines
			Malaysia	Gambia, The	Romania
			Maldives	Georgia	Russia
			Mexico	Ghana	Sierra Leone
			Pakistan	Guatemala	South Africa
			Poland	Guyana	Sudan
			Sao Tome & Principe	Haiti	Sweden
			Singapore	Honduras	Switzerland
			Slovenia	India	Tanzania
			Somalia	Iran, Independent Republic of	Trinidad and Tobago
			Sri Lanka	Italy	Uganda
			Tunisia	Jamaica	Ukraine
			Turkey	Japan	United Kingdom
			Uruguay	Kyrgyz Republic	United States
			Venezuela		Zaire
			Vietnam		Zambia

crisis. Mexico was soon joined by Brazil and Argentina. In total, more than 40 countries in Asia, Africa, and Latin America sought relief from their external debts. Negotiations among the debtor countries, creditor countries, private banks, and international organizations continued throughout the rest of the 1980s.

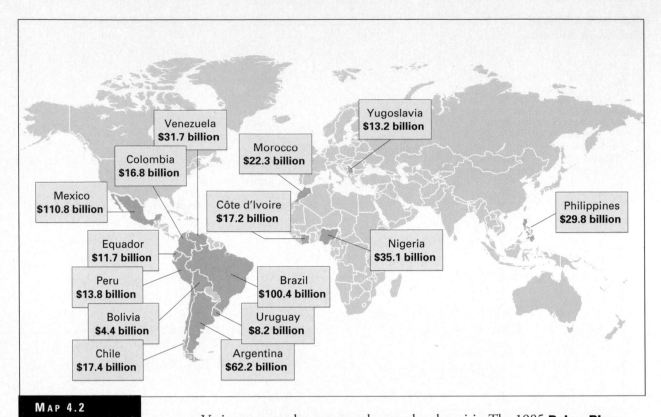

Venezuela
$31.7 billion

Colombia
$16.8 billion

Mexico
$110.8 billion

Equador
$11.7 billion

Peru
$13.8 billion

Bolivia
$4.4 billion

Chile
$17.4 billion

Morocco
$22.3 billion

Côte d'Ivoire
$17.2 billion

Yugoslavia
$13.2 billion

Nigeria
$35.1 billion

Philippines
$29.8 billion

Brazil
$100.4 billion

Uruguay
$8.2 billion

Argentina
$62.2 billion

M A P 4.2

**External Debt of 15
Baker Plan Countries,
January 1993**

Various approaches were used to resolve the crisis. The 1985 **Baker Plan** (named after U.S. Treasury Secretary James Baker) stressed the importance of debt rescheduling, tight IMF-imposed controls over domestic monetary and fiscal policies, and continued lending to debtor countries in hopes that economic growth would allow them to repay their creditors. (Map 4.2 shows the 15 countries affected by the Baker Plan at the beginning of 1993.) In Mexico's case, the IMF agreed to provide a loan package only if private foreign banks holding Mexican debt agreed to reschedule their loans and provide Mexico with additional financing. However, the debtor nations made little progress in repaying their loans. Debtors and creditors alike agreed that a new approach was needed. The 1989 **Brady Plan** (named after the Bush administration's treasury secretary, Nicholas Brady) focused on the need to reduce the debts of the troubled countries by writing off parts of the debts or by providing the countries with funds to buy back their loan notes at below face value. (See also "Going Global.")

The international debt crisis is receding in the 1990s as the debt servicing requirements of debtor countries have been made more manageable via a combination of IMF loans, debt rescheduling, and changes in governmental economic policies (see the discussion of economic reforms in Mexico, Argentina, and Brazil in Chapter 2). The impact of the crisis cannot be overstated. Many experts consider the 1980s the "lost decade" for economic development in Latin America. Yet the international debt crisis should not have come as a surprise. The BOP accounting system provided clear warning of the deteriorating competitiveness of the countries in crisis and the increasing riskiness of their overextended external debt positions. A careful reading of BOP statistics could have protected international bankers from bad investments and risky loans. Because the BOP accounting system provides such valuable economic intelligence information, the next section discusses it in detail.

GOING GLOBAL

Buying Bad Debts for Good Causes

It may come as a surprise that during the international debt crisis of the 1980s, an active market sprang up in the bad debts of countries. As prospects for repayment of these debts dimmed, some creditors were willing to accept less than full payment for their loan notes, happy to get at least some of their money back. Third parties often bought up this debt at a discount, speculating that it would ultimately be repaid. Discounts varied by country, depending on the market's assessment of the likelihood and the timing of debt repayment. In May 1988, for example, Peruvian debt was selling for 6 cents on the dollar, Bolivian debt for 13 cents on the dollar, and Mexican debt for about 54 cents on the dollar.

The international debt crisis was aided by the use of **debt-equity swaps** that resulted from the existence of this secondary market for bad debt. Some far-sighted entrepreneurs bought up discounted loan notes and swapped them for equity in companies in the host country. From the entrepreneur's perspective, the debt-equity swap was often a low-cost way of entering the host market. The host country gained in two ways: its debt burden was reduced, and it gained new investment capital.

Innovative environmentalists designed a different type of swap: **debt-for-nature swaps** that reduced the debt burden of the debtor countries while helping the environment. The Rainforest Alliance, for example, purchased Costa Rican debt at a 40 percent discount and swapped it

Many threatened habitats, such as this Costa Rican rain forest, were preserved as a result of the international debt crisis. Environmental groups purchased bonds issued by deeply indebted governments and swapped the bonds for land in danger of being developed.

for environmentally sensitive forest acreage in Costa Rica. It then deeded the land back to the Costa Rican government in return for a pledge to convert it into a national park to be forever unthreatened by developers. The Worldwide Fund for Nature purchased $9 million of Ecuadorian debt at 12 cents on the dollar to protect vital rain forest areas. The Dutch and Swedish governments used their foreign-aid dollars in similar debt-for-nature swaps.

Source: Stephen Fidler, "Trade-off of a heavy burden," *Financial Times*, May 22, 1991, p. 9.

The Balance of Payments Accounting System

Each year, countries purchase trillions of dollars of goods, services, and assets from each other. The BOP accounting system is a double-entry bookkeeping system designed to measure and record all economic transactions between residents of one country and residents of all other countries during a particular time period. It helps policymakers understand the performance of each country's economy in international markets. It also signals fundamental changes in the competitiveness of countries and assists policymakers in designing appropriate public policies to respond to these changes.

International businesspeople also need to pay close attention to countries' BOP statistics for several reasons, including the following:

1 BOP statistics help identify emerging markets for goods and services.

2 They can warn of possible new policies that may alter a country's business climate, thereby affecting the profitability of a firm's operations in that country. For example, sharp rises in a country's imports may signal an overheated economy and portend a tightening of the domestic money supply. In this case, attentive businesspeople will shrink their inventories in anticipation of a reduction in customer demand.

3 They can indicate reductions in a country's foreign-exchange reserves, which may mean that the country's currency will depreciate in the future. Exporters to that country may find that domestic producers will become more price competitive.

4 As was true in the international debt crisis, BOP statistics can signal increased riskiness of lending to particular countries.

Four important aspects of the BOP accounting system need to be highlighted:

1 The BOP accounting system records international transactions made during some time period, for example, a year.

2 It records only economic transactions, those that involve something of monetary value.

3 It records transactions between *residents* of different countries. Residents can be individuals, businesses, government agencies, or nonprofit organizations, but defining residency is sometimes tricky. Persons temporarily located in a country—tourists, students, and military or diplomatic personnel—are still considered residents of their home country for BOP purposes. Businesses are considered residents of the country in which they are incorporated. An unincorporated branch of an MNC is a resident of its home country, while an incorporated subsidiary is considered a resident of the host country.

4 It is a *double-entry system*. Each transaction produces a credit entry and a debit entry of equal size. In most international business dealings, the first entry in a BOP transaction involves the purchase or sale of something—a good, a service, or an asset. The second entry records the payment or receipt of payment for the thing bought or sold. Figuring out which is the BOP debit entry and which is the BOP credit entry is not a skill that most people are born with. Many experts compare a BOP accounting statement to a statement of sources and uses of funds. Debit entries reflect *uses* of funds; credit entries measure *sources* of funds. Under this framework, buying things creates debits, and selling things produces credits.

The Major Components of the BOP Accounting System

The BOP accounting system can be divided conceptually into four major accounts. The first two accounts—the current account and the capital account—record purchases of goods, services, and assets by the private and public sectors. The official reserves account reflects the impact of central bank intervention in the foreign-exchange market. The last account—errors and omissions—captures mistakes made in recording BOP transactions.

Current Account. The **current account** records four types of transactions among residents of different countries:

1 Exports and imports of goods (or merchandise)

2 Exports and imports of services

3 Investment income

4 Gifts

Table 4.4 summarizes debit and credit entries for transactions involving the current account.

For example, to Germany, the sale of a Mercedes-Benz automobile to a doctor in Marseilles is a **merchandise export**, and the purchase by a German resident of Dom Perignon champagne from France is a **merchandise import**. (The British use the term **trade in visibles** to refer to merchandise trade.) The difference between a country's exports and imports of goods is called the **balance on merchandise trade**. For example, the United States, which has been importing more goods than it has been exporting, has a *merchandise trade deficit*; Japan, which has been exporting more goods than it has been importing, has a *merchandise trade surplus*.

The services account records sales and purchases of such services as transportation, tourism, medical care, telecommunications, advertising, financial services, and education. The sale of a service to another country is a **service export**, and the purchase of a service from another country is a **service import**. (The British use the term **trade in invisibles** to denote trade in services.) For example, for Germany, a German student spending a year studying at the Sorbonne in Paris is an import of services, and the telephone call home that an Italian tourist makes during the Oktoberfest in Munich represents a service export. The difference between a country's exports of services and its imports of services is called the **balance on services trade**.

The third type of transaction recorded in the current account is investment income. Income German residents earn from their foreign investments is viewed as an **export of the services of capital** by Germany. This income takes the form of either interest and dividends earned by German residents on their investments in foreign stocks, bonds, and deposit accounts or profits that are repatriated back to Germany from incorporated subsidiaries in other countries that are owned by German firms. On the other hand, foreigners also make investments in Germany. Income earned by foreigners from their investments in Germany is viewed as an **import of the services of capital** by Germany. This income includes interest

TABLE 4.4

BOP Entries, Current Account

	DEBIT	CREDIT
Goods	Buy	Sell
Services	Buy	Sell
Dividends and interest (investment income)	Pay	Receive
Gifts	Give	Receive

and dividends paid by firms in Germany on stocks, bonds, and deposit accounts owned by foreign residents, as well as profits that are repatriated by foreign-owned incorporated subsidiaries in Germany back to their corporate parents.

The fourth type of transaction in the current account is **unilateral transfers**, or gifts between residents of one country and another. Unilateral transfers include private and public gifts. For example, a Pakistani-born resident of Kuwait who sends part of his earnings back home to feed his relatives is engaging in a private unilateral transfer. In contrast, governmental aid from the United Kingdom used for a flood control project in Bangladesh is a public unilateral transfer. In either case, the recipient need not provide any compensation to the donor.

The **current account balance** measures the net balance resulting from merchandise trade, service trade, investment income, and unilateral transfers. It is closely scrutinized by government officials and policymakers because it broadly reflects the country's current competitiveness in international markets.

Capital Account. The second major account in the BOP accounting system is the **capital account**, which records capital transactions—purchases and sales of assets—between residents of one country and those of other countries. Capital account transactions (summarized in Table 4.5), can be divided into two categories: foreign direct investment (FDI) and portfolio investment. (Recall that we discussed both of these in Chapter 1.)

FDI is any investment made for purpose of controlling the organization in which the investment is made, typically through ownership of significant blocks of common stock with voting privileges. Under U.S. BOP accounting standards, control is defined as ownership of at least 10 percent of a company's voting stock. A portfolio investment is any investment made for purposes other than control. Portfolio investments are divided into two subcategories: short-term and long-term. **Short-term portfolio investments** are financial instruments with maturities of one year or less. Included in this category are commercial paper; checking accounts, time deposits, and certificates of deposit held by residents of a country

---

TABLE 4.5

Capital Account Transactions

	MATURITY	MOTIVATION	TYPICAL INVESTMENTS
Portfolio (short-term)	One year or less	Investment income or facilitation of international commerce	Checking account balances Time deposits Commercial paper Bank loans
Portfolio (long-term)	More than one year	Investment income	Government bills, notes, and bonds Corporate stocks and bonds
Foreign direct investment	Indeterminate	Active control of organization (own at least 10 percent of voting stock)	Foreign subsidiaries Foreign factories International joint ventures

in foreign banks or by foreigners in domestic banks; trade receivables and deposits from international commercial customers; and banks' short-term international lending activities, such as commercial loans. **Long-term portfolio investments** are stocks, bonds, and other financial instruments issued by private and public organizations that have maturities greater than one year and that are held for purposes other than control. For example, when IBM invests excess cash balances overnight in a Paris bank to earn a higher interest rate than it could earn in New York, it is making a short-term portfolio investment. When the California Public Employers Retirement System Pension Fund buys stock in British Airways, it is making a long-term portfolio investment. When British Airways purchases 23 percent of the common stock of USAir, it is making an FDI.

Current account transactions invariably affect the short-term component of the capital account. Why? Well, as noted earlier in the chapter, the first entry in the double-entry BOP accounting system involves the purchase or sale of something—a good, a service, or an asset. The second entry typically records the payment or receipt of payment for the thing bought or sold. In most cases, this second entry involves a change in someone's checking account balance, which in the BOP accounting system is a short-term capital account transaction. "Building Global Skills" at the end of this chapter walks you through this linkage between the current account and the capital account in more detail.

Capital inflows are credits in the BOP accounting system. They can occur in two ways:

1 *Foreign ownership of assets in a country increases.* One highly publicized example of a capital inflow into the United States was the Mitsubishi Estate Co.'s 1989 purchase of 51 percent of the Rockefeller Group, owner of Rockefeller Center, for $846 million.[23] A capital inflow also occurs if a foreign firm deposits a check in a U.S. bank. In this case, the asset being purchased is a claim on a U.S. bank, which of course is all that a checking account balance represents.

2 *Ownership of foreign assets by a country's residents declines.* When the now defunct Pan American World Airways sold its West Berlin operations to Lufthansa for $158 million in 1990, the United States experienced a capital inflow. Similarly, when IBM pays a Japanese disk drive supplier with a check drawn on IBM's account at a Tokyo bank, IBM's Japanese checking account balance declines and the United States experiences a capital inflow because IBM is partially liquidating its ownership of foreign assets.

Capital outflows are debits in the BOP accounting system. They also can occur in two ways:

1 *Ownership of foreign assets by a country's residents increases.* Ford's £1.5 billion purchase of the British firm Jaguar Motor Company in 1990 represented a capital outflow from the United States. A U.S. capital outflow also occurs when Delta Air Lines deposits a check from a London businessperson into an account it holds in an English bank.

2 *Foreign ownership of assets in a country declines.* A German mutual fund that sells 100,000 shares of GM common stock from its portfolio causes a capital outflow from the United States. A U.S. capital outflow also occurs if Japan Air Lines writes

TABLE 4.6

BOP Entries, Capital Account

	DEBIT (OUTFLOW)	CREDIT (INFLOW)
Portfolio (short-term)	Receiving a payment from a foreigner	Making a payment to a foreigner
	Buying a short-term foreign asset	Selling a domestic short-term asset to a foreigner
	Buying back a short-term domestic asset from its foreign owner	Selling a short-term foreign asset acquired previously
Portfolio (long-term)	Buying a long-term foreign asset (not for purposes of control)	Selling a domestic long-term asset to a foreigner (not for purposes of control)
	Buying back a long-term domestic asset from its foreign owner (not for purposes of control)	Selling a long-term foreign asset acquired previously (not for purposes of control)
Foreign direct investment	Buying a foreign asset for purposes of control	Selling a domestic asset to a foreigner for purposes of control
	Buying back from its foreign owner a domestic asset previously acquired for purposes of control	Selling a foreign asset previously acquired for purposes of control

a check drawn on its account at a Hawaii bank to pay its fuel supplier at Honolulu Airport. In both cases, foreigners are liquidating a portion of their U.S. assets.

Table 4.6 summarizes the impact of various capital account transactions on the BOP.

Official Reserves Account. The third major account in the BOP accounting system is the official reserves account. The **official reserves account** records holdings of the official reserves held by a national government. These reserves are used to intervene in the foreign-exchange market and in transactions with other central banks. Official reserves comprise four types of assets:

1 Gold
2 Convertible currencies
3 SDRs
4 Reserve positions at the IMF

Official gold holdings are normally valued using prices determined in the London gold market. Convertible currencies are currencies that are freely exchangeable in world currency markets. The convertible currencies most commonly used as official reserves are the U.S. dollar, the deutsche mark, and the yen. The last two types of reserves—SDRs and reserve positions (quotas minus IMF borrowings) at the IMF—were discussed earlier in this chapter.

Errors and Omissions. The last account in the BOP accounting system is the errors and omissions account. One truism of the BOP accounting system is that the BOP must balance. In theory the following equality should be observed:

$$\text{Current Account} + \text{Capital Account} + \text{Official Reserves Account} = 0.$$

However, this equality is never achieved in practice because of measurement errors. The account called **errors and omissions** is used to make the BOP balance in accordance with the following equation:

$$\text{Current Account} + \text{Capital Account} + \text{Errors and Omissions} \\ + \text{Official Reserves Account} = 0.$$

The errors and omissions account can be quite large. In the chaotic year 1990, for example, the U.S. errors and omissions account totaled a record $73 billion. Experts suspect that a large portion of the errors and omissions account balance is due to underreporting of capital account transactions. Such innovations as instantaneous, round-the-clock foreign-exchange trading, sophisticated monetary swaps and hedges, and international money-market funds have made it difficult for governmental statisticians to keep up with the growing volume of legal short-term money flowing between countries in search of the highest interest rate. Sometimes, errors and omissions are due to deliberate actions by individuals who are engaged in illegal activities such as drug smuggling, money laundering, or evasion of currency and investment controls imposed by their home governments. Politically stable countries, such as the United States, are often the destination of **flight capital**, money sent abroad by foreign residents seeking a safe haven for their assets, hidden from the sticky fingers of their home governments. Given the often illegal nature of flight capital, persons sending it to the United States often try to avoid any official recognition of their transactions. For example, after Alberto Fujimori was elected president of Peru in July 1990, an estimated $600 million of previously unreported flight capital was repatriated back to Peru as citizens' confidence in their economy was restored.[24] Similarly, in the early 1990s governmental statisticians estimated that as much as $15 billion worth of U.S. dollar bills were tucked under mattresses of Middle Easterners and Eastern Europeans distrustful of their own currencies. Much of this hoarding would go unreported in the U.S. BOP accounts.[25] Germany faced a similar problem in 1991, when the former Soviet Union and former Yugoslavia were breaking up politically. The Bundesbank became alarmed, fearing increased inflation, because cash in circulation was expanding at 8.5 percent annually. Yet much of the increased holdings of deutsche marks was later attributed to their use by Soviet and Yugoslavian citizens distrustful of their own currencies in politically chaotic times.[26]

Some errors may crop up in the current account as well. Statistics for merchandise imports are generally thought to be reasonably accurate because most countries' customs services scrutinize imports to ensure that all appropriate taxes are collected. This scrutiny generates paper trails that facilitate the collection of accurate statistics. However, few countries tax exports, so customs services have less incentive to assess the accuracy of statistics concerning merchandise exports.

Statistics for trade in services also may contain inaccuracies. Many service trade statistics are generated by surveys. For example, U.S. tourism exports are measured by surveying foreign tourists on how many days they spent in the United States and how many dollars they spent per day. If tourists underestimate their daily spending, then U.S. service exports are underestimated. To help you gain a better understanding of the BOP accounts, we next review the international transactions of the United States in 1993.

The U.S. Balance of Payments in 1993

The first component of the current account is merchandise (goods) exports and imports. As shown in Table 4.7, U.S. merchandise exports totaled $456.9 billion in 1993, or approximately 7.2 percent of 1993's GDP of $6.377 trillion. Figure 4.5(a) presents a more detailed picture of the leading U.S. exports. Automobiles and auto parts were the largest component of U.S. merchandise exports, generating $52.4 billion in sales. Of U.S. automobile exports, 53 percent were to Canada, a reflection of the integrated nature of North American automobile production that resulted from the 1965 Auto Pact between the United States and Canada. (Canada—meaning primarily GM, Ford, and Chrysler plants that are located in Canada—exported $37.3 billion in automobiles and auto parts to the United States.) The six industries shown in Fig. 4.5(a) accounted for 45 percent of U.S. merchandise exports in 1993.

From Table. 4.7, you can see that U.S. merchandise *imports* totaled $589.4 billion in 1993.[27] From Fig. 4.5(b), you can see that the leading import was automobiles and auto parts, at $102.4 billion, or 17.4 percent of imports. Six industries accounted for $274 billion, or 46.5 percent of total U.S. merchandise imports.

The second component of the current account is trade in services. U.S. exports of services totaled $184.8 billion in 1993, with travel and tourism being the largest portion ($57.6 billion). U.S. service imports equaled $128.0 in 1993, with travel and tourism again being the largest portion ($40.6 billion). The United States had a positive balance on services trade of $56.8 billion (see Table 4.7).

Figure 4.6 shows exports and imports for the major trading partners of the United States. Unlike Figs. 4.5(a) and (b), this figure includes trade in both goods and services. While the United States tends to import more *goods* from its major trading partners than it exports to them, Fig. 4.6 shows it tends to export more *services* to them than it imports from them.

The third component of the current account is investment income (see Table 4.7). In 1993 U.S. residents received $113.9 billion from foreign investments and paid out $109.9 billion to foreigners for a net balance on investment income of $4.0 billion. The United States had a net deficit of $32.1 billion in the fourth component of the current account, unilateral transfers. Summing up the four components yielded a 1993 current account deficit of $103.9 billion.

The capital account is the second major BOP account (see Table 4.7). In 1993 new U.S. FDI abroad (outflows) totaled $57.9 billion, while new FDI in the U.S. (inflows) totaled $21.4 billion. New U.S. long-term international portfolio investments were $120.0 billion in 1993, while new foreign long-term portfolio investments in the United States were $162.0 billion, resulting in a net portfolio investment balance of $42.0 billion. There was also a net inflow of short-term portfolio investment in the United States, totaling $78.7 billion.

TABLE 4.7

U.S. BOP, 1993 (in billions of dollars)

Current Account

Goods		
Exports	+$456.9	
Imports	−589.4	
Balance on Merchandise Trade	−132.6	
Services		
Exports	+184.8	
Imports	−128.0	
Balance on Services Trade	+56.8	
Investment Income		
Received	113.9	
Paid	−109.9	
Balance on Investment Income	+4.0	
Unilateral Transfers (net)	−32.1	
(− means outward gifts greater than inward)		
Balance on Current Account		−103.9

Capital Account

Portfolio, Short-Term (Net Inflow)	+78.7	
Portfolio, Long-Term		
New Foreign Investment in U.S.	+162.0	
New U.S. Investment Abroad	−120.0	
Foreign Direct Investment		
New FDI in U.S.	+21.4	
New U.S. FDI Abroad	−57.9	
Balance on Capital Account		+84.2

Official Reserves Account	−1.4
Errors and Omissions	+21.1
Net Balance	0

The capital account balance was $84.2 billion in 1993, as foreigners bought more U.S. assets than U.S. residents did foreign assets.

U.S. official reserves account transactions were reported as −$1.4 billion, meaning the United States increased its official holdings. (Although that may seem backwards to you, the negative sign means that the U.S. government "purchased" official reserves from other countries.) If the BOP statistical data net were perfect, the current account balance plus the capital account balance plus the official reserves account balance should equal zero. Any discrepancy is put into the errors and omissions account. In 1993 there was a discrepancy of $21.1 billion. So for the U.S. BOP in 1993, the following equation applies:

$$\underset{(-\$103.9 \text{ billion})}{\text{Current}} + \underset{(\$84.2 \text{ billion})}{\text{Capital}} + \underset{(-\$1.4 \text{ billion})}{\text{Changes in}} + \underset{(\$21.1 \text{ billion})}{\text{Errors and}} = 0.$$

Defining Balance of Payments Surpluses and Deficits

Every month the federal government reports the performance of U.S. firms in international markets when it releases the monthly BOP statistics. In most months in the past decade, newscasters have solemnly reported on the evening news that the U.S. BOP is in deficit.

What do the newscasters mean? We just said that the BOP always balances (equals zero), so how can there be a BOP deficit? In reality, when knowledgeable people (or even newscasters) talk about a BOP surplus or deficit, they are referring only to a subset of the BOP accounts. Most newscasters are in fact reporting on the balance on trade in goods and services. When a country exports more goods and services than it imports, it has a trade surplus. When it imports more goods and services than it exports, it has a trade deficit.

Because the balance on trade in goods and services is readily understandable and quickly available to the news media, it receives the most public attention. But other balances also exist, for example, the balance on services, the balance on merchandise trade, the current account balance, and the **basic balance**, which is the sum of the current account balance plus net long-term capital investment.

Another BOP balance is the official settlements balance. The **official settlements balance** reflects changes in a country's official reserves and shows the amount of *accommodating* (or *compensatory*) transactions undertaken by the country's central bank. To understand what an accommodating transaction is, you first must know what an autonomous transaction is. An **autonomous transaction** is a transaction undertaken in the economic self-interest of the participants. All transactions that affect the current account or the capital account are autonomous

---

FIGURE 4.5

Leading U.S. Merchandise Exports and Imports, 1993

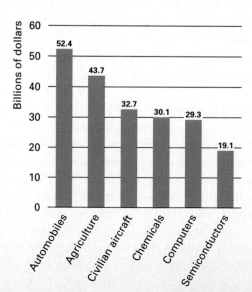

a. Leading U.S. merchandise exports, 1993

(Billions of dollars)

- Automobiles: 52.4
- Agriculture: 43.7
- Civilian aircraft: 32.7
- Chemicals: 30.1
- Computers: 29.3
- Semiconductors: 19.1

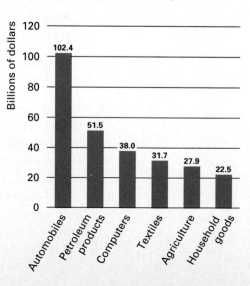

b. Leading U.S. merchandise imports, 1993

(Billions of dollars)

- Automobiles: 102.4
- Petroleum products: 51.5
- Computers: 38.0
- Textiles: 31.7
- Agriculture: 27.9
- Household goods: 22.5

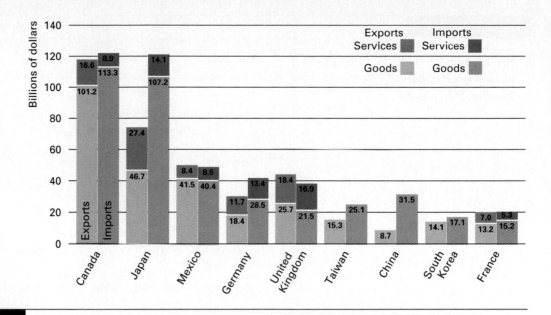

FIGURE 4.6

Exports and Imports Between the United States and its Major Trading Partners, 1993

Note: Data on services exports and imports are not available for Taiwan, China, and South Korea.

because exports and imports of goods or services and international investments are all motivated by the buyers' and sellers' self-interest. An **accommodating transaction**—sometimes called a **compensatory transaction**—is a transaction undertaken solely to accommodate (or compensate) for autonomous transactions. In a flexible exchange-rate system, accommodating transactions reflect the extent of the central bank's intervention in the foreign-exchange market.

Because BOP transactions are either autonomous or accommodating and the BOP accounts must always balance, by definition the following equation holds:

$$\text{Autonomous Transactions} + \text{Accommodating Transactions} = 0.$$

Accommodating transactions thus must equal the negative of autonomous transactions. If current account and capital account transactions are autonomous in nature—and the errors and omissions account is presumed to reflect unmeasured autonomous transactions—then accommodating transactions must equal the official reserves account balance.

Which of these BOP balances is *the* balance of payments? That's a trick question; there is no single measure of a country's global economic performance. Rather, as in the parable of the blind men touching the elephant, each balance presents a different perspective on the nation's position in the international economy. Which BOP concept to use depends on the issue confronting the international businessperson or government policymaker. The balance on merchandise trade reflects the competitiveness of a country's manufacturing sector. The balance on services reflects the service sector's global competitiveness. While the balance on merchandise trade often receives more publicity, the balance on services is growing in importance because of the expansion of the service sector in many national economies. The balance on goods and services reflects the combined international competitiveness of a country's manufacturing and service sectors. The current account balance shows the combined performance of the manufacturing and service sectors and also reflects the generosity of the country's residents (unilateral

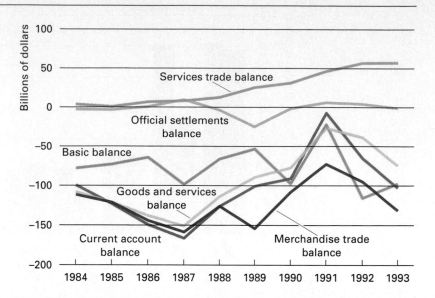

FIGURE 4.7

The U.S. BOP
According to Various
Reporting Measures

transfers) as well as income generated by past investments. The basic balance combines current account transactions with long-term capital investments. Because it excludes short-term capital flows that can be manipulated by the central bank through interest rate changes, some analysts believe the basic balance shows the true underlying private demand for a country's currency. The official settlements balance includes all autonomous transactions (including short-term capital movements) and thus is a record of all demand and supply (other than that of the central bank) for the country's currency.[28] Figure 4.7 shows the U.S. balance of payments for the past decade according to these various measures.

CHAPTER REVIEW

Summary

In their normal commercial activities, international businesses often deal with currencies other than that of their home country. For international commerce to thrive, some system for exchanging and valuing different currencies, preferably at low cost, must exist. The international monetary system accomplishes this by establishing the rules for valuing and exchanging different currencies.

The economic growth of the nineteenth century is attributable in part to the success of the gold standard in providing a stable, reliable international monetary system based on fixed exchange rates. However, the gold standard broke down during World War I and could not be satisfactorily revived in the years between the two world wars.

The Bretton Woods Agreement of 1944 structured the post–World War II international monetary system. In addition to creating the International Bank for Reconstruction and Development (the World Bank) and the International Monetary Fund, it reinstituted a fixed exchange-rate system, with the dollar playing a key role in international transactions. However, as the number of dollars held by foreigners increased, the marketplace began to distrust the ability of the United States to redeem its currency at $35 per ounce of gold as required by the Bretton Woods Agreement. After fending off waves of speculation against the dollar, the United States abandoned the Bretton Woods Agreement in August 1971.

Since then, the international monetary system has relied on a flexible exchange-rate system, although certain countries, such as the EU members, have attempted to maintain fixed exchange rates among their currencies. The system has proven responsive to major shocks to the world economy, such as the shift of wealth from oil-consuming to oil-producing countries after the 1973–1974 oil embargo and the 1980s international debt crisis.

The BOP accounting system, which is used to record international transactions, is important to international businesspeople. The BOP system provides economic intelligence data about the international competitiveness of a country's industries, likely changes in its fiscal and monetary policies, and its ability to repay its international debts.

The BOP accounting system comprises four accounts. The current account reflects exports and imports of goods, exports and imports of services, investment income, and gifts. The capital account records capital transactions among countries and includes FDI and portfolio investments. Portfolio investments in turn can be divided into long-term and short-term investments. The official reserves account is a record of changes in a country's official reserves, which include central bank holdings of gold, convertible currencies, SDRs, and reserves at the International Monetary Fund. The errors and omissions account captures statistical discrepancies that often result from transactions that participants want to hide from government officials.

There are numerous ways to measure a balance of payments surplus or deficit. Each presents a different perspective on a country's global economic performance. The balance on merchandise trade measures the difference between a country's exports and imports of goods. The balance on services is growing in importance because of the rapid expansion of the service sector in many economies. The balance on goods and services measures the nation's trade in goods and services. The current account balance reflects both trade in goods and trade in services, as well as net investment income and gifts. The basic balance is a combination of the current account balance and long-term capital investments. The official settlements balance shows changes in the country's official reserves.

Review Questions

1. What is the function of the international monetary system?

2. Why is the gold standard a type of fixed exchange-rate system?

3. What were the key accomplishments of the Bretton Woods conference?

4. Why was the IFC established by the World Bank?

5. Why are quotas important to IMF members?

6. Why did the Bretton Woods system collapse in 1971?

7. Describe the differences between a fixed exchange-rate system and a flexible exchange-rate system.

8. List the four major accounts of the BOP accounting system and their components.

9. What factors cause measurement errors in the BOP accounts?

10. Differentiate among the different types of balance of payments surpluses and deficits.

Questions for Discussion

1. What parallels exist between the role of the British pound in the nineteenth-century international monetary system and that of the U.S. dollar since 1945?

2. Did the key role that the dollar played in the Bretton Woods system benefit or hurt the United States?

3. Under what conditions might a country devalue its currency today?

4. Are there any circumstances under which a country might want to increase its currency's value?

5. Can international businesses operate more easily in a fixed exchange-rate system or in a flexible exchange-rate system?

6. What connections exist between the current account and the capital account?

This Building Global Skills exercise explains how governmental statisticians account for international transactions. You may want to refer back to Tables 4.4 and 4.6 and to the definitions of capital inflows and capital outflows.

Example 1

Suppose Wal-Mart imports $1 million worth of VCRs from the Sony Corporation of Japan. The debit entry is a merchandise import of $1 million. The import of the Japanese goods means the United States will observe an outflow (or a use) of foreign exchange.

Here's the tough part. What is the offsetting credit entry? The answer is a capital inflow affecting the short-term portfolio account. Recall that a capital inflow occurs because of either an increase in foreign-owned U.S. assets or a decrease of U.S.-owned foreign assets. If Wal-Mart pays Sony with a $1 million check that Sony deposits in its U.S. bank, foreign ownership of assets in the United States increases, which is a short-term capital inflow. If Wal-Mart pays Sony in yen by drawing down a Wal-Mart checking account balance at a Tokyo bank, a decrease of U.S.-owned assets in foreign countries occurs, which is also a short-term capital inflow. Either way, a short-term capital inflow occurs, since the VCRs are being exchanged for a change in a checking account balance.

What if Wal-Mart pays Sony with a $1 million check, but Sony wants yen? Sony will take the check to its U.S. bank and ask the bank to convert the $1 million check to yen. The U.S. bank can accommodate Sony in one of two ways:

1. Give Sony yen that the U.S. bank already owns—this represents a decrease of U.S.-owned foreign assets.

2. Pass the check along to a Japanese bank that keeps the $1 million but gives Sony the equivalent in yen—this represents an increase in U.S. assets owned by foreigners (the Japanese bank).

In either case, a capital inflow occurs.

Thus Wal-Mart's purchase of the VCRs from Sony enters the BOP accounts as follows:

	DEBIT	CREDIT
Merchandise imports account	$1 million	
Short-term portfolio account		$1 million

The merchandise import account is debited to reflect a use of funds. The payment itself is credited because effectively a foreigner has purchased a U.S. asset (either an increase in foreign claims on the United States or a decrease in U.S. claims on foreigners). Note the linkage between the current account and the capital account.

Example 2

A Vietnamese restaurant owner in Los Angeles who escaped Vietnam as a "boat person" in 1984 smuggles $1,000 in cash back to her relatives in Ho Chi Minh City. The U.S. BOP accounts *should* record this transaction as follows:

	DEBIT	CREDIT
Unilateral transfer account	$1,000	
Short-term portfolio account		$1,000

The transaction involves a unilateral transfer, since the $1,000 is a gift. Because the gift is being given by a U.S. resident, it is a debit. The capital account is credited because foreigners have increased their claims on the United States. (A country's currency reflects a claim on its goods, services, and assets.) Had the restaurant owner sent a $1,000 stereo system instead of cash, the credit entry would have been a merchandise export.

Note the use of the qualifier *should* in the previous paragraph. If U.S. governmental statisticians were omniscient, the transaction would be recorded as just explained. However, because the transaction violated Vietnamese law, it is unlikely U.S. statisticians would ever learn of it. When you consider the widespread usage of the dollar in countries suffering political turmoil, it is not surprising that the errors and omissions account is as large as it is.

Example 3

Mitsubishi buys 51 percent of Rockefeller Center for $846 million from a Rockefeller family trust. This transaction will be recorded in the U.S. BOP accounts as follows:

	DEBIT	CREDIT
Foreign direct investment account		$846 million
Short-term portfolio account	$846 million	

In this transaction, two assets are being exchanged. Japan is buying a long-term asset—Rockefeller Center—for purposes of control, and the United States is buying a short-term asset called an "increase of claims on foreigners or a decrease of foreign claims on the United States." The U.S. BOP is credited with a long-term FDI capital inflow of $846 million, because foreign ownership of U.S. assets (for purposes of control) has increased. But the actual payment of the $846 million is debited as a short-term capital outflow:

either Japanese-owned checking account balances in the United States declined by $846 million or U.S.-owned checking account balances in Japan rose by $846 million.

Unlike Examples 1 and 2, this transaction does not involve a current account entry and a capital account entry. Both the debit entry and the credit entry affect the capital account. However, a balance in someone's checking account is affected by this transaction, as was the case in Example 1.

Do the following exercise on your own. How will the following transactions be recorded in the U.S. BOP accounts?

1. A British entrepreneur seeking to sell souvenirs at the 1996 Summer Olympics pays Delta Airlines (a U.S. carrier) £500 (worth $750) for a London-Atlanta round-trip ticket.

2. The British entrepreneur instead pays British Airways (a British carrier) £500 (worth $750) for a London-Atlanta round-trip ticket.

3. Ford Motor Company (U.S.) pays $2.5 billion for the Jaguar Motor Co. (U.K.).

4. Kuwait gives the United States $1 billion in gratitude for its help in the Persian Gulf War.

CLOSING CASE

Recent U.S. BOP Performance: Is the Sky Falling or Not?

During much of the past decade, the U.S. BOP performance could be characterized as follows:

▶ The U.S. current account recorded large annual deficits.

▶ The U.S. capital account recorded large annual surpluses of roughly the same magnitude as the current account deficits.

▶ Changes in the official reserves account were small relative to the magnitude of the current account deficits.

Two scenarios can be developed from these three facts:

1. The sky is falling. U.S. industries are uncompetitive in international markets (as indicated by the first fact), and foreigners are taking over the country by buying up valuable U.S. assets and transforming the country into the largest debtor in international history (as indicated by the second fact).

2. Everything is wonderful. Foreigners are so enthralled with the future prospects of the U.S. market, which is a showcase of economic democracy, that they are eagerly investing in the U.S. economy (the second fact). But the only

way they can do so is by running a current account surplus with the United States (the first fact).

Needless to say, these two scenarios conflict, *even though both are consistent with the data.* They reflect a policy war that is occurring between protectionists and free traders, between Rust Belt firms and Sunbelt firms, between liberals and conservatives, and between export-oriented firms and firms threatened by foreign imports.

People who believe the sky is falling argue that the United States must reduce its balance of trade deficit. They argue that U.S. firms are increasingly uncompetitive in global markets and must be strengthened via aggressive government policies, such as those calling for worker training programs, increased investment in infrastructure, and tax credits for R&D and investment expenditures. They assert that U.S. firms are victimized by the unfair trade practices of foreign firms and governments. They propose stiffer tariffs and quotas on imported goods and believe that the federal government should do more to promote U.S. exports and restrict foreign ownership of U.S. assets.

People who believe everything is wonderful say the best policy is to continue to make the United States an attractive economy in which to invest. By keeping tax rates low and governmental regulation modest, the United States will attract foreign capital. U.S. industries, consumers, and workers will then benefit from increased capital investment and the enhancements in productivity that will ensue from this investment. U.S. consumers will benefit from the availability of low-priced, high-quality imported goods and services. Moreover, U.S. firms will become "leaner and meaner" as they respond to foreign competitors.

A variant of this "everything is wonderful" argument has been offered by Nobel laureate Milton Friedman, the provocative free-market advocate from the University of Chicago. Friedman argues that Japanese workers have been busily producing VCRs, Toyota Camrys, and Sony Walkmans in return for dollar bills from U.S. consumers. If the Japanese are happy voluntarily exchanging their goods for pieces of paper (that is, dollar bills), and U.S. citizens are happy voluntarily exchanging

pieces of paper for goods, why should anyone worry?

As you ponder these divergent perspectives, recognize that they have developed because of two very different views of what represents a BOP deficit. The "sky is falling" crowd is focusing on the balance on merchandise trade and assessing whether U.S. firms are able to sell as many goods to foreigners as foreigners buy from U.S. firms. The "everything is wonderful" folks are focusing on autonomous transactions. In their view, if U.S. citizens find it in their self-interest to be net buyers of foreign goods and foreigners find it in their self-interest to be net buyers of U.S. assets, then what's the problem?

Because BOP statistics affect the ongoing domestic political battle over international trade policy, they are important to virtually every U.S. firm. Export-oriented firms and workers benefit from the free-trade policies promoted by the "everything is wonderful" crowd, as do communities that benefit from jobs created by inward FDI. Firms and workers threatened by imported goods or by the output of new domestic factories built by foreign competitors are more likely to support the "sky is falling" view.

Case Questions

1. What is more important to the U.S. economy—exports or foreign capital inflows?

2. What is the connection between the U.S. current account deficit and capital account surplus?

3. Which of the following groups is likely to endorse the "sky is falling" view of the U.S. BOP?

   ▶ Import-threatened firms such as textile producers
   ▶ Textile workers
   ▶ A cash-starved California biotechnology company
   ▶ Merrill Lynch
   ▶ Boeing Aircraft, one of the country's largest exporters
   ▶ Consumers

Chapter Notes

1. *Wall Street Journal,* June 27, 1994, p. C1.

2. *Wall Street Journal,* June 27, 1994, p. A1.

3. *Wall Street Journal,* June 29, 1994, pp. A2, A8. Reprinted by permission of *The Wall Street Journal,* © 1994 Dow Jones & Company, Inc. All Rights Reserved Worldwide.

4. *Wall Street Journal,* July 1, 1994, p. C21.

5. *Wall Street Journal,* July 5, 1994, p. A7. Reprinted by permission of *The Wall Street Journal,* © 1994 Dow Jones & Company, Inc. All Rights Reserved Worldwide.

6. Del Mar, *A History of Money in Ancient Countries* (New York: Burt Franklin, 1968; originally published in 1885), p. 71.

7. I. Drummond, *The Gold Standard and the International Monetary System 1900–1939* (London: MacMillan Education Group, 1987), p. 10–11.

8. At the turn of the century, the French franc and the German mark were used in addition to sterling for settling private international transactions. For more details, see P. Lindert, "Key Currencies and Gold 1900–1913," *Princeton Studies in International Finance* No. 24 (Princeton: Department of Economics, 1969), p. 1. See also D. Williams, "The Evaluation of the Sterling System," in *Essays in Money and Banking in Honor of R. S. Sayers,* ed. by C. Whittlesley and J. Wilson (Oxford, 1968).

9. B. Cohen, *The Future of Sterling as an International Currency* (London: MacMillan, 1971), pp. 60–61.

10. Drummond, op.cit., p. 31.

11. Ibid., pp. 40ff.

12. Cohen, op.cit., p. 68.

13. The World Bank, *The World Bank Annual Report 1993,* p. 165.

14. The World Bank, *The World Bank* (New York: World Bank, 1991), p. 17.

15. The World Bank, *The World Bank Annual Report 1993,* p. 165.

16. Multilateral Investment Guarantee Agency, *Annual Report 1991,* pp. 13–14.

17. Stephen Riddell, "U.S. set to compromise on World Bank loan policy," *Financial Times,* June 10, 1991, p. 1; "U.S. Agrees to Capital Increase for IFC, Backing Down From Earlier Demands," *Wall Street Journal,* July 1, 1991, p. C14; "New Regime Forming at World Bank That Is Likely to Increase Role of U.S.," *Wall Street Journal,* September 17, 1991, p. B5; "Aid and enterprise," *The Economist,* May 25, 1991, p. 18.

18. The World Bank. *The World Bank* (New York: World Bank, 1991), p. 15.

19. "Poland Passes Budget Bill That Is Approved by IMF," *Wall Street Journal,* June 8, 1992, p. A8.

20. International Monetary Fund, *1990 Annual Report,* p. 133.

21. Eitemann, Stonehill, and Moffett, *Multinational Business Finance,* 6th ed. (Reading, Mass.: Addison-Wesley, 1992), p. 30.

22. *The European Financial Common Market* (Luxembourg: Office for Official Publications of the European Communities, 1989), pp. 43ff.; *The European Community in the Nineties* (Washington, D.C.: EC Delegation to the United States, 1992), pp. 12ff.; Directorate-General for Economic and Financial Affairs, *European Economy,* No. 44 (October 1990), p. 42.

23. "Mitsubishi Estate Resembles Rockefeller," *Wall Street Journal,* November 1, 1989, p. A11.

24. "Suddenly the money goes home to Peru," *The Economist,* June 22, 1991, p. 43.

25. "Off to the Tune of $73 Billion," *Wall Street Journal,* May 24, 1991, p. A2; "Counterfeit Bills Confound Detectors at the Fed, Sleuths at the Secret Service," *Wall Street Journal,* July 3, 1992, p. A8.

26. Norman, Peter, "The mystery of the D-marks that disappear," *Financial Times,* October 10, 1991, p. 17.

27. *Survey of Current Business,* June 1994, pp. 86ff.

28. "Basic truths," *The Economist,* August 24, 1991, p. 68.

CHAPTER

5

Foreign Exchange and International Financial Markets

Chapter Outline

The economics of foreign exchange

The demand for foreign exchange
The supply of foreign exchange
Determination of the equilibrium price

Balance of payments equilibrium

Fixed exchange-rate system
Flexible exchange-rate system
Pros and cons of the two types of
exchange-rate systems

The structure of the foreign-exchange market

The role of banks
Spot and forward markets
Arbitrage and the currency market

The international capital market

Major international banks
The Eurocurrency market
The international bond market
Global equity markets
Offshore financial centers

After studying this chapter you should be able to:

Describe how demand and supply determine the price of foreign exchange.

Analyze how balance of payments equilibrium is reached in a fixed exchange-rate system and a flexible exchange-rate system.

Discuss the role of international banks in the foreign-exchange market.

Assess the different ways firms can use the spot and forward markets to settle international transactions.

Summarize the role of arbitrage in the foreign-exchange market.

Discuss the important aspects of the international capital market.

NEW YORK—"IT'S BEEN BEDLAM—PEOPLE ARE TRYING TO GET prices and can't find them," says Paul Farrell, one of the senior currency traders at Chase Manhattan Bank, on one of the foreign-exchange market's wildest days ever. ■■ Britain has just raised its interest rates twice to defend the pound, but it isn't working. The pound is slipping. The entire European exchange-rate system is in doubt. Rumors are flying, and the dollar is rallying. ■■ Thirty-five floors above Chase Manhattan Plaza yesterday morning, a small army of 50 traders and salespeople is trying to ride the billion-dollar waves sweeping across the currency markets. Hunched over banks of phones and green electronic quote screens, they bark out customer

Exchange-Rate Chaos[1]

orders or price quotes as currency trading machines emit a series of ever-louder, high-pitched beeps, seeking prices from Chase. ■■ "We knew this week would be wild, but not like this," says Geoff Koestner, a European currency trader seated near Mr. Farrell. It's all been unraveling." Now, Chase's traders want to avoid risks and mistakes at all costs. "The whole idea is just be square," Mr. Koestner explains. "Do the deal. Make the money and get out."… ■■ As one trader gets a substantial customer order, he stands up and shouts out for exchange-rate quotes from other Chase traders who specialize in the currencies involved. Then the other traders try to fill the customer's order as quickly as possible—before the market moves or the order is canceled. Usually, one or two traders will be standing at any given time, swapping prices and orders. This day, seven or eight are standing at once, sometimes nearly the entire roomful of traders are on their feet. ■■ Chase, which ranked No. 5 among big U.S. banks with $215 million in 1991 foreign-exchange trading profits, is doing twice its normal trading volume—and making more than twice a normal day's profits, says James Borden, Chase's head of foreign exchange. With the currency market so chaotic, the spread between bids and offering prices is far wider than usual. For Chase, that can be good news, as it makes much of its currency-trading profits from such bid-asked spreads, instead of betting heavily on the market's direction. ■■ At 11:15 a.m., a grave Mr. Farrell stands up and tells other traders: "The central banks are gone here"—meaning the world's central banks appear to have temporarily abandoned their efforts to support the wobbling British pound. A few moments later, Joseph Greene, a sandy-haired bespectacled "sterling-mark" trader, stands and announces that a customer wants to sell £100 million and buy German marks. "There are no prices!" shouts Arnold Neimanis, who trades marks and is on the phone constantly to other brokers who are making price quotes.… ■■ Instead of making a bid—and taking the risk of holding the pounds with the market so disorderly—the Chase traders persuade the customer to allow them to execute the order bit by bit. Over the next few minutes, Chase executes half the trade, £5 million at a time; but the customer decides to stop at £50 million. ▌▌ To veteran currency traders such as Mr. Farrell, the signs of turmoil are everywhere. Normally, he says, currency bid-asked spreads move in orderly progressions, for example, 10–20, then 15–25, then 20–30. The numbers denote the last two digits of a currency's price, such as 1.5220 marks per dollar. Dealers give price quotes without necessarily knowing whether the customer wants to buy or sell, and so must be prepared to buy or sell at the quoted price. At 10–20, the dealer would be offering to buy dollars at 1.5210 or sell at 1.5220. Today, the progression is more like 10–30, then 50–80. ▌▌ Around 11:45, Rick Walsh, a trader who sits opposite Mr. Neimanis, warns him urgently: "Don't be exposed. They're buying dollars on the floor"—meaning the dollar may be moving up sharply against the mark. A few moments later, Mr. Neimanis calls out: "Just buy it, just buy it." Seated next to him, Russell Lascala marvels, "This dollar is going to the moon!" ▌▌ Around noon, Seth Cohen, a salesman, approaches Mr. Neimanis to confer about a rumor that the German central bank is about to hold a news conference. The dollar keeps rising. As the U.S. currency rises through 1.52 marks per dollar, Mr. Neimanis cries out happily, "This thing is bid! I just got paid the figure [meaning 1.5200 exactly]! 152! We're over the figure!" ▌▌ At noon, Chase's traders normally troop outside the trading room for lunch; today, a trader hauls a stack of five large pizza boxes to the window sills. The traders stack pizza slices on paper plates precariously atop their quote machines. ▌▌ With the rumors flying and uncertainty at its peak, Mr. Neimanis gives an indication of an unusually wide market spread of 40–80. "It's so thin that people are afraid to make prices," he explains. When the customer decides to sell at 40, it suddenly appears that the dollar is falling back. "Really?" he says, incredulously. Seconds later, he says, "They just hit a quarter," meaning someone just bought at 25, indicating the dropoff is continuing. ▌▌▌▌▌

One factor that obviously distinguishes international business from domestic business is the involvement of more than one currency in commercial transactions. If Kaufhof, one of Germany's leading department stores, purchases kitchen appliances from Munich-based Siemens AG, that is a domestic transaction that will be done entirely in deutsche marks. But if Kaufhof chooses to purchase the appliances from Iowa-based Maytag Corporation, this international transaction will require some mechanism for exchanging deutsche marks, Kaufhof's home currency, and U.S. dollars, Maytag's home currency. The foreign-exchange market exists to facilitate this conversion of currencies, thereby allowing firms to conduct trade more efficiently across national boundaries. The foreign-exchange market also facilitates international investment and capital flows. Firms can shop for low-cost financing in capital markets around the world and then use the foreign-exchange market to convert the foreign funds they obtain into whatever currency they require.

The Economics of Foreign Exchange

Foreign exchange is a commodity that consists of currencies issued by countries other than one's own. Like the prices of other commodities, the price of foreign exchange—given a flexible exchange-rate system—is set by demand and supply in the marketplace, as the opening case indicates. Let's look more closely at what this means by using the market between U.S. dollars and deutsche marks as an example.

The Demand for Foreign Exchange

Like every other textbook demand curve, the demand curve for deutsche marks (DM) is downward sloping. When the price of marks, P_1, is high, as it is at point A in Fig. 5.1(b), the quantity of marks demanded, Q_1, is low. As the price of marks falls to P_2—as you move from point A to point B in Fig. 5.1(b)—the quantity of marks demanded increases, to Q_2.

But what causes the demand for marks in the first place? Most foreigners don't want marks because they like pieces of colored paper with German writing on them. Rather, the demand for marks derives from foreigners' demand for goods, services, and assets that German residents offer for sale, as suggested by Fig. 5.1(a). For simplicity, we label these goods, services, and assets "German products." When the price of German products, P_1, is high, as it is at point A in Fig. 5.1(a), the quantity of German products demanded by foreigners, Q_1, is low. The quantity of marks demanded, which is derived from foreigners' desires for German products, also is low [see point A in Fig. 5.1(b)]. As the price of German products drops to P_2, the quantity of German products demanded by foreigners rises to Q_2—as shown by a movement from point A to point B in Fig. 5.1(a). The quantity of marks demanded, derived from the demand for German products, also rises—as shown by the movement from point A to point B in Fig. 5.1(b).

FIGURE 5.1

The Demand for Deutsche Marks Is Derived from Foreigners' Demand for German Products

a. Foreigners' demand for German products

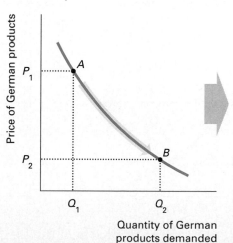

b. Foreigners' demand for DM

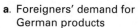
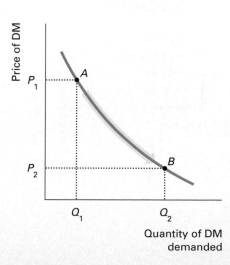

The Supply of Foreign Exchange

Similarly, the supply curve for marks is upward sloping. As with the prices of other goods, when the price of marks is low, the quantity of marks supplied is also low, represented by point *A* in Fig. 5.2(b). As the price of marks rises, the quantity supplied also rises, as you can see when you move from point *A* to point *B* in Fig. 5.2(b). The supply curve for marks thus behaves like most other supply curves: people offer more marks for sale as the price of marks rises.

As Fig. 5.2(a) shows, underlying the supply curve for marks is Germans' desire to buy foreign goods, services, and assets. To buy foreign products, Germans need to obtain foreign currencies, which they do by selling marks and using the proceeds to buy the foreign currencies. Selling marks has the effect of supplying marks to the foreign-exchange market.

Figure 5.2(a) indicates that when the price of foreign products is *high* (as at point *A*), the quantity of foreign products Germans demand is *low*. Correspondingly, point *A* in Fig. 5.2(b) indicates that the amount of marks the Germans are willing to sell in order to buy the foreign goods is also *low*. As the price of foreign products *falls*, the quantity of those products that Germans want to buy *rises*, shown as a movement from *A* to *B* in Fig. 5.2(a). The amount of marks the Germans are willing to sell in order to buy the foreign products also *rises*, shown as the movement from *A* to *B* in Fig. 5.2(b). As with any well-behaved supply curve, the quantity of marks supplied rises as the price of marks rises.[2]

Determination of the Equilibrium Price

Figure 5.3 illustrates the market for marks. Points along the vertical axis show the price of marks in dollars—how many dollars one must pay for each mark purchased. Points along the horizontal axis show the quantity of marks. As in other markets, the intersection of the supply curve (*S*) and the demand curve (*D*) yields the market-clearing, equilibrium price ($0.60/DM1 in this case) and the equilibrium quantity demanded and supplied (DM200). Recall from Chapter 4 that this

---

FIGURE 5.2

The Supply of Deutsche Marks Is Derived from Germans' Demand for Foreign Products

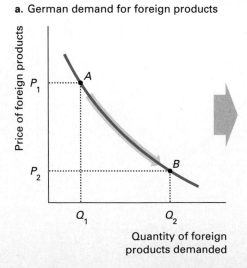

a. German demand for foreign products

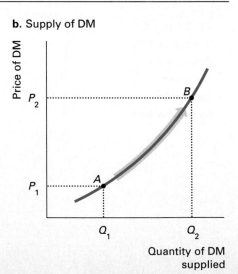

b. Supply of DM

GOING GLOBAL

A Brief Hint

Not everyone reading this book is a finance major. Some readers may have difficulty with the concept of using money to buy money and what is meant by a currency's value rising or falling. If you are having trouble with this, here's a simple trick. In Fig. 5.3, replace the currency that is being bought and sold with the phrase *loaf of bread* (or the name of any other tangible good). If you do this, then the vertical-axis is the price in dollars of one unit of bread and the horizontal-axis is the quantity of bread sold—a standard supply and demand graph that you encountered in your basic economics course. Nothing has changed in the supply and demand graph except the label. Think about this until you feel comfortable with the notion that deutsche marks are merely a good like bread or widgets.

As you read the rest of the book, if you get confused about what is up and what is down when we say a currency is rising or falling in value, you can use the same trick. For example, suppose that on Monday the British pound is worth $1.73 and on Tuesday it is worth $1.74. From Monday to Tuesday, the pound rose in value, while the dollar fell in value. If that's obvious to you, fine. If it isn't, substitute *loaf of bread* for *pound*. A statement about this example would then read "On Monday a loaf of bread is worth $1.73, and on Tuesday a loaf of bread is worth $1.74." The conclusion is that a loaf of bread has gone up in value, because more dollars are needed to buy it on Tuesday. Or, you can say the dollar has gone down in value, because each dollar on Tuesday buys less bread.

equilibrium price is called the *exchange rate*, the price of one country's currency in terms of another country's currency. (See "Going Global" for a better understanding of these processes.)

Although Fig. 5.3 illustrates the dollar-mark foreign-exchange market, a similar figure could be drawn for every possible pair of currencies in the world, each of which would constitute a separate market, with the equilibrium prices of the currencies determined by the supply of and demand for them. Foreign-exchange rates are published daily in most major newspapers worldwide. For example, Fig. 5.4 presents rates for January 10, 1995, published in the *Wall Street Journal*. These rates are quoted in two ways. A **direct exchange rate**

FIGURE 5.3

The Market for Deutsche Marks

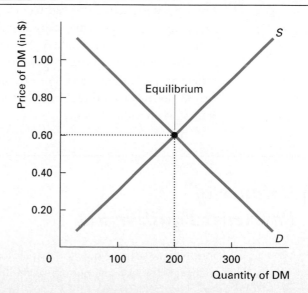

FIGURE 5.4

Direct and Indirect Exchange Rates

Source: *Wall Street Journal*, January 11, 1995, p. C19. Reprinted by permission of *The Wall Street Journal*, © 1995 Dow Jones & Company, Inc. All Rights Reserved Worldwide.

CURRENCY TRADING

EXCHANGE RATES
Tuesday, January 10, 1995

The New York foreign exchange selling rates below apply to trading among banks in amounts of $1 million and more, as quoted at 3 p.m. Eastern time by Bankers Trust Co., Dow Jones Telerate Inc. and other sources. Retail transactions provide fewer units of foreign currency per dollar.

Country	U.S. $ equiv. Tues.	U.S. $ equiv. Mon.	Currency per U.S. $ Tues.	Currency per U.S. $ Mon.
Argentina (Peso)	1.00	1.00	1.00	1.00
Australia (Dollar)	.7668	.7634	1.3042	1.3100
Austria (Schilling)	.09241	.09124	10.82	10.96
Bahrain (Dinar)	2.6524	2.6524	.3770	.3770
Belgium (Franc)	.03169	.03162	31.56	31.63
Brazil (Real)	1.1778563	1.1841323	.85	.84
Britain (Pound)	1.5610	1.5638	.6406	.6395
30-Day Forward	1.5608	1.5635	.6407	.6396
90-Day Forward	1.5605	1.5634	.6408	.6396
180-Day Forward	1.5600	1.5632	.6410	.6397
Canada (Dollar)	.7086	.7101	1.4113	1.4083
30-Day Forward	.7083	.7101	1.4118	1.4083
90-Day Forward	.7074	.7093	1.4137	1.4098
180-Day Forward	.7050	.7075	1.4185	1.4134
Czech Rep. (Koruna)				
Commercial rate	.0359428	.0356328	27.8220	28.0640
Chile (Peso)	.002465	.002472	405.75	404.55
China (Renminbi)	.118460	.118453	8.4417	8.4422
Colombia (Peso)	.001185	.001193	844.00	838.00
Denmark (Krone)	.1653	.1655	6.0495	6.0430
Ecuador (Sucre)				
Floating rate	.000433	.000433	2311.00	2311.00
Finland (Markka)	.20964	.21024	4.7700	4.7565
France (Franc)	.18877	.18834	5.2975	5.3095
30-Day Forward	.18880	.18838	5.2967	5.3083
90-Day Forward	.18893	.18852	5.2931	5.3044
180-Day Forward	.18913	.18875	5.2873	5.2980
Germany (Mark)	.6517	.6509	1.5345	1.5364
30-Day Forward	.6522	.6514	1.5334	1.5351
90-Day Forward	.6537	.6530	1.5296	1.5314
180-Day Forward	.6566	.6558	1.5230	1.5250
Greece (Drachma)	.004199	.004193	238.15	238.50
Hong Kong (Dollar)	.12885	.12894	7.7610	7.7553
Hungary (Forint)	.0089405	.0088754	111.8501	112.6710
India (Rupee)	.03188	.03188	31.37	31.37
Indonesia (Rupiah)	.0004531	.0004541	2207.02	2202.00
Ireland (Punt)	1.5457	1.5480	.6470	.6460
Israel (Shekel)	.3318	.3322	3.0140	3.0103
Italy (Lira)	.0006148	.0006177	1626.50	1619.00

Country	U.S. $ equiv. Tues.	U.S. $ equiv. Mon.	Currency per U.S. $ Tues.	Currency per U.S. $ Mon.
Japan (Yen)	.009990	.010015	100.11	99.86
30-Day Forward	.010021	.010048	99.79	99.53
90-Day Forward	.010089	.010116	99.12	98.86
180-Day Forward	.010210	.010239	97.94	97.67
Jordan (Dinar)	1.4265	1.4225	.7010	.7030
Kuwait (Dinar)	3.3406	3.3322	.2994	.3001
Lebanon (Pound)	.000608	.000608	1645.50	1645.50
Malaysia (Ringgit)	.3913	.3921	2.5553	2.5505
Malta (Lira)	2.7253	2.7021	.3669	.3701
Mexico (Peso)				
Floating rate	.1742160	.1855288	5.7400	5.3900
Netherland (Guilder)	.5819	.5808	1.7185	1.7217
New Zealand (Dollar)	.6370	.6370	1.5700	1.5700
Norway (Krone)	.1487	.1490	6.7231	6.7110
Pakistan (Rupee)	.0324	.0325	30.83	30.77
Peru (New Sol)	.4510	.4545	2.22	2.20
Philippines (Peso)	.04090	.04082	24.45	24.50
Poland (Zloty)	.41050900	.41288190	2.44	2.42
Portugal (Escudo)	.006313	.006333	158.40	157.90
Saudi Arabia (Riyal)	.26662	.26660	3.7507	3.7510
Singapore (Dollar)	.6893	.6906	1.4507	1.4480
Slovak Rep. (Koruna)	.0321027	.0321027	31.1500	31.1500
South Africa (Rand)				
Commercial rate	.2830	.2814	3.5552	3.5552
Financial rate	.2433	.2448	4.1100	4.0850
South Korea (Won)	.0012641	.0012327	791.05	811.22
Spain (Peseta)	.007508	.007524	133.20	132.90
Sweden (Krona)	.1330	.1346	7.5207	7.4320
Switzerland (Franc)	.7794	.7779	1.2830	1.2855
30-Day Forward	.7809	.7794	1.2805	1.2830
90-Day Forward	.7840	.7823	1.2756	1.2782
180-Day Forward	.7895	.7878	1.2666	1.2693
Taiwan (Dollar)	.037995	.037928	26.32	26.37
Thailand (Baht)	.03980	.03979	25.12	25.13
Turkey (Lira)	.0000251	.0000251	39847.00	39885.13
United Arab (Dirham)	.2723	.2723	3.6730	3.6728
Uruguay (New Peso)				
Financial	.173913	.175439	5.75	5.70
Venezuela (Bolivar)	.00588	.00587	169.96	170.40
– – –				
SDR	1.46097	1.45273	.68448	.68836
ECU	1.2375	1.23560	...	...

Special Drawing Rights (SDR) are based on exchange rates for the U.S. German, British, French and Japanese currencies. Source: International Monetary Fund.

European Currency Unit (ECU) is based on a basket of community currencies.

(or **direct quote**) is the price of the foreign currency in terms of the home currency. For example, from the perspective of a U.S. resident, the direct exchange rate between the U.S. dollar and the deutsche mark on Tuesday, January 10, was $0.6517/DM1. An **indirect exchange rate** (or **indirect quote**) is the price of the home currency in terms of the foreign currency. From the U.S. resident's perspective, the indirect exchange rate on Tuesday, January 10, was DM1.5345/$1. Mathematically, the direct exchange rate and the indirect exchange rate are reciprocals of one another. By tradition—and sometimes for convenience—certain exchanges rates are typically quoted on a direct basis and others on an indirect basis. For example, common U.S. practice is to quote British pounds on a direct basis but Japanese yen, German marks, and French francs on an indirect basis.

Balance of Payments Equilibrium

As you saw in Chapter 4, the international monetary system has historically utilized two different types of exchange-rate systems: fixed and flexible. Next we discuss how the market for foreign exchange interacts with each of these exchange-rate systems to produce equilibrium in the balance of payments (BOP).

FIGURE 5.5

Short-Run Equilibrium in a Fixed Exchange Rate System

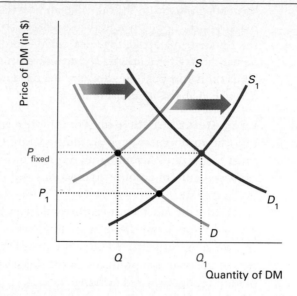

Fixed Exchange-Rate System

We begin by examining how BOP equilibrium was achieved under a fixed exchange-rate system, which existed under the gold standard (1821–1914) and under the Bretton Woods system (1945–1971). For ease of analysis, we assume that the market initially is in equilibrium at the fixed exchange rate, P_{fixed}. The foreign-exchange market for deutsche marks is shown in Fig. 5.5, where D represents the demand curve for marks and S the supply curve for marks. The intersection of D and S yields an equilibrium dollar price for marks of P_{fixed}.

Short-Run Equilibrium. Now suppose that as a result of quality improvements in U.S.-made multipurpose automobiles like Ford Explorers and Chrysler minivans, German consumers increase their demand for U.S. automobiles. To obtain dollars to buy them, Germans must sell more marks, thus shifting the supply curve for marks in Fig. 5.5 from S to S_1. But the new intersection of D and S_1 yields a new equilibrium price of P_1. This price, if allowed to stand, will violate the responsibility of both Germany and the United States to maintain a fixed exchange rate of P_{fixed}. Thus the central banks of Germany (the Bundesbank) and the United States (the Federal Reserve Bank, or FRB) must act to restore P_{fixed} as the equilibrium price. They can do this in one of three ways:

1 The Bundesbank may act alone.

2 The FRB may act alone.

3 The Bundesbank and the FRB may act together.

The Bundesbank, acting alone, can sell gold or dollars from its official reserves and use the proceeds to buy marks. This accommodating transaction will cause the demand curve for marks in Fig. 5.5 to shift to the right. When the Bundesbank sells enough gold (and/or dollars) and buys enough marks to shift the demand curve for marks from D to D_1, P_{fixed} will be restored as the equilibrium exchange rate. Or the FRB, acting alone, can sell enough gold and/or dollars and buy enough marks to shift the demand curve for marks from D to D_1. The new market price, P_{fixed}, would then equal the fixed exchange rate. Or the FRB and the Bundesbank, acting together, could coordinate their policies to shift the demand curve for marks to D_1, again restoring market equilibrium at P_{fixed}. Thus short-run BOP equilibrium in a fixed exchange-rate system is reached through changes in official reserves.

Long-Run Equilibrium. For long-run equilibrium to occur, all transactions must be autonomous, and accommodating transactions by the central banks must fall to zero. Assuming no errors and omissions, capital account transactions and current account transactions will thus sum to zero at the fixed exchange rate.

Under the nineteenth-century gold standard, long-run equilibrium was reached through the effects of gold inflows or outflows on a country's money supply, which in turn affected domestic price levels and the international competitiveness of the country's products. In the previous example, the Bundesbank's sale of gold to restore the fixed exchange rate, P_{fixed}, would cause a deflationary contraction in the German money supply. As the German economy deflated, the prices of German products would fall relative to the prices for foreign goods. The lower prices of German products would make them more attractive to foreigners, thereby increasing German exports. The demand for marks would increase as foreigners demanded more marks to buy the attractively priced German products. Similarly, lower prices for German products would make foreign goods less attractive to German consumers, thereby reducing imports and reducing the supply of marks (German consumers need to buy less foreign currency because they desire fewer foreign goods). The deflation-induced increase in exports and decrease in imports will eventually lead to sufficient shifts in the demand for and supply of marks to restore the exchange rate to P_{fixed}.

The process is reversed for a country enjoying gold inflows. The inflows should increase the domestic money supply, thereby causing inflation in the domestic economy. Higher domestic prices reduce the foreign demand for domestic goods—thus reducing the demand for the home currency in the foreign-exchange market—and increase the domestic demand for foreign goods—thus increasing the supply of the home currency in the foreign-exchange market. As long as the BOP imbalance remains, the inflation will continue until shifts in the supply and demand curves restore the exchange rate to P_{fixed}. When this occurs, the foreign-exchange market is in long-run equilibrium and the country's BOP surplus equals zero. Figure 5.6 summarizes these movements.

While this automatic adjustment process worked reasonably well under the nineteenth-century gold standard, it did not under the postwar Bretton Woods fixed exchange-rate system. Recall that gold played only a minor role in the Bretton Woods system. Only the United States agreed to convert its currency into gold. Other countries merely promised to maintain the par value of their currencies against the dollar. The Bretton Woods system did not rely on automatic gold inflows and outflows to correct BOP surpluses and deficits. Rather it relied on the willingness of national governments to use macroeconomic policies to deflate or inflate their economies to solve BOP adjustment problems. But often domestic political forces constrained a country's central bank from carrying out the necessary but unpopular economic deflation or inflation. On the one hand, correction of a BOP deficit required a contraction of the money supply, which led to domestic

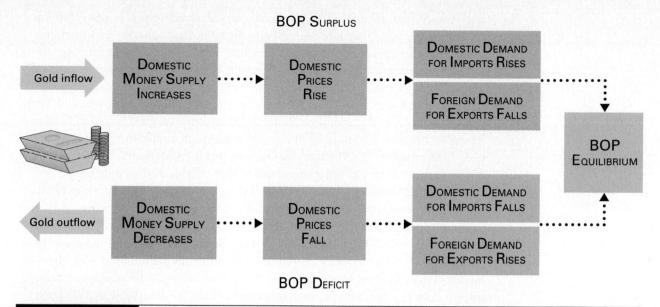

BOP SURPLUS

			DOMESTIC DEMAND FOR IMPORTS RISES	
Gold inflow	DOMESTIC MONEY SUPPLY INCREASES	DOMESTIC PRICES RISE	FOREIGN DEMAND FOR EXPORTS FALLS	BOP EQUILIBRIUM
Gold outflow	DOMESTIC MONEY SUPPLY DECREASES	DOMESTIC PRICES FALL	DOMESTIC DEMAND FOR IMPORTS FALLS	
			FOREIGN DEMAND FOR EXPORTS RISES	

BOP DEFICIT

FIGURE 5.6

Long-Run Adjustment under the Gold Standard

deflation, economic recession, job losses, high unemployment rates, and much political grief. So, politicians usually tried to avoid implementing policies that would end the outflow of reserves. On the other hand, countries running a BOP surplus needed to inflate their economy to eliminate the surplus. But domestic voters, who dislike inflation, and export-dependent firms and their workforces, who dislike the prospect of losing their foreign markets, pressured local politicians to avoid an inflationary policy. Politicians looking forward to the next election often chose to minimize the economic difficulties imposed on their constituents, at least until the election was over.

In practice, the adjustment process under the Bretton Woods fixed exchange-rate system was asymmetric. On the one hand, a country with a BOP surplus did not need to do anything, provided it was willing to accumulate foreign exchange or gold. On the other hand, a country suffering a BOP deficit saw a continuing decrease in its official reserves. It had to cure its BOP problems well before it ran out of reserves. If the country did nothing, other countries (and investors), seeing its reserves dwindling, would begin to distrust its ability to honor its pledge to maintain its currency's par value. These foreigners would rush to sell their holdings of the currency, thereby worsening the drain on the country's reserves. Ultimately the government would have to renege on its promise to convert at the fixed rate and would resort to devaluing its currency. This is what happened to the United Kingdom in 1967, France in 1969, and the United States in 1971. Thus, in practice, the Bretton Woods adjustment burden fell more heavily on deficit countries than on surplus countries.

Flexible Exchange-Rate System

Since the collapse of the Bretton Woods system in 1971, the world economy has relied primarily on the second type of exchange-rate system—the flexible system. Under a flexible exchange-rate system, the exchange rate is determined by the forces of supply and demand for each currency. Assuming a country's central bank is willing to live with the outcome of these market forces, all transactions are autonomous, the result of current and capital account transactions. Official reserves need not be depleted because consumers and investors are determining the currency's value through their self-interested transactions. As we noted in Chapter 4, the United States has run very large current account deficits over the past decade, yet has suffered very little change in its official reserves over the same period.

Consider Fig. 5.7, where D represents the initial demand for marks and S represents the supply of marks. The exchange rate between dollars and marks is determined by the intersection of D and S, which yields an equilibrium exchange rate of P. Now suppose U.S. demand for German products increases. U.S. residents will need more marks in order to purchase those products, thus shifting the demand curve for marks from D to D_1. The equilibrium exchange rate between dollars and marks rises to P_1, where the new demand curve D_1 and the unchanged supply curve S intersect. If the FRB and the Bundesbank choose not to intervene in the foreign-exchange market, the exchange rate will remain at its new level of P_1. But if one or both of the central banks are unhappy with the market-determined exchange rate, they are free to intervene by selling or buying foreign currency. Such accommodating transactions are observable as changes in the official reserves held by the central bank(s) and will shift either the supply or the demand curve, thereby altering the equilibrium price.

BOP Adjustments in the 1990s. As discussed in Chapter 4, the existing international monetary system relies on a combination of fixed and flexible exchange-rate systems. Most EU members participate in the exchange rate mechanism (ERM) of the European Monetary System (EMS) and have agreed to maintain their currencies within a narrow band of a designated par value. ERM participation has in turn forced many EU members to alter their monetary and fiscal policies in order to stay within this band. As a practical matter, for example, most EU central banks in the first half of the 1990s have followed the anti-inflationary, high-interest-rate policies of Germany's Bundesbank in order to avoid capital outflows that would lead to BOP difficulties and a loss of official reserves. The Bundesbank's power over the interest rates that a British driver must pay for his car loan or an Italian entrepreneur must pay for her working capital loan generated some resentment within the EU and led to British and Italian withdrawal

---

FIGURE 5.7

Exchange-Rate Adjustments in the Market for Deutsche Marks in a Flexible Exchange-Rate System

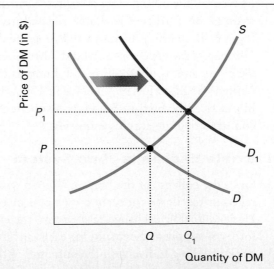

from the ERM in 1992. Other fixed exchange-rate arrangements exist between the French franc and the currencies of many of France's former African colonies, between the Russian ruble and the currencies of several former Soviet republics, and between the U.S. dollar and the currencies of Panama and other countries (see Table 4.3).[3]

Aside from these currency groupings, flexible exchange rates exist between the U.S. dollar and the currencies of major trading countries, including the Canadian dollar, the British pound, the German mark, the Japanese yen, and the Australian dollar. As Fig. 4.4 showed, exchange rates have varied widely over time, thereby causing significant problems for international businesses. For example, as discussed in Chapter 3, the wild fluctuations in the yen-dollar exchange rate in the 1980s first favored Komatsu in its attempts to dethrone Caterpillar in the U.S. construction equipment market. When the value of the dollar fell from ¥251 in 1984 to less than ¥100 at the end of 1994, the shoe was on the other foot. Komatsu suffered erosion of its profit margins as each dollar of sales in the United States produced fewer yen to cover the costs of its Japanese production.

When the value of the domestic currency increases because of changes in supply and demand in the foreign-exchange market, firms such as Komatsu find it harder to export their goods, more difficult to protect their domestic markets from the threat of foreign imports, and more advantageous to shift their production from domestic factories to foreign factories. A decrease in the domestic currency's value has the opposite effects. Savvy international businesspeople are mindful of the impact of these currency fluctuations on their business opportunities.

Pros and Cons of the Two Types of Exchange-Rate Systems

International policymakers have debated the value of reconstructing the Bretton Woods system. Proponents of the system believe fixed exchange rates offer international businesses several advantages. For example, exchange rates are not subject to wide daily, weekly, and yearly fluctuations. The riskiness of international trade transactions is thus reduced, and firms have greater assurance of stability in the values of foreign currencies. Also, fixed exchange rates are an important anti-inflationary tool, since the loss of official reserves forces a country to counteract inflationary tendencies in its economy. Bretton Woods proponents also are distressed because the wild swings in the values of key currencies that occur in flexible exchange-rate systems can disrupt sound international investment decision making.

Advocates of flexible exchange rates look at the other side of the coin. If BOP equilibrium can be reached through changes in exchange rates, then domestic policymakers are free to focus on domestic economic concerns without worrying about the BOP consequences of their actions. Flexible exchange rates also reduce the need for international coordination of domestic economic policies and free each country to follow its own economic destiny. For example, if Mexico's monetary authorities choose more inflationary, growth-oriented economic policies than those adopted by its major trading partners, changes in exchange rates will bring about BOP equilibrium. Flexible exchange rates can absorb the impact of damaging external economic events, such as occurred during the two oil embargoes in the 1970s. Proponents of flexible exchange rates also suggest that fixed exchange-rate systems are not invulnerable to disorderly changes in currency values and cite the depreciation of the pound in 1967, of the French franc in 1969, and of the U.S. dollar in 1971.

The Structure of the Foreign-Exchange Market

The foreign-exchange market comprises buyers and sellers of currencies issued by the world's countries. Anyone who owns money denominated in one currency and wants to convert that money to a second currency participates in the foreign-exchange market. Pakistani tourists exchanging rupees for deutsche marks at the Frankfurt airport utilize the foreign-exchange market, as does Toyota when it exports automobiles to Canada from its factory in Toyoda City, Japan, and the British government when it arranges a multimillion-pound loan to rebuild the monsoon-ravaged economy of Bangladesh. The worldwide volume of foreign-exchange trading is estimated at $1 trillion *per day*. Approximately 83 percent of the transactions involve the U.S. dollar, a dominance stemming from the dollar's role in the Bretton Woods system.[4] Because the dollar is used to facilitate most currency exchange, it is known as the primary **transaction currency** for the foreign-exchange market.

Foreign exchange is traded by bankers, brokers, businesses, and speculators somewhere in the world every minute of the day (see Map 5.1). Traditionally,

These Tokyo-based traders play an important role in the global foreign-exchange market. Linked electronically to traders in Hong Kong, London, New York, and other major cities, they offer to buy or sell the currencies of the major trading nations, for delivery now or in the future.

the trading day begins in Auckland, New Zealand, which lies just west of the International Date Line. As the Earth rotates, foreign-exchange markets open in turn in Sydney, Tokyo, Hong Kong, Singapore, Bahrain, Frankfurt, Zurich, Paris, London, New York, Chicago, and San Francisco. The most important of these markets is in London, followed by New York and Tokyo. The British, U.S., and Japanese markets account for 57 percent of global foreign-exchange volume.[5]

The Role of Banks

Recall from the chapter opening that the foreign-exchange departments of large international banks such as Chase Manhattan in major financial centers such as New York, London, Frankfurt, and Tokyo play a dominant role in the foreign-exchange market. These banks stand ready to buy or sell the major traded currencies. They profit from the foreign-exchange market in several ways, but much of their profits comes from the spread between the bid and asked prices for foreign exchange. For example, if Chase Manhattan buys DM10 million from one customer at a price of DM1.5220/$1 and sells those marks to a second customer at DM1.5210/$1 (as it offered to do in the chapter opening), it makes $4319.73. (Get out your calculator

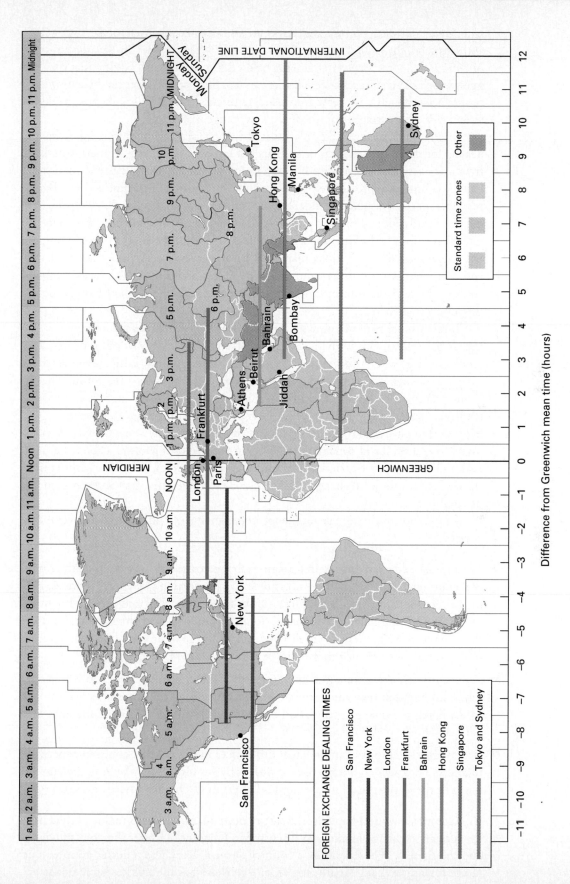

Difference from Greenwich mean time (hours)

FOREIGN EXCHANGE DEALING TIMES

San Francisco
New York
London
Frankfurt
Bahrain
Hong Kong
Singapore
Tokyo and Sydney

Standard time zones

Other

A Day of Foreign-Exchange Trading

MAP 5.1

and do the arithmetic! It buys the marks for 10,000,000 ÷ 1.5220, or $6,570,302.23, and sells them for 10,000,000 ÷ 1.5210, or $6,574,621.96, thereby earning a profit of $4319.73.) Sometimes international banks act as speculators, betting that they can guess which direction exchange rates are headed. Such speculation can be enormously profitable, although it is always risky. And, as discussed later in this chapter, banks also may act as arbitrageurs in the foreign-exchange market.

International banks are key players in the wholesale market for foreign exchange, dealing for their own accounts or on behalf of large commercial customers. Interbank transactions, typically involving at least $1 million (or the foreign-currency equivalent), account for approximately 83 percent of foreign-exchange transactions. Banks may rely on the assistance of independent foreign-exchange brokers, who provide current information about the prices of different foreign currencies and who facilitate transactions by linking buyers and sellers of foreign exchange.[6] Using computers, telephones, telexes, and fax machines, banks and brokers in one market are in constant contact with their counterparts in other markets in order to seek the best currency prices. Telecommunications link foreign-exchange markets worldwide into one global market.

International banks also play a key role in the retail market for foreign exchange, dealing with individual customers who want to buy or sell foreign currencies in large or small amounts. Typically, the price paid by retail customers for foreign exchange is the prevailing wholesale exchange rate plus a premium. The size of the premium is in turn a function of transaction size and the importance of the customer to the bank. For example, a German music store chain that needs $100,000 to pay for 20,000 compact discs of Pearl Jam's latest release will pay a higher premium for its foreign currency than will General Motors when it needs £20 million to repay British investors. And, of course, foreign tourists cashing in a traveler's check for local currency at a bank or exchange office pay an even higher premium.

The clients of the foreign-exchange departments of banks fall into several categories:

▶ *Commercial customers* engage in foreign-exchange transactions as part of their normal commercial activities, such as exporting or importing goods and services, paying or receiving dividends and interest from foreign sources, and purchasing or selling foreign assets and investments. Some commercial customers may also use the market to hedge (reduce) their risks due to potential unfavorable changes in foreign-exchange rates for monies to be paid or received in the future.

▶ *Speculators* deliberately assume exchange-rate risks by acquiring positions in a currency, hoping that they can correctly predict changes in the currency's market value. Foreign-exchange speculation can be enormously profitable if one guesses correctly, but it is also extremely risky.

▶ *Arbitrageurs* attempt to exploit small differences in the price of a currency between markets. They seek to obtain riskless profits by simultaneously buying the currency in the lower-priced market and selling it in the higher-priced market.

Countries' central banks and treasury departments are also major players in the foreign-exchange market. As discussed in Chapter 4, under the gold standard and the Bretton Woods system, a country's central bank was required to intervene in the foreign-exchange market in order to ensure that the market value of the country's currency approximated the currency's par value. A similar requirement applies to ERM members. And, of course, central banks of countries that allow their currencies to float are free to intervene in the foreign-exchange market to influence the market values of their currencies if they so desire.

Active markets exist for relatively few pairs of currency other than those involving the U.S. dollar, the German mark, the British pound, and the Japanese yen.[7] Suppose an Irish knitting mill needs New Zealand dollars to pay for a purchase of 100,000 pounds of merino wool. The foreign-exchange market between the Irish punt and the New Zealand dollar is very small—in fact, no active market exists for the direct exchange of these two currencies. Usually, the U.S. dollar would be used as an intermediary currency to facilitate this transaction. The knitting mill's Irish banker would obtain the necessary New Zealand dollars by first selling Irish punts to obtain U.S. dollars and then selling the U.S. dollars to obtain New Zealand dollars. Such transactions are routine for international banks.

Domestic laws may constrain the ability to trade a currency in the foreign-exchange market. Recall from Chapter 4 that currencies that are freely tradable are called **convertible currencies**. Also called **hard currencies**, these include the German mark, the British pound, the Japanese yen, and the U.S. dollar. Currencies that are not freely tradable because of domestic laws or the unwillingness of foreigners to hold them are called **inconvertible currencies**, or **soft currencies**. The currencies of many developing countries fall in the soft category.

Spot and Forward Markets

Many international business transactions involve payments to be made in the future. These include lending activities and purchases on credit. Because changes in currency values are common, such international transactions would appear to be risky in the post–Bretton Woods era. How can a firm know for sure the future value of a foreign currency? Fortunately, in addition to its geographical dimension, the foreign-exchange market also has a time dimension. Currencies can be bought and sold for immediate delivery or for delivery at some point in the future. The **spot market** consists of foreign-exchange transactions that are to be consummated immediately. ("Immediately" is normally defined as two days after the trade date, because of the time necessary for payment to clear the international banking system.) Spot transactions account for 47 percent of all foreign-exchange transactions.[8]

The **forward market** consists of foreign-exchange transactions that are to occur some time in the future. Organized markets exist for foreign exchange that will be delivered 30 days, 90 days, and 180 days in the future. For example, the following *Wall Street Journal* excerpt indicates that on Tuesday, January 10, 1995, the spot price of the British pound was $1.5610, while the forward price for pounds for delivery in 30 days was $1.5608 and for delivery in 180 days was $1.5600.

	U.S. $ equiv.		Currency per U.S. $	
	Tues.	Mon.	Tues.	Mon.
Britain (Pound)	1.5610	1.5638	.6406	.6395
30-Day Forward	1.5608	1.5635	.6407	.6396
90-Day Forward	1.5605	1.5634	.6408	.6396
180-Day Forward	1.5600	1.5632	.6410	.6397

Pure forward transactions account for 7 percent of total foreign-exchange volume.

Most users of the forward market engage in swap transactions. A **swap transaction** is a transaction in which the same currency is bought and sold simultaneously but delivery is at two different points in time. For example, in a typical "spot against forward" swap, a U.S. manufacturer borrowing £10 million from a British bank for 30 days will sell the £10 million in the spot market in order to obtain U.S. dollars and simultaneously buy £10 million (plus the number of pounds it owes in interest payments) in the 30-day forward market in order to repay its pound-denominated loan. Swaps account for 39 percent of all foreign-exchange transactions.

Normally an international business that wants to buy or sell foreign exchange on a spot or forward basis will contract with an international bank to do so. The bank will charge the firm the prevailing wholesale rate for the currency, plus a small premium for its services. Because of the bank's extensive involvement in the foreign-exchange market, it is typically willing and able to customize the spot, forward, or swap contract to meet the customer's specific needs. For example, if Chrysler expects to receive 10.7 million schillings from its Austrian affiliate in 42 days, its bank will usually agree to enter into a forward contract to buy those schillings from Chrysler with delivery in 42 days.

The foreign-exchange market has developed two other mechanisms to allow firms to obtain foreign exchange in the future. Neither, however, provides the flexibility in amount and in timing that international banks offer. The first mechanism is the currency future. Publicly traded on many exchanges worldwide, a

Computerized automatic trading systems are used to improve the efficiency of the foreign-exchange market. Pictured here is Globex, a 24-hour-a-day global electronic market for trading options and futures contracts. The $75 million Globex system can execute transactions in a mere 3 seconds.[9]

currency future is a contract that resembles a forward contract. However, unlike the forward contract, the currency future is for a standard amount (for example, ¥12.5 million or SwF125,000) on a standard delivery date (for example, the third Wednesday of the contract's maturity month). As with a forward contract, a firm signing a currency-future contract must complete the transaction by buying or selling the specified amount of foreign currency at the specified price and time. This obligation is usually not troublesome, however; a firm wanting to be released from a currency-future obligation can simply make an offsetting transaction. In practice, 95 percent of currency futures are settled in this manner. Currency futures represent only 1 percent of the foreign-exchange market.

The second mechanism, the **currency option**, allows, but does not require, a firm to buy or sell a specified amount of a foreign currency at a specified price at any time up to a specified date. A **call option** grants the right to *buy* the foreign currency in question; a **put option** grants the right to *sell* the foreign currency. Currency options are publicly traded on organized exchanges worldwide. For

FIGURE 5.8

Foreign-Exchange Options on the Philadelphia Exchange

Source: *Wall Street Journal*, January 11, 1995, p. C19. Reprinted by permission of *The Wall Street Journal*, © 1995 Dow Jones & Company, Inc. All Rights Reserved Worldwide.

PHILADELPHIA OPTIONS
Tuesday, January 10, 1995

Strike	Month	Calls Vol.	Calls Last	Puts Vol	Puts Last
CDollr					**70.84**
50,000 Canadian Dollar EOM-European style					
70½	Jan	...	...	4	0.29
71	Jan	4	0.23	...	...
Australian Dollar					**76.72**
50,000 Australian Dollars-European Style.					
76	Mar	20	0.86	...	...
50,000 Australian Dollars-cents per unit.					
75	Mar	...	...	50	0.36
76	Feb	...	...	50	0.49
76	Mar	...	...	50	0.68
77	Feb	200	0.38	...	...
78	Feb	200	0.14	...	...
British Pound					**156.18**
31,250 British Pounds-cents per unit.					
152½	Feb	22	3.60	18	0.40
152½	Mar	...	...	210	0.90
155	Mar	...	...	240	1.70
157½	Mar	50	1.55	10	2.93
160	Mar	550	0.68	...	...
162½	Mar	110	0.34	...	...
British Pound-GMark					**239.40**
31,250 British Pound-German Mark cross.					
238	Feb	30	2.56	200	0.86
238	Mar	...	...	80	1.40
Canadian Dollar					**70.84**
50,000 Canadian Dollars-European Style.					
70	Feb	...	...	10	0.20
72	Jan	...	...	4	1.31
50,000 Canadian Dollars-cents per unit					
71	Mar	5	0.68	84	0.89
71½	Feb	10	0.30	...	...
72	Mar	...	...	8	1.49
ECU					**123.37**
62,500 European Currency Units-cents per unit.					
120	Jan	10	2.98	10	0.02
120	Feb	...	...	32	0.29
122	Jan	16	1.22	16	0.08
122	Feb	...	...	32	80
124	Feb	64	0.90	...	...
French Franc					**188.65**
250,000 French Francs-10ths of a cent per unit.					
18½	Feb	86	3.76	...	...
18½	Mar	...	...	50	1.84
18¾	Feb	108	2.56	...	...
250,000 French Francs-European Style.					
18½	Mar	6227	4.88	...	...
18¾	Mar	6144	3.40	...	...
German Mark					**65.20**
62,500 German Marks EOM-cents per unit.					
62½	Mar	...	...	200	0.34
63	Mar	...	...	2000	0.45
64½	Jan	...	...	56	0.31
65	Jan	...	...	5	0.48
65½	Jan	15	0.43	...	...
66	Jan	475	0.23	...	...
62,500 German Marks-European Style.					
63	Mar	...	...	20	0.30
63½	Feb	25	1.80	...	...
64½	Feb	...	...	15	0.11
65½	Feb	212	0.56	...	...
66	Feb	400	0.41	...	...
66	Mar	200	0.73	...	...
67½	Mar	32	0.34	...	...
62,500 German Marks-cents per unit.					
61	Jan	8	4.40	...	...
61	Feb	7	4.06	...	...
62	Jan	...	...	10	0.01
62	Mar	...	...	100	0.17
63	Jan	10	2.02	...	...
63	Feb	...	...	33	0.11
63½	Jan	2	1.48	...	...
63½	Feb	...	...	30	0.24
63½	Mar	...	...	300	0.45
64	Jan	40	1.16	10	0.03
64	Feb	8	1.45	5	0.35
64	Mar	4	1.85	101	0.54
64½	Jan	33	0.73	33	0.10
64½	Feb	2	1.13	6	0.53
64½	Mar	28	1.40	22	0.73
65	Jan	...	...	8	1.50
65	Feb	...	...	7	1.68
65½	Jan	1021	0.16	...	...
65½	Feb	63	0.61	3	0.88
65½	Mar	80	0.90	...	...
66	Jan	100	0.05	...	...
66	Feb	33	0.42	...	...
66	Mar	82	0.77	8	1.57
67	Mar	304	0.44	...	...
Japanese Yen					**99.93**
6,250,000 Japanese Yen EOM-100ths of a cent per unit.					
98	Jan	...	...	20	0.49
100	Jan	7	0.75	...	...
6,250,000 Japanese Yen EOM.					
101½	Jan	10	0.25	...	...
6,250,000 Japanese Yen-100ths of a cent per unit					
95	Jan	10	4.93	...	...
95	Feb	10	5.19	...	...
98	Jan	...	...	95	0.05
98	Feb	...	...	70	0.32
98½	Feb	...	...	30	0.45
99	Mar	...	...	25	1.04
99½	Jan	1	0.39	21	0.24
99½	Feb	4	1.40	...	...
100	Jan	103	0.36	20	0.41
100	Feb	45	1.10	10	0.96
100	Mar	10	1.73	38	1.49
100½	Jan	22	0.17	...	...
101	Feb	7	0.67	...	...
101	Mar	10	1.32	3	2.00
101½	Feb	22	0.51	...	...
102	Jan	...	...	3	2.31
102	Feb	33	0.38	...	...
Swiss Franc					**77.89**
62,500 Swiss Francs EOM.					
78½	Jan	...	...	8	0.99
62,500 Swiss Francs-European Style.					
75	Jan	80	2.59	...	...
76	Jan	80	1.63	...	...
62,500 Swiss Francs-cents per unit.					
71	Mar	...	...	55	0.07
73	Mar	...	...	9	0.11
75	Mar	...	...	1	0.31
76	Feb	10	1.97	...	...
76	Mar	...	...	70	0.59
76½	Feb	...	...	100	0.06
76½	Feb	...	...	25	0.42
77	Jan	...	...	10	0.16
77	Feb	13	1.37	30	0.48
77	Mar	1330	1.93	1	0.81
77½	Feb	49	1.10	...	...
78	Jan	...	...	10	0.56
78	Mar	...	...	11	1.23
78½	Jan	15	0.19	...	...
78½	Feb	319	0.67	...	...
78½	Mar	10	1.10	...	...
79	Feb	38	0.45	...	...
79	Mar	1	0.98	1	2.08
79½	Feb	200	0.45	...	...

Call Vol ... 20,642   Open Int ... 218,826
Put Vol ... 6,701   Open Int ... 256,226

example, put and call options are available for Canadian dollars on the Chicago Mercantile Exchange (in contract sizes of Can$100,000) and on the Philadelphia Exchange (in contract sizes of Can$50,000). Figure 5.8 lists some of the options available on the Philadelphia Exchange on January 10, 1995. Because of the inflexibility of publicly traded options, international bankers often are willing to write currency options customized as to amount and time for their commercial clients. Currency options account for 5 percent of foreign-exchange market activity.

The forward market, currency options, and currency futures facilitate international trade and investment by allowing firms to hedge, or reduce, the foreign-exchange risks inherent in international transactions. Suppose Toys 'R' Us wants to purchase Super Nintendo game cartridges for ¥140 million for delivery 90 days in the future, with payment due at delivery. Rather than having to buy yen today and hold them for 90 days, Toys 'R' Us can simply go to its bank and contract to buy the ¥140 million for delivery in 90 days. The firm's bank will in turn charge Toys 'R' Us for those yen based on the yen's current price in the 90-day forward wholesale market . Toys 'R' Us could also protect itself from increases in the yen's price by purchasing a currency future or a currency option. We discuss the advantages and disadvantages of these different hedging techniques more thoroughly in Chapter 18.

The forward price of a foreign currency often differs from its spot price. If the forward price (using a direct quote) is less than the spot price, the currency is selling at a **forward discount**. If the forward price is higher than the spot price, the currency is selling at a **forward premium**. For example, as Fig. 5.4 indicates, the *Wall Street Journal* reported that the spot price of the British pound on January 10, 1995 was $1.5610. On the same day, the 90-day forward price was $1.5605, indicating that the pound was selling at a foward discount. The annualized forward premium or discount on the pound can be calculated by using the following formula:

$$\text{Annualized forward premium or discount} = \frac{P_f - P_s}{P_s} \times n$$

where, using our example,

$$P_f = \text{90-day forward price} = \$1.5605$$

$$P_s = \text{spot price} = \$1.5610$$

$$n = \text{the number of periods in a year} = 4$$

(Because the example calls for a 90-day forward rate, n equals 4; there are four 90-day periods in a year.) Thus

$$\text{Annualized forward discount} = \frac{\$1.5605 - \$1.5610}{\$1.5610} \times 4$$

$$= -0.0013 = -0.13\%$$

Had the forward price of the pound been higher than the spot price (using the direct quote), the formula would have yielded the annualized forward premium for the pound.

The forward price represents the marketplace's aggregate prediction of the spot price of the exchange rate in the future.[10] Thus, the forward price helps international businesspeople forecast future changes in exchange rates. These changes can affect the price of imported components as well as the competitiveness and profitability of the firm's exports. If a currency is selling at a forward discount, the foreign-exchange market believes the currency will depreciate over time. Firms may want to reduce their holdings of assets or increase their liabilities denominated in such a currency. The currencies of countries suffering BOP deficits or high inflation rates often sell at a forward discount. Conversely, if a currency is selling at a forward premium, the foreign-exchange market believes the currency will appreciate over time. Firms may want to increase their holdings of assets and reduce their liabilities denominated in such a currency. The currencies of countries enjoying BOP surpluses or low inflation rates often sell at a forward premium. Thus the difference between the spot and forward prices of a country's currency often signals the market's expectations regarding that country's economic policies and prospects.

Arbitrage and the Currency Market

Another important component of the foreign-exchange market is arbitrage activities. **Arbitrage** is the riskless purchase of a product in one market for immediate resale in a second market in order to profit from a price discrepancy. We explore two types of arbitrage activities that affect the foreign-exchange market: arbitrage of goods and arbitrage of money.

Arbitrage of Goods—Purchasing Power Parity. Underlying the arbitrage of goods is a very simple notion: if the price of a good differs between two markets, people will tend to buy the good in the market offering the lower price, the "cheap" market, and resell it in the market offering the higher price, the "expensive" market. Under the *law of one price*, such arbitrage activities will continue until the price of the good is identical in both markets (excluding transactions costs, transportation costs, taxes, and so on). This notion induced purchasing agents for Galeries Lafayette to buy clock radios in Japan and export them to France in the example in Chapter 3.

The arbitrage of goods across national boundaries is represented by the theory of **purchasing power parity (PPP)**. This theory states that the prices of tradable goods, when expressed in a common currency, will tend to equalize across countries as a result of exchange-rate changes. PPP occurs because the process of buying goods in the cheap market and reselling them in the expensive market affects the demand for, and thus the price of, the foreign currency. For example, assume the exchange rate between U.S. and Canadian dollars is U.S.$0.80/Can$1. Suppose Levi's jeans sell for U.S.$24 in the United States and Can$30 in Canada. PPP would exist in this case. At the existing exchange rate,

$$\frac{\text{U.S.\$0.80}}{\text{Can\$1}} \times \text{Can\$30} = \text{U.S.\$24}$$

Thus the Levi's jeans are the same price in both markets (expressed in either U.S. or Canadian dollars), and neither U.S. nor Canadian residents would have any reason to cross their shared border to purchase the jeans in the other country.

Now suppose Canada undergoes an inflation that raises all Canadian prices 20 percent. The Levi's jeans in Canada would now cost Can$36. PPP would no longer exist. At the current exchange rate of U.S.$0.80/Can$1, Canadians could cross the border, exchange Can$30 for U.S.$24, and buy their Levis in the United States, thereby saving themselves Can$6. This behavior affects the foreign-exchange market. By buying their jeans in the United States, Canadians increase the supply of Canadian dollars in the foreign-exchange market, thereby lowering the exchange rate between the Canadian dollar and the U.S. dollar. This process will continue until the exchange rate falls to U.S.$0.67/Can$1. At that exchange rate, PPP will be restored because the price of Levi's jeans will be the same in both countries:[11]

$$\frac{\text{U.S.\$0.67}}{\text{Can\$1}} \times \text{Can\$36} = \text{U.S.\$24}$$

Does this really happen? Obviously, teenagers from Calgary, Alberta, don't fly to Miami, Florida, just to save Can\$6 on a pair of jeans. But consider the residents of Sault Ste. Marie, Ontario, who in the early 1990s paid the equivalent of U.S.\$25 for a case of Canadian-brewed Labatt's beer and U.S.\$2.50 for a gallon of gasoline on their side of the border. They eagerly crossed the bridge to Sault Ste. Marie, Michigan, in order to buy a case of Labatt's for \$12 and a gallon of U.S. gasoline for \$1.20. It takes little imagination to predict the impact of such price differences on the health of the retail sector, on employment opportunities, and on the local tax bases of the two communities. Merchants in the Ontario Sault Ste. Marie lost an estimated Can\$100 million in retail sales annually to Michigan stores because of PPP imbalances.[12]

Of course, the Canadian-U.S. exchange rate is determined by much more than the relative price of jeans in the two countries and border trade between the two Sault Ste. Maries. Nonetheless, if PPP doesn't exist in the two countries for jeans (or any other tradable good), people will buy the good in the cheap market and transport it to the expensive market, thereby affecting supply and demand in the foreign-exchange market and influencing the equilibrium exchange rate. That's why the PPP theory states that prices of tradable goods will *tend* to equalize. Even if prices don't equalize, the effects can be significant. In a typical month in the early 1990s, for example, Canadians made almost 5 million same-day automobile trips to U.S. border communities, and U.S. residents made approximately 1.6 million such trips to Canada. Although not all such trips were for shopping, they indicate the importance of purchasing power imbalances to the Canadian economy—a problem well-known to Canadian merchants and provincial economic development authorities. Overall, cross-border shopping is estimated to have siphoned Can\$3.1 billion from the Canadian economy in 1991.[13]

International economists use PPP to help them compare standards of living across countries. Consider, for example, Japan and the United States. Converting Japan's 1992 per capita income measured in yen into U.S. dollars using the average 1992 exchange rate between the yen and the dollar would yield \$29,485. U.S. per capita income for 1992 was \$23,180. These figures suggest that the average Japanese citizen enjoys a higher income than the average American citizen. However, this comparison fails to take into account differences in price levels between the two countries. After adjusting for purchasing power, Japan's dollar-dominated per capita income falls to \$19,820, indicating that the average Japanese is worse off than the average American. Because of such distortions due to price levels, international businesspeople who use international income data to make decisions, such as which market to enter or how to position a product, must pay close attention to whether the data are reported with or without PPP adjustments.

Foreign-exchange analysts also use the PPP theory to forecast long-term changes in exchange rates. They believe that broad purchasing power imbalances between countries signal possible changes in exchange rates. As a quick and dirty way of assessing misalignments in exchange rates, the British business weekly *The Economist* periodically reports the prices of McDonald's Big Macs around the world; see "Going Global." As the article suggests, even the prices of Big Macs may signal whether currencies are overvalued or undervalued in the foreign-exchange market.

Arbitrage of Money. While we do not want to diminish the long-run importance of the arbitrage of goods, its impact on the foreign-exchange market is dwarfed by that of the short-term arbitrage of money. Much of the demand and supply of foreign currencies stems from financial arbitrage. Professional traders employed by money-market banks and other financial organizations seek to profit from small differences in the price of foreign exchange in different markets. Although not all of the volume in currency markets reflects arbitrage activities, the importance of financial activities relative to real activities (purchases of goods and services) in foreign-exchange markets is indicated by the ratio of daily foreign-currency trading ($1 trillion) to daily international trade ($9 billion).

Whenever the foreign-exchange market is not in equilibrium, professional traders can profit through arbitraging money. Numerous forms of foreign-exchange arbitrage are possible, but we discuss three common examples: two-point, three-point, and covered-interest.

Two-point arbitrage, also called **geographic arbitrage**, involves profiting from price differences in two geographically distinct markets. Suppose £1 is trading for $2.00 in New York City and $1.80 in London. A profitable arbitrage opportunity is available. A foreign-exchange trader at Chase Manhattan, such as those depicted in the chapter opening, could take $1.80 and use it to buy £1 in London's foreign-exchange market. The trader could then take the pound and sell it for $2.00 in New York's foreign-exchange market. Through this two-point, or geographic, arbitrage, the trader at Chase Manhattan magically converts $1.80 into $2.00 at no risk whatsoever.

Of course, currency traders at other banks will also note the opportunity for quick profits. As arbitrageurs sell dollars and buy pounds in London, the dollar falls in value relative to the pound there. As arbitrageurs buy dollars and sell pounds in New York, the pound falls in value relative to the dollar in that market. This process will continue until the pound-dollar exchange rate is identical in both markets. Only when there is no possibility of profitable arbitrage will the foreign-exchange market be in equilibrium.

We add one caveat: if the costs of making an arbitrage transaction were large, there would be differences in the exchange rates in the two markets that reflected the size of the transaction costs. However, for major currencies, foreign exchange is sold in large amounts by very large, well-known international banks. Accordingly, transaction costs are extremely small, and two-point arbitrage generally will cause exchange rates between any two major currencies to be identical in all markets.

Consider another example. Suppose that £1 can buy $2 in New York, Frankfurt, and London, $1 can buy DM1.5 in those three markets, and £1 can buy DM2.5 in all three. Because the exchange rate between each pair of currencies is the same in each country, no possibility of profitable two-point arbitrage exists. However, profitable three-point arbitrage opportunities exist. **Three-point**

Going Global

Big Mac Currencies

The Big Mac index was launched in 1986 as a light-hearted guide to whether currencies are at their correct level.

Burgernomics is based upon the theory of purchasing-power parity (PPP)—the notion that a dollar should buy the same amount in all countries. In the long run, argue PPP supporters, the exchange rate between two currencies should move towards the rate that would equate the price of an identical basket of traded goods in the respective countries.

Our "basket" is a McDonald's Big Mac, which is produced locally in 68 countries. The Big Mac PPP is the exchange rate that would leave hamburgers costing the same in America as in, say, Japan.

The first column of the table shows the local-currency price of a Big Mac. The second column shows prices in dollar terms. The cheapest is in China, where a burger costs a bargain $1.03. Switzerland's Big Mac is the most expensive, at $3.96. These figures imply that the yuan is the most undervalued currency, the Swiss franc the most overvalued.

The average price of a Big Mac in four American cities is $2.30 (including sales tax). Dividing the Swiss price (SFr5.70) by the American price gives a Big Mac PPP for the dollar of SFr2.48 (i.e., at this exchange rate a Swiss burger would cost the same as an American one). This compares with a current exchange rate of SFr1.44, implying that the Swiss franc is overvalued against the dollar by a hefty 72 percent. On the same basis, the yen is overvalued by 64 percent, the deutsche mark by a modest 17 percent.

Compared with a year ago, European currencies have moved closer to their PPPs: they are now less overvalued against the dollar. The yen, however, is more overvalued. In general, rich countries' currencies are overvalued against the dollar (Canada and Australia are the notable exceptions).

Most developing countries' currencies, however, seem to be undervalued according to the Big Mac standard. The currencies of Brazil, China, Hong Kong, Malaysia, and Poland are all undervalued by more than 30 percent. The Mexican peso, however, is more or less at its "correct" level against the dollar. Only two emerging-market currencies are noticeably overvalued: the South Korean won (by 24 percent) and the Argentine peso (57 percent).

According to the Big Mac index, the dollar has been undervalued against the other main currencies for many years. Some readers have therefore had the temerity to complain that the theory of burger-nomics is flawed because:

▶ It assumes that there are not trade barriers. However, price differences between countries may, in part, reflect different levels of farm support. The currencies of places which keep out cheap beef—e.g., Western Europe and Japan—will appear overvalued; Hong Kong and Singapore, which import food at world prices, will seem to have undervalued currencies.

▶ High rates of value-added tax in countries such as Sweden and Denmark inflate prices and so exaggerate the degree of overvaluation.

▶ Profit margins vary with the strength of competition. In Buenos Aires, for example, McDonald's restaurants are in prime spots and appeal to upper middle-class families, who are eager to pay a big premium to enjoy the American way of life.

arbitrage is the buying and selling of three different currencies to make a riskless profit. Figure 5.9 shows how this can work:

Step 1: Convert £1 into $2.

Step 2: Convert the $2 into DM3.

Step 3: Convert the DM3 into £1.2.

Through these three steps, £1 has been converted into £1.2, for a riskless profit of £0.2.

Professional currency traders can make profits through three-point arbitrage whenever the price of buying a currency directly (such as using pounds to buy

Yet the Big Mac does provide a rough and ready measure of PPP. Using far more sophisticated methods, Goldman Sachs, an investment bank, estimates the dollar's PPP to be ¥189 (compared with our ¥170). This suggests that the dollar is even more undervalued than the Big Mac suggests.

	BIG MAC PRICES		Actual Exchange Rate 4/5/94	Implied PPP† of the Dollar	Local Currency Under(-)/over(+) Valuation**(%)
	In Local Currency	In Dollars			
United States‡	$2.30	2.30	—	—	—
Argentina	Peso3.60	3.60	1.00	1.57	+57
Australia	A$2.45	1.72	1.42	1.07	-25
Austria	Sch34.00	2.84	12.0	14.8	+23
Belgium	BFr109	3.10	35.2	47.39	+35
Brazil	Cr1,500	1.58	949	652	-31
Britain	£1.81	2.65	1.46‡‡	1.27‡‡	+15
Canada	C$2.86	2.06	1.39	1.24	-10
Chile	Peso948	2.28	414	412	-1
China	Yuan9.00	1.03	8.70	3.91	-55
Czech Republic	CKr50	1.71	29.7	21.7	-27
Denmark	DKr25.75	3.85	6.69	11.2	+67
France	FFr18.5	3.17	5.83	8.04	+38
Germany	DM4.60	2.69	1.71	2.00	+17
Greece	Dr620	2.47	251	270	+8
Holland	F15.45	2.85	1.91	2.37	+24
Hong Kong	HK$9.20	1.19	7.73	4.00	-48
Hungary	Forint169	1.66	103	73.48	-29
Italy	Lire4,550	2.77	1,641	1,978	+21
Japan	¥391	3.77	104	170	+64
Malaysia	M$3.77	1.40	2.69	1.64	-39
Mexico	Peso8.10	2.41	3.36	3.52	+5
Poland	Zloty31,000	1.40	22.433	13,478	-40
Portugal	Esc440	2.53	174	191	+10
Russia	Rouble2,900	1.66	1,775	1,261	-29
Singapore	$2.98	1.90	1.57	1.30	-17
South Korea	Won2,300	2.84	810	1,000	+24
Spain	Ptas345	2.50	138	150	+9
Sweden	Skr25.5	3.20	7.97	11.1	+39
Switzerland	SFr5.70	3.96	1.44	2.48	+72
Taiwan	NT$62	2.35	26.4	26.96	+2
Thailand	Baht48	1.90	25.3	20.87	-17

*Prices vary locally †Purchasing-power parity: local price divided by price in United States **Against dollar
‡Average of New York, Chicago, San Francisco and Atlanta ‡‡Dollars per pound
Source: McDonald's

Source: *The Economist*, April 9, 1994, p. 88. © The Economist Newspaper Group, Inc. Reprinted with permission. Further reproduction prohibited.

marks) differs from the cross rate of exchange. The **cross rate** is an exchange rate between two currencies calculated through the use of a third currency (such as using pounds to buy dollars and then using the dollars to buy marks). Because of the depth and liquidity of dollar-denominated currency markets, the U.S. dollar is the primary third currency used in calculating cross rates. In the earlier example, the direct quote between pounds and marks is £1/DM2.5, while the cross rate is

$$\frac{£1}{$2} \times \frac{$1}{DM1.5} = \frac{£1}{DM3}$$

FIGURE 5.9

Three-Point Arbitrage

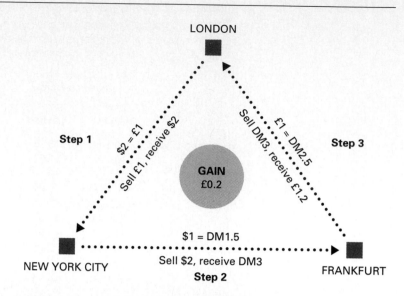

The difference between these two rates offers arbitrage profits to foreign-exchange market professionals. The market for the three currencies will be in equilibrium only when arbitrage profits do not exist, which occurs when the direct quote and the cross rate for each possible pair of the three currencies are equal.

The real significance of three-point arbitrage is that it links together individual foreign-exchange markets. Changes in the pound/dollar market will affect the mark/pound market and the dollar/mark market because of the direct quote–cross rate equilibrium relationship. But these changes will in turn affect other markets, such as the dollar/franc market, the mark/franc market, and the pound/franc market. Because of three-point arbitrage, changes in any one foreign-exchange market can affect prices in all other foreign-exchange markets.

The third form of arbitrage we discuss here is covered-interest arbitrage. **Covered-interest arbitrage** is arbitrage that occurs due to geographical differences in interest rates and differences in foreign-exchange rates over time. In practice, it is the most important of the three types of arbitrage discussed here. Because of the globalization of capital markets resulting from telecommunications and information management innovations, international bankers, insurance companies, and corporate treasurers can scan money markets worldwide to obtain the best returns on their short-term excess cash balances and the lowest rates on short-term loans. But in so doing, they often want to protect, or *cover* (hence the term *covered-interest arbitrage*), themselves from exchange-rate risks.

A simple example demonstrates how covered-interest arbitrage works. Suppose the annual interest rate for 90-day deposits is 12 percent in London and 8 percent in New York. New York investors will be eager to earn the higher returns available in London. To do so, they must convert their dollars to pounds today in order to invest in London. However, the New York investors ultimately want dollars, not pounds, so they must reconvert the pounds back to dollars at the end of 90 days. But what if the pound's value were to fall during that period? The extra interest the New Yorkers will earn in London might then be wiped out by losses suffered when they exchange pounds for dollars in 90 days.

The New York investors can capture the higher London interest rates but avoid exchange-rate dangers by covering in the forward market their exposure to potential drops in the pound's value. Suppose they have $1 million to invest, the spot pound is selling for $1.80, and the 90-day forward pound is selling for $1.79. They have two choices:

1 They can invest their money in New York at 8 percent interest.

2 They can convert their dollars into pounds today, invest in London at 12 percent interest, and in 90 days liquidate their London investment and convert it back to dollars.

If the New York investors choose the first option and invest their funds in the New York money market for 90 days at 8 percent annual interest (or 2 percent for 90 days), at the end of the 90 days their investment will be

$$\$1,000,000 \times 1.02 = \$1,020,000.$$

Or they can invest their money in London for 90 days. To do so, they first convert their $1,000,000 into £555,555.55 at the spot rate of $1.80/£1. At the 12 percent annual interest rate available in London (or 3 percent for 90 days), their investment will grow in 90 days to

$$£555,555.55 \times 1.03 = £572,222.22.$$

If they want to avoid exposure to exchange-rate fluctuations, they can sell the £572,222.22 today in the 90-day forward market at the current 90-day forward rate of $1.79/£1, thereby yielding at the end of 90 days

$$£572,222.22 \times \$1.79/£1 = \$1,024,277.78.$$

The New Yorkers thus earn more money by investing in London than they would at home ($24,277.78 versus $20,000). Covered-interest arbitrage allows them to capture the higher interest rate in London while covering themselves from exchange-rate fluctuations by using the forward market. So, short-term investment money, seeking the higher, covered return, will flow from New York to London.

What happens in the two lending markets and the foreign-exchange market when such arbitrage occurs? Because funds are transferred from New York to London, interest rates will rise in New York, since the supply of loanable money in New York decreases. Interest rates will fall in London, since the supply of loanable money increases there. In the spot market, the demand for pounds increases, thereby raising the spot price of pounds. In the 90-day forward market, the supply of pounds increases, thereby lowering the forward price of pounds. Loanable funds will continue to flow from New York to London until the return on the covered investment is the same in London as it is in New York. Only then will all possibilities for profitable covered-interest arbitrage be exhausted.

Returns to international investors will be equal—and arbitrage-driven, short-term international capital flows will end—when the interest-rate difference between the two markets equals the 90-day forward discount on the pound. Said another way, covered-interest arbitrage will end if the gains investors capture from the higher interest rates in the London market are just offset by the exchange-rate losses they suffer from the conversion of their dollars to pounds today and reconversion of their pounds back to dollars in 90 days. (Note that the pound's forward discount measures the exchange-rate loss on the dual conversion.)

The short-term capital flows that result from covered-interest arbitrage are so important to the foreign-exchange market that in practice the short-term interest-rate differential between two countries determines the forward discount or forward premium on their currencies.[14]

This last statement raises another question: why should interest rates vary among countries in the first place? Addressing this question in 1930, Yale economist Irving Fisher demonstrated that a country's nominal interest rate reflects the real interest rate plus expected inflation in that country. National differences in expected inflation rates thus yield differences in nominal interest rates among countries, a phenomenon known as the **international Fisher effect**. Because of the international Fisher effect and covered-interest arbitrage, an increase in a country's expected inflation rate will lead to higher interest rates in that country. This in turn will lead to either a shrinking of the forward premium or a widening of the forward discount on the country's currency in the foreign-exchange market. Because of this linkage between inflation and expected changes in exchange rates, international business-people and foreign-currency traders carefully monitor countries' inflation trends. The connection between inflation and exchange rates also impacts the international monetary system. For example, a fixed exchange-rate system functions poorly if inflation rates vary widely among countries participating in the system.

In summary, arbitrage activities are important for several reasons. Arbitrage constitutes a major portion of the $1 trillion in currencies traded globally each working day. It affects the supply and demand for each of the major trading currencies. It also ties together the foreign-exchange markets, thereby overcoming differences in geography (two-point arbitrage), currency type (three-point arbitrage), and time (covered-interest arbitrage). Arbitrage truly makes the foreign-exchange market global.

The International Capital Market

Not only are international banks important in the functioning of the foreign-exchange market and arbitrage transactions, but they also play a critical role in financing the operations of international businesses, acting as both commercial bankers and investment bankers (as local law permits). As commercial bankers, they finance exports and imports, accept deposits, provide working capital loans, and offer sophisticated cash management services for their clients. As investment bankers, they may underwrite or syndicate local, foreign, or multinational loans and broker, facilitate, or even finance mergers and joint ventures between foreign and domestic firms.

Major International Banks

The international banking system is centered in large money-market banks headquartered in the world's financial centers—Japan, the United States, the United Kingdom, Germany, and France. These banks are involved in international commerce on a global scale. Of the world's 30 largest banks, 17 are located in

TABLE 5.1

The World's 30 Largest Banks

RANK BY ASSETS 1993	1992			ASSETS ($ MILLIONS)	PERCENTAGE CHANGE FROM 1992
1	2	Fuji Bank	(Japan)	538,243.2	9.9
2	1	Dai-Ichi Kangyo Bank	(Japan)	535,356.5	9.3
3	3	Sumitomo Bank	(Japan)	531,835.3	9.1
4	4	Sanwa Bank	(Japan)	525,126.8	9.0
5	5	Sakura Bank	(Japan)	523,730.6	12.0
6	6	Mitsubishi Bank	(Japan)	487,547.2	6.5
7	7	Norinchukin Bank	(Japan)	435,599.1	15.7
8	8	Industrial Bank of Japan	(Japan)	414,295.5	12.9
9	9	Credit Lyonnais	(France)	337,503.0	(3.8)
10	17	Bank of China	(China)	334,752.7	19.8
11	12	Mitsubishi Trust & Banking	(Japan)	330,478.7	13.5
12	13	Tokai Bank	(Japan)	328,695.4	13.4
13	10	Deutsche Bank	(Germany)	319,997.7	4.4
14	14	Long-Term Credit Bank of Japan	(Japan)	315,026.1	9.2
15	16	Sumitomo Trust & Banking	(Japan)	305,347.4	9.5
16	19	HSBC Holdings	(U.K.)	304,521.3	18.1
17	18	Mitsui Trust & Banking	(Japan)	298,910.5	12.7
18	11	Credit Agricole	(France)	281,787.3	(5.5)
19	23	Asahi Bank	(Japan)	277,688.1	11.0
20	21	Bank of Tokyo	(Japan)	273,864.3	8.3
21	24	Daiwa Bank	(Japan)	262,567.4	17.9
22	20	Societe Generale	(France)	259,128.7	0.9
23	22	ABN Amro Holding	(Netherlands)	252,167.7	(0.4)
24	15	Banque Nationale de Paris	(France)	249,110.3	(12.2)
25	25	Barclays Bank	(U.K.)	245,283.7	10.1
26	28	Yasuda Trust & Banking	(Japan)	238,527.6	13.6
27	30	Cie Financiere de Paribas	(France)	229,025.0	12.8
28	26	National Westminster Bank	(U.K.)	225,859.9	4.2
29	29	Dresdner Bank	(Germany)	218,887.9	7.6
30	27	Citicorp	(U.S.)	216,574.0	1.3

Source: From "The 100 Largest Commercial Banking Companies," *Fortune*, August 22, 1994.

Japan (see Table 5.1), a reflection in part of that country's global financial power and in part of the key role Japanese banks play in financing the business needs of members of Japanese keiretsu.

International banking takes many forms. Originally, most international banking was done through reciprocal correspondent relationships among banks located in different countries. A **correspondent relationship** is an agent relationship whereby one bank acts as a correspondent, or agent, for another bank in the first bank's home country. For example, a U.S. bank could be the correspondent for a French bank in the United States, while the French bank could be the U.S. bank's correspondent in France. Services performed by correspondent banks include paying or collecting foreign funds, providing credit information, and honoring letters of credit. To facilitate these transactions, each bank maintains accounts at the other that are denominated in the local currency.

As the larger banks have internationalized their operations, they have increasingly provided their own overseas operations, rather than utilizing correspondent banks, in order to improve their ability to compete internationally. A bank that has its own foreign operations is better able to access new sources of deposits and profitable lending opportunities. Equally as important, as its domestic clients internationalize, it can better meet those clients' international banking needs. Thus, it retains the international business of its domestic clients and reduces the risk that some other international bank will steal them away.

An overseas banking operation can take several forms. If it is separately incorporated from the parent, it is called a **subsidiary bank**; if it is not separately incorporated, it is called a **branch bank**. Sometimes an international bank may choose to create an **affiliated bank**, an overseas operation in which it takes part ownership in conjunction with a local or foreign partner.

U.S. banks may also use either of the following two techniques to establish international banking operations while operating in the United States:

1 The Edge Act of 1919 allows U.S. banks to establish an **Edge Act corporation**, a bank set up outside of the parent bank's home state (thus circumventing federal prohibitions against interstate banking) for the sole purpose of providing international banking services. Because much of the international financial services infrastructure is located in large cities, Edge Act corporations are an attractive way for banks headquartered outside of financial centers to participate in international lending. For example, an Ohio bank can, through an Edge Act corporation, locate its international operations in New York City, continue to serve its local clients in Cleveland, and yet not violate interstate banking restrictions.

2 A bank can create an international banking facility. This alternative is discussed in detail later in this chapter.

Commercial Banking Services. Tourists utilize international banking services when they exchange their home currency or traveler's checks for local currency. While the physical exchange of one country's paper currency for another's is part of international banking operations, a far more important part involves financing and facilitating everyday commercial transactions. For example, when J.C. Penney orders $10 million worth of high-tech running shoes from Adidas, the German footwear manufacturer, with payment due in 90 days, J.C. Penney may require any of the following:

▶ Short-term financing of the purchase

▶ International electronic funds transfer

▶ Forward purchases of deutsche marks

▶ Advice about proper documentation for importing and paying for the athletic shoes

The international department of the firm's bank will provide any or all of these services as part of its normal commercial banking operations.

Investment Banking Services. In addition to commercial banking services, most international banks also provide investment banking services.[15] Corporate clients hire investment bankers to package and locate long-term debt and equity funding and to arrange mergers and acquisitions of domestic and foreign firms. As the capital market has internationalized, competition has forced investment bankers to globalize their operations in order to secure capital for their clients at the lowest possible cost.

In most of the world, international banks provide both commercial banking services and investment banking services. In the United States, however, the 1934 Glass-Stegall Act restricts commercial banks from providing investment banking services. As a result, investment banking services in the United States are supplied predominantly by securities firms, such as Salomon Brothers, Goldman Sachs, and Merrill Lynch. The foreign subsidiaries of U.S.-based banks are free to provide investment banking services outside the United States, however.

The Eurocurrency Market

Another important facet of the international financial system is the Eurocurrency market. Originally called the Eurodollar market, the Eurocurrency market originated in the early 1950s when the communist-controlled governments of Central and Eastern Europe needed dollars to finance their international trade but feared the U.S. government would confiscate or block their holdings of dollars in U.S. banks for political reasons. The communist governments solved this problem by using European banks that were willing to maintain dollar accounts for them.[16] Thus the Eurodollar was born—U.S. dollars deposited in European bank accounts. As other banks worldwide, particularly in Canada and Japan, began offering dollar-denominated deposit accounts, the term **Eurodollar** evolved to mean U.S. dollars deposited in any bank account outside the United States. As other currencies became stronger in the postwar era—particularly the yen and the deutsche mark—the Eurocurrency market broadened to include Euroyen, Euromarks, and other currencies. Today a **Eurocurrency** is defined as a currency on deposit outside of its country of issue. Some $6 trillion worth of Eurocurrencies are on deposit in banks worldwide; roughly two thirds of these deposits are in the form of Eurodollars.[17]

The Euroloan market has grown up with the Eurocurrency market. The Euroloan market is extremely competitive, and lenders operate on razor-thin margins. Euroloans are often quoted on the basis of the **London Interbank Offer Rate (LIBOR)**, the interest rate that London banks charge each other for short-term Eurocurrency loans. The Euroloan market is often the low-cost source of loans for large, creditworthy borrowers, such as governments and large MNCs, for three reasons. First, Euroloans are free from costly government banking regulations, such as reserve requirements, that are designed to control the domestic money supply but that drive up lending costs. Second, Euroloans involve large transactions, so the average cost of making the loans is less. And, third, since only the most creditworthy borrowers use the Euroloan market, the risk premium that lenders charge also is less.

In the 1970s U.S. banks complained that reserve requirements and other expensive regulations imposed by the Federal Reserve Board prevented them from competing with European and Asian banks in issuing dollar-denominated international loans. These loans account for 60 percent of the Euroloan market. Foreign banks lending in Eurodollars were not subject to the regulations. To counter this problem, the Federal Reserve Board in 1981 authorized the creation of international banking facilities. An **international banking facility (IBF)** is an entity of a U.S. bank that is legally distinct from the bank's domestic operations and that may offer only international banking services. IBFs do not need to observe the numerous U.S. domestic banking regulations. Of course, the Federal Reserve Board has issued various regulations to ensure IBFs do not engage in domestic banking services. For example, IBFs may only accept deposits from or make loans to non-U.S. residents. Nonetheless, they enable U.S. banks to compete with other international bankers on a more equal footing in the critical Eurodollar market.

The International Bond Market

The international bond market represents a major source of debt financing for the world's governments, international organizations, and larger firms. This market has traditionally consisted of two types of bonds: foreign bonds and Eurobonds. **Foreign bonds** are bonds issued by a resident of country A but sold to residents of country B and denominated in the currency of country B. For example, the Nestlé Corporation, a Swiss resident, might issue a foreign bond denominated in yen and sold primarily to residents of Japan. A **Eurobond** is a bond issued in the currency of country A but sold to residents of other countries. For example, American Airlines could borrow $500 million to finance new aircraft purchases by selling Eurobonds to residents of France and Germany. The U.S. dollar is the dominant currency in the Eurobond market (see Table 5.2.)

TABLE 5.2

Eurobond Issues by Currency

1994* RANK	CURRENCY	TOTAL RAISED ($ BILLIONS)	NUMBER OF ISSUES	1993* RANK	TOTAL RAISED ($ BILLIONS)	NUMBER OF ISSUES
1	U.S. dollar	79.81	367	1	75.34	374
2	Yen	26.39	209	5	20.88	92
3	British pound	20.49	88	3	25.20	119
4	French franc	17.78	62	4	22.24	83
5	Deutsche mark	14.94	56	2	30.83	82
6	Canadian dollar	9.27	71	6	17.63	96
7	Lira	9.10	70	8	5.90	39
8	Guilder	6.90	39	7	6.31	27
9	Ecu	4.93	19	9	3.23	9
10	Australian dollar	2.84	36	10	2.05	24

*First six months

Source: Adapted from "Merrill Lynch races to top spot," *Financial Times*, July 4, 1994. Reprinted with permission.

As the global capital market has evolved, the international bond market has grown increasingly sophisticated. Syndicates of investment banks, securities firms, and commercial banks put together complex packages of international bonds to serve the borrowing needs of large, creditworthy borrowers, such as major MNCs, national governments, and international organizations. For example, in 1989 the World Bank lowered its borrowing costs by issuing a new type of financing instrument, the global bond. A **global bond** is a large, liquid financial asset that can be traded anywhere at any time. The World Bank simultaneously sold $1.5 billion of U.S.-dollar denominated global bonds in North America, Europe, and Japan and succeeded in lowering its interest costs on the bond issue by about 0.225 percentage points. While 0.225 percentage points may not seem much, multiplying that amount by $1.5 billion reveals that the Bank reduced its annual financing costs by $3,375,000. Attracted by the World Bank's success, other large organizations, such as Matsushita Electric, the Province of Ontario, Citicorp, and Household Finance, have also issued global bonds in the past three years.[18]

Other innovative opportunities exist in the bond market. For example, at the borrower's option, bond interest may be paid in one currency with the principal paid in a second. Or the borrower may secure a lower interest rate by offering inflation protection through pegging the principal repayment to the value of gold or the SDR.

Like the Euroloan market, the international bond market is highly competitive and borrowers are often able to obtain funds on very favorable terms. Large transaction sizes, creditworthy borrowers, and freedom from annoying regulations imposed on domestic capital markets all lower the interest rates charged on such loans.

Global Equity Markets

The growing importance of multinational operations and improvements in telecommunications technology have also made equity markets more global. MNCs are no longer restricted to raising new equity solely from domestic sources. For example, Japanese venture capitalists are a major source of equity capital for new U.S. biotechnology firms. Established firms also tap into the global equity market. When expanding into a foreign market, a firm may choose to raise capital for its foreign subsidiary in the foreign market. For example, the Walt Disney Company initially sold 49 percent of its Euro Disney project (located outside of Paris) to French investors. Numerous MNCs also cross-list their common stocks on multiple stock exchanges. British Airways, for example, is listed on both the London Stock Exchange and the New York Stock Exchange, thereby enabling both European and American investors to purchase its shares conveniently.

Another innovation is the development of country funds. A **country fund** is a mutual fund that specializes in investing in a given country's firms. As Fig. 5.10 shows, the importance of non-U.S. stocks to the world's investors has increased dramatically since 1970.

The globalization of equity markets has been facilitated by the globalization of the financial services industry. Most major financial services firms, such as Merrill Lynch, Daiwa Securities, and Deutsche Bank, have expanded their operations from their domestic bases into the major international financial centers. These internationalized financial services firms are eager to raise capital, provide investment advice, offer stock market analyses, and put together financing deals for clients anywhere around the world. The closing case analyzes the recent for-

FIGURE 5.10

Market Value of the World's Publicly Traded Stocks, 1970 and 1993
Source: Merrill Lynch Research.

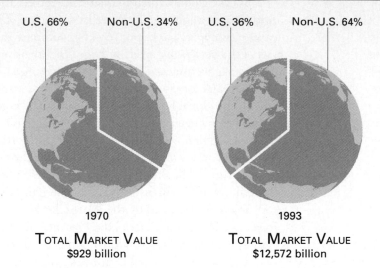

U.S. 66%   Non-U.S. 34%   U.S. 36%   Non-U.S. 64%

1970
TOTAL MARKET VALUE
$929 billion

1993
TOTAL MARKET VALUE
$12,572 billion

tunes of the world's largest securities firm, Nomura Securities of Tokyo, as it tries to adjust to the rapid innovation that characterizes this industry.

Offshore Financial Centers

Offshore financial centers focus on offering banking and other financial services to nonresident customers. Many of these centers are located on island states, such as the Bahamas, Bahrain, the Cayman Islands, Bermuda, the Netherlands Antilles, and Singapore. Luxembourg and Switzerland, although not islands, are also important "offshore" financial centers.

MNCs often use offshore financial centers to obtain low-cost Eurocurrency loans. Many MNCs locate financing subsidiaries in these centers to take advantage of the benefits they offer: political stability, a regulatory climate that facilitates international capital transactions, communications links to other major financial centers, and availability of legal, accounting, financial, and other expertise needed to package large loans. The efficiency of offshore financial centers in attracting deposits and then lending these funds to customers worldwide is an important factor in the growing globalization of the capital market.[19]

CHAPTER REVIEW

Summary

A currency's price in the foreign-exchange market is determined by the interaction of the demand for and supply of the currency. Underlying the demand is foreigners' desire to buy goods, services, and assets of the country. Underlying the supply is residents' desire to purchase goods, services, and assets owned by foreigners.

Two types of exchange-rate systems exist: fixed and flexible. BOP equilibrium is achieved differently in the two types of systems. In a fixed exchange-rate system, short-run equilibrium is achieved via changes in the official reserves owned by central banks. Long-run equilibrium results from the inflationary or deflationary consequences of changes in the domestic money supply on the competitiveness of the country's exporters. Under a flexible exchange-rate system, equilibrium is reached by allowing a currency's price to change until the quantity of currency demanded equals the quantity supplied.

Major international banks in financial centers such as London, Frankfurt, Tokyo, and New York City play a critical role in the functioning of the foreign-exchange market. Key players in the wholesale market, they account for 83 percent of foreign-exchange transactions. In servicing their clients' needs, they are also an important component of the retail market. Banks assist commercial customers, speculators, and arbitrageurs in acquiring foreign currency on both the spot and forward markets.

An important feature of the foreign-exchange market is its time dimension. International businesses may buy currency in the spot market for immediate delivery or in the forward market for future delivery. The forward market, currency futures, and currency options enable firms to protect themselves from unfavorable future exchange-rate movements.

Arbitrage activities affect the demand for and supply of foreign exchange. The theory of purchasing power parity says the prices of tradable goods will tend to equalize among countries. Arbitrage of foreign exchange itself is even more important. Two-point arbitrage implies that the exchange rate between two currencies will be the same in all geographic markets. Three-point arbitrage links individual foreign-exchange markets together. Covered-interest arbitrage causes geographic differences in interest rates to equal differences between spot and forward exchange rates.

The international capital market is growing in sophistication as a result of technological advances in telecommunications and computers. Major international banks still utilize their traditional correspondent relationships, but are increasingly engaged in overseas bank operations themselves. The development of the Eurocurrency market allows banks of any country to conduct lending operations in whatever currencies their clients require. MNCs now commonly raise capital, both debt and equity, on a global basis, wherever its cost is lowest.

Review Questions

1. How are prices established in the foreign-exchange market?

2. How is equilibrium achieved in a fixed exchange-rate system?

3. How is equilibrium reached in a flexible exchange-rate system?

4. What are the advantages and disadvantages of the two types of exchange-rate systems?

5. What is the role of international banks in the foreign-exchange market?

6. Explain the different techniques firms can use to protect themselves from future changes in exchange rates.

7. List the major types of arbitrage activities that affect the foreign-exchange market.

8. Describe the various forms a bank's overseas operations may take.

9. What are Eurocurrencies?

10. What are the major characteristics of offshore financial centers?

Questions for Discussion

1. Suppose the Federal Reserve Board unexpectedly raises interest rates in the United States. How will this impact the foreign-exchange market?

2. How important is communications and computing technology to the smooth functioning of the foreign-exchange market? If the technological advances of the past four decades were eliminated—for example, no PCs or satellite telecommunications—how would the foreign-exchange market be affected?

3. Chapter 4 discusses the attempt by EU members to maintain a fixed exchange-rate system among themselves. If this system is to survive, will these countries need to coordinate their monetary and fiscal policies? (You may want to consider the implications of the international Fisher effect in formulating your answer.)

4. How important is the creation of international banking facilities to the international competitiveness of the U.S. banking industry?

5. What would be the impact on world trade and investment if there were only one currency based on the SDR?

BUILDING GLOBAL SKILLS

Please refer back to Fig. 5.4 in order to answer the following questions:

1. What is the spot rate for the British pound on Tuesday in terms of the U.S. dollar? (Or, stated differently, how many dollars does a pound cost? Or, from the U.S. perspective, what's the direct quote on pounds?)

2. What is the spot price for the dollar on Tuesday in terms of the French franc? (Or, from the U.S. perspective, what is the indirect rate on French francs?)

3. Calculate the cross rate of exchange between the British pound and the French franc.

4. Calculate the annualized forward premium or discount on 180-day yen.

5. If you're planning to go to Japan this summer, should you buy your yen today? Why or why not?

6. According to covered-interest arbitrage theory, is the United States or Japan expected to have higher interest rates?

7. According to covered-interest arbitrage theory, what is the expected difference between interest rates in the United States and Japan?

8. According to the international Fisher effect, is expected inflation higher in Japan or the United States?

CLOSING CASE

Can Nomura Remain Number One?[20]

Technological innovation in telecommunications and computer systems has played a major role in the development and growth of the international capital market. Telecommunications make it easier to monitor changes in individual domestic capital markets and to obtain information about stock market prices, trends in interest rates, and the performance of individual firms anywhere in the world. Computers ease the task of acting on this information and utilizing the sophisticated investment and risk-reduction strategies developed from modern finance theory.

Commercial banks, investment banks, securities brokers, and large institutional investors such as pension funds and insurance companies are well aware of these innovations. They shop for the best advice, the best deals, and the best execution of their orders in a worldwide market. As a result, the financial services industry is becoming globalized. Although firms located in other cities participate in the industry, the major players are concentrated in three cities: London, New York, and Tokyo. London's preeminence stems from the pound's role in the nineteenth-century international monetary system. The "City of London," as London's financial district is known, developed expertise in international banking from managing and financing Britain's far-flung colonial empire. Despite its relatively small economy, the United Kingdom is still the world's leading center of international bank lending activities. Over 300,000 people are directly employed in the financial services industry in the Greater London area.

The second great center for financial services is New York City. U.S. financial service firms, benefiting from their location in the world's largest economy, are aggressive underwriters of equity and debt offerings by firms worldwide. U.S. firms are well-known for their innovative approaches to providing financial services, developing such products as money-market funds, automatic teller machines, and computer-executed program trading of complex bundles of stocks.

However, the dominance of British and U.S. financial services firms is increasingly being challenged by their Japanese counterparts, who are benefiting from Japan's growth into the world's second largest economy. As Table 5.1 showed, 17 of the world's 30 largest banks are in Japan. Furthermore, Japanese banks enjoyed a 15 percent share of the international bank lending market in 1991, second only to British banks. Tokyo is also the third-largest center for foreign-exchange trading.

Tokyo's Nomura Securities Company, Ltd., the world's largest securities firm, is a major force in Japan's financial services sector. Like other securities firms, it buys and sells stocks and bonds on organized stock exchanges and in over-the-counter trading. It also engages in highly profitable underwriting activities in which it helps firms raise capital through public and private placements of debt and equity offerings. Its 156 retail branches span Japan and serve 5 million clients. Nomura's retail salesforce is notoriously aggressive in pushing to those clients stocks and bonds favored by the firm's upper management, particularly ones underwritten or sponsored by Nomura's investment banking operations. Insulated from competition by a fixed commission system and governmental restrictions on domestic and foreign competitors, Nomura benefited substantially from the excellent performance of the Japanese economy in the 1980s. The firm's revenues grew at a compounded rate of 16.3 percent annually, while its income soared at an annual compounded rate of 20.9 percent. Today roughly 80 percent of its revenues are generated in Japan.

During the 1980s, Nomura used its strong domestic base to expand its operations internationally. Currently it operates 41 offices in 27 foreign countries. It purchased a seat on the New York Stock Exchange in 1981 and one on the London Stock Exchange in 1986. During this boom decade for Japan, Nomura became a leading underwriter of Eurobonds (particularly dollar-denominated bonds sold by Japanese companies) and samurai bonds (foreign bonds denominated in yen). In 1988, attracted to the enormous profits earned by investment advisors in the 1980s takeover craze, it purchased a 20 percent share of the Wasserstein Perella Group, one of the

world's leading merger and acquisitions specialists. By luring high-priced, talented investment bankers from other Wall Street firms, Nomura's North American operations have been profitable, although its activities have been limited to niche markets such as those for mortgage-based securities and junk bonds. In the year ending March 1994, for example, it earned $140 million, primarily by packaging and trading securities based on commercial mortgages. But in the North American market, Nomura has not yet succeeded in becoming a major player like Goldman Sachs and Merrill Lynch.

Nomura's situation in Europe is not as profitable. Its European operations have been plagued by high costs and their profits have been disappointing. In the 1980s, Nomura primarily used its 16 European offices to peddle Japanese financial products to European investors. But Japanese stocks and bonds fell out of favor with foreign investors after Japan's "bubble" economy burst, starting in 1989. Suddenly Nomura's glaring weaknesses in Europe were exposed: it lacked both an extensive salesforce and knowledge of the local market. Moreover, U.S. and European securities brokers and investment bankers were well ahead of Nomura in developing the complex financial products, such as derivatives, warrants, and hybrid securities, that appealed to European money managers.

To address these problems, Nomura began in April 1994 to reorganize its European operations. Previously, the heads of its European offices reported directly to an executive in Tokyo. Now they report to the director of European operations headquartered in London. Their power was further weakened when their sales staffs were made members of teams directed by executives in London. For example, a bond salesperson in Zurich who previously reported to Nomura's Swiss country manager now reports to the division head in London who is in charge of fixed-income products. Through this restructuring, Nomura hopes to make its European operations less Japanese and more European in spirit and practice. Moreover, the restructuring improves the promotion opportunities available to its European staff (particularly in London); previously the highest position in Nomura's European operations was that of country manager, and such slots were reserved for Japanese executives.

In the 1990s, Nomura also has run into troubles in its home market. The crash of the Tokyo Stock

Market, in which the Nikkei Stock Average fell as low as 57 percent (in 1991) of its high in 1989, reduced trading volumes, which cut into Nomura's lucrative flow of commission income. And as the domestic recession in the early 1990s reduced corporate Japan's needs for new capital, Nomura's profits from underwriting new debt and equity issues plummeted. For example, its underwriting activities fell from 1201 in 1990 to 12 in the first half of 1991. More threatening to the firm's long-run prospects is the average Japanese household's extreme distrust of investing in stocks. This reaction resembles that of U.S. investors, who shied away from the New York Stock Exchange after the 1929 crash. Confidence in the Japanese market was also disrupted by the news that Nomura, along with other leading Japanese securities firms (including the second-largest firm, Daiwa Securities), reimbursed large Japanese companies over $471 million for their stock market losses, but did not extend the same courtesy to little investors.

Nomura also has to overcome several facets of the Japanese business environment. Savings rates are high in Japan—the average household has accumulated ¥10.9 million in savings (about $100,000)—but most savings are in safe, sedate forms such as postal savings accounts. Nomura needs to lure those yen into investments that yield commissions for Nomura. But Japan's rigid regulation of its financial services sector makes it difficult to develop new financial instruments to accomplish this.

As a result of trade conflicts between Japan and its major trading partners—the United States and the EU—the Japanese Ministry of Finance has increasingly allowed foreign competitors access to the domestic Japanese securities market. Nomura has had difficulties responding quickly to innovations introduced by these foreign competitors, in part because of Japanese business culture. As we discuss in Chapter 9, this culture is very consensus-oriented, and pay scales tend to reward the achievements of the group rather than those of individuals. U.S. securities firms, on the other hand, seek to hire high-achieving superstars and are happy to reward their individual achievements. While Nomura was willing to adopt Western pay practices in its North American and European operations, it has been hesitant to do the same in Japan, thereby leaving itself vulnerable to raids on its personnel by Western securities firms operating in Japan.

As a result, despite the lackluster performance of the Japanese stock market in the past several years, foreign brokers have expanded their share of the Japanese market from 3 percent in 1988 to 20 percent in 1994. Three American firms—Salomon Brothers, Goldman Sachs, and Morgan Stanley—have been reaping record profits in Japan. They have done this by transferring to the Japanese stock market their U.S.-developed expertise in computerized arbitrage trading between the stock market and stock market index futures. Nomura and its fellow Japanese securities firms have been unable to match this success. What annoys the Japanese brokers most is their inability to harness their competitive advantages—their extensive retail branch networks and their understanding of the Japanese customer—to beat back the foreign invasion. As stated by one observer, the Americans' use of computerized arbitrage trading means there is "no need for customers. Nor for Japanese-speaking staff. Nor, indeed, for anyone who knows anything about Japanese companies."

Given the strengths of the Japanese economy, no doubt the Japanese stock market will eventually rise again. Japanese investors will return to the stock market, thereby allowing Nomura to benefit from its strong network of retail branches in Japan. But Nomura will face tougher competition from foreign securities firms in its domestic market in the 1990s than it did in the 1970s and 1980s. The firm must also respond more quickly to the innovations of its foreign competitors if it wants to retain its position as the world's largest securities firm.

Case Questions

1. Nomura's North American operations have been profitable, but the firm's presence in the market has been limited to specific niches. Should Nomura attempt to broaden its participation in the North American market even if it means sacrificing profits in the short run?

2. Is reorganization the solution to improving Nomura's profitability in Europe? If not, what other steps should it take?

3. Can Nomura survive if it doesn't have a presence in all areas of the Triad?

4. How can Nomura protect itself from the U.S. invasion of the Japanese securities market?

5. What can Nomura do to restore the confidence of small Japanese investors in the stock market? Is this a critical task for the firm?

6. What can Nomura do to become an innovator of new financial instruments that serve the needs of large international organizations?

CHAPTER NOTES

1. "European Exchange Rate Chaos Is Bedlam for Currency Traders at Chase Manhattan," *Wall Street Journal,* September 17, 1992, p. C1. Reprinted by permission of *The Wall Street Journal,* © 1992 Dow Jones & Company, Inc. All Rights Reserved Worldwide.

2. To simplify the exposition, we assumed the foreign-exchange supply curve is upward-sloping like most supply curves. Unfortunately, foreign-exchange supply curves may bend backward, a complication that can be left for graduate students in economics and finance to deal with.

3. Ungerer et al., *The European Monetary System: Developments and Perspectives,* Occasional Paper 73 (Washington, D.C.: International Monetary Fund, 1990), p. 95.

4. Eiteman, Stonehill, and Moffett, *Multinational Business Finance,* 6th ed. (Reading, Mass.: Addison-Wesley, 1992), p. 88.

5. Bank for International Settlements, *Central Bank Survey of Foreign Exchange Market Activity in April 1992* (Basle, 1993).

6. Rudi Weisweiller, *How the Foreign Exchange Market Works* (New York: New York Institute of Finance, 1990), p. 12.

7. *Euromoney, The 1991 Guide to Currencies* (London: Euromoney, 1991), p. 105.

8. Bank for International Settlements, *Central Bank Survey of Foreign Exchange Market Activity in April 1992* (Basle, 1993) is the source of this and subsequent market share data.

9. Barbara Durr and Tracy Corrigan, "The future comes into focus on screen," *Financial Times,* June 25, 1992, p. 15; Thomas McCarroll, "Futures Shock," *Time,* June 29, 1992, p. 69.

10. Boris Antl and Richard Ensor, *Management of Foreign Exchange Risk* (London: Euromoney Publications, 1982), p. 43.

11. To simplify our example, we assumed the domestic price of the jeans in Canada and in the United States remained constant. But consider the market for Levis in Canada. As Canadians travel to the United States to buy their jeans, the demand for jeans in Canada decreases, which should decrease the price of jeans in Canada. Similarly, the demand for jeans in the United States should increase, which should increase the price of jeans in the United States. Thus, PPP might occur as a result of changes in the price of the product as well as changes in the price of foreign exchange.

12. "Canada Suffers Exodus of Jobs, Investment and Shoppers to U.S.," *Wall Street Journal,* June 20, 1991, p. A1.

13. "Canadians' Shopping Trips to U.S. Decline," *Wall Street Journal,* July 15, 1992, p. A2.

14. Antl and Ensor, op.cit., p. 112.

15. The Glass-Stegall Act, which restricts U.S. commercial banks from providing investment banking services, is a major source of friction between the United States and other governments because the United States will not allow foreign banks operating in the United States to provide both commercial and investment banking services.

16. Paul Einzig, *The Euro-Dollar System* (New York: St. Martin's Press, 1973), p. 3.

17. Paul R. Krugman and Maurice Obstfeld, *International Economics,* 3rd ed. (New York: HarperCollins, 1994), p. 642f.

18. "Matsushita Electric's Planned $1 Billion Issue May Open Up Access to Issuance of Global Bonds," *Wall Street Journal,* June 8, 1992, p. C1.

19. Eiteman, Stonehill, and Moffett, op.cit., p. 281.

20. John Wyles, "London to Rival New York, Tokyo as Financial Center," *Europe,* Jan./Feb. 1986 (No. 253), p. 22; "Financial Centres: Rise and Fall," *The Economist,* June 27, 1992, p. 4 of survey; "Unchain Japan's Financial Markets," *Wall Street Journal,* June 26, 1991, p. A10; "Chapman Says 'No' To Nomura Units Based in Europe," *Wall Street Journal,* May 18, 1994, p. B4; "Regulatory grip that has cost Tokyo dear," *Financial Times,* June 29, 1994, p. 9; Hoover et al., *Hoover's Handbook of World Business 1992* (Austin, Tex.: Reference Press, 1991), p. 249; Stefan Wagstyl, "Japan's scandal-hit traders may lose fixed commissions," *Financial Times,* August 10/11, 1991, p. 3; "Unfair Advantage," *Wall Street Journal,* June 25, 1991, p. A1; "Nomura Securities Fights to Regain the Confidence of Japanese Investors," *Wall Street Journal,* July 6, 1992, p. 3; Emiko Terazono, "Tokyo offers riches to foreign brokers," *Financial Times,* June 23, 1992, p. 19; "Gaijin, gaijin, gone," *The Economist,* December 22, 1990, p. 96.

The
National
Environment

3

Protecting Workers from Unfair Trade Practices

Countries often try to protect domestic industries from unfair trade practices by their foreign competitors. Unfortunately, because of the complexity of the world economy, protecting jobs in one industry often means the loss of jobs in another. Production of these Macintosh laptop computers was shifted from Colorado to Ireland after the U.S. government decided to protect domestic producers of the display screens used in laptops. (See "Point/ Counterpoint" on pages 230–231.)

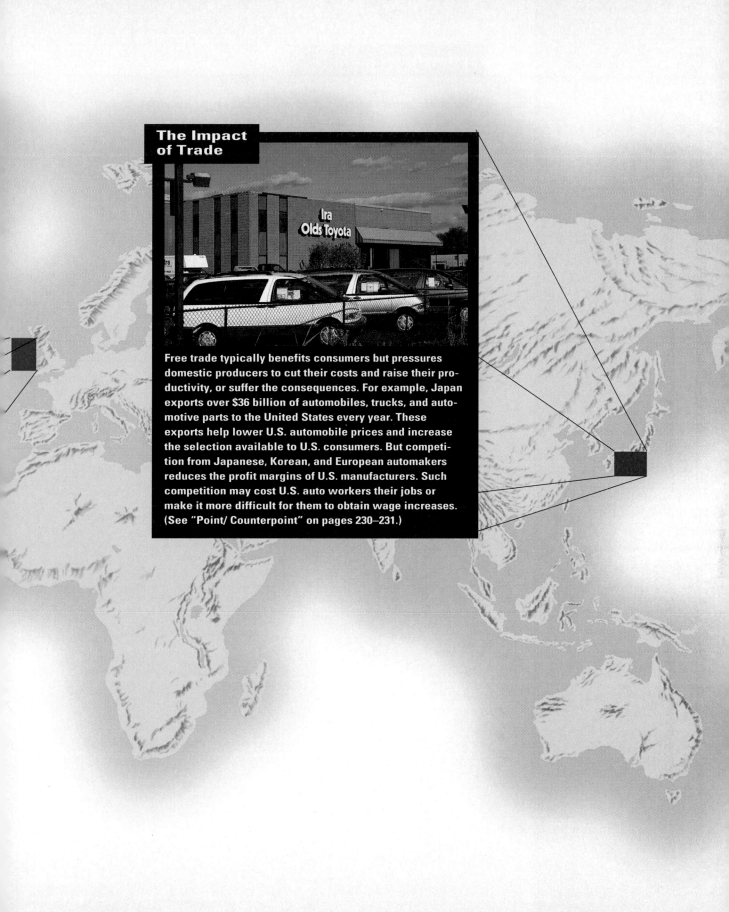

The Impact of Trade

Free trade typically benefits consumers but pressures domestic producers to cut their costs and raise their productivity, or suffer the consequences. For example, Japan exports over $36 billion of automobiles, trucks, and automotive parts to the United States every year. These exports help lower U.S. automobile prices and increase the selection available to U.S. consumers. But competition from Japanese, Korean, and European automakers reduces the profit margins of U.S. manufacturers. Such competition may cost U.S. auto workers their jobs or make it more difficult for them to obtain wage increases. (See "Point/ Counterpoint" on pages 230–231.)

6

Formulation of National Trade Policies

Chapter Outline

Rationales for trade intervention

Industry-level trade policies
National trade policies

Barriers to international trade

Tariffs
Nontariff barriers

Promotion of international trade

Subsidies
Foreign trade zones
Export financing programs

Controlling unfair trade practices

Countervailing duties
Antidumping regulations
Super 301

After studying this chapter you should be able to:

Present the major arguments in favor of and against governmental intervention in international trade.

Discuss the advantages and disadvantages of adopting an industrial policy.

Analyze the role of domestic politics in formulating a country's international trade policies.

Describe the major tools countries use to restrict trade.

Specify the techniques countries use to promote international trade.

Explain how countries protect themselves against unfair trade practices.

A T FIRST GLANCE, DESMARAIS & FRÈRE, LTD. (DESMARAIS), A Longueuil, Quebec, manufacturer founded in 1951, would appear to be in an enviable position. It employs as many as 400 workers during peak production periods and is Canada's largest producer of photo albums that have self-adhesive pages. Its albums retail at $15 to $50 and are sold through mass marketers such as Kmart, Zellers, Woolworths, and Metropolitan. In fact, ten customers account for 70 percent of Desmarais's annual sales, keeping its marketing costs low. And all but three small domestic competitors have fallen by the wayside. Thus Desmarais captured 50 to 90 percent of the Canadian market for these photo albums in the 1970s and 1980s—an enviable market share level in any industry. ■■ But in truth the firm's situation is not so rosy. For 20 years, it has been plagued by import competition

Desmarais Is Tired of Being Dumped On[1]

from low-priced photo albums produced in Asia. One response Desmarais considered to counter this threat was to focus on quality. Yet its major discount-chain customers pride themselves on providing the lowest possible prices for consumers and are willing to use whatever supplier is cheapest, whether foreign or domestic. Further, the photo albums are typically shrink-wrapped in clear plastic, which makes it impossible for a retail customer to compare the quality of different producers' albums. Also, such albums are bought infrequently by the average consumer, so developing brand loyalty among consumers is difficult. ■■ Desmarais believed it was being victimized by a practice known as dumping. **Dumping** is the selling by a firm of its products outside its domestic market at prices below those it charges in its domestic market. Fortunately for Desmarais, Canadian law protects Canadian businesses from dumping. In 1975 Desmarais petitioned the Canadian Import Tribunal (CIT), which has jurisdiction over such cases, for relief from the low prices charged by Japanese and Korean photo album manufacturers. The CIT determined that firms from these two countries were indeed dumping their albums in Canada, thereby causing material injury to Desmarais and its smaller Canadian rivals. The CIT then imposed an **antidumping duty**—a tax on the dumped imported goods—on Korean and Japanese photo albums. This duty was equivalent to the difference between the lower price the Asians were charging in the Canadian market and the higher prices they charged in their home markets. In theory, the duty would eliminate any price advantage the Asian producers gained from the dumping. ■■ However, the new duty did not solve Desmarais's problem because it applied only to Japanese and Korean producers. The production of photo albums simply shifted to other Asian locations, which were not covered by the duty. By 1984 Desmarais's share of the Canadian market had fallen to an all-time low of 50 percent. The foreign competition had hurt the company's profit margins, profits, and financial performance, for it could not raise its prices to compensate for increases in its costs. In 1985 it filed a second successful complaint with the CIT against dumping by Hong Kong, South Korea, and the United States. (The United States entered the picture because Korean manufacturers were shipping the photo albums to the United States and then re-exporting them from there to Canada.) Desmarais then filed dumping complaints against China in 1986, against Singapore, Malaysia, and Taiwan in 1987, and against Indonesia, Thailand, and the Philippines in 1991. ▌▌ In all these cases, the CIT or its successor, the Canadian International Trade Tribunal (CITT), determined that dumping had occurred. The antidumping duties imposed by the CIT and the CITT were not trivial. For example, as a result of the 1991 complaint, antidumping duties were imposed ranging from 35.1 percent (on self-adhesive pages) to 78 percent (on photo albums with self-adhesive pages). Yet Desmarais cannot rest easy. For 20 years, its home market has been targeted by Asian producers. As soon as the firm obtains relief from the CIT or the CITT, production of photo albums shifts to a country not covered by an antidumping duty. Desmarais has little reason to be optimistic that it will be able to raise its prices to recover its cost increases over the past two decades. ▌▌▌▌▌

In today's global economy, firms must deal with both domestic and foreign competitors. The problem facing Desmarais & Frère, Ltd., exemplifies the plight of domestic manufacturers threatened by competition from low-priced foreign producers. And its reaction typifies that of similar firms: it asked its national government for protection against the foreigners. However, many firms benefit from international trade, finding foreign markets a rich source of additional customers. Exports generate domestic jobs, so many national governments promote the success of their countries' domestic firms in international markets. In this chapter we discuss the development of national trade policies that protect domestic firms from foreign competition and help promote the country's exports. We also explore the rationale for these policies and how governments implement them.

Rationales for Trade Intervention

Politicians, economists, and businesspeople have been arguing for centuries over government policy toward international trade. Two principal issues have shaped the debate on appropriate trade policies:

1 Whether a national government should intervene to protect the country's

domestic firms by taxing foreign goods entering the domestic market or constructing other barriers against imports

2 Whether a national government should directly help the country's domestic firms increase their foreign sales through export subsidies, government-to-government negotiations, and guaranteed loan programs

These two issues are the subject of this chapter.

In the United States, the trade policy debate has recently focused on the issue of whether the government should promote "free" trade or "fair" trade. **Free trade** implies that the national government exerts minimal influence on the exporting and importing decisions of private firms and individuals. **Fair trade**, sometimes called **managed trade**, suggests that the national government should actively intervene to ensure that exports of domestic firms receive an equitable share of foreign markets and that imports are controlled to minimize losses of domestic jobs and market share in specific industries. Some participants in this debate argue that the government should ensure a "level playing field" on which foreign and domestic firms can compete on equal terms. While sounding reasonable, the "level playing field" argument is often used to justify policies that restrict foreign competition.

The outcome of this debate is critical to firms. The policies individual countries adopt affect the size and profitability of foreign markets and investments, as well as the degree to which firms are threatened by foreign imports in their domestic markets. Governments worldwide are continually pressured by successful and efficient firms that produce goods for export, as well as by their labor forces and the communities in which their factories are located, to adopt policies supporting freer trade. Companies such as Sony (consumer electronics), Daimler-Benz (automobiles), and Caterpillar (earth-moving equipment) gain increased sales and investment opportunities in foreign markets when international trade barriers are lowered. At the same time governments are petitioned by firms beleaguered by foreign competitors, as well as by their labor forces and the communities in which their factories are located, to raise barriers to imported goods by adopting fair-trade policies. Companies such as Desmarais and French automakers Renault and Peugeot gain increased sales opportunities in their domestic markets when international trade barriers exist.

Industry-Level Trade Theories

The argument for free trade follows Adam Smith's analysis outlined in Chapter 3: voluntary exchange makes both parties to the transaction better off and allocates goods to their highest valued use. In Smith's view, the welfare of a country and its citizens is best promoted by allowing self-interested individuals, regardless of where they reside, to exchange goods, services, and assets as they see fit. However, many businesspeople, politicians, and policymakers believe that, under certain circumstances, deviations from free trade are appropriate. In this section we review the primary arguments against free trade and for government intervention and we discuss trade policies that focus on the needs of individual industries. In the next section we explore broader, national-level policies aimed at meeting the needs of the economy and society as a whole.

The National Defense Argument. National defense has often been used as a reason to support governmental protection of specific industries. Since world events can suddenly turn hostile to a country's interests, the **national defense argument** holds that a country must be self-sufficient in critical raw materials, machinery, and technology or else be vulnerable to foreign threats. For example, the vulnerability of Japan's supply lines was demonstrated by the extensive damage done to its merchant marine fleet by Allied submarines in World War II. After the war Japan banned the importation of rice as a means of promoting domestic self-sufficiency in its dietary staple. Similarly, the United States, to retain shipbuilding skills and expertise within the country in case of war, has developed numerous programs to support its domestic shipbuilding industry. For example, all U.S. naval vessels must be built in U.S. shipyards, and ocean transportation between U.S. ports must be conducted by U.S.-built ships. Many of the 120,000 jobs in the U.S. shipbuilding industry would be lost without these federal protections, for U.S. shipyards are not competitive with those of Japan, Korea, Norway, Denmark, or Germany. A recent federal study found that the average bid by U.S. shipyards on commercial contracts was 97 percent higher than the lowest foreign bid.[2]

The national defense argument appeals to the general public, which is concerned that its country will be pushed around by other countries that control critical resources. Many special-interest groups have used this politically appealing argument to protect their industries from foreign competition. For example, the U.S. mohair industry produces wool that was once used in military uniforms. It has benefited from federal subsidies since the passage of the 1954 National Wool Act, which purported to protect the industry in the country's strategic interest. Even though the military has long since replaced mohair garments with synthetic ones, the subsidy remained in effect until 1995. Other U.S. industries receiving favorable treatment for national defense reasons include steel, electronics, machine tools, and the merchant marine.[3]

The Infant Industry Argument. Alexander Hamilton, the first U.S. Secretary of the Treasury, articulated the **infant industry argument** in 1791. He believed that the newly independent country's infant manufacturing sector possessed a comparative advantage that would ultimately allow it to thrive in international markets. However, he feared that the young nation's manufacturers would not survive their infancy and adolescence because of fierce competition from more mature European firms. Hamilton thus fought for the imposition of tariffs on numerous imported manufactured goods to give U.S. firms temporary protection from foreign competition until they could fully establish themselves. His philosophy has since been adopted by countries worldwide. Japan, for example, has been particularly effective in nurturing its domestic industries. Despite its lack of significant natural resources, Japan has developed since the end of World War II thriving metal fabrication industries (iron and steel, aluminum, copper, and zinc) by eliminating tariffs on imports of raw ores and ore concentrates while imposing high tariffs on processed and fabricated metals. For example, in 1970 no tariff was imposed on copper ore imported in Japan, but fabricated copper products bore tariffs as high as 22 percent. As its metal fabrication industry matured, Japan reduced the level of import protection. Today its tariffs on copper products are negligible.[4]

Governmental nurturing of domestic industries that will ultimately have a comparative advantage can be a powerful economic development strategy, as Japan's postwar economic success indicates. However, determining which industries deserve infant industry protection is often done on a political, rather than an economic, basis. Firms, workers, and shareholders are not shy about using the infant industry argument to bolster support for import protection or export subsidies for their industries. Moreover, once an industry is granted protection, it may be reluctant to give it up. Many infant industries end up being protected well into their old age.

Maintenance of Existing Jobs. Well-established firms and their workers, particularly in high-wage countries, are often threatened by imports from low-wage countries, as shown in the case of Desmarais. To maintain existing employment levels, firms and workers often petition their governments for relief from foreign competition. Government officials, eager to avoid the human and economic misery inflicted on workers and communities when factories are shut down, tend to lend a sympathetic ear to such pleas. Assistance may come in the form of tariffs, quotas, or other barriers that we discuss in more detail in the next section. The assistance may be temporary in nature, as demonstrated in this chapter's closing case, which deals with a request by Harley-Davidson for temporary protection against Japanese imports. Or it may be long-lived, as in the case of governmental protection of the U.S. commercial shipbuilding industry, which has extended that industry's life by over 30 years.

Strategic Trade Theory. When firms and labor union officials plead for government intervention to help them compete internationally, their efforts are usually criticized by economists, who claim that such intervention ultimately harms the economy. The economists base that claim on the theoretical predictions of the classical trade theories—absolute advantage and comparative advantage—discussed in Chapter 3. But these trade theories assume that firms operate in perfectly competitive markets of the sort that exist only in economics textbooks. They also assume that each country's consumers are able to buy goods and services at the lowest possible prices from the world's most efficient producers. According to the classical theories, any governmental intervention that denies consumers these buying opportunities will make the country as a whole worse off, although it could make certain groups within the society better off.

In the early 1980s, however, new models of international trade—known collectively as **strategic trade theory**—were developed. These models provide a new theoretical justification for government trade intervention, thereby supporting firms' requests for protection. Strategic trade theory makes very different assumptions about the industry environment in which firms operate than do the classical theories. Strategic trade theory considers those industries capable of supporting only a few firms worldwide, perhaps because of high product development costs or strong experience curve effects. A firm can earn monopoly profits if it can succeed in becoming one of the few firms in such a highly concentrated industry. Strategic trade theory suggests that a national government can make its country better off if it adopts trade policies that improve the competitiveness of its domestic firms in such oligopolistic industries.[5]

FIGURE 6.1

**Payoff Matrix:
Profits from
Developing a
Nuclear Power
Plant Design (in
billions of dollars)**

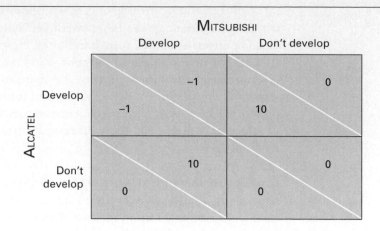

For example, consider the potential market for a new nuclear power plant design, one that could safely and cheaply supply electrical energy. Assume that because of economies of scale, the market will be extremely profitable if one—and only one—firm decides to enter it. Further assume that only two firms, France's Alcatel Alsthom and Japan's Mitsubishi, have the engineering talent and financial resources to develop the new plant design and both are equally capable of successfully completing the project. Figure 6.1 shows the payoff matrix for the two firms. If Mitsubishi decides to develop the plant design and Alcatel decides not to (see the lower left-hand corner), Mitsubishi profits by $10 billion, while Alcatel makes nothing. If Alcatel decides to develop the plant design and Mitsubishi doesn't, Alcatel profits by $10 billion, while Mitsubishi makes nothing (see the upper right-hand corner). If neither firm chooses to develop the design, they both make nothing (see the lower right-hand corner). If both decide to develop the design, both will lose $1 billion, for the market is too small to be profitable for both of them. Neither firm has a strategy that it should follow regardless of what its rival does.

Now suppose the French government learns of the large profits that one of its country's firms could earn if that firm were the sole developer of the new plant design. If France were to offer Alcatel a subsidy of $2 billion to develop the new nuclear technology, the payoff matrix would change to that shown in Fig. 6.2. Because of the subsidy, Alcatel's payoff is increased by $2 billion if and *only* if it develops the technology (see the first row). With the subsidy, Alcatel will develop the technology regardless of what Mitsubishi does, because it makes more money by developing than by not developing. If Mitsubishi chooses to develop, Alcatel makes nothing if it doesn't develop and $1 billion if it does develop. If Mitsubishi doesn't develop, Alcatel makes nothing if it doesn't develop and $12 billion if it does develop. Thus Alcatel will always choose to develop. But if Mitsubishi knows Alcatel will always choose to develop, then the best strategy for Mitsubishi is not to develop.

What has the French government accomplished with its $2 billion subsidy?

1 It has induced Alcatel to develop the new nuclear power plant technology.

2 It has induced the Japanese firm to stay out of the market.

3 It has succeeded in allowing a French firm to make a $12 billion profit at a cost to French taxpayers of only $2 billion.

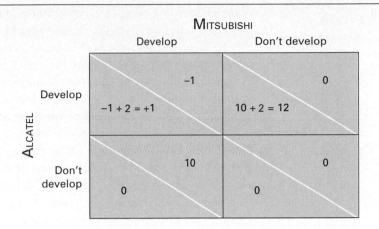

FIGURE 6.2

Payoff Matrix: Profits
Resulting from a
$2 Billion Subsidy
to Alcatel (in billions
of dollars)

By adopting a strategic trade policy in a market where monopoly profits are available, the French government has made French residents as a group better off by $10 billion ($12 billion in profits minus $2 billion in subsidies).

However, strategic trade theory applies only to markets that are incapable of supporting more than a handful of firms on a worldwide basis. Most global industries are more competitive than this. A country's wholesale adoption of strategic trade policies to cover a broad group of industries may actually reduce the country's overall international competitiveness, since favoring certain industries inevitably hurts others. For example, if the French government chooses to subsidize the nuclear power industry, the demand for and salaries paid to the mechanical engineers, computer programmers, and systems analysts needed by the nuclear power industry will rise, thereby reducing the international competitiveness of other French industries requiring such skilled personnel. Further, the benefit of the subsidy could be neutralized if another country adopts a similar strategy. If Japan responded to France's $2 billion subsidy by giving a $3 billion subsidy to Mitsubishi, the payoff matrix would change: Mitsubishi would be encouraged to develop the power plant as well. Any anticipated monopoly profits might be dissipated if the two countries engaged in an all-out subsidy war.[6]

National Trade Policies

The policies just discussed address the needs of individual industries. A national government also may develop trade policies that begin by taking a broader perspective on the needs of the economy and society as a whole. After assessing these needs, the government then adopts industry-by-industry policies to promote the country's overall economic agenda.

Economic Development Programs. An important policy goal of many governments, particularly those of developing countries, is economic development. International commerce can play a major role in economic development programs. Countries dependent on a single export often choose to diversify their economies in order to reduce the impact of, say, a bad harvest or falling prices for the dominant export. For example, the West African country of Ghana, which once depended heavily on cocoa, began an industrialization program to protect itself from fluctuations in cocoa prices. Also, Kuwait chose to diversify from its heavy dependency on oil sales, electing to do so through investment rather than trade. It used cash from its oil revenues to build up its investment portfolio, a strategy so successful that much of its resistance to the 1990 Iraqi invasion was financed by its overseas investments.

As discussed in Chapter 2, some countries, such as Japan, Korea, and Taiwan, based their post–World War II economic development on heavy reliance on exports. According to this **export-promotion strategy**, a country encourages firms to compete in foreign markets by harnessing some advantage the country possesses, such as low labor costs. Other countries, such as Australia, Argentina, India, and Brazil, adopted an **import-substitution strategy** after World War II; such a strategy encourages the growth of domestic manufacturing industries by erecting high barriers to imported goods. Many MNCs responded by locating production facilities within these countries in order to avoid the costs resulting from the high barriers. In general, the export-promotion strategy has been more successful than the import-substitution strategy, as Chapter 2 indicated.

Industrial Policy. In many countries, the government plays an active role in managing the national economy. Often an important element of this task is determining which industries should receive favorable governmental treatment. Bureaucrats within Japan's Ministry of International Trade and Industry (MITI), for example, identify emerging technologies and products and, through subsidies, public statements, and behind-the-scenes maneuvering, encourage Japanese firms to enter those markets. During the 1950s and 1960s, MITI actively diverted scarce credit and foreign exchange from low-value-added, labor-intensive industries such as textiles into high-value-added, capital-intensive heavy industries such as steel and automobiles. In the 1970s and 1980s, MITI targeted industries with high growth potential, such as semiconductors, aerospace, biotechnology, and ceramics. The Taiwanese and Korean governments patterned their economic development strategies after the successful Japanese model.

Because of the postwar economic successes of these Asian countries, the governments of most other Quad countries face the major issue of whether to adopt **industrial policy**, by which the national government identifies key domestic industries critical to the country's future economic growth and then formulates programs that promote their competitiveness. Ideally, industrial policy assists a country's firms in capturing large shares of important, growing global markets, as MITI has done for Japanese MNCs.

Many experts, however, do not view industrial policy as a panacea for improving the global competitiveness of a country's firms. They argue that government bureaucrats cannot perfectly identify the right industries to favor under such policy. As an example, they cite France, where industrial policies targeting automobiles, computers, military and commercial aircraft, and telecommunications have created some spectacularly unprofitable enterprises that require large government subsidies. These industries became a drag on the French economy, rather than a generator of new wealth. Even Japan has not been infallible. In the early 1980s, MITI bureaucrats encouraged domestic consumer electronics firms to develop high-definition television (HDTV) that relied on Japan's lead in analog-based TV technology. Although HDTV is viewed as the wave of the future for television, the technical transmission standards for HDTV products likely to be adopted by U.S. and European regulators will rely on more sophisticated digital technology being developed by Western firms rather than the dated analog technology imposed on Japanese firms by MITI. Consequently, the multibillion-dollar investment of the leading Japanese consumer electronics firms in HDTV is predicted to be a total loss.

Opponents of industrial policy also fear that the determination of which industries will receive governmental largesse will depend on the domestic political clout of those industries rather than on their potential international competitiveness. Instead of future winners in the international marketplace being selected, opponents say, industrial policy will become a more sophisticated-sounding version of pork-barrel politics.

At the heart of the industrial policy debate is the question of what is the proper role of government in a market economy. The Reagan and Bush administrations chose not to adopt formally a strategy of industrial policy on the grounds that the government should limit its role in the economy.[7] Yet others disagree, including key players in the Clinton administration such as Labor Secretary Robert Reich. These advocates argue that improving the global competitiveness of the country's firms is too important to be left to the private sector. In furtherance of this belief, the Clinton administration announced in April 1994 five emerging technologies for which it would increase federal R&D support: genetics, health care information systems, electronics, automobiles and highway systems, and computer software.[8]

Public Choice Analysis. While many arguments favoring governmental trade intervention are couched in terms of national interest, such intervention typically helps some special-interest groups but invariably hurts other domestic interests and the general public. For example, the CIT's decision to impose antidumping duties helped Desmarais and its Quebec workforce. However, it reduced the work available to dockworkers who unload foreign cargos in British Columbia's Port of Vancouver and raised the prices that Canadian consumers had to pay for photo albums.

Why do national governments adopt public policies that hinder international business and hurt their own citizenry overall, even though the policies may benefit small groups within their societies? According to **public choice analysis**, a branch of economics that analyzes public decision making, the special interest will often dominate the general interest on any given issue because special-interest groups are willing to work harder for the passage of laws favorable to their interests than the general public is willing to work for the defeat of laws unfavorable to its interest. For example, under the 1920 Jones Act the United States restricts foreign ships from providing transportation services between U.S. ports. This restriction is supported by owners of U.S. oceangoing vessels, who gain increased profits estimated at $630 million per year. But the Jones Act is also estimated to increase the transportation costs consumers pay by $10.5 billion annually, or $40 per person. Further, like other restrictions on free trade, the Jones Act has had unintended consequences, as Map 6.1 suggests.

Public choice analysis suggests few consumers will be motivated either to learn about the impact of the Jones Act on them or to write or call their elected officials to save a trivial sum like $40. The special interests, such as shipowners and members of U.S. maritime unions, however, are motivated to know all the ins and outs of the Jones Act and to protect it from repeal, because the gains to them

MAP 6.1

An Effect of the Jones Act

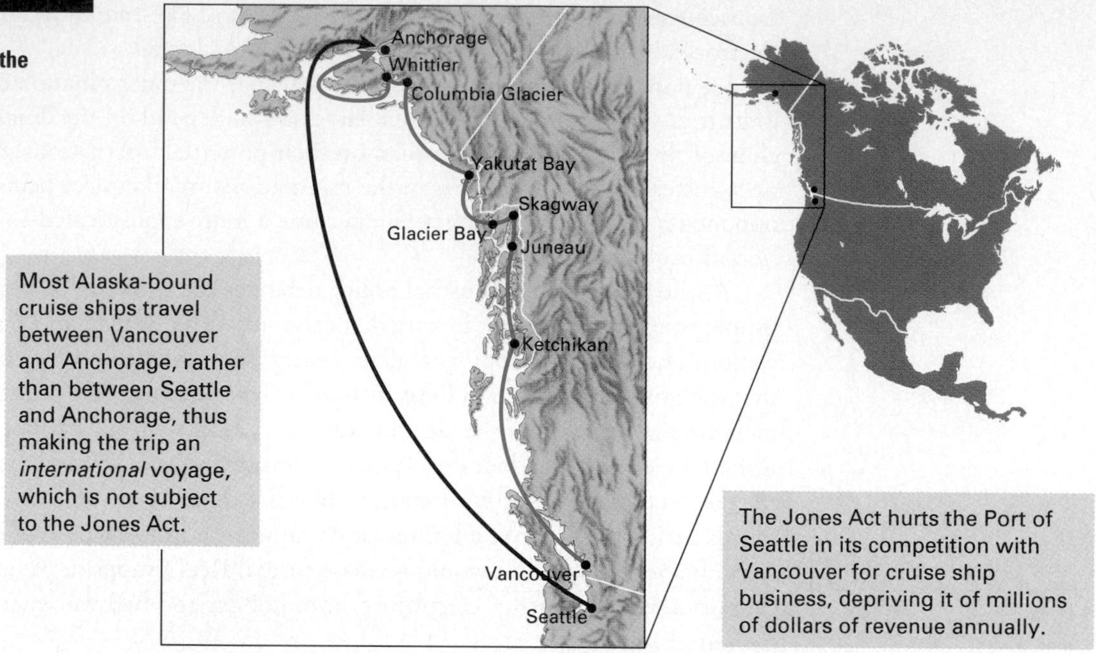
Anchorage
Whittier
Columbia Glacier
Yakutat Bay
Skagway
Glacier Bay
Juneau
Ketchikan
Vancouver
Seattle
Most Alaska-bound cruise ships travel between Vancouver and Anchorage, rather than between Seattle and Anchorage, thus making the trip an *international* voyage, which is not subject to the Jones Act.
The Jones Act hurts the Port of Seattle in its competition with Vancouver for cruise ship business, depriving it of millions of dollars of revenue annually.

make it worth their while to do so. As a result, members of Congress constantly hear from special-interest groups about the importance of preserving the Jones Act, while the average consumer is silent on the issue.[9] Knowing that they will be harmed by the special-interest groups and will not be rewarded by the general public if they repeal the Jones Act, members of Congress will rationally vote with the special interests on this issue.

According to public choice analysis, domestic trade policies that affect international business do not stem from some grandiose vision of a country's international responsibilities but rather from the mundane interaction of politicians trying to get elected. And who elects the politicians? The people in their legislative districts. Hence former Speaker of the House of Representatives Tip O'Neill's brilliant insight: "All politics is local." For example, Japan's unwillingness to open its markets to imported rice stems from the need of Japan's ruling party in parliament to retain the votes of local farmers. Similarly, French politicians restrict the importation of Japanese automobiles in order to win the votes of workers at Renault and Peugeot factories. The impact of these policies on Texas rice farmers, Yokohama autoworkers, or the world economy is of little concern to the domestic politicians.

Smart international businesspeople recognize these political realities. Often a foreign firm needs to find domestic political allies to run interference for it. For example, Nissan and Toyota received much criticism for the size of their exports to the U.S. market, so in the 1980s they built new factories in the United States. The congressional delegations of Tennessee and Kentucky, where these factories are located, can now be expected to support the firms legislatively in order to protect the jobs of constituents working for the Japanese firms. The not-so-subtle political message of the advertisement depicted in Fig. 6.3 is that if you mess with Toyota, you mess with the jobs, lives, and votes of thousands of U.S. workers. Clearly, Toyota understands that "all politics is local."

If you think our DX, LE AND SE are impressive then take a look at our CA, NJ, MO...

FROM our American research and design centers to our U.S. manufacturing plants, Toyota is committed to job growth in all the communities where we operate. Our more than $5 billion investment in America is paying off in the form of thousands of jobs right across the country. It's an investment in people and that's an investment in the future. *INVESTING IN THE THINGS WE ALL CARE ABOUT.* **TOYOTA**

For more information about Toyota in America write Toyota Motor Corporate Services, 9 West 57th Street, Suite 4900, New York, NY 10019.

Barriers to International Trade

As the previous section indicated, domestic politics often cause countries to try to protect their domestic firms from foreign competitors by erecting barriers to trade. Such forms of government intervention can be divided into two categories: tariffs and nontariff barriers. Countries have been erecting trade barriers since the creation of the modern nation-state in the sixteenth century in hopes of increasing national income, promoting economic growth, and/or raising their citizens' standards of living. Sometimes, as you just saw, national trade policies that benefit special-interest groups are adopted at the expense of the general public or society at large.

Tariffs

A **tariff** is a tax placed on a good involved in international trade. Some tariffs are levied on goods either as they leave the country (an **export tariff**) or as they pass through one country bound for another (a **transit tariff**). Most, however, are collected on imported goods (an **import tariff**). Three forms of import tariffs exist:

1 An **ad valorem tariff** is assessed as a percentage of the market value of the imported good. For example, in Table 6.1 (which is drawn from the existing U.S. tariff code) a 3.4 percent ad valorem tariff is levied against imported pineapples preserved by sugar.

2 A **specific tariff** is assessed as a specific dollar amount per unit of weight or other standard measure. As Table 6.1 shows, imported citrus fruit preserved by sugar bears a specific tariff of 7.5¢ per kilogram.

3 A **compound tariff** has both an ad valorem component and a specific component. Imported cherries preserved in sugar are levied a 10 percent ad valorem tariff and a 15.4¢ per kilogram specific tariff.

In practice, most tariffs imposed by developed countries are ad valorem in nature. The tariff applies to the product's value, which is typically the sales price at which it enters the country. For example, suppose Kmart buys a large shipment of

TABLE 6.1

A Section of the Harmonized Tariff Schedule of the United States

HEADING/ SUBHEADING	STAT. SUFFIX	ARTICLE DESCRIPTION	UNITS OF QUANTITY	RATES OF DUTY
2006.00		Fruit, nuts, fruit-peel and other parts of plants, preserved by sugar (drained, glacé or crystallized):		
2006.00.20	00	Cherries	kg	15.4¢/kg + 10%
2006.00.30	00	Ginger root	kg	5.4%
2006.00.40	00	Pineapples	kg	3.4%
		Other, including mixtures:		
2006.00.50	00	Mixtures	kg	20%
2006.00.60	00	Citrus fruit; peel of citrus or other fruit	kg	7.5¢/kg
2006.00.70	00	Other fruit and nuts	kg	10%
2006.00.90	00	Other	kg	20%

Source: U.S. International Trade Commission, *Harmonized Tariff Schedule of the United States* (Washington, D.C.: U.S. Government Printing Office, 1993), p. IV, 20–7.

canned pineapples preserved by sugar from a Filipino food processor at $400 a ton. When the pineapples are delivered to the Port of Los Angeles, Kmart will have to pay the U.S. Customs Service a duty of 3.4 percent of $400, or $13.60, for each ton it imports, a cost Kmart will pass on to its customers.

Most countries have adopted a detailed classification scheme for imported goods called the **harmonized tariff schedule (HTS)**. Because of its complexity, the HTS can sometimes be difficult to use. The first problem facing an importer is anticipating what customs officials will decide is the appropriate tariff classification for an imported good. For example, leather ski gloves imported into the United States are assessed a 5.5 percent ad valorem tariff. But if the leather ski gloves are specifically designed for cross-country skiing, then the ad valorem tariff is only 3.5 percent. Porcelain figurines imported into the United States generally bear a 9 percent ad valorem tariff. But if they are valued at over $2.50 and are produced by professional sculptors, they fall into a separate tariff classification and carry only a 3.1 percent ad valorem tariff.

An importer's expected profit margin on a transaction can shrink or disappear if a customs official subjects the imported good to a higher tariff rate than the importer expected. To reduce this risk, U.S. importers can request an advance tariff classification on prospective importations by writing the U.S. Customs Service in Washington or New York.[10] For example, toy distributor Dakin, Inc., requested such a clarification for four types of stuffed toys it wanted to import from Korea. The Customs Service's reply to this request is shown in Fig. 6.4. The Customs Service determined that the two stuffed toys that depicted *human beings*—Santa and the Paddy Wack Clown—fell under subheading 9502.10.8000 of the HTS and would be subject to an ad valorem

tariff of 12 percent. The two stuffed toys representing *animals*—the Reindeer and the ever-popular Tutu Bunny—belonged under subheading 9503.49.0040 and so would be subject to an ad valorem tariff of 6.8 percent.[11] Based on this written decision of the Customs Service, Dakin can import its goods with full knowledge of their landed cost.

Tariffs historically have been imposed for two reasons:

I Tariffs raise revenue for the national government. As Fig. 6.5 shows, tariff revenues account for a significant portion of government revenues of developing countries such as The Gambia, Ghana, and Sierra Leone. Such countries depend heavily on subsistence agriculture and so find it difficult to collect significant tax revenues from domestic sources. Customs duties, however, are reasonably easy to collect. Further, imported goods tend to be purchased by the wealthier members

Like tariffs, questions of what products fall under specific quotas cause difficulties for international businesses. The EU imposed a quota on imports of nonhuman dolls from China but allowed unlimited human dolls to be imported. Soon the best legal minds in Europe had to wrestle with the question of whether Mr. Spock was human or nonhuman. As any Trekkie knows, while Spock claims Vulcan origins, his mother, Amanda, was in fact an earthling. However, trade bureaucrats ruled that Spock dolls fell under the nonhuman quota, noting that "You don't find a human with ears that size." While others may find it humorous, such decisions by customs officials can cause havoc for international businesses, disrupting supplier relationships and raising the costs of doing business. (See page 210 for a further discussion of quotas.)

DEPARTMENT OF THE TREASURY
U.S. CUSTOMS SERVICE
NEW YORK, NY

NY 834016

JAN 0 5 1989

CLA-2-95:S:N:N3D:225-834016

CATEGORY: Classification

TARIFF NO.: 9502.10.8000; 9503.49.0040

Ms. Laura Fumagalli
Dakin Inc.
Post Office Box 7746
San Francisco, Ca. 94120

RE: The tariff classification of musical dolls and animals from Korea

Dear Ms. Fumagalli:

In your letter dated November 7, 1988 you requested a tariff classification ruling.

Submitted with your inquiry were four samples. The samples are item #46-2530, the "Paddy Wack Clown," item # 15-8830, the "Santa," item # 41–0180, the "Tutu Bunny" and item # 15–8800, the "Reindeer." Each of the items are plush with a large, well-featured stuffed head. Inside the head is a music box device. The bodies of the articles are unstuffed plush, with an internal cord and a plastic loop on the bottom. When the body is in a non-active position it is approximately 7 inches long and has a squashed appearance. When the ring on the bottom of the article is pulled, the body elongates to approximately thirteen inches and activates the musical device in the head. As the music plays the body slowly returns to the original position at which time the music ceases to play.

The applicable subheading for the clown and the Santa will be 9502.10.8000, Harmonized Tariff Schedule of the United States (HTS), which provides for dolls, whether or not dressed: not stuffed: other. The rate of duty will be 12 percent ad valorem. The applicable subheading for the bunny and the reindeer will be 9503.49.0040, Harmonized Tariff Schedule of the United States (HUTS), which provides for toys representing animals or non-human creatures: other: toys having a spring mechanism: other. The rate of duty will be 6.8 percent ad valorem.

This ruling is being issued under the provisions of Section 177 of the Customs Regulations (19 C.F.R. 177).

A copy of this ruling letter should be attached to the entry documents filed at the time this merchandise is imported. If the documents have been filed without a copy, this ruling should be brought to the attention of the Customs officer handling the transaction.

Sincerely,

Jean F. Maguire
Area Director
New York Seaport

FIGURE 6.4   **U.S. Customs Service Letter to Dakin, Inc.**

Tariff Revenues as a Percentage of Total Government Revenues for Selected Countries, 1990

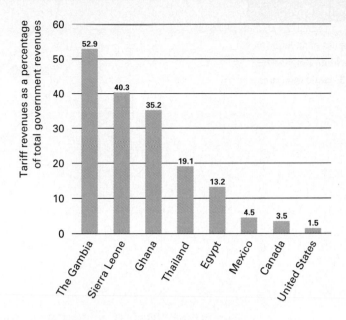

of society, so heavy reliance on import tariffs adds progressivity to the domestic tax system. Conversely, taxes on international trade form a relatively small percentage of government revenues in more developed economies that have broader tax bases such as Thailand, Egypt, and Mexico.

2 A tariff acts as a trade barrier. Because tariffs raise the prices paid by domestic consumers for foreign goods, they increase the demand for domestically produced substitute goods.

Tariffs affect both domestic and foreign special-interest groups. For example, suppose the U.S. government imposes a $2000 specific tariff on imported minivans. Foreign producers of minivans will be forced to raise their U.S. prices, thereby reducing their U.S. sales. But foreign-made minivans and U.S.-made minivans are substitute goods. Thus the higher prices of foreign minivans will increase the demand for U.S.-made minivans, as is shown in Fig. 6.6 by the shift in the demand for U.S.-made minivans from D to D_1, resulting in more domestic vehicles being sold at higher prices. The $2000 specific tariff creates both gainers and losers. Gainers include GM, Ford, and Chrysler automobile dealerships selling domestic minivans; suppliers to domestic producers; workers at domestic GM, Ford, and Chrysler minivan assembly plants; and the communities in which domestic minivan factories are located. Domestic consumers are losers because they pay higher prices for both domestic and foreign minivans. Foreign producers also lose, as well as people and firms that depend on them including Toyota and Mazda automobile dealerships in the United States, workers and suppliers in Japan, and communities in Japan in which the minivans are manufactured.

Nontariff Barriers

Nontariff barriers are the second category of governmental controls on international trade. Any government regulation, policy, or procedure other than a tariff

FIGURE 6.6

Impact of an Import
Tariff on Demand for
U.S.-made Minivans

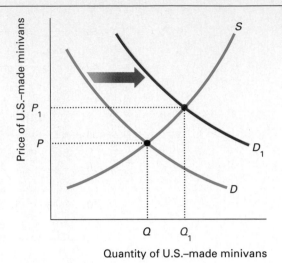

that has the effect of impeding international trade may be labeled a **nontariff barrier (NTB)**. In this section we consider these NTBs:

▶ Quotas

▶ Numerical export controls

▶ Other nontariff barriers

Quotas. Countries may restrain international trade by imposing quotas. A **quota** is a numerical limit on the quantity of a good that may be imported into a country during some time period, such as a year. Most countries use quotas to protect politically powerful industries, such as agriculture, automobiles, and textiles, from the threat of foreign competition. For example, Japan imposes quotas on imports of leather footware and agricultural products such as wheat, rice, barley, and peanuts, and South Korea subjects a wide range of agricultural imports to quotas. Canada imposes quotas on chickens, turkeys, and eggs in order to protect its poultry industry, thereby causing Canadians to pay 46 percent more than their southern neighbors for these products.[12]

A quota helps domestic producers of the good in question but invariably hurts domestic consumers. Consider, for example, the impact of a sugar quota on the U.S. market. The U.S. government restricts the amount of foreign sugar that can be imported to about 2.5 million tons annually. (Domestic producers normally produce about 7 million tons each year.) The price of sugar in the United States is higher than that elsewhere in the world because the quota prevents more imports from flowing into the U.S. market to equalize the prices. In March 1995, for example, the U.S. price for sugar was 22.6¢ per pound, while the average world price was only 15.5¢ per pound.

Who gains from the quota? Domestic sugar producers, such as sugar cane growers in Louisiana and sugar beet growers in North Dakota, benefit because domestic production is increased and the price that domestic suppliers receive rises. Producers of sugar substitutes, such as Archer Daniels Midland, the largest domestic producer of corn-based fructose sweeteners, and corn-belt farmers who supply the corn for the fructose sweeteners also gain as manufacturers of sweetened products substitute lower-cost fructose sweeteners for sugar. Losers from the policy include domestic candy manufacturers and soft-drink makers, which must

The Collin Street Bakery attracts over 250,000 visitors a year to the small Texas town of Corsicana. International sales are an important component of the Bakery's success. Twenty-five percent of the 1.5 million fruitcakes it makes each year are sold overseas, many to repeat customers. But U.S. quotas on sugar and tariffs on imported inputs raise the Bakery's costs, making it more difficult for it to compete in international markets.

pay higher prices for sugar, as well as U.S. consumers, who pay a higher price for all goods containing sugar. U.S. firms such as San Francisco's Ghiardelli Chocolate Company (premium chocolates) or Corsicana, Texas's Collin Street Bakery (fruitcakes) that export goods with high sugar content become less competitive in world markets because the sugar quota increases the cost of their ingredients.

Some foreign exporters of sugar will be losers, others gainers. Foreign firms that do not obtain rights to export sugar to the United States will lose, since they cannot sell their product in the United States. Anyone with the right to import sugar gains, since a quota holder can buy sugar at the lower world price and resell it in the United States at the higher U.S. price. For this reason, the U.S. government uses these rights as an instrument of foreign policy and foreign aid. Countries that are politically sympathetic to the United States or that the United States is trying to woo often receive generous quotas, while countries hostile to the United States find their quotas reduced or eliminated.

An extreme form of a quota is a total ban on a product's importation. Some countries have totally prohibited imports of specific goods as a means of developing a local industry. For example, the 1984 Brazilian Informatics Law banned the importation of personal computers, microchips, and fax machines in order to stimulate the Brazilian electronics industry. The Brazilian economy paid a high price for nurturing this infant industry: obsolescent technology, a computer-illiterate workforce, and higher production costs throughout the economy. For example, in the early 1990s, prices of personal computers in Brazil averaged 2.5 times U.S. prices. And Brazilian petrochemical producer Poliolefinas paid $4 million in 1991 for domestically produced process-control equipment that was inferior to that available at half the price in the United States. Paying the higher price raised the firm's costs and made it more difficult for it to compete with foreign petrochemical companies able to buy state-of-the-art process-control computers. Faced with these problems, Brazil lifted the ban effective October 1992.[13]

Numerical Export Controls. A country also may impose quantitative barriers to trade in the form of numerical limits on the amount of a good it will export. An extreme form of this barrier is a limit of zero. For example, in order to support local sawmills, British Columbia bans the exportation of logs from provincially owned forests.[14] Export controls may also be adopted to punish the country's political enemies. An **embargo**—an absolute ban on the exporting (and/or importing) of goods to a particular destination—is adopted by a country or international governmental authority to discipline another country. For example, after Iraq invaded Kuwait in 1990, the United Nations imposed an embargo on trade with Iraq.

Exporting countries may adopt voluntary export restraints in order to maintain a friendly economic environment with their trading partners. A **voluntary export restraint (VER)** is a promise by a country to limit its exports of a good to another country to a pre-specified amount or percentage of the affected market. The economic impact of a VER closely resembles that of a quota. For example, in 1981 Japan's MITI adopted a VER for Japanese automobile exports destined for the United States after U.S. politicians called for the imposition of quotas on imported Japanese autos. MITI chose this path so that its officials, rather than U.S. politicians, would control the implementation of the program. President Ronald Reagan accepted this gesture by MITI, and domestic political pressures for U.S.-imposed import quotas died.

Initially, the United Auto Workers (UAW) and the U.S. automakers were pleased with the results of Japan's VER. In the short run, Japan's share of the U.S. market stabilized and the quantity of U.S.-made cars sold increased. Consumers suffered, however, as the Japanese raised prices and Detroit then followed suit. The program was controversial in Japan because MITI's allocation of export rights favored the larger Japanese firms that were well established in the U.S. market. Smaller Japanese firms that were trying to crack the U.S. automobile market received export quotas too small to support extensive dealership networks and marketing campaigns in the United States.

To escape the impact of these quantitative controls, the Japanese began to operate assembly plants, often using non-UAW labor, in the United States, even though initially they could produce cars cheaper in Japan. However, as the yen's value rose subsequent to the 1985 Plaza Accord, their foreign factories made economic, as well as political, sense. The Japanese now find it less expensive to serve the U.S. market from these U.S. factories than from their home factories.

Other Nontariff Barriers. Countries also use various other NTBs to protect themselves from foreign competition. Some NTBs are adopted for legitimate domestic public policy reasons but have the effect of restricting trade. Most NTBs, however, are blatantly protectionist in nature. As we discuss in Chapter 7, international negotiations in the post–World War II era have reduced the use of tariffs and quotas. For this reason, nonquantitative NTBs have now become major impediments to the growth of international trade. These NTBs are more difficult to eliminate than tariffs and quotas because they often are embedded in bureaucratic procedures and are not quickly changeable. Among the most common forms of nonquantitative NTBs are the following:

▶ Product and testing standards

▶ Restricted access to distribution networks

▶ Public-sector procurement policies

▶ Local-purchase requirements

▶ Regulatory controls

▶ Currency controls

▶ Investment controls

We discuss these in the following subsections.

GOING GLOBAL

An Unlevel Playing Field

Of the major trading countries, Japan has received the most criticism for using product and testing standards as an NTB. In Japan, government-sponsored committees offer a mark of excellence (called the JIS) for goods produced in factories that adopt specified production techniques and quality control measures. Many public agencies may purchase only goods that have been awarded the JIS. Until 1983 foreign goods were not eligible to receive the JIS, effectively excluding foreign firms from selling to Japanese public agencies. The Japanese government eliminated the JIS as a formal NTB in 1983, but Japanese consumers still regard it as an important indicator of quality. Foreign firms are thus well advised to seek the JIS for marketing purposes. Obtaining JIS certification, however, is not always easy.

The saga of aluminum baseball bat exports to Japan illustrates the use of technical standards as a trade barrier. After several accidents caused by broken bats in the mid-1970s, the Japanese government required all aluminum bats to meet specific safety standards, which were set cooperatively between the government and Japan's baseball league and which excluded foreign-made bats. In 1980 U.S. bat manufacturers asked for permission to market their products in Japan. In 1981 the Japanese government agreed but required U.S. bats to be inspected on a batch-by-batch basis, whereas Japanese manufacturers could meet the safety standards through the simpler and cheaper factory inspection method. After U.S. protests over this discriminatory treatment, the Japanese government dropped its safety standards. However, Japanese baseball officials privately adopted those same standards, thereby frustrating foreign firms' attempts to quickly enter the Japanese market. So far, foreign bats have less than a 1 percent share of the Japanese market.

Source: Edward J. Lincoln, *Japan's Unequal Trade* (Washington, D.C.: The Brookings Institution, 1990), p. 146.

Product and Testing Standards. A common form of NTB is a requirement that foreign goods meet a country's domestic product standards or testing standards before they can be offered for sale in that country. Foreign firms often claim these standards discriminate against their products. For example, under purity laws that date back to 1516, beer marketed in Germany could be made only with water, yeast, barley, and hops. As most other beers have additional ingredients, the effect was to restrict imports of foreign beer (this law was overturned by the EU in the 1980s).[15] While this purity law was not originally explicitly designed as an NTB, such is not the case for many other product-testing regulations. For example, China requires extensive and expensive testing of foreign automobiles, machinery, electronics goods, and pesticides before they may enter its market, yet it does little or no testing of competing domestic products. For example, to certify an automobile for export to China, the automaker must first ante up a fee of $40,000; then it must provide the Chinese government with two free samples and finance an inspection of its assembly plants by Chinese officials.[16] "Going Global" provides another example of the use of product standards as an NTB.

Restricted Access to Distribution Networks. Restricting access of foreign goods to the normal channels of distribution may also act as an NTB, particularly if the distribution network is owned by the government. For example, Ontario's liquor board controls the distribution and sale of all imported beers. U.S. brewers claimed in the early 1990s that the board favored locally produced products by imposing fees on U.S. beers that caused them to sell at prices 18 percent higher than those of comparable Canadian beers. After a series of diplomatic negotiations between Canada and the United States, the Canadians agreed in 1992 to end the discriminatory fee structure.[17]

This problem extends into the private sector as well. South Korea's distribution network was closed to foreigners until July 1991, when a limited number of foreign firms were allowed to enter certain wholesale and retail sectors. But foreigners are still excluded from wholesale distribution in 26 sectors of the economy. Foreign producers of such important products as automobiles and consumer electronics are forced to sell their goods through distribution networks owned by South Korea's chaebol, which in many cases produce competing products and have little incentive to promote foreign brands to their customers.[18]

Japan has borne the brunt of world criticism over the issue of access to distribution networks. Foreigners' access to Japan's networks is often restricted because of the tight corporate and cultural ties among domestic manufacturers, wholesalers, and retailers. For example, Michigan-headquartered Guardian Industries, one of the world's largest producers of flat glass, has had trouble penetrating the Japanese market despite offering prices 25 percent less than those of its Japanese competitors. Guardian's problem has been finding Japanese intermediaries to handle its product line. Often, Japanese glass fabricators and wholesalers fear retribution from the three large Japanese flat glass producers, which dominate the domestic market, if they handle a competitor's products.[19] In several cases, Japan's keiretsu system has been explicitly blamed for restricting foreigners' access to the Japanese market. For example, AIG, a leading multinational insurance company, has been selling consumer-oriented insurance in the Japanese market since 1946 but still finds it difficult to sell industrial risk insurance because most major Japanese firms buy such insurance from an insurance company affiliated with their keiretsu. Of course, these close corporate ties, while acting as a NTB, may not be discriminatory, since they hurt both foreign and domestic newcomers in the Japanese market.

Public-Sector Procurement Policies. Public-sector procurement policies that give preferential treatment to domestic firms are another form of NTB. In the United States, "Buy American" restrictions are common at the federal, state, and local levels. The City of Los Angeles, for example, biased its procurement of mass transit equipment in favor of U.S. producers.[20] And the federal government requires that international air travel paid for by U.S. government funds occur on U.S. carriers.

Despite its own discriminatory policies, the U.S. government has loudly criticized similar policies in other countries. For example, the United States has fought a long battle with the Japanese government over the right of U.S. construction firms to bid on public construction projects in Japan. The U.S. claimed that the Japanese policy of excluding foreign firms from the bidding process unless they had previous construction experience in Japan created a burdensome chicken-or-egg dilemma for U.S. firms.[21] The United States has also criticized Argentina for allowing a government-sponsored cartel, Edcadassa, to block foreign firms such as Federal Express from competing for public express delivery contracts.[22]

Public-sector procurement policies are particularly important in countries that have extensive state ownership of industry and in industries in which state ownership is common. If a national government adopts procurement policies that favor local firms, then foreigners are locked out of much of the market. In Europe, for example, virtually all of the telephone systems are owned by national governments. Under Article 29 of the EU's Utilities Directive, firms from member countries are given a 3 percent bidding preference over firms from other countries in utilities projects. Thus a U.S. or Japanese firm must bid at least 3 percent less than a European firm does to remain eligible for a utilities contract. Also, the governments of EU members may reject any bid when less than 50 percent of the value of the goods and services embodied in the project are produced inside of the EU.[23] Under such circumstances, foreign telecommunications equipment suppliers, such as Northern Telecom and Western Electric, find it more difficult to penetrate the EU market. Because of the importance of the EU utilities market, U.S. trade officials are negotiating with EU counterparts to modify Article 29.

Local-Purchase Requirements.   Host governments may hinder foreign firms from exporting to or operating in their countries by requiring them to purchase goods or services from local suppliers. For example, the Italian government requires foreign air carriers to purchase ground-handling services from a subsidiary of Alitalia, the government-owned Italian airline. Foreign carriers, unhappy about having to buy these essential services from their main rival at Italian airports, complain bitterly that they are overcharged for the poor service they receive. The French government requires local TV services, such as privately owned TF1 or Canal Plus SA, a pay-TV channel, to show French-made films at least 40 percent of the time and European-made films at least 60 percent of the time, thus restricting the market available to non-European films.[24] Similarly, the EU requires that the majority of programming broadcast by European television stations be of European origin. The U.S. government has strongly protested the French and EU requirements, arguing that they are designed to restrict competition from U.S. movie and television producers.[25] Local-purchase requirements also plague MNCs' attempts to develop global advertising campaigns using commercials that can be played in any market. For example, Poland requires that all lyrics in commercials be sung only in Polish, thereby forcing firms to dub over their commercials. And Australia limits imported TV ads, thus forcing firms to reshoot ads in Australia using local actors, directors, and film crews.[26]

Regulatory Controls.   Governments can create NTBs by adopting regulatory controls, such as conducting health and safety inspections, enforcing environmental regulations, requiring firms to obtain licenses before beginning operations or constructing new plants, and charging taxes and fees for public services that affect the ability of international businesses to compete in host markets. Recall from Chapter 2, for example, Cargill's three-and-a-half-year delay in obtaining a license from the South Korean government to build a soybean processing plant in Korea. Similarly, in the early 1980s the French government was upset about the flood of imported Japanese video cassette recorders (VCRs) that were threatening to destroy the French VCR industry. To protect domestic production, France required that all VCR imports clear customs at a small, understaffed, and inconveniently located facility in the city of Poitiers where imports backed up awaiting customs clearance. Faced with these expensive bureaucratic delays, the Japanese agreed to limit their VCR exports to France.

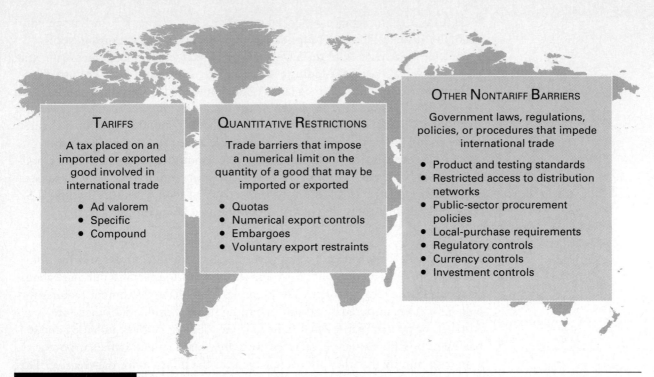

TARIFFS	QUANTITATIVE RESTRICTIONS	OTHER NONTARIFF BARRIERS
A tax placed on an imported or exported good involved in international trade	Trade barriers that impose a numerical limit on the quantity of a good that may be imported or exported	Government laws, regulations, policies, or procedures that impede international trade
• Ad valorem • Specific • Compound	• Quotas • Numerical export controls • Embargoes • Voluntary export restraints	• Product and testing standards • Restricted access to distribution networks • Public-sector procurement policies • Local-purchase requirements • Regulatory controls • Currency controls • Investment controls

FIGURE 6.7

Types of Barriers to International Trade: A Summary

Seemingly innocent laws may affect international trade. For example, in the early 1990s Ontario imposed a 10¢ per bottle fee on all beer sold in nonrefillable containers. Although this regulation might appear to be part of the pro-environment movement, Anheuser-Busch and the Miller Brewing Company believed it was designed to hurt the sales of imported U.S. beers, most of which are sold in recyclable aluminum cans, in favor of Canadian beers, most of which are bottled. Noting that the 10¢ tax did not apply to all beverages sold in aluminum cans (such as soft drinks), the United States retaliated by imposing a 50 percent duty on Canadian exports of beer to the United States, triggering yet another round of beer negotiations.[27]

Currency Controls. Many countries, particularly developing countries and those with centrally planned economies, raise barriers to international trade through currency controls. Exporters of goods are allowed to exchange foreign currency at favorable rates, so as to make foreign markets attractive sales outlets for domestic producers. Importers are forced to purchase foreign exchange from the central bank at unfavorable exchange rates, thus raising the domestic prices of foreign goods. Tourists may be offered a separate exchange rate that is designed to extract as much foreign exchange as possible from free-spending foreigners.

Uganda, for example, uses two exchange rates. An official rate, established by government officials, is used for all governmental imports, debt service payments, oil imports, imports associated with projects sponsored by the World Bank and other official lending agencies, coffee exports, and other government-authorized trade. A free-market rate is used for all other transactions. This rate is established by supply and demand and yields a lower value for the Ugandan shilling than the official rate does. By using this dual exchange-rate system in which the official rate overvalues its currency, Uganda uses less foreign exchange for its official transactions than it would need if it relied solely on the free-market rate. Most private imports, on the other hand, must use the higher market rate, which raises the cost in Uganda of foreign goods, discourages imports, and helps domestic producers compete against foreign goods. Guyana, Somalia, the Sudan, Syria, Zambia, and numerous other countries use similar dual or multiple exchange-rate systems to encourage exports and discourage imports.[28]

Investment Controls. Controls on investment and ownership are common. Before the 1991 dissolution of the former Soviet Union, for example, the Soviet government restricted foreign investment and ownership. These regulations have since been relaxed in order to attract much-needed capital. Countries also may impose controls on investment within key industries in their economies, such as banking, transportation, telecommunications, and defense contracting. For example, Mexico severely limited foreign participation in its financial services industries until 1994, when, as part of its economic liberalization program, it licensed 52 foreign companies to provide banking, insurance, brokerage, and factoring services.[29] Brazil restricts foreign ownership of utilities to 49 percent.[30] The United States similarly restricts foreign ownership of airlines and broadcast stations.

These NTBs are now more important impediments to international trade than tariffs are. And because they are sometimes imposed for sound domestic policy reasons but affect the competitiveness of foreign firms, NTBs can quickly cause intense international conflicts. International businesses whose operations are affected by NTBs often need the support of their home governments to help resolve these problems. "Building Global Skills" at the end of the chapter will acquaint you with some of the U.S. government agencies that can help such firms.

Figure 6.7 summarizes the various forms that trade barriers can take.

Promotion of International Trade

The previous section discussed techniques that governments use to restrict foreign business activity. In this section we discuss government policies to promote international business, including

▶ Subsidies
▶ Establishment of foreign trade zones
▶ Export financing programs

Typically, these programs are designed to create jobs in the export sector or to attract investment to economically depressed areas.

Subsidies

Countries often offer a variety of subsidies to firms operating within their borders in order to increase economic activity and job creation. These subsidies include

▶ Favorable tax breaks for investment, R&D spending, and employee training

▶ Direct payments to producers

▶ Product price supports

▶ Sales of publicly owned property at less than fair market value

▶ Public services provided at below cost

National, state, and local governments often provide economic development incentives—another type of subsidy—to entice firms to locate or expand facilities in their communities in order to provide jobs and increase local tax bases. These incentives may be in the form of property tax abatements, free land, training of workforces, reduced utility rates, new highway construction, and so on. Competition among different localities can be fierce. For example, Alabama beat out a host of states competing to attract a new Mercedes-Benz plant by offering the firm a $300 million incentives package.

Because subsidies reduce the cost of doing business, they may affect international trade by artificially improving a firm's competitiveness in export markets or by helping domestic firms to fight off foreign imports. Subsidies, however, can grow so large as to disrupt the normal pattern of international trade. The international wheat market is a notorious example. The International Wheat Council estimates that governmental export subsidies influence two thirds of international wheat sales. Thus wheat exports often reflect the size of a country's subsidies, not the forces of comparative advantage. In the early 1990s, for example, the EU captured 20 percent of the international wheat market through its extensive sales of heavily subsidized wheat. In retaliation, the U.S. government sold wheat to China for $75 a ton and to Algeria for $65 a ton, even though U.S. production costs averaged $125 a ton. Even a desert country can compete in the wheat market when the game includes subsidies: Saudia Arabia sold wheat to New Zealand for $100 a ton, even though its production costs were $600 a ton. In the past decade, the United States has spent over $6 billion subsidizing its wheat exports, as has the EU. The big losers in the subsidy wars are farmers in wheat-exporting countries that lack large-scale subsidies, such as Argentina, Canada, and Australia.[31]

Foreign Trade Zones

A **foreign trade zone (FTZ)** is a geographical area in which imported or exported goods receive preferential tariff treatment. An FTZ may be as small as a warehouse or a factory site (such as Caterpillar's diesel engine facility in Mossville, Illinois) or as large as the entire city of Shenzhen, China (which neighbors Hong Kong).[32] FTZs are used by governments worldwide to spur regional economic development. For example, an FTZ has played a key role in the economic development of the small African island nation of Mauritius (see Map 6.2). Through utilization of an FTZ a firm typically can reduce, delay, or sometimes totally eliminate customs duties. Generally a firm can import a component into an FTZ, process it further, and then export the processed good abroad and avoid paying customs duties on the value of the imported component.

In the United States, FTZs are extremely popular. Their numbers have grown from approximately 25 in the early 1970s to several hundred today. Of particular importance is the growth of FTZs that specialize in assembling automobiles, which

MAP 6.2

Foreign Trade Zone on Mauritius

Mauritius, which was once a French naval base, is a tropical island, roughly 10½ times the area of Washington, D.C. For much of its history, Mauritius's economy depended on sugar cane, and even today 90 percent of its cultivated land is devoted to this crop.

Mauritius has created a foreign trade zone to diversify its economy and encourage manufacturing. Today the country exports over $500 million of textiles and apparel to Europe and the U.S. Because of the FTZ's success, the country's population (roughly 1 million) enjoys low unemployment — only 2.4 percent.

now account for 85 percent of all goods produced in U.S. FTZs and for most U.S. automobile production. The automobile-based FTZs developed from an inverted tariff structure in which tariffs on imported auto parts, ranging from 4 percent to 11 percent, are higher than the 2.5 percent tariff on imported assembled automobiles. A manufacturer can import parts to the FTZ duty-free and assemble them into an automobile. When the assembled automobile leaves the FTZ and enters the jurisdiction of the U.S. Customs Service, the firm pays a tariff on the foreign parts used in the automobile at the lower 2.5 percent rate. Chrysler, GM, and Ford are estimated to save customs duties of $5 to $10 on each automobile assembled in a U.S. FTZ, while the savings of Japanese-owned automobile factories in U.S. FTZs range from $40 to $50 per auto.[33] (Japanese-owned assembly plants enjoy higher FTZ savings because they tend to use more imported components than do U.S.-owned plants.) As one might expect, automakers are pleased with this arrangement. However, U.S. auto parts producers view this use of FTZs as a means of avoiding the high tariffs on imported auto parts.[34]

The maquiladora system on the U.S.-Mexican border represents another important use of FTZs. A **maquiladora** is a factory located in an FTZ in Mexico near the U.S. border. These factories import unfinished goods or component parts from the United States, further process the goods or parts, and re-export them to the United States. The goods produced by maquiladoras enjoy preferential customs and tax treatment by both countries' governments. Mexico levies no customs duties on unfinished goods imported by a maquiladora, provided the goods are re-exported to the United States after having been further processed in Mexico. Machinery imported into Mexico used by a maquiladora is also exempt from customs duties. U.S. customs duties on maquiladoras' exports are applied only to the value of the processing performed in Mexico.

The maquiladora industry, which was established in 1965 as part of Mexico's Border Industrialization Program, takes advantage of Mexico's low labor costs and its proximity to the United States. Today the maquiladora industry is the second-largest sector of the Mexican economy (after oil production) and the second-largest source of Mexico's foreign-exchange earnings.

However, many ethical issues have been raised regarding the maquiladora industry. The maquiladoras have been criticized by environmentalists, who claim the factories allow firms to escape tough U.S. environmental laws by shifting their operations to Mexico, where enforcement of environmental regulations is lax. U.S. union officials object to maquiladoras because they threaten the jobs of the unions' members and the health of the union movement. Critics also complain that firms utilizing maquiladoras have ignored the social disruption that the maquiladora program has created. The rapid influx of workers into the border area has placed heavy demands on the public infrastructure of Mexico's northern states, overburdening the area's roads, utilities, schools, and housing facilities.

Ironically, the biggest threat to the maquiladoras may be the North American Free Trade Agreement (NAFTA). As a result of NAFTA, many tariff advantages once enjoyed only by the maquiladoras are now available to factories throughout Mexico. Thus interior cities such as Monterrey and Saltillo have been put on an even footing with border communities such as Nuevo Laredo and Matamoros in terms of attracting new plants to serve the North American market.

Export Financing Programs

For many big-ticket items such as aircraft, supercomputers, and large construction projects, success or failure in exporting depends on a firm's producing a high-quality product, providing reliable repair service after the sale, and—often the critical factor—offering an attractive financing package. For example, Boeing competes with Airbus Industrie to sell Singapore Airlines 200-seat short-range aircraft. When Singapore Airlines is deciding which firm's aircraft to buy, it carefully weighs price, after-sale technical support, aircraft operating costs, and financing expenses. All other things being equal, the financing terms offered it may be critical in its decision of which firm wins the contract.

Because of the importance of the financing package, most major trading countries have created government-owned agencies to assist their domestic firms in arranging financing of export sales, both large or small. The **Export-Import Bank of the United States (Eximbank)** provides financing for U.S. exports through direct loans and loan guarantees; in 1994 it financed $12.7 billion of U.S. exports. Large firms like Boeing are important clients, but the Eximbank also services small U.S. exporters. For example, it guaranteed $7.9 million in bank loans for the family-owned De Francisci Machine Corporation, thereby allowing this small New York manufacturer of food-processing equipment to export noodle-drying and pasta-making equipment to two factories in Poland. But government aid often goes beyond mere financing. Eximbank or its subcontractors also provide routine commercial insurance services for Eximbank-supported exports.[35] Another U.S. government sponsored organization, the **Overseas Private Investment Corporation (OPIC)**, provides a very different type of insurance—political-risk insurance—a subject we cover in Chapter 8. If a foreign country confiscates an insured firm's goods or assets, OPIC will compensate the firm for its losses. Other countries have similar organizations that provide export financing, commercial insurance, and political-risk insurance.

Controlling Unfair Trade Practices

With governments around the world adopting programs designed to protect domestic industries from imports and other programs to promote their exports, it should not be surprising that competitors often cry foul. In response to these complaints, many countries have implemented laws protecting their domestic firms from unfair trade practices.

In the United States, complaints from firms affected by alleged unfair trade practices are first investigated by the International Trade Administration (ITA), a division of the U.S. Department of Commerce, which determines whether an unfair trade practice has occurred. The Department of Commerce transfers confirmed cases of unfair trading to the U.S. International Trade Commission (ITC), an independent government agency. If a majority of the six ITC commissioners decide that U.S. producers have suffered "material injury," the ITC will impose duties on the offending imports to counteract the unfair trade practice. The ITC, like Canada's CITT in the case of Desmarais and like similar government agencies worldwide, focuses on two types of unfair trade practices: government subsidies that distort trade and unfair pricing practices.

Countervailing Duties

Most countries protect local firms from foreign competitors that benefit from subsidies granted by their home governments. A **countervailing duty (CVD)** is an ad valorem tariff on an imported good that is imposed by the importing country to counter the impact of foreign subsidies. The CVD is calculated to just offset the advantage that the exporter obtains from the subsidy. In this way, trade can still be driven by the competitive strengths of individual firms and the laws of comparative advantage rather than by the level of subsidies governments offer domestic firms.

Not all government subsidies give a foreign firm an unfair advantage in the domestic market. Most countries impose CVDs only when foreign subsidization of a product leads to a distortion of international trade.[36] For example, the U.S. government, in administering its CVD rules, tries to determine whether a particular subsidy is generally available to all industries in a country, in which case CVDs will not be applied, or restricted to a specific industry, in which case CVDs may be imposed. If a foreign government grants a tax credit to all employers for training handicapped workers, a CVD will not be applied, for the tax credit is available to all the country's firms. If the tax credit is restricted to the footware industry, however, a CVD may be imposed on imported footware equal to the value of the tax credit.

CVDs are often controversial and may lead to international conflict. In one highly publicized case initiated in 1991, the U.S. lumber industry complained that the low stumpage fees Canadian provinces charged lumber firms for the right to harvest timber in provincially owned forests constituted an unfair subsidy to the Canadian lumber industry, as did a British Columbian law restricting exports of logs from that province. The Canadian lumber industry responded that the low stumpage fees represented the fair market value of the timbering rights, and thus were not a subsidy to it. The Canadian loggers further claimed that the restriction on log exports was of little benefit to them. The ITC disagreed and slapped 6.5 percent CVD on Canadian softwood exports to the United States, an amount that the ITC determined was equal to the two supposed subsidies.[37]

Economic development incentives may also trigger complaints of unfair trade. For example, in the early 1990s, the Austrian government (at the time, Austria was not an EU member) wanted to attract a Chrysler minivan assembly plant to a depressed region in the country. It offered $96 million in economic development incentives to Eurostar Automobil Fabrik GmbH, a joint venture between Austria's Steyr-Daimler Puch AG and a European subsidiary of Chrysler. In response, the EU threatened to impose a 10 percent CVD on Eurostar minivans exported to its members. It argued that the incentives were an unfair subsidy that lowered the cost of producing minivans in Austria and therefore distorted trade. After many months of negotiations, Austria agreed to lower the incentives offered to Eurostar and the EU agreed not to impose the CVD.[38]

Antidumping Regulations

Many countries are also concerned about their domestic firms being victimized by discriminatory or predatory pricing practices of foreign firms, such as dumping. Recall from the chapter opening that dumping occurs when a firm sells its goods in a foreign market at a price below what it charges in its home market. This type of dumping is a form of international price discrimination. Another type of dumping involves the firm's selling its goods below cost in the foreign market, in which case the dumping is a form of predatory pricing. Antidumping laws protect local industries from dumping by foreign firms. As Table 6.2 shows, in the decade ending June 1993, Australia, the United States, Canada, and the EU initiated over 1400 legal actions against dumping, including that discussed in the Desmarais case.[39]

TABLE 6.2

Antidumping Cases Initiated, 1983–1993

	1983–84	1984–85	1985–86	1986–87	1987–88	1988–89	1989–90	1990–91	1991–92	1992–93	TOTAL
Australia	70	63	54	40	20	19	23	46	76	61	472
Canada	26	35	27	24	20	14	15	12	16	36	225
EU	33	34	23	17	30	29	15	15	23	33	252
U.S.	46	61	63	41	31	25	24	52	62	78	483
Other developed countries	1	0	2	5	9	12	5	9	21	8	72
Developing countries	0	0	3	4	13	14	14	41	39	38	166
TOTAL	176	193	172	131	123	113	96	175	237	254	1670

Source: From "Negotiations down in the dumps over U.S. draft," *Financial Times*, November 25, 1993. Reprinted with permission.

Determining whether the first type of dumping—price discrimination—has actually occurred is not always easy. For example, many Western politicians incorrectly accuse Japanese automakers of dumping, noting that Japanese automobiles retail for higher prices in Tokyo than in New York City. Retail prices, however, are irrelevant in determining whether dumping has occurred. The comparison should be between the prices charged foreign customers and domestic customers at the factory gate; these prices are often difficult to obtain. The higher retail prices in Tokyo might reflect the inefficient Japanese distribution system or higher costs of doing business rather than dumping by the automaker.

In the second type of dumping—predatory pricing—defining costs is complicated, particularly when dealing with a large, multidivisional MNC such as Toyota or Nissan. For example, when the ITA is determining the "cost" of a Toyota Previa minivan, should it measure cost as the marginal cost of producing one more Previa? Should it include some of Toyota's minivan-related R&D expenses, or should it simply recognize that these R&D costs would have been incurred whether or not the U.S. market existed? Should it include charges for Toyota's corporate overhead? Foreigners' guilt or innocence in dumping cases often turn on the answers to such accounting questions.

Super 301

Another weapon available to the U.S. government to combat unfair trading practices of foreign countries is Section 301—so-called Super 301—of the 1974 Trade Act. **Super 301** requires the U.S. trade representative, a member of the executive branch, to publicly list those countries engaging in the most flagrant unfair trade practices. The U.S. trade representative is then required to negotiate the elimination of the alleged unfair trade practices with the listed countries. If the negotiations are unsuccessful, the executive branch must impose on the recalcitrant offenders appropriate retaliatory restrictions such as tariffs or import quotas. Super 301 gives U.S. negotiators a big club in their dealings with foreign governments. For example, the U.S. government determined in the early 1990s that U.S. firms were having difficulty obtaining contracts for large-scale construction projects in Japan, despite their success and experience in managing major construction projects around the world. U.S. Trade Representative Carla Hills threatened to prohibit Japanese firms from bidding on federally funded construction projects in the United States. The Japanese government then agreed to improve the access of U.S. construction firms to major Japanese building projects.[40]

Section 301 technically expired in 1994. However, President Clinton resuscitated it via executive order, and it remains a powerful, though controversial, weapon in the U.S. trade arsenal. The use of Super 301 has not won the United States many friends internationally. Because Super 301 provides relief solely for U.S. firms, EU members have been particularly displeased with it, arguing that it hinders the development of global trade and promotes unilateral, rather than multilateral, attempts to redress problems facing international commerce. Many targets of Super 301 actions are similarly resentful. They believe its use represents bullying by the United States and pandering to those special-interest groups that have the ear of Congress at any point in time.[41]

CHAPTER REVIEW

Summary

Formulating trade policies that advance the economic interests of their citizens is an important task facing most national governments. While some policymakers suggest that free trade is the most appropriate policy, numerous firms, government bureaucrats, and other interested parties argue for active governmental intervention in international trade.

Some rationales for governmental intervention focus on the specific needs of an industry (national defense, infant industry, maintenance of existing jobs, and strategic trade arguments), while others focus on the country's overall needs (economic development and industrial policy).

Over the centuries, governments have developed a variety of trade barriers. Import tariffs raise revenues for the government as well as help domestically produced goods compete with imported goods. Quotas and VERs place a numerical limitation on the amount of a good that can be imported or exported. Other NTBs may also disadvantage foreign products in the market. These barriers include product and testing standards, restricted access to distribution systems, public procurement policies that favor local firms, local-purchase requirements, regulatory powers, and currency and investment controls.

National governments also seek to promote the interests of domestic firms in international trade through other programs. They may subsidize local production of goods and services in order to make them more competitive in international markets. They also may authorize the establishment of FTZs to help domestic firms export goods. Export financing programs have been developed to assist exporters in marketing their goods.

National governments protect local producers from unfair foreign competition by enacting unfair trade laws. CVDs are imposed on foreign products that benefit from government subsidies that distort international trade. Antidumping laws protect domestic producers from being victimized by predatory pricing policies of foreign firms. Super 301 strengthens the bargaining power of U.S. negotiators in international trade conflicts.

Review Questions

1. What is free trade? Who benefits from it?

2. What is the infant industry argument?

3. What is the difference between the export-promotion and import-substitution economic development strategies?

4. What are the different types of tariffs?

5. Why is it useful for an importer to seek out an advance tariff classification from the U.S. Customs Service?

6. Why might a country adopt a VER?

7. What are the major forms of NTBs?

8. What is an FTZ?

9. What is the role of the Eximbank?

10. What is the purpose of a CVD?

11. Which U.S. government agencies administer laws regarding unfair trade practices?

Questions for Discussion

1. What are the advantages and disadvantages of an industrial policy? What impact would industrial policy have on firms and employees in industries threatened by low-priced imports?

2. Because of Japan's success in competing in international markets, it has been the target of numerous complaints that it restricts foreign access to its local markets. As Japan reduces its barriers to imported goods, who is likely to gain from lowered barriers? Who is likely to lose from them?

3. The U.S. Congress authorized the creation of FTZs in order to stimulate U.S. exports. Given the discussion of FTZs in the text, do you believe FTZs are accomplishing Congress's goal? Does the FTZ law need to be changed?

4. Are the ethical issues raised by the critics of maquiladoras valid? To what extent should managers of international businesses consider these issues in deciding whether or not to operate a maquiladora factory?

BUILDING GLOBAL SKILLS

In the United States, at least 18 separate government agencies have some responsibility for promoting exports of U.S. firms. The ITA coordinates the export development efforts of these federal agencies. The U.S. and Foreign Commercial Service (US&FCS), a branch of the ITA, staffs offices throughout the United States and in foreign countries with international trade experts available to help U.S. firms export their products. These experts can help firms assess their products' export potential, identify the most likely markets for their goods, and locate promising overseas partners and distributors. To promote exports, US&FCS experts also work with 51 District Export Councils, 107 field offices of the Small Business Administration (SBA), the Foreign Agricultural Service (part of the Department of Agriculture), commercial banks, chambers of commerce, and state governments. These groups provide seminars on exporting and information about exporting opportunities in different countries and product lines. A quick listing of these services can be found in the Department of Commerce's accurately titled publication, *A Basic Guide to Exporting*, which provides an informative overview of the exporting process.

Assignment

The U.S. government has so many sources of information available to help first-time exporters that managers are often overwhelmed by deciding where to begin. Put yourself in the shoes of a neophyte exporter who wants to learn about the exporting process.

1. Find out which branch office of the US&FCS serves your local market. You can do this by using *A Basic Guide to Exporting* in your library, looking in your local phone book, calling your congressperson's office (the staff there are experts about the federal bureaucracy), asking a local banker, or chatting with local chambers of commerce. Ask the local US&FCS office to send you literature on its activities and a list of its "Country Desk Officers" (experts knowledgeable about the markets in specific countries) and "Industry Desk Officers" (experts knowledgeable about the international markets for individual products).

2. Find out which state agencies in your state are responsible for promotion of exports from local firms. Ask them about their export development programs.

3. Identify the SBA district office in your area. Ask how it can help local firms identify promising export markets.

4. Locate any private organizations in your area (profit and nonprofit) that provide trade development services. Ask them about the types of services they offer their members and newcomers like yourself.

CLOSING CASE

Harley-Davidson: Back in Hog Heaven[42]

When Marlon Brando rolled into town at the head of a leather-clad biker gang in the 1957 movie *The Wild One*, he symbolized the freedom and the power at the heart of the American love affair with the motorcycle. And one firm, above all its competitors, conjures up the romance between biker and bike: Harley-Davidson (Harley), maker of the world's biggest, most powerful motorcycles, affectionately called "hogs" by their owners and wannabe owners.

Despite its strong brand image and core of loyal customers, Harley had its back against the wall in the mid-1980s. The last survivor of a once-proud U.S. motorcycle industry, it had suffered through an unprofitable 1981 and 1982. Its troubles resulted in part from competition from high-quality, technologically dominant Japanese manufacturers such as Honda and Suzuki that threatened to wipe out the company just as they had all other U.S. motorcycle manufacturers.

But Harley's problems had actually started two decades earlier. The firm had not been too concerned when Japanese motorcycles were first imported into the United States in the 1950s. They were tiny things—scooters really—that posed little challenge to the mighty hogs that were churned out in Harley's Wisconsin and Pennsylvania plants. As late as 1973, Harley enjoyed a 75 percent domestic market share for super-heavyweight bikes (those with engines over 850cc). Unfortunately, the Japanese motorcycles got bigger and better. In 1975, Honda introduced its large touring bike, the Gold Wing, which matched Harley's best bike in size and performance but sold for only $7000, underpricing Harley by $2000. Suzuki and Yamaha soon marketed comparable products. By 1979 Harley's domestic market share for cycles bigger than 850cc had fallen to 39 percent. By 1982 it had shrunk to 29 percent as the value of Japanese imports rose to $450 million.

However, in the late 1970s Harley finally recognized the Japanese threat. Acknowledging the technical superiority and manufacturing excellence of the Japanese, Harley launched a multidimensional revitalization program. To stem its financial losses, it slashed its costs by laying off 40 percent of its workforce, freezing salaries, and cutting the benefits of its remaining workers. It also petitioned the U.S. government in 1982 for temporary relief from import competition under a section of U.S. trade law that protects domestic manufacturers from the threat of injury from imported goods even when no unfair trade practice has taken place. In its petition, Harley-Davidson noted that U.S. dealers of Japanese motorcycles had 18 months of inventory on hand. Harley expected U.S. dealers and the Japanese factories to trim these bloated inventory levels by slashing prices. The firm knew that because of its precarious financial situation, it could not survive such a price war.

The ITC determined that domestic motorcycle manufacturers—which included Harley-Davidson, Honda (with a motorcycle assembly plant in Marysville, Ohio), and Kawasaki (with a plant in Lincoln, Nebraska)—were indeed threatened by injury from imported goods. It devised a complicated schedule of declining tariffs on large motorcycles (those with engines larger than 700cc) to give the domestic industry temporary protection, as Harley had requested. The then existing 4.4 percent tariff applied to the first 6000 motorcycles exported by Japan in 1983, with this ceiling rising by 1000 vehicles each year over the five years that the temporary protection program was to last. But stiff tariffs were levied on Japanese imports over the ceilings: 49.4 percent in 1983, declining to 39.4 percent in 1984, and continuing to fall in steps until 1987, when the ad valorem tariff would be 14.4 percent. The temporary protection was to end in 1988. The high tariffs imposed the first two years were to discourage further imports and allow domestic dealers to work off their excess inventories of imported Japanese motorcycles. Effectively, Harley was given a five-year window in which to turn itself around.

But Harley knew its biggest problem was not the Japanese, but itself. The hard-won loyalty of Harley owners would quickly disappear if the firm didn't improve the quality of its cycles. For example, when ready to sell its new Cafe Racer motorcycle in the late 1970s, Harley discovered huge quality problems. It spent $100,000 fixing the first 100 bikes as they came off the production line—$1000 per unit for a bike set to sell for $4000. This debacle served as a wake-up call to the firm.

Harley also swallowed its pride and decided to learn more about how to manufacture motorcycles from the world's leading expert—Honda. Senior managers toured Honda's plant in Marysville, Ohio. They quickly noted that Honda's JIT inventory methods eliminated the need for purchasing and maintaining complex materials-handling equipment, such as the 3.5-mile conveyor system that circled Harley's main factory in York, Pennsylvania. Harley adopted JIT inventory controls, thereby eliminating storage and interest charges on its parts inventory. It simultaneously adopted a quality-audit program and a new employee involvement program in order to attack its quality problems. Engineers, managers, and assembly workers teamed up to improve employee communication, lower manufacturing costs, and raise quality. Harley invested more heavily in its employees, teaching them modern statistical quality control methods, and it encouraged its parts suppliers to do the same with their employees. It also changed the way it designed new products by adopting the "simultaneous engineering" approaches pioneered by Japanese automakers. In simultaneous engineering, designers and production engineers work together from the start on any new product idea, thereby speeding up product development and lowering manufacturing costs by eliminating potential production glitches in the design phase. In an attempt to regain technological leadership among motorcycle manufacturers, Harley also invested heavily in R&D, developing new suspension systems, steering mechanisms, and computerized solid-state ignitions.

The firm also strengthened its marketing efforts, by concentrating on rebuilding the former fanatical loyalty of Harley owners. Senior managers hopped on their hogs to tour the country's back roads and attend motorcycle rallies in order to hear their customers' complaints and ideas in person. The firm sponsored a new club, the Harley Owners Group (HOG), which presented weekly events nationwide for Harley owners. It also strengthened its dealership network by upgrading the factory training offered its dealers and financing the modernization of their retail stores.

Harley's efforts paid off. By 1986 its share of the large motorcycle market had risen to 33 percent from a low of 23 percent in 1983. In early 1987 it held a widely publicized press conference asking that the last year of the ITC's increased tariff protection be eliminated. By 1988 it had reclaimed 45 percent of the U.S. large motorcycle market.

Of the 150 U.S. firms that produced motorcycles, only Harley remains. The firm obviously handled its domestic competitors well but was unprepared to meet the challenges of foreign manufacturers. Low labor costs gave Japanese manufacturers an initial entrée into the U.S. market, but their sales increased because of favorable word-of-mouth advertising and Harley's inattention to maintaining its technological and quality leadership. However, the firm, with the help of the temporary protection offered by the ITC, clearly has turned around its operations and beaten back the initial challenges of Honda, Suzuki, Yamaha, and Kawasaki. Because of its well-known brand name and loyal customers, Harley is likely to survive. Yet its managers and employees know the fight is not over. The firm will continue to be pressured to improve quality, develop innovative products, and trim costs. Harley-Davidson almost died in the 1980s. Unless it maintains its commitment to quality and its customers, the next crisis could be fatal.

Case Questions

1. How critical to Harley's eventual turnaround was the ITC's decision to impose high tariffs on motorcycle imports in 1983?

2. The Japanese firms assaulted Harley's control over the large motorcycle market by first building their reputations and financial strength in the market for smaller motorcycles. Was Harley wise to allow them to dominate that market? Should it have launched its own competing products in the small motorcycle market?

3. The initial U.S. market penetration by Japanese manufacturers was based on Japan's low labor costs, an advantage that Japanese workers no longer have over U.S. workers as the yen has risen in value relative to the U.S. dollar. What will be the future nature of competition in the motorcycle industry?

4. The ITC developed a unique tariff to protect Harley for five years. Is there a less costly or more beneficial instrument that would have achieved the same results?

CHAPTER NOTES

1. Information for this case was obtained from various decisions of the Canadian Import Tribunal and the Canadian International Trade Tribunal, including: "Photo Albums Originating in or Exported from Singapore, Malaysia, and Taiwan," Inquiry No. CIT-5–87; CITT Review No. RR-89–012; and CITT Inquiry No. NQ–90–003.

2. U.S. International Trade Commission, *Shipbuilding Trade Reform Act of 1992: Likely Economic Effects of Enactment*, USITC Publication 2495 (June 1992), Washington, D.C. The U.S. shipbuilding industry is so uncompetitive in world markets that from 1960 to 1994 the industry exported no commercial oceangoing vessels (p. 6).

3. "The trough," *The Economist*, June 27, 1992, p. 22.

4. Edward J. Lincoln, *Japan's Unequal Trade* (Washington, D.C.: The Brookings Institution, 1990), p. 112.

5. Brander and Spencer, "International R&D Rivalry and Industrial Strategy," *Review of Economic Studies* 50 (1983), 707–722. See also Paul R. Krugman and Maurice Obstfeld, *International Economics* (Glenview, Ill.: Scott, Foresman/Little Brown College Division, 1988), pp. 261ff.

6. Paul R. Krugman, "Is Free Trade Passe?" *Economic Perspectives* (Fall 1987), pp. 131–144.

7. Krugman and Obstfeld, op.cit., Chapter 11.

8. "U.S. Picks Areas of Technology It Wants to Back," *Wall Street Journal*, April 26, 1994, p. A4.

9. "Torpedo Shipping Protectionism," *Wall Street Journal*, November 26, 1991, p. A14.

10. U.S. Customs Service, *Importing into the United States* (Washington, D.C.: Department of the Treasury, January 1989), p. 19.

11. U.S. Customs Service, *Commodity Classifications Under the Harmonized System: The Harmonized System Rulings Packet*, (January/February 1989), vol. 1, no. 2, pp. 414–415.

12. Office of the United States Trade Representative, *Foreign Trade Barriers* (Washington, D.C.: U.S. Government Printing Office, 1992).

13. "Brazil Set to Lift Electronics Import Ban," *Wall Street Journal*, August 8, 1991, p. A7; Office of the United States Trade Representative, *Foreign Trade Barriers* (Washington, D.C.: U.S. Government Printing Office, 1992), p. 20.

14. U.S. International Trade Commission, *Softwood Lumber from Canada*, USITC Publication 2530 (Washington, D.C.: July 1992), p. A–15.

15. European Court Reporter (1987–3 at 1227), *Commission of the European Communities v. Federal Republic of Germany.*

16. Office of the United States Trade Representative, *Foreign Trade Barriers* (Washington, D.C.: U.S. Government Printing Office, 1992), pp. 30 and 47.

17. U.S. International Trade Administration, *International Economic Review*, May 1992, p. 11; "Beer Battle Erupts Between U.S., Canada After Efforts to Reach Settlement Fizzle," *Wall Street Journal*, July 27, 1992, p. C13; Nancy Dunne and Bernard Simon, "Canada-US beer war gets green tinge," *Financial Times*, July 31, 1992.

18. "South Korean Protectionism," *Wall Street Journal*, August 6, 1992, p. A10; Office of the United States Trade Representative, *Foreign Trade Barriers* (Washington, D.C.: U.S. Government Printing Office, 1992), p. 164.

19. "Japan Glass Market Proves Hard to Crack," *Wall Street Journal*, August 7, 1991, p. A4.

20. "Los Angeles Proposal Gives Preference to Local Bids," *Wall Street Journal*, February 7, 1992, p. A7.

21. "White House Again Says Japan Uses Unfair Tactics to Aid Building Industry," *Wall Street Journal*, November 24, 1989, p. 2A.

22. "Now That Argentina's Stable, It's Time for a Revolution," *Wall Street Journal*, August 28, 1992, p. A13.

23. Nancy Dunne, "U.S. moves to drop 'Buy Local' Policy," *Financial Times*, August 23, 1991, p. 6.

24. "France Eases Film Quota," *Wall Street Journal*, July 23, 1992, p. A6.

25. "U.S. Criticizes EC's TV-Content Stance, Seeks Arbitration," *Wall Street Journal*, October 11, 1989, p. A15.

26. "Global Ad Campaigns, After Many Missteps, Finally Pay Dividends," *Wall Street Journal*, August 27, 1992, p. A1.

27. "Beer Blast," *Wall Street Journal*, August 4, 1992, p. A14.

28. International Monetary Fund, *Developments in International Exchange and Payment Systems* (Washington, D.C.: June 1992).

29. Debra Beachy, "A Lumpy Playing Field?" *Houston Chronicle*, August 28, 1991, p. B1; "Mexico's Finance Ministry Awards Foreign Licenses," *Wall Street Journal*, October 19, 1994, p. A13.

30. Victoria Griffith, "Brazil rings the changes to telecoms market," *Financial Times*, August 2, 1991, p. 3.

31. "Arable parable," *The Economist*, August 24, 1991, p. 60; Laurie Morse, "U.S./China wheat deal shows trade war is still on," *Financial Times*, January 11, 1994, p. 30.

32. Committee on Ways and Means, *Operation of the Foreign Trade Zones Program of the United States and its Implications for the U.S. Economy and U.S. International Trade*, October, 1989, Serial 101–56, pp. 281 and 326.

33. Ibid., pp. 75 and 166.

34. Ibid., p. 327.

35. Export-Import Bank of the United States, 1991 *Annual Report* (Washington, D.C.: Eximbank, 1992); *1992 Annual Report* (Washington, D.C.: Eximbank, 1993); *1994 Annual Report* (Washington, D.C.: Eximbank, 1995).

36. Richard Boltuck and Robert E. Litan, "America's 'Unfair' Trade Laws," in Boltuck and Litan, eds. *Down in the Dumps* (Washington, D.C.: The Brookings Institution, 1991), p. 9.

37. U.S. International Trade Commission, "Softwood Lumber from Canada," USITC Publication 2530 (July 1992), Washington, D.C.

38. "EC Delays Ruling on Grants by Austria for Minivan Plant," *Wall Street Journal*, August 4, 1992, p. B9; *Wall Street Journal*, July 30, 1992, p. A8.

39. Nancy Dunne, "Brisk Business for U.S. anti-dumping agencies," *Financial Times*, August 16, 1991, p. 3.

40. "U.S., Japan Failing in Talks to Expand Construction Trade," *Wall Street Journal*, May 24, 1991, p. A8.

41. "EC Criticizes U.S. on Trade Barriers in War of Words," *Wall Street Journal*, May 4, 1989, p. A3.

42. Sources for this case include Peter C. Reid, "How Harley Beat Back the Japanese, *Fortune*, September 25, 1989, p. 155; Vaughn L. Beals, "Operation Recovery," *Success*, January/February, 1989, p. 16; "Ganging Up on the Motorcycle Gangs," *Fortune*, May 16, 1983, p. 101; Rod Willis, "Harley-Davidson Comes Roaring Back," *Management Review*, March 1986, pp. 20–27; "Stiff Motorcycle Duties Said to Be Aimed at Spurring Japan to Help U.S. Industry," *Wall Street Journal*, April 4, 1983, p. 23; "Motorcycle Imports Could Hurt Makers In U.S., Panel Rules," *Wall Street Journal*, January 20, 1983, p. 14; "Trade Panel Urges Import Duty Boost For Motorcycles," *Wall Street Journal*, January 26, 1983, p. 2.

SHOULD UNFAIR TRADE LAWS BE ENFORCED?

Unfair Trade Laws Should Be Enforced

Advocates of strong CVD and antidumping policies believe that government subsidies and dumping reduce the efficiency of the global economy by distorting international trade flows and rewarding inefficient firms. According to the country-based and firm-based trade theories discussed in Chapter 3, international trade not only makes both parties better off but also allocates resources efficiently across national economies because goods are (1) bought by those consumers that value them most highly, and (2) produced by those firms that can produce them at lowest cost. Unfair trade practices thus reduce global economic efficiency because the level of government subsidy or the degree of dumping, not efficiency, will determine which firms will produce which goods.

Enforcement of unfair trade laws also protects domestic jobs and firms. Subsidies by foreign governments and dumping by foreign firms will cause price reductions in the domestic market and lower the profits of domestic producers. Domestic producers will be forced to cut their costs in order to survive. Workers may bear the brunt of these cost-cutting measures as the affected firms reduce wages, fire workers, and/or close down factories. To restore their profitability, domestic firms may be forced to relocate their factories to other countries where wages are lower or to go out of business entirely.

Other experts believe foreign firms may use unfair trade practices to gain a long-run competitive advantage. For example, a firm may dump output in the home markets of its worldwide competitors in order to weaken those competitors and thereby gain a strategic edge in the global competitive battle. For example, the three major U.S. automakers filed a complaint in 1992 against Mazda and Toyota, claiming that they were dumping minivans in the U.S. market. Chrysler, which makes a majority of its profits from selling minivans, charged that Toyota's and Mazda's minivan pricing was designed to rob Chrysler of the cash flow it needed to regain its status as a world-class competitor in automotive markets. (However, the ITC ruled that Japan had not dumped minivans in the U.S. market.)

Advocates of aggressive enforcement of unfair trade laws also believe unfair trade practices hurt consumers. Without such laws, they fear, foreign firms will adopt predatory pricing practices, forcing down domestic prices by dumping their goods in the domestic market and driving domestic firms out of the market. The foreigners will then raise prices, earn monopoly profits, and gouge domestic consumers.

U.S. consumers benefit from price competition among U.S. and Japanese manufacturers. But U.S. automakers argued that Toyota dumped Previa vans on the U.S. market to cripple the long-run viability of the U.S. automobile industry.

The Unfair Trade Law Cure Is Worse Than the Illness

Advocates of free trade argue that unfair trade laws do more damage than good: while they sound reasonable in theory, in practice they are thinly concealed attempts to promote protectionism. Free trade advocates maintain that Department of Commerce (DOC) and ITC procedures are biased against foreign firms. For example, a foreign firm typically has only 30 days to reply to a DOC information request, which may run 100 pages. By the deadline it must supply comprehensive documents detailing in English its pricing and cost accounting procedures. Its failure to do so means that the DOC can use the costs of its U.S. competitors to construct an estimate of its direct costs. To calculate the foreign firm's average costs, the DOC then arbitrarily marks up the direct cost estimate by 10 percent for overhead expenses and adds to that an 8 percent profit margin, much higher than many firms ever earn. As a result of these arbitrary calculations, foreign firms often find it difficult to win unfair trade practices cases and are forced to raise their prices. This benefits domestic producers but harms domestic consumers.

Some economists go even further in their disdain for unfair trade laws. They believe the laws make no sense either in theory or in practice because of the harm to consumers. These economists are skeptical of the predatory pricing argument, contending that decades of economic research have failed to find many real examples of such behavior.

Apple shifted production of laptops from Colorado to Ireland to avoid the 62.67 percent duty on imported active-matrix LCDs, which did not apply to imported laptops containing such displays. The result was a loss of U.S. jobs.

Other critics argue that unfair trade laws may damage the U.S. economy. For example, in 1991 the federal government received a complaint from seven small U.S. manufacturers of active-matrix liquid crystal displays (LCDs) that Japanese manufacturers of this product were dumping it in the U.S. market. The ITC imposed a 62.67 percent duty on the imported active-matrix LCDs. However, imported displays account for as much as 30 percent of the cost of a laptop computer. Not surprisingly, the ITC's action was vigorously resisted by U.S. computer manufacturers such as Apple, IBM, and Compaq, which feared that the duty would dramatically increase the costs of U.S.-made laptops, thereby giving imported Japanese laptops a huge advantage in the U.S. market. They also claimed that saving a few hundred jobs in the U.S. active-matrix LCD industry by imposing the duty would jeopardize thousands of jobs in the U.S. laptop computer industry.

Wrap-up

1. The case involving imported active-matrix LCDs posed a dilemma for the ITC: it could protect jobs in the small LCD industry at the cost of threatening a much larger number of jobs in the laptop computer industry. Was the ITC's decision correct?

2. Do you agree that enforcing unfair trade laws hurts the economy, rather than helps it? Why or why not?

International Cooperation among Nations

Chapter Outline

The General Agreement on Tariffs and Trade

How the GATT works
The Uruguay Round
The future of the World Trade Organization

Regional economic integration

Forms of economic integration
The impact of economic integration on firms

The European Union

Completing the Common Market—EC '92
The creation of the European Union
Governing the European Union

Other regional trading blocs

The North American Free Trade Agreement
Other free trade agreements

International commodity arrangements

Organization of Petroleum Exporting
    Countries
The Multifibre Arrangement

After studying this chapter you should be able to:

Explain the importance of the GATT to international businesses.

Contrast the different forms of economic integration among cooperating countries.

Analyze the opportunities for international businesses created by completion of the EU's internal market.

Describe the other major trading blocs in today's world economy.

Discuss the role of commodity cartels in international trade.

THE 38-TONNE LORRY SWEPT THROUGH ANOTHER FRENCH VILLAGE riven in two by the N136 highway. Traffic was queueing ahead and Gerard Gibeaux, the driver, relaxed his grip on the steering wheel and gave a shrug as he pulled to a halt. ▌▌"Farmers," he said. The southbound long-distance lorry drivers had been warned before leaving Portsmouth for Le Harve that French farmers were once more on the warpath with roadblocks around Paris. Today it appeared that some were converging on Le Mans. A tractor could be seen moving slowly at the head of the snake a mile or so up the road. Just six months from the advent of the single market the movement of goods across borders appears as fraught as ever to the lorry drivers. ▌▌Our load was 154 cases of office furniture made by Herman Miller of Bath. The customer was the savings bank, Caja de Madrid. The freight haulage company was Cave Wood Transport

On the Road to the New EC[1]

of High Wycombe and the driver was French—open borders at least have arrived in the trucking business itself. We caught the final night crossing from Portsmouth. At Le Harve Gerard extended his bottom lip as only a Frenchman can and looked depressed. "We loose much time. Plenty traffic," he said in his best broken English. ▌▌We turned out of the traffic queue to bypass Le Mans and made Bordeaux by nightfall. Trucks crowded into the lorry park just outside the city and the drivers made a beeline for the adjoining hotel and a meal that puts the British transport cafe to shame. The drivers entertain each other with travelers' tales spiced with Chaucerian bawdiness. ▌▌Only the names have changed over the centuries. The lorry driver sees himself as the verray, parfit gentil knyght bedeviled by police and customs officers. Asked how the movement of goods had improved in 1992, Nigel Hainsworth, a British driver, said: "It hasn't changed one bit. No one has yet come up with a solution to the VAT problem. As long as every country has different rates we are going to have to pay duty and that will mean paperwork." ▌▌The main difference for drivers after next January should be the disappearance of documents such as the T2 which needs to be stamped by customs. And VAT will be dealt with by deferred accounting.... ▌▌We approached the Spanish border town of Irun around 11 a.m. and Gerard, one of Cave Wood's most experienced drivers, was worried. "We might be waiting until six o'clock tonight," he said. Drivers who come to Irun discuss one of the most taxing questions. "If the customs controls are going to disappear as we are told," said Nigel Hainsworth, "why are the Spanish building another big lorry park and customs offices on the border?" It was a question to which no one had an answer. ▌▌Gerard was surprised. At 3:30 p.m. his documents were back in his hands. The goods were not physically examined. We never saw a customs officer.... ▌▌ The red-capped Basque police were out in force beyond the border but they were not stopping lorries today. One driver spoke of a convoy of three British lorries carrying a consignment of computers a few weeks ago whose drivers could not produce their permits when stopped by the Basque police. The supplying company was forced to pay £28,000. "The Basque fines are like telephone numbers," he said. ▌▌ In France the fines are lower but seem more frequent. "I had two Fr900 and one Fr600 fines for tachograph offenses in the same month," said Steve Jones, a British driver.... ▌▌ By mid-morning we were heading for Coslada, the customs clearance park for Madrid in hope of finding some freight for the return journey. Coslada is a truckers' grave yard. They come, they hand in their papers and they wait. A British driver parked a refrigerated lorry and walked into the customs offices. His peaches were ruined. Would anyone help him? No one moved. He swore and left. Brussels seemed a long way from Coslada. ▌▌▌▌▌

In Chapter 6, we explored the ways in which national governments intervene in international trade and investment. When a country adopts restrictions on international commerce, it can benefit at least some of its producers and workers. But other countries may retaliate with similar restrictions, thinking that they, too, will gain. As restrictions proliferate, international trading opportunities decline and all countries end up losing. They often then realize that each is better off if they cooperate and agree to forswear trade restrictions. This chapter is about the outcomes of those realizations.

International cooperative agreements form a major part of the economic environment in which international businesses operate. To be successful, international businesspeople must be knowledgeable about these agreements and use them to create business opportunities for their firms and to counteract competitors' actions. Of particular importance is the growth of regional trading blocs, such as the EU and NAFTA, which are designed to reduce trade barriers among their members. Although the truck drivers' experience in the chapter opening would seem to belie it, economic integration is the way of the future.

The General Agreement on Tariffs and Trade

The collapse of the international economy between the two world wars has been blamed in part on countries' imposing prohibitive tariffs, quotas, and other protectionist mechanisms on imported goods. Trading and investment opportunities for international businesses dried up as country after country adopted such "beggar-thy-neighbor" policies. By raising tariff and quota barriers, each nation believed that it could help its own industries and citizens, even though in doing so it might harm the citizens and industries of other countries.

For example, in 1930 the United States sought to protect domestic industries from import competition by raising tariffs under the Smoot-Hawley Tariff Act to an average of 53 percent.[2] However, as other countries, such as the United Kingdom, Italy, and France, constructed similarly high tariff walls, the cumulative effect was that each country was worse off rather than better off. None gained a competitive advantage over another, and as international trade declined, all suffered from the contraction of export markets.

To ensure that the post–World War II international peace would not be threatened by such trade wars, representatives of the leading trading nations met in Havana, Cuba, in 1947 to create the International Trade Organization (ITO). The ITO's mission was to promote international trade; however, it never came into being. Instead the ITO's planned mission was taken over by the General Agreement on Tariffs and Trade (GATT), which had been developed as part of the preparations for the Havana Conference. As of December 1994, 125 countries signed the GATT treaty, and many other nations apply GATT principles to their trade policies without having formally subscribed to the treaty. The GATT is administered by a small, permanent staff headquartered in Geneva, Switzerland, and provides an institutional forum for trade ministers to discuss policies and problems of common concern. However, as a result of international negotiations discussed later in this chapter, GATT's functions are scheduled to be taken over in 1995 by a new international agency, the World Trade Organization (WTO), whose workings will likely follow those of the GATT.

How the GATT Works

Many MNCs strongly support GATT's objectives, for its goal is to promote a free and competitive international trading environment that benefits efficient producers. The GATT accomplishes this by sponsoring international negotiations to reduce tariffs, quotas, and other NTBs. Because high tariffs were initially the most serious impediment to world trade, the GATT first focused on reducing the general level of tariff protection. A series of negotiating "rounds," generally named after the location where each round of negotiations began (see Table 7.1), has been conducted since 1947. The cumulative effect of the GATT's eight rounds

TABLE 7.1

GATT Negotiating Rounds

ROUND	DATES	NUMBER OF PARTICIPANTS	AVERAGE TARIFF CUT (%)
Geneva	1947	23	35
Annecy	1949	13	NA
Torquay	1950–1951	38	25
Geneva	1956	26	NA
Dillon	1960–1962	45	NA
Kennedy	1964–1967	62	35
Tokyo	1973–1979	99	33
Uruguay	1986–1994	117	36

VOLUME OF WORLD TRADE: 1950 = 100 (semi-log scale)

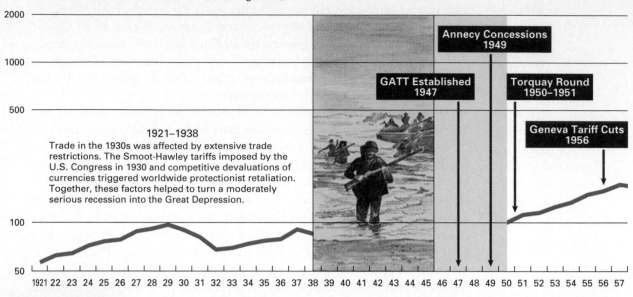

FIGURE 7.1

The History of GATT's Effect on World Trade

Source: From *Financial Times*, December 16, 1993, p. 5. Reprinted with permission.

has been a substantial reduction in tariffs. Tariffs imposed by the developed countries have fallen from an average of over 40 percent in 1948 to approximately 3 percent in 1995.[3] As Fig. 7.1 shows, the GATT negotiations have led to dramatic growth in world trade over the past 50 years.

To help international businesses compete in world markets regardless of their nationality, the GATT seeks to ensure that international trade is conducted on a nondiscriminatory basis. This is accomplished through use of the most favored nation principle. The **most favored nation (MFN) principle** requires that any preferential treatment granted to one country must be extended to all countries. Under GATT rules, all members must utilize the MFN principle in dealing with other members. For example, if the United States cuts the tariff on imports of British trucks to 20 percent, it must also reduce its tariffs on imported trucks from all other members to 20 percent. Because of the MFN principle, multilateral, rather than bilateral, trade negotiations have been encouraged, thereby strengthening GATT's role. (Members are also free to extend MFN status to nonmembers, as "Going Global" on page 238 indicates.)

There are two important exceptions to the MFN principle:

1 To assist poorer countries in their economic development efforts, the GATT permits members to lower tariffs to developing countries without lowering them for more developed countries. In the U.S. tariff code such reduced rates offered to developing countries are known as the **Generalized System of Preferences (GSP)**. Other developed countries have similar exemptions. Obviously, by reducing these tariffs, the GSP increases the pressures on domestic firms that are vulnerable to import competition from the developing countries. In contrast, MNCs can reduce their input and production costs by locating factories and assembly facilities in countries benefiting from the GSP.

2 The second exemption is for regional arrangements that promote economic integration, such as the EU and NAFTA, both of which we discuss soon.[4]

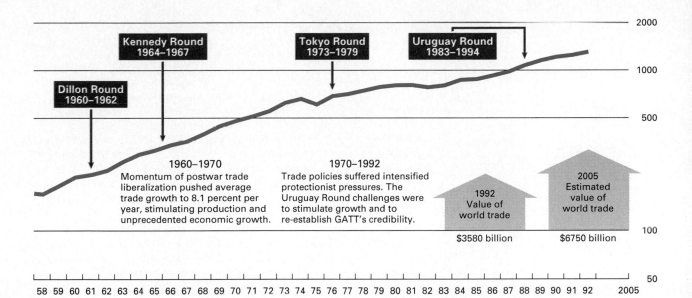

While GATT's underlying principles are noble, its framers recognized that domestic political pressures often force countries to retreat from pure free trade policies. The GATT permits countries to protect their domestic industries on a nondiscriminatory basis, although under GATT rules countries are supposedly restricted to the use of tariffs only. Quotas and other NTBs can often be applied discriminatorily, and they are less "transparent"—that is, it is often hard to judge their impact on competition. However, there are loopholes in these rules, so many countries can adopt quotas and other NTBs and still comply with the GATT. For example, U.S. quotas restricting imports of peanuts, sugar, and other agricultural products that were granted a "temporary" waiver from GATT rules in 1955 remain in effect today.[5] Countries are allowed exemptions to preserve national security or to remedy balance of payments (BOP) problems. The GATT also permits them in certain circumstances to protect themselves against "too much" foreign competition.

The Uruguay Round

The eighth, and most recent, round of GATT negotiations began in Uruguay in September 1986. Ratified by GATT members in Morocco in March 1994, the Uruguay Round agreement took effect in 1995. Like its seven predecessors, the Uruguay Round cut tariffs on imported goods—in this case, from an average of 4.7 percent to 3 percent. Most countries viewed NTBs as the major obstacles to trade, so the Uruguay Round also addressed the more difficult task of reducing their use. The controversies faced by the Uruguay Round negotiators highlight precisely the sorts of trade issues plaguing international businesses today. As you read about GATT deliberations, you will see why international managers follow the GATT closely: outcomes of these deliberations influence both the opportunities and the threats faced by firms in their domestic and foreign markets.

Agricultural Policy. Virtually all governments provide some sort of subsidy or support programs for their farmers that are designed to increase income levels

GOING GLOBAL

MFN and Human Rights

The United States often extends MFN status to non-GATT members, such as China, as part of its overall trade policy. The ethical implications of continued granting of MFN status to China have been the subject of vigorous debate in the United States. Human rights advocates accuse China of exploiting prison labor and squelching democracy. They argue that the United States should withdraw China's MFN status because of these violations of human rights. In the eyes of human rights activities, China's profitable trade with the United States strengthens the political popularity of the existing regime. Withdrawing MFN status would raise the tariffs on many Chinese exports and shrink China's trade surplus with the United States, putting pressure on the Beijing government to reform its policies.

Defenders of the status quo argue that the United States has more leverage with Beijing policymakers if trading relations between the two countries remain friendly. These defenders note that countries often are more likely to honor human rights when their economic futures look prosperous. Thus, over the long run, human rights are more likely to improve in China if the United States adopts policies that aid that country's economic growth. Defenders of the current policy also worry that U.S. jobs would be lost should China retaliate against U.S. firms if the United States withdrew China's MFN status.

of this politically powerful group. For example, in Japan rice farmers provide critical support for the Liberal Democratic Party, which has fought against rice imports for the past 50 years. And, as the opening case suggests, when French farmers thought their subsidies might end as a result of GATT negotiations, they resorted to one of their favorite protest methods—blocking motorways with their tractors. Such domestic governmental policies rob efficient agricultural exporters of potential markets, by closing domestic markets, by artificially lowering prices in domestic markets so that foreign goods cannot compete, or by subsidizing domestic farmers so that they can sell their surplus goods at artificially low prices in international markets.

The leading proponent of agricultural policy reform was the so-called **Cairns Group**, a group of major agricultural exporters led by Argentina, Australia, Canada, and the United States. Opposing the group were Japan, South Korea, India, and the EU. The Uruguay Round negotiators agreed to slash domestic agricultural price supports by 20 percent and export subsidies by 36 percent. These subsidy reductions, coupled with the relaxation of Japanese and Korean rice import quotas, will benefit major food exporters such as Australia, Canada, New Zealand, Thailand, and the United States.

Trade in Services. Previous GATT negotiations devoted little energy to dealing with trade in services. The Uruguay Round developed a set of principles under which trade in services should be conducted. For example, government controls on services trade should be administered in a nondiscriminatory fashion. However, service industries are very diverse, and few concrete agreements regarding specific industries were included in the Uruguay Round. Regarding many industries, GATT members agreed to disagree or to continue to negotiate. For example, the United States pressed for free trade in recorded entertainment.

To David Hasselhoff's delight, *Baywatch* is currently the most popular syndicated TV program in the world. However, the ability of the U.S. entertainment industry to sell its products overseas is hurt by restrictions imposed by the EU, China, and other countries on imports of recorded music, films, and TV programs.

However, the EU, led by France, feared the power of the U.S. movie and record industries and so resisted attempts by the United States to eliminate EU quotas on non-European movies and recorded music. Ultimately both sides agreed to delete recorded entertainment from the Uruguay Round agreement and to attempt to resolve their differences later. Similarly, the United States, seeking to protect its merchant marine, refused to relax its Jones Act restrictions against the use of foreign-owned ships in U.S. domestic transportation markets.

Intellectual Property Rights. Intellectual property rights include patents, copyrights, trademarks, and brand names. Entrepreneurs, artists, and inventors have been hurt by inadequate enforcement by many countries of laws prohibiting illegal usage, copying, or counterfeiting of intellectual property. In China, for example, state-owned factories are allegedly churning out millions of illegal compact discs for export to other Asian markets without paying royalties to the musical artists and copyright holders. The Uruguay Round agreement substantially strengthened the protection granted to owners of intellectual property rights. However, because most such owners reside in the developed countries and many violators live in developing countries, the Uruguay Round negotiators agreed to phase in intellectual property protections over a decade. Not all industries were happy with this concession. For example, the Pharmaceutical Manufacturers Association believes that it grants developing countries carte blanche to continue pirating patented drugs for another ten years.[6]

Creation of the World Trade Organization. Another important facet of the Uruguay Round was the creation of the **World Trade Organization (WTO)**, which is charged with the implementation of the Uruguay Round. In 1995 the WTO is scheduled to subsume the activities of the GATT and serve as the world's advocate and monitor of more open and free international trade in goods, services, and technology. The establishing of the WTO is not without controversy, however. Some politicians are concerned that national governments will have less control over their trade policies. Environmental and human rights advocates are worried that in the interests of promoting trade, the WTO will override national laws protecting the environment and workers' rights.

Overall, World Bank experts believe that the Uruguay Round will result in $274 billion being added to the world's GDP by the year 2002, or about 1.3 percent of its current GDP. Table 7.2 shows in greater detail the provisions of the Uruguay Round.

TABLE 7.2

What the Uruguay Round Accomplished

AREA	STATUS PRIOR TO URUGUAY ROUND	PROVISIONS OF URUGUAY ROUND	MAIN IMPACT
Industrial Tariffs	This is the backbone of previous GATT rounds. Tariffs on manufactures average 4.7 percent in rich countries, down from 40 percent in the late 1940s.	Tariffs on industrial goods cut by rich countries by more than one third. Over 40 percent of imports enter duty-free. Key traders scrap duties for pharmaceuticals, construction equipment, medical equipment, steel, beer, furniture, farm equipment, spirits, wood, paper, and toys.	Easier access to world markets for exporters of industrial goods. Lower prices for consumers. Higher-paying jobs through promotion of competitive industries.
Agriculture	High farm subsidies and protected markets in Europe and the United States lead to overproduction and dumping of cut-price surpluses, thereby squeezing exports of more efficient producers. Farm supports by OECD countries amount to $354 billion in 1992.	Trade-distorting subsidies and import barriers cut over six years. Domestic farm supports reduced 20 percent. Subsidized exports sliced 36 percent in value and 21 percent in volume. All import barriers converted to tariffs and cut 36 percent. Japan's and South Korea's closed rice markets gradually open.	Restraint of farm subsidies war. Lower food prices for consumers in currently protected countries. Better market opportunities for efficient producers. Special treatment for developing countries, although higher world prices could hurt poor food-importers.
Services	No international trade rules cover services such as banking and insurance, transportation, tourism, consultancy, telecommunications, construction, accountancy, films and television, and labor. Countries protect industries from foreign competition.	Rules framework set for basic fair-trade principles such as nondiscrimi-nation. Special provisions made for financial services, telecommunica-tions, air transportation, and labor movement. Individual countries pledge market opening in wide range of sectors.	Boost for trade in services, currently worth $900 billion a year in cross-border trade and another $3000 billion in business of foreign subsidiaries. Further liberalization to be negotiated.
Intellectual Property	Standards of protection for patents, copyrights, and trademarks vary widely. Trade in counterfeit goods reaches alarming levels.	Extensive agreement reached on patents, copyright, performers' rights, trademarks, geographical indications (wine, cheese, etc.), industrial designs, microchip layout designs, trade secrets. International standards of protection, and require-ments for effective enforcement.	Boost for foreign investment and technology transfer, though poor countries with weak patent protec-tion fear higher prices for drugs and seeds.

The Future of the World Trade Organization

The GATT is generally given high praise for its success in lowering tariffs on a wide range of goods over the past 50 years. In the Uruguay Round, GATT negotiators made significant progress in addressing subsidies, trade in services,

continued

AREA	STATUS PRIOR TO URUGUAY ROUND	PROVISIONS OF URUGUAY ROUND	MAIN IMPACT
Textiles and Clothing	Rich countries restrict since 1974 imports of textiles and clothing through bilateral quotas under Multifibre Arrangement (MFA). Countries maintain high textile import tariffs. Protection raises prices but fails to protect jobs.	MFA quotas progressively dismantled over ten years and tariffs reduced. Developing countries reduce trade barriers. Normal GATT rules apply at end of ten years.	Developing countries able to sell more textiles and clothing abroad. Reduced prices for consumers worldwide because of fairer textiles and clothing trade (worth $248 billion in 1992).
Anti-dumping	Countries allowed to combat dumping (exports priced below domestic prices) with anti-dumping duties. Anti-dumping actions proliferate and are increasingly seen as disguised form of protectionism.	Clearer rules for conduct of investigations and criteria for determining dumping and injury to industry. Duties lapse after five years. Rules covering circumvention of anti-dumping duties by relocating production.	More difficult to use anti-dumping actions for trade harassment. Harder to dodge duties by relocating.
Subsidies	Subsidized exports can be met with countervailing duties but these, like anti-dumping duties, are cause of growing trade tensions and increased disputes.	Definition of which subsidies are legal or not: some prohibited, some nonactionable (e.g. research or regional development). Others actionable if they harm competitors.	Tighter curbs on subsidy use, especially for exports. More difficult to use anti-subsidy actions for trade harassment.
Technical Barriers	Product regulations and standards are extensively used by governments to ensure products are safe for consumers and the environment. Varying standards can be disguised trade barriers.	Better rules to ensure that technical norms and testing and certification procedures do not create unnecessary obstacles to trade and to encourage harmonization around international standards but not preclude governments' opting for higher standards.	Reduction in costs of complying with different standards and regulations. Environmental and consumer groups fear higher standards than international norms may be discouraged.
World Trade Organization	GATT originally envisaged as part of the International Trade Organization (third pillar of Bretton Woods institutions alongside World Bank and IMF). ITO not ratified and GATT still applied provisionally.	World Trade Organization implements results of Uruguay Round. It becomes permanent world trade body covering goods, services, and intellectual property rights with a common disputes procedure.	Boost to the status of international trading rules, and more effective advocacy and policing of the open trading system.

Source: Adapted from *Financial Times*, December 16, 1993. Reprinted with permission.

and protection of intellectual property rights. Experts recognize, however, that much work remains to be done in eliminating NTBs. Other analysts argue that GATT's multilateral philosophy is disintegrating as individual countries bargain bilaterally to resolve their trade conflicts. The United States in particular has borne the brunt of sharp criticism that its Super 301 actions are undermining the GATT's multilateral framework. Finally, many international trade experts are concerned that the strengthening of regional trading blocs, such as the EU and NAFTA, may promote international trade among their members but diminish trade among the regions of the world.

Regional Economic Integration

Regional alliances to promote liberalization of international trade are an important feature of the postwar international landscape. They present international businesses with myriad opportunities and challenges. The past decade in particular has seen a rise in the number and strengthening of trading blocs, as countries seek to integrate their economies more closely in order to open new markets for their firms and lower prices for their consumers. Regional trading blocs are designed to stimulate trade among their members, although, as the previous section suggested, perhaps at the expense of trade among the world's regions.

Forms of Economic Integration

Regional trading blocs differ significantly in form and function. The characteristic of most importance to international businesses is the extent of economic integration among a bloc's members, because this affects exporting and investment opportunities available to firms from member and nonmember countries. There are five different forms of regional economic integration:

1 Free trade area

2 Customs union

3 Common market

4 Economic union

5 Political union

We next discuss these in order of ascending degree of economic integration.

Free Trade Area. A **free trade area** encourages trade among its members by eliminating trade barriers (tariffs, quotas, and other NTBs) among them. An example of such an arrangement is NAFTA, which reduces tariff and nontariff barriers to trade among Canada, Mexico, and the United States.

Although a free trade area reduces trade barriers among its members, each member is free to establish its own trade policies against nonmembers. As a result, members of free trade areas are often vulnerable to the problem of **trade deflection**, in which nonmembers reroute (or deflect) their exports to the member nation with the lowest external trade barriers. Canada, for example, may use high tariffs or quotas to discourage imports of a given product from nonmembers, while the United States may impose few restrictions on imports of the same good from nonmembers. Taking advantage of the latter's low barriers, nonmembers may deflect their Canada-destined exports by first shipping the good to the United States and then re-exporting it from the United States to Canada. In Chapter 6 we noted that Desmarais & Frère, well before NAFTA was signed, was victimized by trade deflection as Korean manufacturers first shipped photo albums to the United States and then re-exported them from the United States to Canada in order to avoid Canada's antidumping duty on Korean photo albums. To prevent trade deflection from destroying their members' trade policies toward nonmembers, most free trade agreements specify **rules of origin**, which detail the conditions under which a good is classified as a member good or a nonmember good. For example, under NAFTA rules of origin, photo albums qualify for preferential treatment as a North American product only if they undergo substantial processing or assembly in Mexico, Canada, or the United States.

Customs Union. A **customs union** combines the elimination of internal trade barriers among its members with the adoption of common external trade policies toward nonmembers. Because of the uniform treatment of products from nonmember countries, a customs union avoids the trade deflection problem. A firm from a nonmember country pays the same tariff rate on exports to any member of the customs union.

Historically the most important customs union was the *Zollverein,* created in 1834 by several independent principalities in what is now Germany. The eventual unification of Germany in 1870 was hastened by this customs union, which tightened the economic bonds among the Germanic principalities and facilitated their political union. A more contemporary example of a customs union is that existing between Switzerland and Liechtenstein, the tiny (160 square kilometers) mountainous country nestled between Austria and Switzerland.

Common Market. A **common market** is a third step along the path to total economic integration. As in a customs union, members of a common market eliminate internal trade barriers among themselves and adopt a common external trade policy toward nonmembers. A common market goes a step further, however, by eliminating barriers that inhibit the movement of factors of production—labor, capital, and technology—among its members. Workers may move from their homeland and practice their profession or trade in any of the other member nations. Firms may locate production facilities, invest in other businesses, and utilize their technologies anywhere within the common market. Productivity within the common market is expected to rise because factors of production are free to locate where the returns to them are highest.

The best example of a common market is the EU, which achieved this status in the 1990s as a result of a 35-year struggle to end barriers to the free movement of labor, capital, and technology. (We discuss the EU in the next section.)

Economic Union. An **economic union** represents full integration of the economies of two or more countries. In addition to eliminating internal trade barriers, adopting common external trade policies, and abolishing restrictions on the mobility of factors of production among members, an economic union requires its members to coordinate their economic policies (monetary policy, fiscal policy, taxation, and social welfare programs) in order to blend their economies into a single entity.

The Belgium-Luxembourg Economic Union, founded in 1922, is the best existing example of this form of economic integration. The economic union of these two European neighbors has been facilitated by the tight bonds between their two currencies. The two nations coordinate their monetary policies and

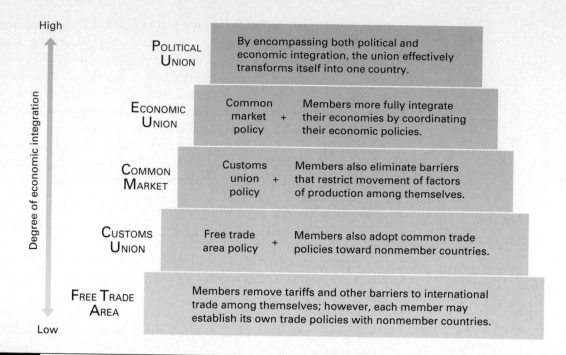

FIGURE 7.2

Forms of Economic Integration

maintain a fixed exchange rate of one Luxembourg franc to one Belgian franc; the Belgian franc is commonly used to conduct business in Luxembourg. However, a much larger economic union is struggling to be born. As we discuss later in the chapter, the EU is attempting to convert its common market into an economic union by the end of this century as a result of the 1992 signing of the Maastricht Treaty.

Political Union. A political union is the complete political as well as economic integration of two or more countries, thereby effectively making them one country. An example of a political union is the integration of the 13 separate colonies operating under the Articles of Confederation into a new country, the United States of America.

Figure 7.2 summarizes the five forms of economic integration.

The Impact of Economic Integration on Firms

From the viewpoint of an individual firm, regional integration is a two-edged sword. Consider elimination of internal trade barriers, a feature common to all five forms of economic integration. Lowering tariffs within the regional trading bloc opens the markets of member countries to all member country firms. Firms can lower their average production and distribution costs by capturing economies of scale as they expand their customer base within the trading bloc. The lower cost structure will also help the firms compete internationally outside the trading bloc. For example, many Canadian manufacturers supported their country's free trade agreements with the United States. They believed that improved access to the large U.S. market would allow longer production runs in Canadian factories, thereby lowering their average costs and making Canadian goods more competitive in international markets inside and outside the free trade area. However, elimination of trade barriers also exposes a firm's home market to competition from firms located in other member countries, thus threatening less efficient firms. A regional trading bloc may also attract FDI from nonmember countries, as firms outside of the bloc seek the benefits of insider status by establishing manufacturing facilities within the bloc. Most non-European MNCs, including General Mills, Toyota, and Samsung, have invested heavily in the EU to take advantage of Europe's increased economic integration. These investments bolster the productivity of European workers and increase the choices available to European consumers but threaten established European firms such as Unilever, Renault, and Siemens.

Typically each form of economic integration confers benefits on the national economy as a whole but often hurts specific sectors and communities within the economy. As a result, negotiating any form of economic integration is not easy. The special-interest groups that will be damaged will lobby against any agreement. For example, U.S. and Canadian auto workers lobbied against NAFTA, fearing that Ford, GM, and Chrysler would shift production to Mexico to take advantage of its lower-cost labor. As a result of such internal political pressures, few economic integration treaties are "pure"; most contain some exemptions to quiet politically powerful domestic special-interest groups.

As noted in the discussion of the Uruguay Round, the growth of regional trading blocs has been controversial because of their uncertain impact on the global market. Trading blocs promote the efficiency of the world economy to the extent that they reallocate production from high-cost producers to lower-cost producers within the trading bloc, a phenomenon called **trade creation**. Efficiency is hurt, however, by **trade diversion**, the shifting of production to higher-cost internal producers from lower-cost external producers, whose products become uncompetitive in the internal market after being subjected to higher tariff walls. The extent of trade creation relative to trade diversion determines whether the regional trading bloc benefits international trade.[7]

For example, suppose that prior to the formation of the EU, apples grown in French orchards cost $1.00 a kilogram, while those grown in German orchards cost $1.20. If Germany were to impose a $0.25 per kilogram specific tariff on imported apples, lower-cost French apples would be excluded from the German market because there they would cost $1.25 a kilogram ($1.00 + $0.25 for the tariff). Under the EU, however, the German tariff would be abolished. Trade would be created because apple production would shift from high-cost Germany to lower-cost France.

But to complicate matters, assume Chilean orchards can produce apples for only $0.85 a kilogram, thereby making Chile a lower-cost producer than either France or Germany. Prior to the formation of the EU, Chilean apples would thus be cheaper than French apples in the German market. (For simplicity, we assume transportation costs are zero.) Chile's crop could be successfully sold in the German market; it would cost $1.10 a kilogram ($0.85 + $0.25 for the tariff), or $0.10 less than German-grown apples and $0.15 less than French-grown apples. Under the EU, however, Germany's tariff on French apples would be eliminated but not its tariff on Chilean apples. As a result, French apples would be cheaper in the German market (at $1.00 a kilogram) than would Chilean apples (at $1.10 a kilogram.) Trade would be diverted from the low-cost external producer, Chile, to a higher-cost internal producer, France, thereby reducing the overall efficiency of the global economy.

The European Union

The most important regional trading bloc in the world today is the European Union (EU). The EU's 15 member countries, with a combined population of 368.7 million, compose the world's richest market, which has a total GDP of $7.2 trillion, or 31 percent of the world economy. (See Table 7.3 and Map 7.1.)

The EU's beginnings stem from the 1952 creation of the European Coal and Steel Community, which was designed to restore those two industries to profitability after World War II. The European Economic Community (EEC) was established in 1957 when six countries (see Table 7.3) signed the **Treaty of Rome**. Under the treaty, they pledged to create a common market by eliminating internal trade barriers, developing common external trade policies, and improving mobility of labor, capital, and technology within the EEC. A third organization, the European Atomic Energy Community, was created in 1958. Officially

---

TABLE 7.3

The European Union, 1992 Data

MEMBERS	POPULATION (MILLIONS)	GDP (BILLIONS)	PER CAPITA GDP*	DATE OF ENTRY
Original Six				
Belgium	10.0	$ 218.8	$20,880	1957
France	57.4	1,319.9	22,260	1957
Luxembourg	0.4	8.5	21,700	1957
Germany	80.6	1,789.3	23,030	1957
Italy	57.8	1,223.0	20,460	1957
Netherlands	15.2	320.3	20,480	1957
Later Entrants				
Denmark	5.2	123.5	26,000	1973
Ireland	3.5	43.3	12,210	1973
United Kingdom	57.8	903.1	17,790	1973
Greece	10.3	67.3	7,290	1981
Spain	39.1	574.9	13,970	1986
Portugal	9.8	79.5	7,450	1986
Total, 12 Members	347.1	$6,671.4	$19,220	
Recent Entrants				
Austria	7.9	$ 185.2	$22,380	1995
Finland	5.0	93.9	21,970	1995
Sweden	8.7	220.8	27,010	1995
Total	21.6	$499.9	$23,193	
Total, 15 Members	368.7	$7,171.3	$19,450	

*GDP per capita adjusted by World Bank staff to smooth out changes in exchange rates.
Source: World Bank, *World Development Report*, 1994.

MAP 7.1

The European Union, 1995

Note: Data not available for the three 1995 entrants.

Source: World Bank, *World Bank Development Report,* 1994.

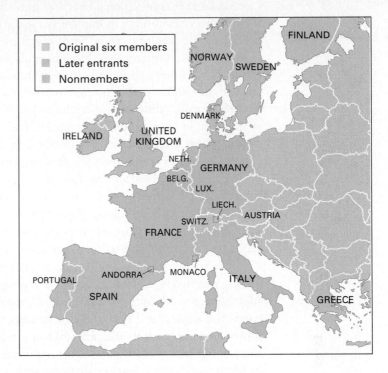

Original six members
Later entrants
Nonmembers

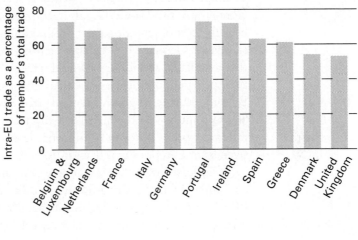

these three communities formed the European Communit*ies* (EC), although the singular form of the noun was often used unofficially. In November 1993, the name of the EC was changed to the European Union (EU) as a result of the Maastricht Treaty.

Completing the Common Market—EC '92

For most of the EC's history, the Treaty of Rome's vision of a common market permitting free movement of goods, services, labor, and capital was nothing more than a cruel mirage. The reality through the 1980s was that most firms wanting to serve the entire EC market continued to have to meet numerous, and sometimes contradictory, sets of national laws and regulations. In practice, the member nations moved cautiously in implementing the common market because of political pressures from domestic special-interest groups.

As a result, numerous conflicting regulations adopted by the members, which affected nearly every good and service purchased by Europeans, hindered trade and the completion of the common market. For example, the United Kingdom defined chocolate differently than the rest of the EC did, causing British chocolates to be illegal in several member countries. Italy required pasta to be made of durum wheat, a requirement not imposed by other EC members. And Belgium allowed yogurt to be colored with dyes extracted from beetroot, but cherries in the yogurt could not be so colored; Germany, in contrast, allowed the cherries to be colored using beetroot dyes, but not the yogurt. The conflicting regulations restricted the ability of Belgian yogurt producers to sell cherry yogurt in Germany and German producers to sell cherry yogurt in Belgium unless a producer established two different production processes to sell yogurt in the two countries.

The EC initially relied on a process of **harmonization** to eliminate such conflicting national regulations. The EC encouraged member countries to voluntarily adopt common, EC-wide ("harmonized") regulations affecting intra-EC trade in goods and services and movement of resources. The harmonization process moved slowly, however, as domestic political forces within the member states resisted change. For example, Belgian yogurt manufacturers balked at Belgium's agreeing to adopt Germany's yogurt regulations; such a concession would raise the level of competition they would face in the domestic yogurt market and force them to bear the cost of retooling their production processes to meet German regulatory standards. German yogurt manufacturers were unwilling to adopt Belgian regulatory standards, because they would have to bear the costs incurred in changing their production processes as well as increased competition in their home market. EC producers of all goods spent an estimated $260 billion (in 1988 dollars) annually to comply with the different national regulations.[8] These increased costs raised the prices European consumers had to pay and reduced the global competitiveness of European manufacturers.

Displeased with the slow progress toward the creation of the common market envisioned by the Treaty of Rome, in 1985 the European Commission (one of the EC's four governing bodies) issued the *White Paper on Completing the Internal Market*. The *White Paper* called for accelerated progress on ending all trade barriers and restrictions on the free movement of goods, services, capital, and labor among members. Accepting the vision of the *White Paper*, the members in February 1986 signed the Single European Act, which took effect on July 1, 1987. The act was intended to help complete the formation of the internal market by December 31, 1992, a goal labeled by the popular press **EC '92**. In the act, the internal market was defined as "an area without internal frontiers in which the free movement of goods, persons, services, and capital is ensured." The implications of completing the internal market were more directly expressed by Ernest Bevin, former British Foreign Secretary. When asked about his vision of Europe without frontiers, he replied: "To be able to take a ticket at Victoria Station and go anywhere I damn well please."[9]

Under the Single European Act, 282 broad regulatory changes had to be made to complete the internal market. While not all have been completely implemented, substantial progress toward EC '92 has been made. These changes can be grouped in three categories:

▶ Physical

▶ Technical

▶ Fiscal

Physical Barriers. The first goal of EC '92 was the removal of physical barriers to the free flow of goods, services, capital, and people. As the opening case suggested, these physical barriers significantly raised the costs of doing business within the EC. Prior to EC '92, shipments among members were stopped at each national border for tax collection, statistics collection, confirmation of compliance with national quotas, administrative checks for plant and animal diseases, and other bureaucratic necessities. On New Year's Day 1993, these requirements were eliminated for intra-EC trade. Most passport controls were also ended at this time, although Denmark, Ireland, and the United Kingdom continued scrutinizing passports in order to control immigration, terrorism, and illegal activities. Abolishing these border formalities—a task that is substantially completed—should save Europeans between ECU13 billion and ECU24 billion a year. This is a worthy achievement, as the truck drivers in the opening case would be the first to affirm.

Technical Barriers. According to the Treaty of Rome, goods, services, labor, and capital were supposed to move freely among members. But differing national product standards restricted trade because manufacturers had to either abandon certain markets or modify their products to meet members' conflicting regulations. The harmonization of technical standards resulting from EC '92 means that a manufacturer has to meet only one set of standards in order to legally sell its goods in each member country. For example, British chocolates and Belgian cherry yogurt can now be sold anywhere within the EU.

The technical standards being adopted by the EU are important to firms of nonmember countries. These firms may be shut out of the European market or face expensive modifications if they fail to meet EU product standards. The EU is working through several European standards-setting organizations, such as the European Committee for Standardization, to establish EU-wide product certification and testing standards. The process is open: representatives of other international organizations, such as the Geneva-based International Standards Organization, and national organizations, such as the American National Standards Institute, may make presentations to the EU's standards setters. Nonmember countries, such as the United States, are also trying to ensure that the standards adopted do not limit their firms' access to the EU market. However, governmental negotiators are often unaware of the impact of technical standards and act only if affected firms notify them of prospective problems. Firms that ignore the EU's deliberations now may pay the price later if standards are imposed that are expensive to meet. A 1992 survey of medium-sized U.S. firms, for example, indicated that 48 percent had not even heard of ISO 9000, a set of quality standards adopted by the EU and commonly used in Asia as well. Only 8 percent were planning to adopt these standards. The remaining 92 percent will have difficulty marketing their goods internationally because of their ignorance and inattention.[10]

Fiscal Barriers. European countries rely on value-added taxes (VAT) as a primary source of revenue. In assessing a VAT, a country taxes each firm in the production-distribution process based on the value it adds to the product. The EU has been concerned that if VAT rates differ substantially among members, consumers will travel to buy goods in countries with lower VAT rates, thereby eroding the tax base of the high-tax country. For example, because French alcohol and tobacco prices are lower than British prices because of tax differences, British citizens have been flocking to Calais and other French ports to stock up on low-priced liquor and cigarettes, to the chagrin of British Inland Revenue officials who are losing an estimated $1.5 million daily in taxes. Similarly,

The EU is sometimes willing to bend its rules to protect local interests. For example, it allowed the United Kingdom to halve the VAT tax on imported artwork in order to protect prestigious British auction houses such as Christie's from U.S.-based competitors.

Fleggaard, a Danish household goods retailer, ships its goods to domestic customers out of Danish warehouses but invoices those customers out of a small office located in Germany. Because the goods are technically sold in Germany, the firm bills its customers the 15 percent German VAT rate, rather than Denmark's 25 percent rate.[11] Unless the gaps between VAT rates are reduced, border controls may need to be reinstituted in high-VAT countries in order to collect additional VAT taxes from their residents, thereby defeating EC '92's goal of eliminating physical barriers among members. The EU is proposing that all national VAT taxes fall within certain narrow bands: 14 to 20 percent for most goods and a reduced rate of 4 to 9 percent for basic necessities. Controlling VATs in this way would reduce the incentives for EU residents to travel to countries with lower VAT rates to purchase goods.[12]

The Benefits of EC '92. The EU's substantial progress towards completing its internal market offers the opportunity for firms both in Europe and elsewhere to sell their goods in a large, rich market. While firms in EU member countries have gained improved access to a larger market, they also face increased competition in their home markets from other members' firms. This increased competition benefits consumers throughout the EU. Marketing, production, and R&D costs have been reduced, since firms have to comply with only one, EU-wide set of regulations instead of 15 separate sets of national regulations. Many firms have been able to restructure their European manufacturing operations to capture economies of scale and lower their production costs. For example, Samsung shifted its European color television production, which was previously split between factories in Portugal and Spain, to its plant in Billingham, England. It dedicated its Spanish factory to producing VCRs for the entire EU market and its Portuguese factory to supplying parts for all of its European operations. Also, in 1992 the firm purchased an East German picture tube manufacturer, Werk für Fernsehelektronik, to supply its European operations. Samsung determined that the economies of scale obtained by this realignment of its operations would lower its manufacturing costs, improve the quality of its products, and create new jobs for European workers.[13]

Member countries have attracted new investment from foreign firms eager to enter the lucrative European market and benefit from EC '92. For example, the Maytag Corporation, headquartered in Iowa, purchased the Hoover Company in 1989 in order to use the latter's factories in Scotland and Wales to supply the European market for white goods (refrigerators, ranges, and so on). Adoption of a single set of regulations for these goods meant Hoover could supply the entire EU market from its British plants.[14] Similarly, Bandag, Inc., the world's leading tire retreader, viewed EC '92 with delight. It expected European trucking firms, which were facing increased competition due to EC '92, to purchase more retreaded tires as a cost-cutting measure. So it developed an innovative distribution system to replace worn tires at a truck terminal: a $60,000 Mercedes truck full of equipment and replacement tires that functioned as a rolling warehouse. By going to its customers' places of business, Bandag estimated that it could save the trucking firms $500 per year per truck from reduced downtime on their vehicle fleets.[15] All told, U.S. FDI in the EU has risen from $84 billion in 1985, when the *White Paper* was first issued, to $233 billion in 1993. Similarly, over 500 Japanese companies have established operations in the EU since 1985.[16]

The Creation of the European Union

Going beyond the initial concept of the EC as a common market, many Europeans argued for the creation of an economic union with common military and foreign policies.[17] Heeding this call, the EC's Council of Ministers met in the Dutch city of Maastricht in December 1991 to discuss the EC's economic and political future. The result was a new treaty that amended the Treaty of Rome; this new treaty was known formally as the **Treaty on European Union** and informally as the **Maastricht Treaty**. After ratification by the twelve EC members, the Maastricht Treaty came into force on November 1, 1993.

The Maastricht Treaty rests on three "pillars" designed to further Europe's economic and political integration:

1 A new agreement to create a common foreign and defense policy among members

2 A new agreement to cooperate on police, judicial, and public safety matters

3 The old familiar EC, with new provisions to create an economic and monetary union among member states

Additionally, the Maastricht Treaty granted citizens the right to live, work, vote, and run for election anywhere within the EC and strengthened the powers of the EC's legislative body, the European Parliament, in budgetary, trade, cultural, and health matters. The treaty also created a new **cohesion fund**, a means of funneling economic development aid to countries whose per capita GDP is less than 90 percent of the EC average (these countries are Greece, Ireland, Portugal, and Spain). In recognition of the increasing integration of Europe, the treaty also changed the name of the European Community to the European Union.

Without a doubt, the most important and most controversial aspect of the Maastricht Treaty is the creation of the **economic and monetary union (EMU)**. The ultimate goal of the EMU is to create a single currency for the EU, thereby eliminating exchange-rate risks and the costs of converting currencies for intra-EU trade. European financial services firms hope that the planned single currency, the ECU, which currently serves as the EU's unit of account, will become as important in international commerce as the U.S. dollar or the yen. Ultimately, the EU will establish a single European central bank in charge of monetary policy for the entire union.

Creation of the EMU is proceeding in three steps:

1 Full membership in the exchange-rate mechanism (ERM) of the European Monetary System by all EU members. This step is deemed to have been reached, even though the United Kingdom and Italy were forced to withdraw "temporarily" from the ERM in September 1992.

2 The creation of the European Monetary Institute in January 1994. The **European Monetary Institute (EMI)** is charged with overseeing members' monetary policies to ensure that they promote the eventual creation of a single currency. Upon successful completion of this step, the EMI will be transformed into the European Central Bank.

3 Complete economic and monetary union, which is to occur no earlier than January 1, 1997, and no later than January 1, 1999. At this time "the ECU will be transformed from a basket of individual moneys to a single medium of exchange based on fixed exchange rates"[18] among EU member currencies. By the year 2000, Europeans may be able to pay for their purchases with ECU-denominated banknotes and coins.[19]

However, in order to participate in the EMU, members must meet certain **convergence criteria**, which include the following:

1 A country's inflation rate must be no more than 1.5 percentage points higher than that of the EU country with the lowest inflation rate.

2 A country's long-term interest rates must be no more than 2 percentage points higher than that of the EU country with the lowest long-term interest rates.

3 A country must not have devalued its currency in the two years prior to joining the EMU.

4 A country's government budget deficit must be no more than 3 percent of its GDP.

5 A country's outstanding government debt must be no more than 60 percent of its GDP.

Effectively, these conditions require convergence of the monetary and fiscal policies of the participating countries. This is a necessary condition for the long-term survival of any fixed exchange-rate system. Only those EU members that meet these criteria will be allowed to join the EMU. As part of the Maastricht negotiations, the United Kingdom was given the right not to participate in the EMU at its option.

Creating a single EU currency will not be easy. Its development implies members will lose the ability to control their own domestic money supplies and economic destinies. National governments facing recessions will be deprived of one tool for reviving their economies and will become more vulnerable to losing elections because of short-term pocketbook issues. The allure of a single currency was called into question in the summer of 1992 when the Bundesbank raised German interest rates to almost 10 percent in order to limit the inflationary impact of German reunification. The United Kingdom was obligated under the ERM to maintain the pound's value relative to the deutsche mark. To do this, the Bank of England was forced to raise British interest rates, thereby plunging the country into its worst recession since World War II. In September 1992, the United Kingdom withdrew from the ERM rather than cripple its economy by continuing to follow the Bundesbank's monetary policies. Further, many EU members have not yet met the convergence criteria and thus are ineligible to join the EMU. By the time the EMU is scheduled to be implemented, optimists believe seven EU members will have met the convergence criteria, while pessimists fear only Luxembourg will.[20]

Governing the European Union

The EU members have created a supranational government that develops, implements, and administers its programs and resolves conflicts among members' diverse interests. The EU is governed by four organizations that perform its executive, administrative, legislative, and judicial functions:

▶ The Council of the European Union (headquartered in Brussels)

▶ The European Commission (also Brussels-based)

▶ The European Parliament (which normally meets in Strasbourg, France)

▶ The European Court of Justice (sitting in Luxembourg)

Because these governmental bodies establish the rules by which international businesses compete within the EU, we discuss them in some detail.

The Council of the European Union. The **Council of the European Union** is composed of 15 representatives, each selected directly by and responsible to his or her home government. Normally, a country's foreign minister represents his or her country at the Council meetings. However, a country's representative may differ depending on the Council's agenda. For example, if the Council is dealing with farm policies, each country may send its minister of agriculture to the Council meeting. The Council presidency rotates among the members every six months. In Council decisions, France, Germany, Italy and the United Kingdom have 10 votes each; Spain has 8; Belgium, Greece, the Netherlands, and Portugal, 5 each; Austria and Sweden, 4 each; Denmark, Finland, and Ireland, 3 each; and Luxembourg, 2. The allocation of votes is in rough proportion to the population and economic importance of the members.

The Council is the EU's most powerful decision-making body. Each representative pursues the interests of his or her home government. The Council's strong powers reflect the hesitancy of the member states to surrender power to Brussels (shorthand for the EU government) on issues they view as vital to their national interests. As a result, some council decisions require unanimous approval. On matters perceived to be less threatening to national interests, Council decisions require only a qualified majority (62 out of a total 87 votes) for passage.

Effectively, a coalition of two large countries and three smaller countries can block a decision. However, the EU strives to create consensus on all issues and often slows its deliberations in order to develop compromises amenable to all the members, even when unanimity is not required.

The European Commission. The **European Commission** is composed of 20 people selected for five-year terms. The smaller EU countries each nominate one citizen to serve on the Commission; the larger countries select two. However, once these individuals are in office, their loyalty is to the EU itself, not to their home countries. The Commission's primary mandate is to be the "guardian of the Treaties." The Commission also acts as the EU's administrative branch. Its functions include the following:

► It proposes legislation to be considered by the Council.

► It implements the provisions of the Treaty of Rome and other EU treaties.

► It protects the EU's interests in political debates, particularly in Council deliberations.

► It has extensive legislative powers in implementing the EU's customs union, the Common Agricultural Policy (CAP), and the completion of the internal market.

► It administers the EU's permanent bureaucracy, which employs about 16,000 people—popularly known as "Eurocrats"—two thirds of whom work at Commission headquarters in Brussels. (Because the EU has eleven official languages, over 2700 of the Commission's employees are engaged in translation services!)

The European Parliament. The **European Parliament** comprises 626 representatives elected in national elections to serve five-year terms. Seats are allocated in rough proportion to a country's population, but the allocation also reflects political jockeying among members. For example, Germany has 99 seats, while France, Italy, and the United Kingdom are allocated 87 seats each, even though Germany's population is at least 39 percent larger than that of any of the other three (see Table 7.3). Of the EU's governing bodies, the Parliament is the weakest. Initially it possessed only a consultative role in EU policymaking. However, it has used its budgetary powers to enlarge its influence within the EU's governing institutions, and it also gained additional powers under the Maastricht Treaty.

The European Court of Justice. The **European Court of Justice** consists of 16 judges who serve six-year terms. It interprets EU law and ensures that members follow EU regulations and policies. Because national governments carry out the EU's policies, many cases reaching the Court are referred from national courts asking it to interpret EU law. For example, as noted in Chapter 6, the Court declared Germany's 450-year-old beer purity law regulating beer additives illegal, ruling that the law unreasonably restricted imports into Germany.

The Legislative Process. To say the least, the EU legislative process is complex (see Fig. 7.3 for a simplified overview). The following steps are needed to pass new EU laws:

I In most cases, the Commission has the sole right to initiate legislation. Normally, the Commission's staff proposes legislation to the Commission, which it may adopt, amend, or kill.

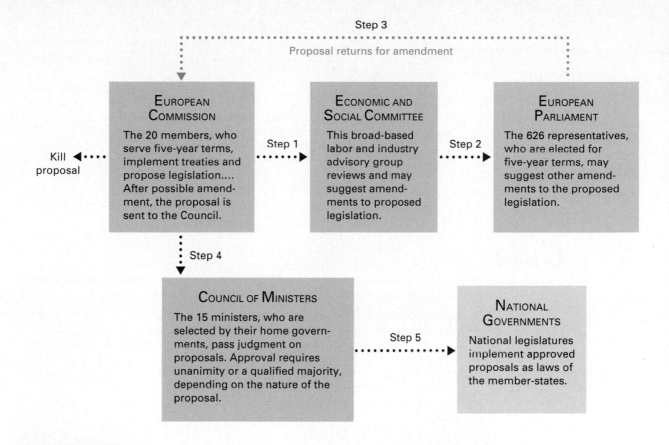

Step 3

Proposal returns for amendment

EUROPEAN COMMISSION

The 20 members, who serve five-year terms, implement treaties and propose legislation.... After possible amendment, the proposal is sent to the Council.

Kill proposal

Step 1

ECONOMIC AND SOCIAL COMMITTEE

This broad-based labor and industry advisory group reviews and may suggest amendments to proposed legislation.

Step 2

EUROPEAN PARLIAMENT

The 626 representatives, who are elected for five-year terms, may suggest other amendments to the proposed legislation.

Step 4

COUNCIL OF MINISTERS

The 15 ministers, who are selected by their home governments, pass judgment on proposals. Approval requires unanimity or a qualified majority, depending on the nature of the proposal.

Step 5

NATIONAL GOVERNMENTS

National legislatures implement approved proposals as laws of the member-states.

FIGURE 7.3

Flowchart of the EU's Legislative Process

2 Legislation approved by the Commission is sent to the Parliament and a broad-based labor and industry advisory group, the Economic and Social Committee, for their opinions on the matter. The Commission may amend its proposal based on the opinions of these two bodies.

3 The legislation is sent to the Council of Ministers. Each representative sends the proposed legislation to senior officials of his or her home government to determine if the legislation is in the member's best interests.

4 Having heard all the diverse views on the proposed legislation, the Council then votes on the issue. Depending on the nature of the proposal, unanimity or a qualified majority of the Council's votes is needed to pass new legislation.

5 Each member's government must pass national legislation to implement the new EU policy.

Because the EU prefers to develop a strong consensus on issues among its members before it adopts new legislation, transforming a Commission proposal into an EU law and then implementing that law into national legislation often takes years. The complicated governance arrangements of the EU reflect the ongoing struggle between the members' desire to retain their national sovereignty and their desire to create a supranational government with an international political and economic stature equal to those of the United States and Japan. (As "Going Global" suggests, many MNCs exploit this power struggle to their benefit.)

GOING GLOBAL

Lobbying the European Union

The EU's government is engaged in many activities that affect international businesses. For example, the EU has decided that at least 50 percent of the programs broadcast on TV stations in its member countries must be European in origin. The effect of this regulation is to shrink the market for movies and TV shows produced in the United States, Mexico, Australia, and other countries. Because of the impact of the EU's decisions on the opening or closing of the enormous European market to international businesses, most countries maintain diplomatic relationships with the EU to ensure the EU does not disregard their economic interests. The United States, for example, maintains a United States Mission to the European Union, led by a senior state department official with ambassadorial status.

But savvy international businesspeople do not rely solely on their home governments to protect them from adverse EU regulations. The first step is understanding the power relationships within the EU—particularly between the Council, which defends national interests, and the Commission, which promotes the interests of an integrated Europe. Firms threatened by pending EU regulations can adopt two strategies:

1 They may lobby the Commission and its elaborate bureaucracy to adopt regulations more beneficial to their interests. Because the Commission must continually balance the often diverse interests of EU members, firms can often influence the Commission to add their interests to the long list of other factors that it will consider in proposing legislation to the Council. Because of the commitment of the Commission to the completion of the EU's internal market, firms have found that arguments promoting increased European integration are particularly well-received by Eurocrats. For example, the Commission dropped proposed franchising regulations after U.S. firms convinced its staff that the pending regulations would hinder European integration.

2 Firms may lobby an ally on the Council. For example, remembering that "all politics is local," Japanese automakers that built assembly plants in the United Kingdom were able to enlist the help of the British representative on the Council—who was interested in preserving jobs in his country—when French and Italian automakers were urging the EU to adopt regulations prejudicial to those U.K. assembly plants.

Sources: James N. Gardner, "Lobbying, European-Style," *Europe*, November 1991 (Number 311), pp. 29–30; "European Bureaucrats Are Writing the Rules Americans Will Live By," *Wall Street Journal*, May 17, 1989, p. A1; "Lobbying Brussels in Anticipation of 1992," *Wall Street Journal*, March 6, 1989, p. A12.

The member countries have granted EU governing bodies power over trade and agricultural policy. The EU and its members share responsibility for formulating transportation policy and environmental policy. Many other areas of responsibility remain with members' governments. The debate over national sovereignty versus supranational government is manifested in another way: while EU policies are formulated supranationally, they must be implemented by members at a national level.[21]

Other EU Controversies. Other political conflicts remain within the EU. Germany, whose workers enjoy high wages and lucrative benefits, lobbied for the implementation of the EU's **Social Policy**. This policy promotes extensive EU-wide job-related benefits, including maternity leave, job training, and pension benefits. But it also reduces the potential loss of jobs from richer countries such as Germany to countries with lower wages and poorer benefit programs, such as Portugal, Greece, and Spain. The United Kingdom, however, fears surrendering its economic destiny to EU bureaucrats in Brussels and so won the right in the

Maastricht negotiations to exempt itself from the Social Policy. In another conflict, the poorer members, led by Spain, successfully argued for increasing the EU's spending on economic development in its poorer regions, against the wishes of the United Kingdom. And France and the United Kingdom continue to squabble over the EU's CAP, which disproportionately benefits French farmers to the detriment of British interests and hurts European MNCs by poisoning relationships between the United States and the EU. Other countries, such as Denmark, are concerned about the lack of democracy within the EU. They believe more power should be given to the EU's only directly elected governing body, the European Parliament.[22]

Still another major point of contention among EU members is state aid to industry. Under EU rules, governments may not provide subsidies to firms that "distort" competition. Yet countries such as France that support governmental direction of the economy are loath to give up their policies. For example, Groupe Bull, the government-owned computer manufacturer, suffered multibillion franc losses in 1990 and 1991 because of high costs and technologically inferior products. Direct subsidies from the French government would likely have been vetoed by the Commission as a distortion of competition. The French solution was to have the state-owned telephone company, France Telecom, inject capital into Groupe Bull, thereby skirting the power of the Eurocrats to intervene.[23]

Other Regional Trading Blocs

The EU's success in enriching its members through trade promotion has stimulated the development of other regional trading blocs. Every continent, except for Australia (which is home to only one country) and Antarctica (home to none), now contains at least one regional trading group. Europe, for example, has two trading blocs; the second one is the **European Free Trade Association (EFTA)**. Its members are Iceland, Liechtenstein, Norway, and Switzerland. EFTA works closely with the EU on economic issues of common concern.

The North American Free Trade Agreement

Another important example of regional economic integration is the North American Free Trade Agreement (NAFTA). Implemented in 1994 to reduce barriers to trade and investment among Canada, Mexico, and the United States, NAFTA builds on the 1988 Canadian-U.S. Free Trade Agreement. A significant amount of trade already existed among the three countries prior to NAFTA. Canada and the United States enjoy the world's largest bilateral trading relationship, with two-way trade totaling $253.1 billion in 1993. The United States is Mexico's largest trading partner, while Mexico is the third-largest trading partner of the United States (after Canada and Japan). However, trade between Canada and Mexico is rather small.

NAFTA reflects the continuation of a decade-long process of opening up the economies of Canada and Mexico. Former Canadian Prime Minister Brian Mulroney worried in the 1980s that Canada's small domestic market limited the ability of Canadian firms to capture economies of scale, raised their costs, and hurt their international competitiveness. In 1985 he sought to strengthen economic ties between Canada and the United States. After several years of negotiation, Mulroney and President Ronald Reagan signed the Canadian-U.S. Free Trade Agreement on January 2, 1988. While U.S. and Canadian negotiators were hammering out the details of this agreement, President Carlos Salinas de Gortai of Mexico was undertaking substantial reforms of the Mexican economy after his election in 1988, including dismantling the high tariff walls that had protected Mexican manufacturers and promoting foreign investment. Salinas also undertook massive privatization of state-owned businesses, selling off key firms in the transportation, banking, and telecommunications industries. As part of this economic development and modernization program, Salinas proposed broadening the Canadian-U.S. Free Trade Agreement to include Mexico. After three years of negotiations and then ratification by the participating governments, NAFTA became effective in January 1994.

The agreement promises an increasing integration of the North American economies. Over 15 years, tariff walls will be lowered, NTBs reduced, and investment opportunities increased for firms located in the three countries. Table 7.4 shows NAFTA's main features. However, note from the table that many industries have received special treatment in the agreement. Negotiators from all three countries recognized the political sensitivity of certain issues and industries and chose to compromise on their treatment within NAFTA to ensure the agreement's ratification. For example, because Canada fears being dominated by U.S. media, NAFTA allows Canada to continue to bar foreign investments in its culture industries (publishing, music, television, radio, cable, and film). Similarly, Mexico may maintain control over foreign investments in its energy sector, while the United States may bar foreign ownership in its airline and broadcasting industries.

U.S. and Canadian negotiators also were concerned that firms from nonmembers might locate so-called screwdriver plants in Mexico as a means of evading U.S. and Canadian tariffs. A **screwdriver plant** is a factory in which very little transformation of the product is undertaken. Speaking metaphorically, in such factories the only tool workers need is the screwdriver they use to assemble a product. So the negotiators developed detailed rules of origin that defined whether a good was North American in origin and thus qualified for preferential tariff status. In the automobile industry, for example, U.S. and Canadian labor unions worried that European and Asian automakers would exploit the treaty by producing major components elsewhere and then establishing a North American factory merely to assemble motor vehicles, thereby causing the loss of jobs at Canadian and U.S. parts-producing factories. To diminish this problem, NAFTA specifies that for an automobile to qualify as a North American product, 62.5 percent of its value must be produced in Canada, Mexico, or the United States. Similarly, to protect textile industry jobs, clothing and other textile products must use North American–produced fibers in order to benefit from NAFTA's preferential tariff treatment.

Nonetheless, consumers in all three countries should benefit from increased competition among members' firms. Opportunities presented by NAFTA are already attracting the attention of North American firms, both large and small. Retailers such as Wal-Mart, J.C. Penney, and 7-Eleven have expanded their operations in Mexico. And, seeking opportunities in the NAFTAlife, the Loewen

TABLE 7.4

What Is NAFTA?

GENERAL PROVISIONS	INDUSTRIES	SIDE AGREEMENTS	OTHER DEALS
Tariffs reduced over fifteen years, depending on sector.	Agriculture: Most tariffs between the United States and Mexico to be removed immediately. Tariffs on 6 percent of products—corn, sugar and some fruits and vegetables—fully eliminated only after fifteen years. For Canada, existing agreement with the United States applies.	Environment: The three countries can be fined, and Mexico and the United States sanctioned, if a panel finds a repeated pattern of their not enforcing environment laws.	The United States and Mexico to set up a North American Development Bank to help finance clean-up of the U.S. border.
Investment restrictions lifted in most sectors, with the exception of oil in Mexico, culture in Canada, and airline and radio communications in the United States.			
Immigration excluded, except some movement of white-collar workers to be eased.	Cars: Tariffs removed over ten years. Mexico's quotas on imports lifted over the same period. Cars eventually to meet 62.5 percent local content rule to be free of tariff.	Labor: Countries are liable for penalties for nonenforcement of child, minimum wage, and health and safety laws.	The United States to spend about $90 million in the first eighteen months retraining workers that will lose their jobs because of the treaty.
Any country can leave the treaty with six months notice.			
Treaty allows for the inclusion of any additional country.	Energy: Mexican ban on private-sector exploration continues, but procurement by state oil firm opened up to the United States and Canada.		
Government procurement opened up over ten years, mainly affecting Mexico, which reserves some contracts for Mexican firms.	Financial Services: Mexico gradually to open financial sector to the United States and Canadian investment, eliminating barriers by 2007.		
Dispute resolution panels of independent arbitrators to resolve disagreements arising out of treaty.	Textiles: Treaty eliminates Mexican, U.S., and Canadian tariffs over ten years. Clothes eligible for tariff breaks to be sewn with fabric woven in North America.		
Some snap-back tariffs if surge of imports hurts a domestic industry.	Trucking: North American trucks could drive anywhere in the three countries by the year 2000.		

Source: Adapted from "What is NAFTA?" *Financial Times*, November 17, 1993. Reprinted with permission.

Group, a British Columbia–based operator of over 600 funeral homes, crematoriums, and cemeteries in Canada and the United States, spread its empire into Mexico after the treaty relaxed Mexican controls on foreign investment.[24]

Other Free Trade Agreements

Many other countries are negotiating or implementing free trade agreements on a bilateral or multilateral basis. For example, Mexico and Chile, with annual bilateral trade of $150 million, negotiated a free trade agreement in 1991. This agreement provided for eliminating NTBs and setting a 10 percent tariff on most products, to be phased in over four years. Also in 1991, Mexico, Venezuela, and Colombia hammered out a trilateral agreement that called for relaxing trade barriers against each other's goods. Mexico is also negotiating free trade pacts with its five Central American neighbors.[25]

The Caribbean Basin Initiative. In 1983 the United States initiated the Caribbean Basin Initiative in order to facilitate the economic development of the countries of Central America and the Caribbean Sea. The **Caribbean Basin Initiative (CBI)** overlaps two regional free trade areas: the Central American Common Market (CACM) and the Caribbean Community and Common Market (CARICOM), the members of which are listed in Table 7.5 and shown in Map 7.2. The CBI, which acts as a uni-directional free trade agreement, permits duty-free import into the United States of a wide range of goods that originate in Caribbean Basin countries or that have been assembled there from U.S.-produced parts. However, numerous politically sensitive goods, many of which are traditional exports of the area, have been excluded from the CBI, including textiles, canned tuna, luggage, apparel, footware, petroleum, and petroleum products. Through this pattern of duty-free access to the U.S. market, the United States hopes to stimulate investment by domestic, U.S., and other foreign firms in new industries in the Caribbean Basin countries.[26]

The Mercosur Accord. In March 1991, the governments of Argentina, Brazil, Paraguay, and Uruguay signed the **Mercosur Accord** (*Mercosur* is Spanish for "southern cone"), an agreement to create a customs union among themselves. By doing so, these four countries will give their firms preferential access to a combined market of 195 million people and total GDP of $607 billion. They agreed to establish common external tariffs and to cut over four years their internal tariffs on goods that account for 85 percent of intra-Mercosur trade. Full implementation of the customs union began in 1995. In Mercosur's first three years, trade among the four countries more than doubled, from $4.1 billion in 1990 to $9.5 billion in 1993.[27]

The Mercosur Accord is a direct response to the growth of other regional trading blocs. But it is also a key element of the free-market–oriented economic reforms adopted by the Argentinian and Brazilian governments elected in 1989 to revitalize their stagnating economies. By opening up their countries' economies, these governments hope to stimulate new flows of FDI, which will enhance the productivity of their workforces and make their goods more competitive in world markets. As noted by Argentina's President Carlos Menem, "There aren't many options. Either we work out a joint strategy in line with our development needs, or we will be the objects of outside strategies."[28]

TABLE 7.5

Major Regional Trade Associations

ACRONYM	FULL NAME/MEMBERS
AFTA	ASEAN Free Trade Area Brunei, Indonesia, Malaysia, Philippines, Singapore, Thailand
ANCOM	Andean Pact Bolivia, Colombia, Ecuador, Peru, Venezuela
CACM	Central American Common Market Costa Rica, El Salvador, Guatemala, Honduras, Nicaragua
CARICOM	Caribbean Community and Common Market Antigua and Barbuda, Bahamas, Barbados, Belize, Dominica, Grenada, Guyana, Jamaica, Montserrat, St. Kitts and Nevis, St. Lucia, St. Vincent and the Grenadines, Trinidad and Tobago
CEEAC	Economic Community of Central African States Burundi, Cameroon, Central African Republic, Chad, Congo, Equatorial Guinea, Gabon, Rwanda, Sao Tome and Principe, Zaire
ECOWAS	Economic Community of West African States Benin, Burkina Faso, Cape Verde, Gambia, Ghana, Guinea, Guinea-Bissau, Ivory Coast, Liberia, Mali, Mauritania, Niger, Nigeria, Senegal, Sierra Leone, Togo
EU	European Union Austria, Belgium, Denmark, Finland, France, Germany, Greece, Ireland, Italy, Luxembourg, Netherlands, Portugal, Spain, Sweden, United Kingdom
EFTA	European Free Trade Association Iceland, Liechtenstein, Norway, Switzerland
GCC	Gulf Cooperation Council Bahrain, Kuwait, Oman, Qatar, Saudi Arabia, United Arab Emirates
MERCOSUR	Southern Cone Customs Union Argentina, Brazil, Paraguay, Uruguay
NAFTA	North American Free Trade Agreement Canada, Mexico, United States
SADCC	Southern African Development Coordination Conference Angola, Botswana, Lesotho, Malawi, Mozambique, Namibia, Swaziland, Tanzania, Zambia, Zimbabwe

Many firms in the four countries reacted quickly to the Mercosur Accord, striking deals to position themselves to take better advantage of it. For example, Renault's Argentinian subsidiary agreed to import needed parts from Cofab, one of Brazil's leading auto parts manufacturers. By building bridges to Brazilian manufacturers, Renault-Argentina hoped to improve its access to the much larger Brazilian market. Volkswagen, Ford, and GM, each with Brazilian production facilities, have aggressively introduced new models and expanded production in anticipation of substantial sales increases in the Mercosur region.[29] Yet, other firms are wary of the agreement. Brazil's computer industry, which had

UNITED STATES

BERMUDA

MEXICO

BAHAMAS

CUBA　HAITI

BELIZE　DOMINICAN REPUBLIC
HONDURAS　JAMAICA　PUERTO RICO
GUATEMALA　NICARAGUA
EL SALVADOR
COSTA RICA　VENEZUELA
PANAMA　COLOMBIA

GUYANA
SURINAME
FRENCH
GUIANA

ECUADOR

PERU　BRAZIL

BOLIVIA

PARAGUAY
CHILE

URUGUAY
ARGENTINA

■ ANTIGUA AND
　BARBUDA
■ BARBADOS
■ DOMINICA
■ GRENADA
■ MONTSERRAT
■ ST. KITTS
　AND NEVIS
■ ST. LUCIA
■ ST. VINCENT AND
　THE GRENADINES
■ TRINIDAD AND
　TOBAGO

Andean Pact
CACM
CARICOM
MERCOSUR

MAP 7.2

**Free Trade
Agreements in
Central and South
America and the
Caribbean**

been protected by the 1984 Infomatics Law that discouraged imports, fears that inexpensive Paraguayan-built personal computers will flood the Brazilian market once the Mercosur Accord is fully implemented.[30]

Andean Pact. The **Andean Pact** is a 1969 agreement to promote free trade among five small South American countries—Bolivia, Chile, Columbia, Ecuador, and Peru—in order to make them more competitive with the continent's larger countries. Venezuela joined the Pact in 1973, but Chile dropped out in 1976. During its first 20 years, the agreement was not very successful; trade among members totaled only 5 percent of their total trade. Geography played a role in this failure: the Andes mountain range, from which the agreement got its name, makes land transportation of goods between some members costly. More important, most members adopted protectionist, import-substitution policies that hindered trade.

The Andean Pact members agreed in 1991 to reinvigorate their agreement. The new resolve resulted from Chile's economic successes that followed its adoption of free-market, export-oriented economic policies in the 1980s and from the threat posed by the Mercosur Accord. In January 1992, the members established a customs union that provided for phased elimination of tariffs among themselves on most goods, a common external tariff, and harmonized regulations on capital movements, immigration, and agriculture. So far, the free trade portion of the Pact is progressing well, with trade among members increasing by 20 percent in 1992 and by another 30 percent in 1993. Creation of a common external tariff, however, has been stalled by political squabbling over the appropriate tariff level and structure.[31]

ASEAN
CEEAC
SADCC

MAP 7.3

Free Trade Agreements in Africa and Asia

Association of South East Asian Nations. The **Association of South East Asian Nations (ASEAN)** comprises Brunei, Indonesia, Malaysia, Philippines, Singapore, and Thailand and was founded in 1967 to promote regional political and economic cooperation (see Map 7.3). These countries are by no means homogeneous: oil-rich Brunei had a 1992 per capita income of $17,000, while Indonesia's was only $670. Nonetheless, the ASEAN economy has been developing rapidly because its poorer members—Indonesia, Malaysia, Philippines, and Thailand—provide large pools of low-cost labor, receive preferential tariff rates under the U.S. GSP and those of other GATT members, and have attracted significant Japanese, European, and U.S. investment.

To promote intra-ASEAN trade, members established the ASEAN Free Trade Area (AFTA), effective January 1993. They agreed to slash tariffs on goods manufactured by members to 5 percent or less over a 15-year period ending in 2008. As with the Mercosur Accord and Andean Pact, the desire for creation of the ASEAN trading bloc stems from two factors: a decrease in governmental control of national economies that has stimulated local entrepreneurs and attracted FDI and a defensive response to the growth of other regional trading blocs such as the EU and NAFTA.[32] And as with other new trading blocs, firms have reacted quickly to take advantage of opportunities created by AFTA. For example, shortly after the agreement was negotiated, Filipino brewer San Miguel, which controls 90 percent of its home market, purchased Jakarta-based Delta Brewery, which controls 40 percent of the Indonesian beer market. By moving quickly, San Miguel hoped to dominate the entire ASEAN market prior to the fall of tariff rates triggered by AFTA.[33]

African Initiatives. The African countries are also attempting to create regional trading blocs. As shown in Table 7.5 and Map 7.3, ten of them created the **Southern African Development Coordination Conference (SADCC)** in 1980 to promote the development of their regional economy. The SADCC also announced plans to develop an 18-member Preferential Trade Area of Eastern and

Southern Africa that would serve as a regional common market.[34] In 1975, 16 African countries along the Atlantic coast formed the **Economic Community of West African States (ECOWAS)** to promote cooperation on regional economic development programs. The **Economic Community of Central African States (CEEAC)**, established in 1983, has similar goals for its region of the continent. However, these initiatives have not been very successful because of poor transportation facilities in most African countries and the failure of most domestic governments to create economic and political systems that encourage significant regional trade. Intra-Africa trade to date accounts for less than 7 percent of the continent's total exports.[35]

International Commodity Arrangements

Countries may also cooperate with one another to control the production, pricing, and sale of goods that are traded internationally. A **commodity cartel** is a group of producing countries that want to protect themselves from the wild fluctuations that often occur in prices of some commodity that is traded internationally, such as crude oil, coffee, rubber, or cocoa. Cartel members may also seek higher, as well as more stable, prices for their good. By assigning production quotas to individual countries and limiting overall output, a commodity cartel can raise the price of its good in international markets. A **commodity agreement** is an agreement among representatives from both producing and consuming countries who jointly negotiate production levels and target prices for the commodity. Membership in a commodity agreement is voluntary, but to be successful it normally must include representatives from countries that produce most of the good in question.

Organization of Petroleum Exporting Countries

The **Organization of Petroleum Exporting Countries (OPEC)** is the most important and successful commodity cartel in the world's history. OPEC is composed of 12 members, which account for 40 percent of the world's oil production. OPEC attempts to control the price of oil in world markets by assigning to its members production quotas that limit the overall amount of crude oil supplied internationally. OPEC first rose to prominence as a result of the Arab oil embargo that followed the 1973 Arab-Israeli War. By restricting the flow of oil to the market, OPEC succeeded in tripling the price of oil from $4 a barrel to $12 a barrel in a few short months in 1973–74. OPEC stabilized world oil prices at these higher levels until the fall of the Shah of Iran in 1978, when it took advantage of the ensuing political chaos to elevate crude oil prices further. By 1981, crude oil was selling for $35 a barrel on world markets.

However, OPEC's control over the world crude oil market gradually lessened during the 1980s. Higher prices for petroleum products motivated consumers to reduce their consumption of such goods, thereby lessening the demand for crude oil. Higher crude oil prices also prompted a shift to other forms of energy, including natural gas, coal, nuclear energy, and renewable sources such as wind and geothermal power. Finally, the higher prices for crude oil attracted increased production from non-OPEC countries, such as Mexico, Norway, and Russia. OPEC's control over oil prices was further weakened by political infighting among its members for increased production quotas in the face of falling prices, as well as by claims that members were producing more than their assigned quotas. By early 1995, crude oil prices had fallen to half their 1981 peak.

The Multifibre Arrangement

The **Multifibre Arrangement (MFA)**, originally signed in 1972, is an agreement between exporting and importing countries to control exports of textiles and apparel from developing countries to developed countries. The MFA takes advantage of an exemption in GATT rules that allows individual importing countries to establish quotas and other restrictions on textile and apparel exports on a country-by-country basis. Approximately 65 percent of the $248 billion of textile and apparel products that are traded internationally are covered by the MFA.[36] Under it, the United States currently imposes quotas on imports from 41 countries; these imports account for 88 percent of U.S. apparel imports.[37]

Trade in textiles and apparel represents one major area in which the philosophy of free trade has broken down. The MFA is only the last in a long line of international agreements dealing with international textile and apparel trade. In 1961 the major textile exporting and importing countries agreed to the Short Term Arrangement, which imposed restrictions on shipments of cotton textiles. The Short Term Arrangement was followed by the Long Term Arrangement in 1962 and finally the MFA in 1972.

The MFA has been renewed several times for lack of a better solution to the conflict between developing and developed nations over the textile and apparel trade.[38] This clash results from the nature of the production of these goods: it requires much labor, little capital, and simple technology. Thus it presents one of the major opportunities for less-developed, low-wage countries to export manufactured goods to developed countries. Unfortunately, because it is labor-intensive, domestic political forces in developed countries often organize to protect domestic jobs from low-wage foreign competition. As a result, many developed countries have imposed high tariffs or low quotas on the importation of textiles and apparel, thereby severely restricting trade. The MFA's complex barriers to trade are set to be dismantled by the year 2005 as a result of the Uruguay Round. It remains to be seen whether the WTO will actually be able to eliminate the MFA by then.[39]

CHAPTER REVIEW

Summary

Countries have joined to create numerous international organizations to promote their joint interests in international commerce. One of the most important is the GATT. This agreement took effect in early 1948 to promote global prosperity by reducing international trade barriers. Through a series of negotiating rounds over the past 45 years, the GATT has significantly reduced the average level of tariffs facing exporters. The most recent series of GATT negotiations, the Uruguay Round, continued the trend of reductions in tariffs and NTBs.

Countries may also band together in various ways to integrate their economies regionally. Free trade areas promote economic integration by abolishing trade barriers among their members. Members of a customs union carry regional economic integration a step further by adopting common external trade barriers as well as abolishing internal barriers to trade. A common market combines the characteristics of a customs union with the elimination of controls on the free movement of labor, capital, and technology among its members. An economic union adds to the features of a common market the coordination of economic policies in order to promote regional economic integration. A political union involves complete political as well as economic integration of two or more countries.

The most important example of a regional trading bloc is the EU, a market of 368.7 million consumers and a combined GDP of $7.2 trillion. Spurred by the passage of the Single European Act of 1987, EU members dismantled the physical, technical, and fiscal trade barriers among themselves in an initiative labeled EC '92. Under the Maastricht Treaty, the EU is attempting to create a true economic union, an effort that goes beyond the common market originally envisioned by the 1957 Treaty of Rome.

A second, but much newer, regional integration effort is occurring in North America. The United States, Mexico, and Canada have instituted NAFTA, which came into effect in January 1994. NAFTA's implementation signals a commitment to tightening the economic bonds among the North American countries.

The development of regional trading blocs in Europe and North America has stimulated efforts to promote regional economic integration on other continents. South America is home to two such agreements, the Mercosur Accord and the Andean Pact. The chances of their future success have been increased by the economic reforms many South American countries have adopted, which have increased the competitiveness of their products in international markets. The ASEAN countries have similarly created a free trade area to promote regional economic integration. Several regional economic integration agreements negotiated by various African countries have yet to show much promise.

International agreements have also been made to manage trade in individual commodities. OPEC has attempted to control the price and production of crude oil. While successful in raising oil prices in the 1970s, OPEC has found its influence over the oil market reduced in the 1980s and 1990s because of energy conservation efforts and increased production from non-OPEC countries. The Multifibre Agreement and its predecessors have imposed restrictions on the production and sales of textiles and apparel in world markets since 1961.

Review Questions

1. What were the major issues facing GATT negotiators during the Uruguay Round?

2. What is the WTO's expected role?

3. How do the various forms of economic integration differ?

4. Why do free trade areas develop rules of origin?

5. What was the goal of the Treaty of Rome?

6. Describe the four major organizations governing the EU.

7. What are NAFTA's major provisions?

8. What is the Caribbean Basin Initiative? What is its goal?

9. What efforts have South American countries made to regionally integrate their economies?

10. What are the goals of international commodity agreements?

Questions for Discussion

1. How does the GATT affect the operations of large MNCs? Did MNCs benefit from the successful completion of the Uruguay Round?

2. Should international businesses promote or fight the creation of regional trading blocs?

3. What strategies can North American and Asian firms adopt to ensure access to the enormous EU market?

4. Is the abandonment of import-substitution policies by South American governments a necessary condition for the success of the Andean Pact and the Mercosur Accord?

5. Do regional trading blocs help or hurt world trade?

6. Of what importance are rules of origin to international businesses?

7. Why does the MFN principle promote multilateral, rather than bilateral, negotiations among GATT members?

8. To stay a member in good standing of the ERM, why did the United Kingdom have to raise its interest rates in 1992 after the Bundesbank raised German interest rates? (*Hint:* You may want to refer to Chapter 5's discussion of the relationships among interest rates, capital flows, and market exchange rates.)

BUILDING GLOBAL SKILLS

NAFTA has been lauded by some as creating a major new market opportunity for U.S. businesses, and criticized by others because of the potential loss of domestic jobs as firms relocate production to Mexico to take advantage of lower-cost labor. This exercise will help you to learn more about the effects of NAFTA on various firms.

Your instructor will divide the class up into groups of four to five students each. Working with your group members, identify four products made by firms in each of the three countries that are part of NAFTA. The four products should include two that would seem to benefit from NAFTA and two that would seem to face increased threats from competitors in the other countries as a result of NAFTA. For example, identify two Canadian-made products that have considerable market potential in the United States and/or Mexico and two other Canadian-made products that would seem to face new competition from U.S. and/or Mexican firms. Each group should identify a total of twelve different products.

Next, work with your group members to determine and assess the appeal of each product in the NAFTA market. Investigate for each the current market share, domestic competitors, foreign competitors, and so forth. Research how well each was doing before and since NAFTA's passage. Carefully discuss exactly how NAFTA has and/or may potentially affect each product.

Follow-up Questions

1. Has NAFTA provided new market opportunities for some of the products you identified? Why or why not?

2. Has it increased competition from other producers?

3. Have the effects of NAFTA on each product been consistent with what either advocates or critics of NAFTA might have predicted?

CLOSING CASE

Will Whirlpool Clean Up in Europe?[40]

For years, international businesses have looked forward to the EU's emergence as a single, integrated market. Among these are firms that produce so-called white goods, or appliances such as refrigerators, dishwashers, ovens, washers, and dryers. (In the past, these kitchen and laundry room appliances predominantly came in white, hence the industry's name. Consumer electronics such as radios, televisions, and stereos came in brown, so these consumer durables are called *brown goods*. The widespread use of color in appliances today makes these labels somewhat anachronistic.)

While the European market has always been large, the peculiarities of each European country kept the white goods market fragmented into many different, often relatively small, markets. For example, different countries use different outlets for plugging in electrical appliances, and there are also differences in the voltage supplied to homes. Consumer tastes vary as well. For example, French consumers tend to prefer top-loading washing machines, whereas many others in Europe prefer front-loading machines. German cooks prefer different types of burner arrangements and heat sources on stoves than French cooks do. And many European homemakers still like to hang their wash out to dry.

About the only constant across Europe is product size. U.S. consumers are used to large appliances; homebuilders there usually construct separate utility rooms with plenty of room for washers and dryers. But homes in Europe are much smaller, with much more limited appliance space. Moreover, many Europeans buy fresh foods daily, thereby decreasing the need for refrigerated storage. As a result, home appliances in Europe are much smaller than their U.S. counterparts. And in some product lines, the European market is underdeveloped by U.S. standards. For example, fewer than 20 percent of European homes have a dishwasher or clothes dryer. Even as consumer tastes change, size still remains an issue. In the United Kingdom, for example, one popular appliance is a combined clothes washer and dryer.

White goods manufacturers believe the emergence of a single market in Europe will change the way they will (and must) do business. Previously, they had to customize their products to meet the often conflicting standards of the EU's 15 national governments. Harmonized product standards resulting from EC '92 allow them to standardize their products, thus permitting them to cut product development and production costs. Reduced barriers to internal trade allow them to concentrate production in one factory that can serve markets throughout the EU. Reduced impediments to cross-border advertising make it easier to develop pan-European brands, which in turn reduce marketing and distribution

costs. And EC '92's elimination of physical barriers at border crossing points and restrictions on trucking competition by national governments leads to productivity gains in logistics and physical distribution management.

But the challenges of operating in the EU's single, integrated white goods market are not for the fainthearted. Firms that fail to adjust are doomed. One of the most aggressive firms seeking to conquer the new European market is Whirlpool, the world's largest white goods manufacturer. Whirlpool currently controls 13 percent of the European white goods market. The firm's managers have a clearly defined view of this market:

> Among the truths about the European home-appliance market, there are two whose net effect Whirlpool has a particular interest in: first, consumers in Europe spend up to twice as many days of household income for appliances as do their U.S. counterparts, creating ... a consumer "value gap"; second, industry profit margins in the region are traditionally much lower than those of North American manufacturers. The reason for this truth is cultural: historically, the industry was organized to do business in individual, national markets, an approach with inherent cost inefficiencies. Now, however, with barriers to pan-European business disappearing, Whirlpool believes that it can use its unique regional position to deliver greater home-appliance value to customers and, in turn, establish a competitive advantage for itself. A strategy to do so suggests that the opportunity to eliminate costs which do not add to consumers' perceptions of value—and invest some of the savings into product and service characteristics that *do* add perceived value—will be substantial.[41]

For the past decade, Whirlpool's managers have been attacking the European white goods market by translating these words into concrete actions. One key element of the firm's strategy was the purchase of the appliance business of Philips Industries, the large Netherlands-based MNC. Whirlpool acquired a 53 percent interest in Philip's European white goods operations in 1989 and the remainder in 1991, thereby obtaining control over Philip's European white goods production facilities and distribution systems. To build brand recognition among European consumers, Whirlpool initially marketed its appliances using the brand name Philips

Whirlpool. It is gradually phasing out the Philips label on its products, as its rights to use that name terminate in 1999.

But Whirlpool has also sought many other operating and marketing economies:

1. It produces and markets three well-established pan-European brands purchased from Philips: Bauknecht, a premium upscale product; Philips Whirlpool, for the broad middle segment of the white goods market; and Ignis, its low-price "value" brand aimed at price-sensitive consumers. This comprehensive product strategy allows Whirlpool to fully utilize its European production facilities and distribution systems and market its goods to Europeans at all income levels.

2. It consolidated 13 separate national sales offices for these three product lines into 5 regional operations in order to cut costs, coordinate pan-European promotional campaigns, and enhance the productivity of its salesforce.

3. It centralized Whirlpool Europe's logistics, information technology, and consumer services operations to take advantage of EC '92. For example, reduced barriers to free trade in trucking services ease the task of warehousing products and distributing them throughout the EU.

4. It has redeployed its manufacturing capacity to take advantage of the elimination of national trade barriers. For example, it concentrates its production of refrigerators for its European customers in Trento, Italy, and that of automatic washers in Schondorf, Germany, thus allowing it to achieve significant manufacturing economies of scale.

5. It has encouraged technology transfer between its European and North American operations, a task made easier by the centralization of its European operations. For example, Whirlpool Europe now produces a line of clothes dryers that feature easier loading and unloading and gentler treatment of clothes, features first developed by Whirlpool's Marion, Ohio, division.

Conversely, European engineers are helping Whirlpool's U.S. engineers adapt energy-efficient horizontal-axis washing machines, which are common in Europe, for the North American market in order to meet pending federal energy-efficiency standards. Clearly Whirlpool is leveraging its European operations in ways that substantiate the benefits of globalization suggested by Kenichi Ohmae and others.

Whirlpool's European strategy seems on track. In 1993 its European operations generated $2.2 billion in sales, approximately 30 percent of the firm's total revenues. Profits from its European appliance business rose that year by 9 percent, to $123 million.

However, Whirlpool knows that competing firms see the same opportunities in Europe as it does. Whirlpool's chief competitor in Europe is the Swedish firm AB Electrolux. Electrolux's brand names in the United States include Frigidaire and Kelvinator; in Europe, it sells these products under the names Electrolux and Zanussi. Electrolux recently purchased the appliance business of AEG Hausgerate from Daimler-Benz. Already controlling a 20 to 25 percent market share in Europe, Electrolux increased its market share by about 6 percentage points through the acquisition of Hausgerate. Even more important, the acquisition put Electrolux on a near-equal footing with Whirlpool in the global white goods market.

Whirlpool's U.S.-headquartered rivals have moved more slowly or more clumsily in Europe. While GE has been a major player in the United States and in certain other countries, it moved cautiously in Europe until its managers had a clearer sense of how the market was going to shape up. The managers believe they now have that understanding and are planning to launch major initiatives in the home appliance market throughout Europe over the next few years. Because of GE's financial strength, Whirlpool must prepare to defend its European market from this formidable competitor.

One key U.S. rival, Maytag, stumbled badly in its initial European efforts. A producer of premium washers, dryers, and dishwashers in the U.S. market, it took a financial bath when its British subsidiary, Hoover, offered free airline tickets in 1993 to any purchaser of £100 worth of its appliances. So many British consumers jumped on the deal that Hoover first tried to modify the terms of the promotion. Forced by public pressure to live up to its offer, Hoover lost over $72 million on the promotion and suffered a public relations disaster throughout the United Kingdom. In May 1995 Maytag announced it would sell off its European operations, taking a loss of 130 million in the process, in order to concentrate on its core North American operations.

Case Questions

1. What are the advantages of consolidating production of product lines at single factories in the EU? What are the disadvantages?

2. Should Whirlpool continue to produce and market in Europe its three product lines (Bauknecht, Whirlpool Philips, and Ignis), which span the entire white goods market, or should it focus on one market niche?

3. What benefits will Whirlpool gain by broadening the Whirlpool brand name from a North American brand to a global one?

4. Is the European market for appliances unique?

5. Do you think it is possible to design and sell the same basic appliance around the world?

CHAPTER NOTES

1. Richard Donkin, "Uphill all the way in drive from Portsmouth to Madrid," *Financial Times*, July 1, 1992, p. 11.

2. H. Grubel, *International Economics* (Homewood, Ill.: Richard D. Irwin, 1981), p. 172.

3. B. Zepter, "Prospects for the Uruguay Round: the Declaration of Punta del Este," in R. Rode, ed., *GATT and Conflict Management* (Boulder, Colo.: Westview, 1990), p. 103.

4. S. Golt, *The GATT Negotiations 1986–90: Origins, Issues & Prospects* (London: British-North American Committee, 1988), p. 4.

5. J. Schott, "U.S. Policies towards the GATT: Past, Present, Prospective," in R. Rode, ed., *GATT and Conflict Management* (Boulder, Colo.: Westview, 1990), p. 26.

6. John Maggs and Keith M. Rockwell, "Hollywood Scuffle: US Concession Stuns Experts," *Journal of Commerce*, December 16, 1993.

7. Jacob Viner, *The Customs Union Issue* (New York: Carnegie Endowment for International Peace, 1950).

8. *Consumer Policy in the Single Market* (Luxembourg: Office for Official Publications of the European Communities, 1991), pp. 7–8.

9. *Europe Without Frontiers—Completing the Internal Market* (Luxembourg: Office for Official Publications of the European Communities, 1989), p. 29.

10. Delegation of the European Communities, *Sources for Standards* (mimeo, November 1991); Mary Saunders, "EC Testing and Certification Procedures: How Will They Work?" *Business America*, February 25, 1991, p. 27; "Not Many Firms Stand Up," *Wall Street Journal*, September 17, 1992, p. A1.

11. "Europe's Borders Fade, And People and Goods Can Move More Freely," *Wall Street Journal*, May 18, 1993, p. A1f; "Still separated by 24 miles," *Houston Chronicle*, May 7, 1994, p. 24A.

12. *Taxation in the Single Market* (Luxembourg: Office for Official Publications of the European Communities, 1990), p. 14; *Opening Up the Internal Market* (Luxembourg: Office for Official Publications of the European Communities, 1991), p. 51.

13. "Daewoo, Samsung, and Goldstar: Made in Europe?" *Business Week*, August 24, 1992, p. 43.

14. "Hoover to use UK plants as base for European production," *Financial Times*, June 7, 1991, p. 2.

15. "Breaking into European Markets by Breaking the Rules," *Business Week*, January 20, 1992, p. 88.

16. *Opening Up the Internal Market* (Luxembourg: Office for Official Publications of the European Communities, 1991), p. 6.

17. "France, Germany Initiate EC Plan for Defense Role," *Wall Street Journal*, October 18, 1991, p. A18.

18. "After Maastricht," *Europe*, January/February, 1992, p. 16a.

19. Commission of the European Communities, *European Union* (Brussels: Office for Official Publications of the European Communities, 1992), p. 42.

20. Charles Goldsmith, "Maastricht Notebook," *Europe*, January/February, 1992, p. 16c.

21. Richard Hay, *The European Commission and the administration of the Community* (Luxembourg: Office for Official Publications of the European Communities, 1989), p. 26.

22. Leonard Bierman, James Kolari, and Michael Pustay, "Denmark and the Maastricht Treaty: A Market Analysis," *Duke Journal of Comparative & International Law*, Vol. 3, No. 1 (Fall 1992), pp. 147–171; "The Battle of 1992," *Wall Street Journal*, March 16, 1989, p. A16.

23. "Plan B, for bull," *The Economist*, January 4, 1992, p. 64.

24. "In Mexico's Naftalife, They'll Sing 'Swing Sweet, Loewen's Chariot,'" *Wall Street Journal*, December 9, 1993, p. B1.

25. "Mexico and Chile to sign free trade agreement next month," *Financial Times*, August 2, 1991, p. 3; "Chile and Mexico display the pioneer spirit," *Financial Times*, September 19, 1991, p. 8; "Mexico, Venezuela and Colombia conclude free trade pact," *Financial Times*, December 7, 1993, p. 10.

26. Maritza Castro-Gershberg, *Global Trade Talk*, Vol. 1, No. 4 (July–August 1991), pp. 13ff; U.S. International Trade Commission, *U.S. Market Access in Latin America: Recent Liberalization Measures and Remaining Barriers*, USITC Publication 2521 (June 1992), pp. 4–6.

27. "Four into one might go," *The Economist*, August 13, 1994, pp. 58–59; "Mercosur four limp to customs union signing," *Financial Times*, August 5, 1994, p. 4.

28. In an address to the Brazilian Congress, as reported by the *Houston Chronicle*, November 6, 1989, p. B1.

29. "Brazil Swiftly Becomes Major Auto Producer as Trade Policy Shifts," *Wall Street Journal*, April 20, 1994, pp. A1, A4.

30. "South America's Mercosur trade zone leaps ahead," *Financial Times*, October 30, 1991, p. 6.

31. "Andean Pact still split on outside tariff," *Financial Times*, May 12, 1994, p. 6; "Andean five put common back into market," *Financial Times*, May 30, 1991, p. 4; "Andean Trade Zones Formed," *Wall Street Journal*, December 6, 1991, p. A5; "Bolivia puts Andean pact in doubt," *Financial Times*, July 7, 1992, p. 5.

32. "Asean discusses plan for regional free trade zone," *Financial Times*, September 5, 1991; "ASEAN to Create Trade Area, *Wall Street Journal*, January 29, 1992, p. A8.

33. "San Miguel's Purchase of Delta Brewery Gives Firm a Stronghold in Indonesia," *Wall Street Journal*, September 11, 1992, p. B14.

34. "African Nations Act on Trade," *Wall Street Journal*, February 3, 1992, p. A6.

35. The General Agreement on Tariffs and Trade, *International Trade Statistics 1993* (GATT: Geneva, 1993), p. 8.

36. "MFA extended for 17 months," *Financial Times*, September 17, 1991, p. 11.

37. Congressional Budget Office, *Trade Restraints and the Competitive Status of the Textile, Apparel, and Nonrubber-Footware Industries*, Congress of the U.S. (December 1991), p. 6.

38. H. Kitamura, "Japan in the GATT," in R. Rode, ed., *GATT and Conflict Management* (Boulder, Colo.: Westview, 1990), p. 52.

39. "GATT Agreement's Biggest Winners May Turn Out to Be Developing Nations," *Wall Street Journal*, December 27, 1993, p. A8.

40. Thomas A. Stewart, "A Heartland Industry Takes on the World," *Fortune*, March 12, 1990, pp. 110–112; "Whirlpool Goes Off on a World Tour," *Business Week*, June 3, 1992, pp. 98–100; "A chance to clean up in european white goods," *Financial Times*, December 13, 1993, p. 23; "If You Can't Stand the Heat, Upgrade the Kitchen," *Business Week*, April 25, 1994, p. 35; Rahul Jacob, "The Big Rise," *Fortune*, May 30, 1994, pp. 74–90; "Whirlpool to Build Washing Machines With European, Fuel-Efficient Design," *Wall Street Journal*, August 19, 1994; Maytag, *1993 Annual Report*, p. 20.

41. Whirlpool Corporation, *1993 Annual Report*, p. 15.

Legal and Political Forces

Chapter Outline

Differences in legal systems

Common law
Civil law
Religious law
Bureaucratic law

Home country laws

Restrictions on trading with unfriendly
    countries
Indirect effects on international
    competitiveness
Extraterritoriality

The impacts of MNCs on host countries

Economic and political impacts
Cultural impacts

Host country laws

Ownership issues
Intellectual property rights
Other host country controls

**Dispute resolution in international
business**

The political environment

Political risk
Doing business in centrally planned
    economies
Doing business in formerly centrally planned
    economies

**After studying this chapter
you should be able to:**

Describe the major types of legal systems
confronting international businesses.

Explain how home country laws can affect
the international marketplace.

Describe the impacts MNCs may have on a
host country.

Discuss the major types of controls that host
countries place on international businesses.

List the ways firms can resolve international
business disputes.

Explain how firms can protect themselves
from political risk.

Analyze the risks facing international firms
doing business in centrally planned
economies and in formerly centrally planned
economies.

I N 1948 CHARLES LAZARUS INVESTED $4000 TO START A CHILDREN'S furniture store in Washington, D.C. But the budding enterprise began to catch on only after Lazarus added a line of toys to the store's merchandise mix. Finally realizing that his fortune lay in toys rather than furniture, he opened in 1958 the first "superstore" devoted solely to toys and related merchandise. And the rest (as they say) is history. Renamed Toys 'R' Us, the firm grew rapidly through the next three decades, eventually becoming the largest toy retailer in the United States. Lazarus's firm proved so successful that stock market analysts developed a new term to describe Toys 'R' Us: *category killer*, a niche retailer so successful that few opportunities remain for

Toys 'R' Us Takes on the World[1]

other merchants selling the same category of goods. ▋▋ The Toys 'R' Us formula for success is really quite simple. The firm builds large, free-standing stores in the suburbs, maintains a large inventory of virtually every toy available, and sells the toys at discount prices. The firm also sells baby products such as disposable diapers at a very low price as a way of building the loyalty of new parents (who will soon be buying toys). It also has built considerable loyalty from toy manufacturers by proving their products could be sold all year, not just at Christmas, thereby allowing them to smooth their production runs over the course of the year. ▋▋ By 1984, prime locations in the U.S. market were getting harder to find. Lazarus and his managers realized that they needed to venture outside the United States if the firm was to continue to grow and prosper. The firm opened its first foreign store in Canada, where it met a receptive Canadian government and a marketplace that was familiar with the firm, since Canadians were used to traveling to Detroit, Buffalo, and other U.S. border cities to buy discounted Barbie dolls and Nintendo Game Boys at Toys 'R' Us stores. As a result, Toys 'R' Us encountered few problems in successfully utilizing its money-making formula in its first international venture. ▋▋ The firm's first tough international test came when it decided to open stores in the United Kingdom. Its market research found that British customers were accustomed to excellent service, did not want to travel far to shop, and distrusted discounting because they thought it indicated poor quality. But the real roadblocks were legal. Small retailers throughout the country had long before fought for and won passage of regulations that prohibit most retailers from being open in the evenings and on Sundays. Even tougher were the zoning laws. The United Kingdom has some of the world's most complex zoning requirements, and local firms are often able to take advantage of them to keep foreign competitors from setting up shop. For example, apparel retailers have used zoning laws in some areas of England to keep new Toys 'R' Us stores from selling children's clothing. Still, the firm has cornered 10 percent of the British market, and continues aggressively and successfully to pursue opportunities not only in the United Kingdom but in other European countries. ▮▮ But the United Kingdom was a cakewalk compared to Japan. For several years, Toys 'R' Us was thwarted in its efforts to build in Japan. That country's Large-Store Law gives the Ministry of International Trade and Industry (MITI) and local communities the ability to slow or stop the building of large stores that threaten to take business from smaller ones. The part of the law that really hurt foreign firms was the ten-year application process it requires. Local Japanese toy retailers, wary of the reputation of Toys 'R' Us as a category killer, exploited every provision of the Large-Store Law to deny the firm access to their market. ▮▮ In the late 1980s, two events turned the tide for the firm. The first was the signing of the Structural Impediments Initiative, one of several agreements between the U.S. and Japanese governments designed to help U.S. firms enter the Japanese market and therefore ease the U.S.-Japanese trade imbalance. The other was the partnership Toys 'R' Us formed with savvy Japanese entrepreneur Den Fujita. ▮▮ Fujita is president of McDonald's Corporation (Japan). Several years earlier, he had gained vast experience in dealing with the Japanese government when he helped McDonald's launch its Japanese restaurants. In return for Fujita's assistance to Toys 'R' Us, McDonald's was given a 20 percent stake in the Toys 'R' Us Japanese operation. Fujita fiercely lobbied his Japanese contacts and took advantage of the Structural Impediments Initiative. As a result, he was able to drastically shorten the application process for the firm. ▮▮ Toys 'R' Us opened its first store in Japan in 1991. President George Bush attended the ribbon-cutting ceremony, and over 60,000 customers made purchases during the first three days. Other stores opened soon after, and today, Toys 'R' Us finally appears to be on its way to becoming a major player in the Japanese market. ▮▮ But the firm still has hurdles to overcome in Japan. Its stores must close every evening by 8:00 p.m. and must remain closed all day for 30 days each year. Further, many Japanese toymakers have been unwilling to sell to the firm. Of course, U.S. toymakers greet this news gleefully, because it means new export opportunities for them. ▮▮▮▮▮

A domestic firm must follow the laws and customs of its home country. An international business faces a more complex task: it must obey the laws not only of its home country but also of all the host countries in which it operates, as Toys 'R' Us has discovered. Both home and host country laws can critically affect the profitability of international commercial transactions. They determine the markets firms may serve, the prices they can charge for their goods, and the cost of necessary inputs such as labor, raw materials, and technology. This chapter focuses on the impact of home and host country laws and political processes on international business operations. We begin by discussing the different types of legal systems and then examine the rules and regulations that home and host countries may impose on domestic and foreign firms—and the problems created for international managers when these laws conflict. Next we talk about the approaches that international businesses may take in resolving disputes with host countries. Finally, we discuss political risk assessment and explore the opportunities and challenges international businesses face in the risky but growing markets in centrally planned economies and in the newly emerging free markets of Central and Eastern Europe.

Differences in Legal Systems

National legal systems vary dramatically. The rule of law, the role of lawyers, the burden of proof, the right to judicial review, and, of course, the laws themselves differ from country to country for historical, cultural, political, and religious reasons. International businesspeople must be aware of the legal systems of the host countries in which their firms operate, for the firms' legal obligations in those countries will likely differ from those in their home countries. In the United States, for example, corporate shareholders have limited liability. In Belgium, however, founders of a start-up firm that has insufficient capital may be personally liable for losses suffered by third parties in the event the firm goes bankrupt within two or three years after its birth.[2] Access to the legal system also may vary from country to country, as suggested by Fig. 8.1. While many people in the United States believe their country has too many

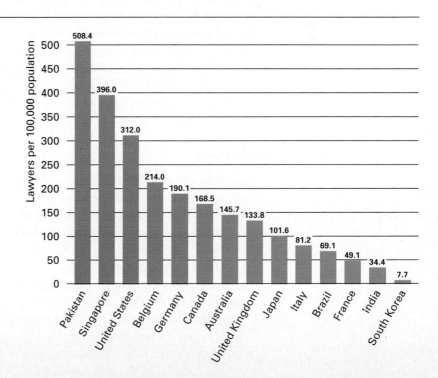

FIGURE 8.1

Lawyers per 100,000 Population

Source: University of Wisconsin, Institute for Legal Studies, from *The Economist*, March 5, 1994, p. 36. © The Economist Newspaper Group, Inc. Reprinted with permission. Further reproduction prohibited.

lawyers (it is blessed with about 39 percent of the world's lawyers), availability of lawyers and nondiscriminatory access to the host country's legal system are important to international businesses in settling disputes with suppliers and customers.[3] South Korea, in contrast, suffers from a shortage of lawyers because of its tough bar exam—only 2 percent of the candidates taking it pass. Thus, many international businesses are forced to resolve disputes privately rather than utilize South Korea's courts.

Common Law

Common law is the foundation of the legal systems in the United Kingdom and its former colonies, including the United States, Canada, Australia, India, New Zealand, Barbados, Saint Kitts and Nevis, and Malaysia. **Common law** is law based on the cumulative wisdom of judges' decisions on individual cases through history. These cases create legal precedents, which other judges use to decide similar cases. Because common law is based on the cumulative effect of judicial decisions over centuries, it has evolved differently in each common law country. Thus laws affecting business practices vary somewhat among these countries, creating potential problems for the uninformed international businessperson. For example, manufacturers of defective products are more vulnerable to lawsuits in the United States than in the United Kingdom as a result of evolutionary differences in the two countries' case law.

In addition to evolutionary differences in case law, **statutory laws**—those enacted by legislative action—also vary among the common law countries. For example, many business transactions between firms and the British government are shielded from public scrutiny—and the prying eyes of competitors—by that country's Official Secrets Act. In contrast, more information about transactions between firms and the U.S. federal government is publicly available because of that country's Freedom of Information Act. Even the administration of the law may vary. For example, in the United States the plaintiff and the defendant in a lawsuit generally pay their own legal fees. Often, defendants agree to quick settlements regardless of the strength of their cases in order to avoid expensive litigation. In the United Kingdom, the losers in trials pay the legal expenses of both parties. Thus the British have less incentive to file frivolous lawsuits. By lowering the amount and overall cost of litigation, the British system reduces the legal costs of firms operating in the United Kingdom.[4]

Civil Law

Civil law, the world's most common form of legal system, is law based on a codification, or detailed listing, of what is and is not permissible. The civil law system originated with the Romans in biblical times, who spread it throughout the Western world. Its dominance was reinforced by the imposition of the Napoleonic Code on territories conquered by French emperor Napoleon Bonaparte during the early nineteenth century.

One important difference between common law and civil law systems concerns the roles of judges and lawyers. In a common law system, the judge serves as a neutral referee, ruling on various motions by the opposing parties' lawyers. These lawyers are responsible for developing their clients' cases and choosing which evidence to submit on their clients' behalf. In a civil law system, the judge takes on many of the tasks of the lawyers, determining, for example, the scope of evidence to be collected and presented to the court.

Religious Law

Religious law is law based on the officially established rules governing the faith and practice of a particular religion. A country that applies religious law to civil and criminal conduct is called a **theocracy**. In Iran, for example, a group of mullahs, or holy men, determine legality or illegality through their interpretation of the Koran, the holy book of Islam. Religious laws can create interesting problems for firms. Consider the impact of the Koran on the capital market. It denounces charging interest on loans as an unfair exploitation of the poor; thus Muslim firms and financial institutions have had to develop alternative financing arrangements. For example, Muslim businesses often rely on leasing arrangements, rather than borrowing money, to obtain long-term assets.[5] In Iran, banks charge up-front fees that act as a substitute for loan interest payments, and owners of bank deposits receive shares of the bank's profits rather than interest payments. Family-owned firms are often influential in legal systems based on the Koran, since members of the owners' extended family may be the best available source of capital, given the costs of circumventing the prohibition on interest.

But countries relying on religious law often have other features that should make outsiders cautious, such as an absence of due process and appeals procedures. In Saudi Arabia, for example, all foreign firms must have a local representative, or sponsor, typically a government agency or a person well connected to the royal family. Should a commercial dispute arise between a foreign businessperson and the local representative, the local representative can have the foreigner detained by the local police. Because no independent judiciary exists in the country to protect the foreigner's rights, the foreigner is in a weak bargaining position.[6]

Bureaucratic Law

The legal system in communist countries and in dictatorships is often described as bureaucratic law. **Bureaucratic law** is whatever the country's bureaucrats say it is, regardless of the formal law of the land. Protections that may appear in the country's constitution—such as the right to an attorney and the right to hear witnesses against one—may be ignored if government officials find them inconvenient. For example, under the regime of terror of dictator Idi Amin in the 1970s, the formalities of Ugandan law afforded Ugandans and foreigners little protection. Similarly, the elaborate protections detailed in the constitution of the former Soviet Union offered little solace to the victims of Joseph Stalin's political purges in the 1930s.

In countries relying on bureaucratic law, an MNC's ability to manage its operations is often compromised by bureaucrats. International managers are often confronted with arbitrary rules or decisions that have the force of law. Steven Spielberg, for example, received permission from Shanghai city officials to film parts of *Empire of the Sun* in that city's dirty, rundown downtown area. However, these same officials later arbitrarily fined Spielberg's movie company $10,000, claiming that smoke from the movie's battle scenes had degraded Shanghai's environment.[7] Thus Spielberg, like numerous international businesspeople before him, learned that an unfortunate by-product of bureaucratic law is the lack of consistency, predictability, and appeal procedures.

International businesspeople often find dealing with bureaucratic legal systems a frustrating experience. In such a system many of the laws seem to be arbitrary and capricious, and appeal procedures may be nonexistent. The moral dilemma faced by actress Michelle Pfeiffer while filming *The Russia House* in Moscow (see "Going Global") typifies the problems encountered by many foreigners when working in countries that use bureaucratic law.

International businesspeople must be aware of these general differences in legal systems to avoid unfortunate misunderstandings, as "Going Global" illustrates. They should also rely on the expertise of local lawyers in each country in which they operate to help them comply with the specific requirements of local laws and to counsel them on substantive differences in due process, legal liabilities, and procedural safeguards.

Home Country Laws

Home country laws affect all facets of a firm's domestic operations: managing its workforce (recruitment, compensation, and labor relations laws); financing its operations (securities, banking, and credit laws); marketing its products (advertising, distribution, and consumer protection laws); developing and utilizing technology (patent, copyright, and trademark laws).

But home country laws may also affect a firm's international operations as well as those of its international competitors. Home country laws may

► Directly regulate international business activities that originate inside the country's borders

► Indirectly affect the ability of domestic firms to compete internationally

► Directly or indirectly affect business activities occurring outside the country's borders

GOING GLOBAL

The Law Is the Law

International businesspeople are often forced to operate in legal and political settings that they may find personally offensive. When actress Michelle Pfeiffer was in Moscow for the filming of the John Le Carré spy novel *The Russia House* a year before the collapse of the former Soviet Union, she was outraged that the U.S. film crew could gorge themselves at tables full of food while the Soviet extras hungrily watched, forbidden by Soviet law from joining in. Eager to help their plight, Pfeiffer walked off the set, vowing not to return until the extras were fed. The result of her protest? Nothing. After receiving a lecture from Soviet film commission officials, the actress realized that her efforts would not help; Soviet law would not change merely because it offended a foreigner's sense of fairness or ethics. Pfeiffer nicely summed up the dilemma facing many international businesspeople dealing with different laws, ethical standards, cultures, and political systems when she said, "I realized . . . this is so typically American. . . .This is what, as a country, we're accused of all the time. Now, whether I was right or wrong isn't the issue. The issue was, do I have the right, as an outsider, to come in and force my sensibilities on this culture?"

Source: Hal Hinson, "Michelle Pfeiffer as a Work in Progress," *Esquire*, December 1990, p. 122.

Restrictions on Trading with Unfriendly Countries

Many home country laws are explicitly designed to regulate international business activities occurring within the home country's borders. Such laws are often politically motivated and designed to promote the country's foreign policy or military objectives. A country may attempt to induce a second country to change an undesirable policy by imposing **sanctions**—restraints against commerce with that country. Sanctions may take many forms, such as restricting access to high-technology goods, withdrawing preferential tariff treatment, boycotting the country's goods, and denying new loans. For example, the United States used these weapons against Poland in 1981 to protest human rights violations directed against the Solidarity trade union movement by Poland's then-communist government. The United States also imposed sanctions against China in 1989 to protest the Tienanmen Square massacre and against Haiti in 1994 as part of its program to restore to power the democratically elected government of Jean-Bertrand Aristide. An **embargo**—a comprehensive sanction against commerce with a given country—may be imposed by countries acting in unison or alone. For example, the United Nations embargoed trade with Iraq after its 1990 invasion of Kuwait. Most countries embargoed goods to or from South Africa in the 1980s to protest its apartheid policies. The United States has unilaterally embargoed trade with Cuba since 1961, when the attempted U.S.-supported overthrow of Fidel Castro died on the beaches of the Bay of Pigs. Similarly, India acted alone in the early 1990s when it embargoed trade with Nepal because it believed that country's prime minister was favoring China's interests over India's (see Map 8.1).

A particularly important form of sanction is export controls on high-technology goods. Typically such controls are imposed multilaterally. For example, 17 Western countries established the **Coordinating Committee for Multilateral**

MAP 8.1

Northern India and Neighboring Countries

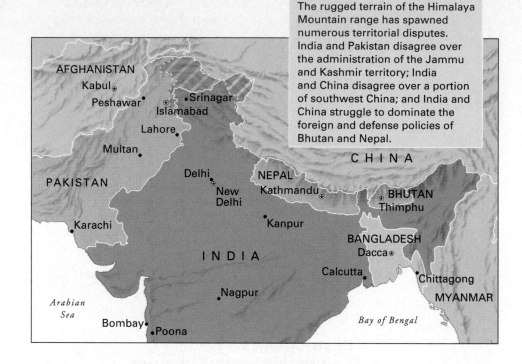

The rugged terrain of the Himalaya Mountain range has spawned numerous territorial disputes. India and Pakistan disagree over the administration of the Jammu and Kashmir territory; India and China disagree over a portion of southwest China; and India and China struggle to dominate the foreign and defense policies of Bhutan and Nepal.

Export Controls (COCOM) in 1949 to prevent exportation to the Soviet Union and its military allies of Western goods and technology that could be used to give the Soviets a military advantage. COCOM also required that firms secure a license to export high-technology goods to neutral countries in order to prevent such goods from being re-exported to the Soviets.[8] After the Soviet Union broke apart and tensions between the East and West diminished, COCOM's mission ended and the organization was dissolved.[9]

Although the Cold War is over, many technologically advanced countries continue to collectively impose export controls in order to promote certain commonly shared foreign policy objectives. To combat world terrorism, most members of the Western alliance, including the United States, restrict military and high-technology exports to countries such as Libya and Iran which have provided havens and staging areas for terrorist organizations. To combat the proliferation of nuclear and biological weapons, these Western nations apply similar restrictions to exports of technology and equipment that may be used to produce such weapons.

These export controls are sometimes controversial because they diminish firms' ability to sell their products in foreign markets. Often firms affected by these regulations complain that goods of similar quality are available from other sources, thereby making the export restrictions ineffective. When U.S. firms believe comparable goods are available from foreign vendors, they may request a relaxation of the export controls from the Office of Foreign Availability within the U.S. Department of Commerce. Often, however, these requests get bogged down in bureaucratic warfare between the Department of Commerce, which generally is sympathetic to the firm's arguments, and the Department of Defense, which generally argues against the sale of high-technology goods.[10]

Indirect Effects on International Competitiveness

Domestic laws may also indirectly affect the abilities of domestic firms to compete internationally by increasing their costs, thus reducing their price competitiveness relative to foreign firms. For example, labor costs for manufacturers in Germany, France, and the Benelux countries are among the world's highest as a result of government-mandated benefits packages. Thus those manufacturers find that their products are less price-competitive in export markets; many of them that compete internationally stress their products' quality rather than their price.

Increased public interest in the industrialized countries in protecting the environment has also affected the international marketplace. For example, Germany passed a strict packaging law to reduce the environmental costs caused by excess packaging. Under this so-called Green Dot law, manufacturers, distributors, and retailers must either accept all returned packaging materials or, through the use of a green dot, signify that consumers should recycle the packaging at facilities established locally by the seller.[11] Increasing the costs borne by German manufacturers through this law makes them less competitive internationally in the short run, since many of their competitors operate in countries with lesser commitments to environmental protection. However, as German firms invent new environmentally friendly packaging technologies in response to this law, they are likely to find ready markets for those technologies in countries that later adopt similar packaging laws.

Many experts are particularly concerned about the impact of U.S. tort laws, particularly regarding product liability, on the international competitiveness of U.S. goods. **Tort laws** cover wrongful acts, damages, and injuries caused by an action other than a breach of contract. The costs imposed by tort laws include payments made by guilty parties to injured parties as well as the costs of pursuing such cases and defending oneself from lawsuits. Various features of the U.S. legal system encourage numerous lawsuits and large awards. These include easy availability of lawyers, the use of contingency fees, generous compensation for pain and suffering and punitive damages, strict liability standards, and opportunities to file class action suits. Tort costs as a percentage of GNP are in fact three to four times higher in the United States than in other developed countries (see Fig. 8.2).

Some U.S. manufacturers are being driven out of their markets, despite their technological superiority, because of their vulnerability to product liability suits. The small-aircraft manufacturing industry is a good example of this phenomenon. U.S. juries have tended to make large awards to plaintiffs in crashes of small aircraft, regardless of whether the product itself was defective. As a result, the cost of aircraft liability insurance has skyrocketed. For example, the price of each aircraft sold by Cessna Aircraft now includes over $90,000 to cover insurance costs. Non-U.S. aircraft manufacturers are less vulnerable to product liability lawsuits than are U.S. firms, for reasons we discuss later in the chapter. As a result, Beech, Cessna, and other leading U.S. small aircraft manufacturers have abandoned the low end of this market to non-U.S. firms and now focus on expensive corporate jets. U.S. manufacturers produced only 613 small aircraft in 1991, down from 17,000 in 1978.[12]

Extraterritoriality

Countries often attempt to regulate business activities that are conducted outside their borders, a practice known as **extraterritoriality**. For example, many countries

FIGURE 8.2

Tort Costs Relative to GNP

Source: Tillinghast, from *The Economist*, July 18, 1992, p. 13. © The Economist Newspaper Group, Inc. Reprinted with permission. Further reproduction prohibited.

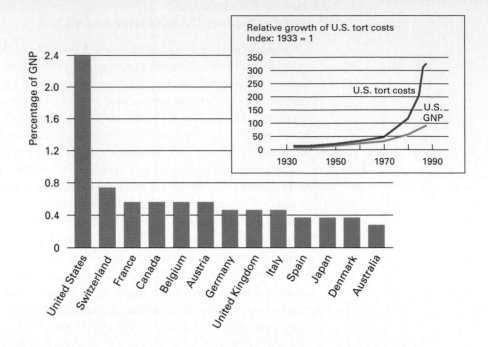

monitor international **transfer prices**—prices that one subsidiary of a firm pays for goods purchased from a second subsidiary—to ensure that firms are not evading income taxes owed them. How could a firm use transfer prices to evade taxes? Suppose subsidiary A, located in a country that imposes low corporate income taxes, overcharges subsidiary B, located in a country that imposes high corporate income taxes, for goods transferred between the two subsidiaries. As a result, reported profits are raised in the low-tax country and lowered in the high-tax country. By manipulating these transfer prices, the parent corporation lowers its overall tax bill. Most countries, including Japan and the United States, claim the right to reject the transfer prices used by a parent corporation to calculate its tax bill, even if they are associated with transactions outside of the country's borders.

Antitrust laws may be applied in an extraterritorial manner. Firms are vulnerable to antitrust lawsuits if they engage in activities outside the United States that diminish competition in the U.S. market. For example, the United States successfully sued Pilkington PLC, the British owner of the most important patents for producing flat glass, for limiting the ability of its U.S. licensees to use the technology in international markets. U.S. authorities claimed that Pilkington's policies hurt U.S. exports and reduced the incentive of U.S. flat glass producers to invest in R&D, thereby lessening competition.[13]

Antiboycott provisions in U.S. trade law also have an extraterritorial reach. U.S. antiboycott law prohibits U.S. firms from complying with any boycott ordered by a foreign country that prohibits trade with a country friendly to the United States. This law is primarily directed against a 1954 resolution adopted by the League of Arab States that calls for a boycott of any firm that does business with Israel. Briggs and Stratton, a U.S. small-engine manufacturer, typifies the plight of firms caught in the middle of this political struggle. Because of the Arab boycott, Briggs was blacklisted in 1977 from doing business in Syria because it had previously done business in Israel. However, U.S. antiboycott law prevented Briggs and

GOING GLOBAL

The Ethics of Bribery

In many countries a small payment to government officials such as customs officers, immigration authorities, and building inspectors is an accepted part of doing business. If they want to succeed in such countries, international businesspeople are often faced with the ethical problem of whether or not to make such payments. Such payoffs to government officials are often frowned upon in the Quad countries. In other countries, however, if a firm's employees fail to make such payments, its goods may face long delays in customs, its newly hired employees may be unable to obtain work permits, or government contracts may go to its competitors.

The U.S. Congress, in another application of the principle of extraterritoriality, passed in 1977 the **Foreign Corrupt Practices Act (FCPA)** to regulate payments to government officials in other countries. The FCPA prohibits U.S. firms, their employees, and agents acting on their behalf from paying or offering to pay bribes to any foreign government official in order to influence the official actions or policies of that official to gain or retain business. This prohibition applies even if the transaction occurs entirely outside U.S. borders.

In congressional hearings preceding the passage of the FCPA, U.S. firms expressed concern that such a law would interfere with the normal conduct of business in foreign countries and reduce their ability to compete with foreign competitors, who would not be bound by the same rules. In response to this lobbying, the FCPA does not outlaw routine payments, regardless of their size, made to government officials to expedite normal commercial transactions, such as issuance of customs documents or permits, inspection of goods, or provision of police services. But as a result of this compromise, the FCPA provides little ethical guidance to international businesses. Some payments to government officials are legal and others are not, depending on their impact. U.S. officials believe the FCPA does unfairly disadvantage U.S. firms in the international marketplace. Accordingly, the Clinton administration has been lobbying the other Quad countries to adopt similar legislation. Its efforts so far have been unsuccessful.

Sources: "U.S. Campaign Against Bribery Faces Resistance From Foreign Governments," *Wall Street Journal*, February 4, 1994, p. A6; George Graham, "U.S. seeks OECD foreign bribes ban," *Financial Times*, December 6, 1993, p. 3.

Stratton from complying with Syrian law and refusing to do business with Israel.[14] Baxter International, one U.S. MNC that did get dropped from the Arab blacklist, found itself in deep trouble after a U.S. grand jury investigated it for selling discounted hospital supplies to Syria, allegedly as a bribe for being delisted. Baxter pleaded guilty to violating the antiboycott law and paid a fine of $6.6 million.[15]

Extraterritorial application of laws often creates conflicts among friendly countries, as well as ethical problems for international businesses (see "Going Global"). Consider the issue of trade with Cuba. U.S. firms are banned by the U.S. government from trading with Cuba. This exercise by the United States of its sovereign power is uncontroversial; other countries recognize the right of the U.S. government to control the activities of its citizens. However, the U.S. government also restricts foreign subsidiaries of U.S. firms from doing business with Cuba unless they first receive permission to do so from the U.S. Treasury Department. The host countries of these subsidiaries believe that the United States has no right to regulate the economic activities of firms incorporated outside the United States. Recall from Chapter 4 that such firms are legally citizens of the country in which they are incorporated. Several of these host countries explicitly forbid resident subsidiaries of U.S. MNCs from complying with the U.S. embargo of Cuba. The business at stake is not trivial: foreign subsidiaries of U.S. firms typically sell over $500 million each year of such goods as automobiles, chemicals, elevators, and grains to Cubans.[16]

A country may also impose rules specifically designed to affect the business practices of foreign firms operating outside the country's borders. For example, the 1972 U.S. Marine Mammal Protection Act forbids the sale in the United States of tuna caught by fishing vessels using techniques that kill large numbers of dolphins. In enforcing this law, the United States forbids the importation of tuna processed at foreign canneries that purchase tuna from such vessels. The governments of Mexico and the EU have denounced the restrictions as thinly disguised attempts to protect U.S. canneries, and GATT officials have twice ruled that the ban violates U.S. obligations under the GATT.[17] The United States so far has refused to alter its policy.

Domestic laws may also inadvertently affect the business practices of foreign firms operating outside the country's borders. For example, firms whose products are geared to the export market often alter their production techniques to meet the regulations of the importing countries, even though their operations are legal within their home country. For example, Ceramica Santa Anita, a china manufacturer in Saltillo, Mexico, exports 30 percent of its output to the United States. Because of the importance of the U.S. market, the firm adheres in its manufacturing processes to the more restrictive U.S. regulations regarding the lead content of dishware.[18] Similarly, Grupo Herdez was forced to alter its production processes in Mexico in order to sell its goods in the U.S. market. Grupo Herdez is one of Mexico's largest producers of mole, a spicy but sweet sauce made from chocolate and chili peppers. The firm's traditional way of preparing the chilies for production—laying them out to dry in the sun for several days—failed to meet hygiene standards of the U.S. Food and Drug Administration (FDA). To receive the necessary FDA approval and benefit from the growing U.S. market for Mexican foods, Grupo Herdez had to develop a new technology that uses electronic dryers to prepare the chilies for mole production.[19]

The Impacts of MNCs on Host Countries

Firms establishing operations beyond the borders of their home country affect and are affected by the political, economic, social, and cultural environments of the host countries in which they operate. To compete effectively in these markets and maintain productive relationships with the host country governments, managers of MNCs must recognize how they and their firms should interact with the national and local environments.[20]

Economic and Political Impacts

MNCs affect every local economy in which they compete and operate. Many of their effects are positive. They may make direct investments in new plants and factories, thereby creating local jobs. In 1992 U.S. subsidiaries of foreign MNCs employed 4.7 million people.[21] Such investments also provide work for local contractors, builders, and suppliers. MNCs also pay taxes, which benefit the local economy, helping to improve educational, transportation, and other municipal services. For example, when Toyota began operating in Georgetown, Kentucky, the

$1.5 million in property taxes it paid represented almost one quarter of the town's municipal budget. Technology transfer can also have positive local effects. For example, a main benefit to the Beijing municipal government of its joint venture with American Motors was access to the latest U.S. automotive technology. And General Electric raised the productivity of Hungary's largest light bulb manufacturer by transferring technological knowledge to the Hungarian firm.

However, MNCs may also have negative effects on the local economy. To the extent MNCs compete directly with local firms, they may cause those firms to lose both jobs and profits. Also, as the local economy becomes more dependent on the economic health of an MNC, the financial fortunes of that firm take on increasing significance. When retrenchment by the MNC is accompanied by lay-offs, cutbacks, or a total shutdown of local operations, the effects can be devastating to the local economy.

MNCs also may have a significant political impact, either intentionally or unintentionally. Their sheer size, for example, often gives them tremendous power in each country in which they operate. And, as is always the case, there is the possibility that this power may be misused. Even when it is not, MNCs are often able to counter efforts by host governments to restrict their activities. They simply threaten to shift production and jobs to other locations. For example, when Spain passed new laws in the early 1990s that raised labor costs, MNCs such as Colgate-Palmolive, S.C. Johnson & Son, Kubota, and Volkswagen closed some of their Spanish factories and/or slashed payrolls. The result was soaring unemployment that reached 24.5 percent in the mid-1990s.[22]

Cultural Impacts

MNCs also can exert a major influence on the cultures in which they operate. As they raise local standards of living and introduce new products and services previously unavailable locally, people in the host cultures develop new norms, standards, and behaviors. Some of these changes are positive, such as the introduction of safer equipment and machinery, better health care and pharmaceuticals, and purer and more sanitary food products. Others are not. While Toyota's locating a plant in Kentucky induced local grocers to stock bean curd and tempura batter, it also encouraged a local entrepreneur to open the "Osaka Health Spa," a massage parlor located within a block of city hall.[23] A more important example is Nestlé's heavy promotion of infant formulas in the world's developing countries. Mothers in such countries were allegedly enticed into buying the products but were not trained in their proper use. They diluted the formula in order to make it go further and often were unable to follow adequate sanitation procedures. As a result, critics argue, infant mortality in those countries increased significantly.

Host Country Laws

Countries have broad discretion to pass and enforce within their borders whatever laws they want, free from legal interference by other countries. While most laws adopted by a host country affect both domestic and foreign firms equally, some are explicitly directed against foreign firms. Because countries are sovereign entities, international businesses have little recourse except to abide by local laws.

Ownership Issues

In most countries, there is ongoing debate between the political left and right regarding the appropriate balance between governmental control of the economy and reliance on market forces to allocate resources. Often when leftist governments obtain power, they choose to transfer ownership of resources from the private to the public sector, a process known as **nationalization**. Most vulnerable to such actions are industries that lack mobility: natural resource industries such as crude oil production and mining and capital-intensive industries such as steel, chemicals, and oil refining. When the host government compensates the private owners for their losses, such a transfer is called **expropriation**. When the host government offers no compensation, the transfer is called **confiscation**. Most governments, including that of the United States, recognize the right of other national governments to mandate the transfer of private property within their borders to the public sector, although they do expect that foreign owners will receive suitable compensation for their lost property. For example, many Arab oil-producing countries nationalized the properties of Western oil firms after 1973. However, they offered those firms a combination of compensation, continuing operating agreements, and future drilling rights that the firms found acceptable.

Privatization. **Privatization** is the conversion of state-owned property to privately owned property. Although not strictly an issue of host country control, it is the opposite of nationalization and creates opportunities for international businesses. Most state-owned enterprises sold to the private sector are unprofitable, undercapitalized, and overstaffed. Nevertheless, they are often attractive to international businesses seeking to expand their operations into new markets located in key sectors of a national economy, such as telecommunications, transportation, and manufacturing.

Privatization, which gained momentum in the 1980s, stems from two primary forces: political ideology and economic pressure. Political ideology prompted Margaret Thatcher, the prime minister of the United Kingdom from 1979 to 1990, who is widely seen as the "mother of privatization," to call for diminishing the role of the state in the economy. During the 1980s, the British government sold off its interests in British Airways, British Telecom, the British Airport Authority, and British Petroleum. Brian Mulroney, head of Canada's Progressive Conservative Party, followed a similar agenda during his tenure as Canada's prime minister from 1984 to 1993, as have the leaders of Argentina, Brazil, Chile, Mexico and many other countries in the past decade.[24]

Privatization has also resulted from competitive pressures that firms face in global markets. The telecommunications industry provides a perfect example of this phenomenon. That industry has benefited from rapid technological change. Yet many national governments, facing enormous budgetary pressures and deficits, have found it difficult to raise the capital required to upgrade and expand state-owned telecommunications systems. As a result, countries such as Argentina, Mexico, Chile, Venezuela, and the United Kingdom have privatized telecommunications services.[25]

Privatization, coupled with a political shift toward policies favoring competition, has created numerous business opportunities for telecommunications firms.

Southwestern Bell, for example, purchased a 20 percent minority ownership of Telefonos de Mexico in order to benefit from the booming domestic Mexican market. Similarly, MCI Communications Corporation licensed the use of its network technology to Stentor, a consortium of Canadian telecommunications firms, for $150 million so that Stentor could upgrade communications services between the United States and Canada.[26] In countries with inadequate telephone service, cellular telephone vendors have found golden opportunities. For example, in Hungary, which has only 96 telephone lines per 1000 people (compared to 545 per 1000 in the United States), getting a new telephone line installed entails a five-year wait. US West's cellular telephone subsidiary entered the Hungarian market in 1990 and was immediately inundated with 10,000 requests for cellular service.

Constraints on Foreign Ownership. Many governments—for example, that of India, until 1991—limit foreign ownership of domestic firms in order to avoid control of their economies by foreigners. Alternatively, a country's government may restrict foreign ownership because of a fear that a large community of foreign-owned firms with easy access to foreign capital could undermine its industrial policy. South Korea used this rationale to restrict foreign ownership of its firms for almost half a century. Modest reforms initiated in 1992 now permit foreigners to own up to 10 percent of the shares in most firms listed on the Seoul Stock Exchange and 8 percent of public utilities and other "strategic industries."[27] South Korea also has controlled foreign participation in its economy via its banking policies. Foreign bankers have difficulty obtaining Korean currency, thus making it hard for them to compete with Korean bankers. Also controls on the banking sector allow the government to funnel credit at preferential interest rates to the country's 30 chaebol, the family-owned conglomerates that account for three quarters of Korea's GNP. Other Korean and foreign firms must pay much higher interest rates in the so-called curb (informal) market. These barriers hinder the ability of foreign firms to expand their Korean operations or act independently of the government's industrial policy.[28]

Other countries focus their ownership controls on key sectors of the economy, such as air transportation, financial services, and telecommunications. For example, Mexico restricts foreign ownership in its energy industry, believing that the benefits of its oil reserves, which it views as part of its "national patrimony," should accrue only to its citizens. Foreign firms are often excluded from the radio and television broadcasting industries. For example, the United States limits foreigners to 25 percent ownership of U.S. television and radio stations. Similar rules exist in Europe. Germany, when allocating commercial television licenses, gives preference to firms owned at least 50 percent by Germans. Greece restricts foreign ownership of its television stations to 25 percent, and Portugal to 15 percent. And Belgium requires 51 percent of commercial television broadcasting to the Flemish (Dutch-speaking) market be owned by publishers of Dutch-language newspapers.[29]

Intellectual Property Rights

Intellectual property—patents, copyrights, trademarks, brand names—is an important asset of most MNCs. The value of intellectual property can be quickly damaged unless countries enforce firms' ownership rights. Several international treaties exist to promote protection of such rights, including the International Convention for the Protection of Industrial Property Rights (more commonly known as the Paris Convention), the Berne Convention for the Protection of Literary and Artistic Works, and the Universal Copyright Convention. These treaties provide some protection to owners of intellectual property rights. However, not all countries have signed them. Further, their enforcement by many signatories is lax. Generally, countries that are net exporters of intellectual property protect it strongly, while net importing countries protect it weakly, if at all.

Weak protection for intellectual property rights can have high costs for international businesses. For example, India's laws provide foreign pharmaceutical firms with five to seven years of patent protection for the process by which a drug is manufactured, but not for the drug itself. By slightly modifying the production process, Indian firms can produce low-priced substitutes for the patented foreign pharmaceuticals while complying with the country's weak drug-patenting law. Consequently, U.S. drug firms lose over $100 million in annual sales.[30] In China the situation is worse. U.S. film, music, and software firms lose over $800 million a year in sales because of copyright infringements by Chinese enterprises. Even more distressing to the U.S. firms is the fact that many of the factories churning out pirated copies of the latest CDs and movies are owned by the Chinese government.[31] As Map 8.2 shows, protection of intellectual property rights in many Asian nations is weak.

International conflicts may also develop because intellectual property laws are not consistent. The United States follows a "first to invent" patent policy, as do Canada and the Philippines.[32] The U.S. system focuses on protecting the rights of the "true" inventor. Unfortunately, it also encourages much litigation as competing patent applicants attempt to prove they were the first to invent the product. The "first to file" system adopted by other countries avoids this litigation by unambiguously assigning rights to the first patent applicant. However, it also puts a premium on speed in applying and favors larger firms with deeper pockets.

Registration of trademarks and brand names can also cause problems for international businesses. Generally, most countries follow a "first to file" approach, which often lends itself to abuses against foreigners. A firm may invent a product

---

MAP 8.2

Annual Trade Losses of U.S. Firms to Copyright Piracy in Asian Countries

Source: *Far Eastern Economic Review,* May 19, 1994, p. 55.

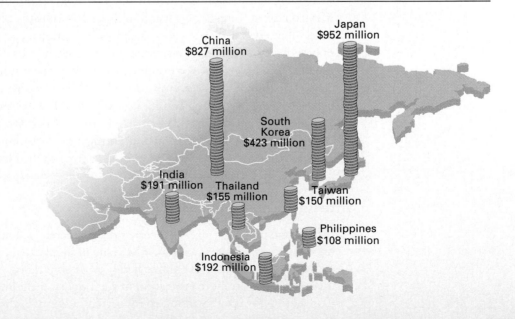

Japan $952 million

China $827 million

South Korea $423 million

India $191 million

Thailand $155 million

Taiwan $150 million

Philippines $108 million

Indonesia $192 million

or popularize a brand name or trademark in its home market, only to find when it attempts to export its product to a second country that some clever entrepreneur has already applied for the intellectual property rights in that country. For example, Nike, while preparing its marketing campaign for the 1992 Summer Olympics in Barcelona, discovered to its horror that its trademarks in Spain applied only to footware, not to sports apparel. Cidesport, the Spanish firm that possessed the rights to use the Nike name on wearing apparel, generously offered to sell those rights to Nike—for $30 million.[33] Similarly, J.C. Penney, which had registered its trademark in most markets to avoid such blackmail, lost the rights to its name in Singapore to a small entrepreneur who adopted the name "J C Penney Collections" for her two clothing stores. The High Court of Singapore, while acknowledging that J.C. Penney had validly registered its trademark in that country, determined that the U.S. firm had lost the right to its company name for failure to exercise its use there.[34]

Administrative delays may also hurt the rights of intellectual property owners. In Japan, approval of a trademark application often takes four times as long for a foreign firm as for a Japanese firm.[35] Approval of foreign patent applications may also take a long time. For example, three decades elapsed before Japanese courts in 1989 recognized Texas Instruments's original patents on integrated circuits. But the value of the royalty payments Texas Instruments will collect in Japan has been substantially reduced as a result of the rapid evolution of technology during the 30-year delay.

Finally, countries' lax enforcement of intellectual property rights may keep foreign firms from doing business within those countries. For example, China is unwilling to recognize copyrights on foreign computer software unless the owner fully discloses its workings. Given the extensive pirating of software in China, few MNCs are trusting enough to hand over such information to the Chinese government. Also, before 1992 China refused to recognize trademarks, thus prompting the Walt Disney Company to withdraw in 1989 from the Chinese market because of trademark piracy. After China agreed in 1992 to protect intellectual property rights, Disney re-entered the market with television programming, a children's magazine, three hundred apparel stores, and a major manufacturing facility in Guangzhou as part of an overall strategy to conquer China's huge children's merchandise market.[36]

Other Host Country Controls

International businesses must comply with numerous other host country laws and regulations that affect their ability to compete with domestic firms in the host country. At times, these requirements may become so onerous that the international firm will choose to withdraw from the market rather than comply.

Offset Obligations. Foreign governments may impose **offset obligations**— whereby a foreign MNC must agree to "offset" the revenues it gains from the country by providing some economic benefit to the country. For example, in order to clinch a $1.5 billion aircraft sale to Spain, McDonnell Douglas pledged to drum up U.S. investment in Spain that would introduce new technologies and techniques to the Spanish manufacturing sector. As part of this offset obligation, McDonnell Douglas facilitated the creation of a joint venture between Spanish investors and California snack food producer Cornnuts.[37]

Repatriation of Profits. A host country often is concerned that foreign MNCs will destabilize its balance of payments by shipping profits to their home countries. To encourage a foreign MNC to reinvest its earnings in the local economy, the host country may restrict its ability to **repatriate**, or return to its home country, profits earned in the host country. For example, until October 1992, Chile restricted the ability of foreign firms to remit capital or dividends home, sometimes delaying repatriation for as much as ten years. Chile subsequently has allowed foreign investors to purchase foreign exchange in the "informal" market to repatriate funds, although they are forced to pay a 3 percent commission on any funds above their initial investment.[38]

Restrictions on repatriation of profits may be imposed specifically to discourage foreign MNCs from investing in the local economy in the first place. For example, Taiwan, which enjoyed a large current account surplus during the last decade, has little need for capital and wants to reduce foreign presence in its economy. It does this by making repatriation difficult—allowing firms to repatriate earnings only once a year and only by converting their Taiwanese dollars on the central bank–controlled spot market. Until 1992 the Taiwanese government also forbade the development of a forward market in Taiwanese dollars, thereby increasing the riskiness of repatriation by foreign firms and discouraging new foreign investments in its economy.

The capital-starved countries of Eastern and Central Europe, on the other hand, need to encourage foreign investments. Poland allows foreign firms to repatriate 15 percent of their earnings from sales to the domestic market and all of their profits from export operations.[39] In this way, Poland encourages foreign firms to promote exports from their Polish factories. The Czech Republic allows repatriation of all profits in hard currency and offers firms with more than 30 percent foreign ownership a lower income tax rate.[40]

Difficulties Exiting the Country. Many countries have adopted plant closing laws that raise the costs of shutting down a factory. Laws in Western European countries such as Belgium, France, Germany, and Spain that protect employees' rights make plant closings expensive. Spanish law, for example, requires that if a plant closes, each worker receives 45 days of severance pay for each year of service.[41] While most such laws apply equally to domestic and foreign-owned factories, a few countries have adopted plant closing laws that discriminate against foreign-owned facilities. For example, under Chinese law, foreigners involved in a joint venture with Chinese partners must receive government approval as well as a unanimous vote of the joint venture's board of directors in order to terminate the venture. This law places the foreign firm at a decided disadvantage when partners conflict. For example, in 1990 Italian sunglass maker Sover SpA accused its Chinese joint venture partner, Suzhou Spectacles No. 1 Factory, of selling sunglasses bootlegged from the jointly owned factory. It tried to close the factory. The Chinese partner denied the charge and refused to agree to liquidate the joint venture. Sover was forced to continue as a partner. Similarly, Occidental Petroleum was denied government permission to rid itself of a 25 percent share of the An Tai Bao coal mine. Occidental made the mistake of announcing its decision before consulting with its Chinese partners. Embarrassed by Occidental's announcement, those partners subsequently lobbied the Chinese government to deny permission to Occidental to terminate the joint venture.[42]

Dispute Resolution in International Business

As in purely domestic transactions, conflicts often arise in international business. Resolving disputes in international commerce can be very complicated. Typically, four questions must be answered for an international dispute to be resolved:

1 Which country's law applies?

2 In which country should the issue be resolved?

3 What technique should be used to resolve the conflict—litigation, arbitration, mediation, or negotiation?

4 How will the settlement be enforced?

Many international business contracts specify answers to these questions in order to reduce uncertainty and expense in resolving disputes. The courts of most of the major trading countries will honor and enforce the provisions of these contracts, as long as they are not contrary to other aspects of the country's public policy. For example, a contract could not include a waiver of the right of a third party to seek damages for injuries caused by a product defect in his or her home country. If a contract contains no answer to the first two questions above, each party to the transaction may seek to hear the case in the court system most favorable to its own interests—a process known as **forum shopping**. Forum shopping is alleged to place some U.S. manufacturers, such as Cessna, at a disadvantage in international markets. Monetary awards are higher in U.S. courts, so many plaintiffs' lawyers attempt to use those courts to adjudicate foreign lawsuits for product defects in U.S.-made goods sold internationally. In contrast, a foreign manufacturer of a good sold outside the United States would not face the threat of having to defend its product in a U.S. court because of the lack of a tie to that forum.

The leakage of poisonous gas at Union Carbide's Indian affiliate in Bhopal, India, in December 1984 led to an instance of attempted forum shopping. Negligence at a plant owned by Union Carbide–India, which was 51 percent owned by the U.S. MNC Union Carbide, was allegedly responsible for the death of 2800 people and injury to thousands more (22 percent of the Indian firm's stock was owned by the Indian government and the remaining 27 percent by thousands of Indian investors). After hearing of the accident, several U.S. trial lawyers flew to India, signed up Indian clients, rushed back to the United States, and filed a class action lawsuit against Union Carbide in U.S. courts, arguing that the U.S. parent effectively controlled the Indian affiliate and that therefore U.S. courts were the appropriate forum in which to try the case. Union Carbide claimed that, as only part owner of Union Carbide–India, it did not have effective control of the Indian operations. It therefore countered that Indian courts were the appropriate forum to adjudicate responsibility and damages for the accident. Both Union Carbide and the U.S. trial lawyers (who typically get a **contingency fee** equal to one third of all monetary damages awarded) were fully aware that U.S. courts would be likely to award higher monetary damages than Indian courts. However, both U.S. and Indian courts determined that damage suits against the firm should be heard in Indian courts. The settlements ultimately received by the Indian plaintiffs were small by U.S. judicial standards.[43]

Whether a foreign court order is enforced is determined by the principle of comity. The **principle of comity** provides that a country will honor and enforce within its own territory the judgments and decisions of foreign courts, with certain limitations. For the principle to apply, countries commonly require three conditions to be met:

1 Reciprocity is extended between the countries; that is, country A and country B mutually agree to honor each other's court decisions.

2 Proper notice is given the defendant.

3 The foreign court judgment does not violate domestic statutes or treaty obligations.[44]

Because of the costs and uncertainties of litigation, many international businesses seek less expensive means of settling disputes over international transactions. Often business conflicts will be resolved through alternative dispute resolution techniques, such as arbitration. **Arbitration** is the process by which both parties to the conflict agree to submit their cases to a private individual or body whose decision they will honor. Because of the speed, privacy, and informality of such proceedings, disputes can often be resolved more cheaply than through the court system. For example, a five-year-old conflict between IBM and Fujitsu over the latter's unauthorized use of proprietary IBM software that was moving slowly through the U.S. judicial system was settled in 1987 with the help of two neutral arbitrators from the American Arbitration Association.[45]

Another set of issues arises when an international business is in a dispute with a national government. The legal recourse available to international businesses in such disputes is often limited. For example, the **Foreign Sovereign Immunities Act of 1976** of the United States provides that the actions of foreign governments against U.S. firms are generally beyond the jurisdiction of U.S. courts. Thus if France chose to nationalize IBM's French operations or to impose arbitrary taxes on IBM computers, IBM could not use U.S. courts to seek redress against the sovereign nation of France. However, the Foreign Sovereign Immunities Act does not grant immunity for the *commercial* activities of a sovereign state. For example, if the French government contracted to purchase 2000 personal computers from IBM and then repudiated the contract, IBM could sue France in U.S. courts.

Countries, including the United States, often seek to protect their firms from arbitrary actions by host country governments by negotiating bilateral treaties. These treaties commonly require the host country to agree to arbitrate investment disputes involving that country and citizens of the other country. For example, the United States and Jamaica have such a treaty. When the Jamaican government announced an increase in taxes on Alcoa's aluminum refining plant despite a contract between that government and Alcoa that prohibited such an increase, Alcoa was able to force the Jamaican government to submit its decision to arbitration.[46]

The Political Environment

An important part of any business decision is assessing the political environments in which the firm operates. Laws and regulations passed by governments at any level can affect the viability of a firm's operations in the host country. For example, minimum wage laws affect the price the firm must pay for labor, zoning regulations affect the way in which it can use its property, and environmental protection laws affect the production technology it can use as well as the costs of disposing of waste materials. Adverse changes in tax laws can slowly destroy a firm's profitability. But civil wars, assassinations, or kidnappings of foreign businesspeople and expropriation of a firm's property are equally as dangerous to the viability of a firm's foreign operations.

Political Risk

Most firms are comfortable assessing the political climate in their home countries. However, assessing the political climate in other countries is far more problematic. Experienced international businesses engage in **political risk assessment**, a systematic analysis of the political risks they face in foreign countries. **Political risks** are defined as any changes in the political environment that may adversely affect the value of the firm's business activities. As Table 8.1 shows, political risks may result from governmental actions such as passage of laws that expropriate private property, raise operating costs, devalue the currency, or constrain the repatriation of profits. They may also arise from nongovernmental actions, such as kidnappings, extortion, and acts of terrorism.

Political risks may affect all firms equally or focus on only a handful. A **macropolitical risk** affects all firms in a country; examples are the civil wars that tore apart Somalia, Bosnia, and Rwanda in the mid-1990s. A **micropolitical risk** affects only a specific firm or firms within a specific industry. Saudia Arabia's nationalization of its oil industry in the 1970s is an example of a governmentally imposed micropolitical risk. Nongovernmental micropolitical risks are also important. For example, EuroDisney has been the target of numerous symbolic protests by French farmers, who view it as a convenient target for venting their disgust with U.S. international agricultural policies.

Most MNCs continually monitor the countries in which they do business for changes in political risk. Often the best sources of information are internal to the firm. Employees of a foreign subsidiary, whether they are citizens of the home country or of the host country, possess first-hand knowledge of the local political environment and are a valuable source of political risk information. The views of local staff should be supplemented by those of outsiders. Embassy officials and international chambers of commerce are often rich sources of information. Numerous consulting firms specialize in political risk assessment to help firms evaluate the risks of doing business in a particular country. And several international business publications annually print surveys of political risk around the world. Map 8.3 depicts the results of one such survey published in *Euromoney* magazine.

The types of information and the level of detail firms need in order to assess political risk depend on the type of business and its likely duration in the host

TABLE 8.1

Examples of Political Risks

TYPE	IMPACT ON FIRMS
Expropriation	Loss of future profits
Confiscation	Loss of assets Loss of future profits
Campaigns against foreign goods	Loss of sales Increased costs of public relations campaigns to improve public image
Mandatory labor benefits legislation	Increased operating costs
Kidnappings, terrorist threats, and other forms of violence	Disrupted production Increased security costs Increased managerial costs Lower productivity
Civil wars	Destruction of property Lost sales Disruption of production Increased security costs Lower productivity
Inflation	Higher operating costs
Currency devaluations	Reduced value of repatriated earnings
Increased taxation	Lower after-tax profits

country. The greater and longer-lived a firm's investment, the broader its risk assessment should be. A Singapore toy manufacturer that subcontracts with a Chinese firm to assemble toy trucks needs to know about politically influenced factors such as trends in exchange rates, reliability of customs procedures, and the legal recourse available to it in the event the Chinese subcontractor fails to deliver products that meet contract specifications and deadlines. If the Singapore toy manufacturer wants to build and operate its own toy factory in China, its political risk assessment must be broadened. It needs to scrutinize its vulnerability to changes in laws dealing with labor relations, environmental protection, currency controls, and profit repatriation, as well as the likelihood the Chinese government may nationalize foreigners' property or split into warring factions and trigger a civil war.

Some degree of political risk exists in every country. But obviously the nature and importance of these risks change by country. The French farmers' protests merely inconvenienced EuroDisney's managers, whereas bombardment of Bosnia's capital of Sarajevo by Serbian nationalists destroyed the economic viability of

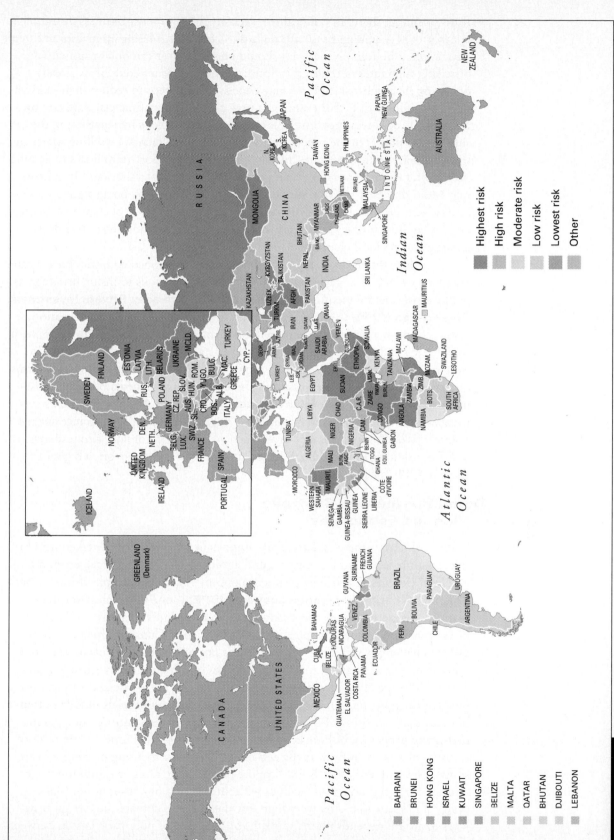

MAP 8.3   **Countries' Relative Political Riskiness, 1993**   Source: Euromoney's Annual Survey of Country Risk, *Euromoney*, September 1993, pp. 363–366.

firms operating there. In political risk assessment, as in most business decisions, it is a matter of matching risks with rewards. A firm considering an investment in an environment high in political risk should be sure that it can obtain sufficiently offsetting high rates of return if it decides to enter that market. Firms already operating in a high-risk country may choose to take steps to reduce their vulnerability to political risks. For example, a firm can reduce its financial exposure by reducing its net investment in the local subsidiary, perhaps by repatriating the subsidiary's profits to the parent through dividend payments, by selling shares in the subsidiary to host country citizens, or by utilizing short-term leases to acquire new capital equipment rather than purchasing it outright. Alternatively, a firm may build domestic political support in the host country by being a good corporate citizen, for example, by purchasing inputs from local suppliers where possible, employing host country citizens in key management and administrative decisions, and supporting local charities.

To reduce the risk of foreign operations, most developed countries have created government-owned or government-sponsored organizations to insure firms against political risks. As we mentioned in Chapter 6, the **Overseas Private Investment Corporation (OPIC)** insures U.S. overseas investments against nationalization, insurrections or revolutions, and foreign-exchange inconvertibility. For example, it sold Texaco $28 million in insurance to cover its investment in 150 oil wells in western Siberia in the mid-1990s.[47] However, OPIC insurance is limited to firms operating in countries with which the United States has signed a bilateral investment treaty. The **Multilateral Investment Guarantee Agency (MIGA)**, a subsidiary of the World Bank established in 1988, provides similar insurance against political risks. Private insurance firms, such as Lloyd's of London, also underwrite political risk insurance, although the premiums they charge are often higher than those of OPIC or MIGA.[48]

Doing Business in Centrally Planned Economies

Political risk assessment is particularly important when governmental control of the economy is high or a country is undergoing substantial political, economic, and legal changes. A centrally planned economy is a good example of the former situation. A **centrally planned economy (CPE)** is one in which government planners determine prices and production levels for individual firms. Managers of international businesses operating in CPEs such as Cuba or China confront unique challenges. Often the government is not only their business partner, but also the one making and interpreting the rules by which the partnership is governed. CPEs are often ideologically hostile to private enterprise and suspicious of people driven by the profit motive. Further, government officials in CPEs often have no understanding of the importance of management information systems, marketing programs, or human resource management techniques to the smooth running of a modern firm, as the end of the book case focusing on Beijing Jeep shows. Government officials may impose new income taxes or minimum wage rates on foreign production facilities without warning or consultation. Macro-political risks are also often very high, for the business climate the foreign firm faces in a CPE depends on the warmth (or coolness) of political relations between the home and the host countries. For example, after the massacre of several thousand unarmed prodemocracy demonstrators at Beijing's Tienanman Square in June 1989, the financial credits offered to China by public and private sources from the capitalist countries dried up. The Chinese economy was devastated, as was the rosy future anticipated by Western investors. Chinese goods fell out of favor with Western consumers, and the value of foreign investments in China plummeted.

Because government and industry are so closely intertwined in CPEs, the organizational structures of these economies can be very complex. Western firms need to spend some time deciphering the organizations with which they do business to understand how they are run and how decisions are made within them. For example, most Western firms are eager to enter the large Chinese market, in which many consumer needs remain unmet. Yet dealing with government bureaucracies in China is quite difficult. The Chinese government is organized vertically; each ministry, such as the ministry of telecommunications, is an empire unto itself. And ministries often conflict with one another, as each competes to secure power, prestige, and resources. Each ministry owns and operates its own factories, distribution centers, housing, hospitals, even universities. Further, many government agencies have responded to China's promarket reforms by hatching new for-profit businesses. For example, the largest business conglomerate in China—some 20,000 firms—is controlled by the People's Liberation Army, which owns and operates such diverse enterprises as mines, construction firms, warehouses, karaoke bars, massage parlors, and Baskin-Robbins ice cream parlors.[49] Little coordination exists between the ministries. An international firm needing permission to conduct business from more than one ministry is on its own. It must seek separate permissions from each ministry involved, rather than assume that one ministry will consult with the others to reach a joint governmental position.

International businesses operating in CPEs may also have difficulty obtaining hard currency and repatriating their profits because the currencies of most CPEs are not freely convertible in foreign-exchange markets. Also, most of these countries suffer from foreign-exchange shortages. Thus, before establishing operations in such a country, international businesses must negotiate their rights to obtain and utilize foreign exchange and to repatriate their earnings. For example, American Motors failed to adequately protect itself in its initial joint venture agreement with Beijing Automotive Works. It assumed that it would be able to obtain foreign exchange to import vital automotive parts, but parts deliveries were delayed because permission from the government agency in charge of allocating foreign exchange was not forthcoming. Only after the joint venture nearly went bankrupt in 1985 was American Motors able to renegotiate more favorable access to foreign exchange in a revised contract with Beijing Automotive Works.

Doing Business in Formerly Centrally Planned Economies

Political risks may also be high when a country is undergoing substantial political, economic, and legal changes. Nowhere are such changes more evident than in the formerly CPEs of Central and Eastern Europe. From 1945 until 1990, the world was politically split between the democratic, market-oriented countries of Western Europe and North America and the communist countries of Eastern and Central Europe. As a result of the political revolution that swept the communist countries in 1989 and 1990, these countries now face the challenge of changing their economies from centrally planned to free market.

Creating a modern market economy from the remains of a centrally planned system is an enormous and complex challenge. It produces concomitant

TABLE 8.2

Western Investors' Problems in Central and Eastern Europe (as percentages of respondents)

PROBLEM	BULGARIA	CZECHO-SLOVAKIA	HUNGARY	POLAND	ROMANIA	FORMER SOVIET UNION	FORMER YUGOSLAVIA
Finding a suitable partner	35	39	58	37	26	36	21
Political environment too volatile	40	40	15	38	54	75	80
Economic environment too uncertain	60	49	63	53	85	99	53
Legal system too ambiguous	32	37	38	40	26	72	18
Environmental liabilities	13	19	20	13	9	10	6
Restructuring costs too high	11	24	34	12	6	11	4

Source: From "Political worries fail to deter western investors," *Financial Times*, October 12, 1992. Reprinted with permission.

micropolitical and macropolitical risks for international businesses. A survey carried out by Business International and the Austrian bank Creditanstalt evaluated the biggest risks perceived by investors (see Table 8.2). A primary source of political risk is the instability of countries' political systems. Democratic traditions are weakly rooted in many of the countries of Central and Eastern Europe, particularly those that emerged from the former Soviet Union and its Czarist history of one-person rule. Russia, for example, survived two major coup attempts in the 1990s, and the constitutional relationship between its president and its parliament is not yet fully resolved. Even the borders of these countries are not yet certain. For example, ownership of the Crimean peninsula is a point of contention between Ukraine and Russia, and separatist groups are trying to carve out ethnic enclaves in Azerbaijan and Armenia. Such instabilities raise the political and economic risks of doing business in these countries. For example, British Petroleum, Pennzoil, and Norway's Statoil may lose hundreds of millions of dollars invested in the Baku oilfields because of Azerbaijan's domestic civil wars and its political conflicts with neighboring Armenia and Russia.[50] Further, political instability may lead to threats by organized criminals against the physical safety of firms' owners, managers, and employees. In Russia, many firms have resorted to providing bodyguards for their higher-paid employees or making protection payments to the local mafia to lessen the physical dangers to their staffs.

Closely tied to the instability of the political systems of these newly emerging market economies is the instability of their economic policies. Most Eastern and Central European countries have adopted expansionary monetary and fiscal policies to keep their electorates contented. However, the impacts of these policies have been high inflation rates, rapidly depreciating currencies, and large governmental budget deficits, all of which raise the operating and financial risks of firms operating in those markets. Often government tax collectors have focused their revenue-raising efforts on foreign firms, creating another set of risks for those firms. Foreign investment in Russian oil fields slowed considerably, for example, after that country's tax authorities imposed a series of export, excise, income, and payroll taxes that totaled over $10 a barrel at a time when oil was selling for $15 a barrel in world markets.[51]

Privatization adds to the uncertainty of operating in these countries. Before the breakdown of communism in Eastern and Central Europe, the governments of Hungary, Poland, East Germany, Czechoslovakia, Romania, Bulgaria, and the Soviet Union controlled most of the means of production (stores, factories, equipment, and so on), consistent with Marxist ideology. Afterward, they chose to reduce the state's role in their economies by privatizing productive assets. Implementing this seemingly simple policy has been rather complicated in practice, however. Numerous questions, including the following, had to be answered in order to successfully privatize these economies:

▶ Who owns state property—the city government, the government of the republic, the federal government, the ministry in charge of the property, or the pre–World War II owners? Potential buyers cannot be provided clear title to the property until the ownership question is settled. To deal with such problems, Hungary created the State Property Agency, which was granted the legal right to sell all state-owned property after ensuring that the sales price was appropriate. In Czechoslovakia, ownership of state-owned enterprises undergoing privatization was allocated to the federal, republic, or municipal governments as a result of political negotiations among the various levels.[52]

▶ How should the shares be sold? When the Western nations of Canada and the United Kingdom wanted to sell state-owned enterprises such as Air Canada and British Steel, their governments simply sold shares to willing buyers through a public offering underwritten by investment bankers. But in the former communist countries, investment bankers did not exist. The Czech Republic has followed a mixed model. Small state-owned enterprises have been given back to their original owners, or, where no former owner has filed a claim, sold at public auction. In other cases, enterprises have been directly privatized through foreign investment in the enterprises. For example, Volkswagen purchased a 31 percent share and management control of Skoda, the dominant Czech automaker, for DM620 million.[53] Belgium's Glaverbel similarly gained control of Sklounion, the largest Czech glass manufacturer, in exchange for capital and technology.[54] For its remaining state-owned enterprises, the Czech Republic, like Poland and Russia,

The Russian government distributed vouchers to its citizens as part of its efforts to create a market economy. Russians use these privatization vouchers to buy shares in newly privatized companies. These new enterprises face many challenges, however, including the need to modernize factories and raise the productivity of their workers.

adopted a complicated voucher scheme. This scheme entails issuing to citizens at a low cost vouchers that they use to buy shares of state-owned enterprises.

▶ Who should the shares be sold to? One simple solution is to give them to the country's residents—the nominal collective owners of the assets. This philosophy underlies the voucher schemes adopted by the Czech Republic, Poland, and Russia.[55] Unfortunately, this approach does not yield the additional funds these capital-starved enterprises need in order to modernize their plants and equipment. Thus modernization often requires selling shares to foreigners—an action seldom politically palatable but often economically necessary.

Foreign firms participating in the transition of former communist economies to capitalism have found it far riskier than they originally assumed. In addition to confronting political risks, they have also encountered operational difficulties. The public infrastructures of many Eastern and Central European countries have been neglected for the past 40 years. Highways, airports, and distribution systems for electricity, water, and natural gas are often overtaxed and unreliable. Deficiencies in communications systems have proven to be particularly troublesome to Western firms used to telephone conference calls and overnight package deliveries—remember, the communist governments wanted to control communication among their populations, not encourage it.

The executive education and management training needs of these countries are also huge. Under the communist system, capital was allocated to businesses according to a central plan. Production quotas were assigned to factories, whose output was distributed to state-owned retail stores. Given the scarcity of consumer goods, the stores quickly sold whatever was given them to sell. Under this system, there was no need for entrepreneurs or specialists in finance or marketing. Accounting and management information systems were designed to monitor production, not costs or sales or inventory levels. As a result, multiple layers of managers must be trained in the skills needed to run a business in a competitive market economy.

These training needs extend below the managerial level. Many communist factories were plagued by low production levels. Workers' attitudes could be summed up by this remark: "They pretend to pay us and we pretend to work." Attitudes in service industries were anything but service-oriented. Because of the lack of consumer goods, most sales personnel treated customers as beggars pleading for the right to buy what few goods were available. As a result, international businesses beginning operations in Eastern and Central Europe must thoroughly train their employees in the behaviors and attitudes required in a competitive market economy. Fortunately, many of these Europeans are eager to learn about the free-market system and to work for Western firms. For example, when McDonald's was preparing to open its first Moscow restaurant, it received 27,000 job applications. McDonald's put the 600 applicants it hired through a thorough training program to teach them its systems and procedures.

Nonetheless, many Western firms have recognized the potentially rich market the region offers. The consumer goods market is particularly attractive for Western firms because of the poor quality and scarcity of such goods under state control. As one businessperson noted, "The late Soviet Union could awe the world by putting men in space, but it couldn't make decent detergents, soaps, and shampoos."[56] Many Western firms are creating joint ventures in order to quickly enter the region. For example, S.C. Johnson & Son (commonly known as Johnson Wax) created a joint venture in Kiev, Ukraine, to produce household cleaning products. The superiority of its products over Soviet cleaners was noted by one Ukrainian woman, who wrote the firm, "Please produce more of this product and bring some happiness to women at this difficult time. God bless you for your work, which brings spiritual peacefulness."[57] Despite such testimonials, Johnson's first several years have not been easy: it has suffered from Ukraine's high inflation, credit squeezes, and public corruption. But it has quickly captured a dominant share of what will ultimately be a huge market. As the Eastern and Central European economies revive, Johnson will benefit immeasurably from the goodwill of such satisfied customers.[58]

Other Western firms are purchasing control of existing enterprises. Doing this conveys advantages unique to these countries. Most Central and Eastern European enterprises had monopoly positions in their countries' economies. Not only did consumers lack choices, but the scarcity of consumer goods made production, not marketing, the chief challenge facing these enterprises. Their acquisition by Western firms provides the Westerners with the opportunity to purchase market share easily. Normally, Western firms spend enormous sums fighting for a point or two of market share. Yet Procter and Gamble (P&G) paid only $20 million for Rakovnik, which enjoys a near monopoly of the Czech detergent market; German detergent manufacturer Henkel purchased Palma, which dominates the Slovak market. Henkel and P&G have effectively bought out all the existing detergent production and distribution systems in what was Czechoslovakia.[59] Western rivals that want to compete in this market must start from ground zero. A Western purchaser also gains a first-mover advantage in building brand loyalty in a market unused to being wooed by consumer goods producers. As one consultant explained, "It is an advertising executive's dream—people actually remember advertisements."[60] Of course, such acquisitions are not trouble free. Manufacturing operations, distribution systems, and staffing policies all may need upgrading. We demonstrate this in a book-closing case that deals with Tungsram, one of the few Soviet bloc firms to successfully penetrate Western consumer goods markets.

CHAPTER REVIEW

Summary

The legal systems used by the world's countries vary dramatically. The former British colonies follow the common law tradition of the United Kingdom, while most other Western countries use the civil law system that originated with the Romans. A few countries, such as Iran and Saudia Arabia, use religious law, while centrally planned economies use bureaucratic law.

Laws adopted by the home countries of international businesses can influence the global marketplace in many ways. The home country can impose restrictions on the ability of firms to conduct business internationally, as well as indirectly affect their competitiveness by raising their costs of doing business. Home country laws may also have extraterritorial reach, that is, affecting transactions conducted beyond the country's borders.

MNCs operating in a host country can influence that country's economic, political, and cultural environments. Often these changes are positive. For example, FDI generates new employment opportunities and raises the productivity of local workers. But MNCs can also impact the host country negatively by increasing competition for workers or introducing products or practices incompatible with the local culture.

Host countries also shape the environment in which international businesses must operate. A host country can control ownership of firms within its borders and enforce (or fail to enforce) the intellectual property rights of foreign firms. The host country may also control the ability of MNCs to repatriate their profits home.

Resolution of international disputes is also important to international businesses. Because of the costliness of international litigation, firms often attempt to resolve disputes through dispute resolution techniques such as arbitration. When U.S. MNCs are dealing with sovereign countries, however, their ability to resolve conflicts is often hindered by the terms of the Foreign Sovereign Immunities Act.

International businesses operating in foreign environments are also subject to political risks. To protect themselves from changes in the political environment, firms should continually monitor the political situations in the countries in which they operate by consulting with local staff, embassy officials, and, where appropriate, consulting firms specializing in political risk assessment.

Firms doing business in CPEs face a unique set of challenges. Because of the government's ownership role, firms operating in CPEs often deal with government officials who serve as their business partners, as well as their judge and jury should disputes arise. Because CPEs often lack a convertible currency, obtaining foreign exchange is a frequent impediment to business operations in them.

Central and Eastern European countries in the 1990s are in the process of transforming themselves from CPEs to free-market economies. Privatization in these countries poses special problems, for they must determine who owns formerly state-owned property, how the property should be sold, and to whom it should be sold. The lack of skills necessary to operate a business in a free-market economy is also an impediment to the revitalization of these economies, as are deficiencies in the public infrastructures.

Review Questions

1. Describe the four different types of legal systems with which international businesses must deal.

2. What is extraterritoriality?

3. How does forum shopping affect the competitiveness of U.S. firms in international markets?

4. How can an MNC affect its host country?

5. How do expropriation and confiscation differ?

6. Why do countries impose restrictions on foreign ownership of domestic firms?

7. What is the difference between "first to invent" and "first to file" patent systems?

8. How do restrictions on repatriation of profits affect MNCs?

9. What is OPIC's role in promoting international business activity?

10. What special problems face foreign firms conducting operations in centrally planned economies?

11. What difficulties do countries with centrally planned economies have in transforming them into free-market economies?

Questions for Discussion

1. What options do firms have when caught in conflicts between home country and host country laws?

2. What is the impact of vigorous enforcement of intellectual property rights on the world economy? Who gains and who loses from strict enforcement of these laws?

3. The Foreign Corrupt Practices Act places U.S. MNCs at a competitive disadvantage against firms from other Quad countries because the latter can use bribery to attract business and U.S. MNCs cannot. The Clinton administration has tried to get the other Quad countries to adopt similar antibribery statutes. If it fails, should the United States abandon the Foreign

Corrupt Practices Act in order to boost U.S. exports and jobs? Why or why not?

4. Some critics have argued that the restrictions of the Marine Mammal Protection Act against imported tuna caught by dolphin-endangering techniques are motivated by protectionism rather than environmentalism; that is, the United States is trying to block a comparative advantage possessed by other countries. Defenders of the law reply that the United States is merely trying to "level the playing field": if U.S. canners are forced to pay high prices for tuna caught by dolphin-friendly means, then foreign canners exporting to the United States should be forced to play by the same rules. What do you think? If the U.S. did not apply the provisions of the 1972 law to imported tuna, what would be the impact on the various market participants—U.S. fishermen, U.S. canneries, foreign fishermen, foreign canneries, as well as tuna and dolphins?

5. Suppose your firm is contemplating a major investment in a country that is undergoing tough economic times. (Pick a real one, if you like.) Conduct a political risk assessment of this investment. What can you do to reduce your firm's political risks?

6. Map 8.3 presents countries' relative political riskiness as of 1993. For which countries has political riskiness changed significantly since 1993?

7. Union Carbide's U.S. managers fought to have the Bhopal case decided in Indian courts, knowing that plantiffs would receive lower damage awards than if the case were adjudicated in the United States. Was such behavior ethical?

BUILDING GLOBAL SKILLS

This exercise will help you better understand the role of legal and political forces on a firm that is entering a foreign market. Your instructor will divide the class into groups of four or five members each and then assign a different type of firm to each group. Example firm types include food retailers, general merchandisers, auto parts makers, steel producers, paper recyclers, computer manufacturers, beer manufacturers, cigarette makers, filmmakers, and petroleum refineries.

Assume your group is a top management team of a foreign firm of the type you've been assigned. Your firm has decided to expand into the United States and has selected the local community as its first point of entry. Your task is to find out what legal and political barriers the firm may encounter and to develop a general strategy for dealing with them. Use whatever resources are available. For example, you could interview a member of the city council or a representative from the area's economic development committee. You could also identify potential competitors and discuss what strategies they might adopt to block your entry. As you identify potential barriers, try to determine if they are industry-specific or applicable only to foreign firms.

Finally, carefully assess each potential political or legal barrier and determine how difficult or easy it might be to address it.

Follow-up Questions

1. How easy or difficult was it to identify political or legal forces affecting your firm's proposed entry?

2. What other political or legal barriers might exist that you were unable to identify?

3. Are the potential barriers so great so as to keep your firm out altogether? Why or why not?

4. Do different levels of government (city, state, and federal) pose different political and legal barriers to your firm? If so, describe these differences.

CLOSING CASE

The Best Little Creamery in Texas[61]

When the short Texas winter gives way to spring, two things inevitably follow. Bluebonnets, indian paintbrush, and other wildflowers pop up along Texas's highways. So do TV commercials starring Belle, the 950-pound strawberry-blond bovine sex symbol for Blue Bell Creameries, the largest employer in the small Texas town of Brenham. The "Little Creamery in Brenham," as Blue Bell calls itself in its advertisements, dominates the ice cream market in Texas, selling half of all the ice cream sold in the state year after year. Nationally, Blue Bell's market share is 6 percent, a remarkable achievement for a regional brand.

Blue Bell's success rests on strict attention to maintaining its product quality and its wholesome country image. To maintain freshness, Blue Bell stays "close to the cow." Milk from 50,000 local cows is delivered to the Brenham creamery every morning. To eliminate the possibility that inattentive handling could cause product quality to deteriorate through melting and refreezing, Blue Bell operates its own fleet of trucks that deliver directly to retailers. Blue Bell drivers stock the retailers' freezers themselves. The firm's advertising, prepared by an in-house agency, stresses the freshness and hometown origin of its product, creating a nostalgia for a time when life was simpler and less stressful.

Despite its down-home marketing image, Blue Bell is a well-run, savvy corporation. Blue Bell's executives believed they had to expand ice cream distribution beyond Texas's borders if the firm was to continue to grow. In the past decade, Blue Bell has built distribution centers in Mobile, Kansas City, New Orleans, Baton Rouge, and Oklahoma City to serve ice cream lovers in these areas. In 1988 another opportunity presented itself—Japan. The Japanese firm of Ezaki Glico approached Blue Bell that year about distributing its ice cream in Japan after the pending 1990 elimination of Japan's quotas on imported ice cream. Exporting to Japan had great appeal to Blue Bell, for Japanese consumers have a worldwide reputation for paying high prices for premium goods—exactly Blue Bell's market niche.

In December 1988 Blue Bell provided the Japanese company's managers with extensive tours of the "Little Creamery in Brenham," showcasing its sophisticated production and distribution facilities. Although talks between the two companies ended in early 1989, the Japanese market still had great appeal for Blue Bell, so it began negotiations with other potential distributors. As part of these efforts, Blue Bell filed a Japanese trademark application in June 1989. This application was rejected by the Japanese government in August 1991 because, without informing Blue Bell, Ezaki Glico had filed a trademark application for the use of the Blue Bell trademark in Japan while the two companies were holding their talks in 1988.

Coming at a time of increased economic tensions between the United States and Japan, Blue Bell's plight and Ezaki Glico's behavior were the subject of ominous headlines and vitriolic editorials in Texas newspapers. Twenty-four hours after U.S. Senator Lloyd Bentsen of Texas (then head of the Senate Finance Committee) made his displeasure known, Ezaki Glico officials explained that this was all a misunderstanding and they would be pleased to give Blue Bell all rights to its trademarks in Japan.

This story had a happy ending, but most firms in this kind of situation do not have the benefit of senatorial intervention and are often blackmailed into buying back their intellectual property if they wish to use it in the foreign country. Far too often a firm that has invented a product or popularized a brand name in its home market finds when it attempts to export to another country that some opportunistic entrepreneur has already applied for the intellectual property rights there.

Case Questions

1. Ezaki Glico's officials argued this whole incident was a misunderstanding. From their perspective, it made good business sense to apply for the trademark to ensure that somebody else didn't claim it first. Blue Bell executives were upset that Ezaki Glico management never men-

tioned the trademark application to them. Given Japan's "first to file" system, was Ezaki Glico's application appropriate? How can such misunderstandings be avoided?

2. What can firms do to avoid similar problems?

3. If Blue Bell were to export its ice cream to Japan, what problems would it have in maintaining the freshness of its product? What techniques would it have to adopt to overcome these problems?

CHAPTER NOTES

1. "Guess Who's Selling Barbies in Japan?" *Business Week*, December 9, 1991, pp. 72–76; "Toys 'R' Us Goes Overseas—And Finds That Toys 'R' Them, Too," *Business Week*, January 26, 1987, pp. 71–72; "A New Game Plan: Toys 'R' Us Ups Ante in Global Market," *Atlanta Constitution*, June 27, 1993, p. R1; "U.S. Discount Retailers Are Targeting Europe and Its Fat Margins," *Wall Street Journal*, September 20, 1993, pp. A1, A4.

2. Speech of Dr. Professor Marc Huybrechts, University of Antwerp-UFSIA, Antwerp, Belgium, May 17, 1994.

3. *The Economist*, August 14, 1993; *The Economist*, July 18, 1992, Survey, p. 4.

4. Joseph Flom, "'Home Court' is best advantage," *Financial Times*, June 27, 1991, p. 12; "American Competitiveness," *Wall Street Journal*, August 14, 1991, p. A8.

5. Ken Brown, "Banking on laws of Islam," *Houston Chronicle*, April 10, 1994, p. 4F.

6. Peter Waldman, "Alleged Victims of Saudi Brutality Think the U.S. Brushes Aside Charges," *Wall Street Journal*, October 26, 1992, p. A10.

7. Jim Mann, *Beijing Jeep* (New York: Simon and Schuster, 1989, p. 267).

8. Alison Maltland, "COCOM eases rules on hi-tech exports," *Financial Times*, August 13, 1991, p. 15; "Licensing Regulations in Exports Are Lifted for Four Countries," *Wall Street Journal*, May 22, 1991, p. A4.

9. "Sales to Soviets of Technology Are Broadened," *Wall Street Journal*, May 28, 1991, p. A8.

10. United States General Accounting Office, *Economic Sanctions: Effectiveness as Tools of Foreign Policy*, Report GAO/NSIAD-92–106 (February 1992); United States General Accounting Office. *Export Controls: Multilateral Efforts to Improve Enforcement*, Report GAO/NSIAD-92–167 (May 1992).

11. "Germany's New Packaging Laws: The 'Green Dot' Arrives," *Business America*, February 24, 1992, p. 36.

12. Nikki Tait, "Textron takes the controls of an overhauled Cessna," *Financial Times*, February 18, 1992, p. 21. Recent changes in product liability laws affecting small aircraft may lead to a resurgence in U.S. production of light aircraft.

13. George Graham, "Pilkington bows to U.S. pressure on process licensing," *Financial Times*, May 27, 1994, p. 1; George Graham, "Washington's new anti-trust vigor," *Financial Times*, May 27, 1994, p. 6.

14. *Briggs and Stratton Corp v. Baldridge*, 539 F. Supp. 1307 (E.D. Wis. 1982) aff'd., 728 F. 2d 915 (1984) United States Court of Appeals (7th Cir.).

15. Thomas M. Burton, "Baxter Agreed to Cut-Rate Shipments of Supplies to Syria, U.S. Probe Finds," *Wall Street Journal*, December 22, 1992, p. A3; "How Baxter Got Off the Arab Blacklist and How It Got Nailed," *Wall Street Journal*, March 23, 1993, p. A1.

16. "Sales to Cuba Sought by Units of U.S. Firms," *Wall Street Journal*, October 24, 1991, p. A12.

17. "A fishy story," *The Economist*, May 4, 1991, p. 69; "GATT members set to oppose U.S. on tuna import curb," *Financial Times*, February 19, 1992, p. 6; Timothy Noah and Bob Davis, "Tuna Boycott Is Ruled Illegal By GATT Panel," *Wall Street Journal*, May 23, 1994, p. A2.

18. "Foreign industries may strain Saltillo's services," *Bryan-College Station Eagle*, January 28, 1992, p. A1.

19. "U.S. Appetite for Mexican Food Grows, Cooking Up Hotter Sales for Exporters," *Wall Street Journal*, February 5, 1992, p. A6.

20. Richard J. Barnet and Ronald E. Muller, *Global Reach— The Power of the Multinational Corporation* (New York: Simon and Schuster, 1974).

21. *Survey of Current Business*, July 1994, p. 154.

22. "With Boom Gone Bust, Spain's Social Agenda Still Haunts Economy," *Wall Street Journal*, June 13, 1994, p. A1.

23. "To Georgetown, Ky., Toyota Plant Seems a Blessing and a Curse," *Wall Street Journal*, November 26, 1991, p. A1.

24. Christina Lamb, "Brazil's sell-off gathers pace as field widens," *Financial Times*, January 21, 1992, p. 24.

25. John Barham. "Argentina scours the world for investors," *Financial Times*, August 22, 1991, p. 17; "The Deals Are Good, but the Dial Tone Isn't," *Business Week*, April 6, 1992, p. 86.

26. "MCI Licenses Canadian Carriers to Use Its Network Technology," *Wall Street Journal*, September 11, 1992, p. B20.

27. John Ridding, "Seoul to allow 10% foreign holdings," *Financial Times*, September 4, 1991, p. 4.

28. "Spoiled rotten," *Financial Times*, June 8, 1991, p. 76.

29. Raymond Snoddy, "EC television ownership rules—a fuzzy picture," *Financial Times*, January 20, 1992, p. 3.

30. "Warning Shots," *The Economist*, May 9, 1992, p. 38; "U.S. Says It Fails to Get Protection on Patents in India," *Wall Street Journal*, February 27, 1992, p. C12.

31. "Trade Friction with China Looms Despite MFN Status," *Wall Street Journal*, May 27, 1994, p. A6.

32. Masaaki Kotabe, "A Comparative Study of U.S. and Japanese Patent Systems," *Journal of International Business Studies*, Vol. 23, No. 1 (First Quarter 1992), p. 150.

33. Peter Bruce, "Spanish ban means Nike can't just do it," *Financial Times*, July 17, 1992, p. 4.

34. "Trademark Piracy at Home and Abroad," *Wall Street Journal*, May 7, 1991, p. A20.

35. "Blue Bell frosted as Japanese freeze trademark," *Houston Chronicle*, September 5, 1991, p. 1B.

36. Yvonne Preston, "China inches along copyright path," *Financial Times*, June 20, 1991, p. 6; "Disney Plans to Re-enter China Market as Beijing Promises Copyright Reforms," *Wall Street Journal*, March 24, 1992, p. C19.

37. "How Small Firms Can Get Free Help from Big Ones," *Wall Street Journal*, July 30, 1991, p. B2.

38. "Chile Eases Remittance Rules," *Wall Street Journal*, August 24, 1992, p. A6.

39. "American Entrepreneurship in Poland Is Picking Up," *Wall Street Journal*, April 8, 1991, p. B2.

40. Anthony Robinson, "Czechs hang 'for sale' sign on 50 of republic's key companies," *Financial Times*, June 14, 1991, p. 2.

41. "With Boom Gone Bust, Spain's Social Agenda Still Haunts Economy," *Wall Street Journal*, June 13, 1994, p. A8.

42. "For China's Foreign Investors, the Door Marked "Exit" Can Be a Tight Squeeze," *Wall Street Journal*, March 12, 1991, p. A4.

43. In re: *Union Carbide Corporation Gas Plant Disaster at Bhopal*, 809 F. 2d 195 (1987) United States Court of Appeals (2d. Cir.).

44. Richard Schaffer, Beverley Earle, and Filiberto Agusti, *International Business Law and Its Environment* (St. Paul, Minn.: West Publishing, 1990), p. 196.

45. Ibid., pp. 196–197.

46. Ibid., pp. 429–430.

47. "Texaco Receives U.S. Assistance For Russian Project," *Wall Street Journal*, September 3, 1993, p. A3.

48. Schaffer, Earle, and Agusti, op. cit., pp. 410–421.

49. "Chinese Army Fashions Major Role for Itself as a Business Enterprise," *Wall Street Journal*, May 24, 1994, p. A1.

50. "Big Oil's Return to Baku Proves Slippery," *Wall Street Journal*, April 26, 1994, p. A15.

51. "Russia Is Expected to Ease Taxes on Oil and Foreign Investors, U.S. Aide Says," *Wall Street Journal*, May 23, 1994, p. A8.

52. Anthony Robinson, "Czech detergent group finds U.S. purchaser," *Financial Times*, June 20, 1991, p. 6; interview with Professor Milan Maly, vice-rector of the Prague University of Economics, April 7, 1992; speech by Professor Maly delivered at Texas A&M University, April 10, 1992.

53. Andrew Fisher and Ariane Genillard, "Eastern Promise," *Financial Times*, February 27, 1992, p. 16.

54. Anthony Robinson, "Czechs hang 'for sale' sign on 50 of republic's key companies," *Financial Times*, June 14, 1991, p. 2.

55. Speech by Professor Milan Maly, vice-rector of the Prague University of Economics, delivered at Texas A&M University, April 10, 1992.

56. "Ukraine's Women Love These Two Firms," *Wall Street Journal*, February 6, 1992, p. A10.

57. Ibid.

58. Jane Perlez, "Johnson Wax tries to conquer Ukraine," *Houston Chronicle*, May 31, 1994, p. 5C.

59. Anthony Robinson, "Czech detergent group finds U.S. purchaser," *Financial Times*, June 20, 1991, p. 6.

60. Guy De Jonquieres, "Home-grown produce on the multinationals' shopping list," *Financial Times*, August 8, 1991, p. 8.

61. "New Texas Rivals seek to Lick Blue Bell," *Wall Street Journal*, August 3, 1994, p. T3; Danya Huling, Kevin Kessler, Heather Marshall, and Brian Walker, "An Analysis of Blue Bell Creameries, Inc." unpublished mimeo, Texas A&M University, December 1993; "Blue Bell regains name in Japan," *Houston Chronicle*, September, 6, 1991, p. 1B; Bill Mintz, "Blue Bell frosted as Japanese freeze trademark," *Houston Chronicle*, September 5, 1991, p. 1B; "Blue Bell hijack," *Houston Chronicle*, September 6, 1991, p. 24A; "The ice cream man cometh," *Forbes*, January 22, 1990, p. 72.

Chapter Outline

Characteristics of culture

Elements of culture

Social structure
Language
Communication
Religion
Values and attitudes

Cultural differences and ethics

Cultural clusters

A final word

CHAPTER

9

The Role of Culture

After studying this chapter you should be able to:

Discuss the primary characteristics of culture.

Describe the various elements of culture and provide examples of how they influence international business.

Identify the means by which members of a culture communicate with each other and how international businesses can prevent intercultural communication problems.

Discuss how religious and other values affect the domestic environments in which international businesses operate.

Explain how ethical conflicts may arise when international businesspeople conduct business with persons from other cultures.

Describe the major cultural clusters and their use to international businesspeople.

I

NTERNATIONAL BUSINESS OPPORTUNITIES ARE WHERE YOU FIND them. On a visit to Russia a few years ago, Mike Cegelsky saw a U.S. executive give the traditional "A-OK" sign to his dinner companion, by forming a circle with his thumb and index finger. What the visiting executive did not realize is that in some parts of Eastern Europe, this sign is a vulgar insult. But Cegelsky, a native of Poland, clearly understood this alternative meaning. And he just as clearly saw a business opportunity for himself. ▐▐ As a young man, Cegelsky had emigrated from Poland to Denmark but eventually found his way to the United States. Even though he and his wife arrived with only $157 in their pockets, he managed to become a U.S. citizen, get a college degree, and become an officer in the U.S. Air Force. Because of his Central European background and because he spoke four languages (English,

Finding a Cross-Cultural Tour Guide[1]

Polish, Russian, and Danish), Cegelsky was frequently called on to accompany high-ranking military officers when they traveled to Europe. He essentially helped them function in an unfamiliar cultural setting and served as a translator. ▐▐ On his many trips, Cegelsky came to realize that traveling U.S. business executives were approaching him more and more often for help. They had noticed that he knew how to function and communicate in Central Europe, even though his U.S. military uniform clearly showed that he was not a local citizen. These executives frequently asked him questions about language, customs, local business practices, religious customs and norms, and just about anything else they could think of involving the local culture that could affect their business success. ▐▐ After he observed the dinner incident in Russia, Cegelsky realized that there was a clear and growing need for **cultural attachés**—experts in local culture and language—who could help foreign businesspeople make contacts, adapt to local customs, and avoid insulting potential customers, partners, or government officials. Cegelsky resigned his military post (although he remains in the Air Force Reserve) and started International Business Protocol Services, Inc., in Colorado Springs. ▐▐ He specializes in making U.S. businesspeople feel comfortable in Poland and Russia by teaching them the customs, culture, and basic business vocabulary they need to function in those countries. Even though his firm has been in existence only a short time, Cegelsky's clients already include a major oil pipeline firm, a training firm, a construction firm, a fruit-processing firm, and several other international businesses. ▐▐ Of course, Cegelsky is not the only person to take advantage of his cultural heritage. The need and opportunity for people who understand different cultures are greater today than ever before. Just a few years ago, some people may have assumed that they needed to understand only three basic cultures in order to function effectively in international business: those of English-speaking North America, Japan, and Western Europe. But with the opening of Central and Eastern Europe and the rapid growth of Brazil, China, Korea, Mexico, and other markets, the need for cultural understanding is exploding. People able to function effectively in different cultures are finding their services in high demand. ▪▪ Another Cegelsky-type success story is that of Yuri Radzievsky. Radzievsky came to the United States in 1973 from what was then the Soviet Union and set up a communications agency called Euramerica. Euramerica's basic product is multilingual advertising services. In many unfortunate cases, naive executives seeking to sell their firms' products in foreign markets simply have the domestic advertising translated word-for-word into the foreign language, which can lead to unintended messages being sent to potential customers. For example, PepsiCo's initial entry into the Chinese market suffered because its slogan "Come Alive with Pepsi," when translated into Chinese, became "Pepsi brings you back from the grave." Similar translation mistakes have resulted in a sign in a Copenhagen airline ticket office that says, "We take your bags and send them in all directions"; one in an Austrian ski lodge that asks guests, "Not to perambulate the corridors in the hours of repose in the boots of ascension"; and one in a Bucharest hotel that says, "The lift is being fixed for the next day. During that time we regret that you will be unbearable." Radzievsky's firm has become quite successful by first learning about its clients' products and services and then translating the meaning of their advertising in ways that make sense in terms of both the language and the culture of the targeted country. ▪▪ Even government agencies are getting into the act, especially in the EU. The 15-nation EU recognizes eleven official languages. While many Europeans speak more than one language, few speak more than two or three. Thus multilingual experts who want employment in EU offices can often take their pick of assignments. EU staff translators start out at $47,300 per year and potentially can earn as much as $147,700. Why such demand? One reason is that every official EU document has to be accurately translated and released in all eleven official languages at the same time. Similarly, all verbal briefings and press releases must be translated simultaneously. Little wonder, then, that the expansion of international business creates new opportunities for cross-cultural experts like Mike Cegelsky. ▪▪▪▪▪

Firms and businesspeople venturing beyond their familiar domestic markets soon recognize that foreign business customs, values, and definitions of ethical behavior differ vastly from their own. They often need someone like Mike Cegelsky to steer them past cultural pitfalls and problems. Virtually all facets of an international firm's business—including contract negotiations, production operations, marketing decisions, and human resource management policies—may be affected by cultural variations. Reliance on a firm's familiar culture in order to survive in a new culture can seriously harm its international success. This chapter highlights some of the kinds of cultural differences among countries and explains how familiarity with those differences can prove invaluable for international businesspeople.

Characteristics of Culture

Business, like all other human activities, is conducted within the context of society. **Culture** is the collection of values, beliefs, behaviors, customs, and attitudes that distinguish a society. A society's culture determines the rules that govern how firms operate in the society. As firms expand their sales into foreign markets, locate production facilities abroad, and search the world for the most productive and talented employees, they are increasingly challenged by the cultural differences among countries and among the people with whom they do business. Improvements in communications technology and reductions in transportation costs have raised the frequency of cross-cultural contacts and increased the importance of a firm's understanding the role of culture in business activities if it wants to remain competitive internationally.

Several characteristics of culture are worth noting:

- ▶ Culture reflects *learned behavior* that is transmitted from one member of a society to another. Some elements of culture are transmitted intergenerationally, as when a father teaches his child table manners. Other elements are transmitted intragenerationally, as when upperclassmen educate incoming freshmen about a school's traditions.

- ▶ The elements of culture are *interrelated*. For example, one element of British culture is its class system. Consistent with this system, British education is very elitist and focuses on training a relatively small number of students extremely well. In contrast, the U.S. educational system is more democratic, a reflection of its cultural heritage. It tries to equalize the educational opportunities available to all even if doing so reduces the quality of training offered to the very brightest students.

- ▶ Because culture is learned behavior, it is *adaptive;* that is, the culture changes in response to external forces that affect the society. For example, after World War II, Germany was divided into free-market–oriented West Germany and communist-controlled East Germany. Despite a common heritage developed over centuries, this division created large cultural differences between *Ossis* (East Germans) and *Wessis* (West Germans). The differences resulted from adaptions of the East German culture to the dictates of communist ideology regarding attitudes toward work, risk taking, and fairness of reward systems.

- ▶ Culture is *shared* by members of the society and indeed *defines the membership* of the society. Individuals who share a culture are members of a society; those who do not are outside the boundaries of the society.

When dealing with a new culture, many international businesspeople make the mistake of relying on the **self-reference criterion**, the unconscious use of one's own culture to help assess new surroundings. For example, a U.S. salesperson who calls on a German customer in Frankfurt and asks about the customer's family is acting politely according to U.S. culture—the salesperson's reference point—but rudely according to German culture, thereby generating ill will and the potential loss of a customer.[2] In behaving as expected in the United States, the salesperson forgot the answer to a critical question: "Who is the foreigner?"

The successful international businessperson traveling abroad must remember that he or she is the foreigner and must attempt to behave according to the rules of the culture at hand. There are numerous ways to obtain knowledge about other cultures in order to achieve **cross-cultural literacy**. The best and most common means, not surprisingly, is personal experience that results from conducting business abroad—as part of either a business trip or a long-term assignment—or from nonbusiness travel.[3] Many firms, such as Motorola, offer cross-cultural training programs to their employees headed for foreign assignments.[4] Information about specific cultures can also be obtained from various published sources. For example, Brigham Young University publishes a series of highly regarded *Culturegrams* on over 125 countries, and the U.S. government publishes detailed descriptions and analyses of the economies, political systems, natural resources, and cultures of the world's countries in a series of volumes called *Country Studies*.

Cross-cultural literacy is the first step in **acculturation**, the process by which a person not only understands a foreign culture but also modifies and adapts his or her behavior to make it compatible with that culture. Acculturation is of particular importance to home country managers who frequently interact with host country nationals—for example, a home country plant manager or marketing director working overseas at a foreign subsidiary.

To complicate matters further, many countries have more than one culture, although the level of such cultural diversity varies by country. Japan, with a population consisting of 99.4 percent ethnic Japanese, is extremely homogeneous. The United States, on the other hand, is culturally heterogeneous, with significant Caribbean, Latin American, Middle Eastern, Hispanic, African, and Asian communities complementing the dominant Anglo-Saxon culture. Successful international businesspeople must recognize the attributes of the primary national culture as well as any important subcultures in culturally heterogeneous societies.

Elements of Culture

A society's culture determines how its members communicate and interact with each other. The basic elements of culture (see Fig. 9.1) are

► Social structure

► Language

► Communication

► Religion

► Values and attitudes

The interaction of these elements affects the local environment in which international businesses operate.

FIGURE 9.1

Elements of Culture

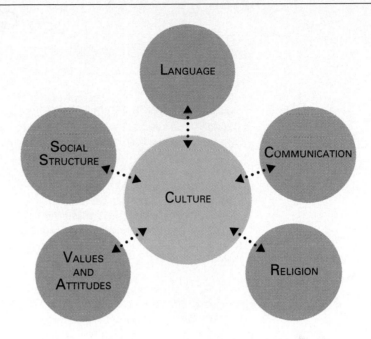

Social Structure

Basic to every society is its social structure, the overall framework that determines the roles of individuals within the society, the stratification of the society, and individuals' mobility within the society.

Individuals, Families, and Groups. All human societies involve individuals living in family units and working with each other in groups. Societies differ, however, in how the family is defined and in the relative importance they place on the individual's role within groups. The U.S. view of family ties and responsibilities focuses on the nuclear family (father, mother, and offspring). In other cultures, the extended family is far more important. Arabs, for example, consider uncles, brothers, cousins, and in-laws as parts of their family unit to whom they owe obligations of support and assistance. Other societies utilize an even broader definition of family. For example, Somalia's society is organized in clans, each of which comprises individuals of the same tribe who share a common ancestor.

These social attitudes are reflected in the importance of the family to business. In the United States, firms forbid nepotism, and the competence of a man who married the boss's daughter is routinely questioned by coworkers. But in Arab-owned firms, family ties are crucial, and hiring relatives is common, accepted practice. Similarly, in Chinese-owned firms, family members fill critical management positions and supply capital from personal savings to ensure the firm's growth.[5]

Cultures also differ in the importance of the individual relative to the group. U.S. culture, for example, promotes individualism. Schools try to raise the self-esteem of each child and encourage each one to develop individual talents. Because respect for individual authority and responsibility is so strong in the United States, children are trained to believe their destinies lie in their own hands. Conversely, in group-focused societies such as China and Japan and in

GOING GLOBAL

The Impact of Japanese Culture on Business

Because of Japan's economic successes since World War II, many critics of U.S. and European industry have argued that Western firms should adopt Japanese business techniques. Other experts believe that Japanese business practices are strongly impacted by Japanese culture and that Western firms should be aware of these cultural differences when contemplating the adoption of Japanese techniques. Let's briefly review some key elements of Japanese culture and how the culture affects Japanese business practices. Note how this culture is learned, interrelated, and shared and how it defines group membership.

The first cultural element that plays a major role in Japanese business practices is the *hierarchical structure* of Japanese society. The social hierarchy strictly defines how people deal with each other. In fact, speaking the Japanese language requires that one know one's position relative to the person to whom one is talking. Different forms of language are used depending on whether one is conversing with a superior or a subordinate. Thus, when two Japanese businesspeople meet, they immediately exchange business cards in order to determine their relative status so that they can know which form of address to use.

A second cultural element is *groupism*. A person is identified as a member of a group, rather than as an individual. This group identity is ingrained in Japanese children at an early age. Watching the differences between children in a U.S. preschool and those in a Japanese preschool is interesting. The U.S. school focuses on nurturing the individual by praising individual accomplishments and working to raise the child's self-esteem. The Japanese school concentrates on transforming spoiled preschoolers, whose every wish to date has been met by their doting mothers, into members of a cohesive group. Strong group identity is reinforced by Japan's ethnic homogeneity and its relative isolation from the rest of the world until the 1850s.

A third element of Japanese culture is *wa*, or social harmony. The goal of each group member is to promote harmony, or consensus, within the group. Decisions are not made within Japanese organizations by upper-management fiat, for that would upset the *wa*. Rather, group members must discuss and negotiate until consensus is reached. The need to preserve *wa* is one reason many Japanese firms encourage after-work socializing and partying by Japanese salarymen. These parties are a means of building trust among group members and allowing them to develop consensus on issues facing their firm.

A fourth cultural element is *obligation*, or duty. The individual, once hired, becomes indebted to the firm. The debt owed the firm for agreeing to employ the person is so great that the person can never extinguish it. The person owes everything to the firm, and the firm's needs come first, even before personal and familial needs. The strong cultural disapproval of an employee's moving to another firm stems from this facet of Japanese culture. At the same time, the firm accepts certain responsibilities toward the employee, much as a feudal lord accepted the obligation to protect the peasants, serfs, craftsmen, and merchants in the lord's realm. The lifetime (until age 55) employment practices of major Japanese firms stem from this cultural element, which in turn affects other Japanese business practices. Because of the lifetime employment relationship, Japanese firms take considerable care in selecting employees and force job applicants to undergo rigorous testing and interviewing prior to being hired. Once hired, employees recognize that their jobs depend on the long-term survival of their employer, but also that their jobs are secure as long as the firm is secure. Thus Japanese managers focus on the long-term impact of their actions, rather than worrying about short-term fluctuations in the firm's reported profits.

Source: Richard G. Newman and K. Anthony Rhee, "Self-Styled Barriers Inhibit Transferring Management Methods," *Business Horizons*, May–June 1989, pp. 17–21.

Israel's kibbutzim, children are taught that their role is to serve the group (see "Going Global"). Virtues such as unity, loyalty, and harmony are highly valued in such societies. These characteristics often are more important in hiring decisions than are personal accomplishments or abilities.[6]

Social Stratification. Societies differ in their degree of **social stratification**. All societies categorize people to some extent on the basis of their birth, occupation, educational achievements, and/or other attributes. But the importance of these categories in defining how individuals interact with each other within and between these groups varies by society. For instance, in medieval Europe the roles and obligations of peasants, craftsmen, tradesmen, and nobles were carefully delineated by custom and law. The strong British class structure and the Indian caste system provide contemporary examples of the same phenomenon, in which one's social position affects all facets of one's dealings with other people. In other societies, social stratification is less important. For example, a U.S. bank president may haughtily bark orders at his janitorial staff on the job yet meekly take orders from those same individuals when cleaning up after a church fundraiser.

MNCs operating in highly stratified societies often must adjust their hiring and promotion procedures to take into account class or clan differences among supervisors and workers. Hiring members of one group to do jobs traditionally performed by members of another group may lower workplace morale and productivity. In less stratified societies, firms are freer to seek out the most qualified employee, regardless of whether that person went to the right school, goes to the proper church, or belongs to all the best clubs. In highly stratified societies, advertisers must more carefully tailor their messages to ensure that those messages reach only the targeted audience and do not spill over to another audience that may be offended by receiving a message intended for the first group. In less stratified societies, such concerns may be less important.

Social mobility is the ability of individuals to move from one stratum of society to another. Social mobility tends to be higher in less stratified societies. It is higher in the United States, for example, than in the United Kingdom or India. Social mobility (or the lack thereof) often affects individuals' attitudes and behaviors toward such factors as labor relations, human capital formation, risk taking, and entrepreneurship. The rigid class system and relatively low social mobility in the United Kingdom have created an "us versus them" attitude among many British industrial workers, causing them to eye suspiciously any management efforts to promote workplace cooperation. Even today, many British working-class youth drop out of school, believing that their role in society is preordained and thus investment in education is a waste of time. In more socially mobile societies, such as those of the United States, Singapore, and Canada, individuals are more willing to seek higher education or to engage in entrepreneurial activities, knowing that if they are successful, they and their families are free to rise in society.

Language

Language is a primary delineator of cultural groups because it is an important means by which a society's members communicate with each other. Experts have identified some 3,000 different languages and as many as 10,000 distinct dialects worldwide (see Map 9.1).[7]

Language organizes the way members of a society think about the world. It filters observations and perceptions and thus affects unpredictably the messages that are sent when two individuals try to communicate. In one famous experiment in Hong Kong, 153 undergraduate students, bilingual in English and Chinese, were divided into two groups. One group was given a class assignment

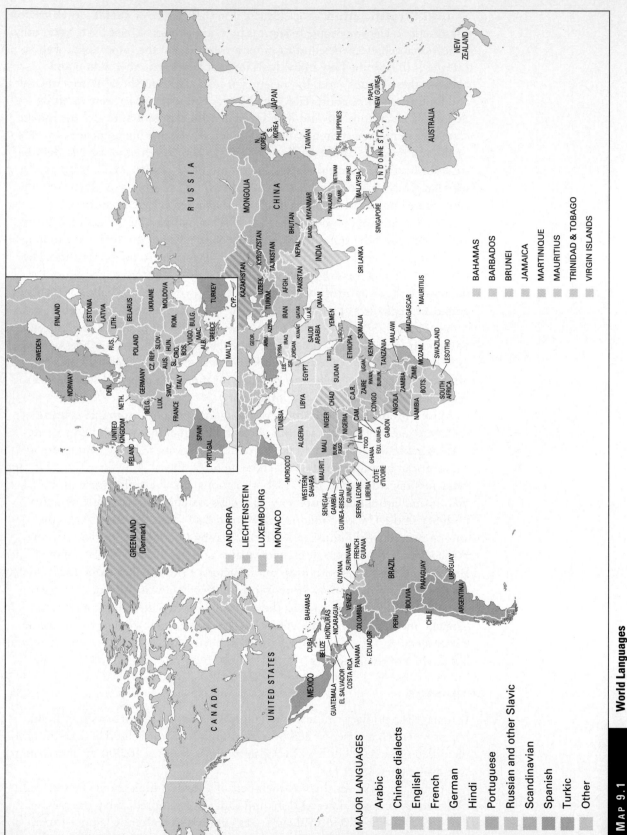

MAP 9.1 World Languages

MAJOR LANGUAGES

Arabic
Chinese dialects
English
French
German
Hindi
Portuguese
Russian and other Slavic
Scandinavian
Spanish
Turkic
Other

BAHAMAS
BARBADOS
BRUNEI
JAMAICA
MARTINIQUE
MAURITIUS
TRINIDAD & TOBAGO
VIRGIN ISLANDS

ANDORRA
LIECHTENSTEIN
LUXEMBOURG
MONACO

written in English; the second was given the same assignment written in Chinese. The professor in charge of the experiment took every precaution to ensure that the translations were perfect. Yet the answers given by the two groups differed significantly, indicating that the language itself altered the nature of the information being conveyed.[8]

In addition to shaping one's perceptions of the world, language provides important clues about the cultural values of the society and aids acculturation. For example, many languages, including French, German, and Spanish, have informal and formal forms of the word for "you," the use of which depends on the relationship between the speaker and the person addressed.[9] Existence of these language forms provides a strong hint that one should take care in maintaining an appropriate level of formality when dealing with businesspeople from countries in which those languages predominate.

The presence of more than one language group is an important signal about the diversity of a country's population and suggests that there may also be differences in income, work ethic, and/or educational achievement. For example, India recognizes 16 official languages, and approximately 3000 dialects are spoken within its boundaries, a reflection of the heterogeneity of its society. In several mountainous countries of South America, such as Bolivia and Paraguay, most of the poor rural population speak local Indian dialects and have trouble communicating with the Spanish-speaking urban elites. Generally, countries dominated by one language group tend to have a homogeneous society, in which nationhood defines the society. Countries with multiple language groups tend to be heterogeneous, with language providing an important means of identifying cultural differences within the country.

Savvy businesspeople operating in heterogeneous societies adapt their marketing and business practices along linguistic lines to account for cultural differences among their prospective customers. For example, market researchers discovered that English Canadians favor soaps that promise cleanliness, while French Canadians prefer pleasant- or sweet-smelling soaps. Thus Procter & Gamble's English-language Canadian ads for Irish Spring soap stress the soap's deodorant value, while its French-language ads focus on the soap's pleasant aroma.[10] Generally, advertisers should seek out the media—newspapers, radio, cable television, and magazines—that allow them to customize their marketing messages to individual linguistic groups. For example, in the United States the development of Spanish-language cable television channels such as Univision has allowed advertisers to more easily customize their advertisements to reach the Hispanic market, without confusing their marketing messages to the larger English-speaking audience.

The presence of multiple major linguistic groups within a country should also alert international businesspeople to potential political conflicts within the country that may threaten the stability of a firm's investments or affect its hiring practices. For example, political conflict exists between Canada's Francophone (French-speaking) province of Quebec and the rest of Canada, which speaks English predominantly. Also, for the past century a political fault line has existed between Belgium's Flemish (Dutch-speaking) citizens in the north and its Walloon (French-speaking) citizens in the south. Unfortunately, linguistic differences may boil over into actual conflict, which sadly has been the case in the former Soviet Union and Yugoslavia.

Same Language, Same Business Culture? Differences in language within a country signal cultural differences among its populace, but one cannot conclude that countries that share a language also share a culture. It is often said, for example, that the United States and the United Kingdom are two countries divided by a common language. Sometimes the meanings of words in British English differ from those in American English. For example, in American English, tabling an item on a business agenda means the group chooses to delay taking action, often because its members were unable to reach a consensus. In British English, tabling an item means the exact opposite—that action was taken on it.

National differences in laws, political systems, social structure, and economic wealth create differences in culture (and vice versa) among countries that share a language. For example, the current British culture has been influenced by a strong class system, which has existed since feudal times. The country's governmental structure reflects the quality of noblesse oblige expected among the upper classes and concentrates much political power in the hands of one person, the prime minister. U.S. culture has rejected the British class system and stresses instead the importance of individual achievement. The checks and balances contained in the U.S. Constitution embody the distrust U.S. citizens have of concentrating power in any one person or institution.

However, researchers have found that countries that share a language often are culturally similar, although not identical. (See the section titled "Cultural Clusters" later in this chapter). Because cultural similarities ease the task of doing business internationally, a domestic firm's initial efforts to expand abroad often focus on countries that speak the firm's home language. For example, the U.S. and British markets are often the first export targets of Canadian firms.

Language as a Competitive Weapon. Linguistic ties often create important competitive advantages because the ability to communicate is so important in conducting business transactions. Commerce among Australia, Canada, New Zealand, the United Kingdom, and the United States is facilitated by their common use of English. For example, Giro Sport Design, a Soquel, California, manufacturer of bicycle helmets, decided in the early 1990s to manufacture its product in Europe rather than export it from the United States. The firm told the consultants hired to find a plant location that the plant had to be located in an English-speaking country. William Hanneman, Giro's president, noted, "With all the problems you have in running a business abroad, we didn't want to be bothered by language."[11] The firm located its European production facilities in Ireland, where it has enjoyed a plentiful supply of low-cost English-speaking labor, economic development incentives, and tax benefits. Similarly, Taiwan, Singapore, and Hong Kong have expanded their economic ties with China, not only because of their proximity to that country but also because of their common ethnic heritage and shared language. For example, over 74 percent of Hong Kong's trade involves re-exports to and from China. And Western firms often find it easier to hire Hong Kong firms to act as intermediaries in dealing with China, rather than dealing directly with that country themselves.

The linguistic legacy of colonialism also affects international business today. For example, French firms possess competitive advantages in former French colonies in Africa (see Map 9.2), such as Algeria, Chad, and Côte d'Ivoire, because much of the local business elite has been taught French as a second language and because government officials often receive their undergraduate and graduate training

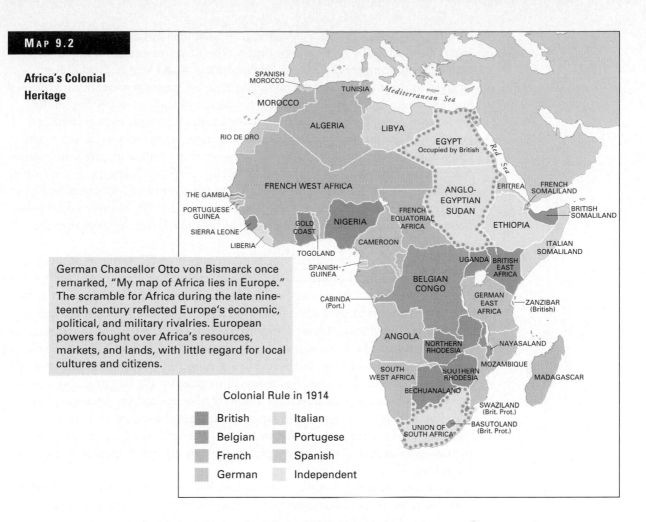

MAP 9.2

Africa's Colonial Heritage

German Chancellor Otto von Bismarck once remarked, "My map of Africa lies in Europe." The scramble for Africa during the late nineteenth century reflected Europe's economic, political, and military rivalries. European powers fought over Africa's resources, markets, and lands, with little regard for local cultures and citizens.

Colonial Rule in 1914

- British
- Belgian
- French
- German
- Italian
- Portugese
- Spanish
- Independent

in French universities. Also, the infrastructures of these countries were developed using French technology, creating a demand for French-made spare parts. Strong banking, communications, and transportation links remain from the colonial period. For similar reasons, British firms possess competitive advantages in former British colonies such as Kenya, India, and Zimbabwe.

Linguistic and cultural ties often help international businesses in their struggles for customers. For example, in the market for international air services, airlines often successfully lure home country citizens to their flights because of the increased cultural comfort the passengers feel from flying the home country carrier.[12] Some carriers have explicitly exploited linguistic ties as part of their strategy for dealing with the ongoing globalization of the international airline industry. For example, most European carriers have focused on expanding their services within Europe or across the North Atlantic (to and from the United States and Canada). However, Iberia Airlines, Spain's state-owned national carrier, has placed its bets on the Spanish-speaking regions of the Americas. It has purchased controlling interests in the South American carriers Aerolineas Argentinas, Ladeco, and VIASA and acquired additional landing rights in Hispanic-rich areas of the United States, particularly Puerto Rico and Miami. Iberia has deliberately chosen to concentrate its resources on Spanish speakers in the New World and to let British Airways, KLM, and Air France duke it out with Air Canada, Delta, American, and United Airlines for the English-speaking portion of the North American market.

Lingua Franca. To conduct business, international businesspeople must be able to communicate. As a result of British economic and military dominance in the nineteenth century and U.S. dominance since World War II, English has emerged as the predominant common language, or **lingua franca**, of international business. Most European and Japanese public school students study English for many years. Some countries that have many linguistic groups, such as India and Singapore, have adopted English as an official language in order to facilitate communication among the diverse groups. Similarly, firms with managers from many different countries may use English as the official corporate language. For example, Philips, the Dutch-based electronics MNC (and the world's 32nd largest firm), has used English for intracorporate communications since 1983. Switzerland's Brown Boveri and Sweden's Asea adopted English as their corporate language after their merger in 1987.[13]

But the widespread usage of English does not solve all communications problems of international businesspeople. As noted earlier, the meanings of some common English words vary among English-speaking countries. English also may be used in ways not understandable to native English speakers. For example, one international negotiator, whose native tongue is English, was asked to redraft a proposed contract between Japanese and Soviet firms written in English. To the negotiator, the contract was full of incoherent language and incomprehensible sentence fragments. But when he attempted to clean up the language and rewrite the contract in more standard English, both the Soviets and the Japanese objected. *They* knew what the words meant, and *they* had agreed to them. Because the contract conveyed the information the two parties wanted it to, the text stayed as written, even though it was meaningless to the native English speaker or any other English-speaking third party.[14]

The dominance of English seemingly confers an advantage on native English speakers in international commerce, particularly when transactions are done in Canada, the United Kingdom, or the United States. However, failure by English speakers to learn a second language puts them and their firms at a decided disadvantage when negotiating or operating on foreign turf. For example, a few years ago Lionel Train Company moved its manufacturing facilities to Mexico to take advantage of lower labor costs. But it could not find enough bilingual managers to run the plant. As a result, the firm eventually shut down the plant and moved its operations back to the United States.[15]

Because language serves as a window onto the culture of a society, many international business experts argue that students should be exposed to foreign languages, even if they are unable to master them. Although mastery is best, even modest levels of language training provide students with clues about cultural norms and attitudes that prove helpful in international business.

Translation. Of course, some linguistic differences may be overcome through translation. An area in which most international businesses must adjust their practices to account for cultural differences is the translation of advertising, operating instructions, and other printed material. While companies sometimes will hire local specialists to develop new materials for the local market, they often choose simply to translate written materials created in the home country into the language of the host country. Yet the translation process requires more than merely substituting words of one language for those of a second. Translators must be sensitive to subtleties in the connotations of words and focus on the translating of ideas, not the words themselves. Far too often, translation problems create marketing disasters. A classic case is GM's marketing of the Chevrolet Nova in Spanish-speaking countries. In Spanish, *no va* means "it doesn't go"—not the best message to link with an automobile. Also, the original translation of Pillsbury's Jolly Green Giant for the Saudi Arabian market was "intimidating green ogre"—a very different image from what the firm intended (although it still might encourage children to eat their peas).

Some translation problems can be eliminated by hiring local native speakers as translators. However, problems may remain if the translators have not mastered all the idioms and connotations of the two languages involved. Firms can reduce the chances that they are sending the wrong message to their customers by using a technique known as backtranslation. In **backtranslation**, after one person translates a document, a second person is hired to translate the translated version back into the original language. This technique provides a check that the intended message is actually being sent, thus avoiding communication mistakes.

When communications to non–native speakers must be made in the home country language, speakers and writers should use common words, use the most common meanings of those words, and try to avoid idiomatic phrases. For example, Caterpillar is faced with the problem of communicating with the diverse international users of its products. It developed its own language instruction program called Caterpillar Fundamental English (CFE), which it uses in its overseas repair and service manuals. CFE is a simplified, condensed version of English that can be taught to non-English speakers in 30 lessons. It consists of 800 words that are necessary to repair Cat's equipment: 450 nouns, 70 verbs, 100 prepositions, and 180 other words.[16] The following "Going Global" presents some other hints for communicating internationally.

Saying No. Another cultural difficulty international businesspeople face is that words may have different meanings to persons with diverse cultural backgrounds. North Americans typically translate the Spanish word *mañana* literally to mean "tomorrow." But in parts of Latin America, the word is used to mean "soon—within the next several days."

Even the use of *yes* and *no* differs across cultures. In contract negotiations, Japanese businesspeople often use *yes* to mean "Yes, I understand what is being said." Foreign negotiators often assume that their Japanese counterparts are using *yes* to mean "Yes, I agree with you" and are disappointed when the Japanese later fail to accept contract terms the foreigners had assumed were agreed to. Misunderstandings can be compounded because directly uttering *no* is considered very impolite in Japan. Japanese negotiators who find a proposal unacceptable will, in order to be polite, suggest that it "presents many difficulties" or requires "further study."[17] Foreigners waiting for a definitive no may have to wait a long time. Such behavior may be considered evasive in U.S. business culture, but it is the essence of politeness in Japanese business culture.

Understanding the subtleties of the Japanese language is a problem not restricted to foreigners. The emphasis on politeness is so important, the multiple meanings of words so common, and the emotional orientation of the language so strong that two Japanese will often have trouble communicating clearly with each other in business settings. Repetition of points of agreement is often needed in order to avoid misunderstandings.[18]

Another mode of business communication is the face-to-face meeting. Distance makes this mode more difficult for MNCs than for domestic firms. But international travel is a necessity in many cases. For example, when Ford and Mazda worked together to design the new Ford Escort, Ford managers on the project made over 150 trips to Japan within a three-year period for meetings.

Nonverbal Communication. Members of a society communicate with each other using more than words. In fact, some researchers believe 80 to 90 percent of all information is transmitted among members of a culture by means other than language.[23] This nonverbal communication includes facial expressions and hand gestures, intonation, eye contact, body positioning, and body posture. While most members of a society quickly understand nonverbal forms of communication common to their society, outsiders may find these difficult to comprehend. Table 9.1 lists some of the many common forms of nonverbal communication.

Because of cultural differences, nonverbal forms of communication often can lead to misunderstandings. For example, in the United States, people discussing

---

TABLE 9.1

Forms of Nonverbal Communication

Hand gestures, both intended and self-directed, such as nervous rubbing of hands

Facial expressions, such as smiles, frowns, and yawns

Posture and stance

Clothing and hair styles (hair being more like clothes than like skin, both subject to the fashion of the day)

Walking behavior

Interpersonal distance

Touching

Eye contact and direction of gaze, particularly in "listening behavior"

Architecture and interior design

"Artifacts" and nonverbal symbols, such as lapel pins, walking sticks, and jewelry

Graphic symbols, such as pictures to indicate "men's room" or "handle with care"

Art and rhetorical forms, including wedding dances and political parades

Smell (olfaction), including body odors, perfumes, and incense

Speech rate, pitch, inflection, and volume

Color symbolism

Synchronization of speech and movement

Taste, including symbolism of food and the communication function of chatting over coffee or tea, oral gratification, such as smoking or gum chewing

Cosmetics: temporary, such as powder and lipstick; permanent, such as tattoos

Drum signals, smoke signals, factory whistles, police sirens

Time symbolism: what is too late or too early a time to telephone or visit a friend or too long or too short a time to make a speech or stay for dinner

Timing and pauses within verbal behavior

Silence

Source: Reprinted with permission of Simon & Schuster Inc. from the Macmillan College text *An Introduction to Intercultural Communication* by John C. Condon and Fathi Yousef. Copyright © 1975 by Macmillan College Publishing Company, Inc.

business at a party typically stand 20 inches from each other. In Saudi Arabia, the normal conversational distance is only 9 to 10 inches. A U.S. businessperson conversing with a Saudi counterpart at a party will respond to the Saudi's polite attempts to move in closer by politely moving back. Each is acting politely within the context of his or her own culture—and insulting the other in the context of that person's culture.[24]

Differences in the meanings of hand gestures and facial expressions also exist among cultures. Nodding one's head means "yes" in the United States but "no" in Bulgaria. Joining the thumb and forefinger in a circle while extending the remaining three fingers is the signal for "okay" in the United States. However, it symbolizes money to the Japanese, worthlessness to the French, male homosexuals to the Maltese, and, as noted in the opening case, a vulgarity in many parts of Eastern Europe.[25] Needless to say, international businesspeople should avoid gesturing in a foreign culture unless they are sure of the gesture's meaning in that culture.

Even silence has meaning. People in the United States tend to abhor silence at meetings or in private conversation, believing that silence reflects an inability to communicate or to empathize. In Japan, silence may indicate nothing more than that the individual is thinking or that additional conversation would be disharmonious. U.S. negotiators have often misinterpreted the silence of their Japanese counterparts and offered contract concessions when none were needed, simply to end the lull in the discussion.[26] Attitudes toward silence also affect management styles. In the United States, good managers solve problems. Thus U.S. managers often attempt to dominate group discussions in order to signal their competence and leadership abilities. In Japan, good managers encourage their subordinates to seek solutions that are acceptable to all parties involved. A Japanese manager therefore will demonstrate leadership by silence, thereby encouraging full participation by subordinates attending the meeting and promoting group consensus.[27]

Cross-cultural differences also are reflected in the spatial arrangements and furnishings of offices. In a typical U.S. firm, large, windowed corner offices on the highest floors of the firm's headquarters are the most prestigous. Most U.S. offices are partitioned to allow each employee private space and to restrict socializing with coworkers. In Japan, the group orientation of the society results in private offices being nonexistent for all but the most senior managers. Japanese offices are open and public with double rows of desks to encourage cooperation and communication between members of a group. The desk of the group leader is positioned at one end of the row to facilitate supervision and group cohesion.[28] In Germany, offices are designed for privacy. The closed-door policy adopted by many German managers suggests their belief that subordinates may be trusted to do their jobs competently without constant monitoring by their supervisor.[29]

Gift Giving and Hospitality. Gift giving and hospitality are important means of communication in many business cultures. Japanese business etiquette requires solicitous hospitality. Elaborate meals and after-hours entertainment serve to build personal bonds and group harmony among the participants. These personal bonds are strengthened by the exchange of gifts, which vary according to the occasion and the status of the giver and the recipient. However, business gifts are opened in private, so as not to cause the giver to lose face should the gift be too expensive or too cheap relative to the gift offered in return.[30] As the rules for gift giving can be quite complicated, even to native Japanese, etiquette books are available that detail the appropriate gift for each circumstance.[31]

Arab businesspeople, like the Japanese, are very concerned about their ability to work with their proposed business partners; the quality of the people one deals with is just as important as the quality of the project. Thus the business culture of Arab countries also includes gift giving and elaborate and gracious hospitality as a means of assessing these qualities. Unlike in Japan, however, business gifts are opened in public so that all may be aware of the donor's generosity.[32]

Norms of hospitality even affect the way bad news is delivered in various cultures. In the United States, bad news is typically delivered as soon as it is known. In Korea, it is delivered at day's end so it will not ruin the recipient's whole day. Further, in order not to disrupt personal relationships, the bad news is often only hinted at. In Japan, maintaining harmony among participants in a project is emphasized. Bad news often is communicated informally from a junior member of one negotiating team to a junior member of the other team. Even better, a third party may be used to deliver the message in order to preserve the harmony within the group.[33]

Negotiation. Firms negotiating contracts with foreign partners must recognize that different cultures have different negotiating styles, as Table 9.2 indicates. Managers of such firms must adapt their negotiating styles and expectations to meet the cultural needs of their foreign counterparts. U.S., Canadian, and British firms rely on binding legal contracts to ensure contract fulfillment, and lawyers are often present at negotiations to ensure that their clients' interests are protected. In contrast, cultures such as those of Saudi Arabia, Japan, and Egypt rely on trusting personal relationships. In these countries, the presence of a lawyer, particularly at the initial meeting of the participants, is viewed as a sign of distrust. Because these cultures value long-term relationships, an assumption by a potential partner that one cannot be trusted may be sufficient grounds to end the negotiations.

Religion

Religion is an important aspect of most societies. It affects the ways in which members of a society relate to each other and to outsiders. Approximately 80 percent of the world's 5.3 billion people claim some religious affiliation. As reflected in Map 9.3, 69 percent of the world's population adheres to one of four religions:

▶ Christianity, comprising Roman Catholic (18.8 percent), Protestant (10.1 percent), and Eastern Orthodox (3.1 percent)

▶ Islam (17.7 percent)

▶ Hinduism (13.3 percent)

▶ Buddhism (5.7 percent)

Religion shapes the attitudes its adherents have toward work, consumption, individual responsibility, and planning for the future. Sociologist Max Weber, for example, has attributed the rise of capitalism in Western Europe to the **Protestant ethic**, which stresses individual hard work, frugality, and achievement as means of glorifying God. The Protestant ethic makes a virtue of high savings rates, constant striving for efficiency, and reinvestment of profits to improve future productivity, all of which are necessary for the smooth functioning of a capitalist economy.

TABLE 9.2		

Differences in Negotiating Styles across Cultures

JAPANESE	NORTH AMERICAN	LATIN AMERICAN
Emotional sensitivity highly valued.	Emotional sensitivity not highly valued.	Emotional sensitivity valued.
Hiding of emotions.	Dealing straightforwardly or impersonally.	Emotionally passionate.
Subtle power plays; conciliation.	Litigation not as much as conciliation.	Great power plays; use of weakness.
Loyalty to employer. Employer takes care of its employees.	Lack of commitment to employer. Breaking of ties by either if necessary.	Loyalty to employer (who is often family).
Group decision-making consensus.	Teamwork provides input to a decision maker.	Decisions come down from one individual.
Face-saving crucial. Decisions often made on basis of saving someone from embarrassment.	Decisions made on a cost benefit basis. Face-saving does not always matter.	Face-saving crucial in decision making to preserve honor, dignity.
Decision makers openly influenced by special interests.	Decision makers influenced by special interests but this often not considered ethical.	Execution of special interests of decision maker expected, condoned.
Not argumentative. Quiet when right.	Argumentative when right or wrong, but impersonal.	Argumentative when right or wrong; passionate.
What is down in writing must be accurate, valid.	Great importance given to documentation as evidential proof.	Impatient with documentation as obstacle to understanding general principles.
Step-by-step approach to decision making.	Methodically organized decision making.	Impulsive, spontaneous decision making.
Good of group is the ultimate aim.	Profit motive or good of individual ultimate aim.	What is good for the group is good for the individual.
Cultivate a good emotional social setting for decision making. Get to know decision makers.	Decision making impersonal. Avoid involvements, conflicts of interest.	Personalism necessary for good decision making.

Source: From Pierre Casse, *Training for the Multicultural Manager: A Practical and Cross-Cultural Approach to the Management of People.* Washington, D.C.: SIETAR International, © 1982. Reprinted with permission of the author.

In contrast, Hinduism emphasizes spiritual accomplishment rather than economic success. The goal of a Hindu is to achieve **nirvana**, a state of spiritual perfection, by leading progressively ascetic and pure lives as one's reincarnated soul goes through cycles of death and rebirth. The quest for material possessions may delay one's spiritual journey. Thus Hinduism provides little support for capitalistic activities such as investment, wealth accumulation, and the constant quest for higher productivity and efficiency.

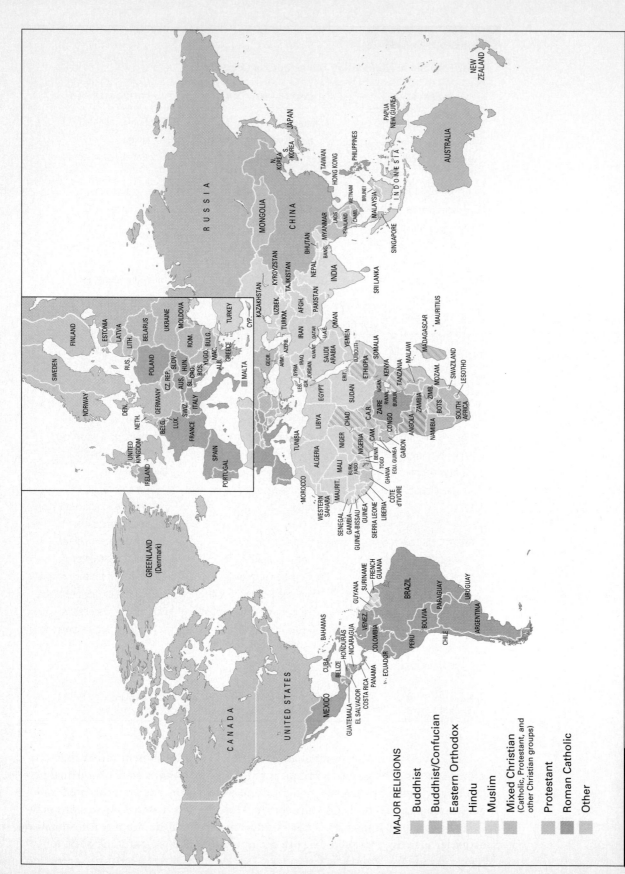

MAJOR RELIGIONS

Buddhist

Buddhist/Confucian

Eastern Orthodox

Hindu

Muslim

Mixed Christian
(Catholic, Protestant, and
other Christian groups)

Protestant

Roman Catholic

Other

MAP 9.3   **Major World Religions**

Islam, while supportive of capitalism, places more emphasis on the individual's obligation to society. According to Islam, profits earned in fair business dealings are justified, but a firm's profits may not result from exploitation or deceit, for example, and all Muslims are expected to act charitably, justly, and humbly in their dealings with others. The Islamic prohibition against payment or receipt of interest noted in Chapter 8 results from a belief that the practice represents exploitation of the less fortunate.

Religion affects the business environment in other important ways. Often religions impose constraints on the roles of individuals in society. For example, the caste system of Hinduism traditionally has restricted the jobs individuals may perform, thereby affecting the labor market and foreclosing business opportunities. For example, only members of the Dom subcaste may provide cremation services.[34] Countries dominated by strict adherents to Islam, such as Saudi Arabia and Iran, limit job opportunities for women, in the belief that their contact with adult males should be restricted to relatives.

Religion also affects the types of products consumers may purchase as well as seasonal patterns of consumption. In most Christian countries, for example, the Christmas season represents an important time for gift giving, yet very little business is done on Christmas Day itself. While consumption booms during the Christmas holidays, production plummets as employees take time off to visit friends and family.

The impact of religion on international businesses varies from country to country, depending on the country's legal system, its homogeneity of religious beliefs, and its toleration of other religious viewpoints. Consider Saudi Arabia, home of the holy city of Mecca, to which all Muslims are supposed to make a pilgrimage sometime in their lives. The teachings of the Koran form the basis of the country's theocratic legal system, and 99 percent of the Saudi population is Muslim. Strong political pressure exists within the country to preserve its religious traditions. It is impossible to overstate the importance to foreign businesspeople of understanding the tenets of Islam as they apply to exporting, producing,

Firms often adapt their products to meet the needs of local cultures. Blonde-haired Barbie dolls are a popular item in any North American toy store. But Barbie's features change from market to market. The dark-haired Barbie dolls produced by these Indonesian workers will be marketed to little girls throughout Asia.

marketing, or financing goods in the Saudi market. For example, work stops five times a day when the faithful are called to pray to Allah. A non-Muslim manager would be foolish to object to the practice even though it seemingly leads to lost production. Foreigners must also be considerate of their Saudi hosts during the holy month of Ramadan, when the Muslim faithful fast from sunrise to sunset. Female executives of Western firms have additional obstacles because of Saudi attitudes toward the appropriate roles for women, which stem from their religion. Even actions taken outside of Saudi borders may affect commercial relations with the country. For example, McDonald's made a major faux pas when, as part of its British marketing campaign during the 1994 World Cup, it printed the flags of the 24 participating soccer teams, including that of Saudi Arabia, on its paper takeout bags. But the Saudi flag includes a sacred inscription that reads, "There is no God but Allah, and Mohammed is His Prophet." Muslims in Saudi Arabia and in other countries were outraged by McDonald's actions, believing that Islam had been insulted by including the name of Allah on a container that would be thrown into garbage cans. McDonald's quickly apologized and pledged to stop using the bags, thereby diffusing a controversy that would have otherwise affected its business in Saudi Arabia and other Muslim countries.

In many other countries, however, religion, while important, does not permeate every facet of life. For example, in many South American countries most of the population is Roman Catholic. But other religions are also practiced, and tolerance of those religions is high. The Catholic Church is an important pillar of these societies, but only one of many institutions that affect and shape the daily lives of the citizens. Yet public holidays reflect Christian theology (Easter, Christmas), as does the work week (Sunday is the day of rest). A firm operating in these countries thus needs to adjust its production and employee scheduling to meet the expectations of its workers and customers. Firms operating in Sweden, which is 97 percent Lutheran, must make similar adjustments.

Ironically, countries characterized by religious diversity may offer even greater challenges. Firms that operate in the cosmopolitan cities of London and New York, such as Barclays Bank, Hoffman-LaRoche, and IBM, must accommodate the religious needs of their Jewish, Christian, Muslim, and Hindu employees and customers by taking into account differences in religious holidays, dietary restrictions or customs, and sabbath days. Firms that fail to adjust to these needs will suffer from absenteeism, low morale, and lost sales.

Values and Attitudes

Culture also affects and reflects the values and attitudes of members of a society. Values are the principles and standards accepted by members of a society; attitudes encompass the actions, feelings, and thoughts that result from those values. Cultural values often stem from deep-seated beliefs about the individual's position in relation to his or her deity, the family, and the social hierarchy that we discussed earlier. Cultural attitudes about such factors as time, authority, education, and rewards reflect these values and in turn shape the behavior of and opportunities available to international businesses operating in a given culture.

Time. Attitudes about time differ dramatically across cultures. In Anglo-Saxon cultures, the prevailing attitude is "time is money." U.S. and Canadian business-people expect meetings to start on time. Keeping a person waiting is considered extremely rude. This cultural attitude toward time is interrelated with other aspects of these cultures. In the United States, pay is linked to time and to one's productivity, so it is not surprising that time is valued highly. Time represents the opportunity to produce more and to raise one's income; so it is not to be wasted. Underlying this attitude is the Protestant ethic, which encourages one to better one's position in life through hard work, and the puritanical belief that "idle hands are the Devil's workshop."

In Latin American cultures, however, few participants would think it unusual if a meeting began 45 minutes after the appointed time.[35] In Arab cultures, meetings not only often start later than the stated time, they also may be interrupted by family and friends who wander in to exchange pleasantries. Westerners may interpret their host's willingness to talk to these unscheduled visitors as a sign of rudeness and as a subtle device to undermine their dignity. Nothing could be further from the truth. This open-door policy reflects the hospitality of the host and the respect he offers to all guests—just the sort of person with whom the Arab presumes the Westerner wants to do business.[36]

Even the content of business meetings can vary by country. If a meeting is scheduled for 2:00 p.m., U.S., Canadian, and British businesspeople arrive at 1:55 p.m. and expect the meeting to start promptly at 2:00 p.m. After exchanging a few pleasantries, they then get down to business, following a well-planned agenda that has been distributed in advance to the participants. At the meeting, the positions of the parties are set forth and disagreement is common. In contrast, in high-context cultures like those of Japan and Saudi Arabia the agenda of an initial meeting will be quite different. Time must be expended to determine whether the parties can trust each other and work together comfortably. The initial meeting does not focus on the details of the proposed business at hand but rather on assessing the character and integrity of the potential business partners. But note that this time is not being wasted. Because these cultures trust personal relationships more than legal documents, time is being utilized for a valuable purpose—assessing the qualities of potential business partners.

Authority. Attitudes toward authority differ dramatically among cultures. Canadian and U.S. businesspeople believe hierarchies exist in order to solve problems and organize tasks within organizations. Some other business cultures, such as those in Indonesia and Italy, assume that hierarchies are developed so that everyone knows who has authority over whom. In approaching a new project, U.S. businesspeople will first define the tasks at hand and then assemble the project team. Indonesians, on the other hand, will first determine who is to be in charge and then assess whether the project is feasible under that manager's leadership.

To assess how different cultures view hierarchy, one survey asked international managers to respond to the following statement: "In order to have efficient work relationships, it is often necessary to bypass the hierarchical line." Swedish, British, and U.S. managers agreed with the statement. They believed that superiors do not necessarily have all the information subordinates need to make decisions and that it is efficient for the subordinate to seek out the person who has the relevant information regardless of the firm's formal hierarchy. Italian managers, on the other hand, disagreed: bypassing a superior is a sign of insubordination, not efficiency, in the Italian business culture. The managers were also asked whether they should be able to provide precise answers to most questions raised by subordinates. French, Italian, and Indonesian managers said yes; most Swedish, British, and U.S. managers said no. The former group viewed the manager as an expert, while the latter viewed the manager as a problem solver. To a U.S. businessperson, a manager who failed to refer a subordinate to a more knowledgeable authority would be viewed as an egomaniac. To an Indonesian, a manager who referred a subordinate to someone else would be demonstrating incompetence.[37]

The attributes of leaders also differ cross-culturally. In the United States, a leader is often someone who makes the tough decisions and makes sure things get done. In Japan, a leader is one who nurtures group harmony and consensus by skillfully listening to the members of the group.[38]

Age. Important cultural differences exist in attitudes toward age. Youthfulness is considered a virtue in the United States. Many U.S. firms devote much time and energy to identifying young "fast-trackers" and providing them with important, tough assignments, such as negotiating joint ventures with international partners. However, in Asian and Arab cultures, age is respected and a manager's stature is correlated with age. These cultural differences can lead to problems. For example, many foreign firms mistakenly send younger, fast-track executives to negotiate with government officials of China. The Chinese view this as a double insult. They prefer to deal with older and more senior members of the firm.

In Japan's corporate culture, age and rank are highly correlated. Yet senior (and by definition, older) managers will not grant approval to projects until they have achieved a consensus among junior managers. Many foreign firms mistakenly focus their attention in negotiations on the senior Japanese managers, failing to realize that their goal should be to persuade the junior managers. Once the junior managers consent to the project, the senior manager will grant his approval as well.

Education. A country's formal system of public and private education is an important transmitter and reflection of the cultural values of its society. For example, U.S. primary and secondary schools emphasize the role of the individual and stress the development of self-reliance, creativity, and self-esteem. The United States prides itself on providing widespread access to higher education. Research universities, liberal arts colleges, and community colleges coexist in order to meet the educational needs of students with disparate incomes and intellectual talents. In contrast, the United Kingdom, reflecting its class system, provides an elite education to a relatively small number of students. And Germany has well-developed apprenticeship programs that train new generations of skilled craftspeople and machinists for its manufacturing sector. The Japanese and French educational systems share a different focus. Their primary and secondary schools concentrate on rote memorization to prepare students to take a nationwide college entrance exam. The top-scoring students gain entry to a handful of prestigious universities—such as Tokyo University or Kyoto University in Japan and the five *grandes écoles* in France—which virtually guarantee their graduates placement in the most important corporate and governmental jobs in their societies.[39]

Status. The means by which status is achieved also vary across cultures. In some societies, status is inherited as a result of the wealth or rank of one's ancestors. In others, it is earned by the individual through personal accomplishments or professional achievements. In some European countries, for example, membership in the nobility ensures higher status than does mere personal achievement, and persons who inherited their wealth look down their noses at the *nouveau riche*. In the United States, however, hard-working entrepreneurs are honored, and their children are often disdained if they fail to match their parents' accomplishments.

In Japan, a person's status depends on the status of the group to which he or she belongs. Thus Japanese businesspeople often introduce themselves by announcing not only their name but also their corporate affiliation. Attendance at elite universities such as Tokyo University or employment in elite organizations such as Toyota Motor Corporation or the Ministry of Finance grant one high status in Japanese society.

In Germany, educational achievement is highly valued. Thus a German executive who has earned the appropriate degree expects to be addressed by the honorific title "Doctor." Such a request by a U.S. executive might be viewed as a bit snobby.

In India, status is determined by one's caste. The caste system, on which much of India's social hierarchy is based, divides the society into various groups such as Brahmins (priests and intellectuals), kshatriyas (soldiers), vaishyas (businesspeople), sudras (farmers and workers), and untouchables, who perform the dirtiest and most unpleasant jobs. According to Hinduism, one's caste reflects the virtue (or lack of virtue) that one exhibited in a previous life. Particularly in rural areas, caste affects every facet of life, from the way a man shapes his mustache to the food the family eats to the job a person may hold.[40]

These differences in how status is acquired affect job attitudes and performance. A U.S. manager may demonstrate her worth and commitment to the firm's goals by rolling up her shirt sleeves and going down to the factory floor to expedite a shipment. This behavior reflects the "can-do" mentality much admired in the United States. An Indian manager would find performance of such a menial task beneath his dignity. Such behavior also would diminish his stature among his peers and subordinates.

Reward Systems. A country's reward system reflects its cultural values. In the United States, employees believe they should be compensated according to their individual achievements. They judge the fairness of any compensation system by whether it achieves this objective. U.S. firms thus spend much time and resources assessing individual performance in order to link pay and performance. A firm that fails to do this will likely lose employees to firms that do.

Such behavior would seem strange within the group-oriented Japanese culture. In Japan, a person's compensation reflects the group to which he or she belongs, not any personal achievements. For example, all individuals who joined Nissan Motor's engineering staff in 1993 receive the same compensation, regardless of their individual talents, insights, and efforts. The salaries received by each cohort within the corporation reflect seniority: engineers who joined Nissan in 1993 receive higher salaries than do engineers who joined the firm in 1994 but lower salaries than do engineers who started in 1992. This compensation structure, which lasts for the first six to eight years the employee works for the firm, encourages employees to focus on group goals.

These cultural differences affect the job mobility of workers. Because of the group orientation of Japanese society, a job switcher is considered disloyal and may have difficulty finding a similar job in another Japanese firm. In the United States, a person's failure to accept a better paying job at another firm raises suspicions about the person's ambition, motivation, and dedication to his or her career.

These cultural differences help explain the widely publicized differences in CEO pay between the United States and Japan. In group-oriented Japan, the CEO's pay symbolically reflects the performance of the group. In the United States, the CEO's pay is presumed to measure the CEO's contribution to the firm. Even the way the issue is framed reflects the cultural values of the United States: the question "How can President Smith of the XYZ Corporation be worth $10 million?" implicitly assumes that the CEO's pay should measure his or her individual contribution to the organization.

Cultural Differences and Ethics

Cultural differences often create ethical problems. Acceptable behavior in one culture may be viewed as immoral in another. For example, in many poorer countries low-paid workers often expect a small payment in return for stamping a passport or finding a "lost" hotel reservation. Such behavior may appear inappropriate to members of richer countries like the United States or Germany, where such a payment would be considered a bribe. And recall Michelle Pfeiffer's dilemma presented in Chapter 8: should she have stood her ground and refused to return to the set until the Soviet extras were fed, or did she do the right thing by obeying local law and custom?

Consider the following scenarios:

▶ To assist the sale of your products in a particular foreign market, it is suggested that you pay a 10 percent commission to a "go-between" who has access to high-ranking government officials in that market. You suspect, but do not know, that the go-between will split the commission with the government officials who decide which goods to buy. Should you do it? Does it make a difference if your competitors routinely pay such commissions?

▶ You have a longstanding client in a country that imposes foreign-exchange controls. The client asks you to pad your invoices by 25 percent. For example, you would ship the client $100,000 of goods, but would invoice the client for $125,000. On the basis of your invoice, the client would obtain the $125,000 from the country's central bank. He then would pay you $100,000 and have you put the remaining $25,000 in a Swiss bank account in his name. Should you do it? Would it make a difference if your client is a member of a politically unpopular minority who may have to flee the country at a moment's notice?

Needless to say, your answers to these questions will reflect your culture as well as your personal circumstances.

Cultural Clusters

Cultural differences provide challenges to international business-people in marketing products, managing workforces, and dealing with host country governments. Fortunately, similarities do exist among many cultures, thereby reducing some of the need to customize business practices to meet the demands of local cultures. Anthropologists, sociologists, and international business scholars have analyzed such factors as job satisfaction, work roles, and interpersonal work relations in an attempt to identify clusters of countries that share similar cultural values that can affect business practices. Map 9.4 shows the eight country clusters developed by one such team of researchers, Ronen and Shenkar. (In their study, four countries—Brazil, India, Israel, and Japan—were not placed in any cluster.) A **cultural cluster** comprises countries that share many cultural similarities, although differences do remain. Many clusters are based on language similarities, as is apparent in the Anglo, Germanic, Latin American, and Arab clusters and, to a lesser extent, in the Nordic and Latin European clusters. Of course, one can disagree with some placements of countries within clusters. Israel, for example, shares many cultural values with the United States, as do Spain and the countries of Latin America.

Many international businesses instinctively utilize the country-clustering approach in formulating their internationalization strategies. Many U.S. firms' first exporting efforts focus on Canada and the United Kingdom. Hong Kong firms have been very successful in exploiting China's markets. And we noted earlier in this chapter how Spain's Iberia Airlines has chosen to focus its international expansion efforts on Spanish-speaking areas in the Americas.

Closeness of culture may affect the form firms use to enter foreign markets. Recent research has found, for example, that Canadian firms are more likely to

enter the British market by establishing joint ventures with British firms, while Japanese firms are more likely to enter the British market via a **greenfield investment**, that is, a brand new one. The likely reason for the difference? Because of the relative closeness of their national cultures, Canadian firms are more comfortable working with British partners than are Japanese firms.[41]

Some experts believe the world's cultures are growing more similar as a result of improvements in communication and transportation. Thanks to MTV and CNN, teenagers worldwide can enjoy the wit and wisdom of Beavis and Butthead, while their parents can learn about politics, scandals, disasters, and culture in other countries. Lower airfares generated by increased airline competition means that more tourists can learn about other cultures firsthand. MNCs facilitate this process of **cultural convergence**, for better or worse, through their advertisements that define appropriate lifestyles, attitudes, and goals and by bringing new management techniques, technologies, and cultural values to the countries in which they operate.

Growth in international business activity, which has been promoted by technological changes in transportation and communication, is a primary force behind the convergence of the world's cultures.

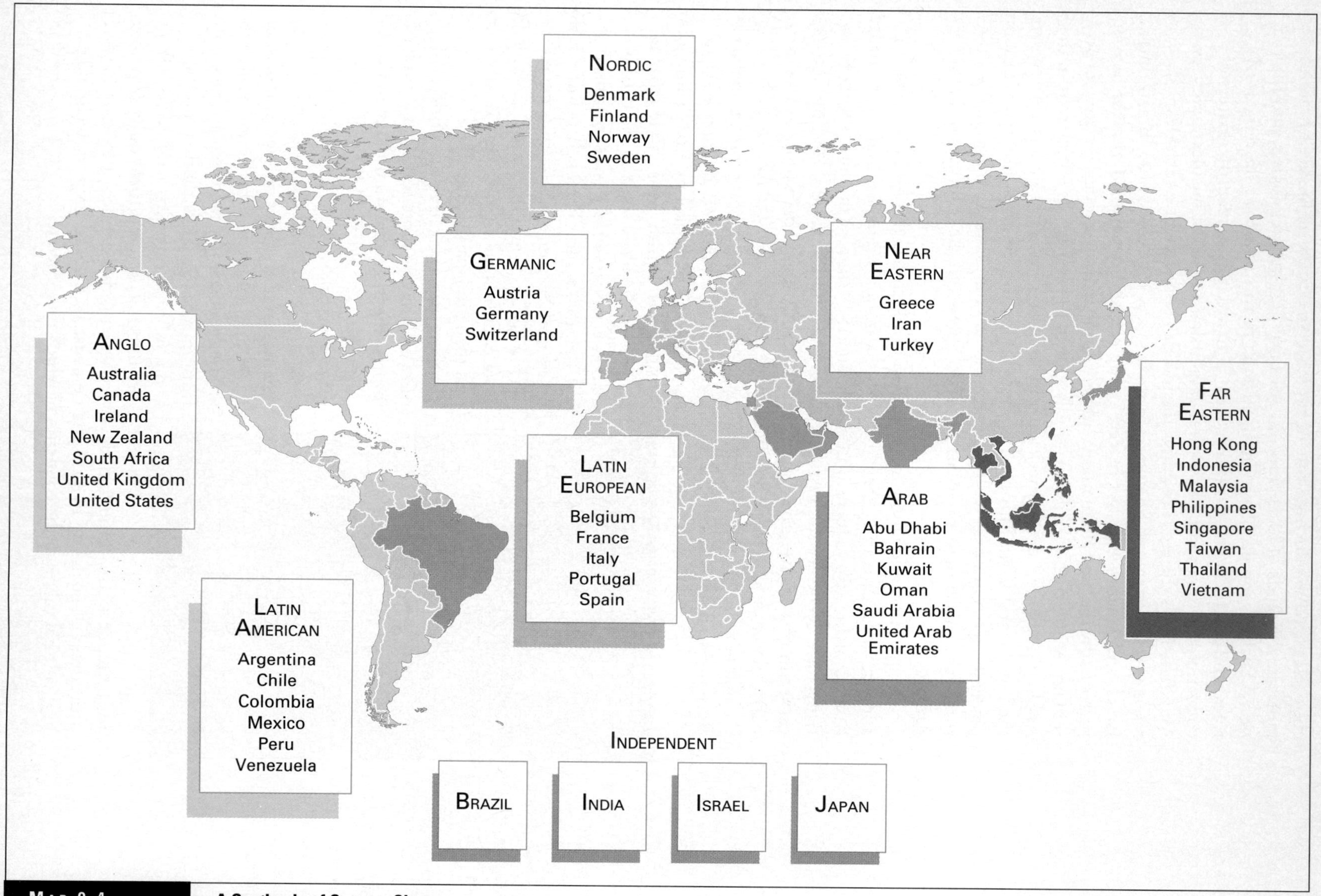

FAR EASTERN
Hong Kong
Indonesia
Malaysia
Philippines
Singapore
Taiwan
Thailand
Vietnam

NEAR EASTERN
Greece
Iran
Turkey

ARAB
Abu Dhabi
Bahrain
Kuwait
Oman
Saudi Arabia
United Arab
Emirates

JAPAN

ISRAEL

NORDIC
Denmark
Finland
Norway
Sweden

LATIN EUROPEAN
Belgium
France
Italy
Portugal
Spain

INDEPENDENT

INDIA

GERMANIC
Austria
Germany
Switzerland

BRAZIL

LATIN AMERICAN
Argentina
Chile
Colombia
Mexico
Peru
Venezuela

ANGLO
Australia
Canada
Ireland
New Zealand
South Africa
United Kingdom
United States

A Synthesis of Country Clusters

Source: From Simcha Ronen and Oded Shenkar, "Clustering Countries on Attitudinal Dimensions: A Review and Synthesis," *Academy of Management Review,* Vol. 10, No. 3 (1985), p. 449. Reprinted with permission.

MAP 9.4

A Final Word

Parts 1, 2, and 3 of this book have discussed the external environments in which international businesses operate. Part 1 provided a general introduction to the world economy. Parts 2 and 3 described the international environment and host country environments, respectively, as the framework in which international business occurs. Part 4, which begins with the next chapter, focuses on the firm itself. Part 5 examines the functional areas within the firm—marketing, operations management, finance, accounting, and human resource management.

As you read Parts 4 and 5, note how often the external environment shapes the opportunities available to international businesses. A firm's strategic choices and operating decisions are often influenced by such external factors as the international monetary system, international treaties, national trade policies, domestic laws, and cultural values. Particularly striking is the importance of politics and culture. As you read the rest of this book, note how often political and cultural factors influence the opportunities available to and the decisions made by international businesses.

CHAPTER REVIEW

Summary

Understanding cultural differences is critical to the success of firms engaging in international business. A society's culture affects the political, economic, social, and ethical rules a firm must follow in its business dealings within that society.

A society's culture also reflects its values, beliefs, behaviors, customs, and attitudes. Culture is learned behavior that is transmitted from one member of a society to another. The elements of culture are inter-related and reinforce each other. These elements are adaptive, changing as outside forces affect the society. Culture not only is shared by the society's members but also defines the society's membership.

A society's culture comprises numerous elements. The social structure reflects the culture's beliefs about the individual's role in society and the importance of mobility within that society.

Language is another important cultural element, for it allows members of the society to communicate with each other. Communication can also take non-verbal forms, such as facial expressions and hand gestures, voice intonation, and use of space. These nonverbal forms of communication are often difficult for outsiders to master.

Approximately 80 percent of the world's population claims some religious affiliation. Religion influences attitudes toward work, investment, consumption, and responsibility for one's behavior. Religion may also influence the formulation of a country's laws.

A society's culture reflects and shapes its values and attitudes, including those toward time, authority, age, status, and education. These affect business operations in numerous ways, such as in hiring practices, job turnover, and the design of compensation programs.

Cultural differences often create ethical dilemmas for international businesspeople. Behaviors that are acceptable in the home country culture may be deemed inappropriate by the host country culture. Such cultural conflicts commonly arise among persons from different cultural backgrounds, and international businesspeople must be prepared to deal with any resultant ethical conflicts.

The existence of cultural clusters eases to some extent the difficulties of doing business internationally. Researchers have discovered that many countries share similar attitudes toward work roles, job satisfaction, and other work-related aspects of life. Often countries within a cultural cluster share a common language.

Review Questions

1. What is culture?

2. What are the primary characteristics of culture?

3. How does *wa* affect Japanese business behavior?

4. What is the self-reference criterion?

5. What is acculturation? Why is it important to international businesspeople?

6. What is a *lingua franca*? Why has English become a lingua franca?

7. What is backtranslation? What problem is it designed to solve?

8. Describe the difference between high-context and low-context cultures.

9. How do differences in attitudes toward time affect international businesspeople?

10. Discuss the differences in pay systems between U.S. and Japanese firms. To what extent are these differences culturally determined?

11. What are cultural clusters?

Questions for Discussion

1. How can international businesspeople avoid relying on the self-reference criterion when dealing with people from other cultures?

2. How important is it for native English speakers to learn a second language? Should all business students whose native tongue is English be required to learn another language? Why or why not?

3. U.S. law protects women from job discrimination, but many countries do not offer women such protection. Suppose several important job opportunities arise at overseas factories owned by your firm. However, these factories are located in countries that severely restrict the working rights of women. You fear that female managers thus will be ineffective there. Should you adopt gender-blind selection policies for these positions? Does it make a difference if you have good reason to fear for the physical safety of your female managers? Does it make a difference if the restrictions are cultural rather than legal in nature?

4. Under what circumstances should international businesspeople impose the ethics of their culture on foreigners with whom they do business? Does it make a difference if the activity is conducted in the home or the host country?

5. Is nonverbal communication more important or less important when two people speak different languages? What are the pitfalls of trying to use only nonverbal communication to "talk" to someone from another country?

BUILDING **G**LOBAL **S**KILLS

This exercise will help give you insights into how cultural and social factors affect international business decisions. Your instructor will divide the class into groups of four or five people. Each group then picks any three products from the first column of the following list and any three countries from the next column. (Or, your instructor may assign each group three products and three countries.)

Products	Countries
swimsuits	France
CD players	Singapore
desks and bookcases	Poland
men's neckties	Saudi Arabia
women's purses	Taiwan
throat lozenges	Italy
film	South Africa
shoes	Russia

Assume that your firm already markets its three products in the United States. It has a well-known trademark and slogan for each product, and each product is among the market leaders. Assume further that your firm has decided to begin exporting each product to each of the three countries. Research the cultures of those three countries to determine how, if at all, you may need to adjust packaging, promotion, advertising, and so forth in order to maximize your firm's potential for success.

Do not worry too much about whether a market truly exists (assume that market research has already determined one does). Focus instead on how your product will be received in each country given that country's culture.

Follow-up Questions

1. What were your primary sources of information about the three countries? How easy or difficult was it to find information?

2. Can you think of specific products that are in high demand in the United States that would simply not work in specific other countries because of cultural factors?

3. How do you think foreign firms assess American culture as they contemplate introducing their products into the U.S. market?

CLOSING CASE

Hollywood Abroad[42]

Movies tend to reflect the culture in which their stories are set. *Forrest Gump*, *The Flintstones*, *Jurassic Park*, *Interview with the Vampire*, and *E.T.*, for example, were all clearly set in a U.S. cultural and social context. *The Crying Game* (a British movie) and *The Piano* (made in New Zealand) were also clearly set within their own specific cultural contexts.

Yet film making has long been an international business. Hollywood movies have played to foreign markets since the 1920s. And indeed, the ultimate profitability of a particular movie has often depended on its foreign revenues. But film makers have considerable difficulty predicting how domestic audiences will respond to any given movie. Predicting how it will do abroad is even more difficult. For example, *Ishtar*, starring Dustin Hoffman and Warren Beatty, was a flop at home but a hit in Europe. On the other hand, *A Few Good Men* was expected to do well in Europe but ended up faring poorly. Likewise, *The Crying Game* had limited success in Europe but was a

commercial hit and a nominee for Best Picture of the Year in the United States.

The foreign success of a Hollywood movie also varies by country. As a general rule of thumb, Hollywood has the easiest time selling its movies in English-speaking markets such as those of the United Kingdom and Australia. The movie's content usually translates well, and language is seldom an issue. When the movie must be dubbed or subtitled, however, things can be a bit more complicated. Literal translations can be confusing, and the pace of the movie may be disrupted if audiences need time to read subtitles.

Film makers have grown accustomed to tailoring their movies to foreign audiences even as they are being shot. For example, nudity is much more acceptable in Europe than in the United States. For years, directors making films like *Basic Instinct* have shot two (or more) versions of love scenes. More extended and explicit scenes are edited into European versions, while shorter and less explicit scenes are used in the U.S. version.

A recent trend has been also to make other accommodations. For example, during the filming of *Demolition Man*, officials at PepsiCo contracted with the film makers to have all restaurants shown in the movie called Taco Bell as a way of promoting one of the firm's restaurant chains in the United States. But there are few Taco Bells abroad; the firm realized it would lose its marketing angle when the film was exported. However, PepsiCo has many Pizza Hut restaurants abroad. Thus it also contracted with the film maker to shoot pertinent scenes a second time, showing Pizza Hut instead of Taco Bell, for a version to be shown outside the United States. As a result, the firm got twice as much promotional payoff for its advertising investment.

While it's tricky to predict which movies will work in specific foreign markets, some experts do think preference patterns exist. For example, U.S. movies about racial or diversity issues do not play well in foreign markets. Visual comedies like *Home Alone* are almost universal in their appeal, but comedies based on social patterns or stereotypes may not travel as well. Action adventures with Arnold Schwartzenegger and Sylvester Stallone and martial arts flicks starring Steven Segal and Jean-Claude Van Damme also do well in foreign countries, no doubt because the viewer does not have to have a firm grasp of the subtleties of the English language in order to follow the plot. The German market, in particular, seems to be very much like the U.S. market. The French market, however, is among the hardest to crack, in part because the French tend to be suspicious of things that are too "American."

Sometimes a movie is derailed for unusual reasons. Many movie theaters in Europe, for example, are not air-conditioned. *The Hand That Rocks the Cradle* was expected to be a big hit in Italy. Just as it opened, however, an extended heat wave struck the country, causing moviegoers to stay home in droves. By the time temperatures had cooled down, the film's opening momentum had dissipated and box office receipts continued to be disappointing.

Political issues are also becoming more of a consideration. Steven Spielberg's *Schindler's List* was a big success in Japan because moviegoers there are attracted to stories about oppression. But the movie's distributor, Universal Studios, ran into trouble in Malaysia. The government there thought the story was too one-sided and insisted on revisions before they would approve it for local release. Spielberg refused, however, and withdrew the movie from consideration.

Case Questions

1. If you were making a movie, what issues would you consider in advance to ensure its successful exportation?

2. Why do you think Hollywood dominates the world movie market?

3. What industry changes are occurring today that may affect future international movie distribution?

4. What recent foreign movies have done well in the United States? Why?

CHAPTER NOTES

1. "Americans Saved from Business Blunders: Springs Firm Guides Businessmen Abroad," *Denver Post,* February 16, 1993, p. C1; "Selling Through a Babel of Tongues," *Business Marketing,* May 1991, pp. 24–26; "The New Europe: A Boom Market—For Linguists," *Business Week,* May 9, 1994, pp. 22A–22D.

2. Kathleen K. Reardon, "It's the thought that counts," *Harvard Business Review,* September–October 1984, pp. 136–141.

3. Stephen Kobrin, *International Expertise in American Business* (New York: Institute of International Education, 1984), p. 38.

4. "Firms Grapple with Language," *Wall Street Journal,* November 7, 1989, pp. B1, B10.

5. "The Overseas Chinese: A Driving Force," *The Economist,* July 18, 1992, pp. 21–24.

6. Nancy Adler, *International Dimensions of Organizational Behavior* (Boston: Kent Publishing, 1986), p. 19.

7. Vern Terpstra and Kenneth David, *The Cultural Environment of International Business* (Cincinnati: South-Western Publishing, 1985), p. 20.

8. John R. Schermerhorn, Jr., "Language Effects in Cross-Cultural Management Research: An Empirical Study and a Word of Caution," *Proceedings of the Academy of Management*, 1987, p. 103.

9. John C. Condon and Fathi Yousef, *An Introduction to Intercultural Communication* (New York: Bobbs-Merrill, 1975), p. 174; Jon P. Alston, *The American Samurai: Blending American and Japanese Business Practices* (New York: Walter de Gruyter, 1986), p. 325.

10. Adler, op. cit., p. 11.

11. Julie Amparano Lopez, "Going Global," *Wall Street Journal*, October 16, 1992, p. R20.

12. Edward Bruning, "The Role of Consumer Ethnocentrism in the Choice of International Air Carrier," *Journal of the Transportation Research Forum*, Vol. 34, No. 2, 1995, pp. 1–12.

13. Trenholme J. Griffin and W. Russell Daggatt, *The Global Negotiator* (New York: Harper Business, 1990), p. 40.

14. Ibid., pp. 39–40.

15. "Some Firms Resume Manufacturing in U.S. after Foreign Fiascoes," *Wall Street Journal*, October 14, 1986, pp. 1, 27.

16. Terpstra and David, op. cit., p. 37.

17. Alston, op. cit., p. 331.

18. Boye De Mente, *The Japanese Way of Doing Business: the Psychology of Management in Japan* (Englewood Cliffs, N.J.: Prentice Hall, 1981), p. 105.

19. Henry W. Lane and Joseph J. DiStefano, *International Management Behavior* (Boston: PWS-Kent Publishing, 1992), p. 214.

20. Edward T. Hall, *Beyond Culture* (Garden City, N.Y.: Anchor Press, 1976).

21. Edward T. Hall and Mildred Reed Hall, *Understanding Cultural Differences* (Yarmouth, Me.: Intercultural Press, 1990), pp. 72–73.

22. Edward T. Hall and Mildred Reed Hall, *Hidden Differences* (Garden City, N.Y.: Doubleday, 1987), pp. 9–10.

23. Ibid., p. 3.

24. Gary P. Ferraro, *The Cultural Dimension of International Business* (Englewood Cliffs, N.J.: Prentice Hall, 1990), p. 82.

25. Ferraro, op. cit., p. 76.

26. "For Japanese, silent negotiation is golden," *Houston Chronicle*, December 14, 1992, p. 2B.

27. Alston, op. cit., pp. 305–306.

28. Ibid., pp. 162–163.

29. Hall and Hall, *Understanding Cultural Differences,* p. 41.

30. Gavin Kennedy, *Doing Business Abroad* (New York: Simon and Schuster, 1985), p. 92.

31. Hall and Hall, *Hidden Differences*, p. 109.

32. Marlene L. Rossman, *The International Businesswoman* (New York: Praeger Publishers, 1986), p. 40.

33. Jon P. Alston, "Wa, Guanxi, and Inhwa: Managerial Principles in Japan, China, and Korea," *Business Horizons*, March–April 1989, pp. 26–31.

34. "The reincarnation of caste," *The Economist*, June 8, 1991, pp. 21–23.

35. Ferraro, op. cit., p. 99.

36. Kennedy, op. cit., pp. 97–98.

37. Adler, op. cit., pp. 32–33; Andre Laurent, "The Cultural Diversity of Western Conceptions of Management," *International Studies of Management and Organization*, Vol. XIII, No. 1–2 (Spring–Summer 1983), pp. 75–96.

38. Hall and Hall, *Hidden Differences*, p. 78.

39. "Miyazawa, Making Waves, Seeks to Cut the Clout of Tokyo University's Alumni," *Wall Street Journal*, March 5, 1992, p. A12.

40. "The reincarnation of caste," *The Economist*, June 8, 1991, pp. 21 23.

41. Bruce Kogut and Harbir Singh, "The Effect of National Culture on the Choice of Entry Mode," *Journal of International Business Studies*, Fall 1988, pp. 411–432.

42. Minda Zetlin, "Hollywood Looks for Marketing Cues in Europe," *The Journal of European Business*, May/June 1993, pp. 28–33.

MANAGING IN THE INTERNATIONAL ENVIRONMENT

4

Protesting against U.S. Investments in South Africa

IUE SAYS STOP U.S. INVESTMENT IN SO. AFRICA

Many activists believe that international businesses should have little involvement in South Africa until that country's racial problems are solved. These students are protesting investments by U.S. companies in South Africa. (See "Point/ Counterpoint" on pages 440–441.)

Whitney Houston as a South African Entrepreneur

The singer Whitney Houston and other prominent African Americans are active in developing new business ventures in South Africa. Ms. Houston, for example, shown here greeting children at a South African museum, is an investor in a soft drink bottling company. (See "Point/ Counterpoint" on pages 440–441.)

International Strategic Management

Chapter Outline

What is international strategic management?

Components of an international strategy
Scope of operations
Resource deployment
Distinctive competence
Synergy

Developing international strategies
Mission statement
Environmental scanning and the SWOT
    ₎analysis
Strategic goals
Tactics
Control framework

Levels of international strategy
Corporate strategy
Business strategy
Functional strategies

Foreign market analysis
Assessing alternative foreign markets
Evaluating costs, benefits, and risks of
    foreign markets

After studying this chapter you should be able to:

Describe the nature of international strategic management.

Identify and discuss the components of international strategy.

Describe the international strategic management process.

Identify and describe levels of international strategies.

Discuss how firms go about analyzing foreign markets.

T O MANY PEOPLE AROUND THE WORLD, MICKEY MOUSE IS A purely American icon. But Mickey's corporate parent, The Walt Disney Company, is a $8.6 billion MNC pursuing a global strategy. For years the firm, founded in 1923, was best known for its animated movies such as *Snow White*, *Pinocchio*, and *Fantasia*. From the firm's beginning, Disney creations proved to be as popular abroad as in the United States. Disney movies attract huge audiences worldwide, and merchandise featuring Mickey and other Disney characters is sold to millions. Today, Disney earns almost $40 million a year from royalties and licensing fees on its products sold abroad. ▌▌Another critical component of the Disney organization is its theme park operations. The firm's first theme park,

Global Mickey[1]

Disneyland, opened in Anaheim, California in 1955 and was soon generating huge profits. Indeed, in 1957 *Time* magazine dubbed Disneyland the biggest tourist attraction in the United States. The firm's next major theme park development, Walt Disney World, opened near Orlando, Florida, in 1971; it also was a major success. Because the two parks generate enormous profits, Disney has continued to invest in them by building new attractions and on-site hotels and by opening new parks adjacent to the existing ones. For example, Epcot Center opened in 1982, the Disney–MGM Studios Theme Park in 1988, and Blizzard Beach in 1995. ▌▌Given the enormous popularity of Disney characters abroad, the firm saw opportunities to expand its theme park operations there. Its first venture into a foreign market, Tokyo Disneyland, opened in 1984. The Japanese have always been keen fans of Disney characters, and many Japanese tourists visit Disneyland and Disney World. Market research showed the Japanese enthusiastically supported the idea of a Disney park in Japan. To limit its risk, the firm did not directly invest in the park. Instead, a Japanese investment group called the Oriental Land Company financed and owns Tokyo Disneyland entirely. Disney oversaw the park's construction and manages it, but receives only royalty income from it. Tokyo Disneyland has been an enormous success from the day it opened its gates: it greeted its 100 millionth visitor after only eight years, a milestone that Disneyland took twice as long to reach. ▌▌The success of Tokyo Disneyland inspired the firm to seek other foreign market opportunities. This time, though, Disney decided to participate more fully in both the park's ownership and profits. Disney officials knew where the next foreign park belonged—Europe. After careful consideration of sites throughout the continent, they narrowed their choice to two: one in France (just outside Paris) and one in Spain (close to Barcelona). The Spanish site held the advantage of a more favorable climate, similar to Florida's. However, the French site, although subject to harsher winter weather conditions, is closer to Europe's major population centers. Three hundred and fifty million people live within a two-hour plane ride of Paris. After careful consideration of the two locations, Disney chose the French site and made its plans public in 1988. ▌▌The

French government's offer of numerous economic incentives also played a role in Disney's decision. The government sold the land for the park to Disney at bargain-basement prices and agreed to extend the Parisian rail system to the proposed park's front door. The government also decreed that Disney could own up to 49 percent of the stock in its new venture, with the remaining 51 percent made available for trade on European stock exchanges. (The French government had traditionally mandated greater local ownership of projects when it was providing economic incentives.) ▌▌ But as Euro Disneyland took shape, storm clouds loomed. The cultural elite in Paris lambasted the project as an affront to French cultural traditions. One vocal critic called the project "a cultural Chernobyl," as threatening to French culture as that disastrous nuclear power plant meltdown was to the health and environment of Europe. Farmers protested the manner in which the French government condemned their land so that it could be sold

As part of an incentive package to convince The Walt Disney Company to build its European theme park near Paris, the French government condemned farmland and sold it to Disney at a bargain-basement price. Resenting the manner in which their land had been taken, French farmers protested by blockading entrances to the park shortly after it opened.

to Disney. And the firm found itself defending its conservative employee dress codes, regimented training practices, and plans to ban alcohol from park facilities. ▌▌ Amid the controversy, Euro Disney opened its doors to the public on April 12, 1992. So far, the results have been mixed. Early visitors seemed happy with their experience, and the park's attendance is generally in line with Disney's projections—approximately 11 million visitors a year. But financially the project has had major difficulties. Disney's quest for perfection raised construction costs. For example, CEO Michael Eisner ordered the removal, at a cost of $300,000, of two steel staircases that obscured the view of the Star Tours ride. Also, visitors have spent 12 percent less on food and souvenirs than expected. ▌▌ Particularly troublesome has been the lower than planned occupancy rates at Disney-owned hotels. Disney planners presumed hotel guests would stay an average of three days, as they do in Orlando. But Euro Disney visitors typically stay at most only two days. These shorter stays lowered occupancy rates and placed an unanticipated burden on the hotel's computer operations because of the unexpectedly high volume of check-in and check-out activity. Disney had to add new computer terminals and staff to handle the flow of guests. Further, the firm had planned to sell the hotels shortly after the park's opening and to use the proceeds to finance expansion in other areas. Unfortunately, the low occupancy rates made the properties less attractive, and Disney found no eager buyers. ▌▌ After 18 months of operation, Euro Disney faced a major financial crisis. The park was not earning enough revenue to cover its expenses, and the bad press about these financial problems was hurting its stock price. The banks that financed the project feared that the park would default on its loans. Everyone agreed new capital was needed to keep the park in operation, but Disney was unwilling to put up new funds without concessions from the local banks, and vice versa. In March 1994, Disney and the banks finally agreed to a complex rescue package that included injection of new capital by Disney, suspension of royalty payments and management fees due to the parent corporation from Euro Disney, forgiveness on interest payments to the banks for 18 months, a new public rights offering, and the sale and lease-back of the Temple of Doom and Discovery Mountain attractions. These efforts halved Euro Disney's debt burden to Fr10 billion and saved the park Fr800 million in interest payments. Finally, in the summer of 1994 Prince Al-Walid bin Talal of Saudi Arabia bought $400 million in Euro Disney stock. His investment gave him about 20 percent ownership and provided Euro Disney with much needed capital. ▪▪ Euro Disney executives remain optimistic about the park's long-term prospects. They argue that it has been a tougher sell than Tokyo Disneyland because Europeans are less attracted to foreign cultures than are the Japanese. They also believe bad timing played a part. An economic recession swept through Europe just as Euro Disney was opening. As a result, the firm scotched its plan to reduce its debt by selling off to local developers land it owned near the park. And the carrying cost of its debt rose further as French interest rates climbed. The 1992 collapse of the EU's exchange rate mechanism added to the problem, since the devaluation of the British pound, the Italian lira, and the Spanish peseta raised the cost of vacationing in France for citizens from those countries. ▪▪ As the European economies rebound, however, Disney executives believe that discretionary income will rise and bring with it a greater interest in leisure activities. The new investment gave the park at least two years of solid footing to get itself on track. A recently opened terminal connecting the park with the French high-speed rail system and the channel tunnel between England and France should also make traveling to and from the park more convenient. And, Disney's managers note, consumers' awareness of the park is high. Euro Disney quickly established itself as Europe's number one vacation resort: in its first 18 months, 17 million people visited Mickey, Donald, and Blanche Neige et les Sept Nains (Snow White and the Seven Dwarfs). ▪▪▪▪

To survive in today's global marketplace, firms must be able to quickly exploit opportunities presented them anywhere in the world and respond to changes in domestic and foreign markets as they arise. This requires them to fully understand why, how, and where they intend to do business. They need a cogent definition of their corporate mission, a vision for how they intend to achieve that mission, and an unambiguous understanding of how they intend to compete with other firms. To obtain this understanding, they must carefully compare their strengths and weaknesses to those of their worldwide competitors; assess likely political, economic, and social changes among their current and prospective customers; and analyze the impact of new technologies on their ways of doing business.

Disney's decisions to build Tokyo Disneyland and Euro Disney are consistent with its strategy to be a global entertainment firm. So, too, is its lucrative worldwide licensing of its characters for T-shirts, school lunchboxes, toys, and other items. While these ventures have generally been successful—Disney has enjoyed a 20 percent compound annual growth rate over the past five years—

the firm must develop effective responses to the poor financial performance of Euro Disney.[2] Further, Disney knows its competitors will continue to fight for market share. European vacationers can enjoy other amusement parks, such as Copenhagen's Tivoli Gardens or France's Cipal–Parc Asterix. Mickey Mouse lunchboxes compete for the attention of the world's schoolchildren with those featuring England's Paddington Bear, France's Babar the Elephant, and Belgium's Smurfs. Disney's top managers know that they are in a continuous battle for the entertainment dollars (and yen and marks) of the world's consumers and that it is up to them to deploy the firm's resources to achieve desired levels of profitability, growth, and market share.

What Is International Strategic Management?

Disney's managers, like those of other international businesses, utilize strategic management to address these challenges. More specifically, **international strategic management** is a comprehensive and ongoing management planning process aimed at formulating and implementing strategies that enable a firm to compete effectively internationally. The process of developing a particular international strategy is often referred to as **strategic planning**. Strategic planning is usually the responsibility of top-level executives at corporate headquarters and senior managers in domestic and foreign operating subsidiaries.[3] Most larger firms also have a permanent planning staff to provide technical assistance for top managers as they develop strategies. Disney's five-person planning staff, for example, gathered demographic and economic data that the firm's decision makers used to select the French site for Euro Disney.

International strategic management results in the development of various **international strategies**, which are comprehensive frameworks for achieving a firm's fundamental goals. Conceptually, there are many similarities between developing a strategy for competing in a single country and developing one for competing in multiple countries. In both cases, the firm's strategic planners must answer the same fundamental questions:

▶ What products and/or services does the firm intend to sell?

▶ Where and how will it make those products or deliver the services?

▶ Where and how will it sell them?

▶ Where and how will it acquire the necessary resources?

▶ How does it expect to outperform its competitors?[4]

But developing an international strategy is far more complex than developing a domestic one because the cultural, political, and geographical differences among countries are almost certain to be much greater than the same differences among areas of a single country. Planning a strategy for a single country allows managers to deal with known levels of governmental control, a single currency, and, often, a single language. Planning a strategy for multiple countries involves dealing with variations in governmental control, multiple curren-

TABLE 10.1

Differences between Domestic and International Operations That Affect Strategic Management for U.S. Firms

FACTOR	U.S. OPERATIONS	INTERNATIONAL OPERATIONS
Language	English used almost universally.	Use of local language required in many situations.
Culture	Relatively homogeneous.	Quite diverse, both between countries and within countries.
Politics	Stable and relatively unimportant.	Often volatile and of decisive importance.
Economy	Relatively uniform.	Wide variations among countries and among regions within countries.
Governmental interference	Minimal and reasonably predictable.	Extensive and subject to rapid change.
Labor	Skilled labor available.	Skilled labor often scarce, requiring training or redesign of production methods.
Financing	Well-developed financial markets.	Poorly developed financial markets; capital flows subject to government control.
Market Research	Data easy to collect.	Data difficult and expensive to collect.
Advertising	Many media available; few restrictions.	Media limited; many restrictions; low literacy rates rule out print media in some countries.
Money	U.S. dollar used universally.	Must change from one currency to another; problems created by changing exchange rates and governmental restrictions.
Transportation/ communication	Among the best in the world.	Often inadequate.
Control	Always a problem, but centralized control will work.	A worse problem—centralized control won't work; must walk a tightrope between overcentralizing and losing control through too much decentralizing.
Contracts	Once signed, are binding on both parties even if one party makes a bad deal.	Can be voided and renegotiated if one party becomes dissatisfied.
Labor relations	Collective bargaining; layoff of workers easy.	Layoff of workers often not possible; may have a mandatory worker participation in management; workers may seek change through political process rather than collective bargaining.

Source: Adapted from R. G. Murdick, R. C. Moor, R. H. Eckhouse, and T. W. Zimmerer, *Business Policy: A Framework for Analysis* (Columbus, Ohio: Grid, 1984), p. 275; as found in Pearce and Robinson, *Strategic Management: Formulation, Implementation, and Control*, 5th ed., © 1994 (Burr Ridge, Ill.: Richard D. Irwin, Inc. Reprinted with permission.

cies, and several languages. These and other differences are summarized in Table 10.1.

Components of an International Strategy

A firm's international strategies are developed within the context of its overall strategy, which encompasses both domestic and international operations. Regardless of whether a particular strategy focuses on domestic or international operations, however, it generally has four basic components. These components of any strategy are

▶ Scope of operations

▶ Resource deployment

▶ Distinctive competence

▶ Synergy[5]

Scope of Operations

The **scope of operations** answers the question "Where are we going to conduct business?" Scope may be defined in terms of geographical regions, such as countries, regions within a country, and/or clusters of countries. Or it may focus on market or product niches within one or more regions, such as the premium-quality market niche, the low-cost market niche, or other specialized market niches. Because all firms have finite resources and because markets differ in their relative attractiveness for various products, managers must decide which markets are most attractive to their firm.

For example, the geographical scope of Disney's theme park operations consists of the United States, Japan, and France, while the geographical scope of its movie distribution and merchandise sales operations is more than one hundred countries. In the semiconductor industry, most firms have chosen to limit the scope of their operations to specific product niches. Japanese semiconductor manufacturers such as NEC, Toshiba, and Hitachi have focused their efforts on producing standardized memory chips. U.S. and European semiconductor firms have found it difficult to compete against the Japanese in this market and so have altered the scopes of their operations. For example, California-based Intel focuses on producing microprocessors, such as the 486 and pentium chips that power most IBM-compatible personal computers. Siemens concentrates on chips that have automotive applications, and Philips specializes in the development of multimedia semiconductors, which bridge consumer electronics and computers.[6] Thus, strategic planning results in some international businesses choosing to compete in only a few markets, some to compete in many, and others (such as Disney) to vary their operations across the different types of business operations in which they are involved.

Resource Deployment

Resource deployment answers the question "Given that we are going to compete in these markets, how will we allocate our resources to them?" For example, even though Disney has theme park operations in three countries, the firm does not have an equal resource commitment to each market. Disney invested nothing in Tokyo Disneyland and limited its investment in Euro Disney to 49 percent. But it continues to invest heavily in its U.S. theme park operations and in filmed entertainment.

Resource deployment might be specified along product lines, geographical lines, or both. This part of strategic planning determines relative priorities for a firm's limited resources. For example, in 1989 Sony spent around $5 billion to buy Columbia Pictures. Sony already had a considerable presence in the U.S. market for its electronic products. It clearly could have found other uses for the $5 billion. However, its managers had decided to increase the firm's resource deployment along geographical lines in the United States. The relative strengths and weaknesses of Columbia, and the complementary nature of its products (entertainment "software") with Sony's product lines (entertainment "hardware"), fit within the parameters of the type of additional deployment Sony was seeking.

Some large MNCs choose to deploy their resources worldwide. For example, Osaka-based Sharp Corporation manufactures its electronic goods in 33 plants in 26 countries. Similarly, Hachette SA, a Paris-based media conglomerate that publishes such popular titles as *Car & Driver*, *Woman's Day*, *Elle* (U.S. and French versions), *France Dimanche*, and *Grolier* encyclopedia, controls 300 firms operating in 40 countries.

While many firms have chosen to deploy resources across a variety of countries, others have opted to focus their production in one. Boeing, the leading U.S. exporter, concentrates final assembly of commercial aircraft in the Seattle, Washington region. And Daimler-Benz concentrates production of Mercedes-Benz automobiles in Germany; even after its Alabama plant begins operations, nine out of ten Mercedes will still be German-built.[7] Although these firms have a global scope regarding the markets in which they buy materials and sell products, they have limited most of their production resource deployment to their home countries.

Distinctive Competence

Distinctive competence answers the question "What do we do exceptionally well, especially as compared to our competitors?" A firm's distinctive competence may be cutting-edge technology, efficient distribution networks, superior organizational practices, or well-respected brand names. Based on this distinctive competence, the firm attempts to develop a **sustainable competitive advantage**— an advantage over its competitors that can be maintained over time. For example, lowering prices is not likely to create a sustainable competitive advantage because competitors can usually lower their own prices in response. The Disney name, image, and portfolio of characters, however, comprise a sustainable competitive advantage that other firms cannot easily duplicate.

As our discussion of Dunning's eclectic theory in Chapter 3 suggested, a firm's possessing a distinctive competence (what Dunning called an ownership advantage) may be necessary for it to compete successfully outside its home market. Having developed a distinctive competence, a firm often then wants to exploit this advantage by expanding its operations into as many markets as its resources allow. To a large degree, the international strategies a firm adopts reflect the interplay between its distinctive competence and the business opportunities available to it in different countries.[8]

For example, Stuttgart-based Robert Bosch GMBH, the world's largest automotive electronic equipment supplier, was the first company to develop and sell electronic fuel injection and antilocking brake systems. This head start resulted in a distinctive competence that other firms have found difficult to match. Bosch still enjoys a 50 percent share of these lucrative markets, selling to automobile manufacturers in all six inhabited continents.[9] Similarly, Frankfurt's Glasbau Hahn constructs glass showcases with self-contained climate controls and fiber-optic lighting. Because the showcases are perceived to be the world's best, museums pay Glasbau Hahn as much as $100,000 for a case in which to display priceless art, sculpture, or artifacts. Exploiting its distinctive competence in this specialized market, Glasbau Hahn has built a $12 million international business.[10]

An international firm may have the same distinctive competence in every market or a unique distinctive competence in each market. Coca-Cola's distinctive competencies—its well-known brand name and product image—are the same worldwide. In contrast, Foster's Brewing Group, Ltd., sells traditional lager beers in Australia, stout and bitter beers in the United Kingdom, and milder beers in North America, thus employing a different distinctive competence in each market. Foster's has still other distinctive competencies in other markets, such as wool production in Scotland and investment and property management in Australia.

Synergy

Synergy answers the question "How can different elements of our business benefit each other?" Sony found Columbia Pictures an attractive investment in part because it believed it could use the film studio's video library to help with international sales of Sony electronic video products. For example, by making available a large library of Columbia movies in 8mm format, it can spur sales of its Sony 8mm video players. But the world's expert in utilizing synergy is Disney. People know the Disney characters from television, so they plan vacations to Disney theme parks, see new Disney movies, and buy merchandise featuring Disney characters. "Going Global" details Disney's exploitation of synergy opportunities associated with the worldwide success of *Aladdin*.

Developing International Strategies

Developing international strategies is not a one-dimensional process. In fact, firms generally carry out international strategic management in two broad stages. These stages into which international strategic management is divided are strategy formulation and strategy implementation:

1 In *strategy formulation*, the firm establishes its goals and the strategic plan that will lead to the achievement of those goals. In international strategy formulation, managers develop, refine, and agree on which markets to enter (or exit) and how best to compete in each. Much of what we discuss in the rest of this chapter and in the next two chapters primarily concerns international strategy formulation.

2 In *strategy implementation*, the firm develops the tactics for achieving the formulated international strategies. Disney's decisions to build Euro Disney and to build it in France were part of strategy formulation. But deciding which attractions to include, when to open, and what to charge for admission is part of strategy implementation. In essence, strategy formulation is deciding what to do and strategy implementation is actually doing it. Strategy implementation is usually achieved via the organization's design, the work of its employees, and its control systems and processes. Chapters 13 through 15 deal primarily with implementation issues.

With this distinction in mind, we now turn to the actual steps managers use to formulate an international strategy. These steps, shown in Fig. 10.1, are as follows:

1 Develop a mission statement.

2 Analyze the firm and its environment to determine its strengths, weaknesses, opportunities, and threats (called a **SWOT analysis**).

GOING GLOBAL

Disney Is Synergy

1993 was "The Year of *Aladdin*" for The Walt Disney Company ... for millions of reasons.

If *Aladdin* had *only* been the animated motion-picture hit that it was ... and nothing else, it would have been wildly successful. The film ultimately earned $218 million at the box office in the United States and $100 million through year-end internationally, where it is still in distribution.

But because one plus one often equals three at The Walt Disney Company, *Aladdin* became a great deal more than a hit movie.

People didn't just want to *see* the movie. They wanted to read it, wear it, listen to it and play with it ... and Disney's many operating units made those things happen.

To meet this demand, Disney Consumer Products licensed a full line of books, apparel, recordings and toys that, more than a year after the release of the movie, are still selling briskly. During 1993, *Aladdin* merchandise provided the largest percentage of The Disney Stores' total business. To date, more than 4000 *Aladdin* products have been created worldwide.

Subscribers to The Disney Channel got an insider's look at the film, thanks to a 30-minute special on the making of *Aladdin*. The channel also broadcast segments that promoted the film between its regularly scheduled shows....

Soon after the movie came out, a new *Aladdin* parade was unveiled at the Disney–MGM Studios and at Disneyland. Then, in July, Aladdin's Oasis opened at Disneyland. This is a popular new restaurant and stage show in Adventureland themed after the movie....

On Oct. 1, *Aladdin* was released on home video. After its first weekend release, it had sold an astounding 10.6 million units. By November more than 20 million units had been sold. ...

Original artwork from the film was auctioned by Sotheby's for more than $1.35 million.... For the more budget conscious, limited-edition seriograph images reproducing scenes from the film were sold at The Disney Stores, the parks and through a network of Preferred Galleries.

In October, the *Aladdin* video game for Sega Genesis was released. This landmark event marked the first time that Disney was an active partner in the creation of a video game....

In the fall of 1994, *Aladdin* will return as the newest entry in *The Disney Afternoon*....

All of this synergistic interaction is possible because The Walt Disney Company continues to focus on entertainment, the common thread that weaves through all of Disney's far-flung enterprises. As a result, opportunities constantly arise in one area of the company that in turn ignite additional opportunities in other areas. This is why one plus one will continue to equal at least three as Disney maintains its leadership in worldwide entertainment.

Source: The Walt Disney Company, *Annual Report 1993*, pp. 18–19.

3 Set strategic goals.

4 Develop tactical goals and plans.

5 Develop a strategic control framework.

Mission Statement

Firms may use a mission statement as the starting point for their international strategic planning process or develop one after the process is complete. A **mission statement** defines the firm's values, purpose, and directions. Most firms that develop a mission statement also commit it to writing, thus allowing them to use the statement as a way of communicating with external constituents and of ensuring employees fully understand corporate goals. Other firms do not write down

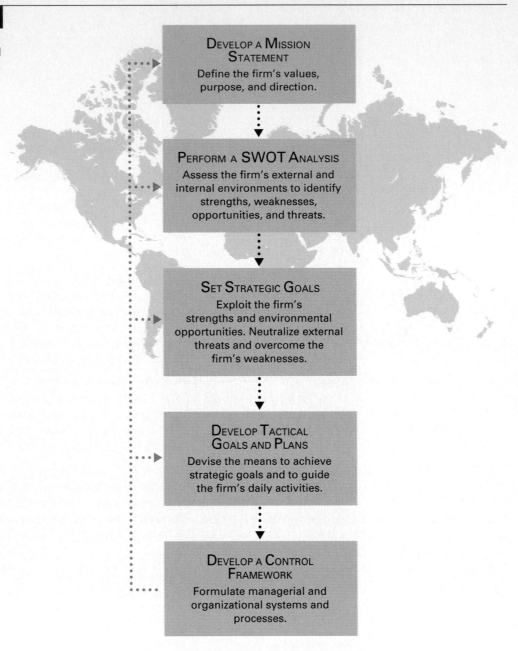

FIGURE 10.1

Steps in International Strategy Formulation

DEVELOP A MISSION STATEMENT
Define the firm's values, purpose, and direction.

PERFORM A SWOT ANALYSIS
Assess the firm's external and internal environments to identify strengths, weaknesses, opportunities, and threats.

SET STRATEGIC GOALS
Exploit the firm's strengths and environmental opportunities. Neutralize external threats and overcome the firm's weaknesses.

DEVELOP TACTICAL GOALS AND PLANS
Devise the means to achieve strategic goals and to guide the firm's daily activities.

DEVELOP A CONTROL FRAMEWORK
Formulate managerial and organizational systems and processes.

their mission statement, preferring instead to rely on informal understanding and the firm's culture to keep employees properly focused.

Most mission statements, which many firms include in their annual reports, specify some or all of the following for the firm:

► Target customers and markets
► Principal products or services
► Geographical domain
► Core technologies
► Concerns for survival

► Plans for growth and profitability
► Basic philosophy
► Desired public image[11]

For example, the mission statement of Hershey Foods includes the goal of being the "No. 1 confectionery company in North America, moving toward worldwide confectionery market share leadership," and MCI specifies its mission as including "leadership in the global telecommunications service industry." MNCs may have multiple mission statements, one for the overall firm, as well as one for each of its various foreign subsidiaries. Of course, a firm that has multiple mission statements must ensure that they are compatible.

Environmental Scanning and the SWOT Analysis

The second step in developing a strategy is conducting a SWOT analysis. SWOT is an acronym for "Strengths, Weaknesses, Opportunities, and Threats." The firm identifies these through the process of environmental scanning. Environmental scanning involves the systematic collection of data about all elements of the firm's external and internal environments, including data about markets, regulatory issues, competitors' actions, production costs, and labor productivity.

When members of a planning staff scan the external environment, they try to identify both *opportunities* (the O in SWOT) and *threats* (the T in SWOT) confronting the firm. They obtain data about economic, financial, political, legal, social, and competitive changes in the various markets the firm serves or might want to serve. (Such data are also used for political risk analysis, discussed in Chapter 8, as well as the country market analysis discussed in Chapter 16.) For example, Boeing continuously monitors changes in political and economic forces that affect air travel. In China, political shifts in the early 1990s to allow more competition in the air travel market led the government to split the giant state-owned carrier CAAC into competing regional carriers and to allow Hong Kong's Cathay Pacific airline to offer air travel within China. Boeing's environmental scanning suggested that booming demand for air travel would make the Chinese market a particularly appealing opportunity. Accordingly, the firm chose to locate a new sales office in Beijing. So far, the move has paid off: in 1994, one out of every seven jets sold by Boeing was to China.

Disney's decision to build Euro Disney was also the result of environmental scanning that suggested that many Europeans were interested in the sort of vacation opportunities the firm provides. Bayerische Motoren Werke (BMW), the manufacturer of BMW cars and motorcycles, has taken advantage of such external factors as a weak U.S. dollar, low U.S. labor costs, and NAFTA to build a new automobile assembly plant in Spartanburg, South Carolina.

External environmental scanning also yields data about environmental threats to the firm, such as shrinking markets, increasing competition, the potential of new government regulation, political instability in key markets, and the development of new technologies that could make the firm's manufacturing facilities or product lines obsolete. Threats to Disney include increased competition in the U.S. market from Universal Studios, Six Flags, and other theme parks, potential competition in Europe from theme parks there, potential French resentment of

U.S. intrusion in France, and fluctuating exchange rates. Threats to BMW include changing U.S. automobile fuel-efficiency standards, a crowded luxury car market, and the rising value of the deutsche mark in the foreign-exchange market. The threats Federal Express faces include not only competition in the international express package delivery market from firms such as DHL Worldwide and TNT, but also the rapidly growing usage of fax machines to send messages internationally.

In conducting a SWOT analysis, a firm's strategic managers must also assess the firm's internal environment, that is, its *strengths* and *weaknesses* (the S and W in SWOT). Organizational strengths are skills, resources, and other advantages the firm possesses relative to its competitors. Potential strengths, which form the basis of a firm's distinctive competence, might include an abundance of managerial talent, cutting-edge technology, well-known brand names, surplus cash, a good public image, and strong market shares in key countries. Disney's strengths include low corporate debt and the international appeal of its characters. BMW's strengths include its skilled workforce, innovative engineers, and reputation for producing high-quality automobiles.

A firm that is formulating strategic plans also needs to acknowledge its organizational weaknesses. These weaknesses reflect deficiencies or shortcomings in skills, resources, or other factors that hinder the firm's competitiveness. They may include poor distribution networks outside the home market, poor labor relations, a lack of skilled international managers, or product development efforts that lag behind competitors'. Disney's organizational weaknesses regarding Euro Disney include high capital costs, negative publicity, and underutilized hotel capacity. BMW's weaknesses include its extremely high domestic labor costs, which make it difficult for it to compete on the basis of price.

One technique for assessing a firm's strengths and weaknesses is the value chain. Developed by Harvard Business School Professor Michael Porter in 1985, the **value chain** is a breakdown of the firm into its important activities—production, marketing, human resource management, and so forth—to enable its strategists to identify its competitive advantages and disadvantages. Each primary and support activity depicted in Fig. 10.2 can be a source of an organizational strength (distinctive competence) or weakness. For example, the quality of Caterpillar's

---

FIGURE 10.2

The Value Chain

Source: Adapted with the permission of The Free Press, a Division of Simon & Schuster, from *Competitive Advantage: Creating and Sustaining Superior Performance,* by Michael E. Porter. Copyright © 1985 by Michael E. Porter.

Primary activities →

| Manufacturing | Marketing & Sales | Service |

Company Infrastructure

Information Systems

Human Resources

Research & Development

Sourcing & Logistics

↑ Support activities

products (Research and Development in the figure) and the strength of its worldwide dealership network (Marketing, Sales and Service in the figure) are among its organizational strengths, but poor labor relations (Human Resources in the figure) represent one of its organizational weaknesses.

Managers use information derived from the SWOT analysis to develop specific effective strategies. Effective strategies are ones that exploit environmental opportunities and organizational strengths, neutralize environmental threats, and protect or overcome organizational weaknesses. For example, BMW's decision to build automobiles in South Carolina took advantage of its strong brand image in the United States. This decision also neutralized the firm's internal weakness of high German labor costs and its vulnerability to loss of U.S. customers due to the increasing value of the deutsche mark relative to the U.S. dollar.

Strategic Goals

With the mission statement and SWOT analysis as context, international strategic planning is largely framed by the setting of strategic goals. **Strategic goals** are the major objectives the firm wants to accomplish through pursuing a particular course of action. By definition, they should be measurable, feasible, and time-limited (answering the questions "how much, how, and by when?"). For example, Disney set strategic goals for Euro Disney for projected attendance, revenues, and so on. But, as the Scottish poet Robert Burns noted, "the best laid plans of mice and men" often go awry. Part of the park's resultant problems arose from the firm's goals not being met. Disney's strategic managers had to revise the firm's strategic plan and goals, taking into account the new information painfully learned from the first years of the park's unprofitable operation.

Another example is provided by Playmates, the Hong Kong toymaker best known for its line of Teenage Mutant Ninja Turtle action figures. Playmates manufactures most of its toys in China but derives 84 percent of its sales from the United States. As part of a recent SWOT analysis, the firm identified this dependence on U.S. sales as a threat. It feared political conflict between China and the United States might lead the U.S. government to revoke most favored nation (MFN) status for China, thereby raising U.S. tariffs on Chinese manufactured goods and hurting Playmate's U.S. profit margins. Therefore, Playmates established the strategic goal of increasing its penetration of the European toy market. It did so by buying 35 percent of the common stock of Ideal Loisirs, France's leading toymaker and the owner of licensing rights to Babar, the famous Parisian-educated pachyderm.[12]

Tactics

As shown in Fig. 10.1, after a SWOT analysis is performed and strategic goals are set, the next step in strategic planning is to develop specific tactical goals and plans, or **tactics**. Tactics usually involve middle managers and focus on the details of how to implement strategic plans. For example, when Sony decided to acquire CBS Records, its middle managers were assigned tactical duties to help facilitate the financing arrangements and to integrate managers at CBS Records into Sony's corporate structure. Other tactics were developed to help guide the day-to-day activities and processes of CBS Records. For example, accountants at

CBS Records had to learn Sony's financial control system and reporting requirements. Disney develops tactical plans for designing, constructing, and promoting new attractions at each of its theme parks.

Control Framework

A final aspect of strategy formulation is the development of a control framework. A **control framework** is the managerial and organizational processes used to keep the firm on target toward its strategic goals. For example, Euro Disney had a first-year attendance goal of 12 million visitors. When it became apparent that this goal would not be met, the firm increased its advertising to help boost attendance and temporarily closed one of its hotels to cut costs. Had attendance been running ahead of the goal, the firm might have decreased advertising and extended its operating hours. Each set of responses stems from the control framework established to keep the firm on course. As shown by Fig. 10.1's feedback loops, the control framework can prompt revisions in any of the preceding steps in the strategy formulation process. We discuss control frameworks more fully in Chapter 15.

Levels of International Strategy

Given the complexities of international strategic management, many international businesses—especially MNCs—find it useful to develop strategies for three distinct levels within the organization. These levels of international strategy, illustrated in Fig. 10.3, are

▶ Corporate
▶ Business
▶ Functional[13]

Corporate Strategy

Corporate strategy attempts to define the domain of businesses the firm intends to operate. Consider three Japanese electronics firms: Sony competes in the global market for consumer electronics and entertainment but has not broadened its scope into home and kitchen appliances. Matsushita competes in all these industries. Pioneer Electronic Corporation focuses on electronic audio and video products. Each firm has answered quite differently the question of what constitutes its business domain. The divergent activities of each firm reflect their differing corporate strengths and weaknesses, as well as their differing assessments of the opportunities and threats produced by the global economic and political environments.

A firm might adopt any of three forms of corporate strategy:

1 Single-business
2 Related diversification
3 Unrelated diversification

FIGURE 10.3

Three Levels of
Strategy for MNCs

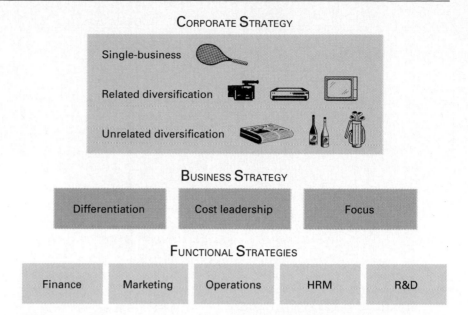

The Single-Business Strategy. The **single-business strategy** calls for a firm to rely on a single business, product, or service for all its revenue. The most significant advantage of this strategy is that the firm can concentrate all its resources and expertise on that one product or service. However, this strategy also increases the firm's vulnerability to its competition and to changes in the external environment. For example, for a firm producing only phonograph players, a new innovation such as the CD player makes the firm's single product obsolete, and the firm may be unable to develop new products quickly enough to survive.[14]

Marks and Spencer PLC, the British department store chain, pursues a single-business strategy. It concentrates on providing high-quality merchandise at moderate prices. The firm has reduced its vulnerability to changes in its environment by expanding beyond its home base. It purchased several retail operations in Canada and the United States in the 1970s and 1980s. It also capitalized on the emerging European market by launching new stores in Belgium, France, the Netherlands, and Spain.[15]

Related Diversification. **Related diversification**, the most common corporate strategy, calls for the firm to operate in several different businesses, industries, or markets at the same time. However, the operations are related to each other in some fundamental way. This strategy allows the firm to leverage a distinctive competence in one market in order to strengthen its competitiveness in others. The goal of related diversification and the basic relationship linking various operations are often defined in the firm's mission statement.[16]

Disney uses the related diversification strategy. Each of its operations (theme parks, filmed entertainment, and consumer products) are linked to the others via Disney characters, the Disney logo, a theme of wholesomeness, and a reputation for providing high-quality family entertainment. Disney movies and TV shows help sell Disney theme parks, which in turn help sell Disney merchandise. Accor SA, the world's second-largest hotel operator, also uses a related diversification strategy. Originally the operator of a chain restaurant, this Paris-based firm began

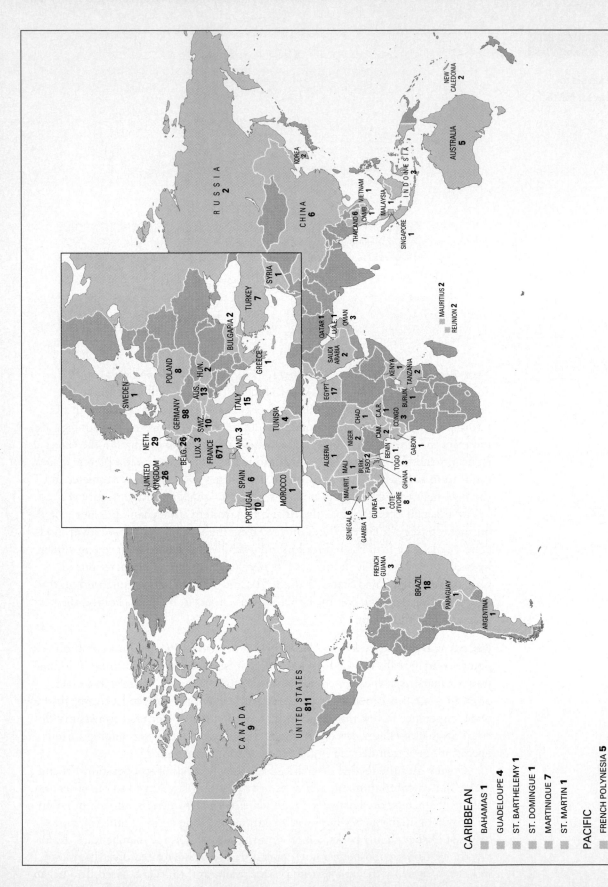

MAP 10.1   **Accor's Worldwide Chain of Hotels**

acquiring luxury hotel chains such as Sofitel and budget chains such as Motel 6 (see Map 10.1). To keep its dining rooms and hotel beds full, Accor then branched out into the package tour business. To promote tourism, the firm even opened its own theme park north of Paris based on the French cartoon character Asterix the Gaul.[17] Sony, too, uses the related diversification strategy, apparent in the interrelationships among the firm's consumer electronics (such as 8mm video players) and entertainment products (movies that can be sold in 8mm format).

Related diversification has several advantages. First, the firm depends less on a single product or service, so it is less vulnerable to competitive or economic threats. For example, if Disney faces increased competition in the theme park business, its movie, television, publishing, and licensing divisions can offset potential declines in theme park revenues. Moreover, these related businesses may make it more difficult for an outsider to compete with Disney in the first place. For example, non-Disney animated movies aimed at children, such as *We're Back* and *Thumbelina*, have trouble competing against new animated releases from the Disney Studios. Makers of these movies must buy advertising at commercial rates, while Disney can inexpensively promote its new releases to families waiting in line at its theme parks and to viewers of shows on the Disney Channel. Similar problems confront rival theme park operators, who have to contend with the constant exposure that Disney's theme parks receive on network television and the Disney Channel and on T-shirts and caps worn by kids of all ages worldwide.

Second, related diversification may produce economies of scale for a firm. For example, The Limited, Inc., takes advantage of its vast size to buy new clothing lines at favorable prices from Far Eastern manufacturers and then divides the purchases among its Limited, Express, and Lerner divisions.

Third, related diversification may allow a firm to use technology or expertise developed in one market to enter a second market more cheaply and easily. For example, Pirelli SpA used its expertise in producing rubber products and insulated cables, refined over 100 years ago, to become the world's fifth largest producer of automobile tires. More recently, Casio Computer Company transferred the knowledge it gained in making hand-held electric calculators in the 1970s to the production of inexpensive electronic digital watches, musical synthesizers, and pocket televisions. Such potential synergies are a major advantage of the related diversification strategy.

One potential disadvantage of related diversification is the cost of coordinating the operations of the related divisions. A second is the possibility that all the firm's business units may be affected simultaneously by changes in economic conditions. For example, Accor can create synergies by steering travel customers to its hotels and restaurants. Yet all of Accor's divisions are vulnerable to a downturn in tourism. If another oil crisis erupts or an increase in terrorist actions keeps travelers at home, all Accor businesses will suffer.

Unrelated Diversification. A third corporate strategy international businesses may use is **unrelated diversification**, whereby a firm operates in several unrelated industries and markets. For example, General Electric (GE) owns such diverse, and unrelated, business units as a television network (NBC), a lighting manufacturer, a medical technology firm, an aircraft engine producer, a semiconductor manufacturer, and an investment bank.

During the 1960s, unrelated diversification was the most popular investment strategy. Many large firms, such as ITT, Gulf and Western, LTV, and

Textron became **conglomerates**, the term used for firms comprising unrelated businesses. The unrelated diversification strategy yields several benefits. First, the corporate parent may be able to raise capital more easily than any of its independent units can separately. The parent can then allocate this capital to the most profitable opportunities available among its subsidiaries. Second, overall riskiness may be reduced because a firm is less subject to business cycle fluctuations. For example, temporary difficulties facing Gulf and Western's sugar plantations might be offset by a hit movie produced by its movie studio. Third, a firm is less vulnerable to competitive threats, since any given threat is likely to affect only a portion of the firm's total operations. Fourth, a firm can more easily shed unprofitable operations because they are independent. It also can buy new operations without worrying about how to integrate them into existing businesses.

Nonetheless, the creation of conglomerates through the unrelated diversification strategy is out of favor today primarily because of the lack of potential synergy across unrelated businesses. Since the businesses are unrelated, any one operation cannot regularly sustain or enhance the others. For example, GE managers cannot use any of the competitive advantages they may have developed in the lighting business to help offset low ratings at the firm's television network. Further, it is difficult for staff at corporate headquarters to effectively manage diverse businesses because it must understand a much wider array of businesses and markets than if operations are related. This complicates the performance monitoring of individual operations.

Business Strategy

Whereas corporate strategy deals with the overall organization, business strategy focuses on specific businesses, subsidiaries, or operating units within the firm. Business strategy seeks to answer the question "How should we compete in each market we have chosen to enter?"

Firms that pursue corporate strategies of related diversification or unrelated diversification tend to bundle sets of businesses together into **strategic business units (SBUs)**. In firms that follow the related diversification strategy, the products and services of each SBU are somewhat similar to each other. For example, Disney defines its SBUs as Theme Parks and Resorts, Filmed Entertainment, and Consumer Products. In firms that follow unrelated diversification strategies, products and services of each SBU are dissimilar. For example, Westinghouse Electric Corporation organizes its businesses into the following SBUs: Broadcasting, Electronic Systems, Financial Services, Environmental Systems, Industries, The Knoll Group, and Power Systems. As these names suggest, the businesses are relatively unrelated (electronics, financing, the environment, and so forth).

By focusing on the competitive environment of each business or SBU, business strategy helps the firm improve its distinctive competence for that business or unit. Once a firm selects a business strategy for an SBU, it typically uses that strategy in all geographical markets the SBU serves. The firm may develop a unique business strategy for each of its SBUs, or it may pursue the same business strategy for all of them. The three basic forms of business strategy are

1 Differentiation

2 Overall cost leadership

3 Focus

Differentiation. Differentiation strategy is the most commonly used business strategy. It attempts to establish and maintain the image (either real or perceived) that the SBU's products or services are fundamentally unique from other products or services in the same market segment. Many international businesses today are attempting to use quality as a differentiating factor. If successful at establishing a high-quality image, they can charge higher prices for their products or services. For example, Rolex sells its timepieces worldwide for premium prices. The firm limits its sales agreements to only a few dealers in any given area, stresses quality and status in its advertising, and seldom discounts its products. Other international firms that use the differentiation strategy effectively include Coca-Cola (soft drinks), Nikon (cameras), Calvin Klein (fashion apparel), and Waterford Wedgewood (fine china and glassware).

Other firms adopt value as their differentiating factor. They compete on the basis of charging reasonable prices for quality goods and services. Marks and Spencer has used the value factor to thrive in the department store market in the United Kingdom. Lands' End, a Wisconsin mail-order clothing seller, has also used this differentiation strategy to grow into a $750 million firm. It is establishing operations in the United Kingdom, as a test of whether its domestic mail-order strategy will succeed internationally. Ironically, this effort may put Marks and Spencer and Lands' End in direct competition with each other, with each stressing the value factor. The differentiation factor they may have to switch to then is distribution mode—catalog versus retail outlet sales.

Overall Cost Leadership. The **overall cost leadership strategy** calls for a firm to focus on achieving highly efficient operating procedures so that its costs are lower than its competitors'. This allows it to sell its goods or services for lower prices. A successful overall cost leadership strategy may result in lower levels of unit profitability due to lower prices but higher total profitability due to increased sales volume. For example, France's Bic Pen Company makes approximately 3 million pens every day. By concentrating on making those pens as cheaply as possible, the firm is able to sell them for a very low price. Taken together, volume production and a worldwide distribution network have allowed Bic to flourish. Other firms that use this strategy are Timex (watches), Fuji (film), Hyundai (automobiles), the Lucky-Goldstar Group (consumer electronics), and NEC (semiconductors).

Focus. A **focus strategy** calls for a firm to target specific types of products for certain customer groups or regions. Doing this allows the firm to match the features of specific products to the needs of specific consumer groups. These groups might be differentiated by geographical region, ethnicity, purchasing power, tastes in fashion, or any other characteristic that influences their purchasing patterns. For example, Cadbury Schweppes PLC markets Hires Root Beer only in the United States because root beer does not appeal to people elsewhere. In other countries, Cadbury sells other flavors of soft drinks, including Solo (mixed-fruit–flavored) and Trina (grapefruit-flavored), that do not appeal to U.S. consumers. Honda sells Accord station wagons only in the United States because U.S. consumers like station wagons more than do consumers in other countries. It concentrates on selling its low-priced Civic in less-developed countries because consumers there have less discretionary income and emphasizes its faster Prelude in Europe because highways there tend to have higher speed limits. Sony's business strategy for its Consumer Electronics SBU focuses on continually upgrading and refining the products through extensive R&D while maintaining its reputation for producing high-quality products.

Disney has different business strategies for each of its SBUs. For its Theme Parks and Resorts SBU, strategies include making the businesses comprehensive destination resorts, stressing quality and cleanliness, and continually upgrading and adding to them. For its Filmed Entertainment SBU, strategies include targeting children with movies with the Buena Vista imprint and adults with the Touchstone and Hollywood Pictures imprints and making at least one new animated movie per year. Its Consumer Products SBU follows the strategy of producing high-quality products based on popular Disney characters in a variety of price groups.

Functional Strategies

Functional strategies attempt to answer the question "How will we manage the functions of finance, marketing, operations, human resources, and research and development (R&D) in ways consistent with our international corporate and business strategies?" We briefly introduce each common functional strategy here, but leave more detailed discussion to later chapters.

International *financial* strategy deals with such issues as the firm's desired capital structure, investment policies, foreign-exchange holdings, risk-reduction techniques, debt policies, and working-capital management. Typically, an international business develops a financial strategy for the overall firm as well as for each SBU. We cover international financial strategy more fully in Chapter 18.

International *marketing* strategy concerns the distribution and selling of the firm's products or services. It addresses questions of product mix, advertising, promotion, pricing, and distribution. International marketing strategy is the subject of Chapter 16.

International *operations* strategy deals with the creation of the firm's products or services. It guides decisions on such issues as sourcing, plant location, plant layout and design, technology, and inventory management. We return to international operations management in Chapter 17.

International *human resource* strategy focuses on the people who work for an organization. It guides decisions regarding how the firm will recruit, train, and evaluate employees and what it will pay them, as well as how it will deal with labor relations. International human resource strategy is the subject of Chapter 20.

Finally, a firm's international *R&D* strategy is concerned with the magnitude and direction of the firm's investment in creating new products and developing new technologies.

Foreign Market Analysis

Regardless of their strategies, most international businesses have the fundamental goals of expanding market share, revenues, and profits. They often achieve these goals by entering new markets or by introducing new products into markets in which they already have a presence. A firm's ability to do this effectively hinges on its developing a thorough understanding of a given geographical or product market. Thus, to successfully increase market share, revenue, and profits, firms must follow these steps:

▶ Assess alternative markets
▶ Evaluate the respective costs, benefits, and risks of entering each
▶ Select those that hold the most potential for entry or expansion

Assessing Alternative Foreign Markets

In assessing alternative foreign markets, a firm must consider a variety of factors, including

▶ Market potential
▶ Levels of competition
▶ Legal and political environments
▶ Sociocultural influences[18]

Table 10.2 summarizes some of the most critical of these factors.

Information on some of these factors is relatively objective and easy to obtain. For example, a country's currency stability is important to a firm contemplating exporting to or importing from that country or analyzing investment opportunities there. Information about this topic can be objectively assessed and can be easily obtained from various published sources in the firm's home country. Other information about foreign markets is much more subjective and may be quite difficult to obtain. For example, information on the role of local government officials in setting tax rates and providing utility permits may be very hard to acquire in the firm's home country. Obtaining such information often entails visiting the foreign location early in the decision-making process to talk to local experts, such as embassy staff and chamber of commerce officials, or contracting with a consulting firm to obtain the needed data.[19]

Market Potential. The first step in foreign market selection is assessing market potential. Many publications, such as those listed in "Building Global Skills" in Chapter 2, provide data on population, GDP, per capita GDP, public infrastructure, and ownership of such goods as automobiles and televisions. Such data permit firms to conduct a preliminary, "quick and dirty" screening of various foreign markets. If the population is highly concentrated in urban areas, has strong purchasing power, and shows high usage of products such as automobiles and televisions, the market may be highly attractive to a firm selling consumer goods such as stereo equipment. But if most of the country's population is rural, has weak purchasing power, and purchases few consumer durables, the market may be much more attractive to a manufacturer of low-cost farm tools and equipment than to stereo equipment manufacturers. The firm must also consider the positioning of its products relative to those of its competitors. A firm producing high-quality products at premium prices will find richer markets attractive but may have more difficulty penetrating a poorer market. Conversely, a firm specializing

TABLE 10.2

Critical Factors in Assessing New Market Opportunities

TOPIC OF APPRAISAL	ITEMS TO BE CONSIDERED
Product-market dimensions	How big is the product market in terms of unit size and sales volume?
Major product-market "differences"	What are the major differences relative to the firm's experience elsewhere in terms of customer profiles, price levels, national purchase patterns, and product technology?
	How will these differences affect the transferability of the firm's capabilities to the new business environment and their effectiveness?
Structural characteristics of the national product market	What links and associations exist between potential customers and established national competitors currently supplying these customers?
	What are the major channels of distribution (discount structure, ties to present producers, levels of distribution separating producers from final customers, links between wholesalers, links between wholesalers and retailers, finance, role of government)?
	What links exist between established producers and their suppliers?
	Do industry concentration and collusive agreements exist?
Competitor analysis	What are major competitor characteristics (size, capacity utilization, strengths and weaknesses, technology, supply sources, preferential market arrangements, and relations with the government)?
	What is competitor performance in terms of market share, sales growth, and profit margins?
Potential target markets	What are the characteristics of major product-market segments?
	Which segments are potential targets upon entry?
Relevant trends (historic and projected)	What changes have occurred in total size of product-market (short-, medium-, and long-term)?
	What changes have occurred in competitor performance (market share, sales, and profits)?
	What is the nature of competition (e.g., national or international)?
	What changes have occurred in market structure?
Explanation of change	Why are some firms gaining and others losing?
	Are foreign firms already operating here gaining or losing?
	Is there some general explanation of observed change, for example, product life cycle, change in overall business activity, and shift in nature of demand?
	What is the future outlook?
Success factors	What are the key factors behind success in this business environment, the pressure points that can shift market share from one firm to another?
	How are these different from those we have experienced in other countries?
	How do these success factors relate to our firm?
Strategic options	What elements emerge from the above analysis which point to possible strategies for this country?
	What additional information is required to identify our options more precisely?

Source: Reprinted with the permission of Lexington Books, an imprint of The Free Press, a Division of Simon & Schuster, from *Multinational Corporate Strategy: Planning for World Markets* by James C. Leontiades. Copyright © 1985 by Lexington Books.

in low-priced, lower-quality goods may find the poorer market even more lucrative than the richer market.[20]

A firm must then collect data relevant to the specific product line under consideration. For example, if Pirelli SpA is contemplating exporting tires to Thailand, its strategic managers must collect data about that country's transportation infrastructure, transportation alternatives, gasoline prices, and growth of vehicle ownership. Pirelli would also need data on the average age of motor vehicles and the ratio of new car prices to used car prices in order to assess whether to focus its marketing efforts on the replacement market or the OEM (original equipment manufacturer) market. In some situations, a firm may have to resort to using proxy data. For example, Whirlpool, in deciding whether to enter the dishwasher market in South Korea, could examine sales of other household appliances, per capita electricity consumption, or the number of two-income families.

But such data reflect the past, not the future. Firms must also consider the potential for growth in a country's economy by using both objective and subjective measures. Objective measures include changes in per capita income, energy consumption, GDP, and ownership of consumer durables such as private automobiles. More subjective considerations must also be taken into account when assessing potential growth. For example, following the collapse of communist economies in Central and Eastern Europe, many Western firms ignored the data indicating negative economic growth in these countries. Instead they have focused on the prospects for future growth as these countries adopt new economic policies and programs. As a result, firms such as P&G and Unilever are establishing production facilities, distribution channels, and brand recognition in order to seize first-mover advantages when these economies recover.

Map 10.2 highlights just a few of the market differences between China and Luxembourg—one of the world's largest countries and one of the smallest. A firm attempting to sell its products in each of these markets would clearly have a very different set of considerations to address for each.

Levels of Competition. Another factor a firm must consider in foreign market selection is the level of competition in the market—both the current level and the likely future level. As the marketplace becomes more global, noncompetitive markets are becoming increasingly rare. Shortly after Euro Disney opened, MCA announced plans to build a Universal Studios theme park in Europe, probably close to the Disney site. Disney had expected that this might occur, but the firm's managers no doubt believed that its head start, combined with the power of the Disney name, would put it in such a strong position that MCA's effort would not be a serious threat.

For a firm to assess its competitive environment, it should identify the number and sizes of firms already competing in the potential market, their relative market shares, their pricing and distribution strategies, and their relative strengths and weaknesses, both individually and collectively. It must then weigh these factors against actual market conditions. For example, a small market already characterized by severe competition may not be able to sustain new competitors. However, a market that is large and prosperous may still hold opportunities for new firms, particularly if they can identify underserved market niches to exploit. For example, the poor-quality image of U.S.-made small cars in the 1970s made GM, Ford, and Chrysler vulnerable to a competitor such as Honda that offered a product of superior quality. Honda's successful entry into the U.S. automobile market was based on its exploiting this vulnerability by offering a high-quality product at a low cost. However, a foreign automaker entering the U.S. market today would be faced with enormous competition not only from the three dominant U.S. automakers but also from such well-entrenched Japanese and European firms as Toyota, Nissan, and BMW.

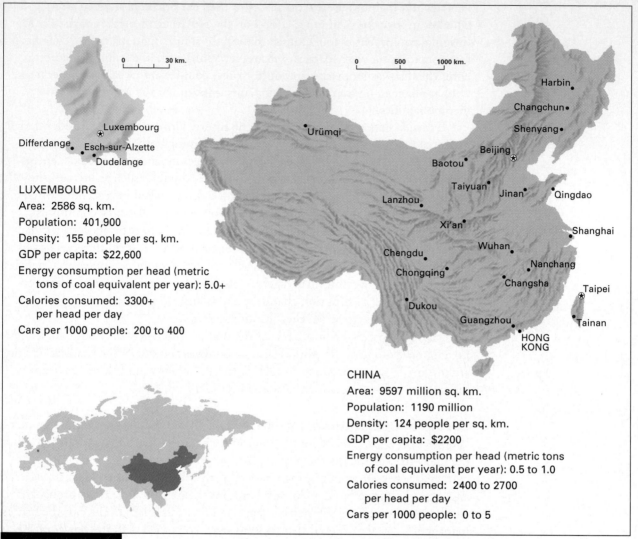

LUXEMBOURG

Area: 2586 sq. km.

Population: 401,900

Density: 155 people per sq. km.

GDP per capita: $22,600

Energy consumption per head (metric tons of coal equivalent per year): 5.0+

Calories consumed: 3300+ per head per day

Cars per 1000 people: 200 to 400

CHINA

Area: 9597 million sq. km.

Population: 1190 million

Density: 124 people per sq. km.

GDP per capita: $2200

Energy consumption per head (metric tons of coal equivalent per year): 0.5 to 1.0

Calories consumed: 2400 to 2700 per head per day

Cars per 1000 people: 0 to 5

MAP 10.2

Differences between a Large and a Small Market

Most successful firms continually monitor major markets in order to exploit opportunities as they become available. In the early 1990s, for example, many U.S. banks reduced their domestic lending activities because of increased regulatory scrutiny of their lending practices. At the same time, major Japanese banks decreased their presence in the U.S. market because of financial problems caused by the collapse of the speculative Japanese land and stock markets. Deutsche Bank, Germany's largest financial services firm, took advantage of this temporary weakness in the competition to increase its corporate lending activities in the United States beginning in 1992. Deutsche Bank's North American branch currently controls $14 billion in assets and employs 1200 people in the United States.[21] Similarly, liberalization of the European telecommunications market resulting from EC '92 has attracted investments by AT&T, MCI, Sprint, and other firms.

Legal and Political Environment. A firm contemplating entry into a particular market also needs to understand the host country's trade policies and its general legal and political environments, which we discussed in Chapters 6 and 8.[22]

For example, a firm may choose to forgo exporting its goods to a country that has high tariffs and other trade restrictions in favor of exporting to one that has fewer or less significant barriers.[23] Conversely, trade barriers may induce a firm to enter a market via FDI. For example, one reason Japanese automakers built plants in the United States in the 1980s was to bypass trade barriers on foreign-built motor vehicles.

Other legal and political issues relate to ownership. Some countries require foreign firms wanting to establish local operations to work with a local joint-venture partner; this requirement may reduce the attractiveness of such a strategy. Barriers to the repatriation of profits may also limit the appeal of operating local production facilities.

Tax policies are also important. Some countries tax foreign firms at a higher rate than they do domestic firms. Others, wanting to promote domestic economic development, are willing to offer economic incentives to firms to locate within their borders. For example, the state of Kentucky offered Toyota $125 million in free land as well as road and other improvements in order to induce the firm to locate a new factory in Georgetown, Kentucky. The government of Austria offered a similar set of incentives to persuade Chrysler to build a mini-van factory within its borders.

Government stability is also an important factor in foreign market assessment, as our discussion of political risk analysis in Chapter 8 indicated. Governmental transitions in countries such as the United States are relatively smooth, so stability is not an issue. But in some less-developed countries prone to military coups and similar disruptions, it is a serious problem. Government regulation of pricing and promotional activities also creates important legal and political issues to consider. For example, the U.S. government restricts advertising for tobacco and alcohol products, so foreign manufacturers of those products must understand how those restrictions will affect their ability to introduce their products in the U.S. market. Still another important legal and political factor to consider is the extent to which the government establishes and enforces health and safety standards for both consumers and employees.[24]

Sociocultural Influences. Managers assessing foreign markets must also consider sociocultural influences. We discussed the role of culture in international business in Chapter 9. To reduce the uncertainty associated with sociocultural factors, firms often focus their initial internationalization efforts in countries culturally similar to their home markets.[25] As with legal and political factors, firms must carefully assess relevant sociocultural factors in deciding whether to enter a particular market. Because of their subjective nature, these factors are often difficult to quantify.

A firm must carefully evaluate the legal and political environment of a foreign market in order to control risk. While Russia provides tremendous opportunities, its legal and political environment also carries considerable risk. Thus Mars has entered the market carefully through the use of kiosks and other low-cost facilities.

If the proposed strategy is to export goods from another country and sell them in the market under consideration, the most relevant sociocultural factors are those associated with consumers. Firms that fail to recognize the needs and preferences of host country consumers often run into trouble. For example, Denmark's Bang & Olufsen, a well-known stereo system manufacturer, has floundered in some markets because its designers stress style rather than function. Japanese competitors, meanwhile, stress function and innovation over style and design. Bang & Olufsen's Danish managers have failed to realize that consumers in markets such as the United States are generally more interested in function than in design and that they are more willing to pay for new technology than for an interesting appearance.[26]

A firm considering FDI in a factory or distribution center must also evaluate sociocultural factors associated with potential employees.[27] It must understand the motivational basis for work in that country, the norms for working hours and pay, and the role of labor unions. By hiring—and listening to—local managers, foreign firms can often avoid or reduce cultural conflicts.

Evaluating Costs, Benefits, and Risks

The next step in foreign-market assessment is a careful evaluation of the costs, benefits, and risks associated with doing business in a particular foreign market.

Costs. Two types of costs are relevant at this point: direct and opportunity. Direct costs are those the firm incurs in entering a new foreign market and include costs associated with setting up a business operation (leasing or buying a facility, for example), transferring managers to run it, and shipping equipment and merchandise. The firm also incurs opportunity costs. Because a firm has limited resources, entering one market may preclude or delay its entry into another. The profits it would have earned in that second market are its opportunity costs— the organization has forfeited or delayed its opportunity to earn those profits by choosing to enter another market first. Thus the firm's planners must carefully assess all the alternatives available to it.

Benefits. Entering a new market presumably offers a firm many potential benefits; otherwise, why do it? Among the most obvious potential benefits are the expected sales and profits from the market. Others include lower acquisition and manufacturing costs (if materials and/or labor are cheap), foreclosing of markets to competitors (which limits competitors' ability to gain strategic advantage), competitive advantage (which allows the firm to keep ahead of or abreast with its competition), access to new technology, and the opportunity to achieve synergy with other operations.

Risks. Of course, few benefits are achieved without some degree of risk. Many of the earlier chapters provided overviews of the specific types of risks facing international businesses. Generally, a firm entering a new market incurs the risks of opportunity costs, additional operating complexity, and direct financial losses due to misassessment of market potential or exchange rate fluctuations. In extreme cases, it also faces the risk of loss through government seizure of property or due to war or terrorism.

This list of factors a firm must consider when assessing foreign markets may seem onerous. Nonetheless, successful international businesses carefully develop their international strategies in order to uncover and exploit any and all opportunities available to them. At best, poor strategic judgments may rob a firm of profitable opportunities. At worst, a continued inability to reach the right strategic decisions may threaten the firm's existence.

For any given firm, different circumstances will dictate the markets it enters. Some choices are easy; virtually all MNCs today have operations in North America, Europe, and Pacific Asia. But complex questions surround the decision to enter various markets in South America, Africa, and other regions. In most cases, firms are sophisticated enough to have a general idea of any given market's potential. However, to exploit a firm's strengths and opportunities effectively, detailed analyses and careful, well-conceived strategic assessments are necessary, often combined with multiple site visits so that managers can witness first-hand the environment in which they may be competing.

CHAPTER REVIEW

Summary

International strategic management is a comprehensive and ongoing management planning process aimed at formulating and implementing strategies that enable a firm to compete effectively in different markets.

A well-conceived strategy has four essential components:

1. Scope of operations—the array of markets in which the firm plans to operate

2. Resource deployment—how the firm will distribute its resources across different areas

3. Distinctive competence—what the firm does exceptionally well

4. Synergy—the degree to which different operations within the firm can benefit each other

International strategy formulation is the process of creating a firm's international strategies. The process of carrying out these strategies via specific tactics is called international strategy implementation. In international strategy formulation, a firm follows three general steps:

1. Develop a mission statement that specifies its values, purpose, and directions.

2. Thoroughly analyze its strengths and weaknesses, as well as the opportunities and threats that exist in its environment.

3. Set strategic goals, outline tactical goals and plans, and develop a control framework.

Most firms develop strategy at three levels:

1. Corporate strategy answers the question "What businesses will we operate?" Basic corporate strategies are single-business, related diversification, and unrelated diversification.

2. Business strategy answers the question "How should we compete in each market we have chosen to enter?" Fundamental business strategies are differentiation, overall cost leadership, and focus.

3. Functional strategy deals with how the firm intends to manage the functions of finance, marketing, operations, human resources, and R&D.

Several factors affect a firm's international expansion. To assess foreign markets, a firm must look closely at several important factors, including market potential, competition, legal and political environments, and sociocultural influences. It must also carefully assess the costs, benefits, and risks associated with each prospective market.

Review Questions

1. What is international strategic management?

2. How do international strategy formulation and international strategy implementation differ?

3. What are the steps in international strategy formulation? Are these likely to vary among firms?

4. Identify the four components of an international strategy.

5. What are the three levels of international strategy? Why is it important to distinguish among the levels?

6. Identify and distinguish among three common approaches to corporate strategy.

7. Identify and distinguish among three common approaches to business strategy.

8. What are the basic types of functional strategies most firms use? Is it likely that some firms have different functional strategies?

9. What are the steps in conducting a foreign market analysis?

Questions for Discussion

1. What are the basic differences between a domestic strategy and an international strategy?

2. Should the same managers be involved in both formulating and implementing international strategy, or should each part of the process be handled by different managers? Why?

3. Study mission statements from several international businesses. How do they differ, and how are they similar?

4. How can a poor SWOT analysis affect strategic planning?

5. Why do relatively few international firms pursue a single-product strategy?

6. How are the components of international strategy (scope of operations, resource deployment, distinctive competence, and synergy) likely to vary across different types of corporate strategy (single-business, related diversification, and unrelated diversification)?

7. Is a firm with a corporate strategy of related diversification more or less likely than a firm with a corporate strategy of unrelated diversification to use the same business strategy for all its SBUs ? Why or why not?

8. Identify products you use regularly that are made by international firms that use the three different business strategies.

9. Do you think it is possible for someone to make a decision about entering a particular foreign market without having visited that market? Why or why not?

10. How difficult or easy do you think it is for managers to gauge the costs, benefits, and risks of a particular foreign market?

BUILDING GLOBAL SKILLS

Form a group with three or four of your classmates. Your group represents the planning department of a large MNC that has been pursuing a corporate strategy of unrelated diversification. Currently, the firm makes four basic products, as follows:

1. *All-terrain recreational vehicles.* This product line consists of small two- and three-wheeled recreational vehicles, the most popular of which is a gasoline-powered mountain bike.

2. *Color televisions.* The firm concentrates on large-screen projection-type televisions.

3. *Luggage.* This line is aimed at the low end of the market and comprises pieces made from inexpensive aluminum frames covered with ballistics material (high-strength, tear-resistant fabric). Backpacks are especially popular.

4. *Writing instruments.* The firm makes a full line of mechanical pens and pencils pitched to the middle market segment, between low-end products such as Bic and high-end ones such as Montblanc.

Your firm's CEO is contemplating international expansion. At present, the firm does well in North America, Europe, and Pacific Asia but has no presence in Africa, Central Asia, and Latin America. The countries the firm is most interested in are India, Pakistan, South Africa, Sri Lanka, and Venezuela. Your job is to conduct a preliminary market analysis for each of your firm's four businesses for any two of these five countries. Follow these steps:

1. Decide what is the most important information you need in order to make decisions.

2. Find this information in the library.

3. Evaluate the information relative to the four products.

4. Make a recommendation regarding the comparative attractiveness of the selected two countries for each product line.

CLOSING CASE

Motorola[28]

In some ways Motorola, Inc., is an anomaly. For years it and other U.S. firms such as RCA, Magnavox, Philco, and Zenith were among the world's most successful consumer electronics firms. In the face of withering competition from the Japanese, however, these firms began to fall by the wayside. Motorola has remained the exception, however. It has been a leader in microchip and semiconductor production for years. Today it is a world leader in mobile communication technology, ranking as the leading maker of cellular telephones, paging devices, automotive semiconductors, and microchips used to operate devices other than computers. In first attaining and then maintaining this lofty position, Motorola has taken on the Japanese head-to-head. And while it may have lost a few battles here and there, the firm has won many more.

Motorola heard the call to battle in the early 1980s. The firm then controlled the emerging U.S. market for cellular telephones and pagers but, like many other firms at the time, was a bit complacent and not aggressively focused on competing with the Japanese. Meanwhile, Japanese firms began to flood the U.S. market with low-priced, high-quality telephones and pagers. Motorola was shoved into the background.

Managers at Motorola at first were unsure how they should respond. They abandoned some business areas and even considered merging the firm's semiconductor operations with those of Toshiba. Finally, however, after considerable soul searching, they decided to fight back and regain the firm's lost market position. This fight involved a two-part strategy: first learn from the Japanese and then compete with them.

To carry out these strategies, executives set a number of broad-based goals that essentially committed the firm to lowering costs, improving quality, and regaining lost market share. Managers were sent on missions worldwide, but especially to Japan, to learn how to compete better. Some managers studied Motorola's own Japanese operation to learn more fully how it functioned; others focused on learning about other successful Japanese firms. At the same time, the firm dramatically boosted its budget for R&D and for employee training worldwide.

One manager who visited Japan learned an especially important lesson. While touring a Hitachi plant north of Tokyo, he noticed a flag flying in front of the factory emblazoned with the characters *P200*. When he asked what it meant, he was told by the plant manager that the factory had hoped to increase its productivity by 200 percent that year. The manager went on to note somewhat dejectedly that it looked like only a 160 percent increase would be achieved. Since Motorola had just adopted a goal of increasing its own productivity by 20 percent, the firm's managers soberly realized they had to forget altogether their old ways of doing business and to reinvent the firm from top to bottom.

Old plants were shuttered as new ones were built. Workers received new training in a wide range of quality-enhancement techniques. The firm placed its new commitment to quality at the forefront of everything it did. It even went so far as to publicly announce what seemed at the time to be an impossible goal: to achieve *Six Sigma* quality—less than 3.4 defects per million, or a perfection rate of 99.9997 percent. And indeed, Motorola has achieved this level of quality in many areas of its operations. This achievement was rewarded when it received the prestigious Malcolm Baldrige National Quality Award.

Even more amazing, however, have been Motorola's successes abroad, especially in Japan. The firm has 20 offices and more than 3000 employees there. It is currently number three in market share there in both pagers and cellular telephones but is closing in fast on number two. Worldwide, Motorola controls 45 percent of the total market for these products, has regained its number two position in semiconductor sales, and is furiously launching so many new products that its rivals seem baffled.

Today, Motorola generates over 56 percent of its revenues abroad. Major new initiatives are underway in Asia, Latin America, and Eastern Europe. The firm has also made headway in Western Europe against entrenched rivals Philips and Thomson. But not content to rest on its laurels, Motorola has set new—and staggering—goals for itself. It wants to take quality to the point where defects will be counted in relation to billions, rather than millions. It wants to cut its cycle times tenfold every five years (cycle times include the time required to produce a new product, the time to fill an order, and/or the time necessary to change a production system from one product to another). And it wants over three quarters of its revenues to come from foreign markets by the end of this decade.

Case Questions

1. What are the components of Motorola's international strategy?

2. Describe how Motorola might have arrived at its current strategy as a result of a SWOT analysis.

3. Discuss Motorola's primary business strategy.

4. What market factors are most important for Motorola?

CHAPTER NOTES

1. "Euro Disney—Oui or Non?" *Travel & Leisure*, August 1992, pp. 80–115; "An American in Paris," *Business Week*, March 12, 1990, pp. 60–64; "Mouse Fever Is About to Strike Europe," *Business Week*, March 30, 1992, p. 32; "The Mouse Isn't Roaring," *Business Week*, August 24, 1992, p. 38; The Walt Disney Company *1993 Annual Report*, p. 6; "Fans Like Euro Disney But Its Parent's Goofs Weigh the Park Down," *Wall Street Journal*, March 10, 1994, p. A1; "Walt Disney prepares to share the pain," *Financial Times*, March 15, 1994, p. 25; "Euro Disney Rescue Package Wins Approval," *Wall Street Journal*, March 15, 1994, p. A3; "How Disney Snared a Princely Sum," *Business Week*, June 20, 1994, pp. 61–62; "Euro Disney's Prince Charming?" *Business Week*, June 13, 1994, p. 42.

2. The Walt Disney Company *1993 Annual Report*, inside front cover.

3. Daniel Sullivan and Alan Bauerschmidt, "The 'Basic Concepts' of International Business Strategy: A Review and Reconsideration," *Management International Review*, Vol. 31, 1991, pp. 111–121.

4. See Charles W. L. Hill and Gareth R. Jones, *Strategic Management: An Analytical Approach*, 2nd ed. (Boston: Houghton Mifflin, 1992) for an overview of strategy and strategic management.

5. Ibid.

6. Stephen Kreider Yoder, "Intel, Backing Its Bets with Big Chips, Wins," *Wall Street Journal*, September 24, 1992, p. B1; Michiyo Nakamoto, "Looking for smaller worlds to conquer," *Financial Times*, September 2, 1992.

7. "European Auto Makers Show Signs of Bouncing Back," *Wall Street Journal*, September 15, 1994, p. B4.

8. Bruce Kogut, "Designing Global Strategies: Comparative and Competitive Value-Added Chains," *Sloan Management Review* (Summer 1985), pp. 15–28.

9. Gary Hoover, Alta Campbell, Alan Chai, and Patrick J. Spain (Eds.), *Hoover's Handbook of World Business 1992* (Austin, Tex.: Reference Press, 1991), p. 270.

10. "Think Small," *Business Week*, November 4, 1991, p. 58.

11. John A. Pearce II and Fred David, "Corporate Mission Statements: The Bottom Line," *The Academy of Management Executive*, May 1987, pp. 109–115.

12. Simon Holberton and Alice Rawsthorn, "Playmates buys stake in French toymaker," *Financial Times*, August 4, 1992.

13. Hill and Jones, op. cit.

14. Michael Porter, *Competitive Strategy* (New York: Free Press, 1980).

15. Hoover et al., op. cit., p. 232.

16. Oliver E. Williamson, *Markets and Hierarchies* (New York: Free Press, 1975).

17. Hoover et al., op. cit., p. 145.

18. See George S. Yip and George A. Coundouriotis, "Diagnosing Global Strategy Potential: The World Chocolate Confectionery Industry," *Planning Review*, January–February 1991, pp. 4–14 for an example of how this can be done.

19. William H. Davidson, "The Role of Global Scanning in Business Planning," *Organizational Dynamics*, Winter 1991, pp. 4–16.

20. John H. Dunning, "Governments, Markets and Multinational Enterprises: Some Emerging Issues," *The International Trade Journal*, Vol. 7, No. 1 (Fall 1992), pp. 1–14.

21. Fred R. Bleakley and Amal Kumar Naj, "Deutsche Bank's North American Unit Gets John Rolls of United Technologies," *Wall Street Journal*, September 30, 1992, p. B14.

22. Peter Smith Ring, Stefanie Ann Lenway, and Michele Govekar, "Management of the Political Imperative in International Business," *Strategic Management Journal*, Vol. 11, 1990, pp. 141–151.

23. C. Fred Bergsten and Edward M. Graham, "Needed: New International Rules for Foreign Direct Investment," *The International Trade Journal*, Vol. 7, No. 1 (Fall 1992), pp. 15–44.

24. J. Behrman and R. Grosse, *International Business and Governments* (Columbia, S.C.: University of South Carolina Press, 1990).

25. M. Krishna Erramilli, "The Experience Factor in Foreign Market Entry Behavior of Service Firms," *Journal of International Business Studies*, Vol. 22, No. 3 (Third Quarter 1991), pp. 479–501.

26. "A Beautiful Face Is Not Enough," *Forbes*, May 13, 1991, pp. 105–106.

27. Susan C. Schneider and Arnoud De Meyer, "Interpreting and Responding to Strategic Issues: The Impact of National Culture," *Strategic Management Journal*, Vol. 12 (1991), pp. 307–320.

28. Ronald Henkoff, "Keeping Motorola on a Roll," *Fortune*, April 18, 1994, pp. 67–78; "Motorola: Training for the Millennium," *Business Week*, March 28, 1994, pp. 158–161; "The Rival Japan Respects," *Business Week*, November 13, 1989, pp. 108–118; Ronald Henkoff, "What Motorola Learns from Japan," *Fortune*, April 24, 1989, pp. 157–168.

CHAPTER

II

Modes
of Entry
into
International
Business

Chapter Outline

Choosing a mode of entry

Exporting to foreign markets
Forms of exporting
Additional considerations
Export intermediaries

International licensing
Basic issues in international licensing
Advantages and disadvantages of
    international licensing

International franchising
Basic issues in international franchising
Advantages and disadvantages of
    international franchising

Specialized entry modes for
international business
Management contract
Turnkey project

Foreign direct investment
The greenfield strategy
The acquisition strategy
Joint ventures

After studying this chapter
you should be able to:

Analyze the process by which firms choose their mode of entry into a foreign market.

Describe forms of exporting and the types of intermediaries available to assist firms in exporting their goods.

Identify the basic issues in international licensing and discuss the advantages and disadvantages of licensing.

Identify the basic issues in international franchising and discuss the advantages and disadvantages of franchising.

Describe management contracts and turnkey projects as specialized entry modes for international business.

Discuss greenfield strategies and acquisition strategies as forms of FDI.

HEINEKEN NV IS THE WORLD'S THIRD-LARGEST BEER PRODUCER, after Anheuser-Busch and Miller. But these two large U.S. brewers have a relatively small international presence: more than 95 percent of their sales are made to U.S. customers. Heineken sells more beer outside the United States than either of them. Of its $5.2 billion in 1993 sales, only 12 percent were in its home market of the Netherlands. Not only is Heineken a market leader in every European country, it also sells its products throughout North and South America, Africa, and Asia—150 countries in all. ■■ Heineken was started in Amsterdam by Gerald Heineken in 1864. Almost from the start, the firm was successful. Within a few years of its founding, it was export-

Heineken Brews Up a Global Strategy[1]

ing beer to France, Italy, Spain, Germany, and even the Far East. In 1914 Heineken's managers decided to export beer to the United States. Gerald Heineken's son Henri, who

was running the firm at the time, sailed to the United States to set up the operation. On board the ship, he met a young bartender named Leo van Munching. Impressed with van Munching's knowledge of beer, Heineken contracted with him to import and distribute the firm's products in North America under the name Van Munching & Company. ■■ Despite Heineken's success, it ceased its U.S. operations during Prohibition. After Prohibition's repeal in 1933, it reestablished those operations, again granting Van Munching & Company of New York exclusive rights to import Heineken products into the United States. After World War II, Henri Heineken sent his son, Alfred, to New York to study marketing and advertising from Van Munching. Alfred returned to the Netherlands in 1948 with knowledge he used to help launch Heineken into other foreign markets worldwide. ■■ Heineken has continued to grow steadily. It has breweries in over 50 countries. Some of the largest are in Canada and France; however, the firm also produces in New Guinea, Australia, and Brazil. Heineken bought its largest Dutch competitor, Amstel, in 1968. In the early 1970s, seeing its bottling technology and global distribution networks as distinctive competencies, the firm entered the soft drink and wine businesses. For example, Heineken is licensed to manufacture and sell Pepsi-Cola and Seven-Up in the Netherlands. ■■ Recently Heineken has stepped up its European expansion plans in order to compete more effectively as the EU completes the formation of its internal market. The firm wants to establish the same sort of overwhelming market dominance in Europe that Anheuser-Busch has in the United States. Thus, during the 1980s, Heineken bought breweries in France, Greece, Ireland, Italy, and Spain as a way of expanding its product lines and facilitating distribution throughout Europe. It also bought a controlling interest in Hungarian brewer Komaromi Sorgyar. Further, to cut its operating costs, it closed ten of its older breweries and modernized six others. ▊▊Interestingly, Heineken has refused to establish a brewery in the United States. Why? Consider a case in point. Several years ago Miller, owner of rights to distribute Lowenbrau in the United States, was selling as much of that Munich-brewed beer in the United States as it could import from Germany. To help keep pace with demand, Miller renegotiated its contract with Lowenbrau and began brewing the beer in Texas under license. Sales soon began to drop, in part because the beer was no longer an import and was perceived to have lost its cachet as an authentic Bavarian beer. To avoid Lowenbrau's mistake and retain its product's image as a true "imported" beer, Heineken continues to ship its beer into the U.S. market even though it might be cheaper to make it there. ▊▊Heineken has recently made one important strategic decision regarding the U.S. market: it bought Van Munching & Company and now owns its U.S. distribution arm outright. While Van Munching continues to operate independently of its parent, its being under Heineken's control has helped cut costs and added additional profit to each bottle of beer sold in the United States. Heineken also can now more easily coordinate its U.S. marketing campaigns with its global promotional efforts for its world-famous beer. ▊▊▊▊▊

Chapter 10 focused on the process by which a firm formulates its international strategy. It also explored the factors a firm considers in selecting the international markets it will enter. This chapter discusses the next step in the implementation of strategy: choosing the mode of entry the firm will use to enter and compete in the international markets it has targeted. As the opening case indicates, MNCs such as Heineken are not restricted to using a single method for participating in international business. For example, Heineken exports its products to a variety of markets. In other markets, it uses licensing agreements with independent firms to promote its business interests. And in New Guinea, Australia, and Brazil, Heineken-owned subsidiaries produce, distribute, and sell Heineken beer. In fact, as we discuss in this chapter, in deciding how to enter a market, a well-managed firm will match its internal strengths and weaknesses to the unique opportunities and needs of that market. Heineken has successfully done this in each of the national markets in which it participates.

Choosing a Mode of Entry

How does a firm decide which mode of entry to use in penetrating a foreign market? Dunning's eclectic theory, discussed in Chapter 3, provides useful insights into the factors that affect the choice among either home country production (exporting), host country production in firm-owned factories

(FDI and joint venture), or host country production performed by others (licensing and franchising). Recall that the eclectic theory considers three factors: ownership advantages, location advantages, and internalization advantages.[2] Other factors a firm may consider include the firm's need for control, the availability of resources, and the firm's global strategy. The role of these factors in the entry mode decision is illustrated in Fig. 11.1.

Ownership advantages are resources owned by a firm that grant it a competitive advantage over its industry rivals. These firm-specific ownership advantages may be tangible or intangible. For example, the ownership by Toronto-based Inco, Ltd., of rich, nickel-bearing ores has allowed the firm, formerly known as International Nickel, to dominate the production of both primary nickel and nickel-based metal alloys. The luxury appeal of Dom Perignon champagne and Christian Dior perfumes—both products of France's LVMH Moet Hennessy Louis Vuitton—although a more intangible resource than a nickel ore mine, similarly grants the Parisian firm a competitive advantage over its rivals in international markets. Assuming that local firms know more about their home turf than foreigners do, a foreign firm contemplating entry into a new market should possess some ownership advantage in order to overcome the information advantage of local firms. As discussed later in this chapter, the nature of the firm's ownership advantage affects its selection of entry mode. Imbedded technology, for example, can best be transferred through an equity mode, while a simple technology is perhaps more suited to a licensing mode. Further, firm advantages are primary determinants of bargaining strength; thus they can influence the outcome of entry mode negotiations.

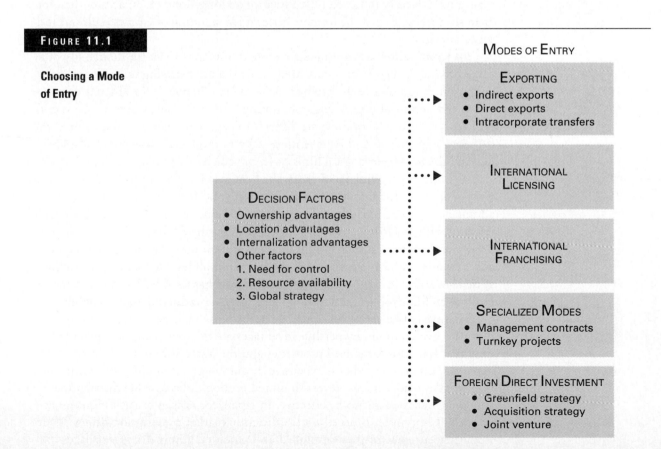

FIGURE 11.1

Choosing a Mode of Entry

MODES OF ENTRY

EXPORTING
- Indirect exports
- Direct exports
- Intracorporate transfers

INTERNATIONAL LICENSING

INTERNATIONAL FRANCHISING

DECISION FACTORS
- Ownership advantages
- Location advantages
- Internalization advantages
- Other factors
  1. Need for control
  2. Resource availability
  3. Global strategy

SPECIALIZED MODES
- Management contracts
- Turnkey projects

FOREIGN DIRECT INVESTMENT
- Greenfield strategy
- Acquisition strategy
- Joint venture

Location advantages are those factors that affect the desirability of host country production relative to home country production. Firms routinely compare economic and noneconomic characteristics of the home market with those of the foreign market in determining where to site their production facilities. If home country production is found to be more desirable than host country production, the firm will chose to enter the host country market via exporting. For example, Siam Cement, one of the world's lowest-cost producers, has relied on exports from its modern Thailand factories to serve the Cambodian, Vietnamese, and Laotian markets rather than setting up production facilities in those countries.[3] But if host country production is more desirable, the firm may invest in foreign facilities or license the use of its technology and brand names to existing host country producers.

The desirability of home country versus host country production is affected by many factors. Relative wage rates and land acquisition costs in the countries are important, but firms may also consider surplus or unused capacity in existing factories, access to R&D facilities, logistical requirements, the needs of customers, and the additional administrative costs of managing a foreign facility. Government policies can also have a major influence.[4] For example, high tariff walls, like those imposed by Argentina and Brazil in the 1970s and the early 1980s, discourage exporting and encourage local production, while high corporate taxes may inhibit FDI.[5] Also, restrictions on licensing fees imposed by host country governments, such as Pakistan's 3 percent limit on pharmaceutical sales or India's 8 percent cap on royalty payments, may deter firms from using licensing as an entry mode.[6] Location advantages may also be culture-bound. For example, locating (and then managing) a factory in China is far easier for a Hong Kong manufacturer than for a Spanish firm because of the former's better understanding of Chinese cultural and social norms.

Internalization advantages are those factors that affect the desirability of a firm's producing a good or service itself rather than contracting with a local host country firm to produce the product. As noted in Chapter 3, the amount of transaction costs (costs of negotiating, monitoring, and enforcing an agreement) is critical to this decision. If contracts are difficult to negotiate, monitor, and enforce, the firm may rely on FDI and joint ventures as entry modes. If transaction costs are low and the firm believes local firms can more efficiently produce the good or service without jeopardizing its interests, the firm may use franchising and licensing as entry modes. In deciding, the firm must consider both the nature of the ownership advantage it possesses and its ability to ensure productive and harmonious working relations with any local firm with which it does business. Toyota, for example, possesses two important ownership advantages: efficient manufacturing techniques and a reputation for producing high-quality automobiles. Neither asset is readily saleable or transferable to other firms; thus Toyota has used FDI and joint ventures rather than franchising and licensing for its foreign production of automobiles.

Pharmaceutical firms routinely use licensing as their entry mode. In this industry, two common ownership advantages are the ownership of a patented drug that has unique medical properties and the ownership of local distribution networks. Obtaining either is expensive; researching, developing, and testing a new wonder drug can cost several hundred million dollars, while distribution networks must be large to be effective. In Japan, for example, a sales force of at least 1000 employees is necessary to efficiently market prescription drugs.[7] Once a pharmaceutical firm has developed and patented a new drug, it is eager to amortize its R&D costs in both domestic and foreign markets. Many such firms prefer to forgo the expensive and time-consuming process of setting up overseas production facilities and foreign distribution networks. Instead they grant existing local firms the right to manufacture and distribute the patented drug in return for royalty payments. For example, Israel's Teva Pharmaceutical Industries, Ltd., granted Du Pont Merck Pharmaceutical Company the rights to distribute its products in the United States rather than establishing its own U.S. sales force.[8] Licensing is also attractive because the risk that the local licensee will cheat the pharmaceutical firm or damage its reputation is minimal, since the costs of monitoring the sales and product quality of patented drugs sold in the host country are relatively low.

Other factors may also affect the choice of entry mode. For example, a firm is likely to consider its need for control and the availability of resources.[9] A firm's lack of experience in a foreign market may cause a certain degree of uncertainty. To reduce this uncertainty, some firms may prefer an initial entry mode that offers them a high degree of control.[10] However, firms short on capital or thin in executive talent may be unable or unwilling to commit themselves to the large capital investments this control entails; they may prefer an entry mode that economizes on their financial commitments, such as licensing. Cash-rich firms may view FDI more favorably, believing that it offers high profit potential and the opportunity to more fully internationalize the training of their young, fast-track managers.

A firm's overall global strategy also may affect the choice of entry mode. Firms such as Ford that seek to exploit economies of scale and synergies between their domestic and international operations may prefer ownership-oriented entry modes. Conversely, firms such as Microsoft, Compaq, and Apple, whose competitive strengths lie in flexibility and quick response to changing market conditions, are more likely to use any and all entry modes warranted by local conditions in a given host country.[11] A firm's choice may also be driven by its need to coordinate its activities across all markets as part of its global strategy. For example, IBM has for this reason traditionally favored ownership-oriented entry modes as part of its globalization strategy.[12]

In short, like most business activities, the choice of entry mode is often a tradeoff between the level of risk borne by the firm, the potential rewards to be obtained from a market, the magnitude of the resource commitment necessary to compete effectively, and the level of control the firm seeks.[13]

The first entry modes we discuss, which require no firm ownership of foreign assets, are

▶ Exporting
▶ Licensing
▶ Franchising
▶ Management contract
▶ Turnkey project

We then discuss two types of FDI—greenfield strategy and acquisition strategy—and touch on a third type—joint venture—that is covered in more detail in Chapter 12.

Exporting to Foreign Markets

Perhaps the simplest mode of internationalizing a domestic business is exporting, the most common form of international business activity. Recall from Chapter 1 that exporting is the process of sending goods or services from one country to other countries for use or sale there. In that chapter we noted that merchandise exports in the world economy totaled $3.6 trillion in 1992, or 16 percent of the world's total economic activity. Service exports amounted to $1 trillion in 1992. Table 11.1 lists the top 20 U.S. exporters.

Exporting offers a firm several advantages. First, it often involves less financial exposure than do some other entry modes. Little or no capital investment is normally necessary, although the firm may incur some startup costs associated with market research, establishment of distribution networks, and/or local advertising. In most cases, the dollar amount of the firm's exporting risks is limited to the value of the goods or services involved in a given transaction plus these startup costs.

Second, exporting permits a firm to enter a foreign market gradually, thereby allowing it to assess local conditions and fine-tune its products to meet the idiosyncratic needs of host country consumers. If its exports are well received by foreign consumers, the firm may use this experience as a basis for a more extensive entry into that market. Thus, through exporting, the firm can gain experience in operating internationally and obtain information about particular markets without incurring any significant capital expenditures. For example, Space-Lok, Inc., a small, 40-person Burbank, California, manufacturer of high-stress fasteners for the aerospace industry, decided in the late 1980s that it needed to expand internationally because of likely decreases in the U.S. defense budget. Because of the simplicity and low risk of exporting, Space-Lok is internationalizing its operations through that mode. Should its initial efforts succeed, Space-Lok might expand beyond exporting and choose to establish its own foreign factories.[14]

Firms may have proactive or reactive motivations for exporting. Proactive motivations are those that *pull* a firm into foreign markets, as a result of opportunities available there. For example, San Antonio's Pace, Inc., a maker of Tex-Mex food products, began exporting proactively to Mexico in the early 1990s after discovering that Mexican consumers enjoy its picante sauce as much as its U.S. customers do.[15] A firm also may export proactively in order to exploit a technological advantage or to spread fixed R&D expenses over a wider customer base, thereby allowing it to price its products more competitively in both domestic and foreign markets. For example, the breakeven price of commercial airliners produced by Boeing, McDonnell Douglas, and Airbus Industrie would skyrocket if these firms limited their sales to either domestic or foreign customers.

Reactive motivations for exporting are those that *push* a firm into foreign markets, often because opportunities are decreasing in the domestic market. Some firms turn to exporting because their production lines are running below capacity or because they seek higher profit margins in foreign markets in the face of downturns in domestic demand. Space-Lok's motivation to internationalize, for example, is clearly reactive—based on fears that domestic customers will curtail their orders as the U.S. defense budget is trimmed. Similarly, when Japanese retailer Yaohan International was challenged domestically in the early 1970s by far

TABLE 11.1

The Top 20 U.S. Exporters

RANK 1992	RANK 1991	COMPANY (HEADQUARTERS)	MAJOR EXPORTS	U.S. EXPORTS 1992 (Millions of dollars)	U.S. EXPORTS Percent Change from 1991	U.S. EXPORTS As Percentage of Total Sales %	U.S. EXPORTS As Percentage of Total Sales Rank
1	1	Boeing (Seattle)	Commercial aircraft	17,486.0	(2.1)	57.5	1
2	2	General Motors (Detroit)	Motor vehicles and parts	14,045.1	(6.8)	10.6	35
3	3	General Electric (Fairfield, Conn.)	Jet engines, turbines, plastics, medical systems	8,200.0	(4.8)	13.2	27
4	4	IBM (Armonk, N.Y.)	Computers and related equipment	7,524.0	(1.9)	11.6	31
5	5	Ford Motor (Dearborn, Mich.)	Motor vehicles and parts	7,220.0*	(1.6)	7.2	45
6	6	Chrysler (Highland Park, Mich.)	Motor vehicles and parts	7,051.8	14.3	19.1	14
7	7	McDonnell Douglas (St. Louis)	Aerospace products, missiles, electronic systems	4,983.0	(19.1)	28.5	6
8	12	Philip Morris (New York)	Tobacco, beverages, food products	3,797.0	24.0	7.6	42
9	11	Hewlett-Packard (Palo Alto, Calif.)	Measurement and computation products and systems	3,720.0	15.4	22.6	10
10	8	E.I. Du Pont de Nemours (Wilmington, Del.)	Specialty chemicals	3,509.0	(7.9)	9.4	38
11	14	Motorola (Schaumburg, Ill.)	Communications equipment, semiconductors	3,460.0	18.2	25.9	8
12	10	United Technologies (Hartford, Conn.)	Jet engines, helicopters, cooling equipment	3,541.0	(3.8)	15.7	17
13	9	Caterpillar (Peoria, Ill.)	Heavy machinery, engines, turbines	3,341.0	(9.9)	32.8	4
14	13	Eastman Kodak (Rochester, N.Y.)	Imaging, chemicals, health products	3,220.0	6.6	15.6	18
15	15	Archer Daniels Midland (Decatur, Ill.)	Protein meals, vegetable oils, flour, grain	2,700.0	3.8	28.9	5
16	17	Intel (Santa Clara, Calif.)	Microcomputer components, modules, and systems	2,339.0	21.3	39.1	3
17	16	Digital Equipment (Maynard, Mass.)	Computers and related equipment	1,900.0	(13.6)	13.5	24
18	18	Allied-Signal (Morristown, N.J.)	Aircraft and automotive parts, chemicals	1,810.0	4.7	15.0	21
19	20	Unisys (Blue Bell, Pa.)	Computers and related equipment	1,795.8	12.4	21.3	11
20	19	Sun Microsystems (Mountain View, Calif.)	Computers and related equipment	1,783.6	11.1	49.2	2

Fortune estimate

larger rivals, it shifted its focus to serving the Southeast Asia market. Although Yaohan is only a midget at home—Japan's 59th largest retailer—today it is one of the largest chain store operators in Hong Kong and is busily extending its empire to Malaysia, Singapore, Taiwan, and Thailand.[16] In addition, Yaohan recently announced a joint venture in China that will ultimately result in as many as 1000 outlets in that country by 2010.[17]

Forms of Exporting

Export activities may take several forms (see Fig. 11.2):

► Indirect exporting
► Direct exporting
► Intracorporate transfers

Indirect Exporting. Indirect exporting occurs when a firm sells its product to a domestic customer, which in turn exports the product, in either its original form or a modified form. For example, if Hewlett-Packard (a U.S. firm) buys microchips from Intel (also a U.S. firm) to use in manufacturing computers, and then exports those completed computers to Europe, Intel's chips have been indirectly exported. Or, a firm may sell goods to a domestic wholesaler who then sells them to an overseas firm. A firm also may sell to a foreign firm's local subsidiary, which then transports the first firm's products to the foreign country.

Some indirect exporting activities reflect conscious actions by domestic producers. For example, the Association of Guatemala Coffee Producers sells bags of coffee to passengers boarding international flights in Guatemala City in order to gain export sales and to build consumer awareness of its product. In most cases, however, indirect exporting activities are not part of a conscious internationalization strategy by a firm. Thus they yield the firm little experience in conducting international business. Further, for firms that passively rely on the actions of others, the potential short-term and long-term profits available from indirect exporting are often limited.

Direct Exporting. Direct exporting involves sales to customers—either distributors or end-users—located outside the firm's home country. Research suggests that in one third of cases, a firm's initial direct exporting to a foreign market is the result of an unsolicited order. However, its subsequent direct exporting typically results from deliberate efforts to expand its business internationally. In such cases, the firm actively selects the products it will sell, the foreign markets it will service, and the means by which its products will be distributed in those markets. Through direct exporting activities, the firm gains valuable expertise about operating internationally and specific knowledge concerning the individual countries in which it operates. And export success often breeds additional export success. Increasing experience with exporting often prompts a firm to become more aggressive in exploiting new international exporting opportunities.[18] Such experience also often proves useful if the firm later engages in FDI.

Intracorporate Transfers. A third form of export activity is the intracorporate transfer, which has become more important as the sizes of MNCs have

FIGURE 11.2

Forms of Exporting

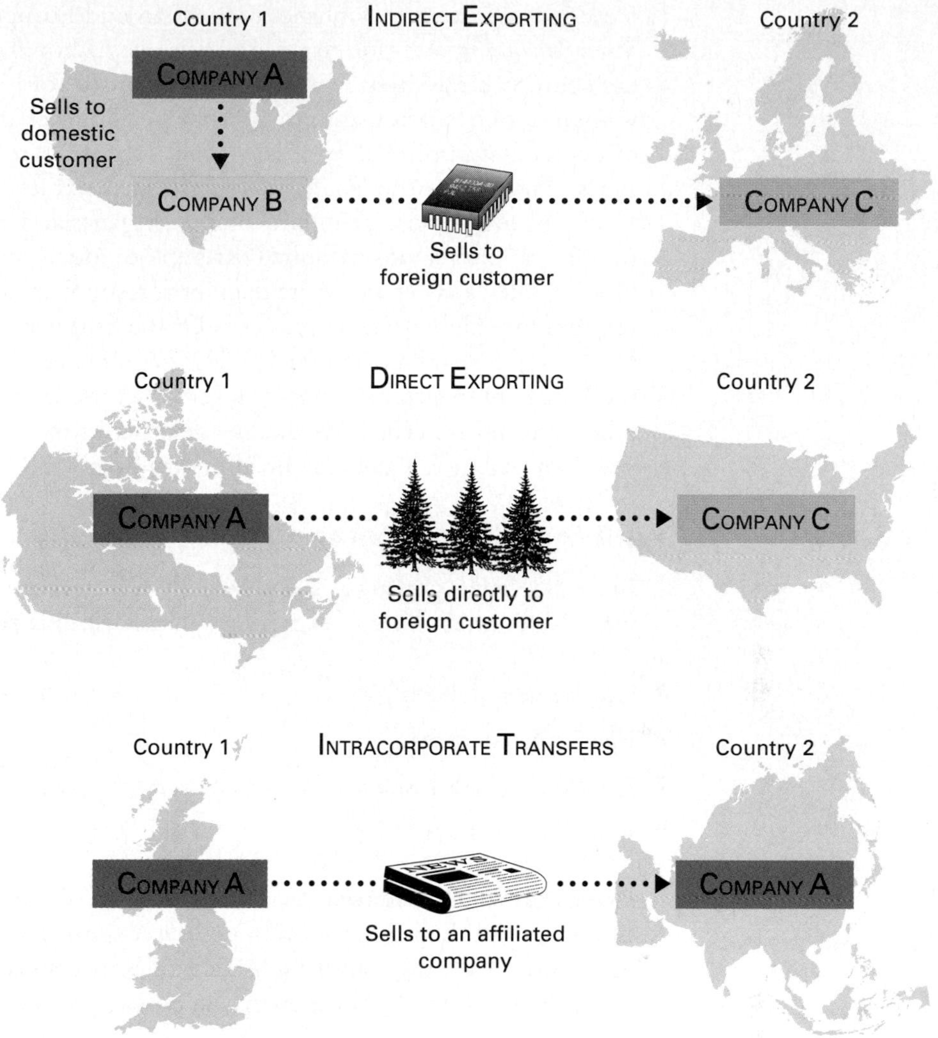

INDIRECT EXPORTING

Country 1

COMPANY A

Sells to
domestic
customer

COMPANY B

Sells to
foreign customer

Country 2

COMPANY C

DIRECT EXPORTING

Country 1

COMPANY A

Sells directly to
foreign customer

Country 2

COMPANY C

INTRACORPORATE TRANSFERS

Country 1

COMPANY A

Sells to an affiliated
company

Country 2

COMPANY A

increased. An **intracorporate transfer** is the selling of goods by a firm in one country to an affiliated firm in another. For example, when British Petroleum ships surplus crude oil from its storage facilities in Kuwait to its Australian subsidiary, the transaction is counted as a Kuwaiti export and an Australian import, but the revenues for the transaction remain within the same firm.

Intracorporate transfers are an important part of international trade. They account for about 35 percent of all U.S. merchandise exports and imports.[19] Many MNCs constantly engage in such transfers, importing and exporting semifinished products and component parts in order to lower their production costs and use their existing factories more efficiently. For example, consider the Ford Crown Victoria automobile. Ford's U.S. assembly plant imports the automobile's fuel tank, windshield, instrument panel, and seats from Ford factories in Mexico, its wheels from a Ford factory in England, its electronic engine control system from a Ford factory in Spain, and its electronic control system for its antilock brakes from a Ford factory in Germany.[20] Ford's intricate meshing of inputs produced at various locations is typical of the behavior of many MNCs.

Such transfers are also common in the service sector. For example, the Dow-Jones Company publishes both Asian and European versions of the *Wall Street Journal* in addition to its U.S. edition. Although some of the stories in each edition are written locally and are intended for local audiences, others are written in one location and printed in all editions of the newspaper. The usage of stories first published by a Dow-Jones subsidiary in one country by Dow-Jones affiliates in other countries is an intracorporate transfer of services.

Firms may choose to import component parts and products from other countries for various reasons. Required parts and products may be unavailable locally, local suppliers may charge more than foreign suppliers do, or foreign suppliers may produce higher-quality products. Or the firm may use the productive capacity of both its domestic and foreign factories more efficiently by concentrating production of individual inputs at specific factories and shipping these inputs to other factories as needed. We discuss these factors more thoroughly in Chapter 17 when we analyze the global sourcing strategies of MNCs.

Additional Considerations

In considering exporting as its entry mode, a firm must consider many other factors besides which form of exporting to use, including the following:

► Government policies
► Marketing concerns
► Logistical considerations
► Distribution issues

Government Policies. Government policies may influence a firm's decision to export. Export promotion policies, export financing programs, and other forms of home country subsidization encourage exporting as an entry mode. Host countries, however, may impose tariffs and NTBs on imported

Levi Strauss has been exporting its popular line of jeans to foreign markets for years. In some parts of the world, a pair of Levis sells on the black market for many times its normal retail price. The firm recently launched a chain of retail outlets called the American Store to sell its products in Europe.

goods, thereby discouraging the firm from relying on exports as an entry mode. For example, as noted in Chapter 6, Japan's imposition of voluntary export restraints (VERs) on Japanese automobiles reduced Japanese exports, but also encouraged Japanese automakers to construct assembly plants in the United States.

Marketing Concerns. Marketing concerns, such as image, logistics, distribution, and responsiveness to the customer, may also affect the decision to export. Often foreign goods have a certain product image or cachet that domestically produced goods cannot duplicate. For example, buyers of Dom Perignon champagne are purchasing, at least in part, the allure of France's finest champagne. This allure would be lost should LMVH choose to produce the product in Lubbock, Texas, even though Lubbock vineyards yield a regionally acclaimed wine, Llano Estacado. Also, recall Lowenbrau's U.S. marketing disaster, described in the opening case. Produced in Munich, Lowenbrau was a premium product to U.S. consumers; produced in the United States, it was just another beer. Swiss watches, German automobiles, Italian shoes, Cuban cigars, and Scottish wool are among the other product groups whose allure is closely associated with specific countries.

The choice of exporting is also influenced by a firm's need to obtain quick and constant feedback from its customers. Such feedback is less important for standardized products whose designs change slowly, if at all, such as toothbrushes and coffeemakers. On the other hand, producers of goods such as personal computers must continually monitor the marketplace to ensure that they are meeting the rapidly changing needs of their customers. For example, Korean manufacturer Hyundai shifted its production of personal computers from Korea to the United States because it needed to be closer to its U.S. customer base.

Logistical Considerations. Logistical considerations also enter into the decision to export. The firm must consider the physical distribution costs of warehousing, packaging, transporting, and distributing its goods, as well as its inventory carrying costs and those of its foreign customers. Typically, such logistical costs will be higher for exported goods than for locally produced goods. But logistical considerations go beyond mere costs. Because exporting means longer supply lines and increased difficulties in communicating with foreign customers, firms choosing to export from domestic factories must ensure that they maintain competitive levels of customer service for their foreign customers.

Fortunately, for the firm that decides to export, various transportation modes are available, including ship, airplane, train, truck, and electronic transmission. Table 11.2 summarizes the relative advantages and disadvantages of each mode and also gives examples of products most likely to be shipped by each.

Also, note that many exports may require multiple modes of transportation to get them to their destinations. For example, Exxon uses pipelines to transport crude oil from its storage facilities to port cities. Tanker ships then carry the oil to foreign ports. From there, pipelines transport the oil to storage facilities and eventually carry it to local refineries. Similarly, as Map 11.1 shows, when Nissan exports automobiles from Japan to the United States, it uses rail transportation to get them from its plant to the shipyard. It then loads them onto a ship, which carries them to the United States. Rail is used again to transport the automobiles to centrally located distribution and storage facilities. Trucks then transport them to individual Nissan dealerships.

> **TABLE 11.2**
>
> **Advantages and Disadvantages of Different Modes of Transportation for Exports**
>
> | TRANSPORTATION MODE | ADVANTAGES | DISADVANTAGES | SAMPLE PRODUCTS |
> |---|---|---|---|
> | Train | Safe
Reliable
Inexpensive | Limited to rail routes
Slow | Automobiles
Grains |
> | Airplane | Safe
Reliable | Expensive
Limited access | Jewelry
Medicine |
> | Truck | Versatile
Inexpensive | Size | Consumer goods |
> | Ship | Inexpensive
Good for large products | Slow
Indirect | Automobiles
Furniture |
> | Electronic media | Fast | Limited access | Information |

Distribution Issues. A final issue that may influence a firm's decision to export is distribution. A firm often lacks the expertise to market its products abroad, so it will seek a local distributor to handle its products in the target market. Critical to the firm's success is the selection of this distributor. The distributor must have sufficient expertise and resources (capital, labor, facilities, and local reputation) to successfully market the firm's products. However, often the best local distributors already handle the products of the firm's competitors. Consequently, the firm must decide between an experienced local distributor and a less-experienced one that will handle the firm's products exclusively.

The profitability and growth potential of exporting to a foreign market will be affected by the firm's agreement with the local distributor. The local distributor must be compensated for its services, of course. This compensation will potentially reduce the exporter's profit margin. Further, the exporter and its local distributor depend on each other to ensure that a satisfactory business relationship is established and maintained. For example, if the host country distributor inadequately markets, distributes, and/or services the exporter's products, it is the exporter that will suffer lost sales and damaged reputation. For example, Apple's initial share of the Japanese personal computer market was hurt by the performance of a Canon subsidiary hired to market and distribute the firm's products in Japan. Apple took over these tasks in the early 1990s and quickly quintupled its market share.[21]

The business judgments of the local distributor and the exporter may differ. The exporter may want its distributor to market its products more aggressively in hopes of building sales volume; the distributor may believe that the additional sales generated by this strategy will not cover the increased expenses incurred. For example, GM set the goal of increasing European sales of its products made in North America from 17,500 vehicles in 1991 to 250,000 vehicles by 2000. But it was concerned that paperwork and red tape discouraged its European dealers from buying North American–made GM vehicles. Thus in

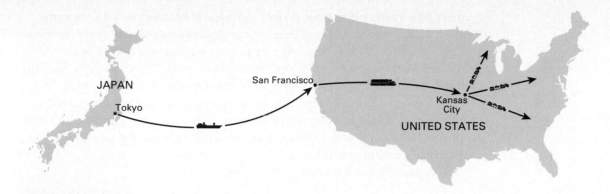

MAP 11.1

Nissan's Distribution Process

1992 it shifted the responsibility of importing such cars from its individual dealers in Europe, which predominantly handle vehicles produced by GM's German subsidiary, Adam Opel AG, to a new GM subsidiary, General Motors Import & Distribution Company GmbH. The new subsidiary in turn distributes the North American–made vehicles to European GM dealerships. GM hopes that easing the administrative burden on individual dealerships will encourage them to sell more of its North American–made products.[22]

The exporter and distributor also may differ on pricing strategies, with the exporter preferring lower retail prices and the distributor favoring higher prices that produce fatter profit margins. For example, Toyota has been displeased by the decision of some of its U.S. distributors to include high-profit add-ons such as "consumer protection packages" on all Toyotas they handle. Toyota feels the distributors essentially are raising the prices of its cars, thereby lowering the number of units sold. The U.S. distributors, meanwhile, earn higher profits for themselves on each car they sell. Such problems can be avoided, of course, if the exporter handles its own distribution in the foreign country.

Because of the importance of distributors in the exporting process, many governments assist their domestic firms in the selection of foreign distributors. For example, overseas officers of the U.S. and Foreign Commercial Service regularly report back to the U.S. Department of Commerce about foreign firms interested in acting as distribution agents for U.S. exporters. The National Trade Data Bank, discussed in the Building Global Skills section of Chapter 2, incorporates a list of potential distributors in its data files.

Export Intermediaries

An exporter may also market and distribute its goods in international markets by using one or more **intermediaries**, third parties that specialize in facilitating imports and exports.[23] These specialists may offer limited services such as handling only transportation and documentation. Or they may perform more extensive roles, including taking ownership of foreign-bound goods and/or assuming total responsibility for marketing and financing exports.[24] Types of intermediaries that offer a broad range of services include the following:

▶ Export management companies
▶ Webb-Pomerene associations
▶ International trading companies

Export Management Company. An **export management company (EMC)** is a firm that acts as its client's export department. Smaller firms often use an EMC to handle their foreign shipments. Several thousand EMCs operate in the United States. Most are small operations that rely on the services of a handful of professionals. An EMC's staff typically is knowledgeable about the legal, financial, and logistical details of exporting and importing and so frees the exporter from having to develop this expertise in-house. The EMC may also provide advice about consumer needs and available distribution channels in the foreign markets the exporter wants to penetrate.

EMCs usually operate in one of two ways:

1 Some act as commission agents for exporters. They handle the details of shipping, clearing customs, and document preparation in return for an agreed-upon fee. In this case, the exporter normally invoices the client and provides any necessary financing it may need.

2 Others take title to the goods. They make money by buying the goods from the exporter and reselling them at a higher price to foreign customers. Such EMCs may offer customer financing and design and implement advertising and promotional campaigns for the product.

Webb-Pomerene Association. A **Webb-Pomerene association** is a group of U.S. firms that operate within the same industry and that are allowed by law to coordinate their export activities without fear of violating U.S. antitrust laws. First authorized by the Export Trade Act of 1918, a Webb-Pomerene association engages in market research, overseas promotional activities, freight consolidation, contract negotiations, and other services for its members. It may also directly engage in exporting by buying goods domestically from members and selling the goods in foreign markets on the association's behalf. Although such associations were originally designed to allow smaller, related firms to cooperate in promoting exports, most are now dominated by larger firms. In general, Webb-Pomerene associations have not played a major role in international business. Fewer than 25 such associations exist today, and they tend to be concentrated in raw materials such as wood pulp, sulfur, and phosphate rock.

International Trading Company. An **international trading company** is a firm directly engaged in importing and exporting a wide variety of goods for its own account. It differs from an EMC in that it participates in both importing and exporting activities. By buying goods in one country and selling them in a second, an international trading company provides the gamut of necessary exporting and importing services. These include market research, customs documentation, international transportation, domestic distribution, marketing, and financing. Typically international trading companies have agents and offices worldwide. The economic intelligence information they glean from these far-flung operations is one of their most potent competitive weapons.

The most important international trading companies in the global marketplace are Japan's sogo sosha. Recall from Chapter 2 that sogo sosha acquire goods by importing them from other countries or by having the goods manufactured and then reselling them in both domestic and foreign markets. The sogo sosha are an integral part of Japan's keiretsu system, often providing exporting, importing, marketing, distribution, and financial services for fellow keiretsu members. The Mitsubishi Corporation, for example, is the trading arm of the Mitsubishi Group, Japan's largest keiretsu. It works with the Mitsubishi Bank (the world's sixth-largest bank and the banking arm of the Mitsubishi keiretsu) to provide trading services for the keiretsu's 160 affiliates, including Mitsubishi Motors, Nikon, Kirin Brewery, Mitsubishi Electric, Asahi Glass, and the Mitsubishi Estate Company (which owns 51 percent of New York City's Rockefeller Center).[25] The sogo sosha also provide trading services for numerous firms that are not keiretsu members.

The sogo sosha have prospered for several reasons. Because of their far-flung operations, they continuously obtain information about economic conditions and business opportunities in virtually every corner of the world. As part of a keiretsu, a sogo sosha enjoys ready access to financing (from the keiretsu's lead bank) and a built-in source of customers (its fellow keiretsu members). This customer base reduces the sogo sosha's costs of soliciting clients and builds up its business volume, thereby allowing it to reap economies of scale in its transportation and information-gathering roles. Nonmembers of the keiretsu are then attracted to doing business with the sogo sosha because of its low cost structure and international expertise. Japan's international trading companies have been so successful that, measured by sales volume, the world's five largest service companies are all sogo sosha.[26] These five are featured in Table 11.3.

As is normal in business, the sogo sosha's success has attracted imitators. In the mid-1970s, South Korea's government ordered its chaebol to create their own trading companies in order to promote Korean exports. This effort has been successful: as discussed in Chapter 2, chaebol such as Samsung, Hyundai, and Lucky-Goldstar are now a major presence in the world market. Similarly, in 1982, under the Export Trading Company Act, the United States authorized the creation of export trading companies to stimulate exports from smaller U.S. firms. An **export trading company (ETC)** is a firm that may engage in various cooperative business practices without fear of violating U.S. antitrust laws. Members of an industry may create an ETC to provide necessary exporting services, such as market research, warehousing, and/or foreign distribution. ETCs may be organized on a product basis or on a geographical basis. U.S. commercial banks also may create ETCs to facilitate the financing of U.S. exports. ETCs may engage in importing services and help U.S. firms arrange international barter transactions. So far, however, ETCs have been only modestly successful. It remains to be seen whether they will become an important component of the importing and exporting sector of the U.S. economy.

Other Intermediaries. In addition to the intermediaries that provide a broad range of services to international exporters and importers, numerous other types of intermediaries, including the following, offer more specialized services:

► **Manufacturers' agents** solicit domestic orders for foreign manufacturers, usually on a commission basis.

► **Manufacturers' export agents** act as an export department for domestic manufacturers, selling those firms' goods in foreign markets.

► **Export and import brokers** bring together international buyers and sellers of such standardized commodities as coffee, cocoa, and grains.

TABLE 11.3

The Five Largest Sogo Sosha

RANK	FIRM	1991 SALES ($ Millions)	KEY SUBSIDIARIES AND AFFILIATES
1	ITOCHU Corporation	156,968	American Isuzu Motors (wholesaling) ATR Wires & Cable Company (steel tire cords) Century 21 Real Estate of Japan, Ltd. (real estate brokerage) Dunhill Group Japan, Inc. (men's clothing and accessories) Mazda Motor of America (wholesaling) Time Warner Entertainment of Japan (25 percent limited partnership) VIDEOSAT, Inc. (satellite transmission of video signals)
2	Sumitomo Group	150,814	Asahi Breweries, Ltd. (alcoholic beverages) NEC Corp. (electronics) Nippon Sheet Glass Company The Sumitomo Bank, Ltd. Sumitomo Cement Company, Ltd. Sumitomo Chemical Company, Ltd. Sumitomo Coal Mining Company, Ltd. Sumitomo Forestry Company, Ltd. Sumitomo Metal Industries, Ltd. Sumitomo Realty & Development Company, Ltd.
3	Marubeni	140,675	Archer Pipe and Tube Company (steel pipe sales) Bactec Corporation (insecticides) Columbia Grain International (grain trading) Fremont Beef Company (meat processing) Kubota Tractor Company (farm equipment) Precision Tools Service, Inc. (machine tools)
4	Mitsubishi Group	136,268	Kirin Brewery (alcoholic beverages) The Mitsubishi Bank, Ltd. Mitsubishi Heavy Industries, Ltd. (construction) Mitsubishi Motor Corporation (automobiles) Nikon Corporation (cameras and video equipment) The Tokyo Marine and Fire Insurance Company
5	Mitsui & Company	133,848	Japan Steel Works, Ltd. (steel manufacturing) Mitsui Construction Company, Ltd. (construction) Mitsukoshi, Ltd. (department stores) Mitsui Mutual Life Insurance Company, Ltd. Onoda Cement Company, Ltd. (construction materials) Sakura Bank

▶ **Freight forwarders** specialize in the physical transportation of goods, arranging customs documentation and obtaining transportation services for their clients.

This list is by no means complete. Indeed, specialists are available to provide virtually every service needed by exporters and importers in international trade. "Going Global" summarizes the suggestions of one successful exporter, including his advice for taking advantage of various services provided by others.

International Licensing

Another means of entering a foreign market is **licensing**, in which a firm, called the **licensor**, sells the right to use its intellectual property—technology, work methods, patents, copyrights, brand names, or trademarks—to another firm, called the **licensee**, in return for a fee. This process is illustrated in Fig. 11.3. The use of licensing as an entry mode is affected by host country policies. Firms are not advised to use licensing in countries that offer weak protection for intellectual property, since they may have difficulty enforcing licensing agreements in the host country's courts. On the other hand, the use of licensing may be encouraged by high tariffs and NTBs, which discourage imports, or by host country restrictions on FDI or repatriation of profits.

In the absence of host country restrictions, licensing is a popular mode for entering foreign markets. Many international firms choose it because it involves little out-of-pocket costs. A firm has already incurred the costs of developing the intellectual property to be licensed; thus revenues received through a licensing agreement often go straight to the firm's bottom line. Licensing also allows a firm to take advantage of any locational advantages of foreign production without incurring any ownership, managerial, or investment obligations.

For example, as the popularity of Japanese foods such as sushi and tempura increased and the number of Japanese expatriates worldwide rose, Kirin Brewery, Japan's largest beer producer, decided to expand internationally. Kirin wanted to maintain the beer's freshness, so exporting the beer from Japan was not an option. Its solution was to sign licensing agreements with host country producers. Molson now produces Kirin beer for the Canadian market, and the Charles Wells brewery does the same for the British market.[27]

Basic Issues in International Licensing

Of course, as in any international business arrangement, a firm involved in licensing negotiations must carefully consider the terms of the proposed license as well as its advantages and disadvantages. The terms of a licensing agreement usually reflect the relative bargaining power and negotiating skills of the licensor and the licensee. Nearly every international licensing arrangement is unique because of variations in corporate strategy, the levels of competition, the nature of the product, and the interests of the licensor and licensee. However, each licensing arrangement must

GOING GLOBAL

"Easier Done Than Said"

Many small firms are overwhelmed at the thought of trying to export their products to foreign markets. They often resist taking the plunge, using arguments such as "It's too complicated," "It's too risky," or "We don't have time." One successful firm that took the plunge anyway was Electronic Liquid Fillers (ELF), a small liquid-packaging equipment manufacturer based in Indiana. ELF increased its exports from $150,000 in 1988 to $6 million in 1992, almost half the firm's total current sales. Jeffrey Ake, ELF's vice president of sales and marketing, offers this advice to other would-be exporters:

1. Name somebody—probably the top sales or marketing executive in the firm—to take responsibility for international sales. Doing this signals to everyone in the firm that international business is now important.

2. Announce far and wide that your firm's products exist and that they are available for sale. For example, mail letters and product information to prospective customers in foreign markets, advertise in local trade publications, attend local trade shows, and set up product demonstration exhibits.

3. Go abroad and sell directly. This helps managers learn firsthand about the foreign market, local conditions that exist there, what competitors are doing, and so on.

4. Stick to what you know works. While some local modifications may be necessary, retain your same fundamental products, use the same approach to selling, and so on.

5. Consider raising your prices. In many areas, price equals quality. You also may need the extra revenue to cover shipping costs.

6. Rely on experts to handle the details. Your customers are likely to be familiar with importing products into their country. Let them show you the ropes and how to handle the paperwork.

7. Emphasize service. When the firm gets a new customer in a foreign market, provide exemplary service to keep it.

8. Keep market-entry costs as low as possible. For example, resist opening a foreign office until you are sure it is necessary.

While there are no guarantees of success, ELF has certainly done well in international markets and is committed to continued expansion of markets worldwide.

Source: Based on Jeffrey J. Ake, "Easier Done Than Said," *Inc.*, February 1993, pp. 96–99.

also address a number of basic issues. Because of the complexities and uncertainties associated with licensing, such arrangements are usually specified in a detailed legal contract. Issues this contract typically addresses include the following:

▶ Boundaries of the agreement

▶ Compensation

▶ Rights, privileges, and constraints

▶ Dispute resolution

▶ Duration of the contract

Specifying the Agreement's Boundaries. The first step in negotiating a licensing contract is to specify the boundaries of the agreement. The firms involved must determine which rights and privileges are and are not being conveyed in the agreement. For example, Heineken is exclusively licensed to

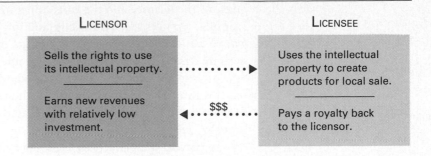

FIGURE 11.3

The Licensing Process

BASIC ISSUES
1. Set the boundaries of the agreement.
2. Establish compensation rates.
3. Agree on the rights, privileges, and constraints conveyed in the agreement.
4. Specify the duration of the agreement.

manufacture and sell Pepsi-Cola in the Netherlands. To implement this agreement, PepsiCo must either provide Heineken with the formula for its soft drink or supply concentrated cola syrup. Heineken is then allowed to add carbonated water to create the beverage, package it in appropriate containers, and distribute and sell it in the Netherlands. But PepsiCo cannot withhold both the formula and the syrup and cannot enter into a competing licensing agreement with another firm to sell Pepsi-Cola in the Netherlands. Similarly, Heineken cannot begin duplicating other products owned by PepsiCo (such as Lays Potato Chips) without a separate agreement. Nor can it alter PepsiCo's formula, market the firm's products as its own, or ship them outside the Netherlands.

Determining Compensation. Compensation is another basic issue that is specified in a licensing contract. Obviously, the licensor wants to receive as much compensation as possible, while the licensee wants to pay as little as possible. Yet each also wants the agreement to be profitable for the other so that both parties will perform their contractual obligations. Licensees must be careful to ensure that they can reach their target levels of profitability after paying licensing fees; the licensor will attempt to establish a rate that allows it to recoup its costs of negotiating the licensing agreement plus a profit on sales. Licensors also want to recover part of their initial R&D costs. In some cases, the licensor may be willing to help pay the licensee's costs of setting up operations.

Compensation under a licensing agreement is called a **royalty**. The royalty is usually paid to the licensor in the form of a flat fee, a fixed amount per unit sold, or, most commonly, a percentage of the sales of the licensed product or service. Although the royalty amount is often determined by prevailing market forces, royalties of 3–5 percent of sales are typical and have long been viewed as reasonable and appropriate. Some licensing agreements also guarantee a minimum royalty payment to ensure that the foreign licensee will take full advantage of the market value of whatever has been licensed rather than merely acquiring and then shelving it to keep domestic rivals from obtaining it.

Establishing Rights, Privileges, and Constraints. Another basic issue to be addressed in licensing agreements concerns the rights and privileges given to the licensee and the constraints imposed on it by the licensor. For example, if a licensee began using inferior (and hence cheaper) materials as a way to boost its profit margin, the image of the licensor's product could be severely damaged. Similarly, if the agreement involved the transfer of technology, production processes, or work methods, the licensee might be tempted to sell this information to another firm, thereby harming the licensor. Or the licensee could simply underreport licensed sales as a means of reducing its licensing fees.

To prevent these practices, licensing agreements usually limit the licensee's freedom to divulge information it has obtained from the licensor to third parties, specify the type and form of records the licensee must keep regarding sales of the licensed products or services, and define standards that will be adhered to regarding product and service quality.

Resolving Disputes. The licensing agreement should also detail how the parties will resolve disputes and disagreements. For example, suppose the licensor feels the materials the licensee uses are inferior but the licensee argues that they meet minimum quality standards. It could be expensive and time-consuming for the two parties to reconcile their differences if they wind up in court. The costs of such conflicts can be reduced if the licensing agreement requires, for example, that disagreements be resolved through the use of a third-party mediator.

Specifying the Agreement's Duration. The last part of the licensing agreement usually specifies its duration. The licensor may view the licensing agreement as a short-term strategy designed to obtain low-cost, low-risk data about the foreign market. If sales of its products and services are strong, it may want to enter the market itself after the agreement has ended. Thus the licensor may seek a short-term agreement. However, if the contract's duration is too short, the licensee may be unwilling to invest in necessary consumer research, distribution networks, and/or production facilities, believing that it will be unable to amortize its investment over the life of the licensing contract. Normally the licensor wants the licensee to undertake these market development efforts. Accordingly, the greater the investment costs incurred by the licensee, the longer is the likely duration of the licensing agreement. For example, the licensees that built Tokyo Disneyland insisted on a 100-year licensing agreement with The Walt Disney Company before agreeing to invest the millions of dollars necessary to build the park.

Licensing is an important element of the strategies of many international firms. Consider the Nintendo Company. The firm manufactures electronic video games and game cartridges. It also licenses 53 U.S. firms to design and, in some cases, to manufacture game cartridges to be used in its game players. As part of its licensing arrangements, Nintendo provides game designers with technical specifications for how its game players work. The design firms create the games and then pay Nintendo a fee to manufacture those games. A few firms manufacture the games themselves, but they must still pay a licensing fee to Nintendo. Through licensing, Nintendo not only generates new revenues; it also inspires the development of new video games, which in turn stimulate demand for Nintendo game players. Similar arrangements are used by most video game and software firms.[28]

Advantages and Disadvantages of International Licensing

Like importing and exporting, licensing has its advantages and disadvantages. One advantage is that licensing carries relatively low financial risk, provided the licensor fully investigates its market opportunities and the abilities of its licensees. It also allows the licensor to learn more about the sales potential of its products and services in a new market without significant investment in financial and managerial resources. Licensees benefit through the opportunity to make and sell, with relatively little R&D cost, products and services that have been successful in other international markets. Nintendo game designers, for example, have the relative safety of knowing there are millions of game system units available that will play their games.

However, licensing does have opportunity costs. Licensing agreements limit the market opportunities for both parties. For example, as long as the licensing agreement between PepsiCo and Heineken is in effect, PepsiCo cannot enter the soft-drink market in the Netherlands and Heineken cannot sell competing soft drinks such as Coca-Cola. Further, licensor and licensee mutually depend on each other to maintain product quality and to promote the product's brand image. Improper actions by one party can damage the other party. For example, if the licensor damages the image and reputation of its products as a result of bad publicity, the licensee will also suffer. If the licensee damages the product's reputation in its market through poor quality control, the adverse publicity can spill over into the licensor's other markets. Further, if the licensee or licensor does not adhere to the agreement, costly and tedious litigation may hurt both parties.

No matter how carefully worded a licensing agreement may be, there is always the risk of problems and misunderstandings. For example, several years ago Oleg Cassini licensed Jovan, the U.S. subsidiary of Beecham of Great Britain, to market the Cassini beauty products line in the United States. After signing the agreement, Jovan was approached by Diane Von Furstenberg Cosmetics with a similar proposal but better terms. Jovan subsequently signed a licensing agreement with Von Furstenberg to make and market its products instead of Cassini's. Cassini was left without a licensee in the United States. To complicate things even further, a clause in the contract between Jovan and Cassini prevented Cassini from licensing its name to any other U.S. firm. Cassini sued Jovan for $789 million. The dispute was eventually settled out of court, but it was more than three years beyond Cassini's original target date before the firm finally got its products into the United States.[29]

A final concern involves the long-term strategic implications of licensing a firm's technology. Many firms are concerned that sharing their technology will inadvertently create a future competitor. The licensee, by producing under the licensing agreement, may be able to learn the manufacturing secrets of the licensor or to develop new production tricks of its own. The licensee can also build an independent reputation for manufacturing quality and service excellence while operating under the contract. Although the licensing agreement may restrict the geographical area in which the licensee can manufacture and sell the product, once the licensing agreement expires, the former licensee may choose to expand its operations into the licensor's existing territory. This is a risk the licensor must take if it feels the benefits of licensing outweigh the risk.

International Franchising

Still another popular strategy for internationalizing a business is franchising. Essentially a special form of licensing, **franchising** allows the licensor more control over the licensee and provides for support from the licensor to the licensee. International franchising is among the fastest-growing forms of international business activity today. A franchising agreement allows an independent entrepreneur or organization, called the **franchisee**, to operate a business under the name of another, called the **franchisor**, in return for a fee. The franchisor provides its franchisees with trademarks, operating systems, and well-known product reputations, as well as continuous support services such as advertising, training, reservation services (for hotel operations), and quality assurance programs.

Basic Issues in International Franchising

International franchising is likely to succeed when certain market conditions exist:

► The franchisor has already achieved considerable success in franchising in its domestic market. For example, there were hundreds of franchised McDonald's restaurants in the United States before the first was built abroad.

► The firm has been successful domestically because of unique products and advantageous operating procedures and systems. McDonald's was successful initially because it provided a popular menu that was consistently prepared and service that was quick and efficient.

► The factors that contributed to domestic success should be transferable to foreign locations. For McDonald's, "American" food is popular in other countries, efficiency and lower prices are valued by consumers worldwide, and foreign visitors to the United States usually seem to want to visit a McDonald's restaurant.

► There must be foreign investors who are interested in entering into franchise agreements. For well-established franchisors, this is typically not a problem.

Like licensing agreements, franchising agreements are almost certain to be spelled out in formal contracts with terms typically as follows:

► The franchisor receives a fixed payment plus a royalty based on the franchisee's sales for the rights to use the franchisor's name, trademarks, formulas, and operating procedures.

► The franchisee agrees to adhere to the franchisor's requirements for appearance, financial reporting, and operating procedures. However, franchisors are likely to allow some degree of flexibility in order to meet local customs and tastes. In fact, as with other licensing arrangements, one of the services the franchisee offers the franchisor is knowledge about the local market's culture and customs. For example, McDonald's restaurants sell beer in Germany and Switzerland and wine in France.

► The franchisor helps the franchisee establish the new business, provides expertise, advertising, and a corporate image, and is usually able to negotiate favorable arrangements with suppliers.

Fast-food restaurants like McDonald's have been very successful in franchising their operations in foreign markets. As this German menu shows, McDonald's food looks the same just about everywhere. But beer is sold in McDonald's German restaurants and wine in its French ones.

Franchising is more common in the United States than in other countries, and U.S. firms are among the leaders in international franchising. One out of three U.S.-based franchisors have at least one foreign franchisee, and half of those without foreign units plan to grow internationally in the next five years.[30] Fast-food firms such as McDonald's, Dairy Queen, Domino's, Pizza Hut, and KFC have franchised restaurants worldwide. Hotels such as Hilton and Marriott and rental car firms such as Hertz and Avis are also successful international franchisors. U.S. franchisors heavily populate Canada, the United Kingdom, and Japan.

Of course, a number of non-U.S. firms have also been successful in franchising. Accor SA has spread its chain of Ibis, Sofitel, and Novetel hotels throughout Europe. It entered the North American market in 1979 and boosted its presence there with the $1.3 billion purchase of Motel 6 in 1990.[31] Benetton, the Italian clothing retailer, has franchised outlets in many countries. Allied-Lyons PLC, a British firm, owns and franchises Baskin-Robbins 31 Flavors and Dunkin' Donuts. And Bridgestone Corporation, a Japanese firm, franchises both Bridgestone and Firestone tire retail outlets in the United States as well as several other countries.

Advantages and Disadvantages of International Franchising

International franchising has both advantages and disadvantages. On the plus side, franchisees can enter a business that has an established and proven product and operating system, and franchisors can expand internationally with relatively low risk and cost. A franchisor also can obtain critical information about local market customs and cultures from host country entrepreneurs that it otherwise might have difficulty obtaining. It further can learn valuable lessons from franchisees that apply to more than the host country. McDonald's managers in the United States believed that the firm's restaurants would be successful only if they were free-standing entities located in suburbs and smaller towns. A Japanese franchisee convinced the firm to allow him to open a restaurant in an inner-city office building. It quickly became one of the firm's most popular restaurants. Because of the insight of its Japanese franchisee, McDonald's now has restaurants in downtown locations in many U.S. cities.

On the negative side, as with licensing, both parties to a franchising agreement must share the profits earned at the franchised location. International franchising may also be more complicated than domestic franchising. For example, when McDonald's expanded to Moscow, it had to teach local farmers how to grow potatoes that met its standards. Moreover, control is also an issue in international franchising. McDonald's was once forced to revoke the franchise it had awarded a French investor because his stores were not maintained according to McDonald's standards.

Specialized Entry Modes for International Business

A firm may also use any of several specialized strategies to participate in international business without making long-term investments. Two of these are the management contract and the turnkey project.

Management Contract

A **management contract** is an agreement whereby one firm provides managerial assistance, technical expertise, or specialized services to a second firm for some agreed-upon time in return for a fee. For its services the first firm may receive either a flat fee or a percentage of sales. The management contract may also specify performance bonuses based on profitability, sales growth, or quality measures. Often such contracts arise as a result of governmental activities. For example, after the Saudi Arabian government nationalized Aramco in the 1970s, it hired Aramco's former owners to manage the firm. Exxon and the other former owners of Aramco, eager to maintain good ties with the Saudi government and access to Saudi oil reserves, were happy to oblige. Sometimes, a government may forbid foreign ownership of firms in certain industries but lack the technical expertise to manage those firms. Major airlines such as Delta, Air France, and KLM often sell their management expertise to small state-owned airlines headquartered in developing countries.

Management contracts allow firms to earn additional revenues without incurring any investment risks or obligations. A subsidiary of Hilton Hotels, for example, offers hotel management and reservation services to hotels that bear the Hilton logo but that are not company-owned. The benefits of Hilton's approach were so pronounced that in 1992 the Marriott Corporation decided to separate its hotel management operations (Marriott International) from its hotel ownership activities (Host Marriott). Marriott believed that doing this would increase its market value because professional investors would recognize the high profitability and low risks associated with its global hotel management services.[32] Similarly, in the 1990s Italy's ENI (Ente Nazionale Idrocarburi) used its knowledge of the European energy industry to aid the Algerian national oil firm, which sought to increase its presence in the European petroleum market. Under a management contract, ENI agreed to construct a network of pipelines for the Algerians and to oversee the distribution of Algerian petroleum in Europe for a predetermined but undisclosed number of years.[33]

Turnkey Project

Another specialized strategy for participating in international business is the turnkey project. A **turnkey project** is a contract under which a firm agrees to fully design, construct, and equip a facility and then turn the project over to the purchaser when it is ready for operation. The turnkey contract may be for a fixed price, in which case the firm makes its profit by keeping its costs below the fixed price. Or, the contract may provide for payment on a cost plus basis, which shifts the risk of cost overruns from the contractor to the purchaser.

International turnkey contracts often involve large, complex, multiyear projects such as construction of a nuclear power plant, an airport, or an oil refinery. Managing such complex construction projects requires special expertise. As a result, most are administered by large construction firms such as Bechtel, Brown and Root, Hyundai Group, New Zealand's Fletcher Challenge Ltd., and Germany's Friedrich Krupp GmbH. The awarding of lucrative turnkey projects is often based on the availability of home government financing, such as through the Eximbank of the United States, or on political ties between the host and home countries. U.S. construction engineering firms have secured many contracts in Saudi Arabia because of the friendly relations between the two countries.

Turnkey projects also may be used when a firm fears that difficulties may arise in procuring resources locally. For example, when PepsiCo wanted to open its first bottling plant in the former Soviet Union, it was concerned about its ability to deal with local suppliers, local building regulations, and the pervasive government bureaucracy. To get around these problems, it contracted with the Soviet government to build the plant to PepsiCo's specifications. When the plant was completed and ready for start-up, PepsiCo managers took over.

Foreign Direct Investment

Exporting, licensing, franchising, and the specialized strategies just discussed all allow a firm to internationalize its business without investing in foreign factories or facilities. However, many firms prefer to enter international markets through ownership of assets in host countries. Other firms may first establish themselves in a foreign market through exporting, licensing, or franchising. After gaining knowledge of and expertise in operating in the host country, they may then want to expand in the market through ownership of production or distribution facilities.

Such FDI affords the firm increased control over its international business operations, as well as increased profit potential. A firm may want such control for either of two reasons:

1 It needs to closely coordinate the activities of its foreign subsidiaries to achieve strategic synergies, as IBM has long done.

2 It determines that the control is necessary in order to fully exploit the economic potential of proprietary technology, manufacturing expertise, or some other intellectual property right.

In one study, for example, British subsidiaries of U.S.-headquartered MNCs were found to be more effective and successful competitors in the United Kingdom than a matched set of British-owned firms, primarily because the U.S. parents were able to transfer their technological and managerial expertise to their British affiliates.[34]

On the other hand, FDI carries with it much greater risk and far more complexity than the other modes of entry. It exposes the firm to greater economic and political risks, as well as the potential erosion of the value of its foreign investments if exchange rates change adversely. A firm's decision to engage in FDI may also be influenced by government policies. As noted in Chapter 8, host countries may discourage FDI through direct controls on foreign capital or through restrictions on repatriation of dividends and capital; home countries can promote FDI through such devices as political risk insurance. Firms using FDI must also meet the standard challenges of managing, operating, and financing their foreign subsidiaries while facing the additional hurdle of doing so in political, legal, and cultural milieus different from their own.

There are three methods for FDI:

1 Build new facilities (called the **greenfield strategy**).

2 Buy existing assets in a foreign country (called the **acquisition strategy**).

3 Participate in a joint venture.

The Greenfield Strategy

The greenfield strategy involves starting a new operation from scratch (the word *greenfield* arises from the image of starting with a virgin green site and then building on it). The firm buys or leases land, constructs new facilities, hires and/or transfers in managers and employees, and then launches the new operation. Kodak's recently opened R&D laboratory in Japan represents a greenfield investment, as does Honda's automobile assembly plant in Marysville, Ohio, and Nissan's factory in Sunderland, England.

The greenfield strategy has several advantages:

▶ The firm can select the site that best meets its needs and construct modern, up-to-date facilities. Local communities often offer economic development incentives to attract such facilities because they will create new jobs; these incentives lower the firm's costs.

▶ The firm starts with a clean slate. Managers do not have to deal with existing debts, nurse outmoded equipment, or struggle to modify ancient work rules protected by intransigent labor unions. For example, GM's managers consider a major advantage of its new Eisenach factory in former East Germany to be its ability to implement Japanese-style production techniques and labor policies without having to battle workers wedded to the old way of doing things.

▶ The firm can acclimate itself to the new national business culture at its own pace, rather than having the instant responsibility of managing a newly acquired, ongoing business. Recent research, for example, indicates that the greater the cultural differences between the home and host countries, the more likely a firm is to choose to build a new factory rather than purchase an existing firm.[35]

However, the greenfield strategy has some disadvantages:

▶ Successful implementation takes time and patience.

▶ Often land in the desired location is unavailable or very expensive.

▶ In building the new factory, the firm must comply with various local and national regulations and oversee the factory's construction.

▶ The firm must recruit a local workforce and train it to meet the firm's performance standards.

▶ The firm, by constructing a new facility, may be more strongly perceived as a foreign enterprise.

Disney managers faced several of these difficulties in building Euro Disney. Although the French government sold the necessary land to Disney at bargain prices, Disney was not fully prepared to deal with French construction contractors. For example, Disney executives had numerous communications difficulties with a painter that applied 20 different shades of pink to a hotel before the firm approved the color. The park's grand opening was threatened when local contractors demanded an additional $150 million for extra work allegedly requested by Disney. And Disney continues to clash with its French employees, who have resisted the firm's attempt to impose its U.S. work values and grooming standards on them.[36]

The Acquisition Strategy

A second FDI strategy is acquisition of an existing firm conducting business in the host country. Although the actual transaction may no doubt be very complex—involving bankers, lawyers, regulators, and mergers and acquisitions specialists from several countries—the basic motivation for this strategy is quite simple. By acquiring a going concern, the purchaser quickly obtains control over the acquired firm's factories, employees, technology, brand names, and distribution networks. The acquired firm can continue to generate revenues as the purchaser integrates it into its overall international strategy.

For example, as part of the growing globalization of the food-processing industry, numerous multinational food processors in the early 1990s purchased existing firms in order to acquire their brand names, trademarks, production facilities, and/or distribution networks. Phillip Morris purchased Europe's largest chocolate producer, Scandinavia's Freia Marabou, for $1.5 billion to acquire its successful brand names. RJR Nabisco purchased Italy's Stella D'Oro Company in 1992, thereby enhancing its existing lines of cookies. Bermuda's Bacardi, Ltd., acquired Luxembourg's Martini and Rossi for $1.4 billion in 1992, giving it Martini and Rossi's valuable brand names as well as its excellent European distribution networks.[37] Pacific Asia also attracted attention: in 1992 Campbell Soup paid $860 million for Arnotts, Ltd., a major Australian food processor, to increase its presence in the Pacific market.[38] That same year, H. J. Heinz Company purchased New Zealand's Wattie Foods, Ltd., for $300 million with the intention of using Wattie's 15 New Zealand manufacturing plants as the base for serving the large and growing Pacific Asia market.[39] In early 1995, Cadbury Schweppes PLC, a British firm, bought Dr. Pepper/Seven-Up Companies, Inc., the third-largest U.S. soft drink company, in order to acquire its brand names, bottling network, and distribution system.

However, the acquiring firm also assumes all the liabilities—financial, managerial, and otherwise—of the acquired firm. For example, if the acquired firm has poor labor relations, unfunded pension obligations, or hidden environmental cleanup liabilities, the acquiring firm becomes financially responsible for solving the problem. The acquiring firm usually must also spend substantial sums up front. For example, when Matsushita purchased U.S. entertainment conglomerate MCA for $6.6 billion in 1991, it had to pay out this vast sum shortly after the deal was closed. The greenfield strategy, in contrast, may allow a firm to grow slowly and spread its investment over an extended period. For example, Honda developed its Ohio operations gradually, beginning with a motorcycle factory in 1972 and adding an automobile assembly plant in 1982. Since 1984, Honda has added an engine factory and expanded its manufacturing capacity as its strategy for succeeding in the U.S. market has evolved. An international acquisition may also reveal unexpected local issues that must be subsequently resolved. For example, after Matsushita bought MCA, it discovered that one of MCA's subsidiaries operated concessions at several U.S. national parks, including Yosemite National Park. Some U.S. government officials expressed concerns that such activities should not be controlled by foreigners. MCA eventually sold the subsidiary to a U.S. firm in order to placate critics.

Joint Ventures

Another form of FDI is the joint venture. **Joint ventures** are created when two or more firms agree to work together and create a jointly owned separate firm to promote their mutual interests. The number of such arrangements is burgeoning as rapid changes in technology, telecommunications, and government policies outstrip the ability of international firms to exploit opportunities on their own. Because of the growing importance of international intercorporate cooperation, as well as the unique set of challenges it offers international firms, we devote Chapter 12 to this subject.

CHAPTER REVIEW

Summary

Once a firm has decided to expand its international operations and assessed potential foreign markets, it must decide how to enter and compete most effectively in the selected foreign markets. An array of strategic options is available for doing this. Choosing an entry mode involves careful assessment of firm-specific ownership advantages, location advantages, and internalization advantages.

Exporting, the most common initial entry mode, is the process of sending goods or services from one country to other countries for use or sale there. Exporting continues to grow rapidly. There are several forms of exporting, including indirect exporting, direct exporting, and intracorporate

transfer. In deciding whether to export, a firm must consider such factors as government policies, marketing concerns, consumer information needs, logistical considerations, and distribution issues. Export intermediaries are often used to facilitate exporting. These include export management companies, Webb-Pomerene associations, international trading companies, and export trading companies.

International licensing, another popular entry mode, occurs when one firm sells the right to use its intellectual property to another firm. Basic issues in international licensing include negotiating mutually acceptable terms, determining compensation, defining the rights and privileges of and the constraints imposed on the licensee, and specifying the duration of the agreement.

International franchising is also growing rapidly as an entry mode. International franchising is an arrangement whereby an independent organization or entrepreneur operates a business under the name of another. Several market conditions must exist in order for a firm to successfully franchise. As with licensing agreements, the terms of a franchising agreement are usually quite detailed and specific.

Two specialized entry modes are the management contract and the turnkey project. A management contract calls for one firm to provide managerial assistance, technical assistance, or specialized services to another firm for a fee. A turnkey project involves one firm agreeing to fully design, construct, and equip a facility for another.

The most complex entry mode is FDI. FDI involves the ownership and control of assets in a foreign market. The greenfield strategy for FDI calls for the investing firm to start a totally new enterprise from scratch. The acquisition strategy, in contrast, involves buying an existing firm or operation in the foreign market. In joint ventures, a third form of FDI, ownership and control are shared by two or more firms.

Review Questions

1. What are some of the basic issues a firm must confront when choosing an entry mode for a new foreign market?

2. What is exporting? Why has it increased so dramatically in recent years?

3. What are the primary advantages and disadvantages of exporting?

4. What are three forms of exporting?

5. What is an export intermediary? What is its role?

6. What are the various types of export intermediaries?

7. What is international licensing? What are its advantages and disadvantages?

8. What is international franchising? What are its advantages and disadvantages?

9. What are two specialized entry modes for international business, and how do they work?

10. What is FDI? What are its three basic forms? What are the relative advantages and disadvantages of each?

Questions for Discussion

1. How does each advantage in Dunning's eclectic theory specifically affect a firm's decision regarding entry mode?

2. Why is exporting the most popular initial entry mode?

3. What specific factors could cause a firm to reject exporting as an entry mode?

4. What conditions must exist for an intracorporate transfer to be cost-effective?

5. Given that most exporting arrangements are likely to involve multiple forms of transportation, what steps could a firm undertake to minimize its transportation costs?

6. Your firm is about to begin exporting. In selecting an export intermediary, what characteristics would you look for?

7. Do you think trading companies like Japan's sogo sosha will ever become common in the United States? Why or why not?

8. What factors could cause you to reject an offer from a potential licensee to make and market your firm's products in a foreign market?

9. Do you think more foreign firms will begin franchising in the United States? Why or why not?

10. Under what conditions should a firm consider a greenfield strategy for FDI? An acquisition strategy?

BUILDING GLOBAL SKILLS

When Heineken enters a new market, it follows a basic set of steps designed to maximize its potential profits in that market:

1. It begins to export its beer into that market as a way to boost brand familiarity and image.

2. If sales look promising, it then licenses its brands to a local brewer. Doing this allows Heineken to build its sales further while simultaneously becoming more familiar with local distribution networks.

3. If this relationship also yields promising results, Heineken then either buys partial ownership of the local brewer or forms a new joint venture with that brewer.

The end result is a two-tier arrangement with the more-expensive Heineken label at the top end of the market and the lower-priced local brands at the bottom, all sharing a common brewery, sales force, and distribution network.

After reading and thinking about Heineken's approach, break up into groups of four or five people each and proceed as follows:

1. Identify at least five products or brands you are familiar with that could use the same three-step approach perfected by Heineken for entering foreign markets. Develop a clear rationale to support each example.

2. Identify at least five products or brands that probably could not use that strategy. Develop a clear rationale to support each example.

3. Randomly list the ten examples you identified, keeping the rationale for each hidden. Exchange lists with another group. Each group should discuss the list given to it by the other group and classify the various products or brands into one of two categories: "can copy Heineken's approach" and "cannot copy Heineken's approach." Be sure to have some rationale for your decision.

4. Each pair of groups that exchanged lists should form one new group. Compare lists and note areas in which the smaller groups agreed and disagreed on their classifications. Discuss the reasons for any disagreements in classification.

Follow-up Questions

1. What are the specific factors that enable Heineken to use the approach described and simultaneously make it difficult for some other firms to copy it? What types of firms are most and least likely to be able to use this approach?

2. What does this exercise teach you about international business?

CLOSING CASE

Blockbuster Fast-Forwards Overseas[40]

The video store that would eventually spawn Blockbuster Entertainment Corporation opened in 1985. In fewer than ten years, Blockbuster has grown to become the market leader in the home video rental industry, with annual revenues exceeding $1 billion. Indeed, the firm today is larger than its ten biggest

rivals combined. It succeeded by combining small video stores into video supermarkets and bringing to the marketplace those efficiencies that come from a large-scale network of buying and advertising operations. It seeks the best locations and offers customers convenient hours and a large selection of videos. About half the Blockbuster outlets in the United States are company-owned; the others are franchises.

Despite Blockbuster's success, some experts worry about its future. They note, for example, that the video rental market faces formidable competition from such alternative products as pay-per-view movies through local cable companies and the potential for broadcasting movies directly over fiber-optic cable from the telephone company. Some critics also argue that Blockbuster depreciates its videos too slowly, resulting in higher short-term profits, and that a substantial portion of its revenues comes from mass video purchases by new franchisees to stock new stores. As the firm's growth slows, they argue, this income flow will gradually end.

But Blockbuster's managers aren't worried. They have confounded their critics before, and they point out that they recognize and understand the challenges they must overcome. Indeed, Blockbuster has recently undertaken a massive effort to expand internationally. The firm's managers believe much of its future growth will come from abroad.

Their immediate goal is to build international sales to 25 percent of total sales by 1995. Their first big push has been in the United Kingdom, which until recently had only a few Blockbuster stores. With so few outlets, the firm had no identity in that market. Thus in 1992 Blockbuster bought Citivision PLC, the largest video rental chain in the United Kingdom, bringing to 790 Blockbuster's stores in that country. It plans to systematically convert each Citivision store into a Blockbuster outlet and then turn those outlets over to franchisees.

Blockbuster is also franchising in other countries. Half of its 51 stores in Canada are franchised, as are all of its 17 stores in Mexico, 47 stores in Chile, 4 in Australia, 3 in Spain, and 2 in Venezuela. But Japan is the firm's next big hope. By enlisting the assistance of large franchisees to help overcome the notorious Japanese bureaucracy, Blockbuster opened 17 stores in Japan in 1992 and 30 in 1993. It plans to have 1000 stores in operation there by the end of the decade.

But Blockbuster is also hedging its video bets. The firm has had ongoing talks with Philips, the Dutch electronics firm, about several direct investment strategies. One scenario has Blockbuster selling Philips products in massive video and music superstores. Another involves using new video technology developed by Philips, such as virtual reality, to construct rides and other amusement devices that would be used in miniparks operated by Blockbuster. The firm also has a joint venture with IBM that will allow customers to record their own music selections on IBM equipment in Blockbuster music stores.

Case Questions

1. What entry modes is Blockbuster using to penetrate foreign markets?

2. What are the advantages and disadvantages of each entry mode for Blockbuster?

3. What competitive factors must Blockbuster consider when entering a particular foreign market?

4. In retailing, which is likely to be most successful: the greenfield strategy or the acquisition strategy?

5. What concerns or obstacles do you think Blockbuster should be worrying about as it pursues its strategy of international growth?

CHAPTER NOTES

1. "Heineken's Battle to Stay Top Bottle," *Business Week*, August 1, 1994, pp. 60–62; Gary Hoover, Alta Campbell, Alan Chai, and Patrick J. Spain (eds.), *Hoover's Handbook of World Business 1994* (Austin, Tex.: Reference Press, 1993), p. 250; Brett Duval Fromson, "Cheers to Heineken," *Fortune*, November 19, 1990, p. 172.

2. John H. Dunning, "Trade, Location of Economic Activity and the MNE: A Search for an Eclectic Approach," in Bertil Ohlin et al., eds., *The International Allocation of Economic Activity* (London: Macmillan, 1977); Alan M. Rugman, "A New Theory of the Multinational Enterprise: Internationalization versus Internalization," *Columbia Journal of World Business*, 1980, pp. 23–29.

3. "Siam Cement Looks Solid to Analysts Despite Building Slump, New Rivalry," *Wall Street Journal*, October 13, 1992, p. C21.

4. Jean J. Boddewyn, "Political Aspects of MNE Theory," *Journal of International Business Studies*, Vol. 19, No. 1 (1988), pp. 341–363; Thomas L. Brewer, "Effects of Government Policies on Foreign Direct Investment as a Strategic Choice of Firms: An Expansion of Internalization Theory," *The International Trade Journal*, Vol. 7, No. 1 (Fall 1992), pp. 111–129.

5. Franklin R. Root and Ahmed A. Ahmed, "The Influence of Policy Instruments on Manufacturing Direct Foreign Investment in Developing Countries," *Journal of International Business Studies*, Vol. 9, No. 3 (1978), pp. 81–93.

6. Ming-Je Tang and Chwo-Ming Joseph Yu, "Regulating the Entry of Multinational Enterprises: Models and Practices," *The International Trade Journal*, Vol. 7, No. 1 (Fall 1992), pp. 131–150; Office of the U.S. Trade Representative, *Foreign Trade Barriers* (Washington, D.C.: U.S. Government Printing Office, 1992).

7. Kenichi Ohmae, "The Global Logic of Strategic Alliances," *Harvard Business Review*, March–April 1989, p. 151.

8. "Company, Du Pont Merck Enter Rights Arrangement," *Wall Street Journal*, October 6, 1992, p. C9.

9. John M. Stopford and Louis T. Wells, *Managing the Multinational Enterprise: Organization of the Firm and Ownership of the Subsidiaries* (New York: Basic Books, 1972).

10. M. Krishna Erramilli, "The Experience Factor in Foreign Market Entry Behavior of Service Firms," *The Journal of International Business Studies*, Vol. 22, No. 3 (Third Quarter 1991), pp. 479–502.

11. Bruce Kogut, "Designing Global Strategies: Profiting from Operational Flexibility," *Sloan Management Review*, Fall 1985, pp. 27–38; Edward W. Desmond, "Byting Japan," *Time*, October 5, 1992, pp. 68–69.

12. W. Chan Kim and Peter Hwang, "Global Strategy and Multinationals' Entry Mode Choice," *Journal of International Business Studies*, Vol. 23, No. 1 (First Quarter 1992), pp. 29–54; see also Sumantra Ghoshal, "Global Strategy: An Organizing Framework," *Strategic Management Journal*, Vol 8. (1987), pp. 425–440.

13. Sanjeev Agarwal and Sridhar N. Ramaswami, "Choice of Foreign Market Entry Mode: Impact of Ownership, Location, and Internalization Factors," *Journal of International Business Studies*, Vol. 23, No. 1 (First Quarter 1992), pp. 1–28.

14. "Small U.S. Companies Try to Soar at Foreign Air Shows," *Wall Street Journal*, October 12, 1992, p. B2.

15. "Latin Links," *Wall Street Journal*, September 24, 1992, p. R6.

16. "A Japanese Retailer Finds Southeast Asia Is the Place to Grow," *Wall Street Journal*, September 4, 1992, p. A1.

17. "Retailer and Chinese Partner to Form Supermarket Chain," *Wall Street Journal*, October 9, 1992, p. B3.

18. Geir Gripsud, "The Determinants of Export Decisions and Attitudes to a Distant Market: Norwegian Fishery Exports to Japan," *The Journal of International Business Studies*, Vol. 21, No. 3 (Third Quarter 1990), pp. 469–494.

19. F. Steb Hipple, "Multinational Companies and International Trade: The Impact of Intrafirm Shipments on U.S. Foreign Trade 1977–1982," *Journal of International Business Studies*, Vol. 21, No. 3 (Third Quarter 1990), pp. 495–504.

20. Alex Taylor III, "Do You Know Where Your Car Was Made?" *Fortune*, June 17, 1991, pp. 52–56.

21. Desmond, op. cit.

22. "German Unit Is Established for Importing, Distribution," *Wall Street Journal*, October 8, 1992, p. C15.

23. See *A Basic Guide to Exporting* (Washington, D.C.: U.S. Department of Commerce, 1986) and *Importing into the United States* (Washington, D.C.: U.S. Department of the Treasury, 1986) for general introductions to exporting and importing.

24. For a discussion of the theory of export intermediaries, see Anne C. Perry, "The Evolution of the U.S. International Trade Intermediary in the 1980s: a Dynamic Model," *Journal of International Business Studies*, Vol. 21, No. 1 (First Quarter 1990), pp. 133–153.

25. "The World's 100 Largest Banks," *Wall Street Journal*, September 24, 1992, p. R27; Hoover et al., op. cit., p. 238.

26. *Forbes*, July 20, 1992, p. 242. Because sogo sosha are involved primarily in buying and selling goods on very small profit margins, they are often excluded from lists of the world's largest firms. Table 1.1, for example, listed the world's largest industrial MNCs, a ranking on which the sogo sosha would do poorly.

27. "Creating a worldwide yen for Japanese beer," *Financial Times*, October 7, 1992, p. 20.

28. "Nintendo to Ease Restrictions on U.S. Game Designers," *Wall Street Journal*, October 22, 1991, pp. B1, B4.

29. "Oleg Cassini, Inc., Sues Firm Over Licensing," *Wall Street Journal*, March 28, 1984, p. 5.

30. *Wall Street Journal*, November 13, 1992, pp. 132.

31. Hoover et al., op. cit., p. 145.

32. "Hospitality Split," *Time*, October 19, 1992, p. 22.

33. "Can a Pumped-Up ENI Get into Fighting Trim?" *Business Week*, May 27, 1991, pp. 76–77.

34. J. H. Dunning, *American Investment in British Manufacturing Industry* (London: George Allen and Unwin, 1958).

35. Bruce Kogut and Harbir Singh, "The Effect of National Culture on the Choice of Entry Mode," *Journal of International Business Studies*, Vol. 19 (Fall 1988), pp. 411–432.

36. "Disney's Rough Ride in France," *Fortune*, March 23, 1992, p. 14.

37. "Bacardi to Buy Martini & Rossi Majority Stake," *Wall Street Journal*, September 11, 1992, p. A7.

38. "U.S. food giants shopping overseas," *Houston Chronicle*, October 13, 1992, p. 12C.

39. "H. J. Heinz Buys New Zealand Firm for $300 Million," *Wall Street Journal*, October 8, 1992, p. B8.

40. "They Don't Call it Blockbuster for Nothing," *Business Week*, October 19, 1992, pp. 113–114; "Fast-Forward Video King," *Business Week*, January 22, 1990, p. 47; "Will This Video Chain Stay on Fast-Forward?" *Business Week*, June 12, 1989, pp. 72, 75; "Blockbuster Is Tuning In to Music," *USA Today*, October 22, 1992, p. 3B.

CHAPTER

12

International Strategic Alliances

Chapter Outline

International corporate cooperation

Comparison of joint ventures and other types of strategic alliances
Growth in strategic alliances

Benefits of strategic alliances

Ease of market entry
Shared risk
Shared knowledge and expertise
Synergy and competitive advantage

Scope of strategic alliances

Comprehensive alliances
Functional alliances

Management of strategic alliances

Selection of partners
Form of ownership
Joint management considerations

Pitfalls of strategic alliances

Incompatibility of partners
Access to information
Distribution of earnings
Potential loss of autonomy
Changing circumstances

After studying this chapter you should be able to:

Compare joint ventures and other forms of strategic alliances.

Discuss the benefits of strategic alliances.

Describe the scope of strategic alliances.

Discuss the forms of management used for strategic alliances.

Describe the limitations of strategic alliances.

THE BREAKFAST CEREAL MARKET IN EUROPE HOLDS ENORMOUS potential. Consumption of cereal is increasing rapidly, and the reduction of trade barriers makes it easier than ever to do business there. Some experts predict that the market could quadruple by the end of this decade. Thus it is extremely attractive, with the potential to generate enormous profits for firms wise enough to seize the opportunity. ▮▮ Kellogg virtually created the market for breakfast cereals in Europe. The maker of such popular brands as Kellogg's Corn Flakes, Rice Krispies, and Frosted Flakes, Kellogg began introducing its products in the United Kingdom in the 1920s and on the continent in the 1950s. However, Europeans traditionally favored bread, fruit, eggs, and meats for breakfast, so the firm had a tough sell on its hands. Indeed, it has taken decades for Europeans to accept cereals as a viable breakfast

The European Cereal Wars[1]

choice. ▮▮ During the last several years, demand for breakfast cereals in Europe has begun to increase faster as European consumers have become more health-conscious and started looking for breakfast alternatives to eggs and meat. Also, the busy schedules of the increasing numbers of dual-career families have spurred demand for prepackaged foods. Another contributing factor has been the emergence of supermarkets in Europe. Traditionally most food products in Europe were sold at small specialty stores. Those stores were often reluctant to stock cereals because they take up so much shelf space. In recent years, however, more full-line supermarkets have opened in Europe, and shelf space is now available for a wider array of products. Finally, the growth of commercial TV networks in Europe has helped firms increase demand through advertising. Thus the stage was set for Kellogg's competitors to move into the European breakfast cereal market. ▮▮ One of Kellogg's biggest competitors in the United States is General Mills. General Mills, which makes Cheerios, Golden Grahams, and other popular brands, has traditionally concentrated on the North American market. But in 1989 General Mills's managers decided it was time to enter the European market. However, they also recognized that taking on Kellogg, which controlled 50 percent of the worldwide cereal market and dominated the European market, would be a monumental battle. ▮▮ After careful consideration, General Mills's CEO Bruce Atwater decided that the firm could compete most effectively in Europe if it worked with a strategic ally located there. And it didn't take him long to choose one: Nestlé, the world's largest food-processing firm. Nestlé is a household name in Europe, has a well-established distribution system, and owns manufacturing plants worldwide. One major area in which

Nestlé had never succeeded, however, was the cereal market. Thus Atwater reasoned that Nestlé would be a logical and willing partner. ▮▮ When he approached his counterpart at Nestlé, he was amazed to discover that that firm had already been considering approaching General Mills about just such an arrangement. From Nestlé's perspective, General Mills could contribute its knowledge of cereal technology, its array of proven cereal products, and its expertise in marketing cereals to consumers, especially children. ▮▮ Top managers of the two firms met and quickly outlined a plan of attack. Each firm contributed around $80 million to form a new firm called Cereal Partners Worldwide (CPW). General Mills agreed to install its proprietary manufacturing systems in existing Nestlé factories, oversee the production of cereals, and help develop advertising campaigns. Nestlé, in turn, agreed to use its own corporate name on the products and to handle sales and distribution throughout Europe. ▮▮ So far, CPW seems like a success. Its strategic goal was to capture 20 percent of the European cereal market by 2000; it seems almost certain that it will easily surpass that goal. Nestlé has struck a deal on behalf of CPW to supply breakfast cereal to restaurants and hotels at Euro Disney and has licensed the use of Disney characters to promote CPW products. Looking ahead, CPW also sees tremendous possibilities in other markets. Nestlé is a household name in Asia, Africa, and Latin America, for example, and CPW expects to enter breakfast cereal markets in those regions soon. ▮▮ Of course, there are obstacles ahead. Kellogg is aggressively defending its European market share. For example, it has introduced new cereal products that look and taste like CPW products and is even packaging them in look-alike boxes. Also, Nestlé poses a potential threat to General Mills. Nestlé has a reputation for acquiring other firms rather than collaborating with them. Although Nestlé maintains that it has no interest in buying General Mills and it would take billions of dollars to complete such an acquisition, managers at General Mills certainly are keeping the threat of a takeover in the back of their minds. ▮▮▮▮▮

As should be obvious by now, firms throughout the world are globalizing. But globalization can be a very expensive process, particularly when a firm must perfectly coordinate R&D, production, distribution, marketing, and financial decisions in order to succeed. A firm may discover that it lacks all the necessary internal resources to effectively compete against its rivals internationally. The high costs just for researching and developing new products often stretch corporate budgets. Thus a firm may seek partners to share these costs. For example, Boeing has enlisted the support of Japanese partners to help offset the high development costs of the next generation of jumbo jets. Or a firm may develop a new technology but lack a distribution network or production facilities in all the national markets it wants to serve. Accordingly, the firm may seek out other firms with skills or advantages that complement its own and negotiate agreements to work together. As the chapter opener indicates, General Mills possesses extensive manufacturing knowledge and valuable brand names for breakfast cereals. It wanted to enter the European cereal market but lacked distribution networks and marketing clout with European grocery retailers. Nestlé, on the other hand, has well-established distribution and marketing expertise in Europe but lacked General Mills's extensive knowledge about manufacturing ready-to-eat cereals.

International Corporate Cooperation

Cooperation between international firms can take many forms, such as cross-licensing of proprietary technology, sharing of production facilities, cofunding of research projects, and marketing of each other's products using existing distribution networks. Such forms of cooperation are known collectively as **strategic alliances**, business arrangements whereby two or more firms choose to cooperate for their mutual benefit.[2] The partners in a strategic alliance may agree to pool R&D activities, marketing expertise, and/or managerial talent.

American Motors Corporation (now a part of Chrysler Motor Corporation) was able to enter the Chinese market through a joint venture with the municipally owned Beijing Automotive Works. The new venture, called Beijing Jeep, produced Jeeps and other vehicles for the Chinese market.

For example, Kodak and Fuji—two fierce competitors in the film market—recently agreed to work together, along with Canon, Minolta, and Nikon, to develop a new standard for camera film.[3]

A **joint venture** is a special type of strategic alliance in which two or more firms join together to create a new business entity that is legally separate and distinct from its parents. Joint ventures are normally established as corporations and owned by the founding parents in whatever proportions they negotiate. Many are owned equally by the founding firms, although unequal ownership is also common. The joint venture agreement may even provide for changes in ownership shares. For example, initial ownership of the joint venture Beijing Jeep was divided equally between its owners, American Motors Corporation and the municipally owned Beijing Automotive Works. However, the joint venture agreement allows American Motors to increase its ownership stake in Beijing Jeep to 70 percent by using its share of the profits to purchase additional shares.

Comparison of Joint Ventures and Other Types of Strategic Alliances

A strategic alliance is only one method by which a firm can enter or expand its international operations. As Chapter 11 discussed, other alternatives exist: exporting, licensing, franchising, and FDI. Each of these alternatives, however, involves a firm acting alone or hiring a second individual or firm—often one further down the distribution chain—to act on its behalf. In contrast, a strategic alliance results from cooperation among two or more firms. Each participant in a strategic alliance is motivated to promote its own self-interest but has determined that cooperation is the best way to achieve its goals.

Some means for managing any cooperative agreement is required. For example, a joint venture, as a separate legal entity, must have its own set of managers and board of directors. A joint venture may be managed in any of three ways:

1 The founding firms may jointly share management, with each appointing key personnel who report back to officers of the parent.

2 One parent may assume primary responsibility.

3 An independent team of managers may be hired to run it.

Often the third approach is preferred, for independent managers focus on what is best for the joint venture rather than attempting to placate bosses from the founding firms.[4] Other types of strategic alliances, on the other hand, may be managed more informally—for example, by a coordinating committee, composed of employees of each of the partners, which oversees the alliance's progress.

Creation of a formal organization to manage a joint venture allows the venture to be broader in purpose, scope (or range of operations), and duration than other types of strategic alliances. A non–joint venture strategic alliance may be formed merely to allow the partners to overcome a particular hurdle that each faces in the short run. A joint venture will be more helpful if the two firms plan a more extensive and long-term relationship. A typical non-joint venture strategic alliance has a narrow purpose and scope, such as marketing a new videophone system in Canada. A joint venture might be formed if firms wanted to cooperate in the design, production, and sale of a broad line of telecommunications equipment in North America. Non-joint venture strategic alliances are often formed for a specific purpose that may have a natural ending. For example, the agreement among the camera manufacturers Canon, Minolta, and Nikon and the film manufacturers Fuji and Kodak to jointly develop new standards for camera film will terminate once this specific project is finished. But because joint ventures are separate legal entities, they generally have a longer duration.

Because of their narrow mission and lack of a formal organizational structure, non-joint ventures strategic alliances are relatively less stable than joint ventures. For example, in 1988 United Airlines and British Airways entered into an agreement to form a strategic marketing alliance involving their North American and European routes. At the time, United was offering limited service to Europe and was losing market share to archrivals Delta and American Airlines, both of which offered more extensive service there. To solve its problem, United agreed to coordinate its flight schedules with British Airways, thereby making it more convenient for a Europe-bound U.S. traveler to board a domestic United flight and then transfer to a transatlantic British Airways flight. United and British Airways both prominently described the arrangement in their marketing campaigns and in the visits of their marketing reps to U.S. and European travel agencies. Within a year, however, Pan Am's routes to London were placed on the auction block.

United quickly purchased those routes from Pan Am and severed relations with its strategic ally. British Airways was of little use to United once United could operate in London on its own.

Growth in Strategic Alliances

Strategic alliances reflect a desire by international firms to achieve their independent business objectives cooperatively. Because these alliances are such an effective way to compete in international markets, their numbers have skyrocketed. In 1980, their growth rate was around 6 percent per year. By the end of the decade, it had nearly quadrupled to 22 percent per year.[5] IBM, for example, at one time shunned collaborative arrangements of any form. Today it has over 40 active strategic alliances with partners that include such firms as Toshiba, Siemens, and Apple. And AT&T continues to develop linkages with most of the world's largest telephone and electronics firms, including Northern Telecom, Matsushita, and Novell.

Benefits of Strategic Alliances

Firms that enter into strategic alliances usually expect to benefit in one or more ways. As summarized in Fig. 12.1, there are four potential benefits that international business may realize from strategic alliances:[6]

1 Ease of market entry
2 Shared risk
3 Shared knowledge and expertise
4 Synergy and competitive advantage

Ease of Market Entry

Chapter 10 discussed some of the basic factors a firm must consider when assessing potential foreign markets. Even if those factors are all favorable and the firm decides to enter a particular market, it may still face major obstacles, such as

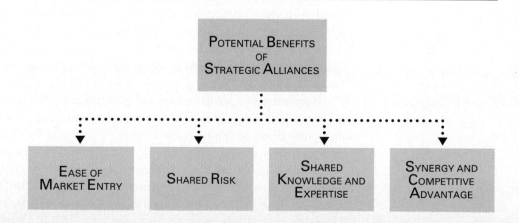

FIGURE 12.1

Benefits of Strategic Alliances

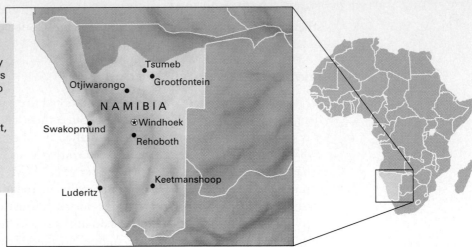

Namibia's government has promoted development of the country's fishing industry by requiring foreign investors who wish to fish its waters to join with local partners in establishing onshore fish-processing plants. As a result, joint ventures have created jobs, both onshore and offshore, for some 10,000 Namibians.

Desert and desert shrub

Wooded savanna

MAP 12.1

Namibia and Joint Ventures

entrenched competition and hostile government regulations. Choosing a strategic alliance as the entry mode may overcome some of these obstacles or reduce the costs of entry.

Advances in telecommunications, computerization, and transportation have made it easier for international firms to enter new foreign markets. Further, economies of scale and scope in marketing and distribution confer benefits on firms that aggressively and quickly enter numerous markets.[7] Yet the costs of doing this are often large and beyond the capabilities of a single firm. Strategic alliances may allow a firm to achieve the benefits of rapid entry while keeping costs down.

Consider the challenges facing TNT, Ltd., an Australian air express firm engaged in a global battle with Federal Express, United Parcel Service (UPS), and DHL Worldwide Express for the lucrative corporate express package-delivery market. Many large MNCs prefer to concentrate their business with one carrier; thus express package-delivery firms have been rapidly expanding globally. But TNT was concerned that its rivals had already grabbed a large share of the European market. This concern was shared by many postal services, which were upset over losing control of this valuable market to package-delivery specialists. As a result, TNT and the post offices of Canada, France, Germany, the Netherlands, and Sweden agreed to establish a joint venture to compete against their mutual rivals. TNT's aircraft will transport the joint venture's parcels internationally, and the five post offices will use their employees to collect and deliver packages. TNT gets quick entry into these markets; the post offices regain the local package-delivery business they were losing to Federal Express, UPS, and DHL Worldwide.[8]

Regulations imposed by national governments also influence the formation of joint ventures. For example, many countries are so concerned about the influence of foreign firms on their economies that they require MNCs to work with a local partner if they want to operate in these countries.[9] For example, the government of Namibia, an African nation, requires foreign investors operating fishing fleets off its coast to work with local partners (see Map 12.1). India also used this approach until 1991, when it liberalized its restrictions on FDI by foreign MNCs. However, many firms continue to choose joint ventures as the preferred mode of entering the Indian market. For example, IBM, which left the Indian market in the 1970s because of India's restrictions on foreign MNCs, reentered it in 1991 via a joint venture with local entrepreneurs.

Similarly, China's communist rulers often allow capitalist firms to enter the Chinese market only as part of a cooperative arrangement. For example, Wal-Mart recently announced the formation of a joint venture with Hong Kong–based Ek Chor Distribution System to open several discount stores in China and Hong Kong. The discount stores will be called Value Clubs and will be smaller versions of Wal-Mart's successful Sam's Wholesale Clubs.[10]

Many Western firms have chosen to enter the markets of the formerly communist Central and Eastern European countries in cooperation with existing domestic firms, in order to obtain information about local customers, distribution networks, and suppliers. For example, Bristol-Myers Squibb joined with the Akrihin Chemical Company in 1992 to create a joint venture that uses Akrihin's existing plant in Kupavna, Russia, to produce and package pharmaceuticals.[11] And CPC International, Inc., a food-processing firm that sells such brands as Hellmann's mayonnaise and Mazola corn oil, has several cooperative arrangements with firms in Eastern European countries to market its products there.[12]

In Mexico, President Salinas's economic reforms encouraged numerous new joint ventures in that country. For example, Toronto's Cambridge Shopping Centres, Ltd., a leading mall developer, has joined with Grupo ICA, Mexico's largest construction firm, to build shopping malls in Mexico. The Canadian company brings to the joint venture its knowledge of mall development, leasing, and management, and Grupo ICA contributes its knowledge of the Mexican construction industry and land use requirements.[13]

Shared Risk

Another common rationale for entering into cooperative arrangements is risk sharing. Today's major industries are so competitive that no firm has a guarantee of success when it enters a new market or develops a new product. Strategic alliances can be used to either reduce or control individual firms' risks. For example, a firm that independently undertakes a new venture requiring an investment of $10 million stands to lose its entire investment if the venture fails. But if it undertakes the same size project as a joint venture instead, with a 50/50 split of the $10 million investment, its greatest potential loss is equal to only $5 million. The $5 million not spent enables the firm to expand in other areas or diversify into other, lower-risk activities, thereby reducing its average risk.

For example, as mentioned earlier in the chapter, Boeing developed a strategic alliance with several Japanese firms to reduce its financial risk in the development and production of its new widebody jet, the Boeing 777. Researching, designing, developing, and safety-testing a new aircraft model costs billions of dollars, much of which must be spent before the manufacturer can establish how well the airplane will be received in the marketplace. Even though Boeing is the world's most successful commercial aircraft manufacturer, it wanted to reduce its financial exposure on the 777 project. Thus it is collaborating with three Japanese partners—Fuji, Mitsubishi, and Kawasaki—which are building 20 percent of the airframe for the new jet. Boeing, the controlling partner in the alliance, also hopes its allies will help sell the new aircraft to large Japanese customers such as Japan Air Lines and All Nippon Airways.

Or consider the strategic alliance involving Kodak and Fuji and three Japanese camera firms. At face value, it might seem odd for Kodak to agree to collaborate with Fuji, its biggest competitor, to develop a new film that both will be able to make and sell. Closer scrutiny, however, suggests that the arrangement reduces Kodak's risks considerably. Kodak managers realized that if they developed the film alone, Fuji would aggressively fight the innovation in the marketplace and Kodak would have to work hard to gain consumer acceptance of its new standard for film. Still worse, Fuji might decide to develop its own new standard film, thereby jeopardizing Kodak's R&D investment should the predominantly Japanese camera-manufacturing industry adopt Fuji's approach rather than Kodak's. Mindful of the financial losses incurred by Sony when VHS rather than Betamax became the standard format for VCRs, Kodak chose to include Fuji in the deal. Through this strategic alliance, Kodak reduces its risks. It also can compete on a playing field of its own choosing, free to harness its marketing clout, distribution networks, and formidable brand name against the efforts of its rivals.

Shared Knowledge and Expertise

Still another common reason for strategic alliances is the potential for the firm to gain knowledge and expertise that it lacks. A firm may want to learn more about how to produce something, how to acquire certain resources, how to deal with local governments' regulations, or how to manage in a different environment— information that a partner often can offer.[14] The firm can then use the newly acquired information for other purposes.

One of the more successful joint ventures in the United States has been that between Toyota and GM. In 1982, GM closed an old automobile manufacturing plant in Fremont, California, because it was inefficient. In 1984, Toyota agreed to reopen the plant and manage it through a joint venture called Nummi (New United Motor Manufacturing, Inc.). Although Nummi is owned equally by the two partners, Toyota manages the facility and makes automobiles for both. Each firm entered into the deal primarily to acquire knowledge. Toyota wanted to learn more about how to deal with labor and parts suppliers in the U.S. market; GM wanted to observe Japanese management practices firsthand.[15] Toyota used its newly acquired information when it opened its own manufacturing plant in Georgetown, Kentucky, in 1988. GM used lessons learned from Nummi in developing and operating its newest automotive division, Saturn.

Synergy and Competitive Advantage

Firms may also enter into strategic alliances in order to attain synergy and competitive advantage. These related advantages reflect combinations of the other advantages discussed in this section: the idea is that through some combination of market entry, risk sharing, and learning potential, each collaborating firm will be able to achieve more and to compete more effectively than if it had attempted to enter a new market or industry alone.[16]

For example, creating a favorable brand image in consumers' minds is an expensive, time-consuming process, as is creating efficient distribution networks and obtaining the necessary clout with retailers to capture shelf space for one's products. These factors led PepsiCo, the world's second-largest soft drink firm, to establish a joint venture with Thomas J. Lipton Co., a division of Unilever, to produce and market ready-to-drink teas in the United States. Lipton, which has a 50 percent share of the $400 million worldwide market for ready-to-drink teas, provides the joint venture with manufacturing expertise and brand recognition in teas. PepsiCo supplies its extensive and experienced U.S. distribution network. This joint venture is a competitive response to a similar arrangement between Coca Cola and Nestlé signed in 1990.[17]

Table 12.1 reports the results of a detailed study of strategic alliance activity in the 1980s. As you can see, the reasons for entering into a strategic alliance varied across industries. For example, in the medical instruments industry, in which rich rewards accrue to the firm that first markets a new technology, reducing the innovation time span and accessing complementary technology were the primary motivations for creating a strategic alliance. In more technologically stable industries such as chemicals, automobiles, and consumer electronics, market access was often a more important reason.

TABLE 12.1

Distribution of Strategic Alliances by Sectors and Fields, 1980–1989

		MAIN REASON FOR ALLIANCE (as percentage)						
	Number of Alliances	High-Cost Risks	Lack of Financial Resources	Technology Complementary	Reduction of Innovation Time Span	Sharing of Basic R&D	Market Access/ Structure	Monitoring Technology/ Market Entry
Biotechnology	847	1	13	35	31	10	13	15
New materials technology	430	1	3	38	32	11	31	16
Information technology	1660	4	2	33	31	3	38	11
Computers	198	1	2	28	22	2	51	10
Industrial automation	278	0	3	41	32	4	31	7
Microelectronics	383	3	3	33	33	5	52	6
Software	344	1	4	38	36	2	24	11
Telecommunications	366	11	2	28	28	1	35	16
Other	91	1	0	29	28	2	35	24
Automobiles	205	4	2	27	22	2	52	4
Aviation/defense	228	36	1	34	26	0	13	8
Chemicals	410	7	1	16	13	1	51	8
Consumer electronics	58	2	0	19	19	0	53	9
Food and beverages	42	1	0	17	10	0	43	7
Heavy electric/power	141	36	1	31	10	4	23	11
Medical instruments technology	95	0	4	35	40	2	28	10
Other	66	35	0	9	6	0	23	8
Total	4182	6	4	31	28	5	32	11

Source: From John H. Dunning, *Multinational Enterprises and the Global Economy*. Wokingham, England: Addison-Wesley Publishers Ltd., 1993. Reprinted with permission.

Scope of Strategic Alliances

The scope of cooperation among firms may vary significantly, as Fig. 12.2 illustrates. For example, it may consist of a comprehensive alliance, in which the partners participate in all facets of conducting business, ranging from product design to manufacturing to marketing. Or it may consist of a more narrowly defined alliance that focuses on only one element of the business, such as R&D. The degree of collaboration will depend on the basic goals of each partner.

Comprehensive Alliances

Comprehensive alliances arise when the participating firms agree to perform together multiple stages of the process by which goods or services are brought to the market: R&D, design, production, marketing, and distribution. Because of the broad scope of such alliances, the firms involved must establish common procedures for intermeshing such functional areas as finance, production, and marketing for the alliance to succeed. Yet integrating the different operating procedures of the parents over a broad range of functional activities is difficult in the absence of a formal organizational structure. As a result, most comprehensive alliances are organized as joint ventures. As an independent entity, the joint venture can adopt

FIGURE 12.2

The Scope of Strategic Alliances

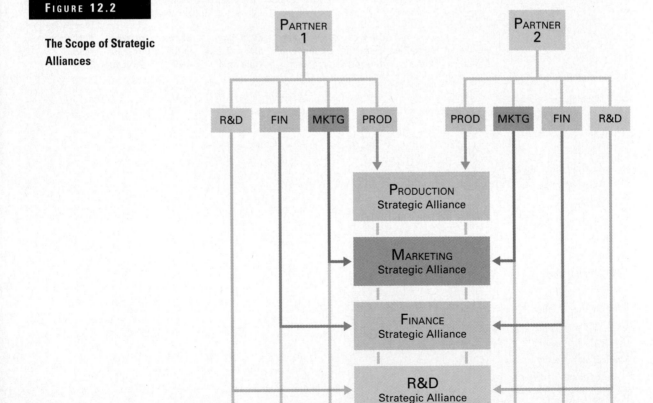

Going Global

Small Alliances Can Be Profitable

It seems that international behemoths dominate the popular press accounts of strategic alliances. For example, the success of arrangements such as General Mills and Nestlé versus Kellogg or Ford and Mazda versus everyone else is frequently mentioned. But a firm need not be big to benefit from international partnerships. Indeed, many smaller firms are finding strategic alliances to be the key to opening the door to foreign markets.

Consider, for example, the case of Acucobol. Acucobol is a San Diego software firm that specializes in software products that modernize business applications written in COBOL. Although COBOL, an early-generation computer language, seems like ancient history to computer buffs, there are thousands of COBOL-based programs still in use and COBOL continues to be a popular language in such far-flung markets as Brazil, India, and Italy. Acucobol's products make these COBOL-based programs more user-friendly and allow them to interface with Windows and other more contemporary applications.

When Acucobol wanted to introduce its products in Europe, its owner, Pamela Coker, knew the firm lacked the resources to launch a full-scale international expansion. So she started in Germany by finding a local partner that had strong connections with German firms and an existing sales and distribution network. This alliance worked so well that Acucobol quickly used the same strategy to enter markets in Italy, the United Kingdom, and Scandinavia.

Mid-sized firms can also benefit from strategic alliances and joint ventures. Diebold is a Canton, Ohio, firm that makes bank vaults, security systems, and automated teller machines (ATMs). The firm decided to begin selling ATMs in Europe. It knew it needed a strong ally to help it make the right connections and to develop the technology necessary to compete in different European countries. IBM agreed to a joint venture with Diebold. It took the two firms a while to figure out how to compete in Europe, but recent successes suggest that they solved the puzzle. For example, Diebold-IBM recently sold 30 ATMs to a Russian bank and helped install them in selected Moscow subway stations. If the idea works, the firm will install ATMs throughout the entire Moscow subway system.

Source: Rob Norton, "Strategies for the New Export Boom," *Fortune*, August 22, 1994, pp. 125–130.

operating procedures that suit its specific needs, rather than attempting to accommodate the often incompatible procedures of the parents, as might be the case with another type of strategic alliance.

Comprehensive alliances are perhaps the most rapidly growing form of strategic alliance between MNCs. By fully integrating their efforts, participating firms are able to achieve greater synergy through sheer size and total resources. For example, General Mills would still have had a major uphill battle in the European cereal market if its joint venture with Nestlé had involved only a single function such as marketing. But a complete meshing of each firm's relative strengths (General Mills's cereal-making expertise and Nestlé's European distribution network and name recognition) resulted in a business unit that emerged as a formidable competitor for Kellogg from its beginning. However, as "Going Global" reveals, large size is not a necessary ingredient for success in forming a strategic alliance.

Not surprisingly, comprehensive alliances are very complex to arrange. This complexity stems from the numerous areas of collaboration that must be addressed and negotiated. As a result, such alliances usually involve only two firms and may evolve over time. The two firms invest more, both tangibly and intangibly, and they become partners in the truest sense of the word. For example, the Fuji Photo Film Company joined in 1962 with Rank Xerox, the British affiliate of Xerox, to create a joint venture known as Fuji Xerox. Initially created solely to market

U.S.-made photocopiers in Japan, Fuji Xerox over time has worked with Xerox to design and produce photocopiers and market them worldwide.

Functional Alliances

Strategic alliances may also be narrow in scope, involving only a single functional area of the business. In such cases, integrating the needs of the parent firms is less complex. Thus functionally based alliances often do not take the form of a joint venture, although joint ventures are still the more common form of organization. Types of functional alliances include the following:

▶ Production alliances
▶ Marketing alliances
▶ Financial alliances
▶ R&D alliances

Production Alliances. A **production alliance** is a functional alliance in which two or more firms each manufacture products or provide services in a shared or common facility. The Nummi joint venture between Toyota and GM fits this model. Each firm has designed its automobiles autonomously, is generally responsible for procuring its own materials, and so on. However, the shared plant, under Toyota's management, makes automobiles for both firms. Similarly, in 1990, Volvo, Mitsubishi, and the government of the Netherlands created a joint venture, Volvo Car BV, to design and produce automobiles for the European market. The joint venture, based in Borne, the Netherlands, gives Volvo access to the latest Japanese automobile manufacturing techniques. It gives Mitsubishi its first European production facilities, thereby allowing it to benefit from EC '92 and to deflect growing criticism from European politicians about the rise in Japanese imports.[18]

Production alliances may call for utilizing a facility one partner already owns or constructing a new facility. For example, IBM and Siemens agreed in 1991 to produce IBM's newly designed 16 megabit DRAM computer chip. Profit margins on new computer chips are highest during the first year or two of availability, so quick production of the new chip was critical to the joint venture's success. IBM supplied the new chip design and manufacturing technology. It also provided an existing chip factory near Paris, France, thereby enabling production to start quickly. Siemens supplied its engineering talent and the bulk of the several hundred millions of dollars needed for the chip's manufacture.[19]

Marketing Alliances. A **marketing alliance** is a functional alliance in which two or more firms share marketing services or expertise. In most cases, this involves one partner introducing its products or services into a market in which the other partner already has a presence. The established firm helps the newcomer by promoting, advertising, and/or distributing its products or services. The established firm may negotiate a fixed price for its assistance or may share in a percentage of the newcomer's sales or profits. For example, AT&T and Olivetti had a strategic alliance that called for AT&T to market Olivetti office equipment in the United States and Olivetti to market AT&T telecommunications equipment in Europe. (This alliance was not successful and was eventually terminated for reasons we discuss later in the chapter.) Many book publishers share marketing services and expenses in foreign countries. Setting up a specialized sales force to market one publisher's products in foreign markets is often inefficient. Thus, in countries such as Canada and the United Kingdom there are firms that handle domestic marketing and promotion for several foreign publishers, some of which are in direct competition with each other.

Financial Alliances. A **financial alliance** is a functional alliance of firms that want to reduce the financial risks associated with a project. Partners may share equally in contributing financial resources to the project, or one partner may contribute the bulk of the financing while the other partner (or partners) provides special expertise or makes other kinds of contributions to partially offset its lack of financial investment. The strategic alliance between Boeing and its three Japanese partners was created primarily for financial purposes—Boeing wanted the other firms to help cover R&D and manufacturing costs. Those firms, in turn, saw a chance to gain valuable experience in commercial aircraft manufacturing as well as profits.

Similarly, BMW and Rolls-Royce agreed in 1990 to create a joint venture to design and manufacture engines for the next generation of aircraft with 100 to 130 seats planned by aircraft manufacturers. Sharing the financial risk is an important motive for creating this joint venture. The two firms expect to invest $900 million in the project. However, the market for the specific type of engines needed for these jets will probably support only one manufacturer profitably, and rival suppliers GE, Pratt & Whitney, and Germany's MTU are already developing competing engines for this market segment.[20] In another example, the British firm Majestic Films, with financial interests in Oscar winners *Dances with Wolves* and *Driving Miss Daisy,* teamed up with Japanese investors (including the Japanese Broadcasting Corporation) to create Newcomm, Ltd., to produce and distribute new movies selected by Majestic's executives. This joint venture blends

In the movie industry, joint ventures are allowing partners from different countries to share the financial risks associated with making and distributing films. *Dances with Wolves,* for example, was a joint production of Orion Pictures (a U.S. company) and Majestic Films (a British company).

Majestic's experience in the film-making business with the financial resources of the Japanese investors to develop new movies.[21]

Research and Development Alliances. Rapid technological change in high-technology industries and the skyrocketing cost of staying abreast of that change have prompted an increasingly common type of functional alliance that focuses on R&D. In an **R&D alliance**, the partners agree to undertake joint research to develop new products or services. These alliances are usually not formed as joint ventures, since scientific knowledge can be transmitted among partners through private research conferences, the exchange of scientific papers, and laboratory visits. Moreover, forming a separate legal organization and staffing it with teams of researchers drawn from the partners' staffs might disrupt ongoing scientific work in each partner's laboratory. Instead each partner may simply agree to cross-license whatever new technology is developed in its labs, thereby allowing its partner (or partners) to use its patents at will. Each partner then has equal access to all technology developed by the alliance, an arrangement that guarantees the partners will not fall behind each other in the technological race. Partners also are freed from legal disputes among themselves over ownership and validity of patents. For example, the alliance among Kodak, Fuji, and the three Japanese camera makers focuses solely on R&D. Both Kodak and Fuji will be licensed to make the new type of film they are working on (if and when they create it); the three camera makers will design the cameras to use it.

Because of the importance of high-tech industries to the world economy, many countries are supporting the efforts of R&D consortia as part of their industrial policies. An **R&D consortium** is a confederation of organizations that band together to research and develop new products and processes for world markets. It represents a special case of strategic alliance in that governmental support plays a major role in its formation and continued operation. The EU has developed a wide array of joint research efforts with clever acronyms—such as ESPRIT, RACE, BRITE, EURAM, JOULE, and SCIENCE—to ensure that its firms can compete against U.S. and Japanese firms in high-tech markets. Until the past decade, R&D consortia were virtually forbidden in the United States because of antitrust concerns. However, a new federal law passed in 1984 makes it easier for U.S. firms to create such consortia. For example, 14 electronics firms, including IBM, Intel, and Motorola, along with the U.S. government, founded a basic R&D laboratory, Sematech, in Austin, Texas. Each firm contributes 1 percent of its annual revenues from sales of semiconductors, and the Department of Defense matches their total contributions. The initial success of Sematech is causing other U.S. industries to consider creating research consortia to share R&D costs.

Japanese firms have successfully practiced this type of arrangement for a long time. For example, over two decades ago the Japanese government, Nippon Telephone and Telegraph, Mitsubishi, Matsushita, and three other Japanese firms agreed to work together to create new types of high-capacity memory chips. They were so successful that they now dominate this market. However, such consortia are not always successful. A similar consortium formed in 1981, called the Fifth Generation Computer Systems Project, has yet to dislodge U.S. firms from their leadership in the high end of the supercomputer market.[22]

Management of Strategic Alliances

The decision to form a strategic alliance should develop from the firm's strategic planning process, discussed in Chapter 10. After a firm's top managers analyze the firm's goals, strengths and weaknesses, and market opportunities, they may decide that a strategic alliance with one or more other firms is the preferred mode for entering a foreign market. Having made this decision, they then must address several significant issues, which set the stage for how the arrangement will be managed. Some of the most critical of these issues are

▶ Selection of partners

▶ Form of ownership

▶ Joint management considerations

Selection of Partners

The success of any cooperative undertaking depends on choosing the appropriate partner(s). Research suggests that strategic alliances are more likely to be successful if the skills and resources of the partners are complementary—each must bring to the alliance some organizational strength the other lacks.[23] A firm contemplating a strategic alliance should consider at least four factors in selecting a partner (or partners):[24]

1 Compatibility

2 Nature of the potential partner's products or services

3 The relative safeness of the alliance

4 The learning potential of the alliance

Compatibility. The firm should select a compatible partner with which it can work effectively and that it can trust. Without mutual trust, a strategic alliance is unlikely to succeed.[25] But incompatibilities in corporate operating philosophies may also doom an alliance. For example, an alliance between General Electric Corporation (a U.K. firm unrelated to the U.S. firm of the same name) and the German firm Siemens failed because of incompatible management styles. The former firm is run by financial experts and the latter by engineers. General Electric Corporation's financial managers continually worried about bottom-line issues, short-term profitability, and related financial considerations. Siemens's managers, in contrast, wanted to worry less about financial issues and pay more attention to innovation, design, and product development.[26]

Nature of a Potential Partner's Products or Services. Another factor to consider is the nature of a potential partner's products or services. It is often hard to cooperate with a firm in one market while doing battle with that same firm in a second market. Under such circumstances, each partner may be unwilling to reveal all its expertise to the other partner for fear that doing so will give that partner a competitive advantage. Most experts believe a firm should ally itself with a partner whose products or services are complementary to but not directly competitive with its own. The joint venture between General Mills and Nestlé is an example of this principle in action: both are food-processing firms, but Nestlé does not make cereal, the product on which it is collaborating with General Mills. Similarly, PepsiCo and Lipton complement but do not compete with one another, thus raising the likelihood that their joint venture to market ready-to-drink tea in the United States will succeed.

Sometimes, however, a firm may receive a rude surprise. For example, JVC, a subsidiary of the Japanese firm Matsushita, wanted to enter the European VCR market. It formed a joint venture with a small German firm. The new venture, a 50/50 partnership, had only limited success because the German firm lacked the necessary marketing expertise to help JVC gain a foothold. Thomson SA, a large French electronics firm, bought out the German firm and learned the tricks for producing VCRs from JVC. JVC was unconcerned about the potential gift of its technology to Thomson, however, because its worldwide sales totaled over 5 million VCRs compared to a mere 800,000 units for its European joint venture. Then, in the late 1980s, Thomson purchased General Electric's consumer electronics business. That purchase boosted its VCR sales to 5 million a year—making the access to JVC's technology gained through the joint venture a very valuable commodity indeed.[27]

The Relative Safeness of the Alliance. Firms should move slowly in selecting, negotiating with, and contracting with a partner. Strategic alliances should be undertaken cautiously and deliberately as part of the firm's strategic plan. Given the complexities and potential costs of failed agreements, managers should gather as much information as possible about a potential partner before proceeding with an agreement.[28] For example, managers should assess the success or failure of previous strategic alliances formed by the potential partner. Also, it often makes sense to analyze the prospective deal from the other firm's side. What does the potential partner hope to gain from the arrangement? What are the partner's strengths and weaknesses? How will it contribute to the venture? Does the proposed arrangement meet its strategic goals? The probability of success rises if the deal makes good business sense for both parties.[29]

For example, Corning, Inc., created a joint venture—Asahi Video Products Company—in 1988 by integrating its television glass production with the operations of Asahi Glass, a producer of large television bulbs. Corning believed this joint venture would be a sound one for several reasons:

▶ Asahi Glass's expertise in large television bulb technology complemented Corning's strength in other bulb sizes.

▶ The joint venture would benefit from Asahi Glass's ongoing business connections with the increasing number of Japanese television manufacturers that were establishing North American facilities.

▶ The combined strengths of the two firms would help both keep abreast of technological innovations in the video display industry.

▶ Asahi Glass would benefit from Corning's technology and marketing clout in the U.S. market.

▶ Corning had successfully operated another joint venture with Asahi Glass since 1965.

In fact, Corning is so good at developing joint ventures that almost half its profits are generated by joint ventures with PPG, Dow Chemical, Samsung, Siemens, Ciba-Geigy, IBM, and, of course, Asahi Glass.[30]

The Learning Potential of the Alliance. Before establishing a strategic alliance, partners should also assess the potential to learn from each other. Areas of learning can range from the very specific—for example, how to manage inventory more efficiently or how to train employees more effectively—to the very general—for example, how to modify corporate culture or how to manage more strategically. At the same time, however, each partner should carefully assess the value of its own information and not provide the other partner with any that will result in competitive disadvantage for itself should the alliance dissolve—a point we revisit in the next section.

Form of Ownership

Another issue in establishing a strategic alliance is the exact form of ownership that is to be used. Recall from earlier in the chapter that the most common type of strategic alliance is the joint venture.[31] A joint venture almost always takes the form of a corporation, and a joint venture is usually incorporated in the country in which it will be doing business. In some instances, it may be incorporated in a different country, such as one that offers tax or legal advantages. The Bahamas, for example, are sometimes seen as a favorable tax haven for the incorporation of joint ventures.

The corporate form enables the partners to arrange a beneficial tax structure, implement novel ownership arrangements, and better protect their other assets. This form also allows the joint venture to create its own identity apart from those of the partners. Of course, if either or both of the partners have favorable reputations, the new corporation may choose to rely on those, perhaps by including the partners' names as part of its name.

A new corporation also provides a neutral setting in which the partners can do business. As we discuss later in the chapter, strategic alliances sometimes lead to conflict among partners. The probability of conflict and related problems increases if the partners are doing business within the facilities or organization of one of them. However, the potential for conflict may be reduced if the interaction between the partners occurs outside their own facilities or organizations. It may also be reduced if the corporation does not rely on employees identified with either partner and instead hires its own executives and workforce whose first loyalty is to the joint venture. For example, a joint venture formed by Corning and Genentech was not performing as well as expected. Corning soon discovered one source of the difficulties: managers contributed by Genentech to the joint venture were actually on leave from Genentech. To ensure that these managers' loyalties were not divided between Genentech and the joint venture, Corning requested that they resign from Genentech. Once they did, the performance of the joint venture improved rapidly.[32]

In isolated cases, incorporating a joint venture may not be possible or desirable. For example, local restrictions on corporations may be so stringent or burdensome that incorporating is not optimal. The partners in these cases usually choose to operate under a limited partnership arrangement. In a limited partnership, one firm, the managing partner, assumes full financial responsibility for the venture, regardless of the amount of its own investment. The other partner (or partners) has liability limited to its own investment. Obviously, such arrangements are riskier for the managing partner.

Public-Private Venture. A special form of joint venture, a **public-private venture**, is one that involves a partnership between a privately owned foreign firm and a government. Such an arrangement may be created under any of several circumstances:

1 When the government of a country controls a resource it wants developed, it may enlist the assistance of a foreign firm that has expertise related to that resource. For example, South American countries have used several foreign lumber firms, such as Weyerhaeuser, to assist in the development of their rain forests and surrounding lands. A similar pattern exists in the discovery, exploration, and development of oil fields. National governments that control access and ownership of oil fields may lack the technical expertise to drill for and manage the extraction of crude oil reserves. International oil firms, on the other hand, possess the requisite knowledge and expertise but may lack the necessary drilling rights. A common result is a joint venture for which the government grants drilling rights and private oil firms provide capital and expertise. For example, the government of newly independent Azerbaijan contracted in 1992 with a group of Western oil firms, led by Amoco, British Petroleum, and Norway's Statoil, to harvest the 1.75-billion barrel Azeri field in order to hasten drilling and alleviate the government's revenue needs.[33]

2 A firm may pursue a public-private venture if a particular country does not allow wholly owned foreign operations. If the firm cannot locate a suitable local partner, it may invite the government itself to participate in a joint venture. Or, the government may request an ownership share. Public-private ventures are typical in the oil industry. In assessing the opportunities and drawbacks to such a venture, a firm should consider and evaluate the various aspects of the political and legal environment it will be facing. Foremost among these is the stability of the government. In a politically unstable country, the current government may be replaced with another, and the firm may face serious challenges. At best, the venture will be considered less important by the new government because of its association with the old government. At worst, the firm's investment may be completely wiped out, its assets seized, and its operation shut down. However, if negotiations are handled properly and if the local government is relatively stable, public-private ventures can be quite beneficial. The government may act benignly and allow the firm to run the joint venture. It may also use its position to protect its own investment—and therefore that of its partner—by restricting competing business activity.

3 A firm entering a centrally planned economy may have no choice but to enlist governmental support. Precisely because these economies are centrally planned, their governments limit the freedom of both domestic and foreign firms. Thus a foreign firm entering into a joint venture with a business partner in a centrally planned economy must carefully assess the advantages and disadvantages of the

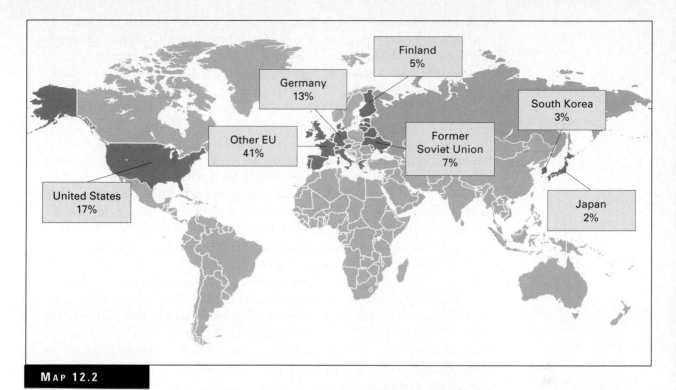

Finland
5%

Germany
13%

South Korea
3%

Other EU
41%

Former
Soviet Union
7%

United States
17%

Japan
2%

MAP 12.2

**Primary Partners
in Public-Private
Ventures with Russia,
1993 (as percentages
of total)**

market before committing itself. It also should ensure that it thoroughly understands the expectations and commitments of both the host country's government and its prospective business partner. These concerns are most obvious in China, the world's largest remaining centrally planned economy. Because of the vast size (over a billion people) and growth prospects of the Chinese market, many firms are interested in investment opportunities there. Yet Westerners can run into problems if they don't understand the needs and incentives facing Chinese managers or how China's economic and political system operates. This happened to American Motors in its initial dealings over Beijing Jeep, its joint venture with the Beijing municipal government (discussed in one of the cases at the end of the book). Yet China remains an attractive market. For example, Gillette established a personal care products joint venture in China in 1983. Buoyed by the venture's profitability, the firm reinforced its commitment to the Chinese market in 1992 by announcing the formation of a new $29.5 million joint venture to produce blades and razors for the Chinese market in partnership with the Shanghai Razor Blade Factory, China's largest producer of razor blades. The joint venture, which Gillette controls, combines Gillette's technology and manufacturing know-how with Shanghai's factory and distribution networks.

When Central and Eastern Europe were under communist control, public-private ventures were the primary means by which Western firms could invest there. Surprisingly, this entry mode has remained popular despite the opening up of these economies to Western firms. Map 12.2 highlights the home countries of Russia's largest partners in 1993. Although existing facilities—whether state-owned or recently privatized—in Central and Eastern Europe may be outmoded by Western standards, Western firms wanting to quickly enter the region often find them to be the only game in town. For example, PepsiCo sought to support its rapid expansion (and its battle with archrival Coca Cola) by creating a joint venture in Belarus. It joined with state-owned MPO Khimvolokno to produce plastic bottles for PepsiCo's 42 bottling operations in the former Soviet Union. PepsiCo provided capital and technology; Khimvolokno supplied its underutilized factory in Mogilev, Belarus.[34]

A joint venture with a state-owned firm often gives a Western firm access to that firm's existing customers—and these have often dealt exclusively with the state-owned firm. For example, Glavunion, a joint venture formed in 1990 between Glaverbel, Belgium's largest glass manufacturer, and Sklo Union, Czechoslovakia's largest glass manufacturer, inherited all of Sklo Union's domestic customers. This investment has been a bonanza for Glaverbel. Glavunion has benefited from increased vehicle production by VW-Skoda, itself a joint venture between Volkswagon and Czechoslovakia's monopolist automaker under the old communist system. Glavunion's production costs are much lower than Glaverbel's costs in its Belgian factories or those of its main rivals—St. Gobain, Pilkington, and Guardian Glass. Because its main factories are located in Bohemia, near the German border, Glavunion has also benefited from eastern Germany's postunification building boom.[35] Although such public-private ventures may decline in importance in Central and Eastern Europe over time, they currently represent a popular way of entering these promising but chaotic markets for firms that can withstand the political risks.

Joint Management Considerations

Further issues and questions are associated with how a strategic alliance will be managed. In general, there are three obvious means that may be used to jointly manage a strategic alliance (see Fig. 12.3):

▶ Shared management agreement
▶ Assigned arrangement
▶ Delegated arrangement

Under a **shared management agreement**, each partner fully and actively participates in managing the alliance. The partners run the alliance, and their managers regularly pass on instructions and details to the alliance's managers. The alliance managers have limited authority of their own and must defer most decisions to managers from the parent firms. This type of agreement requires a high level of coordination and near-perfect agreement between the participating partners. Thus it is the most difficult to maintain and the one most prone to lead to conflict among the partners.

Under an **assigned arrangement**, one partner, such as that owning the majority of a joint venture's stock, assumes primary responsibility for the operations of the strategic alliance. For example, GM, with a 67 percent stake in a joint venture with Raba, a Hungarian truck, engine, and tractor manufacturer, has assumed management control over the venture's operations.[36] Boeing controls the

FIGURE 12.3

**Managing Strategic
Alliances**

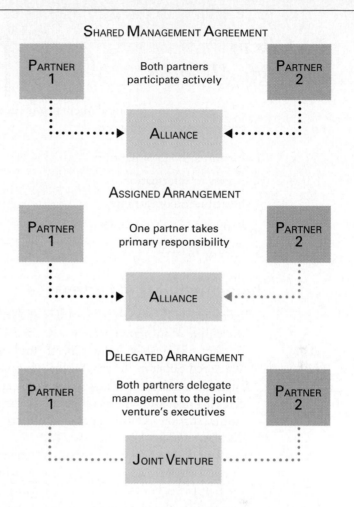

SHARED MANAGEMENT AGREEMENT

PARTNER 1 — Both partners participate actively — PARTNER 2

ALLIANCE

ASSIGNED ARRANGEMENT

PARTNER 1 — One partner takes primary responsibility — PARTNER 2

ALLIANCE

DELEGATED ARRANGEMENT

PARTNER 1 — Both partners delegate management to the joint venture's executives — PARTNER 2

JOINT VENTURE

overall operations of its strategic alliance with Fuji, Mitsubishi, and Kawasaki for the design and production of its new 777 commercial aircraft. Under an assigned arrangement, management of the alliance is greatly simplified because the dominant partner has the power to set its own agenda for the new unit, break ties among decision makers, and even overrule its partner(s). Of course, these actions may create conflict, but they keep the alliance from becoming paralyzed, which may happen if equal partners cannot agree on a decision.

Under a **delegated arrangement**, which is reserved for joint ventures, the partners agree not to get involved in ongoing operations and so delegate management control to the executives of the joint venture itself. These executives may be specifically hired to run the new operation or may be transferred from the participating firms. They are responsible for the day-to-day decision making and management of the venture and for implementing its strategy. Thus they have real power and the autonomy to make significant decisions themselves and are much less accountable to managers in the partner firms (at least in the short term). For example, both American Motors and the Beijing Automotive Works contributed experienced managers to the operation of Beijing Jeep so that its management team could learn both modern automobile assembly operations and operating conditions in China. Moreover, these managers were given responsibility for the joint venture's operations.

Pitfalls of Strategic Alliances

Regardless of the care and deliberation a firm puts into constructing a strategic alliance, it still must consider limitations and pitfalls. Figure 12.4 summarizes five fundamental sources of problems that often threaten the viability of strategic alliances:

1 Incompatibility of partners
2 Access to information
3 Distribution of earnings
4 Potential loss of autonomy
5 Changing circumstances

Incompatibility of Partners

Incompatibility among the partners of a strategic alliance is a primary cause of the failure of such arrangements. At times, incompatibility can lead to outright conflict, although typically it merely leads to poor performance of the alliance. We noted earlier in the chapter the example of the conflict between Siemens's engineering-oriented management and General Electric Corporation's financially oriented management. Incompatibility can stem from differences in corporate culture, national culture, goals and objectives, or virtually any other fundamental dimension linking the two partners.

In many cases, incompatibility problems can be anticipated if the partners carefully discuss and analyze the reasons why each is entering into the alliance in the first place. For example, a useful starting point may be a meeting between top managers of the two partners to discuss their mutual interests, goals, and beliefs about strategy. The manner in which the managers are able to work together during such a meeting may be a critical clue to their ability to cooperate in a strategic alliance. Obviously, if the partners cannot agree on such basic issues as how much decision-making power to delegate to the alliance's business unit, what the alliance's strategy should be, how it is to be organized, or how it should be staffed, compromise will probably be difficult to achieve and the alliance is unlikely to succeed.

For example, recall the strategic alliance between AT&T and Olivetti mentioned earlier in the chapter. This alliance failed because the two firms could not agree on a marketing strategy. Managers from both had failed to negotiate an agreement on such a strategy before beginning the alliance and thus had almost immediately clashed over what they wanted to accomplish and how they wanted to work together. The more the managers tried to reach agreement, the more severe the conflict became. They eventually realized they were simply not going to be able to agree on what to do and so abandoned the alliance.

Access to Information

Access to information is another drawback of many strategic alliances. For a collaboration to work effectively, one partner (or both) may have to provide the other with information it would prefer to keep secret. It is often difficult to identify

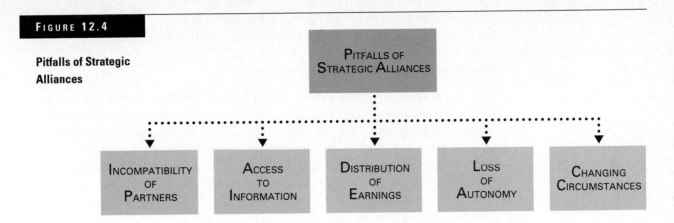

FIGURE 12.4

Pitfalls of Strategic Alliances

information needs ahead of time; thus a firm may enter into an agreement not anticipating having to share certain information. When the reality of the situation becomes apparent, the firm may have to be forthcoming with the information or else compromise the effectiveness of the collaboration.[37]

For example, Unisys, a U.S. computer firm, negotiated a joint venture with Hitachi, a Japanese electronics firm. Only after the venture was well underway did Unisys realize that it would have to provide Hitachi with most of the technical specifications it used to build computers. Although Unisys managers reluctantly gave Hitachi the information, they feared they were potentially compromising their own firm's competitiveness. And a recent alliance between Ford and Mazda to work on the design of the new Ford Escort almost stalled when Mazda officials would not allow their Ford counterparts to visit their research laboratory. After several weeks of arguing, a compromise was eventually reached whereby Ford engineers could enter the facility but only for a limited time.

Distribution of Earnings

An obvious limitation of strategic alliances relates to the distribution of earnings. Because the partners share risks and costs, they also share profits. For example, General Mills and Nestlé split the profits from their European joint venture on a 50/50 basis. Of course, this aspect of collaborative arrangements is known ahead of time and is virtually always negotiated as part of the original agreement.

However, there are other financial considerations beyond the basic distribution of earnings that can cause disagreement. For example, the partners must also agree on the proportion of the joint earnings that will be distributed to themselves as opposed to being reinvested in the business, the accounting procedures that will be used to calculate earnings or profits, and how transfer pricing will be handled.

For example, British Airways is reconsidering a number of its strategic alliances because of financial issues. In 1993 the firm invested several hundred million dollars in USAir as part of a strategic alliance between the two carriers. After British Airways made its investment, USAir suffered mounting losses because of increased competition from low-fare carriers in its core Northeastern U.S. markets. British Airways became concerned about the increased risk to its investment and the viability of USAir as a partner. In 1994 it announced that it was suspending further investment in USAir until that carrier returned to profitability. Other partners in strategic alliances with British Airways have also been warned that their respective agreements are in danger of termination unless profits begin to increase.[38]

Potential Loss of Autonomy

Another pitfall of a strategic alliance is the potential loss of autonomy. Just as firms share risks and profits, they also share control, thereby limiting what each can do. Most attempts to introduce new products or services, change the way the alliance does business, or introduce any other significant organizational change first must be discussed and negotiated. For example, as part of its contract with General Mills, Nestlé had to agree that if the joint venture is ever terminated, it cannot enter the North American cereal market for at least ten years. Similarly, Fuji Xerox, the long-lived and successful joint venture between Rank Xerox and Fuji Photo Film, was originally limited to selling copiers only in Indonesia, Japan, South Korea, the Philippines, Taiwan, and Thailand, although that restriction was later eliminated.[39]

At the extreme, a strategic alliance may even be the first step toward a takeover. In the early 1980s, the Japanese firm Fujitsu negotiated a strategic alliance with International Computers, Ltd. (ICL), a British computer firm. After nine years of their working together, Fujitsu bought 80 percent of ICL. One recent survey of 150 terminated strategic alliances found that over three fourths ended because a Japanese firm had taken over its non-Japanese partner.[40] In other cases, partners may accuse each other of opportunistic behavior, that is, trying to take advantage of each other. For example, a joint venture between the Walt Disney Company and Sky Television, a British pay-TV channel operator, broke down after Sky accused Disney of deliberately delaying the supply of promised programming. Disney, in turn, accused Sky of proceeding too hastily and without consulting it.[41]

Changing Circumstances

Changing circumstances may also affect the viability of a strategic alliance. The economic conditions that motivated the cooperative arrangement may no longer exist, or technological advances may have rendered the agreement obsolete. For example, GM and the Daewoo Group initiated a joint venture, Daewoo Motors, in 1986 to build automobiles in South Korea for export to the United States, with the Daewoo Group given operating control over the project. GM hoped to take advantage of low labor costs in South Korea, and the Daewoo Group hoped to use GM's marketing clout to promote the sales of the joint venture's automobiles. But rising wages in South Korea and the decline in the U.S. dollar eroded the cost savings GM hoped to gain from Korean production. Also, faced with its own quality problems in the U.S. market, GM was unhappy at the prospect of selling the defect-ridden autos coming off Daewoo's assembly lines to U.S. consumers already skeptical of GM's products. Conflict continued as the Daewoo Group lobbied GM to incorporate the latest technological advances into the Daewoo automobiles, but GM was unwilling to invest more money in the joint venture until the quality of its products improved. Trust between the partners was not strengthened when Daewoo Motors signed an agreement to acquire automotive technology from the Suzuki Motor Company. As it turned out, even the decision-making styles of the two firms clashed. The Daewoo Group, a tightly knit, family-owned chaebol, was used to making decisions quickly, while GM's elaborate bureaucracy is fully capable of studying even the simplest problem for years.[42]

CHAPTER REVIEW

Summary

Strategic alliances, in which two or more firms agree to cooperate for their mutual benefit, are becoming increasingly popular in international business. A joint venture, a common type of strategic alliance, involves two or more firms joining together to create a new entity that is legally separate and distinct from its parents.

Strategic alliances offer several benefits to firms that use them. First, they facilitate market entry. Second, they allow the partners to share risks. Third, they make it easier for each partner to gain new knowledge and expertise from the other partner(s). Finally, they foster synergy and competitive advantage among the partners.

The scope of strategic alliances can vary significantly. Comprehensive alliances involve a full array of business activities and operations. Functional alliances involving only one aspect of the business, such as production, marketing, finance, or R&D, are also common.

The decision to form a strategic alliance needs to be based on a number of different considerations. Selecting a partner is, of course, critically important and must take into account compatibility, the nature of the potential partner's products or services, the relative safety of the alliance, and the learning potential of the alliance. Selecting a form of organization is also very important to the success of the alliance. A special form of strategic alliance involves public and private partners. The management structure of the strategic alliance must also be given careful consideration.

Partners in a strategic alliance must be aware of several pitfalls that can undermine the success of their cooperative arrangement. These include incompatibility of the partners, access to information, distribution of earnings, potential loss of autonomy, and changing circumstances.

Review Questions

1. What are the basic differences between a joint venture and other types of strategic alliances?

2. Why have strategic alliances grown in popularity in recent years?

3. What are the basic benefits partners are likely to gain from their strategic alliance? Briefly explain each.

4. What are the basic characteristics of a comprehensive alliance? What form is it likely to take?

5. What are the four common types of functional alliances? Briefly explain each.

6. What is an R&D consortium?

7. What factors should be considered in selecting a strategic alliance partner?

8. What are the three basic ways of managing a strategic alliance?

9. Under what circumstances might a strategic alliance be undertaken by public and private partners?

10. What are the potential pitfalls of strategic alliances?

Questions for Discussion

1. What are the relative advantages and disadvantages of joint ventures compared to other types of strategic alliance?

2. Assume you are a manager for a large international firm, which has decided to enlist a foreign partner in a strategic alliance and has asked you to be involved in the collaboration. What effects, if any, might the decision to structure the collaboration as a joint venture have on you personally and on your career?

3. What factors could conceivably cause a sharp decline in the number of new strategic alliances formed?

4. Could a firm conceivably undertake too many strategic alliances at one time? Why or why not?

5. Can you think of any foreign products you use that may have been marketed in this country as a result of a strategic alliance? What are they?

6. What are some of the issues involved in a firm's trying to learn from a strategic alliance partner without giving out too much valuable information of its own?

7. Why would a firm decide to enter a new market on its own rather than using a strategic alliance?

8. What are some of the similarities and differences between forming a strategic alliance with a firm from the same country and forming one with a firm from a foreign country?

9. The joint venture between General Mills and Nestlé was worked out in only 23 days. Most experts, however, argue that a firm should spend a long time getting to know a prospective partner before proceeding with an alliance. What factors might account for CPW being an exception to this general rule?

10. Kellogg is doing a reasonably good job of countering CPW in Europe. But as CPW branches out into Asia and Africa, Kellogg will be at a greater disadvantage. What might Kellogg be forced to do in order to remain competitive in those markets?

BUILDING GLOBAL SKILLS

Break into small groups of four to five people. Assume your group is the executive committee (that is, the top managers) of Resteaze, Inc. Resteaze is a large manufacturer of mattresses, box springs, and waterbeds. The publicly traded firm is among the largest in the U.S. bedding market. It operates 15 factories, employs over 10,000 people, and last year generated $10 million in profits on sales of $280 million. Resteaze products are sold through department stores, furniture stores, and specialty shops and have the reputation of being of good quality and medium-priced.

Your committee is thinking about entering the European bedding market. You know little about the European market, so you are thinking about forming a joint venture. Your committee has identified three possible candidates for such an arrangement.

One candidate is Bedrest. Bedrest is a French firm that also makes bedding. Unfortunately, Bedrest products have a poor reputation in Europe and most of its sales stem from the fact that its products are exceptionally cheap. However, there are possibilities for growth in Eastern Europe. The consultant who recommended Bedrest suggests that your higher-quality products would mesh well with Bedrest's cheaper ones. Bedrest is known to be having financial difficulties because of declining sales. However, the consultant thinks the firm will soon turn things around.

A second candidate is Home Furnishings, Inc., a German firm that manufactures high-quality furniture. Its line of bedroom furniture (headboards, dressers, chests, and so on) is among the most popular in Europe. The firm is also known to be interested in entering the U.S. furniture market. Home Furnishings is a privately owned concern that is assumed to have a strong financial position. Because of its prices, however, the firm is not expected to be able to compete effectively in Eastern Europe.

Finally, Pacific Enterprises, Inc., is a huge Japanese conglomerate that is just now entering the European market. The firm does not have any current operations in Europe but has enormous financial reserves to put behind any new undertaking it might decide to pursue. Its major product lines are machine tools, auto replacement parts, communications equipment, and consumer electronics.

Your task is to assess the relative advantages and disadvantages of each of these prospective partners for Resteaze. The European market is important to you, this is your first venture abroad, and you want the highest probability for success. After assessing each candidate, rank the three in order of their relative attractiveness to your firm.

Follow-up Questions

1. How straightforward or ambiguous was the task of evaluating and ranking the three alternatives?

2. Determine and discuss the degree of agreement or disagreement among the various groups in the class.

CLOSING CASE

Ford and Mazda Share the Driver's Seat[43]

Ford Motor Company and Mazda Motor Corporation have one of the more unusual working relationships in the automobile industry. Ford is a major U.S. firm; Mazda is based in Japan. But even though they are obviously competitors, the two have collaborated on several different projects, and each agrees that the partnership has paid off. Indeed, the Ford-Mazda alliance is among the most successful in the global automobile market.

It all started in 1979. Mazda, a relatively small player in the world automobile market at the time, wanted a strong international partner in order to make the transformation from being a small niche player to becoming a major global automaker. At the same time, Ford was looking for a foreign partner to help it design and produce smaller automobiles. The two firms agreed that they were logical partners. Mazda sold approximately 25 percent of its stock to Ford, and the two firms have since collaborated on various projects.

One significant success story emerging from the alliance involves the Ford Probe and the Mazda MX-6. Mazda engineers design the basic platform, engine, and drive train for the cars. Mazda then designs the outside of the MX-6, and Ford does the same for the Probe. Finally, both cars are assembled at a factory in Flat Rock, Michigan, that was owned by the two firms. Thus consumers who buy a Ford Probe or a Mazda MX-6 are getting essentially the same car but with a different appearance. And both cars sell quite well.

Another successful collaboration between Ford and Mazda has been the Ford Escort. Again, Mazda engineers design the car, and Ford makes it. With the Escort, however, Mazda's involvement started at the very beginning of the process, and the Japanese firm played the dominant role in establishing a detailed schedule for getting the car into production. Engineers in U.S. firms like Ford have a reputation for continually raising problems and issues during design that result in delays and extensions. Mazda, however, refused to bow to scheduling delays and kept everyone involved focused on moving ahead and staying on schedule. As a result of this occasionally cumbersome but ultimately effective arrangement, the first new Escorts rolled off a Ford assembly line almost to the day of the production target—a target that had been set seven years earlier! Further, the Escort came in under budgeted cost and with higher EPA gas mileage estimates than had been projected at the start of the project. So successful was the collaboration that managers at Ford estimated Mazda's contributions saved the firm over $1 billion on the automobile's design and production.

There have been some rough spots in the alliance, however. For example, the popular Mazda Navaho recreational vehicle, launched in 1990, was actually made by Ford, based on the also popular Ford Explorer. Unfortunately for Mazda, however, Ford announced in 1994 that demand for its Explorer was so great that it would soon cease providing Navahos for its Japanese partner. More importantly—and ultimately more threatening to the otherwise successful alliance—Mazda fell into severe financial difficulties in the mid-1990s due to overexpansion of capacity, costly proliferation of its vehicle models, and a recession in its home market. To restore Mazda's financial health, its chief creditor, Sumitomo Bank Ltd., has given effective management control of Mazda to Ford. Ford now manages that Flat Rock plant—after sending 320 Mazda executives back home to Japan—and has changed the name of Mazda's chain of

Japanese dealerships from Autorama to Ford. To conserve cash, Ford executives also canceled Mazda's plans to start manufacturing in Europe. Instead, Mazda's European dealers will focus on marketing imports from Mazda's Japanese plants and Ford-made products sold under the Mazda nameplate.

Case Questions

1. Is the arrangement between Ford and Mazda a joint venture rather than a more general strategic alliance? Why or why not?

2. What fundamental questions might managers at Ford and Mazda have asked themselves before becoming strategic allies?

3. What are the apparent benefits each firm derives from this relationship?

4. What might eventually cause Ford and Mazda to dissolve their alliance?

5. Why don't more automakers follow the lead of Ford and Mazda and create partnerships for automobile design and manufacturing?

6. Will Mazda's recent financial problems—and Ford's reaction to them—cause their 15-year-old alliance to break up?

CHAPTER NOTES

1. Christopher Knowlton, "Europe Cooks Up a Cereal Brawl," *Fortune*, June 3, 1992, pp. 175–179; "Cafe au Lait, A Croissant—and Trix," *Business Week*, August 24, 1992, pp. 50–52.

2. Refik Culpan, *Multinational Strategic Alliances* (New York: International Business Press, 1993).

3. "Kodak Joins Fuji, Others for Project," *USA Today*, March 26, 1992, p. B1.

4. Peter J. Killing, "How to Make a Global Joint Venture Work," *Harvard Business Review* (May–June 1982), pp. 120–127.

5. Jeremy Main, "The Winning Organization," *Fortune*, September 26, 1988, pp. 50–60.

6. David Lei and John W. Slocum, Jr., "Global Strategic Alliances: Payoffs and Pitfalls," *Organizational Dynamics* (Winter 1991), pp. 44–62.

7. Michael E. Porter, *Competitive Strategy* (New York: Free Press, 1980), p. 275.

8. "TNT Ltd.'s Joint Venture in Europe Could Hurt Its Competitors in the U.S.," *Wall Street Journal*, July 26, 1991, p. C8.

9. Farok J. Contractor, "Ownership Pattern of U.S. Joint Ventures Abroad and the Liberalization of Foreign Government Regulations in the 1980s: Evidence from the Benchmark Surveys," *Journal of International Business Studies*, Vol. 21, No. 1 (First Quarter 1990), pp. 55–73.

10. "MGM Grand, Wal-Mart Venture into China," *USA Today*, August 22, 1994, p. 4B.

11. Gregg Laskoski, "U.S. pharmaceutical companies compete for CIS foothold," *We*, September 7–20, 1992, p. 7.

12. Maile Hulihan, "Into the Fray," *CFO, The Magazine for Senior Financial Executives* (June 1992), pp. 18–26.

13. "Cambridge Shopping, Grupo ICA to Build Retail Malls in Mexico," *Wall Street Journal*, September 25, 1992, p. A5.

14. Bruce Kogut, "Joint Ventures: Theoretical and Empirical Perspectives," *Strategic Management Journal*, Vol. 9 (1988), pp. 319–332; Sanford V. Berg and Philip Friedman, "Causes and effects of joint venture activity: knowledge acquisition vs. parent horizontality," *The Antitrust Bulletin* (Spring 1980), pp. 143–168.

15. Jeremy Main, "Making a Global Alliance Work," *Fortune*, December 17, 1990, pp. 121–126.

16. Kenichi Ohmae, "The Global Logic of Strategic Alliances," *Harvard Business Review* (March–April 1989), pp. 143–154.

17. "PepsiCo Planning Tea-Drink Venture with Unilever Unit," *Wall Street Journal*, December 4, 1991, p. B8.

18. "Volvo, Mitsubishi and Dutch Government Agree to Form Three-Way Joint Venture," *Wall Street Journal*, May 7, 1991, p. A13; Ronald van de Krol, "Mitsubishi in Netherlands carmaking deal with Volvo," *Financial Times*, May 4–5, 1991, p. 12.

19. "IBM, Siemens Reach Agreement to Make DRAM Computer Chip," *Wall Street Journal*, July 5, 1991, p. A4.

20. "BMW/Rolls-Royce unveils plan for East German plant," *Financial Times*, June 15–16, 1991, p. 12.

21. "Majestic Films' Modest Investments Prove Serendipitous," *Wall Street Journal*, June 17, 1991, p. B5.

22. Herbert I. Fusfield and Carmela S. Haklisch, "Cooperative R&D for Competitors," *Harvard Business Review* (November–December 1985), pp. 60–76.

23. J. Michael Geringer, "Strategic Determinants of Partner Selection Criteria in International Joint Ventures," *Journal of International Business Studies,* Vol. 22, No. 1 (First Quarter 1991), pp. 41–62; Kathryn R. Harrigan, *Strategies for joint venture success* (Lexington, Mass.: Lexington, 1985).

24. Main, "Making a Global Alliance Work."

25. The question of trust reflects a larger class of issues revolving around the size of transaction costs. See Paul W. Beamish and John C. Banks, "Equity Joint Ventures and the Theory of the Multinational Enterprise," *Journal of International Business Studies*, Vol. 18 (Summer 1987), pp. 1–16.

26. Main, "Making a Global Alliance Work."

27. Ibid.; Joseph E. Pattison, "Global Joint Ventures," *Overseas Business* (Winter 1990), pp. 24–29.

28. Peter Lorange and Johan Roos, "Why Some Strategic Alliances Succeed and Others Fail," *The Journal of Business Strategy* (January/February 1991), pp. 25–30.

29. Stephen J. Kohn, "The Benefits and Pitfalls of Joint Ventures," *The Bankers Magazine* (May/June 1990), pp. 12–18.

30. Corning, Inc., *1988 Annual Report*, p. 7.

31. Richard N. Osborn and C. Christopher Baughn, "Forms of Interorganizational Governance for Multinational Alliances," *Academy of Management Journal* (September 1990), pp. 503–519.

32. Joseph E. Pattison, "Global Joint Ventures," *Overseas Business* (Winter 1990), pp. 24–29.

33. "Amoco to develop Azerbaijan oil field," *Houston Chronicle*, September 5, 1992, p. 4D.

34. "PepsiCo, Kodak to Produce Plastic with Belarus Firms," *Wall Street Journal*, May 29, 1992, p. A6.

35. Anthony Robinson, "Czech deal with clear attractions," *Financial Times*, June 5, 1992, p. 18.

36. Nicholas Denton, "GM puts further DM100m into its Hungary venture," *Financial Times*, November 6, 1991, p. 7.

37. Karen J. Hladik and Lawrence H. Linden, "Is an International Joint Venture in R&D for You," *Research Technology Management* (July–August 1989), pp. 11–13.

38. "Sky Anxiety," *Business Week*, March 21, 1994, p. 38.

39. "An angry young warrior," *Financial Times*, September 19, 1994, p. 11.

40. Main, "Making a Global Alliance Work."

41. "Murdoch Firm Sues Disney, Alleges Violation of Pact for Pay TV in Britain," *Wall Street Journal*, May 17, 1989, p. B6.

42. James B. Treece, "Why GM and Daewoo Wound Up on the Road to Nowhere," *Business Week*, September 23, 1991, p. 55.

43. "One World, One Ford," *Forbes*, June 20, 1994, pp. 40–41; "How Ford and Mazda Shared the Driver's Seat," *Business Week*, March 26, 1990, pp. 94–95; Thomas A. Stewart, "Brace for Japan's Hot New Strategy," *Fortune*, September 21, 1992, pp. 62–74; Alan Chai, Alta Campbell, and Patrick J. Spain (eds.), *Hoover's Handbook of World Business 1993* (Austin, Tex.: Reference Press, 1993), p. 326; "In a Cultural U-Turn, Mazda's Creditors Put Ford Behind the Wheel," *Wall Street Journal*, November 21, 1994, p. A1.

What Role Should Foreign MNCs Play in South Africa?

Foreign MNCs Should Protect and Nurture South African Businesses

For decades, the government of South Africa openly discriminated against that country's black residents. For example, the government outlawed land ownership by blacks in 1912. After World War II, conditions worsened. Following a change in government leadership, the apartheid system was put into place, creating separate pay scales, career tracks, and living areas for blacks and prohibiting them from voting. By 1970 white South Africans, comprising only 13 percent of the country's population, controlled 87 percent of the land.

Despite its policies of repression and discrimination, South Africa has long been among the most affluent countries on the continent. Not surprisingly, then, many MNCs set up operations there years ago. However, growing opposition to the apartheid system caused some, such as Kodak, Mobil, Coca-Cola, and Ford, to pull out of South Africa during the 1980s.

Apartheid was officially abolished prior to the country's first free and open election in April 1994, but foreign MNCs should proceed cautiously in entering (or reentering) the South African market. Even though apartheid no longer exists, its vestiges remain. Many workers in low-skill jobs complain that their white employers treat them more poorly than before, in part out of resentment. These workers are paid minimal wages, have no employee rights, and are frequently the victims of abuse.

Further, foreign-owned MNCs that move too quickly into South Africa are likely to trample on the efforts of long-suffering local entrepreneurs to build a strong, black-owned business community, which many experts believe is vital if South Africa is to grow economically. Many black business owners struggled for years with poor supplier networks, weak financing, and customers who could not afford to pay full price. Now, just as purchasing power is starting to rise, MNCs are likely to crush existing black-owned firms and wipe out South Africa's small black middle class. Thus if a foreign MNC does enter this market, it has a moral obligation to do so by forming joint ventures and other cooperative arrangements with local partners rather than by creating wholly owned subsidiaries. In this way, foreign MNCs will help develop the skills and abilities of South African citizens.

One positive sign for South Africa is that many foreign MNCs are sensitive to this problem. In recent years, Digital Equipment, Apple, Nike, and Reebok have all announced their reentry into South Africa with local black partners, creating numerous jobs.

With the abolishing of apartheid, investors are again becoming sympathetic to South African investment. Whitney Houston (shown here visiting a Johannesburg children's museum) is one of the partners in a joint venture to create a Pepsi-Cola distribution network in South Africa.

Foreign MNCs Can Best Help South Africa by Helping Consumers

No one can defend the policies of apartheid that repressed the black population of South Africa for decades. The firms that left the South African market in protest—regardless of their motives—did the right thing. Indeed, that very action was no doubt a major catalyst for the eventual elimination of apartheid.

And now that apartheid has been eliminated, it is time for foreign MNCs to reenter the market. Several reasons can be cited in support of this viewpoint. First, businesses should be as nonpolitical as possible. They exist to serve the interests of their owners, not to influence political and social climates. Because the South African market is so large and developed, a business that fails to exploit opportunities there is not acting in the best interests of its owners. And given that many firms, such as Siemens and Mercedes-Benz, have announced plans to start operations in South Africa, other firms run the risk of being left behind if they wait too long.

Foreign MNCs also should enter the South African market to help the country's black residents gain a more competitive position in the local economy. The presence of large MNCs creates jobs and opens new opportunities for everyone. By recruiting and training qualified black South Africans for managerial and executive positions, these firms can promote economic equality in the country. Equally important, foreign MNCs can benefit black South Africans by providing them with high-quality goods at low prices. For example, the September 1994 opening of the first modern shopping mall in Soweto township, complete with an air-conditioned supermarket, a multiplex movie theater, and ATM machines, freed black families from having to pay inflated prices for goods from local convenience stores.

In short, competition among fast-food chains, grocery stores, and other retailers is the best way to promote economic equality in South Africa. Some foreign MNCs may choose to work with local black businesspersons, but others may choose to go it alone. Regardless of how they enter, foreign MNCs will lower prices paid by South Africans, generate employment opportunities, and improve the economy.

The role of business in South Africa has long been controversial. U.S. college students such as these have frequently launched formal protests against business interests in South Africa.

Wrap-up

1. Which is more important to the economic development of South Africa, nurturing the growth of the black business community or lowering the prices paid by black consumers?

2. What ethical concerns face international firms operating in South Africa today?

Organization Design for International Business

Chapter Outline

The nature of international organization design

Initial impacts of international activity on organization design

The corollary approach
The export department
The international division

Global organization designs

Global product design
Global area design
Global functional design
Global customer design
Global matrix design
Hybrid global designs

Related issues in global organization design

Centralization versus decentralization
Role of subsidiary boards of directors
Coordination in the global organization

Corporate culture in international business

Creating the corporate culture in
    international business
Managing the corporate culture in
    international business

Managing change in international business

Reasons for change in international
    business
Types of change in international business

After studying this chapter you should be able to:

Summarize the nature of international organization design.

Identify and describe the initial impacts of international business activity on organization design.

Identify and describe five advanced forms of international organization design and discuss hybrid global designs.

Identify and summarize related issues in global organization design.

Discuss the role of corporate culture in international business.

Describe the management of change in international business.

F ROM ITS EARLIEST DAYS ALMOST A CENTURY AGO, FORD MOTOR Company has sold its automobiles worldwide. Besides its obvious success in the United States, Ford also has had a significant presence in Europe since the 1920s and was a major player in Japan prior to World War II. Today, in addition to its U.S. workforce of 167,000 employees, the firm has almost 100,000 employees in Europe, over 27,000 in Latin America, 15,000 in Canada, and 12,000 in Pacific Asia. ▪▪ U.S. automakers have traditionally followed a strategy that calls for tailoring their products to the individual markets in which the products are sold. For example, both GM and Ford design, manufacture, and sell automobiles in Europe that differ from any

Ford's New Global Design[1]

models they offer in the United States. Product variations are intended to account for differences in consumer tastes, price sensitivity, government regulations, and other factors. For example, many European consumers want relatively small automobiles because of narrow city streets and limited parking facilities, but they want them to have powerful engines to take advantage of the relatively high speed limits. Also, air conditioning and automatic transmissions are not as common in Europe as they are in the United States. ▪▪ For years, Ford aspired to create what it called a "world car"—an automobile that could be sold anywhere in the world with little or no modification for different markets. Such a car would minimize duplication, reduce development costs, and allow the use of common components. Each of these conditions, in turn, would result in lower costs and higher profits. The 1994 version of the Ford Escort (discussed in the closing case in Chapter 12) was originally planned as a world car but ended up requiring much more modification for different markets than was intended. Although the Escort has done well in the marketplace, it does not measure up to Ford's standards for a world car. ▪▪ Ford finally succeeded in its quest for a world car with its newest mid-sized models, the Ford Contour and Mercury Mystique. These automobiles were jointly designed and engineered in Europe and the United States. Regardless of where they are sold, they use the same basic engines and transmissions and have the same basic body style and interior. The only substantive modification across markets is to place the steering wheel on the right in cars to be sold in the United Kingdom and other markets where people drive on the left side of the road. ▪▪ Although Ford is happy with its new world car, it is less than thrilled with the process used to get it. For example, the development costs for the Mystique and Contour exceeded $6 billion. This was more than four times what Chrysler needed to design and develop its new Neon. Indeed, some industry experts believe these development costs are the highest in history for a single model. A large portion of the costs was attributed to coordination problems and duplication of effort in different areas. The automobiles also took much longer to get into production than was originally intended. ▋▋ To help avoid such astronomical development costs and delays in the future, Ford announced plans to overhaul its basic organization structure and change its whole approach to doing business. Its previous structure was based on geographic area: Ford of Europe, Ford of Pacific Asia, and Ford's U.S. operation generally functioned as autonomous units. Each unit designed, manufactured, and marketed its own automobiles. The result was considerable duplication of effort. Further, since each unit sold automobiles only in its own area, there were fewer sales against which to amortize development costs. ▋▋ Ford's new structure adds a truly global perspective to the firm's organization. For example, it calls for one top manager to have global responsibility for engine and transmission development. This executive coordinates the design and manufacturing of engines and transmissions that can be used in Ford automobiles worldwide. Similar positions have been established on a global basis to oversee product design and development, production, marketing, and other functions. The result, Ford hopes, will be a more integrated worldwide strategy that will lower costs for each functional activity and speed development cycles so that automobiles will get to dealer showrooms faster. ▋▋▋▋▋

Ford is clearly a multinational firm—and a very large one at that, with over 320,000 employees worldwide and major operations in the United States, Canada, Europe, Latin America, and Pacific Asia. One of its greatest challenges today is the restructuring of its organization in order to compete more effectively in a global marketplace and to ensure that its overall strategies will be efficiently and effectively implemented. Such structural relationships between the parts of a firm constitute the firm's organization design.

In this chapter, we discuss the various organization designs that international businesses use to achieve their strategic goals. Because these designs typically evolve along a well-defined path as firms become more international, we first discuss the initial forms of organization design firms use as they begin to internationalize their operations.[2] We then analyze the more advanced forms of organization design adopted as firms broaden their participation in international business to become true MNCs. Next we discuss several related issues in global organization design. We conclude by describing two other aspects of organization design: corporate culture and change.

The Nature of International Organization Design

Organization design (sometimes called *organization structure*) is the overall pattern of structural components and configurations used to manage the total organization. Organization design is the basic vehicle through which strategy is ultimately implemented and through which the work of the organization is actually accomplished.

A firm cannot function unless its various structural components are appropriately assembled.[3] Through its design, the firm:[4]

▶ Allocates organizational resources

▶ Assigns tasks to its employees

▶ Instructs those employees concerning the firm's rules, procedures, and expectations about their job performances

▶ Collects and transmits information necessary for problem solving and decision making.

This last task is of particular importance for large MNCs, which must manage the sharing of vast amounts of information between corporate headquarters and subsidiaries and staff spread worldwide.[5]

Early studies of organization design sought to identify the single best design that all organizations should use. The pioneering work of the German sociologist Max Weber, for example, described a so-called **bureaucratic design**, which was based on rational rules, regulations, and standard operating procedures.[6] Later research, however, suggested that there was no one best way to design an organization. Eventually managers, stimulated by British researchers Joan Woodward, Tom Burns, G. M. Stalker, Derek Pugh, and David Hickson, came to learn there are many different ways to effectively design organizations.[7] Managers must carefully assess their situation and context and then develop an appropriate design to fit both. Certain key elements determine the appropriate design for any given organization:

▶ Size

▶ Strategy

▶ Technology

▶ Environment

▶ Cultures of the countries in which it operates

For example, a firm that sells brand-name consumer goods customized for markets in different host countries will structure itself geographically so that regional managers knowledgeable about the idiosyncratic needs of local customers will be empowered with appropriate decision-making authority. Nestlé is an example of a firm with this type of structure. In contrast, a firm that seeks manufacturing efficiencies may organize itself along product lines in order to utilize its lowest-cost production facilities, regardless of their geographical location. Black & Decker has done this.

However, an organization's structure is not created and then left alone; organization design is an ongoing process. Indeed, managers change the design of their firms almost continually. One study found that most firms and divisions of large firms make moderate design changes about once a year and one or more major design changes every four to five years.[8] These changes often result from changes in the firm's strategy, since an important characteristic of a successful firm is its ability to match its strategy with a compatible organization design.[9]

Initial Impacts of International Activity on Organization Design

As a domestic firm expands internationally, it will change its organization design to accommodate its increased international activities. To see how this happens, we'll start by considering a domestic firm that has no international sales. This is not an unreasonable starting point. Many entrepreneurs, particularly in larger economies such as those of the United States, Japan, and Germany, start new firms in response to some perceived need in the local market; they give little immediate thought to the international marketplace. And many small, domestically oriented firms enter international markets passively through indirect exporting, as discussed in Chapter 11. Such a firm may sell its product to a domestic customer, and that customer then incorporates the product into a good that it distributes in foreign markets. Or, a domestic customer may purchase the firm's product for one of its foreign subsidiaries, or a domestic purchasing agent of a foreign wholesaler may order the firm's product. Because such indirect exporting occurs as a routine part of the firm's domestic business, the firm's organization design need not change at all.

For example, Texas-based O.I. International was started in 1969 to produce highly specialized equipment to analyze and monitor oil-drilling activities. In its early years, it had little need to think internationally because oil-drilling activity in Texas and elsewhere in the United States was booming. However, as oil field activity slowed in the United States, O.I. needed new sources of revenue. One day, CEO John Huey was reading a trade magazine and noticed an announcement of an industrial exhibition in Japan. He quickly made arrangements to attend the show to promote O.I. products. During the show, he contracted with JASKO International, a Japanese equipment firm, to distribute O.I. products in Pacific Asia. Because initial sales were relatively small, and because Huey had negotiated the agreement himself, he initially handled sales to JASKO through his own office. There was certainly no need to overhaul the firm's structure in order to deal with this level of international involvement.

As indirect export sales grow, however, a firm may realize the value of more actively pursuing the international market. For example, one small Santa Clara, California, firm began its international sales by accident when its president unexpectedly bumped into officials from Banco National de Mexico at a 1992 New Orleans trade fair. This chance encounter led to a $200,000 order for the firm's software for managing debt collection. Once the firm learned the tricks of doing business in Mexico, it soon expanded its marketing efforts there.[10]

The Corollary Approach

A firm may initially respond to international sales and orders by following the **corollary approach**, whereby it delegates responsibility for processing such orders to individuals within an existing department, such as finance or marketing. Under this approach, the firm continues to use its existing domestic organization design. This approach is typical of a firm that has only a very small level of international activity.

Wal-Mart offers another example of the corollary approach. Wal-Mart has limited international operations and few stores outside the United States. But the firm does buy some products from foreign manufacturers. Because all of its buying is centralized in Bentonville, Arkansas, its buyers simply handle international

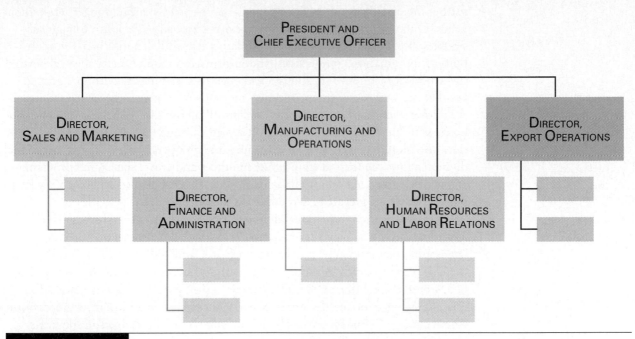

FIGURE 13.1

An Export Department in a Small Manufacturing Firm

purchases as part of their regular jobs. Most transactions are in U.S. dollars, and shipping and transportation are the responsibility of the seller. Thus, for the Wal-Mart buyer the international transaction of purchasing 10,000 VCRs from Sony for a unit cost of $200 (with freight arranged for and paid by the shipper) is fundamentally no different from buying 10,000 televisions from Emerson Electric (a U.S. firm) for a unit cost of $200 (with freight again arranged for and paid by the shipper). However, in response to NAFTA, Wal-Mart has recently entered the Mexican market in a joint venture with Mexico's largest retail chain, Cifra. As its international operations increase, Wal-Mart will probably undergo restructuring in order to accommodate a larger international scope.

The Export Department

As a firm's export sales become more significant, its next step is usually to create a separate, internal export department. The export department takes responsibility for overseeing international operations, marketing products, processing orders, working with foreign distributors, and arranging financing when necessary. Initially, the head of the export department may report to a senior marketing or finance executive. As exports grow in importance, however, the export department may achieve equality on the organization chart with finance, marketing, human resources, and the other functional areas of the firm. O.I., for example, eventually created a small export department—comprising one manager and an assistant—to handle its exports to Japan. Figure 13.1 illustrates how an export department fits into a typical small firm.

The International Division

On a small scale, where selling to foreign customers may not be fundamentally different from selling to domestic ones, the small export department may need little or no familiarity with foreign markets. However, as international activities further increase, firms often find that an export department no longer serves their needs. Once a firm begins to station employees abroad or establish foreign subsidiaries to produce, distribute, and/or market its products, managerial responsibilities, coordination complexities, and information requirements all swell beyond the export department's capabilities and expertise. Familiarity with foreign markets becomes more important and new methods for organizing may be required.

Firms respond to the challenges of controlling their burgeoning international business by changing their organization design through the creation of an international division that specializes in managing foreign operations.[11] The international division allows the firm to concentrate resources and create specialized programs and activities targeted on international business activity while simultaneously keeping that activity segregated from the firm's ongoing domestic activities.

Kmart uses the international division design, in contrast to the corollary approach used by its biggest competitor, Wal-Mart. Kmart has extended its retailing empire internationally; it operates stores in Canada, Puerto Rico, Mexico, and the U.S. Virgin Islands. Although its foreign outlets are outnumbered by its 2200 U.S. stores, the volume of its Canadian business in particular is quite large. To successfully manage the foreign stores, Kmart has established an international division whose managers coordinate their activities with those of managers in the firm's domestic operations. Canadian managers communicate their buying needs to regular Kmart buyers, who add the Canadian requests to their normal purchases and then route the Canadian portion to a distribution center in that country.

Brazil's Banco Economico SA, the oldest private bank in Latin America, also uses the international division approach. As Fig. 13.2 shows, Banco Economico's organization design emphasizes its product lines—corporate finance and nonfinancial investments, retail banking, and corporate banking. The international banking division has equal status with each of these product groups on the organization chart. International division managers are responsible for operating the bank's international branches and foreign-exchange operations and for providing corporate banking and corporate financial services to meet the needs of foreign customers, as well as the international needs of domestic customers.[12]

Global Organization Designs

As a firm evolves from being domestically oriented with international operations to becoming a true multinational corporation with global aspirations, it typically abandons the international division approach. In place of that division, it usually creates a global organization design to achieve synergies among its far-flung operations and to implement its organizational strategy.[13] The five most common forms of global organization design are product, area, functional, customer, and matrix. The global design the MNC chooses will reflect its need for coordination among its units, the source of its firm-specific advantages, and its managerial philosophy about its position in the world economy.[14] MNCs typically adopt one of three managerial philosophies that guide their approach to such functions as organization design and marketing. The **ethnocentric approach** is used by firms that operate internationally the same way they do domestically. The **polycentric approach** is used by

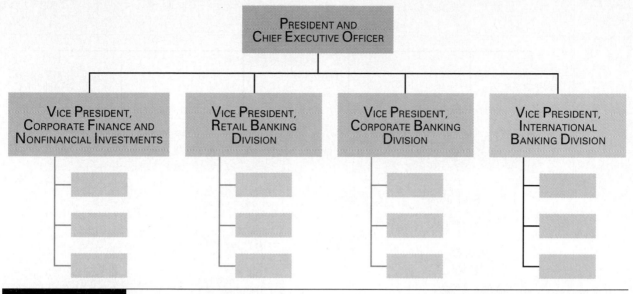

FIGURE 13.2

**Banco Economico
S.A.'s International
Division Design**

firms that customize their operations for each foreign market they serve. Finally, the **geocentric approach** is used by firms that analyze the needs of their customers worldwide and then adopt standardized operations for all markets they serve. (We discuss these concepts more fully in Chapter 16.)

Global Product Design

The most common form of organization design adopted by MNCs is the global product design. The **global product design** assigns worldwide responsibility for specific products or product groups to separate operating divisions within a firm.[15] This design works best when the firm has diverse product lines or when its product lines are sold in diverse markets, thereby rendering the need for coordination between product lines relatively unimportant. If the products are related, the organization of the firm takes on what is often called an **M-form design**; if the products are unrelated, the design is called an **H-form design**.[16] The M in M-form stands for "multidivisional"—the various divisions of the firm are usually self-contained operations with interrelated activities. The H in H-form stands for "holding," as in "holding company"—the various unrelated businesses function with autonomy and little interdependence. The global product design adopted by Daimler-Benz is shown in Fig. 13.3 and discussed more fully in the following "Going Global." This firm's various businesses are relatively unrelated; thus it uses the H-form design.

Another MNC that uses the global product approach is Philip Morris. This firm makes a wide variety of products, ranging from Marlboro cigarettes to Cool Whip to Jell-O to Oscar Mayer bologna to Toblerone chocolate to Miller beer. As a result, Philip Morris uses the global product design, organizing its operations along product lines. Its major divisions include tobacco, brewing, and food processing. Although most of its manufacturing and processing are done in the United States in order to achieve economies of scale, separate groups of product-oriented managers are then responsible for marketing a single product or related group of products to all markets the firm serves.[17] Because each group is somewhat related to the others, Philip Morris exemplifies the M-form design.

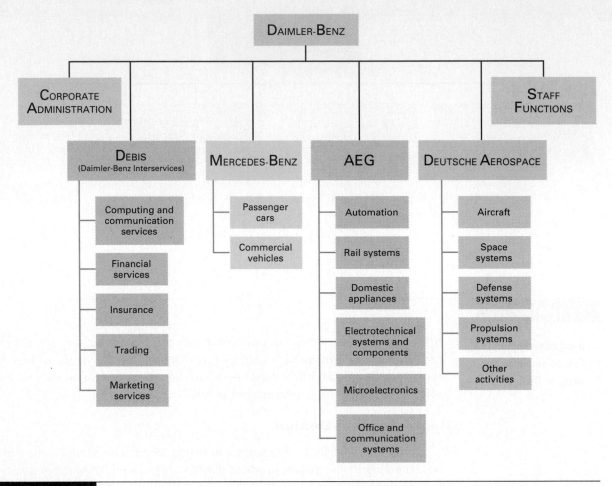

FIGURE 13.3

Daimler-Benz's Global Product Design

Pennsylvania's Harsco Corporation, too, is organized according to its major product groups—industrial services and building products, engineered products, and defense. Each group is responsible for managing domestic and international production, marketing, and distribution for its individual product lines.[18]

The global product design has several advantages:

1 Because a division focuses on a single product or product group, the division managers gain expertise in all aspects of the product or products.

2 It facilitates efficiencies in production because managers are free to manufacture the product wherever manufacturing costs are the lowest.

3 It allows managers to coordinate production at their various facilities, shifting output from factory to factory as global demand or cost conditions fluctuate.

4 Because managers have extensive product knowledge, they are more able to incorporate new technologies into their product(s) and respond quickly and flexibly to technological changes that affect their market.

Not surprisingly, as competition in their industry intensified in the 1990s, two major personal computer manufacturers—IBM and Siemens Nixdorf—

GOING GLOBAL

Daimler-Benz Is More Than Mercedes

Daimler-Benz is Germany's largest firm. Many people associate it with its line of luxury automobiles, the Mercedes-Benz. But today Daimler-Benz is far more than just an automaker; it is a worldwide diversified firm with businesses in everything from aerospace to insurance to software to microelectronics.

As Germany's economy boomed after World War II, demand for the firm's automobiles grew rapidly. Daimler-Benz exported vehicles and engines to virtually every market in the world. Further, its pricing strategy and the luxury image of its products largely protected it against economic downturns. However, Daimler-Benz also has encountered some problems. Automobiles have become more complicated. Managers realized that if they were to maintain the Mercedes image, they needed to look beyond mechanical engineering expertise. They also had to contend with the growing threat posed by Japanese automakers.

Accordingly, Daimler-Benz managers developed a strategy that called for diversification. Edzard Reuter, then vice chairman and today chairman of the firm, spearheaded first the formulation and then the implementation of this strategy. Starting in 1985, the firm bought several major new businesses, including Dornier (aerospace), AEG (electrical equipment), MTU (propulsion systems), and several others in the aerospace and services industries.

After this period of rapid acquisition, Daimler-Benz faced another challenge—how to bring the new businesses under the existing corporate "umbrella." Managers quickly realized they couldn't do this. Instead, they had to restructure the entire organization in order to make it work more efficiently and effectively. After careful analysis, Reuter and his associates decided to organize Daimler-Benz into four basic product groups. Under German law, Daimler-Benz AG became a holding company comprising four legally independent product groups.

One product group, called simply Mercedes-Benz, is responsible for making passenger cars and commercial vehicles. Another product group, called AEG, handles industrial automation, rail systems and transportation technology, electrotechnical systems and components, electrical consumer products, microelectronics, and office and communications technology. The third product group, called Deutsche Aerospace, is responsible for the firm's aircraft, space systems, defense systems, and propulsion systems operations. The fourth group, called Debis (for Daimler-Benz InterServices), handles software, financial, insurance, trading, and marketing services.

Sources: "Daimler-Benz Half-Year Profit DM 462 Million," *Wall Street Journal*, August 31, 1994, p. A15; Alan Chai, Alta Campbell, and Patrick J. Spain (eds.), *Hoover's Handbook of World Business 1993* (Austin, Tex.: Reference Press, 1993), p. 204; "Why Daimler-Benz Has to Win Its Big Gamble in Chips," *Business Week*, June 22, 1992, pp. 53–54; "Daimler's Drive to Become a High-Tech Speedster," *Business Week*, February 12, 1990, pp. 55–58.

switched to the global product design. These firms operate in an industry environment characterized by vicious price competition, global sourcing of inputs, and rapid technological change. Within months of IBM's restructuring, the firm noticed a significant difference in its ability to respond to its competitors. For example, when Compaq launched a price war in summer 1992, IBM was able to counterattack within two hours with its own price cuts, a decision that would have taken several weeks under its old structure.[19]

The global product design offers other advantages:

I It facilitates global marketing. The firm gains flexibility in how it introduces, promotes, and distributes each product or product group. Rather than being tied to one marketing plan that encompasses the whole firm, individual product-line managers may pursue their own plans.

2 It enables the firm to develop specific expertise needed to compete globally. In Harsco's case, one of the firm's competitive advantages lies in its specialized knowledge of how to convert steel mill waste into useful products. Using the global product design, Harsco can focus this expertise within its industrial services and building products group, which can then use this knowledge to compete internationally for contracts with steel mills.

3 Because the global product design forces managers to think globally, it facilitates geocentric corporate philosophies. This is a useful mind-set as firms work to develop greater international skills internally.

The global product design also has disadvantages:

1 It may encourage expensive duplication, since each product group needs its own functional-area skills such as marketing, finance, and information management and sometimes even its own physical facilities for production, distribution, and R&D.

2 Each product group must develop its own knowledge about the cultural, legal, and political environments of the various regional and national markets in which it operates.

3 It makes coordination and corporate learning across product groups more difficult. If such coordination is an important part of the firm's international strategy, it may want to adopt a different global design, such as the global area design.

Global Area Design

The second most common form of global design is the global area design. The **global area design** organizes the firm's activities around specific areas or regions of the world. This approach is particularly useful for firms with a polycentric or multidomestic corporate philosophy.[20] Figure 13.4 illustrates a part of Nestlé that is organized by area. Note that the president and chief operating officer of the firm's food division oversees five directors, each of whom is responsible for a specific geographical area. Thus, while the top level of the firm is organized by product, the food division itself is organized by area.

A global area design is most likely to be used by a firm whose products are not readily transferable across regions. For example, Bertelsmann AG is the world's largest media firm; it publishes newspapers and magazines and records music and video materials. Because of language differences and cultural preferences, however, a Bertelsmann magazine published in the United States cannot be exported in large quantities for sale in Germany or Japan. Thus the firm has separate headquarters in each country in which it operates. The U.S. headquarters, for example, oversees publication of books under the mastheads of Bantam, Dell, and Doubleday and of magazines such as *Parents* and *Young Miss* and records music under such labels as Arista and RCA. Similarly, Bertelsmann's German operation publishes books under the label Bertelsmann Club, publishes magazines such as *Der Spiegel*, and records music under the label BMG Ariola.

Cadbury Schweppes PLC, a British soft drink and candy firm, also uses the global area design. Cadbury owns such brand names as Canada Dry, Hires, Holland House, Cadbury Chocolate, and Beechnut. The firm has five basic divisions, each representing a different area of the world—the United Kingdom, Other Europe, the Pacific Rim, North and South America, and Other Countries. Mana-

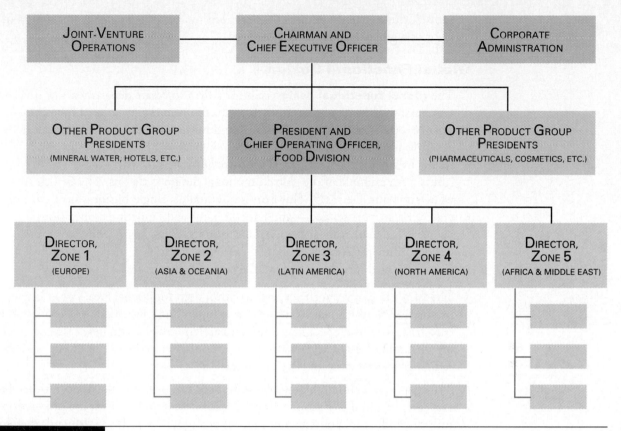

FIGURE 13.4

**Global Area Design
of Nestlé's Food
Division**

gers in each area division handle distribution, promotion, advertising, and other functions for all Cadbury Schweppes products that fit their particular markets.[21]

The global area design is particularly useful for a firm whose strategy is marketing-driven rather than predicated on manufacturing efficiencies or technological innovation or a firm whose competitive strength lies in the reputation of its brand-name products. Both conditions apply to Cadbury Schweppes. Further, the geographical focus of this design allows a firm to develop expertise about the local market. Area managers can freely adapt the firm's products to meet local needs and can quickly respond to changes in the local marketplace. They also can tailor the product mix they offer within a given area. For example, Cadbury managers do not sell all of the firm's products in all areas but instead promote only those that match local tastes and preferences.

The global area design does have disadvantages, however:

1 By focusing on the needs of the area market, the firm may sacrifice cost efficiencies that might be gained through global production.

2 Diffusion of technology is slowed, for innovations generated in one area division may not be adopted by all the others. Thus this design may not be suitable for product lines undergoing rapid technological change.

3 The global area design results in duplication of resources because each area division must have its own functional specialists, product experts, and, in many cases, production facilities.

4 It makes coordination across areas expensive and discourages global product planning.

Indeed, these were the reasons that led Ford to abandon its global area design in favor of a global functional design.

Global Functional Design

The **global functional design** calls for a firm to create departments or divisions that have worldwide responsibility for the common organizational functions—finance, operations, marketing, R&D, and human resources management. This design is used by MNCs that have relatively narrow or similar product lines.[22] It results in what is often called a **U-form organization,** where the U stands for "unity." An example of the global functional design is that used by British Airways, shown in Fig. 13.5. This firm is essentially a single-business firm—it provides air transport services—and has company-wide functional operations dedicated to marketing and operations, public affairs, engineering, corporate finance, human resources, and other basic functions.

The global functional design offers several advantages:

1 The firm can easily transfer expertise within each functional area. For example, production skills learned by Exxon's crews operating in the Gulf of Mexico can be used by its offshore operations in Malaysia's Jerneh field, and new catalytic cracking technology tested at its Baton Rouge, Louisiana, refinery can be adopted by its refineries in Singapore and Trecate, Italy.[23]

2 Managers can maintain highly centralized control over functional operations. For example, the head of Exxon's refinery division can rapidly adjust the production runs or product mix of refineries to meet changes in worldwide demand, thereby achieving efficient usage of these very expensive corporate resources.

3 The global functional design focuses attention on the key functions of the firm. For example, managers can easily isolate a problem in marketing and distinguish it from activities in other functional areas.

These advantages led Ford to adopt the global functional design. Despite these advantages, however, this design is inappropriate for many businesses. In particular, this oganization design has three major shortcomings:

1 It is practical only when the firm has relatively few products or customers.

2 Coordination between divisions can be a major problem. For example, the manufacturing division and the marketing division may become so differentiated from each other that each may start pursuing its own goals to the detriment of the firm as a whole.

3 There may be duplication of resources among managers. For example, the finance, marketing, and operations managers may each hire an expert on Japanese regulation, when a single expert could have served all three functional areas just as effectively.

Because of these problems, the global functional design has limited applicability. It is used by many firms engaged in extracting and processing natural resources, such as in the mining and energy industries, because in their case the ability to transfer expertise is important. Firms that need to impose uniform standards on all of their operations may also adopt this approach. For example, to assure safety, British Airways standardizes its maintenance and flight procedures regardless of whether a flight originates in London, Hong Kong, or Sydney.

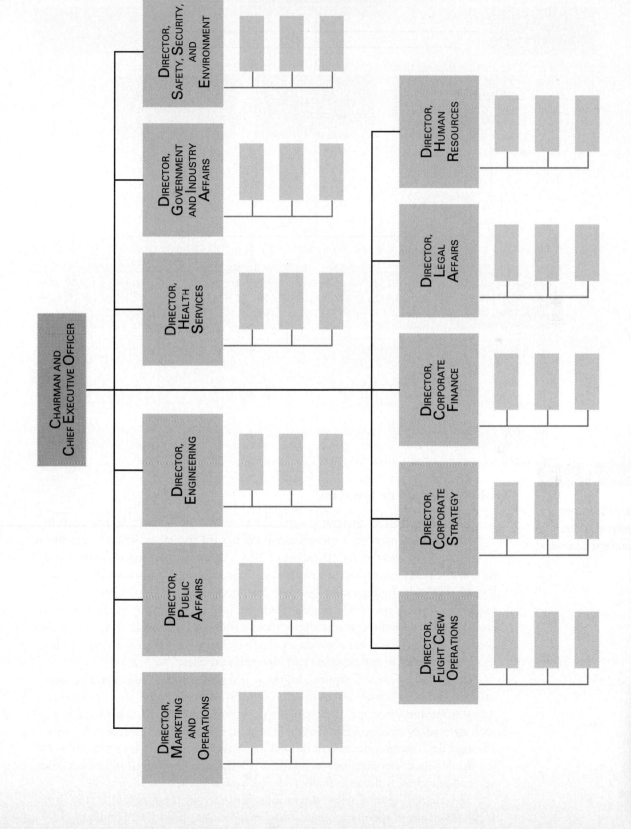

British Airways's Global Functional Design

FIGURE 13.5

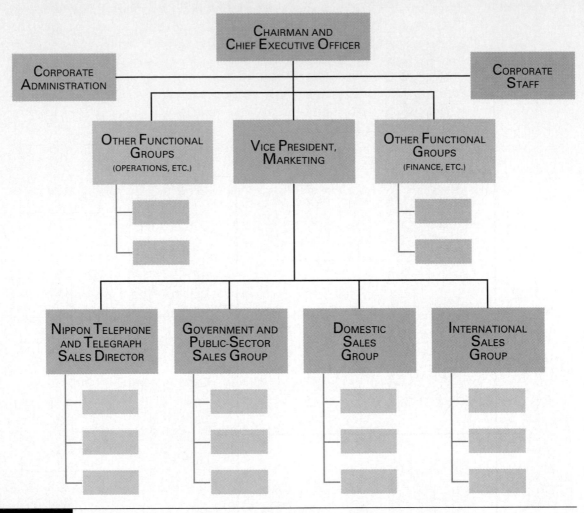

FIGURE 13.6

Global Customer
Design of NEC's
Marketing Operation

Global Customer Design

The **global customer design** is used when a firm serves different customers or customer groups, each with specific needs calling for special expertise or attention. For example, the marketing operation of NEC, Japan's largest manufacturer and supplier of telecommunications equipment, uses the global customer design (see Fig. 13.6). As the figure shows, Nippon Telephone and Telegraph, Japan's public telephone service and NEC's largest customer, is so important to the firm that it has a separate sales director and department dedicated exclusively to servicing the account. The firm also has separate marketing groups for government and public-sector sales, other domestic sales, and international sales.[24]

Japan's Bridgestone Corporation, the world's third-largest tire manufacturer, uses the global customer design in selling tires worldwide under its brand names Bridgestone and Firestone. One division deals with automobile manufacturers such as Ford, Nissan, and BMW, which buy tires as original equipment for new automobiles. Another deals with individual consumers and markets tires through the firm's network of automotive retail outlets. Still another division markets tires to agricultural users through firms such as Deere and Case.

This design is useful when the various customer groups targeted by the firm are so diverse as to require totally distinct marketing approaches. For example, selling four replacement tires to an individual is a completely different task from selling 4 million tires to an automaker. The global customer approach allows the firm to meet the specific needs of each customer segment and track how well its products or services are doing among those segments. On the other hand, the global customer design results in a significant duplication of resources, since each customer group needs its own area and functional specialists. Coordination between the different divisions is also difficult, since each is concerned with a fundamentally different market.

Global Matrix Design

The most complex form of international organization design is the global matrix design.[25] A **global matrix design** is the result of superimposing one form of organization design on top of an existing, different form. The resulting design is usually quite fluid, with new matrix dimensions being created, downscaled, and eliminated as needed. For example, the global matrix design shown in Fig. 13.7 was created by superimposing a global product design (shown down the side) on an existing global functional design (shown across the top). Using a global matrix design, a firm can form specific product groups comprising members from

FIGURE 13.7

A Global Matrix Design

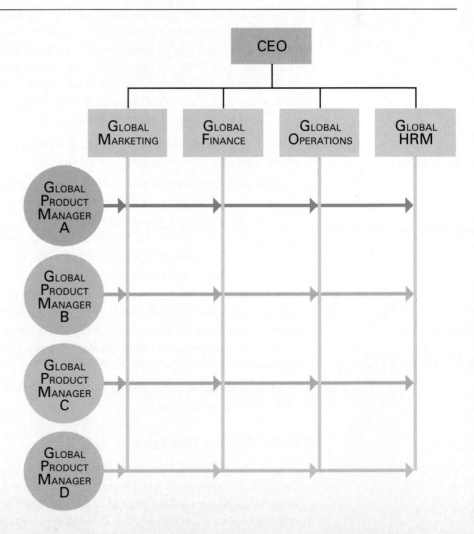

existing functional departments. These product groups can then plan, design, develop, produce, and market new products with appropriate input from each functional area. In this way, the firm can draw on both the functional and the product expertise of its employees. After a given product development task is completed, the product group may be dissolved; its members will then move on to new assignments. And, of course, other matrix arrangements are possible. For example, an area design could be overlaid on a functional design, thereby allowing area specialists to coordinate activities with functional experts.

The global matrix design has the advantage of helping to bring together the functional, area, and product expertise of the firm into teams that develop new products or respond to new challenges in the global marketplace. For example, Texas Instruments (TI) often uses a global matrix design for new product development, although its underlying organization design is based on function. At any time, it has several product development groups in operation. Within any given country in which TI operates, the groups draw members from relevant functional groups and work toward creating new products or new uses for existing ones. When and if such breakthroughs are achieved, matrix-based product groups are used to transfer the new technology throughout the rest of the firm.[26] After the task assigned to the product group is completed (for example, after the new product is launched), the group may be dissolved.

The global matrix design thus promotes organizational flexibility. It allows firms to take advantage of functional, area, customer, and product organization designs as needed while simultaneously minimizing the disadvantages of each. Members of a product development team can be added or dropped from the team as the firm's needs change. The global matrix design also promotes coordination and communication among managers from different divisions.

The global matrix design has disadvantages, however:

1 It is not appropriate for a firm that has few products and that operates in relatively stable markets.

2 It often puts employees in the position of being accountable to more than one manager. For example, at any given time an employee may be a member of his or her functional, area, or product group as well as of two or three product development groups. As a result, the individual may have split loyalties—caught between competing sets of demands and pressures as the area manager the employee reports to wants one thing and the product-line manager wants another.

3 The global matrix design creates a paradox regarding authority. On the one hand, part of its purpose is to put decision-making authority in the hands of those managers most able to use it quickly. On the other hand, because reporting relationships are so complex and vague, getting approval for major decisions may actually be slower.

4 It tends to promote compromises or decisions based on the relative political clout of the managers involved.[27]

Hybrid Global Designs

A final point to consider is that each global form of international organization design described in this section represents an ideal. Most firms create a hybrid design that best suits their purposes, as dictated in part by size, strategy, technology, environment, and culture. Most MNCs, in particular, are likely to blend elements of all these designs. A firm may use a basic product design as its overall approach, but it may have different levels of functional orientation or area focus in some of its product groups than in others. As noted earlier, for instance, this is the approach used by Nestlé. Special customer groups and specific markets may also have divisions or support groups that span all areas in a firm. In fact, if it were possible to compare the designs used by the world's 500 largest MNCs, no two would look exactly the same. A firm's managers start with the basic prototypes discussed here, merge them, throw out bits and pieces, and create new elements unique to their firm as they respond to changes in the organization's strategy and competitive environment.

Figure 13.8 illustrates how Nissan Motor Corporation uses a hybrid design to structure its U.S. operations. At the top level of the firm, Nissan has some managers dedicated to products (such as the vice president and general manager for the Infiniti division) and others dedicated to functions (such as the vice president and chief financial officer). The marketing function for Nissan automobiles is broken down by product, with specific units responsible for sedans, sports cars, and trucks and utility vehicles. Both the Infiniti and Nissan divisions also have regional general managers organized by area. In similar fashion, all large international firms mix and match forms of organization in different areas and at different levels to create hybrid organization designs that their managers believe best serve the firm's needs.

Related Issues in Global Organization Design

In addition to the fundamental issues of organization design we have already addressed, MNCs also face a number of related organizational issues that must be carefully managed. We discuss several of these issues next:

▶ Centralization versus decentralization
▶ The role of subsidiary boards of directors
▶ Coordination among the firm's various operations

Centralization versus Decentralization

When designing its organization, an MNC must make a particularly crucial decision, one that involves the level of autonomy, power, and control it wants to grant its subsidiaries. Suppose it chooses to decentralize decision making by allowing individual subsidiaries great discretion over strategy, finance, production, and marketing decisions, thereby allowing those decisions to be made by managers closest to the market. These managers may then focus only on the subsidiary's needs rather than the firm's overall needs. An MNC can remedy this deficiency by tightly centralizing decision-making authority at corporate headquarters. Decisions made by the corporate staff can then take into account the firm's overall needs. However, these decisions often hinder the ability of subsidiary managers to quickly and effectively respond to changes in their local market conditions. Because both centralization and decentralization offer attractive benefits to the

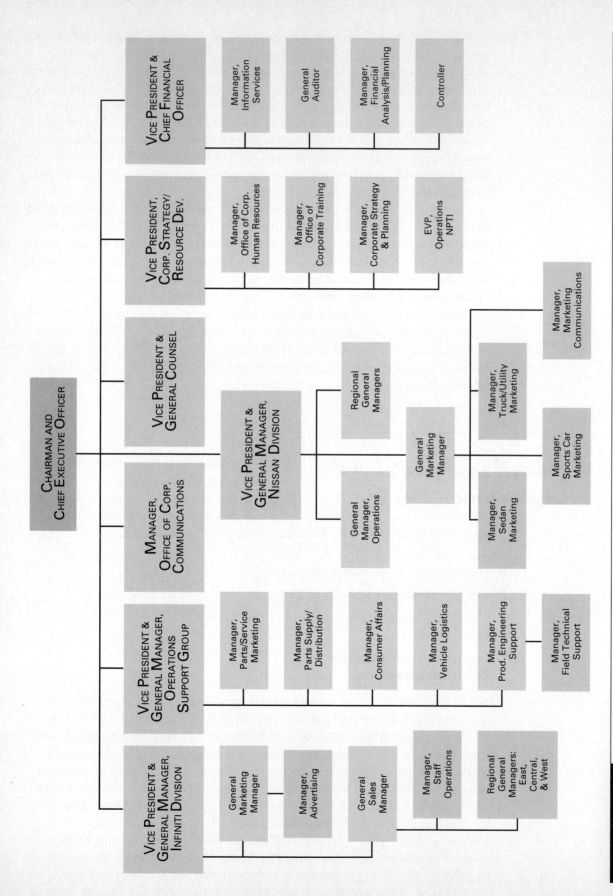

FIGURE 13.8 Nissan USA's Hybrid Design

MNC, most firms use a blend of the two and constantly tinker with the blend to achieve the best outcome in terms of overall strategy.

There seems to be a trend among some MNCs toward greater centralization. While the need to address local factors in different markets is best handled by decentralizing control to local managers, some managers have come to believe it is more important to address the specific needs of different customer groups across many markets, a task best handled via centralization. For example, Europcar International SA, Europe's largest car-rental firm, used to be very decentralized. High-ranking local managers in nine countries held great authority and ran their local operations with virtual autonomy. However, the firm's new CEO decided that business customers, tourists, and local individual renters each represented a clear market segment whose needs could better be handled via centralization. He thus fired the country managers—replacing them with lower-level managers—and centralized operations at headquarters.[28]

Role of Subsidiary Boards of Directors

An MNC typically incorporates each of its subsidiaries in that subsidiary's country of operation in order to limit the subsidiary's liability and to allow it to attain legal status as a local citizen. Most countries require each corporation, including a wholly owned subsidiary of a foreign MNC, to have a board of directors. This board is elected by corporate shareholders (which is the MNC), is responsible to those shareholders for the effective management of the subsidiary (which is owned by the MNC), and oversees the activities of top-level managers (who are hired by the MNC). The issue facing most MNCs, then, is whether to view the creation of a subsidiary board of directors as a pro forma exercise and therefore give the board little real authority or to empower the board with substantial decision-making authority.

Empowering the subsidiary's board has a primary advantage of promoting decentralization. Foreign subsidiaries may need the authority to act quickly and decisively without having to always seek the parent's approval. Also, if the MNC decentralizes authority to local levels, an active board provides a clear account-ability and reporting link back to corporate headquarters. Some MNCs have also found that appointing prominent local citizens to the subsidiary's board is helpful to conducting business in a foreign country. These members can help the subsidiary integrate itself into the local business community and can be an effective source of information for both parent and subsidiary about local business and political conditions. For example, prominent local business officials on the board of Apple's Japanese subsidiary were key to the firm's success in the Japanese market in the early 1990s. They enhanced the credibility of Apple's products in a market in which corporate connections and status are an important marketing tool, while their appointment demonstrated Apple's long-term commitment to the Japanese market.[29] A subsidiary board also can help monitor the subsidiary's ethical and social responsibility practices. Among the MNCs that make frequent use of such boards are Honda, Matsushita, Hewlett-Packard, and Dow.

A potential disadvantage of empowering a subsidiary's board is that the subsidiary may become too independent as its board assumes too much authority and thereby fails to maintain the desired level of accountability to the parent.

In general, a subsidiary board is most useful when the subsidiary has

- ▶ A great deal of autonomy
- ▶ Its own self-contained management structure
- ▶ A business identity separate from the parent's

In such a case, the board can provide substantial guidance and oversight to the subsidiary's managers. Most likely to have active subsidiary boards is an H-form organization, since a holding company's subsidiaries often benefit from being run independently of each other. However, an M-form organization may also have active subsidiary boards. And in some cases a firm that uses the global product or area structure may have subsidiary boards with significant decision-making powers.[30]

Coordination in the Global Organization

Finally, as part of creating an effective design for itself, an international firm must also address its coordination needs. In this sense, **coordination** is the process of linking and integrating functions and activities of different groups, units, or divisions. Coordination needs vary as a function of interdependence among the firm's divisions and functions.[31] There are three levels of interdependence:

1 The highest coordination needs are found in organizations that have *reciprocal interdependence;* that is, each division or activity is dependent on all other divisions or activities because work flows back and forth between divisions in a reciprocal fashion. Examples are U-form organizations and firms that use global functional and matrix designs.

2 Firms with moderate coordination needs are characterized by *sequential interdependence;* that is, each division or activity is dependent on only some of the others because work flows between divisions in a one-way or sequential fashion. Examples are M-form organizations and firms that use global area or customer designs.

3 Organizations that have less need for coordination have *pooled interdependence;* that is, each division or activity functions with relatively little dependence on the others because it does its own work and its results are pooled with the others' at the corporate level. Examples are H-form organizations and firms that use the global product design.

MNCs use any of several strategies to achieve and manage their desired level of coordination. The organizational hierarchy itself is one way to manage interdependence and promote coordination. An organization design that clearly specifies all reporting relationships and directions of influence facilitates coordination because each manager knows how to channel communications, decision making, and so on. Rules and procedures also facilitate coordination. For example, a standard operating procedure that requires the reporting of monthly and quarterly revenue, cost, and profit data to headquarters allows corporate staff to coordinate the firm's cash flows and to quickly identify troublesome markets.

MNCs also adopt somewhat more temporary or ad hoc coordination techniques.[32] Using employees in liaison roles is one such technique. For example, suppose two divisions of an MNC are collaborating on an activity or function. Each may designate a specific manager as its liaison with the other. If any manager in one unit has information or questions that involve the other unit, it is channeled through the liaison to the appropriate person or unit. Toyota, for example, frequently uses this technique for managing relatively small-scale joint efforts.

Coordination is a major challenge for international firms with far-flung operations. Advances in communications technology, especially e-mail and computer-based communications networks, have made it easier for managers to keep in touch with one another and to coordinate their activities.

When the magnitude of the collaboration is significant, task forces may be used for coordination. Here, each participating unit or division assigns one or more representatives to serve on the task force. The assignment may be either full-time or part-time. Ford and Mazda, for example, used a task force when they collaborated on the design of the 1994 Ford Escort. Each firm designated members of its design, engineering, operations, and finance departments to serve on the task force. Employees of the two firms rotated on and off the task force depending on its needs and the stage of development of the automobile. When the final design was complete and the automobile was put into production, the task force was dissolved.

Task forces may also be used to resolve intraorganizational conflicts or to build commitment to new projects. For example, in the early days of the personal computer industry (the early 1980s), Toshiba had to decide which operating system its personal computers would use. To the managers of its U.S. affiliate, Toshiba America, there was only one choice: IBM-compatible. However, the firm's Japanese engineers and marketing staff resisted this choice. So Toshiba created a task force composed of Toshiba America managers, Japanese R&D staff, and Japanese marketers, who, with the aid of a consulting firm, interviewed computer users, distributors, and dealers. In the end, the task force decided that Toshiba's personal computers should be IBM-compatible. Although this decision was obvious to the U.S. managers, the task force was still invaluable because it resulted in the Japanese employees' being fully committed to the use of the IBM-compatible operating system.[33]

Many international firms also rely heavily on informal coordination mechanisms. Informal management networks can be especially effective. An **informal management network** is simply a group of managers from different parts of the world who are connected to one another in some way. These connections often form as a result of personal contact, mutual acquaintances, and interaction achieved via travel, training programs, joint meetings, task force experiences, and so on. Informal management networks can be very powerful for short-circuiting bureaucracy that may delay communication and decision making. They also can be effective for getting things done more quickly and more effectively than if normal and routine procedures were always followed.[34]

Corporate Culture in International Business

While the structural components of an organization design can be somewhat objectively specified and drawn in an organizational chart, there also are informal elements of an organization that are more subjective and amorphous. This informal organization, which also plays a critical role in coordination, is called the corporate culture. **Corporate culture** is the set of shared values that defines for its members what the organization stands for, how it functions, and what it considers important.[35] Most managers agree that it is important to develop a clearly defined and consistent culture to help guide the behavior of managers. Such a culture not only helps managers make sense of the organization and facilitates their understanding of their own jobs but also contributes to overall competitiveness.[36]

Creating such a culture is difficult for any organization. Success in doing so is considerably more important for an MNC, however, than for a purely domestic firm. Each unit within the MNC will naturally have its own culture. This unit culture will be partially defined by the national culture within which that unit functions. At the same time, however, there also needs to be an overall corporate culture that permeates the entire organization. At Sony, for example, the firm's Japanese units have one culture, while its U.S. units have a different one. Each culture was developed from the context of the national culture of the units. But there is also the overall culture—"Sony's Way"—that permeates the entire firm ("Sony's Way" is explored in a case in Chapter 14).

Creating the Corporate Culture in International Business

The creation of a corporate culture for an MNC usually starts with the firm's mission statement. As discussed in Chapter 10, the mission statement spells out the firm's values, goals, and basic operating philosophy. But managers throughout the firm must also accept and enact the corporate culture if it is to become a reality. Contributing to the development of a strong and accepted corporate culture are

▶ Symbols, such as the corporate logo

▶ Heroes, usually successful and distinctive managers

▶ Legends, including stories about past successes and failures that get passed from manager to manager

▶ Shared experiences, such as working together toward shared goals

For example, Sony's chairman, Akio Morita, was one of the firm's founders, and his personal values and beliefs permeate the entire organization. He is given credit for much of the firm's success today and is revered by many of the firm's employees, who look to him for leadership and direction. Thus his influence is indelibly felt throughout the firm.

When Helmut Maucher became CEO of Nestlé, he soon decided that the firm was too bureaucratic and not sufficiently interested in innovation. Maucher is a tough-minded executive who abhors bureaucracy. He hates to read reports and thinks most firms spend too much time processing paperwork instead of carrying out their business. He adopted the slogan "Let's have more pepper and less paper" to let people know he wanted them to spend less time on paperwork and more time communicating, stimulating innovation, and generating new ideas. He repeatedly used this slogan in conversations and meetings with Nestlé managers worldwide. As a result, it gradually became embedded in the firm's corporate culture.

Of course, there is no one best culture toward which international firms should aspire. For example, TI, Honda, and Daimler-Benz each have a distinctive corporate culture that helps everyone understand how the firm functions. TI has what its managers call a "shirt sleeve" culture in which people "roll up their sleeves" and work hard; there are few status differences among its managers. Honda, on the other hand, has a culture that stresses teamwork and togetherness. Each Honda employee understands that he or she is to take responsibility for doing whatever is necessary to enhance quality. Daimler-Benz's culture centers around technology. The firm and its managers have always focused on applying technology as efficiently and effectively as possible. As a result, Daimler-Benz managers put a premium on technological innovation and refinement. The firm also considers its German operations to be superior to its operations in other countries, and so it concentrates its highest-profile and highest-profit activities in its German factories.

Managing the Corporate Culture in International Business

Managing the corporate culture is best approached from the standpoints of consistency and communication. Managers should take every opportunity to communicate the firm's culture to others so as to keep it in the forefront of decision making and other activities. Frequent contact and interaction between managers and other employees are also useful for transmitting and reinforcing the corporate culture. Still another way to spread the culture throughout the organization is to transfer key managers to different units.

When corporate culture is not properly managed, the firm is likely to stumble and its effectiveness diminish. For example, Bond Corporation Holdings, Inc., an Australian conglomerate, has suffered serious setbacks in the last few years, in part because of its disjointed and vague culture. During the 1980s, Bond amassed a collection of businesses ranging from breweries to newspapers to banks to resorts. Some units thought cost control was paramount;

A strong corporate culture can help transmit a firm's values and beliefs to operations around the world. For example, Pizza Hut worked hard to ensure that its foreign restaurants would have the same entrepreneurial culture as its successful outlets in the United States. The firm discovered how well it had succeeded when the manager of the Moscow Pizza Hut passed out free food to demonstrators fighting a failed coup attempt.

others thought they were supposed to expand aggressively with little regard for costs; still others believed their mandate was to earn profits regardless of the methods employed. Because of such diverse approaches and the poorly articulated corporate vision, the Bond empire began to crumble and its various units to self-destruct. Today, Bond is a shell of its former self, in large part because its managers failed to develop a strong, clearly defined culture.[37]

In contrast, Pizza Hut, a division of PepsiCo, has a strong, coordinated culture. PepsiCo managers have worked long and hard to instill throughout their varied businesses a consistent and clearly defined culture that stresses competitiveness and social consciousness. For example, when Pizza Hut opened its first restaurant in Moscow, managers in the United States fretted about how to imbue their new partners abroad with their own entrepreneurial and aggressive spirit. They told them about it and tried to serve as role models, but they were not sure their message was understood. They found out during the failed Soviet coup in 1991. The local Pizza Hut manager in Moscow went out among the demonstrators fighting the coup attempt and passed out free pizza and Pepsi to everyone. This action created much good will for the firm. It also is exactly what executives back in the United States would have advised him to do. But they did not have to tell him because he had learned enough about the corporate culture to know how the firm wanted him to respond.[38]

Managing Change in International Business

Another critical facet of organization design in international firms is change management. In this context, **organization change** is any significant modification or alteration in the firm's strategy, organization design, technology, and/or employees. The process of internationalizing the firm's design, discussed earlier in the chapter, is an important example of organization change. Because the international environment in which a firm operates is never static, managing change in ways that enhance the firm's productivity and profitability is a continual challenge confronting international managers. Because managing change is both complex and important, international managers must understand the reasons for change, the varieties of change they may confront, and how to implement change most effectively.[39]

Reasons for Change in International Business

Change in the firm may be necessitated by any number of external factors, including changes in:

▶ External environment
▶ Technology
▶ Cultural values and mores[40]

Among the most significant forces for internal change are changes in the environment in which the firm operates. As new markets open or existing markets shrink, for example, the firm must develop appropriate responses. Consider the completion of the EU's internal market in 1992. Literally thousands of firms changed their strategy for doing business in that market. Some rearranged their production among their existing factories, hoping to benefit from economies of scale. Unilever, for example, restructured its detergent product line by replacing autonomous, nearly independent national operations with a new subsidiary, Lever Europe, which was charged with treating Europe as one big market.[41] Other firms bought out their competitors in order to broaden their presence within the EU. For example, Air France prepared for the EU's deregulation of air services by purchasing Air Inter, the leading provider of internal air services in France, as well as a share of Belgium's national carrier, Sabena. In addition, firms headquartered outside the EU, such as Samsung, Toshiba, Maytag, and Peat Marwick Mitchell, have increased their direct investments in that area. But as non-EU firms increase their presence, existing firms must respond. For example, entrenched European automakers such as Fiat, BMW, and Ford of Europe all must confront increased competition in this market from non-EU firms such as Toyota, Nissan, and Mitsubishi.

Organization change can also result from changes in technology. New technology may redefine work roles and reporting relationships among employees. For example, the spread of personal computers in the workplace has reduced the need for mainframe computers, altered the role of corporate MIS staff, and offered customer service employees far more information than their counterparts possessed two decades ago, thereby raising their stature as well as their educational requirements. Advances in telecommunications technology have also affected organization design. U.S. computer firms, for example, have established joint ventures in India to supply software, which is then transported electronically via satellite to program developers in the United States.

Changes in cultural values and mores also can prompt organization change. For example, decreased consumption of tobacco products in the United States has caused makers of such products to diversify into other products. Philip Morris purchased General Foods in 1985 and Kraft in 1988. It is now aggressively attacking the European market, acquiring chocolate and coffee marketer Jacob Suchard as well as the leading cigarette company in former East Germany. However, Philip Morris has had to admit to at least one failure: it cannot get French consumers to buy Kraft Velveeta cheese.[42]

Types of Change in International Business

Change in a firm can take many forms, including change in:

▶ Corporate strategy
▶ Organization design
▶ Employees

One significant change occurs when a firm alters its corporate strategy, which results when an international firm moves among the single-product, related diversification, and unrelated diversification strategies discussed in Chapter 10. A firm entering a new market via exporting, licensing, franchising, and management contracts is undertaking strategic change, as is one that adopts a new entry mode such as FDI or a joint venture. Even more dramatic strategic changes include acquiring or being acquired by another firm.[43]

As such changes in corporate strategy develop, compensating changes in organization design are often necessary in order to implement the new strategy successfully.[44] Design changes may involve how the firm configures itself, how it delegates authority to its subsidiaries abroad, how it engages in coordination, and how it establishes reporting relationships. Market conditions may also prompt changes in organization design. For example, Siemens Nixdorf had trouble attaining profitability in its core computer businesses, in part because it could not keep pace with rapid technological and marketing changes in this industry. In order to improve profits and innovation, in 1992 the firm split its computer operations into three autonomous divisions: personal computer, computer printer, and corporate computer systems. By so doing, Siemens Nixdorf hopes to make each division more responsive to changes in the competitive environment.[45]

A final type of organization change involves a firm's employees. A firm sometimes wants to change the attitudes of its employees, for example, enhance their morale or improve their job satisfaction. It also may find it useful to improve its employees' ability or performance levels. For example, Collins & Aikman implemented a systematic program of improving its employees' reading and math skills to ensure they can efficiently operate the firm's increasingly sophisticated textile machinery.

In other cases, the firm effects employee change via transfers, promotions, terminations, or the hiring of more qualified people. For example, the board of directors of Beecham Group PLC, a British consumer products firm, wanted a CEO who had a strong commitment to and understanding of global competitiveness. However, it did not think any current Beecham executive had those qualities, so it hired an experienced U.S. manager, Robert P. Bauman, who had demonstrated his abilities in several previous positions.[46] Similarly, in the early 1990s GM became increasingly concerned that its automobiles' old-fashioned appearance was endangering its short-term profitability and long-term viability. So it transferred the chief designer at its German subsidiary to Detroit to head its worldwide design programs.[47]

CHAPTER REVIEW

Summary

Organization design is the overall pattern of structural components and configurations used to manage the total organization. Early attempts to identify the one best way to design organizations included the bureaucratic design. However, managers now realize that the most appropriate design of an organization depends on its situation. Managers today also realize

that organization design is an evolutionary process.

When a firm first begins to operate internationally, it usually must change its design in one or more ways. Such change may involve following the corollary approach, then establishing an export department, and then creating an international division.

After a firm has established a significant international presence, however, it will usually develop a global organization design. The most common approaches to global organization design are the global product design, the global area design, the global functional design, the global customer design, and the global matrix design. Each of these approaches has unique advantages and disadvantages, and one or more may be more appropriate for some firms than for others. Indeed, many firms actually use a hybrid global design best suited to their needs.

MNCs also must make other decisions related to organization design. Particularly important are those regarding centralization versus decentralization, the role of subsidiary boards of directors, and which coordination mechanisms to use. Informal management networks are especially powerful mechanisms for coordination.

Whereas a firm's design is relatively formal and objective, its culture is more informal and subjective. Corporate culture is the set of values that defines for members what the firm stands for, how it functions, and what it considers important. Culture is shaped by such things as the firm's mission statement, symbols, heroes, legends, past successes and failures, and shared experiences. A strong, clearly defined, and well-managed culture can be a major contributor to the firm's success.

Organization change is any significant modification or alteration in the firm's strategy, organization design, technology, and/or employees. Most firms find they must change regularly for various reasons. The key is to keep change properly focused on specific objectives and in line with other aspects of the firm.

Review Questions

1. What is organization design?

2. What are some of the initial impacts of international activity on organization design?

3. What is the global product design? What are its strengths and weaknesses?

4. What is the global area design? What are its strengths and weaknesses?

5. What is the global functional design? What are its strengths and weaknesses?

6. What is the global customer design? What are its strengths and weaknesses?

7. What is the global matrix design? What are its strengths and weaknesses?

8. What are three issues related to organization design that MNCs face?

9. What is corporate culture? Why is it important in international business?

10. What is organization change? Why do managers of international firms need to understand organization change?

Questions for Discussion

1. Why does a firm's organization design depend on its situation? Why is the design evolutionary?

2. If a new organization starts out with a global perspective, will it necessarily experience any of the initial impacts of international activity on organization design? Why or why not?

3. Do managers of international firms need to approach organization design differently from their counterparts in domestic firms? Why or why not?

4. How do the global product, area, functional, and customer approaches to organization design differ? How are they similar?

5. Why is a global matrix design almost always transitional in nature?

6. Why do international firms need to develop a unique organization design rather than simply model themselves after other firms?

7. Why is coordination important in international business?

8. Can a strong corporate culture be bad? If not, why? If so, give an example.

9. How are national culture and corporate culture likely to be related?

10. Under what circumstances might a firm need to change its design from one of the global designs to a different one?

Form small groups of three or four students. Assume that your group is the board of directors of a large firm, Unipro Incorporated, which until recently followed a single-product strategy. It manufactured small jet aircraft and sold them worldwide. Its products are market leaders in North America, Asia, and Europe and also sell well in South America and Africa. Because of the single-product strategy, Unipro set up a global functional organization design, which it still uses.

The board has been concerned about the firm's dependence on a single product, so several years ago it decided to diversify the firm. Over four years, the firm has bought several other businesses:

▶ General Chemical (based in England; almost 90 percent of its revenues come from Europe)
▶ Total Software (based in Canada; most of its revenues come from North America and Europe)
▶ Pleasure Park (an amusement park in Japan)
▶ Fundamental Foods (a large food-processing firm with strong operations in the United States, Europe, and Japan)

Now that Unipro's diversification strategy has been fully implemented, the board (your group) sees that it needs to change the firm's organization design to better fit the new business mix. Based solely on the information you have, sketch a new organization design for the firm. When you are finished, draw your organization design on the blackboard.

Follow-up Questions

1. How is your group's organization design similar to and different from those of other groups?

2. What do you see as the biggest advantages and disadvantages of your group's organization design?

3. What additional information would have made it easier for you to develop a new organization design for Unipro?

CLOSING CASE

Unilever's Unique Design[48]

Unilever has a unique corporate structure. Unilever has not one but two parent firms, one based in London (Unilever PLC) and the other in Amsterdam (Unilever NV). Unilever is primarily a packaged consumer goods firm with major brands in several businesses: cosmetics (Chesebrough-Ponds, Elizabeth Arden), processed foods (Lipton, Ragu), personal care (Vaseline, Close-Up), and soap and laundry (Dove, All, Sunlight).

Unilever was created in 1927 by a merger of the Margarine Union (a cartel specializing in food prod-

ucts) and Lever Brothers (a consumer products firm). Its unique corporate structure was adopted for tax purposes. For the next several decades, Unilever expanded through aggressive promotion and through acquisition of other related businesses. However, Europe remained its stronghold, with almost two thirds of its revenues and profits coming from European operations.

Unilever gradually created separate operating units for each country in Europe. For example, its subsidiary in the United Kingdom was totally responsible for producing, packaging, and marketing Unilever products in that market. Similar units were set up in other countries. This approach enabled the firm to meet the unique marketing needs of each of the 17 European countries in which it sold its products.

As the integrated European market gradually emerged, however, Unilever's traditional organization design both slowed its ability to compete with foreign firms and increased its costs. For example, because each national subsidiary was allowed to develop its own design and marketing strategy, it took each longer to implement company-wide changes dictated by corporate headquarters. Further, each activity was being duplicated in 17 different markets. In the meantime, Procter & Gamble (P&G) was capitalizing on the shortcomings of Unilever's organization design to beat it to market and capture market share in many product lines.

Unilever decided in 1990 that it needed to change its organization design to more effectively compete with P&G and other firms in the integrated European market. Unilever's detergent operation was among the first to be changed. The firm began by creating a new operating unit called Lever Europe and based in Brussels. The 17 national units in Europe now report directly to Lever Europe rather than to Unilever itself.

Lever Europe, in turn, has established areas of expertise for the largest of the national units. For example, the Unilever subsidiary in the United Kingdom is now totally responsible for all European marketing. Other large national units have similar responsibility for operations, human resources, finance, and so on. The result has been reduced resistance to change: while each national unit has given up some autonomy over its local operations, each also has been given more autonomy in developing and implementing parts of the firm's overall European strategy.

Unilever expects these changes to pay immediate benefits. For example, Lever Europe has already lowered production costs by producing larger quantities of products at fewer locations. Further, it expects to get new products to market much faster than previously. But the firm also intends to maintain local brand names, a practice some experts believe will give P&G a continuing competitive advantage.

Case Questions

1. What form of organization design did Unilever use before its recent changes?

2. What form of organization design does Unilever appear to be using today?

3. What are the strengths and weaknesses of its new organization design?

4. How well do you think Unilever has managed the change in its organization design?

5. Research how P&G structures its European operation and compare it to Lever Europe.

CHAPTER NOTES

1. "Ford to Realign with a System of Global Chiefs," *Wall Street Journal*, March 31, 1994, pp. A3, A4; "Have You Driven a Ford Lately—In Japan?" *Business Week*, February 21, 1994, p. 37; "World Car Rolls Out in USA Tuesday," *USA Today*, July 18, 1994, pp. 1B, 2B; "Fire Tested Ford Exec Directs Historic Reorganization," *Detroit News*, August 21, 1994, p. 1.

2. J. M. Stopford and L. T. Wells, *Managing the Multinational Enterprise* (New York: Basic Books, 1972).

3. Alfred Chandler, Jr., *Strategy and Structure* (Cambridge, Mass.: MIT Press, 1962).

4. Gareth Jones, *Organization Theory* (Reading, Mass.: Addison-Wesley, 1995).

5. William G. Egelhoff, "Strategy and Structure in Multinational Corporations: An Information Processing Approach," *Administrative Science Quarterly*, Vol. 27 (1982), pp. 435–458.

6. Max Weber, *Theory of Social and Economic Organizations*, translated by T. Parsons (New York: Free Press, 1947).

7. See John Woodward, *Industrial Organization: Theory and Practice* (London: Oxford University Press, 1965); Tom Burns and G. M. Stalker, *The Management of Innovation* (London: Tavistock, 1961); Derek S. Pugh and David J. Hickson, *Organization Structure in Its Context: The Aston Program* (Lexington, Mass.: D.C. Heath, 1976).

8. John P. Kotter and Leonard A. Schlesinger, "Choosing Strategies for Change," *Harvard Business Review* (March-April 1979), pp. 106–119.

9. Chandler, op. cit.

10. Jane Applegate, "Don't wait for free trade to do Mexican deals," *Houston Chronicle,* October 19, 1992, p. 1B.

11. John D. Daniels, Robert A. Pitts, and Marietta J. Tretter, "Strategy and Structure of U.S. Multinationals: An Exploratory Study," *Academy of Management Journal,* Vol. 27, No. 2 (1984), pp. 292–307.

12. Banco Economico, *1991 Annual Report* (Salvador, Brazil: Banco Economico, 1992).

13. Anant K. Sundaram and J. Stewart Black, "The Environment and Internal Organization of Multinational Enterprises," *Academy of Management Review,* Vol. 17, No. 4 (1992), pp. 729–757.

14. Kendall Roth, David M. Schweiger, and Allen J. Morrison, "Global Strategy Implementation at the Business Unit Level: Operational Capabilities and Administrative Mechanisms," *The Journal of International Business Studies,* Vol. 22, No. 3 (Third Quarter 1991), pp. 369–402.

15. Arvind V. Phatak, *International Dimensions of Management,* 3rd ed. (Boston: PWS-Kent, 1992).

16. Bruce T. Lamont, Robert J. Williams, and James J. Hoffman, "Performance During 'M-Form' Reorganization and Recovery Time: The Effects of Prior Strategy and Implementation Speed," *Academy of Management Journal,* Vol. 37, No. 1 (1994), pp. 153–166.

17. Patricia Sellers, "Can He Keep Philip Morris Growing?" *Fortune,* April 6, 1992, pp. 86–92.

18. Harsco Corporation, *1991 Annual Report* (Camp Hill, Pa.: Harsco Corporation, 1992).

19. Laurence Hooper, "IBM Set to Unveil Restyled PC Business That Could Operate as a Separate Unit," *Wall Street Journal,* September 3, 1992, p. A3; "Siemens AG," *Wall Street Journal,* October 9, 1992, p. B6; Kyle Pope, "PC Marketers Punch Up Combative Ads," *Wall Street Journal,* October 21, 1992, p. B1.

20. Christopher A. Bartlett, "Organizing for Worldwide Effectiveness: The Transnational Solution," *California Management Review* (Fall 1988), pp. 54–74.

21. Alan Chai, Alta Campbell, and Patrick J. Spain (eds.), *Hoover's Handbook of World Business 1993* (Austin, Tex.: Reference Press, 1993), pp. 172–173.

22. Phatak, op. cit.

23. The Exxon Corporation, *1990 Annual Report* (Irving, Tex.: Exxon, 1991).

24. Phatak, op. cit.

25. Christopher A. Bartlett and Sumantra Ghospal, "Matrix Management: Not a Structure, A Frame of Mind," *Harvard Business Review* (July-August 1990), pp. 138–145.

26. Jeremy Main, "How to Go Global—And Why," *Fortune,* August 28, 1989, pp. 70–76.

27. Lawton R. Burns and Douglas R. Wholey, "Adoption and Abandonment of Matrix Management Programs: Effects of Organizational Characteristics and Interorganizational Networks," *Academy of Management Journal,* Vol. 36, No. 1 (1993), pp. 105–138.

28. "Power at Multinationals Shifts to Home Office," *Wall Street Journal,* September 9, 1994, pp. B1, B4.

29. Edmund W. Desmond, "Byting Japan," *Time,* October 5, 1992, pp. 68–69.

30. Mark P. Kriger, "The Importance of the Role of Subsidiary Boards in MNCs: Comparative Parent and Subsidiary Perceptions," *Management International Review,* Vol. 31 (1991), pp. 317–331.

31. James Thompson, *Organizations in Action* (New York: McGraw-Hill, 1967).

32. Jon I. Martinez and J. Carlos Jarillo, "The Evolution of Research on Coordination Mechanisms in Multinational Corporations," *The Journal of International Business Studies,* Vol. 20 (Fall, 1989), pp. 489–514.

33. John Rehfeld, "What Working for a Japanese Company Taught Me," *Harvard Business Review* (November-December 1990), pp. 167–176.

34. Sumantra Ghospal and Christopher A. Bartlett, "The Multinational Corporation as an Interorganizational Network," *Academy of Management Review,* Vol. 15, No. 4 (1990), pp. 603–625.

35. See Terrence E. Deal and Allan A. Kennedy, *Corporate Culture: The Rites and Rituals of Corporate Life* (Reading, Mass.: Addison-Wesley, 1982), for one of the most influential treatments of corporate culture.

36. Jay Barney, "Organizational Culture: Can It Be a Source of Sustained Competitive Advantage?" *Academy of Management Review* (July 1986), pp. 656–665.

37. Chai, Campbell, and Spain, op. cit., p. 154.

38. "Victualler to the Resistance," *Forbes,* December 9, 1991, pp. 172–173.

39. See Roy McLennan, *Managing Organizational Change* (Englewood Cliffs, N.J.: Prentice-Hall, 1989).

40. Rosabeth Moss Kanter, "Transcending Business Boundaries—12,000 World Managers View Change," *Harvard Business Review* (May-June 1991), pp. 151–164.

41. Guy de Jonquieres, "Unilever adopts a clean sheet approach," *Financial Times,* October 21, 1991, p. 13.

42. Sellers, op. cit.

43. Kotter and Schlesinger, op. cit.

44. William G. Egelhoff, *Organizing the Multinational Enterprise* (Cambridge, Mass.: Ballinger, 1988).

45. "Siemens AG," *Wall Street Journal,* October 9, 1992, p. B6.

46. "Beecham's Chief Imports American Ways," *Wall Street Journal,* October 27, 1988, p. B9.

47. "GM Selects Cherry as Vice President of Company's World-Wide Design Staff," *Wall Street Journal,* September 16, 1992, p. B9.

48. "Procter Outpacing Unilever," *Cincinnati Enquirer,* May 14, 1994, p. 5; "Unilever Adopts Clean Sheet Approach," *Financial Times,* October 21, 1991, p. 13; Floris A. Maljers, "Inside Unilever: The Evolving Transnational Company," *Harvard Business Review,* September–October 1992, pp. 46–52.

Managing Behavior and Interpersonal Relations

Chapter Outline

Basic perspectives on individual differences

Social orientation
Power orientation
Uncertainty orientation
Goal orientation
Time orientation

Motivation in international business

Need-based models across cultures
Process-based models across cultures
The reinforcement model across cultures

Leadership in international business

Decision making in international business

Models of decision making
The normative model across cultures
The descriptive model across cultures

Groups and teams in international business

The nature of group dynamics
Managing cross-cultural teams

After studying this chapter you should be able to:

Identify and discuss basic perspectives on individual differences in different cultures.

Discuss basic views of employee motivation in international business.

Describe basic views of managerial leadership in international business.

Discuss the nature of managerial decision making in international business.

Describe group dynamics and discuss how teams are managed across cultures.

Characterize the role of corporate culture in international business.

SONY CORPORATION IS PERHAPS THE BEST-KNOWN JAPANESE FIRM in the world. It seems that virtually everybody has a Walkman, for example, and the Sony Trinitron is among the best-selling televisions in the United States, Europe, and Asia. But relatively few people know much about the firm itself. And even fewer understand how its unique approach to dealing with its employees has contributed so much to its success. Indeed, Sony's creation of an internal culture unique within its surrounding social culture has been a major ingredient in its ability to grow and prosper. ▌▌While many international firms have aggressively expanded their operations abroad, Sony has resisted this trend. The firm's managers believe that it is vitally

The Sony Way[1]

important for them to understand and appreciate the behavior of the firm's employees and that this can best be accomplished by maintaining most critical operations within Japan. Thus they don't have to worry about integrating people from diverse cultural backgrounds. However, they also are reluctant to hire people who have experience at other Japanese firms. They worry that these people will not easily adapt to the Sony way of doing things and will not adopt the firm's basic philosophies. ▌▌Sony was founded in 1946 by three young Japanese engineers. From the very beginning, one of the firm's fundamental goals was innovation. For example, Sony introduced the first tape recorder in Japan in 1950. It licensed transistor technology from the U.S. firm Western Electric in 1953 and used it to launch one of the world's first transistor radios. Other early innovations included the first transistor television in 1959 and the first solid-state video tape recorder in 1961. ▌▌Today the firm remains a world leader in consumer electronics and earns more than 70 percent of its revenues outside Japan (around 30 percent come from the United States and another 25 percent from Europe). Sony engineers develop about 1000 new products every year—an average of 4 each business day! Approximately 800 of these are extensions and refinements of existing products, but the other 200 or so are totally new products. ▌▌One key to Sony's success at innovation is the kind of people it hires. Like other Japanese electronics firms, Sony recruits most of its new employees from the engineering schools at major Japanese universities. But while many of those firms seek out the top graduates (a common practice not only in Japan but in many other countries as well), Sony looks for innovators, people who are *neyaka*—optimistic, open-minded, and wide-ranging in their interests. The firm believes the people most likely to thrive in its culture are those who want to move around in different product groups and who are interested in working in areas they didn't study in school. ▌▐ Another ingredient in Sony's success is how it treats its employees. Most other firms—including U.S., European, and other Japanese firms—are very rigid in their approach to allowing employees to transfer to different jobs. An employee who wants to transfer must first convince his or her boss to find a new position and then work with the head of that department to expedite the transfer. At Sony, however, employees are encouraged to seek out new projects and convince the head of that department to accept him or her as a transfer. Only after the details have been worked out does the employee's present boss learn of the impending move. Sony believes that this practice allows employees to gravitate to projects they will be most motivated by and encourages managers to maintain stimulating, challenging, and enjoyable projects so as to attract new people. ▌▐ Sony also believes that employees can make greater contributions to the firm if they are kept fully informed as to what it is doing, why, and how it expects to succeed. Thus Sony goes to great lengths to provide information to everyone in the organization. While most firms provide information to those managers and employees who clearly need it, Sony goes far beyond that minimal level and broadly disseminates information to everyone, whether or not they have a clear and immediate need to know. ▌▐ Insight into how people contribute to Sony's success comes from its recent breakthroughs in computer technology. For example, in 1985 the firm assembled a group of engineers to develop its first entry into the computer market. The group's leader, Toshi T. Doi, was concerned that the firm had grown too large and bureaucratic to function as quickly as he would like. So he chose a group of highly individualistic engineers who were not fitting in well with the rest of the firm. He gave them a separate work area, a general charge, and a targeted completion date, and then left them alone. For six months they worked day and night to develop the computer prototype. Team members literally moved into the office; most slept in chairs at night. When they finished the job—two days ahead of schedule—everyone in the firm applauded their efforts. And the new computer, called the News, quickly captured a big chunk of the Japanese market. ▌▐ These and many other similar experiences and stories have resulted in a strong Sony culture. People are hired and promoted on the basis of their talents and skills. No one advances because of their personal contacts or their university pedigree (again, unlike organizational practices in many firms). Everyone is expected to work for the benefit of the firm, yet they can still maintain their individuality. Encouraging people to be entrepreneurial while remaining under the organizational umbrella creates a big challenge for the firm but also helps maintain enthusiasm, motivation, and drive. Although the firm's employees may not know about the abstract concept of a "corporate culture," most do know exactly what is meant by the firm's internal slogan, "Sony's Way." ▌▐▌▐▌

Virtually all definitions of an organization include some reference to the people who make up the organization. Managers in firms like Sony recognize that an organization's people are the most significant contributors to its effectiveness and that each person in the organization has the potential to help carry it closer to its goals.

Motivating each employee to work in the best interests of the organization is a critical task for all organizations. Consider the case of a Texas Instruments (TI) manager who supervises a group of electrical engineers at the firm's factory in Dallas. Most of the engineers were born, raised, and educated in the United States. One is fascinated by technology and loves nothing more than to tinker. One needs to make as much money as possible to support his extravagant lifestyle. One wants to advance into the ranks of management and is highly motivated to succeed. One has worked at the firm for 30 years, is burned out, and resents having a young woman for a boss. One does a great job but often calls in sick. And one does just enough to get by without being fired. The manager of this group clearly has to understand human nature and behavior if she is to get the most out of her people. Now suppose she gets transferred to the TI plant in Lubbock, Texas. Many of the individual characteristics of people she must deal with there will be different, but many will be fundamentally the same. She should be able to adjust to her new setting relatively easily. But suppose she gets transferred again, to a TI plant in Japan. The behavioral complexity she must deal with increases dramatically. This additional complexity stems from her unfamiliarity with the cultural context in which she and the employees she supervises function.

No two people are exactly the same. On the surface, each individual has her or his unique appearance. But aside from physical appearance, people also differ in terms of their personalities, goals, and motives and in how they perceive and interpret their environments. They differ in terms of their values, emotions, and priorities and in what they want from their work. They differ in terms of how they respond to various types of supervision, rewards, feedback, and work settings. And they exhibit different levels of job satisfaction, commitment, absenteeism, turnover, and stress. People also behave differently when they are put into groups. Take a group of five people with a well-developed and understood set of behavioral profiles. Remove one member, add another, and the behavior of each member shifts, if only a little.[2]

Managers who operate in a domestic firm must understand and contend with a complex set of behavioral and interpersonal processes. Managers in a multicultural firm have the additional complexity of managing people with even more diverse frames of reference and perspectives on work and organizations. International managers who develop insights into dealing with people from different cultural backgrounds will be far ahead of those who do not.

In Chapter 9, we discussed national culture and its implications for firms with international operations. We now look more closely at the actual behaviors of managers and employees in different cultures and how those behavioral differences affect the conduct of international business. We start by discussing the nature of individual differences in different cultures. Then we introduce and discuss four aspects of behavior that are especially important for international businesses: motivation, leadership, decision making, and groups and cross-cultural teams. Finally, we analyze how these factors are integrated in a corporate culture, which helps build consensus and commitment for the firm's international activities.

Basic Perspectives on Individual Differences

The term *individual differences* refers to specific dimensions or characteristics of a person that influence that person's perceptions, attitudes, values, or behaviors.[3] Psychologists who study individual differences focus primarily on personality traits and need structures. However, these factors are influenced by the culture in which a person grew up. International businesspeople, who face the challenge of managing and motivating employees with different cultural backgrounds, need to understand what these personality traits and need structures are and how they differ across cultures. Fortunately, an increasing number of studies by industrial psychologists and organizational behavior specialists are identifying these cultural differences, thereby helping international business managers manage their people more effectively.

Among the most influential of these studies is that performed by Geert Hofstede, a Dutch researcher who studied 116,000 people working in dozens of different countries.[4] (Hofstede's research has been criticized for methodological weaknesses and his own cultural biases but remains the largest and most comprehensive work of its kind.) Hofstede's initial work identified four important dimensions along which people seem to differ across cultures. More recently, he added a fifth dimension. These dimensions, which are shown in Fig. 14.1, are as follows:

▶ Social orientation

▶ Power orientation

▶ Uncertainty orientation

▶ Goal orientation

▶ Time orientation

Note that these dimensions do not represent absolutes, but instead reflect tendencies within cultures. Within any given culture, there are likely to be people at every point on each dimension.

Social Orientation

The first dimension identified by Hofstede is social orientation.[5] (We have altered Hofstede's terminology a bit for the sake of clarity.) **Social orientation** is a person's beliefs about the relative importance of the individual and the groups to which that person belongs. The two extremes of social orientation, summarized in Table 14.1, are individualism and collectivism. **Individualism** is the cultural belief that the person comes first. People who hold this belief tend to put their own interests and those of their immediate families ahead of those of others. Key values of individualistic people include a high degree of self-respect and independence but a corresponding lack of tolerance for opposing viewpoints. These people often put their own success through competition over the good of the group, and they tend to assess decisions in terms of how those decisions affect them as individuals. Hofstede's research suggested that people in the United States, the United Kingdom, Australia, Canada, New Zealand, and the Netherlands tend to be relatively individualistic.

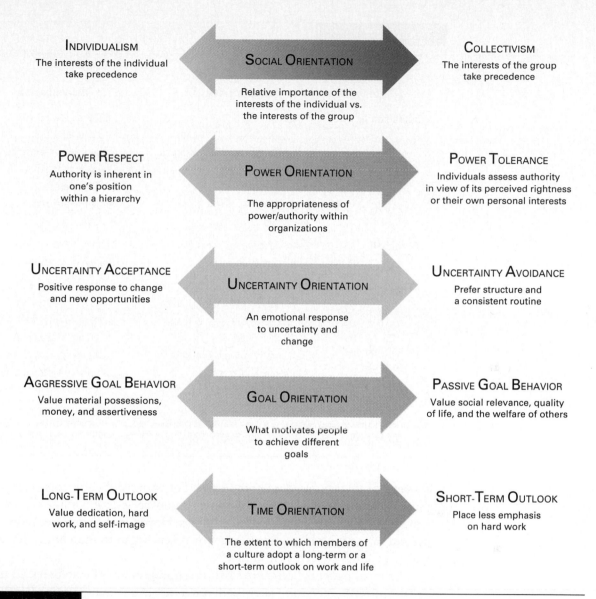

FIGURE 14.1

Individual Differences across Cultures

Collectivism, the opposite of individualism, is the belief that the group comes first. Societies that tend to be collectivistic are usually characterized by well-defined social networks, including extended families, tribes, and coworkers. People are expected to put the good of the group ahead of their own personal freedom, interests, or success. Individual behavior in such cultures is strongly influenced by the emotion of shame; when a group fails, its members take that failure very personally and experience shame. In addition, group members try to fit into their group harmoniously, with a minimum of conflict or tension. Hofstede found that people from Mexico, Greece, Hong Kong, Taiwan, Peru, Singapore, Colombia, and Pakistan tend to be relatively collectivistic in their values.

International firms must be aware of differences in the cultural orientations of countries along the social orientation dimension. In countries such as the United States, where individualism is a cultural norm, many workers prefer reward systems that link pay with individual performance. In a more collectivistic culture, such as China prior to the implementation of its economic reforms, such a reward

TABLE 14.1

Extremes of Social Orientation

	COLLECTIVISM	INDIVIDUALISM
In the family	Education toward "we" consciousness	Education toward "I" consciousness
	Opinions predetermined by group	Private opinion expected
	Obligations to family or in-group:	Obligations to self:
	▶ Harmony	▶ Self-interest
	▶ Respect	▶ Self-actualization
	▶ Shame	▶ Guilt
At school	Learning is for the young only	Continuing education
	Learn how to do	Learn how to learn
At the workplace	Value standards differ for in-group and out-groups: particularism	Same value standards apply to all: universalism
	Other people seen as members of their group	Other people seen as potential resources
	Relationship prevails over task	Task prevails over relationship
	Moral model of employer-employee relationship	Calculative model of employer-employee relationship

Source: Reprinted from Geert Hofstede, "The Business of International Business Is Culture," *International Business Review*, Copyright 1994, page 3, with kind permission from Elsevier Science Ltd., The Boulevard, Langford Lane, Kidlington OX5 1GB, UK.

system may, in fact, be counterproductive. For example, Beijing Jeep once promoted a productive and promising young employee, granting him a raise of $2.70 a month (a 5 percent increase) for his efforts. However, the employee found this 5 percent raise a mixed blessing after his coworkers began to shun him. The raise violated China's collectivistic norms.[6]

A similar pattern characterizes the career progression of employees. In individualistic societies, a person's career path often involves switching employers in a search for higher-paying and more challenging jobs so that the person can prove his or her capabilities in new and changing circumstances. But in collectivistic cultures, even those that are only moderately so, such as Japan, a person's changing jobs reflects disloyalty to the collective good (the firm) and may brand the person as unworthy of trust.[7] Similarly, nepotism is often frowned on in individualistic cultures but may be a normal hiring practice in collectivistic ones.

Power Orientation

The second dimension Hofstede proposed is power orientation. **Power orientation** refers to the beliefs that people in a culture hold about the appropriateness of power and authority differences in hierarchies such as business organizations. The extremes of the dimension of power orientation are summarized in Table 14.2.

Some cultures are characterized by **power respect**. This means that people in a culture tend to accept the power and authority of their superiors simply on the basis of the superiors' positions in the hierarchy and to respect the superiors'

TABLE 14.2

Extremes of Power Orientation

	POWER TOLERANCE	POWER RESPECT
In the family	Children encouraged to have a will of their own	Children educated toward obedience to parents
	Parents treated as equals	Parents treated as superiors
At school	Student-centered education (initiative)	Teacher-centered education (order)
	Learning represents impersonal "truth"	Learning represents personal "wisdom" from teacher (guru)
At workplace	Hierarchy means an inequality of roles, established for convenience	Hierarchy means existential inequality
	Subordinates expect to be consulted	Subordinates expect to be told what to do
	Ideal boss is resourceful democrat	Ideal boss is benevolent autocrat (good father)

Source: Reprinted from Geert Hofstede, "The Business of International Business Is Culture," *International Business Review,* Copyright 1994, page 3, with kind permission from Elsevier Science Ltd., The Boulevard, Langford Lane, Kidlington, OX5 1GB, UK.

right to that power. People at all levels in a firm accept the decisions and mandates of those above them because of their implicit belief that those higher-level positions carry with them the right to make those decisions and issue those mandates. Hofstede found people in France, Spain, Mexico, Japan, Brazil, Indonesia, and Singapore to be relatively power respecting.

In contrast, people in cultures characterized by **power tolerance** attach much less significance to a person's position in the hierarchy. These people are more willing to question a decision or mandate from someone at a higher level or perhaps even refuse to accept it. They are willing to follow a leader when that leader is perceived to be right or when it seems to be in their own self-interest to do so, but not because of the leader's intangible right to issue orders. Hofstede's work suggested that people in the United States, Israel, Austria, Denmark, Ireland, Norway, Germany, and New Zealand tend to be more power tolerant.

Differing cultural attitudes toward power orientation can lead to misunderstandings in business. For example, when firms are negotiating with each other, a firm from a power-tolerant country will often send a team composed of experts on the subject, without concern for rank or seniority. But a team composed of junior employees, no matter how knowledgeable they are about the problem at hand, will be taken as an insult by managers from a power-respecting culture, who expect to deal with persons of rank equal to their own. Also, the quick adoption of informalities by U.S. managers—for example, calling a counterpart by that person's first name—may be misinterpreted by managers from power-respecting cultures as an insulting attempt to diminish another's authority. Similarly, the willingness of a U.S. manager to roll up his or her sleeves and pitch in on the factory floor in an emergency is likely to win praise from U.S. production workers. In Kenya, a superior who exhibited such behavior would be demonstrating his contempt for the management role. A manager so lacking in self-respect would be deemed unworthy of respect or obedience from Kenyan workers.[8]

You can gain a different perspective on Hofstede's dimensions by viewing them in combinations. For example, when social orientation and power orientation are superimposed, individualistic and power-tolerant countries seem to cluster, as do collectivistic and power-respecting countries (see Map 14.1).

Uncertainty Orientation

The third basic dimension of individual differences Hofstede studied is uncertainty orientation. **Uncertainty orientation** is the feeling people have regarding uncertain and ambiguous situations. The extremes of this dimension are summarized in Table 14.3

People in cultures characterized by **uncertainty acceptance** are stimulated by change and thrive on new opportunities. Ambiguity is seen as a context within which an individual can grow, develop, and carve out new opportunities. In these cultures, certainty carries with it a sense of monotony, routineness, and overbearing structure. Hofstede suggested that many people from the United States, Denmark, Sweden, Canada, Singapore, Hong Kong, and Australia are uncertainty accepting.

In contrast, people in cultures characterized by **uncertainty avoidance** dislike and will avoid ambiguity whenever possible. Ambiguity and change are seen as undesirable. These people tend to prefer a structured and routine, even bureaucratic, way of doing things. Hofstede found that many people in Israel, Austria, Japan, Italy, Columbia, France, Peru, and Germany tend to avoid uncertainty whenever possible.

The uncertainty avoidance aspect of German culture spills over into politics. In the 1994 campaign for the EU Parliament, both major parties stressed security. The Socialist Party (SPD) poster on the left focuses on providing jobs for German workers so that they can enjoy economic "security instead of fear." The Christian Democratic Union (CDU) poster on the right stresses a future secure against threats of war, violence, and terrorism.

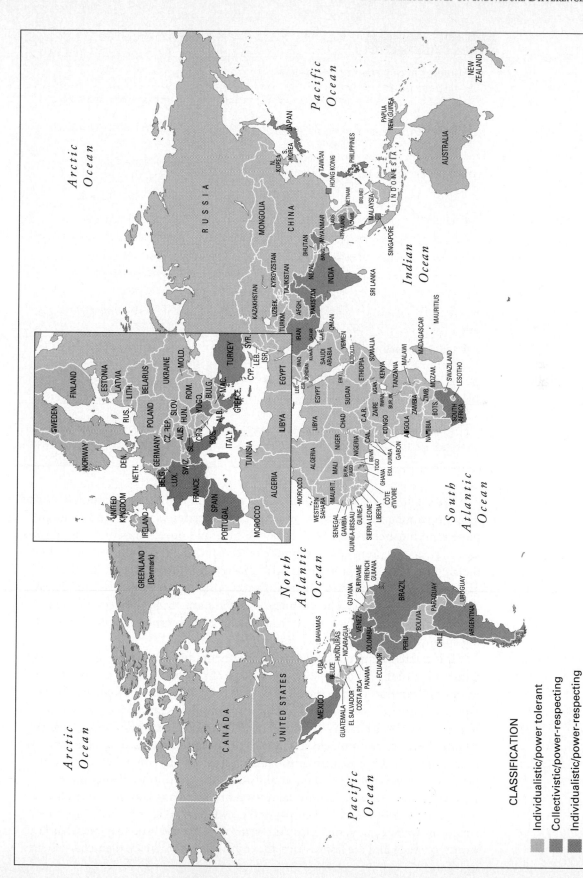

 MAP 14.1 **Classification of Countries by Social Orientation and Power Orientation**

TABLE 14.3

Extremes of Uncertainty Orientation

	UNCERTAINTY ACCEPTANCE	UNCERTAINTY AVOIDANCE
In the family	What is different is ridiculous or curious	What is different is dangerous
	Ease, indolence, low stress	Higher anxiety and stress
	Aggression and emotions not shown	Showing of aggression and emotions accepted
At school	Students comfortable with	Students comfortable with
	▶ Unstructured learning situations	▶ Structured learning situations
	▶ Vague objectives	▶ Precise objectives
	▶ Broad assignments	▶ Detailed assignments
	▶ No timetables	▶ Strict timetables
	Teachers may say "I don't know"	Teachers should have all the answers
At the workplace	Dislike of rules, written or unwritten	Emotional need for rules, written or unwritten
	Less formalization and standardization	More formalization and standardization

Source: Reprinted from Geert Hofstede, "The Business of International Business Is Culture," *International Business Review*, Copyright 1994, page 3, with kind permission from Elsevier Science Ltd., The Boulevard, Langford Lane, Kidlington OX5 1GB, UK.

Uncertainty orientation affects many aspects of managing international firms. Those operating in uncertainty-avoiding countries, for example, tend to adopt more rigid hierarchies and more elaborate rules and procedures for doing business. Uncertainty-accepting cultures, on the other hand, are more tolerant of flexible hierarchies, rules, and procedures. Risk taking ("nothing ventured, nothing gained") is highly valued in uncertainty-accepting countries such as the United States and Hong Kong, whereas preserving the status and prestige of the firm through conservative, low-risk strategies is more important in uncertainty-avoiding countries such as Spain, Belgium, and Argentina.

It is interesting to consider uncertainty orientation along with the social orientation dimension. For example, job mobility is likely to be higher in uncertainty-accepting countries than in those characterized by uncertainty avoidance. Some Japanese firms have traditionally used lifetime employment practices partly in response to the uncertainty-avoiding and collectivistic tendencies of the Japanese culture. Yet lifetime employment—as well as the seniority-based pay and promotion policies used by Japanese firms—may not be an effective policy when transplanted to individualistic and uncertainty-accepting countries. For example, Japanese firms operating in uncertainty-accepting Canada and the United States have been forced to modify their pay and promotion policies because North American workers are more oriented toward an individualistic "pay me what I'm worth" attitude and are less worried about job security than are their counterparts in Japan.

Goal Orientation

The fourth dimension of cultural values Hofstede measured is goal orientation. In this context, **goal orientation** is the manner in which people are motivated to work toward different kinds of goals. One extreme on the goal orientation continuum is aggressive goal behavior (see Table 14.4). People who exhibit **aggressive goal behavior** tend to place a high premium on material possessions, money, and assertiveness. At the other extreme, people who adopt **passive goal behavior** place a higher value on social relationships, quality of life, and concern for others.

According to Hofstede, cultures that value aggressive goal behavior also tend to define gender-based roles somewhat rigidly, whereas cultures that emphasize passive goal behavior do not. For example, in cultures characterized by extremely aggressive goal behavior, men are expected to work and to focus their careers in traditionally male occupations; women are generally expected not to work outside the home and to focus more on their families. If they do work outside the home, they are usually expected to pursue work in areas traditionally dominated by women. According to Hofstede's research, many people in Japan tend to exhibit relatively aggressive goal behavior, whereas many people in Germany, Mexico, Italy and the United States exhibit moderately aggressive goal behavior. Men and women in passive goal behavior cultures are more likely both to pursue diverse careers and to be well represented within any given occupation. People from the Netherlands, Norway, Sweden, Denmark, and Finland tend to exhibit relatively passive goal behavior.

These cultural attitudes affect international business practices in many ways. For example, one study showed that decisions made by Danish managers (a passive goal behavior culture) incorporate societal concerns to a greater extent than those made by more profit-oriented U.S., British, and German executives (from

---

TABLE 14.4

Extremes of Goal Orientation

	PASSIVE GOAL BEHAVIOR	AGGRESSIVE GOAL BEHAVIOR
In the family	Stress on relationships	Stress on achievement
	Solidarity	Competition
	Resolution of conflicts by compromise and negotiation	Resolution of conflicts by fighting them out
At school	Average student is norm	Best students are norm
	System rewards students' social adaptation	System rewards students' academic performance
	Student's failure at school is relatively minor problem	Student's failure at school is disaster; may lead to suicide
At the workplace	Assertiveness ridiculed	Assertiveness appreciated
	Undersell yourself	Oversell yourself
	Stress on life quality	Stress on careers
	Intuition	Decisiveness

Source: Reprinted from Geert Hofstede, "The Business of International Business Is Culture," *International Business Review*, Copyright 1994, page 3, with kind permission from Elsevier Science Ltd., The Boulevard, Langford Lane, Kidlington OX5 1GB, UK.

more aggressive goal behavior cultures).[9] Similarly, studies of the Swedish work-force indicate that that country's egalitarian traditions, as well as workers' desires to maintain a comfortable work schedule, often make promotions less desirable than in other countries. The Swedish tax code, which until recently taxed higher-income workers with marginal tax rates of 97 percent, reinforced this cultural norm by diminishing the value of any pay raise that accompanied a promotion. Many Swedish workers prefer more fringe benefits rather than higher salaries.[10] Or consider the impact of the role of women in business. In Sweden, the high proportion of dual-career families makes it difficult for many workers to accept a promotion if it entails moving. And, not surprisingly, Swedish firms are among the world's leaders in providing fringe benefits such as maternity and paternity leave and company-sponsored child care.

Differences in goal orientation may also affect production techniques. For example, Volvo sought to maintain its product quality and competitiveness by pioneering the use of flexible work groups to produce automobiles. This tech-nique is a means of promoting job satisfaction and reflects Sweden's passive goal behavior, as well as its uncertainty acceptance. Japanese manufacturers, on the other hand, developed quality circles. This practice, inaugurated to promote qual-ity, mirrors the more aggressive goal behavior and the collectivistic aspects of Japanese culture.[11]

Time Orientation

Hofstede recently introduced a fifth dimension into his framework.[12] This dimen-sion, called **time orientation**, is the extent to which members of a culture adopt a long-term versus a short-term outlook on work, life, and other aspects of society. Some cultures, such as those of Japan, Hong Kong, Taiwan, and South Korea, have a long-term orientation that values dedication, hard work, perseverance, and the importance of self-image. Other cultures, including Pakistan and West Africa, are more likely to have a short-term orientation. These cultures put considerably less emphasis on work, perseverance, and similar values. Hofstede's work suggests that the United States and Germany tend to have an intermediate time orientation.

Motivation in International Business

All international businesses face the challenge of motivating their workforces to reduce costs, develop new products, enhance product quality, and improve customer service. Yet, as just discussed, the factors that influence an individual's behavior at work differ across cultures. An apprecia-tion of these individual differences is an important first step in understanding how managers can better assess and address behavioral and interpersonal processes in different cultures.

Motivation is the overall set of forces that cause people to choose certain behaviors from a set of available behaviors.[13] Most modern theoretical approaches to motivation fall into one of three categories:

I   *Need-based models of motivation*, which attempt to identify the specific needs or set of needs that result in motivated behavior

2 *Process-based models of motivation*, which focus more on the conscious thought processes people use to select one behavior from among several

3 *The reinforcement model of motivation*, which deals with how people assess the consequences of their behavioral choices and how that assessment affects the future choice of behaviors and incorporates the roles of rewards and punishment in maintaining or altering existing behavioral patterns

Given the different orientations of national cultures explored by Hofstede and others, an international manager could very well believe that the factors motivating Japanese, Mexican, or Chinese workers differ fundamentally from those found to be important in the United States. Not surprisingly, that manager would be right.[14]

Need-Based Models across Cultures

Hofstede's work provides some useful insights into how need-based models of motivation are likely to vary across cultures.[15] Common needs incorporated in most models of motivation include the needs for security, for being part of a social network, and for opportunities to grow and develop. By relating these need categories to Hofstede's original four dimensions—social orientation, power orientation, uncertainty orientation, and goal orientation—several inferences can be drawn about differences in motivation across cultures.

For example, managers and employees in countries that are individualistic may be most strongly motivated by individually based needs and rewards. Opportunities to demonstrate personal competencies and to receive recognition and rewards as a result may be particularly attractive to such people. In contrast, people from collectivistic cultures may be more strongly motivated by group-based needs and rewards. Indeed, they may be uncomfortable in situations in which they are singled out for rewards apart from the group with which they work, as in the case of the young worker at Beijing Jeep discussed earlier.

Conflicts can easily arise when an international firm's mechanisms for motivating workers clash with cultural attitudes. For example, many U.S. managers working for Japanese MNCs have difficulty with the seniority-based, group-performance–oriented compensation systems of their employers. Similarly, Michigan autoworkers resisted the attempts by Mazda officials to get them to "voluntarily" wear Mazda baseball caps as part of their work uniforms.[16] Tom Selleck's 1992 movie *Mr. Baseball* depicted still other aspects of the cultural clashes arising from these motivational differences between the individual-oriented U.S. culture and the group-oriented Japanese culture. In particular, U.S. baseball players, accustomed to the "star system" that accords them status, prestige, and special privileges, are often shocked by the team-based approach in Japan, which discourages attention to individuals.

Power-respecting individuals are those who accept their boss's right to direct their efforts purely on the basis of organizational legitimacy. As a consequence of this power respect, they may be motivated by the possibility of gaining their boss's approval and acceptance. Thus they may willingly and unquestioningly accept and attempt to carry out directives and mandates. In contrast, power-tolerant people attach less legitimacy to hierarchical rank. Thus they may be less motivated by gaining their boss's approval than by opportunities for pay raises and promotions.

The use of management by objectives also reflects the importance of cultural differences. **Management by objectives (MBO)** is a motivational technique whereby subordinates and managers agree on the subordinates' goals over some period of evaluation. Developed in the United States, a power-tolerant country, it appeals to the U.S. cultural value of individualism in that the employee is made responsible for achieving goals agreed to by the employee and the employee's boss. Exported to Japan, MBO shifted from a focus on individual goals to an evaluation of group goals. However, the MBO concept was a failure in France; it was not compatible with the strong hierarchical nature of French bureaucracy, in which superiors dictate orders to their subordinates.[17]

Managers and employees in uncertainty-avoiding cultures may be highly motivated by opportunities to maintain or increase their perceived levels of job security and job stability. Any effort to reduce or eliminate that security or stability may be met with resistance. In contrast, people in uncertainty-accepting cultures may be less motivated by security needs and less inclined to seek job security or stability as a condition of employment. They also may be more motivated by change and by new challenges and opportunities for personal growth and development. For example, recent studies comparing U.S. and German workers reveal substantial differences in their preferences regarding job values. Job security and shorter work hours were valued more highly by the German workers than the U.S. workers. Income, opportunities for promotion, and the importance of one's work were much more highly valued by the U.S. workers than by their German counterparts.[18]

Finally, people from more aggressive goal behavior cultures are more likely to be motivated by money and other material rewards. They may pursue behavioral choices that they perceive as having the highest probability of financial payoff. They also may be disinclined to work toward rewards whose primary attraction is mere comfort or personal satisfaction. In contrast, workers in passive goal behavior cultures may be more motivated by needs and rewards that can potentially enhance the quality of their lives. They may be less interested in behavioral choices whose primary appeal is a higher financial payoff. For example, Swedish firms provide generous vacations and fringe benefits, while firms operating in China, where wage rates are low by world standards, normally provide workers with housing, medical care, and other support services.

Various studies have tested specific motivation theories in different cultural settings. The theory receiving the most attention has been Abraham Maslow's hierarchy of five basic needs: physiological, security, social, self-esteem, and self-actualization.[19] International research on Maslow's hierarchy provides two different insights. First, managers in many different countries, including the United States, Mexico, Japan, and Canada, usually agree that the needs included in Maslow's hierarchy are all important to them. Second, the relative importance and preference ordering of the needs vary considerably by country.[20] For example, managers in less developed countries such as Liberia and India place a higher priority on satisfying self-esteem and security needs than do managers from more developed countries.[21]

Results from research based on another motivation theory, David McClelland's learned needs framework, have been slightly more consistent. In particular, the need for achievement (to grow, learn, and accomplish important things) has been shown to exist in many different countries. McClelland has also demonstrated that the need for achievement can be taught to people in different cultures.[22] However, given the role of Hofstede's cultural differences, it follows that McClelland's needs are not likely to be constant across cultures. In particular, individualistic, uncertainty-accepting, power-tolerant, and aggressive goal behavior cultures seem most likely to foster and promote the needs for achievement and power (to control resources) but not the need for affiliation (to be part of a social network). In contrast, collectivistic, uncertainty-avoiding, power-respecting, and passive goal behavior cultures may promote the need for affiliation more than the needs for achievement and power.[23]

Frederick Herzberg's two-factor theory is another popular need-based theory of motivation.[24] This theory suggests that one set of factors affects dissatisfaction and another set affects satisfaction. It, too, has been tested cross-culturally with varied results. For example, research has found different patterns of factors when comparing U.S. managers with managers from New Zealand and Panama.[25] Results from U.S. employees suggested that supervision contributed to dissatisfaction but not to satisfaction. But supervision did contribute to employees' satisfaction in New Zealand. Unfortunately, Herzberg's theory often fails to yield consistent results even within a single culture.[26] Thus, even though the theory is well known and popular among managers, managers should be particularly cautious in attempting to apply it in different cultural contexts.

Process-Based Models across Cultures

In contrast to need-based theories, expectancy theory takes a process view of motivation.[27] The theory suggests that people are motivated to behave in certain ways to the extent that they perceive that such behaviors will lead to outcomes they find personally attractive. The theory acknowledges that different people have different needs—one person may need money, another recognition, another social satisfaction, and still another prestige. But each will be willing to improve his or her performance if he or she believes the result will be fulfillment of the needs he or she most prefers.

There has been relatively little research that explicitly tests expectancy theory in countries other than the United States. It does seem logical, however, that the basic framework of the theory should have wide applicability. Regardless of where people work, they are likely to work toward goals they think are important. However, cultural factors will partially determine both the nature of those work goals and people's perceptions of how they should most fruitfully pursue them.

One particularly complex factor that is likely to affect the expectancy process is the cultural dimension of social orientation. The expectancy theory is essentially a model of individual decisions regarding individual behavioral choices targeted at individual outcomes. Thus it may be less able to explain behavior in collectivistic cultures, but otherwise may be one of the most likely candidates for a culturally unbiased explanation of motivated behavior. For example, the expectancy theory helps explain the success Sony has enjoyed. People who go to work for Sony know they will be able to pursue diverse opportunities and will be kept informed about what is happening in the firm. People who see these conditions as especially important will be most strongly motivated to work for Sony.

The Reinforcement Model across Cultures

Like the expectancy theory, the reinforcement model has undergone relatively few tests in different cultures. Basically, this model says that behavior that results in a positive outcome (reinforcement) will be likely to be repeated under the same circumstances in the future. Behavioral choice that results in negative consequences (punishment) will result in a different choice under the same circumstances in the future. As this model makes no attempt to specify what people will find reinforcing or punishing, it may also be generalizable to different cultures.

Like the expectancy theory, the reinforcement model has exceptions. In Muslim cultures, for example, people tend to believe that the consequences they experience are the will of God rather than a function of their own behavior. Thus neither reinforcement nor punishment will have much effect on their future behavioral decisions. Aside from relatively narrow exceptions such as this, however, the reinforcement model, like the expectancy theory, warrants careful attention from international managers, provided they understand that what constitutes rewards and punishment will vary across cultures.

Leadership in International Business

Another important behavioral and interpersonal consideration in international business is leadership. **Leadership** is the use of noncoercive influence to shape the goals of a group or organization, to motivate behavior toward reaching those goals, and to help determine the group or organizational culture.[28] Leadership has been widely studied by organizational scientists for decades. Early studies attempted to identify physical traits or universal behaviors that most clearly distinguished leaders from nonleaders. More recently, attention has focused on matching leadership with situations.[29] Although some studies still focus on traits, most leadership models suggest that appropriate leader behavior depends on situational factors.[30]

Contemporary leadership theories recognize that leaders cannot succeed by always using the same set of behaviors in all circumstances. Instead, leaders must carefully assess the situation in which they find themselves and then tailor one or more behaviors to fit that situation. Common situational factors that affect appropriate leader behavior include individual differences among subordinates; characteristics of the group, the organization, and the leader; and subordinates' desire to participate.

Clearly, cultural factors will affect appropriate leader behavior, and the way in which managers spend their workday will vary among cultures.[31] Indeed, several implications for leaders in international settings can be drawn from the cultural factors identified in Hofstede's work. For example, in individualistic cultures, leaders may need to focus their behavior on individual employees rather than the group. The development of MBO in the United States reflects this characteristic of individualistic cultures. MBO promotes employee involvement and participation by allowing each employee to set individual goals that he or she is best suited to pursue.

In contrast, in a collectivistic culture, leader behaviors will clearly need to focus on the group rather than on individual group members. In a group-oriented culture such as that of Japan, an effective leader must guide subordinates while preserving group harmony. At Sony, for example, managers are expected to allow their employees to transfer at will to more interesting job settings because such transfers are believed to be in the firm's overall best interests. The Japanese management system focuses on consensus-building efforts to ensure that both leader and subordinates reach a common decision. A leader would destroy group harmony if he dictatorially commanded his subordinates to implement his decisions. One problem that may develop, however, is that junior managers attempt to anticipate what their boss's preferred strategy is and then offer it as their own. A leader confronted with such a strong tendency toward conformity must seek ways to encourage creative solutions from subordinates to new problems as they arise. A Japanese manager may thus distance himself from pending decisions, thereby encouraging subordinates to discuss a variety of options among themselves. Only then will the manager lead by dropping subtle hints regarding what he sees as the correct solution to an issue.[32]

Power orientation carries even more direct implications for situational leadership. In power-respecting cultures, for example, employees may expect leaders to take charge, to make decisions, and to direct their efforts. Leaders may therefore need to concentrate on performance-oriented behaviors, avoid employee-oriented behaviors, and make little attempt to foster participation. But if power tolerance is the more pervasive cultural value, a leader should spend less time on performance-oriented behaviors. Instead, employee-oriented behaviors and more employee participation may result in higher levels of effectiveness.

Attempts at blurring the distinctions between managers and workers may not be well received in more authoritarian, hierarchical societies. For example, one U.S. firm exported the "company picnic" concept to its Spanish subsidiary, complete with company executives serving food to the Spanish employees. However, this informality was not well received by the employees, who were embarrassed at being served by their "superiors."[33]

Uncertainty orientation is also an important situational factor to consider. Where uncertainty avoidance is the rule, employees will have a strong desire for structure and direction. Thus performance-oriented behaviors (direct, structured, and goal-oriented behaviors) are likely to be more successful, whereas employee-oriented behaviors (caring, concern, and interpersonally oriented behaviors) and attempts to use participation may be less so. For example, German managers tend to be autocratic and task-oriented, making decisions with reference to existing corporate rules and procedures. Having determined departmental objectives, they then confidently delegate tasks to subordinates, whom they expect to competently carry out the tasks necessary to achieve the objective.[34]

In contrast, employees more prone toward uncertainty acceptance may respond more favorably to opportunities for participation. They may even prefer participative behaviors on the part of their leaders. But performance-oriented leadership may be undesirable or unnecessary, while employee-oriented leadership may have little impact. That is, employees may have such a strong desire to participate and be involved in their work that they see performance-oriented or employee-oriented behaviors from their supervisor as being redundant with or even negating their own opportunities for participation.

Finally, differences in goal orientation also have implications for leadership. Because of the differences in gender-role acceptance along this dimension, male leaders should face relatively little difficulty in either cultural profile. On the other hand, female leaders in an aggressive goal behavior culture may encounter considerable resistance and even outright hostility if their subordinates are predominantly male. The rewards valued in aggressive versus passive goal behavior cultures also affect leader behavior. For example, recall that people in aggressive goal behavior cultures tend to value money and other material rewards. If performance-oriented leadership or higher levels of participation are perceived by followers to result in higher rewards, those behaviors will be more acceptable. In contrast, outcomes enhancing quality of life are more desirable in passive goal behavior cultures. To the extent that employee-oriented leader behaviors may cause followers to feel more satisfied with their work and the organization, such behaviors may be more effective in these settings.

The overriding lesson is that leaders in international settings need to consider a wide array of situational factors that may determine how effective their behavior will be. For example, when Bridgestone (a Japanese firm) bought Firestone (a U.S. firm), it wanted Firestone's CEO, John Nevin, to stay on and run the operation. Nevin's leadership style is blunt and straightforward, with little time wasted on subtleties. His new Japanese bosses, unfortunately, did not react very well to these behaviors. In their country, leaders are expected to be more polite and reserved. Even though both sides appear to have made an honest effort to adjust, Nevin eventually had to leave the firm.[35]

Cultural factors are among the most difficult and complex to assess and understand. They may also be among the most critical in determining leader effectiveness. It is important that leaders attempt to match their behaviors with the context—the people they are leading and the organization in which they are functioning. For example, one study analyzed the productivity of U.S. and Mexican factories owned by the same MNC. Cultural differences clearly exist between the two countries. Mexico ranks high on power respect relative to the United States. U.S. residents are far more individualistic than those of Mexico, while the family is more highly valued in Mexico than in the United States. Mexican cultural values translate into the paternalistic, authoritarian management style adopted by managers of the MNC's Mexican facilities. Managers of its U.S. facilities, however, adopted less paternalistic and more participative styles in managing their employees. By allowing management styles to adapt to national culture, the MNC enjoyed equally high levels of productivity from both facilities.[36]

Decision Making in International Business

Another area of international business in which large cultural differences exist is how decisions are made. **Decision making** is the process of choosing one alternative from among a set of alternatives in order to promote the decision maker's objectives.

Models of Decision Making

There are two very different views of how managers go about making decisions (see Fig. 14.2):

1 The *normative model of decision making* suggests that managers apply logic and rationality in making the best decisions.[37]

FIGURE 14.2

**Models of the
Decision-Making
Process**

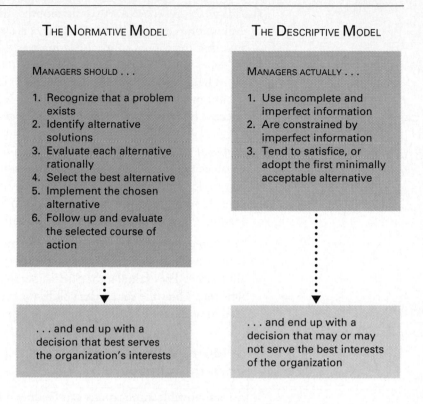

THE NORMATIVE MODEL

MANAGERS SHOULD . . .

1. Recognize that a problem exists
2. Identify alternative solutions
3. Evaluate each alternative rationally
4. Select the best alternative
5. Implement the chosen alternative
6. Follow up and evaluate the selected course of action

. . . and end up with a decision that best serves the organization's interests

THE DESCRIPTIVE MODEL

MANAGERS ACTUALLY . . .

1. Use incomplete and imperfect information
2. Are constrained by imperfect information
3. Tend to satisfice, or adopt the first minimally acceptable alternative

. . . and end up with a decision that may or may not serve the best interests of the organization

2 In contrast, the *descriptive model of decision making* argues that behavioral processes limit a manager's ability to always be logical and rational.[38]

The normative model suggests that decision making involves six steps:

1 *Recognize that a problem exists and a decision has to be made.* For example, a Shell refinery manager recently noticed that turnover among a certain group of workers had increased substantially.

2 *Identify potential alternative solutions.* The Shell manager determined that high turnover could be caused by low wages, poor working conditions, or poor supervision; thus the alternative solutions were raising wages, improving working conditions, or changing the group's supervisor.

3 *Evaluate each alternative in light of the original problem.* The Shell manager knew that the group's wages were comparable to what others in the refinery were making. The manager also knew that the group's work area had been refurbished recently, so working conditions were probably not a problem. However, a new supervisor had recently been appointed for the group.

4 *Select the best alternative.* The Shell manager felt the problem was one of poor supervision and so looked more closely at that particular part of the situation. After scrutinizing the new supervisor's records, the manager saw that the supervisor had been promoted during a very hectic period and had not gone through the refinery's normal supervisory training program.

5 *Implement the chosen alternative.* The Shell manager arranged for the new supervisor to complete the full training program.

6 *Follow-up and evaluate.* After six months, the Shell manager did a follow-up and evaluation. Turnover in the group had dropped significantly, and the manager was sure that the chosen course of action was the correct one.

The descriptive model acknowledges that this is perhaps how managers should make their decisions. But this model notes that, in reality, managers are affected by two important behavioral processes:

1 *Bounded rationality* suggests that decision makers are constrained in their ability to be objective and rational by limitations of the human mind. Thus they often use incomplete and imperfect information. Notice that the Shell manager did not consult with the members of the group to find out why turnover had increased. Had he done so, he might have gained additional information.

2 *Satisficing* suggests that managers sometimes adopt the first minimally acceptable alternative they identify, although a further search might suggest an even better alternative. For example, the Shell supervisor had gained some experience on the new job. Thus, the supervisor's skills may have been improved from an abbreviated or accelerated training program, rather than completion of the full program.

The Normative Model across Cultures

Several possible implications can be drawn from applying a basic understanding of the normative and descriptive models to decision making in other cultures.[39] To explore those implications, we first walk through the steps in the normative model.

Step 1: Problem Recognition. People from different cultures are likely to recognize and define problem situations in very different ways. For example, in individualistic cultures, problems are likely to be defined in terms of individual scenarios and consequences. In collectivistic cultures, the focus will be more on group-related issues and situations. In an uncertainty-accepting culture, managers are more likely to take risks in solving problems and making decisions. In uncertainty-avoiding cultures, they may be much more cautious and strive to reduce uncertainty as much as possible before making a decision. As a result, they may fall back on firm policies and rules to provide a course of action ("We can't do that because it's against company policy").

Step 2: Identifying Alternatives. The processes through which alternatives are identified will also vary across cultures. For example, in power-respecting cultures, managers may be much less willing to consider an alternative that potentially threatens the hierarchy—for example, that a suggestion from a subordinate might be valid or that a problem might exist at a higher level in the organization. But in power-tolerant cultures, such hierarchical issues are more likely to be considered possible remedies to organizational problems. In collectivistic societies, the desire for group harmony and conflict avoidance may be so strong that decision making is approached in unique ways.

For example, the Japanese concern for maintaining group harmony has given rise to the ringi system for identifying alternatives and making decisions. The

ringi system provides that decisions cannot be made unilaterally; doing that would be too individualistic and therefore destructive of group harmony. To encourage creative solutions, a manager may draw up a document, called the *ringisho*, which defines the problem and sets out a proposed solution. The Japanese corporate belief is that those who implement a solution should be those most affected by the problem, since they understand the problem and are motivated to solve it. Thus most ringisho originate from middle managers. Although the ringisho originates from an individual, it is soon subsumed by the group. The document is circulated to all members of the originator's work group, as well as to other groups affected by it. As the ringisho passes through the workplace, it may be accepted, rejected, or modified. Only a document that is approved by all its reviewers is passed to a more senior manager for approval or disapproval. But before the ringisho reaches this stage, any senior manager worth his salt will have already dropped hints if he had any objections to any parts of it. Appropriate changes then would have been incorporated into the document by some subordinate before the ringisho arrived at the senior manager's desk. Through the ringi system, creativity, innovation, and group harmony are all promoted.[40]

In contrast, the German business structure is both strongly hierarchical and compartmentalized. Decision making tends to be slow and drawn out, designed to build consensus within a department of a firm. Data are painstakingly gathered, then communicated to the appropriate employees within the hierarchy. However, information often does not flow easily between departments, and a decision, once reached, may be difficult to change. Also, established operating procedures are followed carefully. These factors substantially reduce the firm's flexibility and responsiveness to rapidly changing conditions. The resulting inflexibility often hinders the performance of foreign subsidiaries of German MNCs, which have difficulty getting the home office to acknowledge that their operating conditions may differ from those in Germany.[41]

Step 3: Evaluating Alternatives. Evaluating alternatives can also be affected by cultural phenomena. For example, an alternative that results in financial gain may be more attractive in an aggressive goal behavior culture than in a passive goal behavior culture, which may prefer an alternative that results in improved quality of work life. Uncertainty avoidance will also be a consideration; alternatives with varying levels of associated uncertainty may be perceived to be more or less attractive.

Evaluating alternatives is further complicated in countries such as China because people there tend to avoid taking responsibility for making decisions. Because China's economic policies have changed so quickly and drastically over the past four decades, those supporting today's economic policies may find themselves in political difficulties tomorrow. A Chinese proverb, "The tall tree gets broken off in the wind," suggests the tendency of many Chinese officials to avoid association with any decision that could haunt them later. Group decision making reduces the potential blame an individual bureaucrat may suffer.[42]

Step 4: Selecting the Best Alternative. Cultural factors can affect the actual selection of an alternative. In an individualistic culture, for example, a manager may be prone to select an alternative that has the most positive impact on him or her personally; in a collectivistic culture, the impact of the alternative on the total group will carry more weight. Not surprisingly, a manager trained in one culture will often use the same techniques when operating in a different culture, even though they may be ineffective there. In one recent study comparing U.S. managers operating in the United States with U.S. managers operating in Hong Kong, the managerial behaviors of the two groups were found to be the same. These behaviors included managerial supportiveness of subordinates, problem solving, openness of communication, disciplining of subordinates, and so on. However, although these behaviors positively affected firm performance in the United States, they had no effect on firm performance in Hong Kong.[43]

Cultural differences in problem solving and decision making may be particularly troublesome for partners in a joint venture or other strategic alliance because they must develop mutually acceptable decisions. U.S. managers often deliberately use conflict (in the form of devil's advocate or dialectical inquiry techniques) as a means of improving the decision-making process. Managers from more consensus-oriented societies, such as Japan, find this disharmonious approach very distasteful and unproductive.[44]

Step 5: Implementation. In a power-respecting culture, implementation may be mandated by a manager at the top of the organization and accepted without question by others. But in a power-tolerant culture, participation may be more crucial in order to ensure acceptance. In an uncertainty-avoiding culture, managers may need to carefully plan every step of the implementation before proceeding so that everyone knows what to expect. In an uncertainty-accepting culture, however, managers may be more willing to start implementation before all the final details have been arranged.

Step 6: Follow-Up and Evaluation. Follow-up and evaluation also have cultural implications, most notably regarding power orientation. In a power-respecting culture, a manager may be unwilling to find fault with an alternative suggested by a higher-level manager. Also, too much credit may be given to a higher-level manager purely on the basis of his or her position in the hierarchy. But in a power-tolerant culture, responsibility, blame, and credit are more likely to be accurately attributed.

The Descriptive Model across Cultures

The behavioral processes of bounded rationality and satisficing are more difficult to relate to cultural differences. Few research efforts have specifically explored these phenomena in different cultures, and their very nature makes it hard to draw reasonable generalizations. Thus, while it is likely that they do have some impact on business decisions made in different cultures and therefore need to be understood by managers, more research needs to be conducted on their

The Dunes Hotel and Casino is owned by a group of Japanese investors. A few years ago, they tried to implement the methodical, consensus-oriented approach to decision making that works so well in Japan. They soon discovered, however, that their U.S. workers found this approach ineffective for the dynamic and fluid environment in which they worked.

precise influence. In particular, all managers need to understand the potential limitations of applying different modes of decision making in different cultural settings. For example, a few years ago the Japanese owners of the Dunes Hotel and Casino in Las Vegas tried to implement a variety of Japanese management practices in the casino operation. One was decision making by consensus. They quickly recognized, however, that it was far too slow for the intensely competitive, fast-changing casino industry.[45]

Groups and Teams in International Business

Other important behavioral processes that international managers should understand are those associated with groups and teams. Regardless of whether a firm is a small domestic company or a large MNC, much of its work is accomplished by people working together as a part of a team, task force, committee, or operating group.

The Nature of Group Dynamics

Firms use groups frequently because, in theory, people working together as a group can accomplish more than they can working individually. Most managers generally use the word *team* instead of *group*, so this discussion also uses that term. Remember, however, that a team is a specific type of group.

A mature team in a firm generally has certain characteristics:

1 It develops a well-defined role structure; each member has a part to play on the team, accepts that part, and makes a worthwhile contribution.

2 It establishes norms for its members. Norms are standards of behavior, such as how people should dress, when team meetings or activities will begin, the consequences of being absent, how much each member should produce, and so on.

3 It is cohesive. That is, team members identify more and more strongly with the team, and each member respects, values, and works well with the others.

4 Some teams identify informal leaders among their members—individuals whom the team accords special status and who can lead and direct the team without benefit of formal authority.

If a team's role structure promotes efficiency, its norms reinforce high performance, it truly is cohesive, and its informal leaders support the firm's goals, then it can potentially reach maximum effectiveness. Sony's computer development group took on all of these characteristics, which no doubt helped contribute to the group's ability to reach its goal ahead of schedule. However, if the team's role structure is inefficient, its performance norms are low, it is not cohesive, and/or its informal leaders do not support the firm's goals, then it may become very ineffective from the firm's standpoint.

Managing Cross-Cultural Teams

The composition of a team plays a major role in the dynamics that emerge from it. A relatively homogeneous team generally has less conflict, better communication,

GOING GLOBAL

The Best and the Brightest

And it seemed like such a good idea at the time! A couple of years ago, IBM, Siemens, and Toshiba entered into a strategic alliance to develop an advanced new type of computer chip. Each firm identified a set of research scientists for the project; the group of around 100 people assembled for work at an IBM facility in East Fishkill, a small Hudson River Valley town in New York. The idea was that the best and brightest minds from three diverse firms would bring such an array of knowledge, insight, and creativity to the project that it was bound to succeed.

Unfortunately, things have not gone as smoothly as expected, and the project has met with only modest success, at least so far. The biggest reason cited for the lack of progress has been the cultural differences and barriers that exist among the group members. For example, the Japanese scientists are accustomed to working in one big room where everyone can interact with everyone else and it's easy to overhear what others are saying. The IBM facility has small, cramped offices that can hold only a few people at a time. The Germans have also been unhappy because most of their offices lack windows. They claim that back home no one would be asked to work in a windowless office.

Interpersonal styles have also caused some conflict. Both the U.S. and Japanese scientists criticize their German colleagues for planning and organizing too much. The Japanese have been criticized for their unwillingness to make clear decisions. And the German and Japanese scientists have complained that their U.S. hosts do not spend enough time socializing with them after work.

There have also been problems with employee privacy and workplace rights. The office doors at the IBM facility all have small windows that visitors can use to peek in to see if the occupant is busy before knocking. Both the Germans and Japanese see this as an invasion of their privacy and often hang their coats over the windows. They also object to IBM's strict no-smoking policy, which mandates that they go outside to smoke, regardless of weather conditions.

While the group's lack of progress has been discouraging, all three firms believe the alliance will eventually yield a positive payoff. Managers feel that part of the problem was inadequate training of group members before they were transferred to the project and that better cultural training in particular would have been useful. They also think the group is now essentially training and socializing itself. The three firms have committed to continuing the project at least through 1997.

Sources: "Computer Chip Project Brings Rivals Together, But the Cultures Clash," *Wall Street Journal*, May 3, 1994, pp. A1, A8; Alan Chai, Alta Campbell, and Patrick J. Spain (eds.), *Hoover's Handbook of World Business* 1993 (Austin, Tex: Reference Press, 1993), pp. 440, 478; Gary Hoover, Alta Campbell, and Patrick J. Spain (eds.), *Hoover's Handbook of American Business* 1994 (Austin, Tex.: Reference Press, 1993), p. 640.

less creativity, more uniform norms, higher cohesiveness, and clear informal leadership. A more heterogeneous team often has more conflict, poorer communication, more creativity, less uniform norms, a lower level of cohesiveness, and more ambiguous informal leadership.

Managers charged with building teams in different cultures need to assess the nature of the task to be performed and, as much as possible, match the composition of the team to the type of task. For example, if the task is relatively routine and straightforward, a homogeneous team may be more effective. Similarities in knowledge, background, values, and beliefs can make the work go more smoothly and efficiently. But if the task is nonroutine, complex and/or ambiguous, a heterogeneous team may be more effective because of members' diverse backgrounds, experiences, knowledge, and values.

Other cultural factors may also play a role in team dynamics. For example, in an individualistic culture, establishing shared norms and cohesiveness may be somewhat difficult, while in a collectivistic culture, team cohesiveness may emerge naturally. In a power-respecting culture, team members should probably be from the same level of the organization, since members from lower levels may be intimidated and subservient to those from higher levels. In a power-tolerant culture, variation in organizational level may be less of a problem. Uncertainty avoidance and team dynamics may also interact as a function of task. If a task is vague, ambiguous, or unstructured, an uncertainty-avoiding group may be unable to function effectively; in contrast, an uncertainty-accepting group may actually thrive. Finally, teams in an aggressive goal behavior culture may work together more effectively if their goal has financial implications, whereas teams in a passive goal behavior culture may be more motivated to work toward attitudinal or quality-of-work outcomes. "Going Global" provides some additional interesting insights into cross-cultural teams.

Much of the competitive strength of Japanese firms is due to their incorporation of Japanese cultural norms into the workplace. Japanese culture emphasizes the importance of group harmony and respect for superiors. "Silent leaders," ones who guide rather than command subordinates and who preserve group harmony, are more admired than are authoritarian managers. The ringi system ensures that new approaches are granted group approval before being implemented. The traditional lifetime employment practices that some major Japanese firms use promote employee loyalty to the organization. All these features are reinforced by careful selection of new employees. Only those persons who are willing to subordinate their individual goals to the needs of the group are hired. This corporate philosophy carries over to foreign operations of Japanese MNCs. For example, many U.S. newspapers have reported on the extraordinary amounts of testing and interviewing that such firms operating in North America do before hiring an employee.

CHAPTER REVIEW

Summary

Behavioral and interpersonal processes are vitally important in any organization. Both their importance and their complexity are magnified in international firms. The pioneering research of Geert Hofstede has identified five basic cultural dimensions along which people may differ: social orientation, power orientation, uncertainty orientation, goal orientation, and time orientation.

Motivation is the overall set of forces that cause people to choose certain behaviors from a set of available behaviors. Need-based, process-based, and reinforcement models of motivation each explain different aspects of motivation. While none of these models is generalizable to all cultures, each can provide insights into motivation in similar cultures.

Leadership is the use of noncoercive influence to shape the goals of a group or organization, to moti-vate behavior toward reaching those goals, and to help determine the group or organizational culture. People from different cultures react in different ways to each type of behavior. These different reactions are determined partially by cultural dimensions and partially by the individuals themselves.

Decision making is the process of choosing an alternative from among a set of alternatives designed to promote the decision maker's objectives. People from different cultures approach each step in the decision-making process differently. Again, variation along cultural dimensions is a significant determinant of variations in decision-making processes.

Groups and teams are part of all organizations. A team's role structure, cohesiveness, norms, and informal leadership all contribute to its success or failure. Culture plays a major role in determining the team's degree of heterogeneity or homogeneity, which in turn helps determine its overall level of effectiveness.

Review Questions

1. What are individualism and collectivism? How do they differ?

2. What is power orientation?

3. What is uncertainty orientation?

4. What are aggressive and passive goal behaviors? How do they differ?

5. What are some of the basic issues managers must confront when attempting to motivate employees in different cultures?

6. What are the three basic sets of leadership behaviors? How does each relate to international business?

7. What are the steps in the normative model of decision making? How does each relate to international business?

8. Why are teams so important? What variations in teams are likely in an international business?

Questions for Discussion

1. Do you agree with Hofstede's findings regarding cultural characteristics in the United States? Why or why not?

2. How would you evaluate yourself on each of Hofstede's dimensions?

3. Assume you have just been transferred by your firm to a new facility in a foreign location. How would you go about assessing the country's culture along Hofstede's dimensions? How would you incorporate your findings into conducting business there?

4. Do you think it will ever be possible to develop a motivation framework that is applicable in all cultures? Why or why not?

5. What advice would you give a Japanese, an Australian, and an Italian manager just transferred to the United States?

6. Assume you are leading a team composed of representatives from British, Mexican, Brazilian, and Egyptian subsidiaries of your firm. The team must make a number of major decisions.

   a. What guidelines might you develop for yourself for leading the team through its decision-making process?

   b. What steps might you take to enhance the team's cohesiveness? How successful do you think such an effort would be?

BUILDING GLOBAL SKILLS

Select a country in which you have some interest and about which you can readily find information (for example, Japan as opposed to Bhutan). Go to your library and learn as much as you can about the behavior of people from the country you selected. Concentrate on such culturally based social phenomenon as the following:

▶ The meaning people from the country attach to a few common English words

▶ The meaning they attach to common gestures
▶ How they interpret basic colors
▶ The basic rules of business etiquette they follow
▶ Their preferences regarding personal space
▶ How the country is characterized along Hofstede's dimensions

Team up with a classmate who chose a different country. Each of you should pick a product or commodity that is produced in the country you studied (such as stereos, bananas, oil, or machine parts). Attempt to negotiate a contract for selling your product or commodity to the other. As you negotiate, play the role of someone from the country you studied as authentically as possible. For example, if people from that culture are offended by a certain gesture and your counterpart happens to make that gesture while negotiating, act offended!

Spend approximately 15 minutes negotiating. Then spend another 15 minutes discussing with your classmate how the cultural background each of you adopted affected (or could have affected) the negotiation process.

Follow-up Questions

1. How easy or difficult is it to model the behavior of someone from another country?

2. What other forms of advance preparation might a manager need to undertake before negotiating with someone from another country?

CLOSING CASE

People Propel Rank Xerox [46]

Rank Xerox was founded in 1956 as a joint venture between the U.S. firm Xerox Corporation and the British firm The Rank Organisation PLC. Rank provided the funding, while Xerox supplied the technology. Headquartered in London, the venture's mission was to manufacture electronic copiers for the European marketplace. Xerox, which controls 51 percent of the venture, is the managing partner, while Rank has played the role of a silent investor.

Rank Xerox grew rapidly throughout the 1970s, but floundered a bit during the 1980s as worldwide competition in the copier industry increased and demand decreased. Late in the 1980s the firm regained its footing, and both sales and profits began to increase once again. For example, in 1991 the firm generated almost £2.5 billion in revenues and made £140 million in profits.

From the start, one of Rank Xerox's most formidable challenges has been melding a workforce from diverse countries. The firm has sales, service, and distribution centers throughout Europe. Each local unit is primarily staffed by local managers and employees, although there are also a few managers from headquarters on-site most of the time at each location.

Variation in basic work norms and employee expectations across countries adds complexity to the task of managing Rank Xerox's workforce. For example, its English employees are accustomed to secure jobs, four or five weeks of vacation per year, and working at a moderate but not strenuous pace. Its German employees are somewhat more mobile and expect even more paid vacation time but also expect to work harder. And its Italian employees are even more mobile and expect less vacation time but much shorter workdays and a somewhat leisurely work pace.

Rank Xerox has for years been positioning itself for the unified European market. At first, its managers saw its diverse workforce as an obstacle that had to be overcome. Their goal was to establish consistent and uniform procedures for dealing with employees at all work sites. Eventually, however, these managers conceded that the firm's very future depended on that diverse workforce. After all, Rank Xerox's customers were just as diverse as its workforce. How could the managers be expected to understand and appreciate those customers if they did not understand and appreciate their own workers? Thus they saw the need to accommodate, rather than eliminate, differences in employees' needs and expectations.

To underscore their newly enlightened approach to managing their workforce, the managers added a new component to the firm's mission statement—to develop and maintain motivated and satisfied employees. To implement this new effort, the firm launched new training and orientation programs designed to better enable its diverse employees to work together more effectively. And by formally adding this concern to its mission statement, Rank Xerox sent a message to everyone in the firm—from clerks to technicians to scientists to managers—that each employee is important and each is entitled to respect.

Corporate headquarters has worked closely with each of the firm's foreign affiliates to help implement this new mission and to instill its importance throughout the corporate culture. For example, senior managers regularly visit Rank Xerox facilities in different countries, meet with their local managers, listen to their problems and ideas, and share with them their own problems and ideas. The firm believes these interchanges have greatly improved everyone's understanding not only of the business itself but also of his or her colleagues throughout the firm.

Case Questions

1. Why do you think it took Rank Xerox so long to modify its approach to dealing with its employees?

2. What might be some of the difficulties Rank Xerox has faced in its efforts to value diversity?

3. Would Rank Xerox's approach have worked if the firm had also had affiliates scattered throughout Asia? Why or why not?

4. Does Rank Xerox's status as a joint venture have any effect on its efforts to manage its employees? Why or why not?

CHAPTER NOTES

1. Brenton R. Schlender, "How Sony Keeps the Magic Going," *Fortune*, February 24, 1992, pp. 76–84; "How Sony Pulled Off Its Spectacular Computer Coup," *Business Week*, January 15, 1990, pp. 76–77; "The Sound and the Fury at Sony and Philips," *Business Week*, June 15, 1992, p. 42; "Sony's Lean New Manufacturing Machine," *Financial Times*, December 10, 1992, p. 14; Alan Chai, Alta Campbell, and Patrick J. Spain (eds.), *Hoover's Handbook of World Business 1993* (Austin, Tex.: Reference Press, 1993), p. 448.

2. For a review of behavioral processes in organizations, see Gregory Moorhead and Ricky W. Griffin, *Organizational Behavior*, 4th ed. (Boston: Houghton Mifflin, 1995).

3. Lawrence A. Pervin, "Persons, Situations, Interactions: The History of a Controversy and a Discussion of Theoretical Models," *Academy of Management Review*, (July 1989), pp. 350–360.

4. Geert Hofstede, *Culture's Consequences: International Differences in Work Related Values* (Beverly Hills, Calif.: Sage, 1980).

5. We have taken the liberty of changing the actual labels Hofstede applied to each dimension. The terms we have chosen are more descriptive, simpler, and more self-evident in their meaning.

6. Jim Mann, *Beijing Jeep* (New York: Simon and Schuster, 1989), p. 253.

7. Gary P. Ferraro, *The Cultural Dimension of International Business* (Englewood Cliffs, N.J.: Prentice-Hall, 1990), p. 157.

8. Ibid., p. 162.

9. B. Bass and L. Eldridge, "Accelerated Managers' Objectives in Twelve Countries," *Industrial Relations*, Vol. 12 (1973), pp. 158–171.

10. Susan C. Schneider, "National versus Corporate Culture: Implications for Human Resource Management," *Human Resource Management*, Vol. 27, No. 2 (Summer 1988), pp. 231–246.

11. Nancy Adler, *International Dimensions of Organizational Behavior*, 2nd ed. (Boston: PWS-Kent, 1991), p. 43.

12. Geert Hofstede, "The Business of International Business Is Culture," *International Business Review*, Vol. 3, No. 1 (1994), pp. 1–14.

13. Craig Pinder, *Work Motivation* (Glenview, Ill.: Scott, Foresman, 1984).

14. For a review, see Nancy Adler, op. cit.

15. Geert Hofstede, "Motivation, Leadership, and Organization: Do American Theories Apply Abroad?" *Organizational Dynamics* (Summer 1980), pp. 42–63.

16. Joseph J. Fucini and Suzy Fucini, *Working for the Japanese: Inside Mazda's American Auto Plant* (New York: Free Press, 1990).

17. Vern Terpstra and Kenneth David, *The Cultural Environment of International Business*, 2nd ed. (Cincinnati: South-Western, 1985), p. 180.

18. Charles Weaver and Michael Landeck, "Cross-National Differences in Job Values: a Segmented Comparative Analysis of United States and West German Workers" (Laredo State University, 1991), mimeo.

19. Abraham Maslow, "A Theory of Human Motivation," *Psychological Review* (July 1943), pp. 370–396.

20. Adler, op. cit., pp. 127–133.

21. P. Howell, J. Strauss, and P. F. Sorenson, "Research Note: Cultural and Situational Determinants of Job Satisfaction among Management in Liberia," *Journal of Management Studies* (May 1975), pp. 225–227.

22. David McClelland, *The Achieving Society* (Princeton, N.J.: Van Nostrand, 1961).

23. Adler, op. cit., pp. 127–133.

24. Frederick Herzberg, Bernard Mausner, and Barbara Snyderman, *The Motivation to Work* (New York: Wiley, 1959).

25. G. H. Hines, "Achievement, Motivation, Occupations and Labor Turnover in New Zealand," *Journal of Applied Psychology*, Vol. 58, No. 3 (1973), pp. 313–317.

26. Pinder, op. cit.

27. Victor Vroom, *Work and Motivation* (New York: Wiley, 1964).

28. Gary Yukl, *Leadership in Organizations*, 2nd ed. (Englewood Cliffs, N. J.: Prentice-Hall, 1989).

29. Bernard M. Bass, *Bass & Stogdill's Handbook of Leadership*, 3rd ed. (Riverside, N. J.: Free Press, 1990).

30. David A. Ralston, David J. Gustafson, Fanny M. Cheung, and Robert H. Terpstra, "Differences in Managerial Values: A Study of U.S., Hong Kong, and PRC Managers," *Journal of International Business Studies* (Second Quarter, 1993), pp. 249–275.

31. Robert H. Doktor, "Asian and American CEOs: A Comparative Study," *Organizational Dynamics*, Vol. 18, No. 3 (1990), pp. 46–56.

32. Jon P. Alston, *The American Samurai* (New York: Walter de Gruyter, 1986), pp. 103–113.

33. "The Spanish-American Business Wars," *Worldwide P & I Planning* (May–June 1971), pp. 30–40.

34. Arvin Parkhe, "Interfirm Diversity, Organizational Learning, and Longevity in Global Strategic Alliances," *Journal of International Business Studies*, Vol. 22, No. 4 (Fourth Quarter 1991), pp. 592–593; Edward T. Hall and Mildred Reed Hall, *Understanding Cultural Differences* (Yarmouth, Maine: Intercultural Press, 1990), pp. 55–62.

35. David Ricks, *Blunders in International Business* (Cambridge, Mass.: Blackwell, 1993).

36. Tom Morris and Cynthia M. Pavett, "Management Style and Productivity in Two Cultures," *Journal of International Business Studies*, Vol. 23, No. 1 (First Quarter 1992), pp. 169–179.

37. George P. Huber, *Managerial Decision Making* (Glenview, Ill.: Scott, Foresman, 1980).

38. Herbert A. Simon, *Administrative Behavior*, 3rd ed. (New York: Free Press, 1976).

39. Adler, op. cit.

40. Jon P. Alston, op. cit., pp. 181–186.

41. Hall and Hall, op. cit., pp. 33–84.

42. Lawrence C. Wolken, "Doing Business in China," *Texas A&M Business Forum* (Fall 1987), pp. 39–42.

43. J. Stewart Black and Lyman W. Porter, "Managerial Behaviors and Job Performance: A Successful Manager in Los Angeles May Not Succeed in Hong Kong," *Journal of International Business Studies*, Vol. 22, No. 1 (First Quarter 1991), pp. 99–113.

44. Arvin Parkhe, op. cit., pp. 579-601.

45. Ricks, op. cit.

46. Gary Hoover, Alta Campbell, Alan Chai, and Patrick J. Spain (eds.), *Hoover's Handbook of World Business 1992* (Austin, Tex.: Reference Press, 1991), p. 264; *Rank Xerox 1991 Overview* (Rank Xerox undated publication); *Rank Xerox—The European Dimension* (Rank Xerox undated publication); *Rank Xerox—Policy and Practice* (Rank Xerox undated publication).

CHAPTER

15

Controlling the International Business

Chapter Outline

Levels of control in international business

Strategic control
Organizational control
Operations control

Managing the control function in international business

Establishing international control systems
Essential control techniques
Behavioral aspects of international control

Controlling productivity in international business

Productivity around the world
Managing productivity

Controlling quality in international business

The meaning of quality
Quality around the world
Total quality management

Controlling information in international business

The role of information
Managing information

After studying this chapter you should be able to:

Describe the general purpose of control and the levels of control in international business.

Discuss how international firms manage the control function.

Describe the meaning of productivity and discuss how international firms work to improve it.

Describe how firms control quality and discuss total quality management in international business.

Discuss how international firms control the information their managers need to make effective decisions.

SIEMENS AG IS GERMANY'S THIRD-LARGEST FIRM, BEHIND ONLY Daimler-Benz and Volkswagen. Siemens can trace its roots to 1847, when Werner von Siemens teamed up with Johann Halske to make telegraph equipment. Halske left the fledgling firm a few years later, while Siemens stayed on and led it to become a major player in the German market for electrical products such as elevator equipment, electric railways, and electric power transmission facilities. ■■ The firm also has long been involved in international business. For example, Siemens himself licensed the technology for the incandescent light bulb from Thomas Edison in 1881, and the firm entered into its first joint venture with Furukawa Electric of Japan in 1923.

Remaking Siemens[1]

■■ In the years immediately following World War II, Siemens grew and prospered, in part because of its unswerving commitment to technological perfection. The firm moved aggressively into new electronics markets, perfecting the silicates that would become the building blocks for semiconductors and developing the world's first implantable pacemaker. But Siemens also benefited from Germany's protectionist policies for the country's domestic telecommunications industry. Indeed, the firm had such little domestic competition and its earnings were so securely guaranteed by the government that it felt little pressure to innovate. It also amassed a huge capital surplus and allowed its corporate bureaucracy to expand so much that at one point a job at Siemens was viewed as being as secure as one in the German civil service. ■■ During the 1980s, CEO Karlheinz Kaske decided to take Siemens global. He restructured the firm into a collection of relatively autonomous profit centers and allowed each to chart its own course for growth and expansion. His mandate to them was clear—expand, branch out, and grow. Siemens was soon operating in 150 countries, had doubled its sales volume, and had added over 100,000 new jobs. Among the firm's more ambitious efforts were the purchase of Bendix Electronics in the United States, the acquisition of Plessey's telecommunications operations in the United Kingdom, and the formation of a new computer business in a joint venture with Nixdorf. Siemens also was quick to exploit the collapse of communism. Today, it has 21 new joint ventures in Central and Eastern Europe, 7 of them in the former Soviet Union. ■■ Kaske retired in 1992 and was replaced by Heinrich von Pierer. Before stepping into his new job, von Pierer decided to take some time to thoroughly examine every facet of Siemens's operations. His purpose was to ensure that the firm was indeed performing as well as everyone seemed to think. Von Pierer wanted to find any potential problems before they became real ones. ■■ To the surprise of many managers at Siemens, his analysis led him to conclude that the firm was, in fact, performing much poorer than thought. Its costs were growing faster than its revenues, and profitability varied too widely among the profit centers. Von Pierer also became convinced that Siemens was more vulnerable to foreign competitors than anyone had thought. Completion of the EU's internal market, for example, will open to other European producers formerly closed German markets in several of the firm's key product lines, such as telecommunications and electric power transmission equipment. ▮▮Von Pierer's agenda, therefore, was to design and implement significant new control systems throughout the firm. His stated goal was to enhance Siemens's ability to more effectively compete with other global firms such as GE, Matsushita, and Philips. One of his first acts was to scrap company plans to build a new plant in Munich to manufacture 64-megabit computer chips. The firm's semiconductor business was operating at a loss, he argued, and the new plant would add new costs while not generating commensurate new revenues. ▮▮Von Pierer also announced the elimination of 6000 jobs at the Siemens-Nixdorf computer subsidiary, again to reduce high costs, and he warned that an additional 25,000 to 30,000 jobs throughout the firm would go by the end of the decade. These announcements came as quite a shock to those who had relied on job security at the firm. Von Pierer also expressed his personal dissatisfaction with Siemens's pre-tax profit margin of 2.4 percent and vowed to boost it to 4 percent. Finally, von Pierer decided that the firm would actually reduce its commitment to technological perfection. He felt the firm was spending too much time and resources on making products that were extremely high-quality but were also too expensive and overly complicated. Von Pierer believes that quality, while important, must be balanced against cost and simplicity. ▮▮Von Pierer also wants to make the firm more flexible. He fears that the Siemens bureaucracy has slowed decision making too much and that the firm is less responsive to its environment than are its major competitors. His challenge is to optimize the decentralized decision making necessary to maximize flexibility against the need for a company-wide control network that will enable him and other top managers to keep better informed on the performance of the firm's various units. ▮▮▮▮▮

Heinrich von Pierer and other managers at Siemens confront a major challenge as they continue their attempts to reorient how that firm does business. To increase their chances of success, they are focusing on one of the fundamental tasks of management: controlling the things the firm is trying to do and how it is trying to do them. Because of the complexity of dealing with different cultures, laws, and currencies, control in international firms is obviously more challenging than in purely domestic ones. For an international firm, control can be focused on activities within a given market, within several markets, or across the entire organization.

Control is the process of monitoring and regulating activities in a firm so that some targeted measure of performance (for example, meeting sales goals or cost limits) is achieved or maintained.[2] The control process begins with the establishment of a goal or other performance target. Managers then monitor progress toward meeting that goal or target and take appropriate actions to keep the firm on-track. Control activities may focus on direct financial performance (such as the profit margin achieved by an individual manager, business unit, or foreign subsidiary) or on some other aspect of performance (such as cutting costs or eliminating resource waste).

For example, suppose the European purchasing manager of a Canadian manufacturing firm has an annual travel budget of $36,000. Based on previous experience, the manager expects travel costs to be spread evenly throughout the year, or around $3000 per month. So travel expenses of $2900 in January lead him to assume that costs are about where they should be. However, if his February travel expenses are $6000, he may need to cut back in March or, if he feels more travel is needed, request an increase in his travel budget from headquarters. The manager is controlling his travel costs by monitoring his monthly expenses to keep them within an expected range and then taking action if they fall too far outside that range.

In this chapter we introduce the three basic levels in international firms at which control systems may be used: strategic, organizational, and operational. We also discuss some methods by which control can be more effectively managed. Then we describe three important aspects of international management that are in fact forms of control systems: the management of productivity, quality, and information.

Levels of Control in International Business

As illustrated in Fig. 15.1, there are three main levels at which control can be implemented and managed in an international business. These three key levels of control are as follows:

▶ Strategic
▶ Organizational
▶ Operational

Strategic Control

Strategic control is intended to monitor both how well an international business formulates strategy and how well it goes about implementing it.[3] Thus strategic control focuses on how well the firm defines and maintains its desired strategic alignment with its environment and how effectively it is setting and achieving its strategic goals. For example, Sony bought Columbia Pictures as part of its strategy of related diversification. At the time Sony management thought that, in addition to generating revenues at the box office, Columbia's movies could be a rich source of software for Sony video equipment and that other synergies between Sony and Columbia could be developed. So far, however, Sony has invested almost $5 billion in the Hollywood studio, yet has little to show for it.

FIGURE 15.1

Levels of
International
Control

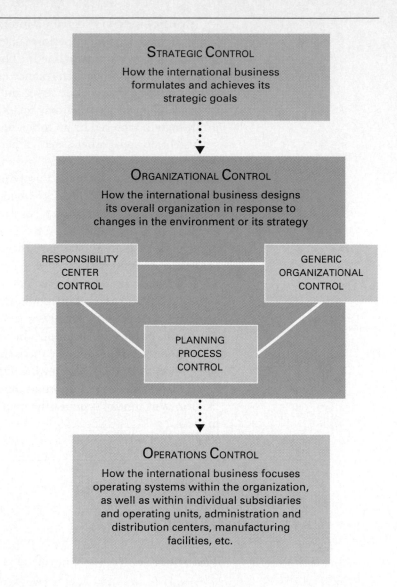

STRATEGIC CONTROL

How the international business
formulates and achieves its
strategic goals

ORGANIZATIONAL CONTROL

How the international business designs
its overall organization in response to
changes in the environment or its strategy

RESPONSIBILITY
CENTER
CONTROL

GENERIC
ORGANIZATIONAL
CONTROL

PLANNING
PROCESS
CONTROL

OPERATIONS CONTROL

How the international business focuses
operating systems within the organization,
as well as within individual subsidiaries
and operating units, administration and
distribution centers, manufacturing
facilities, etc.

Columbia's costs have skyrocketed, its profits have dropped, and its managers have produced a long string of box-office disappointments. Anticipated synergies between Columbia and Sony did not materialize. As a result, in 1994 Sony wrote off as a loss $2.7 billion of its investment in Columbia and is rumored to be giving serious thought to selling the studio.[4] Strategic control is what caused Sony to buy Columbia to begin with, to make investments to help the firm grow, and now to consider divestiture because of disappointing results.

Strategic control also plays a major role in the decisions firms make about foreign-market entry and expansion. This is especially true when the market holds both considerable potential and considerable uncertainty and risk. For example, in the wake of India's recent overtures for FDI, many firms are expanding their operations in that country. Hindustan Lever, Unilever's Indian subsidiary, is increasing its capacity for soap and detergent manufacturing and plans to enter food processing in India as well. These steps represent a strategic commitment by the firm to the Indian market. As this strategy is implemented, strategic control systems will be used to ensure a smooth process.[5] If opportunities in the Indian market continue to unfold, Unilever will no doubt continue to expand there. But if uncertainty and risk become too great, the firm will become increasingly cautious, perhaps even going so far as to reduce its involvement in India.

Often the most critical aspect of strategic control is control of an international firm's financial resources. Money is the driving force of any organization, whether it is in the form of profits or of cash flow to ensure that ongoing expenses can be covered. And if a firm has surplus revenues, managers must ensure that those funds are invested wisely in order to maximize their payoff for the firm and its shareholders. Thus it is extremely important that an international firm develop and maintain effective accounting systems. Such systems should allow managers to fully monitor and understand where the firm's revenues are coming from in every market in which it operates, to track and evaluate all its costs and expenses, and to see how its parts contribute to its overall profitability.

Poor financial control can cripple a firm's ability to compete globally. For example, Mantrust, an Indonesian firm, bought Van Camp Seafood, packager of Chicken of the Sea tuna, for $300 million. Most of that money was borrowed from Indonesian banks. But Mantrust's owner, Teguh Sutantio, was unskilled at managing debt, and the firm had difficulties making its loan payments. Mantrust eventually got itself back on track by selling off part of its other assets and restructuring its loans. But the poor financial management is likely to set back its performance for years.[6] The following "Going Global" provides another vivid illustration of the problems poor financial control can create.

Financial control is generally a separate area of strategic control in an international firm. Given the overall importance of control, as noted earlier, one or more special managerial positions are usually created to handle financial control. Such a position is usually called *controller*. Large international firms often have a corporate controller responsible for the financial resources of the entire organization. Each division within the firm is likely to have a divisional controller who is based in a country in which the firm operates and who oversees local financial control. Divisional controllers are usually responsible both to the heads of their respective divisions and to the corporate controller. These control relationships are managed primarily through budgets and financial forecasts.

A special concern of an international controller is managing the inventory of various currencies needed to run the firm's subsidiaries and to pay its vendors.[7] For example, Coca-Cola has to manage its holdings of over 150 currencies as part of its daily operations. Each foreign subsidiary of an international firm needs.to maintain a certain amount of local currency for its domestic operations. Each also needs access to the currency of the parent corporation's home country in order to remit dividend payments, reimburse the parent for the use of intellectual property, and pay for other intracorporate transactions. The subsidiary further must be able to obtain other currencies in order to pay suppliers of imported raw materials and component parts as their invoices are received.

Given the importance of exchange-rate fluctuations, as discussed in Chapter 5, the controller needs to oversee the firm's holdings of diverse currencies in order to avoid losses when exchange rates change. Many MNCs centralize the management of exchange-rate risk at the corporate level. However, others, such as the Royal Dutch-Shell Group, allow their foreign affiliates to use both domestic and international financial and commodity markets to protect their costs and prices against exchange-rate fluctuations. Firms that decentralize this task need to maintain

GOING GLOBAL

The Importance of Control

Control is an important management responsiblity in any organization. In an international business with far-flung operations, however, the need for effective control becomes even more important. The recent financial disaster at Baring Brothers provides a vivid illustration of this fact.

Baring Brothers is one of the oldest and most respected banks in England. During its 233-year history, the venerable firm financed the Napoleonic Wars for Great Britain and the Louisiana Purchase for the United States and was banker to the House of Windsor. Like many major banks, Baring Brothers opened offices in many major cities around the world in recent years.

One of the bank's subsidiaries was Baring Futures PLC, an investment firm specializing in complex futures trading. In 1992, Baring Futures sent a young broker named Nick Leeson to work in its Singapore office. Leeson performed admirably for the firm, earning vast sums of money with his impressive understanding of Asian financial markets and winning accolades from his superiors for his ability to run a tight operation.

In early 1995, however, disaster struck. Leeson had made a number of questionable, highly leveraged investments in 1994, which would have been very profitable had the Tokyo stock market remained stable. However, the earthquake that struck Kobe, Japan, clobbered Japanese stock prices and Leeson's deals fell apart—bringing Baring to its knees and forcing it into bankruptcy.

The reason Leeson was able to inflict so much damage singlehandedly was that Baring allowed him to function with virtually no controls over his actions. In most investment houses, one person or group handles all trading, and another person or group serves as overseer. This latter function is for control—to ensure that the traders are not taking unnecessary risks and that they have financial backing to cover any losses they might incur.

Leeson, however, was allowed to perform both functions. He made trades, confirmed them himself, and then authorized the funds to cover them. As his deals went sour following the Kobe disaster, he made riskier and riskier investments in a desperate attempt to recoup the losses. Without anyone checking on his work, he eventually suffered trading losses of $1.4 billion.

After the disaster was discovered, Leeson fled but was soon apprehended in Germany. Baring, meanwhile, could find no investors to cover its losses and was taken over by the Bank of England. It was eventually sold to a Dutch finance group, Internationale Nederlanden Groep, which agreed to inject $1.3 billion to return the firm to solvency.

Sources: "Busted!" *Newsweek*, March 13, 1995, pp. 36–47; "The Lesson from Barings' Straits," *Business Week*, March 13, 1995, pp. 30–32; "Barings Debacle: High-Finance Thriller Laced with Greek Tragedy," *Associated Press News Story*, March 5, 1995; "Barings Is Back in Business," *USA Today*, March 7, 1995, p. 2B.

---

adequate financial controls on their subsidiaries or face financial disaster. For example, in the early 1990s Shell's Japanese affiliate, Showa Shell Seikiyu KK, engaged in widespread speculative trading in foreign-currency markets, a practice forbidden by Shell. That is, rather than trying to hedge against exchange-rate fluctuations, the Japanese affiliate was trying to earn profits through exchange-rate fluctuations. Knowledge of this speculative trading was brought to light only when the Japanese group reported a loss of over $1 billion. Clearly, Shell's internal controls had broken down and failed to detect the speculative activities. As a result, corporate officials implemented new procedures and tighter controls to better manage the firm's financial resources.[8]

Managers in international firms must have access to the information they need to engage in strategic control. Information networks and systems should be designed to provide as much relevant, current, and accurate information as possible to managers so they can make the most informed decisions. For example, the Mitsui Construction Company was seeking a site in London on which to build a new office complex. Rather than gather their own information on potential sites, Mitsui managers relied on a British consulting firm to provide such information. The consultants convinced Mitsui to bid on the site of an old building, indicating that the property would sell for no more than $250 million and that the old building could be cheaply demolished. After Mitsui bought the property, it discovered that its bid of $255 million was $90 million more than the next highest bid. Even worse, a few days later the British government declared the building a historic site, so it could not be demolished. Clearly, Mitsui had acted on inaccurate and misleading information.[9]

Another type of strategic control that is increasingly important to international firms is control of joint ventures and other strategic alliances.[10] As we discussed in Chapter 12, strategic alliances, particularly joint ventures, are being used more often by and becoming more important to international firms. It follows then that strategic control systems must also account for the performances of such alliances. Because by definition a joint venture or other strategic alliance is operated as a relatively autonomous enterprise, most partners agree to develop an independent control system for each one in which they participate. The financial control of these alliances then becomes an ingredient in the overall strategic control system for each partner firm. That is, the alliance maintains its own independent control systems, but the results are communicated not only to the managers of the alliance but also to each partner.

Organizational Control

Organizational control focuses on the design of the organization itself. As discussed in Chapter 13, there are many different forms of organization design that an international firm can use. But selecting and implementing a particular design does not necessarily end the organization design process. For example, as a firm's environment or strategy changes, managers may need to alter the firm's design to better enable it to function in the new circumstances. Adding new product lines, entering a new market, or opening a new factory—all can dictate the need for a change in design. For example, IBM's overhaul of its European operations represents an effort to improve its organizational control, as does Ford's major reorganization, discussed in Chapter 13.

International firms generally use one or more of three types of organizational control systems:[11]

▶ Responsibility center control
▶ Generic organizational control
▶ Planning process control

The first two types are based on the **locus of authority**, or where the power to make various decisions resides within the organization. If it is appropriate for individual subsidiaries to call the shots in an MNC, then many of their controls logically can be decentralized. In other cases, it may be more appropriate for headquarters or some other centralized location to maintain more direct control over various decisions. The third type of control system is based on the planning process.

Responsibility Center Control. The most common type of organizational control system is a decentralized one called **responsibility center control**. Using this system, the firm first identifies fundamental responsibility centers within the organization. Strategic business units are frequently defined as responsibility centers, as are geographical regions or product groups. Regardless of how the firm specifies and defines them, however, it then evaluates each center on the basis of how effectively it meets its strategic goals. Thus a unique control system is developed for each responsibility center. These systems are tailored to meet local accounting and reporting requirements, the local competitive environment, and other circumstances.

For example, Nestlé uses responsibility center control for each of its units, such as Carnation, Lean Cuisine, and Stouffer's Hotels (see Map 15.1). These subsidiaries regularly provide financial performance data to corporate headquarters. Managers at Carnation, for example, file quarterly reports to Nestlé headquarters in Switzerland so that headquarters can keep abreast of how well its U.S. subsidiary is doing. By keeping each subsidiary defined as a separate and distinct unit and allowing each to use the control system that best fits its own competitive environment, corporate managers in Switzerland can see almost at a glance how each unit is performing within the context of its own market. Each report must contain certain basic information, such as sales and profits, but each also has unique entries that best reflect the individual subsidiary and its market.

Generic Organizational Control. A firm may prefer to use **generic organizational control** across its entire organization; that is, the control systems used are the same for each unit or operation, and the locus of authority generally resides at the firm's headquarters. Generic organizational control is most commonly used by international firms that pursue similar strategies in each market in which they compete. Because there is no strategic variation between markets, responsibility center control would be inappropriate. The firm is able to apply the same centralized decision making and control standards to the strategic performance of each unit or operation. Moreover, because international firms that use the same strategy in every market often have relatively stable and predictable operations, the organizational control system they use can also be relatively stable and straightforward. For example, United Distillers PLC markets its line of bourbon products in the United States, Japan, and throughout Europe. But because the product line is essentially the same in every market and the characteristics of its consumers vary little across markets, the firm uses the same control methods for each market.[12]

Planning Process Control. A third type of organizational control, which could be used in combination with either responsibility center control or generic organizational control, focuses on the strategic planning process itself rather than on outcomes. **Planning process control** calls for a firm to concentrate its organizational control system on the actual mechanics and processes it uses to develop strategic plans. This approach is based on the assumption that if the firm controls its strategies, desired outcomes are more likely to result. And each business unit may then concentrate more on implementing its strategy, rather than worrying as much about the outcomes of that strategy.

For example, Northern Telecom uses this approach for part of its organizational control process. Whenever a unit fails to meet its goals, the head of that unit meets with the firm's executive committee. The meeting focuses on how the

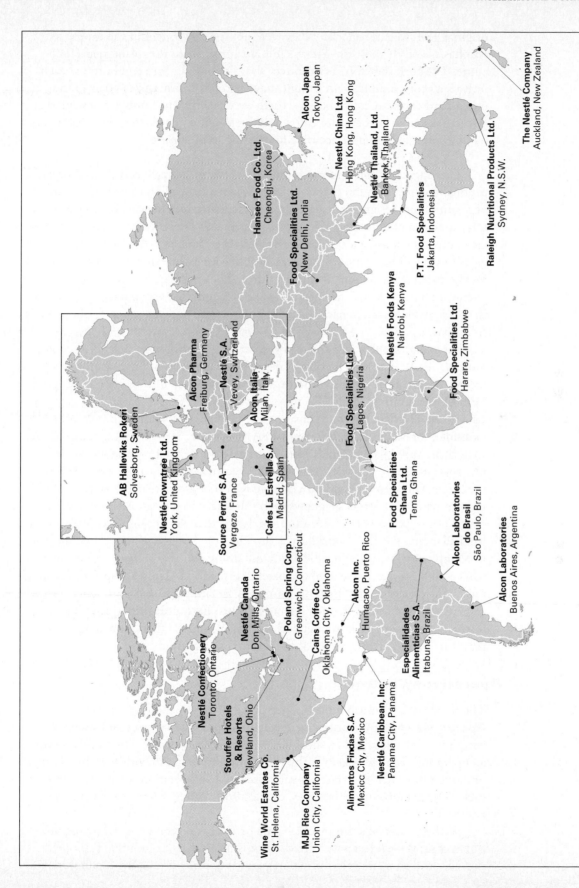

A Sampling of Nestlé's Global Holdings, Subsidiaries, and Affiliates

Alcon Japan
Tokyo, Japan

Nestlé China Ltd.
Hong Kong, Hong Kong

Nestlé Thailand, Ltd.
Bankok, Thailand

The Nestlé Company
Auckland, New Zealand

Hanseo Food Co. Ltd.
Cheongju, Korea

Food Specialities Ltd.
New Delhi, India

P.T. Food Specialties
Jakarta, Indonesia

Raleigh Nutritional Products Ltd.
Sydney, N.S.W.

Nestlé Foods Kenya
Nairobi, Kenya

Food Specialities Ltd.
Harare, Zimbabwe

Alcon Pharma
Freiburg, Germany

Nestlé S.A.
Vevey, Switzerland

Alcon Italia
Milan, Italy

Food Specialities Ltd.
Lagos, Nigeria

AB Halleviks Rokeri
Solvesborg, Sweden

Nestlé-Rowntree Ltd.
York, United Kingdom

Source Perrier S.A.
Vergeze, France

Cafes La Estrella S.A.
Madrid, Spain

Food Specialities
Ghana Ltd.
Tema, Ghana

Alcon Laboratories
do Brasil
São Paulo, Brazil

Alcon Laboratories
Buenos Aires, Argentina

Nestlé Confectionery
Toronto, Ontario

Nestlé Canada
Don Mills, Ontario

Poland Spring Corp.
Greenwich, Connecticut

Cains Coffee Co.
Oklahoma City, Oklahoma

Alcon Inc.
Humacao, Puerto Rico

Especialidades
Alimenticias S.A.
Itabuna, Brazil

Stouffer Hotels
& Resorts
Cleveland, Ohio

Wine World Estates Co.
St. Helena, California

MJB Rice Company
Union City, California

Alimentos Findas S.A.
Mexico City, Mexico

Nestlé Caribbean, Inc.
Panama City, Panama

MAP 15.1

original goals were set and why they were not met. Throughout the meeting, the emphasis is on the process that was followed that led to the unsuccessful outcome. The goal, therefore, is to correct shortcomings in the actual process each unit uses. For example, a unit might have based its unmet sales goals on outdated market research data because there were insufficient funds for new market research. Planning process control would focus not on correcting the sales shortfall, but on enabling more accurate forecasting in the future.

There are clear and important linkages between strategic control and organizational control in an international firm. When a firm adopts a centralized form of organization design, strategic control is facilitated as a logical and complementary extension of that design. But when a firm uses a decentralized design, strategic control is not as logically connected with that design.[13] A decentralized design gives foreign affiliates more autonomy and freedom while making it more difficult for the parent to maintain adequate control. The challenge facing managers of the parent, then, is to foster the autonomy and freedom that accompany a decentralized design while simultaneously maintaining effective parent control of operating subsidiaries.

For a large international firm, organizational control must be addressed at multiple levels. At the highest level, the appropriate form of organization design must be maintained for the entire firm. At a lower level, however, the appropriate form of organization design also must be maintained for each subsidiary or operating unit. The firm also must ensure that these designs mesh with each other. Consider, for example, France's Sogeti SA, the world's fourth-largest computer services firm. Sogeti uses organizational control as an overarching framework for managing its entire array of control systems scattered across more than 20 countries. The firm's founder and CEO, Serge Kampf, has structured Sogeti as a holding company. This structure allows each subsidiary in the various countries in which Sogeti operates to create a unique design that works most effectively in the particular country. Each subsidiary is run by a top manager who reports directly to Kampf and who is responsible for maintaining effective control within the unit while still being accountable to the parent corporation. Thus Kampf can maintain tight control over all the firm's operations by isolating group performance, growth, and costs within clearly defined operating units. Each unit manager is also instructed to create a control network within the unit so that the manager can report to Kampf on any aspect of the business at any time.[14]

Operations Control

The third level of control in an international firm is operations control. **Operations control** focuses specifically on operating processes and systems within both the firm and its subsidiaries and operating units. Thus a firm needs an operations control system within each business unit and within each country or market in which it operates. It may also need an operations control system for each of its manufacturing facilities, distribution centers, administrative centers, and so on.

Strategic control often involves time periods of several years, while organizational control may deal with periods of only a few years or months. But operations control concerns relatively short periods of time, dealing with components of performance that need to be assessed on a regular—perhaps even daily or hourly—basis. An operations control system is also likely to be much more specific and focused than are strategic and organizational control systems.

For example, a manufacturing firm may monitor daily output, scrappage, and worker productivity within a given manufacturing facility, while a retail outlet may measure daily sales. A firm that wants to increase the productivity of its workforce or enhance the quality of its products or services will primarily use operations control to pursue these goals. Operations control usually focuses on the lower levels of a firm, such as first-line managers and operating employees.

While people in the United States are used to sprawling, full-line supermarkets that carry everything from apples to zippers, typical European grocery stores tend to be smaller and less service-oriented, to carry fewer product lines, and to charge higher prices. Aldi, a German grocery firm, has prospered in Europe through an elaborate operations control system that relies heavily on cost control and efficiency. Aldi stores do not advertise or even list their numbers in telephone directories. Products are not unpacked and put on shelves but are instead sold directly from crates and boxes. These no-frills stores are located in low-rent districts. Customers bring their own sacks (or pay Aldi 4 cents each for sacks) and bag their own purchases. Aldi does not accept checks or coupons and provides little customer service. But this austere approach allows the firm to charge rock bottom prices—25 cents for a loaf of bread and 90 cents for a six-pack of cola, for example. Aldi has effectively transferred its control methods to its U.S. operation. The result? Aldi's net profit margins in the United States run about 1.5 percent of sales, double the industry norm, and sales average $350 per square foot, compared to an industry norm of $275. With almost 400 stores operating in the United States, Aldi has become one of the country's most profitable grocery chains.[15]

Managing the Control Function in International Business

Given the obvious complexities in control, it should come as no surprise that international firms must address a variety of issues in managing the control function. To effectively manage control, managers in such firms need to understand how to establish control systems, what the essential techniques for control are, why some people resist control, and what managers can do to overcome this resistance.

Establishing International Control Systems

As illustrated in Fig. 15.2, control systems in international business are established through four basic steps:

1 Set control standards for performance

2 Measure actual performance

3 Compare performance against standards

4 Respond to deviations

FIGURE 15.2

Steps in International Control

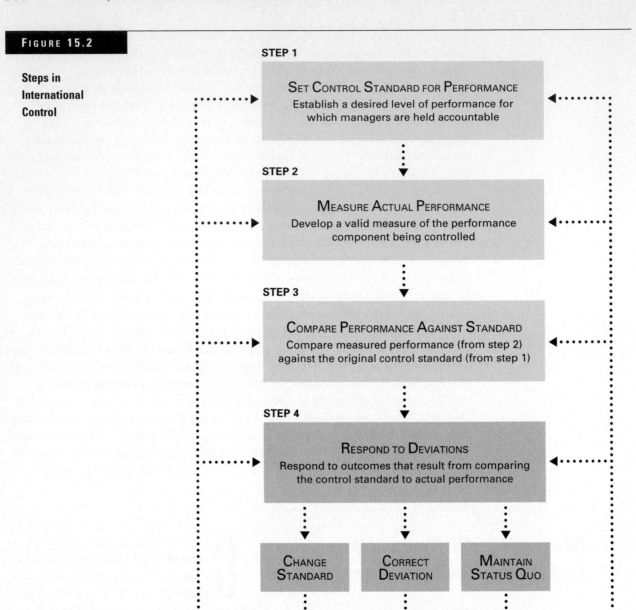

STEP 1

SET CONTROL STANDARD FOR PERFORMANCE
Establish a desired level of performance for which managers are held accountable

STEP 2

MEASURE ACTUAL PERFORMANCE
Develop a valid measure of the performance component being controlled

STEP 3

COMPARE PERFORMANCE AGAINST STANDARD
Compare measured performance (from step 2) against the original control standard (from step 1)

STEP 4

RESPOND TO DEVIATIONS
Respond to outcomes that result from comparing the control standard to actual performance

CHANGE STANDARD

CORRECT DEVIATION

MAINTAIN STATUS QUO

There obviously will be differences in specificity, time frame, and sophistication, but these steps are applicable to any area and any level of control.

Set Control Standards for Performance. The first step in establishing an international control system is to define relevant control standards. A **control standard** in this context is a target, a desired level of the performance component the firm is attempting to control. For example, if a firm anticipates selling 10,000 units of a new product in a particular market next year, 10,000 units sold becomes the control standard for which managers in that market become accountable. Siemens's intent to boost pre-tax profit margins from 2.4 percent to 4 percent is also a control standard.

Control standards need to be objective and consistent with the firm's goals. Suppose a firm is about to open its first manufacturing facility in Thailand. It might set the following three control standards for the plant:

I Productivity and quality in the new plant will exceed the levels in the firm's existing plants.

2 After an initial break-in period, 90 percent of all key management positions in the plant will be filled by local managers.

3 The plant will obtain at least 80 percent of its resources from local suppliers.

These control standards help provide a roadmap for managers involved in opening and running the new plant. Managers can readily see that productivity and quality are critical and that the firm expects them to hire and buy locally. Where did these standards come from? The firm set them on the basis of its objectives for the new plant, its experience with similar operations, and its overall goals.[16] The second and third goals may have resulted from a conscious strategy of reducing political risk or the parent firm's desire to be a good corporate citizen in each country in which it operates.

For example, Laura Ashley, an international retailer discussed in this chapter's closing case, recently established two control standards: to double sales in five years and to achieve and maintain a 12 percent return on investment. But the firm does not apply these standards uniformly across all stores. Some specific stores in certain locations (such as New York and Seoul) may be expected to more than double their sales because of growing markets, while stores in different locations may be expected to attain a smaller increase because of shrinking markets or stiffer competition. Some of the sales increase also would be met by opening new stores.

In another example, when Welsh entrepreneurs Charles and Patricia Lester started a fashion design firm in Cardiff, they knew that they would need to succeed quickly or else suspend operations. They also determined they had to achieve at least half their sales outside the United Kingdom. The Lesters had limited cash reserves and did not want to bankrupt themselves if their venture did not succeed. Thus they set a deadline of becoming profitable within two years. If they did not meet this target, they intended to shut down their business and resume their previous careers. This target of a two-year window for profitability served as their control standard.[17]

Measure Actual Performance. The second step in creating an international control system is to develop a valid measure of the performance component being controlled. For the firm introducing a new product in a foreign market, performance is based on the actual number of units sold. For the new plant in Thailand used as an example earlier, performance would be assessed in terms of productivity, quality, and hiring and purchasing practices.

Some elements of performance are relatively easy and straightforward to measure; examples are actual output, worker productivity, product quality, unit sales, materials waste, travel expenses, hiring practices, and employee turnover. Considerably more difficult is measuring the effectiveness of an advertising campaign to improve a firm's public image, ethical managerial conduct, or employee attitudes and motivation.

For example, after the Lesters got their fashion design firm up and running, they carefully monitored their incoming revenues and outgoing expenditures on a monthly basis. Even though they had given themselves a two-year time frame to start turning a profit, they did not want to use up all their cash reserves too quickly. When expenses grew too large, due in large part to selling trips to the United States and Canada, they cut back on their personal living expenses. When expenses were below average and they moved ahead of projections, they occasionally treated themselves to a bonus.[18]

Compare Performance Against Standards. The next step in establishing an international control system is to compare measured performance (obtained in step 2) against the original control standards (defined in step 1). Again, when control standards are straightforward and objective and performance is relatively easy to assess, this comparison is easy. For example, comparing actual sales of 8,437 units against a target sales level of 10,000 is easy. Likewise, comparing the actual hiring of 20 Thai managers against a target of hiring 19 Thai managers is also straightforward. But when control standards and performance measures are less concrete, comparing one against the other is considerably more complicated. Suppose a manager established a control standard of "significantly increasing market share" and now finds that market share has increased by 4 percent. Is this significant? Obviously, this comparison is ambiguous and difficult to interpret. Managers are advised to use specific and objective standards and performance measures whenever possible.

Responding to Deviations. The final step in establishing an international control system is responding to deviations observed in step 3. Three different outcomes can result when comparing a control standard and actual performance:

1 The control standard has been met.

2 It has not been met.

3 It has been exceeded.

For example, if the standard is sales of 10,000 units, actual sales of 9,998 units probably means the standard has been met, while sales of only 6,230 means it has not. But actual sales of 14,329 clearly surpasses the standard.

Depending on the circumstances, managers have many alternative responses to these outcomes. If a standard has not been met and the manager believes it is because of performance deficiencies on the part of employees accountable for the performance, the manager may mandate higher performance, increase incentives to perform at a higher level, or discipline or even terminate those employees.[19] Of course, the actual course taken depends on the nature of the standard versus performance expectations, the context within which the failure has occurred, and myriad other factors.

But sometimes standards are not met for unforeseen reasons, such as unexpected competition, an unexpected labor strike, unpredictable raw material shortages, or local political upheavals. Or the original control standard may have been set too high to begin with, in which case it may be possible to adjust the standard downward or to make additional allowances.

Finally, actual performance occasionally exceeds the control standard. Again, there may be multiple explanations: Managers and employees may have expended

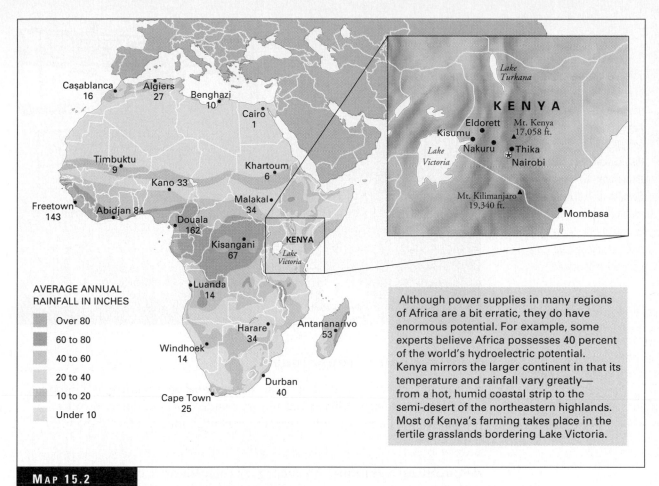

MAP 15.2

Kenyan Rainfall

Although power supplies in many regions of Africa are a bit erratic, they do have enormous potential. For example, some experts believe Africa possesses 40 percent of the world's hydroelectric potential. Kenya mirrors the larger continent in that its temperature and rainfall vary greatly—from a hot, humid coastal strip to the semi-desert of the northeastern highlands. Most of Kenya's farming takes place in the fertile grasslands bordering Lake Victoria.

AVERAGE ANNUAL RAINFALL IN INCHES

- Over 80
- 60 to 80
- 40 to 60
- 20 to 40
- 10 to 20
- Under 10

extra effort, the original standard may have simply been too low, or competitors may have bungled their own opportunities. In this case, managers may need to provide additional rewards or bonuses, adjust their control standards upward, or aggressively seize new opportunities for growth. For example, the Lesters turned their first profits two years after starting their fashion design business, just as they had predicted. Although during the last month they were down to eating rations bought from a bankrupt supermarket, they knew higher revenues and profits were coming very soon. And sure enough, today they have annual revenues of over $500,000—and more than enough profits to live comfortably.

Kenya Power & Lighting (KP&L) often finds it must react to deviations between control standards and actual performance in its distribution of electric power throughout Kenya. Businesses and municipalities in Kenya are more heavily dependent on hydroelectric power than are those in most other countries. Whenever the country experiences inadequate rain or prolonged dry spells (see Map 15.2), KP&L's water-powered electric plants have to ration electricity. Twice in the last decade, the government-run utility has been forced to enact nationwide rationing to ensure adequate power. It has also used smaller-scale rationing on numerous other occasions. During each rationing period, continued supplies of electricity were guaranteed to hospitals and security installations, while big businesses were required to cut energy consumption by 30 percent and homeowners were subjected to two-hour black-out periods each day. As soon as energy supplies reached an acceptable limit, rationing was phased out.[20]

These workers are helping to monitor power usage in Kenya so that Kenya Power & Lighting can effectively control the distribution of electricity throughout the country. Some degree of rationing must be implemented when a dry spell adversely affects hydroelectric generation of power.

Essential Control Techniques

Because of the complexities of both the international environment and international firms themselves, those firms rely on a wide variety of different control techniques. We do not describe them all here but introduce a few of the most important ones.

Accounting Systems.   Accounting is a comprehensive system for collecting, analyzing, and communicating data about a firm's financial resources. Accounting procedures are heavily regulated and must follow prescribed methods dictated by national governments. Because of these regulations, investors, government agencies, and other organizational stakeholders within a given country can better compare the financial performance of different organizations, have a common understanding of what various kinds of information mean, and place reasonable trust in the accuracy and meaning of that information.

International firms face more difficulties in establishing their accounting procedures than do purely domestic firms. International businesses must develop accounting systems to control and monitor the performance of the overall firm and each division, operating unit, or subsidiary. These systems enable managers to keep abreast of the financial performance of every part of the firm. As we discuss in the closing case, managers at Laura Ashley overhauled their accounting system to help facilitate better control. They did this in part because the financial reporting from foreign stores was too slow to enable the parent company's executives to make timely decisions.

But problems can arise when the accounting standards or procedures of the countries in which a firm operates are incompatible with each other, as is frequently the case. Each subsidiary must maintain its accounting records in accordance with local procedures and denominate its accounts in the local currency, in order to satisfy local government regulations and meet the needs of local managers. Yet the parent needs the local accounting records of each subsidiary translated into the parent's currency using accounting procedures dictated by the parent's home country in order to meet the needs of investors, regulators, and tax collectors in that country. The parent further must decide whether it will evaluate the performance of its subsidiaries and the subsidiaries' managers on the basis of their performance using the local accounting system, the parent's home country accounting system, or some combination of the two. We discuss international accounting in more detail in Chapter 19.

Procedures. Firms also use various procedures to maintain effective control. Policies, standard operating procedures, rules, and regulations all help managers carry out the control function. For example, as part of a manufacturing firm's political agreement with its host country, the firm may establish a policy that at least 75 percent of the raw materials it buys must be obtained from local suppliers. This policy guides plant managers in making purchasing decisions and allocations. A firm also could have a rule that each employee transferred to a foreign unit must attain basic proficiency in the local language within six months. This rule would serve as an ongoing and easily referenced measure of what is expected.

Firms often alter these procedures in the face of adversity. For example, consider Singapore Technologies Holdings (STH), a government-controlled R&D firm. STH recently incurred huge losses on several high-risk ventures. Following accepted practice, the firm's management had undertaken those ventures without getting the government's authorization. The government of Singapore traditionally gave the managers of its state-owned businesses considerable latitude in making decisions on their own. But the losses at STH, plus similar ones at other government-controlled firms, caused governmental officials to rethink this approach. They created a new set of policies, rules, regulations, and standard operating procedures that such firms must now follow. For example, any capital expenditure over $5 million must now be approved by a governmental official.[21]

Performance Ratios. International firms also use various performance ratios to maintain control. A **performance ratio** is a numerical index of performance that the firm wants to maintain. A common performance ratio used by many firms is inventory turnover. Holding excessive inventory is dysfunctional because the inventory ties up resources that could otherwise be used for different purposes and because the longer materials sit in inventory, the more prone they are to damage and loss. Based on a firm's unique circumstances, it may decide that it does not want anything to sit in inventory for more than 30 days. That is, it wants to turn its inventory over 12 times a year, and the performance ratio for inventory management, then, is 12. For example, Laura Ashley uses inventory turnover ratios to more effectively manage its stock of garments and household design accessories. But the ratio is likely to differ among different types of retailers and among different countries depending on the amount of floor space, the sophistication of inventory management systems, and the reliability of suppliers. For example, because rents are so high in Tokyo, convenience stores like 7-11 have little room for storage. They must maintain high inventory turnover ratios to remain profitable. Often vendors resupply the 7-11s four or five times a day to ensure that goods are available for customers. Sophisticated electronic linkages allow the stores to communicate their inventory needs to suppliers on a real-time basis.

Indonesia's Garuda Air also uses performance ratios to maintain control of its airline operations. One key ratio for an airline is the percentage of seats filled on specified flights. If this ratio falls below a set minimum, the firm looks into alternative ways to generate passenger demand, such as discounts or additional promotional activity. Another ratio of interest to Garuda is the percentage of its flights that arrive and depart on time. If this ratio slips too much, managers try to identify and eliminate the reasons for delays.[22]

Behavioral Aspects of International Control

Regardless of how well formulated and implemented a control system may be, managers must understand that human behavior plays a fundamental role in how well control works. Essential to this understanding is the awareness that some people resist control. Also essential is the recognition that resistance can be minimized. While resistance to control is likely to exist within most cultures, its magnitude will vary across cultures.

Resistance to Control. People in international firms may resist control for various reasons. One potential reason is overcontrol, whereby the firm tries to exert more control over individuals than they think is appropriate. By definition, control regulates and constrains behavior. And most people accept this within what they perceive to be reasonable limits (with the limits being partially determined by the cultural context). But if attempts to control behavior begin to exceed those perceived limits, people may balk and begin to resist. For example, when Disney first opened Euro Disney outside of Paris, it attempted to apply the same grooming standards for its employees there that it uses in the United States. It banned beards and mandated trimmed hair. However, French employees saw this as overcontrol. They complained about the standards, vented their grievances in the media, and occasionally ignored the standards altogether. The resistance grew to the point where Disney eventually backed off and developed standards that were more acceptable to its European employees.

Organizations that exert too much control over their employees are likely to encounter resistance and other behavioral problems. Because the government of Venezuela heavily restricts the actions of managers at its national oil company, PDV, those managers experience frustration as they attempt to make the company globally competitive.

Another firm that has to deal with problems of overcontrol is Petroleos de Venezuela (PDV), the state-owned national oil enterprise of Venezuela. Experts see PDV as an efficient and well-run organization capable of competing with private-sector rivals from other countries. But the government of Venezuela continually restricts the firm's plans to expand, to invest in capital equipment, and to enter new markets. As a result, managers at PDV feel overly constrained and frustrated in their efforts to compete internationally.[23]

People may also resist control because it may be inappropriately focused; that is, the firm may be inadvertently trying to control the wrong things. For example, if a firm places so much emphasis on lowering costs that quality is compromised and employee morale suffers, employees may become indignant and attempt to circumvent the control system. Whistler Radar, a U.S.

firm, encountered this problem in its assembly of radar detectors. Its control system focused on quality control only at the end of the assembly process. When managers discovered that 100 of the firm's 250 employees were doing nothing more than reworking defective units assembled by the other 150, they realized that control should have been focused on quality throughout the assembly process.

Finally, people may resist control because control increases their accountability. In the absence of an effective control system, employees may be able to get by with substandard performance because managers do not understand what the employees are doing relative to what they should be doing. For example, if a foreign branch manager has to submit financial performance data only annually, the manager may not be doing as good a job on a day-to-day basis as the firm would like. If the firm were to request performance reports more frequently, it could increase the manager's accountability. At the same time, of course, if the firm demands too much reporting, it becomes prone to overcontrol. Thus it is important to strike a balance between appropriate and acceptable levels of accountability without edging over into a condition of overcontrol.

Foster's Brewing Group, an Australian conglomerate, recently suffered because of a clear lack of accountability. Philip Morris Company's Miller Brewing unit bought 20 percent of Foster's Canadian joint venture with Molson. Japan's Asahi Breweries Ltd. already owned a stake in Foster's. Several banks on whose loans Foster's had failed to make payments made substantial claims against the firm's assets. The Australian government, too, made claims against Foster's assets because of past-due taxes, and it began to monitor and regulate the firm's activities. This complex network of ownership linkages and financial claims created a situation in which no one at Foster's home office knew who was in charge or how to proceed. It was hard to tell who made a particular decision, since Philip Morris, Molson, Asahi, banks, and the Australian government were all making decisions about different aspects of the organization. But when Edward T. Kunkel, formerly head of Molson Breweries, a division of Foster's, took over, he began to set things straight. One of his first actions was to define accountability by clarifying reporting relationships among the firm's top executive team and establishing clear performance benchmarks against which managers would be evaluated.[24]

People from different cultures will respond in different ways to control. Using the framework discussed in Chapter 14, for example, individuals from power-tolerant cultures may be more likely to resist control, since they are inclined to discount power relationships within their organization. Conversely, people from power-accepting cultures may perceive control to be a normal part of organizations. Uncertainty acceptance will also be important. People who want to avoid uncertainty may accept more control than will people who do not mind uncertainty.

Overcoming Resistance to Control. Although there are no guaranteed methods for eliminating resistance to control, there are a few that can help minimize it. The appropriate method, as well as its likely effectiveness, will vary by culture.

For many settings—especially those with low power acceptance—a particularly important method is to promote participation. Involving employees who are going to be affected by control in its planning and implementation will enable them to better understand the goal of the control system, how and why the system works, and how their jobs fit into the system. They may as a result be less prone to resist it.

Another obvious method to reduce resistance that works well in most cultures is to create a control system that has a clearly appropriate focus and creates reasonable accountability without overcontrolling. Glaxo Holdings, Great Britain's largest pharmaceutical firm and the world's second largest, uses this method. The firm is very receptive to allowing scientists to explore ideas and possibilities for new prescription drugs, thereby motivating those scientists to pursue ideas and creating an atmosphere of creativity and innovation. At the same time, Glaxo managers carefully monitor the progress of new product development. If costs start becoming excessive or if development begins to lag too far behind the competition, managers may choose to curtail a given project. Employees see this as a viable strategy because it gives them the opportunity to contribute while simultaneously keeping costs in check.[25]

A firm may also overcome resistance to control by providing a diagnostic mechanism for addressing unacceptable deviations. Suppose a plant manager reports productivity levels far below those expected by headquarters. Top managers should avoid jumping to a potentially wrong conclusion, such as simply assuming the manager has done a poor job and reprimanding him, or worse. Instead they should first learn why the poor performance occurred. For example, it may have resulted from the corporate purchasing manager's having bought inferior materials for the plant.

Again, it is important to account for cultural factors when planning how to deal with resistance to control. People from power-accepting cultures, for example, may be reluctant to actively participate in planning and implementing control because they view such activities as the domain of management.

Finally, behavioral aspects of control can be approached and managed from a cultural perspective. The firm may attempt to replace behaviors resulting from national culture with those more consistent with its corporate culture. Being careful to hire people with values, experiences, work habits, and goals that are consistent with the firm's can go a long way toward this goal. Managers of Japanese-owned automobile factories in the United States, for example, spend thousands of dollars per worker selecting U.S. employees who will be receptive to the Japanese way of working. Further refinements in behavior can be expedited through training and management development programs designed to help impart the firm's cultural values and business methods.

Controlling Productivity in International Business

A key consideration in the control systems of many international firms is productivity. Productivity is distinct from control, yet it is also closely related in that the ultimate aim of most control systems is to ensure high levels of productivity. An understanding of productivity allows a better grasp of all the means of attaining it. Thus, in this section we define productivity, examine productivity around the world, and discuss how firms manage productivity.

At its simplest level, **productivity** is an economic measure of efficiency that summarizes the value of outputs relative to the value of the inputs used to create them.[26] Productivity is important for various reasons. For one thing, it helps determine a firm's overall success and contributes to its long-term survival. For another, productivity contributes directly to the overall standard of living of people within a particular country. If the firms within a country are especially productive, the country's citizens will have more products and services to consume. And the firm's goods and services can be exported to other countries, thereby bringing additional revenues back into the country of origin. Each of these factors positively impacts GDP and thus benefits the whole country.

Productivity can be measured in many ways. **Overall productivity** (also called **total factor productivity**) is determined by dividing total outputs by total inputs. But this summary index is often of little direct value to managers, who are likely to be more interested in productivity relative to specific outputs and/or specific inputs. For example, **labor productivity**, a measure of how efficiently the firm is using its workforce, is determined by dividing output by direct labor (either hours or dollars). Comparing labor productivity for different subsidiaries may help managers identify problems before they become excessively costly.

Productivity around the World

While calculating productivity is relatively easy, finding the data to use in the calculations is another matter altogether. Few firms divulge their productivity statistics, and countries often report their data in such different terms that comparisons are difficult. Nevertheless, there is good evidence regarding productivity in the United States, Japan, Germany, and most other Quad countries. Among these countries, clear differences exist between absolute levels of productivity and productivity growth rates. In absolute terms, the United States is the world's most productive major economy. The average U.S. worker produces $45,100 of goods and services each year. In contrast, the average German worker produces $37,850, while the average Japanese worker produces around $34,500.[27]

But while U.S. workers are more productive than their foreign counterparts, U.S. productivity growth has fluctuated. For example, throughout the 1980s productivity growth rates were greater in both Germany and Japan than in the United States. More recently, productivity growth in the United States has begun to accelerate, while productivity growth in Japan has stalled, due at least in part to that country's economic recession. Germany's productivity growth also slowed due to the difficulties of integrating the previously independent economies and political systems of East Germany and West Germany. Figure 15.3 shows productivity rates for four countries for the period 1980–1994 (Germany is not included because of noncomparability due to its reunification). While the United States maintains a clear lead, that lead is shrinking.[28]

Managing Productivity

Regardless of where a firm operates, one of its fundamental goals must be to continue to monitor and control its productivity. There are several general strategies it can pursue in its efforts to maintain and/or boost productivity. Three approaches in particular often help firms become more productive:[29]

1 Spend more on R&D

2 Improve operations

3 Increase employee involvement

FIGURE 15.3

**Some International
Productivity Trends**
Source: DRI/McGraw-Hill,
Business Week.

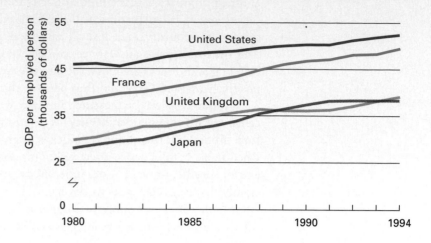

Spend More on R&D. The starting point in improving productivity is often to invest more heavily in R&D. Through R&D, firms identify new products, new uses for existing products, and new methods for making products. Each of these outcomes, in turn, contributes directly to higher productivity. U.S. firms spend more on R&D than do their foreign competitors, but the gap is narrowing as more foreign firms increasingly invest in R&D.[30] Moreover, U.S. firms have a long and painful history of achieving significant scientific breakthroughs but then being ineffective in getting them to market.

Improve Operations. Another important way to increase productivity is to improve operations. This is where control comes in; a firm seeking to increase productivity needs to examine how it does things and then look for ways to do them more efficiently.[31] Replacing inefficient equipment, automating selected tasks, training workers to be more efficient, and simplifying manufacturing processes are all ways to improve operations and boost productivity. Japanese manufacturers have been especially successful at increasing productivity through improved operations. JIT manufacturing and inventory control techniques, consistent investments in technology, and a concentration on efficiency have paid big dividends for many of them. U.S. firms are also paying more attention to operations. For example, until recently General Electric required three weeks to fill an order for a custom-made industrial circuit-breaker box. Further, the firm had six plants making the boxes. Through improved operations—more efficient manufacturing methods and product simplification, among other improvements—the firm can now fill such an order in only three days and makes all its circuit-breaker boxes in a single facility.[32]

Boliviana de Energia Electrica SA, known in the United States as Bolivia Power, has worked continuously for years to improve its operations. As one of the few foreign-owned utility firms in Latin America (it is a subsidiary of a British utility), Bolivia Power has repeatedly escaped attempts at nationalization by demonstrating that it produces electricity more efficiently as a privately owned firm than it could if it were state-owned. Its general manager, Kenneth Lyons, has consistently sought ways to be more efficient, cut costs, and boost output. For example, he has always stressed the value of using the newest technology. By continuing to invest in new equipment and machinery, he has consistently increased productivity. This strategy and his attention to other areas of operations have streamlined the firm's operations to the point that it is among the world's most productive utility firms.[33]

Increase Employee Involvement. Finally, productivity can be improved by increasing employee involvement, particularly in power-tolerant cultures. The idea is that if managers give employees more say in how they do their jobs, those employees will become more motivated to work and more committed to the firm's goals. Further, because they are the ones actually doing the jobs, the employees probably have more insights than anyone else into how to do them better. Increased involvement is generally operationalized through the use of self-managed teams. Groups of workers are formed into teams, each of which has considerable autonomy over how it does its job. Self-managed teams were pioneered in Sweden and the United Kingdom, refined in Japan, and are now used extensively worldwide.[34]

For example, Lufthansa currently uses employee participation in its efforts to cut costs. The firm's overhead had grown out of control, and it needed to be reduced for the firm to remain competitive. Lufthansa wanted to cut its payroll in Germany but was stymied because of two strong national unions. So the firm enlisted the assistance of the unions to meet its cost-cutting goals. Representatives from the firm and both unions now meet regularly to devise ways to trim payroll costs without resorting to massive layoffs. So far, the cuts have focused on reducing work rules and eliminating jobs through attrition and early retirement.[35]

Controlling Quality in International Business

Control also helps firms maintain and enhance the quality of their products and/or services. Indeed, quality has become such a significant competitive issue in most industries that control strategies invariably have quality as a central focus.[36] The American Society for Quality Control has defined **quality** as the totality of features and characteristics of a product or service that bear on its ability to satisfy stated or implied needs.[37] The International Organization for Standardization (ISO) has been working to develop and refine an international set of quality guidelines. These guidelines, called collectively ISO 9000, provide the basis for a quality certification that is becoming increasingly important in international business. Indeed, major companies in more than 50 countries, including the United States and all EU members, have agreed to adopt ISO 9000 guidelines as they are developed.[38]

Quality is of vital importance for several reasons. First, many firms today compete on the basis of quality. Firms whose products or services have a poor reputation for quality are unlikely to succeed. For example, Daewoo, Samsung, and Goldstar, three Korean firms, are each having difficulty competing in Europe because their products are not perceived by Europeans as being of the same quality as those made by European firms. As we explain in Chapters 16 and 17, such country-of-origin factors play a major role in the marketing and location decisions of international firms. The South Korean chaebol are attempting to overcome this shortcoming by opening plants in Europe, establishing strategic alliances with European firms, and working to meet ISO 9000 guidelines and standards.[39]

Second, quality is important because it is directly linked with productivity. Higher quality means increased productivity because of fewer defects, fewer resources devoted to reworking defective products, and fewer resources devoted to quality control itself. Recall, for example, how Whistler Radar, by improving its product quality, also improved the productivity of its workers. Higher quality also serves to lower the costs associated with customer returns and warranty service.

Finally, higher quality helps firms develop and maintain customer loyalty. Customers who buy products and services they feel fulfill their quality expectations will probably buy again from the same firm.[40]

Quality consists of eight dimensions:[41]

1 **Performance** comprises the product's primary operating characteristics, such as an automobile's ability to transport its driver.

2 **Features** include supplementary characteristics, such as power windows on an automobile.

3 **Reliability** refers to the dependability of a product, such as the probability of an automobile's starting.

4 **Conformance** is how well the product meets normal standards.

5 **Durability** refers to the product's expected lifespan.

6 **Serviceability** refers to how fast and easily the product can be repaired.

7 **Aesthetics** refers to how the product looks, feels, tastes, and/or smells.

8 **Perceived quality** is the level of quality as seen by the customer. Perceived quality can be viewed in terms of price and expectations. For example, Sony manufactures and sells a variety of color televisions ranging in price from as little as $300 to well over $2000. For $300 a customer might expect a fairly reliable, small-screen television with basic features and good picture clarity. But for $2000 the same customer is likely to expect an extremely reliable, big-screen television with numerous features and exceptional picture clarity. It is difficult to compare the quality of the two televisions without understanding the price and expectations for each. That is, they may be of equal perceived quality based on actual quality adjusted for price and expectations.

Quality around the World

As with productivity, measuring quality may seem to be a reasonably straightforward task, but obtaining valid and reliable data is not as easy as might be imagined. Nevertheless, two recent studies provide insights into quality in different countries. One surveyed perceptions of managers; the other focused on consumers' perceptions.

Managerial Perceptions of International Quality. A major study of managers' perceptions of international quality was conducted in the early 1990s by Ernst & Young and the American Quality Foundation.[42] This study involved teams of executives from more than 500 firms in the automotive, banking, computer, and health care industries in Canada, Germany, Japan, and the United States. Table 15.1 summarizes the study's major findings.

Two findings are particularly noteworthy. First, the Japanese firms studied indicated that they do not use work teams nearly as much as many people think, but *overall* more of their employees participated in decision making. This suggests that Japanese firms have done a better job of institutionalizing participation throughout their organizations, whereas firms in other countries still tend to use structural dimensions like work teams to achieve participation. Second, the Japanese are far ahead of the rest of the world in using process simplification (finding easier and simpler ways of doing things) and cycle time reduction (doing things faster). These activities are a part of improving operations, which was identified earlier in this chapter as a method for boosting productivity. German firms, however, use these practices far less than do U.S. and Canadian firms.

TABLE 15.1

Management Perceptions of International Quality

1. Japanese firms do not organize the majority of their workforce into teams that focus on quality programs, but they do have the highest rate of employee participation in regularly scheduled meetings about quality.

2. Firms in Canada, Germany, and the United States expect to increase their involvement of employees in quality-related teams. Firms in Japan expect little change in their use of quality teams.

3. More than half the firms in all four countries evaluate the business consequences of quality performance at least monthly. However, almost 20 percent of the U.S. firms review quality less than annually or not at all.

4. Although quality performance was used only on a limited basis in the past, its use as a criterion for compensating senior management is expected to increase substantially in all four countries; in the United States, more than half the firms plan to use this measure.

5. About 40 percent of firms in Canada, Japan and the United States place primary importance on customer satisfaction in strategic planning; 22 percent of German firms do so.

6. German and Japanese firms are far ahead of Canadian and U.S. firms in incorporating customer expectations into the design of new products and services.

7. Japanese firms currently use technology twice as much as U.S. firms in meeting customer expectations. Although firms in all four countries expect to substantially increase the use of technology in meeting customer expectations over the next three years, Japanese firms will still lead the others.

8. German firms rarely place primary emphasis on competitors in the strategic planning process; however, almost one third of Japanese and U.S. firms do. In Canada, only one fourth do.

9. Japan dramatically leads the other countries in the routine use of process simplification and cycle time reduction. About half of Japanese firms use both of these practices more than 90 percent of the time.

10. About 20 percent of Canadian and U.S. firms always or almost always use process simplification techniques or process cycle time analyses to improve business processes; only six percent of German firms do so.

Source: Data from the Ernst & Young and American Quality Foundation study of managerial perceptions of international quality among U.S., Japanese, Canadian, and German executives. Adapted from Karen Bemowski, "The International Quality Study," *Quality Progress* (November 1991), pp. 33–37.

Consumers' Perceptions of International Quality. The consumer quality survey was conducted by the Gallup organization and the American Society for Quality Control.[43] The survey results, released in 1991, are based on interviews with 1008 U.S. consumers, 1446 Japanese consumers, and 1000 German consumers. Each consumer was asked various questions about his or her understanding of the meaning of quality and was asked to evaluate the quality of various products from each of the three countries. Table 15.2 summarizes some of the survey findings.

One clear finding is that domestic consumers in each country generally perceive the quality of products from their own country to be superior to the quality of products from the other two countries. Indeed, "TVs and VCRs" and "personal computers" were the only categories in which consumers picked products from another country (Japan) as being of higher quality than those made domestically.

Beyond these basic findings, the survey also revealed other interesting patterns. For one thing, Japanese and German consumers generally believe U.S. workers are not committed to quality. For another, U.S. firms have a better reputation abroad for services and soft goods than they do for hard goods. While U.S. firms do lag in quality, they are seen as the world's style leader—consumers in both Japan and Germany agreed that products made or introduced by U.S. firms tended to be more visually appealing than those made in their own countries. Finally, consumers in all three countries indicated that they are willing to pay higher prices for higher-quality products and services.

Total Quality Management

Because of the increasing importance of quality, firms worldwide are putting more and more emphasis on improving the quality of their products and services. Many of those firms call their efforts total quality management. **Total quality management (TQM)** is an integrated effort to systematically and continuously improve the quality of an organization's products and/or services.[44]

Components of TQM. TQM programs vary by firm and must be adapted to fit each firm's unique circumstances. However, experts agree that successful TQM programs generally include five essential components:[45]

▶ Strategic commitment to quality

▶ Employee involvement

▶ High-quality materials

▶ Up-to-date technology

▶ Effective methods

As shown in Fig. 15.4, TQM must start with a strategic commitment to quality. This means the quality initiative must start at the top of the firm, and top managers must be willing to commit the resources necessary to achieve continuous improvement. Firms that only pay lip service to quality and try to fool customers into believing they care about it are almost certain to fail.[46]

TABLE 15.2

Consumer Perceptions of International Quality

	PERCENTAGES OF RESPONDENTS CHOOSING EACH COUNTRY		
	U.S. Consumers	Japanese Consumers	German Consumers
Best-quality autos			
United States	41	1	2
Japan	36	71	18
Germany	18	23	78
Don't know	5	5	2
Best-quality personal computers			
United States	48	12	14
Japan	39	80	45
Germany	1	1	33
Don't know	12	7	8
Best-quality TVs and VCRs			
United States	28	2	2
Japan	66	91	59
Germany	1	1	37
Don't know	5	6	2
Best-quality clothing			
United States	89	17	7
Japan	3	75	3
Germany	2	2	87
Don't know	6	6	3
Best-quality cosmetics			
United States	81	21	23
Japan	2	68	4
Germany	2	3	67
Don't know	15	8	6
Best-quality financial services			
United States	79	21	12
Japan	8	63	7
Germany	2	4	75
Don't know	11	12	6
Best-quality health care services			
United States	75	23	8
Japan	6	52	4
Germany	9	12	84
Don't know	10	13	4
Number of interviews	1008	1446	1000

Source: From "Looking for Quality in a World Marketplace," 1991 ASQC/Gallup survey. © 1991 American Society for Quality Control. Reprinted with permission.

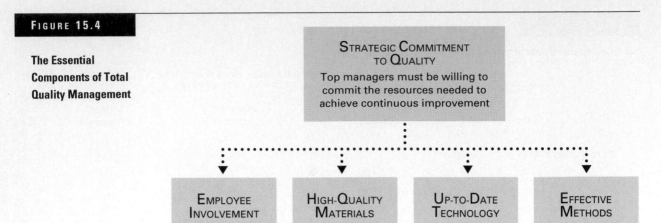

FIGURE 15.4

The Essential
Components of Total
Quality Management

With a strong strategic commitment as a foundation, TQM programs rely on four operational components to implement quality improvement. Employee involvement is almost always cited as a critical requirement in quality improvement. All employees must participate in helping to accomplish the firm's quality-related objectives. Materials must also be scrutinized. Firms can often improve the quality of their products by requiring higher-quality parts and materials from their suppliers. The firm also must be willing to invest in new technology in order to become more efficient and to achieve higher-quality manufacturing processes. And, finally, the firm must be willing to adopt new and improved methods of getting work done.[47]

Quality Improvement Tools. Firms using TQM have a variety of tools and techniques they can draw on, including statistical process control and benchmarking.

Statistical process control is a family of mathematically-based tools for monitoring and controlling quality. Its basic purposes are to define the target level of quality, specify an acceptable range of deviation, and then ensure that product quality is hitting the target.

For example, Source Perrier SA uses statistical process control to monitor its bottling operations. Managers there have determined that a large bottle of Perrier water should contain 23 fluid ounces. Of course, regardless of how careful managers are, few bottles will have exactly 23 ounces—some will have a bit more, some a bit less. However, if too many bottles are filled with either too much or too little, adjustments must be made. An acceptable range for this situation might be an actual content of between 22.8 and 23.2 ounces, with a target of 99.9 percent of all bottles having content within this range. Samples of finished products are taken, and their actual content measured. As long as 99.9 percent of all samples have between 22.8 and 23.2 ounces, production continues. But if only 97 percent of one sample falls within the acceptable range, managers may stop production and adjust their bottling equipment.

Another important TQM technique is benchmarking. **Benchmarking** is the process of legally and ethically studying how other firms do something in a high-quality way and then either imitating or improving on their methods.[48] The managerial quality perception study summarized earlier in the chapter found that 31 percent of all U.S. firms engage in regular benchmarking, while only 7 percent never use benchmarking. Japanese and German firms also engage in benchmarking, but not to the same extent as U.S. firms.

Xerox started the benchmarking movement in the United States as a result of competitive pressures from foreign rivals. In 1979, Canon, a Japanese firm, introduced a mid-sized copier that sold for less than $10,000. Xerox was sure that Canon was selling below cost in order to gain market share. To learn more about what was going on, Xerox sent a team of managers to Japan to work with Fuji-Xerox, a joint venture that a Xerox affiliate had established with Fuji to make copiers in Asia. While there, the managers bought a Canon copier and took it apart. To their surprise, they found the Canon copier to be of both higher quality and lower cost than those Xerox was making. By imitating Canon's materials and methods, Xerox was able to begin making its own higher-quality and lower-cost equipment. But Xerox did not stop there. It has subsequently benchmarked L.L. Bean's warehousing and distribution operation, Disney's equipment maintenance operation, and Corning's employee involvement program. As a result, the firm has regained its global competitive position and is again a formidable competitor against Japanese firms.[49]

Controlling Information in International Business

A final and increasingly important aspect of control in international business involves information. **Information** is data in a form that is of value to a manager in making decisions and performing related tasks.[50]

The Role of Information

Information is vitally important to any firm. Managers use it in every phase of their work, since it is necessary to the decision-making process. Obtaining accurate and timely information is of particular importance to international firms. Managers use information to better understand their firm's environment—its customers, competitors, and suppliers; the government policies that affect its hiring, producing, and financing decisions; and virtually every other element of its environment.

Managers also use information to help them decide how to respond to the environment. Meetings, reports, data summaries, telephone calls, and electronic mail messages are all used as managers set strategic goals and map out strategic plans. Information is also critical to implementing those strategic plans. For example, top managers must communicate their goals and expectations to managers of their foreign operations. Information is needed continually as managers make decisions daily and provide feedback to others in the firm about the consequences of those decisions. And, finally, information is an important part of the control process itself as managers monitor and assess how well they are meeting goals and executing plans. No manager likes to be taken by surprise. Having ready access to information that can be used to gauge ongoing performance and actual accomplishments is an important part of a manager's ability to function effectively.

The importance of information management depends on the type of strategy and organization design the firm uses. For example, if a firm is using related diversification, it is very important that various parts of the firm be able to communicate with other parts so that the firm can most effectively capitalize on the potential synergies of this strategy. If the firm is highly centralized, information systems are vital for top managers so that they can maintain the control they seek from using this particular design.[51] On the other hand, if a firm is using unrelated diversification, its information systems needs will be quite different. For example, communication among the various businesses within the firm will be far less important. And if the firm uses a decentralized form of organization design, its top managers will need and expect somewhat less information reporting by managers of various divisions and units.

Managing Information

The nature of international business adds considerable complexity to information and its role in a firm. In a domestic firm, information is almost certain to be in a common language, within the same legal context (the same accounting standards, financial reporting requirements, and so on will apply), and stored, manipulated, and accessible through common computer software and hardware configurations. But in an international firm, information is likely to be in different languages and subject to different legal contexts. For example, foreign partners and foreign governments may constrain the flow of information into and/or out of their countries. And computer software and hardware configurations are not always compatible. Thus managing information is not only very important for an international firm; it also is more complex than for a domestic firm.

Firms increasingly are working to develop integrated information systems in order to more effectively manage their information.[52] An **information system** is a methodology created by a firm to gather, assemble, and provide data in a form or forms useful to managers. Most information systems are computerized, although they do not necessarily have to be—routing slips, files, and file storage systems can effectively manage information in small firms. But larger firms today almost always use computerized systems to manage their information.[53] For example, managers at Laura Ashley are developing a computerized information system to help the firm manage its information more effectively. Each sale will be electronically recorded and used by managers to make decisions about reordering hot-selling merchandise.

To the extent possible, international firms would like to use information systems to link their operations so that their managers in any part of the world can access information and communicate with counterparts from any of the firm's operations.[54] The sheer size of this undertaking, however, along with computer software and hardware limitations, means that no firm has yet achieved true global integration of its information systems. Thus most firms develop information subsystems for specific functional operations or divisions.[55]

Texas Instruments (TI) is farther along the path toward a truly global system than most firms are. One of its subsidiaries, Tiris (Texas Instruments Registration and Identification Systems), is headquartered in the United Kingdom; its product development units are in Germany and the Netherlands; and its manufacturing facilities are in Japan and Malaysia. Managers and engineers at each facility communicate with each other over an integrated computer-based information system that enables them to function as if they were across the hall from each other rather than thousands of miles apart. For example, a manager in England might respond to a new customer order by sending a request electronically to a designer in

Germany to make a small modification in a part to meet the customer's specifications. After the modification is made, the design specifications and order information can be sent electronically to Japan where the products will be manufactured. The original manager in England receives verification that the parts have been made and shipped and can call the customer with the news. And at any time during the entire process, any manager or designer can electronically monitor what is being done with the order and where it will be sent next. This approach helps TI compete internationally by enabling it to reduce its costs and meet differing needs of customers in different countries.

CHAPTER REVIEW

Summary

Control is the process of monitoring and regulating activities of a firm so that some targeted component of performance is achieved or maintained. For an MNC, control must be managed both at the corporate level and within each subsidiary.

Most MNCs usually address control at three levels. Strategic control monitors how well an international firm formulates strategy and then goes about trying to implement it. Financial control is an especially important area of strategic control in international business. Poor financial control can cripple a firm's ability to compete globally. Most MNCs have a corporate controller as well as controllers within each subsidiary. Organizational control involves the design of the firm. Three basic forms of organizational control are responsibility center control, generic strategic control, and planning process control. Operations control focuses specifically on operating procedures and systems within the firm.

When international firms establish control systems, they first set control standards, then measure actual performance. Next they compare performance against the standards and respond to deviations. Essential control techniques include accounting systems, procedures, and performance ratios. International managers also need to understand behavioral aspects of control, such as why people resist control and how to overcome that resistance. Cultural factors are an important ingredient in addressing behavioral aspects of control.

Productivity is an economic measure of efficiency that summarizes the value of outputs relative to the value of inputs used to create them. Productivity can be assessed at a variety of levels and in many different forms. U.S. workers are the world's most productive, but Japan and Germany have greater productivity growth rates. Experts agree that a firm can improve productivity by spending more on R&D, improving operations, and increasing employee involvement.

Quality is the total set of features and characteristics of a product or service that bears on its ability to satisfy stated or implied needs. Quality has become a critical factor in both domestic and global competition. Most domestic consumers see products made in their own country as being of high quality. To improve quality, many firms are relying on TQM. TQM starts with a strategic commitment and is based on employee involvement, high-quality materials, up-to-date technology, and effective methods. Quality improvement tools include statistical process control and benchmarking.

Information is data in a form that is of value to a manager. It plays a major role in international business. Managers use information to understand their environment and to make decisions. It is also an important element in effective control. Managing information in an international firm is complex, and many firms use sophisticated electronic information systems to do so more effectively.

Review Questions

1. What are the three levels of control in international business?

2. Why is financial control so important?

3. What are three types of organizational control? Describe them.

4. What is the basic difference between responsibility center control and generic strategic control?

5. What is the basic focus of organizational control in international business?

6. What are the four basic steps in establishing an international control system?

7. Identify and discuss several essential control techniques.

8. Why is it important for organizations to control productivity?

9. What is quality? Why is it an important area of control for international firms?

10. How do firms manage information as part of control?

Questions for Discussion

1. Why is control an important management function in international business?

2. Do you think the three common types of international organizational control are mutually exclusive? Why or why not?

3. What are the advantages and disadvantages of each type of international organizational control?

4. Which form of control system would you most and least prefer for your own work? Why?

5. Which control techniques are most likely to be tailored to international settings? Which can be merely extensions of domestic operations?

6. What role do ethics play in control?

7. Why is it more common for developing countries to report dramatic increases in productivity, while more developed countries usually report much smaller increases?

8. List ten products you use for which quality is important in your purchasing decision. Which countries, if any, have reputations (good or bad) for each of those particular products?

9. Which of the findings in Table 15.1 do you think are most expected? Which are least expected?

10. What types of information are particularly important to an international firm?

 BUILDING GLOBAL SKILLS

This exercise is to help you learn more about control in international business. To begin, read the following introduction about your firm and your role in it. Then complete the small-group exercise that follows.

Wahner, Inc., is a moderately large international holding company with subsidiaries in eight countries. Until recently the firm was managed by its founder, Pete Wahner, who got his start by using his inheritance to buy an importing firm. Over the years,

Wahner bought and sold various businesses until he accumulated the current set of subsidiaries. In total, Wahner, Inc., consists of fifteen subsidiaries operating around the world. Wahner died of cancer two years ago, and the firm has been run by his former assistant, Thomas Henderson. However, Wahner's heirs have become concerned that the firm is not being effectively managed and that Henderson may not have the skills necessary to manage a complex international business. An audit of the firm revealed several significant problems, and your consulting firm has been hired to straighten things out. After four weeks of learning the business, you have developed the following impressions:

▶ A French subsidiary that exports wine has been operating at a loss for three years. Because the firm was required to report revenues only annually, no one paid much attention to what was happening until recently. You now see that the losses are excalating.

▶ An Australian subsidiary that makes beer containers has been steadily losing market share because of deteriorating product quality. Three of its largest customers recently took their business to alternative suppliers.

▶ A manager at an Argentinean subsidiary has allegedly been stealing money from the firm, although this allegation is only in the form of a confidential report submitted by two of his subordinates. These subordinates are known to be trustworthy, however, and you believe the allegations are true.

▶ A German subsidiary has been enormously profitable but has several millions of surplus marks sitting idly in checking accounts. These funds are not drawing interest and have been accumulating for at least three years.

▶ Two subsidiaries in the United States, as well as one in Mexico and one in Egypt, have been performing effectively. Each is making a good profit and seems to be effectively managed.

▶ The audits of the remaining seven subsidiaries have not yet been completed, but a preliminary report suggests that there are few major problems in any of them. All seven of these subsidiaries are based in Canada and report to a single executive vice-president, Nancy Gleason. Gleason is currently considering leaving Wahner for the top position in another firm.

Your task is to develop a control framework for getting Wahner, Inc., back on track. Working in small groups, do the following:

1. Develop preliminary ideas as to why and how the current state of affairs has emerged.

2. Outline control-related issues that need to be addressed.

3. Determine how you will go about establishing control at Wahner.

CLOSING CASE

A New Face for Laura Ashley[56]

A Laura Ashley shop is part of the landscape in the fashion districts of most major cities around the world. Laura Ashley (the business) was started in England by Laura Ashley (the person) in 1953. She provided personal decorating and design services before opening her first retail outlet in London in 1969. Featuring almost exclusively her widely recognized floral motifs, Laura Ashley fashions and home furnishings have become a staple for those with stately, traditional lifestyles. By the mid-1980s, the firm had 475 retail stores in 15 countries, concentrated in the fashion centers of Paris, Rome, Salzburg, Tokyo, Seoul, Sydney, Boston, New York, Houston, and Chicago.

When Laura Ashley died in 1985, the firm was thrown into turmoil. Her husband, Sir Bernard Ashley, retained control of 60 percent of the firm's stock but had neither the interest nor the skill to manage the business. Over the next several years, managers jockeying for power within the firm nearly tore it apart. Some managers wanted to introduce new fashion lines, while others wanted to adhere to the traditional Laura Ashley look. Some wanted to expand aggressively, while others wanted to retrench. Some wanted to broaden the firm's customer base by cutting prices and selling to department stores, while others wanted to maintain the firm's policies of premium pricing and exclusivity—floral motif designs, limited availability, and English cachet.

Any international retail firm has to contend with varying consumer tastes and buying patterns, different laws regulating business practices, and a diverse sales force. But the internal strife at Laura Ashley made it even more difficult to manage the firm. By 1990, sales and profits had plummeted, and the firm was on the brink of bankruptcy. Only the infusion of $70 million by a Japanese firm, retailer Jusco Co., in return for 15 percent ownership, enabled Laura Ashley to survive. But Bernard Ashley and the firm's creditors knew that big changes were necessary if the firm was going to turn itself around and regain profitability. After a worldwide search, Bernard Ashley hired James Maxmin, an American, to take over management of the firm and lead it back to success. Maxmin was a surprise choice, in part because he had no fashion experience (his previous job was running a chain of specialty stores) and in part because he was a vocal critic of much of what had made Laura Ashley so successful to begin with (he argued that retailers needed to keep pace with new tastes and styles and to broaden their product lines to reach more customers).

After being hired, Maxmin announced a strategy for getting the firm back on track. One of the first things he did was set two goals: double sales in five years, and achieve and maintain a 12 percent return. To accomplish these goals, he announced, the firm needed to develop a more professional image. Better-qualified and better-trained managers and a stronger and clearer accounting system were two specific areas

he stressed. In the past the firm had hired experienced local managers whenever it opened a new store and allowed them to function the way they had been trained in their local retail industries. Maxmin mandated that all managers complete an intensive training program in London and that each store report more complete financial data to headquarters more often.

Maxmin also felt the firm's designers had been too restricted by previous management to traditional fabrics and prints. One of his first actions was to give the green light for designers to develop new fashion lines aimed at younger customers and working women. These new fashions represented a more contemporary look and supplemented the traditional Laura Ashley floral patterns. Maxmin also indicated that he intended to license more home furnishings, such as linens and tableware, partly to generate more profits and partly to increase the firm's visibility. He also felt that such products would increase consumer awareness of the firm's other products.

He also recognized that to monitor these various changes, the firm needed to better manage its information. Previously, Laura Ashley had conducted little market research, and its existing information system provided very poor feedback about which products were selling and which were not. To counter these shortcomings, Maxmin set about creating an entirely new accounting system. This system was designed not only to enable him and other managers to keep better informed about sales of individual products at individual stores, but also to provide much needed market research data directly from the marketplace. The firm would also be able to use this information for more timely reordering of hot-selling merchandise. His goal, he said, was to better inform everyone in the firm about what was going on and to give them more opportunities for input on how things were done.

Maxmin's efforts slowly began to pay dividends for the firm. Losses continued for a while, but the firm returned to profitability in 1993, with pretax profits of approximately $2.7 million. The firm's new home furnishings products and contemporary clothing lines led the way, becoming increasingly more important to the firm as sales of its traditional product lines remained constant. Several new store openings also contributed to the bottom line, and investors began to believe the firm's prospects were looking up. Unfortunately, however, they were soon to be disappointed yet again. In 1994 Maxmin resigned, and the firm had to announce that its profits again would be too meager to enable it to pay a meaningful dividend. One reason noted for this problem was that costs were still too great and additional cuts were needed. Managers vowed to keep pursuing Maxmin's program and to continue to turn things around.

Case Questions

1. Identify as many illustrations of control (good and bad) as you can in this case.

2. Which do you think is most important for Laura Ashley—strategic, organizational, or operations control?

3. Which specific control techniques do you think are most relevant at Laura Ashley?

4. Do you think managers at Laura Ashley will encounter any resistance to their efforts to increase control?

5. What does this case suggest about the long-term process of organizational control?

6. What implications regarding information control can be drawn from this case?

CHAPTER NOTES

1. Alan Chai, Alta Campbell, and Patrick J. Spain (eds.), *Hoover's Handbook of World Business 1993* (Austin, Tex.: Reference Press, 1993), p. 440; "Siemens, the 'Sleepy Giant,' Gets a Rude Awakening from Its New CEO," *Profiles* (March 1993), pp. 23–24; "Siemens Is Starting to Look Like a Chipmaker," *Business Week*, February 7, 1994, pp. 43–44.

2. Robert N. Anthony, *The Management Control Function* (Boston: Harvard Business School Press, 1988).

3. David Asch, "Strategic Control: A Problem Looking for a Solution," *Long Range Planning* (February 1992), pp. 120–132.

4. *Entertainment Weekly*, October 14, 1994, pp. 14–15.

5. Rahul Jacob, "India Is Open for Business," *Fortune*, November 16, 1992, pp. 128–130.

6. "Pains of Indigestion," *Far Eastern Economic Review* (March 1992), pp. 51–52.

7. Lane Daley, James Jiambalvo, Gary Sundem, and Yasumasa Kondon, "Attitudes Toward Financial Control Systems in the United States and Japan," *Journal of International Business* (Fall 1985), pp. 91–110.

8. "Royal Dutch-Shell Posts Profit Despite Japanese Affiliate's Loss," *Houston Chronicle*, February 26, 1993, p. 2B.

9. Carla Rapoport, "Great Japanese Mistakes," *Fortune*, February 13, 1989, pp. 108–111.

10. J. Michael Geringer and Louis Hebert, "Control and Performance of International Joint Ventures," *Journal of International Business Studies* (Summer 1989), pp. 235–254.

11. Asch, op. cit., pp. 120–132.

12. "Sweet Sales for Sour Mash—Abroad," *Business Week*, July 1, 1991, p. 62.

13. Michael Goold, "Strategic Control in the Decentralized Firm," *Sloan Management Review* (Winter 1991), pp. 69–81.

14. "The Napoleon of Software," *Forbes*, June 24, 1991, pp. 112–116.

15. "Bag Your Own," *Forbes*, February 1, 1993, p. 70.

16. Robert S. Kaplan and David P. Norton, "The Balanced Scoreboard—Measures That Drive Performance," *Harvard Business Review* (January-February 1992), pp. 71–79.

17. "Welsh Couture," *Forbes*, July 20, 1992, pp. 100–103.

18. Ibid.

19. Robert H. Schaffer, "Demand Better Results—and Get Them," *Harvard Business Review* (March-April 1991), pp. 142–149.

20. "Elaborate Plans for Power Cut-Back," *The Weekly Review*, April 10, 1992, pp. 19–20.

21. "Call to Account," *Far Eastern Economic Review*, March 1992, pp. 45–46.

22. "When the Dust Settles," *Far Eastern Economic Review*, February 27, 1992, pp. 36–37.

23. "How not to run an oil company," *The Economist*, January 11, 1992, pp. 65–66.

24. "Soap Opera Down Under," *Forbes*, February 15, 1993, pp. 140–146.

25. "Why to Kill New Product Ideas," *Fortune*, December 14, 1992, pp. 91–94.

26. John W. Kendrick, *Understanding Productivity: An Introduction to the Dynamics of Productivity* (Baltimore: Johns Hopkins, 1977).

27. Thomas A. Stewart, "U.S. Productivity: First But Fading," *Fortune*, October 21, 1992, pp. 54–57.

28. "The Good Life Isn't Only in America," *Business Week*, November 2, 1992, p. 34.

29. "How to Regain the Productive Edge," *Fortune*, May 22, 1989, pp. 92–104.

30. Gene Bylinsky, "Turning R&D into Real Products," *Fortune*, July 2, 1990, pp. 72–77.

31. Jeremy Main, "Manufacturing the Right Way," *Fortune*, May 21, 1990, pp. 54–64.

32. Brian Dumaine, "How Managers Can Succeed Through Speed," *Fortune*, February 13, 1989, pp. 54–59.

33. "Stiff Upper Lip," *Forbes*, February 15, 1993, pp. 54–56.

34. Brian Dumaine, "Who Needs a Boss?" *Fortune*, May 7, 1990, pp. 52–60; Brian Dumaine, "The Trouble with Teams," *Fortune*, September 5, 1994, pp. 86–92.

35. "Even Lufthansa Is Carrying Too Much Baggage," *Business Week*, September 7, 1992, p. 80.

36. Richard J. Schonberger, "Total Quality Management Cuts a Broad Swath—Through Manufacturing and Beyond," *Organizational Dynamics* (Spring 1992), pp. 16–28.

37. Ross Johnson and William O. Winchell, *Management and Quality* (Milwaukee: American Society for Quality Control, 1989).

38. Ronald Henkoff, "The Hot New Seal of Quality," *Fortune*, June 28, 1993, pp. 116–120.

39. "Daewoo, Samsung, and Goldstar: Made in Europe?" *Business Week*, August 24, 1992, p. 43.

40. Genichi Taguchi and Don Clausing, "Robust Quality," *Harvard Business Review* (January-February 1990), pp. 65–75.

41. David A. Garvin, "Competing on the Eight Dimensions of Quality," *Harvard Business Review* (November-December 1987), pp. 101–109.

42. Karen Bemowski, "The International Quality Study," *Quality Progress* (November 1991), pp. 33–37; Stephen L. Yearout, "The International Quality Study Reveals Which Countries Lead the Race for Total Quality," *The Journal of European Quality* (March/April 1992), pp. 27–30.

43. *Looking for Quality in a World Marketplace* (Milwaukee: American Society for Quality Control, 1991).

44. "Quality," *Business Week*, November 30, 1992, pp. 66–75.

45. Lloyd Dobyns and Clare Crawford-Mason, *Quality or Else* (Boston: Houghton Mifflin, 1991).

46. Marshall Sashkin and Kenneth J. Kiser, *Putting Total Quality Management to Work* (San Francisco: Berrett-Koehler, 1993).

47. Charles C. Poirer and William F. Houser, *Business Partnering for Continuous Improvement* (San Francisco: Berrett-Koehler, 1993).

48. Jeremy Main, "How to Steal the Best Ideas Around," *Fortune*, October 19, 1992, pp. 102–106.

49. "Beg, Borrow—and Benchmark," *Business Week*, November 30, 1992, pp. 74–75.

50. George W. Reynolds, *Information Systems for Managers* (St. Paul, Minn.: West, 1988).

51. Raja K. Iyer, "Information and Modeling Resources for Decision Support in Global Environments," *Information & Management*, Vol. XX (1988), pp. 67–73.

52. Albert L. Lederer and Raghu Nath, "Making Strategic Information Systems Happen," *The Academy of Management Executive* (August 1990), pp. 76–83.

53. Carolyn V. Woody and Robert A. Fleck Jr., "International Telecommunications: The Current Environment," *Journal of Systems Management* (December 1991), pp. 32–36.

54. Jeremy Main, "Computers of the World, Unite!" *Fortune*, September 24, 1990, pp. 113–122.

55. Charlene A. Dykman, Charles K. Davis, and August W. Smith, "Turf Wars: Managing the Implementation of an International Electronic Mail System," *Journal of Systems Management* (October 1991), pp. 10–35.

56. "A Pennsylvania Yankee in Laura Ashley's Court," *Business Week*, December 23, 1991, pp. 80–82; "Laura Ashley Distribution," *New York Times*, March 20, 1992, p. D10; "Laura Ashley Bursts Its Seams—with Growth," *Textile World*, June 1988, pp. 83–84; "Laura Ashley: Life After Laura," *House & Garden*, April 1991, p. 212; "Laura Ashley Holdings Announces First Profitable Year Since Fiscal 1989," *PR Newswire*, March 15, 1993; "Laura Ashley Plans Restructuring," *Financial Times*, September 23, 1994, p. 22; "Wilted Flowers," *Forbes*, April 10, 1995, p. 94.

MANAGING INTERNATIONAL BUSINESS OPERATIONS

5

Many international businesses work diligently to protect their workers around the world and to provide the same basic level of safety, health, and compensation for everyone. These IBM employees in Brazil, for example, would be wearing the same protective clothing and be working in the same secure environment if they were at IBM facilities in Japan or the United States. (See "Point/Counterpoint" on pages 610–611.)

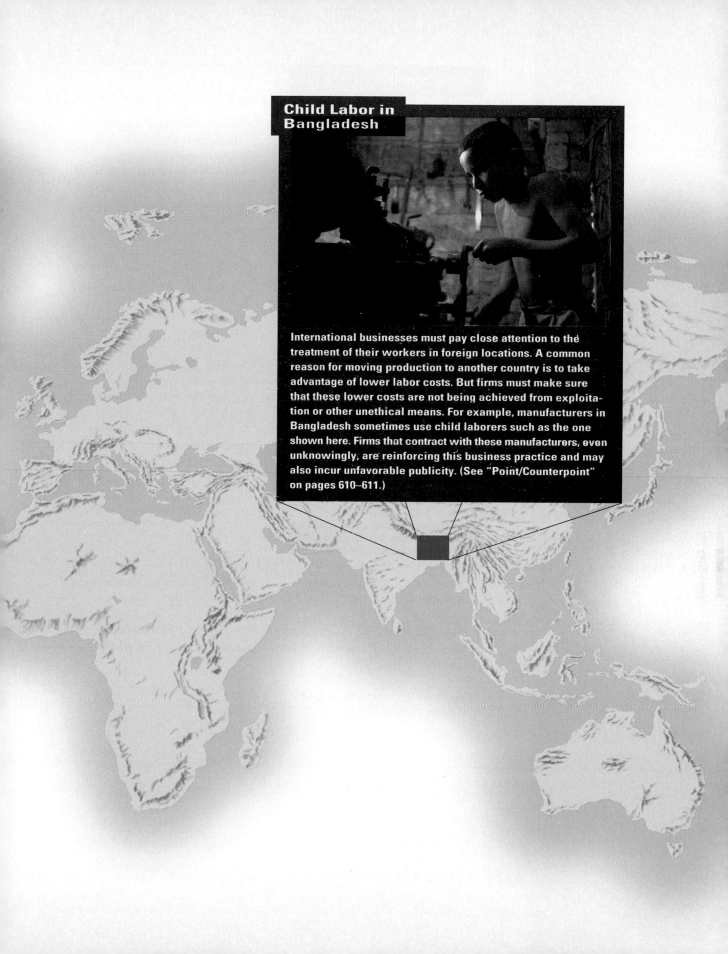

Child Labor in Bangladesh

International businesses must pay close attention to the treatment of their workers in foreign locations. A common reason for moving production to another country is to take advantage of lower labor costs. But firms must make sure that these lower costs are not being achieved from exploitation or other unethical means. For example, manufacturers in Bangladesh sometimes use child laborers such as the one shown here. Firms that contract with these manufacturers, even unknowingly, are reinforcing this business practice and may also incur unfavorable publicity. (See "Point/Counterpoint" on pages 610–611.)

CHAPTER

16

International Marketing

Chapter Outline

International marketing management
International marketing and business
    strategies
The marketing mix
Standardization versus customization

Product policy
Standardized products or customized
    products?
Legal forces
Cultural influences
Economic factors
Brand names

Pricing issues and decisions
Pricing policies
Market pricing

Promotion issues and decisions
Advertising
Personal selling
Sales promotion
Public relations

Distribution issues and decisions
International distribution
Channels of distribution

After studying this chapter you should be able to:

Characterize the nature of marketing management in international business.

Discuss the basic kinds of product policies and decisions made in international business.

Identify and describe pricing issues and decisions in international business.

Identify and describe promotion issues and decisions in international business.

Discuss the basic kinds of distribution issues and decisions in international business.

ESTLÉ SA IS ONE OF THE LARGEST GLOBAL FIRMS. THE SWISS GIANT has operations spanning the globe; it employs almost 200,000 people outside of Switzerland and operates 423 factories world-wide. It is the world market leader in confections, instant coffee, frozen foods, condensed milk, and infant food. The firm's 1993 annual sales exceeded $36 billion. ▮▮ But Nestlé isn't resting on its laurels. Indeed, its CEO, Helmut Maucher, recently announced a goal of doubling the firm's annual sales to $72 billion over a ten-year period. And this sales increase is projected to come purely from existing operations; it doesn't include any future acquisitions the firm may make. ▮▮ How does Nestlé intend to achieve such dramatic growth?

Nestlé: The Swiss Giant[1]

Maucher has outlined several strate-gies for boosting the company's sales. First, he is seeking ways to extend products across different markets. In the past, Nestlé's general approach was to develop, produce, and market clearly defined product lines within a spe-cific market such as the United States or Western Europe. If a particular product happened to sell well in multiple markets, that was fine, but the firm did not emphasize this sort of market expansion. ▮▮ Now, however, managers are encour-aged to identify products that will sell in multiple markets and then to expand aggressively into each of those markets. For example, after Nestlé bought the British candymaker Rowntree Mackintosh PLC, managers began to expand its product sales more aggressively to the Continental market. As a result, exports from the United Kingdom to the Continent of such products as After Eight din-ner mints and Smarties candies have increased by 60 percent in only two years. ▮▮ The firm is also paying more attention to its pricing policies. Its goal used to be ensuring that its prices were comparable to its competitors'. Now, however, managers think that they must lower prices to gain market share and thus enhance future revenues. For example, a bloody price war with ConAgra in the frozen dinner and entree market has brought Nestlé's Lean Cuisine and Stouffer brands from the number three spot to a near tie for number one. Nestlé has also been engaged in a tough price war in the coffee market, with P&G's Folgers pro-viding the strongest competition. ▮▮ Nestlé also is concentrating more on adver-tising. Until recently, it paid little attention to global exploitation of the value of its brand names. The same or similar products might be sold in different markets under different names, with little or no connection to the Nestlé corporate name. Now the firm is ensuring that, whenever possible, it uses the same name when it extends products into new markets, thereby allowing its products to develop a stronger and clearer global identity. In the United States, for example, products previously sold only under the Carnation label now are more likely to bear both the original label and the Nestlé name. ▮▮ Maucher also is looking for ways to improve distribution. Getting products from factories to retailers is a major challenge for any firm, but it is even more complicated for MNCs. Improved distribution efficiency can boost revenues (by getting more products to more places more quickly), while simultaneously cutting the costs involved in having many intermediaries. In the United States, for example, Nestlé has cut the number of its distribution centers from 20 to 8, with each carrying full product lines and having larger and more productive receiving and shipping capabilities. ▮▮ Finally, Nestlé has also gone into direct selling in some markets. For example, many stores in Indonesia and Malaysia are not air-conditioned, so candymakers often have to provide air-cooled display cases to keep their products from melting. Because Nestlé had to provide such cases to individual stores anyway, it found that it was also easy to sell and ship its products directly to those outlets. ▮▮▮▮▮

Nestlé managers are aggressively seeking to launch new products more effectively, find new markets for existing products, price their products more competitively, advertise and promote their products to wider audiences, and distribute their products more efficiently. Indeed, Nestlé is expanding and growing worldwide by concentrating on one of the most important functions for any consumer products firm—marketing. People sometimes equate marketing with advertising, but, as we will see, advertising is actually only one part of a firm's overall marketing strategy.

Marketing is the process of planning and executing the conception, pricing, promotion, and distribution of ideas, goods, and services to create exchanges that satisfy individual and organizational objectives. **International marketing** is the extension of these activities across national boundaries. Firms expanding into new markets in foreign countries must deal with differing political, cultural, and legal systems, as well as unfamiliar economic conditions, advertising media, and distribution channels. For example, an international firm accustomed to promoting its products on television will have to alter its approach when entering a less developed market in which relatively few people have televisions. Advertising regulations also vary by country. In the United States, for example, firms may not advertise cigarettes or hard liquor on television. But many other countries have no such restrictions; firms such as RJR Nabisco and Seagram adjust their advertising and promotional tactics to take advantage of those less restrictive regulatory environments.

In addition to dealing with national differences, international marketing managers have two tasks their domestic counterparts do not face: capturing synergies among various national markets and coordinating marketing activities in those markets. Synergies are important because they provide opportunities for additional revenues and for growth and cross-fertilization. Coordination is important because it can help lower marketing costs and create a unified marketing effort.

International Marketing Management

An international firm's marketing activities are often organized as a separate and self-contained function within the firm. Yet that function both affects and is affected by virtually every other organizational activity, as shown in Fig. 16.1, and so must be integrated and coordinated with all those activities.[2] For this reason we open Part IV, which deals with the specific functional areas of international business operations, with marketing.

If an international firm's marketing managers intend to promote a particular product on the basis of its high quality, the production and operations managers must be prepared to ensure that quality is indeed high. And if the firm's controller plans to slash operating budgets across the board, its marketing managers must be prepared to deal with fewer resources in carrying out their tasks. Thus international marketing management encompasses a firm's efforts to ensure that its international marketing activities comply with the firm's corporate strategy, business strategy, and other functional strategies. A primary task facing international marketing managers is to operationalize the firm's international strategy by selecting appropriate markets to enter and then developing an appropriate approach for competing in those markets.[3]

International Marketing and Business Strategies

A key challenge for a firm's marketing managers is to adopt an international marketing strategy that supports the firm's overall business strategy.[4] As discussed in Chapter 10, business strategy can take one of three forms:

1 Differentiation

2 Cost leadership

3 Focus

A business strategy of differentiation requires marketing managers to develop products and pricing, promotional, and distribution tactics that differentiate the

FIGURE 16.1

International Marketing as an Integrated Functional Area

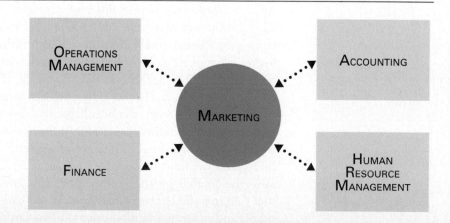

firm's products or services from its competitors' in the eyes of customers. Differentiation can be based on perceived quality, fashion, reliability, or other salient characteristics, as the marketing managers of such products as Rolex watches, BMW automobiles, and Montblanc pens have successfully shown. Assuming that the differentiation can be adequately communicated to customers, the firm will be able to charge higher prices for its product or insulate itself from price competition from lesser brands. For example, Rolex, which follows a successful differentiation strategy, does not need to cut the price for its diamond-encrusted $15,000 watches whenever Kmart features Timex quartz watches for $39.95.

Alternatively, a firm may adopt an international business strategy that stresses its overall cost leadership. Cost leadership can be pursued and achieved through systematic reductions in production and manufacturing costs, reductions in sales costs, the acceptance of lower profit margins, the use of less expensive materials and component parts, or other means. Marketing managers for a firm adopting this strategy will concentrate their promotional efforts on advertising the low prices of the product and will utilize channels of distribution that allow the firm to keep the retail price low—for example, by selling through discounters rather than through fashionable boutiques. Texas Instruments calculators, Hyundai automobiles, and Bic pens are all marketed using a cost leadership strategy. And Timex's cost leadership approach has allowed it to dominate much of the large market for low-price watches.

A firm also may adopt a focus strategy. In this case, marketing managers will concentrate their efforts on particular segments of the consumer market or on particular areas or regions within a market. International marketing managers will therefore need to concentrate on getting the appropriate message regarding the firm's products or services to the various selected target markets. For example, many U.S. cigarette makers focus their marketing efforts on young people in other countries; they advertise and promote their products at high schools, video arcades, and other places where young people congregate.[5] Similarly, the Swiss watchmaker Ste. Suisse Microelectronique et d'Horlogerie SA (SMH), which manufacturers the popular Swatch watches, focuses its marketing efforts on selling this inexpensive line of watches to young, fashion-oriented consumers in Europe, North America, and Asia.

A critical element for a firm's success is the congruency of its international marketing efforts with its overall business strategy. Timex, Rolex, and SMH—all watchmakers—have chosen different strategies, yet all are successful internationally because they match their international marketing efforts with their business strategies. Timex's cost leadership strategy implies that the firm must seek out low-cost suppliers globally and sell its watches in discount stores such as Wal-Mart and Woolworth rather than in fashionable department stores such as Saks Fifth Avenue and Harrod's. Rolex's differentiation strategy, based on its carefully nurtured worldwide image, might collapse if it distributed its watches through armies of street corner vendors stationed in front of subway stations throughout the world instead of through a handful of very expensive and very chic horologists located on the most fashionable avenues of large cities. Similarly, SMH does not advertise Swatch watches to the upper-class, middle-aged audiences of *Town and Country* and *Architectural Digest* in the United States while simultaneously marketing to young, fashion-oriented Parisian readers of *Elle*. It does advertise its wares in both the U.S. and French editions of *Elle*, which are read by demographically similar young, trendy female audiences—the target of its focus strategy.

Having adopted an overall international business strategy, firms must assess where they want to do business. Decisions about whether to enter a particular foreign market are derived from and must be consistent with the firm's overall business strategy. For example, the rapid growth in the past decade of the Indonesian economy, which is large (184 million people) but low-income (1992 per capita income of $670), offers exciting new business opportunities for Timex, but not necessarily for Rolex.

Chapter 10 discussed the techniques used by international managers to analyze the potential of foreign markets. Because of budget and resource limitations, international firms must carefully assess countries and rank them according to which will offer the greatest potential markets for their products. Influencing this process may be factors such as culture, levels of competition, channels of distribution, and availability of infrastructure. Depending on the nature of the product and other circumstances, a firm may choose to enter simultaneously all markets that meet certain acceptability criteria. For example, consumer goods marketers like Nike and Coca-Cola often introduce new products broadly throughout North America or Europe in order to maximize the impact of their mass media advertising campaigns. Or, a firm may choose to enter markets one by one, in an order based on their potential to the firm. Caterpillar, for example, uses this approach, since its marketing strategy is based on the painstaking development of strong local dealerships, not glitzy TV campaigns highlighting the endorsements of the latest music and sports stars.

The Marketing Mix

After an international firm has decided to enter a particular foreign market, further marketing decisions must be made.[6] In particular, international marketing managers must address four issues:

1 How to develop the firm's product(s)

2 How to price those products

3 How to sell those products

4 How to distribute those products to the firm's customers

These elements are collectively known as the **marketing mix** and colloquially referred to as the *four P's of marketing*: product, pricing, promotion, and place (or distribution). The marketing mix reflects the firm's decisions regarding how it will actually market its goods. The role of the four P's in international marketing is illustrated in Fig. 16.2.

International marketing mix issues and decisions parallel those of domestic marketing in most ways, although they are more complex. The array of variables international marketing managers must consider is far broader, and the interrelationships among those variables far more intricate, than is the case for domestic marketing managers. Before we discuss these complexities, we need to focus on another important issue in international marketing—the extent to which an international firm should standardize its marketing mix in all the countries it enters.

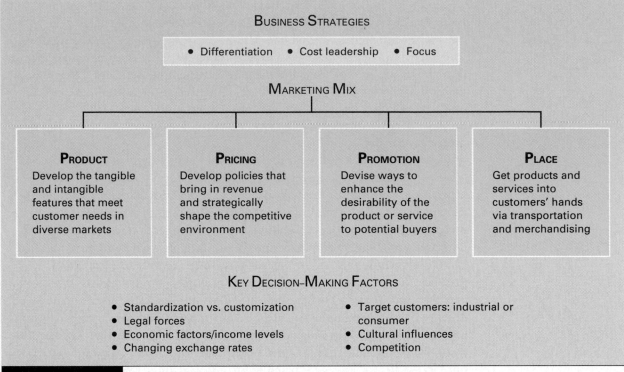

FIGURE 16.2

The Elements of the Marketing Mix for International Firms

Standardization versus Customization

A firm's marketers must decide which of the following approaches to take:

▶ Should the firm adopt an *ethnocentric approach*, that is, simply market its goods internationally the same way it does domestically?

▶ Should it adopt a *polycentric approach*, that is, customize the marketing mix to meet the specific needs of each foreign market it services?

▶ Should it adopt a *geocentric approach*, that is, analyze the needs of customers worldwide and then adopt a standardized marketing mix for all the markets it serves?[7]

The **ethnocentric approach** is relatively easy to adopt. The firm simply markets its goods in international markets using the same marketing mix it uses domestically, thereby avoiding the expense of developing new marketing techniques to serve foreign customers. This approach may not be desirable, however, if as a result the firm loses sales because it failed to take into the account the needs of customers abroad. Because of this significant shortcoming, few successful international firms adopt this approach.

The **polycentric approach** is far more costly because the international marketers attempt to customize the firm's marketing mix in each market it enters in order to meet the idiosyncratic needs of customers in that market. However, while more expensive, customization may increase the firm's revenues if its marketers successfully match its marketing mix with the needs of local customers. Often, international firms that view themselves as multidomestic adopt this approach.

The **geocentric approach** calls for standardization of the marketing mix, thereby allowing the firm to provide essentially the same product or service in different markets and to use essentially the same marketing approach to sell that product or service globally. Coca-Cola was one of the first international businesses to adopt this approach. It sells its popular soft drink worldwide and uses essentially the same packaging, product, and advertising themes everywhere. Indeed, the contoured shape of a Coca-Cola bottle is one of the world's most recognized images. The firm has even gone so far as to add the contour shape to its plastic bottles.[8] Standardization became a popular buzzword in the 1980s, as proponents such as Kenichi Ohmae (then managing director of McKinsey & Company's Tokyo office) argued that customers in the Triad are becoming increasingly so much alike, with similar incomes, educational achievements, lifestyles, and aspirations, that expensive customization of the marketing mix by country is less necessary.[9] Similarly, Harvard Business School marketing guru Theodore Levitt believes that standardization of the firm's products and other elements of its marketing mix creates huge economies of scale in production, distribution, and promotion. By transforming these cost savings into reduced world prices, Levitt argues, a firm that adopts standardization can easily outperform its international competitors.[10]

The tradeoffs between standardization and customization are clear. Standardization allows a firm to achieve manufacturing, distribution, and promotional efficiencies and to maintain simpler and more streamlined operations. Customization allows a firm to gain specific advantages within given markets that it might not otherwise be able to achieve.[11] In practice, most firms avoid the extremes of either approach.[12] Many successful firms have adopted a strategy of "think globally, act locally" in order to gain the economies of scale of a global marketing mix while retaining the ability to meet the needs of customers in differing national markets.

The home appliance market provides a useful example of this strategy. U.S. kitchens tend to be large and spacious, and consumers prefer large stoves, refrigerators, and washing machines. But the smaller kitchens of Europe and Japan dictate the use of much smaller appliances. Further, within Europe there are marked differences in power supply characteristics and in consumer preferences for various design features and alternatives. Thus appliance manufacturers must develop specific and unique product lines for each country in which they do business. Whirlpool has tried to reduce some of the costs of customization by designing its products to meet the needs of market niches that cross national boundaries. For example, Whirlpool designers have developed a "World Washer"—a small, stripped-down automatic washing machine targeted to meet the needs of the emerging middle classes in such countries as Brazil, Mexico, and India. But Whirlpool stands ready to customize even the World Washer when needed. For example, the agitators of World Washers sold in India have been modified to ensure that the machines won't shred or tangle the delicate saris traditionally worn by Indian women.[13]

The degree of standardization or customization a firm adopts depends on many factors, including product type, the cultural differences between the home country and the host countries, and the host countries' legal systems. The firm may adopt one approach for one element of the marketing mix and another for a second element. Often firms standardize product designs to capture manufacturing economies of scale but customize advertisements and the channels of distribution to meet specific local market needs. The degree of standardization may also be influenced by the firm's perception of the global marketplace—which is similar to the conundrum "Is the glass half full or half empty?" A firm tilting toward standardization assumes that consumers around the world are basically similar but then adjusts for differences among them. A firm tilting toward customization assumes that consumers are different but then adjusts for similarities among them.

In deciding where to locate on the standardization/customization spectrum, an international firm also must consider organizational structure and organizational control implications. Standardization implies that power and control must be centralized at the firm's headquarters, while customization suggests that headquarters must delegate considerable decision-making power to local managers. Thus a strongly centralized firm (see Chapter 13) can more easily standardize its international marketing mix than can a decentralized one. Often international firms address these organizational issues by adopting a two-step process:

1 The decision to standardize some elements of the marketing mix, such as product design, brand name, packaging, and product positioning, is made centrally.

2 Then local managers are called on to critique the global marketing program and to develop plans to implement customized elements of the marketing mix, such as promotion and distribution.[14]

Table 16.1 summarizes some factors that may lead a firm to adopt standardization or customization for all or part of its international marketing efforts.

TABLE 16.1

Standardization versus Customization of the International Marketing Approach

FACTORS FAVORING STANDARDIZATION	FACTORS FAVORING CUSTOMIZATION
Allows efficiency in R&D	Reflects varying conditions of product use
Results in economies of scale in production	Allows for local differences in laws or regulations
Promotes lower marketing costs	Takes account of differences in buyers' behavior patterns
Allows centralized control of marketing program	Promotes local initiative and motivation when implementing marketing program
Reflects the trend toward a single world market	Allows for closer adherence to needs of individual markets

Source: Adapted from Michael R. Czinkota, Iikka Ronkainen, and Michael Moffat, *International Business*, 3rd ed. (Fort Worth, Tex.: Dryden, 1994), p. 456.

Product Policy

The first P of the international marketing mix is the product itself. Here, **product** comprises both the set of tangible factors (the physical product and its packaging) that the consumer can see or touch and numerous intangible factors (such as image, installation, warranties, and credit terms). Critical to a firm's ability to compete internationally is its success in developing products with tangible and intangible features that meet the wants and needs of customers in diverse national markets.[15] For example, Toyota's success in selling its automobiles in Europe, Asia, and the Americas reflects its product-related achievements in designing and producing mechanically reliable vehicles, offering competitive warranties, building a solid brand name for its products, providing spare parts and repair manuals, and furnishing financing to its dealers and retail customers.

Standardized Products or Customized Products?

A key product policy decision facing international marketers is the extent to which their firm's products should be standardized across markets or customized within individual markets. For example, Toyota, like many international firms, has adopted a blend of customization and standardization. It has standardized its corporate commitment to build high-quality, mechanically reliable automobiles and to maintain the prestige of the Toyota brand name. But it customizes its products and product mix to meet the needs of local markets. For example, it sells right-hand-drive motor vehicles in Japan, Australia, and the United Kingdom and left-hand-drive vehicles in the Americas and continental Europe. It also adjusts its warranties from country to country based on those offered by its competitors. The name under which it sells a product also may vary by country. For example, the automobile sold as a Lexus Sports Coupe in the United States is sold as a Toyota Soarer in Japan. Toyota will even adjust the products it sells in order to meet local market conditions. For example, its initial entry into the U.S. minivan market suffered from poor handling and a lack of power and therefore failed to make a dent in Chrysler's dominance of this growing market. The firm corrected these problems in its Previa van, which it rushed to the U.S. market in 1990. However, because Chrysler's sales in Asian markets were limited and of little threat Toyota continued to sell its original van model for several years in those markets.

Sometimes firms discover they have customized their products not by design but by accident. For example, in the late 1980s Unilever discovered to its horror that for no apparent reason it was using 85 different recipes for its chicken soups and 15 different shapes for cones for its Cornetto ice creams in Europe. Once the problem was detected, Unilever quickly standardized its ice cream cone design and slashed the number of chicken soup flavors it offered European customers, thereby reducing its production and inventory costs and simplifying its distribution requirements.[16]

The extent to which products should be customized to meet local needs varies according to several factors. One is the nature of the product's target customers—those people, groups, and/or organizations that are likely to purchase the good or service in question. Two broad groups of target customers exist: industrial users and consumers.

Industrial products are goods and services sold primarily for use by organizations. Examples include machinery (used by manufacturers), heavy equipment (construction firms), accounting services (firms without their own accounting systems), and bulk food (hospitals, schools, and the military). Generally speaking, industrial products are more likely to be standardized. For example, Caterpillar's bulldozers and front-end loaders are sold throughout the world without substantial modification. Products sold as commodities are also typically standardized across different markets; for example, agricultural products, petroleum, 1MB computer memory chips, and chemicals. On the other hand, heterogeneous, differentiated goods—which are set apart by their reputation (see Chapter 3)—are often customized to meet local preferences.[17]

Consumer products are goods and services sold for use by individual consumers. Examples include foodstuffs, personal electronics products, clothing, hair care services, and luggage. Consumer products are more likely to be customized to meet local market preferences. For example, McDonald's tailors its menus to local markets—selling pork sandwiches and beer in its German restaurants, wine in its French restaurants, and fish and rice in its Japanese restaurants. Even Coca-Cola modifies the sweetness and flavoring of its soft drinks to meet consumer preferences in different markets.

Legal Forces

The laws and regulations of host countries may also affect the product policies adopted by international firms. For example, countries often impose detailed labeling requirements and health standards on consumer products that firms, both foreign and domestic, must follow strictly. Often international firms must adjust the packaging and even the products themselves to meet these consumer protection regulations. For example, Grupo Modelo SA, the brewer of Corona beer, had to move product content listings from the back of the Corona bottle to the front in order to comply with German law. It also had to reduce the nitrosamine levels of the beer it sells in Germany, Austria, and Switzerland in order to meet those countries' health standards.[18] Countries also may regulate the design of consumer products in order to simplify purchase and replacement decisions. For example, Saudi Arabia requires electrical connecting cords on consumer appliances to be two meters long. GE suffered the embarrassment (and a loss of profits) of having its goods turned back at a Saudi port when an inspector determined its connecting cords were only two yards long.[19] A country's legal requirements also may substantially affect the way a firm can do business. For example, the central bank of Singapore sought to control consumer spending in 1991 by imposing regulations specifying the minimum annual income needed to qualify for a credit card and capping the allowable credit limit on credit cards at two months' salary. These regulations hinder the ability of foreign firms such as American Express and Visa International to market their financial services to Singaporeans.[20]

Countries impose widely varying technical standards on such products as electrical appliances and broadcasting and telecommunications equipment in order to facilitate compatibility and reduce interference. Such standards provide strong incentives for firms to customize their products, while also hindering mass production of a standard product. For example, the electrical plugs of home appliances sold in Europe must be modified on a country-by-country basis to fit the array of electrical outlets found there. Similarly, AT&T's initial attempts in the 1980s to sell telecommunications equipment internationally failed because it insisted on selling equipment adhering to U.S. standards. Since it adjusted its equipment to meet the technical standards of various foreign countries, AT&T has become a major player in the telecommunications network equipment market, particularly in the booming Asian region.[21]

Hayes Microcomputer Products, the standard-setting manufacturer of modems for personal computers, has developed a unique approach to meeting local technical needs while capturing the benefits of standardization. Hayes engineers analyzed the electrical and telecommunications standards of 30 countries, and then designed the firm's new modems so that they could meet any of these diverse national standards through the addition or elimination of specific components. Through this approach, Hayes has accelerated the rate at which it can introduce new products globally.[22]

Cultural Influences

International firms often must adapt their products to meet the cultural needs of local markets. One typical adaptation is to change the labeling on the product's package into the primary language of the host country. However, in some cases, a foreign language may be used to connote quality or fashion. For example, P&G adds German words to the labels of detergents sold in the Czech Republic. Market researchers had determined that products in packages labeled in English or German are viewed by Czechs as being of higher quality than those whose packages are labeled in Czech.[23] Also, the ingredients of food products are often modified to better please local palates. For example, when Domino's Pizza entered the Japanese market in 1986, it assumed Japanese pizza lovers, like their U.S. counterparts, would favor pepperoni pizzas. Its success in the $2.8 billion Japanese pizza market was slow in coming until it broadened its choice of toppings to include some Japanese favorites: squid, tuna, spinach, corn, and grilled chicken. These toppings are readily available in the local market, so Domino's was able to inexpensively customize its product to meet local tastes.[24] Similarly, Heinz adds more spices and less sweeteners to its ketchup in Europe than in the United States.[25] And Big Boy made several changes to its marketing approach in Saudi Arabia in response to the religious dictates of Saudi custom and law. Its restaurants there serve no pork (turkey is used instead of ham in Big Boy's "Slim Jim" sandwich); male waiters are substituted for waitresses; and separate seating areas are provided for men, for families, and for children and women.[26]

Culture may affect product policy in other ways. For example, Japanese consumers are extremely quality-conscious. Bausch & Lomb initially failed in its attempt to sell hard contact lenses produced to U.S. standards in the Japanese market because Japanese ophthalmologists demanded a higher level of perfection in the lenses' optical surfaces than did their U.S. counterparts. The firm developed new technologies to meet the demands of the Japanese market and now enjoys an 11 percent market share there. Many German consumers are very environmentally conscious. As a result, firms often must redesign products they sell in Germany to allow for easier disposal and recycling. In another example, Mattel allowed its Japanese subsidiary to make Barbie dolls more Japanese in appearance. This move boosted the annual sales of Barbie dolls in Japan by 2 million units.[27]

GOING GLOBAL

International Marketing Ethics

Ethics comprise a person's beliefs about what is right or wrong, good or bad, acceptable or unacceptable behavior. Every manager must consider the ethical implications of his or her actions. But managers involved in international marketing face an additional set of ethical dilemmas. Since what constitutes ethical behavior varies from one country to another, these managers must assess the ethics not only of their home country but also of the host country when they adopt a course of action.

For example, Nestlé has been criticized for its aggressive marketing of infant formula in less developed countries. Critics argue that the firm convinces mothers to buy the relatively expensive formula when they really do not have the money. Moreover, there have been reports that infants do not receive proper nourishment from the formula because mothers add too much water to the mix in order to make it last longer or prepare it improperly because they do not understand the directions. Nestlé, on the other hand, argues that consumers are free to choose how they spend their money.

More controversial products have an even more complex ethical context. For example, in the United States advertising for products such as tobacco, alcohol, and guns is heavily regulated. But regulations vary considerably among other countries, and firms that produce these goods may be tempted to take a more aggressive advertising approach in markets where they have more freedom. They argue that it is appropriate for them to work to increase their profits in each market as long as they follow all local laws and customs. (A case at the end of this book looks more closely at tobacco companies' marketing in host markets.)

Source: Michael A. Mayo, Lawrence J. Marks, and John K. Ryans, Jr., "Perceptions of Ethical Problems in International Marketing," *International Marketing Review*, Vol. 8, No. 3 (1991), pp. 61–75.

Still another cultural influence, regarding the ethics of international marketing, is discussed in "Going Global."

Economic Factors

Economic factors also may induce an international firm to customize its products to meet local market needs. A country's level of economic development may affect the desired attributes of a product. Consumers in richer countries often favor products loaded with extra performance features; more price-sensitive consumers in poorer countries typically opt for stripped-down versions of the same products. Sometimes a firm may have to adjust package size or design to meet local conditions. For example, firms selling toothpastes or shampoos in poorer countries often package their goods in single-use sizes in order to make the products more affordable to local citizens. The quality of a country's infrastructure also may affect the customization decision. For example, manufacturers may reinforce the suspension systems of motor vehicles sold in countries where road maintenance is poor. The availability and cost of repair services can affect product design. For example, most automobiles sold in North America use electronic fuel injectors rather than carburetors. In poorer countries, the reverse is true, primarily because of maintenance considerations. Maintaining fuel injectors requires sophisticated electronic test equipment backed up by highly trained technicians; any mechanic can tune up a carburetor.

Brand Names

One element international firms often like to standardize is the brand name of a product. A firm that does this can reduce its packaging, design, and advertising production costs. It also can capture spillovers of its advertising messages from one market to the next. For example, Avon's entry into the China market was made easier because millions of consumers had seen its products advertised on Hong Kong television.[28] Mars, Inc., sought to capture the benefits of standardization by dropping its successful local brand names for the Marathon bar in the British market and the Raider chocolate biscuit on the Continent in favor of the more universally known Snickers and Twix brands.[29] However, sometimes legal or cultural factors force a firm to alter the brand names under which it sells its products. For example, Grupo Modelo SA markets Corona beer in Spain as Coronita because a Spanish vineyard owns the Corona brand name.[30] And Coca-Cola calls its low-calorie soft drink Diet Coke in weight-conscious North America but Coca-Cola Light in other markets.

Pricing Issues and Decisions

The second P of the international marketing mix is pricing. Developing effective prices and pricing policies is a critical determinant of any firm's success.[31] Pricing policies directly affect the size of the revenues earned by the firm. But they also serve as an important strategic weapon by allowing the firm to shape the competitive environment in which it does business. For example, Toys 'R' Us has achieved enormous success in Germany, Japan, the United States, and other countries by selling low-priced toys in low-cost warehouse-like settings. Its low prices have placed enormous pressure on its competitors to slash their costs, alter their distribution systems, and shrink their profit margins. The firm's aggressive pricing strategy has effectively forced its competitors to fight the battle for Asian, European, and American consumers on terms dictated by Toys 'R' Us.

Both domestic and international firms must strive to develop pricing strategies that will produce profitable operations. But the task facing an international firm is more complex than that facing a purely domestic firm. To begin with, a firm's costs of doing business vary widely by country. Differences in transportation charges and tariffs cause the landed price of goods to vary by country. Differences in distribution practices also affect the final price the end customer pays. For example, intense competition among distributors in the United States minimizes the margin between retail prices and manufacturers' prices. In contrast, Japan's inefficient multilayered distribution system, which relies on a chain of distributors to distribute goods, often inflates the prices Japanese consumers pay for goods. Exchange-rate fluctuations can also create pricing problems. If an exporter's home currency rises in value, the exporter must choose between maintaining its prices in the home currency (which makes its goods more expensive in the importing country) and maintaining its prices in the host country (which cuts its profit margins by lowering the amount of home-country currency it receives for each unit sold).

International firms must consider these factors in developing their pricing policies for each national market they serve. They must decide whether they want to apply consistent prices across all those markets or customize prices to meet the needs of each. In reaching this decision, they must remember that competition, culture, distribution channels, income levels, legal requirements, and exchange-rate stability may vary widely by country.

Pricing Policies

International firms generally adopt one of three pricing policies:[32]

1 Standard price policy
2 Two-tiered pricing
3 Market pricing

An international firm following a geocentric approach to international marketing will adopt a **standard price policy**, whereby it charges the same price for its products and services regardless of where they are sold. Firms that adopt this policy are generally of two types:

1 A firm whose products or services are highly visible and allow price comparisons to be readily made. Boeing, for example, sells commercial aircraft for approximately the same price to airlines worldwide, regardless of whether the customer is United Airlines, Japan Airlines, Lufthansa, or some other airline. Relatively few planes are sold each year, and most major sales are reported in the business press. If Boeing charged vastly different prices for its aircraft, some of its favored customers might begin to resell the planes to less favored ones—an easy task, given the mobility of Boeing's product. Thus the nationality of the customer is of little importance in the firm's pricing decisions.

2 A firm that sells commodity goods in competitive markets. For example, producers of crude oil, such as Aramco, Kuwait Oil, and Pemex, sell their products to any and all customers at prices determined by supply and demand in the world crude oil market. Other commodities produced and traded worldwide, such as coal and agricultural goods, are also sold at competitive prices (with suitable adjustments for quality differentials and transportation costs) with little regard to the purchaser's nationality.

An international firm that follows an ethnocentric marketing approach will use a **two-tiered pricing policy**, whereby it sets one price for all its domestic sales and a second price for all its international sales. A firm that adopts a two-tiered pricing policy commonly allocates to domestic sales all accounting charges associated with R&D, administrative overhead, capital depreciation, and so on. The firm can then establish a uniform foreign sales price without having to worry about covering these costs. Indeed, the only costs that need to be covered by the foreign sales price are the marginal costs associated with foreign sales, such as the product's unit manufacturing costs, shipping costs, tariffs, and direct sales costs.

Two-tiered pricing is often used by domestic firms that are just beginning to internationalize. In the short run, charging foreign customers a price that covers only marginal costs may be an appropriate approach for such firms. But the strong ethnocentric bias of two-tiered pricing suggests it is not a suitable long-run pricing strategy. A firm that views foreign customers as marginal to its business—rather than as integral to it—will never develop the international skills, expertise, and outlook necessary to compete successfully in the international marketplace.

Firms that adopt a two-tiered pricing policy are also vulnerable to charges of dumping. Recall from Chapter 6 that dumping is the selling of a firm's products in a foreign market for a price lower than that charged in its domestic market—an outcome that can easily result from a two-tiered pricing system. Most OECD countries have issued regulations intended to protect domestic firms from dumping by foreign competitors. For example, in 1993 Toyota and Mazda were charged with dumping minivans in the U.S. market. Although the Japanese automakers were not penalized in this case, both subsequently raised their minivan prices in order to avoid future dumping complaints.

An international firm that follows a polycentric approach to international marketing will use a **market pricing policy**. Market pricing is the most complex of the three pricing policies and the one most commonly adopted. A firm utilizing market pricing customizes its prices on a market-by-market basis to maximize its profits in each market. Because of the importance and the complexity of this approach, we discuss it in more detail next.

Market Pricing

As you may remember from your microeconomics class, the profit-maximizing output (the quantity the firm must produce to maximize its profit) occurs at the intersection of the firm's marginal revenue curve and its marginal cost curve. The profit-maximizing price is found by reading across from the point on the firm's demand curve where the profit-maximizing output occurs. In Fig. 16.3(a), the intersection of the marginal revenue curve (*MR*) and the marginal cost curve (*MC*) occurs at *Q*, which is the profit-maximizing output. If you read straight up from *Q* until you reach the demand curve (*D*), then move left to the y-axis, you find the profit-maximizing price, *P*, the maximum price at which quantity *Q* of the good can be sold.

With market pricing, the firm calculates and charges the profit-maximizing price in each market it serves. Figure 16.3(b) shows two markets in which a firm has identical demand and marginal revenue curves but faces different marginal cost curves. The firm faces higher marginal costs (MC_1) in country 1 than in country 2 (MC_2). Accordingly, its profit-maximizing price in country 1 (P_1) must be higher than that in country 2 (P_2).

Two conditions must be met if a firm is to successfully practice market pricing:

1 The firm must face different demand and/or cost conditions in the countries in which it sells its products. This condition is usually met, since taxes, tariffs, standards of living, levels of competition, infrastructure costs and availability, and numerous other factors vary by country.

2 The firm must be able to prevent arbitrage, a concept discussed in Chapter 5. The firm's market pricing policy will unravel if customers are able to buy the firm's products in a low-price country and resell them profitably in a high-price country. Because of tariffs, transportation costs, and other transaction costs, arbitrage is usually not a problem if country-to-country price variations are small. But if prices vary widely by country, arbitrage can upset the firm's market pricing strategy.

a. Finding the profit-maximizing price

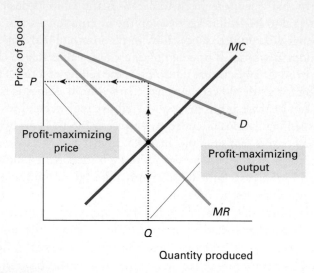

b. Finding the profit-maximizing price
   for two markets

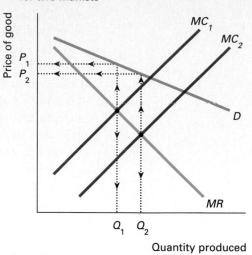

<table>
<tr><td>FIGURE 16.3</td></tr>
</table>

Determining the Profit-Maximizing Price

Assuming these conditions are met, the advantages of this polycentric approach are obvious. For example, the firm can set higher prices where markets will tolerate them and lower prices where necessary in order to remain competitive. It also can directly allocate relevant local costs against local sales within each foreign market, thereby allowing corporate strategists and planners to better allocate the firm's resources across markets. But such flexibility comes with a cost. To capture the benefits of market pricing, local managers must closely monitor sales and competitive conditions within their markets so that appropriate and timely adjustments can be made. Also, the corporate staff must be willing to delegate authority to local managers to allow them to adjust prices within their markets.

Firms most likely to use this approach are those that both produce and market their products in many different countries. For example, Samsung uses market pricing for its line of consumer electronics products. It operates production facilities in almost two dozen countries and sells its products in close to a hundred markets. Samsung has found that market pricing actually makes it easier to export and market its products within such a complex context.[33]

A market pricing policy can, however, expose a firm to dumping complaints (as discussed earlier) as well as to two other risks:

I Damage to its brand name

2 Development of a gray market for its products

The firm needs to ensure that the prices it charges in one market do not damage the brand image it has carefully nurtured in others. For example, suppose Seagram encouraged its North American and European brand managers to market Johnny Walker Red as a premium scotch whiskey sold at a premium price but allowed its Japanese brand managers to peddle it as a nonprestigious brand sold at rock-bottom prices. Because of its marketing approach in Japan, Seagram would risk deterioration of Johnny Walker Red's premium brand image in North America and Europe. Thus any international firm that sells brand-name products and adopts market pricing should review the prices charged by local managers to ensure that the integrity of its brand names and its market images are maintained across all of its markets.

A firm that follows a market pricing policy also risks the development of gray markets for its products as a result of arbitrage. A **gray market** is a market that results when products are imported into a country legally but outside the normal channels of distribution authorized by the manufacturer. A gray market may develop when the price in one market is sufficiently lower than the price the firm charges in another that entrepreneurs can buy the good in the lower-price market and resell it in the higher-price market. Thus the firm that has large price differences among markets is vulnerable to having these differentials undercut by gray markets. Gray markets frequently arise when firms fail to adjust local prices after major fluctuations in exchange rates. Coca-Cola, for example, faced such a problem in 1994 after the yen strengthened relative to the U.S. dollar. Japanese discounters were able to purchase and import Coke made in the United States for 27 percent less than the price of Coke made in Japan, thereby disrupting the firm's pricing strategy in both countries.[34]

Products commonly influenced by gray markets include big-ticket items such as automobiles, cameras, computers, ski equipment, and watches. Gray markets are also more prevalent in free-market economies, where fewer government regulations make it easier for them to emerge. One recent estimate suggests that sales in gray markets in the United States exceed $10 billion each year.[35] Many MNCs have attempted to eliminate or control gray markets through legal action, but few have had much success.

Gray market sales undermine a firm's market pricing policy and often lower its profits. They also cause friction between the firm and its distributors, which lose sales but are often stuck with the costs of either providing customer support and honoring product guarantees on gray market goods or explaining to unhappy customers why they will not do so. For example, Charles of the Ritz reports that over 10,000 retailers sell its Opium perfume, although the firm has authorized only 1,300 to do so. The prices its authorized dealers charge are continually being undercut by those offered by gray market sellers, thereby making it difficult for the authorized dealers to adhere to the firm's suggested pricing schedule. Charles of the Ritz has sought to smooth over the resulting friction by helping its authorized dealers to compete with the gray marketers through additional advertising allowances and special price reductions. This practice, however, harms the firm's profit margins. Similarly, annual sales of "gray" Mercedes-Benz automobiles in the United States are estimated to exceed 25,000 units. But the so-called dealers that import and sell these cars in the gray market usually have no service facilities. The buyers become angry when they cannot get their cars serviced, and Mercedes-Benz usually has to make special arrangements to provide them with service.[36]

Promotion Issues and Decisions

The third P of the international marketing mix is promotion. **Promotion** encompasses all efforts by an international firm to enhance the desirability of its products among potential buyers. While many promotional activities are specifically targeted at buyers, successful firms recognize that they must also communicate with their distributors and the general public to ensure favorable sentiment toward themselves and their products. Because promotion involves communication with audiences in the host country, it is the most culture-bound of the four P's. Thus a firm must take special care to ensure that the message host-country audiences receive is in fact the message the firm intended to send. International marketing managers must therefore effectively blend and utilize the four elements of the **promotion mix**—advertising, personal selling, sales promotion, and public relations—to motivate potential customers to buy their firm's products.

Advertising

The first element of the promotion mix is advertising. For most international firms, especially those selling consumer products and services, advertising is the most important element in the promotion mix. As a firm develops its advertising strategy, it must consider three factors:

1 The message it wants to convey
2 The media available for conveying the message
3 The extent to which the firm wants to globalize its advertising effort

International firms planning advertising campaigns must be attuned to how consumers in different countries will use their products. For example, in the United States, Honda markets its motorcycles as sports and recreation equipment, because that is how they are most often used. But in other countries, motorcycles are a basic form of transportation, and Honda must use a different advertising message there.

At the same time, the firm must take into account relevant cultural, linguistic, and legal constraints found in various national markets.

Message. The message of an advertisement refers to the facts or impressions the advertiser wants to convey to potential customers. An automaker may want to convey a message of value (low price), reliability (quality), and/or style (image and prestige). The choice of message is an important reflection of how the firm sees its own products and services and how it wants them to be seen by customers. Coca-Cola, for example, believes that its products help consumers enjoy life, and its advertising messages consistently stress this theme worldwide. Products that are used for different purposes in different areas will need to be marketed differently. For example, in the United States motorcycles are seen primarily as recreational products, but in many other countries they are seen mainly as a means of transportation. Thus Honda and Kawasaki's ads in the United States stress the fun and cachet of riding. In poorer countries, they stress the reliability and functionalism of motorcycles as a mode of inexpensive transportation.[37]

The country of origin of a product often serves as an important part of the advertising message.[38] For example, among fashion-conscious teenagers and young adults in Europe and Japan, U.S. goods are often viewed as being very trendy. Thus Levi Strauss, KFC, and the National Basketball Association, among others, highlight the U.S. origins of their products. Japanese products, on the other hand, are often perceived to be of high quality, so international marketers stress the Japanese origin of such products as Toyota automobiles and Sony electronics goods. In an interesting twist, when Ford recently introduced its so-called world car—called the Ford Contour in the United States and the Ford Mondeo in foreign markets—it emphasized the automobile's global heritage in its advertising campaign. Its goal is to represent the automobile as the best the world has to offer.

> Automobile manufacturers once took a domestic approach to marketing their products. For example, "Made in America" was a popular refrain. But when Ford introduced its new Contour, it took a different approach—marketing the automobile as a "world car." The premise is that the car is created using the best available resources and sold throughout the world with relatively little modification.

Medium. The **medium** is the communication channel used by the advertiser to convey a message. A firm's international marketing manager must alter the media used to convey its message from market to market based on availability, legal restrictions, standards of living, literacy rates, the cultural homogeneity of the national market, and other factors. In bilingual or multilingual countries such as Belgium, Switzerland, and Canada, international firms must adjust their mix of media outlets in order to reach each of the country's cultural groups. For example, Swissair communicates to its French-speaking Swiss audience by advertising in French-language newspapers, and to its German-speaking Swiss audience via ads in German-language newspapers.

A country's level of economic development may also affect the media firms use. For example, in many less developed countries, television ownership may be limited and literacy rates low. This eliminates television, newspapers, and magazines as useful media but raises the importance of radio advertising.

Price may also come into play. Advertising rates are extremely high on Japanese television and on U.S. network television; thus these media are effectively eliminated for many smaller firms. In the Russian Federation, however, TV advertising rates are very low, as little as $3000 for a 30-second ad on the national nightly news.[39] Since levels of television viewing are high in the Russian market, many Western firms have found television to be not only inexpensive but also extremely effective as a medium for advertising their products in that market.

Legal restrictions may also prompt the use of certain media. Most national governments limit the number of TV stations as well as the amount of broadcast time sold to advertisers. Countries often outlaw the use of certain media for the advertising of products that may be harmful to their societies. For example, South Korea, Malaysia, Hong Kong, China, and Singapore ban cigarette advertising on television. South Korea has extended this ban to magazines read primarily by women and by persons under the age of 20; Hong Kong to radio; China to radio, newspapers, and magazines; and Singapore to all other media.[40] As in the United States, however, this ban has prompted tobacco firms to sponsor athletic events and to purchase display ads at stadiums that will be picked up by TV cameras.[41] Legal restrictions on the advertising of alcoholic products also are common throughout the world.

To help deal with issues related to message and media, many international firms use multinational advertising agencies, which have branch offices or affiliates in various national markets. As listed in Table 16.2, the world's largest advertising agencies are the WPP Group, the Interpublic Group, and Saatchi & Saatchi—all headquartered in the United Kingdom or the United States.[42] International firms sometimes use local advertising agencies, too. Of course, a firm that wants to use a local advertising agency is advised to select a reputable, qualified one. Advertising has become so popular in Russia, for example, that there are as many as 800 agencies in Moscow alone. Many of them, however, are low-rent operations staffed by

TABLE 16.2

The World's 25 Largest Advertising Agencies

RANK	ORGANIZATION	LOCATION OF HEADQUARTERS	1991 SALES (MILLIONS OF $)
1	WPP Group	United Kingdom	2,662
2	Interpublic Group of Cos.	United States	1,799
3	Saatchi & Saatchi Co.	United States/ United Kingdom	1,706
4	Omnicom Group	United States	1,471
5	Dentsu	Japan	1,451
6	Young & Rubicam	United States	1,057
7	Euro RSCG	France	1,016
8	Grey Advertising	United States	659
9	Hakuhodo	Japan	656
10	Foote, Cone & Belding Communications	United States	616
11	Leo Burnett Co.	United States	577
12	D'Arcy Masius Benton & Bowles	United States	535
13	Publicis-FCB Communications	France	513
14	BDDP Worldwide	France	277
15	Bozell, Jacobs, Kenyon & Eckhardt	United States	221
16	Tokyu Agency	Japan	177
17	Daiko Advertising	Japan	174
18	N W Ayer	United States	171
19	Asatsu	Japan	166
20	Dai-Ichi Kikaku Co.	Japan	160
21	TBWA Advertising	United States	145
22	Chiat/Day/Mojo	United States	141
23	Dentsu, Young & Rubicam Partnerships	United States	129
24	Ketchum Communications	United States	127
25	Lopex	United Kingdom	124

Source: Excerpted with permission from *Hoover's Handbook of World Business 1993*, p. 85. Data from *Advertising Age*, April 13, 1992

people with little skill in professional advertising. Firms that use them are likely to be overcharged and/or represented by poor-quality advertising campaigns.[43]

Global versus Local Advertising. A firm must also decide whether advertising for its product or service can be the same everywhere or must be tailored to each local market it serves.[44] Some products, such as Coca-Cola soft drinks, Bic pens, Levi jeans, and McDonald's hamburgers, have almost universal appeal. These firms use the same basic message everywhere, perhaps with a bit of localization and language translation. For example, during the 1992 Winter Olympics, Coca-Cola used the same sing-a-long TV commercials in 12 languages in 131 countries to tout its involvement with national Olympic teams. The firm also uses an ethnically diverse cast in its TV commercials and tries to avoid tying sets to easily identifiable locales. To promote Chivas Regal, Seagram similarly developed a global billboard campaign that emphasized the scotch's snob appeal.[45]

Often firms adopt a global campaign but make subtle adaptations to meet the needs of local markets. For example, Unilever has applied a strategy of "think globally, act locally" to its advertising campaign for Dove soap. Its TV commercials are identical in each market, but the actors are not. On the same stage and set, U.S., Italian, German, French, and Australian models are filmed in succession, each stating in her own language, "Dove has one-quarter cleansing cream."[46] Nestlé used one theme in promoting Kit Kat candy to its European customers— "Have a break, have a Kit Kat"—but changed the backgrounds to better appeal to customers across national markets.

Other firms have opted for a regionalization strategy. IBM, for example, began advertising its PCs in European markets by creating a pan-European advertising campaign. Instead of customizing its ads by country, IBM featured the same text and visual images in all its European ads, altering only the language used for its broadcast and print ads. IBM determined that this approach saved $22–30 million in creative and production expenses (out of a total advertising budget of $150 million). However, maintaining uniformity of the product's image was of paramount concern. The campaign was designed specifically to ensure that IBM's European clients, regardless of the country in which they were located, received the same message regarding its product.[47] Similarly, Levi Strauss used the same TV ad to sell its 501 jeans in six European markets. Since each of its commercials costs about $500,000 to shoot, Levi Strauss would have spent about $3 million on six ads and thus saved $2.5 million in production costs alone by adopting this regional strategy.[48]

Of course, many firms find it useful to use both standard and localized approaches to advertising. Unilever, for example, generally follows a standardized advertising strategy. Thus it developed a national advertising campaign to promote its products in China, calling for the same basic message using the same basic media throughout the country. But Unilever found that clear differences exist within different regions of the country regarding perceptions of soap. Thus it developed 50 specialized commercials for its Lux soap for use in separate markets within China.[49]

Whether to choose a standardized or a specialized advertising campaign also is a function of the message the firm wants to convey. Standardized advertisements tend to contain less concrete information than do more specialized advertisements. Ads for products such as candy and soft drinks often can be standardized because the ads stress the warm, emotional aspects of consuming the good, while ads for products like credit cards, automobiles, and airline services tend to be customized to meet the needs of local consumers.[50]

Personal Selling

The second element of the promotion mix is **personal selling**—making sales on the basis of personal contacts. The use of sales representatives, who call on potential customers and attempt to sell a firm's products or services to them, is the most common approach to personal selling.[51] Because of the close contact between the salesperson and the potential customer, sellers are likely to rely on host-country nationals to serve as their representatives. For a firm just starting international operations, personal selling is often subcontracted to local sales organizations that usually handle product lines from several firms. As the firm grows and develops a sales base in new markets, however, it is likely to establish its own sales force. Colgate-Palmolive, for example, made very effective use of personal selling to gain market share in Central Europe. The firm opened a sales office in Warsaw in 1991 and used it to develop a well-trained professional sales staff. That staff has made Colgate-Palmolive the consumer products market leader in Poland.[52]

The importance of personal selling as an element of the promotion mix differs for industrial products and for consumer products. For industrial products (such as complex machinery, electronic equipment, and customized computer software), customers often need technical information about product characteristics, usage, maintenance requirements, and availability of after-sales support. Well-trained sales representatives are often better able to convey information about the intricacies of such products to customers than are print or broadcast media. For consumer products, personal selling is normally confined to selling to wholesalers and to retail chains. Most consumer products firms find that advertising, particularly in print and broadcast media, is a more efficient means of communicating with consumers than is personal selling. However, personal selling can be used to market some goods, usually in the form of door-to-door selling. Avon and Amway, for example, have successfully exported to the Asian and European markets the personal selling techniques they developed in the United States. But these consumer products firms use personal selling not because of the high level of technical expertise required of the sales representative, but because personal selling provides convenience to the buyer and motivation to the salesperson.

Personal selling has several advantages for an international firm:

▶ Firms that hire local sales representatives can be reasonably confident that those individuals understand the local culture, norms, and customs. For example, a native of India selling products in that country will be better informed about local conditions than will someone sent from Spain to sell products in India.

▶ Personal selling promotes close, personal contact with customers. Customers see real people and come to associate that personal contact with the firm.

▶ Personal selling makes it easier for the firm to obtain valuable market information. Knowledgeable local sales representatives are an excellent source of information that can be used to develop new products and/or improve existing ones for the local market.

On the other hand, personal selling is a relatively high-cost strategy. Each sales representative must be adequately compensated, but each may also reach relatively few customers. An industrial products sales representative, for example, may need a full day or more to see just one potential customer. And after a sale is closed, the sales representative may still find it necessary to spend large blocks of time with the customer explaining how things work and trying to generate new business. Most larger international firms also find it necessary to establish regional sale offices staffed by sales managers and other support personnel, which add still more sales-related costs.

Sales Promotion

The third element of the promotion mix is sales promotion. **Sales promotion** comprises specialized marketing efforts such as coupons, in-store promotions, sampling, direct mail campaigns, cooperative advertising, and trade fair attendance. Sales promotion activities focused on wholesalers and retailers are designed to increase the number and commitment of these intermediaries working with the firm. Many international firms, for example, participate in international trade shows such as the Paris Air Show or the Tokyo Auto Mart in order to generate interest among existing and potential distributors for their products. Participation in international trade shows is often recommended as a first step for firms wanting to internationalize their sales. The U.S. Department of Commerce will often help U.S. small firms participate in overseas trade shows as part of its export promotion efforts. Firms may also develop cooperative advertising campaigns or provide advertising allowances to encourage retailers to promote their products.

Sales promotion activities may be narrowly targeted to consumers and/or offered for only a short time before being dropped or replaced with more permanent efforts. This flexible nature of sales promotions makes them ideal for a marketing campaign tailored to fit local customs and circumstances. For example, British American Tobacco, Rothmans, Philip Morris, and RJR/Nabisco compete in the Taiwanese market by handing out free cigarettes, a practice not utilized in the U.S. market. Also, Philip Morris and RJR/Nabisco built market share by offering Korean consumers free cigarette lighters and desk diaries emblazoned with the firms' logos in return for cigarette purchases.[53] U.S. airlines have effectively used direct mail to lure international travelers away from foreign airlines. By carefully analyzing the travel habits of members of their frequent flyer programs, carriers like American and Continental can target their mailings (and customize the incentives, such as the awarding of bonus frequent flyer miles) to those customers who are most likely to respond to such lures.

Like all international marketing activities, sales promotion efforts must be carefully tailored to the societal context. In Poland, for example, consumers distrust firms that offer free samples because they assume that products that are being given away must not be very good. But in other countries, such as Japan and the United States, free samples are commonly distributed and widely accepted. Note that sales promotions that are not carefully planned can sometimes do more harm than good, as the following "Going Global" illustrates.

Public Relations

The fourth element of the promotion mix is public relations. **Public relations** consists of efforts aimed at enhancing a firm's reputation and image with the general public, as opposed to touting the specific advantages of an individual product or service. The consequence of effective public relations is a general belief that the firm is a good "corporate citizen," that it is reputable, and that it can be trusted.

GOING GLOBAL

Sales Promotions Can Be Too Successful

International firms must ensure that sales promotion efforts have their intended effect. Two of the most well-publicized international marketing disasters in the 1990s involved sales promotion efforts that went awry. In 1992, executives at Hoover Europe, a subsidiary of the Maytag Corporation, decided on a way to boost the firm's British vacuum and home appliance sales. They offered any consumer who bought at least £100 of the firm's home appliances two free round-trip flights to Europe or the United States. Expecting a low consumer response, they had assumed they could buy discount tickets at off-peak times to meet their obligations. To their horror, more than 220,000 consumers took them up on the offer, requiring far more tickets than were available at deep discount. Many customers bought Hoover vacuums and washing machines solely for the airline tickets; they dumped their unused appliances on the second-hand market, further disrupting Hoover's sales efforts. Needless to say, the sales promotion was a financial disaster. It cost Hoover's U.S. parent over $72 million and made the firm a national laughingstock. Three of Hoover Europe's top executives were sacked as a result.

PepsiCo's distributor in the Philippines created a disaster of similar magnitude in a 1992 sales promotion effort. It offered any consumer purchasing a Pepsi with the number 349 on the underside of the bottle cap a prize of a million pesos (about $36,000). A mistake at the bottle cap manufacturer, however, resulted in the generation of 500,000 winning bottle caps. The distributor's financial exposure totaled $18 billion, and it offered the disgruntled winners $19 each, an offer many refused. The firm was hit with 5600 lawsuits, arrest orders were issued for ten of its executives, and its brand name was severely damaged. The fallout did not stop there. The firm also became the target of anti-Pepsi rallies and suffered from sabotage of its plants and trucks and at least one grenade attack.

Sources: "Hoover buyers clean up on air fare," *Houston Chronicle*, April 21, 1994, p. 8D; Maytag Corporation, *1993* Annual Report, p. 20; Gary Mead, "A blunder on a corporate scale," *Financial Times*, May 6, 1993; "PepsiCo Is Facing Mounting Problems in the Philippines," *Wall Street Journal*, July 28, 1993, p. B10; "It sucks," *The Economist*, April 3, 1993, p. 66.

Ineffective public relations can often lead to a public perception that the firm cannot be trusted or that it cares little for the community.

Savvy international firms recognize that money spent on public relations is money well spent because it earns them political allies and makes it easier to communicate their needs to the general public. They also recognize that as "foreigners," they often are appealing political targets; thus they attempt to reduce their exposure to political attacks. Toyota provides a case in point. Japanese firms, unlike their U.S. counterparts, do not have a tradition of corporate philanthropy. Recall from Chapter 8 that Toyota received large financial incentives from the state of Kentucky to build a plant in Georgetown. During the first few years it operated that plant, Toyota received a fair amount of criticism for its lack of community concern. The firm eventually realized that it had to adapt its corporate attitudes to local customs if it wanted to maintain the good will of local politicians. Toyota subsequently became a model corporate citizen, providing grants to local charities, funding college scholarships to graduating high school students, and sponsoring local youth sports teams.

The impact of maintaining good public relations is hard to quantify, but over time an international firm's positive image and reputation are likely to benefit it in a host country. Consumers are more likely to resist "buy local" pitches when the foreign firm is also perceived to be a good guy. Good public relations can also help the firm when it has to negotiate with a host-country government for a zoning permit or an operating license or when it encounters a crisis or unfavorable publicity. For example, Toshiba found itself in deep trouble in 1986 when a Toshiba subsidiary was discovered to have been illegally selling to the Soviet Union advanced technology designed to make the detection of nuclear submarines harder. Normally, few citizens would be aware of the importance of such a breach of security. Unfortunately for Toshiba, one of the best-selling novels of the 1980s, Tom Clancy's *The Hunt for Red October*, had educated U.S. readers about the technological nature of submarine warfare. Fortunately for Toshiba, the firm had been a good corporate citizen in the United States. Relying on the good will it had previously fostered with local government officials, community leaders, and its workforce, it was able to avoid trade sanctions that would have jeopardized its stature in the United States. But this example offers a clear lesson: an international firm cannot rely on good will to bail it out of a crisis if it has no good will with important stakeholders to begin with.

Distribution Issues and Decisions

The fourth P of the international marketing mix is place—more commonly referred to as distribution. **Distribution** is getting products and services from the firm into the hands of customers. (As we discuss in Chapter 17, distribution is one component of international logistics management.) An international firm faces two important sets of distribution issues:

1 Addressing the problems of physically transporting its goods and services from where they are created to the various markets in which they are to be sold

2 Selecting the means by which it will merchandise its goods in the markets it wants to serve

International Distribution

The most obvious issue an international firm's distribution managers must address is the selection of mode(s) of transportation for shipping its goods from their point of origin to their destination. (Modes of transportation were discussed in Chapter 11.) This choice seemingly entails a simple tradeoff between time and money. Faster modes of transportation, such as air freight and motor carrier, are more expensive than slower modes, such as ocean shipping, railroad, pipeline, and barge. However, the transportation mode selected affects the firm's inventory costs and customer service levels, as well as the product's useful shelf life, exposure to damage, and packaging requirements. International air freight, for example, scores high on each of these dimensions, while ocean shipping ranks very low.

Consider the impact of transportation mode on the firm's inventory expenses and the level of customer service. If the firm relies on slower modes of transportation instead of faster ones, it can maintain a given level of inventory at the point of sale only by maintaining higher levels of inventory in transit. If it selects unreliable modes that make it difficult to predict when shipments will actually arrive, it will have to increase buffer stocks in its inventory in order to avoid stock-outs that will lead to disappointed customers. Choosing slower modes of transportation also increases the firm's **international order cycle time**—the time between the placement of an order and its receipt by the customer—for any given level of inventories. Longer order cycle times lower the firm's customer service levels and may induce its customers to seek alternative supply sources.

The product's shelf life affects the selection of transportation mode. Goods that are highly perishable because of physical or cultural forces—such as cut flowers or fashionable dresses—are typically shipped by air freight because of their short shelf life. Less perishable products, such as coal, crude oil, or men's socks, are shipped using less expensive modes. In some cases the transportation mode may affect the product's packaging requirements. For example, goods sent on long ocean voyages may need special packaging to protect them from humidity infiltration and damage due to rough seas; the firm could avoid the extra costs of such packaging if it chose a faster mode such as air freight. Of course, a simple solution is sometimes available: when Calpis, a Colorado-based agricultural goods processor, entered the Japanese orange juice market, it switched its packaging from glass bottles to cans in order to reduce breakage.[54]

Channels of Distribution

An international firm's marketing managers must also determine which distribution channels to use to merchandise the firm's products in each national market it serves. Figure 16.4 shows the basic channel options used by most international manufacturing firms. Note that a distribution channel can consist of as many as four basic parts:

1 The manufacturer that creates the product or service

2 A wholesaler that buys products and services from the manufacturer and then resells them to retailers

---

FIGURE 16.4

Distribution Channel Options

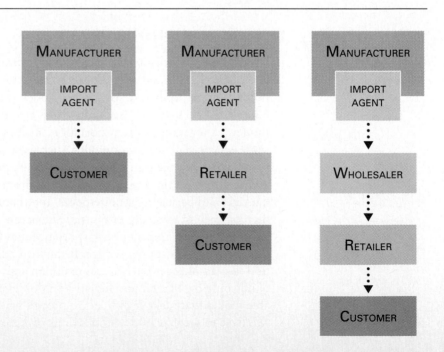

3 The retailer, which buys from wholesalers and then sells to customers

4 The actual customer, who buys the product or service for final consumption.

Import agents (discussed in Chapter 11) may also be used as intermediaries, especially by smaller firms.

One important factor illustrated by Fig. 16.4 is channel length. **Channel length** is the number of stages in the distribution channel. A firm that sells directly to its customers, which then pay the business directly, bypasses wholesalers and retailers and therefore has a very short distribution channel. This approach is called **direct sales** because the firm is dealing directly with its final consumer. Dell Computer started out as a direct sales business, taking customer orders over toll-free, 24-hour telephone lines. The advantage of this approach is that the firm maintains control over retail distribution of its products and retains any retailing profits it earns. Unfortunately, the firm also bears the costs and risks of retailing its products.

A slightly longer channel of distribution involves selling to retailers, which then market and sell the products to customers. This is easiest to do when retailers in a given market are heavily concentrated. When there are relatively few large retailers, selling directly to each is easier for manufacturers; when a larger number of smaller retailers are present, selling to each is more complex. For example, huge supermarkets with vast selections of foods and toiletries exist throughout the United States. But in Europe, many consumers still buy food from small neighborhood stores, and few of these carry toiletries. A consumer products firm, therefore, will have to use very different approaches to distributing its products in the two markets. For example, in the United States, P&G may sell directly to Kroger or Safeway, which will routinely stock several hundred tubes of toothpaste of various sizes on its shelves and store cartons of inventory in its warehouse. But a European retailer may have retail space for only a few tubes and little storage space for backup inventory, thereby making it more difficult for P&G to sell directly to such outlets.

The longest distribution channel involves the use of wholesalers. Wholesalers are separate businesses that buy from manufacturers and then resale to retailers or, in some cases, to other wholesalers. For example, small farmers cannot easily sell their produce to large grocery chains because those chains find it inefficient to deal with large numbers of small suppliers. Instead, farmers sell their produce to wholesalers, which then sell it to grocery stores; thus the grocery stores must deal with only a few large suppliers. Similarly, in markets with little retail concentration, a consumer products firm like P&G generally finds it easier to sell to a few wholesalers rather than attempt to deal with a huge number of small retailers. The use of wholesalers makes it easier to market in countries with little retail concentration and also allows the firm to maintain a smaller sales staff. On the other hand, profit margins tend to be smaller because there are more businesses involved, each of which expects to make a profit. Rather than keeping all the profits for itself, as in the case of direct sales, a firm must share them with wholesalers and retailers.

The challenge for international marketing managers is to find the optimal distribution channel to match the firm's unique competitive strengths and weaknesses with the requirements of each national market it serves. In practice, as with other elements of international marketing, most international firms develop a flexible distribution strategy—they may use a short channel in some markets and a longer channel in others.

The firm's distribution strategy may also be an important component of its promotion strategy. For example, SMH manufactures not only relatively inexpensive Swatch watches but also high-priced watches such as Omega and Tissot. It distributes its expensive watches through exclusive jewelry stores and its Swatch watches through department stores like Macy's and Dillard's.[55] Toyota adopted different distribution strategies for its luxury cars in the United States and Japan. In the United States it named the model Lexus and set up an independent dealership network to strengthen the prestige of that brand name. But in Japan, where the firm had less need to bolster its image, the same model is sold under the Toyota name through existing Toyota dealerships.

As noted in Chapter 11, some international firms, particularly producers of more specialized products, may hire a sales or import agent to distribute their goods. For example, the National Football League contracted with Japan Marketing Services to promote NFL-licensed goods in Japan. Annual Japanese sales of T-shirts, sweatshirts, and other clothing bearing the names of U.S. football teams exceed $50 million.[56] Many governments, as part of their efforts to stimulate exports, have developed programs to help firms locate suitable international import agents. For example, the U.S. and Foreign Commercial Service, a branch of the Department of Commerce, provides lists of foreign firms that have expressed a willingness to distribute given products in their market areas. These data can be obtained by contacting local offices of the U.S. and Foreign Commercial Service or through the CD-ROM–based National Trade Data Bank (see "Building Global Skills," Chapter 2).

Firms should exercise caution when selecting a foreign distributor. The distributor *is* the firm as far as local customers are concerned, so a poor distributor jeopardizes the firm's reputation and performance in that market, often for a very long time. Further, local laws may make it difficult for a firm to terminate the distributor. In Saudi Arabia, for example, a foreign firm must hire a local national to represent it and firing that agent is virtually impossible without his consent. In any case, firing a distributor can cause confusion among the firm's customers. For example, in January 1992 Nissan ended a 21-year distribution arrangement with a British entrepreneur operating under the name Nissan UK. Nissan then faced the nightmarish task of contacting over 400,000 purchasers of its automobiles to explain that they should thereafter deal with Nissan Motors (GB), not Nissan UK. It also had to deal with a possible short-term price war as Nissan UK liquidated its inventory of more than 20,000 Nissan autos, which were in its dealers' showrooms when the distribution agreement expired.[57]

Some international firms attempt to transfer to international markets the distribution systems developed in their home countries. McDonald's, for example, gained its status as the leading food service company in the United States by taking great care in selecting its franchisees and by nurturing their enterprises to the mutual benefit of both the franchisees and McDonald's. The firm has followed a similar distribution strategy to capture fast-food dollars in Europe, Asia, and Central and South America. And Avon has been a smash hit in the Chinese market by pioneering the use there of door-to-door selling for cosmetics, a distribution strategy identical to that used in Avon's home market. Similarly, as shown in Map 16.1, Coca-Cola utilizes a network of subsidiaries and bottlers (in some of

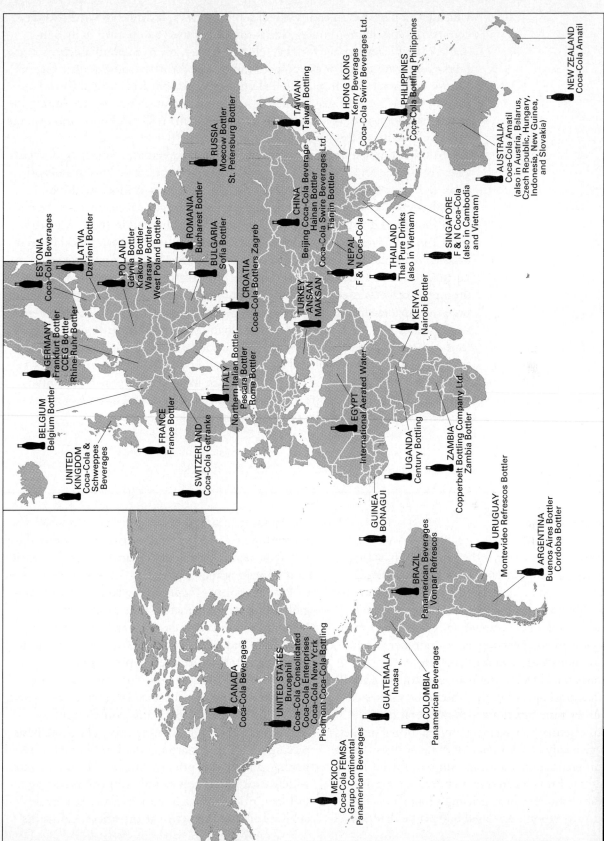

Coca-Cola's Global Distribution Network

Source: Based on *The Coca-Cola Company Annual Report 1993*, pp. 24–25.

MAP 16.1

which Coca-Cola has an equity stake) to market its soft drinks in virtually every country—a distribution strategy identical to that used by the firm in its home market. This extensive network has allowed Coca-Cola to respond quickly to new market opportunities. For example, to exploit the formerly communistic Central European markets, the firm has relied on its regional bottlers to help. Coca-Cola Amatil, which bottles Coke in Austria, was given responsibility for developing the Hungarian, Czech, and Slovak markets, while the firm's Greek bottler took charge of its Bulgarian and Romanian distribution.[58]

At other times, a firm may adapt its distribution practices to match local customs. In Russia, for example, many goods are sold at streetside kiosks; so Pepsi-Cola and Coca-Cola are sold at hundreds of these stands in Moscow alone.[59] Local laws also affect distribution strategies. For example, for many years the ability of foreigners to establish distribution systems was limited in India, Mexico, and China. As a result, most MNCs established joint ventures with local firms in order to distribute their products in those countries. Also, the complexities of Japan's culture and the complicated nature of its distribution networks have prompted many Western firms to seek joint venture partners to help them penetrate the Japanese market. KFC, for example, teamed up with Mitsubishi to create a joint venture to market its products in Japan. Mitsubishi contributed chicken (one of its subsidiaries is a major chicken producer), distribution networks, and an understanding of the cultural nuances of dealing with Japanese consumers. KFC contributed its brand name, an American image that appealed to fashion-conscious Japanese, and its technology and trade secrets—including, of course, the secret spices that make its product so finger-lickin' good.

CHAPTER REVIEW

Summary

International marketing is the process of planning and executing the conception, pricing, promotion, and distribution of ideas, goods, and services across national boundaries to create exchanges that satisfy individual and organizational objectives. Thus international marketing encompasses a number of areas and functions within an organization.

International marketing management is a critical organizational operation that should be integrated with other basic functions such as operations and human resource management. International marketing is generally based on one of three business strategies: differentiation, cost leadership, or focus. Determining the firm's marketing mix involves making decisions about product, pricing, promotion, and place (distribution). A related basic issue that market-

ing managers must address is the extent to which the marketing mix will be standardized or customized for different markets. A variety of factors must be considered in making their decision.

Product policy focuses on the tangible and intangible factors that characterize the product itself. Standardization versus customization is again a consideration. Industrial products and consumer products usually require different types of product policies. Legal, cultural, and economic forces also affect product policy and must be carefully evaluated.

Pricing issues and decisions constitute the second element of the marketing mix. The three basic pricing philosophies are standard pricing, two-tiered pricing, and market pricing. Market pricing, the most widely used and complex policy, involves setting different prices for each market. Basic economic analyses are used to arrive at the prices. Concerns related to gray markets and dumping must be addressed by firms that use this approach. Otherwise, serious problems may result.

Promotion issues and decisions generally concern the use of advertising and other forms of promotion. The promotion mix is a blend of advertising, personal selling, sales promotion, and public relations. Each of these elements is usually carefully tailored for the market in which it will be used and implemented accordingly.

Finally, international marketing managers must also plan for distribution—getting products and services from the firm to customers. International distribution may involve a variety of transportation modes, each with its own unique set of advantages and disadvantages. A firm must also develop appropriate distribution channels, which may involve wholesalers and retailers in addition to the firm and its customers. Effective distribution can have a significant impact on a firm's profitability.

Review Questions

1. What is international marketing?

2. What is the marketing mix?

3. What are the basic factors involved in deciding whether to use standardization or customization?

4. How do legal, cultural, and economic factors influence product policy?

5. Why are brand names an important marketing tool for international business?

6. What are the three basic pricing policies?

7. What are two problems that a firm using market pricing might encounter?

8. What are the four elements of the international promotion mix?

9. What are some of the fundamental issues that must be addressed in international advertising?

10. What is a distribution channel? What options does an international firm have in developing its channels?

Questions for Discussion

1. What are the similarities and differences between domestic and international marketing?

2. Are the four P's of international marketing of equal importance to all firms? What factors might cause some to be more or less important than others?

3. Identify several products you think could be marketed in a variety of foreign markets with little customization. Identify other products that would clearly require customization.

4. How do legal, cultural, and economic factors in the United States affect product policy for foreign firms?

5. What are the pros and cons of trying to use a single brand name in different markets, as opposed to creating unique brand names for various markets?

6. What are the advantages and disadvantages of each pricing policy? Why do most international firms use market pricing?

7. What steps could a firm wanting to use market pricing take to minimize gray market activity and avoid charges of dumping?

8. What are some basic differences you might expect to see in TV ads broadcast in France, Japan, Saudi Arabia, and the United States?

9. Why is the public relations function important to an international firm?

10. What are the advantages and disadvantages of short versus long channels of distribution?

BUILDING GLOBAL SKILLS

Ajax Alarms is a medium-sized U.S. firm that sells alarm clocks. It licenses the production of its clocks to a Korean electronics firm, which handles complete production based on Ajax designs and specifications and then ships the clocks directly to the Ajax warehouse in Kansas. Ajax markets and distributes the clocks throughout the United States and Canada. The clocks themselves are brightly colored novelty items. For example, one of the firm's biggest sellers is a plastic rooster that crows in the morning. Last year Ajax reported profits of around $5 million on total revenues of slightly more than $50 million.

Ajax managers have determined that the firm has few growth opportunities in the United States and so must sell its products internationally if it is to continue to expand. They have decided to start by selling in Mexico. They have hired you, an internationally famous marketing consultant, to advise them.

Your assignment here is to briefly outline a marketing plan for Ajax. (Your instructor may ask you to do this exercise as an outside-of-class assignment, either alone or in a group.) Essentially, Ajax wants you to consider product policy, pricing, promotion, and distribution issues. In developing your marketing plan, be sure to consider the factors discussed in this chapter, including standardization versus customization, legal forces, cultural influences, economic factors, and brand name questions. Note specific areas where you can make recommendations to your client. For example, if you believe that a certain advertising medium will be beneficial to Ajax, make that recommendation (be sure to provide some rationale or justification). If you feel you lack sufficient information to make a recommendation in some area, identify the factors that must be addressed by Ajax in that particular area. For example, if you cannot recommend a pricing policy, describe the information Ajax needs to acquire and evaluate when making that decision.

CLOSING CASE

Levi Strauss: Clothing the World[60]

Many people think of Levi Strauss as a quintessentially American firm that enjoys the same sort of international stature as Coca-Cola and McDonald's—an icon of the American way of life. And, like those other two famous firms, Levi Strauss is a major international firm with operations worldwide.

Levi Strauss was founded in 1847 in San Francisco by a Bavarian immigrant of the same name. Strauss got his start by using extra-strength canvas to make sturdy clothing for gold miners. He later changed to denim for his pants and oversaw his firm as it became one of the world's largest clothing manufacturers. In the 1950s Levi Strauss jeans became the standard uniform for young people—and they still are. Today the firm is controlled by Strauss's descendants, the Haas family.

In the early 1980s, Levi Strauss managers realized that they needed to concentrate more on foreign markets if the firm was to continue to grow. Clothing sales in the United States were leveling off, and competition was increasing. Because Levi's jeans were already known globally, a bountiful international market awaited the firm. Today Levi Strauss has 15 foreign plants and earns 38 percent of its revenues abroad.

The firm has pursued an interesting marketing strategy in its foreign markets. It quickly found that its basic advertising strategy could be applied everywhere. Thus ads emphasizing the comfort and fit of Levi's jeans can be found on televisions and in magazines around the world. These ads also clearly portray jeans to be as American as apple pie—even when they are made in Hungary or Malaysia.

The firm has taken a different approach with respect to price, however. In the United States, Levi

Strauss has allowed a wide variety of retailers to sell its jeans, including discounters; thus competition has kept prices low. But in many foreign markets, customers were used to paying high prices for black market Levi's jeans. Also, the firm was signing up retailers for the first time—and so could be more selective. As a result, in most foreign countries Levi's jeans cost about twice what U.S. customers pay.

Levi Strauss also developed a new approach to distribution as part of its international expansion. Specifically, the firm has launched its own chain of retail stores called Levi's Only Stores. Approximately 600 of these stores dot the landscape of Western Europe and account for about 25 percent of the firm's European sales. Levi Strauss is testing the same concept in the United States and Japan, with six test stores currently open in each of these markets.

One headache for the firm has been the flood of counterfeit products, especially in Central and Eastern Europe. The higher prices the firm charges there have put many of its products out of reach of the average consumer. For example, in the Czech Republic a pair of 501 red-tab jeans retails for $63— nearly a third of the average Czech's monthly salary.

But a pair of relatively high-quality counterfeit Levi's—smuggled in from Asia, Turkey, or Poland— can be had for as little as $12. Nevertheless, Levi Strauss continues its international expansion in its quest to clothe the world.

Case Questions

1. What are the basic elements of Levi Strauss's marketing mix for its international operations?

2. Would you expect the marketing of Levi's jeans to be standardized or customized?

3. What legal, cultural, and economic factors are likely to affect Levi Strauss's product policy?

4. What are the firm's pricing policies?

5. What promotional methods are likely to work best for Levi Strauss in foreign markets?

6. What risks does Levi Strauss run by opening its own stores in the United States?

CHAPTER NOTES

1. Carla Rapoport, "Nestlé's Brand Building Machine," *Fortune*, September 19, 1994, pp. 147–156; "Nestlé: A Giant in a Hurry," *Business Week*, March 22, 1993, pp. 50–54; Gary Hoover, Alta Campbell, Alan Chai, and Patrick J. Spain (eds.), *Hoover's Handbook of World Business 1993* (Austin, Tex.: Reference Press, 1993), p. 342.

2. Adrian Slywotzky and Benson Shapiro, "Leveraging to Beat the Odds: The New Marketing Mind-Set," *Harvard Business Review* (September-October 1993), pp. 97–107.

3. Sandra M. Huszagh, Fredrick W. Huszagh, and Gwen F. Hanks, "Macroeconomic Conditions and International Marketing Management," *International Marketing Review*, Vol. 9, No. 1 (1992), pp. 6–18.

4. David Lei, "Strategies for Global Competition," *Long Range Planning*, Vol. 22, No. 1 (1989), pp. 102–109. See also Yoram Wind and Susan Douglas, "International Portfolio Analysis and Strategy: The Challenge of the 1980s," *Journal of International Business Studies* (Fall 1981), pp. 69–82.

5. "America's New Merchants of Death," *Reader's Digest* (April 1993), pp. 50–57.

6. Nicholas Papadopoulos and Louise A. Heslop (eds.), *Product-Country Images—Impact and Role in International Marketing* (New York: International Business Press, 1993).

7. For an overview, see David McCutcheon, Amitabh Raturi, and Jack Meredith, "The Customization-Responsiveness Squeeze," *Sloan Management Review* (Winter 1994), pp. 89–100.

8. "Behemoth on a Tear," *Business Week*, October 3, 1994, pp. 54–55.

9. Kenichi Ohmae, "The Triad World View," *Journal of Business Strategy*, Vol. 7, No. 4 (Spring 1987), pp. 8–19.

10. Theodore Levitt, "The Globalization of Markets," *Harvard Business Review* (May-June 1983), pp. 92–102.

11. Aysegul Ozsomer, Muzzafer Bodur, and S. Tamer Cavusgil, "Marketing Standardisation by Multinationals in an

Emerging Market," *European Journal of Marketing*, Vol. 25, No. 12 (1991), pp. 50–63.

12. John A. Quelch and Edward J. Hoff, "Customizing Global Marketing," *Harvard Business Review* (May-June 1986), pp. 59–68.

13. "The Right Way to Go Global: An Interview with Whirlpool CEO David Whitwam," *Harvard Business Review* (March-April 1994), pp. 134–145; "A Little Washing Machine That Won't Shred a Sari," *Business Week*, June 3, 1991, p. 100.

14. Quelch and Hoff, op. cit.

15. Judie Lannon, "Developing Brand Strategies Across Borders," *Marketing and Research Today* (August 1991), pp. 160–167.

16. Guy de Jonquieres, "Just One Cornetto," *Financial Times*, October 28, 1991.

17. Frank Cespedes, "Industrial Marketing: Managing New Requirements," *Sloan Management Review* (Spring 1994), pp. 61–70.

18. "Mexico's Corona Brew Wins Back Cachet Lost During the Late '80s," *Wall Street Journal*, January 19, 1993, p. B6.

19. "U.S. Firms Are Letting Saudi Market Slip," *Wall Street Journal*, January 20, 1994, p. A10.

20. "Credit-Card Firms Woo Singaporeans with Cars, Condos," *Wall Street Journal*, January 6, 1993, p. C10.

21. "After Initial Fuzziness, AT&T Clears Up Signal to Asia," *Wall Street Journal*, June 30, 1993, p. B6.

22. Bryan Batson, "The Road Less Traveled," *Sales and Marketing Management* (December 1992), p. 52.

23. "Eastern Europe Poses Obstacles for Ads," *Wall Street Journal*, July 30, 1992, p. B6.

24. "Pizza in Japan Is Adapted to Local Tastes," *Wall Street Journal*, June 4, 1993, p. B1.

25. "Heinz Aims to Export Taste for Ketchup," *Wall Street Journal*, November 20, 1992, p. B1.

26. "Big Boy to set up in Saudi Arabia," *Houston Chronicle*, December 26, 1991, p. 4D.

27. Philip Kotler, "Global Standardization—Courting Danger," *The Journal of Consumer Marketing*, Vol. 3, No. 2 (Spring 1986), p. 14.

28. "U.S. Companies in China Find Patience, Persistence and Salesmanship Pay Off," *Wall Street Journal*, April 3, 1992, p. B1.

29. "In Pursuit of the Elusive Euroconsumer," *Wall Street Journal*, April 23, 1992, p. B1.

30. "Mexico's Corona Brew Wins Back Cachet Lost During the Late '80s," *Wall Street Journal*, January 19, 1993, p. B6.

31. Clive Sims, Adam Phillips, and Trevor Richards, "Developing a Global Pricing Strategy," *Marketing and Research Today* (March 1992), pp. 3–14.

32. William Pride and O. C. Ferrell, *Marketing*, 9th ed. (Boston: Houghton Mifflin, 1995).

33. "The Korean Tiger Is Out for Blood," *Business Week*, May 31, 1993, p. 54.

34. "Coca-Cola Faces a Price War," *Wall Street Journal*, July 7, 1994, p. A1; "Cola Price War Breaks Out in Japan," *Financial Times*, July 14, 1994, p. 1.

35. "A Red-Letter Date for Gray Marketers," *Business Week*, June 13, 1988, p. 30.

36. "The Gray Market: A Threat to Global Marketing?" *The International Executive* (November/December 1991), pp. 46–53.

37. "World Marketing: Going Global or Acting Local? Five Expert Viewpoints," *Journal of Consumer Marketing* (Spring 1986), pp. 5–26.

38. Martin S. Roth and Jean B. Romeo, "Matching Product Category and Country Image Perceptions: A Framework for Managing Country-of-Origin Effects," *Journal of International Business Studies*, Vol. 23, No. 3 (Third Quarter 1992), pp. 477–498; John R. Darling and Van R. Wood, "A Longitudinal Study Comparing Perceptions of U.S. and Japanese Consumer Products in a Third/Neutral Country: Finland 1975 to 1985," *Journal of International Business Studies*, Vol. 21, No. 3 (Third Quarter 1990), pp. 427–450.

39. "Life-Style Pitch Works in Russia Despite Poverty," *Wall Street Journal*, August 21, 1992, p. B1.

40. "U.S. Cigarette Firms Are Battling Taiwan's Bid to Stiffen Ad Curbs Like Other Asian Nations," *Wall Street Journal*, May 5, 1992, p. C25.

41. General Accounting Office, *Advertising and Promoting U.S. Cigarettes in Selected Asian Countries*, Report GAO/GGD-93-38 (December 1992), p. 38f.

42. "World's Top 50 Advertising Organizations," *Advertising Age*, January 6, 1992, p. S6.

43. "Signs of the times," *Financial Times*, September 22, 1994, p. 8.

44. Barbara Mueller, "Multinational Advertising: Factors Influencing the Standardised vs. Specialised Approach," *International Marketing Review*, Vol. 8, No. 1 (1991), pp. 7–18.

45. "Prof. Levitt Stands by Global Ad Theory," *Wall Street Journal*, October 13, 1992, p. B7.

46. "Global Ad Campaigns, After Many Missteps, Finally Pay Dividends," *Wall Street Journal*, August 27, 1992, p. A1.

47. "IBM Strives for a Single Image in Its European Ad Campaign," *Wall Street Journal*, April 16, 1991, p. B12.

48. "A universal message," *Financial Times*, May 27, 1993.

49. "This Time It's for Real, *Forbes*, August 2, 1993, pp. 58–61.

50. Barbara Mueller, "An Analysis of Information Content in Standardized vs. Specialized Multinational Advertisements," *Journal of International Business Studies*, Vol. 22, No. 1 (First Quarter 1991), pp. 23–40.

51. For a review of the issues involved, see Sudhir H. Kale and John W. Barnes, "Understanding the Domain of Cross-National Buyer-Seller Interactions," *Journal of International Business Studies*, Vol. 23, No. 1 (First Quarter 1992), pp. 101–132.

52. "Colgate-Palmolive Is Really Cleaning Up in Poland," *Business Week*, March 15, 1993, pp. 54–56.

53. General Accounting Office, *Advertising and Promoting U.S. Cigarettes in Selected Asian Countries*, Report GAO/GGD-93-38 (December 1992), pp. 37ff.

54. Ashley Blaker, "For global assistance, Dyal a marketer," *San Antonio Business Journal*, August 7, 1989, p. 8.

55. "SMH Leads a Revival of Swiss Watchmaking Industry," *Wall Street Journal*, January 20, 1992, p. B4.

56. Jean Downey, "Touchdown!" *Business Tokyo*, March 1992, p. 34.

57. John Griffiths, "Japanese models queue up for life in the fast lane," *Financial Times*, January 14, 1992.

58. Guy de Jonquieres, "A new red flag flies over eastern Europe," *Financial Times*, June 2, 1992, p. 19.

59. "Coca-Cola to Open Plant in Moscow," *Wall Street Journal*, January 17, 1992, p. A3.

60. "Levi Learns Eastern Europe Legal Protections Are Threadbare," *San Francisco Business Times*, April 1, 1994, p. 1; "Private Firms Profit in Global Markets," *San Francisco Business Magazine* (August 1993), p. 14; "True Fit—What Kind of Texan Are You? The Answer Is in Your Jeans," *Texas Monthly* (September 1993), pp. 120.

Chapter Outline

**The nature of international
operations management**

The strategic context of international
    operations management
Complexities of international operations
    management

Production management

Sourcing and vertical integration
Location decisions
International logistics and materials
    management

International service operations

Characteristics of international services
The role of government in international
    services trade
Managing service operations

After studying this chapter you should be able to:

Characterize the nature of international
operations management.

Describe the sourcing and vertical
integration decisions facing international
production managers.

Identify and discuss the basic location
decisions in international production
management.

Discuss the basic issues in international
logistics and materials management.

Identify and discuss the basic issues in
international service operations.

B ENETTON GROUP SPA, THE TRENDY ITALIAN CLOTHING CHAIN, has grown from a one-knitter operation to a multinational retailer. It started in 1955 near Venice, Italy, when Luciano Benetton convinced his sister, Giuliana, to let him sell the brightly colored sweaters she knit. The low-priced, stylish sweaters sold quickly. Their popularity convinced Luciano to sell his accordion and his younger brother's bicycle to buy his sister a knitting machine so that she could knit even faster. ■■ Over the next few years, Luciano and Giuliana worked together managing their rapidly growing operation. In the beginning, they rented production space in an empty warehouse and hired Giuliana's friends to help produce sweaters as well as other garments.

Coloring the World[1]

Eventually, demand for Benetton products grew beyond what this small workforce could handle. The Benetton family built a new factory near Venice and set up operations as a full-line apparel maker. ■■ The first Benetton retail store opened in a fashionable ski resort in the Italian Alps in 1968. Others quickly followed in the leading fashion capitals of Europe. Between the early 1980s and 1993, the firm opened a new retail store somewhere in the world every day. When the Iron Curtain came down in the early 1990s, Benetton was the first Western European retailer to set up shop in Central and Eastern Europe. It now has hundreds of stores throughout the former communist bloc, as well as stores in such far-flung locations as Turkey, Beijing, and Egypt. ■■ Benetton's greatest problem has been cracking the U.S. market, where fashion is more faddish than in Europe. It also underestimated the power of competitors such as The Gap and The Limited. Although there were almost 1000 Benetton stores in the United States in the mid-1980s, today there are fewer than 400. But in Europe, Benetton remains a leading clothing manufacturer and retailer. In addition to clothing, Benetton now makes cosmetics, toys, eyewear, and watches. ■■ What are the keys to Benetton's success? Italian styling and reasonable prices are certainly two of the main ones. But it is Benetton's operations management that has enabled it to stay a world-class competitor in the fashion industry. Benetton has a commitment to achieving quality and meeting customer needs through its manufacturing and distribution systems. Management of the firm's retail operations is decentralized so that store managers can better understand and respond to local buying preferences and patterns. Design and production, however, are centralized in Italy so that the firm can maintain tight control over manufacturing costs, quality, and related considerations. ■■ The starting point in the Benetton system involves information technology. Each retail transaction in a Benetton store is electronically coded and transmitted to a central information-processing center in Italy. Managers there can constantly track which products are selling where. In particular, they can track three vital pieces of information that are critical to success in any retailing operation: absolute sales levels, sales trends and patterns, and inventory distributions. This information can also be analyzed for individual stores, for clusters of stores in a given city or region, by country, or on a global basis. ▮▮ Managers use this sales information to plan and adjust production activity. Whenever a new sweater or other garment is designed, its creators try to plan for possible variations and alterations. For example, a new shirt will be designed so that it can be produced with short, mid-length, or full-length sleeves and with or without a collar. Early production runs and shipments will include all six possible styles. But a portion of those runs will be devoted to making shirt bodies without sleeves or collars. As sales figures begin to arrive, managers can very quickly tailor production adjustments to these inventoried shirt bodies to finish them out according to customer demand. If shirts with mid-length sleeves and a collar sell much faster than do other variations, more of this type of shirt can quickly be finished and shipped to stores. The same approach is also used for colors. If blue shirts sell twice as quickly as red ones, managers can easily tilt production toward finishing more blue shirts and fewer red shirts. ▮▮ Bar codes and scanners are used throughout Benetton factories and warehouses. Using fully networked computer workstations, managers can plan and initiate production runs based on style and color demand. Partially completed products are pulled from shelves by robots and placed on final production lines. As those products are finished out, bar codes are attached and they are automatically wrapped, packaged, and shipped to those stores that need inventory replenishment. ▮▮▮▮▮

Benetton has flourished for various reasons. Among them are its abilities to track demand for each of its various products and then to take the appropriate steps to satisfy that demand promptly and efficiently. By centralizing its design and manufacturing systems in its home country of Italy, Benetton is able to maintain tight control over those and related functions. By building flexibility into design, production, and distribution, the firm is able to get new inventory to its stores around the world much faster than most of its competitors can. The basis for planning and implementing these activities is operations management.

Some firms, such as Shell, Exxon, and British Petroleum, are concerned with physically transforming natural resources into various products through complex refining processes. Others, such as Compaq, Sony, and Philips, purchase completed component parts from suppliers and then assemble those into electronics products. Still others, such as Air France and JAL, use a global travel network to provide transportation services to people. Regardless of a firm's product, however, the goal of its international operations managers is to design, create, and distribute goods or services that meet the needs and wants of customers worldwide—and to do so profitably.[2]

The Nature of International Operations Management

Operations management is the set of activities an organization uses to transform different kinds of inputs (materials, labor, and so on) into final goods and services. **International operations management** refers to the transformation-related activities of an international firm. Figure 17.1 illustrates the international operations management process. As shown, a firm's strategic context provides a necessary backdrop against which it develops and then manages its operations functions. A key part of international operations management is the activities and processes connected with the acquisition of the resources the firm needs to produce the goods or services it intends to sell. Location decisions—where to build factories and other facilities—are also important. Finally, international operations managers are concerned with logistics and materials management—the efficient movement of materials into, within, and out of the firm. We use this framework to organize this chapter's discussion of international operations management.

Operations management is closely linked with both quality and productivity. (Chapter 15 described how product quality and productivity have become two key elements in international competitiveness.) A firm's operations management system largely determines how inputs are transformed into goods or services. Properly designed and managed operating systems and procedures play a major role in determining product quality and productivity. For example, Benetton is able to squeeze extra measures of productivity from its distribution centers because of its highly efficient and flexible design. Conversely, poorly designed operating systems are a major cause of poor quality and lower productivity. They promote inefficiency and can contribute in various ways to higher costs and suboptimal profit performance.[3]

Successful firms recognize that to survive they must continually adapt and respond to changes in their environments. These include technological advancements, regional and/or local changes in consumer tastes and preferences, shifting pricing levels, and the actions of their competitors in a constantly changing global arena. An operations management system that is properly designed can help managers respond more effectively to these changes. For example, automakers used to shut down for an entire month when they changed equipment to produce a new model or make of automobile. Today, the most efficient automakers can enact that same shift in a matter of hours, thereby losing only a small amount of production time. This capability, in turn, makes it easier and less costly for them to change models or shift production from a low-profit line to a high-profit line. And as already noted, Benetton uses its operating systems to make timely adjustments to sales patterns and consumer preferences. The result is a competitive advantage over many of the firm's competitors around the world.

A poorly designed operations management system can be a barrier to change. For example, just a few years ago, the German firm Metallgesellschaft was hailed as a miniature version of the highly respected Japanese firm Mitsubishi. It was establishing numerous operations and buying subsidiaries in a number of different markets, all intended to complement its core business of metals mining and trading. The firm's goal was to become Europe's largest conglomerate. Soon, however, it

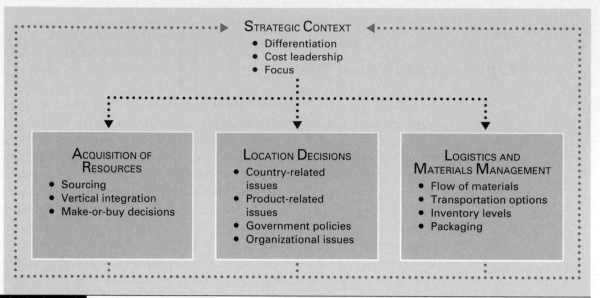

STRATEGIC CONTEXT
- Differentiation
- Cost leadership
- Focus

ACQUISITION OF RESOURCES
- Sourcing
- Vertical integration
- Make-or-buy decisions

LOCATION DECISIONS
- Country-related issues
- Product-related issues
- Government policies
- Organizational issues

LOGISTICS AND MATERIALS MANAGEMENT
- Flow of materials
- Transportation options
- Inventory levels
- Packaging

FIGURE 17.1

The International Operations Management Process

began losing money, and eventually it slid into bankruptcy. The primary reason for Metallgesellschaft's decline was that its managers did a poor job of integrating the operating systems of the firm's 258 separate businesses scattered around the globe.[4]

The Strategic Context of International Operations Management

From Fig. 17.1 you can see that international operations management must be closely aligned with a firm's business strategy. The central role of operations management is to create the potential for achieving superior value for the firm. If operations management can take $2 worth of inputs and create $10 worth of goods or services from them, it has created considerable value. But if it requires $9 worth of inputs to create the same $10 worth of goods or services, it has created very little value. Thus how the firm structures and manages its operations management function both influences and is influenced by its strategy.

Indeed, the business strategy set by top managers both at the corporate and regional levels of a firm should direct the planning and implementation of operations management activities.[5] For example, for a firm pursuing a differentiation strategy, the operations management function must be able to create goods or services that are clearly different from those of the firm's competitors. This effort may require a greater investment in higher-quality resources, equipment, and so on, with cost being a secondary consideration. For a firm following a cost leadership strategy, the operations management function must be able to shave the costs of creating goods or services to the absolute minimum so that the firm can lower its prices while still earning an acceptable level of profits. In this case, cost and price issues are central, while quality may be less critical.

Thus the firm's overall strategy drives many operations management activities, including location decisions, facilities design, and logistics management. For example, if the firm intends to compete on the basis of price, operations managers will need to design procedures and employ technology that minimizes the costs of creating goods or services. As a result, it may be highly appropriate to locate production facilities where labor costs are especially low—Mexico or Malaysia, for example. But if the firm wants to compete on the basis of product quality, costs will be less important than product quality and design. Production facilities, as a result, may need to be located where there is a relatively skilled labor force, even if the cost of employing that labor is relatively high.[6]

Complexities of International Operations Management

International operations management presents one of the most complex and challenging set of tasks managers face today. The basic complexities inherent in operations management stem from the production problem itself—where and how to produce various goods and services. Operations managers typically must decide important and complex issues in three areas:

1 *Resources.* Managers must decide where and how to obtain the resources the firm needs to produce its products. Key decisions relate to sourcing and vertical integration.

2 *Location.* Managers must decide where to build administrative facilities, sales offices, and plants, how to design them, and so on.

3 *Logistics.* Managers must decide on modes of transportation and methods of inventory control.

All firms, whether domestic or international, must address these issues. However, resolving them is far more complicated for international firms. A domestic manufacturer may deal with only local suppliers, be subject to one set of government regulations, compete in a relatively homogeneous market, have access to an integrated transportation network, and ship its goods relatively short distances. An international manufacturer, in contrast, is likely to deal with suppliers from different countries and confront different government regulations wherever it does business, as well as very heterogeneous markets, disparate transportation facilities and networks, and relatively long distances. International operations managers must choose the countries in which to locate production facilities, taking into account factors such as costs, tax laws, resource availability, and marketing considerations. They also must consider potential exchange-rate movements and noneconomic factors such as government regulations, political risk, and predictability of a country's legal system. Further, they must consider the impact of facilities' locations on the firm's ability to respond to changes in customer tastes and preferences. Finally, they must factor in logistical problems. Just as long supply lines doomed Napoleon's invasion of Russia, locating factories far from one's suppliers may impede timely access to resources and materials.

Production Management

While some similarities exist between creating goods and creating services for international markets, there are also major fundamental differences. Operations management decisions, processes, and issues that involve the creation of tangible goods are called **production management**, and those involving the creation of intangible services are called **service operations management**. This section focuses on production management; service operations management is addressed later in the chapter.

Manufacturing involves the creation of goods by transforming raw materials and component parts in combination with capital, labor, and technology. Some examples of manufacturing activities are Sony's production of stereo equipment, BMW's production of automobiles, and Bridgestone's production of tires. BMW, for example, takes thousands of component parts, ranging from sheet metal to engine parts to upholstery to rubber molding, and combines them to make different types of automobiles.

Most successful manufacturers use many sophisticated techniques to produce high-quality goods efficiently. These techniques are best covered in more advanced and specialized production management courses, so we focus here on other important dimensions of international production management:

▶ International sourcing
▶ International facilities location
▶ International logistics

Sourcing and Vertical Integration

Because the production of most manufactured goods requires a variety of raw materials, parts, and other resources, the first issue an international production manager faces is deciding how to acquire those inputs.[7] **Sourcing** is the set of processes and steps a firm uses to acquire the various resources it needs to create its own products (some managers use the term *procuring* instead of *sourcing*).[8] Sourcing clearly affects product cost, product quality, and internal demands for capital. Because of these impacts, most international firms approach sourcing as a strategic issue to be carefully planned and implemented by top management.[9]

The first step in developing a sourcing strategy is to determine the appropriate degree of vertical integration.[10] **Vertical integration** is the extent to which a firm either provides its own resources or obtains them from other sources. At one extreme, firms that practice relatively high levels of vertical integration are engaged in every step of the operations management process as goods are developed, transformed, packaged, and sold to customers. Various units within the firm can be seen as suppliers to other units within the firm, which in turn can be viewed as the customers of the supplying units. At the other extreme, firms that have little vertical integration are involved in only one step or just a few steps in the production chain. They may buy their inputs and component parts from other suppliers, perform one operation or transformation, and then sell their outputs to other firms or consumers.[11]

British Petroleum is an excellent example of a vertically integrated international business. One unit of the firm is engaged in the worldwide exploration for natural gas and petroleum. After oil is discovered, another unit is responsible for its extraction. The oil is then transported through company-owned pipelines and on company-owned tanker ships to company-owned refineries. Those refineries transform the crude oil into gasoline, processed petroleum, and other petroleum-

Logistics and materials management are important for international business. The Alaskan Pipeline provides a case in point. The pipeline was undertaken amid controversy regarding its negative environmental impact and the size of the necessary financial investment. The pipeline, however, has made the transport of petroleum from isolated regions of Alaska much more efficient and cost-effective.

based fuels. Next, the fuel is transported by company-owned trucks to company-owned service stations and convenience stores, where it is sold to individual consumers. Thus British Petroleum's exploration and extraction business supplies its pipeline business, which supplies its refinery business, which supplies its retailing business. While the firm occasionally uses third-party suppliers and may sometimes sell its products to other firms, it primarily seeks to maintain an unbroken and efficient chain of vertically integrated operations from the beginning of the production process to the final sale of the product to individual consumers.[12]

In contrast, Heineken NV, the world's third-largest beer producer, practices relatively little vertical integration. The firm buys the grains and chemicals it needs to brew beer from local farmers and agricultural cooperatives. From various container suppliers it buys the bottles, labels, and cartons it uses to package its beers. After brewing and bottling its beers, Heineken sells them to distributors, which subsequently resell them to retailers, which, in turn, resell them to consumers.

The extent of a firm's vertical integration is the result of a series of sourcing decisions made by production managers.[13] In deciding how to acquire the components necessary to manufacture a firm's products, its production managers have two choices: the firm can make the inputs itself, or it can buy them from outside suppliers. This choice is called the **make-or-buy decision**. The basic make-or-buy options available to an international firm are shown in Fig. 17.2. Note, in particular, that the make-or-buy decision carries with it other decisions as well. For example, a decision to buy rather than make dictates the need to choose between long-term and short-term supplier relationships. A decision to make rather than buy leaves open the option of making by self or making in partnership with others. And if partnership is the choice, yet another decision relates to the degree of control the firm wants to have.

The make-or-buy decision can be influenced by a firm's size, scope of operations, and technological expertise and by the nature of its product. For example,

FIGURE 17.2

Basic Make-or-Buy Options

Source: Reprinted from "Strategic Outsourcing" by James Brian Quinn and Frederick G. Hilmer, *Sloan Management Review*, Summer 1994, p. 50, by permission of the publisher. Copyright 1994 by the Sloan Management Review Association. All rights reserved.

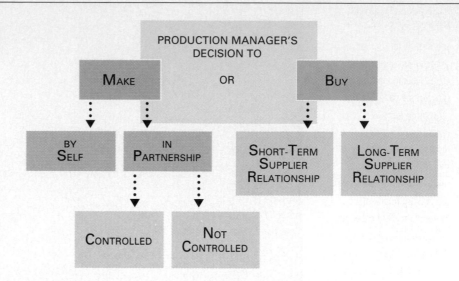

because larger firms are better able to benefit from economies of scale in the production of inputs, larger automakers such as GM and Fiat are more likely to make their parts themselves, while smaller ones such as Saab or BMW are more likely to buy them from outside suppliers. Components embodying relatively new technologies, such as anti-locking braking systems or automotive CD players, are more likely to be purchased from outside suppliers, while more standardized components, such as standard braking systems and AM/FM automotive radios, are more likely to be produced in-house. At other times, the make-or-buy decision will depend on existing investments in technology and manufacturing facilities. For example, personal computer manufacturers such as Compaq and IBM must decide whether they want to make or buy microprocessors, memory chips, disk drives, motherboards, and power supplies. Because of its extensive manufacturing expertise with mainframe computers, IBM is more likely to make a PC component in-house, while Compaq is more likely to rely heavily on outside suppliers.

All else being equal, a firm will choose to make or buy simply on the basis of whether it can obtain the resource cheaper by making it internally or by buying it from an external supplier. But since "all else being equal" seldom actually occurs, strategic issues must also be considered. Figure 17.3 highlights the need to balance competitive advantage against strategic vulnerability when resolving the make-or-buy decision. For example, if a high potential for competitive advantage exists along with a high degree of strategic vulnerability, the firm is likely to maintain strategic control by producing internally. But if the potential for competitive advantage and the degree of strategic vulnerability are both low, the firm will need less control and will therefore be more likely to buy "off the shelf." Finally, when intermediate potential for competitive advantage and moderate degree of strategic vulnerability call for moderate control, special ventures or contract arrangements will be most appropriate.

In addition to these strategic considerations, other factors may play a role with respect to the make-or-buy decision. In particular, international firms typically must make tradeoffs between costs and one or more of the following factors:

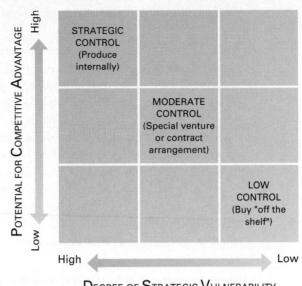

FIGURE 17.3

Competitive Advantage versus Strategic Vulnerability in the Make-or-Buy Decision

Source: Reprinted from "Strategic Outsourcing" by James Brian Quinn and Frederick G. Hilmer, *Sloan Management Review*, Summer 1994, p. 48, by permission of the publisher. Copyright 1994 by the Sloan Management Review Association. All rights reserved.

► Control

► Risk

► Investment in facilities, technology, and people

► Flexibility

Control. Making a component has the advantage of increasing the firm's control over product quality, delivery schedules, design changes, and costs. A firm that buys from external suppliers may become overly dependent on those suppliers. If a given supplier goes out of business, raises its prices, or produces poor-quality materials, the firm will lose its source of inputs, see its costs increase, or experience its own quality-related problems.

Another issue of control relates to the ability to enforce contracts with outside suppliers. Enforcing contracts with foreign suppliers may be difficult or costly because of differences in national legal systems. For example, if laws protecting intellectual property of foreigners are weak in a certain country, entertainment firms such as Sony Records and Warner Brothers may be unwilling to license firms in that country to duplicate their CDs and videotapes. When such considerations are important, a firm may prefer to make rather than buy necessary inputs. One strength of the Japanese keiretsu system, for example, is its ability to reduce the problem of enforcing contracts between a firm and its suppliers. Cross-ownership of shares among keiretsu members, which strengthens trust among members, increases their willingness to enter into long-term contracts and to share intellectual property with each other.[14]

By making rather than buying, the firm may also be able to develop new business opportunities. British Petroleum, for example, has a chemical division that relies in part on petroleum-based ingredients for the production of certain chemical products. This chemical unit has a relatively dependable and cooperative "built-in" supplier for its petroleum needs. This arrangement allows it to more effectively address future price, availability, and delivery schedule questions as it develops its strategic and operational plans.

Risk. Buying a component from an external supplier has the advantage of reducing the firm's financial and operating risks. British Petroleum, for example, has risk associated with its drilling platforms, pipelines, and every other stage in its production chain. If the firm simply bought crude oil from other firms, it would not have to worry about drilling platform injuries or equipment failure because those risks would be assumed by the supplier. It would also not have to worry about earning an adequate rate of return on those assets. Equally important, the firm that buys rather than makes can reduce its political risk in a host country. For example, British Petroleum runs the risk that politicians elected on anti-British or antiforeigner platforms in the United States, Nigeria, Colombia, or elsewhere may some day expropriate its refineries. Indeed, this did happen in 1951, when Iran's rulers seized a major British Petroleum operation in that country.

Investments in Facilities, Technology, and People. Buying from others lowers the firm's level of investment. By not having to build a new factory or learn a new technology, a firm can free up capital for other productive uses. For example, as production at Honda's U.S. manufacturing plant in Ohio grew, the firm needed an increased supply of mirrors for its cars. It convinced a local supplier, Donnelly Corp., to build a new factory to assemble mirrors for its automobiles. Thus Honda obtained a convenient and dependable supplier without having to invest its own money in building a mirror factory.[15] Of course, by buying rather than making the mirrors, Honda surrendered the profits of mirror manufacturing to Donnelly.

Buying from others also reduces a firm's training costs and expertise requirements. By contracting with Donnelly, Honda avoided having to develop expertise in designing, manufacturing, and marketing automobile mirrors. British Petroleum, in contrast, needs a wide range of expertise and talent among the ranks of its manager to take full advantage of its highly vertically integrated global operations.

Flexibility. A firm that buys rather than makes retains the flexibility to change suppliers as circumstances dictate. This is particularly helpful in cases in which technology is rapidly evolving or delivered costs can change as a result of inflation or exchange-rate fluctuations. Most personal computer manufacturers, for example, have chosen to buy disk drives, CD-ROM units, and microprocessors from outside suppliers. By so doing, they avoid the risk of product obsolescence and the large R&D expenditures needed to stay on the cutting edge of each of the technologies embedded in the component parts of personal computers. Similarly, Dallas's Peerless Manufacturing buys components from numerous European subcontractors that produce filters and separators. Peerless can shift its sourcing around the Continent depending on currency fluctuations and flows of orders from its customers.[16]

Of course, sometimes a firm must make tradeoffs that reduce flexibility. In the case of Honda and Donnelly, Donnelly was concerned that it would be at Honda's mercy once it invested in the new mirror factory. To induce Donnelly to agree to build the new factory, the automaker had to assure Donnelly managers that the firm would get all of Honda's mirror business for at least ten years. By so doing, Honda reduced its capital investment but sacrificed the flexibility of changing suppliers during the ten-year period. This example also illustrates a major trend in buyer-supplier relationships. Not long ago, managers assumed that it was useful to use a variety of suppliers in order to avoid becoming too dependent on a single one. A drawback of this approach, however, is the complexity associated with dealing with a large network of suppliers, especially if that network is global. More recently, some firms have come to realize that by engaging in exclusive or semi-exclusive long-term relationships with a few suppliers, they increase the dependence of those suppliers on them as customers to the point that they can virtually dictate product quality, delivery schedules, and even price.

Figure 17.4 highlights how Ford has effectively narrowed its supplier network. When Ford was building its 1994 Tempo, it relied on over 700 suppliers for its North American production facilities alone. Its new 1995 Mercury Mystique, in contrast, is produced worldwide using only 227 suppliers. Indeed, Ford recently overhauled its entire purchasing function. Previously, its North American and European operations had separate purchasing functions. These units are now

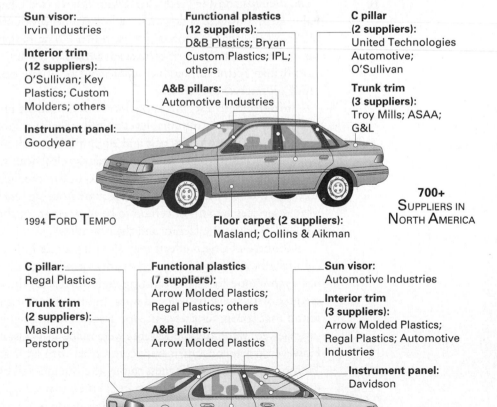

FIGURE 17.4

Ford's Trend toward Fewer Suppliers and a Global Supplier Network

Source: From Alex Taylor, "The Auto Industry Meets the New Economy," *Fortune*, September 5, 1994. © 1994 Time, Inc. All rights reserved.

Sun visor:
Irvin Industries

Interior trim (12 suppliers):
O'Sullivan; Key Plastics; Custom Molders; others

Instrument panel:
Goodyear

Functional plastics (12 suppliers):
D&B Plastics; Bryan Custom Plastics; IPL; others

A&B pillars:
Automotive Industries

C pillar (2 suppliers):
United Technologies Automotive; O'Sullivan

Trunk trim (3 suppliers):
Troy Mills; ASAA; G&L

1994 FORD TEMPO

Floor carpet (2 suppliers):
Masland; Collins & Aikman

700+ SUPPLIERS IN NORTH AMERICA

C pillar:
Regal Plastics

Trunk trim (2 suppliers):
Masland; Perstorp

Functional plastics (7 suppliers):
Arrow Molded Plastics; Regal Plastics; others

A&B pillars:
Arrow Molded Plastics

Sun visor:
Automotive Industries

Interior trim (3 suppliers):
Arrow Molded Plastics; Regal Plastics; Automotive Industries

Instrument panel:
Davidson

1995 MERCURY MYSTIQUE

Floor carpet:
Masland

227 SUPPLIERS WORLDWIDE

consolidated into a single purchasing department charged with the responsibility of buying parts for all Ford operations. The firm estimates that this move will save $3 billion per year, or $500 per automobile. [17]

Location Decisions

An international firm that chooses to make rather than buy inputs faces another decision: where should it locate its production facilities? In reaching a location decision, the firm must consider several sets of factors:[18]

▶ Country-related issues

▶ Product-related issues

▶ Government policies

▶ Organizational issues

Country-Related Issues. Several features of countries can influence the siting location of an international facility. Chief among these are resource availability and cost, infrastructure, and country-of-origin marketing effects.

Resource availability and cost constitute a primary determinant of whether an individual country is a suitable location for a facility. As suggested by the classical trade theories and the Heckscher-Ohlin theory (see Chapter 3), countries that enjoy large, low-cost endowments of a factor of production will attract firms needing that factor of production. For example, China has attracted toy, footwear, and textile manufacturers eager to take advantage of its vast army of low-cost labor. And British Petroleum has little choice but to situate drilling platforms where crude oil reserves are located.

Infrastructure also affects the location of production facilities. Most facilities require at least some minimal level of infrastructural support. To build a facility requires construction materials and equipment as well as materials suppliers and construction contractors. More importantly, electrical, water, transportation, telephone, and other services are necessary to utilize the facility productively. And access to medical care, education, adequate housing, entertainment, and other related services are almost certain to be important for the employees and managers who will work at the facility and their families.

Country-of-origin effects may also play a role in locating a facility. Certain countries have "brand images" that affect product marketing. For example, Japan has a reputation for manufacturing high-quality products, while Italy is often credited with stylishly designed ones. In one interesting experiment, a researcher found that consumer preference for Timex watches fell by only 6 percent when interviewees were told the watches were made in Pakistan rather than Germany. However, when consumers were confronted with an unfamiliar brand called "Tempomax," their willingness to buy the watches fell by 74 percent when they were told the watches were made in Pakistan instead of Germany. All else being equal, it obviously is easier to sell watches made in Germany than ones made in Pakistan to consumers in industrialized countries, particularly if the product is not backed by a strong brand name. Firms must take into account these country-of-origin effects in deciding where to site a production facility. A firm interested in marketing its product as high-quality might choose to locate in Japan or Germany rather than in Pakistan or Indonesia, while a firm competing on the basis of low price might make the opposite choice.[19]

Product-Related Issues. Product-related characteristics may also influence the location decision. Among the more important of these are the product's value-to-weight ratio, the required production technology, and the importance of customer feedback.[20]

The product's value-to-weight ratio affects the fraction of transportation costs in the product's delivered price. Goods with low value-to-weight ratios, such as iron ore, cement, coal, bulk chemicals, and raw sugar and other agricultural goods, tend to be produced in multiple locations in order to minimize transportation costs. Conversely, goods with high value-to-weight ratios, such as microprocessors or diamonds, can be produced in a single location or handful of locations without loss of competitiveness. For example, transportation costs are a trivial part of the cost of producing and distributing Intel's Pentium chip, so Intel is free to locate the chip's production on the basis of nontransportation factors.

The production technology used to manufacture the good may also affect facility location. A firm must compare its expected product sales with the efficient size of a facility in the industry. If a firm's sales are large relative to an efficient-sized facility, the firm is likely to operate many facilities in various locations. If its sales are small relative to an efficient-sized facility, it will probably utilize only one plant. For example, the minimum efficient size of a petroleum refinery is about 200,000 barrels per day. Thus British Petroleum, which can refine up to 5 million barrels per day, has chosen to operate 17 refineries located in such countries as the United Kingdom, Spain, and Colombia.

The relative importance of customer feedback may also influence the location decision. Products for which firms desire quick customer feedback are often produced close to the point of final sale. For example, a general rule of thumb in the U.S. apparel industry is that, all else being equal, the more fashionable the item, the more likely it is that its production will occur near or in the United States so that the manufacturer can quickly respond to market trends. At the beginning of each selling season, women's sportswear buyers for Macy's, Nordstrom's, and Dillards carefully monitor which new items are hot sellers. They quickly reorder the hot items and mercilessly dump goods that fashion-conscious shoppers ignore. Because the selling season for such goods may last only two or three months—and no one can predict with certainty what the fashion fanatics will buy—apparel manufacturers in the United States are better able to respond to the sportswear buyers' demands than are producers in Taiwan or Indonesia. Conversely, low-fashion items are more likely to be produced outside the United States to take advantage of lower production costs. For example, J.C. Penney can predict with great certainty how many athletic socks and white cotton briefs it will sell each summer. And if for some reason it overestimates summer sales of these items, it can continue to sell them in the fall. Accordingly, Penney's menswear buyers often enter into long-term contracts with Asian knitting mills. In this case, cost is a more important variable than speed or flexibility of delivery.

Government Policies. Government policies may also play a role in the location decision. Especially important are the stability of the political process, national trade policies, economic development incentives, and the existence of foreign trade zones.

The stability of the political process within a country can clearly affect the desirability of locating a factory there. Firms like to know what the rules of the game are so that they can make knowledgeable investment, production, and staffing decisions. A government that alters fiscal, monetary, and regulatory policies seemingly on whim and without consulting the business community raises the risk and uncertainty of operating in a country. Unforeseen changes in taxation policy, exchange rates, inflation, and labor laws are particularly troublesome to international firms.

National trade policies may also affect the location decision. To serve its customers, a firm may be forced to locate a facility within a country that has high tariff walls and other trade barriers. For example, Toyota, Nissan, and Mazda built factories in the United States to evade a VER imposed by the Japanese government to limit the exports of Japanese-built automobiles to the United States. Similarly, Compaq Computer located a personal computer manufacturing facility in Sao Paulo to avoid Brazilian import taxes.[21]

Economic development incentives may influence the location decision. Communities eager to create jobs and add to the local tax base often seek to attract new factories by offering international firms inexpensive land, highway improvements, job training programs, and discounted water and electric rates. For example, the city of Paris offered to sell the Walt Disney Company suburban land on which to build Euro Disney at a greatly discounted rate. To lure a Toyota plant and its estimated 4000 jobs in the mid-1980s, Kentucky ponied up subsidies worth tens of millions of dollars. And Tuscaloosa, Alabama, outbid dozens of North American cities for a new Mercedes-Benz factory in 1993, offering the firm a multimillion-dollar package of incentives.[22]

An international firm may also choose a site based on the existence of a foreign trade zone (FTZ). As discussed in Chapter 6, an FTZ is a specially designated and controlled geographical area in which imported or exported goods receive preferential tariff treatment. A country may establish FTZs near its major ports of entry and/or major production centers. It then allows international firms to import products into those zones duty-free for specified purposes, sometimes with express limitations, for example, about allowable types and value of products and the kind of work that may be performed.

A firm may decide to locate in a particular area because the existence of an FTZ gives it greater flexibility regarding importing or exporting and creates avenues for lowering costs.[23] For example, the Port of Houston operates a large FTZ used primarily for storage by non-U.S. automakers. Toyota and Nissan can ship all their automobiles bound for sale in the southern part of North America to Houston, where they are stored without any payment of import tariffs being required. Only when specific automobiles are removed from the zone and shipped to dealerships must the manufacturers pay the duty. However, some automobiles are eventually shipped to Mexico or various Caribbean countries. The firms then pay only whatever duty those countries levy and avoid payment of U.S. duties altogether.

Costs can be lowered through the creative use of FTZs. For example, a firm may be able to import component parts, supplement them with other component parts obtained locally, and assemble them all into finished goods. The duty paid on the imported components incorporated into the products assembled in the FTZ may be lower than the duty imposed on imported components in general. For this reason, most automobiles produced in the United States are assembled in FTZs. Further, some duties are calculated on the basis of the good's total weight, including packaging. So a firm may lower its duties by bringing goods into the FTZ in lightweight, inexpensive packaging, and then, after duties have been paid, repackaging them with heavier, more-substantial materials obtained locally.

Organizational Issues. An international firm's business strategy and its organizational structure may also affect the location decision. Inventory management policies are also important considerations.

A firm's business strategy may affect its location decisions in various ways. A firm that adopts a price leadership strategy must seek out low-cost locations, while one that focuses on product quality must locate facilities in areas that have adequate skilled labor and managerial talent. A firm may choose to concentrate production geographically in order to better meet organizational goals. Benetton does this with its Italian production facilities so as to better control product design and quality. Similarly, Boeing has concentrated its final aircraft assembly operations in the Seattle area in order to take advantage of the skilled machinist and engineering talent in the area. Other firms find that strategic goals can be better met by dispersing facilities in various foreign locations. Most electronics firms take this approach. For example, Intel has manufacturing plants in the United States, Ireland, Puerto Rico, Israel, Malaysia, and the Philippines to take advantage of the relatively low-cost resources available in each of these markets. Further, shipping the firm's computer chips to distant markets from those manufacturing facilities is relatively easy and inexpensive. Multiple production facilities also protect a firm against exchange-rate fluctuations. FMC, for example, often shifts orders for its food-packaging machinery from plants in Chicago to plants in Italy or vice versa, depending on the relative values of the dollar and the lira.

A firm's organizational structure also influences the location of its factories. For example, as noted in Chapter 13, adoption of a global area structure decentralizes authority to area managers. These managers, seeking to maintain control over their area, are likely to favor siting factories within their area to produce goods sold within the area. For example, until 1994 Ford was structured into three area groups: North America, Europe, and Asia Pacific. The firm exported few automobiles from these regions; rather, each area focused on producing automobiles to meet the needs of consumers in its area. (Ford abandoned this organizational structure in 1994, believing that it hindered its ability to truly globalize its automobile production.[24]) Conversely, a firm having a global product structure will locate factories anywhere in the world in order to meet its cost and quality performance goals.

A firm's inventory management policies are affected by plant location decisions. Inventory management is a complex task all operations managers must confront. They must balance the costs of maintaining inventory against the costs of running out of materials and/or finished goods. The costs of maintaining inventory include those associated with storage (operating a warehouse, for example), spoilage and loss (some stored inventory gets ruined, damaged, or stolen), and opportunity costs (an investment in inventory cannot be put to other business uses).

Factory location affects the level of inventory that firms must hold because of the distances and transit times involved in shipping goods. For example, if Wal-Mart purchases private-label televisions for its U.S. stores from a Taiwanese factory, its inventory levels will be higher than if it purchases them from a Mexican factory. Compaq Computer has chosen to locate its primary assembly plants in Houston, Scotland, Singapore, and Brazil in order to improve service to its North American, European, Asian, and South American customers, respectively, while cutting overall inventory levels.

Factory location becomes particularly critical when a firm's customers adopt the popular JIT inventory management system. As "Going Global" discusses, this is a method for holding down the costs of storing materials by arranging to have them delivered directly to the production site as they are needed, or "just in time."

International Logistics and Materials Management

Regardless of the location of an international firm's factories, its operations managers must address issues involving international logistics.[25] **International logistics** is the managing of the flow of:

▶ Materials, parts, supplies, and other resources from suppliers to the firm

▶ Materials, parts, supplies, and other resources within and between units of the firm itself

▶ Finished products, services, and goods from the firm to customers [26]

The first two sets of activities are usually called **materials management**, while the third is often called physical distribution, or, more simply, distribution. Recall that we discussed distribution issues in Chapter 16 because they are often managed as a part of the firm's marketing function. Thus our focus here is on the materials management area of logistics.

Three basic factors differentiate domestic and international materials management functions. The first is simply the distance involved in shipping. Shipments within even the largest countries seldom travel more than a couple of thousand miles, and many travel much less. For example, the road distance between New York City and Los Angeles is around 2800 miles. But the distances between New York and Warsaw, Tokyo, and Sydney are 4300 miles, 6700 miles, and 9900 miles, respectively.[27] Thus assembling component parts in Kansas City, Chicago, and St. Louis and then shipping them to Cincinnati for final assembly is much easier than assembling component parts in San Diego, Montreal, and Cairo and then shipping them to Singapore for final assembly.

The second basic difference between domestic and international materials management functions is the sheer number of transport modes that are likely to be involved. Shipments within the same country often use only a single mode of transportation, such as truck or rail. But shipments that cross national boundaries, and especially those traveling great distances, almost certainly involve multiple modes of transportation. For example, a shipment bound from Kansas City to Berlin may use rail, ship, and then rail again.

Third, the regulatory context for international materials management is much more complex than for domestic materials management. Most countries regulate many aspects of their internal transportation systems—price, safety, packaging,

Going Global

Just-in-Time Inventory Management

A relatively new—and increasingly popular—system for inventory management is called just in time, or JIT. With this approach a firm's suppliers deliver their products directly to the firm's manufacturing center, usually in frequent small shipments, just as they are needed for production. That is, they arrive "just in time" instead of being sent first to a warehouse for storage and later retransported for actual use by the manufacturer. Thus the JIT system requires careful coordination between a firm and its internal and external suppliers.

Honda uses the JIT inventory management system very effectively. In addition to its arrangement with Donnelly for supplying its U.S. plant with mirrors, Honda also uses independent suppliers for stereo speakers, seats, and dozens of other component parts. Each supplier delivers parts to the Honda factory three times a day, with each shipment going directly to the assembly line for immediate use. The advantages of this system to the manufacturer are obvious: it does not need to maintain a large parts inventory and it minimizes spoilage and damage. The suppliers also benefit: they avoid maintaining a finished goods inventory, since they ship directly to the customer as parts are completed. They also can generally establish an exclusive, long-term relationship with the firms they supply.

Many other firms have adopted the JIT system, which was first developed in Japan. For example, an important element of Harley-Davidson's successful struggle to regain supremacy in the heavyweight motorcycle industry, which we discussed at the end of Chapter 6, was its adoption of a JIT system. How did Harley find out about JIT? Its production managers visited Honda's factory in Ohio.

Source: "How to Achieve Worldwide JIT," *Material Handling Engineering* (October 1991), pp. 59–60; Shirley J. Daniel and Wolf D. Reitspergger, "Management Control Systems for J.I.T.: An Empirical Comparison of Japan and the U.S.," *Journal of International Business Studies* (Fourth Quarter 1991), pp. 603–617.

and so on. Shipments that cross through several countries are subject to the regulations of each of those countries. While various economic trade agreements and groups such as NAFTA and the EU have sought to streamline international shipping guidelines and procedures, transporting goods across national boundaries is still complex and often involves much red tape.

Seemingly simple logistics and materials management issues often become much more complex in an international context. Packaging issues, which might at first glance seem minor, are in reality a significant consideration in managing international logistics. Packaging protects the goods in transit, helps make the goods easier to handle, and facilitates delivery and/or sale of finished goods at their final destination. International shipping complicates packaging decisions, however, because of the use of multiple modes of transportation as well as the variation in conditions that will be encountered.[28]

For example, consider the problems encountered by a firm that wants to ship a large quantity of delicate electronics equipment from a plant in California, where the equipment was produced, to a facility in Saudi Arabia, where it will be used. During the course of shipment, the equipment will likely be on trucks, railcars, and a ship. These transport settings will have variations in humidity, temperature, and amount of dust. And each time the equipment is loaded and unloaded, it will be handled with varying degrees of roughness or delicacy. Thus the equipment must be packaged to handle everything it will encounter during its travels.

The weight of the packaging itself is also a consideration, especially for finished goods en route to customers. As noted earlier in the chapter, weight sometimes determines the amount of import duty; so firms frequently repackage goods after shipment. Sometimes customers even go so far as to specify precise total weights they will accept, including packaging, and may require that packaging meet certain preset specifications.

Logistical considerations may play a critical role in the decision of where to locate a factory. Production costs may be lower in a domestic factory than in a foreign one. However, the firm must also consider the materials management costs of

One of the most basic elements of managing international business operations is handling the actual movement of products across national boundaries. Ports of entry such as this one are extremely complex and busy facilities as boxcars of goods arrive from trains to be loaded onto ships or arrive by ship to be loaded onto railcars. Considerable amounts of paperwork accompany each shipment, and government inspections are commonplace as well.

warehousing, packaging, transporting, and distributing its goods, as well as its inventory carrying costs and those of its foreign customers. Typically, such logistical costs will be higher for exported goods than for locally produced goods. And there are logistical considerations other than costs. Because of longer supply lines and increased difficulties in communicating with foreign customers, a firm that chooses to export from domestic factories must ensure that it maintains competitive levels of service for its foreign customers.

International Service Operations

The service sector has emerged in recent years as an increasingly important part of many national economies, especially those of developed countries.[29] For example, the service sector accounts for almost three fourths of the U.S. GNP and is the source of most new U.S. jobs.[30] It should therefore come as no surprise that services are becoming a more integral part of international trade and of the global economy. An **international service business** is a firm that transforms resources into an intangible output that creates utility for its customers. Examples of international services are British Airways's transporting of passengers from London to India, Ernst & Young's assistance with the accounting and auditing functions of a global enterprise, and Dai-Ichi Kangyo Bank's handling of international corporate business accounts.

Figure 17.5 clearly demonstrates the increasing importance of the service sector in the U.S. economy. The relative percentage of agricultural jobs in the U.S. economy has steadily declined for decades. The relative percentage of jobs in the manufacturing sector of the U.S. economy has fluctuated some but has tended to remain relatively flat for the last several decades. But the relative percentage of service-sector jobs in the U.S. economy has steadily increased throughout this century. Figure 17.6 further highlights the importance of the service sector. Note that while the United States was running a merchandise trade deficit with the rest of the world in the early 1990s, its services trade surplus helped to reduce the overall current account deficit.

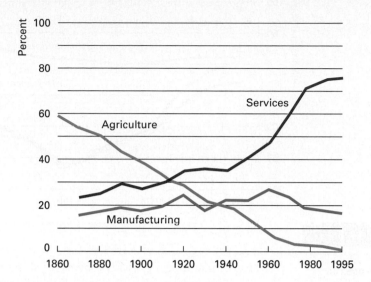

FIGURE 17.5

Relative Importance of Service-Sector Employment in the United States, 1870–1995

Nor are these trends limited to the United States. International services trade among most industrialized countries is increasing at a rate that exceeds other forms of international trade. It plays a major role in the economies of such countries as the United Kingdom, France, and Singapore—in fact, virtually all the world's major industrialized countries. At the same time, because service firms tend to follow the establishment of manufacturing firms, agricultural and manufacturing jobs still play the dominant role in the world's less developed and developing economies.

Characteristics of International Services

Services have several unique characteristics that create special challenges for firms that want to sell them in the international marketplace. In particular, services often are intangible, are not storable, require customer participation, and are linked with tangible goods.

Services are intangible. A consumer who goes to a store and buys a Sony Walkman has a tangible product, one that can be held, manipulated, used, stored, damaged, and/or returned. But a customer who goes to an accountant and gets financial advice leaves with intangible knowledge that cannot be held or seen. (The pieces of paper sometimes associated with services—tax statements, insurance policies, and so on—while tangible themselves, are actually just symbols or representations of the service product itself.) Because of this intangibility, assessing a service's value or quality is often more difficult than assessing that of a good.

Services are also generally not storable. Often they cannot be created ahead of time and inventoried or saved for future usage. A service call to repair a broken washing machine can occur only when the technician is physically transported to the site of the broken appliance—and is wasted if no one is home to unlock the door. An empty airline seat, an unused table in a restaurant, an unsold newspaper—all lose their economic value as soon as their associated window of opportunity closes—that is, after the plane takes off, the restaurant kitchen closes, and the next day's newspaper is printed. The high degree of perishability of services makes

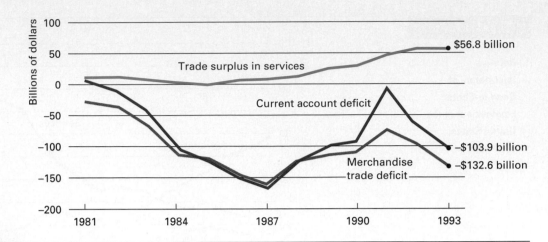

capacity planning a critical problem for all service providers. **Capacity planning** is deciding how many customers a firm will be able to serve at a given time. Failure to provide sufficient capacity often means permanently lost sales, while provision of too much capacity raises the firm's costs and lowers its profits.

Services often require customer participation. International services such as tourism cannot occur without the physical presence of the customer. Because of customer involvement in the delivery of the service, many service providers need to customize the product to meet the purchaser's needs. Thomas Cook, for example, can sell more bus tours in London if it provides Spanish-speaking guides for its Mexican, Venezuelan, and Argentinean clients and Japanese-speaking guides for its Japanese customers. Further, an identical service can be perceived quite differently by each of its customers, thereby creating strategic and marketing problems. The London bus tour, for example, may be viewed with great excitement by Japanese honeymooners on their first trip outside of Osaka but with boredom by a harried Toshiba executive who has visited the city many times.

Many services are tied to the purchase of other products. Many firms offer **product-support services**—assistance with operating, maintaining, and/or repairing products for customers. Such services may be critical to the sale of the related product. For example, Swedish appliance maker AB Electrolux manufactures vacuum cleaners, refrigerators, washing machines, and other appliances under such names as Eureka, Frigidaire, Tappan, and Weed Eater. It also has service operations set up to repair those products for consumers who buy them, to provide replacement parts, and so on. The firm's ability to sell its appliances would be substantially harmed if it did not offer these related services. And it must not only offer them at its corporate home in Stockholm, Sweden. If AB Electrolux wants to compete in the U.S., Canadian, and British markets, it must provide repair and parts distribution services there as well.

The Role of Government in International Services Trade

An important dimension of the international services market is the role of government. Many governments seek to protect local professionals and to ensure that domestic standards and credentials are upheld by restricting the ability of foreigners to practice such professions as law, accounting, and medicine. Government regulations often stipulate which firms are allowed to enter service markets and the prices they may charge. For example, in the United States, foreign banks and insurance firms are heavily regulated and must follow the directives of numerous state and federal regulatory agencies. In many countries, telecommunications, transportation, and utility firms typically need governmental permission to serve individual markets. For example, airline routes between the United States and France are spelled out by a bilateral agreement between those two countries. Air France can fly passengers from Paris to Dallas and from Paris to New York, but it cannot board passengers in New York and fly them to Dallas. U.S. carriers are given similar rights to routes between U.S. and French cities.

On the other hand, the past decade has seen a reduction in domestic and international regulation of many service industries. This deregulation has created opportunities for firms in industries such as banking and telecommunications and spurred them to aggressively seek new domestic markets and expand their operations to foreign markets. For example, the U.S. government deregulated AT&T's activities, thereby giving that firm the opportunity to expand its operations worldwide. In 1985, Japan followed suit by deregulating its largest telephone company, NT&T. As a result, both telecommunications firms are now larger and more profitable than ever before—and competing with each other in dozens of foreign markets. Opportunities for trade in international services are also increasing as a result of the strengthening of regional economic blocs such as the EU and NAFTA.

Managing Service Operations

The actual management of international service operations involves a number of basic issues:

▶ Capacity planning

▶ Location planning

▶ Facilities design and layout

▶ Operations scheduling

Recall that capacity planning is deciding how many customers the firm will be able to serve at one time. Because of the close customer involvement in the purchase of services, capacity planning affects the quality of the services provided to customers. For example, McDonald's first restaurant in Russia was considerably larger than many of its other restaurants in order to accommodate an anticipated higher level of sales volume. Despite this larger size, customer waiting times at the Moscow restaurant are much longer than those in the United States. The lack of restaurant alternatives makes Muscovites more willing to stand in long lines for their "Big Mek." In contrast, if customers had to wait a half-hour to be served in Boulder, Columbus, or even Paris, McDonald's would lose many sales.

As with production management, location planning is important for international service operations. By definition, most service providers must be close to the customers they plan to serve (exceptions might be information providers that rely on electronic communication). Indeed, most international service operations involve setting up branch offices in each foreign market and then staffing each with locals.

International service facilities must also be carefully designed so that the proper look and layout are established. U.S. firms operating internationally typically try to create a look that blends their American heritage with the local culture. At Euro Disney, for example, signs are in both English and French. Many foreign firms, however, try to blend their facilities into the local environment so as to look local. For example, most guests at a Motel 6 in the United States have no idea that the chain is foreign-owned.

Finally, international service firms must schedule their operations to best meet the customers' needs. For example, airlines transporting passengers from the United States to Europe generally depart late in the evening. Doing this gives passengers the opportunity to spend some of the day working before they depart, and they arrive around mid-morning the next day. In contrast, westbound flights usually leave Europe in mid-morning and arrive in the United States late that same afternoon. This scheduling provides an optimal arrangement because it factors in customer preferences, time zones, jet lag, and aircraft maintenance requirements.

CHAPTER REVIEW

Summary

International operations management is the set of activities used by an international firm to transform resources into goods or services. Effective operations management is a key ingredient in any firm's success. A firm's business strategy provides the major direction it will take regarding its operations management activities.

Production management refers to the creation of tangible goods. One of the first decisions production managers must make concerns sourcing and vertical integration. Sourcing, also called procuring, encompasses the set of processes and steps used in acquiring resources and materials. Vertical integration refers to the extent to which a firm either provides its own resources or obtains them externally.

A key decision is whether to make or buy inputs. Several options exist. Production managers attempting to select from among them must consider strategic issues as well as risks, flexibility, investments in facilities, and questions of control.

Location decisions are also of paramount importance to effective international operations management. Country-related considerations include resource availability and costs, infrastructure, and country-of-origin marketing effects. Product-related issues are the value-to-weight ratio, production technology, and the importance of customer feedback. Governmental factors that must be considered include stability of the political process, tariffs and other trade barriers, economic development incentives, and the existence of FTZs. Finally, organizational issues include the firm's strategy, its structure, and its inventory management policies.

International logistics and materials management is also a basic part of production management. Several factors differentiate international from domestic materials management, including shipping distance, transportation modes, and the regulatory context. Packaging, weight, and factory location must also be considered.

Service operations management is concerned with the creation of intangible products. The service sector is an increasingly important part of the global economy. International services are generally characterized as being intangible, not storable, requiring customer participation, and linked with tangible goods. The basic issues involved in managing service operations include capacity planning, location planning, design and layout, and operations scheduling.

Review Questions

1. What is international operations management and how is it accomplished?

2. Why is effective operations management important for an international firm?

3. How does a firm's corporate strategy affect its operations management?

4. How do production management and service operations management differ?

5. What is sourcing? What is vertical integration?

6. What factors must a firm consider when addressing the make-or-buy decision?

7. What basic set of factors must a firm consider when selecting a location for a production facility?

8. How do materials management and physical distribution differ?

9. What trends characterize the service sector of the global economy?

10. What basic factors must be addressed when managing international service operations?

Questions for Discussion

1. How does international operations management relate to international marketing (discussed in Chapter 16)?

2. How are a firm's strategy and operations management interrelated?

3. What constraints do operations impose on strategic options?

4. How do each of the basic business strategies (differentiation, cost leadership, and focus) relate to operations management?

5. What are the basic similarities and differences between production management and service operations management?

6. What are the advantages and disadvantages of being vertically integrated?

7. What are the steps a manager might follow in selecting a site for a new factory?

8. What is the relationship between international operations management and materials management?

9. Why are services most closely associated with developed, industrialized economies?

10. Do you think services will continue to grow in importance?

BUILDING GLOBAL SKILLS

Begin by reading the following, which is adapted from a *Harvard Business Review* case study titled "The Plant Location Puzzle."[31]

Ann Reardon made her way across the crowded trade-show floor, deep in thought and oblivious to the noisy activity all around her. As CEO of The Eldora Company (EDC) for the previous 13 years, she had led her organization through a period of extraordinary success. While larger bicycle makers

had moved their manufacturing operations overseas to take advantage of lower labor costs, Eldora had stuck with a domestic manufacturing strategy, keeping its plant on the same campus as its corporate offices in Boulder, Colorado. Ann felt that her strategy of keeping all the parts of the company in the same location, while unconventional, had contributed greatly to cooperation among various departments and, ultimately, to the company's growth: EDC had become the largest and most profitable bicycle company in the United States. Yet her manufacturing vice president, Sean Andrews, was now urging her to build a plant in China.

"Look at the number of companies here," he had said that morning, as they helped several EDC staffers stack brochures on the exhibit table and position the company's latest models around the perimeter of their area. "There are too many players in this market," he had said. "I've been saying this for two months now, and you know the forecasters' numbers back me up. But if they weren't enough to convince you, just look around. The industry is reaching the saturation point here in the States. We have to break into Asia."...

Ann thought about what Sean had said about the U.S. market. In 1992, EDC's sales and earnings had hit record levels. The company produced almost 30 percent of the bicycles sold in the United States. But U.S. mass-market bicycle sales were growing by only 2 percent per year, while the Asian market for those same bikes was nearly doubling on an annual basis. And Eldora could not competitively serve those markets from its U.S. manufacturing facility. Two of the largest bike manufacturers in the world, located in rapidly growing Asian markets, enjoyed a significant labor and distribution cost advantage....

One of the reasons the company had been so successful was that Boulder, Colorado, was a bicyclists' mecca. Eldora employees at all levels shared a genuine love of bicycling and eagerly pursued knowledge of the industry's latest trends and styles. Someone was always suggesting a better way to position the hand brakes or a new toe grip that allowed for better traction and easier dismounts. And Eldora never had a shortage of people willing to test out the latest prototypes.

Another reason was that all marketing staff, engineers, designers, and manufacturing personnel worked on one campus, within a ten minute walk of one another. Ann had bet big on that strategy, and it had paid off. Communication was easy, and changes in styles, production plans, and the like could be made quickly and efficiently. Mountain bikes, for example, had gone from 0 percent to more than 50 percent of the market volume since 1988, and Eldora had met the increased demand with ease. And when orders for cross-bikes—mountain/road bike hybrids that had enjoyed a spurt of popularity—began to fall off, Eldora had been able to adjust its production run with minimal disruption....

Ann's satisfaction was quickly tempered with thoughts of foreign sales performance. Between 1987 and 1991, EDC's foreign sales had grown at an annual rate of over 80 percent. But during the previous two years, they had been flat.

Sean appeared at Ann's side, jolting her out of her thoughts and into the reality of her surroundings. "Dale just finished up the first round of retailers' meetings," he said. "We'd like to get some lunch back over at the hotel and talk about our options." Dale Stewart was Eldora's marketing vice president. His views of what was best for the company often differed from Sean's, but the two had an amiable working relationship and enjoyed frequent spirited verbal sparring matches....

Over sandwiches, Sean made his case. "Our primary markets in North America and Western Europe represent less than a quarter of the worldwide demand. Of the 200 million bicycles made in the world last year, 40 million were sold in China, 30 million in India, and 9 million in Japan. Historically, bikes sold in Asia's developing markets were low-end products used as primary modes of transportation. But the economic picture is changing fast. There's a growing middle class. Suddenly people have disposable income. Many consumers there are now seeking higher quality and trendier styles. Mountain bikes with suspension are in. And crossbikes are still holding their own. In fact, the demand in those markets for the product categories we produce has been doubling annually, and the growth rates seem sustainable.

"If we're going to compete in Asia, though, we need a local plant. My staff has evaluated many locations there. We've looked at wage rates, proximity to markets, and materials costs, and we feel that China is our best bet. We'd like to open a plant there as soon as possible, and start building our position."

Dale jumped in. "Two of our largest competitors, one from China, one from Taiwan, have been filling the demand so far," he said. "In 1990, 97 percent of the volume produced by these companies was for export. In 1994, they are projecting that 45 percent of their production will be for local markets. We can't compete with them from here. About 20 percent of our product cost is labor, and the hourly wages of the manufacturing workforce in these countries are between 5 percent and 15 percent of ours. It also costs us an additional 20 percent in transportation and duties to get our bicycles to these markets."

He glanced at Sean quickly and continued. "But here's where I disagree with Sean. I think we need a short-term solution. These companies have a big lead on us, and the more I think about it, the more I believe we need to put a direct sales operation in Asia first."

"Dale, you're crazy," Sean said, pouring himself some ice water from the pitcher on the table. "What good would an Asian sales operation do without a manufacturing plant? I know we source components in Asia now, but we could save another 10 percent on those parts if we were located there. Then we would really be bringing Eldora to Asia. If we want to compete there, we have to play from our greatest strength—quality. If we did it your way, you wouldn't be selling Eldora bikes. You'd just be selling some product with our label on it. You wouldn't get the quality. You wouldn't build the same kind of reputation we have here. It wouldn't really be Eldora. Over the long term, it couldn't work."

"We're building bicycles not rocket ships," Dale countered. "There are lots of companies in Asia that could provide us with a product very quickly if we gave them our designs and helped them with their production process. We could outsource production in the short term, until we made more permanent arrangements." He turned to Ann. "We could even outsource the product permanently, despite what Sean says. What do we know about building and running a plant in China? All I know is we're losing potential share even as we sit here. The trading companies aren't giving our products the attention they deserve, and they also aren't giving us the information we need on the features that consumers in those markets want. A sales operation would help us learn the market even as we're entering it. Setting up a plant first would take too long. We need to be over there now, and opening a sales operation is the quickest way."

Ann cut in. "Dale has a good point, Sean," she said. "We've been successful here in large part because our entire operation is in Boulder, on one site. We've had complete control over our own flexible manufacturing operation, and that's been a key factor in our ability to meet rapid change in the local market. How would we address the challenges inherent in manufacturing in a facility halfway around the world?

Would you consider moving there? And for how long?

"Also, think about our other options. If the biggest issue keeping us out of these markets right now is cost, then both of you are ignoring a few obvious alternatives. Right now, only our frame-building operation is automated. We could cut labor costs significantly by automating more processes. And why are you so bent on China? Frankly, when I was there last month touring facilities, a lot of what I saw worried me. You know, that day I was supposed to tour a production facility, there was a power failure. Judging by the reactions of the personnel in the plant the next day, these outages are common. The roads to the facility are in very poor condition. And wastewater and cleaning solvents are regularly dumped untreated into the waterways. We could operate differently if we located there, but what impact would that have on costs?

"Taiwan has a better developed infrastructure than China. What about making that our Asian base? And I've heard that Singapore offers attractive tax arrangements to new manufacturing operations. Then there's Mexico. It's closer to home, and aside from distribution costs, the wage rates are similar to Asia's and many of the other risks would be minimized. You both feel strongly about this, I know, but this isn't a decision we can make based on enthusiasm."...

Walking back to the convention center with Dale and Sean, Ann realized that she wasn't just frustrated because she didn't know which course EDC should pursue. She was concerned that she really didn't know which aspects of the decision were important and which were irrelevant. Should she establish a division in China? If so, which functions should she start with? Manufacturing? Marketing? And what about engineering? Or should she consider a different location? Would China's low labor costs offset problems caused by poor infrastructure?

Growth had always been vitally important to Eldora, both in creating value to shareholders and in providing a work environment that could attract and retain the most talented people. Now it appeared that Ann would have to choose between continued growth and a domestic-only manufacturing strategy that had served her well.

Now that you have read the case study, you are ready to participate in the exercise related to it. First, make sure you completely understand the details of the case. Next, form groups of six people each. One person should adopt the role of Ann Reardon, one the role of Sean Andrews, and one the role of Dale Stewart. The other three group members will constitute the board of directors of The Eldora Company. If the number of people in the class doesn't divide evenly by six, the board of directors can be increased in size. Ann, Sean, and Dale should each summarize for the board—in two minutes or less—the basic issues each sees regarding the firm's potential entry into the Asian market.

The board of directors should then use its own understanding of the background material (in the

case itself) to discuss and debate whether to build a new plant in Asia. Your instructor will then ask each group to summarize its deliberations and report on its final decision.

Follow-up Questions

1. How similar or different were the reports from each group?

2. Why do you think this pattern of similarities or differences occurred?

CLOSING CASE

Principles to Fasten Onto[32]

For the average hard-nosed stock market investor, laudable concepts such as partnership sourcing, just-in-time delivery, and total quality management tend to take second place to cash flow, gearing, and dividend payments.

But for Malcolm Diamond, managing director of Sussex-based Trifast, they are three guiding principles for business. After a decade using them, and persuading customers to work in partnership with Trifast, he is hoping to convince investors of their importance, too.

Trifast is going public next month in a £15 million flotation that will raise £3 million–£4 million for the company—most of the rest will go to its two founders, who are cashing in a big part of their stake....

In financial terms, it is an unexceptional deal, and Trifast's products—some 70,000 different types of industrial fasteners with names like the Binx Nut and the Hank Rivet Bush—are unlikely to get City types salivating. But, apart from offering an investment in a barometer of the U.K. electronics and electrical industry, where most of Trifast's fastenings end up, it is also a rare opportunity to invest in a U.K. pioneer of influential management ideas.

Diamond, who has worked at Trifast for 19 years and been its managing director since 1984, talks

about the three principles with as much commitment and enthusiasm as on the subject of the latest technology for putting heads onto screws. He says they are much more than just a philosophical framework—there is a clear link between their adoption and the financial performance of the company, which trades as TR Fastenings.

The practice for which Trifast has gained most recognition is known as partnership sourcing. This involves it becoming sole supplier to a customer, normally for all its fastener needs, and often supplying direct to the production line.

With a high degree of trust on both sides, paperwork can be cut to a minimum, the customers' stock levels can be reduced and Trifast gets the security of long-term business in return for giving a better overall service.

Up to this point, partnership sourcing has much in common with another new approach known as "fastener management." In this case a supplier such as Trifast takes responsibility for all the customer's fastener needs, in line with the trend towards the contracting out of "non-core" services.

But the partnership approach goes further, as it leads to a cradle-to-grave relationship on each of the customer's products. The supplier gets an early look at planned products so that it can work out its own schedules and make suggestions to the customers, and also receives early warning of when a product is to be replaced.

Partnership sourcing has become increasingly important in the information technology and electronics industry, where short product cycles and the fast pace of change make such a relationship mutually beneficial—if not crucial, especially for the supplier. Other fastener companies, such as Infast, part of Haden MacLellan Holdings, are also developing such arrangements with customers. Partnership sourcing is also being promoted more widely by the Department of Trade and Industry and the Confederation of British Industry.

Roger Hardman of James Capel, Trifast's broker, claims partnership sourcing is part of a virtuous triangle that also comprises JIT and TQM. "None of these philosophies is much use without the others," he says. "It's all indicative of an approach that puts the customer first."

Trifast's involvement with partnership sourcing began a decade ago when IBM UK wanted to reduce costs by thinning its supplier base. "They told us we were an average supplier of fasteners, but our attitudes were better than average," says Diamond. "So we were selected as a guinea pig—because with so many types of fasteners there is so much scope for things to go wrong."

Initially staggered by the demands on quality and delivery made by IBM in return for becoming a single supplier of fasteners, Trifast has now won two of the computer company's "market driven quality" awards and gained sufficiently in confidence to take the concept to other customers.

Diamond likens partnership sourcing to a supermarket that customers use because of the overall package—the convenience of shopping in one place, known reliability, and quality—even though some individual items might be found more cheaply by going round to several shops.

The challenge, says Bob Stevens, group quality director, is to convince purchasing managers to look at overall costs rather than price and to accept that partnership sourcing can lead to savings even if it does not put money in their hands. The costs and time involved in repeatedly contacting a batch of fastener suppliers, asking about price and delivery and choosing the best deal, are frequently overlooked.

"Very rarely do fasteners exceed 1 percent of total purchasing," says Diamond, "but the overheads often exceed that." Once the core relationship is established, however, there are some useful spin-offs for Trifast. Some information technology suppliers are using the fastener supplier to bring in items such as cabling and industrial gloves on its regular trips to fill the fastener bins, says Martin Phillips, director responsible for sales to the information technology and electronics industries.

Partnership sourcing and fastener management have taken off for Trifast in the past five years, comments Stevens, and it now has 70 customers using such arrangements. This represents just 2 percent of its customer base of 3500, but already accounts for about a third of its annual sales and could reach half, says Diamond.

For investors, there are two points about such arrangements. First, the margins on this business are generally higher, says Diamond. Just as importantly, partnership sourcing "locks in" the supplier to the customer, insulating at least part of the business from the vagaries of the traditional customer-supplier battleground.

Case Questions

1. Provide an overview of how Trifast manages its operations function.

2. What are the advantages and disadvantages to Trifast of its partnership approach to sourcing?

3. Why do you think Trifast managers see partnership sourcing as being so closely related to the JIT inventory management system and TQM?

4. Do you think partnership sourcing will become more popular in the future? Why or why not?

5. What should an organization look for when selecting a sourcing partner?

CHAPTER NOTES

1. "Fashionable Tech: How Benetton Keeps Costs Down," *Information Week*, February 12, 1990, pp. 24–25; Alan Chai, Alta Campbell, and Patrick J. Spain (eds.), *Hoover's Handbook of World Business 1993* (Austin, Tex.: Reference Press, 1993), pp. 150–151; "The Faded Colors of Benetton," *Business Week*, April 10, 1995, pp. 87–90.

2. Barrie James, "Reducing the Risks of Globalization," *Long Range Planning*, Vol. 23, No. 1 (1990), pp. 80–88.

3. Scott Young, K. Kern Kwong, Cheng Li, and Wing Fok, "Global Manufacturing Strategies and Practices: A Study of Two Industries," *International Journal of Operations & Production Management*, Vol. 12, No. 9 (1992), pp. 5–17.

4. "The Meltdown at Metallgesellschaft ..." *Business Week*, January 24, 1994, pp. 48–49.

5. Robert H. Hayes and Gary P. Pisano, "Beyond World-Class: The New Manufacturing Strategy," *Harvard Business Review* (January–February 1994), pp. 77–87.

6. Michael McGrath and Richard Hoole, "Manufacturing's New Economies of Scale," *Harvard Business Review* (May–June 1992), pp. 94–103.

7. Masaaki Kotabe and Janet Y. Murray, "Linking Product and Process Innovations and Modes of International Sourcing in Global Competition: A Case of Foreign Manufacturing Firms," *Journal of International Business Studies* (Third Quarter, 1990), pp. 383–408.

8. Ravi Venkatesan, "Strategic Sourcing: To Make or Not To Make," *Harvard Business Review* (November–December 1992), pp. 98–108.

9. James Brian Quinn and Frederick G. Hilmer, "Strategic Outsourcing," *Sloan Management Review* (Summer 1994), pp. 43–55.

10. James A. Welch and P. Ranganath Nayak, "Strategic Sourcing: A Progressive Approach to Make-or-Buy Approach," *The Academy of Management Executive* (February 1992), pp. 23–31.

11. Stephen J. Kobrin, "An Empirical Analysis of the Determinants of Global Integration," *Strategic Management Journal*, Vol. 12 (1991), pp. 17–31.

12. Peter Siddall, Keith Willey, and Jorge Tavares, "Building a Transnational Organization for British Petroleum," *Long Range Planning*, Vol. 25, No. 1 (1992), pp. 18–26.

13. Welch and Nayak, op. cit.

14. David Flath, "Keiretsu Shareholding Ties: Antitrust Issues," *Contemporary Economic Issues*, Vol. 12, No. 1 (January 1994), pp. 24–36.

15. Myron Magnet, "The New Golden Rule of Business," *Fortune*, February 21, 1994, pp. 60–64.

16. "U.S. Companies Move to Limit Currency Risk," *Wall Street Journal*, August 3, 1993, p. A10.

17. Alex Taylor, III, "The Auto Industry Meets the New Economy," *Fortune*, September 5, 1994, pp. 52–60.

18. Alan D. MacCormack, Lawrence J. Newman, III, and Donald B. Rosenfield, "The New Dynamics of Global Manufacturing Site Location," *Sloan Management Review* (Summer 1994), pp. 69–80.

19. Victor V. Cordell, "Effects of Consumer Preferences for Foreign Sourced Products," *Journal of International Business Studies*, Vol. 23, No. 2 (Second Quarter 1992), pp. 251–270; Paul Chao, "Partitioning Country of Origin Effects: Consumer Evaluations of a Hybrid Product," *Journal of International Business Studies*, Vol. 24, No. 2 (Second Quarter 1993), pp. 291–306; Frederick W. Schroath, Michael Y. Hu, and Haiyang Chen, "Country-of-Origin Effects of Foreign Investments in the People's Republic of China," *Journal of International Business Studies*, Vol. 24, No. 2 (Second Quarter 1993), pp. 277–290.

20. Andrew D. Bartmess, "The Plant Location Puzzle," *Harvard Business Review* (March–April 1994), pp. 20–22.

21. Dwight Silverman, "Compaq plans to build $15 million Brazil plant," *Houston Chronicle*, March 23, 1994, p. 1B.

22. "'The Exodus of German Industry Is Under Way,'" *Business Week*, May 25, 1994, pp. 42–43.

23. Patriya S. Tansuhaj and George C. Jackson, "Foreign Trade Zones: A Comparative Analysis of Users and Non-Users," *Journal of Business Logistics*, Vol. 10, No. 1 (1989), pp. 15–30.

24. "Ford Is Expected to Name President of Global Auto Operations This Week," *Wall Street Journal*, April 19, 1994, p. B10.

25. John H. Roberts, "Formulating and Implementing a Global Logistics Strategy," *The International Journal of Logistics Management*, Vol. 1, No. 2 (1990), pp. 53–58.

26. William C. Capacino and Frank F. Britt, "Perspectives on Global Logistics," *The International Journal of Logistics Management*, Vol. 2, No. 1 (1991), pp. 35–41.

27. Walter Zinn and Robert E. Grosse, "Barriers to Globalization: Is Global Distribution Possible?" *The International Journal of Logistics Management*, Vol. 1 (1990), pp. 13–18.

28. Clyde E. Witt, "Packaging: From the Plant Floor to the Global Customer," *Material Handling Engineer* (October 1992), pp. 3–31.

29. Ronald Henkoff, "Service Is Everybody's Business," *Fortune*, June 27, 1994, pp. 48–60.

30. Richard B. Chase and Warren J. Erikson, "The Service Factory," *The Academy of Management Executive* (August 1988), pp. 191–196.

31. Reprinted by permission of *Harvard Business Review*. An excerpt from "The Plant Location Puzzle" by Andrew D. Bartmess, March/April 1994. Copyright © 1994 by the President and Fellows of Harvard College; all rights reserved.

32. "Principles to Fasten On To," from *Financial Times*, January 24, 1994. Reprinted with permission.

SHOULD INTERNATIONAL BUSINESSES PROMOTE HUMAN AND WORKER RIGHTS?

International Businesses Have a Moral Obligation to Protect Human and Worker Rights

It is a common business practice today for firms to move their manufacturing facilities to countries in which production costs are low or to subcontract production to local firms in those countries. Unfortunately, the reasons for the low production costs may be inadequate wages, unsafe or unhealthy working conditions, and disregard for worker rights. For example, two hundred people died in a 1993 fire in a Thai toy factory that lacked basic safety precautions such as fire extinguishers and sprinkler systems.

Businesses that set up shop in foreign countries have an obligation to make the proper treatment of local employees a high priority. Just because an MNC might be able to get away with paying substandard wages and providing poor working conditions by no means suggests that it should do so. Indeed, today's international businesses have a social obligation to improve the quality of life for their employees and those of their subcontractors worldwide.

To do so makes good business sense for several reasons. First, it is simply good public relations. Firms that allow their foreign workers to be treated poorly fare badly themselves when their practices receive media attention. For example, Wal-Mart was recently the focus of a TV news report because it was selling shirts made by Bangladeshi children. Public pressure forced the retailer to alter its buying practices to avoid such problems in the future.

Second, human rights advocates argue that to treat employees poorly violates human rights. This simple premise becomes even more persuasive when it is augmented with stories and examples detailing such abhorrent practices as using what amounts to slave labor and physically abusing workers.

Third, international businesses can make a difference in the world by practicing more humanitarian HRM policies. Levi Strauss is an excellent example of a firm that has taken to heart the importance of treating its foreign workers with dignity and providing them with the proper rewards and working conditions. This firm mandates that all its foreign plants, including those of its subcontractors, must maintain safety and health practices comparable to those in the United States. For example, drinking water purity and bathroom conditions must meet U.S. standards.

When businesses set up operations in foreign countries, they should have the same regard for their workers as they have at home. These IBM workers in Brazil, for example, have safety equipment and procedures comparable to those used by IBM workers around the world.

Such Objectives, While Noble, Are Often Counterproductive

Often the only comparative advantage that developing countries have in the international marketplace is low wage rates. International businesses locating in these countries should be allowed to exploit fully these countries' low-cost production opportunities as long as they adhere to local customs and norms.

If foreign MNCs were required to pay above-market wages or to provide working conditions equal to those in developed countries, the economic development of poorer countries might be crippled. If an international giant moves into a low-cost region and pays higher-than-normal wages, workers will no longer be willing to work for the prevailing wage rate. Thus costs for local businesses increase. In addition, requiring foreign firms to pay above-market wages and benefits will discourage them from locating in developing countries. Such countries need to lure more foreign capital and technology, not drive it away.

Some government officials in developing countries believe the sentiments expressed by worker rights advocates in richer countries are thinly disguised attempts at protectionism. In their view, public pressure to force Western retailers to buy goods only from factories that pay wages and offer working conditions equivalent to those in the Quad countries acts as a NTB against goods from developing countries.

These officials also often resent these pressures as a form of cultural imperialism by Westerners who have little first-hand knowledge of the often harsh economic alternatives facing workers in developing countries. When Levi Strauss recently discovered that one of its Bangladeshi factories was employing young children, it demanded that the factory's practices be changed. The manager pointed out that most of the children were their families' only source of income and to deprive them of a job would bring hardship on entire families. In some regions of Southeast Asia, the situation is far worse: children who are unable to obtain jobs are often sold into prostitution by their families. Critics argue that given these alternatives, foreign MNCs should stick to providing jobs for developing countries and leave the social engineering to local governments.

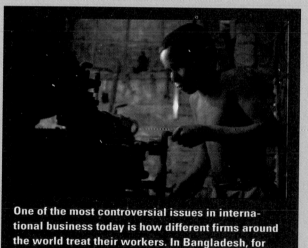

One of the most controversial issues in international business today is how different firms around the world treat their workers. In Bangladesh, for example, children are often used to perform difficult jobs under adverse working conditions while being paid minimal wages.

Wrap-up

1. What ethical responsibilities do MNCs have to their workers in developing countries? Do their ethical responsibilities differ for workers employed at a firm-owned factory and workers employed at a subcontractor's factory?

2. Do you agree that attempts to impose Western-style wage rates and working conditions on factories in developing countries constitute an NTB? Why or why not?

Chapter Outline

Financial issues in international trade
Choice of currency
Credit checking
Methods of payment
Financing trade

Managing foreign-exchange risk
Transaction exposure
Translation exposure
Economic exposure

Management of working capital
Minimizing working capital balances
Minimizing currency conversion costs
Minimizing foreign-exchange risks

International capital budgeting
Net present value
Internal rate of return
Payback period

Sources of international investment capital
Internal sources of investment capital
External sources of investment capital

After studying this chapter you should be able to:

Discuss the major forms of payment in international trade.

Identify the primary types of foreign-exchange risk faced by international businesses.

Describe the techniques used by firms to manage their working capital.

Evaluate the various capital budgeting techniques used for international investments.

Discuss the primary sources of investment capital available to international businesses.

K LM ROYAL DUTCH AIRLINES (KLM) LIVES OR DIES IN THE INTER-national market. It has virtually no domestic market because the physical size of the Netherlands does not lend itself to extensive airline travel: the country is smaller than West Virginia, and its two major cities, Amsterdam and Rotterdam, are only 40 miles apart. KLM is 38.2 percent owned by the Dutch government, and as the world's fifteenth-largest airline, competes head-to-head against other major international carriers, including American, United, Delta, British Airways, Lufthansa, Air France, Japan Air Lines, Qantas, and Singapore Airlines. ■■ The foundation of KLM's global success is its reputation for providing high-quality service. Its service has lured pas-

KLM's Worldwide Financial Management[1]

sengers of all nationalities to its flights, particularly highly valued business travelers, who are willing to pay a premium for luxurious and reliable service. Only 29 percent of its business is done on the friendly turf of Europe. Asian operations account for 19 percent of its revenues, and the critical U.S.-Netherlands market accounts for over 25 percent. ■■ KLM is one of a handful of European carriers that has held its own against the mighty U.S. airlines in the transatlantic market. In 1993, U.S. carriers held 69 percent of the U.S.-France market, 60 percent of the U.S.-Germany market, and 48 percent of the U.S.-U.K. market. However, they captured only 27 percent of U.S.-Netherlands market. KLM's success in this transatlantic market is due in part to its purchase of 22 percent of Minneapolis-based Northwest Airlines, the world's eighth-largest airline. KLM and Northwest coordinate their flight schedules to entice U.S.-Europe travelers to use KLM on the transatlantic leg and Northwest on the U.S. leg of their trips. To heighten their appeal to quality-sensitive passengers, the two airlines jointly market their premium-priced World Business Class service throughout their two route networks. ■■ A truly international carrier, KLM services more than 150 cities on six continents. But its international success brings a major financial challenge—managing its holdings of the 180 or so currencies it uses in the normal conduct of business. KLM receives from its customers a rainbow of currencies, including francs (Belgian, French, and Swiss), crowns (Czech, Danish, Norwegian, Slovak, and Swedish), dollars (Australian, Canadian, Hong Kong, New Zealand and U.S.), as well as yen, marks, and, of course, Dutch guilders. It also must pay in local currency for local services—landing fees, ground handling services, travel agent commissions, and so on—in each country in which it does business. ■■ Further, the firm has had to obtain over $2 billion to pay for aircraft from U.S. manufacturers. To fund its aircraft purchases and other operational needs, KLM has borrowed the equivalent of $1.6 billion from international sources, including 38 billion yen, 780 million Swiss francs, 194 million French francs, 160 million deutsche marks, 412 million U.S. dollars, 900,000 ECUs, and 695 million Dutch guilders. ■■ Managing the firm's revenues, expenses, assets, and liabilities, all denominated in various foreign currencies, is a major task for KLM's financial officers. To pay local expenses, they must maintain local-currency cash balances in each country. They also must search worldwide for sources of low-cost capital in order to modernize the firm's aircraft fleet and thereby maintain its reputation for high-quality service. In addition, they must protect KLM from exchange-rate fluctuations, which will change the value in guilders that it receives for its services and the cost in guilders that it pays for aircraft, fuel, flight services, and ground handling. These officers must thoroughly understand how the contemporary international monetary system operates. They must monitor changes in the foreign-exchange market, be knowledgeable about potential shifts in government economic policies in their major markets, and constantly shop for the best credit terms in such capital markets as Amsterdam, London, Frankfurt, New York, and Tokyo. ■■■■■

In most business transactions, the receipt of goods by the buyer and the receipt of payment by the seller in a form the seller can use immediately do not coincide. Even when a customer pays for goods with a check, the seller will not have access to the funds until the check clears. Until then, the seller risks having the check returned because of insufficient funds. Thus some type of financing and some degree of trust between buyer and seller are necessary to allow business transactions to occur.

While these problems affect both domestic and international business, the problems of financing and credit checking are far greater for international transactions. Differences in laws, customs, financial practices, and currency convertibility among countries mean that an international firm must know the practices both of its home country and of each country in which it does business—or else hire experts who do. A firm also must acquire specific credit information about the foreign firms with which it wants to deal. On top of these problems is that of transacting in a foreign currency—a problem that either the buyer or the seller must face. Financial officers of international businesses like KLM are well aware of the challenges created by using different currencies. How international businesses address these myriad problems is the subject of this chapter.

Financial Issues in International Trade

We begin by considering the problems associated with financing international trade. In any business transaction, the buyer and the seller must negotiate and reach agreement on such basic issues as price, quantity, and delivery date. However, when the transaction involves a buyer and seller from two countries, several other issues arise:

▶ Which currency to use for the transaction

▶ When and how to check credit

▶ Which form of payment to use

▶ How to arrange financing

Choice of Currency

One problem unique to international business is choosing the currency to use to settle a transaction. Exporters and importers usually have clear and conflicting preferences as to which currency to use. The exporter typically prefers payment in its home currency so that it can know the exact amount it will receive from the importer. The importer generally prefers to pay in its home currency so that it can know the exact amount it must pay the exporter. Sometimes an exporter and an importer may elect to use a third currency. For example, if both parties are based in countries with relatively weak or volatile local currencies, they may prefer to deal in a more stable currency such as the deutsche mark, the Japanese yen, or the U.S. dollar. By one estimate, over 70 percent of the exports of less developed countries and 85 percent of the exports of Latin American countries are invoiced using the U.S. dollar.[2] In some industries, one currency is customarily used to settle commercial transactions. For example, in the oil industry, the U.S. dollar serves this function. Among the major exporting countries, however, the most common practice is for the exporter to invoice foreign customers using its home currency.[3] Japan is the one exception to this rule; it invoices most of its exports to the United States in U.S. dollars.

Credit Checking

Another critical financial issue in international trade concerns the reliability and trustworthiness of the buyer. If an importer is a financially healthy and reliable company and one with whom an exporter has had previous satisfactory business relations, the exporter may choose to simplify the payment process by extending credit to the importer. But if the importer is financially troubled or known to be a poor credit risk, the exporter may demand a form of payment that reduces its risk.

In any commercial transactions, it is wise to check customers' credit ratings. For most domestic business transactions, firms have simple and inexpensive mechanisms for doing this. In the United States, for example, firms may ask for credit references or contact established sources of credit information such as Dun & Bradstreet. Similar sources are available in other countries: however, many first-time exporters are unaware of them. Fortunately, an exporter's domestic banker often can obtain credit information on foreign customers through the bank's foreign banking operations or through its correspondent bank in a customer's country. Most national government agencies in charge of export promotion also offer credit-checking services. For example, the International Trade Administration, a branch of the U.S. Department of Commerce, provides financial information about foreign firms for a fee. Numerous commercial credit-reporting services are also available. Country desk officers of the U.S. and Foreign Commercial Service are available to steer new exporters to these services.

The firm that ignores the credit-checking process may run into serious payment problems. In the early 1990s, for example, one small U.S. manufacturer exported $127,000 worth of fan blades to a new customer in Africa. However, it failed to first contact any of the customer's credit references. Frustrated by the subsequent lack of payment, the manufacturer turned the account over to a collection agency, which discovered that the supposed customer had vanished and its credit references were nonexistent.[4]

Implicit in this discussion is an important lesson that many successful international businesspeople have learned the hard way. Because the physical and cultural gaps between the exporter and the importer are often large, finding partners, customers, and distributors with whom to build long-term, trusting relationships is invaluable to any international business.

Method of Payment

As with domestic transactions, firms engaged in international transactions must select the method of payment carefully.[5] The parties to the transaction negotiate a method of payment based on the exporter's assessment of the importer's creditworthiness. Many forms of payment have been developed over the centuries, including the following:

▶ Payment in advance

▶ Open account

▶ Documentary collection

▶ Letters of credit

▶ Credit cards

▶ Countertrade

As with most aspects of finance, each form involves different degrees of risk and cost.

Payment in Advance. From the exporter's perspective, the safest method of payment in international trade is payment in advance: the exporter receives the importer's money prior to shipping the goods. Using this method, the exporter can reduce its risk and also receive payment quickly, which may be important if its working capital balance is low. Exporters prefer payments in advance to be made by wire transfer, which allows immediate use of the funds. Payment by ordinary check may take four to six weeks to clear the banking systems of the two countries involved, depending on the size and sophistication of their financial services sectors.

From the importer's perspective, payment in advance is very undesirable. The importer must give up the use of its cash prior to the receipt of the goods. The importer also bears the risk that the exporter will fail to deliver the goods in accordance with the sales contract. For these reasons, exporters that insist on payment in advance are vulnerable to losing sales to competitors willing to offer more attractive payment terms. Nonetheless, payment in advance may be the preferred form if the importer is a poor credit risk.

Open Account. From the importer's perspective, the safest form of payment is the **open account**, whereby goods are shipped by the exporter and received by the importer prior to payment. The exporter then bills the importer for the goods, stipulating the amount, form, and time at which payment is expected. Open accounts also can be used as a marketing tool because they offer potential buyers short-term financing. Use of an open account enables the importer to avoid the fees charged by banks for alternative means of payment such as letters of credit or documentary collection, which will be discussed shortly. An open account has the further advantage of requiring less paperwork than do these other forms of payment.

From the exporter's perspective, an open account may be undesirable for several reasons. First, the exporter must rely primarily on the importer's reputation for paying promptly. Second, since the transaction does not involve a financial intermediary like a bank, the exporter cannot fall back on such an intermediary's expertise if a dispute arises with the importer. Third, the exporter may pay a price for the advantage of doing less paperwork: if the importer refuses to pay, the lack of documentation can hamper the exporter's pursuit of a claim in the courts of the importer's home country. Finally, the exporter must tie up working capital to finance foreign accounts receivable. Borrowing working capital collateralized by foreign receivables is often expensive, because it is difficult for domestically oriented lenders to evaluate the riskiness of a firm's portfolio of foreign receivables. Such borrowing is not impossible, however. Numerous firms engage in a specialized international lending activity called **factoring**, in which they buy foreign accounts receivable at a discount from face value. The size of the fees these firms charge (in the form of the discount from face value of the receivables) reflect both the time value of money and the factor's assessment of the portfolio's riskiness.

As a result, an open account is best suited for dealing with well-established, long-term customers or larger firms with impeccable credit ratings and reputations for timely payment of their bills. For example, U.S. video film distributors that deal with Blockbuster Video in the United States on an open account basis might offer the same arrangement to Citivision PLC, Blockbuster's subsidiary in the United Kingdom, particularly if Blockbuster pledged to honor Citivision's trade obligations. Similarly, foreign subsidiaries owned by a common parent corporation often deal with each other on an open account basis, since the risk of default in such circumstances is minimal. By some estimates, as much as 35 percent of U.S. international trade involves transactions between subsidiaries of a parent firm.

Payment in advance and an open account share a basic similarity. Both shift the cash flow burden and risk of default to one party in the transaction: to the buyer in the case of payment in advance and to the seller in the case of an open account.

Documentary Collection. To get around the cash flow and risk problems caused by the use of payment in advance and open accounts, international businesses and banks have developed several other methods to finance transactions. One is **documentary collection**, whereby commercial banks serve as agents to facilitate the payment process. To initiate this method of payment, the exporter draws up a document called a **draft** (often called a *bill of exchange* outside the United States), in which payment is demanded from the buyer at a specified time. After the exporter ships its goods, it submits to its local banker the draft and appropriate shipping documents, such as the packing list and the bill

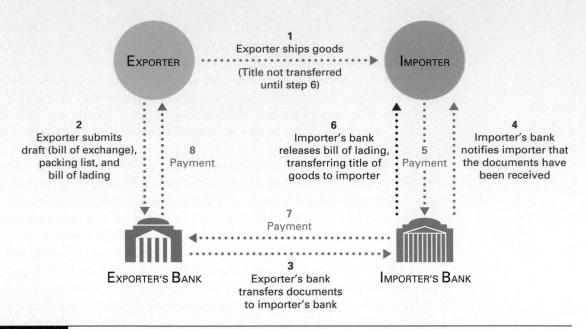

FIGURE 18.1

Using a Sight Draft

Note: In the case of a time draft, the importer makes a promise to pay, not the actual payment, in step 5.

Source: Based on *Dynamics of Trade Finance*, Chase Manhattan Bank, 1989, p. 42.

of lading.[6] The **bill of lading** plays two important roles in documentary collection: it serves as both a contract for transportation between the exporter and the carrier and as title to the goods in question. Acting on the exporter's instructions, the exporter's bank then contacts its correspondent bank in the importer's country (or one of its own branches there, if it has any). The latter bank is authorized to release the bill of lading, thereby transferring title of the goods, when the importer honors the terms of the exporter's draft.[7] This process is shown in Fig. 18.1.

There are two major forms of drafts:

1 A **sight draft** requires payment upon the transfer of title to the goods from the exporter to the importer. When the bank in the importer's country receives the bill of lading and the sight draft from the exporter's bank, it notifies the importer, which then pays the draft. Upon payment, the bank gives the bill of lading to the importer, which can then take title to the goods.

2 A **time draft** extends credit to the importer by requiring payment at some specified time, such as 30 or 60 days, after the importer receives the goods. (A variant of the time draft, the **date draft**, specifies a particular date on which payment will be made.)

To obtain title to the goods when a time draft is used, the importer must write "accepted" on the draft, thereby incurring a legal obligation to pay the draft when it comes due. An accepted time draft is called a **trade acceptance**, which under the laws of most countries is a legally enforceable and negotiable debt instrument. For a fee, the importer's bank may also accept a time draft, thereby adding its own obligation to pay the draft to the importer's. In this case, the time draft becomes a **banker's acceptance**.

The exporter may hold either a trade acceptance or a banker's acceptance until it comes due. But banks and other commercial lenders are often willing to buy acceptances at a discount, thereby allowing the exporter to receive immediate cash. Some acceptances are sold **without recourse**, meaning that the buyer of the acceptance is stuck with the loss if the importer does not pay. Others are sold **with recourse**, meaning that the exporter will have to reimburse the buyer of the acceptance in the case of nonpayment by the importer. Exporters planning to sell their accepted time drafts must balance the prices they will receive for them against the additional banking fees they must pay (in the case of banker's acceptances) and the degree of risk they are willing to bear (in the case of acceptances sold with recourse). Because of their greater riskiness, acceptances sold without recourse are sold at bigger discounts from face value than acceptances sold with recourse. Similarly, since banker's acceptances are guaranteed by the bank as well as by the importer, they are less risky and are usually discounted less than trade acceptances are.

For an exporter, payment through documentary collection has several advantages over the use of open accounts. First, the bank fees for documentary collection are quite reasonable because the banks act as agents, rather than risk-takers (unless a banker's acceptance is involved). Second, a trade acceptance or a banker's acceptance is an enforceable debt instrument under the laws of most countries, thereby solidifying the exporter's legal position if the importer defaults on its promise to pay. Third, using banks simplifies the collection process for the exporter and substitutes the banks' superior expertise in effecting international payments for the exporter's presumably inferior knowledge. Further, because the collection agent is a local bank, and the importer does not want to jeopardize its business reputation with a local lender, the importer is more likely to pay a time draft promptly than a bill sent under an open account. Finally, because of the enforceability of acceptances in courts of law, arranging financing for foreign accounts receivable is easier and less expensive when documentary collection is used than when open accounts are used.

With documentary collection, the exporter still bears some risks, however. Suppose local business conditions change or the importer finds a cheaper supply source. In such a case, an importer may simply refuse the shipment and decline to accept the draft, perhaps under a false pretext that the shipment was late or the goods improperly packed. The importer's default on the sales contract places the exporter in the unenviable position of having its goods piled up on a foreign loading dock (and running up storage fees) while receiving no payment for them. Alternatively, the importer may default on the time draft when it comes due. The exporter may have legal remedies in either case. But pursuing them is often costly in terms of time, energy, and money.

Letters of Credit. To arrange for payment, international businesses often use a **letter of credit**, a document that is issued by a bank and contains its promise to pay the exporter upon receiving proof that the exporter has fulfilled all requirements specified in the document. Because of the bank's pledge, the exporter bears less risk by using a letter of credit than by relying on documentary collection. However, cautious bankers are unlikely to issue a letter of credit unless they fully expect the importer to reimburse them. Thus, using a letter of credit has additional benefits in that the exporter benefits from the bank's knowledge of the importer's creditworthiness, the requirements of the importer's home country customs service, and any restrictions the importer's home country government imposes on currency movements.

Usually, an importer applies to its local bank—in most cases, one with which it has an ongoing relationship—for a letter of credit. The bank then assesses the importer's creditworthiness, examines the proposed transaction, determines whether it wants collateral, and, assuming everything is in order, issues the letter of credit. The bank typically charges the importer a small commission for this service. The letter of credit details the conditions under which the importer's bank will pay the exporter for the goods. The conditions imposed by the issuing bank reflect normal sound business practices. Most letters of credit require the exporter to supply an invoice, appropriate customs documents, a bill of lading, a packing list, and proof of insurance. Depending on the product involved, the importer's bank may demand additional documentation before funding the letter, such as the following:

▶ *Export licenses* are issued by an agency of the exporter's home country. They may be required for politically sensitive goods, such as nuclear fuels, or for high-technology goods that may have military uses.

▶ *Certificates of product origin* confirm that the goods being shipped were produced in the exporting country. They may be required by the importing country so that it can assess tariffs and enforce quotas.

▶ *Inspection certificates* may be needed to provide assurance that the products have been inspected and that they conform to relevant standards. For example, imported foodstuffs often must meet rigorous standards regarding pesticides, cleanliness, sanitation, and storage.

After issuing the letter of credit, the importer's bank sends it and the accompanying documents to the exporter's bank, which advises the exporter of the terms of the instrument, thereby creating an **advised letter of credit**. Alternatively, the exporter can request its bank to add its own guarantee of payment to the letter of credit, thereby creating a **confirmed letter of credit**. This type of instrument is particularly appropriate when the exporter is concerned about political risk. If the importer's home country government later imposes currency controls or otherwise blocks payment by the importer's bank, the exporter can look to the confirming bank for payment.

Another type of letter of credit is the **irrevocable letter of credit**, which cannot be altered without the written consent of both the importer and the exporter. A bank may also issue a **revocable letter of credit**, which it may alter at any time and for any reason. An irrevocable letter of credit offers the exporter more protection than a revocable letter of credit does. However, amending such an instrument can be cumbersome, expensive, and time-consuming.

Banks that issue, advise on, and/or confirm letters of credit charge for their services. Therefore, international firms must determine which of these services they really need in order to avoid paying unnecessary fees.

When goods are sold under a letter of credit, payment does not depend on meeting the terms of the sales contract between the buyer and seller. Rather the bank issuing the letter of credit will make payment only when the terms of that letter have been fulfilled. Thus the exporter must carefully analyze the letter's terms before agreeing to them, to be sure that they are compatible with the sales contract.

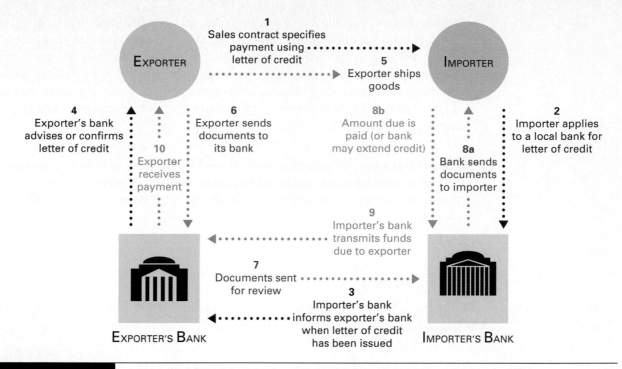

FIGURE 18.2

Using a Letter of Credit

Source: Based on *Dynamics of Trade Finance*, Chase Manhattan Bank, 1989, pp. 62–63.

Surprisingly, it is this feature of letters of credit—that they are paid when their terms are met, not when the sales contract is fulfilled—that makes them so useful in international trade. Once the exporter meets the letter's terms, the importer's bank is obligated to pay the exporter even if the importer refuses the shipment or fails to pay for the goods. Such difficulties become the problem of the importer's bank, not the exporter. But the likelihood of such difficulties arising are reduced because the importer is unlikely to jeopardize its credit lines with its bank. Figure 18.2 shows how a letter of credit is used in a typical international transaction.

Although the issuing bank will not pay the exporter until all the terms of the letter of credit have been met, the exporter often can sell the letter prior to the expected payment date to its bank or another commercial lender at a discount from the face value. The discount will reflect the time value of money, the risk the buyer of the instrument bears if the issuing bank defaults on the transaction, and the buyer's administrative costs. Because confirmed and irrevocable letters of credit reduce the risk of secondary buyers, they sell for higher prices (or lower discounts from face value) than do letters of credit without these features. Thus an exporter planning to sell a letter of credit prior to delivery must trade off the inconvenience or higher fees paid for these less risky types against the higher prices it will receive from secondary buyers of them.

Credit Cards. For small international transactions, particularly those between international merchants and foreign retail customers, credit cards such as American Express, VISA, and MasterCard may be used. A firm may tap into the well-established credit card network to facilitate international transactions, subject to the normal limitations of these cards. The credit card company collects transaction fees (usually 2 to 4 percent) from the merchant and in return assumes the costs of collecting the funds from the customer and any risks of nonpayment. Because credit card companies buy foreign currency in large quantities at wholesale rates, they typically charge only a 1 percent fee for converting currencies. However, they offer exporters and importers none of the help banks do in dealing with the paperwork and documentation requirements of international trade.

Countertrade. An additional method used for payment in international transactions is countertrade. **Countertrade** occurs when a firm accepts something other than money as payment for its goods or services. Forms of countertrade include

▶ Barter

▶ Counterpurchase

▶ Buy-back

▶ Offset purchase

The simplest form of countertrade is **barter**, in which each party simultaneously swaps its products for the products of the other. In 1993, for example, Cuba swapped sugar worth $60 million to Italgrani, a Naples-based food processor, in return for an equivalent value of cereals, pasta, and vegetable oils.[8]

A more sophisticated form of countertrade is **counterpurchase**, whereby one firm sells its products to another at one point in time and is compensated in the form of the other's products at some future time. Boeing, for example, has used counterpurchase to sell aircraft to Saudi Arabia in return for oil.[9]

Another variant of countertrade involves **buy-back**, or compensation arrangements whereby one firm sells capital goods to a second firm and is compensated in the form of output generated as a result of their use. For example, Japan's Fukusuke Corporation sold ten knitting machines and raw materials to Chinatex, a Shanghai-based clothing manufacturer, in exchange for 1 million pairs of underwear to be produced on the knitting machines.[10] Because it links payment with output from the purchased goods, a buy-back is particularly useful when the buyer of the goods needs to ensure the exporter will provide necessary after-sale services such as equipment repairs or instructions on how to use the equipment.[11]

Another important type of countertrade involves **offset purchases**, whereby part of an exported good is produced in the importing country. Offset arrangements are particularly important in sales to foreign governments of expensive military equipment such as fighter jets or tanks. General Dynamics, for example, sold several hundred F-16 military jets to Belgium, Denmark, Norway, and the Netherlands by agreeing to allow those countries to offset the cost of the jets through coproduction agreements. As part of the deal, the countries were allowed to produce 40 percent of the value of the aircraft they purchased from General Dynamics. The firm sweetened the deal by authorizing the European countries to coproduce 10 percent of all F-16s sold to the U.S. military and 15 percent of any F-16s sold to other countries.[12]

Balancing export sales and counterpurchase obligations on a deal-by-deal basis is often cumbersome. To facilitate countertrade, firms may agree to establish **clearinghouse accounts**. Using this approach, as a firm exports goods and services to another, it incurs a counterpurchase obligation of an equivalent value,

Countertrade is often used to finance the purchase of high-technology military equipment such as this F-15 aircraft operated by the Royal Saudi Air Force.

which is recorded in its clearinghouse account. When the firm buys goods from its partner, its clearinghouse obligation is reduced. Thus a firm does not need to balance any single countertrade transaction, although it must honor its cumulative set of obligations by the time its clearinghouse account expires.

Sometimes firms enter into countertrade agreements in order to expand their international sales, without having experience in or desire to engage in countertrade. In this case, countertrade agreements often permit the use of **switching arrangements**, whereby countertrade obligations are transferred from one firm to another. A variety of consulting firms, many headquartered in either London (because of access to capital markets) or Vienna (because of access to the former communist countries), are available to provide financing, marketing, and legal services needed by international businesses engaging in switching arrangements.[13] Japan's soga sosha are particularly skillful in the use of switching arrangements and clearinghouse accounts because of their extensive worldwide operations. A soga sosha might assist in the sale of Mitsubishi trucks in Ghana, taking payment in cocoa, which then can be sold to keiretsu-linked food processors back in Japan or to independent candymakers anywhere in the world.[14]

Some firms specialize in exploiting countertrade opportunities by constructing complicated multiple-market trades as part of their normal business. Consider, for example, Marc Rich & Co., which does over $3 billion in business annually in the former Soviet Union. In 1993 the firm engineered a complicated deal that began with its buying 70,000 tons of Brazilian raw sugar on the open market (see Map 18.1). It then hired a Ukrainian firm to refine the sugar and paid the refinery with part of the sugar. Next, it swapped the rest of the refined sugar to oil refineries in Siberia, which needed the sugar for their workers, in return for gasoline. It then swapped 130,000 tons of gasoline to Mongolia in return for 35,000 tons of copper concentrate. The copper concentrate was shipped to copper refineries in Kazakhstan, which received payment in kind. The refined copper was then sold on the world market. At that point, Marc Rich—after several months of efforts—was able to extract its profits on these countertrades in the form of hard currency.[15]

Countertrade is important to international businesses because of its widespread use. Informed estimates suggest that countertrade accounts for 15–20 percent of world trade, although some published reports claim that the proportion approaches 40 percent.[16] Countertrade is of particular importance to countries

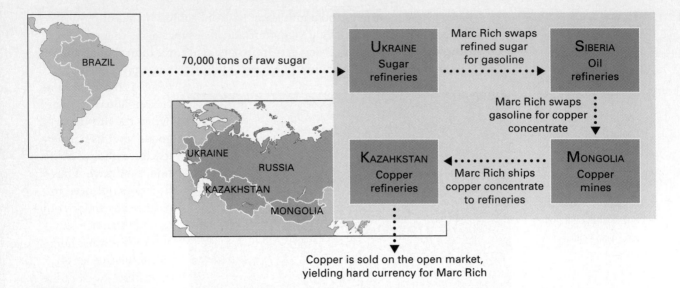

BRAZIL

70,000 tons of raw sugar

UKRAINE
RUSSIA
KAZAKHSTAN
MONGOLIA

UKRAINE
Sugar refineries

Marc Rich swaps refined sugar for gasoline

SIBERIA
Oil refineries

Marc Rich swaps gasoline for copper concentrate

KAZAKHSTAN
Copper refineries

Marc Rich ships copper concentrate to refineries

MONGOLIA
Copper mines

Copper is sold on the open market, yielding hard currency for Marc Rich

MAP 18.1

Countertrade by Marc Rich

that lack a convertible currency and is often used as a means of reducing the drain on scarce holdings of convertible foreign currencies. The former Soviet Union, for example, was a major countertrade user. Often goods were traded between the Soviet Union and the former members of COMECON using clearinghouse accounts. The former communist countries also engaged in countertrade with capitalist countries.

PepsiCo turned the Soviet lack of convertible currencies to its strategic advantage. Always looking for an edge in its worldwide battle against Coca-Cola, PepsiCo struck a deal in 1974 with the Soviets to supply equipment and concentrated soft-drink syrup and to market Stolichnaya vodka in the West. In return, the Soviets agreed to construct three bottling plants. PepsiCo continues to refine its countertrade agreements in order to maintain its market share. In 1989, for example, it agreed to sell ships constructed in Soviet shipyards as countertrade for the soft-drink concentrates it exported to the Soviets. After the dissolution of the Soviet Union, the shipyards became part of the newly independent Ukraine. PepsiCo then agreed to sell additional Ukrainian ships in the West, with the proceeds being used to buy soft-drink bottling equipment, build five new Ukrainian bottling plants, and open 100 PepsiCo-owned Pizza Huts in that country. As a result of its nimble use of countertrade, PepsiCo enjoys a three to one lead over Coca-Cola in the Ukrainian soft-drink market.[17]

Table 18.1 summarizes the benefits and costs of the various methods of payment. Techniques that reduce risk for the exporter generally are more expensive. Thus the exporter must decide how much risk it is willing to bear. In dealing with a new and unknown customer, an exporter may choose a safer, but more expensive means of securing payment. In dealing with well-established clients, less expensive but riskier payment methods may be acceptable.

Financing Trade

Financing terms are often important in closing an international sale. In most industries, standard financing arrangements exist, and an international firm must be ready to offer those terms to its foreign customers. Depending on the product,

TABLE 18.1

Payment Methods for International Trade

METHOD	TIMING OF PAYMENT	TIMING OF DELIVERY OF GOODS	RISK(S) FOR EXPORTER	RISK(S) FOR IMPORTER	AVAILABILITY OF FINANCING FOR EXPORTER	CONDITION(S) FAVORING USE
Payment in advance	Prior to delivery of goods	After payment, when goods arrive in importer's country	None	Exporter may fail to deliver goods	N/A	Exporter has strong bargaining power; importer unknown to exporter
Open account	According to credit terms offered by exporter	When goods arrive in importer's country	Importer may fail to pay account balance	None	Yes, by factoring of accounts receivable	Exporter has complete trust in importer; exporter and importer are part of the same corporate family
Documentary collection	At delivery if sight draft is used; at specified later time if time draft is used	Upon payment if sight draft is used; upon acceptance if time draft is used	Importer may default or fail to accept draft	None	Yes, by discounting draft from its face value	Exporter trusts importer to pay as specified; when risk of default is low
Letter of Credit	After terms of letter are fulfilled	According to terms of sales contract and letter of credit	Issuing bank may default; documents may not be prepared correctly	Exporter may honor terms of letter of credit but not terms of sales contract	Yes, by discounting letter from its face value	Exporter lacks knowledge of importer; importer has good credit with local bank
Credit card	According to normal credit card company procedures	When goods arrive in importer's country	None	Exporter fails to deliver goods	N/A	Transaction size is small
Countertrade	When exporter sells countertraded goods	When goods arrive in importer's country	Exporter may not be able to sell countertraded goods	None	No	Importer lacks convertible currency; importer or exporter wants access to foreign distribution network

industry practice may be to offer the buyer 30 to 180 days to pay after receipt of an invoice. For the sale of complex products such as commercial aircraft, which will be delivered several years in the future, the payment terms may be much more complicated. They may include down payments, penalty payments for cancellation or late delivery, inflation clauses, and concessionary interest rates for long-term financing. Outside of the Quad countries, capital markets are often not well-developed, and local lenders may charge extremely high interest rates, especially to smaller borrowers. Thus exporters with access to low-cost capital can gain a competitive advantage by offering financing to foreign customers that lack access to cheaper financing. Of course, by acting as a lender, the exporter increases the risk of not being paid for its goods. Before deciding to extend credit, the exporter must examine the tradeoff between the benefits of increased sales and the higher risks of default.

As noted earlier in this chapter, banks and other commercial lenders are often willing to finance accounts receivable of exporters by purchasing letters of credit or time drafts or factoring open accounts at a discount from face value. Many developed countries supplement the services of these commercial lenders with government-supported financing programs to promote exports. For example, the Export-Import Bank of the United States (Eximbank) offers a working capital guarantee loan program to encourage U.S. exports. Under this program, commercial loans made to finance exportable inventory and foreign accounts receivable will be reimbursed 90 percent if the importer defaults on its obligations. Eximbank has made a special effort to serve the needs of small businesses; it approves over $2 billion of support annually for exports by U.S. small businesses. For example, in the early 1990s, Ormat, Inc., a small Nevada producer of geothermal power generation equipment, beat out Japanese and Italian competitors for a $33.5 million contract with the National Power Corporation of the Philippines, thanks to Eximbank financing.[18] Eximbank also offers medium-term loan guarantees (up to seven years' duration) and long-term guarantees (over ten years' duration) for telecommunications, electrical generation, and transportation infrastructure projects.

Managing Foreign-Exchange Risk

By using contracts denominated in a foreign currency, KLM and other firms that conduct international trade are exposed to the risk that exchange-rate fluctuations may affect them adversely. Experts have identified three types of foreign-exchange exposure confronting international firms:[19]

1 Transaction

2 Translation

3 Economic

Transaction Exposure

A firm faces **transaction exposure** when the financial benefits and costs of an international transaction can be affected by exchange-rate movements that occur after the firm is legally obligated to complete the transaction. Many typical international business transactions denominated in a foreign currency can lead to transaction exposure, including the following:

► Purchase of goods, services, or assets
► Sales of goods, services, or assets
► Extension of credit
► Borrowing of money

For example, suppose that, in order to meet its Christmas needs, Saks Fifth Avenue agrees on April 1, 1996, to buy 5 million Swiss francs' worth of Rolex watches from Rolex's Swiss manufacturer, payable on delivery in October. Saks now faces the risk that exchange-rate fluctuations will raise the cost of the watches denominated in its home currency—in this case, U.S. dollars—by the time the transaction is completed in October. (Of course, exchange-rate movements could *lower* its costs.) Saks could avoid this risk by contracting in dollars, but then Rolex would face transaction exposure. In an international transaction, one of the parties has to bear transaction exposure.

Saks has several options for responding to this transaction exposure:

► Go naked
► Buy Swiss francs forward
► Buy Swiss francs in the currency options market
► Acquire an offsetting asset

Go Naked. Saks can ignore the transaction exposure and deliberately assume the foreign-exchange risk by choosing to buy the necessary Swiss francs in October when it needs to pay for the watches. By doing so, Saks is betting that the U.S. dollar will rise in value relative to the franc between April and October. This approach has several advantages. First, Saks does not have to tie up any capital in April for the transaction, since its only obligation is to pay 5 million Swiss francs in October. Second, Saks can benefit from any appreciation of the U.S. dollar versus the Swiss franc. If this happens, it can pay its bill in October using fewer dollars than it otherwise would have. This advantage, of course, can turn sour if the dollar falls relative to the franc. In this unfortunate circumstance, Saks would be forced to pay more U.S. dollars for the watches than it had anticipated. But by going naked, Saks avoids paying fees to any intermediaries, an expense that it would incur if it adopted any of the three other strategies, discussed next.

Buy Swiss Francs Forward. Saks has several ways of avoiding the transaction exposure if it wants. For example, it could buy Swiss francs forward in the foreign exchange market for delivery in October, thereby locking in the price in April that it will pay for the 5 million francs in October. This strategy has two advantages. First, Saks guarantees the dollar price it will pay for the imported watches and protects itself from declines in the value of the dollar. Second, it ties up none of its capital until it receives the goods, since its only agreement is to buy the currency in October and pay Rolex the 5 million francs on delivery of the watches. On the other hand, with this strategy, Saks will miss the opportunity to benefit from any appreciation of the U.S. dollar relative to the Swiss franc. It also will bear some transaction costs in the form of fees and markups charged by the bank through which it buys the forward Swiss francs.

A variant of this approach is for Saks to purchase Swiss franc currency futures, as discussed in Chapter 5. Whether the firm chooses to buy currency futures or use the forward market depends on the price of francs in these two markets as well as the relative transaction costs of using the two markets.

Buy Swiss Francs in the Currency Options Market. Alternatively, Saks could buy Swiss francs in the options market. As discussed in Chapter 5, the purchase of an options contract gives the buyer the opportunity, but not the obligation, to buy a certain currency at a given price in the future. By buying an option, Saks can guarantee that it will pay no more for its francs than the price stated in its options contract. When payment for the watches is due in October, Saks can exercise the option if the U.S. dollar has declined in value relative to the franc or let the option expire if the U.S. dollar has increased in value—hence the advantage of an options contract over a forward contract or a futures contract. Saks is equally protected against depreciation of the dollar by all three types of foreign-exchange transactions; however, it can benefit from an appreciation of the U.S. dollar with an options contract (by letting it expire unused), but not with a forward or a futures contract. The options contract's disadvantage is that it is more expensive than other hedging techniques. Options typically cost from 3.0 to 5.5 percent of the transaction's total value. Nonetheless, many major MNCs prefer currency options to currency futures or forward contracts when hedging their transactions risk, because of the "heads I win, tails I don't lose" feature of options.[20]

Acquire an Offsetting Asset. Another option for Saks is for it to neutralize its liability of 5 million Swiss francs pending in October by acquiring an offsetting asset of equivalent size denominated in Swiss francs. For example, suppose the interest rate in April on a six-month certificate of deposit (CD) in Switzerland is 8 percent annually (4 percent for six months). By purchasing a six-month CD in April from a Swiss bank such as Credit Suisse for 4,807,692 francs, Saks will receive 5 million francs ($4,807,692 \times 1.04$) in October when its payment obligation to Rolex comes due. By matching its assets denominated in francs with its liabilities denominated in francs, Saks will suffer no *net* transaction exposure. The disadvantage of this approach is that Saks has to tie up some of its capital in a Swiss bank until October. It will earn interest on the Swiss CD, but it may have been able to earn a higher rate of return if it utilized its capital elsewhere.

Of course, if Saks (or a member of its corporate family) already had an existing franc-denominated CD or receivable due in October, Saks could have used that asset to offset its pending franc-denominated liability to Rolex. Suppose, for example, Saks had licensed a Swiss T-shirt manufacturer to use the Saks logo on its shirts. If Saks expected to receive 5 million Swiss francs in royalties in October from the licensing deal, it could have offset those funds against its October liability to Rolex in order to neutralize its transaction exposure, rather than buying the Swiss CD. If the licensing deal were to yield only 2 million Swiss francs instead of 5 million, Saks could still pair up the two transactions. To eliminate its exposure totally, Saks would then need to cover its *net* transaction exposure of 3 million francs using one of the means just discussed.

Table 18.2 summarizes the various techniques available to manage transaction exposure. (See also the following "Going Global.")

Translation Exposure

As part of reporting its operating results to its shareholders, a firm must integrate the financial statements of its subsidiaries into a set of consolidated financial statements. Problems can arise, however, when the financial statements of a foreign subsidiary are denominated in a foreign currency rather than the firm's home currency. **Translation exposure** is the impact on the firm's consolidated financial statements of fluctuations in exchange rates that change the value of foreign subsidiaries as measured in the parent's currency. If exchange rates were fixed, translation exposure would not exist. (Because translation exposure develops from the need to consolidate financial statements into a common currency, it is often called *accounting exposure*.)

The intricacies of international accounting are covered in Chapter 19, so here we present only a simple example of translation exposure. Suppose GM transfers $10 million to Deutsche Bank to open an account for its new German distribution subsidiary, General Motors Import & Distribution Company GmbH, so that the subsidiary can begin operations.[21] Further assume that the exchange rate on the day of the transfer is DM1.5/$1. Thus the subsidiary's sole asset is a bank account containing DM15 million. If the value of the dollar were to rise to 1.51 deutsche marks per dollar, the subsidiary would still have DM15 million. However, when GM's accountants prepared the firm's consolidated financial statements,

TABLE 18.2

Strategies for Managing Transaction Exposure

STRATEGY	BENEFIT(S)	COST(S)
Go naked	No capital outlay; potential for capital gain if home currency rises in value	Potential for capital loss if home currency falls in value
Buy forward currency	Elimination of transaction exposure; flexibility in size and timing of contract	Fees to banks; lost opportunity for capital gain if home currency rises in value
Buy currency future	Elimination of transaction exposure; ease and relative inexpensiveness of futures contract	Small brokerage fee; inflexibility in size and timing of contract; lost opportunity for capital gain if home currency rises in value
Buy currency option	Elimination of transaction exposure; potential for capital gain if home currency rises in value	Premium paid up front for option because of its "heads I win, tails I don't lose" nature; inflexibility in size and timing of option
Acquire offsetting asset	Elimination of transaction exposure	Effort or expense of arranging offsetting transaction; lost opportunity for capital gain if home currency rises in value

GOING GLOBAL

Financial Derivatives: Blessing or Curse?

The most important change in financial markets in the past decade has been the growth of so-called financial derivatives. A **financial derivative** is a financial instrument whose return derives from some other bond, stock, or other asset. International financial derivatives such as currency forwards, futures, options, swaps, and swaptions (the right to use a swap at some later date) have helped international firms reduce their financial exposure to exchange-rate fluctuations.

Often firms use these contracts to hedge exchange-rate risks, as Saks Fifth Avenue did. Some firms use these instruments to speculate, hoping to make a financial killing by guessing correctly which way exchange rates will move in the future. But sometimes these contracts seem to have been signed by financial officers who just didn't know what they were doing or who were violating company policy. Consider the following examples.

Kashima Oil lost $1.5 billion over several years by purchasing a huge number of forward contracts to buy U.S. dollars—far more than it needed for its actual operations. In effect, Kashima's major business became currency speculation, not petroleum refining. When the value of the U.S. dollar fell, Kashima was stuck with horrendous losses. The firm then used loopholes in the Japanese accounting system to hide the true extent of its losses, thus compounding the damage to its reputation when those losses were ultimately revealed.

Showa Shell Seikiyu K.K., a Japanese oil refiner half-owned by Royal Dutch Shell, lost $1.05 billion in 1993 by speculating in foreign-exchange futures, an action that violated Shell's company policy.

Allied-Lyons, a U.K. food and beverage manufacturer, lost £150 million in 1991 by speculating on changes in the value of the U.S. dollar.

Procter & Gamble (P&G) entered into a series of complex contracts involving interest-rate differentials between German and U.S. treasury bonds in 1993 and 1994. If U.S. interest rates had continued to fall, P&G would have made out handsomely. Unfortunately, those interest rates rose. P&G lost $157 million on the contracts, and its corporate treasurer lost his job.

Nippon Steel & Chemical Co. lost $135 million in the early 1990s through ill-advised trades in the foreign-exchange market. The loss was discovered only when an audit was conducted after the head of the firm's accounting department died in a railway accident.

Obviously, shareholders in these firms were not pleased. However, from the public's perspective, of even greater concern is the fact that trading in such instruments exposes the banking community to similarly large losses. In 1993, for example, Chemical Bank held derivative contracts totaling $2.4 trillion, while Bankers Trust and Citicorp each had contractual obligations of $1.9 trillion. Many other international banks in Europe and Japan have similarly large obligations. Bankers calmly explain, however, that while their gross exposure is quite large, their net exposure is much smaller. For example, a bank may buy British pounds forward in order to accommodate one client and sell an equivalent amount of British pounds forward to meet the needs of another client. Because the two transactions effectively cancel each other out, the bank's net exposure is zero. Further, many transactions in this market are made between banks, so the banking system's net exposure is much smaller than the numbers suggest.

Banking regulators in Europe, Japan, and the United States are less sanguine. They fear mismanagement by just one major bank of its derivative portfolio could lead to chaos in the international financial market. In their doomsday scenario, a failure by one bank to honor its obligations could trigger a series of defaults by other banks, whose ability to honor their obligations depend on the collapsed bank's honoring its own.

Sources: "Beleagured Giant: As Derivative Losses Rise, The Huge Industry Fights to Avert Regulation," *Wall Street Journal,* August 25, 1994, p. A6; "Through a market, darkly," *Financial Times,* May 27, 1994, p. 15; "The beauty in the beast," *The Economist,* May 14, 1994, p. 21; "Just What Firms Do With 'Derivatives' Is Suddenly a Hot Issue," *Wall Street Journal,* April 14, 1994, p. A1; Carol J. Loomis, "The Risk That Won't Go Away," *Fortune,* March 7, 1994, pp. 40ff; "Many Americans Run Hidden Financial Risk From 'Derivatives,'" *Wall Street Journal,* August 10, 1993, p. A1; "Japan Toughens Financial Disclosure Law," *Wall Street Journal,* August 10, 1993, p. C1; "Loss focuses attention on detecting unauthorised trades," *Financial Times,* May 24, 1993; "Tremors follow Showa Shell's futures shock," *Financial Times,* February 23, 1993; "Shell shares slip on big currency losses at Japanese arm," *Financial Times,* February 23, 1993.

its investment in the German subsidiary would be worth only $9,933,775 (15 million marks divided by 1.51 marks per dollar). GM thus would suffer a translation loss of $66,225 ($10,000,000 minus $9,933,775).

Financial officers can reduce their firm's translation exposure through the use of a balance sheet hedge. A **balance sheet hedge** is created when an international firm matches its assets denominated in a given currency with its liabilities denominated in that same currency. This balancing occurs on a currency-by-currency basis, not on a subsidiary-by-subsidiary basis. For example, suppose Volvo of North America, Volvo's marketing arm in the United States, is owed $50 million in the first quarter of 1996 by its U.S. dealers for automobiles it has sold to them but not yet received payment for. Volvo might want to avoid translation exposure when its U.S. subsidiary's accounts are translated into Swedish krona. Volvo could eliminate this translation risk by developing an offsetting liability. For example, the parent might borrow $50 million from Citicorp in New York or 50 million Eurodollars from Credit Anstalt in Vienna to finance improvements to Volvo's paint shop in its plant in Gothenburg. By equalizing its dollar-denominated assets and its dollar-denominated liabilities on a consolidated basis, Volvo can eliminate its translation exposure with regard to the U.S. dollar. Of course, in this case the firm must also consider the relative costs of borrowing in dollars (in the U.S. or the Eurodollar market) versus borrowing monies denominated in other currencies.

Firms find it difficult to avoid both translation and transaction exposure. Translation exposure could be eliminated if a parent firm forced all its subsidiaries to denominate their transactions in the parent's home currency. But foreign subsidiaries would then face transaction exposure as measured by their own local accounting statements. Many experts believe that managers, if given a choice, should weigh in on the side of protecting against transaction exposure, rather than translation exposure. Transaction exposure may produce true cash losses to the firm, while translation exposure produces only paper, or accounting, losses.[22] But translation exposure should not be ignored. For example, firms forced to take writedowns of the value of their foreign subsidiaries may trigger default clauses in their loan contracts if their debt-to-equity ratios fall too low.

Economic Exposure

The third type of foreign-exchange exposure is economic exposure. **Economic exposure** is the impact on the value of a firm's operations of unanticipated exchange-rate changes. From a strategic perspective, the threat of economic exposure deserves close attention from the firm's highest policymakers, for it affects virtually every area of operations, including global production, marketing, and financial planning.

Unanticipated exchange-rate fluctuations may affect a firm's overall sales and profitability in numerous markets. In 1992, for example, the value of the U.S. dollar fell in world currency markets. Exporters that were reliant on the U.S. market faced the unhappy choice of either raising their prices in the United States and seeing their market shares erode *or* holding the line on prices and seeing their profit margins cut. The managers of the U.S. subsidiary of Charles Jourdan Industries, for example, were confronted with this dilemma after a 13 percent drop in the value of the dollar versus the franc. Fearful of customer reaction, Max

Imgruth, CEO of Charles Jourdan USA, decided to hold the line on the firm's U.S. prices. He judged that a price increase would wipe out 20 years of painstakingly building market share for the firm's pricey shoes. On the other hand, French vineyards chose to protect their profit margins by raising their U.S. prices. They lost market share to cheaper Australian and Chilean wines.[23] Japanese firms faced similar problems in 1995 when the value of the yen rose to record levels against most major currencies. Nissan, for example, estimates that it loses seven billion yen of revenue for every one-yen increase vis-a-vis the dollar.

Long term investments in property, plant, and equipment are particularly vulnerable to economic exposure, even if they are located in a firm's home country. For example, the U.S. market is very important to German luxury automobile manufacturers such as Daimler-Benz, Porsche, and BMW. The decline in the U.S. dollar relative to the deutsche mark in the 1980s made upscale German cars increasingly expensive to U.S. motorists. German automakers thus lost market share in the luxury car segment of the U.S. market. To address this problem, both BMW and Daimler-Benz have chosen to build assembly plants in the United States. By diversifying their production to better match the location of their customers, they are reducing their economic exposure to fluctuations in the dollar/mark exchange rate.

Other innovative techniques exist for reducing economic exposure to exchange-rate changes. For example, in 1988 the Walt Disney Company developed a creative financial plan to reduce uncertainty regarding its proceeds from Tokyo Disneyland. Concerned about fluctuations in the value of the U.S. dollar relative to the yen, in 1988 the firm sold 20 years of projected royalties from Tokyo Disneyland to a group of Japanese investors at a time when the value of the yen was high relative to the dollar. The value of the payments was discounted back to 1988 terms at the prevailing 6 percent interest rate on long-term Japanese bonds and then converted from yen to dollars. Disney placed the proceeds ($750 million) in U.S. government bonds, which were yielding 10 percent at the time. By doing so, the firm locked in a favorable exchange rate for its yen earnings, thereby hedging against a drop in the yen's value.[24]

As this Disney example suggests, an important element of managing economic exposure is analyzing likely changes in exchange rates. (Map 18.2 shows exchange-rate changes versus the dollar in the first half of the 1990s.) A wide variety of exchange-rate experts are available to assist international businesses in this task. These range from private consultants to the staffs of international banks to the published forecasts of international organizations such as the World Bank and the International Monetary Fund. These experts scrutinize many of the factors discussed in Chapter 5. The theory of purchasing power parity, for example, provides guidance regarding long-term trends in exchange rates between countries. In the short term, forward exchange rates have been found to be unbiased predictors of future spot rates. Because of the importance of interest arbitrage in establishing equilibrium exchange rates, experts may also forecast countries' monetary policies in order to predict future currency values. BOP performance is also useful because it provides insights into whether a country's industries are remaining competitive in world markets and whether foreigners' short-term claims on a country are increasing. Prospects for inflation are also carefully assessed, since inflation can affect a county's export prospects, demand for imports, and future interest rates.

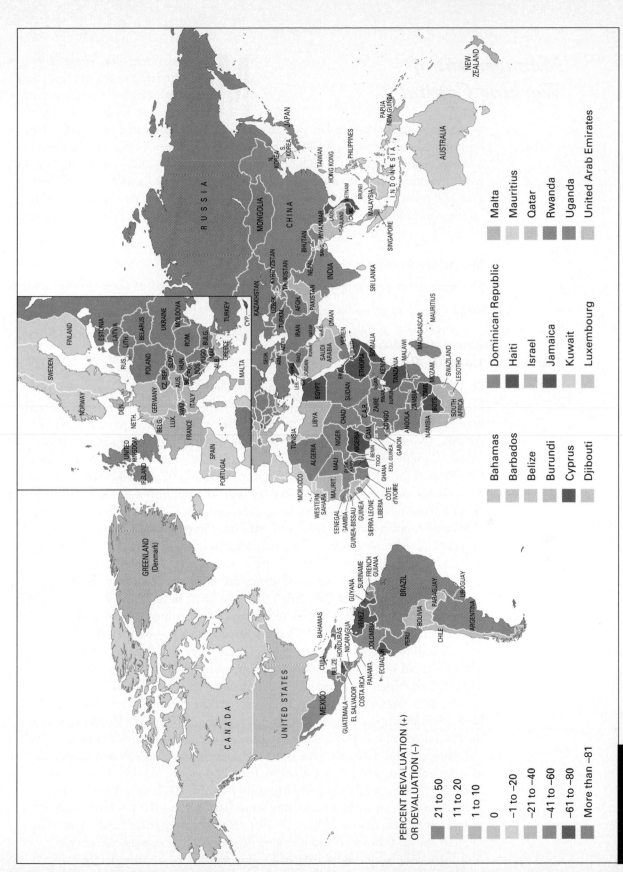

PERCENT REVALUATION (+)
OR DEVALUATION (−)

21 to 50

11 to 20

1 to 10

0

−1 to −20

−21 to −40

−41 to −60

−61 to −80

More than −81

Bahamas	Dominican Republic	Malta
Barbados	Haiti	Mauritius
Belize	Israel	Qatar
Burundi	Jamaica	Rwanda
Cyprus	Kuwait	Uganda
Djibouti	Luxembourg	United Arab Emirates

MAP 18.2   **Changes in Currency Values Relative to the U.S. Dollar, January 1995 versus January 1990**

Management of Working Capital

Managing foreign-exchange exposure is related to another task that financial officers of international businesses perform—managing working capital, or cash, balances. This task is more complicated for MNCs than for purely domestic firms. An MNC's financial officers must consider the firm's working capital position for each of its foreign subsidiaries and in each currency in which the subsidiaries do business, as well as for the firm as a whole. KLM, for example, uses over 180 currencies in its operations, and its financial officers must monitor its holdings of each of these currencies. In the process, they must balance three corporate financial goals:

1 Minimizing working capital balances

2 Minimizing currency conversion costs

3 Minimizing foreign-exchange risks

Minimizing Working Capital Balances

Financial officers seek to minimize the firm's working capital balances. Both domestic and international firms must hold working capital for two reasons: to facilitate day-to-day transactions and to cover the firm against unexpected demands for cash. (Note that the term cash refers here to actual cash, checking account balances, and highly liquid marketable securities that normally carry low yields.) Obviously, a firm does not want to run out of cash on hand. Failure to have sufficient cash to pay workers or suppliers can lead, at a minimum, to expensive emergency borrowings or, in the worst case, to an embarrassing loss of reputation that may cause suppliers and lenders to cut off future lines of credit. However, the rate of return on working capital is extremely low, and financial officers prefer to capture higher rates of return, if possible, by investing surplus funds in some other form than cash. Thus they need to balance the firm's needs for cash against the opportunity cost of holding the firm's financial assets in such low-yielding forms.

One technique MNCs can use to minimize their company-wide cash holdings is the centralized cash depository. A **centralized cash depository** coordinates an MNC's worldwide cash flows and pools its cash reserves. These depositories are usually located in important money market centers such as Tokyo, New York, and London, which have well-developed financial services sectors, excellent worldwide communication links, freely convertible currencies, and laws that facilitate international currency flows. Each of the MNC's subsidiaries sends to the centralized cash depository a daily cash report and an analysis of its expected cash balances and needs over the short run, which may range from a week to a month depending on the parent corporation's operating requirements. These reports are then assembled by the depository's staff, which uses them to plan short-term investment and borrowing strategies for the MNC. The depository may receive excess cash held by each subsidiary and pool these funds, funneling them to subsidiaries when and if emergencies arise. The unexpected need for additional cash by one subsidiary will often be offset by an unexpected excess of cash generated by a second. Thus the central cash depository is able to reduce the

GOING GLOBAL

Colfax and Fowler's Cash Flow Solution

Smaller businesses are also faced with the task of managing working capital and currency conversion costs. For example, U.K.-based Colfax and Fowler sells its high-priced, trendy wallpaper and fabric to upscale customers and distributors throughout Europe. However, its average invoice is only £96, and the bank charges its French and German customers pay for converting their local currencies into pounds typically total £15 per transaction. In the past, these customers often would seek to reduce their currency conversion costs by accumulating their invoices until their total reached some minimum amount. The typical customer paid an average of 86 days after receiving an invoice. This behavior played havoc with Colfax and Fowler's cash flow and increased the size of the working capital loans it needed.

Wanting to improve its cash flow but afraid of losing customers, the firm sought advice from a British financial services consulting firm. That firm recommended that Colfax and Fowler establish bank accounts in each country in which it did significant business. Its customers then could save conversion costs by writing checks denominated in the local currency for deposit in Colfax and Fowler's local accounts.

But Colfax and Fowler ultimately wants pounds, not French francs or deutsche marks. So it hired a Dutch firm, EDM, which specializes in handling large numbers of small payments for firms such as the publishers of *Newsweek* and *National Geographic*. EDM contracts with European banks to provide it with daily information about payments made to its clients' accounts. EDM then faxes this account information to its clients so that they can credit their customers' accounts. In the case of Colfax and Fowler, once local bank balances reach an agreed-upon level, EDM instructs the local banks to transfer funds to Colfax and Fowler's British bank account. Although the British firm now bears the currency conversion costs, the new system encourages its customers to buy more goods more often. And by speeding up the payment process, Colfax and Fowler has saved an estimated £45,000 annually in interest charges on its working capital loans. This savings more than pays for EDM's services.

Source: "Small cheques, big problems," *Financial Times*, June 21, 1994, p. 12.

precautionary cash balances held by the firm as a whole, and thereby reduce the amount of firm assets tied up in such a low-yielding form. Further, the expertise of the depository's staff can be used to seek out the best short-term investment opportunities available for the firm's excess cash holdings and to monitor expected changes in the values of foreign currencies. By transferring these tasks from the subsidiaries to the parent corporation, the centralized cash depository also reduces the number of highly trained, high-salaried financial specialists the corporate family needs. Thus it is more efficient and cost-effective to concentrate such financial information-gathering and decision-making in one unit of the corporation, rather than compelling each subsidiary to develop such expertise in-house. (For an innovative solution to working capital problems facing smaller businesses, see "Going Global.")

Minimizing Currency Conversion Costs

International businesses face another complication. Their foreign subsidiaries may continually buy and sell parts and finished goods among themselves. Ford of Europe, for example, has major assembly plants as well as company-owned parts suppliers and distribution companies in the United Kingdom, Germany, and

FIGURE 18.3

**Payment Flows
without Multilateral
Netting**

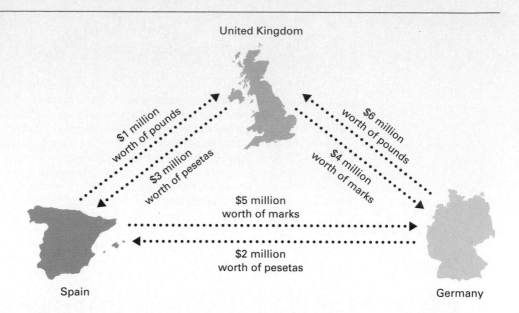

Spain. The constant transfer of parts and finished goods among the Ford subsidiaries in the three countries generates a blizzard of invoices and a constant need to transfer funds among the subsidiaries' bank accounts. Cumulative bank charges for transferring these funds and converting the currencies involved can be high. For large transactions involving two major European currencies, currency conversion fees and expenses may average 0.3 percent of the value of the transaction. For smaller-sized transactions or for transactions involving minor currencies with narrow markets, such fees and expenses can easily be three or four times higher.[25]

As a result, most MNCs use netting operations where possible to minimize the amount of funds that must be converted in the foreign-exchange market to settle transactions between subsidiaries. **Bilateral netting** is done between two business units, and **multilateral netting** is done among three or more business units. Figure 18.3 and Table 18.3 present an example of a multilateral netting operation for an MNC, denominated in a common currency (U.S. dollars) for simplicity. The gross trade among the firm's subsidiaries in the three countries is $21 million (see Fig. 18.3). If the costs of converting currencies total 0.5 percent of the transactions' value, the MNC would pay 0.5 percent times $21 million, or $105,000, to convert the currencies necessary to settle these transactions among its subsidiaries. Through multilateral netting, however, the conversion costs decrease dramatically. In our example, the British subsidiary owes the equivalent of $7 million to the other two subsidiaries but is also owed $7 million by them, as shown in Table 18.3. The German subsidiary is owed $9 million but owes $8 million, for a net receipt of $1 million. The Spanish subsidiary is owed $5 million but owes $6 million, for a net debt of $1 million. When accompanied by the appropriate bookkeeping entries, all transactions among the three subsidiaries can be settled by the Spanish subsidiary transferring $1 million worth of deutsche marks to the German subsidiary. Because only $1 million is physically being converted in the foreign-exchange market and transferred through the banking system, the MNC's conversion costs shrink to $5000 (0.5 percent × $1 million) as a result of the netting operations.

TABLE 18.3

Multilateral Netting in Action (all quantities in millions of U.S. dollar equivalents)

| | | PAYMENTS OWED BY | | | | |
		German subsidiary	Spanish subsidiary	British subsidiary	TOTAL RECEIPTS	NET TRANSFER
RECEIPTS DUE TO	German subsidiary	—	5	4	9	+1
	Spanish subsidiary	2	—	3	5	-1
	British subsidiary	6	1	—	7	0
	TOTAL PAYMENTS	8	6	7	21	

In concept, multilateral netting differs little from what children do on the playground all the time: "David owes Karen a quarter, but Karen owes LaTisha twenty cents, so David owes LaTisha twenty cents and Karen five cents, and Karen owes nobody anything." To complicate matters, however, some countries, such as France, Italy, and Spain, impose restrictions on netting operations in order to support their local banking industries, which benefit from the fees charged for currency exchange.[26] MNCs wanting to engage in netting operations often have to work around such government-imposed barriers.

Minimizing Foreign-Exchange Risk

Financial officers also typically adjust the mix of currencies that comprise the firm's working capital in order to minimize foreign-exchange risk. Often firms use a **leads and lags strategy** to try to increase their net holdings of currencies that are expected to rise in value and to decrease their net holdings of currencies that are expected to fall in value. For example, if the Spanish peseta were expected to decline in value, the financial officers would try to minimize the MNC's peseta-denominated liquid assets, perhaps by demanding quicker (or *leading*) payment on peseta-denominated accounts receivable or by reducing peseta-denominated bank balances. The officers also would try to increase the firm's peseta-denominated short-term liabilities, perhaps by slowing (or *lagging*) payment on peseta-denominated accounts payable or by increasing short-term borrowing from Spanish banks. Conversely, if the Austrian schilling were expected to rise in value, the financial officers would try to maximize the firm's net holdings of schillings through reverse techniques.

In summary, an MNC's financial officers face a complex task. They must ensure each subsidiary maintains sufficient cash balances to meet expected ordinary day-to-day cash outflows, as well as an appropriate level of precautionary balances in order to respond quickly to sudden, unexpected increases in cash outflow. They also must balance each subsidiary's expected and unexpected demands for cash against the opportunity cost of holding the firm's financial assets in such low-yielding forms, while simultaneously controlling working capital-related currency conversion costs and foreign-exchange risk.

International Capital Budgeting

Another task financial officers of any business face is capital budgeting. Firms have limited funds for investment and often a seemingly endless set of projects from which to choose. They must establish mechanisms for developing, screening, and selecting projects in which the firm will make significant new investments. Numerous approaches for evaluating investment projects are available, but the most commonly used methods include the following:

▶ Net present value

▶ Internal rate of return

▶ Payback period

Net Present Value

The net present value approach is based on a basic precept of finance theory that a dollar today is worth more than a dollar in the future. To calculate the net present value of a project, a firm's financial officers estimate the cash flows the project will generate in each time period and then discount them back to the present. For many projects, the cash flow in the early years will be negative, since the firm must outlay cash for the initial investment and be prepared to suffer startup operating losses in the first year or two. In later years, of course, the firm expects cash flows to be positive. Financial officers must decide which interest rate, called the *rate of discount*, to use in the calculation, based on the firm's cost of capital. For example, if the firm's cost of capital is 10 percent, then financial officers will use an annual interest rate of 10 percent to discount the cash flows generated by the project through time in order to calculate the present value. The firm will undertake only projects that generate a positive net present value.

The net present value approach can be used for both domestic and international projects. However, several additional factors must be considered when determining whether to undertake an international project.[27] These factors are risk adjustment, currency selection, and choice of perspective for the calculations.

Risk Adjustment. Because a foreign project may be riskier than a domestic project, international businesses may adjust either the discount rate upward or the expected cash flows downward to account for a higher level of risk. The amount of risk adjustment should reflect the degree of riskiness of operating in the country in question. For example, little if any risk adjustment is needed for Germany because of its political stability, well-respected court system, and superb infrastructure. In contrast, tribal and civil war in Somalia warrant the use of much higher risk adjustment for potential investments in that country.

Choice of Currency. The determination of the currency in which the project should be evaluated depends on the nature of the investment. If the project is an integral part of the business of an overseas subsidiary, use of the foreign currency is appropriate. For example, GM's German subsidiary Adam Opel AG invested millions of deutsche marks to build a new factory in Eisenach, Germany in the early 1990s. Constructing the plant was central to Opel's overall business plan, and the subsidiary's financial officers thus made the net present value calculation in deutsche marks. For foreign projects that are more properly viewed as integrated parts of a firm's global procurement strategy, translation into the home country currency may make sense. For example, Houston-based Compaq Computer allocates production between its U.S. and foreign factories as part of an overall strategy of global reduction of production costs. If Compaq invests £10 million to expand the output of its Scottish production facilities, it should calculate the project's net present value in U.S. dollars instead of pounds. To do this, it must estimate revenues and costs for the project and then convert them into dollars. It also must account for any expected changes in the exchange rate between the dollar and the pound over the life of the project.

Whose Perspective: Parent's or Project's? Another factor is determining whether the cash flows that contribute to the net present value of the capital investment should be evaluated from the perspective of the parent or that of the individual project. In practice, some international businesses analyze the cash flows of the individual project, others focus on the project's impact on the parent, and others do both.[28]

The cash flows to the parent can differ from those to the project for several reasons. MNCs often impose arbitrary accounting charges on the revenues of their operating units for the units' use of corporate trademarks or to cover general corporate overhead. These arbitrary charges may reduce the *perceived* cash flows generated by the project, but not the *real* cash flows returned to the parent. For example, suppose that when the corporate parent's accountants are calculating a subsidiary's profitability, they routinely assess a 5 percent fee against revenues for general corporate and administrative expenses. This technique may be a reasonable mechanism for allocating general corporate expenses across all the firm's operations. But the 5 percent charge does not represent a true drain on the cash flow generated by the subsidiary. Thus it should be ignored in the calculation of the net present value to the parent of a project the subsidiary proposes. Similarly, fees assessed against the subsidiary for the use of corporate trademarks, brand names, or patents should not be considered in the net present value calculation because the parent firm incurs no additional costs regardless of whether the subsidiary undertakes the project.[29]

Financial officers also must consider any governmental restrictions on currency movements that would affect the firm's ability to repatriate profits when it wants. A project proposed by a foreign subsidiary may be enormously profitable, but if the profits can never be repatriated to the parent, the project may not be desirable from the perspective of the parent and its shareholders. The importance of currency controls in determining the attractiveness of a project may also be a function of the parent's overall strategy. For example, consider PepsiCo's investment in Ukraine mentioned earlier in this chapter. Any current Ukrainian restrictions on profit repatriation are of little concern to PepsiCo and its shareholders, since the firm realizes that it will have to increase its investments in the country in the short and medium term. However, PepsiCo's shareholders would be concerned if the firm were never allowed to repatriate profits from its Ukrainian operations.

Internal Rate of Return

A second approach commonly used for evaluating investment projects is to calculate the internal rate of return. With this approach financial officers first estimate the cash flows generated by each project under consideration in each time period, as in the net present value analysis. They then calculate the interest rate—called the *internal rate of return*—that makes the net present value of the project just equal to zero. As with the net present value approach, the financial officers must adjust their calculations for any accounting charges that have no cash flow implications (intracorporate licensing fees, overhead charges for general corporate and administrative expenses, and so on). They then compare the project's internal rate of return with the **hurdle rate**—the minimum rate of return the firm finds acceptable for its capital investments. The hurdle rate may vary by country to account for differences in risk. The firm will undertake only projects for which the internal rate of return is higher than the hurdle rate.

Payback Period

A third approach for assessing and selecting projects is to calculate a project's **payback period**—the number of years it will take the firm to recover, or pay back, from the project's earnings the original cash investment. Vancouver's Placer Dome, Inc., often uses a payback approach to evaluate mining investments, such as a proposed $500 million investment in a Chilean copper mine as part of a joint venture with Finland's Outokumpu OY. After determining that this project's payback period would be less than five years, Placer decided in 1992 to proceed with the deal.[30]

The payback period technique has the virtue of simplicity: all one needs is simple arithmetic to calculate the payback period. This approach ignores, however, the profits generated by the investment in the longer run. A project that earns large early profits but whose later profits diminish steadily over time may be selected over a project that suffers initial startup losses but makes large continuous profits after that.

Because of its simplicity, many firms use the payback period technique for a quick-and-dirty screening of projects and then follow with a more sophisticated method for further analysis of those that pass the preliminary screening.[31] A firm may choose different payback criteria for international projects than for domestic ones. Here, too, adjustments must be made to eliminate intracorporate charges that have no real effect on corporate cash flows.

Before investing $500 million in this Chilean copper mine, the financial officers of Vancouver's Placer Dome Inc. carefully analyzed the risks and rewards of the project using sophisticated capital budgeting techniques drawn from modern finance theory.

Sources of International Investment Capital

Firms use capital budgeting techniques to allocate their financial resources toward those domestic and international projects that promise the highest rates of return. Having identified such profitable opportunities, firms must secure sufficient capital to fund them, from either internal or external sources. In doing so, an international business wants to minimize the worldwide cost of its capital, while also minimizing its foreign-exchange risk, political risk, and global tax burden.[32]

Internal Sources of Investment Capital

One source of investment capital for international businesses is the cash flows generated internally (for example, profits from operations and noncash expenses such as depreciation and amortization) by the parent firm and its various subsidiaries. The amount from such sources is significant: in 1993, foreign subsidiaries of U.S.-owned firms earned $57.5 billion, while U.S. subsidiaries of foreign-owned parents earned $5.1 billion.[33] Internal cash flows thus represent an important source of capital for funding subsidiaries' investment projects.

Subject to legal constraints, the parent firm may use the cash flow generated by any subsidiary to fund the investment projects of any member of the corporate family. The corporate parent may access the cash flow directly via the subsidiary's dividend payments to the parent. The parent then can channel those funds to another subsidiary through either a loan or additional equity investments in that subsidiary. Alternatively, one subsidiary can directly lend funds to a second subsidiary. Figure 18.4 summarizes the various internal sources of capital available to the parent and its subsidiaries.

Two legal constraints may affect the parent's ability to shift funds among its subsidiaries. First, if the subsidiary is not wholly owned by the parent, the parent must respect the rights of the subsidiary's other shareholders. Any intracorporate transfers of funds must be done on a fair market basis. This ensures the parent

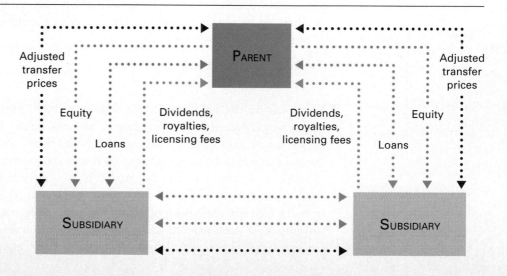

FIGURE 18.4

Internal Sources of Capital for International Businesses

does not siphon off the subsidiary's profits through self-dealing, thereby harming the other shareholders' interests. If the subsidiary is wholly owned, transfers of funds are not a problem. Second, some countries impose restrictions on the repatriation of profits, thus blocking intracorporate transfers of funds. However, a parent may find that while it cannot shift funds in the form of dividends to itself, it can shift funds in the form of loans to other subsidiaries. Or, the parent may be able to recapture funds from the subsidiary by charging licensing fees for the use of the parent's brand names, trademarks, copyrights, or patents or by imposing fees for general corporate or administrative services. Such payments are not trivial. In 1993, foreign subsidiaries paid their U.S.-owned parents $20.4 billion in royalties and licensing fees, while U.S. subsidiaries paid their foreign-owned parents $4.8 billion for the same purpose.[34] (Please note that we do not mean to imply that any of these fees were paid to evade host country restrictions on currency movements.)

A parent corporation also may shift funds between its operating units by adjusting the transfer prices paid for goods and services in intracorporate transactions between a subsidiary and other branches of the corporate family. Suppose subsidiary B operates in a country that restricts profit repatriation, while subsidiary A does not. By raising the price charged by subsidiary A for a good purchased by subsidiary B, the MNC can transfer funds from B to A. (Chapter 19 discusses the income tax implications of these pricing policies and the pitfalls awaiting firms that aggressively manipulate transfer prices.) Firms must be aware that transfer-pricing policies are least controversial when used between two wholly owned subsidiaries. Otherwise, the parent may be placing itself in the position of either defrauding the outside investors (in the case of subsidiary B) or enriching them (in the case of subsidiary A) at the expense of its own shareholders.

While such intracorporate transfers of funds may theoretically benefit the entire firm, they can create serious problems at the subsidiary and managerial level. From the parent's perspective, shifting cash flows from subsidiary to parent may be beneficial. However, it may cause operational problems and increased expenses for the subsidiary. The parent may consider it wise policy to siphon off the subsidiary's working capital and reduce its reported profitability by inflating royalty fees, administrative charges, or other transfer prices. Yet such approaches may result in a misleading picture of the subsidiary's performance in the marketplace. If the parent rewards managerial performance without making adjustments for these financial manipulations, morale among the subsidiary's managers may plummet, to the detriment of the parent.

External Sources of Investment Capital

When raising external financing for their investment projects, international businesses may choose from a rich source of debt and equity alternatives. Investment bankers, such as Goldman Sachs, and securities firms, such as Merrill Lynch and Nomura, can help firms acquire capital from external sources. For example, if a firm wants to increase its equity base, such an intermediary can place the firm's stock with investors in the home country, in the host country, or in other countries. To facilitate the raising of equity internationally, many MNCs list their common stock on stock markets in several different countries. For example, KLM shares are listed in New York and Amsterdam. And Caterpillar's stock is listed not only on the New York Stock Exchange but also on exchanges in Belgium, France, Germany, Switzerland, and the United Kingdom.[35] Through multiple foreign listings, international businesses assure foreign investors that they can easily dispose of their shares should the need arise.

International firms also have many opportunities to borrow funds internationally on either a short-term or a long-term basis. They may shop for the best credit terms in their home country market, in the host country market, or in other markets. For example, consider New Jersey's Baltek Corporation, which annually produces $30 million in balsa wood products at its factory in Ecuador. In the early 1990s, Baltek relied on local Ecuadorian banks to finance its expansion into shrimp farming in the Gulf of Guayaquil. The firm found those banks more eager for its business than U.S. banks were—an example of the advantages of being a big fish in a small pond.[36] Larger MNCs may rely on syndicated short- and medium-term loans in which a consortium of international banks and pension fund managers join together to provide the capital. Often these syndicated loans use Eurocurrencies, since the absence of expensive central bank regulations reduces the cost of Eurocurrency-based loans. MNCs also may secure longer-term loans in the form of home country bonds, foreign bonds, and international bonds, as discussed in Chapter 5.

Securities firms and investment banks are continually developing innovative financing techniques to reduce the costs of borrowing for their MNC clients or to exploit gaps in national financial regulations.[37] For example, an MNC may issue dual-currency bonds, whereby it borrows money and pays interest in one currency but repays the principal in a second currency. Or bonds may be denominated as a basket of several currencies or be redeemable in gold. Some firms get very creative. For example, in October 1992, the Walt Disney Company issued $400 million in Eurobonds that had a different twist: their interest rate depended on the success of 13 Disney movies. Investors were guaranteed at least a 3 percent rate, with a possible return of 13.5 percent. Comparable quality bonds were yielding only 7–8 percent. Eager investors snapped up the bonds, betting that *The Muppet Christmas Carol* and other Disney movies would be box office hits.[38] Pleased with its ability to shift some movie-making risks to the bondholders through low minimum interest rates, in 1994 Disney offered a similar note linked to a new set of motion pictures.[39]

A particularly important facet of the international capital market is the **swap market**, in which two firms can exchange their financial obligations. The global swap market is estimated to total $4.3 trillion.[40] Swaps are undertaken to change the cost and nature of a firm's interest obligations or to change the currency in which its debt is denominated. For example, suppose firm A has a fixed-rate obligation but prefers a floating-rate one, while firm B has a floating-rate obligation and wants a fixed-rate one. The two firms can swap their obligations. As noted by John Grout, a financial officer at Cadbury Schweppes, "The advantage of the swap market is that it allows you to adjust exposure profiles without having to undo the underlying transactions."[41] Often an international bank will facilitate such swaps by acting as a broker or by undertaking half of a swap for its own account.

MNCs also often engage in currency swaps, in order to shift their interest and payment obligations from a less preferred currency to a more preferred one. An MNC may consider its net obligations in one currency to be too large or may expect exchange-rate fluctuations to adversely affect its loan repayment costs. A swap may be arranged between two firms that have differing currency preferences.

International banks play a key role in the currency swap market. Since they continually monitor foreign-exchange markets as well as their net currency exposures, they usually can accommodate any MNC's currency swap needs. Most international banks engage in currency swaps with corporate clients on an ongoing basis.

Through swaps, international businesses can manage both their interest costs and their exposure to exchange-rate fluctuations. For example, the Inco, Ltd., 1990 annual report noted that the firm had swapped SFr200 million in 5.75 percent bonds and ECU70 million in 9.5 percent notes for debt obligations denominated in U.S. dollars bearing interest rates of 10.2 percent and 10.5 percent, respectively. Why would Inco agree to pay higher interest rates on the new bonds than it was paying on the old ones? One reason is that the firm receives much of its revenues in U.S. dollars and wants to match those dollar receipts with offsetting dollar obligations. Inco may also have believed that the U.S. dollar would depreciate in value and relished the prospect of paying off the bonds in the future with depreciated dollars.[42]

Currency swaps are only one technique for controlling exposure to exchange-rate fluctuations. Clearly, however, managing this exposure is critical to international business success, and it should be handled proactively. For example, in 1993, Ford had outstanding currency swaps, forward contracts, and options contracts that totaled $8.6 billion.[43]

CHAPTER REVIEW

Summary

International firms face financial management challenges that are far more complex than those confronting purely domestic firms. Conflicts may arise between exporters and importers over the currency to use in invoicing international transactions. Exporting firms often find it difficult to check the creditworthiness of their foreign customers. Also, obtaining payment for goods from foreign customers may be more difficult because of greater geographical distances, differing legal systems, and unfamiliar business customs. Fortunately, many methods of payment have been developed over the centuries, including letters of credit, documentary collection, credit cards, and countertrade.

International firms must strive to minimize the impact of exchange-rate fluctuations on their operations. Three main types of exchange-rate exposure exist. Transaction exposure refers to the impact of exchange-rate fluctuations on the profitability of a business transaction denominated in a foreign currency. Translation exposure reflects the impact of exchange-rate fluctuations on the value of foreign operations in a firm's accounting records. Economic exposure is the impact unanticipated exchange-rate movements have on the value of the firm's operations.

Management of working capital balances presents international businesses with unique challenges. A firm and each of its operating subsidiaries must have sufficient cash to facilitate day-to-day operations and to meet unexpected demands for cash. Also, the firm must monitor its holdings of each currency in which it and its subsidiaries do business. MNCs often use centralized cash depositories and currency netting operations to control their working capital balances, reduce transaction costs, and minimize their exposure to adverse changes in exchange rates.

Financial officers of international firms must adjust capital budgeting techniques to meet the unique requirements of international business. Standard investment evaluation techniques, such as net present value, internal rate of return, and payback period analysis, must be changed to account for differences in risk, government restrictions on currency movements, and various payments between the parent firm and its foreign subsidiaries that do not affect net cash flows generated by an investment project.

Finally, financial officers must look worldwide for low-cost sources of capital. Ongoing operations of the parent firm and its foreign subsidiaries are often an important internal source of investment capital. Well-developed international debt and equity markets can provide external sources of such capital. Also, international businesses often use the swap market to reduce their exposure to adverse changes in currency values or interest rates.

Review Questions

1. What special problems arise in financing and arranging payment for international transactions?

2. What are the major methods of payment used for international transactions?

3. What are the different types of letters of credit?

4. How do a time draft and a sight draft differ? A trade acceptance and a banker's acceptance?

5. How do the various types of countertrade arrangements differ from each other?

6. What techniques are available to reduce transaction exposure? Discuss each.

7. What is translation exposure? What effect does a balance sheet hedge have on translation exposure?

8. Why do MNCs engage in currency netting operations?

9. What capital budgeting techniques are available to international businesses?

10. What is the difference between an interest rate swap and a currency swap?

Questions for Discussion

1. What are the advantages and disadvantages of each method of payment for international transactions from the exporter's perspective?

2. Which type of letter of credit is most preferable from the exporter's point of view?

3. Why do firms use countertrade? What problems do they face when they do?

4. How does capital budgeting for international projects differ from that for domestic projects?

BUILDING GLOBAL SKILLS

Consider Belgian Lace Products (BLP), a hypothetical table linens manufacturer. BLP consists of a parent corporation, a wholly owned manufacturing subsidiary in Belgium, and four wholly owned distribution subsidiaries in Belgium, Germany, Japan, and the United States. Its manufacturing subsidiary buys inputs from various suppliers, manufactures high quality lace napkins and tablecloths, and sells the output to the four BLP-owned distribution subsidiaries. The four distribution subsidiaries in turn sell the products to retail customers in their marketing areas. The distribution subsidiaries buy certain inputs, such as labor, warehouse space, electricity, and computers, from outside suppliers as well.

The following summarizes typical monthly transactions for each of the BLP operating units (BF = Belgian francs):

Manufacturing Subsidiary

Sales to Belgian distribution subsidiary: BF600,000
Sales to German distribution subsidiary: BF500,000
Sales to Japanese distribution subsidiary: BF700,000
Sales to U.S. distribution subsidiary: BF450,000

Cost of inputs purchased from Belgian suppliers:
BF300,000

Costs of inputs purchased from German suppliers:
DM50,000

Costs of inputs purchased from Japanese suppliers:
¥3,000,000

Costs of inputs purchased from U.S. suppliers:
$5,000

Belgian Distribution Subsidiary

Sales to retail customers: BF2,000,000

Payments to BLP manufacturing subsidiary:
BF600,000

Payments to external suppliers: BF30,000 and
DM20,000

German Distribution Subsidiary

Sales to retail customers: DM150,000

Payments to BLP manufacturing subsidiary:
BF500,000

Payments to external suppliers: DM10,000,
BF40,000, and $9,000

Japanese Distribution Subsidiary

Sales to retail customers: ¥5,000,000

Payments to BLP manufacturing subsidiary:
BF700,000

Payments to external suppliers: ¥3,000,000 and
$8,000

U.S. Distribution Subsidiary

Sales to retail customers: $40,000

Payments to BLP manufacturing subsidiary:
BF450,000

Payments to external suppliers: $10,000 and
¥300,000

Exchange rates

BF20 = DM1

BF30 = $1.00

BF1 = ¥3

Use the above information to answer the following questions:

1. Calculate the profitability of each of BLP's five subsidiaries. (Because BLP is Belgian, perform the calculations in terms of Belgian francs.) Are any of the subsidiaries unprofitable? On the basis of the information provided, would you recommend shutting down an unprofitable subsidiary? Why or why not?

2. Suppose it costs each subsidiary 1 percent of the transaction amount each time it converts its home currency into another currency in order to pay its suppliers. Develop a strategy by which BLP as a corporation can reduce its total currency conversion costs. Suppose your strategy costs BLP BF15,000 per month to implement? Should the firm still adopt your approach?

3. What effect would the creation of a single European currency have on BLP? On the benefits and costs of the strategy you developed to reduce its currency conversion costs?

CLOSING CASE

Janssen Pharmaceutica Cures Its Currency Ills[44]

Janssen Pharmaceutica, started by Dr. Paul Janssen in 1953, is one of the most innovative and successful firms in the pharmaceutical industry. A subsidiary of Johnson & Johnson (J&J) since 1961, Janssen Pharmaceutica today employs 12,000 people worldwide. About 3300 work in or near Beerse, the Belgian city where the firm was born and is headquartered.

Janssen's competitive strength lies in new drug development. Between 1970 and 1992, only one firm in the world ranked higher than Janssen in the number of new drugs developed to cure humankind's ills. The Janssen-developed drugs Risperdal, Propulsid, and Itrizole, for example, combat such diverse medical problems as schizophrenia, nighttime heartburn, and fungal infections.

Janssen is also an important innovator in an area very different from pharmaceuticals: management of corporate treasury operations. Like many European firms, Janssen has production facilities and sales operations throughout Western Europe, the Americas, and Asia. It also purchases inputs and services from a wide variety of suppliers outside Belgium. Before 1984, handling the numerous incoming and outgoing cross-border invoices generated by its operations was very expensive. Much working capital was tied up as each of the firm's 32 far-flung subsidiaries maintained balances in their checking accounts sufficient to handle day-to-day operating needs and to protect against unexpected demands for cash. Further, every time a Janssen subsidiary paid an invoice denominated in a foreign currency, it paid currency conversion charges that averaged 0.5 percent of the amount in question.

In 1983, Belgium sought to improve the international competitiveness of its firms by authorizing the creation of so-called *coordination centers* to reduce the costs of corporate treasury activities. To qualify to establish a coordination center, a company had to have affiliates in at least four countries, to have sales of at least $300 million, and to employ a minimum of ten employees in its Belgian coordination center. Concomitant changes in Belgian tax laws reduced the corporate income tax burdens on coordination centers to near zero. By 1994, over 350 coordination centers had been established in Belgium, employing more than 7500 highly trained professionals. The coordination centers have increased demand in Belgium for such corporate support services as accounting, auditing, legal research, and investment banking. About 30 percent of the coordination centers are owned by U.S. MNCs, 15 percent by Belgian MNCs, and 46 percent by European MNCs headquartered outside of Belgium.

Janssen Pharmaceutica moved quickly to take advantage of the Belgian law by establishing a coordination center in June 1984. This center, a separately incorporated and wholly owned subsidiary of Janssen, provides a variety of financial services for the firm and its subsidiaries. Initially the coordination center focused on **treasury management**—the management of financial flows and of the currency and interest-rate risks associated with these flows. This mission involved three objectives:

1. Identify short- and medium-term financial risks on a worldwide basis.

2. Quantify such risks and recommend appropriate responses to Janssen's executives.

3. Manage and control these financial exposures on a worldwide basis subject to J&J's corporate rules and procedures (which encourage hedging but discourage speculation).

The center's treasury management activities include acting as a centralized cash depository and performing currency netting operations for the Janssen group of companies, thereby lowering the levels of cash balances held by the group and reducing the group's aggregate currency conversion costs. As Janssen has learned to use the center more efficiently, the center's duties have expanded. It now performs all currency and interest-rate exposure management and hedging activities for the Janssen group.

The coordination center has also taken over the bank management function. To benefit the whole group, it established checking accounts in the various countries in which Janssen does business. Suppose Janssen's German subsidiary buys paper and writing instruments from a French office supply wholesaler. The invoice (denominated in French francs) received by the German subsidiary will be sent to the coordination center, which will pay the invoice from its account at a French bank. By dealing with the banking system of only one country, Janssen can predict more reliably when checks will be debited or credited to its accounts. More important, however, this technique reduces currency conversion costs for the group as a whole. The German subsidiary, by shifting the responsibility for obtaining francs to the coordination center, avoids the cost of converting deutsche marks into francs. The coordination center can often obtain the necessary francs to pay French suppliers without converting any currencies. It does this by depositing franc-denominated revenues received by other Janssen subsidiaries into the coordination center's French bank account. This netting of payments and receipts on a corporate basis substantially reduces the need to convert currencies. The cumulative savings of currency conversion fees on hundreds of thousands of incoming and outgoing invoices amount to millions of dollars each year.

The managers of each Janssen subsidiary of course want credit for the revenues their subsidiary generates. Thus, at the end of the monthly accounting period, the coordination center nets out payments and receipts in all the currencies in which the subsidiary does business. It then sends each subsidiary either a *single* check or a *single* invoice, denominated in its local currency, that reflects the subsidiary's net position. And only 35 employees perform this monthly miracle for the Janssen group, although, as you can imagine, they work with an extremely sophisticated computer and telecommunications network.

In addition, the coordination center acts as an internal bank for the Janssen group. Its specialists interact continuously with the banking community worldwide, seeking the highest short-term interest rates for the group's excess cash balances. The center often can locate sources of low-cost loans for the Janssen subsidiaries. If a subsidiary needs to borrow money, the coordination center offers to match the best local terms available to that subsidiary. It uses a standardized loan document and so can offer 24-hour turnaround time on loan approvals. It also allocates to the borrowing subsidiary any tax benefits generated by the transaction.

As Janssen's coordination center honed its treasury management, bank management, and lending skills, J&J's corporate managers recognized that Janssen's expertise could be used to benefit the rest of the corporate family. Today, Janssen's coordination center provides financial services for the entire J&J family, with one significant change. When it served only the Janssen group, the center focused on managing exchange-rate risk in terms of the Belgian franc. However, because J&J is a U.S. firm, the center now manages exchange-rate risk in terms of the U.S. dollar.

Case Questions

1. In essence, to qualify for the tax breaks offered to a Belgian coordination center, a firm must be an MNC. Why would Belgium limit these tax breaks to multinationals? Are Belgian authorities happy that Janssen's coordination center is benefiting all of J&J's worldwide operations?

2. What are the advantages of having the Janssen coordination center act for J&J worldwide? Are there any disadvantages?

3. Can you think of any other strategies for reducing currency conversion costs that could be used by firms operating in Europe?

CHAPTER NOTES

1. *KLM Annual Report 1993/94*; U.S. Department of Transportation, *U.S. International Air Passenger and Freight Statistics Calendar Year 1993*, Vol. 1, No. 5 (July 1994); *Fortune*, August 22, 1994, p. 190.

2. George Alogoskoufis and Richard Portes, "International costs and benefits from EMU," *European Economy*, Special Edition No. 1 (1991), p. 237.

3. S. Black, "International money and international monetary arrangements," in P. B. Kenen and R. W. Jones (eds.), *Handbook of International Economics*, Vol. 2 (Amsterdam: North-Holland, 1985).

4. "Small Firms Hit Foreign Obstacles in Billing Overseas," *Wall Street Journal*, December 8, 1992, p. B2.

5. An overview of methods of paying for international transactions may be found in Chapter 13 of the 1992 edition of *A Basic Guide to Exporting*, published by the U.S. Department of Commerce.

6. Richard Schaffer, Beverley Earle, and Filiberto Agusti, *International Business Law and Its Environment* (St. Paul, Minn.: West Publishing, 1990), pp. 154–155.

7. Chase Manhattan Bank, *Dynamics of Trade Finance*, (New York: Chase Manhattan, 1984), pp. 41–58; Steve Murphy, *Complete Export Guide Manual* (Manhattan Beach, Calif.: Tran Publishing House, 1980).

8. "Cuba barters its sugar," *Financial Times*, April 23, 1994, p. 22.

9. "Saudis Agree to Trade Oil for Aircraft and Missiles," *Aviation Week and Space Technology*, September 20, 1985, p. 19.

10. Pompiliu Verzariu, *Countertrade Practices in East Europe, The Soviet Union and China: An Introductory Guide to Business* (Washington, D.C.: Department of Commerce, International Trade Administration, November 1984), pp. 98, 101.

11. Rolf Mirus and Bernard Yeung, "Economic Incentives for Countertrade," *The Journal of International Business Studies* (Fall 1986), pp. 27–39.

12. Ingemar Dorfer, *Arms Deal: The Selling of the F-16* (New York: Praeger, 1983).

13. Grant T. Hammond, *Countertrade, Offsets and Barter in International Political Economy* (New York: St. Martin's, 1990), p. 75.

14. Max Eli, *Japan Inc.* (Chicago: Probus Publishing, 1991), pp. 101–104.

15. "Marc Rich & Co. Does Big Deals at Big Risk in Former U.S.S.R.," *Wall Street Journal*, May 15, 1993, p. A1.

16. Hammond, op. cit., p. 11.

17. "Pepsi Seeking to Boost Sales to Ukrainians," *Wall Street Journal*, October 23, 1992, p. A10; Guy de Jonquieres, "PepsiCo to finance Ukraine expansion with ship exports," *Financial Times*, October 23, 1992, p. 21.

18. Export-Import Bank of the United States, *1991 Annual Report*, p. 7.

19. Boris Antl, "Measuring foreign exchange risk," in *The Management of Foreign Exchange Risk*, 2nd ed. (London: Euromoney Publications, 1982), p. 7.

20. "Foreign Currency Trades Slow at Merc as Firms Back Away," *Wall Street Journal*, October 20, 1992, p. C1.

21. "German Unit Is Established For Importing, Distribution," *Wall Street Journal*, October 8, 1992, p. C15.

22. David K. Eiteman, Arthur I. Stonehill, and Michael H. Moffett, *Multinational Business Finance*, 6th ed. (Reading, Mass.: Addison-Wesley, 1992), p. 263.

23. "Consumers Still Find Imported Bargains Despite Weak Dollar," *Wall Street Journal*, October 7, 1992, p. A1; "Fine French Vintages Become a Hard Sell in Slumping Economy, *Wall Street Journal*, October 20, 1992, p. A1.

24. Christopher Knowlton, "How Disney Keeps the Magic Going," *Fortune*, December 4, 1989, pp. 111–132.

25. *European Economy*, No. 44 (October 1990), p. 66.

26. Eiteman, Stonehill, and Moffett, op. cit., p. 574.

27. Alan C. Shapiro, "Financial structure and cost of capital in the multinational corporation," *Journal of Financial and Quantitative Analysis* (June 1978), pp. 211–216.

28. Marjorie Stanley and Stanley Block, "An Empirical Study of Management and Financial Variables Influencing Capital Budgeting Decisions for Multinational Corporations in the 1980s," *Management International Review*, Vol. 23, No. 3 (1983), pp. 61–71.

29. Alan C. Shapiro, "Capital budgeting for the multinational corporation," *Financial Management* (Spring 1978), pp. 7–16.

30. "Placer Dome's Revamped Management Strikes Gold," *Wall Street Journal*, October 26, 1992, p. B4.

31. U. Rao Cherukuri, "Capital Budgeting in India," in S. Kerry Cooper, ed., *Southwest Review of International Business Research* (1992), pp. 194–204.

32. Eiteman, Stonehill, and Moffett, op. cit., p. 416.

33. *Survey of Current Business*, June 1994, p. 94.

34. Ibid.

35. Caterpillar Corporation, *Annual Report 1990*, p. 25.

36. "When It's Smart to Use Foreign Banks," *International Business* (January 1992), pp. 17–18.

37. Gunter Dufey and Ian H. Giddy, "Innovation in the International Financial Market," *The Journal of International Business Studies* (Fall 1981), pp. 33–51.

38. "A Eurobond Issue Tied to Film Results," *Wall Street Journal*, October 12, 1992, p. C17.

39. "Walt Disney to Sell Notes Tied to Films' Results, With Initial Yield Linked to U.S. 7-Year Issue," *Wall Street Journal*, February 17, 1994, p. C20.

40. J. Dickson Brown, "Derivatives: Part of the Solution to Global Risk," *Global Finance*, October 1992, p. 25.

41. "Vital tool in minimizing costs," *Financial Times*, November 11, 1992, p. III.

42. Inco Ltd., *Annual Report 1990*, p. 38.

43. Ford Motor Company, *Annual Report 1993*, p. 40.

44. Johnson & Johnson, *1993 Annual Report*; lectures and personal interviews, staff of Janssen Internationaal N.V., May 25, 1994; "Visa plans small payments cross-border service," *Financial Times*, July 12, 1993, p. 1; "One Euro Currency Saves on Accounting But Not on Worries," *Wall Street Journal*, December 9, 1991, p. A9.

CHAPTER

19

International Accounting and Taxation

Chapter Outline

National differences in accounting
The roots of differences
Differences in accounting practices
Impact on capital markets
Impact on corporate financial controls
Accounting in centrally planned economies

Efforts at harmonization

Accounting for international business activities
Accounting for transactions in foreign currencies
Foreign-currency translation

International taxation issues
Transfer pricing
Tax havens

Taxation of foreign income by the United States
Taxation of exports
Taxation of foreign branch income
Taxation of foreign subsidiary income

Resolving international tax conflicts
Tax credits
Tax treaties
"Bashing" of foreign firms

After studying this chapter you should be able to:

Discuss the various factors that influence the accounting systems countries adopt.

Describe the impact these national accounting differences have on international firms.

Analyze the benefits to international firms of harmonizing differences in national accounting systems.

Describe the accounting procedures used by U.S. firms engaged in international business.

Identify the major international taxation issues affecting international businesses.

Discuss the taxation of foreign income by the U.S. government.

Assess the techniques available to resolve tax conflicts among countries.

S O YOU WANT TO INVEST OVERSEAS? THAT MAKES SENSE. AFTER all, foreign stock markets often outperform the U.S. market. Now all you have to do is figure out what you're investing in. ▌▌ It won't be easy: Disclosure and accounting rules overseas differ sharply from those in the United States—and also differ significantly among foreign countries. ▌▌ Only companies in the United States and Canada, for example, issue reports quarterly on profits and other key financial data. And many companies in Japan and … Germany don't consolidate the financial data of majority-owned subsidiaries.… ▌▌ Gary Greenberg, a global analyst with Harris Associates, says that in other nations the lack of a strong enforcement body like the U.S.

There's No Comparison[1]

Securities and Exchange Commission permits overseas companies to be more footloose and fancy-free with disclosures. And insider trading is often greeted with a wink by government regulators. In Holland, Spain, and France, where stock exchanges are relatively small, government regulation and oversight of company disclosures are "very relaxed," Mr. Greenberg says.… ▌▌ Overseas companies don't have to embroider facts, though, to complicate things for the U.S. investor. Differences in accounting rules make for a wide divergence of financial results in various countries.…

▌▌ To illustrate how tough it is to compare such profits, three accounting professors at Rider College in Lawrenceville, N.J., set up a computer model of an imaginary company's financial reports in four nations. Starting with the same gross operating profit of $1.5 million the company had net profit of $34,600 in the United States, $260,600 in the United Kingdom, $240,000 in Australia and $10,402 in … Germany—all because of varying accounting rules in each country. ▌▌ Although many companies have worldwide operations, their financial results in different countries aren't comparable, the professors say. They term this a "serious problem" for "accountants who may be called upon to analyze a foreign company's financial statements." ▌▌▌▌▌

The goal of an accounting system is to identify, measure, and communicate "economic information to permit informed judgements and decisions by users of the information."[2] These users are numerous. The accounting system provides operational information to line managers and financial performance data to top executives to help them make marketing, financial, and strategic decisions. Investors use information about the firm's performance to determine whether to purchase its stock and debt instruments. And the government uses this information to assess the firm's tax burdens and to regulate the issuance of its securities.

Accounting has been called the "language of business." Unfortunately for international firms, it is far from being a lingua franca. The accounting tasks of international businesses are much more complex than those of domestic firms. The accounting system of a purely domestic firm must meet the professional and regulatory standards of its home country. An MNC and its subsidiaries, however, must meet the sometimes contradictory standards of all the countries in which they operate. To effectively manage and control their operations, local managers need accounting information prepared according to local accounting concepts and denominated in the local currency. However, for corporate officers to assess the foreign subsidiary's performance and value, the subsidiary's accounting records must be translated into the parent's home currency using accounting concepts and procedures detailed by the parent. Investors around the world, seeking the highest possible returns on their capital, need to be able to interpret the firm's track record, even though it may be using a currency and an accounting system different from their own. The firm will also have to pay taxes to the countries in which it does business based on the accounting statements it develops in these countries. And when a parent corporation attempts to integrate the accounting records of its subsidiaries to create consolidated financial statements, additional complexities arise because of changes in the value of the host and home currencies over time.

This chapter discusses how international businesses deal with national differences in accounting and taxation systems. It first examines the causes of these differences and describes countries' attempts to reduce them. It goes on to describe how accountants of international businesses treat international business transactions in the firms' income statements and balance sheets. Finally, it discusses the impact of national taxation policies on international business and the strategies international firms adopt to reduce their global tax burdens.

National Differences in Accounting

An international business must develop an accounting system that provides both the internal information required by its managers to run the firm and the external information needed by shareholders, lenders, and government officials in the countries in which the firm operates. Yet, as you will see, differences in national accounting philosophies and practices make such a task easier said than done.

The Roots of Differences

A country's accounting standards and practices reflect the influence of legal, cultural, political, and economic factors, as Fig. 19.1 indicates.[3] Because these systems vary by country, the underlying goals and philosophy of national accounting systems also vary dramatically.

Consider first the difference between common law and code law countries. In common law countries such as the United Kingdom and the United States, accounting procedures normally evolve via decisions of independent standards-setting boards, such as the U.K.'s Accounting Standards Board or the U.S. Financial Accounting Standards Board (FASB). Each board works in consultation with professional accounting groups, such as the U.K.'s various Institutes of Chartered Accountants or the American Institute of Certified Public Accountants.

FIGURE 19.1

Influences on
a Country's
Accounting
System

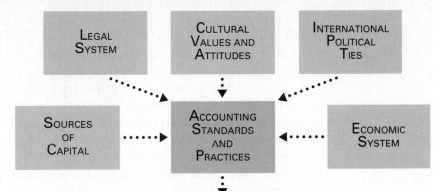

Differences among countries' accounting
practices affect a firm's decisions on:

- Reported income and profits
- Valuations of assets and inventories
- Tax reporting
- Desire to operate in a given country
- Use of accounting reserves

Accountants in common law countries typically follow so-called generally accepted accounting principles (GAAP) that provide a "true and fair view" of a firm's performance based on the standards agreed on by these professional boards. Operating within the boundaries of these principles, accountants have leeway to exercise their professional discretion in reporting a "true and fair" depiction of a firm's performance.

Countries relying on code law, on the other hand, are likely to codify their national accounting procedures and standards.[4] In these countries, accounting practices are determined by the law, not by the collective wisdom of professional accounting groups like the FASB.[5] For example, France's code law system and long tradition of strong central government control over the economy is reflected in its imposition on French firms of a national uniform chart of accounts—the *Plan Comptable Général*. This accounting system, which dates to 1673, creates accounting records designed to serve as proof in legal procedures. To facilitate this legal role, all corporate accounting records must be officially registered with the government. Similarly, German accounting practices adhere strictly to requirements laid down by law or court decisions.

A country's legal system also influences enforcement of accounting practices. Most developed countries rely on both private and public enforcement of business behavior, although the public/private mixture varies by country. Because French and German accounting procedures are laid down by law, the government plays a major role in monitoring accounting practices in those countries. In contrast, the U.S. system relies to a greater extent on private litigation to enforce the accuracy and honesty of firms' accounting practices. Any attempt to mislead private investors or creditors in the United States is likely to prompt a lawsuit; U.S. firms and their accountants have shelled out hundreds of millions of dollars settling such claims.[6] Thus, U.S. firms (and their accountants) are motivated to provide accurate information in their public accounting statements because of this threat of private litigation; French and German firms, in contrast, are more concerned about meeting governmental standards.

A country's accounting system also may reflect its national culture. The detailed accounting procedures laid down by the French government mirror France's statist tradition. Larger French firms also must publish a "social balance sheet" detailing their treatment and compensation of their workforces.[7] Australia's accounting requirements for public firms are generally permissive, reflecting the distrust of government power embedded in that country's individualistic, frontier culture. Strong anti-inflation biases are embedded in German accounting procedures, a reaction to the tragic hyperinflation of the early 1920s that wiped out much of the wealth of the German middle class and helped Adolph Hitler rise to the chancellorship in 1932.

International political ties are also important determinants of a country's accounting procedures. Most members of the British Commonwealth have adopted the accounting principles and procedures of the United Kingdom, while former colonies of France and the Netherlands have adopted those of their colonial rulers. Similarly, the accounting procedures of the Philippines follow those of the United States, which controlled that country from 1898 to 1946.

A country's economic system also influences its accounting practices. In a centrally planned economy (CPE) such as that of China or the former Soviet Union, the accounting system is driven by the need to provide output-oriented information to the state planners. Such accounting systems focus on documenting how state funds are used and whether state-mandated production quotas are being met.[8] In market-oriented systems, on the other hand, managers and investors require profit- and cost-oriented information.

Capital markets may also affect national accounting standards. U.S. firms have historically raised capital by relying on public investors. U.S. accounting standards therefore emphasize the provision of accurate and useful information to help outsiders—private shareholders and bondholders—make appropriate investment decisions. As part of this goal, publicly owned firms must satisfy all the disclosure regulations of the Securities and Exchange Commission (SEC). In Germany, the dominant role of a few large banks in providing capital results in accounting practices that focus on the needs of creditors, for example, by tending to undervalue assets and overvalue liabilities. This conservative approach is favored by the lending banks. The public capital market has been much less important in Germany than in the United States, and German accounting practices provide less information to public investors than do U.S. ones.[9] For example, a German corporation does not need to consolidate the accounts of its subsidiaries if the subsidiaries' activities differ substantially from the parent's or if consolidation would be too expensive for the parent. This lack of consolidation makes it difficult for private investors to assess such a firm's overall performance. This is no problem for its bankers, however, who often sit on its board of directors and who in their role as lenders have access to all its financial information.

The situation is similar in Japan. Most publicly traded Japanese firms are members of a keiretsu. They have relatively few public shareholders because of the pervasive cross-ownership of shares among keiretsu members and the extensive share ownership by banks and other financial institutions. Most Japanese firms also have large debt-to-equity ratios by Western standards. Thus Japanese accounting standards are geared toward meeting the needs of the firm's lenders and keiretsu partners, both of which already have privileged access to the firm's financial records, rather than those of outside investors. Consider Hino Motors, the largest producer of medium- and heavy-duty trucks in Japan, with total sales of $4.8 billion in fiscal year 1992. Approximately 59 percent of its shares are owned by financial institutions. Another 30.5 percent are owned by other Japanese firms, including Toyota Motor Corporation, which owns 11.2 percent. Only 10.5 percent of Hino's shares are owned by "outsiders"—either private individuals or foreign firms—whose primary source of information about the firm is its published financial reports.[10]

Differences in Accounting Practices

Political, cultural, legal, and economic forces affect each country's philosophy and attitude toward its accounting system. They also affect how the country's accountants treat different accounting issues. These differing treatments in turn impact a firm's reported profits, the value of its assets, its tax bill, and its decision to begin or continue to operate in the country. International businesses that rely on foreign accounting records but fail to recognize these differences may make expensive, perhaps fatal, strategic errors and operating mistakes. Let's look at some of the more important national accounting differences that affect international business:

▶ Valuation and revaluation of assets
▶ Valuation of inventories
▶ Relations with tax collectors
▶ Use of accounting reserves

Valuation and Revaluation of Assets. Most countries' accounting systems begin with the assumption that a firm's assets should be valued on an historical cost basis. That is, the asset is carried on the firm's books according to its original cost, less depreciation. Because of inflation, however, the market value of an asset is often higher than its historical cost. The resolution of this problem differs among national accounting systems. For example, Dutch firms are permitted to raise the value of such assets on their balance sheets to reflect their true current value. British accountants may exercise their professional discretion and value assets on an historical cost basis, a current cost basis, or a mixture of the two. Australia, an inheritor of British accounting philosophy, similarly grants a firm's accountants a great degree of professional discretion. Australian firms may alter the value of long-term assets on their balance sheets to take into account inflation or improved economic conditions. In the United States and Japan, however, such upward revaluations are illegal. These differences in asset revaluation procedures suggest the need for caution when comparing the strength of balance sheets of firms from different countries.

Valuation of Inventories. Every introductory accounting course discusses the two principle methods for valuing inventories: LIFO (last in, first out) and FIFO (first in, first out). In times of inflation, LIFO tends to raise the firm's reported costs of goods sold, lower the book value of its inventories, and reduce its reported profits (and, presumably, its taxes) more than FIFO does, while FIFO produces a clearer estimate of the value of the firm's existing inventories than does

LIFO. Thus, in comparing the performance of two firms, one needs to know which technique they use to value their inventories. There are significant international differences in the use of the two methods: U.S., Japanese, and Canadian firms may use either approach, whereas Brazilian and British firms normally use only FIFO.[11]

Dealing with the Taxman. A firm's accounting records form the basis for assessing its income tax burden. In Germany, accounting procedures are explicitly detailed in the German Commercial Code and follow the requirements of German tax laws. A German firm's taxable income is measured by the contents of its financial records. Normally no distinction is made between financial statements reported to shareholders and financial statements reported to German tax authorities. The United States follows a very different approach. U.S. firms commonly report two different sets of financial statements—one to the Internal Revenue Service (IRS) and one to shareholders. Such conduct is authorized by U.S. law and allows firms to take advantage of special tax code provisions to reduce their taxable income. For example, U.S. firms often use accelerated depreciation for tax purposes but not for financial reporting purposes. A German firm normally does not have this option. If it wants to use accelerated depreciation for tax-reporting purposes (to reduce its current-year taxes), it must also use accelerated depreciation in reporting to its shareholders (which reduces its reported income).

Forced to choose between higher taxes and low reported income, most German firms opt for the latter. Managers and investors need to recognize that the reported profits of German firms are thus biased downward. The inflexibility of Germany's accounting system seems to put German firms at a disadvantage in raising capital from outside investors. However, German firms typically obtain most of their capital from large financial intermediaries like banks and insurance firms. These inside investors have access to more detailed information about the firm's performance than is available in its public financial statements published in its annual report.

Tax laws also play a major role in French accounting practices, which follow well-defined procedures detailed by the French government in the national uniform chart of accounts. As in the German system, no deductions for tax purposes may be taken unless they have been entered into the firm's annual accounting records. Because of the dominance of tax law in accounting judgments, French firms are likely to bias their reported earnings and net assets downward in order to reduce their tax burdens.

Use of Accounting Reserves. Another important difference in national accounting systems is in the use of accounting reserves. Firms often use **accounting reserves** to adjust for foreseeable future expenses that affect their operations. An office supplies wholesaler, for example, might establish a reserve account for bad debts and for returned merchandise, knowing that when it ships merchandise, some retailers will ship the goods back and some will fail to pay their bills. The use of accounting reserves by U.S. firms is carefully monitored and limited by the IRS and the SEC. The IRS dislikes them because charges to accounting reserves reduce the firm's taxable income. The SEC fears that firms might manipulate their accounting reserves to provide misleading pictures of their financial performance.

In contrast to the restrictive U.S. system, the German Commercial Code liberally permits German firms to establish accounting reserves for various potential future expenses, such as deferred maintenance, future repairs, or exposure to international risks. Because these reserves reduce reported income on which taxes are based, most German firms use them aggressively. In 1993, for example, Daimler-Benz admitted that its hidden reserves amounted to $2.45 billion.[12]

The use of such reserves hampers outside investors' ability to assess a German firm's performance. Often these firms use reserve accounts to smooth out fluctuations in their earning flows by adding large sums to their reserves in good years and dipping into their reserves in poor years. For example, Lufthansa, the German airline, reported in its 1993 annual report that in fiscal year 1992 it withdrew DM20.9 million from its reserves, and a year later it added DM9.9 million. No explanation was offered in the report for either of these transactions.[13] Because of their use of accounting reserves, the reported earnings of German firms often fluctuate less than those of U.S. firms, giving the misleading appearance that the former are less risky than the latter. These accounting differences complicate investors' decision making regarding how to diversify their portfolios internationally to reduce overall investments risk.[14]

Other Differences. Many other differences exist in how countries treat accounting issues, for example:

▶ *Capitalization of financial leases:* U.S., British, and Swedish firms must capitalize financial leases, while French and Swiss firms may do so but are not required to.

▶ *Preparation of consolidated financial statements:* Consolidation of financial statements is mandatory for U.S. and British firms, while German firms may exclude consolidating subsidiaries if their activities differ substantially from the parent's or if consolidation would be too expensive for the parent.

▶ *Capitalization of R&D expenses:* Most countries permit firms to capitalize R&D expenses, but this practice is forbidden in the United States except in limited circumstances.

▶ *Treatment of goodwill:* A firm that acquires a second firm often pays more than the book value of the acquired firm's stock. The excess payment is called **goodwill**. In the Netherlands, firms typically amortize goodwill over a five-year period, although they may write it off instantaneously or over a period of up to ten years. French firms may amortize goodwill over five to twenty-years. Japan, however, severely limits firms' ability to write off goodwill.

Table 19.1 summarizes important accounting differences among selected countries.

Impact on Capital Markets

The various national differences in accounting practices would be little more than a curiosity were it not for international businesspeople's need for information in order to make decisions. These differences can distort the measured performance of firms incorporated in different countries. As already noted, the earnings of German and French firms are often understated because of the congruency between financial reporting and tax reporting. And the price-to-earnings ratios of

TABLE 19.1

Summary of International Accounting Differences

	UNITED STATES	JAPAN	UNITED KINGDOM	FRANCE	GERMANY	NETHERLANDS	SWITZERLAND	CANADA	ITALY	BRAZIL
Capitalization of research and development costs	Not allowed	Allowed in certain circumstances	Allowed in certain circumstances	Allowed in certain circumstances	Allowed in certain circumstances	Allowed in certain circumstances	Allowed in certain circumstances	Allowed in certain circumstances	Allowed in certain circumstances	Allowed
Fixed asset revaluations stated at amount in excess of cost	Not allowed	Not allowed	Allowed	Allowed	Not allowed	Allowed in certain circumstances	Allowed in certain circumstances	Not allowed	Allowed in rare circumstances	Allowed
Inventory valuation using LIFO	Allowed	Allowed	Allowed but rarely done	Allowed	Allowed in certain circumstances	Allowed	Allowed	Allowed	Allowed	Allowed but rarely done
Finance leases capitalized	Required	Allowed in certain circumstances	Required	Allowed	Allowed in certain circumstances	Required	Allowed	Required	Not allowed	Allowed but seldom done
Pension expense accrued during period of service	Required	Allowed	Required	Allowed	Required	Required	Allowed	Required	Allowed	Allowed
Book and tax timing differences presented on the balance sheet as deferred tax	Required	Allowed in certain circumstances	Required in certain circumstances	Required	Allowed but rarely done	Required	Allowed	Required	Allowed but rarely done	Required
Current rate method used for foreign-currency translation	Required	Generally required	Required	Generally required	Allowed	Required	Allowed	Required in certain circumstances	Required	Required
Pooling method used for mergers	Required in certain circumstances	Allowed in certain circumstances	Allowed in certain circumstances	Not allowed	Allowed in certain circumstances	Allowed but rarely done	Allowed but rarely done	Allowed in rare circumstances	Allowed in rare circumstances	Allowed but rarely done
Equity method used for 20–50 percent ownership	Required	Required	Required	Required	Required	Required	Allowed	Required	Allowed	Required

Source: From Frederick D.S. Choi, *Handbook of International Accounting*. Copyright © 1994 John Wiley & Sons, Inc. Reprinted by permission of John Wiley & Sons, Inc.

Japanese firms are often higher than those of U.S. firms, primarily because Japanese accounting practices often substantially reduce reported profits. For example, Japanese firms report depreciation expenses on an accelerated basis to their shareholders and are allowed to create generous reserve funds for future pension liabilities. Australia's accounting practices allow firms to appear more profitable than identically performing U.S. firms, an advantage that helped such

Australian entrepreneurs have taken advantage of Australia's flexible accounting standards in building their corporate empires. Rupert Murdoch, head of Australia-based News Corporation, is well on his way to establishing the first truly global media company, centered on the Fox Network in North America, STAR-TV in Asia, and Sky Broadcasting in Europe.

Aussie entrepreneurs as Rupert Murdoch and Alan Bond to gain favorable access to additional capital and play the takeover game in the United States in the 1980s.[15] British firms must mingle extraordinary items, such as the one-time disposal of a subsidiary, with their ongoing operations, thereby making it harder for investors to assess the firm's "maintainable" profits.[16] The overall impact of these accounting differences is clear: comparing the financial reports of firms from different countries is exceedingly complex. Thus international investors find it more difficult to assess the performance of the world's businesses.

These differences can affect the global capital market in other ways. The New York Stock Exchange (NYSE), for example, is concerned about SEC-mandated accounting rules that must be followed by publicly traded corporations. Those rules emphasize full and comprehensive disclosure of a firm's financial performance information, and the NYSE fears that they will reduce its competitiveness relative to non-U.S. stock markets by raising the cost to foreign firms that want to list their stocks in New York. Consider the Netherlands-based firm Philips NV. Under Dutch accounting standards, Philips assesses its assets on a current-value basis. To list its stock on the NYSE, Philips must undergo the expense of revaluing its assets on an historical cost basis to meet SEC requirements.[17] Although 2300 non-U.S. firms qualify to be listed on the NYSE, only 108 have chosen to do so. Richard Grasso, NYSE president, believes that the SEC regulations do discourage foreign firms from listing on the exchange, thereby threatening the exchange's global competitiveness.[18] This fear is supported by research that shows higher disclosure requirements reduce firms' incentive to list their stocks on a foreign exchange.[19]

The information-laden accounting practices used by U.S. firms do offer them certain advantages, however. A senior officer of the Long-Term Credit Bank of Japan believes that the United States is the easiest foreign locale in which his firm can lend because of U.S. public disclosure policies. Those policies result in good numbers for assessing the riskiness of potential loans. In contrast, the German accounting system, which allows firms to lump together various cost categories and establish a variety of reserves, are much less helpful for a potential foreign lender. Thus the U.S. accounting requirements allow U.S. firms easier access to international lenders than the German system does.[20]

As globalization of the world's economies increases, the capital requirements of international firms also grow. Firms are relying to a greater extent than ever on the global capital market as a source of funds. As a result, they are being compelled to provide more detailed information about their financial performance and prospects. For example, Daimler-Benz's need to access the U.S. capital market is so great that it agreed to publish a new set of accounting records that use Anglo-American accounting procedures. Investment managers hailed the firm's decision. As one noted, "The poor quality of financial information available from many German companies makes it difficult for investors to buy a stock with confidence, since valuations cannot be clearly established."[21] Despite the NYSE protestations concerning the disadvantage arising from SEC regulations, Daimler-Benz's decision may signal a trend, as more foreign firms adopt Anglo-American reporting procedures to improve their access to the U.S. capital market.[22]

Impact on Corporate Financial Controls

National differences in accounting procedures also complicate an MNC's ability to manage its foreign operations. An MNC's subsidiaries must provide the parent's senior executive officers with timely and uniform financial information prepared on a comparable basis in order to facilitate assessment of the subsidiaries' performances. So the parent typically dictates to the subsidiaries the form and procedures to be used for financial reports submitted to it. Coca-Cola, for example, has carefully developed for its subsidiaries an easy-to-use, standardized accounting manual that incorporates U.S. GAAP.[23]

Senior executives of an MNC must also determine whether to use the parent's or the subsidiary's currency in assessing the performances of foreign subsidiaries and their managers. The choice may seem obvious: translate each subsidiary's financial reports into the parent's currency, thereby allowing easy comparisons by the parent. However, the use of financial reports denominated in the parent's currency may induce the subsidiary's managers to focus their energies on beating the foreign-exchange market rather than on managing the local operations. In practice, there is no uniform answer to the question of which currency to use for performance evaluation: some MNCs choose the host currency and others the home currency, but most appear to use both.[24]

Accounting in Centrally Planned Economies

The accounting systems of CPEs offer special challenges to international businesses operating in those countries. The goals of these systems differ quite a bit from those in market economies. The accounting system used by China's state-owned enterprises, which is a modification of the former Soviet Union's, is designed to provide information about an enterprise's aggregate production. This information is then passed from the enterprise to the central planners so that they can monitor the enterprise's success in fulfilling its performance goals in the economy's central plan and can make mid-plan adjustments as needed.

International businesses must approach financial statements developed in CPEs with great caution. General Electric (GE), for example, ran into several accounting problems in its 1990 purchase of the Hungarian lighting firm

Tungsram. Tungsram was not required by Hungarian law to consolidate its transactions with those of its 17 foreign sales subsidiaries. Because the bonuses of Tungsram's managers were tied to its sales revenues, the firm routinely shipped goods to the subsidiaries even though the subsidiaries might not be able to sell them. By so doing, Tungsram was able to claim increased sales and profits on its accounting statement, and managers were allowed to claim their bonuses. Had Tungsram been forced to consolidate its accounts, these sales to subsidiaries would have been recorded as increased inventory levels instead. In one case, GE discovered that Tungsram's French and German subsidiaries were warehousing $3 million worth of an obsolete automobile headlight that had not been marketed for over a decade.[25] Had GE recognized these accounting differences upfront, it might have either paid substantially less for Tungsram or walked away from the deal.

CPEs' accounting systems are of little use to international businesses trying to meet their own internal managerial and reporting requirements. These systems focus on recording production information needed by central planners but ignore "trivialities" such as revenues, costs, and profits that may be incompatible with Marxist ideology. China's accounting system, for example, ignores bad debts and obsolete inventory but requires foreign-currency transactions to be recorded at the official exchange rate, which often deviates substantially from market rates.[26] A firm involved in a joint venture in a CPE thus needs to modify the host country's accounting system in order to obtain the information needed to manage the joint venture. Consider, for example, American Motors' Beijing Jeep joint venture in China. American Motors' accountants struggled to add standard accounting reports such as income statements, balance sheets, cash flow statements, and budget forecasts to the joint venture's accounting system. While the reports initially were needed for internal control purposes, American Motors soon discovered that they boosted their negotiating clout with Chinese officials. For example, when the Chinese government arbitrarily imposed new taxes that affected Beijing Jeep, American Motors' executives could quickly point out the negative impact on the joint venture and then negotiate concessions from the Chinese. Without an adequate Western cost-accounting system to document the impact of the new tax, American Motors would have been in a weaker bargaining position.[27]

Efforts at Harmonization

Differences in accounting systems are confusing and costly to international businesses. Incompatibilities in these systems make it more difficult for firms to monitor their foreign operations and for investors to comprehend the relative performance of firms based in different countries.[28]

To help solve such problems, many accounting professionals and national regulatory bodies are attempting to harmonize the various national accounting practices. One of the most important of these efforts was the creation of the **International Accounting Standards Committee (IASC)** in 1973. IASC founding members were drawn from the professional accounting societies of the leading trading nations, including the United States, Germany, Japan, the United Kingdom, the Netherlands, Canada, Australia, Mexico, and Ireland. Today, the IASC membership consists of over 100 professional societies from over 70 countries. The IASC has issued a series of standards designed to harmonize national treatment of various accounting issues within its member countries. Among its most important goals is the promotion of comparability of financial statements across countries by establishing standards for inventory valuation, depreciation, deferred income taxes, and other matters. However, the IASC lacks enforcement powers. National governments often ignore its accounting standards if they disagree with them.[29]

The EU has undertaken a separate initiative to harmonize the accounting systems of its member states as part of its drive to complete the formation of its internal market. By so doing, the EU hopes to reduce the total accounting costs of European MNCs. In addition, as national accounting standards of the EU member states become more similar, investors will find it easier to assess the performance of those countries' firms. For example, the EU's Fourth Directive, issued in 1978, mandates that each member require its firms to adopt certain accounting practices and to ensure that financial statements provide a "true and fair view" of operations. The Seventh Directive, issued in 1983, requires firms to publish consolidated financial statements. Each directive, however, allows members a fair amount of discretion in establishing their national accounting standards. For example, inventories may be valued using LIFO, FIFO, actual cost, or weighted cost approaches. Similarly, consolidation is not required if a subsidiary's operations are immaterial to the parent, if the subsidiary's operations are substantially dissimilar from the parent's, or if consolidation would be expensive to perform.

These harmonization efforts have their critics, however. The costs of harmonization are significant. Accountants, firms, and government officials must incur retooling costs if they abandon existing national accounting standards.[30] Some analysts believe that harmonization may affect international competition among accountants. For example, the IASC standards have a strong bias toward British and U.S. accounting procedures. To the extent that the IASC's standards are adopted worldwide, these countries' accounting firms are favored in the international market for accounting services. As a result, other countries are resisting the universal adoption of IASC-endorsed procedures. France, for example, is aggressively promoting the rules developed by its own standards board, the Conseil National de la Comptabilité. So far this board's standards have been adopted by Bulgaria and Romania, thereby giving French accounting firms the inside track in selling accounting services in those countries.[31]

Accounting for International Business Activities

Besides the challenges posed by differences in national accounting systems, most international firms must also deal with two types of specific accounting problems that routinely develop when business is conducted internationally:

1 Accounting for transactions denominated in foreign currencies

2 Reporting the operating results of foreign subsidiaries in the firm's consolidated financial statements

Because of the collapse of the Bretton Woods system in 1971, both problems have become increasingly important to international businesses. Under the Bretton Woods fixed exchange-rate system, the accounting problems raised by international business activities denominated in foreign currencies tended to be minor. In the post–Bretton Woods era, however, currency values can change dramatically. Since 1971, accounting for the impact of exchange-rate changes on the value of international transactions and on the firm's consolidated financial statements has become a significant issue for international businesses.

Accounting for Transactions in Foreign Currencies

Chapter 18 introduced the concept of transaction exposure, which is the effect of exchange-rate fluctuations on the economic benefits and costs of an international transaction. Firms confront the problem of accounting for transactions in foreign currency whenever they agree to pay or receive payment in a foreign currency in settlement of a purchase or sale of goods, services, or assets. Under the existing flexible exchange-rate system, it is very likely that the exchange rate will change between the time a firm enters into an international transaction and the time it receives payment or pays for the goods, services, or assets in question. In accordance with FASB Statement 52, issued in 1981, U.S. firms must account for such international transactions by using a two-transaction approach in their financial statements.[32]

For example, Microsoft Corporation, the Seattle-based computer software giant, faces this problem when it ships copies of its MS-DOS, Windows, and Microsoft Word to a British computer store chain and agrees to accept £30,000 in payment in 90 days. If £1 is worth $1.80 when the contract is signed, making the transaction worth $54,000 (£30,000 × $1.80), Microsoft, by following FASB Statement 52, will account for the transaction as follows:

	DEBIT	CREDIT
Accounts Receivable	$54,000	
Sales Revenues		$54,000

Suppose that in 90 days, when Microsoft receives a check for £30,000, the value of the British pound has dropped to $1.70. In terms of its home currency, Microsoft has received only $51,000 rather than the $54,000 it expected. The actual receipt of the monies is accounted for as follows:

	DEBIT	CREDIT
Cash	$51,000	
Foreign-Exchange Loss	3,000	
Accounts Receivable		$54,000

This accounting procedure highlights any foreign-exchange loss or gain resulting from the sale or purchase. Ultimately, the firm's net income is affected by both the primary transaction and any foreign-exchange gains or losses. But the two-transaction approach has the benefit of separating out information about the success of the firm's core activities—selling its products—from its success in managing its exposure to fluctuations in foreign-currency values. In the example, Microsoft's managers would realize that they need to improve management of their transaction exposure to such fluctuations, perhaps by engaging in hedging operations through the use of the forward market or currency futures (discussed in Chapter 18).

Because the two-transaction approach distinguishes between the firm's core activities and its management of transaction exposure, it is of particular value to stock market analysts, who are often wary of firms that expose themselves to excessive foreign-exchange risk. Dell Computer, for example, lost 10 percent of its market value when it reported $38 million in currency-exchange losses in 1992, an amount equal to roughly one quarter of its annual profits. Stock market analysts believed that the size of the losses meant that Dell was engaging in foreign-currency speculation, rather than merely hedging foreign-currency earnings from its export sales. Dell denied the allegations.[33]

Foreign-Currency Translation

A second type of international accounting problem confronts an MNC when it reports the results of its foreign subsidiaries' operations to its home country shareholders and tax officials. Because its foreign subsidiaries will normally conduct their business using their local currency, the firm must convert its subsidiaries' financial reports into its home currency (an accounting task discussed briefly in Chapter 18).

The process of transforming a subsidiary's reported operations denominated in a foreign currency into the parent's home currency is called **translation**. For most MNCs, the translation process is intertwined with the need to create consolidated financial statements. **Consolidated financial statements** report the combined operations of a parent and its subsidiaries in a single set of accounting statements denominated in a single currency.

Translating financial reports from one currency into another requires the use of an appropriate exchange rate to convert from the first currency to the second. Because the business activities captured in accounting records occur at different times, a question arises as to which exchange rate to use. Should the firm use the exchange rate on the date the transaction occurred (the historical rate), the rate on the date the financial statement is prepared (the current rate), a weighted average over time, or some other rate? For U.S. firms, FASB Statement 52 details the exchange rates and accounting procedures firms are to use in translating and then consolidating subsidiaries' financial statements denominated in a foreign currency.

The treatment of foreign investments under FASB Statement 52 depends upon the size of the parent's ownership stake in the foreign firm, as summarized in Table 19.2. A firm will use one of the following methods:

▶ Cost
▶ Equity
▶ Consolidation

A U.S. firm that has a portfolio investment in a foreign firm (less than 10 percent ownership) must use the **cost method**. With this method, the investment is

TABLE 19.2

Parent's Ownership Stake and Accounting Treatment of Its Foreign Investments

OWNERSHIP STAKE	METHOD USED
Less than 10 percent	Cost method
Between 10 and 50 percent	Equity method
More than 50 percent	Consolidation method

recorded in the U.S. firm's accounting records at cost using the historical exchange rate—the exchange rate at the time the foreign shares were acquired. Any dividends the U.S. firm receives from its portfolio investment are to be reported in its income statement using the exchange rate in effect on the day it received the dividend. Delta Air Lines, for example, uses the cost method to account for its ownership of 5 percent of Singapore Airlines' and Swissair's common stocks, which it bought in the 1980s as part of its global strategic alliance with those carriers.

A U.S. firm that owns between 10 and 50 percent of a foreign firm's stock must use the **equity method** to value its ownership stake. For example, Ford's 23 percent ownership stake in Mazda is entered into Ford's consolidated financial statements using this approach. The equity method calls for the U.S. firm to record its initial investment in the foreign firm at cost using the historical exchange rate. However, when the foreign firm earns profits or suffers losses, the value of the investment carried on the U.S. firm's consolidated financial statements is adjusted to reflect those profits or losses using the exchange rate prevailing when they were reported. Any dividends issued by the foreign firm reduce the value of the U.S. firm's investment in the foreign firm. This adjustment also is made using the exchange rate in effect on the day when the dividends were paid.

The most complicated accounting issues arise when a U.S. firm purchases more than 50 percent ownership of a foreign firm, such as Ford's purchase of all of the stock of the Jaguar Motor Company in 1990. In such cases, the U.S. firm must use the **consolidation method**. This method calls for the accounting records of the two firms to be consolidated when the U.S. firm reports operating results to its shareholders and the SEC. Because the foreign subsidiary uses the accounting rules prescribed by its national government or national professional association, the subsidiary's financial statements must first be restated using U.S. GAAP. The next step is to determine the **functional currency** of the subsidiary, defined as the currency of the principal economic environment in which the subsidiary operates. For example, the functional currency of GM's German subsidiary, Adam Opel AG, is the deutsche mark because Opel produces most of its parts in Germany, assembles its vehicles in Germany, and sells most of its output in Germany. In contrast, Compaq Computer's production facilities in Scotland and Singapore are integrated into the firm's worldwide sourcing program. Thus the functional currency of those two subsidiaries is their parent's currency, the U.S. dollar.

The U.S. firm will use one of two methods for translating a subsidiary's financial statements into the U.S. dollar (the parent's home currency), depending on the subsidiary's functional currency:

TABLE 19.3

Translation of Income Statement of Belgian Subsidiary of U.S. Firm Using the Current Rate Method for the Quarter Ending September 30, 1995

	IN FUNCTIONAL CURRENCY (BELGIAN FRANCS)	IN HOME CURRENCY (U.S. DOLLARS)
Revenues	350,000,000	10,000,000
Expenses		
Cost of goods sold	210,000,000	6,000,000
General and administrative	45,500,000	1,300,000
Depreciation	42,000,000	1,200,000
Income before Taxes	52,500,000	1,500,000
Income Taxes	24,500,000	700,000
Net Income after Taxes	28,000,000	800,000

1 The **current rate method** is used if the subsidiary's functional currency is the host country's currency. This method assumes that the foreign subsidiary is a stand-alone operation. Any gains or losses arising from translation thus reflect the impact of exchange-rate changes, not the subsidiary's operational performance.

2 The **temporal method** is used if the subsidiary's functional currency is the U.S. dollar. This method assumes that the foreign subsidiary's operations are integrated into the parent's. Thus its profitability should be evaluated in terms of the parent's currency.

These two approaches differ mainly in how they treat translation losses and gains. Under the temporal method, translation losses and gains appear on the firm's income statement; under the current rate method, they appear as an adjustment to shareholders' equity. In some cases, a firm may use both approaches because of differences in the functional currencies of various subsidiaries. For example, Federal-Mogul, a $1.1 billion Detroit-based producer of motor vehicle parts, uses the temporal method to translate the results of its Brazilian and Argentinian subsidiaries, whose functional currency is the U.S. dollar. It uses the current rate method to translate the results of its British and German subsidiaries, whose functional currencies are the pound and the deutsche mark, respectively. As a result, in 1991 Federal-Mogul recorded a $4.9 million foreign-exchange loss in its income statement (which reflected its use of the temporal method as well as its transaction gains or losses) and a $8.5 million currency translation adjustment to its shareholders' equity (which resulted from its use of the current rate method).[34] The temporal method is less commonly used and more complicated than is needed for an introduction to international accounting, so we focus on the current rate method for illustrative purposes.

Applying the Current Rate Method to Income Statements. FASB Statement 52 requires a firm using the current rate method to show in its income statement either the exchange rate on the day a transaction occurred or a weighted average of exchange rates during the period the income statement covers. For simplicity's sake, firms often use the latter approach. Dividends, however, are translated using the exchange rate in effect on the day they are paid. Table 19.3

TABLE 19.4

Translation of Balance Sheet of Belgian Subsidiary of a U.S. Firm Using the Current Rate Method for the Quarter Ending September 30, 1995

	IN BELGIAN FRANCS	EXCHANGE RATE (BF/U.S. DOLLAR)	IN U.S. DOLLARS
ASSETS			
Cash	105,000,000	35	3,000,000
Accounts Receivable	70,000,000	35	2,000,000
Inventories	70,000,000	35	2,000,000
Plant and Equipment	140,000,000	35	4,000,000
Total	385,000,000		11,000,000
LIABILITIES AND SHAREHOLDERS' EQUITY			
Current Liabilities	87,500,000	35	2,500,000
Notes Payable	122,500,000	35	3,500,000
Common Stock	50,000,000	50	1,000,000
Retained Earnings	125,000,000	40	3,125,000
Cumulative Translation Adjustment*			875,000
Total	385,000,000		11,000,000

* Needed to make assets = liabilities + shareholders' equity when denominated in U.S. dollars

presents a simple example of the translation of an income statement of a Belgian subsidiary of a U.S. parent. The subsidiary's functional currency is the Belgian franc, and the average exchange rate between the Belgian franc and the U.S. dollar during the three months the statement covers is assumed to be BF35 = $1.

Applying the Current Rate Method to Balance Sheets. The foreign subsidiary's balance sheet also must be translated. Under the current rate method, the assets and liabilities shown on the subsidiary's balance sheet are translated using the exchange rate in effect on the date for which the balance sheet was prepared (September 30, 1995 for the example in Table 19.4). Equity accounts (common stock and retained earnings) are generally treated on an historical basis. Because two or more different exchange rates are being used, the subsidiary's assets are not likely to equal the sum of its liabilities and shareholders' equity when they are translated. To reconcile this discrepancy, the firm makes an accounting entry known as the **cumulative translation adjustment** (see Table 19.4), which makes the firm's assets equal the sum of its liabilities and shareholders' equity, an equality necessary to make the balance sheet balance. FASB Statement 52 requires that when a parent consolidates the subsidiary's balance sheet into its own, it must enter the cumulative translation adjustment as an adjustment to the parent's shareholders' equity. Table 19.5 shows how Johnson & Johnson's used the cumulative translation adjustment in its 1993 annual report to its shareholders.

Using the cumulative translation adjustment significantly benefits both the firm and investors. Under the current rate method, the cumulative translation adjustment is made directly to shareholders' equity rather than first flowing

---

TABLE 19.5

Consolidated Balance Sheet of Johnson & Johnson for 1993 (millions of U.S. dollars)

ASSETS

Current Assets	$5,217
Marketable securities, noncurrent, at cost	437
Property, plant, and equipment, net	4,406
Intangible assets, net	925
Other assets	1,257
Total Assets	$12,242

LIABILITIES AND STOCKHOLDERS' EQUITY

Current Liabilities	$3,212
Long-term debt	1,493
Deferred tax liability	122
Other liabilities	1,847
Total Liabilities	6,674
Stockholders' Equity	
Common stock—par value $1.00 per share (authorized 1,080,000,000 shares; issued 767,372,000 shares)	767
Note receivable from employee stock ownership plan	(84)
Cumulative currency translation adjustments	(338)
Retained earnings	7,727
	8,072
Less common stock held in treasury, at cost (124,391,000 shares)	2,504
Total Stockholders' Equity	5,568
Total Liabilities and Stockholders' Equity	$12,242

Source: Johnson & Johnson 1994 Annual Report

---

through the firm's income statement. Thus, translation gains and losses do not affect the firm's reported net income. Companies are able to avoid the temptation of engaging in expensive efforts to dampen fluctuations in reported earnings resulting from translation gains or losses, a temptation to which many firms succumbed under the FASB accounting requirement that preceded Statement 52.[35] Instead, the current rate method more properly focuses investors' attention on the impact of exchange-rate changes on the home currency value of the firm's equity in its foreign subsidiaries.

The cumulative translation adjustments of U.S. MNCs are often large in absolute terms, as Table 19.6 shows. As a percentage of total shareholders'

TABLE 19.6

Cumulative Translation Adjustment (CTA) and Shareholders' Equity (SE) for Selected U.S. MNCs, 1993 (in millions of U.S. dollars)

FIRM	CTA	SE	CTA AS PERCENTAGE OF SE	FOREIGN ASSETS AS PERCENTAGE OF TOTAL ASSETS
Apple	($20)	$2,026	1.0%	34.3%
Caterpillar	(170)	2,199	7.7	19.8
Coca-Cola	(420)	12,021	3.5	59.6
Disney	(37)	5,031	0.7	N/A
Ford	(1,078)	15,574	6.9	21.1
GM	(330)	5,598	5.9	19.6
Gillette	(415)	1,479	28.1	65.7
Johnson & Johnson	(338)	5,568	6.1	43.8
Maytag	(71)	587	12.1	27.3
PepsiCo	(184)	6,339	2.9	33.7
Whirlpool	(77)	1,648	4.7	N/A

Source: 1993 annual reports of firms listed

equity, however, this adjustment varies widely from company to company. Not surprisingly, firms with more extensive foreign investments tend to have higher cumulative translation adjustments relative to their shareholders' equity. Of the firms listed in Table 19.6, the relative importance of the cumulative translation adjustment is greatest for Gillette. But 65.7 percent of Gillette's assets are located outside the United States, more than for any other firm listed in the table.

International Taxation Issues

A close relationship often exists between national accounting procedures and national taxation policies. A country's tax code affects a variety of business behaviors as firms seek to maximize their after-tax profitability. A country may use its tax code not only to raise revenue but also to stimulate certain activities, such as the hiring of persons with physical disabilities or an increase in firms' R&D expenditures. Location, production, and hiring decisions may all be influenced by the structure and level of taxes.

Like domestic firms, international firms seek to maximize their after-tax income. However, they also are challenged to meet the tax requirements (which unfortunately often are in conflict) of all the countries in which they operate. International businesses typically must navigate a careful path between taking advantage of tax incentives and sidestepping punitive taxes.

Transfer Pricing

Two common means international businesses adopt to reduce their overall tax burden are transfer pricing and tax havens. **Transfer pricing** refers to the prices one branch or subsidiary of a parent charges a second branch or subsidiary for goods or services. Transfer pricing is important to international business for several reasons. Intracorporate transfers of goods, technology, and other resources are common between subsidiaries located in different countries. For example, by one estimate, intracorporate shipments account for 35 percent of the U.S. international trade in goods.[36] Transfer prices also affect an MNC's ability to monitor the performance of individual corporate units and to reward (or punish) managers responsible for a unit's performance. Further, the transfer prices affect the taxes an MNC pays both to its home country and to the various host countries in which it operates.

In practice, transfer prices are calculated in one of two ways:

1. Market-based method
2. Nonmarket-based methods

Market-Based Transfer Prices. The market-based method utilizes prices determined in the open market to transfer goods between units of the same corporate parent. Suppose Hyundai wants to export memory chips from South Korea for use in assembling personal computers at one of its U.S. subsidiaries. It can establish the transfer price for the memory chips between its U.S. and Korean subsidiaries by using the open market price for such chips.

This market-based approach has two main benefits. First, it reduces conflict between the two units over the appropriate price. The higher the price charged in the intracorporate transfer, the better the selling subsidiary's performance appears and the poorer the buying subsidiary's performance appears. To the extent that the parent allocates managerial bonuses or investment capital to its subsidiaries on the basis of profitability, the unit managers have incentives to squabble over the transfer price, because they care about how the MNC's accounting system reports their unit's performance. From the parent's perspective, however, such arguments waste firm resources. Once the firm's accounting records are consolidated, its overall before-tax profits will remain the same regardless of whether the transfer price overstates unit A's profitability and understates unit B's, or vice versa. Assuming both subsidiaries recognize the basic equity of the market-based price, such intracorporate conflict will be reduced.

Second, the market-based approach promotes the MNC's overall profitability by encouraging the efficiency of the selling unit. If the price the unit can charge for intracorporate sales is limited to the market price, its managers know that the unit's profitability depends on their ability to control its costs. Moreover, they recognize that if they successfully produce the product in question more cheaply than their international competitors can, the parent's market-based transfer pricing will acknowledge their efforts in full. Motivated by the prospects of bonuses and lucrative promotions, unit managers have every incentive to improve the efficiency and profitability of their operations.

Nonmarket-Based Transfer Prices. Transfer prices may also be established using nonmarket-based methods. Prices may be set by negotiations between the buying and selling units or on the basis of cost-based rules of thumb, such as production costs plus a fixed markup. Some services of the corporate parent may be assessed as a percentage of the subsidiary's sales, such as charges for general corporate overhead or for the right to use technology or intellectual property owned by the parent.

MNCs commonly use nonmarket-based prices partly because, for some goods and services, no real market exists outside the firm. For example, the sole market for an engine produced in a Ford factory in Spain may consist of Ford automobile assembly plants in Belgium, Germany, and the United Kingdom. Because no external market exists for this engine, Ford may establish a transfer price for the engine based on production costs plus an allowance for overhead and profit. Similarly, Toyota's ability to design and develop new automobile models is not a service that is bought and sold in the open market. Yet Toyota may want to charge its North American, British, and Australian subsidiaries an appropriate fee for the use of its research, design, and development services.

The use of nonmarket-based prices has both disadvantages and advantages. One disadvantage is that managers of the buying and selling units may waste time and energy arguing over the appropriate transfer price, since it will affect their reported profits (even though it will have no overall impact on the parent's consolidated before-tax income). Nonmarket-based transfer prices may also reduce the selling unit's efficiency. A transfer price based on the seller's costs plus some markup may reduce the seller's incentive to keep its costs low because it can pass along any cost increases to other members of the corporate family through the nonmarket-based price.

However, strategic use of nonmarket-based transfer prices may benefit an international business, as Table 19.7 shows. Creative rearranging of intracorporate prices may allow the parent to lower its overall tax bill.[37] For example, an MNC can lessen the burden of an ad valorem import tariff by reducing the price the selling unit charges the buying unit, thereby lowering the basis on which the tariff is calculated. Further, such pricing may enable a firm to slash its total income taxes. Suppose an MNC operates in two countries, one with high corporate income tax rates and the second with low rates. The firm can raise the transfer prices charged to the subsidiary in the high-tax country and lower those charged to the subsidiary in the low-tax country. Doing this will reduce the profitability of the first subsidiary, as measured by its accounting records, while increasing the profitability of the second. The net effect is to shift the location of the MNC's profits from the high-tax country (which would tax them more) to the low-tax country (which taxes them less), thereby reducing the firm's overall tax burden. Ireland, for example, has effectively exempted exports of manufactured goods from Irish corporate taxation in order to give MNCs an incentive to locate factories in that country. But this tax break also encourages MNCs to manipulate the transfer prices charged by their Irish factories so as to increase the profits reported by those factories and lower the profits reported by their non-Irish subsidiaries.[38]

Clever structuring of transfer prices can even allow a firm to evade host country restrictions on repatriation of profits. Suppose, for example, that a host country blocks repatriation by forbidding dividend payments from the subsidiary to the parent. The parent can evade this restriction by raising the transfer prices it charges the subsidiary for goods and services produced by other units of the corporate family or by charging fees for general corporate services. By means of this

TABLE 19.7

Strategic Use of Nonmarket-Based Transfer Prices

GOAL	TECHNIQUE	EFFECT
Decrease tariff paid on components imported from a subsidiary	Lower transfer price charged by the subsidiary	Lowering the price on which an ad valorem tariff is based decreases total amount of import tariff.
Decrease overall corporate income tax	Raise transfer prices paid by subsidiaries in high-tax countries and/or lower transfer prices charged by those subsidiaries; lower transfer prices paid by subsidiaries in low-tax countries and/or raise transfer prices charged by those subsidiaries	Reported profits of subsidiaries in high-tax countries decrease, and reported profits of subsidiaries in low-tax countries increase; total corporate tax burden decreases.
Repatriate profits from a subsidiary located in a host country that blocks repatriation	Raise transfer prices paid by the subsidiary; lower transfer prices charged by the subsidiary	Cash flows from the subsidiary to other units, circumventing restriction on repatriation

technique, cash will flow from the subsidiary to other parts of the firm in the form of payments for goods or services, rather than through the forbidden dividend payments. The net effect is the same, however: funds (in some form) are repatriated from the host country.[39]

A firm's transfer prices often reflect a tradeoff between tax consequences and legal constraints imposed by countries in which the firm operates.[40] Numerous studies conducted by researchers indicate that MNCs routinely engage in tax-shifting behavior through transfer pricing and other devices.[41]

Government agencies, such as the IRS, are well aware of these opportunities to play accounting games. As a result, both home and host countries scrutinize the transfer-pricing policies of MNCs operating within their borders to ensure that the firms do not evade their tax obligations and that the governments receive their "fair share" of taxes from the firms. A common approach is to use an **arm's length test** whereby government officials attempt to determine the price that two unrelated firms operating at arm's length would have agreed on. But in many cases, an appropriate arm's length price is difficult to establish, leading to conflict between international businesses and tax authorities. For example, in 1994 Japan's National Tax Administration billed Coca-Cola $140 million for back taxes, claiming that the royalty rates the firm charged its Japanese subsidiary for the right to use its trademarks were too high. The firm immediately appealed the decision, asserting its royalty rates were reasonable. Of course, determining the appropriate arm's length price for a unique asset like Coca-Cola's trademark is not simple. Thus this kind of conflict will not be resolved easily or quickly.[42]

Tax Havens

A second device international businesses use to reduce their tax burdens is to locate their activities in **tax havens**, countries that impose little or no corporate income taxes. For a relatively small fee, an MNC may set up a wholly owned subsidiary in a tax haven. By manipulating payments such as dividends, interest, royalties, and capital gains between its various subsidiaries, an MNC may divert income from subsidiaries in high-tax countries to the subsidiary operating in the

Many MNCs and international banks establish subsidiaries in tax havens to benefit from those countries' low tax rates, friendly business climates, and excellent communications linkages to world financial centers. In the Bahamas alone, U.S. banks such as Citibank have invested more than $2.7 billion in order to better serve their corporate clients.

tax haven. By booking its profits in the tax haven subsidiary, the MNC escapes the clutches of revenue agents in other countries. For example, an MNC may give ownership of its trademarks to a subsidiary located in the Cayman Islands. That subsidiary can then charge each of the corporation's operating subsidiaries a fee for the use of the trademarks. The fees paid by the operating subsidiaries reduce their profitability and thus the corporate income taxes they must pay to their host governments. The government of the Cayman Islands, however, imposes no income tax on the trademark licensing fees earned by the subsidiary located there—or on income, profits, capital gains, or dividends. Thus the MNC reduces its overall income tax burden. The following "Going Global" explores some of the ethical issues surrounding the use of tax havens and transfer prices to reduce corporate tax burdens.

Several other smaller countries, including Liechtenstein, Luxembourg, and the Netherlands Antilles, also have gone into the business of being tax havens. To attract MNCs, a tax haven must not only refrain from imposing income taxes but also provide a stable political and business climate, an efficient court system, and sophisticated banking and communications industries. In return, the tax haven is able to capture franchising and incorporation fees and provide numerous lucrative professional jobs far beyond what an economy of its size normally could.

Being a tax haven can create a thriving economy. For example, foreign-owned firms outnumber the 32,000 residents of the Cayman Islands. The Cayman Islands' success as a tax haven reflects the high-quality services it provides to international businesses; for example, an MNC can create and incorporate a Cayman Islands subsidiary within 24 hours if needed.[43] The firms create demand for highly paid professionals such as accountants, bankers, and lawyers. As a result, the Cayman Islands is a major world banking and finance center. Its banks have attracted $300 billion in deposits from foreign investors, or about $9.4 million per resident.[44] From the Cayman Islands' perspective, the tax-haven sector of

GOING GLOBAL

The Ethics of Tax Havens and Transfer Pricing

Multinational corporations can save millions of dollars in income and other taxes through the use of tax havens and transfer prices. For example, by manipulating transfer prices, an MNC can shift profits from high-tax countries to low-tax countries. But is such behavior ethical?

Skillful utilization of tax havens and transfer prices obviously benefits the MNC and its shareholders. However, such techniques reduce the revenues available to the home or host country government to solve important social problems such as poverty, homelessness, and drug addiction. An MNC's failure to pay its "fair share" of taxes in the countries in which it operates means that either the resources needed to solve these problems will be unavailable or other taxpayers will be forced to pick up the tab. Because an MNC benefits from various services the local governments provide, such as transportation infrastructure, educational facilities, and police protection, many people claim it is unethical for the MNC to shirk paying for its share of these services.

Others argue that so long as an MNC is engaging in tax avoidance, its use of transfer prices and tax havens to reduce its tax burden is ethical. (Experts distinguish between *tax avoidance*, whereby a firm uses legal tax code loopholes to minimize its tax burden, and *tax evasion*, whereby a firm engages in illegal activities to lessen its tax payments.) Many accountants argue that an MNC's officers are bound by their fiduciary duties to their shareholders to take advantage of tax avoidance opportunities provided by various national tax codes. Indeed, from this perspective a manager's failure to do so could be viewed as unethical.

the local economy represents the ultimate "clean" industry so beloved by economic development officials. But the existence of tax havens creates numerous headaches for the taxing authorities of other countries, as explained in the next section.

Taxation of Foreign Income by the United States

The tax treatment of foreign income varies by country, although some basic similarities exist among many developed countries. As an example, let's review U.S. tax treatment of foreign income from three common sources: exports, foreign branches, and foreign subsidiaries.

Taxation of Exports

Ordinarily the U.S. tax code treats the profits associated with the export of goods and services the same as domestically generated income. Such exports are not trivial: in 1993, U.S. firms exported $457 billion of goods and $185 billion of services.[45] However, to encourage firms to increase their export activities, the U.S. tax code allows firms to establish **foreign sales corporations (FSC)**. The tax code requires that an FSC engage in significant overseas activities, such as marketing, order processing, distribution, invoicing, and financing export sales. If a firm fully complies with all the provisions for establishing an FSC, it can significantly reduce its U.S. federal income taxes on its exporting activities.[46] Compaq, for example, reduced its 1993 tax burden by $7 million through the use of an FSC.[47]

Taxation of Foreign Branch Income

A foreign branch is an unincorporated subsidiary of a corporation. It operates in a foreign country, but because legally it is identical to the parent, its income is treated as if it were the parent's. Thus any earnings of a foreign branch of a U.S. corporation create taxable income for the parent, regardless of whether or not the earnings are repatriated to the parent.

Taxation of Foreign Subsidiary Income

Foreign subsidiaries are incorporated in a foreign country and thus are legally distinct from the home country parent corporation. In general, for U.S. tax purposes, a U.S. parent corporation does not need to include the earnings of its foreign subsidiaries in reporting its profits to the IRS. The **deferral rule** in the U.S. tax code allows such earnings to be taxed only when they are remitted to the parent in the form of dividends, thus allowing the parent to defer paying U.S. taxes on those earnings. For example, the deferral rule saved Compaq $25 million in 1993 U.S. federal corporate income taxes.[48]

The deferral rule is intended to stimulate international business activity by U.S. firms. In Compaq's case, 49 percent of its sales occur outside North America, and the deferral rule has helped it penetrate key markets in Europe and Asia. However, one important exception to the deferral rule ensures that U.S. firms do not establish shell corporations in tax havens that do little but provide the parent with the ability to defer U.S. taxes. U.S. tax law requires a parent corporation to determine whether each of its foreign subsidiaries is a controlled foreign corporation. A **controlled foreign corporation (CFC)** is a foreign corporation in which U.S. shareholders—each of which holds at least 10 percent of the firm's shares— together own a majority of its stock. This definition may seem strange, but it is designed to focus on foreign firms that are controlled by a single U.S. firm or a group of U.S. firms acting in concert, rather than those owned by many small U.S. investors. For example, Ford's wholly owned Jaguar subsidiary is a CFC, but its 23 percent share of Mazda, which is primarily owned by Japanese investors, is not.

According to the U.S. tax code, the income of CFCs is divided into two types: active income and passive income (also called Subpart F income). **Active income** is income generated by traditional business operations such as production, marketing, and distribution. **Subpart F income**, or **passive income**, is generated by passive activities such as the collection of dividends, interest, royalties, and licensing fees—the type of activities typically performed by subsidiaries incorporated in tax havens. U.S. firms may defer active income earned by CFCs they control. In calculating their U.S. taxes, however, they generally may not defer Subpart F income. In the absence of this restriction, U.S. firms could escape federal corporate income taxes on earnings generated by their intellectual property and investment portfolios. They could do this by establishing subsidiaries in tax havens and transferring to those subsidiaries legal title to their trademarks, patents, brand names, and investment portfolios. The U.S. government, by treating active and passive earnings of foreign subsidiaries differently, is walking a fine line between stimulating U.S. firms' international business activities and limiting their ability to evade U.S. taxes through the creation of subsidiaries in tax havens.

Resolving International Tax Conflicts

A cross countries, differences exist in tax rates as well as in the definition of what is to be taxed. International businesses must answer to the tax authorities of each country in which they operate. Often, national tax authorities may be in conflict or may cumulatively impose extremely burdensome levels of taxation on international firms. As a result, resolving international tax conflicts is very important to international businesspeople.

Tax Credits

The home country may reduce the burden of the joint taxation of foreign subsidiary income by the home country and the host country by granting a tax credit to a parent corporation for income taxes paid to the host country. This tax credit reduces the level of home country taxes that the MNC must pay.

The U.S. tax code, for example, allows U.S. firms to reduce their federal corporate income taxes by the amount of foreign income taxes paid by their foreign branches or subsidiaries, subject to certain limitations. The foreign income tax credit cannot be larger than the foreign operation's U.S. tax burden. However, under certain circumstances firms may carry excess tax credits backward or forward for a limited number of years. But many common destinations for U.S. FDI impose higher corporate taxes than the United States does, so the foreign income tax credit offers U.S. MNCs only partial relief from high foreign taxes. For example, Germany's corporate tax rate is 56 percent, Japan's is 43 percent, and France's is 50 percent. The comparable U.S. rate, taking into account state income taxes, is approximately 39 percent.[49] Further, the tax credit may be taken only for income taxes, not for other forms of taxes such as value-added taxes or sales taxes. While these concepts are simple in principle, many provisions of the U.S. tax code dealing with foreign tax credits are far more complicated in practice. International firms generally hire professionals knowledgeable about the intricacies of the tax code's treatment of foreign tax credits.

Tax Treaties

To promote international commerce, many countries sign treaties that address taxation issues affecting international business. For example, the United States has signed over 40 tax treaties with foreign nations. While the details vary, many of these treaties contain provisions for reducing withholding taxes imposed on firms' foreign branches and subsidiaries. Sometimes these treaties reduce the overall tax burden imposed on foreign income earned by home country firms or completely exempt interest and royalty payments from taxation. For example, an August 1991 tax treaty between Germany and the United States reduced taxes on dividends paid by German subsidiaries of U.S. MNCs retroactive to the beginning of 1990. Such savings are not inconsequential. For example, A. Schuman, Inc., an Akron, Ohio, manufacturer of plastic compounds and resins, received a rebate of $2,176,000 from German tax authorities in 1991 as a result of this tax treaty.[50]

Typically, such preferences are granted on a reciprocal basis: country A provides country B's firms with favorable treatment only if country B treats country A's firms the same way.[51]

"Bashing" of Foreign Firms

Another source of international tax conflict involves the "bashing" of foreign firms by domestic politicians who believe that such firms manipulate transfer prices to avoid paying their "fair share" of taxes. In 1989, for example, only 28 percent of foreign-owned firms operating in the United States paid any U.S. income taxes. Yet it is unclear to what extent foreign firms are engaging in illegal tax evasion, as opposed to the legal use of tax code loopholes to avoid taxes. In the late 1980s, the IRS stepped up its enforcement of U.S. transfer-pricing rules. However, because of exemptions in the tax code, it obtained only 26.5 percent of the amount it originally sought. In two significant cases the IRS filed against Merck & Co. and Nestlé during this period, U.S. courts held that the firms were properly following the requirements of the U.S. tax code. Some foreign MNCs, such as Matsushita Electric Industrial Co., seek to avoid costly and lengthy litigation by entering into advance pricing agreements with the IRS, in which both sides agree in advance to the transfer prices the company will charge for intracorporate transactions.[52] Nonetheless, some U.S. politicians have proposed requiring foreign firms to pay some minimum level of income taxes based on the profitability of their U.S. competitors. So far, Treasury Department officials have opposed such proposals, arguing that such taxes would violate existing tax treaties. U.S.-based MNCs have also fought such proposals, believing that unfair treatment of foreign firms by the United States would invite retaliation by foreign governments against foreign subsidiaries of U.S. firms.[53]

CHAPTER REVIEW

Summary

The accounting tasks international businesses confront are more complex than those purely domestic firms face. An international firm must meet the accounting requirements of both its home country and all the countries in which it operates. Unfortunately, significant philosophical and operational differences exist in the accounting standards and procedures of the world's countries.

To reduce the costs that differing national accounting systems impose on international businesses and international investors, several efforts are underway to harmonize the accounting systems of the major trad-

ing nations. The International Accounting Standards Committee (FASB) has played an important role in such efforts, as has the European Union.

Firms engaged in international business typically face two specific accounting challenges: accounting for transactions in foreign currencies and translating the reported operations of foreign subsidiaries into the currency of the parent firm for purposes of consolidation. FASB Statement 52 details the procedures U.S. corporations use to account for such international transactions.

International businesses are also challenged in dealing with various countries' taxation policies. MNCs try to maximize their after-tax profitability by taking advantage of tax breaks and avoiding punitive taxes. They may manipulate transfer prices to shift reported profits from high-tax countries to low-tax countries. A few smaller countries have built strong local economies by providing tax havens to attract MNCs through the elimination of corporate income taxes and the creation of favorable business climates.

Like many countries, the United States offers favorable tax incentives to encourage its firms to participate in international business. The U.S. tax code allows firms to establish foreign sales corporations to reduce the taxes they pay on exports. Under certain conditions, U.S. firms also may defer paying U.S. income taxes on income generated by their foreign subsidiaries. However, foreign branches of U.S. firms enjoy no such tax benefits.

Because of the revenue needs of governments, international businesses often find themselves in conflict with foreign governments. To reduce firms' tax burdens, many home governments offer their firms credits for taxes paid to foreign governments. They also negotiate tax treaties to both reduce firms' tax burdens and promote international commerce. But foreign firms are often the target of "bashing" by domestic politicians who rightly or wrongly believe those firms are not paying their fair share of domestic taxes.

Review Questions

1. What factors influence the accounting procedures a country adopts?

2. How do German firms use accounting reserves?

3. What problems do Western firms and investors face in analyzing the performance of firms in CPEs?

4. What is the impact of differing accounting standards on the international capital market?

5. Which organizations are promoting the harmonization of national accounting standards?

6. What is the two-transaction approach?

7. How do firms establish prices for goods sold by one subsidiary to another?

8. How do U.S. MNCs benefit from the deferral rule?

9. Why are the IRS's rules regarding CFCs so complicated? What kind of behavior is the IRS trying to prevent?

10. What mechanisms have national governments adopted to lessen the burden of foreign governments' taxes on home country MNCs?

Questions for Discussion

1. What impact would harmonization of national accounting standards have on international businesses?

2. What are the benefits of the two-transaction approach to international businesses and international investors?

3. How can an international firm use transfer pricing to increase its after-tax income?

4. The U.S. tax code distinguishes between active and passive income in permitting the deferral of foreign subsidiaries' income. Why has it made this distinction? Why is the distinction important? If tax havens were eliminated, would the tax code need to continue to distinguish between active and passive income?

5. Is the use of transfer pricing in order to reduce a firm's taxes ethical? Why or why not?

6. Are U.S. firms at a competitive disadvantage because they can't use accounting reserves as German firms do?

BUILDING GLOBAL SKILLS

International accounting is complex. As this chapter has shown, a firm's international activities affect its financial statements in many ways. To gain a better appreciation of this impact, obtain the most recent annual report of a publicly traded corporation that engages in international business. Most major firms listed on the NYSE, the American Stock Exchange, or NASDAQ are happy to provide you with their most recent annual report if you write or phone their investor relations department. Your local library or members of your family may also be able to provide you with a report.

Next, answer the following questions regarding the firm you selected. (You may not be able to answer all of them. Some firms provide highly detailed information about their foreign operations, others very little.)

1. How large is the firm's cumulative translation adjustment in absolute terms? How large is the adjustment relative to shareholders' equity?

2. Did the firm use an FSC to save on its taxes? If so, how much did it save?

3. Did the firm benefit from the deferral rule on foreign subsidiary income? If so, by how much?

4. What percentage of the firm's assets are located in foreign countries? What percentage of its profits come from its foreign operations?

5. How much taxes did the firm pay to foreign countries?

6. How important is exporting to the firm?

7. Did the firm enjoy or suffer any foreign-currency transactions gains or losses? Did it engage in any hedging activities to protect itself from exchange-rate changes?

CLOSING CASE

Globalization of Accounting Services[54]

Like businesses in many other industries, accounting firms are undergoing rapid globalization as they attempt to address their clients' international needs. This industry is dominated by six firms—collectively referred to as the Big Six—which together provide accounting and audit services for 494 of the Fortune 500 in the United States and 96 of the 100 largest British firms. The biggest of the Big Six is KPMG, which had 1993 revenues of over $6 billion and has 76,000 employees worldwide.

Like most accounting firms, KPMG is organized as a partnership. Owned by its 6100 partners, the firm operates 820 offices in 125 countries. KPMG was formed in 1987 by the merger of a large U.S.-based accounting firm, Peat Marwick Mitchell, and a large, mainly European firm, Klynveld Main Goerdeler (KMG). KMG, in turn, had been formed by a 1979 merger of the largest accounting firm in the Netherlands, Klynveld Kraayenhoff; Germany's second-largest accounting firm, Deutsche Treuhand; and a smaller U.S. firm, Main Hurdman & Cranstoun.

KPMG's path to number one in the accounting profession is indicative of the process by which this service industry is globalizing. Several others of the Big Six have also grown through mergers in the past decade. In 1989, for example, Deloitte Touche Tohmatsu was created by the merger of Deloitte Haskins & Sells with Touch Ross & Company and its Japanese affiliate, Tohmatsu & Co. Similarly, Ernst & Young resulted from the 1989 merger of Ernst & Whinney and Arthur Young. Ernst & Whinney was the result of a merger between a U.S. and a U.K. accounting firm shortly after the end of World War II.

This trend toward international expansion can be explained in part by the growth of international business. As their clients have globalized, accounting firms have felt compelled to expand their operations in order to meet their clients' needs—as well as to retain their business. To navigate among the various accounting regulations and tax laws of the nations in which its MNC clients do business, an accounting firm needs to be able to offer advice to its clients based on the operating needs of each of their foreign subsidiaries and of the parents themselves. The most effective way of providing this service is to have an office in each country in which the clients do business. By merging with existing accounting firms, the Big Six have gained quick access to many domestic markets as well as to the existing client bases of the acquired firms.

Thus KPMG and its counterparts in the Big Six are well positioned to continue to benefit from the increase in international business activity. Their clients' international activities are booming, and so their international accounting needs are also skyrocketing. However, the picture for the Big Six is not entirely rosy. These firms must deal with conflicting accounting practices in various countries. They also face the task of managing their own global operations and have found that coordinating responsibilities among their subsidiaries is often difficult.

The Big Six accounting firms also face pressures as the role of auditor changes in market-oriented societies. Increasingly, auditors are being sued for malpractice if they fail to uncover fraudulent activities by a firm's management. For example, a U.S. jury found Price Waterhouse liable for $338 million in damages for failure to detect deterioration in the performance of an Arizona bank in 1992. U.S. accounting firms are involved in 4000 lawsuits over malpractice and other issues, with total claims amounting to $30 billion. By some estimates, litigation expenses amount to as much as 9 percent of the audit fees collected by the Big Six.

Another problem is determining compensation for those managers who enter the organization as the result of a merger with another firm. As discussed in Chapters 14 and 20, attitudes toward compensation vary considerably among business cultures. The Big Six must therefore, for example, keep group-oriented Japanese partners happy while simultaneously satisfying "what's in it for me" U.S. partners. This problem is exacerbated because the Big Six have all developed extensive management consulting businesses in addition to their traditional auditing and accounting services. Because the consulting businesses have enjoyed more rapid growth than the accounting businesses in the past decade, many partners on the consulting side have argued that they deserve a bigger slice of the compensation pie, a suggestion not well received by the accounting partners.

Still, the Big Six are pushing ahead aggressively in their quest for global expansion. Within the last few years, for example, Arthur Andersen has bought a Japanese accounting firm, KPMG moved into China and Estonia, and Price Waterhouse acquired a Swiss firm and opened an office in Budapest. Thus, like many businesses, the Big Six accounting firms have globalized their operations to serve the needs of their clients and to exploit new market opportunities. However, managing their operations around the world and motivating employees with very different cultural backgrounds have presented these companies with a series of management challenges.

Case Questions

1. The Big Six have globalized primarily through mergers. What advantages does this growth strategy offer these firms? What are the disadvantages of using mergers to globalize?

2. How can a Big Six firm headquartered in country A protect itself from malpractice by its subsidiary in Country B?

3. How important is it for a Big Six firm like KPMG to maintain uniform compensation practices for its partners in various countries?

CHAPTER NOTES

1. Excerpted from "No Comparisons" by Lee Berton, *The Wall Street Journal*, September 22, 1989, p. R30. Reprinted by permission of *The Wall Street Journal*, © 1989 Dow Jones & Company, Inc. All Rights Reserved Worldwide.

2. American Accounting Association, *A Statement of Basic Accounting Theory* (Evanston, Ill.: AAA, 1966), p. 1.

3. Much of the discussion in this section is taken from Frederick D. S. Choi and Gerhard Mueller, *International Accounting*, 2nd ed. (Englewood Cliffs: Prentice Hall, 1992), Chapters 2 and 3, and from reports of the Working Group on Accounting Standards, Organisation for Economic Cooperation and Development, published in 1987: "Accounting Standards Harmonization, No. 2: Consolidation Policies in OECD Nations" and "Accounting Standards Harmonization, No. 3: The Relationship between Taxation and Financial Reporting."

4. Stephen B. Salter and Timothy S. Doupnik, "The Relationship between Legal Systems and Accounting Practices," in Kenneth S. Most (ed.), *Advances in International Accounting*, Vol. 5 (Greenwich, Conn.: JAI Press, 1992).

5. Hanns-Martin W. Schoenfeld, "International Accounting: Development, Issues, and Future Directions," *The Journal of International Business Studies* (Fall 1981), pp. 83–100.

6. "Accountancy," *The Economist*, October 17, 1992, p. 23.

7. Choi and Mueller, op. cit., p. 95.

8. "Chinese practitioners ready for their great leap forward," *Financial Times*, August 13, 1993, p. 20.

9. Timothy S. Doupnik, "Recent Innovations in German Accounting Practice," in Kenneth S. Most (ed.) *Advances in International Accounting*, Vol. 5 (Greenwich, Conn.: JAI Press, 1992).

10. Hino Motors, Ltd., *Annual Report for the Year Ended March 31, 1992*, Tokyo, 1992.

11. Robert Bloom, Jayne Fuglister, and Jeffrey Kantor, "Toward Internationalization of Upper-Level Financial Accounting Courses," in Kenneth S. Most (ed.) *Advances in International Accounting*, Vol. 5 (Greenwich, Conn.: JAI Press, 1992), pp. 239–253; Frederick D. S. Choi and Richard Levich, *The Capital Market Effects of International Accounting Diversity* (Homewood, Ill.: Dow Jones–Irwin, 1990), pp. 115–117.

12. "Daimler-Benz Discloses Hidden Reserves of $2.45 Billion, Seeks Big Board Listing," *Wall Street Journal*, March 25, 1993, p. A10.

13. Lufthansa, *Annual Report 1993*, p. 30.

14. Donald Lessard, "Principles of International Portfolio Selection," *International Financial Management* (New York: John Wiley and Sons, 1985), pp. 16–30.

15. "Shares of Murdoch's News Corp. are Clouded by Australian Accounting, Critics Contend," *Wall Street Journal*, August 16, 1988, p. 53.

16. "Spot the profit," *The Economist*, October 31, 1992, p. 82.

17. S. J. Gray, J. C. Shaw, and L. B. McSweeney, "Accounting Standards and Multinational Corporations," *The Journal of International Business Studies* (Spring/Summer 1981), pp. 121–136.

18. "Big Board Chief Renews His Pitch on Foreign Stocks," *Wall Street Journal*, January 7, 1992, p. A2.

19. Gary C. Biddle and Sharrokh M. Saudagaran, "The Effects of Financial Disclosure Levels on Firms' Choices among Alternative Foreign Stock Exchange Listings," *Journal of International Financial Management and Accounting* (Spring 1989), p. 81.

20. Presentation of Tetsuo Sakamoto, Senior Vice President, The Long-Term Credit Bank of Japan, Ltd., Texas A&M University, June 1, 1992.

21. "Daimler-Benz gears up for a drive on the freeway," *Financial Times*, April 30, 1993.

22. "US triggers disclosure revolution," *Financial Times*, June 16, 1993, p. 19.

23. Andrew L. Nodar, "Coca-Cola Writes an Accounting Procedures Manual," *Management Accounting*, Vol. 68 (October 1986), pp. 52–53.

24. Istemi S. Demirag, "Assessing Foreign Subsidiary Performance: The Currency Choice of U.K. MNCs," *Journal of International Business Studies*, Vol. 19, No. 2 (Summer 1988), pp. 257–275.

25. Shawn Tully, "GE in Hungary: Let There Be Light," *Fortune*, October 22, 1990, p. 142.

26. "Chinese practitioners ready for their great leap forward," *Financial Times*, August 13, 1993, p. 20.

27. Paul Aiello, "Building a Joint Venture in China: The Case of Chrysler and the Beijing Jeep Corporation," *Journal of General Management*, Vol. 17, No. 2 (Winter 1991), pp. 54–55.

28. John N. Turner, "International Harmonization: A Professional Goal," *Journal of Accountancy* (January 1983), pp. 58–59.

29. Choi and Mueller, op. cit., pp. 262ff.

30. Stephen B. Salter, *Classification of Financial Reporting Systems and a Test of Their Environmental Determinants*, unpublished Ph.D. dissertation, University of South Carolina (1991), p. 5.

31. "France girds itself for an international market," *Financial Times*, June 28, 1991, p. 13.

32. Financial Accounting Standards Board, *Statement of Financial Accounting Standards No. 52: Foreign Currency Translation* (Stamford, Conn.: FASB, December, 1981).

33. "Dell Computer at War with Analyst Critical of Its Currency Trades," *Wall Street Journal*, November 30, 1992, p. A1; "Dell Computer Shares Drop by 9.8% on Analyst's Currency-Trading Report," *Wall Street Journal*, November 11, 1992, p. A5.

34. Federal-Mogul Corporation, *1991 Annual Report*.

35. Robert G. Ruland and Timothy S. Doupnik, "Foreign Currency Translation and the Behavior of Exchange Rates," *Journal of International Business Studies*, Vol. 19, No. 3 (Fall 1988), p. 462.

36. F. Steb Hipple, "Multinational Companies and International Trade: The Impact of Intrafirm Shipments on U.S. Foreign Trade 1977–1982, *Journal of International Business Studies*, Vol. 21, No. 3 (Third Quarter, 1990), pp. 495–504.

37. J. Shulman, "When the Transfer Price Is Wrong—By Design," *Columbia Journal of World Business* (May–June 1967), pp. 69–76.

38. J. C. Stewart, "Transfer Pricing: Some Empirical Evidence from Ireland," *Journal of Economic Studies*, Vol. 16, No. 3, pp. 40–56.

39. D. J. Lecraw, "Some evidence on transfer pricing by multinational corporations," in A. M. Rugman and L. Eden (eds.), *Multinationals and transfer pricing* (New York: St Martin's Press, 1985).

40. Mohammad F. Al-Eryani, Pervaiz Alam, and Syed H. Akhter, "Transfer Pricing Determinants of U.S. Multinationals," *Journal of International Business Studies*, Vol. 21, No. 3 (Third Quarter, 1990), pp. 409–425.

41. David Harris, Randall Morck, Joel Slemrod, and Bernard Yeung, "Income Shifting in U.S. Multinational Corporations," University of Michigan, mimeo, 1991; James R. Hines and Eric Rice, "Fiscal Paradise: Foreign Tax Havens and American Business," N.B.E.R. Working Paper #3477 (Cambridge, Mass., 1990); James Wheeler, "An Academic Look at Transfer Pricing in a Global Economy," *Tax Notes*, July 4, 1988.

42. "Japan Orders 60 Firms to Pay Back-Taxes," *Wall Street Journal*, October 12, 1994, p. A13.

43. "Cleaning Up by Cleaning Up," *Euromoney*, April 1991, pp. 73–77.

44. Howard W. French, "Offshore Banking Gets New Scrutiny with B.C.C.I. Scandal," *New York Times*, September 29, 1991, p. 7.

45. *Survey of Current Business*, (June 1992), p. 79.

46. Bruce W. Reynolds and Alan R. Levenson, "Setting Up a Foreign Sales Corporation Can Cut Your Tax Bill," *Journal of European Business* (July/August 1992), pp. 59–64; Mark A. Goldstein and Arthur I. Aronoff, "Foreign Sales Corporations: Tax Incentives for U.S. Exporters," *Business Credit* (April 1991), pp. 20–23.

47. Compaq Computer Corporation, *1993 Annual Report*, p. 31.

48. Ibid., p. 32.

49. Nigel M. Healey, "Is the United States Turning Protectionist?" *Business and the Contemporary World*, Vol. 4, No. 3 (Summer 1992), pp. 24–29.

50. A. Schulman, Inc., *1991 Annual Report* (Akron, Ohio), p. 20.

51. Choi and Mueller, op. cit., p. 554.

52. "Clinton's Economic Proposal Faces Problem: Taxes of Foreign Companies Won't Meet Goal," *Wall Street Journal*, November 11, 1992, p. A16.

53. "Lawmakers say tax fraud by foreign firms costs U.S. billions," *Houston Chronicle*, April 10, 1992, p. 10F; "Treasury Opposes Legislation to Impose Minimum Tax on Foreign Firms in U.S.," *Wall Street Journal*, July 22, 1992, p. A2.

54. "All Change," *The Economist*, October 17, 1992, pp. 19ff.; Alan Chai, Alta Campbell, and Patrick J. Spain (eds.), *Hoover's Handbook of World Business 1993* (Austin, Tex.: Reference Press, 1993), pp. 134, 194, 206, 220, 300, 386; "Coopers & Lybrand Profit Payout Drops; Litigation Costs Cited," *Wall Street Journal*, November 12, 1992, p. B16; "The Deal of the Century? *FW*, September 27, 1994, pp. 45–46; "The Man with 20/20 Vision," *Accountancy*, September 1993, p. 42.

CHAPTER

20

International Human Resource Management and Labor Relations

Chapter Outline

The nature of human resource management
Strategic significance of HRM

International managerial staffing needs
Scope of internationalization
Centralization versus decentralization of control
Staffing philosophy

Recruitment and selection
Recruitment of managers
Selection of managers
Expatriation and repatriation issues

Training and development
Assessing training needs
Basic training methods and procedures
Developing younger international managers

Performance appraisal and compensation
Assessing performance in international business
Determining compensation in international business

Retention and turnover

Human resource issues for nonmanagerial employees
Recruitment and selection
Training and development
Compensation and performance appraisal

Labor relations
Comparative labor relations
Collective bargaining
Union influence and codetermination

After studying this chapter you should be able to:

Characterize the nature of human resource management in international business.

Discuss how firms recruit and select managers for international assignments.

Describe how international businesses train and develop expatriate managers.

Discuss how international firms conduct performance appraisals and determine compensation for their expatriate managers.

Discuss retention and turnover issues in international business.

Describe basic human resource issues involving nonmanagerial employees.

Describe labor relations in international business.

WHEN AN INTERNATIONAL BUSINESS OPENS A NEW OFFICE, MANU-facturing plant, or other facility in a foreign country, one of its most important tasks is staffing that new facility with managers and operating employees. To do this, the firm must decide how many employees it needs for the new facility, what skills they must have, where they will be hired, how much they will be paid, and many other issues. Most firms think they do a pretty good job in this area. However, when it comes to staffing a foreign operation, Japanese companies are among the most careful and thorough in the world. ▪▪ Consider, for example, how Toyota approached the staffing of its first automobile assembly plant in the United States. In Japan, auto-

Training for the World[1]

makers and other manufacturers have set up special training programs in high schools. Students who are not likely to go to college can enter training and apprenticeship pro-grams financed by these businesses. In the United States, such programs are rare. ▪▪ Toyota managers believe it takes a special kind of employee to succeed in their firm. The firm wants to hire only people who will conform to the Japanese emphasis on teamwork, corporate loyalty, and versatility along the production line. In Japan, prospective employees have been trained and screened along these dimensions while in high school. But to find such people in the United States, Toyota goes to what some observers see as extraordinary lengths. ▪▪ When Toyota was opening its first wholly owned U.S. plant in Kentucky, it received over 100,000 applications for 2,700 production jobs and 300 office jobs. Over half of these applicants were rejected immediately because they lacked the minimum education or experience Toyota deemed necessary. Other applicants were elimi-nated early in the screening process because they lacked one or more other essen-tial qualifications. ▪▪ The thousands of applicants still under consideration were invited to participate in an exhaustive battery of tests. Applicants for even the lowest-level jobs in the plant were tested for over 14 hours. The initial tests cov-ered such areas as manual dexterity, job skills, and technical knowledge. Worker attitudes toward unionization were also assessed during this phase of testing because Toyota did not want its plant to be unionized by the United Auto Workers, the collective bargaining agent for U.S. automakers. ▪▪ Those appli-cants who passed the first level of tests were invited back to participate in an orga-nizational simulation exercise. Although many firms use organizational simula-tion when hiring managers, Toyota uses it for all prospective employees. Results from the simulation eliminated still other applicants from the pool, while those who remained were invited back for still more testing. This third wave of testing involved performing mock production line jobs on a simulated conveyor belt under the observation of trained supervisors. Only 1 of every 20 applicants made it through this test and was invited back yet again, this time for an interview. ■ ■ The interview was conducted by a panel of officials and representatives from each department in the plant. These interviewers were trained to determine how well the applicant would fit into both the overall Toyota culture and the interviewers' specific departments. Finally, applicants who were favorably evaluated by the interviewers were asked to take a physical exam and drug tests. If they passed both, then—and only then—were they deemed to have met Toyota's standards. ■ ■ By the time the selection process is completed and Toyota actually hires a person, it has spent over $13,000 on testing and evaluating that individual. And, of course, it has already spent thousands of dollars more eliminating others at earlier stages. ■ ■ Is Toyota unique in the thoroughness of its selection process in the United States? No. Mazda and Mitsubishi spend about the same amount in selecting employees for their U.S. operations. Each puts a slightly different twist on the process, however. Mazda, for example, uses more tests relating to job skills, while Mitsubishi puts more emphasis on group exercises and simulations. Honda emphasizes tests much less but subjects each applicant to a minimum of three interviews. Nissan takes yet another approach. Applicants who meet its preliminary screening criteria must go through 40 hours of nonpaid pre-employment training. After that training is complete, their ability to meet Nissan's performance standards is assessed on a simulated assembly line. Those who meet the minimum acceptable standards may then be eligible for employment with the firm. ■ ■ ■ ■ ■

At its most basic level, any organization—from a small neighborhood convenience store to the largest MNC—is nothing more than a collection of jobs, clusters of jobs, and interconnections among those jobs. The people who fill the jobs are a vital ingredient in determining how effectively the organization will be able to meet its goals, remain competitive, and satisfy its constituents. Toyota's care in selecting its Kentucky workforce shows that it understands that its employees are among its most important assets.

The Nature of Human Resource Management

Human resource management **(HRM)** is the set of activities directed at attracting, developing, and maintaining the effective workforce necessary to achieve a firm's objectives. HRM includes recruiting and selecting nonmanagers and managers, providing training and development, appraising performance, and providing compensation and benefits. HR managers, regardless of whether they work for a purely domestic firm or an international one, must develop procedures and policies for accomplishing these tasks.

International HR managers, however, face challenges beyond those confronting their counterparts in purely domestic companies.[2] Specifically, differences in cultures, levels of economic development, and legal systems among the countries in which a firm operates may force it to customize its hiring, firing, training, and compensation programs on a country-by-country basis. Particularly troublesome problems develop when conflicts arise between the culture and laws of the home country and those of the host country. For example, prohibitions against gender discrimination in U.S. equal employment opportunity laws conflict with Saudi Arabian custom and law regarding the role of women. Such conflicts cause problems for U.S. MNCs that want to ensure that their female executives receive overseas assignments equivalent to those given to their male executives.

The international firm must also determine where various employees should come from—the home country, the host country, or third countries. The optimal mix of employees may differ according to the location of the firm's operations. A firm is likely to hire more employees from its home country to work in production facilities there than to work in foreign facilities. Local laws must also be considered, because they may limit or constrain hiring practices. For example, immigration laws may limit the number of work visas granted to foreigners, or employment regulations may mandate the hiring of local citizens as a requirement for doing business in a country.

International businesses also face more complex training and development challenges. For example, HR managers must provide cross-cultural training for corporate executives chosen for overseas assignments. Similarly, training systems for production workers in host countries must be adjusted to reflect the education offered by local school systems. For example, because Toyota (like other large Japanese firms) views employment as a lifetime commitment, it goes to great lengths to hire just the right people to work in its factories and offices. As the chapter opener revealed, it has nurtured partnerships with local public school systems in Japan to help train and select future employees. But Toyota cannot rely on this approach in each country in which it does business because local school systems often are not prepared to operate such training partnerships with individual firms. The German secondary school system provides extensive vocational training for its students, but that training is less firm-specific. The United States, on the other hand, emphasizes general education and provides only modest vocational training opportunities through its public schools. And many countries have labor pools that, when measured along any dimension, are uneducated and unskilled. Toyota thus has adjusted its selection, recruitment, and training practices to meet the requirements of the countries in which it does business.

And, finally, because working conditions and the cost of living may vary dramatically by country, international HR managers often must tailor compensation systems to meet the needs of the host country's labor market. They must take into account variations in local laws, which may require the payment of a minimum wage or may mandate certain benefits, such as annual bonuses or health care coverage. These managers must also determine how to compensate executives on overseas assignments, who potentially face higher costs of living, reductions in the quality of their lifestyle, and unhappiness or stress due to separation from friends and relatives.

Strategic Significance of HRM

International HR managers must ensure that the firm's employees are capable of meeting its strategic goals. Just as any organization—domestic or international—develops strategies for each functional area, such as marketing and finance, so too does it develop HRM strategy.[3] In the past, HRM was a low-status organizational function (usually called personnel management) that was perceived to be necessary (such as for hiring people) but not as playing a major role in organizational success. Today, top managers recognize the strategic importance of HRM and incorporate it as an integral part of their overall strategic planning process. The cultural nuances involved in international business make strategic HRM even more important.[4]

The basic elements of the international HRM process are shown in Fig. 20.1, which provides the framework around which this chapter is organized. The starting point is recognizing and appreciating HRM's strategic position within the firm and the interconnection between overall firm strategy and HRM strategy.[5] For example, suppose that a firm decides to adopt a cost leadership strategy and subsequently identifies the opportunity to undercut competing firms by aggressively pricing its products in new international markets. In implementing this

---

FIGURE 20.1

The International Human Resource Management Process

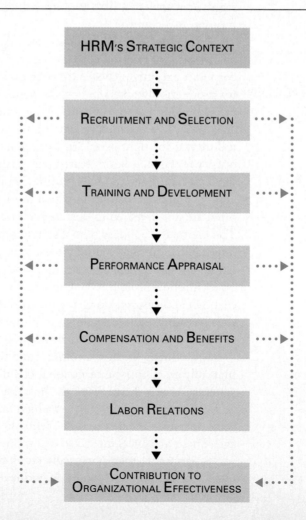

strategy, the firm could decide to purchase more inputs from outside suppliers, or it could shift production to a country with low-cost labor, such as Indonesia or Malaysia. This production location decision could result in less need for home country workers and more need for workers at the foreign facility. The firm's HR managers thus would have to develop severance packages and provide outplacement services for released workers in the home country as well as select, recruit, and train the new workers in the foreign country. Over time, the firm's HR managers would have to adjust their labor relations to meet the conditions in the host country, which are likely to differ from those in the home country.

The decision to shift production overseas has other HR consequences. HR managers have to select key managerial personnel to oversee the transfer of the firm's technology, operating policies, and proprietary skills to its new overseas factories.[6] Regardless of the skills or abilities of the selected international managers, few of them will be able to walk into a foreign operation and know exactly how to do things from the first day they arrive. Thus HR managers must provide them with training to help them function more effectively in a new culture.

HR managers must also be prepared to define performance effectiveness and assess how well each international manager is doing relative to that definition. And international managers must be compensated for their work. Further, firms invest a lot in their international managers, so HR managers must carefully assess the effectiveness of their management of retention and turnover.

International Managerial Staffing Needs

The staffing issues confronting international human resource managers can be divided into two broad categories:

1 Recruiting, training, and retaining managerial and executive employees

2 Recruiting, training, and retaining nonmanagerial employees, such as blue-collar production workers and white-collar office staff

For managerial employees, strategic and developmental issues are of primary importance. For nonmanagerial workers, differences in cultural, political, and legal conditions among countries may be of greater significance.

Scope of Internationalization

We begin by focusing on recruiting, training, and retaining managers. The size of this task depends on the scope of the firm's international involvement. Obviously, a firm's needs in the beginning stages of internationalization, such as in indirect exporting, are far less complex and comprehensive than those confronting an MNC with extensive investments in numerous countries. Consider the evolution of organizational structure discussed in Chapter 13.

1 *Export department.* A firm's initial foray into international business usually involves small-scale exporting using output from existing domestic production facilities. Its international activities are administered by an export department,

whose manager reports to an existing company executive such as the vice president of marketing. The manager is likely to be a citizen of the home country and may or may not have special training in overseas marketing and financing. But as export sales increase, the firm quickly recognizes that it must increase its staff's expertise, so it hires specialists in export documentation, international trade financing, and overseas distribution and marketing. These specialists are often recruited from international banks, international freight forwarders, or export management companies (EMCs).

2 *International division.* As their international operations grow in importance, firms often create a separate international division to administer all of their international activities. Typically, a firm's international division is housed at corporate headquarters in its home country and is headed by a home country citizen in order to facilitate communication and coordination between the domestic and international operations. The heads of the firm's foreign subsidiaries in turn report to the vice president of the international division. These foreign subsidiaries' managers (including their presidents as well as heads of functional departments such as finance, marketing, and production) may be either home country or host country citizens. Use of a home country manager facilitates communication and coordination with corporate headquarters because of shared cultural and educational backgrounds.[7] Use of a host country manager often improves the subsidiary's ability to adjust to changes in local economic and political conditions. As we discuss later in this chapter, cost considerations also play a major role in the choice between home country and host country managers.

3 *Global organization.* Firms further along in the internationalization process often adopt a global organization form. (Chapter 13 discussed the global product, global function, global area, and global customer forms.) Because of the complexity of their operations, global organizations must assemble a team of managers that have the expertise to produce, finance, and market their products worldwide while simultaneously coordinating their activities to achieve global production, financing, and marketing economies and synergies. To operate successfully, a global firm needs a team of managers that collectively possess expertise in and knowledge of the following:

▶ The firm's *product line.* Product managers must be aware of such factors as the latest manufacturing techniques, R&D opportunities, and competitors' strategies.

▶ The *functional skills* (accounting, logistics, marketing, manufacturing management, and so on) necessary to ensure global competitiveness. Functional specialists strive to capture global economies of scale and synergies in a firm's financial, marketing, and production activities.

▶ The *individual country markets* in which the firm does business. Country managers must understand such factors as local laws, culture, competitors, distribution systems, and advertising media. They play a key role in meeting the needs of local customers, ensuring compliance with host country rules and regulations, and enlarging the firm's market share and profitability in the host country.

▶ The firm's *global strategy.* High-level executives at corporate headquarters must formulate a global strategy for the firm and then control and coordinate the activities of the firm's product, functional, and country managers to ensure that its strategy is successfully implemented.[8]

Centralization versus Decentralization of Control

An international business's HRM needs are also affected by whether the firm wants decision making to be centralized at corporate headquarters or delegated (decentralized) to operating subsidiaries. Firms that use a centralized approach often favor employing home country managers; those that follow a decentralized decision-making philosophy are more likely to employ host country managers.

Certain organizational approaches and forms affect the choice of centralization or decentralization. Firms that view themselves as multi*domestic* rather than multi*national* are likely to favor decentralization of decision making. The global area form facilitates delegating responsibility to managers of the firm's foreign subsidiaries. Conversely, the international division form favors centralizing decision making at corporate headquarters.

Recall from Chapter 13 that most international businesses operate somewhere along the continuum from pure centralization to pure decentralization. In managing human resources, most adopt an overall HRM strategy at the corporate headquarters level, but delegate many day-to-day HR issues to local and regional offices. Doing this allows each foreign operation to meet its own needs and to more effectively deal with local conditions, cultures, and HR practices.

Staffing Philosophy

The extent of the firm's internationalization and its degree of centralization or decentralization affects (and is affected by) its philosophy regarding the nationality of its international managers. Firms can hire from three groups:

1 Parent-country nationals

2 Host-country nationals

3 Third-country nationals

Parent-country nationals (PCNs) are residents of the international business's home country. Use of PCNs in an MNC's foreign operations provides many advantages to the firm. Because PCNs typically share a common culture and educational background with corporate headquarters staff, they facilitate communication and coordination with corporate headquarters.[9] If the firm's global strategy involves exploiting new technologies or business techniques that were developed in the home market, PCNs are often best able to graft those innovations to a host country setting. For example, Toyota sent a team of executives from Japan to oversee the startup of its U.S. operations. It wanted to ensure that its manufacturing techniques and corporate commitment to quality were successfully transplanted to Kentucky.

However, using PCNs has several disadvantages. PCNs typically lack knowledge of the host country's laws, culture, economic conditions, social structure, and political processes. Although they can be trained to overcome these knowledge gaps, such training is expensive (particularly when the opportunity cost of the manager's time is considered) and is not a perfect substitute for having been born and raised in the host country. Further, PCNs are often expensive to relocate and maintain in the host country.[10] Finally, many host countries restrict the number of foreign employees who can be transferred in and/or mandate that a certain percentage of an international firm's payroll must be paid to domestic employees. Thus, an international business may not have total freedom to hire whomever it wants for international assignments. Because of these factors, PCNs are most likely to be used in upper-level and/or technical positions in host countries.

Host-country nationals (HCNs) are residents of the host country. HCNs are commonly used by international businesses to fill middle-level and lower-level jobs, but they also often appear in managerial and professional positions. Experienced MNCs such as Intel, Texas Instruments, IBM, DuPont, and AT&T hire HCNs instead of transferring their domestic workers to work in professional positions in their foreign operations.[11] Many smaller firms setting up operations abroad hire HCNs because they do not have enough managerial talent at home to send someone on a foreign assignment.[12]

Using HCNs offers two primary advantages. First, HCNs already understand the local laws, culture, and economic conditions. Second, the firm avoids the expenses associated with expatriate managers, such as relocation costs, supplemental wages paid for foreign service, and private schooling for children. However, using HCNs can have disadvantages. HCNs may be unfamiliar with the firm's business culture and practices, thus limiting their effectiveness. As noted earlier in this chapter, Toyota used Japanese executives to shepherd the development of its Kentucky operations in order to ensure that its new employees understood the firm's emphasis on producing quality automobiles.

Andersen Consulting, the world's largest consulting firm, has developed an innovative approach to training HCNs in its corporate culture. All of Andersen's entry-level consultants, who staff 151 offices in 47 countries, must undergo an intensive three-week education program at its Center for Professional Education in St. Charles, Illinois. The newly recruited professionals learn about the Andersen way of doing business and solving clients' problems. By providing its multinational recruits with common training, the firm transmits its corporate culture throughout its international empire and promotes intracorporate networking of the new employees that transcends national boundaries.[13]

International businesses increasingly recruit new employees from every market they serve. Andersen Consulting, for example, hires new consultants from around the world. Each recruit must complete an intensive training course at the Arthur Andersen Worldwide Organization Center for Professional Education in order to learn how the firm conducts business.

Finally, an international firm may hire **third-country nationals (TCNs)**, who are not citizens of the firm's home country or of the host country. Like PCNs, TCNs are most likely to be used in upper-level and/or technical positions. TCNs and PCNs collectively are known as **expatriates**, or people working and residing in countries other than their native country. In the past, TCNs were likely to be used when they had special expertise that was not available to the firm through any other channel. Today, they are consciously being used by some firms to promote a global outlook throughout their operations. For example, firms such as Nestlé and Philips NV rely heavily on TCNs because they believe those managers bring broader perspectives and experiences to the firm's host country operations. And some firms are recruiting more TCNs to serve on their boards of directors to help bring a more global orientation to the boards.[14]

Most international firms develop a systematic strategy for choosing among HCNs, PCNs, and TCNs for various positions. Some rely on the **ethnocentric staffing model**, whereby they use primarily PCNs to staff higher-level foreign positions. This approach is based on the assumption that home office perspectives should take precedence over local perspectives and that expatriate PCNs will be most effective in representing the views of the home office in the foreign operation. Other international firms follow a **polycentric staffing model**; that is, they emphasize the use of HCNs in the belief that HCNs know the local market best. Finally, the **geocentric staffing model** puts PCNs, HCNs, and TCNs on an equal footing. Firms that adopt this approach want to hire the best person available, regardless of where that individual comes from.[15]

National culture often affects the staffing model chosen by a firm. European MNCs are more likely than U.S. or Japanese ones to adopt the geocentric approach. This approach is encouraged by the EU in order to improve the mobility of workers and managers throughout its member countries. Japanese firms favor the ethnocentric staffing model, in part because their consensus-oriented approach to decision making is facilitated by employing Japanese managers in key roles in their foreign subsidiaries. But Japanese firms sometimes rely too heavily on this model, to their own disadvantage. While they usually hire HCNs for lower-level positions, they are reluctant to use non-Japanese managers in higher-level positions. When they do hire an HCN as a local manager, they have been accused of being too quick to send in a troubleshooter from the home office at the first sign of a problem.[16] Further, the non-Japanese managers often face a glass ceiling because the top positions in the firm are reserved for Japanese managers. Thus, the ethnocentric policy often results in the loss of the best HCN managers, who seek more challenge and responsibility by shifting to non-Japanese employers.

Recruitment and Selection

A firm's scope of internationalization, level of centralization, and staffing philosophy help determine the skills and abilities its international managers need. As shown in Fig. 20.2, these skills and abilities fall into two general categories:

1 Those needed to do the job

2 Those needed to work in a foreign location

The firm first must define the actual business skills necessary to do the job. For example, a firm that has an assembly plant in a foreign market needs a plant manager who understands the technical aspects of what is to be manufactured, what manufacturing processes will be utilized, and so on.[17] The firm's marketing

FIGURE 20.2

Necessary Skills and Abilities for International Managers

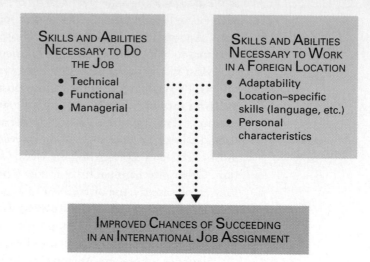

SKILLS AND ABILITIES NECESSARY TO DO THE JOB
- Technical
- Functional
- Managerial

SKILLS AND ABILITIES NECESSARY TO WORK IN A FOREIGN LOCATION
- Adaptability
- Location–specific skills (language, etc.)
- Personal characteristics

IMPROVED CHANCES OF SUCCEEDING IN AN INTERNATIONAL JOB ASSIGNMENT

managers must be knowledgeable about advertising media availability, distribution channels, market competition, and local consumers' demographic characteristics.

The firm next must determine the skills and abilities a manager must have to work and function effectively in the foreign location. These include the manager's ability to adapt to cultural change, ability to speak the local language, overall physical and emotional health, levels of independence and self-reliance, and appropriate levels of experience and education. Obviously, an HCN can meet these requirements far easier than a PCN or TCN can. Firms relying on the ethnocentric or geocentric staffing models thus must devote more resources to selecting and training PCNs and TCNs for foreign assignments than do firms that rely on the polycentric model.

Recruitment of Managers

Once the international business determines the skills and abilities an international manager must have, it next must develop a pool of qualified applicants for the job and then recruit and select the best candidate.[18]

Recruitment of Experienced Managers. International businesses recruit experienced managers through a variety of channels. A common source of recruits is within the firm itself—among employees already working for the firm in the host country or those who, while currently employed in the home country, might be prepared for an international assignment in the host country. The latter group may include both managers who have never held an international assignment and managers who have already completed previous international assignments. For example, when Kal Kan's Canadian subsidiary entered the animal food market in Poland in 1992, the firm relied on a team of Polish-born Canadian executives to start up the new operation.

An international business may also attempt to identify prospective managers who work for other firms. These may be home country managers who are deemed to be qualified for an international assignment or managers already working in an international assignment for another firm.[19] For higher-level positions, firms often rely on so-called headhunters to help them locate prospective candidates. **Headhunters** are recruiting firms that actively seek qualified managers and other professionals for possible placement in positions in other organizations. In many parts of the world, including Japan, switching employers has long been frowned on. And until recently, headhunting in Europe was considered unethical. Both of these views are changing, however. Some firms are now finding that they can even entice highly qualified Japanese employees away from Japanese firms.[20]

One trend seems clear: as a result of the globalization of business, the market for executive talent is also becoming globalized. Firms increasingly value performance more than nationality. For example, fewer than half of the 150 highest-level executives of Imperial Chemical Industries PLC, Britain's largest chemical manufacturer, are British nationals.[21] A few years ago Texas-based Compaq Computer hired a German executive, Eckhard Pfeiffer, for a top position in its European operations. Shortly thereafter, Compaq ousted its president and CEO and promoted Pfeiffer to the position. Similarly, the new president of Esprit de Corp, a U.S. sportswear maker, is Swiss, and Xerox has a new executive vice president from Italy. Current estimates are that between 7 and 10 percent of all newly filled executive positions in U.S. firms go to foreigners.[22]

Recruitment of Younger Managers. It is uncommon for large MNCs to hire new college graduates for immediate foreign assignments. Some firms, however, will hire new graduates they ultimately intend to send abroad and, in the short term, give them domestic assignments. Particularly attractive are graduates with foreign language skills, international travel experience, and a major in international business or a related field.[23] A few firms have started taking a longer-term view of developing international managerial talent. Coca-Cola, for example, has developed an innovative strategy for recruiting managers for future international assignments. It actively seeks foreign students who are studying at U.S. colleges and universities and who intend to return to their home countries after receiving their degrees. The firm recruits and hires the best of these graduates and puts them through a one-year training program. The new managers then return home as Coca-Cola employees and take assignments in the firm's operations in their home countries.[24]

Colgate-Palmolive has mounted perhaps the most aggressive effort of this sort. This firm each year selects 15 new recruits (from an applicant pool of 15,000) to participate in its fast-track globalization program, which provides quick lessons in competing in the global marketplace. Colgate reaps several benefits from this program. It is able to hire excellent young talent because college graduates from around the world seek one of the coveted slots. By exposing management trainees and entry-level managers to a new culture, the firm can forcefully show its young talent the problems inherent in self-referencing one's culture in international markets. For example, a Dutch trainee brought to the United States was shocked by the huge assortment of goods in a typical U.S. supermarket. That visit created a vivid impression of the high level of competitiveness of the U.S. market and forced the trainee to recognize that marketing strategies that might work in the Netherlands could be dismal failures in the United States. A U.S. trainee sent by Colgate to a Romanian store had a similar experience. When the trainee asked Romanian shoppers which brands of soap they preferred—

a perfectly logical question to market researchers in the United States—she was surprised by the response: the Romanian shoppers, accustomed to scarcity, bought whatever soap was available.[25]

Selection of Managers

After the pool of prospective managers has been identified, HR managers must decide which persons from that pool are the best qualified for the assignment. The most promising candidates share the following characteristics:

▶ Managerial competence (technical and leadership skills, knowledge of the corporate culture)

▶ Appropriate training (formal education, knowledge of the host market and its culture and language)

▶ Adaptability to new situations (ability to deal simultaneously with adjusting to a new work and job environment, adjusting to working with HCNs, and adjusting to a new national culture)[26]

The importance of the selection process cannot be overstated when dealing with expatriate managers. The costs to a firm of expatriate failure are extremely high. **Expatriate failure** is the early return of an expatriate manager to his or her home country because of an inability to perform in the overseas assignment.[27] Experts suggest that these costs are between $40,000 and $250,000 (these figures include the expatriate's original training, moving expenses, and lost managerial productivity, but do not include the decreased performance of the foreign subsidiary itself).[28]

Expatriate failure occurs far too often. Failure rates of 20–50 percent are common for many U.S. firms, and rates appear to be much higher for them than for European and Japanese firms. More than 76 percent of U.S. firms experience expatriate failure rates of over 10 percent (that is, at least one out of ten expatriate assignments were deemed failures), while only 14 percent of Japanese firms and only 3 percent of European firms experienced similar failure rates.[29]

The primary cause of expatriate failure is the inability of the manager and/or his or her spouse and family to adjust to the new locale. As a result, international HR managers increasingly are evaluating the nontechnical aspects of a candidate's suitability for a foreign assignment. Assessing certain skills and abilities is relatively easy. For example, measuring a prospect's language proficiency is a straightforward undertaking. But assessing a person's cultural adaptability is more difficult and must be accomplished through a variety of means. Most firms use a combination of tests (such as personality and aptitude tests) and interviews in their selection process. Assessment centers, which offer programs of exercises, tests, and interviews that last several days, are also useful because they provide an in-depth look at a set of prospective candidates under the same circumstances.

Another important consideration is the prospect's motivation for and interest in the foreign assignment. Some managers are attracted to foreign assignments, perhaps because they relish the thought of living abroad or because they see the experience as being useful in their future career plans. But others balk at the thought of uprooting their family and moving to a foreign environment, particularly one that is culturally distant from their own. As noted above, failure of the family to adjust to the new culture is a prominent cause of expatriate failure. Thus, most firms also consider the family's motivation for and interest in the foreign assignment. The manager's job performance will often deteriorate if he or she has to soothe an unhappy spouse cut off from friends and family and frustrated by dealing with a new culture. And clearly a foreign relocation is far more disruptive to the family than a domestic one. Dependent children may face problems integrating into a new school culture—particularly if they do not speak the local language—and may find that material covered in the courses at their new school is well ahead (or well behind) that at their home school. In addition, there's the dual career problem. The trailing spouse may find it difficult to take leave from his or her current position, thereby forcing a disruption in his or her career advancement. Still worse, labor laws in the new country may make it difficult or impossible for the spouse to obtain employment there legally.

Because of the risk of expatriate failure, firms often devote considerable resources to selection and training. AT&T, for example, prides itself on doing an especially thorough job of selecting managers for foreign assignments. The firm has long used personality tests and interviews as part of its selection process. It now also uses psychologists to help assess prospects and is investing more into learning about family considerations. In addition, the prospects complete a self-assessment checklist designed to help them probe their motivations for seeking a foreign transfer. Table 20.1 summarizes sample questions the firm uses to screen potential expatriates and their spouses. AT&T reports that this exercise increases managers' self-awareness. As a result, more managers now remove themselves from consideration for foreign assignments.[30]

General Motors spends almost $500,000 per year on cross-cultural training for 150 or so U.S. managers and their families heading to international assignments in order to reduce the risk of expatriate failure. The firm reports that fewer

---

TABLE 20.1

AT&T's Questionnaire for Screening Overseas Transferees

Would your spouse be interrupting a career to accompany you on an international assignment? If so, how do you think this will [affect] your spouse and your relationship with each other?

Do you enjoy the challenge of making your own way in new situations?

Securing a job upon reentry will be primarily your responsibility. How do you feel about networking and being your own advocate?

How able are you in initiating new social contacts?

Can you imagine living without television?

How important is it for you to spend significant amounts of time with people of your own ethnic, racial, religious, and national background?

As you look at your personal history, can you isolate any episodes that indicate a real interest in learning about other peoples and cultures?

Has it been your habit to vacation in foreign countries?

Do you enjoy sampling foreign cuisines?

What is your tolerance for waiting for repairs?

Source: Consultants for International Living. From "As Costs of Overseas Assignments Climb, Firms Select Expatriates More Carefully," *The Wall Street Journal*, January 9, 1992, p. B1. Reprinted by permission of *The Wall Street Journal*, © 1992 Dow Jones & Company, Inc. All Rights Reserved Worldwide.

than 1 percent of its expatriates request an early return and attributes much of this success to its training efforts.[31]

An international business must determine not only how well a prospective manager will adapt to the foreign culture but also how well he or she will fit into that culture. For example, for years some U.S. firms hesitated to send women managers on foreign assignments to some countries, such as Japan, because they assumed the women would not be accepted in a culture that frowned on women working outside the home. However, recent research indicates that this fear may be overstated. Host country citizens react primarily to these executives' foreignness, rather than their gender.[32]

Expatriation and Repatriation Issues

PCNs on long-term foreign assignments face great acculturation challenges. Working in and coping with a foreign culture can lead to **culture shock**, a psychological phenomenon that may lead to feelings of fear, helplessness, irritability, and disorientation. New expatriates experience a sense of loss regarding their old cultural environment as well as confusion, rejection, self-doubt, and decreased self-esteem from working in a new and unfamiliar cultural setting.[33] Acculturation, as shown in Fig. 20.3, typically proceeds through four phases.[34]

Culture shock reduces an expatriate's effectiveness and productivity, and so international businesses have developed various strategies to mitigate its effects. One simple solution is to provide expatriates (and their families) with pre-departure language and cultural training so that they can better understand and anticipate the cultural adjustments they must undergo. In addition to straightforward training, firms might also make initial foreign assignments relatively brief and make sure that the expatriate understands the role each particular international assignment plays in his or her overall career prospects.[35]

Interestingly, international businesses should pay almost as much attention to **repatriation**—bringing a manager back home after a foreign assignment has been completed—as they do to expatriation. If a manager and his or her family have been successfully expatriated, they become comfortable with living and working in the foreign culture. Returning home can be almost as traumatic to them as was the original move abroad.[36] One reason for the difficulty of repatriation is that people tend to assume that nothing has changed back home. They look forward to getting back to their friends, familiar surroundings, and daily routines. But their friends may have moved or developed new social circles and their coworkers may have been transferred to other jobs. Some expatriates who have returned to the United States have even been denied credit because they have no domestic financial history for several years![37] The repatriated manager also has to cope with change and uncertainty at work. The firm may not be sure what the manager's job is going to entail. Further, the manager may have been running the show at the foreign operation and enjoying considerable authority. Back home, however, he or she is likely to have much less authority and to be on a par with many other managers reporting to more senior managers. Also, the manager and his or her family may have enjoyed a higher social status in the host country than they will after returning home. Thus, readjustment problems may be severe and need the attention of both manager and firm.

FIGURE 20.3

**Phases in
Acculturation**

HONEYMOON

For the first few days or months, the new culture seems exotic and stimulating. Excitement of working in new environment makes employee overestimate the ease of adjusting.

DISILLUSIONMENT

Differences between new and old environments are blown out of proportion. As employee and family face challenges of everyday living, differences become magnified. Many transplanted employees remain stuck in this phase.

ADAPTATION

With time, employee begins to understand patterns of new culture, gains language competence, and adjusts to everyday living.

BICULTURALISM

Anxiety has ended as transplanted employee gains confidence in ability to function productively in new culture.

The repatriation problem can be expensive for a firm. By some estimates, one quarter of all repatriated employees leave their employer within a year after returning home. The average U.S. expatriate costs his or her employer about $300,000 per year and stays 3–4 years on an overseas assignment; thus, each repatriated executive who leaves the firm represents a million-dollar investment walking out the door.[38] One new strategy to help managers cope with repatriation has been successfully used by Nynex Corp. Nynex brings home a manager who is to be repatriated about six weeks before the permanent move. The manager spends a couple of days getting reacquainted with the surroundings before coming back for good. This procedure helps reduce repatriation problems.[39]

The bottom line is that expatriation and repatriation problems can be reduced if international businesses systematically provide organizational career development programs for their expatriate managers. Recent research indicates that the likelihood of a manager being successful at an overseas assignment increases if the manager:

▶ Can freely choose whether to accept or reject the expatriate assignment

▶ Has been given a realistic preview of the new job and assignment

▶ Has been given a realistic expectation of what his or her repatriation assignment will be

▶ Has a mentor back home who will guard his or her interests and provide corporate and social support during the assignment

▶ Sees a clear link between the expatriate assignment and his or her long-term career path

Of these five elements, the last is the most critical in determining expatriate success.[40]

Training and Development

The international firm's HR managers must also provide training and development for its home and host country managers. **Training** is instruction directed at enhancing specific job-related skills and abilities. For example, training programs might be designed to help employees learn to speak a foreign language, to use new equipment, or to implement new manufacturing procedures. **Development** is general education concerned with preparing managers for new assignments and/or higher-level positions. For example, a development program could be aimed at helping managers improve their ability to make decisions or to motivate subordinates to work harder.[41] Training and development help employees perform more effectively. Special acculturation training is important for employees who are given international assignments.

Assessing Training Needs

Before a firm can undertake a meaningful training or development program, it must assess its exact training and development needs. This assessment involves

New technology combined with global business opportunities dictates that international businesses continually train their employees in a variety of areas. Emerging computer-based communication networks are especially important. This Buddhist monk, for example, is conducting research on his computer at a monastery outside Bangkok.

determining the difference between what managers and employees can do and what the firm feels they need to be able to do. For example, suppose a firm that does business in Latin America wants its employees to be able to speak Spanish fluently. If most of its employees are fluent in Spanish, its language training needs may be minimal. But if relatively few employees are, extensive training may be called for. The assessment of training needs is an extremely important element of international HRM. Firms that underestimate training needs can encounter serious difficulties. Indeed, lack of knowledge about foreign customers and markets is a major barrier to successful entry into such markets, as Fig. 20.4 shows.

A firm just moving into international markets has different training and development needs from those of an established global firm. For example, the

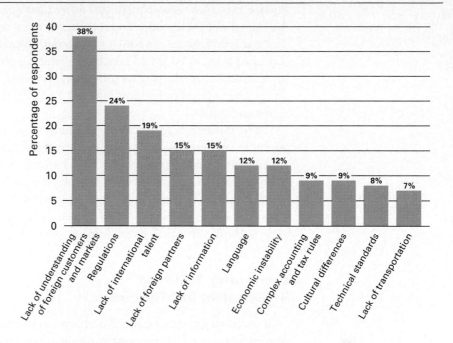

FIGURE 20.4

Barriers to Entering Foreign Markets

Source: From "Cross-cultural training helps in leap abroad," *Houston Chronicle*, September 25, 1994, p. 1E. Reprinted with permission. Data: Ernst & Young survey.

newly internationalizing firm is likely to have few, if any, experienced international managers. Thus, its training and development needs will be substantial.[42] In contrast, a global firm has a cadre of trained and experienced managers with international backgrounds, skills, and abilities.[43]

Basic Training Methods and Procedures

The first issue an international business must consider as it plans its training and development efforts is whether to rely on standardized programs or to develop its own customized programs. Certain kinds of training can be readily obtained in the open market—for example, language-training programs and self-paced language training from cassette tapes. Prudential Insurance even offers packaged training programs for families of expatriates, a good idea in light of the importance of family problems in causing expatriate failure.[44] One advantage of standardized programs is that they tend to be less expensive than customized ones. On the other hand, a standardized program may not precisely fit the firm's needs.

Most training and development programs are customized to a firm's particular needs. Larger MNCs, for example, often have training and development departments that develop customized programs for the unique needs of individual managers and/or business units. Training and development activities may take place in regular classroom settings within the firm, on actual job sites, or off premises in a conference center or hotel. Customized programs are more costly than are standardized ones; however, they ensure that employees get the precise information deemed necessary. Regardless of whether training and development programs are standardized or customized, most use a variety of methods as instructional vehicles. Lectures and assigned readings are common, as are videotaped and software-based instruction. Role playing and other forms of experiential exercises are useful for helping people better understand other cultures. Case studies are also used, although not as frequently as other methods. Training materials must often be altered to fit different cultural contexts. For example, a consultant hired to make training videos for Bally of Switzerland initially assumed that he could use the same basic video for each of Bally's regional offices, with only minor script modifications. As the project progressed, however, he found that so many language and cultural differences affected the video that he essentially had to reshoot it for each office.[45]

The trainers themselves may also need to adapt how they do things. For example, one professional trainer reported difficulties in using her normal style when running a training program in Thailand. She prefers to be informal and to involve the participants through role playing and other forms of interaction. But she found that Thai managers were uncomfortable with her informality and resisted the role-playing approach. She eventually had to adopt a more formal style and use a straightforward lecture approach to get her points across.[46]

Developing Younger International Managers

The increasing globalization of business has prompted most MNCs to recognize the importance of internationalizing their managers earlier in their careers.[47] Until the late 1980s, most U.S. MNCs delayed giving their managers significant overseas assignments until they had spent 7–10 years with the firm. Today many of them are beginning to recognize that they need to develop the international awareness and competence of their managers earlier and to systematically integrate international assignments into individual career plans. For example, GE provides language and cross-cultural training to its professional staff even though they may not be scheduled for overseas postings. Such training is important because these employees, even if they never leave their home countries, are likely to work with GE employees from other countries and to deal with visiting executives from GE's foreign partners, suppliers, and customers. Such training also helps the employees gain a better understanding of the firm's international markets.

Other firms, such as American Express and Johnson & Johnson, have begun posting managers to overseas assignments after only 18–24 months on the job. Honda's U.S. manufacturing subsidiary has been sending U.S. managers to Tokyo for multi-year assignments so that they can learn more about the firm's successful manufacturing and operating philosophies. PepsiCo and Raychem are bringing young managers from their foreign operations to the United States for similar reasons.

U.S. firms aren't the only ones integrating international assignments into career development plans for younger managers. For example, Samsung regularly sends its executives abroad for various assignments. One of its more interesting strategies is to send managers to certain foreign locations for as long as a year with no specific job responsibilities. They are supposed to spend their time learning the local language and becoming familiar with the culture. The idea is that if they are transferred back to that same location in the future—when they are in a higher-level position—they will be able to function more effectively. Even though the program costs Samsung about $80,000 per person per year, executives believe the firm will quickly recoup its investment.[48]

Performance Appraisal and Compensation

Another important part of international HRM consists of conducting performance appraisals and determining compensation and benefits. Whereas recruitment, selection, and training and development tend to focus on pre-assignment issues, performance appraisal and compensation involve ongoing issues that continue to have an effect well past the initial international assignment.

Assessing Performance in International Business

Performance appraisal is the process of assessing how effectively a person is performing his or her job. The purposes of performance appraisal are

▶ To provide feedback to individuals as to how well they are doing

▶ To provide a basis for rewarding top performers

▶ To identify areas in which additional training and development may be needed

▶ To identify problem areas that may call for a change in assignment

Performance appraisals of an international business's top managers must be based on the firm's clear understanding of its goals for its foreign operations. A successful subsidiary in a mature and stable foreign market will have different goals than will a startup operation in a growing but unstable market. Thus, a firm assigning two new managers to head up these different subsidiaries must understand that it cannot expect the same outcomes from each of them. Similarly, managers of foreign subsidiaries that serve as cost centers must be judged by different standards from those used for managers of profit centers.

In assessing a manager's actual performance, the firm may consider sales, profit margin, or market share growth. And if a subsidiary has been having problems, performance may be more appropriately assessed in terms of how well the manager has helped to solve those problems. For example, reducing net losses or halting a decline in market share might be considered good performance, at least in the short term.

Expected and actual performance must be compared, and differences must be addressed. This step needs to have a strong diagnostic component: why and how has the manager's performance been acceptable or unacceptable? Are any problems attributable to the manager's lack of skills? Are some problems attributable to unforeseen circumstances? Is the home office accountable for some of the problems that may have arisen, perhaps because the manager was inadequately trained?

Circumstances will dictate how frequently performance appraisals occur. In a domestic firm, they may occur as often as every quarter. But geographical factors can limit the frequency with which international performance appraisals can occur. Generally, international managers are expected to submit reports on performance-based results to headquarters regularly. As long as these reports fall within acceptable parameters, the firm is likely to conduct a formal performance appraisal perhaps on an annual basis. But if standard reports reveal a problem, performance appraisals may be done more often in an effort to get things back on track.

Determining Compensation in International Business

Another important issue in international HRM is determining managerial compensation. To remain competitive, firms must provide prevailing compensation packages for their managers in a given market. These packages include salary and nonsalary items and are determined by labor market forces such as the supply and demand of managerial talent, occupational status, professional licensing requirements, standards of living, government regulations, tax codes, and similar factors.[49] For example, in Germany, employers customarily reimburse their executives for car expenses. In Japan, the executive may actually get a car plus expenses. Japanese executives also receive generous entertainment allowances and an allowance for business gifts. Similarly, because of high marginal income tax rates in the postwar period, British companies typically provide company cars to managers at all levels. In the United States, firms offer managers health care benefits because such benefits are free from income taxes.

Compensating Expatriate Managers. A more complex set of compensation issues apply to expatriate managers. Most international businesses find it necessary to provide these managers with differential compensation to make up for dramatic differences in currency valuation, standards of living, lifestyle norms, and so on.[50] When managers are on short-term assignments abroad, their salary usually continues to be tied to their domestic currency and home country standard of living. (Of course, the managers are reimbursed for short-term living expenses such as for hotel rooms, meals, and transportation.) But if the foreign assignment is indefinite or longer-term, compensation is routinely adjusted to allow the manager to maintain his or her home country standard of living.[51] This adjustment is particularly important if the manager is transferred from a low-cost location to a high-cost location or from a country with a high standard of living to one with a lower standard of living. Table 20.2 summarizes cost-of-living differences for a number of international business centers.

The starting point in differential compensation is a **cost-of-living allowance**. This allowance is intended to offset differences in the cost of living in the home and host countries. The premise is that a manager who accepts a foreign assignment is entitled to the same standard of living he or she enjoyed at home. If the cost of living in the foreign country is higher than that at home, the manager's existing base pay will result in a lower standard of living and the firm will supplement the base pay to offset this difference. Of course, if the cost of living in the foreign location is lower than at home, no such allowance is needed.

Sometimes firms find they must supplement base pay in order to get a manager to accept an assignment in a relatively unattractive location. While it may not be difficult to find people willing to move to England or Japan, it may be much more difficult to entice people to move to Haiti, Somalia, or Malaysia. Called either a **hardship premium** or a **foreign service premium**, this supplement is essentially an inducement to the individual to accept the international assignment.[52]

TABLE 20.2

Worldwide Costs of Living

PLACE	LIVING COST INDEX*	INFLATION RATE (%)	PLACE	LIVING COST INDEX*	INFLATION RATE (%)
Tokyo, Japan	161.6	1.7	Antigua	92.3	1.0
Oslo, Norway	147.3	2.0	Bridgetown, Barbados	91.9	8.3
Brazzaville, Congo	143.4	0.5	Singapore	90.9	2.4
Stockholm, Sweden	139.2	2.0	Brunei	90.8	2.5
Zurich, Switzerland	133.1	3.5	Manila, Philippines	90.5	8.5
Copenhagen, Denmark	130.6	2.0	Los Angeles, United States	90.2	3.0
Abidjan, Cote d'Ivoire	129.9	2.1	Riyadh, Saudi Arabia	88.0	−2.3
Paris, France	122.9	2.6	Beijing, China	87.6	10.0
Tripoli, Libya	121.9	4.4	Muscat, Oman	87.6	1.6
Vienna, Austria	120.3	3.9	Valletta, Malta	85.8	2.8
Brussels, Belgium	119.9	2.3	Kuala Lumpur, Malaysia	85.3	4.4
Dublin, Ireland	116.5	2.8	Doha, Qatar	85.1	3.0
Amsterdam, Netherlands	113.6	3.5	Manama, Bahrain	84.0	−0.1
Frankfurt, Germany	112.2	3.6	Tunis, Tunisia	83.5	4.4
Helsinki, Finland	111.3	2.3	Sydney, Australia	83.0	0.8
Victoria, Seychelles	111.1	4.6	Bangkok, Thailand	82.7	3.4
Madrid, Spain	109.2	5.8	Toronto, Canada	82.4	1.3
Lisbon, Portugal	108.3	9.3	Amman, Jordan	81.8	6.1
Luxembourg	106.7	3.0	Abu Dhabi, United Arab Emirates	81.8	2.0
Victoria, Hong Kong	105.3	9.2	Accra, Ghana	81.7	10.3
Taipei, Taiwan	104.9	7.6	Dubai, United Arab Emirates	81.4	2.0
Monrovia, Liberia	104.6	4.5	Jakarta, Indonesia	79.6	9.3
Nassau, Bahamas	104.4	6.6	Port of Spain, Trinidad	79.3	2.4
Milan, Italy	103.5	4.7	Suva, Fiji	77.0	7.1
London, United Kingdom	100.0	3.6	Cairo, Egypt	76.2	9.5
New York City, United States	98.6	3.0	Wellington, New Zealand	74.8	1.1
Havana, Cuba	97.7	7.0	Panama	73.7	2.3
Seoul, South Korea	95.3	5.7	Colombo, Sri Lanka	71.3	9.7
Tel Aviv, Israel	93.0	8.3	Prague, Czech Republic	65.3	9.3
Casablanca, Morocco	92.7	6.0	Karachi, Pakistan	62.7	9.9

* Excludes housing; based on London prices at 100.

Source: From Michael Dixon, "How living costs vary across the globe," *Financial Times*, February 5, 1993. Reprinted with permission.

Finally, many international businesses also find they must set up a tax-equalization system. A **tax-equalization system** is a means of ensuring that the expatriate's after-tax income in the host country is similar to what the person's after-tax income would be in the home country. Each country has unique tax laws that apply to the earnings of its own citizens, to earnings within its borders by foreign citizens, and/or to earnings in another country by its own citizens. The most common tax-equalization system has the firm's own accounting department handling

GOING GLOBAL

The American Advantage

Congratulations. The Japanese-owned company down the street has offered you a big job at a big salary. It seems too good to be true.

It probably is.

When you tally your total compensation package, you may discover that you would be better off at a U.S. firm. True, job security is probably greater with a foreign-owned firm, but there is a lot less reward for individual performance. And foreign firms show a great reluctance to give employees any equity stake in the parent company.

In short, the better you are, the wider the pay gap between U.S. firms and foreign companies' U.S. subsidiaries. The gap can be enormous—as much as 40 percent for some comparable high-level positions.

"Europeans and Asians don't believe in the U.S. Pavlovian theory of compensation: the carrot and the stick," says Michael Emig, a principal at Wyatt Co., a compensation-consulting firm.

Only 38 percent of foreign companies' U.S. affiliates offer potentially lucrative incentives such as stock options, compared with nearly 90 percent of Fortune 500 companies, according to a recent survey by Hay Group. These foreign affiliates also are much stingier with annual bonuses. And they are less likely to offer executives often-coveted perquisites such as country-club memberships, company cars and executive dining rooms....

Now for the good news: Intense competition for senior executives is beginning to force foreign owners to sweeten the pot. In 1988, U.S. affiliates of foreign companies employed 3.8 million people—more than twice as many as they did in 1978. The total easily could double again by 1993, consultants say....

The biggest pressure comes in highly competitive industries like health care. Solvay America Inc.'s pharmaceutical division "certainly lost some" hot prospects because it didn't offer long-term incentives, says Frank McKevitt, human-resources vice-president at Solvay America, the Houston subsidiary of Belgium chemical giant Solvay & Cie....

So this year, he is phasing in a deferred-bonus plan for 20 of Solvay's 85 U.S. senior managers. He says the bonus made "compensation discussions a great deal easier" in finding a new head of the automotive-plastics division. The deferred bonus also has curbed management turnover.

Yet it took Mr. McKevitt a full year, six trans-Atlantic trips and a lot of overhead slides before Solvay's top brass accepted deferred bonuses. Mr. McKevitt recalls his bosses asking: "We're a long-term company anyway—why do we have to pay [American executives] twice?" He won over the Belgians in part by

the taxes of its expatriates. A firm accountant determines what a manager's taxes will be where he or she is living and what they would be at home on the same income and then makes the appropriate adjustment to equalize the two.[53] "Going Global" provides additional insights into some of the complexities involved in compensating international managers.

Benefits Packages for Expatriate Managers. International businesses must provide not only salary adjustments, but also special forms of benefits for their expatriate managers in addition to standard benefits such as health insurance and vacation allowances. Special benefits include

▶ Housing
▶ Education
▶ Medical treatment
▶ Travel to the home country
▶ Club memberships

arguing that Americans don't receive generous government benefits that are common in Europe, such as free medical care and college tuition....

Still, Europeans are *eager* to change compared with the Japanese. Nearly 75 percent of European concerns may offer long-term incentives to American executives within five years, compared with under 60 percent today, predicts Annette Rosinski, an international-compensation specialist for Hewitt Associates. Stock options are catching on in Europe, although generally with narrower scope and scale than in the United States.

In contrast, a Hewitt poll shows only a third of Japanese-owned units now provide long-term inducements in the United States. Ms. Rosinski believes the proportion will go no higher than 50 percent in the next couple of years. "Japan will always lag behind," she says.

The reason, Ms. Rosinski says, is cultural. She cites the skepticism of officials at one Japanese toiletries maker who repeatedly quizzed Ms. Rosinski when she suggested so-called phantom stock for two U.S. businesses it had acquired. (Phantom stock usually involves payments reflecting appreciation in a company's shares or other performance measures.) "Why do you [Americans] need long-tem incentives?" the puzzled Japanese asked. "You are going to be here forever." Her reply: Many U.S. executives job hop and need financial motivation to think farther ahead than next quarter's results....

Still, compensation pressures on Japanese companies in the United States are mounting as more Americans move into management positions—and hit a glass ceiling blocking high-level advancement because they aren't Japanese. Americans' frustrations over the lack of upward mobility in Japanese-owned firms is seen in a flurry of job-bias suits filed recently against Japanese corporations.

The need for U.S.-style pay practices at Japan, Inc. "is just something which is emerging now," says Dan Schaul, who joined Sumitomo Trust & Banking Co. in 1988 as one of just a handful of American managers among Sumitomo Trust's 100 U.S. employees. Today, Sumitomo Trust has 250 employees in the U.S., including about 15 Americans, and Mr. Schaul has been trying to Americanize the pay package at the trust company.

Mr. Schaul, now North American vice president for human resources, concedes that his forays have been modest: While he has introduced richer annual bonuses—high-flying traders can earn about 30 percent of their salaries in bonuses, double the previous maximum—Sumitomo Trust still doesn't match the bonuses and stock options common at U.S. rivals. He was able to sell Tokyo on the idea of a retirement savings plan after several senior staff members complained "that they couldn't rely on Social Security to take care of their full retirement needs," Mr. Schaul says.

Source: From Joann S. Lublin, "The American Advantage," *The Wall Street Journal*, April 17, 1991, p. R4. Reprinted by permission of *The Wall Street Journal*, © 1991 Dow Jones & Company, Inc. All Rights Reserved Worldwide.

A common special benefit involves housing. Like other components of living costs, housing expenses vary in different areas. Duplicating the level of housing the executive enjoyed in his or her home country may be expensive, so housing is usually treated as a separate benefit. If a manager is going on permanent or long-term assignment, the firm may buy the manager's existing home at fair market value. It may also help the manager buy a house in the host country if housing costs or interest rates are substantially different from those at home.

If the expatriate manager has a family, the firm may need to provide job location assistance for the spouse and help cover education costs for the children. For example, the children may need to attend private school, which the firm would pay for. Schooling represents a particularly important problem for Japanese expatriate managers, whose children may not do well in the national entrance exams for the most prestigious Japanese universities if their reading and writing skills atrophy as a result of living abroad. Thus, many Japanese firms pay for their expatriates' children to attend private schools that help students cram for those exams.[54]

Medical benefits may also need to be adjusted. For example, some people consider Malaysian health care facilities inadequate. Thus, managers on assignment there often request that their employer send them to Singapore whenever they need medical attention.

Most international businesses provide expatriates with a travel allowance for trips to the home country for personal reasons, such as to visit other family members or to celebrate holidays. The manager and his or her family may be allowed one or two trips home per year at company expense. If the manager's family remains at home during a short-term assignment, the manager may be given more frequent opportunities to travel home.

In some cultures, belonging to a certain club or participating in a particular activity is a necessary part of the business world. In Japan, for example, many business transactions occur during a round of golf. To be effective in Japan, a foreign manager may need to join a golf club. Memberships in such clubs, however, cost thousands of dollars and a single round of golf may cost ten times or more what it costs elsewhere. Because such activities are a normal part of doing business, firms often provide managers transferred to Japan with these benefits.[55]

Equity in Compensation. Thus far our discussion of compensating expatriate managers has not addressed the issue of equity between the compensation granted expatriate managers and that given to HCNs in similar positions. Often, the compensation package offered the expatriate manager is much more lucrative than that offered an HCN occupying an equivalent position of power and responsibility. The equity issue becomes even more complicated when dealing with TCNs. For example, if a U.S. international oil firm transfers a Venezuelan executive to its Peruvian operations, should the Venezuelan be paid according to Peruvian, Venezuelan, or U.S. standards?

Unfortunately there is no simple solution to this problem, and MNCs use a variety of approaches in grappling with it. For example, Hewlett-Packard pays expatriates on short-term assignments according to home country standards and those on long-term assignments according to host country standards. Minnesota Mining & Manufacturing (3M) compares the compensation package it offers in the expatriate's home country with what it normally pays HCNs and then gives the expatriate the higher pay package. Phillips Petroleum pegs a TCN's salary to that of the person's home country, but offers housing allowances, educational benefits, and home leaves based on costs in the host country.[56]

Retention and Turnover

Another important element of international HRM focuses on retention and turnover. **Retention** is the extent to which a firm is able to retain employees. **Turnover**, essentially the opposite, is the rate at which people leave a firm.

People choose to leave a firm for any number of reasons—for example, dissatisfaction with their current pay or promotion opportunities or receipt of a better offer to work elsewhere. Turnover is often a result of job transitions such as those associated with expatriation and repatriation: a worker contemplating changing work locations may also consider changing employers.[57] Turnover is a particular problem in international business because of the high cost of developing managers' international business skills.[58] Managers with strong reputations for having those skills are in high demand. As noted earlier, some firms even rely on headhunters to help them locate prospective managers currently working for other firms. For exactly the same reason—a scarcity of skilled, experienced managers—keeping successful managers should be a high priority for any international business.[59] One way to control managerial turnover is to develop strategies designed to reduce expatriate failure and repatriate failure. These may include providing career development counseling or cross-cultural training to ease the stress of relocation.

A firm also may have to provide special inducements or incentives to its most valuable international managers. For example, they may receive higher salaries or be given a greater say in choosing their assignments. The firm may also make stronger guarantees to them regarding the time frame of their assignments. For example, a firm may want to hire a particularly skillful TCN to run its operation in Italy. Because of the costs and other problems associated with relocation, the individual may consider the assignment only if the firm guarantees it will last for a minimum of, say, five years.[60]

Another important element of turnover management is the exit interview. An **exit interview** is an interview with an employee who is leaving a firm. Its purpose is to find out as much as possible about why the person decided to leave. Given the distances involved in international business, however, firms may be reluctant to do exit interviews. Yet the potential value of the information gleaned is high: managers can use it to reduce future employee losses. Thus, firms should give careful consideration to using such interviews as part of their strategy for reducing turnover.

Human Resource Issues for Nonmanagerial Employees

Next, we shift the focus of our discussion of HR issues to nonmanagerial employees in host countries. The standard HRM tasks associated with nonmanagerial employees—recruitment, selection, training, compensation, and so on—are strongly influenced by local laws, culture, and economic conditions. To prosper in the host country environment, HR managers must not fall prey to their own self-referencing criteria. They must be willing to do things the way the locals want, not the way things are done at home. In short, "When in Rome, do as the Romans do." Thus, many MNCs hire HCNs to staff their HR operations so as to incorporate their local knowledge into the policies and procedures of the HR department.

Recruitment and Selection

In international firms' foreign operations, nonmanagerial employees, such as blue-collar production workers and white-collar office workers, are typically HCNs. In most cases, there are economic reasons for this decision: HCNs are usually cheaper to employ than are PCNs or TCNs. HCNs are also used because local laws often promote the hiring of locals. Immigration and visa laws, for example, typically restrict jobs to citizens and legal residents of the country. A few exceptions to this rule exist. Construction firms in rich countries like Saudi Arabia or Kuwait often use Korean or Pakistani labor because local citizens dislike the working conditions. And oil firms and airlines often employ PCNs and TCNs for high-skilled jobs such as drilling supervisor and pilot.

Nonetheless, an international business must develop and implement a plan for recruiting and selecting its employees in a host country market. This plan should include assessments of the firm's human resources needs, sources of labor, labor force skills and talents, and training requirements and should also account for special circumstances that exist in the local labor market. The chapter opening, for example, detailed how Toyota goes about recruiting and selecting U.S. employees for its U.S. production facilities.

When firms are hiring PCNs for foreign assignments, they must adhere to their home country's hiring regulations, laws, and norms. But when hiring HCNs, they must be aware of those regulations, laws, and norms within the host country. For example, in the United States laws and regulations prohibit a firm from discriminating against someone on the basis of gender, race, age, religion, and assorted other characteristics. Toyota had to ensure that during its selection of its U.S. employees, it did not violate any of those laws and regulations. Because of these restrictions, the selection process in the United States emphasizes job relatedness. Job-related criteria such as skills, abilities, and education can be used to hire employees; non–job-related criteria such as gender or age cannot. In some other countries, however, characteristics such as gender, religion, and skin color are commonly used in hiring decisions. For example, firms in Israel and Northern Ireland often discriminate on the basis of religion, and those in Saudi Arabia discriminate on the basis of gender.

Training and Development

HR managers must also assess the training and development needs of the host country's workforces in order to help them perform their jobs more effectively.[61] The training and development needs of local workforces depend on several factors. An important one is the location of the foreign operation. In highly industrialized markets, firms usually find a nucleus of capable workers who may need only a bit of firm-specific training. But in an area that is relatively underdeveloped, training needs will be much greater. For example, when Hilton began operating hotels in Eastern Europe, it found that waiters, hotel clerks, and other customer service employees lacked the basic skills necessary to provide high-quality service to guests. These employees were so accustomed to working in a planned economy, where there was little or no need to worry about customer satisfaction, that they had difficulty recognizing why they needed to change their workplace behavior. Hilton had to invest much more in training new employees there than it had anticipated.[62]

Training also is a critical element if an international business wants to take full advantages of locating production abroad. For example, in recent years, MNCs have shown a marked tendency to move facilities to certain areas, such as Honduras, Malaysia, and Indonesia, in order to capitalize on inexpensive labor. But often the productivity of this labor is low, unless the firm is willing to invest in workforce training. In Malaysia, for example, only one third of adults have more than a sixth-grade education; thus, training costs there can be quite high.

And the owner of Quality Coils, Inc., a U.S. maker of electromagnetic coils, closed the firm's plant in Connecticut and opened one in Ciudad Juarez, Mexico, because hourly wage rates there were one third as much as in Connecticut. The owner soon discovered, however, that productivity was also only one third of what it had been. This, combined with higher absenteeism and the personal costs of running a facility in Mexico, prompted him to move the operation back to Connecticut.[63]

Japan is the world leader in training and development. Its workers receive more annual training on a regular basis than do workers in any other country.[64] Workers in Germany, South Korea, Singapore, and France also receive more annual training than do their U.S. counterparts. On the other hand, firms in Hong Kong are reputed to do a relatively poor job of training and development.[65] Firms in the United States have begun to recognize the importance of training and development and are closing the gap.

Compensation and Performance Appraisal

Compensation and performance appraisal practices for nonmanagerial employees also differ dramatically among countries, depending on local laws, customs, and cultures. Individualistic cultures such as that of the United States focus on assessing the individual's performance and then compensating the person accordingly. More group-oriented cultures such as Japan's emphasize training and motivating the group and place less emphasis on individual performance appraisal and compensation. The HR manager at each foreign operation must develop and implement a performance appraisal and reporting system most appropriate for that setting, given the nature of the work being performed and the cultural context.[66] For example, while U.S. workers often appreciate feedback from the appraisal system—thereby allowing them to do better in the future—German workers are often resentful of feedback, believing that it requires them to admit failures and shortcomings.[67]

Compensation practices also reflect local laws, culture, and economic conditions. Prevailing wage rates vary among countries, which has caused many labor-intensive industries to migrate to countries such as Malaysia, Indonesia, and Guatemala. To attract workers, HR managers must ensure that their firms' wage scales are consistent with local norms.

But compensation packages entail incentive payments and benefit programs in addition to wages. International business researchers have found that the mix among wages, benefits, and incentive payments varies as a function of national culture. For example, wages on average accounted for 85 percent of the total compensation package for workers in 41 manufacturing industries in four Oriental countries. However, they amounted to only 56 percent of the total compensation package for workers in those same industries in five "Latin European" countries. By adjusting the composition of the compensation package to meet local norms, HR managers ensure that their workers (and the firm) get the maximum value from each compensation dollar spent.[68] Local laws also affect an international firm's compensation policies. For example, Mexican law requires employers to provide paid maternity leave, a Christmas bonus of 15 days' pay, and at least three months' severance pay for dismissed workers.

Labor Relations

A final component of international HRM is labor relations. Because of their complexity and importance, labor relations are often handled as a separate organizational function, apart from human resource management.

Comparative Labor Relations

Labor relations in a host country often reflect its laws, culture, social structure, and economic conditions. For example, membership in U.S. labor unions has been steadily declining in recent years and today constitutes less than 20 percent of the country's total workforce. Labor relations in the United States are heavily regulated by various laws, and both the actions of management toward labor and those of labor toward management are heavily restricted. Further, the formal labor agreement negotiated between a firm and a union is a binding contract enforceable in a court of law. Because of the heavy regulation, most negotiations are relatively formal and mechanical, with both parties relying on the letter of law.

However, a different situation exists in most other countries. For example, in some countries union membership is very high and continues to grow. Over half the world's workforce outside the United States belongs to labor unions.[69] In Europe, for example, labor unions are much more important than in the United States. Labor unions in most European countries are aligned with political parties, and their fortunes ebb and flow as a function of which party currently controls the government. In England, labor agreements are not legal contracts but merely understandings that can be broken by either party with no penalty. Throughout most of Europe, temporary work stoppages are frequently used by unions in a bid for public backing for their demands. For example, the transport workers' union in Paris often calls for daily work stoppages that result in the city's busses, subways, and railroads being totally shut down. The union hopes that the inconvenienced public will call on elected officials to do whatever it takes to avoid such stoppages in the future.

In contrast, labor relations in Japan tend to be cordial. Labor unions are actually created and run by businesses themselves. Unions and management tend to work cooperatively toward their mutual best interests. The Japanese culture discourages confrontation and hostility, and these norms carry over into labor relations. Disputes are usually resolved cordially and through mutual agreement. In the rare event that a third-party mediator is necessary, there is seldom any hard feelings or hostility after a decision has been rendered. Thus, strikes are relatively rare in Japan.

Collective Bargaining

Collective bargaining is the process used to make agreements between management and labor unions. As already noted, collective bargaining in the United States is highly regulated. But aside from passing the laws that regulate the process, government plays a relatively benign role in establishing labor agreements. Union and management representatives meet and negotiate a contract. That contract governs their collective working relationship until it expires, when a new contract is negotiated. Bargaining normally takes place on a firm-by-firm and union-by-union basis. For example, United Air Lines must bargain with a pilots' union, a flight attendants' union, a mechanics' union, and so on, one at a time. And each of these unions negotiates individually with each airline whose employees it represents.

In many other countries, the government is much more active in collective bargaining. For example, collective bargaining in Europe is often undertaken by representatives of several firms and unions, along with government officials. The outcome is an umbrella agreement that applies to entire industries and collections of related labor unions.[70] In Japan, collective bargaining also usually involves government officials, but is done on a firm-by-firm basis. A government official serves more as an observer, recording what transpires and answering any questions that arise during the negotiation.

Union Influence and Codetermination

Union influence can be manifested in various ways, including membership, strikes, and public relations. In Europe, much of the influence of labor unions arises from the premise of **industrial democracy**—the belief that workers should have a voice in how businesses are run. In some countries, most notably Germany, union influence extends far beyond traditional boundaries of labor-management relations. The approach taken in Germany is called **codetermination** and provides for cooperation between management and labor in running the business.

Codetermination is the result of a 1947 German law that required firms in the coal and steel industries to allow unions to have input into how the firms were run. The law has since been amended several times, and today it applies to all German firms with 2000 or more employees. (Firms in what was formerly East Germany are being brought under the codetermination legislation on a staggered basis.[71]) The law requires all covered firms to establish a supervisory board. Half the seats on this board are elected by the firm's owners (much like the board of directors of a U.S. corporation); the other half are appointed or elected by labor. Of the labor seats, one third are union officials and two thirds are elected by the workforce. One seat elected by labor must be occupied by a managerial employee, so management essentially controls a potential tie-breaking vote. The supervisory board oversees another board called the board of managers. This board, composed of the firm's top managers, actually runs the business on a day-to-day basis.

The German model represents the most extreme level of industrial democracy. However, other countries, including Sweden, the Netherlands, Norway, Luxembourg, Denmark, and France, take similar approaches in requiring some form of labor representation in running businesses. In contrast, Italy, Ireland, the United Kingdom, Spain, Greece, and Portugal have little or no mandated labor participation. The EU has advocated the German codetermination model for all its members, but it appears unlikely that most will adopt it anytime soon.[72] However, a clear goal of the EU is to standardize labor practices, employment regulations, and benefits packages throughout its member states.[73] So far, all EU members except the United Kingdom have agreed to a **social charter**, whereby employment conditions and practices will be standardized throughout the community. Worker participation reform is also spreading into Pacific Asia. For example, workers in Singapore have recently been given a considerably stronger voice in how businesses are operated.[74] And even though Japanese workers do not have a particularly strong voice in the management of their firms, they have traditionally enjoyed an abundance of personal power and control over how they perform their own jobs.

CHAPTER REVIEW

Summary

Human resource management is the set of activities directed at attracting, developing, and maintaining the effective workforce necessary to achieve a firm's objectives. Because the human resource function is central to a firm's success, top managers should adopt a strategic perspective on it.

International human resource needs are partially dictated by a firm's degree of internationalization. The relative degree of centralization versus decentralization of control also plays an important role. A basic staffing philosophy should be developed and followed.

Recruitment and selection are important elements of international human resource management. Some firms choose to recruit experienced managers for foreign assignments, while others hire younger, and more likely inexperienced, managers. Various avenues may be used for either approach to recruiting. The selection of managers for foreign assignments usually involves consideration of both business and international skills. Managers and firms must address a variety of expatriation and repatriation issues.

Training and development are also important aspects of international human resource management. The two principal components of this activity are the assessment of training needs and the selection of basic training methods and procedures.

A firm also must assess the performance of its international managers and determine their compensation. Compensation for expatriate managers usually includes a cost-of-living adjustment, as well as special benefits.

Given the high cost of training and development of expatriates, firms need to focus special attention on managing retention and turnover. Each part of international human resource management also must be addressed for the firm's nonmanagerial employees.

Labor relations pose an especially complex task for human resource managers and are often handled by a special department. One key aspect of labor relations is collective bargaining, or negotiating agreements with unions. Germany's practice of codetermination represents one interesting variation on labor relations.

Review Questions

1. What is human resource management?

2. Along what dimensions does domestic HRM differ from international HRM?

3. How does the degree of centralization or decentralization affect international staffing?

4. What are the basic issues involved in recruiting and selecting managers for foreign assignments?

5. What issues are at the core of expatriation and repatriation problems?

6. How does a firm go about assessing its training needs?

7. Why is performance appraisal important for international firms?

8. What special compensation and benefits issues arise in international HRM?

9. How does international HRM for nonmanagerial employees differ from that for managerial employees?

10. What is codetermination?

Questions for Discussion

1. How does HRM relate to other functional areas such as marketing, finance, and operations management?

2. Why and how does the scope of a firm's internationalization affect its HRM practices?

3. How are the different approaches to recruiting and selecting managers for foreign assignments similar and dissimilar?

4. Which are easier to assess, business skills or international skills? Why?

5. If you were being assigned to a foreign position, what specific training requests would you make of your employer?

6. Do you agree or disagree with the idea that some international assignments require special compensation?

7. How easy or difficult do you think it is to handle the equity issue in international compensation?

8. What does the high cost of replacing an international manager suggest regarding staffing philosophy?

9. Which do you think is easier, HRM for managerial employees or HRM for nonmanagerial employees? Why?

10. Do you think codetermination would work in the United States? Why or why not?

BUILDING GLOBAL SKILLS

Assume you are a manager for a growing international business. Your firm is among the leaders in its industry and has recently decided to emphasize its foreign operations even more. You have worked for the firm for ten years, and it is well known that you have been designated for fast-track consideration for top management. You have an MBA from a leading university program and currently earn $150,000 per year. You have two school-aged children, and your spouse has a thriving medical practice. Neither you nor your spouse has ever lived outside the United States.

Your boss has just told you he would like you to get some international experience. He has given you a list of ten possible locations and suggested you relocate to one of them. At the end of two years, you would return home to a new position (which would clearly be a promotion). He implied that a refusal to relocate would be a serious blow to your career with the firm. He has also suggested that you look into each location. While he and other top managers will have veto power, he has indicated that every effort will be made to accommodate your preference.

Finally, he has asked you to make a proposal regarding the compensation package you would request in order for you to accept the international assignment.

First, peruse the following list of ten locations. Select the three that appeal most to you, and then research each at the library. On the basis of your research, select your preferred location and draft a set of compensation and relocation benefits you would like to request.

Brussels	Moscow
London	Rome
Rio de Janerio	Seoul
Kyoto	Sydney
Singapore	Cairo

Bring to class your list of three "finalists," your specific choice (including your justification), and your proposed compensation and relocation package. Form a group with two or three of your classmates and share with them your location choices, the reasons for your choosing them, and the details regarding your compensation and relocation package.

Follow-up Questions

1. How similar or dissimilar were the preferences of the members of your group?

2. What were the most and the least important compensation factors?

3. Faced with the situation and the alternatives described above, would you consider refusing the international assignment and facing the consequences?

4. How interested are you personally in living and working abroad?

CLOSING CASE

"You Americans Work Too Hard"[75]

Andreas Drauschke and Angie Clark work comparable jobs for comparable pay at department stores in Berlin and suburban Washington, D.C. But there is no comparison when it comes to the hours they put in.

Mr. Drauschke's job calls for a 37-hour week with six weeks' annual leave. His store closes for the weekend at 2 p.m. on Saturday afternoon and stays open one evening each week—a new service in Germany that Mr. Drauschke detests. "I can't understand that people go shopping at night in America," says the 29-year-old, who supervises the auto, motorcycle and bicycle division at Karstadt, Germany's largest department-store chain. "Logically speaking, why should someone need to buy a bicycle at 8:30 p.m.?"

Mrs. Clark works at least 44 hours a week, including evening shifts and frequent Saturdays and Sundays. She often brings paperwork home with her, spends her days off scouting the competition, and never takes more than a week off at a time. "If I took any more, I'd feel like I was losing control," says the senior merchandising manager at J.C. Penney in Springfield, Va.

The 50-year-old Mrs. Clark was born in Germany but feels like an alien when she visits her native land. "Germans put leisure first and work second," she says. "In America it's the other way around."

While Americans often marvel at German industriousness, a comparison of actual workloads explodes such national stereotypes. In manufacturing, for instance, the weekly U.S. average is 37.7 hours and rising; in Germany it is 30 hours and has fallen steadily over recent decades. All German workers are guaranteed by law a minimum of five weeks' annual holiday.

A day spent at a German and an American department store also shows a wide gulf in the two countries' work ethic, at least as measured by attitudes toward time. The Germans fiercely resist any incursions on their leisure hours, while many J.C. Penney employees work second jobs and rack up 60 hours a week.

But long and irregular hours come at a price. Staff turnover at the German store is negligible; at J.C. Penney it is 40 percent a year. Germans serve apprenticeships of two to three years and know their wares inside out. Workers at J.C. Penney receive training of two to three days. And it is economic necessity, more than any devotion to work for its own sake, that appears to motivate most of the American employees.

"First it's need and then it's greed," says Sylvia Johnson, who sells full-time at J.C. Penney and works another 15 to 20 hours a week doing data entry at a computer firm. The two jobs helped her put one child through medical school and another through college. Now 51, Mrs. Johnson says she doesn't need to work so hard—but still does.

"My husband and I have a comfortable home and three cars," she says. "But I guess you always feel like you want something more as a reward for all the hard work you've done."

Mr. Drauschke, the German supervisor, has a much different view: Work hard when you're on the job and get out as fast as you can. A passionate gardener with a wife and young child, he comes in 20 minutes earlier than the rest of his staff but otherwise has no interest in working beyond the 37 hours his contract mandates, even if it means more money. "Free time can't be paid for," he says.

The desire to keep hours short is an obsession in Germany—and a constant mission of its powerful unions. When Germany introduced Thursday night shopping in 1989, retail workers went on strike. And Mr. Drauschke finds it hard to staff the extra two hours on Thursday evening, even though the late shift is rewarded with an hour less overall on the job. "My wife is opposed to my coming home late," one worker tells him when asked if he will work until 8:30 on a coming Thursday.

Mr. Drauschke, like other Germans, also finds the American habit of taking a second job inconceivable. "I already get home at 7. When should I work?" he asks. As for vacations, it is illegal—yes, illegal—for Germans to work at other jobs during holidays, a time that "is strictly for recovering," Mr. Drauschke explains. He adds: "If we had conditions like in America, you would have to think hard if you wanted to go on in this line of work."

At J.C. Penney, the workday of the merchandising manager Mrs. Clark begins at 8 a.m. when she rides a service elevator to her windowless office off a stock room. Though the store doesn't open until 10 a.m., she feels she needs the extra time to check floor dis-

plays and schedules. Most of the sales staff clock in at about 9 a.m. to set up registers and restock shelves—a sharp contrast to Karstadt, where salespeople come in just moments before the shop opens.

Case Questions

1. How does HRM in the United States differ from HRM in Germany?

2. What do you see as the basic advantages and disadvantages of each system?

3. If you were the top HRM executive for an international department store chain with stores in both Germany and the United States, what basic issues would you need to address regarding corporate HR policies?

4. Are the issues more or less acute in the retailing industry versus other industries?

5. Under which system would you prefer to work?

CHAPTER NOTES

1. "Toyota Retooled," *Business Week*, April 4, 1994, pp. 54–57; "Toyota Takes Pains, and Time, Filling Jobs at Its Kentucky Plant," *Wall Street Journal*, December 1, 1987, pp. 1, 29; "How Does Japan Inc. Pick Its American Workers?" *Business Week*, October 3, 1988, pp. 84–88; Louis Kraar, "Japan's Gung-Ho U.S. Car Plants," *Fortune*, January 30, 1989, pp. 98–108.

2. Sakhawat Hossain and Herbert J. Davis, "Some Thoughts on International Personnel Management as an Emerging Field," in Albert Nedd (guest editor), Gerald R. Ferris, and Kendrith M. Rowland (eds.), *Research in Personnel and Human Resources Management (Supplement 1: International Human Resources Management)* (Greenwich, Conn.: JAI Press, 1989), pp. 121–136.

3. Gregory D. Chowanec and Charles N. Newstrom, "The Strategic Management of International Human Resources," *Business Quarterly* (Autumn 1991), pp. 65–70.

4. Richard M. Steers, "The Cultural Imperative in HRM Research," in Albert Nedd (guest editor), Gerald R. Ferris and Kendrith M. Rowland (eds.), *Research in Personnel and*

Human Resources Management (Supplement 1: International Human Resources Management) (Greenwich, Conn.: JAI Press, 1989), pp. 23–32.

5. John Milliman, Mary Ann Von Glinow, and Maria Nathan, "Organizational Life Cycles and Strategic International Human Resource Management in Multinational Companies: Implications for Congruence Theory," *Academy of Management Review* (July 1991), pp. 318–339.

6. Ruth G. Shaeffer, "Matching International Business Growth and International Management Development," *Human Resource Planning*, Vol. 12, No. 1 (1992), pp. 29–35.

7. Nakiye Boyacigiller, "The Role of Expatriates in the Management of Interdependence, Complexity, and Risk in Multinational Corporations," *Journal of International Business Studies*, Vol. 21, No. 3 (Third Quarter 1990), pp. 357–382.

8. Christopher Lorenz, "Global executives walk a tightrope," *Financial Times*, October 12, 1992, p. 10.

9. Allan Bird and Roger Dunbar, "Getting the Job Done Over There: Improving Expatriate Productivity," *National Productivity Review* (Spring 1991), pp. 145–156.

10. "The High Cost of Expatriation," *Management Review* (July 1990), pp. 40–41.

11. "Like Factory Workers, Professionals Face Loss of Jobs to Foreigners," *Wall Street Journal*, March 17, 1993, pp. A1, A9.

12. Cynthia Fetterolf, "Hiring Local Managers and Employees Overseas," *The International Executive* (May–June 1990), pp. 22–26.

13. Ronald Henkoff, "Inside Andersen's Army of Advice," *Fortune*, October 4, 1993, pp. 79ff.

14. "More U.S. Companies Venture Overseas for Directors Offering Fresh Perspectives," *Wall Street Journal*, January 22, 1992, pp. B1, B8.

15. Ellen Brandt, "Global HR," *Personnel Journal* (March 1991), pp. 38–44.

16. "Japan should give the locals a chance," *Financial Times*, November 15, 1991, p. 15.

17. Frank Heller, "Human Resource Utilization: A Model Based on East-West Research," *The International Executive* (January-February 1992), pp. 15–25.

18. J. Steward Black, Hal B. Gregersen, and Mark E. Mendenhall, *Global Assignments* (San Francisco: Jossey-Bass, 1992).

19. Jennifer J. Laabs, "The Global Talent Search," *Personnel Journal* (August 1991), pp. 38–44.

20. "Long Frowned Upon, Switching Employers Is Climbing in Japan," *Wall Street Journal*, November 18, 1991, pp. B1, B4.

21. "Firms in Europe Try to Find Executives Who Can Cross Borders in a Single Bound," *Wall Street Journal*, January 25, 1991.

22. "Foreign Accents Proliferate in Top Ranks as U.S. Companies Find Talent Abroad," *Wall Street Journal*, May 21, 1992, pp. B1, B7.

23. Hugh Scullion, "Strategic Recruitment and Development of the Global Manager," in *Proceedings of the Third Conference on International Personnel and Human Resources Management*, Ashridge Management College, Berkhamsted, United Kingdom, 1992. See also "Glut of Graduates Lets Recruiters Pick Only the Best," *Wall Street Journal*, May 20, 1993, p. B1.

24. Richard M. Hodgetts and Fred Luthans, "U.S. Multinationals; Compensation Strategies," *Compensation & Benefits Review* (January-February 1993), pp. 57–62.

25. "Younger Managers Learn Global Skills," *Wall Street Journal*, March 31, 1992, p. B1.

26. J. Stewart Black and Gregory Stephens, "The Influence of the Spouse on American Expatriate Adjustment in Overseas Assignments," *Journal of Management*, Vol. 15 (1989), pp. 529–544.

27. M. G. Harvey, "The Multinational Corporation's Expatriate Problem: An Application of Murphy's Law," *Business Horizons*, Vol. 26 (1983), pp. 71–78.

28. Allan Bird and Roger Dunbar, "Getting the Job Done Over There: Improving Expatriate Productivity," *National Productivity Review* (Spring 1991), pp. 145–156.

29. Rosalie L. Tung, "Selection and training procedures of U.S., European, and Japanese multinationals," *California Management Review*, Vol. 25, No. 1 (1982), pp. 57–71.

30. "As Costs of Overseas Assignments Climb, Firms Select Expatriates More Carefully," *Wall Street Journal*, January 9, 1992, pp. B1, B6.

31. "Companies Use Cross-Cultural Training to Help Their Employees Adjust Abroad," *Wall Street Journal*, August 9, 1992, pp. B1, B6.

32. Nancy J. Adler and Dafna N. Izraeli, *Women in Management* (New York: M.E. Sharp, 1988).

33. Joel D. Nicholson, Lee P. Stepina, and Wayne Hochwarter, "Psychological Aspects of Expatriate Effectiveness," in Ben B. Shaw and John E. Beck (guest editors), Gerald R. Ferris and Kendrith M. Rowland (eds.), *Research in Personnel and Human Resources Management (Supplement 2: International Human Resources Management)* (Greenwich, Conn.: JAI Press, 1990), pp. 127–145.

34. Gary P. Ferraro, *The Cultural Dimension of International Business* (Englewood Cliffs, N.J.: Prentice Hall, 1990), pp. 143-144.

35. L. V. Newman, "A Process Perspective on Expatriate Adjustment," in *Proceedings of the Third Conference on International Personnel and Human Resources Management*, Ashridge Management College, Berkhamsted, United Kingdom, 1992.

36. J. Steward Black and Hal B. Gregersen, "When Yankee Comes Home: Factors Related to Expatriate and Spouse Repatriation Adjustment," *Journal of International Business Studies* (Fourth Quarter 1991), pp. 671–694.

37. "Expatriates Find Long Stints Abroad Can Close Doors to Credit at Home," *Wall Street Journal*, May 17, 1993, pp. B1, B6.

38. Black and Gregersen, op. cit.

39. "As Costs of Overseas Assignments Climb, Firms Select Expatriates More Carefully," *Wall Street Journal*, January 9, 1992, pp. B1, B4.

40. Daniel C. Feldman and David C. Thomas, "Career Management Issues Facing Expatriates," *Journal of International Business Studies*, Vol. 23, No. 2 (Second Quarter 1992), pp. 271–293; J. Stewart Black and Hal B. Gregersen, "The Other Half of the Picture: Antecedents of Spouse Cross-Cultural Adjustment," *Journal of International Business Studies*, Vol. 22, No. 3 (Third Quarter 1991), pp. 461–477.

41. Paul Vanderbroeck, "Long-Term Human Resource Development in Multinational Organizations," *Sloan Management Review* (Fall 1992), pp. 95–99.

42. Stephen H. Rhinesmith, "Going Global From the Inside Out," *Training & Development* (November 1991), pp. 42–47.

43. Joseph A. Petrick and Lisa Russell-Robles, "Challenges in the Education of the Contemporary U.S. International Manager," *The International Executive* (May-June 1992), pp. 251–261.

44. R. D. Albert, "Cultural Diversity and Cross-Cultural Training Approaches in Multinational Organizations: Major Issues and Approaches," in *Proceedings of the Third Conference on International Personnel and Human Resources Management*, Ashridge Management College, Berkhamsted, United Kingdom, 1992. See also "Employers Ignore Expatriate Wives at Their Own Peril," *Wall Street Journal*, March 2, 1992, p. A12.

45. Peter R. Schleger, "Making International Videos: An Odyssey," *Training & Development* (February 1992), pp. 25–32.

46. Michael J. Marquardt and Dean W. Engel, "HRD Competencies for a Shrinking World," *Training & Development* (May 1993), pp. 59–60.

47. Cynthia Lee and Miriam Erez, "Context-Oriented Strategies in Planning Career Promotion: A Cross-Cultural Comparison," in *Proceedings of the Third Conference on International Personnel and Human Resources Management*, Ashridge Management College, Berkhamsted, United Kingdom, 1992.

48. "Korea's Biggest Firm Teaches Junior Execs Strange Foreign Ways," *Wall Street Journal*, December 30, 1992, pp. A1, A4.

49. Wouter van Ginneken and Rolph van der Hoeven, "Industrialisation, Employment, and Earnings (1950–1987): An International Survey," *International Labour Review*, Vol. 128, No. 5 (1989), pp. 571–599.

50. K. S. Law, "A New Perspective on Determining an Organization-Wide Pay Structure," in *Proceedings of the Third Conference on International Personnel and Human Resources Management*, Ashridge Management College, Berkhamsted, United Kingdom, 1992.

51. "What's an Expatriate?" *Wall Street Journal*, April 21, 1993, pp. R1, R5.

52. Michael J. Bishko, "Compensating Your Overseas Executives, Part 1: Strategies for the 1990s," *Compensation & Benefits Review* (May-June 1990), pp. 33–43.

53. Richard M. Hodgetts and Fred Luthans, "U.S. Multinationals' Expatriate Compensation Strategies," *Compensation & Benefits Review* (January-February 1993), pp. 57–62.

54. "Cultural divide," *The Economist*, February 8, 1992, p. 33.

55. "For Executives Around the Globe, Pay Packages Aren't Worlds Apart," *Wall Street Journal*, October 12, 1992, pp. B1, B5.

56. "What's an Expatriate," *Wall Street Journal*, April 21, 1993, pp. R4–R5.

57. Yoram Zeira and Moshe Banai, "Selecting Managers for Foreign Assignments," *Management Decision*, Vol. 25 (1987), pp. 38–40.

58. Beverly Geber, "The Care and Breeding of Global Managers," *Training* (July 1992), pp. 32–37.

59. Richard A. Guzzo, Katherine A. Noonan, and Efrat Elron, "A Model of Organizational HR Practices and Expatriate Retention," in *Proceedings of the Third Conference on International Personnel and Human Resources Management*, Ashridge Management College, Berkhamsted, United Kingdom, 1992.

60. Larry Crump, "Developing Effective Personnel for International Business," *Management Japan* (Autumn 1990), pp. 31–36.

61. Mike Regan, "Developing the Middle Manager for Globalisation," in *Proceedings of the Third Conference on International Personnel and Human Resources Management*, Ashridge Management College, Berkhamsted, United Kingdom, 1992.

62. Robert O'Connor, "Retraining Eastern Europe," *Training* (November 1992), pp. 41–45.

63. "Some U.S. Companies Find Mexican Workers Not So Cheap After All," *Wall Street Journal*, September 15, 1993, pp. A1, A16.

64. Mitsuru Wakabayashi and George Graen, "Human Resource Development of Japanese Managers," in Albert Nedd (guest editor), Gerald R. Ferris and Kendrith M. Rowland (eds.), *Research in Personnel and Human Resources Management (Supplement 1: International Human Resources Management* (Greenwich, Conn.: JAI Press, 1989), pp. 235–256.

65. Paul S. Kirkbride and Sara F. Y. Tang, "Training in Hong Kong," in Ben B. Shaw and John E. Beck (guest editors), Gerald R. Ferris and Kendrith M. Rowland (eds.), *Research in Personnel and Human Resources Management (Supplement 2: International Human Resources Management)* (Greenwich, Conn.: JAI Press, 1990), pp. 293–312.

66. Uco J. Wiersam, Peter T. van den Berg, and Gary P. Latham, "The Practicality of Performance Appraisal Instruments: A Replication and Extension," in *Proceedings of the Third Conference on International Personnel and Human Resources Management,* Ashridge Management College, Berkhamsted, United Kingdom, 1992.

67. Christopher Lorenz, "Learning to live with a cultural mix," *Financial Times,* April 23, 1993, p. 18.

68. Anthony M. Townsend, K. Dow Scott, and Steven E. Markham, "An Examination of Country and Culture-Based Differences in Compensation Practices," *Journal of International Business Studies,* Vol. 21, No. 4 (Fourth Quarter 1990), pp. 667–678.

69. David G. Blanchflower and Richard B. Freeman, "Unionism in the United States and Other Advanced OECD Countries," *Industrial Relations* (Winter 1992), pp. 56–79.

70. David A. MacPherson and James B. Stewart, "The Effect of International Competition on Union and Nonunion Wages," *Industrial and Labor Relations Review* (April 1990), pp. 434–446.

71. K. Volker, U. Hanel, C. Brewster, and A. Hegewisch, "Human Resource Management and the Re-Unification of Germany," in *Proceedings of the Third Conference on International Personnel and Human Resources Management,* Ashridge Management College, Berkhamsted, United Kingdom, 1992.

72. Dennis R. Briscoe, "Coping with the Human Resource Implications of the EC 1992," in *Proceedings of the Third Conference on International Personnel and Human Resources Management,* Ashridge Management College, Berkhamsted, United Kingdom, 1992.

73. Georges Spyropoulos, "Labour Law and Labour Relations in Tomorrow's Social Europe," *International Labor Review,* Vol. 129, No. 6 (1990), pp. 733–750.

74. Cheng Soo May, "Worker Participation in Private Companies in Singapore," in Albert Nedd (guest editor), Gerald R. Ferris and Kendrith M. Rowland (eds.), *Research in Personnel and Human Resources Management (Supplement 1: International Human Resources Management* (Greenwich, Conn.: JAI Press, 1989), pp. 97–120.

75. Daniel Benjamin and Tony Horwitz, "German View: 'You Americans Work Too Hard—and for What' " *The Wall Street Journal,* July 14, 1994, pp. B5–B6. Reprinted by permission of *The Wall Street Journal,* © 1994 Dow Jones & Company, Inc. All Rights Reserved Worldwide.

Comprehensive Cases

Lloyd's of London

Picture a smoky, seventeenth-century, English coffee house echoing with the mingled voices of merchants, farmers, and sea captains. Now picture a gleaming, modern skyscraper housing thousands of executives clustered around humming computers and fax machines. What do these two scenes have in common? Both are snapshots of the same organization, Lloyd's of London.

Today, Lloyd's of London is the world's best-known insurance organization. Athletes' legs and arms, rock singers' voices, and governments' satellites and military hardware are among the more unusual properties insured with Lloyd's. Lloyd's lost over $1 million when Luciano Pavarotti had to cancel a concert in Italy because of a sore throat. But Lloyd's loves to pay out on such claims, for they invariably yield a goldmine of free publicity that the organization's less known competitors envy. Even though Lloyd's is still headquartered in London, the organization does about 75 percent of its business outside the United Kingdom, with 40 percent coming from the United States.

Lloyd's was started in 1688. At that time, coffee houses were a common forum for informal business transactions. Edward Lloyd's coffee house attracted a clientele of merchants, ship's captains, and others interested in foreign trade. These merchants and sea captains began to offer a share of the profits from their voyages in return for investors' sharing the risk of a loss at sea. An individual investor would agree to reimburse, or insure, the captain in the event of a loss (due to a shipwreck or to pirates, for example), and the captain would agree to pay the investor a share of the profits if there were no loss. The primary investor, in turn, would then line up other investors to help him cover his own losses, if any, in return for a share of his profits.

Today, Lloyd's is one of the world's largest insurance organizations, and it still conducts business much as it did 300 years ago. Individual insurance underwriters, called "working Names," accept risk on behalf of a group of outside investors, "external Names." Each collection of Names is called a syndicate. Some syndicates have thousands of members; others have only a few dozen.

Until the mid-1970s, Lloyd's was viewed as one of Britain's most exclusive clubs. One could not simply invest in Lloyd's by buying stock. Rather, one was elected to membership on the basis of one's wealth, and Lloyd's Names represented the cream of British society. A sound reason existed for this method of selection. Unlike many corporations, which limit the personal liability of their shareholders to the actual amount invested, each of the individual Names personally accepts unlimited liability for paying off his or her share of claims on insurance that his or her syndicate has underwritten. Since 1975, however, Lloyd's has become a less exclusive club. To expand its underwriting activities, it needed more capital and thus more Names, so it hired recruiters to attract new blood into its syndicates. These recruiters were quite successful: between 1975 and 1978, the number of Names nearly doubled, from 3,917 to 7,710; by 1989, it was 34,218.

For most of its 300-year existence, the unlimited liability of Lloyd's Names was more a theoretical threat than a real possibility. For example, from 1967 to 1987, Lloyd's enjoyed profitable operations. But in the past decade, the threat has turned into a nightmarish reality for many Names. The net losses (premiums minus claim settlements and operating costs) to date that are attributable to policies written from 1988 to 1991 alone total $10 billion. (Lloyd's accounting system operates three years in arrears in order to match claims, which are filed after the insurance was written, with premium income.) This total is likely to rise because claims against those policies continue to pour into Lloyd's offices. An estimated $7.5 to $13 billion will be needed to settle all claims not yet filed against the organization.

Some of these losses are attributable to what might be considered "normal" events in the insurance industry—hurricanes, earthquakes, floods, destruction of North Sea oil rigs, even the grounding of the *Exxon Valdez*. But the real problem lies in so-called long-tailed risks, where claims are submitted many years after an insurance policy is written. Because of the hidden nature of such risks, they are often underestimated and the premiums therefore underpriced. Lloyd's long-tailed risk problem is centered in the United States, in particular on asbestosis and pollution insurance claims. Asbestosis may develop from exposure to asbestos that occurred decades ago; thus, assessing which firm was actually at fault is difficult. U.S. manufacturers and users of asbestos products settled most asbestosis litigation through a multi-billion-dollar class action suit and then presented their insurance firms, including Lloyd's, with the bill.

But the impact of asbestosis on insurers pales in comparison to that of pollution claims. Legal liabilities under U.S. environmental laws are far reaching. The Superfund, created in 1980, has been particularly troublesome. The Superfund authorizes the U.S. Environmental Protection Agency to file suit against persons responsible for contaminating active or abandoned hazardous waste disposal sites. Usually these persons are the operators of the sites. However, landowners, former landowners, lenders, transporters of the wastes, and even customers of the hazardous waste sites have also been drawn into Superfund litigation because often the original defendant countersues them in order to spread the cost of cleaning up the disposal site. At one disposal site in Ohio, for example, 289 generators and transporters of hazardous wastes were found to be jointly and severally responsible for cleaning up the site. Inevitably, in such cases, the insurance providers of each party get drawn into the litigation as well.

Much of this legal liability was unanticipated by insurance firms. For example, an insurer of a motor carrier specializing in transportation of hazardous wastes would normally price its policy based on the carrier's past safety record, the quality of its employee training programs, and other factors controllable by its managers. Ignorant of its superfund exposure, the insurer would not consider the likelihood that the carrier (and its insurer) would end up paying for the cleanup of the disposal site. Thus, it would, inadvertently, underprice its policies.

Long-tailed insurance risks like asbestosis and pollution liability account for much of the existing and expected losses suffered by Lloyd's Names. Legally, because of their unlimited liability, the Names who participated in insurance syndicates in the 1980s will have to cough up billions of additional dollars to pay these claims. However, many of the Names have already been financially devastated and so have little ability to honor their pledges to pay these claims.

Lloyd's problems have created a new sector of Britain's upper and upper-middle classes: *deficit millionaires,* persons who owe Lloyd's at least £1 million to cover past insurance losses. Titled gentlemen, society matrons, members of parliament, and former RAF officers who valiantly defended their country in its darkest hour face bills for millions of pounds they don't have and so are forced to appear before Lloyd's Hardship Committee. This committee reads them their financial last rights and strips them of all their assets except "a modest and only home," which reverts to Lloyd's after their deaths. So far, over 1400 desperate Names have been forced to place their fate in the hands of the Hardship Committee. Others have filed for bankruptcy, and, sadly, at least seven have ended their own lives as a result of their financial troubles.

The most popular approach, however, is one familiar in the United States: many Names are suing Lloyd's for negligence, fraud, and favoritism. By one estimate, 60 percent of the external Names have filed lawsuits against Lloyd's. Newer Names claim they were duped into investing in the riskier syndicates, while more profitable insurance opportunities were reserved for the working Names and external Names of longer standing. Some external Names are claiming that Lloyd's failed to warn them about the riskiness of its U.S. underwriting activities. They cite a 1981 letter from a Chicago law firm and a 1982 audit report from a London accounting firm warning about the potential liability of asbestosis claims. They say this information was not disseminated to them. And some U.S. Names have tried—so far unsuccessfully—to have their claims heard in U.S. courts, arguing that Lloyd's violated U.S. securities and racketeering laws.

Lloyd's problems do not end there. To continue to underwrite insurance, the organization needs new capital. But many Names are withdrawing, fearing increased financial exposure. Membership has dropped from its peak of 34,218 in 1989 to fewer than 20,000 today. To attract new capital, Lloyd's has been forced to change two of its longstanding traditions. Unlimited liability was effectively ended in 1992 with the creation of a mandatory stop-loss insurance policy, which places a ceiling on individual losses at $3.6 million over a four-year period. Lloyd's also abandoned its reliance on individual investors by changing its rules in 1993 to allow corporate and institutional investors to participate in its underwriting business. It initially attracted 30 firms willing to inject almost $3 billion of new capital into the organization.

Lloyd's faces an uncertain future. At the turn of this century, it controlled over half of the world's insurance underwriting. Today, excluding marine insurance, it has only 2 percent. This dramatic loss of market share has come as a result of fierce worldwide competition throughout the insurance industry. Moreover, the recent crises have cost the organization dearly, damaging its reputation for integrity and financial responsibility, which had been built up over 300 years. No doubt British courts will be tied up with messy lawsuits for the rest of the century as Lloyd's pressures the Names to honor their unlimited liability commitments, while the Names countersue for fraud and negligence. Many observers agree that Lloyd's must continue to make fundamental changes in how it does business or face the very real possibility of going under.

Discussion Questions

1. U.S. courts have determined that U.S. investors in Lloyd's must pursue their legal claims against the organization in British courts. Do you agree with this? Should U.S. citizens always have the right to have their claims against foreigners heard in U.S. courts? Why or why not? As a result of this decision, what precautions should potential U.S. Names take before deciding to invest in Lloyd's?

2. Should Lloyd's have gone further in assessing its exposure to asbestosis and pollution claims in the United States? More generally, what precautions should firms undertake when doing business in foreign markets?

3. How will ending the unlimited liability of Names affect Lloyd's operations?

4. What will be the impact of allowing firms and institutional investors to join Lloyd's? Will they force additional changes in the way Lloyd's is managed?

5. If you were in charge of Lloyd's, what would you do to restore the organization's faded luster?

Sources

"Lloyd's of London—A Sketch History" (London: Lloyd's publications, no date); *United States v. Chem-Dyne Corp.,* 572 F. Supp. 802 (S.D. Ohio 1983); "Why Lloyd's Is Looking for Its Own Safety Net," *Business Week,* September 23, 1991, pp. 84–85; "Lloyd's of London, an Insurance Bulwark, Is a Firm Under Siege," *Wall Street Journal,* October 24, 1989, pp. A1, A18; "The New Broom at Lloyd's at London," *Business Week,* January 14, 1991, p. 54; "Lloyd's Plans to Put Cap on Exposure, Now Open-Ended, of Members to Losses," *Wall Street Journal,* January 16, 1992, p. A8; "Toughing it out," *The Economist,* February 22, 1992, p. 70; "Lloyd's wins one US judgment in dispute over jurisdiction," *Financial Times,* March 3, 1992, p. 22; "Lloyd's to Cap Loss Exposure, Rejects Bailout," *Wall Street Journal,* June 19, 1992, p. A8; Julian Barnes, "The Deficit Millionaires," *The New Yorker,* September 20, 1993, pp. 74ff; "Lloyd's 'Names' Vote to Admit New Investors," *Wall Street Journal,* October 21, 1993, p. A19; "Spurning the lifebelt," *The Economist,* January 22, 1994, p. 86; "Mess at Lloyd's May Have a Darker Side," *Wall Street Journal,* March 17, 1994, p. A10.

The Uphill Climb of Beijing Jeep

Changes in political relationship among countries affect the opportunities available to international businesses. One of the most dramatic examples of this occurred with the 1978 announcement of an "Open Door" policy by the People's Republic of China, followed by the restoration of diplomatic relations between the United States and China in 1979. Every major North American, European, and Asian firm salivated at the prospect of selling its products to China's 1.1 billion citizens. Although the income levels of Chinese consumers were low (only $470 per capita annually), those consumers had little access to consumer goods, particularly high-quality ones of the sort produced by the OECD countries. Further, as foreign firms contemplated the wages paid to Chinese workers—extremely low by Western standards—visions of an infinite supply of cheap, docile workers danced in the heads of corporate cost accountants. Western firms also saw China as a launching pad for invading the Asian market and blunting the competitive strengths of their Japanese rivals.

American Motors Corporation (AMC), the maker of the famous Jeep line of four-wheel-drive vehicles, was one of the firms drawn to the lure of the Chinese market. In January 1979, AMC began negotiations with officials of the Beijing Automotive Works

(BAW), a manufacturer of four-wheel-drive vehicles owned by the Beijing Municipal Government. After four years of seemingly endless and fruitless negotiations, AMC executives flew to Beijing in May 1983 to sign a 20-year contract with BAW and the Beijing government in the Great Hall of the People. When news of the agreement became public, AMC's stock price rose 40 percent.

The agreement called for the creation of a joint venture called the Beijing Jeep Corporation. BAW received a half interest in the joint venture in return for its contribution of $28 million in assets (its factory in Beijing) and $7 million in cash, denominated in the local Chinese currency, the renminbi. AMC, for a mere $8 million in cash and American technology valued at an additional $8 million, received a half interest. The contract gave AMC the right to repatriate its earnings from the joint venture, up to the amount of its original investment, back to the United States. AMC was also given the option of increasing its ownership share of Beijing Jeep to 70 percent by reinvesting its dividends in the joint venture.

Most of what AMC brought to the joint venture was technology and managerial experience. AMC agreed to help Beijing Jeep modernize its existing product, a jeeplike vehicle called the BJ212, and to design a new four-wheel-drive vehicle for sale to domestic and export markets. It also promised to transfer to Beijing Jeep on a continuous basis modern automotive technology and intellectual property. Further, it pledged to provide the joint venture with its know-how in managing the manufacture of automobiles, as well as the managing of R&D for new automotive technology. AMC also consented to distribute and sell Beijing Jeep's output internationally and to help develop a network of automotive parts producers in the Beijing area to supply the joint venture.

Although the venture didn't officially start until the beginning of 1984, shortly after the signing of the contract AMC sent teams of employees to Beijing to scout out potential problems. They quickly noticed that, by U.S. standards, the factory was overstaffed and productivity was low. Workers took extended lunch and tea breaks and often stood around with nothing to do. Production was supposed to end at 5:30 p.m., but many employees quit early in order to shower before bicycling home. AMC's advance team was shocked to observe that the only piece of furniture in the offices of many Chinese managers was a bed, which the managers used for their traditional afternoon nap. They were also disturbed by the nearly equal pay received by workers of all skill and experience levels and a lack of bonuses for extraordinary performance—a clear clash between capitalist incentives and communist ideology.

More important, AMC officials soon discovered that the joint venture document contained troubling ambiguities and that, to their horror, the Chinese viewed the signing of the agreement as an opportunity to reopen negotiations with AMC. For example, shortly before Beijing Jeep was to begin operations, the Chinese demanded an additional $6 million for equipment they had recently added to the factory. AMC officials agreed to allow BAW to be repaid the monies out of Beijing Jeep's future profits.

Another problem arose over managerial compensation. Both U.S. citizens and Chinese citizens were on Beijing Jeep's upper management team. The Chinese managers, as befits a communist society, were paid little more than the production workers—perhaps $100 per month. To the U.S. managers, however, Beijing was a hardship post; so AMC (and Beijing Jeep) had to amply compensate them. As a result, the Chinese argued that Beijing Jeep should pay the five top Chinese managers $40,000 per year so that their pay more closely approximated the $5,000 to $7,000 monthly salaries the U.S. managers would be making. After much arguing, AMC agreed. However, while Beijing Jeep's accounts were charged U.S.-like salaries for the Chinese managers, those managers continued to receive Chinese-level salaries. AMC officials were left to wonder where the excess salary funds were going.

Cultural differences were a constant source of friction. For example, Beijing Jeep was to pay for the housing and incidental expenses of its U.S. managers. The U.S. employees were unhappy with the spartan hotel accommodations they were originally assigned and so moved into more expensive Western-style hotels. All told, the costs of paying and maintaining eight Westerners in Beijing cost $1.3 million a year, a sum that outraged the Chinese officials.

Other cultural problems arose. Shortly after Beijing Jeep's operations began, it became apparent that capital was needed to modernize its factory, which had an inadequate conveyor system and an antiquated paint shop. One AMC executive had the bright idea of inviting the Chinese delegation to the firm's annual August dealer show. In this way, while negotiations for the factory improvements were being held, the Chinese could see how a *real* automaker marketed automobiles. Held at the MGM Grand Hotel in Las Vegas, the million-dollar show was a huge success. After a few drinks, many of the dealers were helping the Beach Boys, who had been brought in for the occasion, sing "Little Deuce Coupe," "409," and other Top Ten hits from their teenage years. Because production, rather than marketing, is of more concern in a command economy, the Chinese negotiators were not quite sure what to make of the Las Vegas festivities. However, when AMC then returned to the bargaining table and, pleading poverty, refused to inject any more cash into Beijing Jeep, the Chinese were disbelieving. They reasoned that if AMC could spend a million dollars so conspicuously on the dealer show, why couldn't they invest more capital in Beijing Jeep?

During 1984, the first year of operations, Beijing Jeep produced 16,400 BJ212s, a substantial increase over BAW's previous annual output. By 1986, production of the BJ212 had risen to 22,000, and the number of workers had been slashed from 10,000 to 4,000. But the Chinese had not entered the joint venture to produce the old-style four-wheel-drive vehicles. They pressured AMC to supply Beijing Jeep with a new vehicle, as AMC had promised. Delivering on that promise quickly became a problem. AMC wanted to minimize design and production costs by making the new vehicle similar to its existing Jeeps. BAW, responsive to the needs of its largest customer, the People's Liberation Army, wanted a vehicle more suitable to the requirements of a military force. After both sides recognized that designing a new vehicle could cost $1 billion—a sum neither wanted to pay—the Chinese agreed that the new vehicle called for in the contract would be the recently introduced Jeep Cherokee. Beijing Jeep would assemble the vehicle from completely knocked down (CKD) kits shipped from AMC's Jeep factory in Toledo, Ohio.

This solution raised problems that neither side fully appreciated at the time. AMC now had an incentive to ship as many CKD kits from Toledo to Beijing as possible, for AMC could control the pricing of the CKD kits. However, the contract made no provision for obtaining the foreign exchange necessary to pay for the kits. AMC, of course, wanted to be paid in U.S. dollars rather than renminbi, which were inconvertible into other currencies and could be used only in China. But the Chinese had entered into the joint venture agreement in anticipation that the project would generate foreign exchange, not drain it from the country. After an initial 400 Cherokee CKD kits had been exported to China in mid-1985, the Beijing Municipal Government recognized the foreign-exchange impact of the Cherokee agreement. Claiming a shortage of foreign exchange, it refused to release additional hard currency to Beijing Jeep, thereby stranding AMC with over a thousand CKD kits ready to be shipped to its joint venture.

To make things worse, Beijing Jeep was fast approaching bankruptcy. The first purchaser of the Chinese-produced Cherokees was a government agency that planned to resell them within China; but it refused to pay Beijing Jeep. The firm also was not receiving any cash for the old Chinese-model BJ212s it was producing; BAW was keeping the sales revenues for itself rather than remitting them to Beijing Jeep as the joint venture agreement required. This was of little concern to the Chinese, however, for the incentives of a centrally planned economy are based on the product's production, not its profitability.

Clearly, AMC and Beijing Jeep were in trouble. AMC put pressure on the Chinese by threatening to make the difficulties public. Fearful of the negative reaction of other foreign investors if this showcase project were to fail, Chinese government officials addressed most of AMC's concerns in a series of negotiations that ended in May 1986. China agreed to guarantee the availability of $120 million in foreign exchange, an amount sufficient to finance the import of 12,500 Cherokee CKD kits over a four-year period. Beijing Jeep was allowed to keep any foreign currency it obtained through domestic sales within China and to convert any renminbi profits it earned on the sale of BJ212s into foreign currency. And BAW agreed to spend $70 million modernizing the Beijing Jeep factory.

Armed with the new agreement, Beijing Jeep saw its Cherokee sales rise from 2,000 in 1986 to 3,000 in 1987. In 1987, Chrysler purchased AMC, thereby becoming the new U.S. partner in Beijing Jeep. Since then, the outlook for Beijing Jeep has steadily improved, although there have been a few rough spots. For example, Chinese customs officials in 1989 arbitrarily announced major increases in import duties imposed on the CKD kits. After bitter negotiations, the Chinese rescinded the new fees. Then, in June 1989, thousands of pro-democracy demonstrators were killed in Tiananmen Square when Chinese troops fired on the crowd. Foreign businesses, shocked and disgusted by the violence, withdrew from the country, as did all of Beijing Jeep's non-Chinese personnel. Chrysler's main Jeep factory in Toledo, Ohio, also attracted some unwanted attention: It became the target of protestors against the Tianenmen Square massacre, who believed the factory's output was being used by the military. Although economic relations between China and the rest of the world have since gradually warmed, that country is not looked on by international businesses as favorably as it was before the events of June 1989.

By all accounts, Beijing Jeep is now a successful operation. It is the second-largest joint venture in China, after Shanghai Volkswagen, and enjoys a 10-percent share of the Chinese automobile market. In 1991, it raised Cherokee production to 13,000, up from 7,500 in 1990. It also produced 35,000 Chinese model jeeps in 1991, on which it earned profits of $40 million on total sales of $400 million. Beijing Jeep invested $225 million from 1992 to 1995 in order to improve its facilities, boost annual output of its Jeep Cherokee to 80,000 units, and design a new vehicle to replace the BJ212.

The foreign-exchange problem still plagues the joint venture, however. Importing the Cherokee CKD kits requires hard currency, which the government unhappily doles out. Beijing Jeep, like other foreign automotive joint ventures, is allowed to sell some of its output in the domestic market for convertible currencies. To reduce its hard currency needs, Beijing Jeep is now assembling its engines in Beijing and is locally producing six key engine parts. However, the local content of the Cherokee is only 45 percent, and the several hundred Cherokees the firm manages to export annually actually create a foreign currency loss for it. But new export opportunities may be opening up. In conjunction with Chrysler's main Jeep factory in Toledo, Ohio, Beijing Jeep is planning to produce right-hand-drive vehicles for export to the Japanese, British, Australian, and New Zealand markets.

Moreover, competition is heating up in the Chinese market. Latecomers such as GM, Mazda, and Daimler-Benz are trying to establish joint ventures of their own. In response to these competitive pressures, Beijing Jeep actually had to advertise in 1993 (for the first time) in order to defend its 10 percent share of the Chinese automobile market. It has also improved its parts supply operations and its dealership network. Previously, dealers drove to Beijing every two or three months to obtain spare parts. Now Beijing Jeep supplies its 20 dealerships weekly. Despite these competitive pressures, the firm's long-run potential remains promising, since on a per capita basis China has one eighth as many cars as Nigeria, even though the average income of the two countries is equivalent.

Discussion Questions

1. AMC was clearly surprised by many facets of doing business in China. How could they have avoided some of these problems?

2. How risky was the original Beijing Jeep joint venture for AMC? If AMC knew then what it knows now, would it have entered into the joint venture agreement in the first place? If it had had more information originally, what modifications in the original agreement might it have sought?

3. AMC seemed surprised by many of the cultural aspects of doing business in China. What suggestions would you have offered its managers to help them avoid these culture-based unpleasant surprises?

4. International and domestic political forces affected the birth and growth of the Beijing Jeep joint venture. What strategies could AMC have adopted to favorably influence these political forces?

Sources

"Chrysler Stays Open in Beijing," *New York Times,* June 29, 1989, p. D4; "Chrysler to Export Axles to China," *New York Times,* February 16, 1989, p. D5; Jonathan Karp, "Back on the road," *Far Eastern Economic Review,* March 26, 1992, pp. 49–50; Robert L. Simison, "Huge Market Potential in China Lures Auto Makers," *Wall Street Journal,* January 11, 1994, p. B4; Tony Walker, "Beijing Jeep is out of the thicket," *Financial Times,* June 16, 1993, p. 5; "Chrysler to Export Special Cherokees," *New York Times,* May 18, 1991, p. A37; Paul Aiello, "Building a Joint Venture in China: The Case of Chrysler and the Beijing Jeep Corporation," *Journal of General Management,* Vol. 17, No. 2 (Winter 1991), pp. 47–64; Jim Mann, *Beijing Jeep* (New York: Simon and Schuster, 1989); Jim Mann, "One Company's China Debacle," *Fortune,* November 6, 1989, pp. 145ff.

Lighting Up Europe

Since the fall of communism at the end of the 1980s, the markets of Central and Eastern Europe present international businesses with intriguing opportunities. These countries represent a major untapped market, affording new exporting opportunities for many international businesses. While most MNCs were happy to sell goods in those countries, they approached warily the prospect of purchasing state-owned enterprises there. By Western standards, the workforces of those countries were both low-paid and low-producing. Further, many of the enterprises were burdened with outmoded facilities, inadequate control systems, and a total lack of marketing knowledge.

A few state-owned enterprises did not fit this mold, however. One was Hungary's Tungsram Company, which employed almost 18,000 workers in twelve factories in Hungary and one in Austria. According to its records, Tungsram was profitable. But more important, Tungsram was a rarity among communist bloc enterprises: it was able to produce goods of sufficient quality to sell in capitalist markets. Of its $300 million in annual sales, 70 percent were made to Western Europe and other Western markets. But Tungsram's financial position began to deteriorate when the Hungarian government started viewing it as a cash cow and taxed 85 percent of its earnings. In 1988, Tungsram's main creditor, the state-owned Hungarian Credit Bank, reduced Tungsram's debt in return for equity in the enterprise as a short-term measure to bolster the enterprise's financial position.

Tungsram was particularly appealing to the General Electric Company (GE). The world's second-largest light bulb manufacturer, GE has suffered an invasion of its profitable domestic lighting industry. The threat came from Philips, the world's leading lighting manufacturer, which dominated Western Europe's lighting industry and which had targeted North America. GE decided it would counter Philips's North American move by assaulting Philips's Western European base. But GE had only a modest 3 percent market share in Western Europe. It knew that increasing that market share would normally be a slow and expensive proposition. For example, building its own European factories might cost $300 million.

The political changes that swept Central and Eastern Europe in the late 1980s provided GE with a rare opportunity. In January 1990, it was able to purchase a 50 percent (plus one share) interest in Tungsram from the Hungarian Credit Bank. For a mere $150 million, GE gained control over Tungsram's 7 percent share of Western Europe's lighting market. That purchase, coupled with its later purchase of the lighting division of Thorne EMI, a British firm, led GE to believe it could become a major player in the European lighting market and accomplish its strategic objective of attacking Philips's home base.

However, when GE executives examined what they had obtained for their $150 million investment in Tungsram, they realized they had much work to do. Their first shock was the state of the enterprise's factories. Like those of many such enterprises, its physical plant was run-down. Some of its equipment was brand-new; some was 30 years old. GE also realized it would have its hands full dealing with a workforce that typified such enterprises: underemployed, unproductive, and unmotivated. Tungsram's labor force was one seventh as productive as GE's U.S. workers. Still, its cost of producing an incandescent light bulb was 30 percent less than that of its U.S. or European competitors because Tungsram workers were paid one tenth as much as their capitalist counterparts.

A bigger shock was the state of Tungsram's financial records. State-owned enterprises in a command economy face different incentives than do firms in free-market economies. The bonuses of managers and workers depend on their meeting output goals imposed by the state's planners; profitability is often of no concern whatsoever. While Tungsram had reported $22 million in profits to its state owners in 1989, GE accountants soon discovered that at least half of those profits were attributable to Tungsram's sloppy accounting procedures. Bills were unpaid. Some cartons ready for shipment were stuffed with rocks instead of the expected light bulbs, so workers could collect bonuses based on volume. And company warehouses were full of cartons that Tungsram had been allowed under the state's accounting system to count as sold.

To address these problems, GE appointed as manager Hungarian-born George Varga, a 28-year GE veteran who had fled Hungary as a college student during the Hungarian Revolution of 1956. Among Varga's first tasks was explaining the meaning and importance of profits to the firm's socialist-trained managers. His initial goals for Tungsram were quite modest. By combining Tungsram's and GE's market shares, he planned to build the firm's European market share to 11 or 12 percent by the end of 1995. He started with a strong base in that half of Tungsram's sales came from producing incandescent light bulbs, for which it had the advantage of being the low-cost producer. But the importance of this market was expected to decline as usage of more energy-efficient forms of lighting increased. Varga expected to attack that problem by investing over $15 million annually for several years in new product development.

Varga and his management team moved slowly to adjust the firm's excess payrolls. They were concerned that quick layoffs would harm the morale of employees used to the lack of unemployment in a socialist system. Moreover, Tungsram's new managers had no idea which of its 18,000 employees should be laid off. While its office staff was enormous by Western standards, in the short run that staff was necessary. Because of the lack of computerization, most bookkeeping entries were made by hand. And few Hungarians had checking accounts, so over 150 employees were dedicated simply to stuffing workers' pay envelopes with Hungarian *forints* every Friday. However, moving slowly and using attrition and early retirements when possible, Tungsram was able to reduce its payroll by 2,700 employees by 1992. The firm was also very aggressive in helping former employees find new jobs with other firms.

GE managers moved more quickly when it came to modernizing production techniques. For example, one Tungsram factory manufacturing outdoor spotlights suffered wastage and breakage of one sixth of its output. GE located a production engineer in its Cleveland plant who knew how to use the Tungsram machinery (which was of a type scrapped in GE's U.S. facilities two decades earlier). After the engineer fine-tuned the machinery, the factory's annual breakage bill fell by $500,000. Various other small, but simple modifications further improved the productivity and profitability of the firm's manufacturing operations. Tungsram also initiated a program of sending Hungarian production managers to GE's U.S. factories to observe state-of-the-art techniques for manufacturing light bulbs.

By 1992, GE's investment in Tungsram had risen to $275 million, as it raised its ownership share to 70 percent and modernized the firm's manufacturing plant. In the first two years of operation, Tungsram's output increased by 20 percent while its workforce shrank by one third. Now, with Tungsram and the lighting operations of Thorne EMI, GE holds 18 percent of the Western European lighting market. Thus, initial indications suggest that Tungsram is meeting GE's strategic objective of boosting its European presence in the lighting market and threatening the home base of arch-rival Philips. Tungsram now occupies a more important role in GE's corporate globalization strategy than was earlier conceived, as suggested by the corporate mission statement Tungsram's board of directors adopted in 1990: "The vision is to make Tungsram a world-class, customer-oriented company by uniting the best attributes of Tungsram and GE. At the same time, it is our goal to have highly productive, well-paid people and provide them with excellent working conditions and a work atmosphere which allows for freedom of initiative, self-determination, and job satisfaction."

Discussion Questions

1. What measures could GE have adopted to reduce the unpleasant surprises it found when it purchased Tungsram?

2. What HRM problems did GE face when it took over Tungsram?

3. Do you agree with the strategic decision of GE's senior management that the purchase of Tungsram was the best way to attack the European market? Why or why not?

4. Reread Tungsram's mission statement. Is the second sentence mere lip service designed to placate workers who grew up under socialism, or does it reflect policies that firms must adopt to be able to compete globally in the next century?

Sources

John McClenahen, "Light in the East," *Industry Week, March 2,* 1992, pp. 14ff; Natalia Wolniansky and Leon P. Garry, "A New Hungarian Spring?" *Management Review* (July 1991), pp. 37ff; "Lighting the Way in Eastern Europe," *Industry Week,* February 18, 1991, pp. 28ff; Shawn Tully, "GE in Hungary: Let There Be Light," *Fortune,* October 22, 1990, pp. 137ff; "GE Carves Out a Road East," *Business Week,* July 30, 1990, pp. 32ff.

The Ethics of Global Tobacco Marketing

Cigarette smoking was once considered to be an elegant and glamorous pastime in the United States. Movie stars, athletes, politicians, and other public figures were often photographed holding or smoking a cigarette, and tobacco companies aggressively pushed their products as a basic commodity in the same way that firms today market soft drinks and fast foods. Driven in part by the allure of fashion and in part by this aggressive marketing, the annual consumption of cigarettes by U.S. smokers increased steadily from 54 per person in 1900 to a high of 4,345 in 1963.

In 1964, however, things began to change. The U.S. Surgeon General released a report that demonstrated a clear link between cigarettes and lung cancer. During the subsequent several years, numerous reforms were put in place that affected the ability of tobacco firms to market their products in the United States. Among the most stringent were bans on television and radio advertising, mandatory warning labels on cigarette packages, high sales taxes, and age restrictions for the legal purchase of cigarettes. These measures, combined with increased public awareness, caused the annual consumption of cigarettes by U.S. smokers to drop to 2,493 per person in 1994.

There are four major international cigarette makers today. Philip Morris, the world's largest, is a U.S. firm that manufactures such brands as Marlboro, Benson & Hedges, Parliament, and Virginia Slims. RJR Nabisco, also a U.S. firm, markets Camel, Doral, Salem, Winston, and other brands. B.A.T. Industries, a British firm, sells such brands as Kool, Raleigh, and Viceroy (B.A.T.'s U.S. operation is called Brown & Williamson). Rothmans International, also a British firm, sells its Rothmans brand cigarette primarily outside the U.S. market.

As pressures to curb cigarette smoking in the United States increased during the 1970s and 1980s, U.S. cigarette makers began to adopt two diversification strategies in an effort to boost their profits. First, they branched into nontobacco markets, using cash flows generated by their tobacco profits to acquire leading firms outside their industry. Their experience in marketing premium-priced, brand-name consumer goods led them to focus on markets where this expertise would be useful. For example, Philip Morris purchased Kraft, General Foods, and Miller Brewing

Company. Within the U.S. market, Philip Morris currently derives less than half of its revenues from tobacco. RJR, previously known as R.J. Reynolds, acquired Nabisco in 1985 and became RJR Nabisco. It now sells a number of food and food-related products that came with that acquisition, including candy, gum, nuts, cookies, crackers, and cereals. And B.A.T. has insurance and financial services operations.

Second, these major tobacco marketers sought to diversify their tobacco sales geographically by focusing their efforts on markets other than the United States. These markets have two major advantages over the U.S. market. First, many of them place fewer restrictions on tobacco sales than is the case in the United States. Second, growth prospects in these markets are higher. Rising incomes and reduction of trade restrictions make such markets as Russia, the Czech Republic, Japan, and South Korea particularly appealing to U.S. tobacco companies. Thus, in one market after another, the four international giants, other international tobacco suppliers, and local tobacco brands are waging aggressive marketing wars in their efforts to increase sales of their products, especially to younger people.

Central and Eastern Europe is one battlefield. Communist government officials actively promoted the use of cigarettes and vodka. These commodities were cheap to make, and their addictive character helped maintain order and discipline in society. Indeed, after the collapse of communism and the move toward an open market in Russia, cigarette shortages caused riots in Moscow. Nor surprisingly, then, cigarette makers are rushing to gain advantage in the former Soviet bloc countries, where total annual cigarette consumption is estimated to be as high as 700 billion, compared to 500 billion in the United States.

Philip Morris, RJR Nabisco, and B.A.T. have discovered that consumers in this region crave affordable, high-quality, Western-style products. Cigarettes seem to fill at least part of the bill. Those firms have plastered cities throughout Central and Eastern Europe with billboards featuring the Marlboro Man—an icon of America, the West, and freedom—or symbols of other Western brands. Not surprisingly, the number of smokers in Central and Eastern Europe continues to escalate. Philip Morris is perhaps the most successful firm in this region so far, in part because it was able to buy the Czech cigarette monopoly, Tabak, in 1992 during that country's privatization program. It has also purchased majority interests in formerly state-owned cigarette factories in Hungary, Kazakhstan, Russia, and Ukraine.

Asia is another major battlefield. The Japanese, for example, have long been heavy smokers. The Japanese market was essentially closed to foreign firms until the Bush administration pressured the Japanese to reduce their high tariffs on imported cigarettes and end Japan Tobacco's monopoly over the domestic market. Because Japanese consumers have long been interested in products that they strongly associate with the United States (such as Levi Strauss jeans, McDonald's restaurants, and Disney films), U.S. cigarette makers are now finding Japan a fertile market for their brands.

The story is similar in the Philippines, Taiwan, Korea, Vietnam, Malaysia, Hong Kong, and Indonesia. Aggressive advertising, often targeted at young consumers and women, is inducing more and more people to become smokers. For example, a 1985 survey of high school students in Taiwan found that only 26 percent of males and 1 percent of females had ever smoked a cigarette. Six years later, a similar survey found 48 percent of males and 20 percent of females had smoked.

But perhaps China holds the greatest opportunity for cigarette makers. There are currently over 300 hundred million smokers in China, most of whom currently smoke local brands. But as the Chinese market continues to open for foreign firms, Philip Morris, RJR Nabisco, and B.A.T. are all poised to move in in a big way. Indeed, each believes that the Chinese market is potentially the world's most lucrative one for their products.

But these efforts and strategies have been very controversial, raising ethical concerns about the behavior of the firms and the U.S. government. Critics argue, for example, that the tobacco giants are being socially irresponsible by taking advantage of uninformed, impressionable consumers who don't fully understand the health risks of smoking. One expert has predicted that lung-cancer deaths among Chinese men will increase from 30,000 in 1975 to 900,000 by 2025. Another observer predicts that if U.S. tobacco firms are allowed full and free access to the Chinese market and can use the aggressive marketing techniques they have perfected elsewhere and if they increase the number of smokers by only 2 percent, more Chinese will be killed by lung cancer than triple the number of Americans killed in wars this century.

The tobacco companies respond that they are doing nothing wrong. For example, they point out that local governments, especially in Central and Eastern Europe, have encouraged their investments. They also point out that they are simply taking advantage of legal market opportunities that already exist. Indeed, failing to do just what they are doing might seem to be a disservice to their stockholders and employees.

Among the most controversial issues are the marketing practices international tobacco companies employ. China again provides a good case in point. That country has a law that prohibits the advertising of cigarettes. But the law bans only the display of and actual mention of a cigarette. Philip Morris actively promotes its Marlboro brand without ever showing a picture of or mentioning cigarettes. One of its radio commercials, for example, proclaims, "This is the world of Marlboro. Ride through the rivers and mountains with courage. Be called a hero throughout the thousand miles. This is the world of Marlboro." And Philip Morris's efforts appear to be paying off: its brand recognition is high among Chinese consumers. One Canton factory manager, when asked by an interviewer why he smokes Marlboros, replied, "Marlboro shows my superior position to others. I'm more privileged."

More controversial has been the role of the U.S. government. Although it discourages cigarette usage at home, it has played an active role in opening foreign markets to U.S. tobacco firms. In the 1980s, the U.S. Trade Representative (USTR) (the government agency in charge of international trade negotiations) successfully hammered out agreements with Japan, South Korea, Taiwan, and Thailand to end their restrictions on the sale of foreign cigarettes. The USTR attacked foreign countries for utilizing public policies that the U.S. government itself had adopted. Taiwan, for example, previously disallowed all cigarette advertising as a means of discouraging cigarette consumption. As a result, most cigarettes were consumed by adult males. In 1986, however, the U.S. government exerted pressure on the Taiwanese government to allow greater access to its market by U.S. firms. Bowing to this pressure, Taiwan not only opened its market to Philip Morris and RJR Nabisco, but also relaxed its regulations on cigarette advertising. These Western firms have focused their marketing efforts on teenagers and females, believing that older males will continue to smoke domestic brands. U.S. brands now sell well among those targeted audiences. When Taiwanese health officials tried to strengthen the warning labels on cigarette packages, ban smoking by those under 18, and prohibit vending machine cigarettes sales, the USTR counterattacked, claiming that these efforts would hurt U.S. tobacco companies. The USTR took similar stances in trade negotiations with Japan, South Korea, and Thailand, threatening these countries with Super 301 retaliation if they did not open their markets to U.S. cigarettes.

All in all, the international marketing efforts of U.S. cigarette makers seem to be working. Exports to Asia alone account for 12 percent of U.S. cigarette production. These firms' primary target markets—teenagers, females, and the affluent—are purchasing U.S. cigarettes in record numbers. But the controversy rages on, however, as more and more critics line up in an effort to curtail the U.S. tobacco companies' efforts to indoctrinate people in other regions toward cigarette smoking.

Discussion Questions

1. Summarize the basic ethical and social responsibility issues that this case illustrates.

2. If you managed an international tobacco firm, what actions would you take today to protect your market opportunities abroad?

3. Do you think other foreign cigarette makers, such as those in Japan, will ever be able to crack the U.S. market? Why or why not?

4. In most Asian cultures, cigarette smoking is restricted to males. Should U.S. cigarette makers respect the cultural values of these countries and restrict their marketing efforts to males? Should females be targeted for marketing as well?

5. The Clinton administration is contemplating changing the sales-oriented cigarette exporting policies of the USTR to ones that are more health-oriented. Should the administration make such a change? In formulating its international trade policies, should the U.S. government focus on protecting the interests of U.S. tobacco growers, workers, and manufacturers, or should it concentrate on protecting the lungs of Asians? More generally, what is the appropriate role of the U.S. government in foreign tobacco marketing?

Sources

Stan Sesser, "Opium War Redux," *The New Yorker,* September 13, 1993, pp. 78–89; "Smoking Level Lowest in 50 Years," *USA Today,* November 17, 1994, p. D1; "Cigarettes May Find New Foe in Trade Rep," *Wall Street Journal,* August 1, 1994, p. B1; "Tobacco Companies Race for Advantage in Eastern Europe While Critics Fume," *Wall Street Journal,* December 28, 1992, pp. B1, B4; "U.S. Cigarette Firms Are Battling Taiwan's Bid to Stiffen Ad Curbs Like Other Asian Nations," *Wall Street Journal,* May 5, 1992, p. C25; "Opiate of the Masses," *Forbes,* April 11, 1994, pp. 74–75.

Glossary

The number in parentheses following each definition gives the page on which the term is introduced.

A

absolute advantage, theory of: theory stating that trade between nations occurs when one nation is absolutely more productive than other nations in the production of a good; according to Adam Smith, nations should export those goods for which they possess an absolute advantage and import goods for which other nations possess an absolute advantage (84)

accommodating transaction: transaction undertaken by a central bank solely to accommodate autonomous transactions; also called compensatory transaction (147)

accounting reserves: reserves used by firms for foreseeable future expenses (656)

acculturation: process of understanding and learning how to operate in a new culture (312)

acquisition strategy: form of foreign direct investment involving the purchase of existing assets in a foreign country (402)

active income: income generated by active business operations such as production, marketing, and distribution (675)

ad valorem tariff: tax assessed as a percentage of the market value of an imported good (206)

adjustable peg: feature of the Bretton Woods system by which a country had a limited right to adjust the value of its currency in terms of gold (127)

advised letter of credit: letter of credit in which the seller's bank advises the seller about the credit-worthiness of the bank issuing the letter of credit (620)

affiliated bank: partly owned, separately incorporated overseas banking operation of a home country bank (182)

aggressive goal behavior: behavior based on the cultural belief that material possessions, money, and assertiveness underlie motivation and reflect the goals that a person should pursue (485)

Andean Pact: customs union composed of Bolivia, Colombia, Ecuador, Peru, and Venezuela (262)

antidumping duty: tax on imported goods designed to protect domestic firms from sales of imported goods at less than their cost of production or at prices less than they sell for in their home markets (195)

arbitrage: riskless purchase of a product in one market for immediate resale in a second market in order to profit from price differences between the markets (173)

arbitration: dispute resolution technique in which both parties agree to submit their cases to a private individual or body for resolution (292)

arm's length test: test imposed by the Internal Revenue Service to determine the appropriateness of transfer prices; reflects the price that one independent company would charge a second for a good or service (672)

assigned arrangement: management arrangement in which one partner in a strategic alliance assumes primary responsibility for the operations of the alliance (430)

Association of South East Asian Nations (ASEAN): organization that promotes free trade among Brunei, Indonesia, Malaysia, the Philippines, Singapore, and Thailand (263)

autonomous transaction: transaction undertaken in the economic self-interest of a market participant (146)

B

backtranslation: technique used to check for translation errors; after one person translates a document from language A to language B, a second person translates the document from B back to A to check if the intended message is actually being sent (321)

Baker Plan: plan developed in 1985 by U.S. Treasury Secretary James Baker to solve the international debt crisis; stressed debt rescheduling, tight controls over domestic monetary and fiscal policies, and continued loans to debtor nations (136)

balance on merchandise trade: difference between a country's merchandise exports and imports (139)

balance of payments (BOP) accounting system: accounting system that records commercial transactions between the residents of one country and residents of other countries (118)

balance on services trade: difference between a country's service exports and imports (139)

balance sheet hedge: technique for eliminating translation exposure in which a firm matches its assets and liabilities denominated in a given currency on a consolidated basis (631)

banker's acceptance: time draft that has been endorsed by a bank, signifying the bank's promise to guarantee payment at the designated time (618)

barter: form of countertrade involving simultaneous exchange of goods or services between two parties (622)

basic balance: sum of the current account balance plus net long-term capital investment (146)

beggar-thy-neighbor policies: domestic economic policies that ignore the economic damage done to other countries (122)

benchmarking: process of legally and ethically studying how other firms do something in a high-quality way and then either imitating or improving on their methods (532)

bilateral netting: netting of transactions between two business units (636)

bill of lading: international trade document that serves (1) as a contract between the exporter and the transporter and (2) as a title to the exported goods (618)

Brady Plan: plan developed in 1989 by U.S. Treasury Secretary Nicholas Brady to solve the international debt crisis; involves writing off a portion of the debtor nations' debts or repurchase of their debts at less than face value (136)

branch bank: overseas banking operation of a home country bank that is not separately incorporated (182)

bureaucratic law: legal system based on interpretations, actions, and decisions of government employees (277)

buy-back: form of countertrade in which a firm is compensated in the form of goods produced by equipment or technology that it has sold to another firm (622)

BV: abbreviation used in the Netherlands to refer to a privately held, limited-liability firm (10)

C

Cairns Group: group of major agricultural exporting nations, led by Argentina, Australia, Canada, and the United States, that lobbies for reductions in agricultural subsidies (238)

call option: publicly traded contract granting the owner the right, but not the obligation, to buy a specific amount of foreign currency at a specified price at a stated future date (170)

capacity planning: deciding how many customers a firm will be able to serve at a given time (600)

capital account: BOP account that records capital transactions between residents of one country and those of other countries (140)

Caribbean Basin Initiative (CBI): program developed by the United States to spur the economic development of countries in the Caribbean Basin; allows duty-free importation of selected goods into the United States from these countries (260)

centralized cash depository: entity controlled by a parent corporation that coordinates worldwide cash flows of its subsidiaries and pools their cash reserves (634)

centrally planned economy (CPE): economy in which government planners determine price and production levels for individual firms (298)

chaebol: any of the large business conglomerates that dominate the Korean economy (60)

channel length: number of stages in a distribution channel (571)

civil law: law based upon detailed codification of permissible and nonpermissible activities; world's most common form of legal system (276)

clearinghouse accounts: accounting system used to facilitate international countertrade; a firm must balance its overall countertrade transactions but need not balance any single countertrade transaction (623)

codetermination: German system that provides for cooperation between management and labor in running a business (713)

cohesion fund: means of funneling economic development aid to countries whose per capita GDP is less than 90 percent of the EU average (251)

collective bargaining: process used to make agreements between management and labor unions (712)

collectivism: cultural belief that the group comes first (479)

comity, principle of: principle of international law that one country will honor and enforce within its own territory the judgments and decisions of foreign courts (292)

commodity agreement: agreement created by major producers and consumers of a good to control production and prices of that good (264)

commodity cartel: cartel created by producers of a good to control production and prices of that good (264)

common law: law that forms the foundation of the legal system in Anglo-American countries; based on cumulative findings of judges in individual cases (276)

common market: form of regional economic integration that combines features of a customs union with elimination of barriers inhibiting the movement of factors of production among members (243)

comparative advantage, theory of: theory stating that trade between countries occurs when one country is relatively more productive than others in the production of a good (85)

compensatory transaction: *see* accommodating transaction

compound tariff: tax that combines elements of an ad valorem tariff and a specific tariff (206)

comprehensive alliance: strategic alliance in which participants agree to perform together multiple stages of the process by which goods or services are brought to market (420)

confirmed letter of credit: letter of credit in which the seller's bank adds its promise to pay should the issuing bank fail to pay the seller (620)

confiscation: involuntary transfer of property, with little or no compensation, from a privately owned firm to the host government (286)

conglomerate: firm that uses a strategy of unrelated diversification (362)

consolidated financial statement: a financial statement combining the accounting records of a parent corporation and all its subsidiaries into a single set of statements denominated in a single currency (664)

consolidation method: technique used to consolidate accounting records of subsidiaries in which the parent company's ownership stake is more than 50 percent (665)

consumer products: goods and services sold for use by individual consumers (554)

contingency fee: type of payment for legal services in which the fee paid is based on the size of monetary payments awarded to the client (291)

control: process of monitoring and regulating activities in a firm so that targeted measures of performance are achieved or maintained (507)

control framework: managerial and organizational processes used to keep a firm on target toward its strategic goals (358)

control standard: desired level of a performance component a firm is attempting to control (516)

controlled foreign corporation (CFC): foreign corporation in which certain U.S. shareholders (each of which must own at least 10 percent of the foreign corporation's stock) cumulatively own at least 50 percent of the foreign corporation's stock (675)

controller: managerial position in an organization given specific responsibility for financial control (509)

convergence criteria: conditions that must be met by EMU members in order to participate in the EU's single currency program, including numerical limits on members' inflation, interest rates, currency values, budget deficits, and outstanding national debts; designed to force convergence of participants' monetary and fiscal policies (252)

convertible currencies: currencies that are freely traded and accepted in international commerce; also called hard currencies (169)

Coordinating Committee for Multilateral Export Controls (COCOM): organization created by the Western allies to control the export of goods and technology with military value to the countries of the Soviet bloc (279)

coordination: process of linking and integrating functions and activities of different groups, units, or divisions (462)

corollary approach: approach whereby a firm delegates responsibility for processing international sales orders to individuals within an existing department, such as finance or marketing (446)

corporate culture: set of shared values that defines for its members what the organization stands for (464)

correspondent relationship: agency relationship whereby a bank in country A acts as an agent for a bank from country B, providing banking services in country A for both the B bank and its clients; typically done on a reciprocal basis (181)

cost-of-living allowance: compensation for managers on international assignment designed to offset differences in living costs (704)

cost method: technique used to consolidate accounting records of subsidiaries in which the parent company's ownership stake is less than 10 percent (664)

Council of the European Union: main decision-making body of the EU; composed of 15 members, who represent the interests of their home governments in Council deliberations (253)

counterpurchase: form of countertrade in which one firm sells its products to another at one point in time and is compensated in the form of the other's products at some future time (622)

countertrade: form of payment in which a seller accepts something other than money in compensation (622)

countervailing duty (CVD): ad valorem tariff placed on imported goods to offset subsidies granted by foreign governments (221)

country fund: mutual fund that specializes in investing in stocks and bonds issued by firms in a specific country (185)

country similarity theory: theory stating that international trade in manufactured goods will occur between countries with similar income levels and at similar stages of economic development (90)

covered-interest arbitrage: arbitrage that exploits geographic differences in interest rates and differences in exchange rates over time (178)

cross-cultural literacy: ability to understand and operate in more than one culture (312)

cross rate: exchange rate between two currencies, A and B, derived by using currency A to buy currency C and then using currency C to buy currency B (177)

cultural attachés: experts in local culture and language who help foreign businesspeople in their dealings with local people and businesses (309)

cultural cluster: group of countries that share many cultural similarities (335)

cultural convergence: convergence of two or more cultures (335)

culture: collection of values, beliefs, behaviors, customs, and attitudes that distinguish and define a society (311)

culture shock: psychological phenomenon arising from being in a different culture; may lead to feelings of fear, helplessness, irritability, and disorientation (698)

cumulative translation adjustment: account created to balance any difference between a subsidiary's assets and its liabilities and stockholder's equity when the current rate method is used to value its balance sheet (667)

currency future: publicly traded contract involving the sale or purchase of a specific amount of foreign currency at a specified price with delivery at a stated future date (170)

currency option: publicly traded contract giving the owner the right, but not the obligation, to sell or buy a specific

amount of foreign currency at a specified price at a stated future date (*see also* call option; put option) (170)

current account: BOP account that records exports and imports of goods, exports and imports of services, investment income, and gifts (138)

current account balance: net balance resulting from merchandise exports and imports, service exports and imports, investment income, and unilateral transfers (140)

current rate method: approach used to consolidate the financial statements of a foreign subsidiary when the subsidiary's functional currency is the subsidiary's home currency (666)

customs union: form of regional economic integration that combines features of a free trade area with common trade policies toward nonmember countries (243)

D

date draft: draft that requires payment at some specified date (618)

debt-equity swaps: reduction of debtor nations' debts in return for equity investments in their domestic companies (137)

debt-for-nature swaps: reduction of debtor nations' debts in return for protection of sensitive environmental habitats (137)

decision making: process of choosing one alternative from among a set of alternatives in order to promote the decision maker's objectives (492)

deferral rule: rule permitting U.S. companies to defer paying U.S. income taxes on profits earned by their foreign subsidiaries (675)

delegated arrangement: management arrangement in which partners in a strategic alliance play little or no management role, delegating responsibility to the executives of the alliance itself (431)

development: general education aimed at preparing managers for new assignments and/or higher-level positions (700)

differentiation strategy: business-level strategy that emphasizes the distinctiveness of products or services (363)

direct exchange rate: price of a foreign currency in terms of the home currency; also called a direct quote (159)

direct exporting: product sales to customers, either distributors or end-users, located outside the firm's home country (384)

direct quote: *see* direct exchange rate

direct sales: selling products to final consumers (571)

dirty float: *see* managed float

distinctive competence: component of strategy that answers the question "What do we do exceptionally well, especially as compared to our competitors?" (351)

distribution: process of getting a firm's products and services to its customers (569)

documentary collection: form of payment in which goods are released to the buyer only after the buyer pays for them or signs a document binding the buyer to pay for them (617)

draft: document demanding payment from the buyer (617)

dumping: sale of imported goods either (1) at prices below what a company charges in its home market or (2) at prices below cost (195)

E

EC '92: common name given to the process of completing the internal market mandated by the Single European Act, which was to be finalized by December 31, 1992 (248)

eclectic theory: theory that foreign direct investment occurs because of location advantages, ownership advantages, and internalization advantages (103)

Economic Community of Central African States (CEEAC): organization promoting regional economic cooperation created by Central African countries (264)

Economic Community of West African States (ECOWAS): organization promoting regional economic cooperation created by 16 West African countries (264)

economic exposure: impact on the value of a firm's operations of unanticipated exchange-rate changes (631)

economic and monetary union (EMU): organization created by the Maastricht Treaty whose goal is to create a single currency for the EU, thereby eliminating exchange-rate risks and the costs of converting currencies for intra-EU trade (252)

economic union: form of regional economic integration that combines features of a common market with coordination of economic policies among its members (243)

economies of scale: conditions that occur when average costs of production decline as the number of units produced increases (95)

economies of scope: conditions that occur when a firm's average costs decline as the number of different products it sells increases (95)

Edge Act corporation: bank that is domiciled outside the parent bank's home state and provides international banking services (182)

embargo: ban on the exporting and/or importing of goods to a particular country (211, 279)

equity method: technique used to consolidate accounting records of subsidiaries in which the parent's ownership stake is between 10 and 50 percent (665)

errors and omissions: BOP account that results from measurement errors; equals the negative of the sum of the current account, the capital account, and the official reserves account (143)

ethnocentric approach: managerial approach in which a firm operates internationally the same way it does domestically (449, 550)

ethnocentric staffing model: approach that primarily uses PCNs to staff upper-level foreign positions (693)

Eurobond: bonds denominated in one country's currency but sold to residents of other countries (184)

Eurocurrencies: currency on deposit in banks outside its country of issue (183)

Eurodollars: U.S. dollars deposited in banks outside the borders of the United States (183)

European Commission: twenty-person group that acts as the EU's administrative branch of government and proposes all EU legislation (254)

European Court of Justice: sixteen-member court charged with interpreting EU law; also interprets whether the national laws of the 15 EU members are consistent with EU laws and regulations (254)

European Currency Unit (ECU): weighted "basket" of EU currencies used for accounting purposes within the EU (131)

European Free Trade Association (EFTA): second major trading bloc in Europe that works closely with the EU to promote intra-European trade and whose current members are Iceland, Liechtenstein, Norway, and Switzerland; has shrunk in size over time as many of its members have joined the EU (257)

European Monetary Institute (EMI): organization created by the Maastricht Treaty as a first step in establishing a European Central Bank; plays a critical role in promoting economic and monetary union among EU members (252)

European Monetary System (EMS): system based on 1979 agreement among members of the European Union to manage currency relationships among themselves (130)

European Parliament: legislature with 626 members elected from districts in member countries that has a consultative role in EU decision making (254)

exchange rate: price of one currency in terms of a second currency (119)

Exchange Rate Mechanism (ERM): agreement among European Union members to maintain fixed exchange rates among themselves within a narrow band (130)

exit interview: interview with an employee who is leaving the organization (709)

expatriate failure: early return of an expatriate manager to his or her home country because of an inability to perform in the overseas assignment (696)

expatriates: collective name for parent-country nationals (PCNs) and third-country nationals (TCNs) (692)

export and import brokers: agents who bring together international buyers and sellers of standardized commodities such as coffee, cocoa, and grains (391)

Export-Import Bank of the United States (Eximbank): U.S. government agency that promotes U.S. exports by offering direct loans and loan guarantees (220)

export management company (EMC): firm that acts as its clients' export department (390)

export of the services of capital: income that a country's residents earn from their foreign investments (139)

export promotion: economic development strategy based on building a vibrant manufacturing sector by stimulating exports, often by harnessing some advantage the country possesses, such as low labor costs (68, 202)

export-promotion strategy: *see* export promotion

export tariff: tax levied on goods as they leave the country (205)

export trading company (ETC): firm that may engage in various cooperative exporting practices without fear of violating U.S. antitrust laws (391)

exporting: selling products made in one's own country for use or resale in other countries (10)

expropriation: involuntary transfer of property, with compensation, from a privately owned firm to a host country government (286)

extraterritoriality: application of a country's laws to activities occurring outside its borders (281)

F

factoring: specialized international lending activity in which firms buy foreign accounts receivable at a discount from face value (617)

fair trade: trade between nations that takes place under active government intervention to ensure that the companies of each nation receive their fair share of the economic benefits of trade; also called managed trade (197)

financial alliance: strategic alliance in which two or more firms work together to reduce the financial risks associated with a project (423)

financial derivative: financial instrument whose return derives from some bond, stock, or other asset (630)

first-mover advantage: competitive advantage gained by the first firm to enter a market, develop a product, introduce a technology, etc. (95)

fixed exchange-rate system: international monetary system in which each government promises to maintain the price of its currency in terms of other currencies (119)

flexible (or floating) exchange-rate system: system in which exchange rates are determined by supply and demand (130)

flight capital: money sent out of politically or economically unstable countries by investors seeking a safe haven for their assets (40, 143)

float: to allow a currency's value to be determined by forces of supply and demand (120)

focus strategy: business-level strategy targeting specific types of products for certain customer groups or regions (363)

foreign bonds: bonds issued by residents of one country to residents of a second country and denominated in the second country's currency (184)

Foreign Corrupt Practices Act (FCPA): U.S. law enacted in 1977 prohibiting U.S. firms, their employees, and agents acting on their behalf from paying or offering to pay foreign government officials in order to influence official actions or policies or to gain or retain business (283)

foreign direct investment (FDI): acquisition of foreign assets for the purpose of controlling them; under U.S. regulations, FDI occurs when an investor owns at least 10 percent of the voting stock of a foreign company (12, 99)

foreign exchange: currencies issued by countries other than one's own (157)

foreign sales corporation (FSC): subsidiary of a U.S. MNC that enjoys substantial income tax savings from profits earned from exporting activities (674)

foreign service premium: *see* hardship premium

Foreign Sovereign Immunities Act of 1976: U.S. law that limits the ability of U.S. citizens to sue foreign governments in U.S. courts (292)

foreign trade zone (FTZ): geographical area in which imported or exported goods receive preferential tariff treatment (218)

forum shopping: attempt to seek a court system or judge that will be most sympathetic to an attorney's client (291)

forward discount: difference between the forward and the spot price of a currency expressed as an annualized percentage (assumes the forward price is *less* than the spot price) (*see also* forward premium) (172)

forward market: market for foreign exchange involving delivery of currency at some point in the future (169)

forward premium: difference between the forward and the spot price of a currency expressed as an annualized percentage (assumes the forward price is *more* than the spot price) (*see also* forward discount) (172)

franchisee: independent entrepreneur or organization that operates a business under the name of another (398)

franchising: special form of licensing allowing the licensor more control over the licensee while also providing more support from the licensor to the licensee (12, 398)

franchisor: firm that allows an independent entrepreneur or organization to operate a business under its name (11)

free trade area: regional trading bloc that encourages trade by eliminating trade barriers among its members (242)

free trade: trade between nations that is unrestricted by governmental actions (197)

freight forwarders: agents who specialize in the physical transportation of goods, arranging customs documentation and obtaining transportation services for their clients (293)

functional currency: currency of the principal economic environment in which a subsidiary operates (665)

G

General Agreement on Tariffs and Trade (GATT): international organization that sponsors negotiations to promote world trade (235)

Generalized System of Preferences (GSP): system of reduced tariff rates offered on goods exported from developing countries (236)

generic organizational control: form of organizational control based on centralized generic controls across the entire organization (512)

geocentric approach: management approach in which a firm analyzes the needs of its customers worldwide and then adopts standardized operating practices for all markets it serves (551)

geocentric staffing model: approach using a mix of PCNs, HCNs, and TCNs to staff upper-level foreign positions (693)

geographic arbitrage: *see* two-point arbitrage (175)

global area design: form of organization design that centers a firm's activities around specific areas or regions of the world (452)

global bonds: large, liquid bond issues designed to be traded in numerous capital markets (185)

global corporation: organization that views the world as a single marketplace and strives to create standardized goods and services to meet the needs of customers worldwide (14)

global customer design: form of organization design centered around different customers or customer groups, each requiring special expertise or attention (456)

global functional design: form of organization design based on departments or divisions having worldwide responsibility for a single organizational function such as finance, operations, or marketing; also called U-form organization (454)

global matrix design: complex form of international organization design created by superimposing one form of design on top of an existing different form (457)

global product design: form of organization design that assigns worldwide responsibility for specific products or product groups to separate operating divisions within a firm (449)

goal orientation: cultural beliefs about motivation and the different goals toward which people work (485)

gold standard: international monetary system based on the willingness of countries to buy or sell their paper currencies for gold at a fixed rate (119)

goodwill: payment in excess of the book value of a firm's stock (657)

gray market: market created when products are imported into a country legally but outside the normal channels of distribution authorized by the manufacturer (561)

greenfield investment: form of investment in which the firm designs and builds a new factory from scratch, starting with nothing but a "green field" (335)

greenfield strategy: form of foreign direct investment that involves building new facilities (402)

gross domestic product (GDP): measure of market value of goods and services produced in a country (42)

gross national product (GNP): measure of market value of goods and services produced by resources owned by a country's residents (42)

H

hard currencies: currencies that are freely tradable; also called convertible currencies (169)

hard loan policy: World Bank lending policy requiring that loans be made only if they are likely to be repaid (124)

hardship premium: supplemental compensation to induce managers to accept relatively unattractive international assignments; also called foreign service premium (704)

harmonization: voluntary adoption of common regulations, policies, and procedures by members of a regional trading bloc to promote internal trade (248)

harmonized tariff schedule (HTS): classification scheme used by many nations to determine tariffs on imported goods (207)

headhunters: recruiting firms that actively seek qualified managers and other professionals for possible placement in positions in other organizations (695)

Heckscher-Ohlin theory: *see* relative factor endowments, theory of

H-form design: form of organization design in which products are unrelated to each other (449)

high-context culture: culture in which the context in which a discussion is held is equally as important as the actual words that are spoken in conveying the speaker's message to the listener (323)

home country: country in which a firm's headquarters is located (12)

host country: country other than a firm's home country in which it operates (12)

host-country nationals (HCNs): employees who are citizens of the host country where an international business operates (692)

human resource management (HRM): set of activities directed at attracting, developing, and maintaining the effective workforce necessary to achieve a firm's objectives (686)

hurdle rate: minimum rate of return a firm finds acceptable for its capital investments (640)

I

IMF conditionality: restrictions placed on economic policies of countries receiving IMF loans (126)

import of the services of capital: payments that a country's residents make on capital supplied by foreigners (139)

import-substitution policy: economic development strategy that relies on the stimulation of domestic manufacturing firms by erecting barriers to imported goods (68, 202)

import tariff: tax levied on goods as they enter a country (206)

importing: buying products made in other countries for use or resale in one's own country (10)

Inc.: abbreviation for *incorporated,* meaning that the liability of the company's owners is limited to the extent of their investments if the company fails or encounters financial or legal difficulties (10)

income distribution: relative numbers of rich, middle-class, and poor residents in a country (43)

inconvertible currencies: currencies that are not freely traded because of legal restrictions imposed by the issuing country or that are not generally accepted by foreigners in settlement of international transactions; also called soft currencies (169)

indirect exchange rate: price of the home currency in terms of the foreign currency; also called indirect quote (160)

indirect exporting: sales of a firm's products to a domestic customer, which in turn exports the product, in either its original form or a modified form (384)

indirect quote: *see* indirect exchange rate (160)

individualism: cultural belief that the person comes first (478)

industrial democracy: system based on the belief that workers should have a voice in how businesses are run (713)

industrial policy: economic development strategy in which a national government identifies key domestic industries critical to the country's economic future and then formulates policies that promotes the international competitiveness of these industries (202)

industrial products: goods and services sold primarily for use by organizations (554)

infant industry argument: argument in favor of governmental intervention in trade: a nation should protect fledgling industries for which the nation will ultimately possess a comparative advantage (198)

informal management network: group of managers from different parts of the world who are connected to one another in some way (463)

information: data in a form that is of value to a manager (533)

information system: methodology created by a firm to gather, assemble, and provide data in a form or forms useful to managers (534)

intellectual property rights: intangible property rights that include patents, copyrights, trademarks, brand names, and trade secrets (239)

interindustry trade: international trade involving the exchange of goods produced in one industry in one country for goods produced in another industry in a different country (90)

intermediaries: third parties that specialize in facilitating imports and exports (389)

internalization advantages: factors that affect the desirability of a firm's producing a good or service itself rather than relying on existing local firms to control production (380)

internalization theory: theory stating that foreign direct investment occurs because of the high costs of entering into

production or procurement contracts with foreign firms (102)

International Accounting Standards Committee (IASC): international organization whose mission is to harmonize the national accounting standards used by various nations (661)

International Bank for Reconstruction and Development (IBRD): official name of the World Bank, which was established by the Bretton Woods agreement to reconstruct the war-torn economies of Western Europe and whose mission changed in the 1950s to aid the development of less developed countries (122)

international banking facility (IBF): entity of a U.S. bank that is exempted from domestic banking regulations as long as it provides only international banking services (184)

international business: business that engages in cross-border commercial transactions with individuals, private firms, and/or public sector organizations; term is also used to refer to cross-border transactions (13)

International Development Association (IDA): World Bank affiliate that specializes in loans to less developed countries (124)

International Finance Corporation: World Bank affiliate whose mission is the development of the private sector in developing countries (124)

international Fisher effect: observation that differences in nominal interest rates among countries are due to differences in their expected inflation rates (180)

international investments: capital supplied by residents of one country to residents of another (11)

international logistics: management functions associated with the international flow of materials, parts, supplies, and finished products from suppliers to the firm, between units of the firm itself, and from the firm to customers (596)

international marketing: extension of marketing activities across national boundaries; *see also* marketing (546)

International Monetary Fund (IMF): agency created by the Bretton Woods Agreement to promote international monetary cooperation after World War II (125)

international monetary system: system by which countries value and exchange their currencies (118)

international operations management: transformation-related activities of an international firm (583)

international order cycle time: time between placement of an order and its receipt by the customer (570)

international service business: firm that transforms resources into an intangible output that creates utility for its customers (598)

international strategic management: comprehensive and ongoing management planning process aimed at formulating and implementing strategies that enable a firm to compete effectively internationally (348)

international trade: voluntary exchange of goods, services, or assets between a person or organization located in one country and a person or organization located in another country (81)

international trading company: firm directly engaged in importing and exporting a wide variety of goods for its own account (390)

intracorporate transfer: selling of goods by a firm in one country to an affiliated firm in another country (385)

intraindustry trade: trade between two countries involving the exchange of goods produced by the same industry (90)

invoicing currency: currency in which an international transaction is invoiced (41)

irrevocable letter of credit: letter of credit that cannot be changed without the consent of the buyer, the seller, and the issuing bank (670)

J

Jamaica Agreement: agreement among central bankers made in 1976, allowing each country to adopt whatever exchange-rate system it wished (130)

joint venture: special form of strategic alliance created when two or more firms agree to work together and jointly own a separate firm to promote their mutual interests (413)

just-in-time (JIT) systems: systems in which suppliers are expected to deliver necessary inputs just as they are needed (9)

K

kabuskiki kaisha (KK): in Japan, term used to represent all limited-liability companies (10)

keiretsu: family of Japanese companies, often centered around a large bank or trading company, having extensive cross-ownership of shares and interacting with one another as suppliers or customers (58)

L

labor productivity: measure determined by dividing output by direct labor hours or costs; used to assess how efficiently an organization is using its workforce (525)

leadership: use of noncoercive influence to shape the goals of a group or organization, to motivate behavior toward reaching those goals, and to help determine the group or organizational culture (490)

leads and lags strategy: money management technique in which an MNC attempts to increase its holding of currencies and assets denominated in currencies that are expected to rise in value and to decrease its holdings of currencies and assets denominated in currencies that are expected to fall in value (637)

Leontief paradox: empirical finding that U.S. exports are more labor-intensive than U.S. imports, which is contrary to the predictions of the theory of relative factor endowments (89)

letter of credit: document issued by a bank promising to pay the seller if all conditions specified in the letter of credit are met (619)

licensee: firm that buys the rights to use the intellectual property of another firm (393)

licensing: transaction in which a firm (called the licensor) sells the rights to use its intellectual property to another firm (called a licensee) in return for a fee (12, 393)

licensor: firm that sells the rights to use its intellectual property to another firm (393)

lingua franca: common language (320)

location advantages: factors that affect the desirability of host country production relative to home country production (380)

locus of authority: where the power to make various decisions resides within the organization (511)

London Interbank Offer Rate (LIBOR): interest rate that London banks charge each other for short-term Eurocurrency loans (183)

long-term portfolio investments: portfolio investments with maturities of more than one year (141)

Louvre Accord: agreement made in 1987 among central bankers to stabilize the value of the U.S. dollar (132)

low-context culture: culture in which the words being spoken explicitly convey the speaker's message to the listener (323)

Ltd.: abbreviation used in the United Kingdom to indicate a privately held, limited liability company (10)

M

Maastricht Treaty: common name given to the Treaty on European Union (251)

macropolitical risk: political risk that affects all firms operating within a country (293)

make-or-buy decision: decision for an organization to either make its own inputs or buy them from outside suppliers (587)

managed float: flexible exchange system in which government intervention plays a major role in determining exchange rates; also called a dirty float (130)

managed trade: *see* fair trade

management contract: agreement whereby one firm provides managerial assistance, technical expertise, or specialized services to a second firm for some agreed-upon time in return for a fee (12, 400)

manufacturers' agents: agents who solicit domestic orders for foreign manufacturers, usually on a commission basis (391)

manufacturers' export agents: agents who act as an export department for domestic manufacturers, selling those firms' goods in foreign markets (391)

maquiladoras: Mexican factories located along the U.S.-Mexico border that receive preferential tariff treatment (219)

market pricing: customization of prices on a market-to-market basis to maximize profits (559)

market pricing policy: pricing policy under which prices are set on a market-by-market basis (159)

market socialism: form of socialism that allows significant private ownership of resources (55)

marketing: process of planning and executing the conception, pricing, promotion, and distribution of ideas, goods, and services to create exchanges that satisfy individual and organizational objectives (546)

marketing alliance: strategic alliance in which two or more firms share marketing services or expertise (422)

marketing mix: how a firm chooses to address product development, pricing, promotion, and distribution (549)

Marshall Plan: massive U.S. aid program following World War II; designed to help European nations rebuild themselves (22)

materials management: part of logistics management concerned with the flow of materials into the firm from suppliers and between units of the firm itself (596)

medium: communication channel used by an advertiser to convey a message (563)

mercantilism: economic philosophy based on the belief that a nation's wealth is measured by its holdings of gold and silver (82)

merchandise export: sale of a good to a resident of a foreign country (139)

merchandise exports and imports: trade involving tangible products (11)

merchandise import: purchase of a good from a resident of a foreign country (139)

Mercosur Accord: customs union composed of Argentina, Brazil, Paraguay, and Uruguay (260)

M-form design: form of organization design in which products are related in some way (449)

micropolitical risk: political risk that affects only specific firms or a specific industry operating within a country (293)

mission statement: definition of a firm's values, purpose, and directions (353)

most favored nation (MFN) principle: principle that any preferential treatment granted to one country must be extended to all countries (236)

motivation: overall set of forces that cause people to choose certain behaviors from a set of available behaviors (486)

multidomestic corporation: firm composed of relatively independent operating subsidiaries, each of which is focused on a specific domestic market (14)

Multifibre Agreement (MFA): commodity agreement among exporting and importing countries of textiles and apparel to control trade in those goods (265)

Multilateral Investment Guarantee Agency (MIGA): World Bank affiliate that offers political-risk insurance to investors in developing countries (124, 298)

multilateral netting: netting of transactions between three or more business units (636)

multinational corporation (MNC): incorporated firm that has extensive involvement in international business, engages in foreign direct investment, and owns or controls value-adding activities in more than one country (13)

multinational enterprise (MNE): business that may or may not be incorporated and has extensive involvement in international business (14)

multinational organization (MNO): any organization—business or not-for-profit—with extensive international involvement (14)

N

national competitive advantage, theory of: theory stating that success in international trade is based upon the interaction of four elements: factor conditions, demand conditions, related and supporting industries, and firm strategy, structure, and rivalry (96)

national defense argument: argument in favor of governmental intervention in trade holding that a nation should be self-sufficient in critical raw materials, machinery, and technology (198)

nationalization: transfer of property from a privately owned firm to the government (286)

neo-mercantilists: modern supporters of mercantilism, who hold that a country should erect barriers to trade to protect its industries from foreign competition; also called protectionists (83)

nirvana: state of spiritual perfection; according to the Hindu faith, one achieves nirvana by leading progressively ascetic and purer lives as one goes through the cycle of life, death, and rebirth (329)

nontariff barrier (NTB): any governmental regulation, policy, or procedure other than a tariff that has the effect of impeding international trade (210)

NV: in the Netherlands, abbreviation used to refer to a publicly held, limited-liability firm (10)

O

official reserves account: BOP account that records changes in official reserves owned by a central bank (142)

official settlements balance: BOP balance that measures changes in a country's official reserves (146)

offset obligations: agreement between an MNC and a host government in which the MNC agrees to provide some economic benefit to the host government in return for purchase of a good or service by the host government (289)

offset purchases: form of countertrade in which a portion of the exported good is produced in the importing country (622)

open account: type of payment in which the seller ships goods to the buyer prior to payment; seller relies on the promise of the buyer that payment will be forthcoming (616)

operations control: level of control that focuses on operating processes and systems within both the organization and its subsidiaries and operating units (514)

operations management: set of activities used by an organization to transform different kinds of resource inputs into final goods and services (583)

opportunity cost: value of what is given up in order to get the good or service in question (85)

organization change: any significant modification or alteration in a firm's strategy, organization design, technology, and/or employees (466)

organization design: overall pattern of structural components and configurations used to manage the total organization; also called organization structure (444)

Organization for Economic Cooperation and Development (OECD): organization whose 25 members are among the world's richest countries and consist of Canada, Mexico, the United States, Japan, Australia, New Zealand, and 19 Western European countries (43)

Organization of Petroleum Exporting Countries (OPEC): commodity cartel created to control production and prices of crude oil (264)

organization structure: *see* organization design

organizational control: level of control that focuses on the design of the organization itself (511)

overall cost leadership strategy: business-level strategy that emphasizes low costs (363)

overall productivity: productivity measure determined by dividing total outputs by total inputs; also called total factor productivity (525)

Overseas Private Investment Corporation (OPIC): U.S. government agency that promotes U.S. international business activities by providing political risk insurance (220, 298)

ownership advantages: resources owned by a firm that grant it a competitive advantage over its industry rivals (379)

ownership advantage theory: theory stating that foreign direct investment occurs because of ownership of valuable assets that confer monopolistic advantages in foreign markets (102)

P

paper gold: *see* special drawing rights

par value: official price of a currency in terms of gold (119)

parent-country nationals (PCNs): employees who are citizens of an international business's home country and are transferred to one of its foreign operations (691)

passive goal behavior: behavior based on the cultural belief that social relationships, quality of life, and concern for others are the basis of motivation and reflect the goals that a person should pursue (485)

passive income: *see* Subpart F income

payback period: number of years it takes a project to repay a firm's initial investment in that project (640)

pegged: tied to, as in "The gold standard created a fixed exchange-rate system because each country pegged the value of its currency to gold" (119)

per capita income: average income per person in a country (42)

performance appraisal: process of assessing how effectively a person is performing his or her job (703)

performance ratio: control technique based on a numerical index of performance that the firm wants to maintain (521)

personal selling: making sales on the basis of personal contacts (566)

planning process control: form of organizational control that focuses on the actual mechanics and processes a firm uses to develop strategic plans (512)

Plaza Accord: agreement made in 1985 among central bankers to allow the U.S. dollar to fall in value (132)

PLC: abbreviation used in the United Kingdom to indicate a publicly held, limited liability company

political risk: change in the political environment that may adversely affect the value of a firm (293)

political risk assessment: systematic analysis of the political risks that a firm faces when operating in a foreign country (293)

political union: complete political as well as economic integration of two or more countries (244)

polycentric approach: management approach in which a firm customizes its operations for each foreign market it serves (550)

polycentric staffing model: approach primarily using HCNs to staff upper-level foreign positions (693)

portfolio investments: passive holdings of stock, bonds, or other financial assets that do not entail active management or control of the securities' issuer by the investor (12, 99)

power orientation: cultural beliefs about the appropriateness of power and authority in hierarchies such as business organizations (480)

power respect: cultural belief that the use of power and authority is acceptable simply on the basis of position in a hierarchy (481)

power tolerance: cultural belief that the use of power and authority is not acceptable simply on the basis of position in a hierarchy (481)

principle of comity: *see* comity, principle of

privatization: sale of publicly owned property to private investors (53, 286)

product: international marketing mix component that comprises both tangible factors that the consumer can see or touch and numerous intangible factors (553)

product-support services: assistance a firm provides for customers regarding the operation, maintenance, and/or repair of its products (600)

production alliance: strategic alliance in which two or more firms each manufacture products or provide services in a shared or common facility (422)

production management: international operations management decisions and processes involving the creation of tangible goods (585)

productivity: economic measure of efficiency that summarizes the value of outputs relative to the value of inputs used to create them (524)

promotion: set of all efforts by an international firm to enhance the desirability of its products among potential buyers (561)

promotion mix: mix of advertising, personal selling, sales promotion, and public relations used by a firm to market its products (562)

protectionists: *see* neo-mercantilists

Protestant ethic: belief that hard work, frugality, and achievement are means of glorifying God (327)

public choice analysis: branch of economics that analyzes public decision making (203)

public-private venture: joint venture involving a partnership between a pri-

vately owned foreign firm and a government (428)

public relations: efforts aimed at enhancing a firm's reputation and image (567)

purchasing power parity (PPP): theory stating that the prices of tradable goods, when expressed in a common currency, will tend to equalize across countries as a result of exchange-rate changes (173)

put option: publicly traded contract granting the owner the right, but not the obligation, to sell a specific amount of foreign currency at a specified price at a stated future date (170)

Q

Quad: economic grouping of countries, consisting of Canada, the European Union, Japan, and the United States (40)

quality: totality of features and characteristics of a product or service that bear on its ability to satisfy stated or implied needs (527)

quota: deposit paid by a member nation when joining the International Monetary Fund (125)

quota: numerical limit on the quantity of a good that may be imported into a country (210)

R

R&D alliance: strategic alliance in which two or more firms agree to undertake joint research to develop new products or services (424)

R&D consortium: confederation of organizations that band together to research and develop new products and processes for world markets (424)

re-exporting: process of importation of a good into a country for immediate exportation, with little or no transformation of the good (61)

regional development banks: banks whose mission is to promote economic development of poorer nations within the region they serve (125)

related diversification: corporate-level strategy in which the firm operates in several different but related businesses, industries, or markets at the same time (359)

relative factor endowments, theory of: theory stating that a country will have a comparative advantage in producing goods that intensively use factors of production it has in abundance; also called Heckscher-Ohlin theory (87)

religious law: law based on officially established rules governing the faith and practice of a particular religion (277)

repatriate: to return to a home country (290)

repatriation: moving a manager back home after a foreign assignment has been completed (698)

resource deployment: component of strategy that answers the question "Given that we are going to compete in these markets, how will we allocate our resources to them?" (350)

responsibility center control: form of organizational control based on decentralized responsibility centers (512)

retention: extent to which a firm is able to retain its employees (708)

revocable letter of credit: letter of credit that can be changed by the bank without the consent of the buyer and the seller (620)

ringi system: Japanese approach to ensuring that decisions are made collectively, rather than by an individual (495)

royalty: compensation paid by a licensee to a licensor (395)

rules of origin: rules to determine which goods will benefit from reduced trade barriers in regional trading blocs (243)

S

sales promotion: specialized marketing efforts using such techniques as coupons and sampling (567)

sanctions: government-imposed restraints against commerce with a foreign country (279)

scope of operations: component of strategy that answers the question "Where are we going to conduct business?" (10)

screwdriver plant: domestic factory that assembles imported parts in which little value is added to the parts (258)

self-reference criterion: unconscious use of one's own culture to assess and understand a new culture (311)

service export: sale of a service to a resident of a foreign country (139)

service exports and imports: trade involving intangible products (11)

service import: purchase of a service from a resident of a foreign country (139)

service operations management: international operations management decisions and processes involving the creation of intangible services (586)

shared management agreement: management arrangement in which each partner in a strategic alliance fully and actively participates in managing the alliance (430)

short-term portfolio investments: portfolio investments with maturities of one year or less (140)

sight draft: draft that requires payment upon transfer of the goods to the buyer (618)

single-business strategy: corporate-level strategy that calls for a firm to rely on a single business, product, or service for all its revenue (359)

Smithsonian Conference: meeting held in Washington, D.C. in December 1971, during which central bank representatives from the Group of Ten agreed to restore the fixed exchange-rate system but with restructured rates of exchange between the major trading currencies (129)

social charter: EU policy promoting common job-related benefits and working conditions throughout the EU; also called Social Policy (256, 713)

social mobility: ability of individuals to move from one stratum of society to another (315)

social orientation: cultural beliefs about the relative importance of the individual and the groups to which an individual belongs (478)

Social Policy: *see* social charter

social stratification: organization of society into hierarchies based on birth, occupation, wealth, educational achievements, and/or other characteristics (315)

soft currencies: *see* inconvertible currencies

soft loans: loans made by the World Bank Group that bear significant risk of not being repaid (124)

sogo sosha: large Japanese trading company (58)

sourcing: set of processes and steps a firm uses to acquire the various resources it needs to create its own products (586)

Southern African Development Coordination Conference (SADCC): free trade area created by ten Southern African countries (263)

special drawing rights (SDRS): credits granted by the IMF that can be used to settle transactions among central banks; also called paper gold (129)

specific tariff: tax assessed as a specific dollar amount per unit of weight or other standard measure (206)

spot market: market for foreign exchange involving immediate delivery of the currency in question (169)

standard price policy: pricing policy under which a firm charges the same price for its products and services regardless of where they are sold (558)

statistical process control: family of mathematically based tools for monitoring and controlling quality (532)

statutory laws: laws enacted by legislative action (276)

sterling-based gold standard: gold standard in which the British pound is commonly used as an alternative means of settlement of transactions (120)

strategic alliance: business arrangement in which two or more firms choose to cooperate for their mutual benefit (413)

strategic business units (SBUs): "bundles" of businesses created by a firm using a corporate strategy of either related or unrelated diversification (362)

strategic control: process of monitoring how well an international business formulates and implements its strategies (507)

strategic goals: major objectives a firm wants to accomplish through the pursuit of a particular course of action (357)

strategic planning: process of developing a particular international strategy (348)

strategic trade theory: theory addressing the optimal policies through which a government may benefit its country by aiding domestic firms in monopolistic or highly oligopolistic industries (199)

Subpart F income: income earned from financial transactions, such as dividends, interest, and royalties; also called passive income (675)

subsidiary bank: separately incorporated overseas banking operation (182)

Super 301: section of U.S. trade law that requires the U.S. trade representative to publicly identify countries that flagrantly engage in unfair trade practices (273)

sustainable competitive advantage: advantage over competitors that can be sustained over time (351)

swap market: facet of international capital market in which two firms can exchange financial obligations (643)

swap transaction: transaction involving the simultaneous purchase and sale of a foreign currency with delivery at two different points in time (170)

switching arrangements: agreement under which firms may transfer their countertrade obligations to a third party (623)

SWOT analysis: analysis of a firm and its environment to determine its strengths, weaknesses, opportunities, and threats (352)

synergy: component of strategy that answers the question "How can different elements of our business benefit each other?" (352)

T

tactics: methods used by middle managers to implement strategic plans (357)

tariff: tax placed on a good involved in international trade (205)

tax havens: countries that charge low, often zero, taxes on corporate incomes and that offer an attractive business climate (673)

tax-equalization system: system for ensuring that an expatriate's after-tax income in the host country is comparable to what the person's after-tax income would be in the home country (705)

temporal method: approach used to consolidate the financial statements of a foreign subsidiary whose functional currency is the U.S. dollar (666)

theocracy: country whose legal system is based upon religious law (277)

theory of absolute advantage: *see* absolute advantage, theory of

theory of comparative advantage: *see* comparative advantage, theory of

theory of national competitive advantage: *see* national competitive advantage, theory of

theory of purchasing power parity: *see* purchasing power parity (PPP)

theory of relative factor endowments: *see* relative factor endowments, theory of

third-country nationals (TCNs): employees of an international business who are not citizens of the firm's home or host country (692)

three-point arbitrage: arbitrage based upon exploiting differences between the direct rate of exchange between two currencies and their cross-rate of exchange using a third currency (175)

time draft: draft that requires payment at some specified time after the transfer of goods to the buyer (618)

time orientation: cultural beliefs regarding long-term versus short-term outlooks on work, life, and other aspects of society (486)

tort laws: laws covering wrongful acts, damages, and injuries (281)

total factor productivity: *see* overall productivity

total quality management (TQM): integrated effort to systematically and continuously improve the quality of an organization's products and/or services (530)

trade: voluntary exchange of goods, services, or assets between one person or organization and another (81)

trade acceptance: time draft that has been signed by the buyer signifying a promise to honor the payment terms (618)

trade creation: shifting of production from high-cost producers to low-cost producers within a regional trading bloc (245)

trade deflection: rerouting of exported goods to the member of a free trade area with the lowest barriers to imports from nonmember countries (242)

trade diversion: shifting of production to higher-cost producers located within a regional trading bloc from lower-cost producers located outside the trading bloc (245)

trade in invisibles: British term denoting trade in services (139)

trade in visibles: British term referring to merchandise trade (139)

training: instruction directed at enhancing job-related skills and abilities (700)

transaction currency: currency in which an international transaction is denominated (166)

transaction exposure: financial risks that occur because the financial benefits and costs of an international transaction may be affected by exchange rate movements occurring after the firm is legally obligated to the transaction (626)

transactions costs: costs of negotiating, monitoring, and enforcing a contract (102)

transfer pricing: prices that one branch or subsidiary of a parent firm charges for goods, services, or property sold to a second branch or subsidiary of the same parent firm (282, 670)

transit tariff: tax levied on goods as they pass through one country bound for another (206)

translation: process of transforming the accounting statements of a foreign subsidiary into the home country's currency using the home country's accounting procedures (664)

translation exposure: impact on a firm's consolidated financial statements of fluctuations in foreign exchange rates that change the value of foreign subsidiaries as measured in the parent's currency (629)

transnational corporation: organization that seeks to combine the benefits of global-scale efficiencies with the benefits of local responsiveness (15)

treasury management: management of financial flows and their associated currency and interest-rate risks (647)

Treaty on European Union: treaty signed in 1992 that came into force on November 1, 1993, furthering economic and political integration of the EC's members; important provisions include the creation of an economic and monetary union, a cohesion fund, a pledge to cooperate on foreign and defense policies, and the renaming of the EC as the European Union; commonly known as the Maastricht Treaty (251)

Treaty of Rome: treaty signed in 1957 that established the European Economic Community; its original six signatories have expanded to 15 over time (246)

Triad: grouping of countries that dominate the world economy, consisting of the European Union, Japan, and the United States (40)

Triffin paradox: paradox that resulted from reliance on the U.S. dollar as the primary source of liquidity in the Bretton Woods system; for trade to grow, foreigners needed to hold more dollars; the more dollars they held, however, the less faith they had in the U.S. dollar, thereby undermining the Bretton Woods system (127)

turnkey project: contract under which a firm agrees to fully design, construct, and equip a facility and then turn the project over to the purchaser when it is ready for operation (400)

turnover: rate at which people leave an organization (708)

two-point arbitrage: riskless purchase of a product in one geographic market for immediate resale in a second geographic market in order to profit from price differences between the markets; also called geographic arbitrage (175)

two-tiered pricing policy: pricing policy under which a firm sets one price for all its domestic sales and a second price for all its international sales (558)

two-transaction approach: approach used by U.S. firms to account on their income statements for transactions denominated in foreign currencies (663)

U

U-form organization: form of organization design based on global functional design

uncertainty acceptance: cultural belief that uncertainty and ambiguity are stimulating and present new opportunities (482)

uncertainty avoidance: cultural belief that uncertainty and ambiguity are unpleasant and should be avoided (482)

uncertainty orientation: cultural beliefs about uncertainty and ambiguity (482)

unilateral transfers: gifts made by residents of one country to residents of another country (140)

unrelated diversification: corporate-level strategy that calls for a firm to operate in several unrelated businesses, industries, or markets (361)

Uruguay Round: GATT negotiations (1986–1994) that created the World Trade Organization, slashed tariff rates, and strengthened enforcement of intellectual property rights (237)

V

value chain: technique for assessing a firm's strengths and weaknesses by identifying its most important activities (356)

vertical integration: extent to which a firm either provides its own resources or obtains them from other sources (586)

voluntary export restraint (VER): promise by a country to limit its exports of a good to another country (212)

W

Webb-Pomerene association: group of U.S. firms that operate within the same industry and that are allowed by law to coordinate their export activities without fear of violating U.S. antitrust laws (390)

with recourse: term signifying that should a trade acceptance or banker's acceptance sold by an exporter to an investor fail to be paid, the exporter will reimburse the investor; the exporter retains the risk of default by the signer of the acceptance (619)

without recourse: term signifying that should a trade acceptance or banker's acceptance sold by an exporter to an investor fail to be paid, the exporter is not obligated to reimburse the investor; the investor retains the risk of default by the signer of the acceptance (619)

World Bank: *see* International Bank for Reconstruction and Development

World Bank Group: organization consisting of the World Bank and its affiliated organizations, the International Development Agency, the International Finance Corporation, and the Multilateral Investment Guarantee Agency (123)

world company: currently hypothetical firm that transcends national boundaries and has no national identity (16)

World Trade Organization (WTO): successor organization to the GATT founded in 1995; created by the Uruguay Round negotiations (239)

Company Index

A. Schuman, Inc., 676
AB Electrolux, 269, 600
Accor SA, 399, 359–361
Acer Inc., 106
Acucobol, 421
Adam Opel AG, 98, 389, 639, 665
Adidas, 182
AEG, 451
AEG Hausgerate, 269
Aerolineas Argentinas, 319
Aeromexico, 47
AIG, 214
Air Canada, 45, 299, 319
Air France, 319, 400, 467, 582, 601, 613
Air Inter, 467
Airbus Industrie, 26, 220, 382
Akrihin Chemical Company, 417
Alcan Aluminum, 22
Alcatel Alsthom, 200
Alcoa, 17, 292
Aldi, 515
Alitalia, 215
All Nippon Airways, 417
Allied-Lyons PLC, 399, 630
Allied Stores, 25
Amatil, 574
American Airlines, 26, 184, 319, 414, 613
American Express, 185, 554, 621, 702
American Motors Corporation, 22, 285, 297, 413, 429, 431, 661
American Telephone & Telegraph. See AT&T
Amoco, 428
Amstel, 377
Amway, 566
An Tai Bao coal mine, 290
Andersen, Arthur. See Arthur Andersen
Andersen Consulting, 692
Anglo-Suisse, 54
Anheuser-Busch, 216, 377
Apple Computer, 93–94, 97, 231, 381, 388, 415, 461
Aramco, 400, 558
Archer Daniels Midland, 210
Arista, 452
Arnotts, Ltd., 403
Arthur Andersen, 680
Arthur Young, 679
Asahi Breweries Ltd., 323
Asahi Glass, 391, 426, 427
Asahi Video Products Company, 426
Asea, 320
Asea Brown Boveri, Ltd. (ABB), 16
Association of Guatemala Coffee Producers, 384

AT&T, 368, 415, 422–423, 432, 555, 601, 692, 697
Avis, 399
Avon, 557, 566, 572
Ayala Corporation, 105

Bacardi, Ltd., 403
Bally of Switzerland, 702
Baltek Corporation, 643
Banco Economico SA, 448
Banco National de Mexico, 446
Bandag, Inc., 251
Bang & Olufsen, 370
Bank of England, 510
Bankers Trust, 630
Bantam, 452
Barclays Bank, 120, 330
Baring Futures PLC, 510
BASF AG, 9
Baskin-Robbins, 297, 399
Bausch & Lomb, 555
Baxter International, 283
Bayerische Motoren Werke (BMW), 98, 132, 355, 356, 357, 367, 423, 456, 467, 586, 588, 632
Bean, L.L. See L.L. Bean
Bechtel, Brown and Root, 401
Beech, 281
Beecham, 397
Beecham Group PLC, 468
Beijing Automotive Works, 297, 413, 431
Beijing Jeep, 296, 479, 487, 661
Bendix Electronics, 505
Benetton Group Spa, 10, 106, 399, 581–582, 583, 595
Bertelsmann AG, 16, 25, 452
Bertelsmann Club, 452
Bethlehem Steel, 22
Bharat Earth Movers, Ltd., 111
Bibby Backhoe. See John Bibby Backhoe Hire
Bic Pen Company, 363, 548
Big Boy, 555
Black & Decker, 445
Blockbuster Entertainment Corporation, 406–407, 617
Bloomingdale's, 25
Blue Bell Creameries, 303–304
BMW. See Bayerische Motoren Werke
Boeing Aircraft Company, 11, 12, 22, 26, 91, 96, 102, 220, 322, 351, 355, 382, 412, 417, 423, 430–431, 558, 595, 622
Bolivia Power, 526
Boliviana de Energia Electrica SA, 526

Bond Corporation Holdings, Inc., 465–466
Borden, 23
Bridgestone Corporation, 399, 456, 492, 586
Briggs and Stratton, 282–283
Brilliance China Automotive Holdings, 72
Bristol-Myers Squibb, 417
BRITE, 424
British Airport Authority, 286
British Airways, 94, 141, 185, 286, 319, 414, 415, 433–434, 454, 455, 598, 613
British American Tobacco, 567
British East India Company, 19
British Leyland Motor Corporation, 34
British Petroleum, 9, 286, 298, 385, 428, 582, 586–587, 589–590, 593
British Steel, 299
British Telecom, 286
Brown Boveri, 320
Burlington Northern, Inc., 10
Business International, 298

CAAC, 355
Cadbury Schweppes PLC, 363, 403, 452–453, 643
Caja de Madrid, 233
Calpis, 570
Calvin Klein, 363
Cambridge Shopping Centres, Ltd., 417
Campbell Soup, 403
Campeau Corporation, 25
Canal Plus SA, 215
Canon, 9, 388, 413, 414, 533
Capel. See James Capel
Cargill, 37, 215
Carnation, 512
Carrefour SA, 10
Case, 456
Casio Computer Company, 361
Caterpillar, 23, 79–80, 81, 98, 100, 102, 111–112, 132, 165, 197, 218, 321, 356–357, 549, 554, 642–643
Cathay Pacific, 355
Cave Wood Transport, 233
CBS Records, 25, 357–358
Celanese, 25
Cementarny a Vapenka Mokra, 124
Ceramica Santa Anita, 284
Cereal Partners Worldwide (CPW), 412
Cessna Aircraft, 281
Charles Jourdan Industries, 631–632
Charles of the Ritz, 561

Charles Wells Brewery, 393
Chase Manhattan Bank, 155, 166
Chemical Bank, 630
Chinatex, 622
Christie's, 250
Chrysler Motor Corporation, 22, 25, 161,
   209, 219, 222, 230, 245, 367, 369,
   413, 553
Chung Shing Textile Company, 72
Ciba-Geigy, 427
Cidesport, 289
Cifra, 447
Cipal-Parc Asterix, 348
Citicorp, 16, 185, 630
Citivision PLC, 407, 617
Citrovita, 105
Clovergem Fish and Food Ltd., 124
Coca-Cola, 6, 7, 62, 95, 107, 351–352,
   363, 419, 430, 509, 549, 551, 557,
   561, 562, 565, 572–574, 576, 624,
   660, 672–673, 695
Cofab, 261
Colfax and Fowler, 635
Colgate-Palmolive, 285, 566, 695
Colin Street Bakery, 211
Columbia Pictures, 350–351, 352,
   507–508
Compaq Computer Corporation, 99,
   117, 231, 381, 451, 582, 588, 594,
   596, 639, 665, 674, 675, 695
ConAgra, 545
Concord Camera, 104
Continental, 94
Cook. See Thomas Cook
Corning, Inc., 426, 533
Cornnuts, 289
CPC International, Inc., 417
Creditanstalt, 298
Crestone Energy Corporation, 70

Daewoo Group, 9, 22, 60, 434
Daewoo Motors, 434, 527
Dai-Ichi Kangyo Bank, 598
Daimler-Benz, 7, 14, 98, 109, 197, 218,
   269, 351, 441, 449, 450, 451, 465,
   505, 632, 657, 660
Daimler-Benz InterServices, 451
Dairy Queen, 399
Daiwa Securities, 185, 190
Dakin, Inc., 207, 208
De Francisci Machine Corporation, 220
Deere, 456
Dell Computer Corporation, 117, 452,
   571, 664
Deloitte Haskins & Sells, 679
Deloitte Touche Tohmatsu, 679
Delta Air Lines, 26, 141, 319, 400, 414,
   613, 665, 713

Delta Brewery, 263
Desmarais & Frere, Ltd., 195–196, 199,
   203, 242–243
Deutsche Aerospace, 451
Deutsche Bank AG, 10, 22–23, 368
Deutsche Treuhand, 679
DHL International, 37
DHL Worldwide Express, 356, 416
Diane Von Furstenberg Cosmetics, 397
Diebold, 421
Dillard's, 47, 572, 593
Disney. See Walt Disney Company
Disney Channel, 353, 361
Disney Consumer Products, 353
Disney Stores, 353
Disney-MGM Studios, 353
Disney-MGM Theme Park, 345
Disneyland, 353
Domino's Pizza, 399, 555
Dong-A Motor Co., 111
Dongbang Corporation, 37
Donnelly Corp., 590–591, 597
Dornier, 451
Doubleday, 452
Dow Chemical, 23, 427, 461
Dow-Jones Company, 386
Dr. Pepper/Seven-Up Companies, Inc.,
   403
Dresser Industries, 111
Dunes Hotel and Casino, 496, 497
Dunkin' Donuts, 399
Dunlop, 19
DuPont, 17, 23, 692
DuPont Merck Pharmaceutical Company,
   381
Dutch East India Company, 19

Eastman Kodak, 6, 7, 25, 72
Edcadassa, 214
EDM, 635
Ek Chor Distribution System, 417
Electronic Liquid Fillers (ELF), 394
Emerson Electric, 447
Ente Nazionale Idrocarburi (ENI), 400
Ericcson, 19
Ernst & Whitney, 679
Ernst & Young, 528, 598, 679
ESPRIT, 424
Esprit de Corp, 695
EURAM, 424
Euramerica, 310
Euro Disney, 293, 294, 345–347, 348,
   355, 357, 403, 412, 522, 594, 601
Europcar International SA, 461
European Broadcasters Union, 6
Eurostar Automobil Fabrik GmbH, 222
Exxon, 28, 387, 400, 582
Ezaki Glico, 304

Federal Express, 214, 356, 416
Federal-Mogul, 666
Federated Department Stores, 25
Fiat Spa, 10, 467, 588
Fifth Generation Computer Systems
   Project, 424
Firestone, 492
First International, 93
Fleggaard, 250
Fletcher Challenge Ltd., 401
FMC, 595
Ford Motor Company, 12, 22, 23, 25,
   33–34, 100, 141, 161, 209, 219, 245,
   261, 367, 381, 385, 421, 433, 437–438,
   443–444, 454, 456, 463, 467, 563,
   591–592, 595, 635, 665, 671, 675
Foster's Brewing Group, 352, 523
Fox Network, 659
France Telecom, 257
Freia Marabou, 403
Friedrich Krupp GmbH, 401
Fuji, 22, 25, 90, 363, 413, 414, 417, 418,
   424, 431
Fuji Photo Film, 421, 434
Fuji Xerox, 421–422, 434, 533
Fujitsu, 292, 434
Fukusuke Corporation, 622
Furukawa Electric, 505

Gap, The, 581
Garuda Air, 521–522
GE. See General Electric
Genentech, 427
General Dynamics, 622
General Electric, 22, 285, 361, 423, 426,
   506, 526, 554, 660–661, 702
General Electric Corporation, 425, 432
General Foods, 467
General Mills, 245, 411–412, 413, 421,
   426, 433, 434
General Motors, 22, 25, 33, 43, 54, 114,
   168, 209, 219, 245, 261, 321, 367,
   388–389, 402, 418, 422, 430, 434,
   443, 468, 588, 665, 697–698
General Motors Import & Distribution
   Company GmbH, 389
Ghiardelli Chocolate Company, 211
Gillette, 429
Giro Sport Design, 318
Glasbau Hahn, 351
Glaverbel, 299, 430
Glavunion, 430
Glaxo Holdings PLC, 10, 524
GM. See General Motors
Goldman Sachs, 183, 189, 190, 642
Goldstar, 527
Goodyear, 23
Groupe Bull, 257

Grupo Herdez, 284
Grupo ICA, 417
Grupo Modelo SA, 554, 557
Guardian Glass, 430
Guardian Industries, 214
Gulf and Western, 361, 362

Hachette SA, 10, 351
Haden MadLellan Holdings, 606
Harley-Davidson, 114, 199, 226–227
Harris Associates, 651
Harrod's, 548
Harsco Corporation, 450, 452
Hay Group, 706
Hayes Microcomputer Products, 555
Heineken NV, 105, 377–378, 394–395, 397, 587
Heinz. *See* H.J. Heinz Company
Henkel KGaA, 10, 301
Hershey Foods, 355
Hertz, 399
Hewlett-Packard, 93, 384, 461, 708
Hilton Hotels, 399, 400, 710
Hindustan Lever, 508
Hino Motors, 654–655
Hitachi, 25, 350, 374, 433
H.J. Heinz Company, 17, 28, 72, 403, 555
Hoechst AG, 25
Hoffman-LaRoche, 330
Honda, 9, 17, 25, 99, 114, 226, 227, 363, 367, 402, 404, 461, 465, 562, 590–591, 597, 686, 702
Hoover Company, 251, 269–270
Hoover Europe, 568
Host Marriott, 400
Household Finance, 185
Hudson's Bay Company, 19
Hughes Network Systems, 54
Hyundai, 60, 93, 363, 387, 391, 548
Hyundai Group, 401

Iberia Airlines, 319, 335
Ibis, 399
IBM, 14, 17, 23, 37, 141, 231, 292, 330, 350, 381, 401, 407, 415, 416–417, 421, 422, 424, 427, 450–451, 463, 498, 565, 588, 610, 692
IBM UK, 606–607
Ideal Loisirs, 357
IKEA, 114
Imperial Chemical Industries PLC, 695
Inco, Ltd., 379, 644
Infast, 606
Intel, 93, 96, 350, 384, 424, 593, 595, 692
International Business Machines. *See* IBM
International Business Protocol Services, Inc., 309

International Computers, Ltd. (ICL), 434
International Nickel. *See* Inco, Ltd.
Internationale Nederlanden Groep, 510
Interpublic Group, 564
Italgrani, 622
ITT, 361

Jacob Suchard, 467
Jaguar Motor Company, 12, 33, 34, 100, 141, 665, 675
JAL, 582
James Capel, 606
Janssen Pharmaceutica, 646–648
Japan Air Lines, 22, 141, 417, 558, 613
Japan Marketing Services, 572
Japanese Broadcasting Corporation, 423
Jardine Matheson Holdings, Ltd., 19
JASKO International, 446
J.C. Penney, 47, 258, 289, 593, 716, 717
John Bibby Backhoe Hire, 79
Johnson & Johnson (J&J), 646, 667, 668, 702
Johnson Wax, *See* S.C. Johnson & Son
Jourdan, Charles. *See* Charles Jourdan Industries
Jordan Marsh, 25
JOULE, 424
Jovan, 397
Jusco Co., 537
JVC, 426

Kal Kan, 694
Karstadt, 716, 717
Kashima Oil, 630
Kaufhof, 156
Kawasaki, 226, 227, 417, 431, 562
Kellogg, 28, 411, 412, 421
Kentucky Fried Chicken. *See* KFC
Kenya Power & Lighting, 519, 520
KFC, 106, 399, 563, 574
Kirin Brewery, 391, 393
KLM Royal Dutch Airlines (KLM), 25, 94, 319, 400, 613–614, 626, 642
Klynveld Kraayenhoff, 679
Klynveld Main Goerdeler (KMG), 108, 679
Kmart, 104, 195, 206, 448, 548
KMG. *See* Klynveld Main Goerdeler
Kodak, 90, 402, 413, 414, 418, 424
Koito Manufacturing, 58
Komaromi Sorgyar, 378
Komatsu Ltd., 80, 102, 111–112, 132, 165
KPMG, 108, 679, 680
Kraft, 467
Kroger, 571
Kubota, 285
Kuwait Oil, 558

LanChile, 319
Lands' End, Inc., 10, 363
Laura Ashley, 517, 520, 534, 537–538
Lazarus, 25
Lean Cuisine, 512
Lever Brothers, 470
Lever Europe, 467, 471
Levi Strauss Company, 108, 563, 565, 576, 610
Levi's Only Stores, 576
Liberty Ships, 96
Limited, Inc., The, 361, 581
Lionel Train Company, 320
Lipton. *See* Thomas J. Lipton Co.
Lloyds of London, 14, 120, 296
L.L. Bean, 533
Lockheed, 22
Loewen Group, 258, 260
Long-Term Credit Bank of Japan, 659
Louis Vuitton, 95
LTV, 361
Lucky-Goldstar Group, 60, 363, 391
Lufthansa, 141, 527, 558, 613, 657
LVMH Moet Hennessy Louis Vuitton, 379

Macy's, 572, 593
Magnavox, 373
Main Hurdman & Cranstoun, 679
Majestic Films, 423
Mantrust, 509
Marc Rich & Co., 623, 624
Margarine Union, 470
Marks and Spencer PLC, 359, 363
Marriott Corporation, 399, 400
Marriott International, 400
Mars, Inc., 557
Martini and Rossi, 403
MasterCard, 621
Matsushita Electric Industrial Co., 26, 27, 97, 185, 358, 404, 415, 424, 426, 461, 506, 677
Mattel, 555
Maytag Corporation, 156, 251, 269, 467
Mazda Motor Corporation, 22, 25, 27–28, 34, 209, 230, 421, 433, 437–438, 463, 487, 559, 594, 665, 675, 686
MCA, 367, 404
McDonald's, 61, 72, 102, 103, 175, 176–177, 274, 300, 330, 398, 554, 572, 576, 601
McDonnell Douglas, 22, 26, 91, 289, 382
McGraw-Hill, 104
MCI Communications Corporation, 287, 355, 368
McKinsey & Company, 40, 551
Mercedes-Benz. *See* Daimler-Benz

Merck & Co., 23, 677
Merrill Lynch, 183, 185, 189, 642
Metallgesellschaft, 583–584
Metropolitan, 195
MG Car Company, 33–34
Michelin Company, 95
Microsoft Corporation, 381, 663
Miller Brewing Company, 216, 377, 378, 523
Minnesota Mining & Manufacturing (3M), 708
Minolta, 413, 414
Mitac International, 93
Mitsubishi Bank, 391
Mitsubishi Corporation, 391
Mitsubishi Electric, 391
Mitsubishi Estate Co., 141, 391
Mitsubishi Group, 391
Mitsubishi Heavy Industries, 79, 100, 111–112
Mitsubishi Motors, 200, 391, 417, 422, 424, 431, 467, 574, 583, 686
Mitsui and Company, 17
Mitsui Construction Company, 511
Molson, 393, 523
Monsanto, 23
Moore Corporation, 9
Morgan Stanley, 190
Motel 6, 361, 399, 601
Motorola, Inc., 25, 72, 96, 312, 373–374, 424
MPO Khimvolokno, 430
MTU, 423, 451

National Power Corporation, 626
National Semiconductor, 93
NBC, 361
NEC, 96, 350, 363, 456
Nestlé Corporation, 14, 16, 27, 28, 184, 285, 411–412, 413, 419, 421, 426, 433, 434, 445, 452, 453, 459, 464–465, 512, 513, 545–546, 556, 565, 677, 693
Newcomm, Ltd., 423
News Corporation, 659
Nike, 549
Nikon, 363, 391, 413, 414
Nintendo Company, 273, 396
Nippon Steel & Chemical Co., 630
Nippon Telephone and Telegraph (NT&T), 424, 456, 601
Nissan Motor Company, 22, 25, 27, 34, 42, 204, 223, 333–334, 367, 387, 402, 456, 459, 460, 467, 572, 594, 632, 686
Nissan Motors (GB), 572
Nissan UK, 572
Nixdorf, 505

Nomura Securities Company, Ltd., 186, 188–190, 642
Nordstrom's, 593
Northern Telecom, 9, 27, 215, 415, 512, 514
Northwest Airlines, 25, 94, 613
Novell, 415
Novetel, 399
NT&T. *See* Nippon Telephone and Telegraph
Nummi (New United Motor Manufacturing, Inc.), 418, 422
Nynex Corp., 699

Occidental Petroleum, 290
O.I. International, 446, 447
Oleg Cassini, 397
Olivetti, 422–423, 432
Opel. *See* Adam Opel AG
Oriental Land Company, 345
Orion Pictures, 423
Ormat, Inc., 626
Outokumpu OY, 640

P&G. *See* Procter & Gamble
Pace, Inc., 382
Palma, 301
Pan American World Airways, 141, 414, 415
Pari Mutuel Urbain (PMU), 107
Pearl Jam, 168
Peat Marwick Mitchell, 108, 467, 679
Peerless Manufacturing, 590
Pemex, 558
Penney. *See* J.C. Penney
Pennzoil, 298
People's Liberation Army, 297
PepsiCo, 6, 95, 107, 310, 340, 397, 401, 419, 426, 430, 440, 466, 568, 624, 639–640, 702
Petroleos de Venezuela (PDV), 522
Peugeot, 197, 204
Philbro, 54
Philco, 373
Philip Morris Company, 28, 403, 449, 467, 523, 567
Philips, 72, 320, 350, 374, 407, 506, 582
Philips Electronics NV, 10, 659, 693
Philips Industries, 268, 269
Phillips Petroleum, 708
Pilkington PLC, 282, 430
Pillsbury, 321
Pioneer Electronic Corporation, 358
Pirelli SpA, 361, 366
Pizza Hut, 340, 399, 465, 466, 624
Placer Dome Inc., 640
Playmates, 357
Plessey, 505

Polaroid, 23
Poliolefinas, 211
Porsche, 98, 632
PPG, 427
Pratt & Whitney, 423
Price Waterhouse, 680
Procter & Gamble (P&G), 37, 301, 317, 367, 471, 545, 555, 571, 630
Prudential Insurance, 701

Qantas, 613
Quality Coils, Inc., 711
Quanta Group, 61

Raba, 430
RACE, 424
Rainforest Alliance, 137
Rakovnik, 301
Rank Organization PLC, 501
Rank Xerox, 421, 434, 501–502
Ray Ban, 6
Raychem, 702
RCA, 22, 373, 452
RCA Records, 25
Reebok, 6
Renault, 197, 204, 245, 261
Reuters, 16
RJR Nabisco, 403, 546, 567
Robert Bosch GMBH, 351
Rockefeller Group, 141
Rolex, 363
Rolls-Royce, 423
Rothmans, 567
Rowntree Mackintosh PLC, 545
Royal Dutch Shell, 19, 509, 630

Saab, 588
Sabena, 467
Safeway, 571
Saks Fifth Avenue, 548
Salomon Brothers, 183, 190
Sam's Wholesale Clubs, 417
Samsung, 60, 93, 245, 250, 391, 427, 467, 527, 560, 702
San Francisco-Moscow Teleport, Inc., 54
San Miguel, 263
SAS, 94
Satachi & Satachi, 564
S.C. Johnson & Son, 285, 301
SCIENCE, 424
Seagram, 546, 565
Seiko, 7
Sematech, 424
7-Eleven, 258, 521
Shanghai Petrochemical, 72
Shanghai Razor Factory, 429
Sharp Corporation, 351

Shell, 493–494, 582. *See also* Royal Dutch Shell

Showa Shell Seikiyu K.K., 510, 630

Siam Cement, 380

Siemens AG, 9, 72, 156, 245, 350, 415, 422, 425, 427, 432, 441, 498, 505–506

Siemens Nixdorf, 450–451, 468

Singapore Airlines, 613, 665

Singapore Technologies Holdings (STH), 521

Six Flags, 355

Sklo Union, 299, 430

Skoda, 299

Sky Broadcasting, 434, 659

Sofitel, 361, 399

Sogeti SA, 514

Solomon, Inc., 54

Solvay America Inc., 706

Solvay & Cie, 706

Sony Corporation, 7, 12, 25, 27, 90, 95, 97, 197, 350–351, 352, 357–358, 364, 418, 447, 464, 475–477, 489, 491, 497, 507–508, 563, 582, 586

Sony Records, 589

Sotheby's, 250

Source Perrier SA, 532

Sover SpA, 290

Space-Lok, Inc., 382

Sprint, 368

St. Gobain, 430

STAR-TV, 659

Statoil, 298, 428

Ste. Suisse Microelectronique d'Horlogerie SA (SMH), 548, 572

Stella D'Oro Company, 403

Stern's, 25

Steyr-Daimler Puch AG, 222

Stouffer's Hotels, 512

Subaru, 6–7

Sumitomo Bank Ltd., 437

Sumitomo Trust & Banking Co., 707

Suzhou Spectacles No. 1 Factory, 290

Suzuki Motor Company, 226, 227, 434

Swire Pacific, Ltd., 10

Swissair, 665

Taco Bell, 340

Tatung, 93

TECO Information Systems, 93

Telefonos de Mexico, 47, 286

Teva Pharmaceutical Industries, Ltd., 381

Texas Instruments (TI), 25, 289, 458, 465, 477, 534–535, 548, 692

Texas Instruments Registration and Identification Systems (Tiris), 534–535

Textron, 362

TF1, 215

Thomas Cook, 120, 600

Thomas J. Lipton Co., 419

Thomson SA, 374, 426

3M, 708

Timex, 363

Tivoli Gardens, 348

TNT, Ltd., 356, 416

Tohmatsu & Co., 679

Tokyo Disneyland, 345, 347, 396, 632

Toshiba, 25, 96, 97, 350, 373, 415, 463, 467, 498, 569

Touche Ross & Company, 679

Toyota Motor Corporation, 9, 14, 17, 22, 25, 27, 58, 102, 109, 114, 166, 204, 205, 209, 223, 230, 245, 284, 285, 333, 367, 369, 380, 389, 418, 422, 463, 467, 553, 559, 563, 568, 594, 655, 671, 685–686, 687, 710

Toys 'R' Us, 171, 273–274

Trifast, 606–607

Triumph Motor Company, 33, 34

Tungsram, 661

Unilever, 14, 19, 37, 245, 367, 419, 467, 470–471, 508–509, 553, 565

Unilever NV, 470

Unilever PC, 470

Union Carbide, 291–292

Unisys, 433

United Airlines, 26, 319, 414, 415, 558, 613

United Distillers PLC, 512

United Parcel Service (UPS), 416

Universal Studios, 355, 367

Univision, 317

U.S. Steel, 22

US West, 287

USAir, 94, 141, 433

Value Clubs, 417

Van Camp Seafood, 509

Van Munching & Company, 377, 378

Varyeganneftegas, 54

VISA, 6, 554, 621

Volkswagen AG, 10, 98, 261, 285, 299, 505

Volvo, 9, 422, 467, 631

Volvo Car BV, 422

Von Furstenberg Cosmetics. *See* Diane Von Furstenberg Cosmetics

VW-Skoda, 430

Wal-Mart, 47, 104, 258, 417, 446–447, 448, 548, 596, 610

Walt Disney Company, 27, 95, 185, 289, 345–348, 350, 353, 355, 356, 357, 358, 359, 361, 362, 364, 367, 396, 403, 434, 522, 533, 594, 632, 643

Walt Disney World, 345

Warner Brothers, 589

Wasserstein Perella Group, 189

Waterford Wedgewood, 95, 363

Wattie Foods, Ltd., 403

WEFA Group, 117

Werk für Fernsehelektronik, 250

Western Electric, 215

Westinghouse Electric Corporation, 362

Weyerhaeuser Co., 117, 428

Whirlpool, 267–270, 367, 551

Whistler Radar, 522–523, 528

White Nights, 54

Woolworths, 195, 548

Worldwide Fund for Nature, 137

WPP Group, 564

Wyatt Co., 706

Xerox, 22, 421, 422, 501, 533, 695

Yamaha, 226, 227

Yaohan International, 382, 384

Young, Arthur. *See* Arthur Young

Zellers, 195

Zenith, 373

Zhejiang Spark Industrial Automatic Meter Industrial Development Group, 63

Brand Name Index

Accord, 363
After Eight, 545
All, 470
Apple II, 93
Asterix the Gaul, 361

Babar, 348, 357
Barbie, 273, 555
Bauknecht, 269
Beechnut, 452
Beijing Jeep, 413, 429, 431
Betamax, 418
Bic, 565
Big Mac, 175, 176
Binx Nut, 606
BMG Ariola, 452
BMW, 90, 132, 355, 548
Boeing, 91, 417 737, 747, 757, 777
Bridgestone, 399, 456
Buena Vista, 364

Cadbury Chocolate, 452
Cafe Racer, 226
Canada Dry, 452
Carnation, 546
Cheerios, 411
Chesebrough-Ponds, 470
Chicken of the Sea, 509
Chivas Regal, 565
Christian Dior, 379
Civic, 363
Close-Up, 470
Coca-Cola, 397, 574
Coca-Cola Light, 557
Contour, 443–444, 563
Cool Whip, 449
Cornetto, 553
Corolla, 22
Corona, 22, 554, 557
Coronita, 557
Crown Victoria, 386

Datsun, 22, 34
DC-8, 91
Diet Coke, 557
Disney, 351

Dom Perignon, 379, 387
Dove, 470, 565
DRAM chip, 422

Electrolux, 269
Elizabeth Arden, 470
Escort, 433, 437, 443, 463
Eureka, 600
Eurostar, 222
Evian, 6
Explorer, 161, 437

Firestone, 399, 456
Folgers, 545
Frigidaire, 269, 600
Frosted Flakes, 411

Game Boy, 273
Gold Wing, 226
Golden Grahams, 411

Hank Rivet Bush, 606
Hellmann's, 417
Hires, 363, 452
Holland House, 452
Hollywood Pictures, 364

Ignis, 269
Infiniti, 459
Irish Spring, 317
Itrizole, 646

J.C. Penney, 289
Jell-O, 449
Jolly Green Giant, 321
JVC, 26

Kellogg's Corn Flakes, 411
Kelvinator, 269
Kit Kat, 565

Lays Potato Chips, 395
Lean Cuisine, 545
Levi's 501 jeans, 565, 576
Lexus, 553, 572
Lipton, 470
Llano Estacado, 387

Lowenbrau, 378, 387
Lux, 565

Marathon, 557
Marlboro, 449
Mazola corn oil, 417
McDonald's, 565
Mercedes-Benz, 351, 451, 561, 594
MG, 33
Miata, 27–28, 34
Mickey Mouse, 345, 348
Microsoft Word, 663
Miller, 449
Mondeo, 563
Montblanc, 548
Morris, 33
MS-DOS, 663
Mustang, 33–34
MX-6, 437
Mystique, 443–444, 591

Navaho, 437
Neon, 443
News, 476
Nike, 289
Nissan, 459
Nova, 321

Omega, 572
OMO detergent, 37
Opium, 561
Oscar Mayer, 449

Paddington Bear, 348
Paddy Wack Clown, 207
Panasonic, 26
Pepsi-Cola, 310, 377, 395, 574
Philips Whirlpool, 269
Prelude, 364
Previa, 230, 553
Probe, 437
Propulsid, 646

Quasar, 26

Ragu, 470
Raider, 557

Ray Ban, 6
Reebok, 6
Reindeer, 207
Rice Krispies, 411
Riley, 33
Risperdal, 646
Rolex, 548, 549

Sana, 207
Saturn, 418
Seven-Up, 377
Slim Jim, 555
Smarties, 545
Smurfs, 348
Snickers, 557
Soarer, 553
Solo, 363
Sony, 98
Stolichnaya, 624
Stouffer, 545
Sunlight, 470
Super Nintendo, 171
Swatch, 548, 572

Tappan, 600
Teenage Mutant Ninja Turtles, 357
Tempo, 591
Timex, 548, 549
Tissot, 572
Toblerone, 449
Touchstone, 364
Toyota, 553, 90
Trinitron, 475
Triumph TR7, 34
Tutu Bunny, 207
Twix, 557

Vaseline, 470
Velveeta, 467

Walkman, 90, 475
Wash & Go shampoo, 37
Weed Eater, 600
Windows, 663
World Washer, 551

Zanussi, 269

Subject Index

Absolute advantage, 83–85
Acceptances
 with recourse, 619
 without recourse, 619
 types of, 618–619
Accommodating transaction, 147
Accounting exposure, 629
Accounting practices, 652–661
 for accounting reserves, 656–657
 for asset valuation/revaluation, 655
 in centrally planned economies, 654,
  660–661
 corporate financial controls and, 660
 harmonization of, 661–662
 for inventory valuation, 655–656
 and taxes, 656
 for transactions, 663–664
 for translation, 664–668
Accounting reserves, 656–657
Accounting Standards Board, 652
Accounting systems, 520–521. *See also*
  Balance of payments (BOP)
  accounting system
Acculturation, 312, 698
Acquisition strategy, 403–404
Active income, 675
Ad valorem tariff, 206
Adjustable peg, 127
Advertising, 562–565. *See also* Promotion
Advertising agencies, 564–565
Advised letter of credit, 620
Affiliated bank, 182
Africa, marketplaces of, 64–66
AFTA, 263
AG liability, 10
Age, cultural views on, 332
Aggressive goal behavior, 485
Agricultural policy, in GATT, 237–238
Ake, Jeffery, 394
Aktiengesellschaft (AG), 10
Aladdin, 352, 353
Albania, 50, 55–56
Algeria, 66
Alternatives identification, 493, 494–495
American Arbitration Association, 292
American Federation of Labor-Congress
  of Industrial Organizations, 83
American Institute of Certified Public
  Accountants, 652
American Quality Foundation, 528
American Society for Quality Control,
  527, 530
Amin, Idi, 277
ANCOM, 261
Andean Pact, 262

Andorra, 50
Angola, 66
Antiboycott provisions, 282–283
Antidumping duty, 195
Antidumping regulations, 222–223, 241
Antitrust laws, 282
Arbitrage
 covered-interest, 178–180
 definition of, 173
 pricing and, 559
 three-point, 175–177
 two-point (geographic), 175
Arbitrage and currency market, 173–180
Arbitrageurs, 168
Arbitration, 292
Area design, global, 452–454
Argentina, 68, 136, 238, 260, 380
Aristide, Jean-Bertrand, 279
Arm's length test, 672
Armenia, 54
ASEAN Free Trade Area, 263
Ashley, Sir Bernard, 537
Asia, marketplaces of, 56–64
Asian Wall Street Journal, 37
Asset(s)
 in official reserves account, 142
 offsetting, 628
 valuation and revaluation of, 655
Assigned arrangement, 430–431
Association of South East Asian Nations
  (ASEAN), 263
Attitudes, cultural, 330–334
Atwater, Bruce, 411–412
Australia, 58, 215, 238, 654, 655, 659
Austria, 50
Authority
 culture and, 331–332
 locus of, 511
 matrix design and, 458
Autonomous transaction, 146–147
Autonomy, 434
Azerbaijan, 54, 428

Background Notes, 70
Backtranslation, 321
Bad news, cultural differences in, 326
Baker, James, 136
Baker plan, 136
Balance of payments
 adjustments in, in 1990s, 164–165
 equilibrium in, 160–166
Balance of payments (BOP) accounting
  system, 118, 137–148
 components of, 138–144
 errors and omissions in, 143

official reserves account, 142
 surpluses and deficits and, 146–148
 United States and, 144–146, 151–152
Balance of Payments Statistics, 71
Balance on merchandise trade, 139
Balance on services trade, 139
Balance sheet, current rate method of
  translating, 667–669
Balance sheet hedge, 631
Bangladesh, 62
Banker's acceptance, 618
Banks
 affiliated, 182
 branch, 182
 foreign-exchange market and,
  166–169
 major international, 180–183
 services of, 182–183
 subsidiary, 182
Barter, 622
Basic Guide to Exporting, A, 71
Bauman, Robert P., 468
Beatty, Warren, 339
Beggar-thy-neighbor policies, 122
Behavior, learned, 311
Belarus, 54
Belgium, 287, 317
Belgium-Luxembourg Economic Union,
  243–244
Benchmarking, 532–533
Benefits, 370, 706–708
Benetton, Giuliana, 581
Benetton, Luciano, 581
Bentsen, Lloyd, 304
Berne Convention for the Protection of
  Literary and Artistic Works, 288
Besloten vennootschop (BV), 10
Bibby, John, 79
Bilateral netting, 636
Bill of exchange. *See* Draft
Bill of lading, 618
Board of directors, subsidiary, 461–462
Bolivar, Simon, 66
Bolivia, 262
Bond, Alan, 659
Bond(s), international, 184–185
Bond market, 184–185
Borden, James, 155
Border Industrialization Program,
  219–220
Bosnia-Herzegovina, 50
Bounded rationality, 494
Brady, Nicholas, 136
Brady Plan, 136
Branch bank, 182

Brand names
  preservation of, 107–108
  pricing policy and, 560
  product policy and, 557
  registration of, 288–289
Brando, Marlon, 226
Brazil
  accounting practices in, 658
  debt crisis of, 136
  investment controls in, 217
  marketplace of, 66, 68
  trade agreements of, 260, 261–262
  trade policies of, 217, 380
Brazilian Informatics Law, 211
Bretton Woods era, 122–129
Bretton Woods fixed exchange-rate
    system, 128–129, 162–163
Bribery, ethics and, 283
Brigham Young University, 312
British pound sterling, 120
Brown goods, 268
Brunei, 263
Bulgaria, 50, 54, 55–56, 325
Bundesbank
  exchange rate and, 161–162
  monetary policy and, 48
Bureaucratic law, 277–278
Burns, Robert, 357
Burns, Tom, 445
Bush, George, 124, 203, 274
Business strategy
  forms of, 362–364
  international marketing and, 547–549
  location issues and, 595
  operations management and, 584–585
  transfer pricing and, 671–672
Buy-back, 622
BV (besloten vennootschop), 10

CACM, 260
Cairns Group, 238
Call option, 170
Canada
  accounting practices in, 658
  cultural differences in, 317, 335
  exchange rate of, 173
  GATT and, 238
  marketplace of, 43, 45–46
  NAFTA and, 257–260
  nontariff barriers in, 213–214, 216
  as Quad partner, 40
  trade policies of, 210, 211, 221–222
Canadian Import Tribunal (CIT), 195,
    203
Canadian International Trade Tribunal
    (CITT), 196
Canadian-U.S. Free Trade Agreement,
    257, 258

Capacity planning, 600, 601
Capital
  management of working, 634–638
  sources of investment, 641–644
Capital account, 140–142
Capital budgeting, 638–640
Capital market, 180–186
  accounting practices and, 654, 657,
    659–660
  equity, 185–186
  Eurocurrency, 183–184
  offshore, 186
Car & Driver, 351
Caribbean, 47–48
Caribbean Basic Initiative, (CBI), 260
Caribbean Community and Common
    Market (CARICOM), 260
CARICOM, 260
Carranza, Venustiano, 47
Category killer, 273
Caterpillar Fundamental English (CFE),
    321
Cayman Islands, 673–674
CEEAC, 264
Cegelsky, Mike, 309, 310
Central America, 47
Central American Common Market
    (CACM), 260
Central Europe
  marketplace of, 54–56
  political risk assessment in, 297–301
Centralization, 459, 461, 691
Centralized cash depository, 634–635,
    647
Centrally planned economy (CPE)
  accounting practices in, 654, 660–661
  business risks in, 296–297
  former, 297–301
  strategic alliances in, 428–429
Chad, 64
Chaebol, 60, 214, 287, 391
Change, managing, 466–468
Channel, distribution, 570–574
Channel length, 571
Chiang, Kai-Shek, 63
Chicago Mercantile Exchange, 170
Chile, 68, 260, 262, 290
China
  accounting practices in, 654
  decision making in, 495
  intellectual property rights in, 239,
    288, 289
  legal restrictions in, 290, 417
  marketplace of, 62–64, 355, 367, 368,
    429
  nontariff barriers in, 213
  political risk in, 296–297
  pros and cons of, as market, 71–72

social orientation in, 479–480
  social structure in, 313, 314, 332
  trade and human rights in, 238, 279
Chretien, Jean, 45
Civil law, 276–277
Clark, Angie, 716–717
Classical trade theories, 82–89
  absolute advantage, 83–85
  comparative advantage, 85–87
  mercantilism, 82–83
Clearinghouse accounts, 623
Clinton, Bill, 203, 223
COCOM, 279–280
Code law, 652–653
Codetermination, 713
Cohesion fund, 251
Coker, Pamela, 421
Collective bargaining, 712–713
Collectivism, social orientation of, 479,
    480
Collis, Don, 117
Colombia, 260, 262
Colonialism, 318–319
Colt, Samuel, 19
Columbus, Christopher, 17
COMECON, 55
Comity, principle of, 292
Commercial banking services, 182
Commercial customers, 168
Commodity agreement, 264
Commodity arrangements, international,
    264–265
Commodity cartel, 264
Commodity Trade Statistics, 70
Common Agricultural Policy, 254
Common law, 276, 652–653
Common market, 243
Commonwealth of Independent States
    (CIS), 50
Communication, cultural differences in,
    322–326
Comparative advantage, 85–87, 88
Compatibility, of firms, 425
Compensation
  determining, 704–708, 711
  equity in, 708
  licensing and, 395
Compensatory transaction, 147
Competence, distinctive, 351–352
Competition, 367–368
Competitive advantage
  FDI and, 106–107
  joint ventures and, 418–419
  make-or-buy decision and, 588
  national, 96–99
  sustainable, 351
Competitive Advantage of Nations, The, 96
Competitive forces, 27

Competitiveness, 281
Compound tariff, 206
Comprehensive alliances, 420–422
Confirmed letter of credit, 620
Confiscation, 286
Conglomerate, 362
Conseil National de la Comptabilité, 662
Consolidated financial statements, 657,
    664
Consolidation method, 665
Consumer products, 554
Consumers, 530, 531
Contingency fee, 291
Control
    accounting practices and, 660
    behavioral aspects of, 522–524
    definition of, 507
    of information, 533–535
    levels of, 507–515
    management of, 515–524
    marketing approach and, 552
    of operations, 514–515
    organizational, 511–514
    of productivity, 524–527
    of quality, 527–533
    resistance to, 522–524
    sourcing and, 589–590
    staffing needs and locus of, 691
    steps in, 515–519
    strategic, 507–511
    techniques for, 520–522
Control framework, 358
Control standards, 516–517, 518
Control systems, 515–524
Controlled foreign corporation (CFC),
    675
Controller, 509–510
Convergence, cultural, 335
Convergence criteria, 252
Convertible currencies, 169
Coordination, 462–463
Coordination centers, 647
Coordination Committee for Multilateral
    Export Controls, 279–280
Corollary approach, 446–447
Corporate cooperation, 413–415
Corporate culture, 464–466
Corporate logo, 464
Corporate strategy
    change in, 467–468
    forms of, 358–362
Corporations
    largest, 13
    types of, 13–16
Correspondent relationship, 181–182
Cost leadership strategy, 363, 547, 548,
    584
Cost method, of translation, 664–665

Cost of living, comparison of, 704, 705
Cost-of-living allowance, 704
Costs, evaluation of, 370
Côte d'Ivoire, 64
Council for Mutual Economic Assistance
    (COMECON), 55
Council of the European Union, 253–254
Counterpurchase, 622
Countertrade, 622–624
Countervailing duty (CVD), 221–222
Country fund, 185
Country-of-origin effects, 592–593
Country similarity theory, 90
Country Studies, 312
Covered-interest arbitrage, 178–180
Credit, letters of, 619–621
Credit cards, 621–622
Credit checking, 615–616
Croatia, 50
Cross-cultural literacy, 312
Cross rate, 177–178
Cuba, 66, 283, 296
Cultural attaches, 309
Cultural cluster, 335–336
Cultural convergence, 335
Cultural Revolution, 63
Culture. *See also* Individual differences
    advertising medium and, 563
    characteristics of, 311–312
    clusters of, 335–336
    communication differences in, 322–
        326
    effect of MNCs on, 285
    elements of, 312
    ethics and, 334–335
    gift giving and, 326
    hospitality and, 326
    international business and, 8
    language and, 315–322
    low-context versus high-context, 322
    negotiating style and, 326
    product policy and, 555–556
    reward systems and, 333–334
    social structure and, 313–315
    status in, 333
    values and attitudes and, 330–334
Culture shock, 698
Culturegrams, 312
Cumulative translation adjustment, 667
Currency(ies)
    choice of, 615, 638–639
    convertible, 169
    functional, 665
    inconvertible, 169
    international business and, 8
    invoicing, 41
    primary transaction, 166
Currency controls, 216–217

Currency conversion, 635–637
Currency future, 170, 628
Currency option, 170, 628
Current account, 138–140
Current account balance, 140
Current rate method of translation,
    666–669
Customer(s), types of, 553–554
Customer access, 106
Customer design, global, 456–457
Customer mobility, 108
Customization, 550–552
Customs union, 243
Czech Republic
    marketplace of, 50, 54, 55
    privatization in, 299–300
    repatriation and, 290
Czechoslovakia, 50, 55, 299

Dances with Wolves, 423
Date draft, 618
Debt-equity swaps, 137
Debt-for-nature swaps, 137
Decentralization, 459, 461, 691
Decision making, 492–497
Deferral rule, 675
Delegated arrangement, 431
Demand, for foreign exchange, 157
Demand conditions, 97
Demolition Man, 340
Denmark, 249, 257
Descriptive model of decision making,
    493, 496–497
Developing countries, 43, 74–75
Der Spiegel, 452
Diamond, Malcolm, 606, 607
Diaz, Porfirio, 46
Differentiation, marketing and, 547–548
Differentiation strategy, 363, 584
Direct exchange rate, 159–160
Direct exporting, 384
Direct quote, 160
Direct sales, 571
Direction of Trade Statistics, 71
Dirty float, 130
Dispute resolution, 291–292, 432
Distinctive competence, 351–352
Distribution. *See also* Materials
    Management
    channels of, 570–574
    exporting and, 388–389
    issues and decisions in, 213–214, 569–
        574
Distribution networks, 213–214
Diversification
    related, 359–361
    unrelated, 361–362
Documentary collection, 617–619

Doi, Toshi T., 476
Draft, types of, 617–618
Drauschke, Andreas, 716–717
Dual-currency bonds, 643
Dumping, 195, 559, 560. *See also*
    Antidumping regulations
Dun & Bradstreet, 615
Dunning, John, 103

Earnings, distribution of, 433–434
East Germany. *See* Germany
Eastern Europe
    countertrade with, 623–624
    marketplaces of, 50, 52–54
    political risk assessment in, 297–
        301
EC '92, 247–251
Eclectic theory
    entry mode and, 378–379
    of investment, 103
    strategic management and, 351
Economic and monetary union (EMU),
    252
Economic and Social Committee of
    European Union, 255
Economic Community of Central African
    States, 264
Economic Community of West African
    States, 264
Economic development incentives
    FDI and, 108–109
    location issues and, 594
    as unfair trade practice, 222
Economic development programs,
    201–202
Economic exposure, 631–633
Economic integration, 242–245
Economic union, 243–244
Economies of scale, 95–96
Economies of scope, 95–96
Economist, The, 175
ECOWAS, 264
Ecuador, 262
Edge Act Corporation, 182
Edge Act of 1919, 182
Education, culture and, 332–333
EFTA, 257
Egypt, 326
Eisner, Michael, 346
Elle, 351
Embargo, 211–212, 279
Emig, Michael, 706
Empire of the Sun, 277
Employee involvement, 527
Employees, individual differences in,
    478–486
Employment, trade policies and, 199
English, variations in, 318

Entry mode
    choosing, 378–381
    strategic alliances and, 415–417
Environment, scanning of, 355–357
Epcot Center, 345
Equilibrium price, of foreign exchange,
    158–160
Equity markets, global, 185–186
Equity method, 665
Errors and omissions in BOP accounting
    system, 143
Estonia, 50, 54
E.T., 339
Ethics
    bribery and, 283
    cultural differences in, 334–335
    marketing and, 556
    tax havens and, 674
    transfer pricing and, 674
Ethnocentric approach
    to marketing, 550, 558–559
    to staffing, 693
EU. *See* European Union
Eurobonds, 184, 643
Eurocurrency market, 183–184
Eurodollar, 183
Euroloan market, 183
Euromoney, 293
Europe, growth of business in, 22–24
European Atomic Energy Community,
    246–247
European Bank for Reconstruction and
    Development, 125
European Central Bank, 252
European Coal and Steel Community, 246
European Commission, 248, 254
European Committee for Standardization,
    249
European Community, 247. *See also*
    European Union
European Court of Justice, 254
European Currency Unit (ECU), 131
European Free Trade Association (EFTA),
    257
European Monetary Institute (EMI), 252
European Monetary System (EMS), 130–
    131, 164–165
European Parliament, 254
European Union (EU), 246–257
    accounting practices and, 662
    creation of, 251–253
    EC '92 changes and, 247–251
    effects of, 467
    GATT and, 238, 239
    governing bodies of, 253–257
    languages in, 310
    legislative process of, 254–256
    members in, 48

R&D consortiums of, 424
    Utilities Directive, 215
    as Triad partner, 40, 48
    unions and, 713
Exchange rate(s). *See also* Exchange-rate
    system, Foreign exchange
    countries' arrangements for, 134–135
    cross, 177–178
    definition of, 119
    direct, 159–160
    equilibrium price and, 158–160
    indirect, 160
Exchange-rate fluctuations, 509–510, 557
Exchange-rate mechanism (ERM), 130,
    164, 252
Exchange-rate systems
    fixed, 119, 161–163, 165–166
    flexible, 130, 163–166
    floating, 130
    pros and cons of, 165–166
Eximbank, 220, 401, 626
Exit interview, 709
Expatriate, 692, 704–708
Expatriate failure, 696–697
Expatriation, 698–700
Expectancy theory of motivation,
    489–490
Experience curve, 96
Export(s). *See also* Exporting
    merchandise, 11
    capital, 139
    service, 11
    taxation of, 674–675
Export agents, manufacturers', 391
Export and import brokers, 391
Export controls, 211–212, 279–280
Export department, 447, 689–690
Export financing program, 220
Export-Import Bank of the United States
    (Eximbank), 220, 401, 626
Export intermediaries, 389–393
Export license, 620
Export management company (EMC),
    390
Export promotion, 68, 202
Export tariff, 205–206
Export Trade Act of 1918, 390
Export Trading Act (1982), 391
Export trading company (ETC), 391
Exporters, top twenty, 383
Exporting, 382–392
    advantages of, 382
    considerations in, 386–389
    definition of, 10
    forms of, 384–386
    intermediaries for, 389–393
Expropriation, 286
Extraterritoriality, 281–284

Facial expressions, 325
Factor conditions, 96–97
Factor endowments, relative, 87–89
Factoring, 617
Fair trade, 197
Family, 313
Fantasia, 345
Farrell, Paul, 155
Fastener management, 606
FDI. *See* Foreign direct investment
Federal Reserve Bank, 161–162
Federal Reserve Board, 184
Few Good Men, A, 339
FIFO, 655
Financial Accounting Standards Board
     (FASB), 652, 663, 664, 666, 667
Financial alliance, 423–424
Financial control, 509
Financial derivatives, 630
Financial issues, 614–626
     choice of currency, 615
     credit checking, 615–616
     financing, 624, 626
     payment method, 616–624
Financial statements, 657, 664
Financial strategy, 364
Firm, strategy and structure of, 98–99
First-mover advantage, 95
Fisher, Irving, 180
Fixed exchange-rate system, 119, 161–
     163, 165–166
Flexible exchange-rate system, 130, 163–
     166
Flight capital, 41, 143
Flintstones, The, 339
Float, 120, 130
Floating exchange-rate system, 130
Focus strategy, 363–364, 547, 548
Foreign bonds, 184
Foreign branch income, 675
Foreign Corrupt Practices Act (FCPA),
     283
Foreign-currency translation, methods of,
     664–668
Foreign direct investment (FDI)
     definition of, 12, 99–100
     demand factors and, 106–108
     factors influencing, 103–109
     methods of, 402–404
     point/counterpoint on, 114–115
     shifts in, since World War II, 20–22
     United States and, 100–101
     use of, 401–404
Foreign exchange
     demand for, 157
     economics of, 157–160
     equilibrium price for, 158–160
     supply of, 158

Foreign-exchange market
     arbitrage and currency, 173–180
     spot and forward, 169–173
     structure of, 166–180
Foreign exchange rate, as trade barrier,
     216–217
Foreign-exchange risk, 626–633
     economic exposure, 631–633
     minimizing, 637–638
     transaction exposure, 626–629
     translation exposure, 629–631
Foreign market
     analysis of, 364–371
     exporting to, 382–392
     mode of entry into, 378–381
Foreign sales corporations (FSC),
     674–675
Foreign service premium, 704
Foreign Sovereign Immunities Act of
     1976, 292
Foreign subsidiary, 675
Foreign trade zone (FTZ), 218–220,
     594–595
Formality, 322
Forrest Gump, 339
Forum shopping, 291
Forward discount, 172
Forward market, 169–173
Forward premium, 172
Four P's of marketing, 549, 550
Four Tigers, 59–62
France
     accounting practices in, 653, 654, 656,
          658, 662
     devaluing of franc in, 163
     education in, 332–333
     EU and, 257
     GATT and, 239
     industrial policies of, 202
     marketplace of, 48
     nontariff barriers in, 215
     productivity in, 526
     training in, 711
France Dimanche, 351
Franchisee, 398, 399
Franchising, 12, 398–400
Franchisor, 398, 399
Free trade, 197
Free trade area, 242–243
Freedom of Information Act, 276
Freight forwarders, 393
Friedman, Milton, 152
Fujimori, Albert, 143
Fujita, Den, 274
Functional alliances, 422–424
Functional currency, 665
Functional design, global, 454–455
Functional strategy, 364

Gabon, 66
Gama, Vasco da, 19
Gambia, 66, 207
GATT. *See* General Agreement on Tariffs
     and Trade
General Agreement on Tariffs and Trade
     (GATT), 234–242
     business growth and, 29
     mechanics of, 235–237
     publications of, 70
     Uruguay Round, 237–241
Generalized System of Preferences (GSP),
     236
Generally accepted accounting principles
     (GAAP), 653
Generic organizational control, 511, 512
Geocentric approach (marketing), 551
Geocentric staffing model, 693
Geographic arbitrage, 175
Georgia, 50
German Commercial Code, 656, 657
Germany
     accounting practices in, 654, 655, 656,
          657, 658
     cultural differences in, 311, 325, 333,
          491, 495, 498
     foreign direct investment by, 20
     labor relations in, 713
     legal restrictions in, 281, 287
     marketplace of, 48, 638
     productivity in, 525
     training and appraisal in, 711
     unions in, 713
Gesellschaft mit beschrankter Haftung
     (GmbH), 10
Ghana, 201, 207
Gibeaux, Gerard, 233
Gift giving, 326
Glass-Stegall Act, 183
Global area design, 452–454
Global bond, 185
Global corporation, 14–15
Global customer design, 456–457
Global functional design, 454
Global matrix design, use of, 457–458
Global product design, 449–452
Global strategic rivalry theory, 94–96
Global strategy, entry mode and, 381
Globex, 171
GmbH liability, 10
Goal orientation
     individual differences in, 485–486
     leadership style and, 491–492
     motivation and, 488
Gold standard
     collapse of, 120–122
     dollar-based, 126–128
     monetary system of, 119–122

Goods, arbitrage of, 173–175
Goodwill, 657
Gorbachev, Mikhail S., 50
Gortari, Carlos Salinas de, 47, 258
Government and policy
  business growth and, 28–29
  exporting and, 386–387
  location decisions and, 593–595
  on trade, 201–204
Government services trade, 600–601
Grasso, Richard, 659
Gray market, 561
Great Depression, 120
Great Leap Forward, 63
Greece, 287
Green Dot law, 281
Greenberg, Gary, 651
Greene, Joseph, 155
Greenfield strategy, 335, 402–403
Gross domestic product (GDP), 42
Gross national product (GNP), 42
Group dynamics, 497
Groupism, 314
Groups, cultural differences in, 497–499
Grout, John, 643
Guyana, 217

H-form design, 449, 462
Hainsworth, Nigel, 233
Haiti, 279
Halske, Johann, 505
Hand gestures, 325
Hanneman, William, 318
Hard currencies, 169
Hard loan policy, 124
Hardman, Roger, 606
Hardship premium, 704
Harley Owners Group (HOG), 227
Harmonization, 248, 249
Harmonized tariff schedule (HTS), 207
Hasselhoff, David, 239
Headhunters, 695
Heckscher, Eli, 87
Heckscher-Olin theory, 87–89, 592
Heineken, Alfred, 377
Heineken, Gerald, 377
Heineken, Henri, 377
Herzberg, Frederick, 489
Hickson, David, 445
Hierarchy of needs, 488
High-context culture, 322
High-income countries, 43
Hills, Carla, 223
Hinduism, 329, 333
Hoffman, Dustin, 339
Hofstede, Geert, 478, 480, 481, 482, 485, 486
Holding company, 449

Home country, 12
Home country laws
  effects of, 278–284
  extraterritoriality and, 281–284
  indirect effects of, 281
Hong Kong, 59, 61–62
Hospitality, 326
Host country
  assessment of, 368–369
  definition of, 12
  ethics and, 556
  impact of MNCs on, 284–285
  location issues and, 592–593
  trade controls of, 289–290
  political environment of, 293–301
Host country laws, 285–290
Host-country nationals (HCNs), 692
Houston, Whitney, 440
Huey, John, 446
Human capital, 74
Human resource management (HRM)
  compensation determination, 704–705, 711
  expatriation and repatriation, 698–700
  labor relations, 712–714
  managerial staffing, 689–693
  nature of, 686–689
  nonmanagerial staffing, 709–711
  performance appraisal, 703–704, 711
  recruitment, 693–696, 709–710
  retention and turnover, 708–709
  selection, 696–698
  staff development, 700, 702, 710–711
  staffing philosophy of, 691–693
  strategic significance of, 688–689
  training, 700–702, 710–711
Human resource strategy, 364
Human rights, 610–611
Hungary, 50, 54, 55, 287, 299, 661
Hunt for Red October, 569
Hurdle rate, 640

Iceland, 50
IMF conditionality, 126
Imgruth, Max, 631–632
Import(s)
  merchandise, 11
  of the services of capital, 139–140
Import-substitution strategy, 68, 202
Import tariff, 206
Importing, 10
Income, active versus passive, 675
Income distribution, 43
Income levels, 42–43
Income statements, 666–667
Inconvertible currencies, 169
India
  Bhopal, 291–292

caste system in, 315, 333
GATT and, 238
intellectual property rights in, 288
marketplace of, 62, 508–509
legal restrictions of, 279, 287, 416–417
Indirect exchange rate, 160
Indirect exporting, 384
Indirect quote, 160
Individual differences, 478–486
  goal orientation and, 485–486
  power orientation and, 480–482
  social orientation and, 478–480
  uncertainty orientation and, 482–484
Individualism, 313, 478
Indonesia, 64, 263
Industrial democracy, 713
Industrial policy, national, 202–203
Industrial products, 554
Industry-level trade theories, 197–201
Infant industry argument, 198–199
Inflation rate
  EMU and, 252
  interest rates and, 180
  in Russia, 53
Infomatics Law, 262
Informal management network, 463
Information
  access to, 432–433
  control of, 533–535
Information system, 534
Infrastructure, 45–46, 74, 592
Input-output analysis, Leontief's, 88–89
Inputs, acquiring, 587–592
Inquiry into the Nature and Causes of the Wealth of Nations, An, 83
Institutes of Chartered Accountants, 652
Institutional Revolutionary Party (PRI), 47
Intellectual property rights
  definition of, 239
  protection of, 287–288
  sourcing and, 589
  strategic rivalry and, 94–95
Interdependence, levels of, 462
Interest, in Muslim countries, 277
Interest rates, 180
Interindustry trade, 90
Intermediaries, export, 389–393
Internal rate of return, 640
Internal Revenue Service, 656–657
Internalization advantage, 103, 380–381
Internalization theory of investment, 102–103
International Accounting Standards Committee (IASC), 661–662
International Bank for Reconstruction and Development (IBRD). *See* World Bank

International banking facility (IBF), 184
International business
  activities of, 10–13
  definition of, 13
  early era of, 16–19
  evolution of, 16–26
  growth in, 19–29
  reasons for, 8
  study of, 9–10
International Convention for the
    Protection of Industrial Property
    Rights, 287–288
International Development Association
    (IDA), 123, 124
International division, 447–448, 690
International Finance Corporation (IFC),
    123, 124
International Financial Statistics, 71
International Fisher effect, 180
International Herald Tribune, 37
International investments, categories of,
    11–12
International logistics, 596–598
International marketing, 546. *See also*
    Marketing
International monetary system
  in Bretton Woods era, 122–129
  debt crisis in, 132–139
  definition of, 118
  history of, 119–136
  performance of, since 1971, 129–136
International Monetary Fund, (IMF), 71,
    125–126, 632
International Olympics Committee, 5–7
International operations management,
    583. *See also* Operations
    management
International order cycle time, 570
International Organization for
    Standardization (ISO), 527
International service business, 598
International Standards Organization, 249
International strategic management. *See*
    Strategic management
International strategy. *See* Business
    strategy; Strategy
International trade, 81
International Trade Administration, 615
International Trade Commission, 221, 231
International Trade Organization (ITO),
    235
International Trade Statistics, 70
International trading company, 390–391
International Wheat Council, 218
Internationalization, 13–14, 689–690
Interpersonal relations
  control and, 522–524
  individual differences and, 478–486

Interview with the Vampire, 339
Intracorporate transfer, 384–386
Intraindustry trade, 90
Inventories, valuation of, 655–656
Inventory management
  just-in-time, 9, 526, 597
  location issues and, 595–596
Inventory turnover, 521
Investment. *See also* Foreign direct
    investment
  greenfield, 335
  level of, and sourcing, 590
  long-term portfolio, 141
  overview of, 99–100
  short-term portfolio, 140
  theories of, 101–103
  types of, 99–100
Investment banking services, 183
Investment capital, 641–644
Investment controls, 217
Invisible trade, 11
Invoicing currency, 41
Iran, 277, 280
Iraq, 212, 279
Ireland, 249
Irrevocable letter of credit, 620
Ishtar, 339
Islam, 329, 330
ISO 9000, 527, 528
Israel, 283
Italy, 658

Jamaica, 292
Jamaica Agreement, 130
Janssen, Dr. Paul, 646
Japan. *See also* Keiretsu, Ringhi system,
    Sogo sosha
  accounting practices in, 658, 659
  cultural context of, 323
  cultural differences between U.S. and,
    321, 322, 323, 325, 498
  distribution networks in, 214
  education in, 332–333
  foreign direct investments by, 20
  GATT and, 238
  gift giving in, 326
  industrial structure in, 58
  labor relations in, 712, 713
  language and, 321
  leadership style in, 490–491
  legal restrictions of, 274
  marketplace of, 56, 58
  mode of entry and, 380–381
  productivity in, 22–24, 525, 526
  social orientation in, 313–314,
    333–334, 487, 499
  trade policies of, 198–199, 202, 210
  training in, 685, 711

as Triad partner, 40
  view of aging in, 332
Jobs, Steve, 93, 97
Johnson, Sylvia, 716
Joint venture(s)
  definition of, 404
  risk sharing in, 417–418
  shared knowledge in, 418
  versus strategic alliance, 413–415
  strategic control of, 511
Jones, Steve, 234
Jones Act, 203–204, 239
Jurassic Park, 339
Just-in-time (JIT) inventory management,
    9, 526, 597

Kabushkiki Kaisha (KK), 10
Kampf, Serge, 514
Kaske, Karlheinz, 505
Keiretsu
  accounting practices and, 654–655
  control and, 589
  definition of, 58
  financing and, 181
  role of, 390–391
  as trade barrier, 214
Kenya, 64, 482, 520
KGaA liability, 10
KK liability, 10
Klaus, Vaclav, 55
Koestner, Geoff, 155
Kommanditgesellschaft auf Aktien
    (KGaA), 10
Krugman, Paul, 94
Kunkel, Edward T., 523
Kuwait, 201–202, 279

Labor productivity, 525
Labor relations, 712–714
Lancaster, Kelvin, 94
Language, culture and, 315–322
Large-Store Law, 274
Latin America, 322
Latvia, 50, 54
Law of one price, arbitrage and, 173
Laws. *See also* Government and policy;
    Legal systems
  distribution channel and, 572
  home country, 278–284
  host country, 285–290
  product policy and, 554–555
Lazarus, Charles, 273
Leadership
  factors affecting, 490–492
  social orientation and, 498–499
Leads and lags strategy, 637
League of Arab States, 282
Learned needs framework, 488–489

Leases, capitalization of, 657
Legal environment, assessment of, 368–369
Legal regulations. *See* Laws; Legal systems
Legal systems
    accounting practices and, 652–653
    differences in, 275–278
Leontief, Wassily, 88
Leontief paradox, 89
Lester, Charles and Patricia, 517, 518, 519
Letters of credit, 619–621
Levitt, Theodore, 551
Liability, types of, 10
Liaison role, 463
Libya, 66, 280
Licensee, 393, 396
Licensing
    advantages and disadvantages of, 397
    definition of, 393
    international, 12, 393–397
    issues in, 393–396
    use of, 380–381
Licensing agreement, 394–395, 396
Licensing fees, 642
Licensor, 393, 396
Liechtenstein, 50, 243
Life cycle, of product, 91–94
LIFO, 655–656
Limited liability, 10
Linder, Steffan, 90
Lingua franca, 320
Lion King, The, 94
Lithuania, 50, 54
Loans, soft, 124
Location, 585, 592–596
Location advantage, 103, 380
Location planning, 601
Locus of authority, 511
Logistics, 105, 596–598
London Interbank Offer Rate (LIBOR), 183
London Stock Exchange, 185
Long run, equilibrium in, 161–162
Long Term Arrangement, 265
Long-term portfolio investments, 141
Los Angeles, 214
Louvre Accord, 132
Low-context culture, 322
Ltd. liability, 10
Luxembourg, 367, 368, 673
Lyons, Kenneth, 526

M-form design, 449, 462
Maastricht Treaty, 244, 251–253
Macedonia, 50
Macropolitical risk, 293
Madero, Francisco, 47

Madred, Miguel de la, 47
Magellan, Ferdinand, 19
Make-or-buy decision, 587–592
Malaysia, 64, 263
Malta, 50
Managed float, 130
Managed trade, 197
Management. *See also* Human resource management
    of change, 466–468
    of control function, 515–524
    of cross-cultural teams, 497–499
    of foreign-exchange risk, 626–633
    of information, 534–535
    of marketing, 547–552
    of productivity, 525–527
    of service operations, 601–602
    of strategic alliances, 425–432
    of working capital, 634–638
Management by objectives (MBO), 488, 490
Management contract, 12, 400
Management network, informal, 463
Managers
    compensation and benefits for, 704–708
    quality perceptions of, 528–529
    recruitment of, 694–696
    selection of, 696–698
    training and development of, 700–702
Mandela, Nelson, 66
Manufacturers' agents, 391
Mao Tse-Tung, 63
Maquiladora, 219–220
Marginal cost curve, 559
Marginal revenue curve, 559
Marine Mammal Protection Act, 284
Market, assessing of alternative, 365–370
Market analysis, foreign, 364–371
Market-based transfer prices, 670
Market entry, 415–417
Market expansion, 27
Market potential, assessment of, 365–367
Market pricing, 559–561
Market socialism, 55
Marketing
    business strategy and, 547–549
    definition of, 546
    distribution issues in, 569–574
    ethics and, 556
    exporting and, 387
    marketing mix, 549
    pricing issues and decisions, 557–561
    product policy, 553–557
    promotion issues and decisions, 561–569
    standardization versus customization, 550–552

Marketing advantages, FDI and, 106
Marketing alliance, 422–423
Marketing management, 547–552
Marketing mix, 549
Marketing strategy, 364
Marketplaces
    Africa, 64–66
    Asia, 56–64
    China, 62–64
    Eastern and Central Europe, 50–56
    global, 24
    India, 62
    major, 25–26
    North America, 41–48
    Western Europe, 48–50
    South America, 66–68
    southeast Asia, 64
Marshall Plan, 22, 123
Maslow, Abraham, 488
Materials management, 596–598
Maturing product stage, 93
Maucher, Helmut, 464–465, 545, 546
Mauritius, 66, 218
Maxmin, James, 537–538
McClelland, David, 488–489
McKevitt, Frank, 706
Medium, advertising, 563–565
Menem, Carlos, 260
Mercantilism, trade theory of, 82–83
Merchandise export, 11, 20, 139
Merchandise import, 11, 139
Merchandise trade, 81
Mercosur Accord, 260–262
Message, advertising, 562–563
Mexico
    debt crisis of, 134–135, 136
    legal restrictions of, 711
    as marketplace, 46
    trade agreements of, 257–260
    trade polices of, 217, 219–220
    U.S. domestic laws and, 284
Micropolitical risk, 293
Middle-income countries, 43
Miller, Herman, 233
Mindanao, 74
Ministry of International Trade and Investment (MITI), 56, 274
Minuet, Peter, 100
Mission statement, 353–355
MNC. *See* Multinational corporation
Monaco, 50
Monetary system. *See* Exchange-rate systems; International monetary system
Money
    arbitrage of, 175–180
    comparative advantage and, 86–87
Montenegro, 50

Morita, Akio, 464
Most favored nation (MFN) principle, 236, 238
Motivation, 486–490
Mozambique, 66
Mr. Baseball, 487
Mulroney, Brian, 45, 257, 258, 286
Multidivisional design. *See* M-form design
Multidomestic corporation, 14
Multifibre Arrangement, 241, 265
Multilateral Investment Guarantee Agency (MIGA), 123, 124, 296
Multilateral netting, 636
Multinational corporation (MNC)
    definition of, 13–14
    host countries and, 284–285
    strategic rivalry and, 94
Multinational enterprises (MNEs), 14
Multinational organization (MNO), 14
Munching, Leo van, 377
Muppet Christmas Carol, The, 643
Murdoch, Rupert, 659
Muslim countries, motivation and, 490

Naamloze vennotschop (NV), 10
NAFTA. *See* North American Free Trade Agreement
Napoleonic Code, 276
National(s), types of, 691–693
National Basketball Association, 563
National competitive advantage, 96–99
National defense argument, 198
National Football League, 572
National Labor Relations Board, 80
National Tax Administration (Japan), 672
National Trade Data Bank, 71, 389, 572
National trade policies, 201–204
National Wool Act, 198
Nationalization, 286
Natural resources, 105
Navigation Act of 1660, 82
Need-based model of motivation, 486, 487–489
Negotiating style, 326
Neimanis, Arnold, 155, 156
Neo-mercantilists, 83
Nepal, 279
Net present value, 638–640
Netherlands, 422, 658
Netherlands Antilles, 673
Netting, bilateral versus multilateral, 636
Nevin, John, 492
New product stage, 91, 93
New York Stock Exchange (NYSE), 185, 659
New Zealand, 58
Neyaka, 475
Nicholas II, 50

Niger, 64
Nigeria, 66
Nirvana, 329
Nixon, Richard M., 129
Nonmanagerial employees, 709–711
Nonmarket-based transfer prices, 670–673
Nontariff barriers (NTB), 209–217
Nonverbal communication, 324–325
Normative model of decision making, 492, 493–496
North American Free Trade Agreement (NAFTA)
    business growth and, 29
    effects of, 220
    Mexico and, 47
    provisions of, 257–260
    ratification of, 45
Norway, 50
NV (naamloze vennotschop), 10

O'Neill, Tip, 204
Obligation
    culture and, 314
    offset, 289
Office, cultural differences in, 325
Office of Foreign Availability, 280
Official reserves account, 142
Official Secrets Act, 276
Official settlements balance, 146
Offset obligation, 289
Offset purchases, 622
Offshore financial centers, 100, 186
Ohlin, Bertil, 87
Ohmae, Kenichi, 40, 48, 269, 551
Oil cartel, 264–265
Olympic games, 5–7, 16
Open account, 616–617
Operations. *See also* Operations management
    improving, 526–527
    scope of, 350
Operations control, 514–515
Operations management
    issues in, 585
    nature of, 583–585
    production, 585–598
    service, 586, 598–602
    strategic context of, 584–585
Operations strategy, 364
Opportunities, analysis of, 355–357
Opportunity cost, 85, 370
Order cycle time, international, 570
Organization change, managing, 466–468
Organization design
    centralization versus decentralization in, 459, 461
    change in, 468

coordination in, 462–463
early studies of, 445
global area design, 452–454
global customer, 456–457
global functional, 454–455
global matrix, 457–458
global product, 449–452
hybrid global, 458–459
impact of international activity on, 446–448
nature of, 444–445
subsidiary boards and, 461–462
Organization for Economic Cooperation and Development (OECD), 43
Organization of Petroleum Exporting Countries (OPEC), 23, 133, 264–265
Organizational control, 511–514
Organizational structure. *See also* Organization design
    location issues and, 595
    staffing needs and, 689–690
Origin, rules of, 243
Ouchi, William, 24
Overall cost leadership strategy, 363
Overall productivity, 525
Overcontrol, 522–523
Overseas Private Investment Corporation (OPIC), 220, 296
Ownership
    constraints on, 287
    host country and, 286–287
    in strategic alliance, 427–430
Ownership advantages, 103, 379
Ownership advantage theory, 102, 103

Packaging, 597
Pakistan, 62
Par value, 119
Paraguay, 260
Parent-country nationals (PCNs), 691–692
Paris Air Show, 567
Paris Convention, 288
Partnership sourcing, 606–607
Passive goal behavior, 485
Passive income, 675
Payback period, 640
Payment methods
    in advance, 616
    countertrade, 622–624
    credit card, 621–622
    documentary collection, 617–619
    letters of credit, 620–621
    open account, 616–617
Pegging, 119
Per capita income, 42

Performance
  comparing to standards, 518
  measuring, 517–518
Performance appraisal, 703–704, 711
Performance ratios, 521–522
Personal selling, 566–567
Peru, 262
Pfeiffer, Eckhard, 695
Pfeiffer, Michelle, 278, 279
Pharmaceuticals, licensing and, 380–381
Philadelphia Exchange, 170–171
Phillipines, 263
Phillips, Martin, 607
Piano, The, 339
Pinocchio, 345
Plan Comptable General, 653
Planning process control, 511, 512, 514
Plant closings, 290
Plaza Accord, 132
PLC, 10
Poland
  economic restructuring of, 50, 54, 55
  nontariff trade barriers in, 215
  repatriation and, 290
  trading restrictions, 279
Political environment
  assessment of, 368–369
  foreign direct investment and, 108–109
  of host country, 293–301
Political risk, 294
Political risk assessment, 293–296
Political union, 244
Polycentric approach
  to marketing, 550–551
  to pricing, 560
  to staffing, 693
Porter, Michael, 96, 98, 356
Portfolio investments
  definition of, 12, 99
  long-term, 141
  short-term, 140
Portugal, 66, 287
Power orientation
  control and, 523, 524
  culture and, 331–332
  decision making and, 494–495, 496
  individual differences in, 480–482
  leadership style and, 491
  marketing approach and, 552
  motivation and, 488
  teams and, 498
Power respect, 480–481
Power tolerance, 481–482
Predatory pricing, 222, 223
Preferential Trade Area of Eastern and
    Southern Africa, 263–264
Price, profit-maximizing, 559
Price discrimination, 222, 223

Price leadership strategy, 595. *See also*
    Cost leadership strategy
Price-to-earnings ratio, 657, 659
Pricing, issues and decisions in, 557–561
Primary transaction currency, 166
Principle of comity, 292
Privatization, 53, 286–287, 298–299
Problem recognition, 493, 494
Procedures, as control technique, 521
Process-based model of motivation, 487, 489
Procurement policies, 214
Product. *See also* Product life cycle,
    Product policy
  location issues and, 593
  standardized versus customized, 553–554
Product design, global, 449–452
Product liability, 281
Product life cycle, 91–94
Product line, 690
Product policy
  economic factors in, 556
  legal standards and, 554–555
  in marketing mix, 553–557
Product standards, 213, 554–555
Product-support services, 600
Production alliance, 422
Production costs, 104
Production management, 585–598
  definition of, 585
  location decisions, 592–596
  sourcing and vertical integration, 586–592
Productivity
  control of, 524–527
  international comparisons of, 525
  management of, 525–527
  operations management and, 583
Profit margins, 176
Profits, repatriation of, 290, 642
Promotion
  advertising, 562–565
  definition of, 561
  issues and decisions in, 561–569
  personal selling, 566–567
  public relations, 567–569
  sales, 567, 568
Promotion mix, 562
Promptness, 331
Protectionists, 83
Protestant ethic, 327, 331
Public choice analysis, 203–204
Public-private venture, 428–430
Public relations, 567–569
Puerto Rico, 66
Pugh, Derek, 445

Purchasing power parity (PPP), 173–175, 176
Purchasing requirements, 215
Put option, 170

Qadhafi, Muammar, 66
Quad, 40, 81
Quality
  control of, 527–533
  dimensions of, 528
  operations management and, 583
  perceptions about, 528–530
  total quality management, 530, 532–533
Quota
  IMF, 125–126
  as trade barrier, 210–211

R&D. *See* Research and development
R&D alliance, 424
R&D consortium, 424
Radzievsky, Yuri, 310
Ramadan, 330
Rate of return, internal, 640
Re-exporting, 61
Reagan, Ronald, 203, 212, 258
Recruitment, 694–696, 709–710
Regional development banks, 125
Regional economic integration, 242–245
Regulatory controls, 215–216
Reich, Robert, 203
Reinforcement model of motivation, 487, 490
Related diversification, 359–361
Relative factor endowments, 87–89
Religion, 277, 326–330
Repatriation
  of employees, 698–700
  of profits, 290, 642
Republic of China. *See* Taiwan
Research and development
  alliances for, 424
  capitalization of, 657
  consortia for, 424
  productivity and, 525, 526
  strategic advantage and, 95
Resource(s)
  endowment of, 87–89
  natural, and FDI, 105
  operations management and, 585
  trade and, 41
Resource acquisition, 27
Resource deployment, 350–351
Responsibility center control, 511, 512
Retailers, 571
Retention, 708
Return, internal rate of, 640
Reuter, Edzard, 451

Revocable letter of credit, 620
Reward system
  culture and, 333–334
  social orientation and, 480, 487
Ricardo, David, 85
Rider College, 651
Ringi system, for decision making, 494–495, 499
Ringisho, 495
Risk
  adjustment of NPV for, 638
  evaluation of, 370–371
  foreign-exchange, 626–633
  pricing policy and, 560
  sharing, in joint venture, 417–418
  sourcing and, 590
  strategic alliances and, 426–427
  uncertainty orientation and, 484
Romania, 50, 54, 55–56
Rosinski, Annette, 707
Royalty, 395
Rules of origin, 243
Russia House, The, 278, 279
Russian Federation (Russia) 50, 53–54, 298, 564–565
Rwanda, 66

SA (societé anonyme), 10
SADCC, 263–264
Sales promotion, 567, 568
Salinas, President, 417
Samurai bonds, 189
Sanctions, 279
Satisficing, 494
Saudi Arabia, 293, 325, 326, 330, 554, 572
Scale, economies of, 95–96
Schaul, Dan, 707
Schwartzenegger, Arnold, 340
Scope
  economies of, 95–96
  of operations, 350
Screwdriver plant, 258
Securities and Exchange Commission (SEC), 654, 656
Segal, Steven, 340
Selection, employee, 696–698, 709–710
Self-reference criterion, 311–312
Selleck, Tom, 487
Servia, 50
Service(s)
  characteristics of, 599–600
  trade in, 238–239
Service business, 598, 600–601
Service export, 11, 139
Service import, 11, 139
Service operations management, 586, 598–602

Service sector, 598–599
Shared management agreement, 430
Shelf life, 570
Shipping industry, 239
Short run, equilibrium in, 161–162
Short Term Arrangement, 265
Short-term portfolio investments, 140
Siemens, Werner von, 505
Sierra Leone, 66, 207
Sight draft, 618
Silence, 325
Singapore, 59, 61, 289, 521, 554, 711
Single-business strategy, 359
Single European Act, 248–249
Six Sigma quality, 374
Sloan, Alfred, 33
Slovakia, 50, 54, 55
Slovenia, 50
Smith, Adam, 83, 197
Smithsonian Agreement, 130
Smithsonian Conference, 129
Smoot-Hawley Tariff Act, 235
Snow White, 345
Social change, 28
Social charter, 713
Social mobility, 315
Social orientation
  decision making and, 495–496
  individual differences in, 478–480
  leadership style and, 490–491
  motivation and, 487, 489
Social Policy, EU, 256–257
Social stratification, 315
Social structure, 313–315
Societé anonyme (SA), 10
Sociocultural influences, 369–370
Soft currencies, 169
Soft loans, 124
Sogo sosha
  definition of, 58
  role of, 390–391, 392
  trade arrangements by, 623
Somalia, 217, 313
Sourcing
  control and, 589–590
  flexibility in, 590–592
  partnership, 606–607
  production management and, 586–592
South Africa, 64, 66, 279, 440–441
South America, 66–68
South Korea
  GATT and, 238
  as marketplace, 59–60
  nontariff barriers in, 214
  ownership policy of, 287
  trade policies of, 202, 210
  training in, 711

Southern African Development Coordination Conference, 263–264
Soviet Union, 50, 52–54, 280, 624
SpA liability, 10
Spain, 66, 257, 285, 289
Special drawing rights (SDRs), 129
Special-interest groups, 203
Specific tariff, 206
Speculators, 168
Spielberg, Steven, 277, 340
Spot market, 169
Spratly Islands, 70
Staffing models, 693
Staffing needs, 689–693
Stalin, Joseph, 277
Stalker, G. M., 445
Stallone, Sylvester, 340
Standard price policy, 558
Standardization, marketing approach of, 550–552
Standardized product stage, 93
State Property Agency, 299
Statistical process control, 532–533
Status, 333
Statutory law, 276
Sterling-based gold standard, 120
Stevens, Bob, 607
Strategic alliance
  benefits of, 415–419
  earnings distribution in, 433–434
  growth in, 415
  joint management considerations for, 430–432
  versus joint ventures, 413–415
  management of, 425–431
  ownership in, 427–430
  pitfalls of, 432–434
  scope of, 420–424
Strategic business units (SBUs), 362
Strategic control, 507–511
Strategic goals, 357
Strategic management, 348–349
Strategic partners, 425–427
Strategic planning, 348
Strategic rivalry, 94
Strategic trade theory, 199–201
Strategy
  business, 362–364
  components of, 349–352
  control framework for, 358
  corporate, 358–362
  development of, 352–358
  firm, 90–99
  formulation of, 352
  functional, 364
  goals and, 357
  implementation of, 352
  mission statement, 353–355

Strategy (cont.)
resource deployment and, 350–351
scope of operations and, 349–350
SWOT analysis and, 355–357
tactics and, 357–358
Strauss, Levi, 576
Strengths, analysis of, 355–357
Structural Impediments Initiative, 274
Subpart F income, 675
Subsidiary, 461–462, 671, 675
Subsidiary bank, 182
Subsidies, to promote trade, 217–218
Suharto, President, 37
Super 301, 223
Supply, of foreign exchange, 158
Supply factors, 103–104
Supporting industries, 97
Survey of Current Business, 70
Sustainable competitive advantage, 351
Sutantio, Teguh, 509
Swap market, 643
Swap transaction, 170
Switching arrangements, 623
Switzerland, 50, 243, 658
SWOT analysis, 352, 355–357
Sudan, 217
Synergy, 352, 418–419
Syria, 217, 283, 284

Tactics, 357–358
Taiwan
marketplace of, 59, 60–61
repatriation and, 290
trade policies of, 202
Talal, Prince Al-Walid bin, 347
Tanzania, 66, 74
Tariff(s)
location and, 380
reasons for, 207–209
types of, 205–209
Tariff schedule, harmonized, 207
Tax credits, 676
Tax-equalization system, 705–706
Tax havens, 673–674
Tax policy, assessment of, 369
Tax treaties, 676–677
Taxation
of foreign income in United States, 674–675
international issues in, 669–674
resolving conflicts about, 676–677
tax havens and, 673–674
transfer pricing and, 670–673
Taxes, accounting practices and, 656
Teams, cross-cultural, 497–499
Technical standards, 249
Technological change, 28
Technology, 106

Temporal method of translation, 666
Testing standards, 213
Textile agreements, 265
Thailand, 64, 263
Thatcher, Margaret, 286
Theocracy, 277
Theory of absolute advantage, 84
Theory of national competitive advantage, 96–99
Theory of relative factor endowments, 87–89
Theory Z, 24
Third-country nationals (TCNs), 692–693
Threats, analysis of, 355–357
Three-point arbitrage, 175–177
Thumbelina, 361
Time, 331, 486
Time, 345
Time draft, 618, 619
Time orientation, 486
Tokyo Auto Mart, 567
Tokyo Stock Exchange, 189–190
Tort laws, 281
Total factor productivity, 525
Total quality management (TQM), 530, 532
Trade. *See also* Trade barriers; Trade policies; Trade theories
definition of, 81
early era of, 16–19
factors affecting, 40, 236
financial issues in, 614–626
financing, 624, 626
free versus fair, 197
promotion of, 217–220
restrictions on, 279–280
unfair, 221–223
Trade acceptance, 618–619
Trade Act, Section 301, 223
Trade associations, regional, 261
Trade barriers, 205–217
FDI and, 108
nontariff, 209–217
purchasing power parity and, 176
tariffs as, 205–209
Trade creation, 245
Trade deflection, 242
Trade diversion, 245
Trade in invisibles, 139
Trade in visibles, 139
Trade intervention, rationale for, 196–204
Trade policies, 196–197, 230–231
national, 201–204
to promote trade, 217–220
Trade routes, ancient, 17, 18
Trade theories
classical, 82–89
industry-level, 197–201

modern, 90–99
strategic, 199–201
Trademarks, 107–108, 288–289
Trading company, 390–391
Training, of employees, 700–702, 709–711
Transaction costs, 102, 380
Transaction exposure
accounting practices and, 663–664
managing, 626–629
Transfer prices, 282
Transfer pricing
as source of investment capital, 642
taxation and, 670–673
Transit tariff, 206
Translation
accounting practices and, 664–668
definition of, 664
language, 320–321
Translation exposure, 629–631
Transnational corporation, 15–16
Transportation, 387–388, 569–570
Treasury management, 647
Treaty of Rome, 246, 247, 248, 249
Treaty on European Union, 251–253
Triad, 40, 48
Triffin, Robert, 128
Triffin paradox, 128–129
Trudeau, Pierre, 43
Turnkey project, 400–401
Turnover, 708–709
Two-factor theory of motivation, 489
Two-point arbitrage, 175
Two-tiered pricing policy, 558–559

U-form design, 454, 455, 462
Uganda, exchange rate in, 216–217
Ukraine, 54, 301
Uncertainty acceptance, 482
Uncertainty avoidance, 482
Uncertainty orientation
individual differences in, 482, 484
leadership style and, 491
motivation and, 488
teams and, 499
Undeveloped countries, 43
Unilateral transfers, 140
Unions, 713–714
United Auto Workers, 80, 212, 685
United Kingdom
accounting practices in, 652, 658
class system in, 311, 315, 332
cultural differences and, 335
devaluing of money of, 163
EU and, 48–50, 250, 253, 256–257
labor relations in, 712, 713
language differences between U.S. and, 318

legal restrictions of, 273–274
mercantilism and, 82–83
privatization in, 286
productivity in, 526
United Nations, 70, 279
United Negro College Fund, 17
United States
accounting practices and, 655, 656
balance of payments in, since 1993, 144–146, 151–152
embargoes by, 279
exchange rate of, 173
foreign direct investment in, 100–101
GATT and, 238, 239
golden business era of, 20, 22
investment controls in, 217
language differences between United Kingdom and, 318
legal restrictions of, 281, 282, 283–284, 287
marketplace of, 41–43
NAFTA and, 257–260
productivity in 525, 526
shifts in foreign direct investments of, 20
taxation of foreign income in, 674–675
trade policies of, 198, 210
Triad partner, 40
United States and Foreign Commerical Service, 389, 572, 615
United States Central Intelligence Agency, 70

United States Department of Commerce, 70, 71, 231, 389, 567, 615
United States International Trade Administration, 221
United States Mission to the European Union, 256
United States State Department, 70
United States Treasury Department, 283
Universal Copyright Convention, 288
Unrelated diversification, 361–362
Uruguay, 260
Uruguay Round agreement, 237–241

Value-added taxes, 176, 250
Value chain, 356
Values, cultural, 330–334
Van Damme, Jean-Claude, 340
Venezuela, 68, 260, 262, 522
Vernon, Raymond, 91
Vertical integration, 586–592
Vietnam, 64
Villa, Pancho, 47
Visible trade, 11
Voluntary export restraint (VER), 108, 212, 387
Von Pierer, Heinrich, 505–506

Wall Street Journal, 159, 172
Walsh, Rick, 156
We're Back, 361
Weaknesses, analysis of, 355–357
Webb-Pomerene Association, 390
Weber, Max, 327, 445

Wheat subsidies, 218
White goods, 267
White Paper on Completing the Internal Market, 248
Wholesalers, in distribution channel, 571
Wild One, The, 226
Woman's Day, 351
Woodward, Joan, 445
Working capital, 634–638
World Bank, 632
formation and organizations of, 122–125
global bonds and, 185
income statistics and, 43
publications of, 70
World Bank Group, 123
World company, 16
World Development Report, 70
World Economic Outlook, 71
World economy, 40–41
World Factbook, The, 70
World Trade Organization (WTO), 235, 239, 240–242
World War I, gold standard and, 120

Yeltsin, Boris, 53
Yew, Lee Kuan, 61

Zaire, 66
Zambia, 66, 217
Zapata, Emiliano, 47
Zimbabwe, 64
Zollverein, 243